THE GREAT
CONTEMPORARY
ISSUES

POLITICAL
PARTIES

THE GREAT CONTEMPORARY ISSUES

THE GREAT
CONTEMPORARY
ISSUES

POLITICAL
PARTIES

The New York Times

ARNO PRESS

NEW YORK / 1977

WILLIAM E. LEUCHTENBURG
Advisory Editor

GENE BROWN
Editor

Library of Congress Cataloging in Publication Data

Main entry under title:

Political parties.

    (The Great contemporary issues)
    Articles originally appearing in the New York
times.
    Bibliography: p.
    Includes index.
    1. Political parties—United States—History—
Addresses, essays, lectures. I. Leuchtenburg,
William Edward, 1922- II. Brown, Gene.
III. New York times. IV. Series.
JK2261.P63   329'.02   76-54572

ISBN 0-405-09866-9

Manufactured in the United States of America

The editors express special thanks to The Associated Press,
United Press International, and Reuters for permission to
include in this series of books a number of dispatches originally distributed by those news services.

Book design by Stephanie Rhodes

Contents

Publisher's Note About the Series

It would take even an accomplished speed-reader, moving at full throttle, some three and a half solid hours a day to work his way through all the news The New York Times prints. The sad irony, of course, is that even such indefatigable devotion to life's carnival would scarcely assure a decent understanding of what it was really all about. For even the most dutiful reader might easily overlook an occasional long-range trend of importance, or perhaps some of the fragile, elusive relationships between events that sometimes turn out to be more significant than the events themselves.

This is why "The Great Contemporary Issues" was created—to help make sense out of some of the major forces and counterforces at large in today's world. The philosophical conviction behind the series is a simple one: that the past not only can illuminate the present but must. ("Continuity with the past," declared Oliver Wendell Holmes, "is a necessity, not a duty.") Each book in the series, therefore has as its subject some central issue of our time that needs to be viewed in the context of its antecedents if it is to be fully understood. By showing, through a substantial selection of contemporary accounts from The New York Times, the evolution of a subject and its significance, each book in the series offers a perspective that is available in no other way. For while most books on contemporary affairs specialize, for excellent reasons, in predigested facts and neatly drawn conclusions, the books in this series allow the reader to draw his own conclusions on the basis of the facts as they appeared at virtually the moment of their occurrence. This is not to argue that there is no place for events recollected in tranquility; it is simply to say that when fresh, raw truths are allowed to speak for themselves, some quite distinct values often emerge.

For this reason, most of the articles in "The Great Contemporary Issues" are reprinted in their entirety, even in those cases where portions are not central to a given book's theme. Editing has been done only rarely, and in all such cases it is clearly indicated. (Such an excision occasionally occurs, for example, in the case of a Presidential State of the Union Message, where only brief portions are germane to a particular volume, and in the case of some names, where for legal reasons or reasons of taste it is preferable not to republish specific identifications.) Similarly, typographical errors, where they occur, have been allowed to stand as originally printed.

"The Great Contemporary Issues" inevitably encompasses a substantial amount of history. In order to explore their subjects fully, some of the books go back a century or more. Yet their fundamental theme is not the past but the present. In this series the past is of significance insofar as it suggests how we got where we are today. These books, therefore, do not always treat a subject in a purely chronological way. Rather, their material is arranged to point up trends and interrelationships that the editors believe are more illuminating than a chronological listing would be.

"The Great Contemporary Issues" series will ultimately constitute an encyclopedic library of today's major issues. Long before editorial work on the first volume had even begun, some fifty specific titles had already been either scheduled for definite publication or listed as candidates. Since then, events have prompted the inclusion of a number of additional titles, and the editors are, moreover, alert not only for new issues as they emerge but also for issues whose development may call for the publication of sequel volumes. We will, of course, also welcome readers' suggestions for future topics.

Introduction

To understand contemporary party warfare, you need to know the historical roots of today's political loyalties. In national elections, the disposition of the great majority of voters is determined by a complex set of influences, some of which have antecedents that reach back over many decades. When he published *Midwest Politics* in 1966, the political scientist John H. Fenton reported that Republicans and Democrats in the Old Northwest diverged "along Civil War lines" a century after that conflict ended, and in the 1970's Abraham Lincoln and Franklin D. Roosevelt still cast their shadows over the polling places.

The era of the Civil War and Reconstruction affected twentieth-century political alignments in one particular respect; it divided party allegiances on a sectional basis. Decades later, the nation showed the same regional cleavages as it had in the disputes over slavery, notably in the strength of the Democrats in the "Solid South" and of Republicans in the Northern countryside. The exceptions are even more illuminating. In the South, pockets of Unionism during the Civil War persisted as enclaves of Republicanism far into the next century, and in the North Copperhead areas continued generations later to vote against the party of Abe Lincoln.

In the political contests of the post-Civil War era, all the obvious advantages lay with the Republicans. Leaders of the Grand Old Party claimed that their organization was nothing less than the party of the union, and for a generation Republican orators urged, "Vote the way you shot." The GOP could count on rural Protestant voters in the New England belt of migration, where abolitionism and temperance had been strongest, and on black voters, wedded to the party of the Great Emancipator. The Democrats, on the other hand, seemed vaguely disrespectable. The reformer Fred Howe recalled: "There was something unthinkable to me about being a Democrat — Democrats, Copperheads and atheists were persons whom one did not know socially. As a boy I did not play with their children." No Democrat would enter the White House with as much as 50 per cent of the vote between Franklin Pierce in 1852 and Franklin D. Roosevelt in 1932, eighty years later.

Yet for a time the Democrats put up a good fight. In 1880, after the last federal troops had been withdrawn from below the Mason-Dixon line, the Democrats swept every state in the former Confederacy, and this phenomenon of the Solid South continued in every election for the next forty years. By combining electoral votes in the monolithic South with their strength in border states, the Southern belt of migration in the Midwest, and among Irish Catholic immigrants in the great Northern cities, the Democrats were able to achieve an equilibrium with the Republicans in the 1870's and '80s. It even proved possible to break the Republican monopoly of the White House by electing Grover Cleveland in 1884, and re-electing him in 1892, though each time he had less than a majority of the vote.

The events of the 1890's shattered this equilibrium. There had been a good number of third parties like the Greenbackers in the post-Reconstruction era, but it was the emergence of the Populists in the 1890's that tore voters from their moorings. For a time it seemed that one of the major parties might yield to a radical farmer-labor party, especially after the Panic of 1893 caused widespread misery. Instead, the electorate took out its anger on the party in power, the Democrats, in the 1894 midterm elections. When McKinley rolled back the class and sectional challenge of William Jennings Bryan in 1896, it became even more clear that the upheavals of the 1890's would end not in a radical realignment but in an era of Republican supremacy. From 1894 to 1930 the

Democrats would win only three Congressional elections, and in some twenty northern and western states, the GOP was almost as certain of victory as the Democrats were in the South.

Only for one brief interval in this age of Republican predominance of 1894-1930 did the Democrats prevail. In 1910, a split in the Republican party over the issues of progressivism permitted the Democrats to gain control of the House and capture a number of governorships, including that of New Jersey, won by the president of Princeton, Woodrow Wilson. Two years later, one of the Republican factions launched a new organization, the Progressive Party, with the former President, Theodore Roosevelt, as its standard bearer. In 1912, the Democratic nominee, Woodrow Wilson, polled only 42 per cent of the ballots cast, but, with the Republicans divided, that earned him enough electoral votes to put him in the White House. Colonel Roosevelt finished second, and the official Republican candidate, President William Howard Taft, ran a pathetic third. (In a lively four-way race, the Socialist favorite, Eugene V. Debs, received nearly a million votes, a respectable showing.) By 1916, the Republicans had reunited, but Wilson, on a platform of peace and progressivism, squeaked through to a second term.

However, the Democratic interregnum proved short-lived. In 1920, partly because they blamed Wilson and the Democrats for failing to live up to the implied pledge to keep the country out of World War I, the voters returned the Republicans to power in an emphatic fashion. Not since James Monroe's virtually uncontested victory in 1820, exactly a century before, had any candidate won by so huge a margin in the Electoral College as did Warren Harding. He also gained the biggest share of the popular vote in the history of party competition. So badly defeated was the Democratic nominee, James Cox, that he lost Manhattan, all but one county in New England, and every county on the Pacific Coast. Through the remainder of the "prosperity decade," Republican supremacy was reaffirmed in the Coolidge landslide of 1924, and Herbert Hoover's triumph in the 1928 election which saw the Democratic choice, Alfred E. Smith, reduced to only eight states in the Electoral College.

This era of Republican predominance came to an abrupt halt with the onset of the Great Depression, which began just seven months after Hoover took office with the Wall Street crash of 1929. When Hoover sought a second term in 1932, he went down to the worst defeat ever suffered by a Republican candidate in a two-party race. The Democratic nominee, Franklin Delano Roosevelt, captured 42 of the 48 states, including every state south and west of Pennsylvania. The Republican party has never fully recovered from that debacle; it continues to be perceived as the party of hard times. From 1932 to the present, the GOP has won control of the House only twice. Throughout that period, the Democrats have been America's majority party.

The success of the Democratic party owed as much to Franklin Roosevelt's skill in forging a new coalition as it did to the trauma of the Great Depression. If section was the hallmark of the era of Republican supremacy, social stratification was the distinguishing feature of the period of Democratic predominance. In 1936, when Roosevelt captured every state but Maine and Vermont, he received 76 per cent of lower income ballots, only 42 per cent of the upper income share of the two-party vote. This transit of lower-income groups to the Democrats took place largely in the great cities, especially in "ethnic" neighborhoods. In 1936, the President rolled up ratios of better than 2-1 in Detroit, 3-1 in San Francisco and New York City (which gave him a stunning 1,367,000 plurality), and 4-1 in Milwaukee. The most notable swing of lower-income groups in the big cities came among black voters, who in 1936 transferred their loyalties from the party of Lincoln to the party of FDR, where they have largely remained ever since. This "Roosevelt coalition" helped win its progenitor two more terms in office, and accounted for the election of Harry Truman in 1948, when the nearly 80 per cent of workers voting Democratic was a higher proportion than that ever recorded by left-wing parties in Europe.

However, though the Democrats remained the majority party after Roosevelt's death, their position deteriorated. In 1948 Truman lost four southern states to a Dixiecrat ticket, and in no election since 1944 has the South been "Solid" for the Democrats. In 1952, and again in 1956, Dwight D. Eisenhower showed that when

Republicans had an immensely popular candidate, they could overcome the advantage the Democrats enjoyed in having many more Americans identify with their party than with the GOP. Still, the fact that Eisenhower's triumphs resulted from his personal allure rather than his party identification was demonstrated when in each subsequent Congressional election during his tenure, the Democrats prevailed.

From 1960 to the present, the cadences of politics have been harder to discern, except that national elections have oscillated rhythmically between exceptionally close contests and runaways. In 1960, John F. Kennedy restored the White House to the Democrats but by the narrowest margin in this century. Four years later, when the Republicans chose a factional leader, they lost overwhelmingly. In 1968, the two sides approached an equilibrium again, but this time the Republicans were the victors. However, in 1972, when the Democrats took a turn at selecting a factional leader, they were routed. In 1976, with a candidate nearer to the center of the party, they were successful, but in another of those every-other-election close affairs. The increasing percentage of independents, voters not allied with either party, contributed to the political instability of this period. Yet even in these years of fluctuating majorities, political competition took place within a historical matrix. Northern Protestant small towns swore fealty to the Republicans in the 1970's as they had in the 1870's, and in 1976 political analysts saw in Jimmy Carter's winning combination — the South plus lower income voters in urban districts — the lineaments of the FDR coalition.

The reader who wants to trace out the historical tapestry of American politics will find no better source than the pages of *The New York Times*. This well-edited sampler from the columns of America's premier newspaper permits us to follow the course of party warfare from the era of the titanic struggle over slavery and sectionalism to the Carter presidency, and the vivid dispatches made available here give a sense of immediacy to more than a century of political struggle.

WILLIAM E. LEUCHTENBURG

CHAPTER 1

The Republican Age
1860-1929

Warren G. Harding and Calvin Coolidge, symbols of an
era of Republican dominance.

Courtesy Compix

Drift of the Republican Party.

We have more than once stated our belief, since the last Presidential election, that the Republican Party could no longer stand exclusively upon the platform which carried it through that canvass. The cardinal feature of their platform then was, resistance, by Congressional legislation, to the extension of Slavery into free territory of the United States. This was the primary, prominent, and controlling object for which the party was organized. The repeal of the Missouri Compromise, and the Pro-Slavery invasion of Kansas had made such resistance necessary, and the organization, therefore, had its basis and its strength in an existing necessity of the times. The great mass of the people of the Free States were opposed to such extension of Slavery, and were ready to take any legitimate action necessary to prevent it. The strength of this principle, and the conviction of imminent danger forced upon the public mind, gave the Republican Party the immense vote which it received in 1856.

This issue has disappeared. Kansas is no longer in jeopardy—it has been secured to Freedom. The principle of Congressional legislation for the exclusion of Slavery from the territories, has been annulled by a decision of the Supreme Court, and, even if it had not, there is no territory so exposed to the danger as to demand its exercise. The principle of Popular Sovereignty, moreover, however it may be questioned in form, has been established in fact, and will hereafter settle all disputes that may arise concerning Slavery in new territories of the United States. The controversy upon this point is over ; and the contest between the Free and the Slave States of the Union for supremacy in the Federal Councils has been decided, as Senator SEWARD declared two years ago, in favor of the North.

The Republicans, therefore, must have a modified platform for the struggle of 1860. And it is becoming a matter of considerable interest to know what will be its leading features. Will Slavery be the cardinal topic on which it will rest ? And what will be the particular phase of Slavery which will be presented for the public judgment ? What will the Republican Party propose *to do* in regard to Slavery, as the reason why they should be placed in power ?

It is alleged by its opponents that the Republican Party is becoming rapidly *Abolitionized ;*—that instead of limiting its aims to preventing the extension of Slavery, it is preparing to wage open war on Slavery itself in the Southern States ;—that it is thus gradually throwing aside its national character, and becoming openly a sectional, Anti-Slavery, Abolition party. Its leading organs deny the charge in words,—but the very terms of the denial involve a substantial admission of its truth.

The *Tribune*, for example, which claims and is acknowledged to be a Republican journal, holds the following language in its issue of yesterday:

"You know that we Anti-Slavery men are *not ' sectional'* in our purposes and aspirations—that, on the contrary, we are seeking to *encourage and inspire the South to cast off the burden* which has caused her to lag so far behind the North in every element of growth and greatness—know that if the South had thrown off Slavery when New-York did, her population, wealth, intelligence, would have been to-day at least double what they are. You know that mistaken Old JOHN BROWN, and his brave sons with him at Harper's Ferry, laid down their lives *not to injure but benefit the South* —that they and their comrades, dead, or about to be killed, *were the least sectional of human beings.* They sacrificed their all in an unlawful but *heroic* effort to benefit those whom they had never seen."

The *Tribune* thus declares that *an armed invasion of Southern States for the purpose of liberating their slaves, is not a sectional movement*;—that men who engage in it cannot be called sectional men ;—and by necessary inference, that a political party which proclaims that to be its purpose, is not a *sectional* party. After such a definition of terms as that, of what possible use is a disclaimer of " sectionality,"—or a proclamation that the party is purely and thoroughly *national* in its motives and its plans? JOHN BROWN and his companions, according to the *Tribune*, were the " least sectional" of human beings." If the Republican Party, therefore, were to imitate the conduct and follow the example of JOHN BROWN, it would also be the " least sectional" of political parties, according to the same authority.

The sophistry of all this scarcely needs to be pointed out. The *Tribune* considers that only sectional which aims at the advantage of one section or the injury of another ; and as the abolition of Slavery would be, in its judgment, a blessing to both sections, Abolitionism itself cannot be considered sectional.

But the important point for the public is, whether the Republican Party accepts this interpretation,—whether it is content to be only as " sectional" as JOHN BROWN, and whether it proposes to plant itself upon the platform thus occupied by the *Tribune*. We need scarcely say that we do not believe it does :— certainly not, unless it has entirely changed its character since 1856, and is prepared to put itself under new leaders, and go into the Presidential canvass under an entirely different flag. But the *drift*, it must be confessed, is distinctly in that direction. The tendency of the party, as indicated by the language of its leading organs, has been towards a much more open and pronounced Abolitionism than was thought of or tolerated during the last campaign. The Republicans will find it necessary before long to define their position on this subject somewhat more distinctly than has been done hitherto : and it may not be amiss for their prominent men to give it some little attention meantime. The *Tribune's* language is certainly not calculated to increase public confidence in the nationality of the party which it represents.

December 10, 1859

BALTIMORE UNION CONVENTION.

A PLATFORM ADOPTED.

Hon. John Bell, of Tennessee, Nominated for President.

Hon. Edward Everett, of Massachusetts, for Vice-President.

Entire Harmony and Unbounded Enthusiasm.

Special Dispatch to the New-York Times.

BALTIMORE, Thursday, May 10.

Before the Convention assembled this morning circulars and handbills were liberally circulated through the Hall, setting forth the availability of Gen. HOUSTON for the Presidency, with EDWARD EVERETT for Vice-President. Though the current had, during the night, set strongly against HOUSTON, his supporters had been very busy. It was understood that a damaging break had been made against HOUSTON in the New-York delegation, and that BELL would receive ten to fifteen votes from that State.

All the States but Michigan, New-Hampshire, California, Oregon and Wisconsin responded in the Convention this morning at roll-call.

JOSEPH R. INGERSOLL, of Pennsylvania, from the Business Committee, reported the following Platform :

Whereas, Experience has demonstrated that Platforms adopted by the partisan Conventions of the country have had the effect to mislead and deceive the people, and at the same time to widen the political divisions of the country, by the creation and encouragement of geographical and sectional parties' therefore,

Resolved, That it is both the part of patriotism and of duty to recognize no political principles other than the Constitution of the country, the Union of the States, and the enforcement of the laws ; and, as the representatives of the Constitutional Union men of the country, in National Convention assembled, we here pledge ourselves to maintain, protect and defend, separately and unitedly, these great principles of public liberty and national safety, against all enemies at home and abroad ; believing thereby that peace may at once be restored to the country, the just rights of the people and of the States be established, and the Government again placed in that condition of justice, fraternity, and equality which, under the example and Constitution of our fathers, has solemnly bound every citizen of the United States to maintain a more perfect union, establish justice, and secure domestic tranquillity ; provide for the common defence ; promote the general welfare, and, secure the blessings of liberty to ourselves and our posterity.

The platform was adopted without dissent, amid great cheering.

After much debate, each State was allowed to cast the number of its electoral vote ; every delegate to vote for himself.

The Convention then proceeded to ballot for a Candidate for the Presidency.

The first ballot indicated beyond question that Hon. JOHN BELL was the preference of a majority of the Convention ; an indication confirmed by the second ballot when Mr. BELL had 138 votes, Gen. HOUSTON 69, and the remainder scattering. One by one the delegations from various States commenced changing their votes to BELL, and finally, speaking for a large majority of the New-York delegation, Mr. ERASTUS BROOKS proposed that the nomination of Mr. BELL be made unanimous.

The motion was carried with exalted enthusiasm, and Mr. BELL was declared to be the candidate.

The first ballot for Vice-President, resulted in the selection of Hon. EDWARD EVERETT.

The hidden break-down of the Houston interest, and the nomination of BELL, is a sore thing to many of the New York Delegates. Nearly a dozen of them refused to make the choice unanimous. It is believed to be the only sore spot in the Convention. The Southern Delegates generally are much elated, and say that he will carry Tennessee, Maryland and North Carolina any way, and, with two Democrats running, a majority of the Southern States. The

Democratic Party in the South is said to be in a more broken condition than in the North. That the election will be carried into the House is confidently predicted. The proceedings attending the nomination of EVERETT were a love feast, which healed all differences. The unmixed Whig character of the ticket does not escape remark. An occasional Democrat suspects that this is little less than a Whig Convention. Nevertheless it is the general belief in and out of the Convention that it is the strongest that could have been made. The Kentucky Delegates express great satisfaction, as do the supporters of Gen. Houston generally, with the election of Mr. EVERETT. A dispatch from New-Orleans, received in the Convention, pledges Louisiana for the ticket.

The New-England delegates are much elated. The Editor of the Boston *Courier* at once telegraphed to have the ticket run up at the head of its columns.

There is no doubt that, if he would have consented Mr. CRITTENDEN would have been nominated, instead of Mr. BELL.

Gen. HOUSTON will remain the candidate in Texas.

It is believed that there will be no third Electoral Ticket run in New-York, but that the Union men of that State will be left to decide between the Democratic and Republican tickets.

Gov. HUNT, in declining the nomination for Vice-President, stated that he would allow nothing to interfere with his purpose to act independently and effectually in his State. The remark was regarded as significant.

The speeches of Maj. HENRY, of Tennessee, and Mr. HILLARD, of Massachusetts, were efforts of great eloquence.   B.

May 11, 1860

FROM CHICAGO.

THE REPUBLICAN TICKET FOR 1860.

Abram Lincoln, of Illinois, Nominated for President.

The Late Senatorial Contest in Illinois to be Re-Fought on a Wider Field.

Hannibal Hamlin, of Maine, the Candidate for Vice-President.

Disappointment of the Friends of Mr. Seward.

INTENSE EXCITEMENT AND ENTHUSIASM

Special Dispatch to the New York Times.
Chicago, Friday, May 18.

The work of the Convention is ended. The youngster who, with ragged trousers, used barefoot to drive his father's oxen and spend his days in splitting rails, has risen to high eminence, and Abram Lincoln, of Illinois, is declared its candidate for President by the National Republican Party.

This result was effected by the change of votes in the Pennsylvania, New Jersey, Vermont, and Massachusetts Delegations.

Mr. Seward's friends assert indignantly, and with a great deal of feeling, that they were grossly deceived and betrayed. The recusants endeavored to mollify New York by offering her the Vice-Presidency, and agreeing to support any man she might name, but they declined the position, though they remain firm in the ranks, having moved to make Lincoln's nomination unanimous. Mr. Seward's friends feel greatly chagrined and disappointed.

Western pride is gratified by this nomination, which plainly indicates the departure of political supremacy from the Atlantic States.

The prominent candidates for Vice-Presidency were Messrs. Hickman, Banks, Clay and Reeder. Pennsylvania desired Hickman. New York, in order to resent the conduct of Pennsylvania, Massachusetts and Kentucky, favored Mr. Hamlin, of Maine; and on the second ballot, cast her whole strength for him, and it was owing to this, and the desire to conciliate New York, that his nomination was so promptly secured.

Immense enthusiasm exists, and everything here would seem to indicate a spirited and successful canvass. The city is alive with processions, meetings, music and noisy demonstrations. One hundred guns were fired this evening.

The Convention was the most enthusiastic ever known in the country, and if one were to judge from appearances here, the ticket will sweep the country.

Great inquiry has been made this afternoon into the history of Mr. Lincoln. The only evidence that he has a history as yet discovered, is that he had a stump canvass with Mr. Douglas, in which he was beaten. He is not very strong at the West, but is unassailable in his private character.

Many of the delegates went home this evening by the 9 o'clock train. Others leave in the morning.

A grand excursion is planned to Rock Island and Davenport, and another to Milwaukee and Madison, and still another over the Illinois Central, over the prairies. These will detain a great many of the delegates and the editorial fraternity.

The Wigwam is as full as ever—filled now by thousands of original Lincoln men, who they "always knew" would be nominated, and who first suggested his name, who are shouting themselves hoarse over the nomination. "What was it Webster said when Taylor was nominated?" ask the opponents of Lincoln. "What was the result of the election?" retorted Lincoln's friends.

Thirty-three guns were fired from the top of the Tremont House.

The dinner referred to in Tuesday evening's dispatch was a private one, and I regret that inaccurate reading of it should have misrepresented the position of the delegation as regards Mr. Greeley. His right to act as he deemed best politically, was not denied, and consequently there was no defense of his career needed.

Massachusetts delegates, with their brass band, are parading the streets, calling at the various headquarters of the other delegations, serenading and bidding them farewell. "Hurrah for Lincoln and Hamlin—Illinois and Maine!" is the universal shout, and sympathy for the bottom dog is the all-pervading sentiment.

The "Wide-Awakes," numbering about two thousand men, accompanied by thousands of citizens, have a grand torch-light procession. The German Republican Club has another. The office of the *Press and Tribune* is brilliantly illuminated, and has a large transparency over the door, saying, "For President, Honest Old Abe." A bonfire thirty feet in circumference burns in front of the Tremont House, and illumines the city for miles around. The city is one blaze of illumination. Hotels, stores and private residences, shining with hundreds of patriotic dips. Enough.

HOWARD.

May 19, 1860

The Charleston Convention.

The Convention made progress yesterday. It took, indeed, a long stride towards the performance of the business which called it together. It adopted a PLATFORM, and thus set forth the basis on which it proposes to conduct the Presidential Canvass. All that remains is the nomination of a candidate : and even that has been greatly facilitated by the action already taken.

The Northern wing of the Democratic party has vindicated its numerical and its   strength in the adoption of a Platform. The resolutions reported by the majority of the Committee have been rejected—and those of the minority adopted in their stead. The former embodied the position held by the Pro-Slavery ultraists, that slaves are property by the Federal Constitution—that they may be taken into the territories, and must be protected there by the Federal authority, and that it is only when they form a State Constitution and are admitted into the Union, that the settlers of a territory have a right to determine whether Slavery shall or shall not exist within its limits. This doctrine was repudiated by the Convention ;—and the platform adopted in its stead was simply the re-affirmation of the Cincinnati Platform, with the additional declaration that " *the Democratic Party will abide by the decision of the Supreme Court of the United States over the institution of Slavery within the Territories.*" This is all that is to be said upon that subject.

It is further declared that we "ought to acquire Cuba, on such terms as shall be honorable to ourselves and just to Spain,"—and that "enactments of State Legislatures to defeat the faithful execution of the Fugitive Slave law, are hostile in character, subversive of the Constitution, and revolutionary in their effect." The first is a decided softening of the Ostend manifesto ; and the last position will scarcely be controverted in theory, whatever may be his practice, by WENDELL PHILLIPS himself.

This is very strong ground for the Democratic Party throughout the Northern States. It leaves but one question open for debate, and that is—*What is* the decision of the Supreme Court on Slavery in the Territories? It can be very plausibly contended that the

Court has given no "decision" whatever upon that subject—that its only decision in the Dred Scott case was, that Scott, not being a citizen of the United States, could not appeal from the decision in the court below; and that this plank, therefore, amounts to just nothing at all. It certainly offers no very salient or exposed points to the enemy, and will be universally hailed by the Democrats of the North, as precisely the Platform needed for the canvass.

How its adoption will affect the nomination is not yet quite clear. On the face of it, it seems to render DOUGLAS certain to be the candidate. Four or five States have apparently seceded. If they do not return, DOUGLAS will doubtless command the votes of two-thirds of the remaining delegates, and thus secure the nomination. If the seceding States should bolt and run a candidate of their own, they may withdraw just so many votes from DOUGLAS; but the very fact of their secession will strengthen him immensely in the North, and may possibly give him Northern States enough to offset their defection. On the other hand, it is not impossible that the seceders may be coaxed back,—either into the Convention, or into the party during the canvass,—by the nomination of a Southern man like GUTHRIE or ORR; and DOUGLAS may be sacrificed by the triumphant North as a peace-offering to the Southern wing. To-day's proceedings in Convention will probably determine this point.

Thus far, the action at Charleston is not calculated to encourage overweening confidence on the part of the Republicans. They will not get the square fight on principle for which they have been hoping, and which the earlier action of the Convention encouraged them to expect. They will have to contend with a dodging foe.

May 1, 1860

PRESIDENTIAL.

The Proceedings of the Disunited Democracy.

TWO TICKETS NOMINATED.

Special Dispatch to the New-York Times.
BALTIMORE, Sunday, June 24.
We have assurances from persons who ought to know that both BRECKINRIDGE and LANE will accept their nominations by the Convention of seceders.

It is the game of the Southern wing to defeat an election by the people and carry it into Congress, where they think they are reasonably certain of electing BRECKINRIDGE. The Douglas men here speak openly of preferring Lincoln's election to such a result.

YANCEY and other extremists are delighted at the prospect. They say that they can either elect BRECKINRIDGE in the House and thus perpetuate their control over the Government, or else elect LINCOLN, which will give them an opportunity to rally the South in favor of dissolution.

The city is entirely deserted.   H.

Dispatch to the Associated Press.
BALTIMORE, Sunday, June 24.
The nominations of both the Democratic and the Seceders Conventions, were received well here by their respective friends, but all the outside enthusiasm is for DOUGLAS. There was much excitement last night about the ballots. The nomination of the Seceding Convention was tendered to Mr. GUTHRIE's friends, as well as to Mr. HUNTER's, but both candidates declined. It is understood that Mr. BRECKINRIDGE will accept.

A challenge has been sent by A. SMITH, of California, to Mr. NESBITT, of Illinois, who was the Delegate who declared in the Convention, during Mr. SMITH's offensive remarks, that if Mr. CUSHING, the President, would not protect the members, they would protect themselves.

A large number of persons went to Washington to-day, both the friends of BRECKINRIDGE and DOUGLAS. Most of the New-York delegation return to-night.

June 25, 1860

THE PRESIDENTIAL ELECTION.

Astounding Triumph of Republicanism.

The North Rising in Indignation at the Menaces of the South.

Abraham Lincoln Probably Elected President by a Majority of the Entire Popular Vote.

The canvass for the Presidency of the United States terminated last evening, in all the States of the Union, under the revised regulation of Congress passed in 1845, and the result, by the vote of New-York, is placed beyond question at once. It elects ABRAHAM LINCOLN of Illinois, President, and HANNIBAL HAMLIN of Maine, Vice-President of the United States, for four years, from the 4th March next, directly by the People: These Republican Candidates having a clear majority of the 303 Electorial votes of the 33 States, over all three of the opposing tickets. They receive, including Mr. LINCOLN's own State, from which the returns have not yet come, in the

New-England States	41
New-York	35
Pennsylvania	27
New-Jersey	7
And the Northwest	61
Total Electoral for LINCOLN	171

Being 19 over the required majority, without wasting the returns from the two Pacific States of Oregon and California.

The election, so far as the City and State of New-York are concerned, will probably stand, hereafter as one of the most remarkable in the political contests of the country; marked, as it is, by far the heaviest popular vote ever cast in the City, and by the sweeping, and almost uniform, Republican majorities in the country.

The State of Pennsylvania, which virtually decided her preference in October, has again thrown an overwhelming majority for the Republican candidates. And New-Jersey, after a sharp contest has, as usual in nearly all the Presidential elections, taken her place on the same side. The New-England majorities run up by tens of thousands.

The Congressional elections which took place yesterday in this State have probably confirmed the probability of an Anti-Republican preponderance in the next House of Representatives, by displacing several of the present Republican members.

The new House of Assembly for New-York will, as usual, be largely Republican.

Of the reëlection of Gov. MORGAN there is little or no question. By the scattering vote thrown for Mr. BRADY in this City, the plurality of Mr. KELLY over Gov. MORGAN is partially reduced; while the heavy Republican majority in the country insures Gov. MORGAN's success.

The rival Presidential candidates against Mr. LINCOLN have probably divided the Southern vote as follows:

FOR MR. BELL.			
Virginia	15	Tennessee	12
Kentucky	12		
FOR MR. BRECKINRIDGE.			
South Carolina	8	Florida	3
North Carolina	10	Mississippi	7
Georgia	10	Texas	4
Alabama	9	Arkansas	4
DOUBTFUL.			
Missouri	9	Delaware	3
Louisiana	6	Maryland	8

November 7, 1860

The Democrats and the Copperheads.

It is said, on apparently good authority, that at least *seventy thousand* Democrats in Pennsylvania voted for Gov. CURTIN at the recent election. In Ohio the number of Democrats who gave their suffrages to JOHN BROUGH was still larger in proportion. Gov. CURTIN was a Republican in his antecedents, JOHN BROUGH a Democrat; but this difference was not thought of in the two canvasses. It was enough that they were both staunch friends of the war, and the regular Union candidates.

The great question here in New-York is— How many of the old Democrats will support the Union ticket? Will there be the same measure of independence of party exhibited here by them as has been so decisively shown in the other two great States? If so, Copperheadism will get an unheard-of smiting in New-York next Tuesday.

New-York gave Mr. LINCOLN, at the Presidential election, a majority of about forty thousand. But an insignificant fraction of those who then voted for him—we believe not one thousand all told—are now found among the opponents of the Administration. Large numbers of them, it is true, have been drawn off to the war, and are practically disfranchised for the time; but the Democrats have lost by the same means in nearly equal proportion. Therefore, an immense Union majority is assured, if there is anything like the same accession to the Union party from the Democratic ranks as has been realized in the other States.

Why should there not be such accessions? Neither in Pennsylvania nor in Ohio have so many prominent leaders of the old Democratic party gone over to the support of the Administration. It would be impossible to name men who, three years ago, had the confidence of the Democratic party of this State to a greater extent than Dickinson, and Dix, and Brady, and Van Buren, and Porter, and Tremain, and Cochrane, and Sickles; and yet these all, as well as many others of perhaps less note, are now found among the staunchest adherents of the Administration. If the old chiefs of the party have thus thrown off their old party trammels, why should not the same influences operate upon the rank and file? If in the other States the rank and file have so largely rallied to the support of the old flag, with comparatively little encouragement upon the part of the old leaders, why should there be any greater holding back here where that encouragement is so very decided?

Besides, the New York Democracy has a peculiar stimulus in this direction, which did not exist in the other States. We mean the mischief and shame of a Copperhead Administration. Gov. Seymour has here practically demonstrated in the eyes of all the people the evil of opposition to the Government in a great national emergency like the present. He has written them out in letters of flame and blood that have horrified every right-minded man from one extremity of the State to the other. The disgrace of it does not attach to him simply; it is necessarily shared also by the Democratic party which put him in power, and which he still professes to represent. The party in Pennsylvania and Ohio, not having been in power, has been subjected to no such brand of faithlessness. Honest Democrats there had comparatively nothing to resent. They occupied much the same position in respect to their candidates that honest Democrats did the last year, when they trusted to the fair promises of Horatio Seymour in reference to the future, without any practical experience of him to make it manifest that he would not make good these promises. We say that with the practical experiences of the past year, the Democrats of this State have a vastly stronger reason to break away from their party than their brethren had in the other States. We are confident that this reason will operate, and that tens of thousands who honestly gave their votes to Horatio Seymour last year, in the belief that he would in good faith do all in his power to promote the vigorous and successful prosecution of the war, will now, with the spirit that becomes undeceived men, repudiate him and his works.

Many well-meaning Democrats cling to the Copperheads, in the vain imagination that they are thus keeping true to their old party organization, and that they are opposing the Republican party of other days. Nothing could be more erroneous. Neither of the old parties exist. The events of the last two years have completely destroyed their identity—and what is more, have completely destroyed the very objects of their former being. The Charleston platform and the Chicago platform are both as totally obsolete, as utterly irrelevant to the present order of things as the Twelve Tables of Rome. The most salient distinction between the two was that the one established Slavery in the territories, while the other prevented Slavery in the territories; and yet there is no man now so mad as to imagine that the time can possibly ever return when that will be a a practical question. Slavery, not only in the territories, but everywhere else, has had its day. The war, by its own inevitable operations, has destroyed it beyond all possibility of recovery. And in like manner the war has broken up all the old issues upon which the parties lived and struggled. It has brought an absolutely new order of things; and one which forces all considerate men, whether they like it or not, into new positions. The sole question now is, *whether the Government, which is struggling against a rebellion which seeks its life, shall be supported, or not?* Those who are for supporting it have, in consistency, no alternative but to support the war, and the constituted authorities which conduct the war. All support which falls short of this, however rightly inclined, is no support at all. Just as a prop, which falls short an inch, however correct its leaning, is no prop at all. There are various degrees of defection; but any defection whatever, in a crisis like this, is a crime. The man who does not come square, plump, up to the maintenance of the war, by which alone the country can be saved, however patriotic he may be in spirit, is no patriot in fact; and however Democratic in sentiment he may have once been, now assumes the name of Democrat but to disgrace it. Truer words were never uttered than by that great Democratic leader, Stephen A. Douglas:

"Patriotism emanates from the heart, fills the soul, infuses itself into the whole man, and speaks and acts the same language. A friend of his country in war will feel, speak and act for his country, revere his country's cause, and hate his country's enemies. America wants no friend, acknowledges the fidelity of no citizen, who, after war is declared, condemns the justice of her cause, and sympathizes with the enemy. All such are traitors in their hearts."

October 30, 1863

PRESIDENTIAL.

Lincoln & Johnson.

THE LOYAL PLATFORM.

Slavery Must Perish by the Constitution.

Emancipation, the Monroe Doctrine, Economy and the Pacific Railroad.

THE PLATFORM.

Mr. Raymond, of New-York, from the Committee on Resolutions, reported the following resolutions:

Resolved, That it is the highest duty of every American citizen to maintain against all their enemies the integrity of the Union, and the paramount authority of the Constitution and laws of the United States, and that laying aside all differences and political opinions, we pledge ourselves as Union men, animated by a common sentiment, and aiming at a common object, to do everything in our power to aid the Government in quelling by force of arms the rebellion now raging against its authority, and in bringing to the punishment due to their crimes the rebels and traitors arrayed against it. [Prolonged applause.]

Resolved, That we approve the determination of the Government of the United States not to compromise with rebels or to offer any terms of peace except such as may be based upon an "unconditional surrender" of their hostility and a return to their just allegiance to the Constitution and laws of the United States; and that we call upon the Government to maintain this position and to prosecute the war with the utmost possible vigor to the complete suppression of the rebellion, in full reliance upon the self-sacrifices, the patriotism, the heroic valor and the undying devotion of the American people to their country and its free institutions. [Applause.]

Resolved, That as Slavery was the cause, and now constitutes the strength, of this rebellion, and as it must be always and everywhere hostile to the principles of Republican Government, justice and the national safety demand its utter and complete extirpation from the soil of the Republic; [applause,] and that we uphold and maintain the acts and proclamations by which the Government, in its own defence, has aimed a death-blow at this gigantic evil. We are in favor, furthermore, of such an amendment to the Constitution, to be made by the people in conformity with its provisions, as shall terminate and forever prohibit the existence of Slavery within the limits or the jurisdiction of the United States. [Applause.]

Resolved, That the thanks of the American people are due to the soldiers and sailors of the army and the navy, [applause,] who have periled their lives in defence of their country and in vindication of the honor of the flag; that the nation owes to them some permanent recognition of their patriotism and their valor, and ample and permanent provision for those of their survivors who have received disabling and honorable wounds in the service of the country; and that the memories of those who have fallen in its defence shall be held in grateful and everlasting remembrance. [Loud applause.]

Resolved, That we approve and applaud the practical wisdom, the unselfish patriotism and unswerving fidelity to the Constitution and the principles of American liberty with which Abraham Lincoln has discharged, under circumstances of unparalleled difficulty, the great duties and responsibilities of the Presidential office; that we approve and indorse, as demanded by the emergency and essential to the preservation of the nation, and as within the Constitution, the measures and acts which he has adopted to defend the nation against its open and secret foes; that we approve especially the proclamation of emancipation and the employment as Union soldiers of men heretofore held in slavery; [applause,] and that we have full confidence in his determination to carry these and all other constitutional measures essential to the salvation of the country into full and complete effect.

Resolved, That we deem it essential to the general welfare that harmony should prevail in the national councils, and we regard as worthy of public confidence and official trust those only who cordially indorse the principles proclaimed in these resolutions and which should characterize the administration of the Government. [Applause.]

Resolved, That the Government owes to all men employed in its armies, without regard to distinction of color, the full protection of the laws of war, [applause,] and that any violations of these laws, or of the usages of civilized nations in the time of war, by the rebels now in arms, should be made the subject of full and prompt redress. [Prolonged applause.]

Resolved, That the foreign immigration which in the past has added so much to the wealth and development of resources and increase of power to this nation—the asylum of the oppressed of all nations—should be fostered and encouraged by a liberal and just policy.

Resolved, That we are in favor of the speedy construction of the railroad to the Pacific.

Resolved, That the national faith pledged for the redemption of the public debt must be kept inviolate, and that for this purpose we recommend economy and rigid responsibility in the public expenditures, and a vigorous and just system of taxation; that it is the duty of every loyal State to sustain the credit and promote the use of the national currency.

Resolved, That we approve the position taken by the Government that the people of the United States can never regard with indifference the attempt of any Euro-

5

pean Power to overthrow by force or to supplant by fraud, the institutions of any Republican Government on the Western Continent; [prolonged applause;] and that they will view with extreme jealousy, as menacing to the peace and independence of this our country, the efforts of any such Power to obtain new footholds for Monarchical Governments, sustained by a foreign military force in near proximity to the United States. [Long-continued applause.]

The reading of the resolution elicited the wildest outbursts of enthusiasm, especially the emancipation and Anti-Slavery sentiments enunciated.

The mention of the name of ABRAHAM LINCOLN was received with tremendous cheering, the whole house rising and waving hats and handkerchiefs.

The resolution indorsing the Monroe doctrine was also received with great applause.

On motion of Mr. BUSHNELL, of Connecticut, the resolutions were adopted by acclamation.

THE NOMINATIONS.

Mr. DELANO, of Ohio—I move that this convention now proceed to the nomination of candidates for President and Vice President of the United States.

The Chairman stated the motion.

Mr. CAMERON—I move the following as a substitute for the motion of the gentleman from Ohio.

The Chairman directed the Secretary to read the resolution.

Resolved, That ABRAHAM LINCOLN, of Illinois, be declared the choice of the Union party for President, [applause,] and HANNIBAL HAMLIN, of Maine, be the candidate for Vice President of the same party.

Cries of "No, no."

A VOICE—Divide the resolution.

Mr. CRESWELL, of Maryland—I call for a division.

Mr. STONE, of Iowa—I ask if I can make an amendment to that resolution.

The Chairman said the resolution of Mr. CAMERON was now the question before the convention.

Mr. STONE—I move to lay it on the table. Carried.

Mr. STONE—I now move that ABRAHAM LINCOLN, of Illinois, be the unanimous nominee of the convention.

Cries of "Question" and great confusion.

The CHAIRMAN—Will the gentleman listen for one moment. The gentleman from Iowa moved that a resolution offered by the gentleman from Pennsylvania (CAMERON) be laid on the table. That has been carried. The Chair then recognized Mr. COOK, of Illinois, as having the floor.

Mr. STEVENS, of Pennsylvania—I called for the vote by States before the vote was declared to the House.

Mr. STONE, of Iowa, claimed the floor.

Mr. STEVENS—I have not yielded the floor.

The CHAIRMAN—Does the gentleman from Pennsylvania insist upon a call of the States, upon the motion to lay on the table the resolution of Mr. CAMERON?

MANY VOICES—State the question.

The CHAIR—The gentleman from Iowa moved to lay upon the table the substitute offered by Gen. CAMERON, of Pennsylvania, and Mr. STEVENS informs the Chair that before that motion was put to the convention he moved a call of the States under the rules. Before the announcement of a vote, a delegate has a right to move a call by States, that being so the convention will now come to the question of laying on the table the substitute offered by Mr. CAMERON. Upon that the States were ordered to be called.

Mr. CRESSWELL, of Maryland—I call for a division of the question.

Mr. GOLDSBOROUGH, of Maryland, also called for a division.

The CHAIRMAN—The question is shall the resolution offered by Gen. CAMERON as a substitute be laid upon the table. The Secretary will proceed with the call.

Mr. BRECKINRIDGE—I wish to make a motion concerning the whole of this subject, and I hope the house will hear me for one moment. I want to modify it so as to lay the resolution on the table for the purpose of declaring ABRAHAM LINCOLN the nominee by acclamation.

Mr. STEVENSON, of Indiana—I desire to know what has become of the vote to lay, the substitute of Mr. CAMERON on the table.

The CHAIRMAN—That is now before the convention. The Secretary will call the roll of the States for the purpose of knowing whether it will be laid upon the table.

Mr. LANE, of Kansas—I appeal to the gentleman from Pennsylvania, with the consent of the convention, to withdraw his resolution. It places us in a very awkward predicament. I hope Gen. CAMERON, consulting the best wishes of the country, will withdraw his resolution. Let us vote upon the motion put by the gentleman from Iowa.

Mr. STONE, of Iowa—Hurrah for LINCOLN.

Mr. CAMERON—To save all this trouble to gentlemen who seem to wish to show their hands here I will withdraw it. [Applause.]

The CHAIRMAN—Mr. COOK, of Illinois, has the floor.

Mr. CAMERON, of Pennsylvania—I will withdraw it, or amend by moving that this convention nominate by acclamation ABRAHAM LINCOLN for a second term.

Mr. STONE, of Iowa—The gentleman is cheating me out of my motion; I object.

Laughter—Cries of "order," "order," "question," "question."

Mr. LANE, of Kansas—Hurrah for STONE.

The CHAIRMAN—Mr. CAMERON's motion to amend is not in order. It must be an absolute withdrawal, or none at all. Does he withdraw his resolution.

Mr. CAMERON—I will modify my resolution to make it "nominate ABRAHAM LINCOLN by acclamation."

Mr. STONE, of Iowa—That won't do. You must withdraw.

The CHAIRMAN—The gentleman from Pennsylvania has not answered the question of the Chair. Has the resolution been withdrawn or not?

Mr. CAMERON—I want to modify.

The CHAIRMAN—That is not a definite answer, and cannot be recognized as such by the Chair. The question before the convention is upon the resolution offered by Mr. CAMERON. A call of the States is demanded.

Mr. RAYMOND, of New-York—I understand that the question before the convention is the substitute offered by Gen. CAMERON for one which he offered and afterward withdrew, and that the motion now is that ABRAHAM LINCOLN be nominated for the Presidency. I desire to say one word upon the manner in which it is proposed to be done. I believe that there is no man in this convention who will not, however the vote may be taken, give his vote in just one way. It can therefore, be from no apprehension of the result of the vote that this particular way of taking it should be proposed, therefore, we may as well look to other considerations in deciding how we will take it. It is very well known that attempts have been made, though with no very great success, to create the impression that the nomination of ABRAHAM LINCOLN has to be pushed through this convention by some demonstration that will not look to the exercise of individual influence. Is it wise under these circumstances to take a vote by acclamation? It cannot possibly change the result. It can add no weight whatever to its earnestness, and it may give rise to false impressions. I suggest, and will move as a substitute a resolution embodying my view. I suggest that the wisest course would be to allow the roll of the States represented in this convention to be called, and let every delegation declare its vote. I believe there will be a unanimous vote from every delegation precisely to the same effect. I think the effect of that vote will be greater than one taken by acclamation. It can be reinforced, as it will be reinforced, by this convention, and throughout the country by the loud acclamations of the American people; and now I move, as a substitute for the motion of the gentleman from Pennsylvania, that the roll of the States be called, and that each delegation be called upon to record its vote. [Applause.]

Mr. CAMERON—I accept the modification.

Mr. COOK, of Illinois—Mr. President, the State of Illinois again presents to the loyal people of this nation, for President of the United States, ABRAHAM LINCOLN—God bless him!

Mr. CAMERON—I desire to accept the modification of the gentleman of New-York.

Cries of "Roll, roll," "Question," &c.

The CHAIR—The gentleman from Ohio moved that this convention proceed to the nomination of candidates for President and Vice-President. Upon that a resolution was offered by Gen. CAMERON that has been discussed. Upon that the gentleman from New-York (RAYMOND) moves we proceed to the nomination of a candidate for President alone. I ask the gentleman from Ohio whether he accepts that as a substitute for his motion.

Mr. DELANO—It was in full comprehension of the necessity of having an individual expression of opinion in favor of ABRAHAM LINCOLN that I made my motion, and that there should be no misapprehension, and no claim that he had been nominated by clamor, that public sentiment had been suppressed, that I desired the nomination as indicated by my resolution. For no man desires his nomination more than I. I accept the resolution offered by the gentleman from New-York as a substitute for my own.

The Chair stated that the question was to proceed to a nomination for President by a call of the States.

After further debate, and great confusion, the question was put on Mr. RAYMOND's substitute, which was adopted.

The convention then proceeded to ballot for President, which resulted as follows:

For Mr. Lincoln—Maine, 14; New-Hampshire, 10; Vermont, 10; Massachusetts, 24; Rhode Island, 8; Connecticut, 12; New-York, 66; New-Jersey, 14; Pennsylvania, 52; Delaware, 6; Maryland, 14; Louisiana, 14; Arkansas, 10; Tennessee, 15; Kentucky, 22; Ohio, 42; Indiana 26; Illinois, 32; Michigan, 16; Wisconsin, 16; Iowa, 16; Minnesota, 8; California, 10; Oregon, 6; West Virginia, 10; Kansas, 6; Nebraska, 6; Colorado, 6; Nevada, 6. Total, 497.

For Gen. Grant—Missouri, 22.

On motion of Mr. HUME, of Missouri, the vote was declared unanimous.

The enthusiasm was perfectly indescribable, the whole convention being on their feet, shouting, and the band playing "Hail Columbia."

After the nomination the Chairman read a dispatch from the Secretary of War, giving the good news from Gen. HUNTER, which was received with great cheering.

The convention resolved to proceed to vote for a candidate for Vice-President.

The following names were presented:

DANIEL MACE, of Indiana, presented the name of ANDREW JOHNSON, of Tennessee.

Mr. STONE, of Iowa, seconded the motion.

Mr. CAMERON, of Pennsylvania, offered the name of HANNIBAL HAMLIN.

Mr. TREMAINE, of New-York, in behalf of a portion of the delegation, presented DANIEL S. DICKINSON.

Mr. MAYNARD, of Tennessee, advocated the claims of ANDREW JOHNSON.

Mr. TREMAINE, of New-York, made an eloquent appeal in favor of the nomination of DANIEL S. DICKINSON. His remarks were received with great enthusiasm.

Great impatience was manifested to vote.

The President announced the following names as being before the convention:

ANDREW JOHNSON, of Tennessee.
HANNIBAL HAMLIN, of Maine.
L. H. ROUSSEAU, of Kentucky.
DANIEL S. DICKINSON, of New-York.

The House then proceeded to ballot.

Maine, New-Hampshire, Vermont, Connecticut, New-York, New-Hampshire, New-Jersey, Pennsylvania, Delaware, Maryland, Louisiana, Arkansas, Missouri, Kentucky, Ohio, Indiana, Illinois, Michigan, Iowa, California, Oregon, West Virginia, Kansas, Nebraska, Colorado and Nevada voted entire for Johnson. Massachusetts voted Johnson 21; Dickinson 3. Rhode Island, Johnson, 7; Dickinson, 1. Wisconsin, Johnson, 2; Dickinson, 10; Hamlin, 4. Minnesota, Dickinson, 3; Hamlin, 5. The total vote was Johnson, 492; Dickinson, 17; Hamlin, 9. Previous to the vote being announced, Johnson had 200; Dickinson, 113; Hamlin, 145; Butler, 28; Rosseau, 21; Burnside, 2; Colfax, 6; Col. Colt, 2; Tod, 2, and King, 1; but the States changed their votes before the announcement was made.

June 9, 1864

CHICAGO CONVENTION.

McClellan Nominated for President.

Pendleton, of Ohio, for Vice-President.

CHICAGO, Wednesday, Aug. 31.

The National Democratic Convention reassembled at 10 o'clock this morning.

The Wigwam is again densely packed, and the crowd outside is greater than ever.

Immediately after the convention had been called to order, a prayer was offered up by Rev. Dr. HALSEY, of Chicago.

Mr. WICKLIFFE then rose and said that the delegates from the West were of the opinion that circumstances may occur between now and the 4th of March next for the Democracy of the country to meet in convention again. He therefore moved the following resolution, which was unanimously adopted:

Resolved, That this convention shall not be dissolved by adjournment at the close of its business, but shall remain organized, subject to the call at any time and place that the Executive National Committee shall designate.

The following communication was then received from the National Democratic Committee, and was presented by Mr. LAWRENCE, of Rhode Island:

At a meeting of the National Democratic Committee, held at the Sherman House, at the City of Chicago, on the 31st day of August, 1864, the following resolution was adopted:

Whereas, A respectful devotion to the memory of STEPHEN A. DOUGLAS, the great statesman of the West, was the crowning motive which induced the committee to concur in calling the convention in the City of Chicago; now, therefore, it is the deliberate conviction of this committee, that had his life been spared his gigantic grasp of mind, taken in connection with his declaration that "War is Disunion," a declaration which time has proved the wisdom of, would long since have restored the power of the Federal compact, and avoided that terrible loss of life for which nothing can compensate, and that bitterness of feeling so much to be deplored, which is the great barrier to the restoration of peace and union.

THOMAS B. FLORENCE, Chairman.

WM. FLINN,
F. A. AIKEN, } Secretaries.

The President then stated the question before the convention to be on ordering the previous question, (nominating a candidate for the Presidency,) and it was ordered without dissent.

The vote was then taken by States, the Chairman of each delegation announcing the vote when the States were called.

Connecticut and Ohio having been passed for the moment, the vote stood as follows:

For McClellan..................................162
Scattering.................................... 64

September 1, 1864

The Presidential Election—Some Facts from the Returns.

The returns of the Presidential election, though not all as yet officially verified, will enable us now to take a broad view of the character of the vote which has shaped the national policy for the next four years.

To the surprise of those foreign enemies of the Republic who have been steadily predicting the separation of the West from the East, and of those British critics who have claimed that the Government works in the Middle States and the high protection to the iron and coal interests, chained these communities to the prosecution of the war, it is discovered from this vote that the extreme East and the Central West are the most united, and that the Middle States give the weakest majorities for the Government.

Eastern New-England, and the rich Central West, are found the most unanimous for Mr. LINCOLN. Ohio and Massachusetts give him his two heaviest majorities, or about 100,000. Illinois, Indiana, Michigan, and the opening Northwest—Wisconsin, Iowa and Minnesota—unite with Maine, Vermont and New-Hampshire, in a tremendous popular majority for the Union candidates. Connecticut shares the sentiment, as she does the vote, of the Middle States, and gives LINCOLN but a slender majority. New-York barely elects him, New-Jersey rejects him, and Pennsylvania shows but a respectable majority; while, to the astonishment of most, the outlying States of the Union roll up, for their population, immense majorities. Kansas has a majority almost as great as her voters; California polls a very large vote for the Union candidate, though it gave the Democracy 40,000 majority in 1860; and Oregon and Nevada, though the former is settled by large numbers of Southern men, present a very fair preponderance for the Union and Republican party.

The apparent inference from these facts, taken in broad, is that the Union and Anti-Slavery sentiment is strongest in the eastern New-England States and the Central West and Northwest, and that, as the Republic extends over the vast plains toward the Pacific, the feeling of loyalty only grows with distance from the centre, while, in the Middle States, it is weakest, and is lowest of all in the large cities of these States.

Before seeking to account for these interesting phenomena, we would call attention to one most encouraging conclusion, which we may draw from them, and that is, the exceeding difficulty of bringing about, under any conspiracy or possible disaster, a disruption of the Free States. With the two extremes so united in sentiment and policy, what could the Middle States do, even if they desired, against the Union? Even if FERNANDO WOOD should succeed in stirring up his ignorant followers to make New-York a "Free City," there would still be force enough all around him to keep them in order. Furthermore, it must be remembered that the great rural population of our State—the intelligent mechanics and farmers—are generally intensely loyal in feeling, and determined on the maintenance of the Union and the institutions of freedom.

The character of the vote which we have noted above, is to be explained by various causes. It will be found that the New-England element everywhere—the descendants and relations of New-Englanders—have formed the strength of the Union and Anti-Slavery party, and that, where they have influenced, there the vote for LINCOLN has been strongest. The Central West, as is well known, in its leading classes, is merely New-England repeated in other circumstances. Ohio, Michigan, Northern Illinois and Northern Indiana are very largely settled by emigrants from the Eastern States. These men and their descendants control the press, the business and the public life of those powerful communities.

Along with them act in the West the more intelligent Germans and other foreign-born citizens; for, it should be borne in mind, that the Irishman or German settling in our rural districts is a very different person from his compatriots among the laboring poor of the great cities. In the West he becomes like any native-born citizen, he is *Americanized*, and he feels the impulse of such ideas as animate the Union party. In the cities he is commonly only a tool of politicians. It is the foreign-born population in our city and Brooklyn, and the river counties, which has brought down LINCOLN's majority in this State from 50,000 in 1860 to some 7,000 in 1864; and this is equally true of Connecticut, where we beheld our majority reduced from 10,000 to some 2,500—the foreign operatives filling now her manufacturing villages. In New-York and Pennsylvania it is not merely the New-England element which supports so ardently the Union cause, but the native population of these States. In some districts the vote could be almost divided by race.

In bringing these facts to public attention, we do not, in the smallest degree, reflect upon any portion of our foreign-born citizens. In the first year of the war they sacrificed nobly for the country. But we have come to that period in which enthusiasm or even pugnacity have little comparative influence in continuing the struggle. To sustain the war now, is needed the most indomitable pluck, and a persistence, which comes from a moral purpose of the highest order, and a will set immovably on distant and well-considered objects. Only the native born could be expected to hold on now, with the tremendous sacrifices demanded, and only a race like the Anglo-American, which is spurred on by obstacles and disasters, could have patience sufficient to secure the victory.

With all the weakness of the majorities for Mr. LINCOLN in the Middle Seaboard States—amounting in three States, inhabited by millions, to barely 25,000—the Union party must feel elated at their magnificent success in the States which have lost the most men for the cause—Ohio, Michigan, Illinois and Indiana—where the united majorities will come close to 100,000, and at the result through the Union, which has increased LINCOLN's majority, after four years of terrible war, by over 400,000 votes.

November 23, 1864

THE NEW PRESIDENT.

The Political History and Antecedents of Andrew Johnson.

ANDREW JOHNSON has been in continuous public life for thirty years. He entered the General Assembly of Tennessee as a member of the House of Representatives the first Monday in October, 1835, from the County of Greene, in East Tennessee. He was reëlected to the succeeding biennial Assembly in 1837, and again in 1839. In 1841 he was transferred to the State Senate by the Counties of Washington, Greene and Sullivan. In 1843 to a seat in Congress from the First Representative District, comprising the same counties and the new County of Johnson. He served the same district, by four successive reelections, until the new apportionment under the census of 1850, in all ten years, when, in 1853, he was made Governor of Tennessee, and was subsequently reëlected in 1855. At the end of his second term, in 1857, he was made United States Senator, his term expiring on the 4th of March, 1863, since when, and until his recent election as Vice-President of the United States, he was Military Governor of Tennessee.

Such, in brief, has been the public service of Mr. JOHNSON. His political antecedents from 1835 to 1865 have been uniformly true to the Federal Union, to rigid public economy, independent labor, free representation and free homesteads. His practice rather than profession has been that of democracy. His democracy was in the acknowledgment and assertion of the right and rule of the people. From 1839 to 1861, he was identified with the so-called Democratic party of Tennessee. He honored the party by his conscientious and upright services as the Representative and Executive of the people, successively, and was honored by it because of these and the additional qualification of consistent and useful not to say able statesmanship. The other prominent leaders of his party did not always love him, especially while Governor, because their democracy was of a different order from his own humble origin, frugal habits, and unpretending walk and conversation in high office. But they early learned to respect him because of the hold which he had upon the people, and because of his inflexible integrity. When, in the early troubles of 1861, they forgot this lesson, and attempted to rush the State out of the Union, against his eloquent and indignant protests in the Senate and on the stump, and against the direct popular protest of the people, on a direct vote for a convention in February, of that year, they were not long in discovering, if not their own great mistake, *his* prescience and consistency as a power in the State, which had abhorred Nullification in, and since the days of JACKSON, and which had made the capital too hot to hold Secession, when attempted by the "fire-eaters" of the other Southern States, at Nashville, in 1850.

A retrospect of Mr JOHNSON's earlier position in the politics of Tennessee may not be uninteresting. The Constitution of the State was remodeled in 1834. Gradual emancipation was petitioned for extensively from the Eastern and other Mountain Districts to the State Convention. but rejected by the larger Slaveholding Delegates. Mr. JOHNSON was not a member of the convention, but that his sympathies were for Free Representation, and with this movement is attested by an earnest subsequent effort in the Legislature for the equal apportionment of the Free White Voting population of the State by Congressional Districts, under the succeeding census of 1840. He held the principle of the three-fifths Slave representation as a constitutional blunder at best, and its application to the Free Mountain Districts of East Tennessee as an iniquity. He was not successful, however, in reforming it.

Mr. JOHNSON was made a member of the first Legislature under the new constitution in 1835. He was then only 27 years of age; young, energetic, and thoroughly imbued with an independent and self-reliant spirit. The year before, a breach had been made in the hitherto dominant and overwhelming Jackson Democracy of the State, as between Mr. VAN BUREN and Judge HUGH L. WHITE for the Presidential election. Mr. POLK and Mr. BELL were the rival leaders, as they had

been rivals for the Speakership of the United States House of Representatives, on the appointment of Mr. ANDREW STEVENSON as Minister to England. Mr. BELL was elected in 1834 to fill this Chair for the remainder of that Congress. But the contest was exceedingly bitter, and was carried into the next Congress, President JACKSON taking part against BELL for Speaker and WHITE for the next Presidency, and openly for POLK and VAN BUREN. Mr. POLK was made Speaker. But BELL and WHITE carried the State for Governor and Legislature in 1835 and the Presidency in 1836. Mr. JOHNSON entered public life as a Bell and White man. He was a favorite of the party in the Legislature of 1835, and their caucus candidate for Speaker of the House in 1837, but was defeated by a coalition between the Van Buren minority and another White delegate from East Tennessee. When WHITE and BELL subsequently became closely identified with the old Whig party, Mr. JOHNSON left them and was the acknowledged leader of the Van Buren Governor (POLK) in the Legislature of 1839.

We have intimated that Mr. JOHNSON, in his highest positions at home and in Washington, was a man of frugal, economical habits. In this he was consistent with his early life as an industrious, hard laboring mechanic, and the provident care of his wife and family. The former had taught him to read and write

after they were married. He subsequently became emulous of public life. He entered upon it with zest and loved it for its fascinations, and faithfully won honors. He had no professional training; was ambitious of none. He was never a lawyer, as we believe has been generally supposed. He was never a huckstering politician; never paid money for a nomination or for an election, beyond the incidental expenses of his *stump* campaigns for Congress and for Governor. He was and is devoted to the public service, for its usefulness and its honors, and content with and systematically economizing its moderate emoluments for the sake of his family. And in this, it is safe to say that parsimony has as little to do with his sense of domestic duty, as expensive tastes or prodigal wastefulness.

Above all, Mr. JOHNSON is a true, as well as a brave man; faithful four years ago among the faithless of his old rivals of the Whig party, and his old colleagues of the Democratic party of Tennessee; true to the Union, when it cost something to be true; to the government in its life struggle against rebellion and insurrection; to free labor and its disenthralment from the incubus of slavery, and to that unswerving line of duty and devotion to hard study, progressive statesmanship and ripening experience which have carried him from the humblest to the topmost round of human ambition.

April 17, 1865

The Democratic Party and the Elections.

We trust the Democratic Party is satisfied with the success of its "little game" in the late elections. If it is, everybody else can well afford to be content. The extreme Radicals, as usual, owe their power to the selfish and unscrupulous partisanship of the Democrats; and the Union men can console themselves for whatever good results they have failed to secure by the fact that the ascendency of the Democratic Party has at all events been averted. It was that ascendency which the Democrats sought, and which the People feared more than anything else. The Democratic leaders in all the States, and most notably in Pennsylvania and New-York,—made the restoration of their party to power the main aim of all their efforts. They held everything everywhere subordinate to this one object. They supported President JOHNSON, partly perhaps because they agreed with him, but mainly to control the patronage and the power at his command for the attainment of this one end. They indorsed the Philadelphia Convention,—partly because its positions and principles defied their assaults,—but mainly because they hoped to make it the stepping stone to party control in State and national affairs. They used both the President and the Convention, remorselessly and recklessly, for their own advantage; and they have been utterly and thoroughly overwhelmed with defeat.

The reason of this result is palpable. The People distrust the patriotism and loyalty of the Democratic Party, and will not trust the restoration of the Union and the reformation of our civil and political institutions to its hands. They see now, more clearly than they could see before the war, that the inherent spirit and temper of that party were

always at war with the best interests of the nation. The party, as such, always allied itself with the worst elements and most perilous influences of the national life. It was the ally of Slavery,—not simply tolerant of its existence, but the active defender of its worst enormities and the open advocate of its ambition. Out of its devotion to Slavery and its craving for the power which Slavery carried with it, it led the South into the rebellion, and lacked nothing but the courage to follow it thither. Throughout the war, its sympathies, as a party, were with the rebellion. It rejoiced in its successes,—it magnified its merits and power, it mourned its defeats, it predicted its triumph,—it crippled and hampered the Government in its struggle against it, it threw out of the party as false and treacherous those men who sought to give vigor and success to the nation's arms, and it evinced in every way and by every means which can indicate the spirit and purpose of party action, the most determined and ingrained sympathy with the rebel movement. Such action in such a crisis makes an abiding impression on the public mind. Neither in the case of individuals nor of a party, is it soon forgotten. The people long for peace, for the restoration of Union, for the resumption of national prosperity and power; but they want all this on the basis of the Union principles vindicated and established by the war.

Whatever differences of opinion have existed in the Union party should have been settled within that party and by its members. President JOHNSON always declared that he so intended,—that he sought only to save the party which carried the country through the war from falling into the hands of extreme men; and that he had no thought or purpose of throwing the power of the Government into the hands of the party which had opposed

the war, and which was now ready to sacrifice its results to securing its own ascendency. If the President had adhered to this purpose he could very easily have secured the result at which he aimed. But he allowed the Democrats to overrule or overbear him. Instead of aiding and strengthening the National sentiment in the Union ranks, and thus checking and thwarting the Disunion element which sought to control it, he invoked the Democratic Party to the rescue. He recognized the nominations of that party everywhere as those for which he sought support,—as those which represented his policy and his Administration,—as those whose success was demanded by the principles he deemed essential to the public good. And even after the Philadelphia Convention had laid down a platform thoroughly national in its principles, upon which the Union could be restored in strict harmony with the results of the war and the principles on which the war had been carried to its triumphant close, he still permitted the Democratic Party to seize upon it for its own advantage,—to climb into power by its aid, to use it for the promotion of its own ends and the reëstablishment in the national councils of its own supremacy. The Democrats in the Albany Convention cared nothing for the Philadelphia Convention,—nothing for President JOHNSON, nothing for the restoration of the Union,—nothing for the patriotic men who were struggling for it, except as it could use them all to bring the old Democratic Party, as it had been organized and controlled for the past five years, again into power. *That* was the object and aim of all their efforts. Everything else was of not the slightest consequence except as it could be made to aid in its attainment.

Their action was rigidly and vigorously partisan throughout. They held their party organization, laid down their party platform, put a party ticket in the field, and aimed openly and avowedly at a party victory. And they made the President believe that the success of his principles depended on giving them a party triumph and the offices in his gift as essential thereto.

The result is now visible, and is precisely what calm and dispassionate observers knew it would be. The direct effect of this policy was to unite the Union Party—to consolidate all its strength against the Democratic Party, whose success was to be the death-knell of its influence on national affairs. No man outside the ranks of the Democratic organization

had the slightest interest, personal or political, in its success. Indeed, everything which Union men had deemed essential to the public good was directly threatened with utter overthrow by the renewed ascendency of the Democratic Party. The people would not tolerate such a result. They would not entrust the restoration of the Union to the party which had sympathized with those who sought its overthrow. Whatever their faults, those who had saved it were the most to be trusted in its redemption. And so they have continued the control of the nation's affairs in the hands of the Union Party. How that control is to be exercised,— whether under the guidance of calm and

patriotic councils, or by passion and the ambition of reckless and unscrupulous men, it is for the future to reveal.

One result has been put beyond further controversy by these elections:—the Democratic Party will not be speedily restored to power in national affairs. It will not be allowed to control the destiny or to shape the policy of the country. The more it strives to seize the reins of authority, the more profound will be the popular distrust of its temper, and the more vigorously will its efforts be resisted.

November 10, 1866

The Political Future.

The political history of the past two years has been little more than a record of the triumphs of what was originally the Abolition Party, and which has since become the ultra, absolutist element in the Republican Party. This element has driven that party from the constitutional position which it held down to 1864,—and from one point to another,—each more "advanced" and extreme than its predecessor—ever since that time.

Where this movement is to stop, or whether it is to stop at all, is matter of conjecture. If it does stop it will be from compulsion and not from choice. Every victory thus far has proved to be only the precursor of new demands : and this is quite as true now as it was a year ago. They have secured universal suffrage for the blacks of the Southern States, with the exclusion from the ballot-box of a large portion of the whites :—they have abrogated wholly the supremacy of law as administered by the civil tribunals, and have subjected the South to military control,—and they have succeeded in giving Congress absolute authority in the National Government. For all this thus far they have had the general acquiescence and support of the people.

It becomes a matter of considerable importance to watch carefully all indications as to what this restless, insatiate and potent element of the dominant party proposes to do next. What they *propose* to-day may be *law* to-morrow. Judging from the past, it is very likely to be so. We publish this morning a letter from Senator SUMNER and an article from the *Anti-Slavery Standard* which will be read with interest in this connection.

Mr. SUMNER's leading object in his letter is to insist upon subjecting suffrage in all the States North and South to the regulation of Congress. He demands that the States shall no longer be left free to define the qualifications of voters within their limits, but that this shall be done by Congress. And he

frankly avows that the specific object of this fundamental change in the practice of the Government, is to secure the negro vote in all the States for the Republican Party. "There are Northern States," he says, "where the votes of the negroes can make the good cause safe beyond question," and he is therefore in favor of giving the negroes the right to vote in every State without consulting the Constitution, laws or will of the people thereof. The fact that the Constitution of the United States recognizes, in express and explicit language, the right of each State to regulate the suffrage, and to prescribe the conditions of its exercise within its limits, is passed over by Mr. SUMNER as utterly unworthy of notice. He condescends not to forget "the hesitations" which have been experienced on the subject, but that is all.

If Mr. Sumner and his friends can make it so, this is to be henceforward a plank in the platform of the Republican Party. Thus far it has not been enforced as a doctrine absolutely essential to political salvation, but we cannot rely on the indefinite indulgence of this gracious and gratuitous toleration. Those Republicans who hesitate to assert and uphold the absolute authority of Congress to control the suffrage in every State, will very soon come to be denounced as the confederates of Copperheads and rebels.

The *Anti-Slavery Standard,* which has been for some time past the fruitful source of inspiration for the "advanced" wing of the Republican Party, is still more sweeping, though not more peremptory, than Mr. Sumner in its demands. It opens by branding the Republican majority in the Fortieth Congress as treacherous and cowardly. It shirked the impeachment of the President, which, with more candor than wisdom, it declares to have been the object for which it was convened. It pronounces the adjournment to July a contemptible trick. It denounces the Republican Congressmen as venal and corrupt,— charging them with having sold themselves for office in the most scandalous and disgraceful manner. It names individual members whom it holds subject to this serious charge,—among them Bingham, Blaine and Banks, while its denunciation of individual Senators is even more direct and emphatic.

After this cheerful opening of its vials of wrath, the *Standard* reads a solemn warning to those Republicans who seek to emancipate the party from the domination of this ultra-radical element. It graciously informs them that the only reason why the Republican Party has been suffered to exist hitherto is the fact that the Radicals found it the "*most available instrument*" for doing *their* work;"—and it warns them that whenever that party *ceases* thus to do the work of the Radicals, it will be abandoned and destroyed.

These pleasant intimations are followed by an invitation to the Democratic Party to come near enough to allow the Radicals and the negroes to reinstate it in power. That such an alliance is by no means impossible would seem evident from the action of the two parties in the last Congress. The ultra Radicals and Democrats coalesced more than once during that Congress, and the Radicals secured more than one of their most signal victories by the help of Democratic votes. Thus the Democrats and Stevens men voted down the proposed qualifications,—and secured *universal* suffrage for the negroes of the District of Columbia. And the same coalition at a later day secured the partial disfranchisement of the whites in the South, while it gave the ballot to the Southern negroes without qualification or distinction of any kind.

What has been, may be. Meantime all we have to do just now is to watch the current of events.

May 3, 1867

The President and the Republicans.

From the Tribune.

"The TIMES assumes that the Republicans in Congress are at variance with Mr. JOHNSON *because of incompatible views touching reconstruction.* We hold, and prove, that *reconstruction is at best but a pretext—that* Mr. JOHNSON had *predetermined to quarrel with and desert the Republicans before any such difference had arisen—that he is warring upon them with all the malignity of one who has requited boundless trust by inconceivable perfidy—all the implacable hate of one whose treachery is aggravated by measureless ingratitude.*"

We can hardly believe the *Tribune* sincere in these declarations. We are confident the

Republicans in Congress will not indorse them. *They* will not confess that their differences with the President grow wholly out of party relations,—that *their* hostility to him has no better basis than that of resentment for intended party treachery,—that Reconstruction is "but a pretext,"—a mere cover for the party objects which really lie at the bottom of this most disastrous conflict between the two great departments of the Government. If the *Tribune's* allegation is true in regard to the President, it must be true also in regard to Congress. If Reconstruc-

tion was "but a pretext" on the one side, it was "but a pretext" on the other also.

We do not believe the *Tribune's* statement, as a matter of fact. And here is the "evidence" which that journal gives us, as conclusive in support of it :

"It is *undoubtedly in evidence that he* [President JOHNSON] *was meditating and intriguing for a revival of the old Democratic Party, with himself at or near its head, before he had taken possession even of that secondary office to which the Republicans elected him.* Before he had been one month in the White House, the Tom Florences, Wendells and other *reliques of the ancien régime,* were each confidentially and joyfully whispering that Andy was 'all right'—that he was a Democrat still, and would soon dispel all doubt on the subject. Their organ intimated this within ten weeks after Mr. JOHNSON's elevation to Mr. LINCOLN's seat. In our ensuing election, though the TIMES' friends had nominated our State ticket, on a platform of unbounded Johnsonism, the TIMES' editor was unable to wrench one word of comfort for its supporters from the lips or pen of the President; while MONTGOMERY BLAIR traversed our State, canvassing for the Democratic ticket, *assuring its supporters that Johnson was with them*, and that they should have the run of the Custom-house and the Federal offices generally if they would only beat the Republicans in the pending contest. These and many kindred facts the TIMES coolly ignores."

What sort of "evidence" is this? The "whisperings" of the Tom Florences and Wendells were never of the slightest consequence to anybody,—were even less important, if possible, than the "assurances" which MONTGOMERY BLAIR is in the habit of giving whenever stumping any State, in support of any ticket. Not one of these men, with all their assurance, ever pretended to have the least authority for anything they saw fit to say about Mr. JOHNSON's intentions or opinions. They undoubtedly said a great deal, for it was the only way they had of increasing their own importance;—but they said it wholly without warrant or authority of any sort. And at the very time when the *Tribune*, in common with other Radical journals, was reporting day after day that "TOM FLORENCE" and company had been holding long confidential interviews with the President, and had arranged everything to their mutual satisfaction, especially the demolition of the Republican Party, the writer of this paragraph was informed by the President himself that he had never seen Mr. FLORENCE for ten minutes at a time, and had never had anything like a confidential political conversation with him in the whole course of his life.

We believe at the time referred to we had quite as good an opportunity of knowing the President's purposes and intentions as the *Tribune* had; and we have no hesitation in expressing, what was our belief then and what is our belief now, that he had no more thought or design of "deserting the Repub-

lican Party" and espousing the Democratic cause, than the Editor of the *Tribune* has now. The *Tribune's* assertion that Mr. JOHNSON had "predetermined to quarrel with and desert the Republican Party before any difference had arisen on the subject of Reconstruction," is, in our judgment, utterly untrue. It finds no shadow of support in anything that he said, or did,—in any assurances he ever gave the Democrats, or in any intimations he ever gave the Republicans who were in frequent intercourse with him.

When Mr. JOHNSON became President, he adopted the policy of Restoration which he believed to be that of Mr. LINCOLN, which was embodied in the North Carolina proclamation drawn by Secretary STANTON, which was indorsed, supported and urged upon him by every member of the Republican Cabinet that Mr. LINCOLN had appointed and which he had continued in office. Opposition to that plan had, indeed, manifested itself in the Republican Party, before Mr. LINCOLN's death as well as after;—but there was no such demonstration of hostile sentiment in advance of the meeting of the Thirty-ninth Congress, as showed the Republican Party to be against it, or as should restrain the President from commending it to their favor in his message at the opening of the session. The Republicans met it, and arrested all effective discussion upon it, by sending the whole subject at once to a joint committee of both Houses, and by declaring, by joint resolution, that no member from States that had been in rebellion should be admitted to his seat until that Committee had made its report. There was nothing in this to indicate any purpose on the President's part to abandon the party that had elected him. No one charged him with any such purpose, or suspected him of it. He himself held no language and did no act which could give warrant for such a charge. But a "difference" then arose between him and the party, which neither took the slightest pains to harmonize, and which grew, by successive acts on both sides, into the bitter hostility which has since been developed.

We do not think the President acted wisely in the early stages of this contest. He made little effort to conciliate the party that held absolute control of Congress, or to concert with them practical measures of restoration, on which both could agree without sacrifice of principle or of the public safety. That common ground for such concert of action could have been found, we have no doubt whatever. That a President of different temper and different views of public duty could have found it, we feel equally sure. That President LINCOLN, if he had lived, entertaining substantially the same opinions as Mr. JOHNSON, and aiming certainly at the same results, *would* have found it, and secured the prompt and peaceful restoration of the Union upon it, we are quite as confident. The trouble with Mr. JOHNSON was—not that he had predetermined to quarrel with any party or anybody — but that he was too strongly wedded, by nature and the habit of his life, to his own convictions—that he was too little accustomed to confer with others on matters of common action—that he overrated the dignity and force of his own office and underrated those of Congress too much, to appreciate aright the necessity of concessions and compromises in the practical affairs of government. He had precisely the temper which made him firm and steadfast during the war, and which is always of the first necessity in conflicts with an open foe, but which is by no means so useful in concerting with colleagues of coördinate power the practical measures of government in time of peace.

The Republican majority cannot in our judgment, evade the responsibility for their action by the plea which the *Tribune* makes on their behalf. The course they pursued was not made necessary by any predetermined purpose of the President to quarrel with and desert the Republican Party. Their measures are to be judged on their merits,—by their bearing and effect upon the restoration of the Union,—and not by the party emergency which the *Tribune* invents in their defence.

January 15, 1868

IMPEACHMENT IN THE COUNTRY.

The Feeling at Albany in Regard to Impeachment — The President's Removal Demanded.

Special Dispatch to the New-York Times.

ALBANY, Monday, Feb. 24.

The impeachment question is the all-absorbing topic here. There is nothing else talked of or apparently thought of. The division is almost strictly party. Radical and Conservative Republicans appear to have found a common platform upon which to stand, and to a man are in favor of a quick and short decisive trial and conviction of the President.

The Democrats, with equal unanimity, are in favor of a quick trial and determination of the matter. They don't appear to have much sympathy for the President, but rather express the desire that the Senate shall make a verdict which will disqualify the President and take him off their hands.

Democratic Meeting in Philadelphia.

PHILADELPHIA, Monday, Feb. 24.

A meeting of the Democrats of the Fourth Ward was held yesterday, at which 117 persons were

present. The following resolution was adopted:

Resolved, That inasmuch as an usurping Congress calls itself the people, when in fact the Congress is not the people, but the servants of people, we, citizens of Philadelphia, who value the Constitution above all party and party tactics, do solemnly resolve that ANDREW JOHNSON, President of the United States, standing as he does for the Constitution and the rights of the people under it, is the true exponent of the feelings of the people, and that we will, if necessary, shoulder our muskets to sustain, not ANDREW JOHNSON alone, but the Constitution which he supports with a vigor and truthfulness that challenge our admiration and respect.

Second—That this is a white man's Government that must be sustained at all hazards.

Another resolution proposed that the meeting adjourn to meet at the railroad depot under arms and proceed to Washington, but before the vote was taken on it the meeting broke up in some confusion.

The New-Jersey Legislature Indorses the President.

TRENTON, N. J., Monday, Feb. 24.

Both Houses passed a resolution this evening, in substance as follows,

Resolved, That the President of the United States, in his struggle against the encroachments of a Radical majority in Congress, has our hearty sympathy; and we hereby request the Joint Committee on Federal Relations to prepare suitable resolutions, to be submitted at the earliest moment, to both Houses of this Legislature, expressive of our feelings in regard to the exigency of public affairs.

The resolutions were adopted by a party majority.

Rejoicing in Pennsylvania.

READING, Penn., Monday, Feb. 24.

The news of the prompt action of the House in the impeachment movement was received here

with great rejoicing. One hundred guns were fired in the Square in honor of the event.

Troops Offered to Preserve the Peace in Washington.

POUGHKEEPSIE, N. Y., Monday, Feb. 24.

Lieut.-Col. EASTMAN has tendered to Adjutant-General MARVIN the services of the Twenty-first Regiment, of this district, to preserve the peace at Washington. He says the regiment can be ready in twenty-four hours' notice.

The Vote on Impeachment—Salute in Philadelphia.

PHILADELPHIA, Monday, Feb. 24.

The Union League of the Nineteenth Ward, in this city, fired a salute of 50 guns this evening in honor of the passage of the impeachment resolution.

A Meeting to be Held in Chicago To-Night.

CHICAGO, Monday, Feb. 24.

A meeting of prominent citizens was held at Tremont Hall to-day to make arrangements for a mass meeting of the citizens to be held to-morrow night to give an expression of the public sentiment in regard to the pending impeachment of the President.

February 25, 1868

IMPEACHMENT.

Final Vote in the Senate on the Eleventh Article.

The President Acquitted of the Offences Charged.

Special Dispatch to the New-York Times.

WASHINGTON, Saturday, May 16.

The great impeachment drama is practically at an end, and the President stands acquitted of the principal charge. Nineteen votes against thirty-five—just enough, and no more, to turn the scale of verdict. Twelve Democrats and seven Republicans—that magical number of seven—against thirty-five Republicans! My calculations since Tuesday are fully verified. Thirty-six was the best vote the friends of conviction could possibly count upon after Tuesday, and ever since then the fight has been to get the one necessary vote for acquittal on the one side and to keep the one necessary vote for conviction on the other. The debate of Monday developed the fact that the President had five Republican votes sure. Senator FOWLER'S course developed the fact on Tuesday that he had six. It has been the work of the week to get the seventh man, and EDMUND G. ROSS, of Kansas, was secured. When Gen. THOS. EWING, Jr., said yesterday that Ross would vote for acquittal *if* necessary to secure it, he knew whereof he spoke.

The excitement last night on the revival of the prospect of conviction was so great that it survived the night, and this morning pervaded the minds of such people as went to bed early to hear of it. While the confidence of both sides were thus great, however, a few busy working spirits were still contesting the great question of the only still wanting vote. The man who bore the brunt of the contest was Mr. Ross. Conviction had him to dinner last night, and pledged him sure; but Acquittal slept with him over night, and this morning he was weak and vacillating, and the few who talked with him gave him up. Two hours before the vote was taken it was known precisely how it would stand.

May 17, 1868

GRANT AND COLFAX.

The Republican Candidates for President and Vice-President.

Gen. Grant Nominated on the First Ballot.

An Exciting Contest for the Vice-Presidency.

Schuyler Colfax Nominated on the Fourth Ballot.

The Platform Received and Indorsed Amid Much Enthusiasm.

THE PLATFORM.

The Hon. RICHARD W. THOMPSON, of Indiana, Chairman of the Committee on Resolutions, advanced to the platform and reported as follows:

"The National Republican Party of the United States, assembled in National Convention in the City of Chicago, on the 20th day of May, 1868, make the following declaration of principles:

1. We congratulate the country on the assured success of the reconstruction policy of Congress, as evinced by the adoption, in the majority of the States lately in rebellion, of Constitutions securing equal civil and political rights to all; and it is the duty of the Government to sustain those Constitutions and to prevent the people of such States from being remitted to a state of anarchy. (Cheers.)

2. The guarantee by Congress of equal suffrage to all loyal men at the South was demanded by every consideration of public safety, of gratitude, and of justice, and must be maintained, while the question of suffrage in all the loyal States properly belongs to the people of those States. [Cheers.]

3. We denounce all forms of repudiation as a national crime, [prolonged cheers,] and the national honor requires the payment of the public indebtedness in the utmost good faith to all creditors at home and abroad, not only according to the letter, but the spirit of the laws under which it was contracted. [Applause.]

4. It is due to the labor of the nation that taxation should be equalized and reduced as rapidly as the national faith will permit.

5. The national debt, contracted, as it has been, for the preservation of the Union for all time to come, should be extended over a fair period for redemption; and it is the duty of Congress to reduce the rate of interest thereon whenever it can be honestly done.

6. That the best policy to diminish our burden of debt is to so improve our credit that capitalists will seek to loan us money at lower rates of interest than we now pay, and must continue to pay, so long as repudiation, partial or total, open or covert, is threatened or suspected.

7. The Government of the United States should be administered with the strictest economy, and the corruptions which have been so shamefully nursed and fostered by ANDREW JOHNSON call loudly for radical reform.

8. We professedly deplore the untimely and tragic death of ABRAHAM LINCOLN, and regret the accession of ANDREW JOHNSON to the Presidency, who has acted treacherously to the people who elected him, and the cause he was pledged to support—who has usurped high legislative and judicial functions—who has refused to execute the laws—who has used his high office to induce other officers to ignore and violate the laws—who has employed his executive powers to render insecure the property, the peace, liberty, and life of the citizen—who has abused the pardoning power—who has denounced the National Legislature as unconstitutional—persistently and corruptly resisted, by every measure in his power, every proper attempt at the reconstruction of the States lately in rebellion—who has perverted the public patronage into an engine of wholesale corruption, and who has been justly impeached for high crimes and misdemeanors, and properly pronounced guilty thereof by the vote of thirty-five Senators.

9. The doctrine of Great Britain and other European Powers, that because a man is once a subject, he is always so, must be resisted at every hazard by the United States, as a relic of the feudal times, not authorized by the law of nations and at war with our national honor and independence. Naturalized citizens are entitled to be protected in all their rights of citizenship as though they were native born, and no citizen of the United States, native or naturalized, must be liable to arrest and imprisonment by any foreign Power, for acts done or words spoken in this country; and if so arrested and imprisoned it is the duty of the Government to interfere in his behalf.

10. Of all who were faithful in the trials of the late war, there were none entitled to more especial honor than the brave soldiers and seamen who endured the hardships of campaign and cruise, and imperiled their lives in the service of the country. The bounties and pensions provided by the laws for these brave defenders of the nation are obligations never to be forgotten. The widows and orphans of the gallant dead are the wards of the people, a sacred legacy bequeathed to the nation's protecting care.

11. Foreign emigration, which in the past has added so much to the wealth, development and resources, and increase of power to this nation, the asylum of the oppressed of all nations, should be fostered and encouraged by a liberal and just policy.

12. This Convention declares itself in sympathy with all the oppressed people which are struggling for their rights.

The PRESIDENT—The resolutions are before the Convention.

Mr. SPENCER, of New-York—I move the report be adopted. I believe it evidences great care, and is a preëminently wise, truthful presentation of the articles of the faith of the Union Republican Party of the country; and, as the great majority of this Convention are anxious and willing, promptly, in my judgment, to vote upon the platform, and as a discussion, in my judgment, would have no other effect than perhaps to place a dot over an i, or alter some word or sentence, leaving the platform substantially intact, I make this my motion and call for the previous question. ["Good."]

Mr. COCHRANE—I rise to a question of order. The question is not moved for by a majority of our delegation.

The PRESIDENT—There is a rule of the Convention that a call for the previous question must come from one delegation and be sustained by another.

Mr. COCHRANE—I move you, Sir, that in the resolution respecting impeachment, after the words "properly convicted by thirty-five votes," there be inserted the words "and improperly acquitted by nineteen." [Great applause and laughter.]

Gen. SCHURZ—I am in favor of the platform as it stands. [Cheers.] I only want to move two additional paragraphs, which I think I shall have the unanimous consent of the Convention to offer. I move to attach to the second resolution a clause in relation to the right of suffrage for the colored race.

Pennsylvania and Rhode Island called the previous question.

The PRESIDENT—Shall the main question be now put?

[Cries of "Yes; question, question."]

The Chair stated the question was on Mr. COCHRANE'S amendment.

Mr. COCHRANE—Upon my individual responsibility I should suffer that amendment to remain. My delegation, however, unanimously appealed to me, in their name, to withdraw it, and I do so. [Cheers.]

Gen. SCHURZ took the floor.

Mr. MCCLURE, of Pennsylvania—I rise to a point of order. The previous question goes to the main question before the Convention, and the Convention can do nothing now but vote upon the platform as a whole. [Cries of "That's it—That's right."] There can be no discussion; we must vote; the main question has been ordered.

The President so ruled, and said: Gentlemen—Are you ready for the question?

VOICES—Aye.

The PRESIDENT—All who are in favor of accepting the resolutions, as offered by the Committee, and adopting them as the voice of this Convention will please signify it by saying "Aye."

The affirmative response was unanimous and enthusiastic.

Mr. MCCLURE moved to reconsider the vote and lay the motion to reconsider on the table, which was adopted.

Mr. THOMPSON, Chairman of the Committee on Resolutions, reported an additional resolution, to the effect that the adjournment of this Convention shall not work a dissolution of the same; but that it shall remain as an organization subject to be called together again at any time and place that the National Republican Executive Committee shall designate.

The resolution was adopted.

Mr. CARL SHURZ—I will now read what I intended to ask the Convention to adopt as an independent resolution:

Resolved, That we highly commend the spirit of magnanimity and forgiveness with which the men who have served in the rebellion, but now frankly and honestly cooperate with us in restoring the peace of the country and reconstructing the Southern States Governments upon the basis of impartial justice and equal rights, are received back into the communion of the loyal people, and we favor the removal of the disqualifications and restrictions placed upon the late rebels in the same measure as the spirit of loyalty will direct and as may be consistent with the safety of the loyal people. [Cries of "Good, good."] That is my first amendment. It seems to me that the platform of the Republican Party ought to contain at least a recognition of the great charter of our rights and liberties—the Declaration of Independence. I would therefore move that the following resolutions be added to these already reported by the Committee.

Resolved, That we recognize the great principles laid down in the immortal Declaration of Independence as the true foundation of Democratic government, and we hail with gladness every effort toward making these principles a living reality on every inch of American soil.

Mr. MCCLURE, by unanimous vote of the Pennsylvania delegation, seconded the motion for the adoption of these resolutions.

Mr. GOOCH, of Massachusetts—I ask, Mr. President, that these resolutions, by unanimous consent, may be made part of the platform which has just been adopted.

Mr. WARNER, of Alabama—As a soldier of the Republic who fought for years to subdue the rebellion and now as an Alabama Republican, I desire to third that resolution as expressing the sentiments of the Republicans of the unreconstructed States.

The resolution was then adopted.

THE PRESIDENCY.

Mr. FRENCH, of North Carolina—I move you, Sir, that we now proceed to ballot for candidate for President. [Cheers.]

Mr. LOGAN—I rise to propose a question to the Chair. According to the order of our business, it is not necessary for a vote in reference to balloting for President.

The PRESIDENT—The rules for the order of business do not prescribe any specific time when the Convention will go to balloting. It may delay it until after the nomination of Vice President, if it chooses. The Convention is at liberty to say whether or not it will now proceed to that business.

Gen. LOGAN—Is it the decision of the Chair that nominations are now in order?

The PRESIDENT—They are.

GEN. GRANT NOMINATED.

Gen. LOGAN—Then, Sir, in the name of the loyal citizens and soldiers and sailors of this great republic of the United States of America; in the name of loyalty, liberty, humanity and justice; in the name of the National Union Republican Party, I nominate as candidate for the Chief Magistracy of this nation ULYSSES S. GRANT.

The greatest enthusiasm prevailed upon the nomination of Gen. GRANT. The members arose to their feet and gave three rousing cheers for the General. Handkerchiefs were waved, and the band played "Hail to the Chief."

A delegate from South Carolina—I move you, Sir, that the vote be taken by acclamation. [Cries of "No! no!"]

THE PRESIDENT.—The rules designate the manner in which the vote shall be taken. The list of States and Territories will be called by the Secretary, and as they are called each delegation will designate its choice for President of the United States. It is understood, under the rules, that the Chairman of the delegations shall announce the vote for their respective States.

The roll was called, when each delegation responded as follows:

Alabama, through the Chairman of her delegation cast 18 votes for ULYSSES S. GRANT.

Arkansas cast 10 votes for U. S. GRANT.

California—We come here, six thousand miles to call our vote for Gen. GRANT. [Cheers.]

COLORADO.—The Rocky Mountains of Colorado say six votes for Gen. GRANT.

CONNECTICUT unconditionally surrenders her twelve votes to Gen. GRANT.

DAKOTAH.—GRANT, two votes.

DELAWARE.—Six votes for GRANT.

DISTRICT OF COLUMBIA gives her two votes for GRANT.

Florida, the land of flowers, gives six votes for Gen. GRANT.

Georgia cast her vote through Gov. BROWN, who said the Republicans of Georgia, many of whom were the original Secessionists, recognizing the wisdom of the maxim, "Enemies in war, in peace friends," and heartily desiring to speed the restoration of the Union, harmony, peace and good government, instruct me through their representatives here to cast eighteen votes for Gen. GRANT.

IDAHO gives two votes for GRANT.

ILLINOIS gives thirty-two votes for GRANT.

INDIANA gives twenty-six votes for GRANT.

IOWA gives sixteen votes for GRANT, and promises to back it up with forty thousand majority.

KANSAS, the John Brown State, gives six votes for GRANT.

KENTUCKY casts twenty-two votes for GRANT.

LOUISIANA gives fourteen votes for GRANT, and we propose to fight it out on that line if it takes all Summer. (Applause.)

MAINE gives fourteen votes for GRANT.

MARYLAND—Believing that our great captain will crush treason in the Cabinet as he crushed it in the field, "Maryland, My Maryland," gives fourteen for GRANT. [Applause.]

MASSACHUSETTS gives twenty-four for GRANT.

MICHIGAN, following the State of Massachusetts, gives sixteen for GRANT.

MINNESOTA, the North Star State, gives all she has, eight votes, for GRANT.

MISSISSIPPI, the home of JEFF. DAVIS, repudiates the traitor, and offers her fourteen votes for GRANT.

MISSOURI was under instruction of the State Convention to vote for GRANT on a Radical platform. We have confidence that GRANT will carry out its principles. Missouri gives GRANT twenty-two votes.

MONTANA. The mountains of Montana, from whence flow the waters of the Columbia and Mississippi, are vocal with the name of GRANT, to whom she gives two votes. [Laughter.]

NEBRASKA, the last State admitted to the Union and the first to adopt impartial suffrage, gives six votes for GRANT.

NEVADA, the silver State, has only six votes, but proposes to give six more next Fall for GRANT.

NEW-HAMPSHIRE—Ten votes for GRANT.

MEW-MEXICO called for, but not present to respond.

NEW-JERSEY—Her delegation, instructed by her Convention which spoke the voice of every man of the Republican Party within her borders, deliver their fourteen votes for GRANT, not only the victorious soldier, but conspicuous for calmness of judgment, sincerity of patriotism and personal honesty.

New-York—Sixty-six votes for GRANT.

North Carolina—Known as the land of the tar-heels, [great laughter,) gives eighteen vetes for GRANT, and will give 36,000 votes for him, all of which will stick. [Applause.]

Ohio has the honor of being the mother of our great leader. Ohio is in line, and "on that line" Ohio proposes, under the captain who never knew defeat, to fight it out through the summer and in the autumn when the great victory will be secured. Ohio casts forty-two votes for GRANT.

RHODE ISLAND.—Little Rhody, small in stature, but great in patriotic impulses, gives her eight votes for GRANT and wishes she had more. [Applause.]

SOUTH CAROLINA.—The birthplace and home of CALHOUN, and the doctrine of State Rights, the first to withdraw herself from the Union, directs her representatives, sent here by a majority of 43,470, [applause,] returning as we do to the counsels of those who desired only to preserve the Union, arm in arm, and in heart to heart, with Massachusetts, [great cheers,] gives her twelve votes for GRANT. [Immense applause.]

TENNESSEE, being one of the Southern States that was forced into rebellion, being the first to reconstruct and be readmitted into the Union, and to-day being in the enjoyment of the most liberal Republican Government in the United States casts twenty votes for GRANT, [cheers,] and with the solemn pledge never again to present the name for President or Vice President of such a traitor as A. JOHNSON, [loud cheers,] casts twelve votes for GRANT.

Texas—The empire State of the South, containing 275,000 square miles, and capable of sustaining 20,000,000 of people, casts eight votes for GRANT. [Applause.]

Verment—Ten votes for GRANT.

VIRGINIA —Rising from the grave that Gen. GRANT dug for her in the Appomattox in 1865, comes up here with twenty votes and enlists under his banner. They propose next November to move on the enemy's works. [Loud applause.]

WEST VIRGINIA—A corner of the rebellion which never gave a Democratic majority, gives freely and willingly her ten votes for GRANT. [Applause.]

WISCONSIN—The last of the roll of States, adds her voice to that of her sister States and gives sixteen votes for GRANT. [Applause.]

The PRESIDENT—The roll is completed. Gentlemen of the Convention you have six hundred and fifty votes, and you have given six hundred and fifty votes for Gen. ULYSSES S. GRANT. [Tremendous applause.

The entire audience arose with three times three for GRANT.

May 22, 1868

The Democratic Nomination.

A nomination by the Democracy seemed at one time probable by which the chances of the Presidential contest would have been rendered comparatively close. There were signs of a disposition to accept those results of reconstruction which are, peaceably, irreversible, and to adapt the future policy of the party to the living questions of finance and administration. The nomination of Mr. CHASE was talked of as at once the symbol and the guarantee of the good faith and practical character of the movement. The rejection of an extreme leadership was urged as essential to success, and a platform was suggested which would have recognized the main features of reconstruction as accomplished facts. Had this view commended itself to the favor of the Democratic Party, the most exciting controversy of the day would have lost its more dangerous characteristics, and the struggle of the parties for the supremacy would have involved nothing inimical to the national peace.

If doubts remained as to the fate of this programme, they were dispelled by the resolutions unanimously adopted by the Democratic Convention. These indicated the predominance of the more extreme element. They affirm a sectional policy of bad faith and confiscation on the financial question, and a bitter though undefined opposition, as well to the means employed for the restoration of the South to the Union, as to the attitude which the reconstructed States are expected to occupy. The financial policy adopted is unmistakably that of PENDLETON. On the reconstruction question, the precise meaning of the Convention remained to be interpreted by the position and purposes of the candidate selected.

Here again the Convention has by its subsequent action obviated uncertainty. It has realized apparently, the growth of an inclination to pursue a moderate course, and has availed itself of the opportunity to put the spirit of the party beyond dispute. There was the chance, by nominating HANCOCK, to conciliate the Union sentiment, and to give a hostage for the party's adherence to the law. Or by elevating HENDRICKS, it might have proclaimed the surrender of Copperheadism to the War Democracy. But the Convention, from the moment of its assembling, treated schemes of moderation and compromise with contempt. Its platform revealed a temper and policy unaffected by experience or responsibility, and it has filled the measure of its determination by nominating for the Presidency HORATIO SEYMOUR.

The meaning of all that was dubious in the platform, and the policy of the party, in relation to the Union, are by this nomination made plain. Mr. SEYMOUR is the exponent of a Democracy that cannot be misunderstood. His late speeches have been suspiciously vague. They were for PENDLETON and against him—for CHASE and against him. They pointed the workman's finger of hate at the bondholder, and lulled the bondholder into a delusive sense of security by representing his interest and the workman's as one. On the reconstruction question he has played the part of demagogue rather than of statesman. He has assailed as intolerable measures which cannot be undone except by revolution, and has pandered to prejudices which can be gratified only at the cost of peace. He has treated as still open matters which in seven States are already closed, and has counseled proceedings which could have no other effect than to rekindle the animosities and revive the perils of the rebellion. A certain haze has hung over these utterances, but their tendency has undoubtedly been to fan the flame of resistance to reconstruction, and to create the conviction that the work of restoring the Union is yet unfinished.

Mr. SEYMOUR will be judged, however, less by the speeches of to-day than by his record as Governor of this State during a critical period of the war. Whether he should be trusted with the administration of the National Government at a time when its whole strength will be needed to solidify and smoothen the work of reconstruction, is a question best answered by reference to what he did when the nation's destinies were in jeopardy. What he may now say amounts to little. What he did as State Executive in 1863 and 1864 affords the best possible means of judging how far he is fitted to perfect the restoration of the Union, and to hold in check the hostile influences which still threaten its permanence.

The one great fact which rises in judgment against Mr. SEYMOUR is, that, as Governor, his whole power was exerted against the National Government. Elected on the distinct ground that the aid of the State should be given to make more vigorous the prosecution of the war, he used the opportunities and influence of his office to foster discontent, to impair the efficiency of Mr. LINCOLN's administration, and so to encourage and prolong the rebellion. His sympathies and plans were on the side of those who would have rendered the continuance of the struggle for the Union impossible. He was an effective ally of the Copperheads, and exerted his energies to array the State against the Republic. He sowed the seeds of sectional quarrels, as between New-York and the West on one hand, and New-England on the other, and for two years was in reality the most formidable enemy of the Government not actually in arms against it. When the cause of the Union triumphed, it was in spite of the adroit, persistent, and most mischievous endeavors of Mr. SEYMOUR.

To make such a man the standard-bearer of the Democratic Party against GRANT is to array that party in an attitude hostile to the pacification of the country. There are many who fought manfully against the Union who are now laboring for its preservation and prosperity. And it is at least possible that a frank acceptance of the situation by Mr. SEYMOUR, before this nomination offered the temptation to dissimulate, would have been treated as in large part an atonement for official acts in the Copperhead service. But coming forth as he does the champion of a party which withholds acquiescence from the results of reconstruction, and menaces these results with threats which may culminate in renewed trouble, we cannot forget that the HORATIO SEYMOUR who is to wrestle with GRANT for the Presidency did what he could

to weaken the Union soldier on the battle-field. It is meet that he who labored, secret-ly, to succor the rebels, should now be the nominee of a party intent upon undoing the results of victory.

The nomination deserves additional significance from the purposes boldly avowed by his associate on the ticket. The alliance of SEYMOUR, who plotted against the Union, with F. P. BLAIR, who gallantly fought to save it, would be most incongruous but for the epistle with which the latter sought to commend himself to the good graces of the Convention. Nothing more revolutionary than his proposition has appeared. It threatens the overthrow of reconstruction, the undoing of all that has been done, and the reëstablishment in power of the old disloyal whites, by sheer usurpation and force. Considering Mr. BLAIR's letter in conjunction with Mr. SEYMOUR's record, and both with the platform adopted by the Convention, we must conclude that the position and policy of the

Democracy are hostile to the peace which above all things the country needs.

Such a ticket, resting on such a platform, inspires no apprehension of success. SEYMOUR, with all his ability, has never filled a national office, and his reputation is not great outside the State. BLAIR, who once stood well with the Western volunteers, has ruined his standing by his recent surrender to the enemy. The ticket, therefore, is not a strong one. It will not bring out even the full Democratic vote, and it will assuredly disgust the non-partisan element, without whose support the Democracy would, under any circumstances, strive in vain. Mr. SEYMOUR was more than usually candid, yesterday, when he told the Convention that "he could not be nominated without putting himself and the Democratic Party in peril." Nothing but a succession of miracles can save it from defeat.

July 10, 1868

The General Result.

Everybody seems to be very well satisfied, on the whole, with the result of the election. The Democrats cared comparatively little for the Presidency, which they despaired of carrying immediately after the October elections; they are abundantly consoled for the defeat of SEYMOUR by the success of HOFFMAN. All they have hoped or sought to do for the last month was to hold the State of New-York. This will give them a chance to reorganize their shattered party, and will make it certain that, whenever it shall again be reconstructed, the Democracy of this State, (meaning thereby the Tammany Ring,) will have the ascendency and control of its councils.

The Erie Railroad is a tool in the hands of the Ring already, and its money and direction are used remorselessly to augment its political power and swell the personal fortunes of its individual members. The patronage and general influence of the Executive branch of the State Government will be in the same hands, and used for the same ends. And whenever the Democratic Party shall again enter the field, it will be rather to confirm the power and advance the fortunes of the Tammany Ring, than to build up and strengthen the Democ-

racy as one of the great political parties of the country. The Ring is at last supreme in the party councils of the nation, and bids fair to extend over the State and Union the same sway it has wielded so long over the affairs and interests of this City.

Tammany has played its game with adroitness and success. By dictating the platform and the candidates it destroyed all chances of a national success; and by bending all its efforts to elect HOFFMAN, it secured all the advantage of such success as the party might achieve, to itself. Its rejoicings over the result confirm the charges of treachery to the party which have been so lavishly heaped on the Ring by the leading organs of the Democracy outside the State. The *National Intelligencer*, which has been conspicuous for its plain-speaking on this subject, will find all its denunciations of the Tammany wire-pullers fully confirmed by the result of their labors.

This election, unless we are mistaken, will put an end to the Democratic Party as at present organized. That party can never again rally on a platform of sympathy with the secession movement. It will be forced to do now, what its wisest and most patriotic members tried to have it do last July—*accept*

the results of the war and make them the starting point in any new political crusade.

The reconstruction measures will now have a fair trial. If they work well and promote harmony and prosperity in the Southern States, they will enter into the fixed policy of those States and become part of their fundamental laws. It not, they will be amended, repealed or replaced by others which will answer the purpose better. Those Southern States, which have resumed their practical relations with the General Government, have now complete control of their own affairs,—as fully and in the same sense as the other States within the Union. The people of the South have no longer any motive for the disorder and violence which prevailed before the election. They can gain nothing, and they may lose much, by continuing it longer. Their alliance with the Democratic Party of the North can no longer be of any service to them; the party is without present power or future hope. If the South is not incapable of profiting by disaster and learning wisdom by experience, it will await hopefully the advent of GRANT's administration, and will give it such support as its practical character may show that it deserves.

November 5, 1868

Gen. Grant and Political Parties—Things to be Remembered.

There are some leading facts which it may be well for those who are so anxious concerning Gen. GRANT's party relations and probable action, to bear in mind. The Republicans, for example, who insist that he ought to be, in the strict sense of the word, a party President,—taking the advice of the leaders of the Republican Party as his sufficient guide and rule of action, because he was nominated and elected by that party,—will do well to remember:

1. That Gen. GRANT never was a member of the Republican Party until after the war.
2. That he was nominated at Chicago not mainly because he was a Republican, but because he had more of the confidence of the people than any other man in the country.
3. That the canvass proved that he was stronger with the country than the party, and received a great many votes and a great moral support from outside the party limits.

4. That his hold on the confidence of the country is quite as strong to-day as it ever was, and is not likely to be forfeited or lessened by any rash or reckless action on his part.

These considerations combine to give Gen. GRANT a degree of independence, in his official action, which few of his predecessors have ever had. The people do not expect or desire him to be a mere party President. His assent to the leading principles and measures of the Republican Party, has been given in the clearest and most explicit manner, and no one doubts that they will form the basis of his Administration. But this fact gives no warrant for the expectation that he will, in all things, consult primarily the wishes or supposed interests of the party as the guide of his action.

On the other hand those Democrats who are predicting that he will turn his back upon the Republican Party and espouse, in any

way, the principles or policy of the Democracy, may do well to call to mind:

1. That throughout the war Gen. GRANT received no support from the Democratic Party, and always regarded its action as hostile to the cause of the Union, which the war was waged to sustain.
2. That after the war, he took more than one occasion to say that no party which, during the war, failed to do its utmost in support of the Government, deserved the confidence of the country.
3. That he has more than once declared that he had far more toleration for Southern men who went into the rebellion, than for Northern men who did not do all in their power to put it down.
4. That he regards efforts to obstruct and embarrass the Government in its endeavors to reorganize Southern society on the basis of existing laws, as hostile to the peace,

which is essential to the prosperity, of the country.

5. That in accepting the nomination of the Republican Party, he evinced and declared his reliance upon that party, rather than any other, to restore harmony to the nation and bring the Government back to its natural and beneficent course of operation.

While Gen. GRANT has a right, therefore, to expect from the Democratic Party such a degree of support as the wisdom and justice of his official action may deserve, there is no reason to suppose that he will look for, or try to get, anything more at its hands. That any part of the patronage of his office, will be offered as a consideration for Democratic support, no one for a moment dreams. And that he will shape his measures with a view to securing Democratic favor, any further than to make them such as will deserve the favor of *all*, there is no more reason to suppose.

Mere party considerations of any kind, we think, will enter much less into Gen. GRANT'S administration than many suppose. His first aim will be to deserve the favor and support of all honest and patriotic men of *all* parties, by doing that which will best promote the welfare and prosperity of the whole country. That there is any better way than this, of securing the support of his own party, none but its enemies will for a moment pretend.

February 10, 1869

THE FINAL ACT.

Detailed Report of the Third and Last Day's Proceedings of the Convention.

CINCINNATI, Ohio, May 3.—The Convention was called to order at 10:10 o'clock. The reading of the journal was dispensed with.

The Chair stated that the statement in a morning paper pretending to give a dispatch from him (SCHURZ) to a candidate was utterly untrue.

Mr. GILMORE, of Missouri, offered a resolution that when the Convention reaches the point of balloting for candidates, there shall be no formal presentation of candidates, but that the Convention proceed to vote.

Mr. DEXTER, of Illinois, sustained the proposition. He said he wanted to proceed to business, and avoid mere personal eulogies.

The resolution was carried.

THE ADDRESS AND RESOLUTIONS.

Mr. HORACE WHITE, from the Committee on Platform, reported a set of resolutions which had been unanimously adopted by the Committee.

Address of the Committee on Resolutions.

The Administration now in power has rendered itself guilty of wanton disregard of the laws of the land and of powers not granted by the Constitution. It has acted as if the laws had binding force only for those who are governed, and not for those who govern. It has thus struck a blow at the fundamental principles of constitutional government, and the liberties of the citizen. The President of the United States has openly used the powers and opportunities of his high office for the promotion of personal ends. He has kept notoriously corrupt and unworthy men in places of power and responsibility to the detriment of the public interest. He has used the public service of the Government as a machinery of partisan and personal influence, and interfered with tyrannical arrogance in the political affairs of States and municipalities. He has rewarded with influential and lucrative offices men who had acquired his favor by valuable presents, thus stimulating demoralization of our political life by his conspicuous example. He has shown himself deplorably unequal to the tasks imposed upon him by the necessities of the country, and culpably careless of the responsibilities of his high office. The partisans of the Administration, assuming to be the Republican Party and controlling its organization, have attempted to justify such wrongs and palliate such abuses, to the end of maintaining partisan ascendancy. They have stood in the way of necessary investigations and indispensable reforms, pretending that no serious fault could be found with the present administration of public affairs, thus seeking to blind the eyes of the people. They have kept alive the passions and resentments of the late civil war to use them for their own advantage. They have resorted to arbitrary measures in direct conflict with the organic law instead of appealing to the better instincts and latent patriotism of the Southern people by restoring to them those rights, the enjoyment of which is indispensable for a successful administration of their local affairs, and would tend to move a patriotic and hopeful national feeling. They have degraded themselves, and the name of their party, once justly entitled to the confidence of the nation, by a base sycophancy to the dispenser of executive power and patronage unworthy of Republican freemen, they have sought to stifle the voice of just criticism, to stifle the moral sense of the people and to subjugate public opinion by tyrannical party discipline. They are striving to maintain themselves in authority for selfish ends by an unscrupulous use of the power which rightfully belongs to the people, and should be employed only in the service of the country. Believing that an organisation thus led and controlled can no longer be of service to the best interests of the Republic, we have resolved to make an independent appeal to the sober judgment, conscience and patriotism of the American people.

We, the Liberal Republicans of the United States, in National Convention assembled at Cincinnati, proclaim the following principles as essential to just government:

First—We recognise the equality of all men before the law, and hold that it is the duty of government in its dealings with the people to mete out equal and exact justice to all, of whatever nativity, race, color or persuasion, religious or political.

Second—We pledge ourselves to maintain the union of the States, emancipation and enfranchisement, and to oppose any reopening of the questions settled by the Thirteenth, Fourteenth and Fifteenth Amendments to the Constitution.

Third—We demand the immediate and absolute removal of all disabilities imposed on account of the rebellion which was finally subdued seven years ago, believing that universal amnesty will result in complete pacification in all sections of the country.

Fourth—Local self-government with impartial suffrage will guard the rights of all citizens more securely than any centralized power. The public welfare requires the supremacy of the civil over the military authority, and freedom of person under the protection of the *habeas corpus*. We demand for the individual the largest liberty consistent with public order, for the State self-government, and for the nation a return to the methods of peace and the constitutional limitation of power.

Fifth—The civil service of the Government has become a mere instrument of partisan tyranny and personal ambition, and an object of selfish greed. It is a scandal and reproach upon free institutions, and breeds a demoralization dangerous to the perpetuity of republican government. We therefore regard such thorough reforms of the civil service as one of the most pressing necessities of the hour; that honesty, capacity and fidelity, constitute the only valid claims to public employment; That the offices of the Government cease to be a matter of arbitrary favoritism and patronage, and that public station become again a post of honor. To this end it is imperatively required that no President shall be a candidate for re-election.

Sixth—We demand a system of Federal taxation which shall not unnecessarily interfere with the industry of the people, and which shall provide the means necessary to pay the expenses of the Government economically administered, the pensions, the interest on the public debt, and a moderate reduction annually of the principal thereof; and, recognizing that there are in our midst honest but irreconcilable differences of opinion with regard to the respective systems of protection and free trade, we remit the discussion of the subject to the people in their Congressional districts and to the decision of Congress thereon, wholly free of Executive interference or dictation.

Seventh—The public credit must be sacredly maintained, and we denounce repudiation in every form and guise.

Eighth—A speedy return to specie payment is demanded alike by highest considerations of commercial morality and honest government.

Ninth—We remember with gratitude the heroism and sacrifices of the soldiers and sailors of the Republic, and no act of ours shall ever detract from their justly earned fame or the full reward of their patriotism.

Tenth—We are opposed to all further grants of land to railroads or other corporations. The public domain should be held sacred to actual settlers.

Eleventh—We hold that it is the duty of the Government, in its intercourse with foreign nations, to cultivate the friendship of peace by treating with all on fair and equal terms, regarding it alike dishonorable either to demand what is not right or to submit to what is wrong.

Twelfth—For the promotion and success of these vital principles, and the support of the candidates nominated by this Convention, we invite and cordially welcome the co-operation of all patriotic citizens, without regard to previous affiliations.

(Signed,) HORACE WHITE,
Chairman of Committee on Resolutions.
G. P. THURSTON, Secretary.

The platform was adopted unanimously.

BALLOTING OF CANDIDATES.

The next order of business was stated by the Chair to be the nomination of candidates for the Presidency, without the formal presentation of candidates.

Before the result of the first ballot was announced, GRATZ BROWN, by unanimous consent, took the stand and thanked his friends for their support of him, but withdrew his name and asked his friends to support HORACE GREELEY. [Great cheers with many persistent hisses.]

Considerable confusion ensued, various delegations asking to change their votes, contention arising in some of them—notably Kentucky—as to what the changes among themselves really were, after which the Chair announced the following result:

First Ballot.

Whole number of votes	714		
Necessary to a choice	358		
Adams	203	Greeley	147
Trumbull	110	Brown	95
Davis	92½	Curtin	62
Chase	2½	Sumner	1

Missouri asked leave to retire for consultation. Mr. MCCLURE withdrew Gov. CURTIN'S name, and asked leave for the Pennsylvania delegation to retire, which request was granted. The proceedings were suspended until the return of the absent delegations.

Second Ballot.

Greeley	245	Adams	243
Trumbull	148	Davis	75
Brown	2	Chase	1

Third Ballot.

Adams	264	Greeley	258
Trumbull	156	Davis	44

Fourth Ballot.

Adams	279	Greeley	251
Trumbull	141	Davis	51

Fifth Ballot.

Adams	309	Greeley	258
Trumbull	91	Davis	30
Chase	24	Chase	2

The announcement of ADAMS' vote was received with great cheers. The sixth ballot was ordered, amid a scene of great confusion. Missouri asked leave to retire for consultation. After an interval of twenty minutes, the call of the roll was proceeded with.

Sixth Ballot.

Greeley	332	Adams	324
Chase	32	Trumbull	19
Davis	6	Palmer	1

Before the vote was formally announced, Minnesota changed 9 from TRUMBULL to GREELEY. Various States changed their votes. A scene of great confusion and noise followed. Mr. MCCLURE changed Pennsylvania to 50 for GREELEY and 6 for DAVIS. Indiana changed to 27 for ADAMS. A stampede of changes to GREELEY here occurred, and the noise and confusion that followed was very great. Illinois changed solid to GREELEY, except one delegate, who insisted that his vote should stand for TRUMBULL.

The Chair finally announced the whole vote as 714; necessary to a choice, 358. ADAMS had 187; GREELEY 482.

Mr. CASEMENT moved to make the nomination unanimous, but it was declared lost, as there were many nays before the vote was announced.

The Chair then announced that Mr. GREELEY was nominated as the candidate for the Presidency by the Convention.

NOMINATING THE VICE-PRESIDENT.

On motion, it was ordered to proceed to the nomination of a Vice-President immediately, and GRATZ BROWN was nominated on the second ballot. During the balloting Gov. KOERNER, of Illinois, stated that he had received a telegram from Mr. TRUMBULL positively declining to be a candidate for Vice-President under any circumstances. Several States offered their votes to CASSIUS M. CLAY, but he declined to be considered a candidate, advising them to vote for Mr. BROWN. Mr. COX, of Ohio, also declined to be considered a candidate. Gov. PALMER, of Illinois, would not accept a nomination under any circumstances. Mr. BROWN'S nomination was then made unanimous, and the President and Vice-President of the Convention were appointed a Committee to announce the nominations to the candidates.

After resolutions of thanks to Cincinnati for her hospitality and to the officers of the Convention were adopted, the roll of the States was called for members of the National Executive Committee.

In response to vehement calls for a speech, Senator SCHURZ said: My fellow-citizens—This Convention has overwhelmed me with kindness, and I have especially to thank them for the indulgence with which they have borne with me while I was endeavoring, to the best of my ability, to conduct with fairness and impartiality the deliberations of this large, and let us confess, a little unruly, body. [Laughter.] We have now accomplished our work. Our duty it will be now to proclaim to all the land the principles we have embodied in our platform, and go forward and solicit, with all entreaties which our minds and hearts are capable of making, the support of the people of the United States for the candidates we have nominated. I have already done so much speaking in this Convention, and, may be, I may have to do so much during the impending campaign, that you will certainly bear with me if I close my speech in the same manner in which I closed my first—then by seconding the motion to adjourn, and now by declaring the Liberal Republican Convention adjourned *sine di.*.

May 4, 1872

Convention Notes.

That a National Convention should cast its vote unanimously for one candidate, and with the deepest earnestness and enthusiasm, is a phenomenon which the out-at-elbows and miserable Greeley faction will find it hard to explain away. Such a scene as that which was witnessed yesterday at Philadelphia is unprecedented in our history. The feeling entertained for Gen. GRANT is far more cordial and affectionate than his best friends have ventured to represent it. The delegates from all the States declare that their fellow-citizens will not hear of anybody mentioned as a rival to GRANT. Pennsylvania undertakes to give him a large majority—the States which have been considered doubtful are now confident of victory. There can be no question that Gen. GRANT is much stronger with the people than the ordinary run of politicians ever supposed. The people understand the value of the opposition which arises from disappointment or personal resentments, and have no sympathy whatever with it. They have more confidence in Gen. GRANT than they had even in 1868, and they will elect him this year by a larger majority than they gave him then.

Senator WILSON owes his nomination in a great measure to his own hard services and high character—but he must also thank Senator SUMNER for some share in bringing about the result. The delegates were determined to express their opinion of the shameful slanders which Mr. SUMNER poured out against the President, and to give his fellow-Senator the second place on the ticket with Gen. GRANT seemed to afford the most effectual means of gratifying this desire. We believe it is a positive fact that Mr. SUMNER was fully convinced that his tirade would prevent the nomination of General GRANT at Philadelphia! It is only another proof of the fact that a man may nurse and "coddle" his vanity until it completely runs away with his judgment. We do not suppose that Mr. SUMNER has any misgivings about his recent course, for in his eyes whatever Mr. SUMNER does must be right. His friends, however, can all see

pretty plainly how irreparable is the mistake he has committed, and if the question of his re-election were to come up just now in Massachusetts, he would find out what the people of that State think of his descending to become a conduit for CHARLES A. DANA's slanders.

Mr. WILSON is very popular with the working classes, and he well deserves the recognition he has received. He is a strong man, and will assist the ticket—if it needed any assistance—in various directions. It is only proper, however, for us to add that Mr. COLFAX has not lost one particle of the respect or confidence of the country. The feeling for him at Philadelphia was of the kindest description, and we wish he could have heard the cordial manner in which the delegations spoke of him. An odd story has crept about to the effect that newspaper correspondents were decidedly against Mr. COLFAX. If they were, it made no difference one way or the other. Journalists are men of little influence when they step out from their papers to advocate any man, and their incapacity for "running" a convention was sufficiently proved at Cincinnati. It the reporters at Philadelphia flatter themselves that they had anything to do with the nomination of HENRY WILSON, they merely afford a fresh application of the fable in which the fly on the wheel expresses prodigious astonishment at the dust he is raising. Newspaper men seldom show to so little advantage as when they are fussing about to get this or that candidate elected; and if they could only get it into their heads how little people respect or care for them, apart from their papers, it would save them a world of trouble, and sometimes prevent them making great fools of themselves.

Mr. COLFAX can scarcely be said to be defeated. The rivalry—if such it was—was conducted on the most friendly terms, and we are far from believing that the public would be contented to see Mr. COLFAX relegated permanently to private life. He will yet occupy a distinguished and useful position in the country. He has done absolutely nothing to forfeit the confidence with which

he has long been regarded. We should have been happy to have seen his name this year again on the Presidential ticket—but it is a satisfaction to know that his successor is a man in every way deserving of the honor paid to him. The sentiment prevailed very generally among the delegates that Mr. WILSON deserved some reward for his services, and that it was not wise to postpone that reward too long. We shall not take leave of Mr. COLFAX when Mr. WILSON succeeds him, but rely confidently on seeing him once more in a prominent position before the nation, and still followed by their cordial respect and good wishes.

Altogether, this Convention will rank as one of the most memorable in our history. The delegations were composed of singularly able and independent men. It is the stupidest of all slanders to represent those gentlemen as "corrupt office-holders," as the *Tribune* does, for that only offends the people of the States from which they come, and does not really deceive anybody. The insults which the *Tribune* has leveled at the Convention are dictated by the merest fatuity, and will go far toward ruining that once powerful paper. There are at least two parties who know how false are the *Tribune's* assertions—the delegates themselves and the people who sent them. What is the good, then, of "telling lies," as GREELEY used to call it, which have not even the negative merit of taking anybody in? The truth is that the Convention was an extremely creditable body of men, and they did their work in a most intelligent and business-like manner. What they have done the people will ratify, as surely as the sun will rise and set today. Let us only work carefully and properly, and while despising the enemy —as we cannot help doing, for he is at once a foolish and dishonest enemy—take care to circumvent his "dodges," and the Democrats, with GREELEY at their head, will be consigned to certain destruction in November. By all means let us get GREELEY and all of them in one pit, so that they may be decently interred with as little expense and trouble as possible.

June 7, 1872

THE INFAMOUS ALLIANCE

"Tammany Responds to Greeley."

"Tammany Does Support Greeley— Tammany is for Greeley."—*New-York Tribune, July 18, 1872.*

Anybody who walks through our streets,

or who takes the trouble to make a few inquiries among Democrats, may see or find out that Horace Greeley is supported by the entire gang of Tammany Democrats.

From Tammany Hall his flag is flying.

The Tammany which supports Greeley is the same as that which robbed the people. Respectable Democrats are everywhere holding aloof from him. Mr. Augustus Schell avows that he only supports Greeley as a means of bringing utter and final ruin upon the Republican Party.

But the Tammany which "is for Greeley" today is identically the same body which so abominably plundered New-York, and which was defended and advocated by the very newspapers now engaged in defending and advocating Greeley.

When the announcement of his nomination at Baltimore reached New-York, Tammany ordered a salute of 100 guns to be fired in his honor. The *Tribune* itself, on the following day, made the following boasts in its most prominent columns:

"In the City Hall Park was displayed a large banner bearing the inscription: TAMMANY RESPONDS TO THE NOMINATION OF THE NATIONAL CONVENTION AT BALTIMORE.' Directly in front of this banner was a four-pounder, from which 100 salutes in honor of the nomination were fired in quick succession. Soon after this small gun began to make itself heard, two ten-pounders were put in position a little to the left of it, each of which added fifty reverberating roars," &c. &c. "Upon the receipt of a dispatch from Baltimore announcing the nomination of the Cincinnati candidates, *a large flag was raised over Tammany Hall.*"

Tweed is working actively for Greeley. So is Sweeny. So is A. Oakey Hall. So is Matthew T. Brennan, who continues to cheat the City yearly out of thousands of dollars. There is not a rascal connected with the Ring which so wickedly plundered New-York who is not vitally concerned in Greeley's success. This is a matter of fact, which no respectable Democrat denies.

All these knaves are well aware that the election for Governor, and that for Mayor and other local officers, take place on the same day as the Presidential election.

Greeley's "Republican" friends must vote the entire Democratic ticket, and in return the Tammany gang will vote for Greeley.

Thus a Tammany Mayor will be secured, and Controller Green will instantly be turned out. The *Herald* is already suggesting Mr. John Kane as a candidate for Mayor. Mr. Kane is merely another edition of Mayor Hall. He is Hall's nominee. He worked hard to prevent Hall's expulsion from the Union Club, and Hall would be scarcely less powerful than he now is if Kane were elected. The City of New-York would once more be handed over to a rule of Thieves, and the Tammany system of government would be carried to Washington.

July 27, 1872

The Result.

Our readers will share with us in the satisfaction with which we regard the close of the Presidential contest. It will now, we hope, be possible to talk about something else besides politics and the "claims" of candidates. There are many social questions which urgently call for attention, and it is very desirable that careful study should be given to the measures which can alone render the Republican Party worthy of the confidence which the public has so long reposed in it. We do not regard our work as finished, although the election is over. We have, as a party, yet to prove that we deserve to retain the control of public affairs, and that can only be done by unremitting care, by a careful consideration of the wishes and interests of the people, and by pursuing a broad and liberal policy, worthy of the period in which we live and of the nation.

In re-electing Gen. GRANT as President, the people have once more shown that intriguing politicians are unequal to the task of deceiving them, and that dishonest combinations of discordant factions are always resented with peculiar intensity. The idea of a party calling itself "Democratic Republican" was too preposterous to mislead the intelligent mass of voters. The men who called together the Cincinnati Convention were chiefly disappointed politicians or *doctrinaires*, who, after all, found themselves in the absurd position of being unable to control the machinery which they had framed. All the wheels turned the wrong way, and produced **the very article** which **they did not want. The old hands** at political roguery ran away with them.

and GREELEY's nomination was admitted to be fatal to the pretensions of "reform" which had been set up. All kinds of miserable tricks were resorted to for the purpose of gaining popularity for a gross imposture. Mr. GREELEY himself went about, masquerading in a white hat and coat, and constantly exhibiting himself as a "wood-chopper" in the act of spoiling good trees, by way of appealing to the "agricultural sentiment" of the country. In the mean while, the *Tribune* was busily occupied in falsifying all the professions it had entertained since its foundation, of repudiating all its principles, praising all the men whom it had denounced, and denouncing all the men whom it had praised. The idols before whom it burnt incense were Democrats like HORATIO SEYMOUR and JAMES BROOKS, and the most violent class of Secessionists. In 1866 it had bitterly opposed any suggestion of reconciliation with the South. Now it tried to convince the people that the men who were prominent in the war for the preservation of the Union were cruel despots; that the South was another Ireland; that every Northern settler in the South was a thief and murderer. No man has ever had to revile so many old friends as HORACE GREELEY during this campaign—no man has ever more completely turned his back on his own principles, or made for himself a record which will occasion him more trouble in the future. It is said that Mr. GREELEY will immediately return to the *Tribune*, determined to "wipe off all scores." He will find that the public have a "score" against him, which it will not be so easy for him to wipe off.

Although much has been said about the "abuse" and "virulence" which have characterized this campaign, it will be found upon a calm review that the inexcusable abuse has all been practiced by one side—that of GREELEY and his Democratic allies. Not only has every crime known to mankind been laid at the door of Gen. GRANT, but his wife and children have also been most wantonly assailed, and nothing has been left undone to bring him into disrepute. The criticisms upon Mr. GREELEY have been almost exclusively directed to his political inconsistencies. We have been among the most uncompromising of his opponents, and we have said nothing of him which is not strictly true—nothing which we could not prove then or now. We have based our comments upon him chiefly upon his own writings, from which we have largely quoted. In his private life and domestic circle he has been untouched—calumnies directed to these quarters have been left to our opponents. In like manner, GREELEY's chief supporters have suffered chiefly from their own misconduct. Senator SCHURZ has done his best to sell out the Republican Party to the Democrats, and in supporting GREELEY he falsified the promises made in his behalf by his best friends. DOOLITTLE was proved to have entered into a transaction utterly ruinous to any man in public life. FENTON has sustained his reputation as an utterly unprincipled and knavish schemer. We might go through the list, but at present it is unnecessary. On our side the contest has been conducted on the basis of appeals to justice and the good sense of the people, and the result justifies us in the attitude we have taken.

November 6, 1872

HAYES AND WHEELER.

AN INVINCIBLE COMBINATION.

EXCELLENT WORK OF THE NATIONAL CONVENTION—NOMINATION OF RUTHERFORD BIRCHARD HAYES, OF OHIO, FOR PRESIDENT, AND WILLIAM A. WHEELER, OF NEW-YORK, FOR VICE PRESIDENT—ENTHUSIASTIC RECEPTION OF BOTH NAMES BY THE CONVENTION AND THE NATION.

The Republican National Convention completed its labors yesterday by nominating Gov. Rutherford B. Hayes, of Ohio, for the Presidency, and Hon. William A. Wheeler, of New-York, for the Vice Presidency. The balloting began as soon as the Convention met in the morning. Before the result of the first ballot was announced, Mississippi wished to correct her vote, which raised a question whether this could be done under the rules adopted the day before on this subject. After a brief explanation, the correction was allowed, and the result of the ballot was announced by the Secretary. There was no choice, the highest number of votes being given for Mr. Blaine, which was 285. Gov. Hayes had 61. The second ballot being taken, a protracted debate occurred on the right of four Pennsylvania delegates to vote independently, the rules under which the delegation acted requiring them to vote as a unit. In the end, the Convention sustained the decision of the Chair, allowing the delegates to vote as they pleased. The result of the ballot was then announced, which still showed no choice. The balloting still went on, until, on the sixth ballot, Blaine had 308 votes. The names of Morton and Bristow were then withdrawn, and the seventh and decisive ballot gave Gov. Hayes 384 and Mr. Blaine 351. Gov. Hayes was then declared the nominee of the Convention amid the wildest enthusiasm. For

Vice President Hon. William A. Wheeler, of New-York; Stewart L. Woodford, of New-York; Joseph R. Hawley, of Connecticut; Theodore Frelinghuysen, of New-Jersey, and Marshall Jewell, of Connecticut,

were successively nominated. The roll was called, and about half the States had responded, giving Mr. Wheeler 366 votes, when, on motion, his nomination was made unanimous. This completed its work, and

the Sixth National Republican Convention adjourned with cheers for the ticket.

June 17, 1876

TILDEN NOMINATED.

A RAILROAD LAWYER AND A RE-PUDIATION PLATFORM.
THE DEMOCRATIC MACHINE AND ITS WORK AT ST. LOUIS—THE REPUTABLE ELEMENT IN THE PARTY IGNORED AND INSULTED—DISGRACEFUL SCENES — DEMOCRATS GAGGED IN A DEMOCRATIC CONVENTION.

The Democratic National Convention reassembled yesterday morning at 11 o'clock. The first business in order was the report of the Committee on Resolutions, but the committee were not ready to report, and a variety of resolutions concerning the order of business and other matters were offered and disposed of. John Kelly offered a memorial from influential

Democrats in New-York, protesting against the nomination of Tilden, but it was declared out of order. Much wrangling took place, but it was finally ended by the announcement that the Committee on Resolutions would be ready to report at 2 o'clock. A recess was taken until that hour. On reassembling the Committee made a majority and minority report, the point of difference being the financial plank of the platform. The majority report condemned the Republicans for their imbecility in not returning to specie payment, accused them of placing hindrances in the way of resumption, denounced these hindrances, and demanded the repeal of the Resumption act. The minority report declared that this act was injurious to the country and demanded its unconditional repeal. After

great confusion on motions and counter-motions, the majority report was adopted by a decisive vote. The nomination of candidates then commenced. Thomas Francis Bayard, of Delaware, was the first nominee; Thomas A. Hendricks of Indiana, came next; Joel Parker, of New-Jersey, followed; then came Samuel J. Tilden, of New-York, who was followed by William Allen, of Ohio, and Gen. Winfield Scott Hancock, of Pennsylvania. This completed the list of nominees, and the balloting ensued. On the first ballot there was no choice; on the second Samuel J. Tilden received more than the necessary two-thirds of the votes, and was declared the candidate of the Democratic Party.

June 29, 1876

EXTRA.

FRIDAY, MARCH 2, 6:30 A. M.

HAYES PRESIDENT.

The Great Contest in Congress Ended.

After a night session, in which the obstructors of the Presidential count exhausted every pretext, fair and unfair, of delay in

reaching a vote, the House, at 3:50 o'clock this morning, voted not to count the vote of the Elector from Wisconsin objected to by the Democrats. This terminated the long struggle to prevent the declaration of the election of the Republican candidate, the Senate having early in the night voted to count the State for Hayes, and notice was sent to that body to meet the House in joint convention to continue the count. The Senators appeared, the President of the Senate took the chair and the action of the two houses was announced. The ten votes of Wisconsin were then counted for Hayes and Wheeler, and these gentlemen were declared President and Vice President of the United States, having received a majority of all the Electoral votes.

March 2, 1877

THE DEAL THAT RESTORED THE SOUTH

REUNION AND REACTION: The Compromise of 1877 and the End of Reconstruction. By C. Vann Woodward. Illustrated. 263 pp. Boston: Little, Brown & Co. $4.

By DUMAS MALONE

IN the present season of political excitement and personal controversy it is a good thing to remind the American public that our generation is not the only one that has had to face dangerous dissension. During the century that ended with World War I, our domestic quarrels were set on no such background of international struggle as they are today, and there was no imperative need to present a united front against a foreign foe. On the other hand, the great sectional conflict,

Professor of History at Columbia. Mr. Malone is joint author of "The Interpretation of History."

A Searching Study of How a Broken Nation Was Brought Together After the Civil War

which created a whole series of major crises, followed geographical lines and thus threatened the very existence of the Union.

Mr. Woodward's illuminating and exciting book deals with the last of this series of crises, and, more particularly, with the compromise that settled it. The end of Reconstruction was also the end of the only period in American history during which the attempt was made to settle disputed domestic questions by force. By returning to traditional policies of expediency and concession our forefathers restored the shattered Union, gaining peace at a

price. The story of the Compromise of 1877 may be regarded as an account of the final peace negotiations.

HOWEVER, as Mr. Woodward says, this was a case of "secret covenants privately arrived at." The terms of the compromise have not been fully known, and many Americans of today may even be unaware that the political situation in 1876-77 was critical. The external facts about the disputed Presidential election between Rutherford B. Hayes and Samuel J. Tilden are that the Democratic candidate received a

popular majority and would have had an electoral majority but for the action of the returning boards in certain Southern states. In two of these, South Carolina and Louisiana, Republican State Governments were still maintained by force of arms. The electoral commission which Congress set up in this unparalleled situation had a Republican majority somewhat by accident and it proved to be strictly partisan. It gave all the disputed states to Hayes, who thus had an electoral majority of one.

The Democrats controlled the House of Representatives, however, and during the last days of the session they were filibustering against the completion of the electoral count. If the country was not on the verge of civil war, it was in danger of anarchy, since this confused session might have ended without the formal election of a President.

The agreement which ended the crisis was not between the Republicans and the Northern Democrats, who were left on a limb, but between representatives of Hayes and Southern Democrats. The traditional account of it is based on what is known of a series of last-minute conferences. According to this, the Southerners, though convinced that Tilden had really been elected, agreed to accept Hayes on the understanding that the Federal troops should be withdrawn from the Southern states and home rule restored. They abandoned the Northern Democrats and bartered the Presidency for the control of their own localities.

Mr. Woodward, a Southern historian who is as frank and fearless as he is competent, has carefully re-examined the settlement and given it a fresh interpretation which may excite some controversy. While recognizing that the restoration of home rule was essential from the Southern point of view and that this was the principle upon which the Southerners as a group were themselves united, he throws a flood of light on the political purposes and economic motives of the most active of the Southern negotiators. He does this by telling a detailed story of negotiations behind the scenes over a period of weeks, and his book deserves high commendation as a detective story.

The "bargain," he believes, had already been made before those conferences were held in the last troubled days of the Grant administration. By that time the retiring President had already pointed the way to a conciliatory Southern policy and Hayes was already committed to one. Since Congress had failed to pass an Army appropriations bill, it would have been difficult for the incoming President to have followed a stern military policy, even if he wanted to. Furthermore, the word had already gone around that the Southerners would not prevent the completion of the electoral count. Thus the conferences merely put the seal of approval on an agreement which had been made already, and Mr. Woodward, like a detective, sets out to discover what lay behind it, believing that more was there than struck the eye.

WITHOUT attempting to retell or even to outline the complicated but engrossing story of informal negotiation and intrigue that he unfolds, we can summarize his main conclusions. Some people on both sides of the old sectional dividing line may regard them as iconoclastic. The particular Southern leaders who were most involved were old-line Whigs in spirit, though nominally Democrats, and they were by no means unwilling to coalesce with the Hayes Republicans.

In other words, Southern political unity against the detested Republicans was less than has been supposed. A considerable body of leaders were ready to join the enemy. The main reasons were economic. Actually, these particular leaders were in the tradition of Henry Clay and Alexander Hamilton rather than that of Andrew Jackson and Thomas Jefferson, and, apart from racial questions, were more sympathetic with conservative Republicans than with Northern Democrats. In order to gain their open or tacit support, however, the Northerners had to sidetrack the racial question. Also, this group not unnaturally wanted financial favors for their section, and the tradition of Federal aid was much stronger at this stage among Republicans than Democrats.

THE bargain which these Southerners worked out with representatives

A contemporary cartoon from Puck.

"To Southerners, the return of home rule was essential."

of Hayes was afterward glossed over, according to Mr. Woodward, because there were things in it which neither side wanted to talk about. As stated in a newspaper at the time, and elaborated in this book, "Democratic apostasy" in the South was to be rewarded by the following guarantees: (1) One or two Cabinet places, especially the Postmaster Generalship, the hope being that an Administration party could be built up in the South with the aid of patronage. (2) The control by the South of its own state governments. (3) A policy of liberal appropriations for Southern internal improvements, such as levees on the lower Mississippi. (4) The passage of the Texas and Pacific Railroad bill, granting favors to a Southern enterprise similar to those granted Northern and Western railroads.

MR. WOODWARD tells the sordid but engrossing railroad story at length. Tom Scott of the Pennsylvania Railroad was deeply involved and Collis P. Huntington of the Southern Pacific was his bitter rival. Among Scott's supporters were some Southerners of sainted memory, like Alexander H. Stephens, former Vice President of the Confederacy, and L. Q. C. Lamar, who served with such dignity in the Senate and later on the Supreme Court. It afterward seemed desirable to forget this part of the "plot."

Certain other parts of the "bargain" have been largely forgotten because they could not be carried out. Hayes appointed a former Confederate general as Postmaster General, and Southerners began to share the patronage, but the attempt to build up a Southern Republican party failed and practically everybody clung to the Democratic label. The President withdrew the support of the Army from the remaining Reconstruction governments and these promptly fell, but the Southerners, despite the agreement of some of them to help the Republican minority organize the House of Representatives, gave the Republicans no help when Congress assembled in the fall, and the Democrats organized the House.

Perhaps it was because of this breach of the agreement that Hayes did not carry out his part of the economic bargain, though there were other reasons why he did not support the dubious railroad bill. More important still was the apparent failure of the Southern bargainers to carry out their own conservative economic purposes at home. As soon as all the states were assured of local self-rule the Southern agrarians joined hand with their Western brethren against the East, clamoring for cheap money.

ON the whole, however, things turned out as the bargainers hoped and expected. The road to reunion was a forked road, as Mr. Woodward aptly says, the right fork leading to the East and the left to the West. Sometimes most of the Southerners took the left fork, but generally they took the right. The so-called "Bourbons" who came into political power

(Wade Hampton of South Carolina is a good example) were thoroughly sympathetic with Eastern conservatism.

The Compromise thus proved to be a fundamentally conservative one, guaranteeing the persistence of the new economic order which had consolidated its power when Southerners had no part in the Government, and making the South, to all practical purposes, a satellite of the Northern industrial and financial system. That was the real price the South paid for reunion. Apparently Mr. Woodward thinks that the degree of acquiescence on the part of the leaders was greater than was necessary.

It seemed to many Northerners in 1877 that the granting of undisputed local control to the Southern states amounted to a repudiation of the more idealistic objects of the war and the virtual abandonment of the freedmen, even though important laws respecting the latter remained on the statute books. Mr. Woodward is convinced that the dominant Northern group were now willing to surrender the guardianship of the freedmen in return for assured eco-

Rutherford B. Hayes.

nomic power, but he does not discuss this aspect of the "bargain" at any length. He talks mostly about the South and so shall I, leaving to others all questions of Yankee idealism, realism and materialism.

TO nearly all Southern white men, home rule has continued to seem indispensable, for reasons which are partly economic but are certainly not wholly so. It is not possible to reduce *everything* to economic terms, and Mr. Woodward is too good a historian to try to. He has contributed to a realistic understanding of past and present problems, however, by his emphasis on the influence of economic attitudes.

He has had to show the seamy side of the Compromise of 1877, since that happens to be the relatively unknown side, but that does not mean that the settlement as a whole was more bad than good. In certain respects it seems to have cost considerably more than was necessary. It was relatively disadvantageous to the poorer whites, and many people are now saying that it was to the Negroes. These are highly controversial questions, however, and no one can draw a fair balance sheet who does not remember that it did preserve the peace and restore the Union.

THE POLITICS OF STALEMATE

BETWEEN THE OLD PARTIES.

All the activity in politics that gives evidence of any genuine vitality at present is to be found in the field of restless discontent that lies between the old parties. The letters which we have recently published, presenting the strength and organized movements of the National Labor-Greenback Party in this State, afford a revelation of what is going on all over the country. It is impossible to ignore the fact that the new party movement is not only showing just now an energy that is lacking in other quarters, but that it is making rapid progress, and threatening the integrity of the old organizations while their leaders are sleeping. This fact is largely due to an almost unconquerable reluctance of the latter to abandon the contests of the past, and address themselves to the living issues that take hold on the feelings and vital interests of the people. The discontented elements, discordant though they may be, and lacking a general principle of cohesion and a well-defined common purpose, are associated about what is really the leading question of the time, and which bids fair to hold them together until they can at least force the great political parties into taking some kind of a decided stand. There is little doubt that if the National Party were to acquire dimensions that gave it any chance of having the responsibility of shaping a policy and dealing with practical affairs, it would fall into fatal disagreements as to its course. The Labor Reformers would discover that there was as little hope of attaining their purposes through the new combination as through those old ones which they are now denouncing, and they would probably fall away and return to their own exclusive platform. But the prospect is not that the results of this movement are to be worked out by the Nationals growing into a majority party, and undertaking the control of affairs, while the old organizations either stand aloof and watch the result or combine in a common opposition. Triangular contests cannot last long in politics.

The issues that are destined to become predominant in our politics have but two sides, and the forces must array themselves sooner or later in direct opposition and settle them. The Greenback movement has begun between the old parties, and taken an independent course thus far, for the simple reason that it could begin in no other way. Neither party has been wholly for it or wholly against it, and the cohesiveness in each, derived from old traditions and former conflicts, has been too strong to admit of a breaking up and a rearrangement on the financial questions. These questions can be definitely and finally settled only by a direct antagonism of parties which shall place the forces face to face, a powerful organization with the people of one faith behind it on one side, and a powerful organization with the people of the other faith behind it on the other side. This necessity has long been seen and felt by those who have appreciated the depth and breadth of this issue and the conditions necessary to its complete solution. And yet the Democrats have hard-money traditions, and some of their strongest men are tenacious of a creed derived from the days of ANDREW JACKSON. They were originally strenuous opponents of the Legal-tender acts, and of all measures for a Government currency. Others have been carried away in these latter days by the paper-money delusion, and so the party could not take its position nowhere, for fear of breaking asunder and thereby losing what, after all, is its supreme aim, the chance of success. The Republicans, on the other hand, while sustaining the legal-tender policy for the sake of the ends which it served in a supreme emergency of the nation, have been in the main for a return to the specie basis, but the party has had its weak constituencies to deal with, and has been afraid of alienating any part of its support by taking and maintaining a decided stand. So it came to pass that the two parties could never squarely face each other when this subject was in hand, and it was impossible for them to break up spontaneously and recombine on a new basis.

It was inevitable that the contest typified by the "greenback" should be fought out between political parties, and that the country should have the education on the questions involved which can only come through a thorough agitation and discussion. That education could come through these means only by having parties brought into antagonism on this line. If they would not or could not range themselves upon it, it was a necessity that a new party should spring up, to draw its strength from both until it attained power to bring one or the other to its platform. When it comes to hold the balance of power, to dictate nominations, to threaten defeat in local contests, in States, and in the nation, there will soon be propositions for a surrender from one side or the other. Conciliation and compromise may be offered on both at once, but these will never serve the purpose. Halfway concessions may be made, in the hope of taking the life out of the new movement, but they are not likely to do it. We see no probable outcome of the business but for the National Party to draw upon the strength of one of the old organizations until it concludes to save itself by going over bodily to the standard. Then the other will find itself in opposition, and will gather up the deserters and those with whom principle and honor have a meaning, and will cease to dally with the enemy. Can there be any doubt as to which party is destined to come to the Greenback platform, when men like VOORHEES, of Indiana, begin to apologize for the fact that the Democrats ever opposed a national legal-tender, and to belittle the dubious credit of the Republican Party as its creator? The Democracy has more than half surrendered already, and only awaits its first occasion for concerted action to make a formal capitulation. In view of the inevitable drift of events, the course of the Republican Party is plain. It has only to adhere to sound principles, to maintain a firm attitude, to take up the live issues of the time with boldness, and place itself on the side of economic truths and national honor, and let the coalition of the scattered and hesitating forces of repudiation and financial ballooning work itself out. With reason, honesty, and the lessons of experience on its side, it ought to have no fear of the result.

July 30, 1878

THE PRESIDENT'S POLICY.

NO CHANGE CONTEMPLATED.

THE PRESIDENT DISAPPOINTED WITH THE SOUTH, BUT NOT WILLING TO ADOPT SEVERE MEASURES—A "RECONCILIATION" BETWEEN THE ADMINISTRATION AND THE REPUBLICAN PARTY LEADERS PROPOSED—THE PRESIDENT READY TO LET BYGONES BE BYGONES.

Special Dispatch to the New-York Times.

WASHINGTON, Nov. 14.—In reference to the recent publication of what purports to be an interview with the President on affairs in the Southern States, the *Star* of this evening prints the following, which is said to have been revised by the President himself:

Two positions of great importance in the politics of the country have, within the past few days, been assigned the President—one that he has abandoned in toto his Southern policy; the other, that he has, by giving way in that policy, brought about a "reconciliation" between his Administration and the so-called "stalwart" wing of the Republican Party, the elements of which have been, since the inauguration of the conciliation policy, alienated from him. Both of these statements are either untrue or are given an improper coloring. As to the reported change of policy regarding the South, there is nothing in it. The method of dealing with the Southern States which the President has seen fit to pursue is the same now as it was when inaugurated. This policy was in no respect whatever an experiment. The President considered, and still considers it, a matter of duty to see that in administering the laws of the land, the constitutional rights of every citizen, in every portion of the country, equally and alike, should be fully respected and guarded. It is pretty generally conceded that the South, under bayonet rule, was not enjoying the free government vouchsafed it by the Constitution. To remove that rule was a duty the President considered devolving upon him, and it was accordingly removed. He has gone on, with the determination of securing, as far as lay in his power, that every citizen shall be protected in the full and free exercise of all his rights and privileges. With this determination has been coupled a very strong desire not to use the military branch of the Government, except to quell insurrection and put down riots. All violations of the law should, he has always held and still holds, be punished by civil processes, if possible. Therefore, when it was learned, prior to the recent elections, that Republican voters in the South, notably in South Carolina, Louisiana, and Alabama, would certainly be interfered with in the exercise of their franchise rights, the Attorney-General ordered the United States District Attorneys for those States to see that all violators of the law in this respect were promptly arrested and brought to trial; and after the elections, notwithstanding the advances for compromise from those arrested, the Attorney-General was last Saturday instructed to prosecute offenders to the utmost limits of the law. Neither of these instructions could be regarded as "a change of policy." They were but the carrying out of the President's determination to see that the laws are enforced everywhere. The statement that the President has recently said that he had tried the plan of conciliation and found it a complete failure is untrue. The President has never made such a statement. It is true that he does not think the South has responded as it should to his good intentions, but, nevertheless, he does not intend to change in any manner whatever, the course of his Administration upon this account. This course, as has previously been said, is not a Southern policy. It is not in any true sense a man policy. It is the enforcement of the laws by civil processes.

As to the other statement, that there has been a reconciliation between the Administration and the dissatisfied leaders of the Republican Party, it may be stated that in order that there might be "a reconciliation," as the phrase is, it would be necessary that the President should come at least partially to the way of thinking held by the leaders of the party with which he is to be "reconciled," the President has never seen any reason why he should cease to do his duty because some portion of his party was dissatisfied with his methods. He has always desired, and still desires, that the utmost harmony should exist in the party. If leaders of the party, after interchanging views with him, see that they have misunderstood his course and conduct, and think that it would be good that past differences should be healed, the President is ready to respond heartily. That such is the case is, no doubt, true, and the party which elected the President to office is certainly, now, with few exceptions, "ready," as Representative White, of Pennsylvania, says, "to look to future results and forget the effete past with its past differences." If this is "reconciliation," well and good."

November 15, 1878

THE REPUBLICAN TICKET

A RETROSPECTIVE VIEW OF THE CONVENTION.

CHICAGO, June 9—The long Convention is ended. Through 36 successive ballots the defenders of the fame of America's greatest living citizen maintained their ranks unbroken, and repelled the assaults of 450 opponents. Deprived of the aid of those who ought to have been beside them, and with whom victory would have been assured, the faithful 300 stood by their colors to the end. There was something peculiarly impressive in the unfaltering allegiance of the colored delegates from the South. They were voting for the man who had led the armies which had overthrown their oppressors; for the man whose name is a household word in every lowly Southern cabin; for the man whose election would preserve the liberty which his victories in the field had gained for them. The name of Grant, the savior of a disorderly and divided Nation, meant to them safety, freedom, an honest ballot-box, and the complete discomfiture of their oppressors; and ignorance had no part in fastening this belief upon their minds, for the colored delegates from the South in this Convention have shown to the Northern Republicans an astonishing familiarity with the political history of what is now their country, and a common sense which has sometimes put white men to shame.

So these men, the white Republicans of the North who saw in Grant's nomination the second defeat of the party which was overthrown at Appomattox, and the emancipated slaves of the South, who saw in his name the safety of their race, joined hands and presented an unbroken front from morning until night. Confident in the excellence of their cause, they fought against the adjournment by which their opponents sought to gain time for a new combination, but they were defeated, and the Republicans who were crying "anybody to beat Grant" secured a dozen hours for consultation. They had discovered that the Senator from Maine had spent his strength, and could hope for nothing but the impossible. Under the cover of the night they might be able to find another leader. But great difficulties confronted them. The Blaine votes could not be delivered to Sherman, nor could the Sherman votes be transferred to Blaine. An attempt to unite the opposition upon Washburne or Edmunds would send a host of votes to Grant. The first transfer of a respectable body of votes to him would be the signal for a stampede, and his nomination would be effected in five minutes. The night was spent in vain efforts to shake the Southern supporters of the ex-President, and in making an agreement to test cautiously the strength of Sherman and Washburne. When the Convention reassembled, there was but little to raise hope in the breasts of the perplexed opposition. The first ballot disclosed no weakness in the column which had so firmly supported the silent soldier of Galena, but unveiled the plans of the opposition.

The strength of Sherman was first to be tested. Massachusetts was the instrument chosen for this purpose. The plan was a complete failure. The vote of Sherman rose to 120, and then began, slowly but surely, to fall. A little movement toward Washburne was no more successful. Where could the man be found? The leaders of the opposition were in close communication by wire with the Secretary of the Treasury and the Senator from Maine. The Secretary saw that his defeat was inevitable, and he directed his lieutenants to lead his supporters to the side of Garfield. The Senator from Maine would not release his men. He preferred to see them abandon him without permission. It became the lot of Wisconsin to turn the tide. She had made a diversion in favor of Washburne, and it had failed. On the thirty-fourth ballot, 16 members of her delegation cast their votes for Garfield, who until that time had been kept before the Convention by Grier, of Pennsylvania, who sometimes had had a companion. The galleries, weary of watching the long and monotonous contest, and caring comparatively little for the great principles involved in its settlement, cheered wildly as they saw an opening which might relieve their suspense. There were only the Territories to be called after the announcement of the vote of Wisconsin, and they sent no reinforcements to the Wisconsin skirmishing party. For the effect of the experiment, for such it was, the audience must look to the next ballot. Nine States were called, and 10,000 persons waited in silence for a response to Wisconsin's offer. The tenth was Indiana. In that State, 1 supporter of Grant, 12 followers of Blaine, 2 of Sherman, and 12 of Washburne hurriedly consulted, and then joined Wisconsin in her support of Garfield. Before the roll-call was ended, half a dozen more had forsaken their old leaders for the new one. The experiment would be successful, but the vote for Grant had risen to 313, and what was to be done by the opposition must be done quickly.

Then were Chairmen of delegations and agents of the Treasury seen running from one seat to another. The next ballot would decide the great question, but if the opponents of Grant should fail to transfer their forces at once, the tide might turn to the ex-President. A great deal of work was done in the five minutes which elapsed between the call of the last Territory on the thirty-fifth ballot and the beginning of the roll-call on the thirty-sixth. Plans which had been formed by the labor of four years were hastily thrown aside; sentiments which had been the motive force in a hard-fought campaign were ignored and forgotten. Considerations of all kinds were thrust into oblivion, for now had come the opportunity for the defeat of Grant.

Connecticut was the first to turn to what promised to be the winning side. Her delegates, with the exception of one of the three supporters of Blaine, cast their votes for Garfield. The most earnest solicitation had done its work with the representatives of the little State, where almost every man had seemed to have a separate candidate. Seven of the delegates from Illinois who had been created by the committee followed these men, and the transfer of the entire delegation of Iowa from Blaine to the coming man betokened a speedy nomination. The stampede had begun. Before the whirlwind of impulse, men who had so steadfastly defended their preference for Blaine, for Washburne, or for Edmunds were powerless. All their carefully-prepared arguments were forgotten, and they struggled only to see who should be first to salute the rising sun. Before the roll-call was ended, Gen. Garfield was the nominee of the Republican Party for President, and the great hall was the scene of a tumult which can hardly be described. Where were the friends of Grant? Through all this excitement they had remained fixed and immovable. They could not desert their best friend and the man by whom they felt that the safety of the Republic and the equality and security of all its inhabitants would be preserved beyond the shadow of a doubt. Like a solid phalanx they maintained their lines to the very end. On the first ballot they had given him 304; on the twenty-ninth, after 12 hours' work, had been directed against them, 305, and on the thirty-sixth, and last, while delegates all around them were deserting their colors and urging them to come with them and conciliate the nominee, they responded with 306 votes for Grant. The pages of our political history contain no record of an act like this. If the votes of which they had been deprived had been restored to them on any one of the 36 ballots, their candidate would have been nominated. A glance at the last ballot shows that 20 of these votes were those of the New-York delegates, who repudiated their obligations; 21 were cast against them by seceders in Pennsylvania; 18 were the creation of the contested seats committee in the Illinois delegation, and 21 were those of men who disobeyed instructions in Alabama, Kentucky, Missouri, South Carolina, Texas, and Virginia. Here were 80 votes which would have raised the total Grant vote on the last ballot to 386, or 7 more than the number necessary for a choice.

There were some incidents in this Convention which can never be forgotten by those who carefully watched the course of the action. They were not the scenes of wild applause, when gray-haired men lost their heads, but among them were the quiet and sometimes pathetic indications of the mental strain caused by injustice, and the defeat of long-cherished hopes. The enforcement of the report of the committee in relation to the Illinois delegation was an act which brought Senator Logan in strong relief. The vote upon one district admitted two of the contestants, and, as the remaining contestants came in two by two, the black-haired Senator stood in his place and announced each time the vote of his delegation. Two by two his strength was slipping away, and each announcement which he made was given in a tone which showed how the injustice of the defeat was inwardly galling him. The eloquence of the Senator from New-York cannot be effaced from the mind of any person who heard his words. In print they express only a small part of the power which marked their delivery. The gloom which settled on the faces of Messrs. Hale, Frye, and Chandler when Blaine's defeat became certain, and their ineffectual attempts to conceal their emotion, were memorable and full of suggestion. But before these, and before all memories of things said and done within those walls, distinct and ineffaceable, will remain the impressions made by the grand and unparalleled support of Grant by his faithful body of delegates.

June 10, 1880

THE BOURBONS STAMPEDED

THEY NOMINATE GEN. HANCOCK AND WILLIAM H. ENGLISH.

THE CONVENTION TRANSFORMED INTO A HOWLING MOB—HANCOCK NOMINATED AFTER THE SECOND BALLOT BY A STAMPEDE—ENGLISH NAMED BY ACCLAMATION—A SHORT PLATFORM—SPEECHES BY SEVERAL DISAPPOINTED PARTISANS IN SUPPORT OF THE NOMINEES—THE OLD CHAIRMAN'S AMUSING BLUNDERS.

CINCINNATI, June 24.—The National Democratic Convention has done its work. By it, Gen. Hancock, who is politically from Pennsylvania, and in the Army Register from Missouri, has been nominated for President of the United States, and Mr. William H. English, of Indiana, for Vice-President. They owe their success, in the first place, to a wild and unreasonable stampede, which could not be controlled, and, secondly, to a union between the ex-rebel Brigadiers and Tammany Hall. During the whole of last night and this morning, the one cry heard on every side here was, "let us nominate a man who will satisfy John Kelly, and who will not be objectionable to the solid South." Such a man was found in the person of Hancock. Kelly favored him, for what reason nobody seems to know, and he was warmly pressed by the ex-Confederates of the South. Why they supported him it is hardly necessary to explain. They are determined to succeed in the present contest. They know it is the very last opportunity for success which they can ever hope for, and they have made a virtue of necessity, and aided by the men of Tammany Hall, have succeeded in nominating for President a man whom they have every reason to detest heartily, and about whose views on public questions they, in common with the rest of the world, know next to nothing. As to his record no man has spoken. If he has a record on any great public question in which the people of this country are now interested, no man here knows anything about it. Gen. Hancock is the candidate of sentiment. He has grown out of a dire Democratic dilemma. He is not the choice of the masses of the party to which he professes to belong; he is not known he has no personal following; he is the last man to attract independent votes; he can only hope for the support of the fraudulently-solid South, and of the political tricksters in the North, who will use him for their own purposes.

June 25, 1880

INTERESTS OF BUSINESS MEN.

The paramount questions in our politics at this time are those which affect the material interests of the country. Questions of control by this party or that or of the predominance of one section or another are to the general comprehension important mainly for their bearing upon the material well-being of the people. After a long struggle with adverse circumstances, we seem to have got clear of the disturbing influences which were the product of a great upheaval that broke the continuity of our prosperous career as a nation. The causes of fierce political agitation in the past have been in a large measure removed. The financial and commercial disasters which were the result of a great civil war have been buried, and at last we are in a position to resume our growth in wealth and power and devote ourselves to a solution of the questions which stand in the way of enlightened progress. Confidence has been restored, business has revived, industries are active and profitable, and all classes are disposed to regard the future with high hope. They are anxious that nothing should happen to disturb the prospects which seem to be opening before them. They want no change that will not make these more secure. After the experience of the last few years it has come to be understood how seriously the welfare of the people and all the conditions on which it depends may be affected by the policy of the Government. It is seen that stability in the currency is essential to confidence and industrial success, and that a firm and steady policy in all that affects commercial interests is of the highest importance.

Resumption has been so far secured as to place our currency for the time being on the unvarying basis of gold and in conformity with the money standard of the commercial world. The advantage is distinctly showing itself, and it must speedily be understood that everything necessary to the completion of the policy which has produced this result should be done. There should be no upsetting or going back. What remains to be done involves no disturbing change, but merely the security of the results already obtained. The treatment of the silver question, or of the issue between Government notes and bank notes, must have in view not a disturbance of the present equilibrium but its permanency, not a change of the basis or the level of the currency but its maintenance. The measures needed are those of prevention, which shall make secure and permanent what we have gained, and make a relapse impossible. On this the continuance of confidence and of the conditions of prosperity depends. Our business men understand this perfectly, and the industrial class, who are business men in their way, have a more or less clear perception of it. The re-funding of the national debt at a lower rate of interest is a work of relief for business and the people, inasmuch as it lightens the weight of taxation. It is not yet complete, but its benefits are observable. It should be carried as far as practicable, and to this end the public faith and credit must be maintained at their highest, and confidence in the stability of the financial policy of the Government must be unshaken. So of other questions which bear upon taxation and affect the material interests of the Nation. What is called for is no radical or violent change, no unsetting or tearing to pieces, but a careful and judicious readjustment, for relief where relief is needed, but not for disturbance and agitation.

What has been done to bring our financial condition thus far on the way to soundness, to restore confidence and promote prosperity, has been done by the Republicans in Congress and the Executive department of the Government. It has been done against Democratic opposition and obstruction. If the course pursued has not always been steady and consistent, that fact has been due to difficulties raised by the opposition to the party. And now threats of reaction, of change and retrogression, of new experiments and the undoing of the work of years of struggle, come from that same opposition. The success of the Republicans in the election of this year promises a continuance and completion of the work whose fruits are already visible in our prosperous condition. Men of capital, men of business, and laboring men alike have an interest in the perpetuity of the favorable conditions of industry and trade. What we have they know, what its continuance means they understand, and they know that the election of Gen. GARFIELD would give assurance of that continuance. What would come of intrusting the Administration to the Democrats, with the record they have made in the last few years, they do not know, but they have every reason to apprehend that it would bring disturbing, if not disastrous, changes. Where the interests of business men lie in this campaign is evident, and there is every indication that they realize it more and more every day.

The most purely political consideration in the present canvass has its bearing upon commercial and industrial interests also. As we have constantly insisted, the success of the Democratic Party must inevitably result in the ascendency of the ex-Confederate leaders of the South in the national councils. This must needs be so, because the strength of the party lies in that section, and these men would have the highest claim to control an Administration of their own making, and they would control it. This would produce a sharp turn in the general policy of the Government, for it would no longer be dominated by the idea of the supremacy of national authority, but with the idea of the independent sovereignty of States. The free, enlightened, and progressive North would find itself put out of control and its place taken by the reactionary South. The result would be distrust, agitation, and trouble, for the course which these Southern rulers of a too trustful people would be sure to take in regard to the claims and pretensions of their section would not be acquiesced in without protest. The politics which we should have for the next four years would not be conducive to the steady and vigorous progress of those material interests which are now uppermost in men's thoughts and hopes. The policy of the people should not be to "let well enough alone," but to make it secure and permanent, and keep it out of the hands of those who would be sure to unsettle and overturn it.

August 21, 1880

THE GREAT TRUST RENEWED

GARFIELD AND ARTHUR THE CHOICE OF THE NATION.

FRAUD AND FORGERY REPUDIATED BY THE AMERICAN PEOPLE.

NEW-YORK GIVES 25,000 REPUBLICAN MAJORITY.

THE HOUSE OF REPRESENTATIVES ONCE MORE REPUBLICAN.

EVERY NORTHERN STATE EXCEPT NEW-JERSEY CARRIED FOR THE REPUBLICAN PRESIDENTIAL CANDIDATES— THE SUPERB SOLDIER AND THE SOLID SOUTH TAKE A BACK SEAT—A CLEAR REPUBLICAN MAJORITY IN THE NEXT HOUSE OF REPRESENTATIVES—A TREMENDOUS FALLING OFF IN THE DEMOCRATIC MAJORITIES IN NEW-YORK AND BROOKLYN.

The country speaks out again as it spoke in 1872. Every Northern State except New-Jersey has declared for Garfield and Arthur, giving them 222 of the 369 votes of the Electoral College, and an overwhelming majority of the popular vote. The Democratic Presidential candidates will receive but 147 Electoral votes. THE TIMES's dispatches tell of heavy Republican gains over the vote of 1876 everywhere except in New-Hampshire, where, however, the Garfield Electors and a Republican Governor have been chosen. The magnitude of the victory in this State surpasses all expectation. The Democratic majority in New-York City has been reduced to 41,000, and in Brooklyn it will not exceed 10,000. Maine redeems herself with a Republican majority of between 4,000 and 5,000. Connecticut gives Garfield 4,200 majority; Massachusetts more than 50,000; Pennsylvania, 45,000; Ohio, 40,000. Indiana fulfills the promise of her October election by giving a Republican majority of about 7,000. From all over the West comes news of increased Republican majorities, even in Kentucky there have been large gains. Nevada has chosen the Garfield Electors. At the hour of going to press it seems probable that the next House of Representatives will contain 157 Republicans, 131 Democrats, and 5 Greenbackers; but this estimate of the Republican strength covers 2 districts in North Carolina, 1 in Massachusetts, 1 in Nevada, and 1 in Pennsylvania which are, at least, doubtful. Conceding all these to the Democrats, however, the House would still have 152 Republicans to 136 Democrats, and 5 Greenbackers.

November 3, 1880

A SENSATION IN POLITICS

SENATORS CONKLING AND PLATT RESIGN.

THE LETTER OF RESIGNATION.

A JOINT LETTER FROM THE TWO SENATORS GIVING REASONS FOR THEIR ACTION.

ALBANY, May 16.—The following is the letter of resignation of Senators Conkling and Platt:

WASHINGTON, D. C., May 14, 1881.

SIR: Transmitting, as we do, our resignations, respectively, of the great trusts with which New-York has honored us, it is fit that we acquaint you, and, through you, the Legislature and people of the State, with the reasons which, in our judgment, make such a step respectful and necessary.

Some weeks ago the President sent to the Senate, in a group, the nominations of several persons for public offices already filled. One of these offices is the Collectorship of the Port of New-York, now held by Gen. Merritt; another is the Consul-Generalship at London, now held by Gen. Badeau; another is Chargé d'Affaires to Denmark, held by Mr. Cramer; another is the mission to Switzerland, held by Mr. Fish, a son of the former distinguished Secretary of State. Mr. Fish had, in deference to an ancient practice, placed his position at the disposal of the new Administration, but, like the other persons named, he was ready to remain at his post if permitted to do so. All of these officers, save only Mr. Cramer, are citizens of New-York. It was proposed to displace them all, not for any alleged fault or for any alleged need or advantage of the public service, but in order to give the great office of Collector of the Port of New-York to Mr. William H. Robertson as a "reward" for certain acts of his, said to have "aided in making the nomination of Gen. Garfield possible." The chain of removals thus proposed was broken by Gen. Badeau's promptly declining to accept the new place to which he was to be sent.

These nominations summoned every member of the Senate to say whether he advised such a transaction. The movement was more than a surprise. We had been told only a few hours before that no removals in the New-York offices were soon to be made or even considered, and had been requested to withhold the papers and suggestions bearing on the subject, which had been sent to us for presentation, should occasion arise, until we had notice from the President of his readiness to receive them. Learning that the Vice-President was equally surprised, and had been equally mislead, we went to Mr. James, the Cabinet officer from our State, and learned that, though he had spent some time with the President on the morning of the day the nominations were sent in, no disclosure of an intention to send them had been made to him, and that he first knew of the matter by hearsay following the event.

After earnest reflection and consultation we believed the proceeding unwise and wrong, whether considered wholly in relation to the preservation and integrity of the public service and the public example to be set, or in relation also to the integrity of the Republican Party. No public utterance of comment or censure was made by either of us in the Senate or elsewhere; on the contrary, we thought that the President would reconsider action so sudden and hasty, and would at least adopt less hurtful and objectionable modes of requiting personal or individual service. In this hope, the following paper was prepared and signed and presented by Mr. James to the President, who was subsequently informed that you had authorized your name to be added also:

To the President:

We beg leave to remonstrate against the change in the Collectorship at New-York by the removal of Mr. Merritt and the appointment of Mr. Robertson. The proposal was wholly a surprise. We heard of it only when the several nominations involved in the plan were announced in the Senate. We had, only two days before this, been informed from you that a change in the Customs offices at New-York was not contemplated, and quite ignorant of a purpose to take any action now, we had no opportunity, until after the nominations, to make the suggestions we now present. We do not believe that the interests of the public service will be promoted by removing the present Collector and putting Mr. Robertson in his stead. Our opinion is quite the reverse, and we believe no political advantage can be gained for either the Republican Party or its principles. Believing that no individual has claims or obligations which should be liquidated in such a mode, we earnestly and respectfully ask that the nomination of Mr. Robertson be withdrawn.

CHESTER A. ARTHUR,
T. C. PLATT,
THOMAS L. JAMES,
ROSCOE CONKLING.

This paper was presented to the President by Mr. James, on Monday, the 28th day of March. Knowing the frequency with which every one of the 20 Presidents of the Republic, and markedly the present incumbent, had withdrawn nominations on less serious representations, we did not apprehend that such a suggestion would be treated as an intrusion or an invasion of any prerogative of the nominating power. We were disappointed. Immediately the public press, especially in articles and dispatches written by those in close and constant association with the President and with an influential member of his Cabinet, teemed with violent denunciations of the Senators from New-York for "opposing the Administration" and "dictating" to the President. Persons who visited the Executive Mansion reported the President resentful and impatient of hesitation to "advise and consent" to what he proposed. We had made, we have made, no assault upon anybody. We have at all times refused to answer questions by representatives of the press, or to make complaint or comment, or even denial of the many truthless charges published against us by the officious champions of "the Administration." Indeed, beyond confidential consultations with brother Senators and officials, we have said nothing until now on the subject, nor have we, or either of us, "promoted the dead-lock in the Senate" in order to prevent or influence action on any nomination, nor have we ever so stated.

May 17, 1881

POLITICAL UNDERCURRENTS.

Events and personalities not in themselves of prime importance are often significant as symptoms of an underlying tendency which may in time produce changes of great moment. The resignation of both the Senators of the leading State in the Union would be a startling event if it could be distinctly and promptly attributed to an adequate cause. If an act of petty personal resentment and of chagrin at a single political defeat, it becomes trivial in its significance, and can produce only a feeling of mingled vexation and disgust. But while the recent act of the New-York Senators cannot be regarded as having any adequate provocation or proper motive, and is therefore neither startling in a serious sense nor impressive in any sense, it is not reasonable to attribute it to mere spleen or peevishness. These men may not be statesmen of broad views and lofty purposes, but they are something more than headstrong school-boys. They are likely to have acted with a purpose and in the exercise of what they at least considered political sagacity. It is by no means certain that they counted on a vindication by re-election or wholly miscalculated the tendencies of public sentiment. They may have decided to make the test with a full consciousness that they were likely to be defeated, and with a deliberate preference for such defeat over a continuance of the political position in which they found themselves.

Ever since the issues of the great contest between slavery and freedom were settled, or put in the way of final settlement, there has been a constant slackening of the cohesive force in our political parties. Again and again one or the other has threatened to go to pieces, involving in its fate the dissolution of its antagonist; but every time a fear of some relapse from the position gained, a menace of dangerous reaction, and an energetic resort to the power of party organization have prevented the catastrophe. More and more the old issues have lost their hold on the minds of men, while new questions have failed so to rouse conviction as to compel a ranging of parties on the lines they present. No one of the important questions of policy that may now be regarded as having real vitality and that divide the opinions of men is strictly a party question. Parties do not face each other on these questions; they run all athwart of party lines. Without a direct antagonism rising out of opposing convictions on some vital principle there can be little cohesion among the elements of parties. There will be a constant tendency to dissolution until the touch comes that once more awakens the spirit of antagonism and rearranges the forces for new contests.

Since the Republican Party lost the unifying influence of its early purposes and its original principles, there have been at work with varying energy two divergent tendencies within its ranks. One of these has been toward reform in policy and in administration and the acceptance of new issues. The other has been directed to the strengthening of organization and the maintenance of a hold upon the Government through the force of leadership and discipline and the use of the public service as an engine of party power. It is evident that the divergence could not go on indefinitely and the party hold together. It is equally manifest that no one man could successfully navigate both diverging currents at the same time. Last year, by dint of strenuous effort and great good fortune, they were brought into one channel and carried Gen. GARFIELD into the seat of power. That accomplished, they diverged again, and the President made the futile effort to keep them together or to go with both at once. Senator CONKLING represented one of the tendencies in the Republican Party distinctly and conspicuously. The President did not represent the other, nor has it yet in public office or in active politics any conspicuous exponent. But it became evident to Mr. CONKLING that the Administration was not with him, and he may possibly have seen that the Republican Party was not with him and could not be carried his way. Possibly he foresaw that a break was coming, and preferred to help it on and to be in a position to take an active part in the rearrangement of political forces that he believed to be impending.

The Senatorial resignations owe their significance not to the personal conflict which gave the occasion for them, but to the tendency in party sentiment which intimated to Mr. CONKLING that he must abandon his motives and his methods in politics or be reduced to insignificance. The one he could not do, the other he could not endure. What will be the result? It requires great temerity to make predictions in American politics, but it does not look as though Mr. CONKLING's case could be bettered by a re-election, or as though he could desire it for the promotion of any comprehensible purpose. But as questions of reform and of practical policy do not as yet clearly divide the political forces into opposing parties, so the political methods which Mr. CONKLING represents are not characteristic of one of the existing parties. They are repudiated by many Republicans, possibly a majority; they are believed in by many Democrats, possibly a majority. Gen. BUTLER's avowed sympathy with Mr. CONKLING, as well as that of certain prominent Southern Democrats, is quite natural. Their ideas as to party government are similar and their differences regarding any vital principle would be difficult to point out. The dissolution and rearrangement of political elements and forces have been long delayed and they certainly must come. It is desirable that they should come, and that as soon as events are ripe for them. They are necessary to renewed political progress for the country. Possibly what the public is just now disposed to regard as itself a disorder in the body politic or in a political party is but a symptom of changes going on or impending in the deeper currents of our political life.

May 22, 1881

A GREAT NATION IN GRIEF

PRESIDENT GARFIELD SHOT BY AN ASSASSIN.

THOUGH SERIOUSLY WOUNDED HE STILL SURVIVES.

THE WOULD-BE MURDERER LODGED IN PRISON.

THE PRESIDENT OF THE UNITED STATES ATTACKED AND TERRIBLY WOUNDED BY A FANATICAL OFFICE-SEEKER ON THE EVE OF INDEPENDENCE DAY—THE NATION HORRIFIED AND THE WHOLE CIVILIZED WORLD SHOCKED—THE PRESIDENT STILL ALIVE AND HIS RECOVERY POSSIBLE.

The appalling intelligence came from Washington yesterday morning that President Garfield had been assassinated and was dead. Later dispatches, however, modified this startling news by the announcement that the President, while dangerously wounded, was still living, and that there was a slight hope of his recovery.

Briefly told, the story of the tragedy is as follows: President Garfield and Secretary Blaine drove from the Executive Mansion, about 9 o'clock yesterday morning, to the depot of the Baltimore and Potomac Railroad, where the President was to join other members of his Cabinet and proceed on a trip to New-York and New-England. As he was walking through the passenger rooms, arm in arm with Mr. Blaine, two pistol-shots were fired in quick succession from behind, and the President sank to the floor, bleeding profusely from two wounds. The assassin was instantly seized, and proved to be Charles J. Guiteau, a half-crazed, pettifogging lawyer, who has been an unsuccessful applicant for office under the Government, and who has led a precarious existence in several of the large cities of the country.

The wounded President was conveyed to the offices of the railroad on the second floor of the depot building. Several physicians were soon in attendance, and after an hour had elapsed it was decided to remove him to the Executive Mansion, where he was made as comfortable as possible. His mind remained perfectly clear all day, notwithstanding the desperate nature of his injuries, and when his wife, who had been summoned from Long Branch, arrived at his bedside, he was able to converse with and encourage her.

During the afternoon the physicians expressed little hope of the President's recovery, but late in the evening their bulletins were more favorable, and there is still hope of a favorable result.

July 3, 1881

THE REFORM BILL.

Now that the bill for the improvement of the civil service has passed both houses of Congress, and must shortly become a law, it will be interesting to recall its exact provisions, that our readers may know what may really be done under it. Some few changes were made in the bill as reported to the Senate, and some additions were also made to it, but the bill went through the House precisely as it came from the Senate.

It authorizes the appointment by the President, with the consent of the Senate, of three Commissioners, not more than two of whom shall be adherents of the same party, and they shall constitute "The United States Civil Service Commission." Their term of office is not defined, but the President may remove any Commissioner; they are to receive an annual salary of $3,500 each and their necessary traveling expenses; any vacancy in their number is to be filled by the President and Senate to conform to the conditions of the first selection. It is to be the duty of the Commissioners to aid the President, at his request, in preparing suitable rules to carry the act into effect. When these rules shall have been promulgated it becomes the duty of every officer in any of the departments and offices to which they shall relate to aid in all proper ways in carrying them out. These rules must provide, as nearly as the conditions of good administration will warrant, as follows: For open competitive examinations for testing the fitness of applicants for the public service, so far as now classified or to be classified under the act; that places coming within the act are to be filled "from among those graded highest as the result of such examinations," that appointments to the public service in Washington must be apportioned among the States and Territories and the District of Columbia upon the basis of population; that promotions shall be from the lower grades to the higher on the basis of merit and competition; that no person in the public service is for that reason under any obligation to contribute to any political

fund or to render any political service, and cannot be removed or otherwise prejudiced for refusing to do so; that there shall be non-competitive examinations in all proper cases before the commission when competent persons, after due notice, do not compete.

The commission is required, subject to the rules that the President may make, to make regulations for the examinations and to have control of them; to make investigations as to the operation of the civil service rules, and to report annually to the President for transmission to Congress, showing the nature and effect of the examinations, the exceptions made to the rules and the reason for them, and any suggestions for the more effectual accomplishment of the purposes of the act. The commission is authorized to employ a Chief Examiner at $3,000, a Secretary at $1,600, a stenographer at $1,600, and a messenger at $600 a year.

It may also designate at Washington and elsewhere where examinations are to take place a suitable number of persons, not less than three, in the service of the United States, to be members of Boards of Examiners. Examinations are to be held at convenient places in the States and Territories, and, where there are persons to be examined, not less than twice in each year. Stringent prohibitions of any favoritism or corrupt action in the examinations, either by the Commissioners, Examiners, or others, are enacted.

Under the present statutes the force in the departments at Washington is classified, and to these the act applies. It is also made the duty of the Secretary of the Treasury and the Postmaster-General within sixty days to make a like classification of the force in all the offices under them having fifty or more employes. Afterward, at the direction of the President, any head of a department is required to classify the offices under him in like manner, and the act then applies to them. After six months no one can be appointed in any office so classified, except after an examination, or unless he be shown to be exempt under

the rules. It is further provided that when two or more persons of the same family are in the service in the grades covered by the act no other person of the same family can be appointed to such grades. No recommendation may be given by any Senator or Representative to applicants for office, and none can be received or regarded in making the examination or appointment, except as to character and residence. No person habitually using intoxicating beverages to excess can be appointed to, or retained in, the offices to which the act applies. There are also four sections of the act prohibiting all officers or employes of the United States, and all Senators and Representatives from soliciting or receiving political contributions from officers or employes of the Government, forbidding the latter to make any such contributions to the former directly or indirectly, and forbidding any one to solicit or collect such contributions in any building or room occupied in the discharge of his official duty by any officer or employe of the United States. A violation of any of these sections is punished by a fine of not more than $5,000, or by imprisonment for not more than three years, or both.

It will be seen by the above very complete abstract of the provisions of the reform act that it is simply permissive. It authorizes the President to appoint a commission to carry out the system of appointment for merit tested by competition and probation. It gives him no actual power that he did not already have, but it furnishes him with adequate means to establish the merit system thoroughly and carefully. It is the declaration of both houses of Congress by an overwhelming majority of their interpretation of the will of the people in this matter. The interpretation is entirely just, and the people are in earnest. It only remains for the President to do his duty.

January 7, 1883

THE CONVENTION'S CHOICE

BLAINE AND LOGAN TO BEAR THE REPUBLICAN STANDARD.

FOUR BALLOTS FOR PRESIDENT TAKEN AMID GREAT CONFUSION AND EXCITEMENT—BLAINE AT LAST GETS A MAJORITY OF 133—NO OPPOSITION MANIFESTED TO LOGAN FOR VICE-PRESIDENT.

FIRST BALLOT.

JAMES G. BLAINE	334½
CHESTER A. ARTHUR	278
GEORGE F. EDMUNDS	93
JOHN A. LOGAN	63½
JOHN SHERMAN	30
JOSEPH R. HAWLEY	13
ROBERT T. LINCOLN	4
W. T. SHERMAN	2

SECOND BALLOT.

JAMES G. BLAINE	349
CHESTER A. ARTHUR	276
GEORGE F. EDMUNDS	85
JOHN A. LOGAN	61
JOHN SHERMAN	28
JOSEPH R. HAWLEY	13
ROBERT T. LINCOLN	4
W. T. SHERMAN	2

THIRD BALLOT.

JAMES G. BLAINE	375
CHESTER A. ARTHUR	274
GEORGE F. EDMUNDS	69
JOHN A. LOGAN	53
JOHN SHERMAN	25
JOSEPH R. HAWLEY	13
ROBERT T. LINCOLN	8
W. T. SHERMAN	2

FOURTH BALLOT.

JAMES G. BLAINE	541
CHESTER A. ARTHUR	207
GEORGE F. EDMUNDS	41
JOHN A. LOGAN	7
JOSEPH R. HAWLEY	15
ROBERT T. LINCOLN	2

From the Special Correspondent of the Times.

CHICAGO, June 6.—The convention's work is done. On the fourth ballot James G. Blaine was nominated by the votes of 544 delegates to be President of the United States. Beginning on the first ballot with 334½ votes—a number which proves the substantial accuracy of the estimates sent from this city to THE TIMES—the Blaine men marched steadily and resistlessly forward to victory. The second roll-call revealed 349 Blaine votes, and the third 375. On the fourth, great States, whose delegations had been divided, closed their broken ranks and wheeled into line for the man from Maine. Favorite sons withdrew from the field and delivered their delegates to him, and the number of his supporters was increased by accessions, large and small, until he had received a majority and had 133 votes to spare.

Blaine's managers were unwilling yesterday that there should be any break in the course of

the balloting. The first ballot would reveal their strength more accurately than it had been shown in the Lynch-Clayton contest, and if a night should intervene between the first ballot or the first two ballots and the succeeding ones they feared that their opponents would be able to outwit them by combining to support a new man, or in some other way. They were confident, but at the same time they remembered the defeat of their candidate in 1876 and 1880. They decided to guard their lines with the utmost care, and to enter the race under the most favorable circumstances if possible.

After all the speeches had been made last night, Judge Foraker, of Ohio, John Sherman's representative, surprised the Blaine men by moving that a ballot should be taken at once. Mr. Stewart, of Pennsylvania, sprang to his feet and moved that if a beginning was to be made the work of balloting should not be interrupted till at least five ballots had been taken. One ballot said an adjournment might ruin his candidate, but five, he believed, would give him the nomination. Mr. Thurston, prompted by Mr. Elkins, moved an adjournment. The Blaine and anti-Blaine men again locked horns on this motion, which was defeated by a vote of 391 to 410. The change of 15 votes, misplaced because the Alabama delegates did not understand the question, would have made the vote 376 to 425. Filibustering would have been continued through the remainder of the night if the Sherman men had not seen the folly of such a course and put an end to the contest. The Blaine men could have afforded to allow one ballot to be taken, for there could have been formed during the night no combination which would have beaten them to-day. But they wanted to be on the safe side.

When the convention reassembled this morning it was apparent that nothing could prevent a Blaine victory. Messrs. Roosevelt and Henry Cabot Lodge had been hard at work through the night trying to take the anti-Blaine vote to some candidate, new or old,

whom Arthur men, Edmunds men, and the independents could heartily support. It had been a hopeless task, but these men had courageously undertaken to accomplish it. Even if the leading Arthur men had been willing to desert the President, and they were not, their votes could not be transferred. Nor would the Edmunds men go to Arthur for reasons that have been given in preceding dispatches. If a transfer of the Arthur vote could have been made, there was no man whom the combination could support against

Blaine with the slightest hope of success. Lincoln was out of the question. His friends discovered that while he had seemed to be theoretically available, because of his character, record, and the universal acceptance of his name to be put in the second place on the ticket, he was practically unavailable in this convention for the first place.

June 7, 1884

THE BOLT AGAINST BLAINE

A GREAT MEETING TO BE HELD IN BOSTON TO-DAY.

THE CALL SIGNED BY HUNDREDS OF INFLUENTIAL REPUBLICANS OF THE OLD BAY STATE.

BOSTON, June 12.—The call for the meeting of Republicans and independents to protest against the Chicago nominations to be held in this city to-morrow is published in the morning papers with the signatures of some of those in sympathy with it. The call is as follows:

"We, the undersigned Republican and independent voters of Massachusetts, believing that only men of high character should be elected to high office, and that the nominations just made at Chicago ought not to be supported in any contingency that now seems likely to arise, invite those who think with us on this point to meet in the

old dining-room at Young's Hotel, Boston, on Friday, June 13, at 3.30 P. M., to consider what action to take in opposition to these nominations."

About 1,500 names are appended to the call. On the list are the names of many Republicans as well as pronounced independents and civil service reformers who are not intimately attached to either party, though leaning toward the Republican. Among the signers are the following: Henry L. Pierce, formerly Congressman from the leading Boston district, and several times Mayor of Boston; Col. Charles R. Codman, who presided at the Republican State Convention which nominated Gov. Robinson; William Endicott, Jr., Martin Brimmer, C. W. Eliot, Col. Henry Lee, James Freeman Clarke, Moorfield Story, Col. T. W. Higginson, Edward Atkinson, Phineas Pierce, Henry L. Higginson, Stanton Blake, George William Bond, Estes Howe, Moses Williams, Darwin E. Ware, Samuel Hoar, son of Judge E. R. Hoar; Hamilton A. Hill, Francis J. Child, C. W. Peabody, William H. Forbes, George S. Hale, William Lloyd Garrison. The meeting is expected to be one of consultation and delegates will be sent to the June 17 conference in New-York.

Among the letters received by the committee are the following, the first from the Rev. Rufus Ellis, Pastor of the first Church, Congregational-Unitarian, and the second from Judge Pitman, of the Superior Court:

I.

MY DEAR SIR: Platform and candidates are both utterly distasteful to me. It is time that we made a start, at least, upon an entirely different basis. The thing is rotten clear through. It was a mistake to go into a convention at all with such probabilities, or even possibilities, as to the outcome. I am ready to throw away my vote upon Independents, as I used to do in Free-Soil days. Yours very truly,
RUFUS ELLIS.

II.

MY DEAR SIR: I send you my name as that of a Republican voter, who in no contingency will support the nomination of James G. Blaine. I have voted for every Republican President from Fremont down. I should not lightly break with the grand old national party, but the time has come for Republicans when to defeat Blaine will be a far greater honor than success. Yours truly,
ROBERT C. PITMAN.

June 13, 1884

MR. THEODORE ROOSEVELT.

HE WILL VOTE THE TICKET BUT TAKE NO PART IN THE CANVASS.

From the Boston Herald, July 2).

Mr. Theodore Roosevelt, of New-York, being in Boston for a few days, a representative of the *Herald* saw him and asked him if he would give an authoritative statement of his position in the present political alignment. Mr. Roosevelt responded as follows:

"In the first place, I would like to say that this is the first time I have said anything whatever for publication; all of the alleged interviews that have appeared so far are absolutely false. I intend to vote the Republican Presidential ticket. While at Chicago I told Mr. Lodge that such was my intention; but before announcing it I wished to have time to think the whole matter over. A man cannot act both without and within the party; he can do either, but he cannot possibly do both. Each course has its advantages, and each has its disadvantages, and one cannot take the advantages or disadvantages separately. I went in with my eyes open to do what I could within the party. I did my best and got beaten, and I propose to stand by the result. It is impossible to combine the functions of a guerrilla chief with those of a Colonel in the regular army; one has greater independence of action, the other is able to make what action he does take vastly more effective. In certain contingencies the one can do most good, in certain contingencies the other; but there is no use in accepting a commission and then trying to play the game out on a lone hand. During the entire canvass for the nomination Mr. Blaine received but two checks—one was at the Utica Convention, the other was the Powell Clayton incident. I had a hand in both, and I could have had a hand in neither had not those Republicans who at Utica elected me as the head of the New-York State delegation supposed that I would in good faith support the man who was fairly made the Republican nominee. I am by inheritance and by education a Republican; whatever good I have been able to accomplish in public life has been accomplished through the Republican Party; I have acted with it in the past and wish to act with it in the future; I went as a regular delegate to the Chicago Convention, and I intend to abide by the outcome of that convention. I am going back in a day or two to my Western ranch, as I do not expect to take any part in the campaign this Fall."

July 21, 1884

A STRONG TICKET CHOSEN

CLEVELAND AND HENDRICKS THE DEMOCRATIC NOMINEES.

AN OVERWHELMING VOTE FOR CLEVELAND ON THE SECOND BALLOT—HENDRICKS CHOSEN FOR VICE-PRESIDENT UNANIMOUSLY—KELLY'S LAST EFFORT—HIS HEELERS DEPART IN DISGUST.

THE SECOND AND LAST BALLOT.

CLEVELAND	683
BAYARD	81 1-2
HENDRICKS	45 1-2
THURMAN	4
RANDALL	4
McDONALD	2

From the Special Correspondent of the Times.

CHICAGO, July 11.—The Democratic Convention completed its work to-day by nominating Grover Cleveland, of New-York, to be President of the United States, and Thomas A. Hendricks, of Indiana, to be Vice-President. Cleveland won on the second ballot. On that ballot he received 475 votes. Before the result was announced opposing States threw aside their candidates and fought among themselves for the honor of being the first to get on the winning side. After all the changes had been made there were 683 votes for the Governor of New-York, and he was nominated by the unanimous voice of the convention.

July 12, 1884

GOV. CLEVELAND ELECTED

A VERY DECIDED MAJORITY IN THE ELECTORAL COLLEGE

NEW YORK GIVES CLEVELAND A PLURALITY OF 10,000.

BOTH CONNECTICUT AND NEW JERSEY DEMOCRATIC.

WISCONSIN VOTES FOR CLEVELAND BY 5,000.

INDIANA DEMOCRATIC BY 5,000 MAJORITY—THE RETURNS FROM THE WEST COMING IN VERY SLOWLY—CLOSE VOTES IN MANY STATES—RETURNS FROM THE SOUTH SHOW NO BREAK IN THE DEMOCRATIC COLUMN.

The returns indicate that Grover Cleveland has been elected President of the United States. The State of New York gives Cleveland a plurality of about 10,000. He has carried Connecticut by a plurality of from 1,500 to 2,500. Indiana is certainly Democratic by more than 5,000 majority. The latest estimates from Wisconsin are to the effect that Cleveland has carried that State by 5,000. Michigan is claimed by both parties, and the vote of the State is close. Both parties claim Virginia, but it is not probable that it has been taken from the Democratic column. The returns from New Jersey are incomplete, but it is believed that Cleveland has carried the State by 6,000 plurality. The Republicans claim Essex County by only 1,300, which indicates a Democratic gain of 1,700.

There is no trustworthy indication that Cleveland has lost any of the 153 votes in the South hitherto assigned to him. If we add to those 153 votes the 36 votes of New York, the 15 votes of Indiana, the 9 votes of New Jersey, and the 6 votes of Connecticut, the total is 219, or 18 more than a majority of the entire number of Electoral votes. But there must be added to this total, according to late returns, the 11 votes of Wisconsin. The total may be therefore 230 instead of 219.

The Democrats will have a large majority in the House of Representatives of the Forty-ninth Congress.

The distinguishing feature of the election in the Southern States was the light vote polled in nearly all places where some local issue did not bring out the voters. Perfect quiet and freedom from all disturbance is generally reported. North Carolina shows large Democratic gains in nearly all localities. In Virginia the Republicans put in their heaviest work in the colored districts and polled a large vote—so large that they claim the State. The Democrats, however, are confident that they have carried it by nearly 10,000 majority. Republican gains are reported in West Virginia, but the indications are that the State has gone Democratic. In Georgia the Republicans gained in the coal and iron districts.

Pennsylvania has, of course, been carried by the Republicans, but by a reduced majority. Of the 28 Congressmen the Republicans elect 20.

In this State the Democrats have elected 17 of the 34 Congressmen, while the Republicans have carried the Assembly, electing three more members than they had last year, when the number was 72. This insures a Republican United States Senator to be elected next Winter.

November 5, 1884

DR. BURCHARD EXPLAINS.

HE TELLS WHAT HE MEANT BY RUM, ROMANISM, AND REBELLION.

Mr. Charles Sutorius writes to the Utica Herald: " Inclosed you will find an answer from Dr. Burchard to my question: ' How under the sun could you make such a remark as " Rum," &c., entirely out of place and damaging Blaine, which you could have foreseen?' I think there are good reasons to print that answer for the public, if you think so too." Following is Dr. Burchard's reply:

NEW-YORK, Nov. 13, 1884.
Mr. Charles Sutorius:
DEAR SIR: As your note of yesterday is both candid and courteous, it shall receive a courteous reply. You ask, " How I could have made use of the expressions which have caused so much excitement and trouble?" In answer, I would say that the words were not premeditated and doubtless unfortunately uttered, especially as they have been totally misunderstood and misapplied. I went to the meeting of ministers at the Fifth-Avenue Hotel as a warm friend of Mr. Blaine and of the Republican Party. In my brief remarks of welcome I designed to characterize the Democratic Party as having manifested, if not friendliness, certainly no hostility to the excessive use of rum. I meant further to be understood that said party has endeavored to use the Roman Catholic population of this country as a factor to promote partisan and political purposes. I meant further to emphasize the fact that the party in question did not frown upon the late rebellion, but rather encouraged and aided the effort to destroy this Republic. Such was the intended meaning and application of the offensive terms used. Could I have foreseen the use and application which might have been made of them to the injury of Mr. Blaine and to the Republican cause they never would have found utterance. While, therefore, I exceedingly regret their misuse and misapplication, I still maintain that the alliterative expressions have a truthful and intended application, and who shall say that they may not have been overrated for good? If Mr. Cleveland is declared to be the successful candidate let us all, as good citizens, be cheerfully submissive and say, " Vox populi est vox Dei." Very respectfully,
S. D. BURCHARD

November 17, 1884

THE PRESIDENT AND HIS PARTY.

There is a curious difference of opinion among Democrats as to how far Mr. CLEVELAND represents his party. There is no doubt about his own position. His convictions are too firmly held and too well defined to leave that open to question. The doubt is as to whether his party is prepared to take the same position. Some of his admirers are tempted to believe that the party is practically in sympathy with his ideas and will in the long run support him. Some of his critics are ready to declare that he has betrayed his party, has adopted ideas and is pursuing a policy quite contrary to those of his party, and is bound to ruin it unless he can be induced to abandon them, of which they have little hope, or can be forced to do so, of which there is plainly no hope at all. Others are content with saying that he has got some pronounced ideas of his own, but that they are not of controlling importance, and that in the main he is a sound Democrat with Democratic principles, to which he will adhere.

There is a modicum of truth in all these opinions. Undoubtedly the President is a Democrat by association. He has always acted with his party, never openly against it. He would doubtless prefer to do so. He has a genuine attachment to the ideas which were once characteristic of the party—the strict construction of the Constitution, respect for the rights and powers reserved to the States and the people, jealousy of centralization, regard for the limitations placed by the Constitution upon the functions of the Executive and the Congress, and for their respective rights and powers. But these ideas are no longer peculiar to the Democratic Party. They are shared by many Republicans, and they are opposed or neglected by many Democrats, and Mr. CLEVELAND is too keen an observer not to be aware of that fact. He would wish to keep his party true to these principles, and will resist—he is constantly resisting—the tendency to depart from them, but he perceives that they are not now distinctive, and that any issue clearly involving them would divide each of the present great parties. On the other hand, he sees that there are certain living questions on which neither party is entirely agreed, and which are of very great importance, on which he has profound convictions, and as to which he will shape his policy quite independent of the mere party support he may receive. The chief of these are civil service reform and the silver coinage. As to each of them the President has taken a stand from which he will not recede, and that is the fact of which his party must take note and with which it must reckon.

Both of these are relatively new questions. Neither of them is related directly to the great questions growing out of the war that have formed the basis of party organization for the past quarter of a century, though the silver question is indirectly related to that of the paper currency of the war. Both questions are of immediate urgency, and both divide each of the great parties. The problem for the Democrats to decide is whether that division in their case is to be temporary or permanent, and that is the same as saying that the problem is whether they will sustain the President. They cannot hope to temporize or to wait until the questions "blow over." They are both so far of an enduring nature that they will agitate the country until they are settled in the right way, which happens to be the way in which the President would settle them. The country is

never going back to the rule of partisan politicians, and will not cease to work at the reform of the civil service until the service is completely and lastingly divorced from partisan politics. The idea of the reform is a strong and genuine American idea. The American people will not rest till they have realized it. In the same way the country will ultimately adopt a currency based on gold as the standard. Whatever use it may make of silver, it will not allow it to become the standard of the currency used in general commerce. We are a rich, prosperous, industrious, and enterprising people. We need the best

implements. We will not accept the poor ones. We may experiment with them. We may hesitate and compromise for a while, but finally we shall take the currency in use by our great rivals in the trade of the world, the currency which will help and not hinder us in making New-York what London now is, the centre of the financial world. If the Democratic Party can be united on these questions by gradually adopting the sound views of the President, so much the better for the party and for the country. If it cannot be united in this way it must be hopelessly divided.

January 18, 1886

THE SOUTHERN ELECTION QUESTION.

Those Republican politicians who still think there is capital for their party in keeping up sectional agitation and firing the Northern heart with Southern outrages are trying desperately to make an issue of the alleged suppression of the Republican vote in Southern States. The difficulty which confronts them lies in the fact that the Northern people want no more sectional agitation and are entirely willing to leave the elections in Southern States to the control of the people of those States. This does not imply a lack of belief in some of the alleged wrongs, but it indicates a lack of faith in the efficacy of Federal interference to right them, and a willingness to leave the South to work out its own political problems. Universal suffrage does not work to perfection in any State. It is beset with evils and abuses against which honest men are constantly contending, but it is generally admitted that the States must be left to cure these evils as best they can.

Most candid men both North and South are forced to admit that much has been done to counteract the effect of the negro vote where it is large enough materially to affect results. The original reason for this is to be found in the deplorable consequences that followed upon the enfranchisement of the colored race. Unprepared to exercise intelligently or conscientiously their newly-acquired rights, the negroes fell under the leadership of unscrupulous men and were arrayed against the people who had the largest interest in the good order and good government of the reconstructed States. The result was incapacity, extravagance and fraud in public affairs, and a burlesque on popular government. The native Southern people, who felt that they had the right to control affairs in their own States, saw no salvation for their public or private interests except in overcoming the power

which was thrust upon them. It could not be done by persuasion, and they were prepared to countenance almost any means by which it could be done. Even the Federal power intrenched in the reconstruction acts could not prevent the violence and the outrages by which the control of three States was recovered by the men who paid the taxes and who had the intelligence and character to maintain decent government.

The North soon admitted that Federal interference to sustain State Governments which rested on the ignorant negro vote and were managed mainly by greedy and unscrupulous adventurers could not be maintained. Public opinion withdrew all support, and nearly a dozen years ago the whole fabric went to pieces. By one means or another the negro vote was to a large extent suppressed, and there is no question that in several States it has since been kept down so far as was necessary to enable the native Southerners, who owned property, who paid taxes, and who controlled intelligent public sentiment in their States, to direct the management of their public interests. This is a fact which no candid Southern man can deny, and which most Southern men will privately admit and defend. On the other hand, most candid Northern men will admit that, given the same situation in any Northern State, the result would have been the same. This is the truth of the history of the last twenty years.

There is no need to go into the circumstances which inevitably arrayed the great mass of intelligent and property-owning citizens in the Southern States against the Republican Party so long as it controlled the National Administration. They were determined to control the political and public affairs of their States, and they were mostly Democrats. Outrage, violence, and election frauds diminished in proportion as the necessity for them ceased. For the last two years little has been heard of them, but election returns show that many votes are

withheld from the ballot box for one reason or another. Colored voters may have become indifferent, after finding that the ills which they were taught to expect from Democratic ascendency did not befall them, and easily induced not to vote. More or less, also, they have begun to divide their votes between the parties. In not voting or in voting for Democratic candidates they are probably influenced by no worse inducements than are used in Northern States to sway the action of voters whose intelligence and honesty are not sufficient to guide their political action.

There is but one hopeful way of dissolving the Democratic solidity of the South. Slowly the political intelligence of the colored citizens increases. Gradually the colored vote is ceasing to be a solid Republican vote. As it divides, the motives which sustain the Democratic solidity will give way, and the questions which divide citizens in the North on national politics will divide them in the South, without regard to race. Every attempt to maintain sectional distinctions, every suggestion of new experiments of Federal intervention, will retard this process, and every such attempt or suggestion will find less and less support in the North. The Republican Party abandons its chance of making gains in the South and loses still more of its support in the North every time it insists anew upon its sectional attitude. The country is weary of the long contest and wishes to see both parties national in spirit and in purpose. There are electoral wrongs in the Southern States. They have been diminishing steadily for years, and the process will go on if no new antagonism is excited. Negro suffrage presents problems and difficulties in those States which cannot be settled at once, but they can only be settled at all by the people of the States in which they exist.

December 18, 1887

CLEVELAND RENOMINATED

AND HIS TARIFF REFORM POLICY INDORSED.

ST. LOUIS, June 6.—The long and tiresome struggle over the tariff between the opposing factions in the Committee on Resolutions came to an end to-night. The resolution which the committee will report to the convention renews the party's pledge of fidelity to Democratic principles, indorses the last annual message of President Cleveland, and declares that message to be a correct interpretation of the tariff platform of 1884, and approves and applauds the efforts of Democratic Representatives in Congress to secure reduced taxation. There will also be offered to the convention a supplementary resolution commending the Mills bill and urging Democrats to vote for it and pass it. Mr. Watterson says: "My original idea did not contemplate a recurrence to the resolution of 1884, and of course I opposed a repetition of that resolution when it was proposed, but as it is coupled with an authoritative interpretation of that ambiguous platform and an indorsement of the work of our party in Congress, the resolution as finally adopted meets my most hearty approval."

It is announced that the committee will present a solid front in support of the tariff plank, and that ex-Gov. Abbett of New-Jersey will move the adoption of the report. Mr. Lehmann of Iowa declares that he will support the report. He regards it as "an advance," but it is not entirely satisfactory to him.

The sub-committee of eleven, to which the work of framing a platform had been referred, was busily engaged until 3 o'clock this morning, and at 9 o'clock that part of the work which related to the tariff was brought back into the whole committee. It is understood that the sub-committee had been unable to agree and that a majority of its members were not in accord with Mr. Watterson, although seven of the eleven had voted to make him Chairman. It is also stated that when the subject came back to the whole committee the sub-committee had taken no steps toward the indorsement of the President's message. The first vote in the whole committee was upon a preamble in which the tariff resolution of 1884 was reaffirmed. Mr. Watterson moved that this be stricken out, and was beaten by a vote of 25 to 21. Thereupon the committee adjourned, and the work was resumed at 6 o'clock this evening. Lawrence T. Neil of Ohio, who had voted to make Gorman Chairman because he admired the man, although his opinions concerning the tariff coincided with those of Watterson. After Watterson's motion to strike out had been lost Neil moved the adoption of additions which were substantially those relating to the message and the Mills bill, which were finally adopted.

Early in the day there was some probability that the contest would be taken into the convention, but the compromise that was reached this evening appears to have prevented any such outbreak. The real tariff reformers made great gains in the closing hours of the fight. As has been shown heretofore, their opponents were determined at first that neither the message nor the Mills bill should be mentioned. But considerable pressure was applied to the committee by means of telegrams from Congressmen and others. Several members who had betrayed their trust were placed under discipline, notably the Missouri member, O'Day, who had surrendered to Gorman, in the face of the strongest State resolutions and the most positive instructions. Early this evening some of the obstructionists were forced to admit that the message would be indorsed, but they declared that an "unqualified" indorsement was neither probable nor expedient. This was the attitude of ex-Senator Davis of West Virginia.

Mr. Morrison expresses satisfaction with the result. One of the reasons which kept him out of the committee was this, that it had become the duty of the Illinois member to urge the adoption of a resolution in support of the proposed Hennepin canal, and this project is not advocated in the southern part of the State, where Mr. Morrison lives. He preferred that the duty should be performed by some other man.

The history of this contest will show that owing to the neglect of leaders of the majority, a committee which ought to have fairly represented the party was at one time almost evenly divided upon the question whether it should indorse or even recognize the most prominent feature of the policy of a President whom a convention gave to the party had actually renominated unanimously for another term. And only in the last hours of the struggle was the influence of protected interests and mischiefmakers overcome. The other work of the convention has been delayed by this struggle in committee. Nothing has been done beyond the nomination of Mr. Cleveland. A nomination for the second place will be made to-morrow.

"He has done his duty; let us do ours," said Mr. McKenzie to-day while seconding the nomination of Mr. Cleveland. If the differences of the Resolutions Committee on the tariff had been carried into the convention to-day the obstructionists would speedily have been routed.

The scene in the convention hall immediately after the closing words of Mr. Dougherty's speech, "I give you a name entwined with victory; I nominate Grover Cleveland of New-York," was one long to be remembered. For nearly 25 minutes the vast crowd applauded. The standard of all the States were taken from their stations and grouped around New-York's uplifted shield. The vote for adjournment appears to have had no special significance with regard to the nomination for second place. F. D. R.

TARIFF REFORM INDORSED.

THE PLATFORM WILL REAFFIRM THAT OF 1884 AND APPROVE PRESIDENT CLEVELAND'S TARIFF REFORM MESSAGE.

ST. LOUIS, June 6.—The Committee on Resolutions, at 8:30 to-night, have agreed upon the tariff plank of the platform by a unanimous vote. The plank is as follows:

"The Democratic Party of the United States in National Convention assembled renews the pledge of its fidelity to Democratic faith, reaffirms the platform adopted by its representatives in the convention of 1884, and indorses the views expressed by President Cleveland in his last annual message to Congress as the correct interpretation of that platform upon the question of tariff reduction, and also indorses the efforts of our Democratic Representatives in Congress to secure a reduction of excessive taxation."

This plank was the outcome of a long fight begun in the sub-committee last night and continued to-day in the meeting of the whole committee. The sub-committee, which was supposed to consist of seven men in accord with Mr. Watterson and four who were in accord with Mr. Gorman, turned out at an early stage of the proceedings to be opposed to Mr. Watterson, who would not consent to a reaffirmation of the tariff plank of 1884. The draft of a platform prepared by Mr. Scott, and which was understood to satisfy the Administration, did not at all meet Mr. Watterson's expectations. The sub-committee gave up its efforts to agree and the full committee took up the subject. Mr. Scott had taken the place of Mr. Mutchler as the member from Pennsylvania, and he appealed to the committee to give careful consideration to the platform offered, as one prepared with the hope of reasonably satisfying all sections of the party. It was not deemed necessary to reiterate the language of the platform of 1884, but to reiterate fidelity to its principles as understood and acted upon by the President and Congress.

Soon after the committee met Mr. Watterson's strength was tested. He made a motion to substitute for the plank offered by Mr. Scott a plank of his own of a more radical character, containing no references to the platform of 1884, but committing the party to tariff reform as the supreme issue. There were 46 members of the committee present. Of these 21 voted with Mr. Watterson and 25 voted against him. Having decided not to follow Mr. Watterson's advice the committee directed its attention to the verbal form of the leading resolution. The plank, as submitted by Mr. Scott, stopped at the words "tariff reduction." Upon the suggestion of Mr. Neal of Ohio the words beginning "We also indorse the efforts of our Democratic Representatives in Congress" were added, as he considered that the platform would be lame and imperfect if it did not directly approve the attempt being made in Congress to reduce taxation. Mr. Cooper of New-York was inclined to split hairs as usual. He contended a long time for a verbal change. It seemed important to him to say that the convention considered the President's message as "in accord with the platform of 1884" instead of characterizing it as "a correct interpretation of the language of the platform of 1884."

Mr. Scott is satisfied with the plank. So is Mr. Watterson, or at least he says it is satisfactory. Mr. Watterson likes it, of course, as he reported the platform of 1884, and his interpretation of it was always the interpretation that the President gave of it in his message to Congress. Mr. Barnum does not know whether he likes it or not. Mr. Kelly of Minnesota thinks that it rather squints both ways, but he does not grumble.

If the plank is not satisfactory to exacting tariff reformers, who had been led to believe that the Democratic Party was ready boldly to take hold of tariff reform in the convention, it will be because the party managers could not see their way to victory with a radical utterance. The representatives of protected industries—Democrats of Pennsylvania of prominence and influence, whose co-operation in the coming campaign was desired—undoubtedly intimated that a radical utterance would compel them to remain indifferent spectators during the coming struggle.

The action of the committee will probably be found to mean that Mr. W. H. Barnum will be at the head of the National Committee; that Mr. Gorman will also be an active worker in the campaign, and that Mr. Davis of West Virginia, Mr. Abbett, and other sensitive Democrats will be kept in the harness and help in the campaign for Cleveland and Thurman.

June 7, 1888

HARRISON AND MORTON

THE REPUBLICAN TICKET AT LAST NOMINATED.

THE BLAINE CONSPIRATORS LOSE THEIR GRIP ENTIRELY AND RETIRE FROM THE FIGHT—HOW HARRISON'S VOTE INCREASED UNTIL HE WAS NOMINATED—LEVI P. MORTON PREFERRED TO PHELPS FOR VICE-PRESIDENT—THE CONVENTION ADJOURNS.

THE FINAL BALLOT.

BENJAMIN HARRISON of Indiana	544
JOHN SHERMAN of Ohio	118
RUSSELL A. ALGER of Michigan	100
WALTER Q. GRESHAM of Indiana	59
JAMES G. BLAINE of Maine	5
WILLIAM McKINLEY of Ohio	4
WHOLE NUMBER OF VOTES	830
NECESSARY TO A CHOICE	416

CHICAGO, June 25.—The Blaine conspirators discovered last night that they had lost their hold upon the convention. The revolt against them had become so formidable that they were forced to withdraw from the field. Having thrust them aside, the delegates this morning took up the problem, and in three ballots solved it by yielding to the judgment of the doubtful States. On the sixth ballot the votes of the great States of New-York and Indiana, that of one delegate excepted, were cast for Harrison, and with these were 14 of New-Jersey's 18 votes. On the eighth ballot the convention acknowledged the force of this recommendation by giving Harrison a majority of 128 votes to spare.

June 26, 1888

A RICH MAN'S PARTY.

When the Republican Party arose, now more than thirty years ago, it was necessarily from the nature of its aims a party of the common people. There was nothing about it to attract the wealthy as such; there was much to attract those whose means were scant, whose struggle in life was hard. It was essentially an anti-slavery party, and though its policy was restricted to the exclusion of slavery from the Territories, it was well understood by the authors of that policy and by those against whom it was directed that such exclusion would be fatal to slavery. Republicanism, therefore, stood in those days for the rights of free labor, for the protection of the oppressed, and all men of the working class sufficiently intelligent to understand how liberty and equality were the very bulwarks of their rights sympathized with the party. It was not, moreover, at that time in any sense a place-hunting party. It had no patronage to bestow, and its best workers throughout the North, in every town and village and on the farms, were men whose convictions were strong and definite and whose conscience was awakened and active. They sought no reward but the triumph of their principles; they spent money rather than gained it in politics, and they felt themselves to be, as in fact they were, the equals of any with whom they were associated.

The condition of the party has since then greatly changed. Rich men, often without too much regard to how their riches were obtained, have come to the front and have taken the lead. Under Republican rule the Senate has come to be looked upon as a "club of rich men," and the possession of wealth has not infrequently opened its doors to those who had very little other qualification, not even party loyalty, as witness the way in which the mine-owning Senators have persistently opposed the long-established policy of the party as to silver until they have finally succeeded in securing its disavowal. Nor has this been the only channel to political advancement opened by mere wealth in the Republican Party. No one supposes for a moment that Mr. MORTON would have been chosen as a candidate for the Vice-Presidency had he been a poor man. A respectable private citizen, he has never given the slightest evidence of being endowed with unusual capacity for public affairs. Indeed, such evidence as is afforded by his brief and obscure career in Congress is all against that conclusion. On the other hand, he has failed conspicuously to secure the confidence of the people of the State in which he lives or of his own party. He has more than once undertaken to secure an election to the United States Senate by methods that demonstrated little but his personal wealth, his ambition, and his liberality in spending his money in order to gratify his ambition. There are, at a moderate estimate, 10,000 men in the Republican Party better fitted by mental equipment, by experience, by reputation for the office to which Mr. MORTON has been nominated. But they have not so much money, or else are unwilling to contribute it.

Two things have combined to bring about this change in the Republican Party. One is the spoils system which the party succeeded to when it came into power, and which it had, when ejected, enormously developed. The other, and more important, is the gradual and finally complete subversion of the party to the influence of the protected interests. This has been extremely and constantly demoralizing, because it has brought into active operation in public life the pecuniary interests that are the most harmful. In business life, where these interests necessarily prevail, they are checked and regulated by the fact that every one is measurably free to contend for his own. But in public life all power is a trust, and the money employed does not belong to and is not furnished by those who handle it. Hence the need of the strictest safeguards and also of the strictest limitations that can be enforced. In the case of protection the evil is worse, because the action of public men enables certain persons to get large gains, not through the Treasury, where they could be watched, but through taxes collected by the parties in interest from the consumers. By giving special advantages to favored persons the protective tariff organizes a large body of active and eager men with whom the perpetuation of the tariff and of the party that will sustain the tariff is a matter of direct personal interest. They may easily think it is also a matter of patriotic principle, but every one knows that judgment complicated with interest is not to be trusted. And, as a matter of fact, the tendency toward something very like corruption and wholly unlike candid and honest politics has grown in the Republican Party with the growth of protection. When men make money by politics, they are ready to use money in politics, and this is the way in which money has come to be more important in the Republican Party than anything else.

August 17, 1888

TARIFF REFORM DEFERRED

THE REPUBLICAN NATIONAL TICKET VICTORIOUS.

CONGRESS DEMOCRATIC BY A SMALL MAJORITY—RE-ELECTION OF GOV. HILL — THE STATE LEGISLATURE REPUBLICAN.

Harrison and Morton have been elected President and Vice-President of the United States. The majority for the Republican candidates in the Electoral College will be fourteen more than that cast in 1884 for Cleveland and Hendricks. Harrison has carried New-York, Indiana, California, Michigan, and Colorado, all of which had been regarded as debatable States. The majority in this State for Harrison will not be far from 11,000. In Indiana it will be very small, but in Minnesota, Iowa, and Michigan, where the interest manifested in the tariff question was relied upon to effect a considerable change in the vote, the Republicans have developed their full strength, and obtained pluralities for the national ticket much larger than those cast for Blaine in 1884.

Connecticut gives a small majority for Cleveland, and shows marked Democratic gains in the manufacturing towns, where the question of tariff taxation was constantly and thoroughly discussed during the long campaign. New-Jersey, a State greatly interested in manufacturing, not only more than doubled its Democratic majority of 1884, but chose a Legislature that will elect a Democratic United States Senator to succeed McPherson.

The returns from the Western States are still very imperfect, but it is apparent that Merriam, (Rep.) has been elected Governor of Minnesota, Hoard (Rep.) in Wisconsin, and Luce (Rep.) in Michigan, and that the legislative contests in those States have resulted to the advantage of the Republicans.

The Congressional elections have been hotly contested, and the outcome of the battles in many districts is surprising. By the latest reports it appears that the Fifty-first Congress will be controlled by the Democrats by an extremely small majority, which may be wiped out altogether by the corrected returns from Virginia, Arkansas, North Carolina, and Michigan, in all of which States there are disputed results. The Democrats secure a solid delegation from West Virginia, including Mr. William L. Wilson, a member of the Ways and Means Committee, who was re-elected by an increased lead. The defeat of Mr. Clifton R. Breckinridge, another member of the Ways and Means Committee, in the Second Arkansas District, is claimed by the allied Wheelers and Republicans, but is not admitted by the Democrats.

Gov. Hill has been re-elected in his State by a majority of about 19,000, and there seems to be no doubt that Lieut.-Gov. Jones has also been re-elected, and that Justice Gray has been retained as a member of the Court of Appeals. The Republicans will have 79 members of the next Assembly and the Democrats 49. Full returns show that there are only a few changes to be made in the tables printed in THE TIMES of yesterday. They are as follows: Peter Schaaf, (Dem.,) in place of John Reits, Seventh Kings; James P. Graham, (Dem.,) in place of D. W. Tallmadge, Twelfth Kings; Moses Dinkelspiel, (Dem.,) in place of Sol D. Rosenthal, Twelfth New-York; William Murray, (Dem.,) in place of T. Irving Burns, First Westchester; Bradford Rhodes, (Rep.,) re-elected, Second Westchester.

A revision of the vote in this city gives Cleveland a plurality of 57,213 and to Hill, for Governor, a plurality of 58,353. The vote cast for Governor was also larger by several thousands than that cast for President, which is unusual. Warner Miller, the Republican candidate for Governor, received 3,198 more votes than Harrison, and Hill 4,238 more than Cleveland.

November 8, 1888

LEADERS AND "BOSSES."

The most strenuous advocates of freedom and independence in political action admit the necessity and the utility of organization. The most earnest believers in the representative principle in party management concede the importance of leadership. The rank and file of a political party have certain convictions or instincts in regard to public policy, certain tendencies of thought and feeling which lead them to one side of the dividing line rather than to the other, but in order to formulate principles and establish a recognized basis of agreement and united action there must be an organization effected and carried on through selected representatives of the mass. The theory of such an organization is that these representatives, whether acting as members and officers of party committees, delegates to conventions and conferences, or elected agents of the people in public positions, reflect the convictions and wishes of those by whom they are chosen. But, necessarily, they must exercise their own judgment in behalf of their constituents. To an extent they must lead and direct, and not merely obey. It is for them to study the conditions of politics and of pending questions and to devise plans of party action, appealing for support to the intelligence and the convictions of those whom they represent.

There must necessarily be leaders in this work of organization, and in a normal state of things these will be men with a clear comprehension of the principles that underlie popular convictions and tendencies, a quick perception of the demands of the time, and a capacity for organizing and directing forces that have their source in the people and not in themselves. Their function will be to guide, to direct, and to give expression to party forces, not to dictate or to control party action for selfish purposes of their own. Those who undertake to do the latter become "bosses" and not leaders. They forget or ignore the representative character in party organization and assume that authority proceeds not from the mass of party membership, but from themselves. They assume to command and to exact obedience, rather than to exercise an authority derived from a constituent body for the promotion of its purposes. They undertake to use an organization, formed to carry out certain principles and to promote certain policies in public affairs, to give effect to their personal designs and to accomplish ends that are not consistent either with the public good or the well-being of the party itself.

We have had in this country two kinds of "bosses." One has flourished chiefly in large cities, where there is a mass of ignorant or indifferent voters and where the more intelligent part of the community is apt to be so absorbed in private interests as to neglect public duties. Political leaders have there found the opportunity of controlling party organization to suit their own plans and purposes, and have depended upon the manipulation of one class of voters, the easy acquiescence of another class, and the general disposition of party men to accept nominations made for them, for the success of their designs. The "boss" of the Tammany type, however, seeks to win support. He may be ready to deceive and manipulate the ignorant, to secure the vicious and indifferent by an appeal to selfish motives, to use the "spoils" of office and of public patronage to enlist in his service those who can control votes, but at the present time, at least, he dare not resort to dictation and coercion and the exercise of autocratic authority.

The Republican "boss" of to-day is a comparatively new type. He finds that his party has drifted into a dependence upon certain combinations of private interests, which derive profit from the policy of the Government and desire to continue doing so. They seek to use politics to increase their advantages and their power. They have obtained practical control of a political party, and their alliances are made directly with the so-called leaders of that party. It is a consolidation of power that has to be maintained on the corporation principle and not on the representative principle. Influence is not proportioned to numbers, but to ownership of stock. Those who command the largest resources have most power, and the springs of action are in the officers and directors and not in the constituent body. The designs contrived by those few in their inner councils must be carried out or the whole scheme will fail. It matters not whether their purposes are understood or not, they must be accepted, and the orders issued must be obeyed, lest the whole party machinery break down. Party fidelity and the fear of the success of the opposition are made an instrument of coercion, and party action becomes subject to "bossism" and not to leadership. "Bossism" of this kind necessarily becomes autocratic and tyrannical. It cannot exist upon any other terms, and the power of a man like TOM PLATT in a party depends wholly upon the ruthless and unscrupulous use of coercion. The combination of interests which he represents cares nothing for the fate of any party unless it can be used to accomplish the ends that the combination has in view. It does not ask or plead, it commands and insists. It will reward those who serve it and it will destroy those who refuse. It is PLATT's readiness to ruin that makes him obeyed, not his power to benefit; his willingness to undermine, to stab in the dark, to wreck and destroy, not his ability to build up. It is a question how long such "bossism" can last in a free country. A party may submit to it, but will the people? If the party submits to it, will it not be at the cost of continual revolts and desertions which will end in a disastrous loss of all power?

February 2, 1890

HARRISON WINS THE PRIZE

BLAINE BEATEN AS HE NEVER WAS BEATEN BEFORE.

THE PRESIDENT RENOMINATED BY A PLURALITY OF 166—WHITELAW REID THE CANDIDATE FOR VICE PRESIDENT — BLAINE FORCES DIVIDED IN THE BALLOT, ABOUT HALF GOING TO M'KINLEY.

For President—BENJAMIN HARRISON of Indiana.

For Vice President—WHITELAW REID of New York.

MINNEAPOLIS, June 10.—The Republican ticket for 1892 is made up.

After three days of preliminary work, and in the first session of the fourth day, Benjamin Harrison of Indiana was nominated on the first ballot, receiving 535 1-6 votes to 182 1-6 for William McKinley of Ohio, and 182 votes for James G. Blaine of Maine, with 4 votes for Thomas B. Reed of Maine and 1 for Robert T. Lincoln of Illinois.

At the second session, Whitelaw Reid of New York was nominated for Vice President by acclamation.

The omen of last night, when the lights went out on the initial conflict between the Harrison and Blaine men, was as true of the beginning of his search for the Presidential nomination as it was of the close of it, for everybody now assumes that Blaine will never again become or allow his friends to cause him to be considered a candidate for President.

Harrison's friends refrained from harsh references to Mr. Blaine, while Mr. Blaine's supporters have indulged in coarse, bitter, vindictive epithets about the President. The Harrison men, with a candidate absolutely without a personal friend or any magnetic qualities of attraction, demoralized the adherents of the Plumed Knight, and have left the once brilliant leader crushed and beaten, after desertion in battle by half of his noisy and vengeance-breathing supporters.

Blaine has been beaten before, but never under such humiliating conditions, or in a way from which so little satisfaction can be gleaned. His supporters, in placing him in nomination, lauded him as little less than a god, and then, with their laudations still ringing in the ears of the thousands to whom they had been addressed, they fled away from the advancing Harrison hosts in a divided body that would have lacked, if united, almost a hundred votes to make a majority.

Blaine's men flung in the faces of the Harrison men the taunt that Harrison was to be nominated by the Solid South, which has no Republican votes, yet in the States of New-York and Pennsylvania he secured more votes from Northern States than either Blaine or McKinley.

June 11, 1892

CLEVELAND AND STEVENSON

TWO STRONG LEADERS FOR ALL DEMOCRATS TO FOLLOW.

THE CONVENTION COMPLETES THE TICKET BY ADDING ADLAI E. STEVENSON OF ILLINOIS—BOTH CANDIDATES WERE SELECTED ON THE FIRST BALLOT—END OF A CONTEST CHARACTERIZED BY MUCH EARNESTNESS AND SOME BITTERNESS.

For President—GROVER CLEVELAND of New York.

For Vice President—ADLAI E. STEVENSON of Illinois.

CHICAGO, June 23.—Grover Cleveland will again lead the Democracy of the United States as candidate for President.

At daybreak to-day, in the presence of the greatest audience that ever witnessed such an event, after a contest characterized by intense earnestness and patriotism, and by bitterness on the side of the opposition, the confidence in the great leader of the Democracy as the fittest candidate was expressed in the nomination of Grover Cleveland on the first ballot and before the roll call of States was fully completed.

Gen. Adlai E. Stevenson of Illinois was chosen for Vice President this afternoon, and also upon the first ballot. His most formidable opponent in the contest was ex-Gov. Isaac P. Gray of Indiana.

Cleveland and Stevenson present a very strong ticket to the country.

The candidate for President, already held in high esteem by every citizen who is capable of feeling pride, is a grand type of Americanism. He is admitted by candid Republicans to be so popular in Illinois as to justify the expectation that his record for personal integrity and executive bravery and efficiency may prove so great an attraction to the voters of this State as to take its Electoral vote out of the Republican column in November.

Gen. Stevenson is in many respects an admirable candidate to strengthen the ticket and to encourage the hope of the Democrats of the country that Illinois may be won upon a low-tariff and sound-money platform. A soldier of the Union, a gentleman of education, with affable manners and possessing decided executive ability, he has, through his administration of a branch of the Postal Service under President Cleveland, become known, by name at least, in every hamlet in the land. This acquaintance has been widened by his recent official connection with the World's Columbian Exposition, so that it will be unnecessary to introduce him to the country. His record is one that offers no mark to the most unscrupulous foe.

June 24, 1892

MR. CLEVELAND'S VICTORY

LATER RETURNS ONLY CONFIRM FIRST REPORTS.

THE DEMOCRATIC MAJORITY IN THE ELECTORAL COLLEGE WILL BE AT LEAST ONE HUNDRED AND FIFTY-SIX — REPUBLICANS AND THIRD-PARTY MEN WELCOME TO THE STATES YET IN DISPUTE — THE "DOUBTFUL" STATES FIRMLY FIXED IN THE DEMOCRATIC COLUMN.

Later reports of Tuesday's election extend the lines of the Democratic conquest. Mr. Cleveland's majority in the Electoral College will be at least 156 votes, and it is possible that it may be still greater.

The official count weakens the Republican column. Colorado, which was admitted to the Union under a Republican Administration, has cast its votes for Weaver Electors. Of the five States the Republicans created in the Northwest in order to preserve their majority in the United States Senate they have assuredly carried three—Washington, Wyoming, and Montana. North Dakota is placed in the Republican column, but the chances are that the People's Party has won it. Kansas and Nebraska, which have voted the Republican Electoral ticket since they were admitted to Statehood, have cast their votes for Weaver. California has been carried by the Democrats for the second time in nine Presidential elections. In Illinois the Republican majority of over 20,000 in 1888 has given place to a Democratic plurality nearly, if not quite, as large, and the State has for the first time since before the war chosen Democratic Electors.

Michigan for the first time in more than thirty years divides its vote and gives at least six Electors to the Democrats, and Wisconsin breaks a line of Republican victories stretching back for a like time by choosing the Democratic Electoral ticket by a plurality of 11,000 or more.

Illinois furnished the surprise of the first news from the West, but it is equaled this morning by that from Ohio. It is reported on what seems to be good authority that McKinley's own State has cast its vote for the Cleveland Electors. Harrison carried the State by nearly 20,000 in 1888, and McKinley, when he ran for Governor, by over 21,000. The State has never before gone Democratic in a Presidential year.

The so-called doubtful States are Democratic. In this State Mr. Cleveland's plurality is over 41,000, in New-Jersey 12,000, in Connecticut over 5,000, in Indiana nearly 10,000, and in West Virginia 7,000. Whatever States are still in doubt are to be divided between the Republicans and the third party. Any changes that may be disclosed by the official figures will not lessen Mr. Cleveland's total vote. On the contrary, it is more likely to be increased.

Yesterday reports of the elections for Representatives in Congress have made several individual changes in the list as presented in THE TIMES of Wednesday, but have not materially affected the strength of the Democrats, who will have more than 80 majority over Republicans and People's Party members combined. These returns make the ante-election predictions of ex-Clerk McPherson and ex-Journal Clerk H. H. Smith appear to have been about as ill considered as the predictions of Clarkson and Platt before the Minneapolis Convention.

November 10, 1892

"THE GREATEST BLUNDER SINCE SECESSION."

We commend to the thoughtful attention of Gov. MCKINLEY and many other prominent Republicans who profess a desire to make the fight again on the old lines the following editorial remarks in the St. Louis *Globe-Democrat*, one of the most influential Republican newspapers in the country, and a journal that supported McKinleyism and the Republican ticket heartily during the recent campaign:

"The Republican Party was beaten because it had taken a wrong position on some of the leading questions of national concern. It was wrong on the Federal election matter; it was emphatically and fatally wrong on the tariff. The passage of the McKinley law of 1890 was the greatest blunder ever committed by any party since the Democratic crime of secession. It overwhelmingly defeated the party in the Congressional election of that year, and it was the leading cause in the overthrow this year. Many Republicans who were never in favor of the act believed after the setback of 1890 that the popular hostility to it would subside by the time the Presidential election came around, and that the party might then retain its supremacy in the executive branch of the Government and regain control of the legislative branch. The returns show how completely and conspicuously those hopes have been blasted.

"This thing called McKinleyism—this advancing of duties on articles which have been on the dutiable list for from a third of a century—has been condemned finally and eternally by the people. This verdict has been rendered twice, and after an interval of two years between the judgments. The first verdict may have been hastily given, and without sufficient examination of the evidence, but the second was recorded after reasonable deliberation, and it was more pronounced and emphatic than the first. If the Republican Party is to win any victories in the future it must drop McKinleyism immediately and permanently, and send all the men who cling to it to the rear. The party must, of course, adhere to the protective policy, but it must be protection of the rational kind—the protection which keeps the interests of consumers as well as those of producers in view."

November 21, 1892

REFORM AND THIRD PARTIES

The Convention at Apollo Hall.

A meeting was held yesterday in Apollo Hall, for the purpose of organizing a new political party, and to nominate candidates for President and Vice-President. The hall, which was decorated with a number of peculiarly-worded banners, was nearly filled with ladies, wearing eye-glasses and short hair in general. There were a few men present. Mr. MADDOX read the call, and the Committee on Permanent Organization made their report, appointing as President Hon. J. D. REYMERT, of New York; First Vice-President, ANNA L. MIDDLEBROOK, and a number of other officers.

The Committee on Platform and Resolutions reported a platform embracing the following points: Complete reconstruction of the functions of the Government of the United States; a new Constitution to meet the present wants of the people, the present Constitution being behind the present age of civilization; a uniform national code of civil and criminal law; important legislation to be submitted to and be approved by the people before becoming law; all monopolies to be abolished, charters revoked, and the Government to take charge of all public enterprises, which are to be for the public use, and not to be charged for at a higher rate than the cost of construction and maintenance; public lands to be for the free use of actual settlers; one system of currency, based on the national faith; direct taxation according to personal property; free trade; general peace; fair remuneration for labor; the Government to employ the unemployed; capital punishment to be abolished; every person, male and female, to be allowed to vote; the Monroe doctrine, and that the new party be called the Equal Rights Party.

A very disturbed and boisterous discussion ensued first on the acceptance of the report, but after a while the document was accepted.

It was then moved to adopt the platform as a whole body; this caused the most angry debate, during which the President nearly knocked his desk to pieces in his endeavors to keep order.

It was then moved to consider it seriatim, and this excited an equally angry debate, during which a motion to adjourn was carried.

The evening session was principally occupied by an address from VICTORIA C. WOODHULL, after which she was nominated for President, and FRED. DOUGLASS for Vice-President. The platform of the afternoon was sprung upon the meeting during the enthusiasm of the nomination, and adopted by acclamation, after which the Convention adjourned until this morning.

May 11, 1872

THE GREENBACK PARTY'S TICKET.

WEAVER FOR PRESIDENT AND CHAMBERS FOR VICE-PRESIDENT — THE CONVENTION'S ALL-NIGHT SESSION.

CHICAGO, June 11.—In the Greenback-Labor Convention last night, after the nomination of Messrs. Weaver, Campbell, Butler, and Woolf for the Presidency, Congressman Yokum, of Pennsylvania, placed in nomination the Hon. Hendrick B. Wright, of Pennsylvania. William R. Dale, of Tennessee, who claimed to be a phenomenon, as the only living Confederate private in the United States, nominated Thompson H. Murch, of Maine, but Mr. Murch being on the floor of the Convention, declined the honor. Wisconsin presented the name of Edward P. Allis, of that State. The call of the States from Alabama to Wisconsin was seized on by delegates to speak on every question connected with the Greenback-Labor Party and the various candidates. At 3:25 A. M. it was moved that the Convention proceed to ballot for a nominee for President of the United States. An informal ballot was first taken, the result of which was announced at 4:10 o'clock A. M., just as daylight was breaking. It stood: Weaver, 224½; Wright, 126½; Dillage, 119; Butler, 95; Chase, 89; Allis, 41; Campbell, 21.

Before the announcement of the first ballot, it became evident that Weaver had a clear majority, and all the delegates hastened to change their votes to that candidate. Motions sprang from every part of the Convention to make his nomination unanimous, and just as the sun shone through the eastern windows, the result of the ballot was announced as 718 for James B. Weaver—the total vote—and without any motion his nomination was made unanimous. In the midst of a perfect pandemonium of shouting delegates, the nominations of candidates for Vice-President were made. Gen. Horace P. Sergeant, of Massachusetts, presented the name of Gen. A. M. West, of Mississippi; B. J. Chambers, of Texas, the nominee of the St. Louis Greenback Convention, was also put in nomination. On the first ballot Chambers received 403, and West 311. Gen. Chambers's nomination was then made unanimous. At 6 A. M. Gen. Weaver came into the hall, apparently fresh after a good night's sleep, and accepted the nomination which a sleepless convention tendered to him. He said that in a most informal manner, and relying on Divine Providence, he accepted the trust reposed in him, and promised to inform the Convention in a more formal manner of his acceptance. After passing the usual votes of thanks, the Convention, at 6:10 A. M., adjourned sine die.

THE CANDIDATES.

Gen. James B. Weaver, the Greenback candidate for President, was born at Dayton, Ohio, June 12, 1833, and after receiving a common school education, studied law with the Hon. S. G. McAckran, of Bloomfield. He was graduated at the Cincinnati Law School in the Spring of 1856, and practiced his profession up to the outbreak of the war. In April, 1861, he enlisted as a private in the Second Iowa Infantry, and was elected First Lieutenant of Company G of that regiment. In October, 1862, he was promoted to the rank of Major, and 10 days later was made Colonel of his regiment, both the Colonel and Lieutenant-Colonel having been killed at the battle of Corinth. In March, 1864, he was brevetted Brigadier-General of Volunteers, "for gallantry on the field." Gen. Weaver was elected District Attorney for the Second Judicial District of Iowa in October, 1866, and was appointed United States Assessor of Internal Revenue in January, 1867, holding that office for six years, when it was abolished. He was elected to the Forty-sixth Congress on the National-Greenback ticket in the Fall of 1878, defeating his Republican opponent by more than 2,000 votes. The main features of his career in Congress have been the introduction and advocacy of the wildest inflation and bounty measures.

Col. B. J. Chambers, of Texas, Gen. Weaver's associate on the Greenback ticket, was born in Montgomery County, Ky., Dec. 5, 1817. During his boyhood he labored on his father's farm, receiving only such an education as could be acquired in the country schools of that day. When 20 years of age he became a volunteer in the Texan-Mexican revolution, and was commissioned Captain on the staff of his uncle, Gen. T. J. Chambers. In 1839 he became a surveyor on the Texas frontier, which business he followed until 1847. Since that time he has been engaged mainly in farming. During the war he was an opponent of the Confederate Exemption laws, and after the close of hostilities took part in the financial discussions of the day, a subject on which he had the most pronounced views.

June 12, 1880

THE PROHIBITIONIST CANDIDATE.

PORTLAND, Me., July 20.—Gen. Neal Dow has written a letter accepting the nomination for the Presidency by the National Prohibitory Party. After commenting at some length on the evils of the liquor traffic and the respectability of the prohibitory movement, he concludes as follows: "I consider the objects of the Prohibitionists of this country to be of supreme importance to the interests of the Nation and the people. Aside from its bearing upon the moral and religious welfare of the people, I consider the suppression of the liquor traffic to be an object of far greater political importance than any other now claiming the attention of the country. My life has been largely devoted to the accomplishment of that purpose. Perhaps I may live to see my dearest hopes in relation to it realized at least in this, my own State. But, however that may be, in the future as in the past, I shall keep that object in view. While I sincerely wish that the choice of a candidate by the Cleveland Convention had fallen upon some other than myself, I accept the nomination willingly, being sure that it will prove to be the humble beginning of a triumphant end."

July 21, 1880

BUTLER'S PRESIDENTIAL BOOM.

THE GREENBACKERS FORMALLY TENDER HIM THEIR NOMINATION.

BOSTON, June 11.—Gen. Butler's campaign for the Presidency advanced a stage this afternoon. The committee appointed by the National Greenback-Labor Convention to notify him of his nomination by that party waited upon him and found him very civil. He received the committee at his Pemberton-square office in this city, and, after what they described as a pleasant conversation, intimated that he would accept the nomination. He will make public by Monday a letter, setting forth at some length his views on the financial question, and discussing in his usual spicy manner other phases of the political situation. A dinner was given the committee before it met Gen. Butler. About 60 more or less prominent Greenbackers were present, and speeches were made by Charles H. Litchman, of Massachusetts; Gen. Innis, of Michigan; Ex-Gov. Sprague, of Rhode Island; E. M. Chamberlain, of Massachusetts, and others. A number of the speakers declared that Butler was the only man who could beat Blaine, and that next to Butler, Blaine was the popular choice. It was urged that the Democrats must nominate Butler if they hoped to win.

June 12, 1884

THE "WHEEL."

A NEW PARTY WHICH IS BECOMING STRONG IN THE SOUTH.

LITTLE ROCK, Ark., Aug. 15.—The candidates recently nominated for State offices by the Agricultural Wheel, have all, excepting the nominee for Attorney-General, the Hon. J. M. Harrell, accepted, and the canvass has opened with three tickets in the field, namely, Democratic, Republican, and Wheeler. As the latter party appears destined in the future to play an important part in the political history of Arkansas, and of other Southern States as well, a history of the organization may be of interest to readers of THE TIMES. The Wheel originated near Des Arc, Prairie County, Ark., in 1882. Three farmers met in a school house and formed it, the object being the amelioration of the farming class. It was decided that none but farmers should be admitted to membership, and this rule has been steadily adhered to. The movement grew in popularity from the outset. Wheel after Wheel was formed. Inside of a year from the date of organization every county in the State was enlisted in the work. In October, 1885, the Wheel and the Brothers of Freedom consolidated under the first-named organization. The Brothers of Freedom was an organization similar to the Grangers. They originated in Eastern and Northern Arkansas. Taking an active part in politics, they carried several counties and elected two or three of their number to the State Legislature. The consolidation strengthened the Wheel greatly, and there are now over 1,200 distinct Wheels throughout the State, with a membership of 55,000.

Although declining to enter politics as a party or body the Wheelers nevertheless are a factor in political matters, and are taking an active part in local elections all over the State. In many counties they have nominated full tickets; in others they are supporting such men as they deem worthy. In June last a State Convention of the Wheel was held here and a State ticket nominated, although many members objected and some bolted and left the convention. The Hon. John G. Fletcher, a leading Democrat, was named for Governor; George Thornburg, Secretary of State, and W. P. Grace, Attorney-General. All these gentlemen declined. Mr. Fletcher, while expressing sympathy with the Wheel movement, felt constrained to decline, owing to various reasons. The general belief is that he would have been elected, provided the full voting strength of the Wheel could have been polled for him. Another convention was held at Litchfield, Ark., July 28, when a grand National Wheel was formed. Representatives were present from Missouri, Tennessee, Texas, and Kentucky. Isaac McCracken was chosen President of the State and National Wheels, and R. H. Morehead, Secretary. McCracken is a reputable farmer, and lives in Johnson County, this State. After the adjournment the Executive Committee of the State Wheel met and nominated a ticket as follows: For Governor—Charles E. Cunningham; Secretary of State—J. J. Bell; Auditor—O. L. James; Treasurer—J. J. Andrews; Superintendent of Education—A. B. Marberry; Land Commissioner—C. E. Tobey. The ticket is not likely to receive a united support, yet Wheelers who are posted claim at least 20,000 votes for it. As to the political preference of the Wheelers the majority are Democrats, and hence the outcry of the politicians that the Wheel by entering politics will destroy the Democratic Party. In future elections, however, it appears very probable that the Wheelers may not only hold the balance of power, but also elect State officers.

August 16, 1886

HEWITT ELECTED MAYOR

MR. ROOSEVELT IS THIRD IN THE CONTEST.

There was a remarkably heavy vote polled in this city yesterday, and it resulted in a complete victory for the united Democratic ticket. The entire vote for Mayor, with two election districts missing, foots up 218,706. Of this Mr. Abram S. Hewitt, the Democratic candidate, obtained 90,199; Henry George, the Labor candidate, 67,581, and Theodore Roosevelt, Republican, 60,352. Mr. Hewitt's plurality over George was 22,618, and over Roosevelt 29,847. The Prohibition candidate received 574 votes.

November 3, 1886

LABOR AND POLITICS.

One of the prominent subjects of discussion since the last elections has been the formation of a labor party in politics. This has been prompted in a great measure by the strength which the George movement in this city developed. Mr. GEORGE was not nominated by any party organization but by the labor unions of the city, and he was supported by many people who did not belong to these unions and are not workingmen in the ordinary acceptation of the word. Since the election some of the leaders in the movement have formed, provisionally at least, what they call the United Labor Party, and in the recent conferences and meetings of labor organizations the question has been mooted of the advisability of going into politics as a party.

In a country like ours, where all citizens, irrespective of occupation or position, are supposed to have the same rights and the same interest in the administration of public affairs, a labor party seems to be as great an absurdity as a business party or a leisure party. Nearly all our people are workers in one line or another. The class of persons who do nothing and live on the income of fixed investments is insignificant in numbers and importance. There are large numbers of people whose working capacity unfortunately lies chiefly in their sinews, who on one account or another seem to be capable only of manual labor directed by others. Their numbers are so great in proportion to the work to be done that they earn no more than a dollar or two a day. There are many others who are capable of a more intelligent direction of their efforts, and who find occupations in which care and skill are required. Their wages are from twice to three or four times those of the other class and vary according to the degree of skill required and attained in their various employments. Others of different constitutions and aptitudes are better fitted for clerical work, or that of selling goods over a counter and the numerous functions involved in trade. They may or may not receive better pay than skilled mechanics. Some do, more do not. What they earn depends upon the capacity

for usefulness to their employers which they can show. Other men who develop a different kind and degree of capacity, as for organizing and directing operations in which much labor is employed, earn larger salaries because their work conduces more to increasing the products of labor. They may, by the possession of capital which they have acquired, or by a valuable capacity for directing industrial operations and making them productive, become employers and share in the general profits of the business in which they are engaged. They are workers nevertheless. Often they work harder than any of those employed under them, and the pay or profit which they obtain is merely the legitimate reward for what they are able to do in making industries productive. Those who by natural aptitude, taste, and education become professional men are doing precisely what the day laborer does. They are trying to do in the community that part of its necessary work which they are best able to do and to get for it what it is worth, considering the amount of it there is to do and the number of persons able and willing to do it to the satisfaction of those having occasion for its employment.

In short, the whole body politic is made up of laborers of one kind and another, all engaged more or less zealously in doing the best they can for themselves. Where is a line of political division to be drawn that will have any meaning? Is it to be determined by the extent to which a man does his work with his muscles and the extent to which he does it with his brains? The variations are infinite, from the man who sweeps the dirt into heaps on the pavement to the man who directs the operations of a great system of transportation. There is no distinct line of demarkation anywhere. Shall it be determined by the pay that men get for their work? This, too, runs through a continuous and unbroken scale from the street cleaner's dollar a day, through the mechanic's four dollars a day, or the clerk's $1,200 a year to the railroad President's or the merchant's $40,000 a year, more or less.

Where, then, is the basis for a labor

party? The interest of an intelligent citizen in public affairs, in the policy or the administration of the Government, is not determined by the kind of work he does or the amount of pay it brings. Intelligence, whether it is handling tools, running machinery, keeping books, selling muslin, carrying on wholesale trade, or directing the operations of a factory or a railroad, finds a common ground of agreement as to the principles and methods on which public affairs are to be conducted. There is not one policy for the man who handles a trowel or a plane and another for the man who handles a yard stick or a pen.

The general assumption of those who advocate the formation of a labor party is that there is a distinct class of men who toil chiefly with their hands in common, unskilled labor or in manufacturing and skilled trades, who are somehow peculiarly affected by Government and are not capable of forming opinions and acting upon intelligent convictions in public matters like their fellow-citizens. The assumption is not flattering, and it is strange that it is not more generally resented. The agitators and organizers go further, and assume that these people need to be kept together in their action and told what to do or they will act against their own interests. They wish to deprive them of their individual independence. This can be accomplished only so far as those with whom they deal are ignorant and submissive to dictation, and we do not believe a very powerful political party can be built up in this country on ignorance and slavishness. If there could be, it would be a very dangerous and pernicious party, and would be sure to become the instrument of despotism. Those are precisely the qualities on which all despotism is maintained, and their prevalence is inconsistent with the working of free institutions. If workingmen, so called, wish to maintain their rights and their interests they must insist upon acting freely in politics upon the same principles that guide other citizens.

December 12, 1886

Reform and Third Parties

October 20, 1889

A MAP SHOWING THE STATES THAT CONTRIBUTED TO DEMOCRATIC SUPREMACY IN THE RECENT TARIFF-REFORM CYCLONE

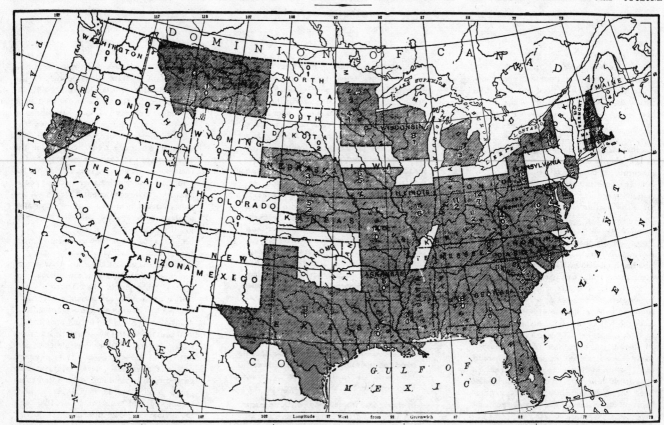

In the accompanying map of the United State THE TIMES presents the results of the recent Congressional elections in a form more effective than tables, because the magnitude of the great victory for Tariff Reform can be seen at a glance. The shaded parts of the map represent those portions of the country which emphatically resented the outrageous McKinley tariff law by voting for Democratic or, in a few instances, Alliance candidates for Congress. In States where the Republicans were able to elect a few Congressmen, less than 100 in all, no effort has been made to indicate by the shaded lines the exact districts which went Democratic, but only to show the proportionate strength of the two parties in the delegations which will represent the various States in the Fifty-second Congress. In New-Jersey, for instance, five of the seven Congressmen elected are Democrats and five-sevenths of the State is covered by the shaded lines.

In each State the numerical strength of the two parties in the Fifty-second Congress is given in figures, the upper number indicating the number of Democrats in such delegation and

the lower the number of Republicans. In the Massachusetts delegation, for instance, there are seven Democrats and five Republicans, and those figures will be found in the shaded portion of Massachusetts on the map. According to the latest returns the Republicans will have only 89 members in the next House, while the combined Democratic and Alliance vote will be at least 242, or probably 243 when the Second District of Rhode Island elects. This will give a majority of at least 153 against the Republicans.

Prior to the election of Nov. 4 five States had chosen Congressmen—Idaho, Maine, Oregon, Vermont, and Wyoming. All of these elections were held before the new tariff law went into effect, and in every instance the Republicans won. But before the elections of Nov. 4 were held the new tariff had been in operation nearly a month and its burdens were beginning to be felt. The result was that in no State did the Republicans make gains, and in only seven States—California, Colorado, Kentucky, Nevada, the two Dakotas, and South Carolina—did they hold their own. Of the States named all but California, Kentucky, and South Carolina are so sparsely settled that the effect of the new tariff has hardly reached them. In the great Republican strongholds the party's loss was appalling. The solid delegation of seven from Kansas is broken, and out of the ruins the Re-

publicans saved only two members. New-Hampshire was lost entirely, as was the hold the party had on Arkansas, Maryland, Virginia, West Virginia, Louisiana, and Missouri. Rhode Island went to the Democrats, and the solid Republican delegation from Nebraska entirely disappeared. Of the solid delegation from Minnesota the Republicans saved only one. Illinois exactly doubled its Democratic representation, Massachusetts and Michigan trebled theirs, Connecticut quadrupled its, and Iowa multiplied its by six. The Democratic delegation from New-York increased 50 per cent., and in Pennsylvania the proportionate gain was nearly as great. In only twelve States in the Union have the Republicans a majority in the Congressional delegations.

An analysis of the sources of the great Democratic majority furnishes some curious facts. The Republicans have always held that the strength of the Democracy lay almost entirely in the "solid South" and in the great cities, and it has sought to break the former by such devices as Sherman and Harrison "machines." It has held that the Democratic vote came from the States which seceded from the Union thirty years ago and has sneered at the Democratic Party as built upon disloyalty. The results of the last election disprove these allegations in a very significant way. Eleven States in all seceded. They were Alabama, Arkansas, Florida, Georgia, Louisiana, Mississippi, North Carolina, South Carolina, Tennessee, Texas, and Virginia. Out of these the Democrats secured at the last election 81 Congressmen, leaving 161 to be otherwise accounted for. The following table shows the number of Democratic Congressmen elected in each of the loyal States which were in existence at the time of the civil war:

California	2	Minnesota	4
Connecticut	3	Missouri	14
Delaware	1	Nebraska	3
Illinois	14	New-Hampshire	2
Indiana	11	New-Jersey	5
Iowa	6	New-York	23
Kansas	5	Ohio	14
Kentucky	9	Pennsylvania	10
Maryland	6	Rhode Island	1
Massachusetts	7	Wisconsin	8
Michigan	8		
Total			156

West Virginia, which was a loyal section during the war, increases this number by four, and Montana, which was admitted into the Union by a Republican Congress that it might strengthen the party, adds another to the Democratic column, making 161 Representatives elected on the 4th inst. by that section of the country which did not secede. That is to say, less than one-half of the Democratic representation in the Fifty-second Congress will come from the States which seceded, and if the delegations from those States were thrown out the Democrats could still organize the House.

As to the charge that the strength of the Democracy lies in the great cities, here is a little table showing the Congressmen returned from the districts either formed iu whole or in part from the five chief cities in the country:

	Dem.	Rep.		Dem.	Rep.
New-York	9	0	Chicago	3	1
Brooklyn	4	0	Boston	3	1
Philadelphia	1	4			
Total				20	6

In a year when the Republicans had deliberately antagonized the city vote by increasing the burdens on the cost of living, particularly on those articles which enter largely into city life, and had devoted its energies to deluding the farmer with false protection of his interests, the party was still able to elect six Congressmen from the chief cities in the country. It must look elsewhere for an explanation of its defeat. Its losses in the great agriculture regions of the West are the losses of the greatest significance.

NOTE.—News was received last night, too late to make the correction in the above map, that two Democrats are elected from California. Instead, therefore, of the figures "1—5" for California, they should be "2—4."

November 19, 1890

WILL A THIRD PARTY COME OF IT?

The Farmers' Alliance of Florida has got up a sort of agricultural fair at the town of Ocala, in that State, under the name of a Semi-Tropical Exposition, and it is accompanied by a convention of the National Farmers' Alliance, the second held by that organization. The chief question that seems to be agitating the assemblage is whether the Alliance is to take the form of a "third party" in politics. The Farmers' Alliance had its origin in the South and set out with the purpose of exerting an organized influence in behalf of agricultural interests without taking part in political warfare as an independent party. It extended up the Mississippi Valley and into the Northwest, where it acquired considerable strength. It is known that it obtained virtual control of the Democratic Party in South Carolina during the past year, and in various parts of the West it made independent nominations for State offices and for members of Congress, and had no little effect upon the November elections. Its power was displayed most conspicuously in Kansas, but it became a political factor of no small importance in several other States. Now, some of the Western delegates at Ocala appear to be pushing with vigor in favor of the third party movement. The plan seems to be to bring the workingmen of other occupations as well as the farmers into the organization.

There is nothing especially novel in this development, and, judging by the experiences of the past, it is likely that later on, if not now, it will take the form of a third political party and meet the fate that has awaited similar efforts heretofore to build parties upon special classes and special interests. It springs from a general discontent at the failure to obtain through the old parties a redress of the grievances which those who feel that they have not their full of prosperity attribute to the policy of the Government. There is considerable haziness in the minds of those engaged in the movement as to the cause of their grievances, real or supposed, and as to the means by which they are to be removed, but the prevailing notion of those who find that their lot is not a happy one seems to be that there is not money enough in circulation. It is the same spirit that animated the old Greenback Party, and, infecting the labor element, brought about the combination that came to be known as the Greenback-Labor Party. The old idea of an unlimited volume of irredeemable notes of the Government is not revived, but there is the same hostility to the national bank system, the same delusion about the control of the currency by Wall Street, and a desire to bring about inflation in some way that shall make money " cheap" and easy to get. The favorite scheme of the Alliance has been what is known as the Sub-Treasury plan, under which circulating notes would be issued upon deposits of the products of labor.

There is no probability that any such scheme of inflation can be forced upon either of the political parties of the country, and it is certain that neither party would gain anything by giving it the least countenance. If it is to be promoted by political action, it must be through a third party, which would not be long in bringing upon itself the fate of the Greenback Party, for the simple reason that it would be founded upon a delusion that could not survive the searching scrutiny of our political contests. A movement of this kind has its source in ignorance of the principles and working of finance and public economy and is sustained by false reasoning, and these are gradually dispelled by popular agitation and enlightenment. It may begin with a good deal of blind enthusiasm and find a ready support among those who are eager for a sweeping remedy for their ills, but its supporters are sure to acquire more sober views in time, and to dwindle away when the real issues of politics come under a fierce debate. Even farmers may be taught that something cannot be had in exchange for nothing, and that volume of money is not in itself wealth. No inflation of the currency can increase the actual value of what they produces or enable them to get greater value for it.

But the agitation may gradually lead them to a better understanding of the real cause of their unsatisfactory condition. The Mayor of Ocala, in his address at the opening of the Semi-Tropical Exposition, touched upon the real source of the farmer's distress. He spoke of the fact that the agricultural interests did not seem to share in the boasted prosperity of the country and that mortgages were banishing sleep from the honest tiller of the soil, and raised the inquiry whether we are not " drifting away from the doctrine of our fathers, which proclaimed equal rights to all and special privileges to none." What the farmer needs to learn is that the prosperity of other industries is built up largely at his expense, that the taxing power of the Government is used to draw his substance from him to enrich favored interests, and that it is impossible for him to escape mortgages so long as the fruits of his labor are sold in competition with all the world, while the cost of what he buys is enhanced by taxation for the benefit of others. When he understands why prosperity attends other pursuits and leaves him to struggle with mortgages, he will learn that the remedy is to be found not in third party movements but in an intelligent choice between the two parties, one or the other of which must prevail in our national politics.

December 3, 1890

BUTLER'S PARTY REVIVED

WITH A MORE COMPREHENSIVE PLATFORM.

DELIBERATIONS OF THE NATIONAL UNION CONFERENCE AT CINCINNATI —THE PEOPLE'S PARTY AND THE PRINCIPLES IT WILL ADVOCATE.

CINCINNATI, May 20.—At noon to-day, after a morning session in which there were some curious manifestations of feeling, the National Union Conference revived the name of the "People's Party" for the organization that is to be the third in the great political contest of 1892. While taking the name with which Gen. B. F. Butler made his campaign of 1884, the party began business with a platform of a much more comprehensive description. There is a plank for everybody except the Prohibitionists, and the Prohibitionists were disregarded, not because there were not many Prohibitionists in the convention, but because it was feared that votes would be lost from many organizations by making prohibition a test of loyalty to the people's movement.

The members of the committee that made the platform, and who have reiterated the St. Louis, Ocala, and Omaha platforms with planks for inflation, for money enough to do the business of the country "on a cash basis," free silver, against alien ownership of lands, against class legislation, for national supervision and perhaps ownership of transportation lines, and for elections of President, Vice President, and Senators by direct vote, may have formulated too much. The wonder is, considering the elements of the convention, that more of the notions entertained by delegates were not put in shape. The Committee on Resolutions was dominated by the visionary Ignatius Donnelly, but Gen. Weaver, who is a practical politician, exerted a regulating power that undoubtedly kept many extravagances out of the declaration of principles.

It might not have been thought difficult to get a convention of farmers and other toilers together at 8:30 o'clock, to which hour this morning an adjournment had been taken last night. As a matter of fact, it was, and it was not until 10 o'clock that the Rev. D. Delamatyr, formerly a Greenback representative from Ohio in Congress, was making the opening prayer to about half the delegates. Then came Capt. Power, who gets the credit for having made this conference, with a report of $36 collected and $365 expended in the cause, when, at the suggestion of Representative Wilkin of Kansas, hats were passed to make up a purse for the service, which Mr. Wilkin declared could not have been secured for $500. While the silver pieces were clinking in the hats, the Committee on Credentials made a report showing that there were present 1,418 delegates. The apportionments were interesting. The four States of Kansas, Ohio, Indiana, and Nebraska had nearly a thousand of these delegates.

A South Dakota delegate created an uproar by attempting to secure consideration of a resolution to give a vote to each State, and an additional vote to each fifty delegates present from any State, but his proposition went to the Committee on Resolutions after a great deal of uproar. There was presently another tumult of a very sensational sort. An invitation was given by Con Burkhauser of the Committee of Arrangements to the entire convention to eat a lunch. There was a breeze at the edge of the convention. Presently it blew clear. Helen D. Gougar, who discovered the convivial horrors of the Hearst funeral train, loomed up over the edge of the stage with her hands clasped behind her and her strong, confident face defiantly set forward. She repudiated the offer of a Secretaryship of the convention in which she was not a delegate because she had found a liquor dealer on the Reception Committee. The convention gave her some applause as she indignantly left. Sam Woods of Missouri explained that the lunch to which the convention was invited was not in a brewery, but in a broom factory, and that there was little danger of getting "full" of brooms.

After this exhilarating incident came the report of the committee on permanent organization, with Senator W. A. Peffer of Kansas as permanent Chairman, and a long list of subordinate officers. Mr. Peffer is not an electrical speaker. His words were a serious warning to the old parties to get out of the way at the same time that they expressed concern about the discordant elements of which the new party is composed. He likened the new party to the Kansas men who went into the army desiring to be cavalry. They had no horses; so they decided to go in the infantry and come out as cavalry.

Mrs. Marion Todd of Chicago was allowed to take the rostrum to present a basket of flowers to the Chairman, and her little speech, soulful with the earnestness of the practiced platform orator, soon led many of the sturdy delegates to mop their eyes with their bandana handkerchiefs. Ben Carvin of Saginaw, who had found a smart negro politician named Savage, who had come all the way from North Carolina to be with "the people," secured a place for him on the rostrum, and he made a "slick" speech, while "Ben" passed the hat for another collection wherewith to pay Savage's fare home again. The clinking of coin was kept up for an hour, suggesting that there was not an absolute scarcity of ready money in the convention.

When the rules were reported one provision only gave rise to hot discussion. That was the rule giving a vote to each delegate and directing that all votes should be by call of States. Several efforts were made to modify it, but it was carried as proposed. The Committee on Rules really usurped the function of the Committee on Plan of Organization, for by providing for the election of a National Executive Committee it created the new party without giving it a name. Chairman Peffer let the speechmaking go on until a tedious delegate from Massachusetts wore out the patience of the convention, and there was a call for the previous question. Mr. Peffer then betrayed his lack of familiarty with parliamentry practice by proposing the main question, but he was helped out, and at 12 o'clock the convention was shouting to celebrate the birth of the third party. Then there was a recess for the lunch at the broom factory.

Soon after reassembling there was another stage ceremony in which a lady figured. The wife of the Rev. Dr. Foster, who publishes a paper in the interest of the new party, made a little speech, and after pushing aside Chairman Peffer's patriarchial beard she pinned upon his breast a badge presented by the Committee on Arrangements. Then came a lot of communications of a suggestive and congratulatory nature, and at last Ignatius Donnelly, with the report of the Committee on Resolutions. Mr. Donnelly prefaced the report with a little speech, in which he told how the committee had worked all night and that the sun rose on its members still at work. This, he hoped, would be a happy augury. The report of the committee was then read. It was as follows:

1. That in view of the great social, industrial, and economical revolution now dawning upon the civilized world and the new and living issues confronting the American people, we believe that the time has arrived for a crystallization of the political reform forces of our country and the formation of what should be known as the People's Party of the United States of America.

2. That we most heartily indorse the demands of the platforms as adopted at St. Louis, Mo., in 1889, Ocala, Fla., in 1890, and Omaha, Neb., in 1891, by industrial organizations there represented, summarized as follows:

(*a*) The right to make and issue money is a sovereign power to be maintained by the people for the common benefit; hence we demand the abolition of national banks as banks of issue, and as a substitute for national bank notes we demand that legal-tender Treasury notes be issued in sufficient volume to transact the business of the country on a cash basis without damage or especial advantage to any class or calling, such notes to be legal tender in payment of all debts, public and private, and such notes when demanded by the people shall be loaned to them at not more than 2 per cent. per annum upon nonperishable products, as indicated in the Sub-Treasury plan, and also upon real estate with proper limitation upon the quantity of land and amount of money.

(*b*) We demand the free and unlimited coinage of silver.

(*c*) We demand the passage of laws prohibiting alien ownership of land, and that Congress take prompt action to devise some plan to obtain all lands now owned by alien and foreign syndicates, and that all land held by railroads and other corporations in excess of such as is actually used and needed by them be reclaimed by the Government and held for actual settlers only.

(*d*) Believing the doctrine of equal rights to all and special privileges to none, we demand that taxation —national, State, or municipal—shall not be used to build up one interest or class at the expense of another.

(*e*) We demand that all revenues—national, State, or county—shall be limited to the necessary expenses of the Government economically and honestly administered.

(*f*) We demand a just and equitable system of graduated tax on income.

(*g*) We demand the most rigid, honest, and just national control and supervision of the means of public communication and transportation, and if this control and supervision does not remove the abuses now existing we demand the Government ownership of such means of communication and transportation.

(*h*) We demand the election of President, Vice President, and United States Senators by a direct vote of the people.

3. That we urge the united action of all progressive organizations in attending the conference called for Feb. 22, 1892, by six of the leading reform organizations.

4. That a national central committee be appointed by this conference, to be composed of a Chairman to be elected by this body and of three members from each State represented, to be named by each State delegation.

5. That this central committee shall represent this body, attend the National Conference on Feb. 22, 1892, and if possible unite with that and all other reform organizations there assembled. If no satisfactory arrangement can be effected, this committee shall call a National Convention not later than June 1, 1892, for the purpose of nominating candidates for President and Vice President.

6. That the members of the central committee for each State where there is no independent political organization conduct an active system of political agitation in their respective States.

The following additional resolutions were also offered:

Resolved, That the question of universal suffrage be recommended to the favorable consideration of the various States and Territories.

Resolved, That while the party in power in 1869 pledged the faith of the nation to pay a debt in coin that had been contracted on a depreciated currency basis and payable in currency, thus adding nearly one billion dollars to the burdens of the people, which meant gold for the bondholders and depreciated currency for the soldier, and holding that the men who imperilled their lives to save the life of a nation should have been paid in money as good as that paid to the bondholders, we demand the issue of legal-tender Treasury notes in sufficient amount to make the pay of the soldiers equal to par with coin, or such other legislation as shall do equal and exact justice to the Union soldiers of this country.

Resolved, That as eight hours constitute a legal day's work for Government employees in mechanical departments, we believe this principle should be further extended so as to apply to all corporations employing labor in the different States of the Union.

Resolved, That this conference condemns in unmeasured terms the action of the Directors of the World's Columbian Exposition on May 19 in refusing the maximum rate of wages asked for by the labor organizations of Chicago.

Resolved, That the Attorney General of the United States should make immediate provision to submit the act of March 2, 1889, providing for the opening of Oklahoma to homestead settlement, to the United States Supreme Court, so that the expensive and dilatory litigation now pending there be ended.

The following resolution, introduced by Mason A. Green of Massachusetts in behalf of the Nationalists, was referred to the various reform bodies for their consideration:

Resolved, That when in the course of business consolidations in the form of trusts or private syndicates it becomes evident that any branch of commerce is used for the behoof and profit of a few men at the expense of the general public, we believe that the people should assume charge of such commerce, through their National, State, or municipal administration.

There were occasional outbursts of applause while the resolutions were read, those touching the money question stirring the convention most deeply. The criticism of the World's Columbian Exposition Managers for neglecting the propositions of the labor organizations for an eight-hour day was gratifying to the representatives of industrial organizations, and they shouted lustily as it was read.

It remained for Texas to get up the scene of the greatest dramatic interest. A tall, slim man in a butternut suit—James Davis, who is called "Methodist Jim" at home—made a shake-hands-across-the-bloody-chasm speech as a member of the committee. "Jim" was not born until 1854, and was but six years of age when the war broke out; but he was hailed by the convention as a reconstructed rebel, and he helped out the illusion by prefacing his speech with a terrific "rebel yell," performed in full sight of the audience, which screamed with childish delight. He was in favor of printing $350,000,000 of money as soon as the third party took possession of all the branches of the Government. This strengthened "Methodist Jim's" hold.

Wadsworth of Indiana, a former Union soldier, was put alongside of Jim, and presently there was a flag in the hands of each. The flags were waved vigorously. The people in the hall went wild with cheering, and there came on one of those scenes witnessed only in enthusiastic conventions. The placards were torn from their places in the hall and carried upon the long poles to which they were attached. They were soon held aloft in a semicircle behind and above the Chairman. All the delegates stood up in their places and yelled. Everybody on the stage stood upon chairs or tables and longed for something higher upon which to climb. Chairman Peffer pounded his desk a long time before he finally restored order. One old man was so affected by the fraternal scene under the flags that he wept copiously.

Speeches were then made by representatives of nearly every one of the organizations taking part in the convention, that of General Lecturer Willetts of the Farmers' Alliance being most important, as indicating the full concurrence of the Alliance in the movement for a third party.

The Prohibitionists here determined to get in a plank committing the convention as an opponent of the liquor traffic. G. M. Miller of California, after persistently claiming a hearing, offered a prohibition amendment and spoke on it. He was received with every manifestation of disapproval, and was only heard after a special plea for fair play by Chairman Peffer. When the amendment came to a vote, Kansas was solidly opposed to it. The People's Party already had political sense enough to see that it would do better by not meddling with prohibition. The vote for the amendment was ridiculously small. The report of the Committee on Resolutions, including the resolutions not made a part of the platform, was then adopted by a rising vote. The approval of the platform was practically unanimous. The number of negative votes was too small even to provoke a remark of contempt.

Chairman Peffer begged to be excused after the platform was adopted, so that he could leave for Washington by an afternoon train. Gen. Weaver was put in his place, and he conducted as expeditiously as possible the collection of names of the National Executive Committee. The convention went to pieces during that process, and when it formally adjourned the attendance was reduced to a mere handful in the great hall.

The following is the National Committee:

Arkansas—L. P. Featherstone, Isaac McCracken, Jo A. Bush.

California—Marion Cannon, H. C. Dillon, A. G. Hinckley.

Connecticut—Robert Pique.

Florida—W. D. Condon, L. Baskins, J. D. Goss.

Georgia—C. C. Post.

Iowa—J. B. Weaver, M. L. Wheat, A. J. Westfield.

Indiana—C. A. Powers, Leroy Templeton, J. D. Comstock.

Illinois—S. N. Norton, A. J. Streator, H. E. Taubeneck.

Kansas—P. H. Elder, Levi Dumbauld, R. S. Osborn.

Kentucky—D. L. Graves, S. F. Smith, T. G. Fallin.

Louisiana—J. J. Mills, Dr. R. B. Paine, John Pickett.

Massachusetts—G. F. Washburn, E. G. Brown, E. M. Boynton.

Michigan—Ben Colvin, Mrs. S. E. V. Emery, John O. Seabel.

Minnesota—Ignatius Donnelly, C. N. Perkins, Andrew Stevenson.

Missouri—Paul J. Dickson, J. W. Rodgers, W. O. Atkinson.

Maine—H. S. Hobbs, F. A. Howard, D. W. Smith.

Nebraska—J. H. Edmonston, William Dysart, W. H. West.

New York—Jacob H. Studer, Joel J. Hoyt.

Ohio—Hugo Prior, J. C. H. Cobb, H. F. Barnes.

Oklahoma—Samuel Crocker, A. E. Light, John Hogan.

Pennsylvania—R. A. Thompson, F. R. Agnew, Lewis Edwards.

South Dakota—J. W. Hardin, H. L. Loucks, Frederick Zeph.

Texas—W. R. Lamb, Thomas Gaines, J. H. Davis.

Tennessee—H. P. Osborne, J. W. J. Kay, John W. James.

Wisconsin—Robert Schilling, Alfred Manheimer, A. J. Phillips.

West Virginia—Luther C. Shinn, George W. Hannment, Thomas C. Keeny.

Wyoming—H. B. Setenstein, James A. Smith, H. D. Merritt.

District of Columbia—Lee Crandall, S. A. Bland, H. J. Schulteis.

The 1,400 delegates are going home from this convention confident in the immediate success of the People's Party. The less sanguine men, who are politicians, do not really see the way to the election of their candidate for President. Most of them are indifferent about the fate of the candidates of both the old parties. Sam Wood of Missouri expressed the feelings of many of his associates when he said: "We will carry Kansas, Michigan, Wisconsin, Nebraska, and Iowa, perhaps Minnesota. Yes, the Alliance in the South will be Democratic. The old party candidates will be Harrison and Cleveland. We may hurt the Republicans by defeating Harrison, but it will not be because we want to elect Cleveland. It is none of our concern who is elected if we cannot elect the candidate of the People's Party."

The alliance effected today may turn out to be more dangerous to the old parties than this talk would indicate. Gompers, the head of the Federation of Labor, has been here observing the course of events. He does not predict, but it is surmised that the federation may decide to join the People's Party in the campaign. That reinforcement would be a menace to the old parties that would make the leaders fearful of the results, as the Federation of Labor is an organization of greater numerical strength and political power than the Knights of Labor, who make much more fuss.

Here in Cincinnati, where a convention of sentimentalists is apt to provoke sneers, the intense earnestness of this one, notwithstanding the fact that "Boss" Power of Terre Haute had so much to do with getting it up, is realized, and the People's Party is accepted as a political force that will give the leaders—particularly the Republican leaders—much trouble. The movement may be guided by schemers, but it is a movement of enthusiasts who do not mind being called "cranks" or "fanatics" or "sentimentalists." The Ohio farmers have not yet been stricken with the Alliance fever, but it is in the air. When the Farmers' Union of the State meets, as it will in a few days, it is predicted by veteran observers that it will be found to have been infected.

THIRD PARTY TICKETS.

BUBBLES THAT HAVE FLOATED FOR A WHILE ON THE POLITICAL SEA.

From the San Francisco Argonaut, July 18.

Third parties are the tramp ships on the ocean of politics. Many become derelicts, and most of them sink to the profound depths of that ocean deeper than ever plummet sounded. The first in the United States to hold convention and nominate Presidential candidates was the Anti-Masonic Party of 1832, with William Wirt for President. The organization had barely one object—the ostracism of Masonry—and it carried the Electoral vote of one State, Vermont, out of the twenty-four States which comprised the Union. That one campaign was its beginning and its end, and it passed into history.

Since that time, of third parties, there have come and disappeared the Abolition Party, the Free-Soil Party, the American Party, and the Greenback Party. The American Party was the only one of them that had votes in every State, and it carried the Electoral vote of one State. The Abolition Party caused the defeat of Henry Clay for President by running the Birney ticket in New-York, which drew away from Clay over 15,000 Whig votes, and gave the Electoral vote of the State to Polk. To rebuke Henry Clay on account of his slavery sentiments, they in effect elected Polk and put in power the Democratic Party, devoted to slavery.

The Free-Soil Party was founded and organized by Democrats who had become dissatisfied with the party. In 1848 the movement was made to defeat Gen. Cass for President by carrying New-York against him. It was not expected to prevail in any other State. With the Democratic vote divided between Cass and Van Buren, the Electoral vote of New-York was cast for the Whig nominee, Gen. Taylor, and made his election sure.

The Free-Soil Party wrought the defeat of Gen. Cass and the Democratic Party in 1848, just as the Abolition Party had effected the defeat in 1844 of Henry Clay and the Whig Party. In each instance it was the work of men who had become disaffected with the party in which they had before held fellowship. In 1844 it was resolute rebuke, in 1848 it was partisan revenge. Neither the Abolitionists nor the Free-Soilers obtained the Electoral vote of a single State, whereas the Anti Masons and the Americans each carried the Electoral vote of a State—the Anti-Masons, of Vermont; the Americans, of Maryland.

In 1880 the Greenback Party and the Prohibition Party entered the field with Presidential candidates. Neither of them carried an Electoral vote of the thirty-eight States. Their candidates for President, Weaver of Iowa and Dow of Maine, were both former Republicans—the one disaffected, the other a crank on his chief hobby.

Again, in 1884, the two organizations put up candidates for the Presidency—Butler, Greenbacker; St. John, Prohibitionist.

The Prohibitionists had again, in 1888, a Presidential ticket in the field, and this year Gen. Bidwell of Chico is their candidate for President. He is a pioneer of California—an honest, upright, conscientious man. He was formerly a Democrat; has since been a Republican member of Congress and an independent candidate for Governor. He is a farmer of great wealth, and is too sensible to imagine that he will be elected President. His candidacy is to attest his devotion to the cold-water cause. The Union Labor Party is in the list of organizations of the period which can never expect direct results.

The Farmers' Alliance, or People's Party, is the most recent of the third-party organizations. It started with local, widely segregated, phenomenal sweeps. It elected nine members of Congress in 1890—five from Kansas, two from Nebraska, and one each from Minnesota and Georgia. It displaced Ingalls, United States Senator from Kansas, and chose Peffer in his place, and Kyle, Senator from South Dakota. It caused the defeat of Senator Wade Hampton in South Carolina, and, with the much inferior Irby to the exalted station. It made Tillman Governor of South Carolina, and, with the Prohibitionists, Boies Governor of Iowa. On this coast, in Oregon, it has elected several members to the Legislature ; but it did not succeed in the election of any State officer.

July 24, 1892

THE OUTCOME IN THE NATION.

Two facts stand out in the returns of Tuesday's elections, one with startling clearness, the other in a manner to challenge intense interest and careful study. The first is the tremendous shrinkage in the straight Democratic vote. Even if we put aside the overwhelming defeat of Mr. Hill in this State, as involving his own exasperating personality as well as the accumulated outrages of the State machine and its complicity with Tammany, and pass to other States, it is to find adverse pluralities only less amazing. Throughout the large States of the North and East and the Central West, these mount through the tens of thousands, and their total is expressed in hundreds of thousands. And the popular branch of the National Legislature, the House of Representatives, elected in 356 districts of fairly equal population, evenly distributed over the territory of the entire Union, will, after the 4th of March next, contain only a pitiful 108 Democrats and 238 Republicans, or exactly two-thirds. This is as striking a revolution in that body as political history records, and the more so as it follows within four years upon the revolution in the opposite direction which took place in 1890. At the same time the Democrats in the Senate will be reduced from 44 to 38; the Republicans will be increased from 37 to 44, and the 6 Populists will stand ready to join the Republicans in seating a Populist-Republican fusionist from Alabama.

The second fact to which we have alluded is the degree of strength developed by the Populists. On the face of the returns so far received, which are confined mainly to the figures of pluralities, the Populists seem to have suffered very complete reverses, that impression being derived chiefly from the defeat of the notorious Waite in Colorado and Lewelling in Kansas. Unquestionably these are instances of the very thorough revolt of two States against Populism in its most aggravated and offensive form. They are encouraging because they indicate that Populism, like some forms of poison, if taken in large enough doses, produces a nausea adequate to dispose of it. But it would be a mistake, and a very serious mistake, to infer that Populism generally, where it is organized and, in fusion or otherwise, plays a distinct part in politics, has failed, as it has failed in these two States. How far it has failed is to be known clearly only when we shall have the full returns and shall be able to tell with reasonable accuracy what has been the Populists' contribution to it. There are general statements, still to be verified, that they have made a strong showing in Illinois and Michigan, and there are results in Iowa, Minnesota, Nebraska, and in some of the Southern States in which their actual part is not yet known. It may be considerable; it may be insignificant; it may prove to be an increasing or a decreasing quantity. We cannot yet know with certainty, and while we have a right to rejoice in the extinction of Waite and Lewelling, we may be misled, both as to feeling and as to policy, by that cheerful incident.

There is, we are convinced, no danger of a Populist national party having any serious rôle as a separate party in this country. There is danger of the influence of the Populists upon the two great parties of the country. The violent fluctuations of public sentiment as to these parties as expressed in the elections of the last four years, show that neither party is secure of preponderance on the issues actually pending, and they are bound to have a very strong effect on the minds of the managers of the respective parties. We see to-day how the Republicans, under the stress of the reverses of 1890 and 1892, made haste to form alliances with the Populists in Alabama and North Carolina, and less formally in other States of the South, while in some Congressional districts in different parts of the country, each party in a minority has more or less courted the Populists, who were supposed to be able to turn the balance. It is quite probable that like temptations will present themselves during the next two years.

The anxiety of the politicians will be the greater because the elections of this year, unlike those of 1890 and 1892, did not turn on the tariff, and no action on that subject will result from them. Every one knew two years ago to-day that the McKinley tariff must be repealed. No one to-day expects that the new tariff will be repealed. It is physically impossible for three years, and when the next national election comes around it is more than probable that neither party will propose any radical change. What, then, will be the issue? That will sorely puzzle all leaders, and in their uncertainty they may do a great many risky things. But one thing the Democratic leaders must remember as a matter of life and death: They cannot fool with the currency question. They have done far too much of this already. It was only the splendid firmness of President Cleveland and the almost unbroken co-operation of the Republicans in Congress that secured the repeal of the Sherman law with no perilous conditions. Ohio and Michigan Democrats have been trying the experiment of fishing with free-silver bait for Populist votes, and have been properly punished. Speaker Crisp thought it expedient to lead a free-silver and anti-Administration fight in Georgia, and will have his reward in sitting under the gavel of Mr. Reed in the next Congress. Whatever is done or left undone before 1896, let there be no mistake about one thing—if the Democratic Party gets squarely on the wrong side of the currency question, that year will see it practically wiped out, and its leaders will look back upon the elections of this year with envy.

November 8, 1894

McKINLEY AND HOBART OF NEW-JERSEY

Nominated at St. Louis by the Republican Party for President and Vice President.

VOTE FOR THE GOLD PLATFORM 812 1-2 TO 110 1-2

Twenty-one Silver Men Bolt the Convention, Led by Teller, Who Weeps Copiously as He Leaves the Hall.

St. Louis, June 18.—William McKinley of Ohio was nominated this afternoon as the candidate of the Republican Party for President, and Garret A. Hobart of New-Jersey was named for Vice President.

This outcome, secured in one prolonged session of the convention, the fourth sitting since it was called to order on Tuesday, was more than half expected last night. Gov. Morton's chances were then very doubtful, partly owing to his reiterated disinclination to accept the nomination for Vice President "under any circumstances," and partly because of the bitter opposition to Gov. Morton in his own State—an opposition that was cultivated with complete disregard of the tarnish that it was putting upon the State and its Chief Executive, and which provoked the contempt of Gov. Morton's opponents in other States.

Hanna came to St. Louis, as has been repeatedly stated in these dispatches, determined to make Hobart the candidate with McKinley. He resented the fight made to put "gold" in the financial plank, and he was alarmed when he found that his resentment was not only futile to keep "gold" out, but that the men who were for the use of the word "gold" were disposed to express their thanks to Mr. Platt and the gold people of New-York by voting for Morton for Vice President if he would present him. Morton's dispatch of declination to Mr. Depew helped Hanna. It assisted the protesting anti-Platt men to fix the impression that Morton could not get the unanimous indorsement of his own State.

Battered though his influence was after the fight for a straddle, Hanna was still influential, and his power was fully restored when Mr. Morton to-day telegraphed Mr. Depew that he could only take the Vice Presidency if nominated unanimously. Hanna, Warner Miller, and Bliss had made that impossible.

The ticket is Hanna's. The platform is the work of the convention. At Hanna's request the declaration on the tariff was allowed to come first. Mr. Lodge had promised that, and Foraker was not enough concerned about the order of the paragraphs to assert his contempt for Hanna by insisting that the most important policy should be asserted in the first paragraph of the platform.

To the people the ticket is not likely to be as interesting as the platform. If the Republicans shall be successful in November it will be the money plank, not the tariff plank nor the names of McKinley and Hobart, that will win the victory.

The thoughtful and well-informed Republicans here know that in the bolt of Teller and his following of silver men to-day lies the menace of a serious breaking of party lines. To such Republicans it is known that the silver fever is higher than generally supposed, and that it is prostrating victims heretofore regarded as sound with the suddenness and completeness with which grip overcomes the subjects of its attacks. The wide distribution of the silver bacilli, as suggested by Teller's elaborate farewell, was ominous and threatening.

The platform makers were alive to the condition of the country and to the general indifference to talk about McKinley duties; otherwise it would not have been possible to secure from a Republican convention a practical denunciation of McKinleyism on the same day that McKinley, for making his unpopular bill, was honored with the nomination for the highest office in the land. It was a tub to a whale, a bait to catch those Republicans who are not so zealous for protection as they were in 1890.

Teller's desertion of his party may make him the candidate of the silver party and the Populists, and if the Chicago Convention, affected to conservative action by the gold stand of the Republicans, shall take the middle course indicated by Hanna, as the one to be followed by the Republicans and shall name a doubtful man, rejecting Bland and Boies, it would not be at all astonishing to see another St. Louis ticket, with Teller and Bland, or Teller and some silver Democrat at its head.

This will not help the Republicans. It will make the selection of McKinley depend very largely upon the nomination of a gold Democrat of character and capacity, the division of the Democratic vote in several States in which the Republican vote is large, but not a majority, and the prevention of a silver success by a reference of the contest to the House of Representatives.

The convention presented no incident so thrilling as that of the bolt of Teller and his silver associates. The noisy demonstrations for candidates were evidently contrived with the properties and music prepared in advance by a political theatrical manager. It was a disorderly convention, badly officered with perhaps the least efficient Sergeant at Arms and the most utterly useless corps of assistants ever collected for a similar purpose. The presiding officer, Senator John M. Thurston, really presided, commanding the noisy body well, speaking briefly when occasion required, and inspiring confidence in the audience by his own composure and by an easy assumption of the authority conferred upon him.

June 19, 1896

THE AMERICAN PROLETARIAT.

The Chicago Convention has given currency to an alluring alliteration which is calculated to startle old-fashioned Americans. It is declared that the contest between the silver and the gold standard is a contest between " proletariat and plutocrat." The application of the word " proletariat " to American society is not new. In his famous address on " Democracy " LOWELL mentioned the change, to him a saddening one, in his own lifetime of the peasantry of New-England from a yeomanry to a proletariat, or words to that effect. But whenever the word is used we think of Europe and not of America, because it denotes, in the first place, a separate class, and, in the second place, a class which is not only down, but has no hope of getting up. It is the class which has a congenital grievance against society. It has been one of our boasts for a hundred years and more that no native American, however poor and humble he might be, was doomed to stay where he was put by birth; that in no older country was there such a facility in passing from one class to another. Nay, it was our boast that in our democracy there were no classes, properly so called; that the individual stood on his own feet and by his own merits. This way of thinking is interrupted when anybody so much as speaks of our proletariat, and forces us to inquire whether there is really such a class in this country.

We are afraid we must admit that there is a larger exception to the old rule of equality, even of equality of opportunity, than we have been accustomed to allow. Of course, " the foreign element " has always been troublesome to assimilate, but heretofore it has been true that in the second generation the children of immigrants have been as " good Americans " as the children of natives, leaving out a sentimental attachment to the Fatherland of their fathers, which is not only a becoming, but really a valuable, sentiment. It is the public-school system upon which we have relied for the fusion of the children of the foreigner with the children of the native. The adult immigrants might compose a proletariat, and have done so. But the children of Irishmen and of Germans and of Scandinavians have been found to be very readily assimilable. Of late years we have come to deal with elements far more foreign and heterogeneous, and with these elements the hereditary sense of oppression has made the task of converting them from a proletariat into an equal body of citizens very much harder. The adult or adolescent immigrant who brings to our shores a hatred of what is constituted and established because it is, is an almost hopeless subject. He is becoming increasingly formidable in numbers and he seems, especially in the Middle West, to be increasingly inaccessible to Americanizing influence. That such a representative of him as ALTGELD should have become the Governor of a great State is a portent and a menace, because unfortunately there can be no doubt that ALTGELD represents what may properly be called a proletariat.

But also it must be owned that we have a native proletariat in part of the country. It is a relic of slavery, and it is composed of the poor whites or crackers who grew up hating and fearing the slave-holding aristocracy, but, until of late years, powerless against it. The overthrow of slavery emancipated not only the negroes, but the poor whites, or crackers, but it left both as ignorant and as helpless as they were before. The crackers, however, being of the Caucasian race, were the first to perceive their political power, and they have revolted against the gentlemen of the South, the " aristocrats " to whom they formerly paid a dogged and reluctant deference. The recent history of Southern politics is a history of this revolt. In those States of which the social composition was most aristocratic the revolt has been most marked. The poor whites have refused any longer to take their politics from the educated classes, and they have set out to devise remedies for themselves for their own condition. Being woefully ignorant, almost or quite as ignorant as their black neighbors, their remedies have been preposterous schemes like those set forth in the Ocala platform. They have found demagogues to lead them, and these demagogues have either displaced the old leaders or have forced the old leaders into a pretense of conformity with their notions. The Senators from North and South Carolina are specimens of the emancipated cracker. The Senators from some other Southern States are examples of the educated men who go in fear of the cracker. When the cracker uprising began in South Carolina, WADE HAMPTON withdrew from the strife. His colleague, Mr. BUTLER, remained and endeavored to conciliate the crackers, but was beaten all the same. The long-oppressed cracker would no more accept his assurances than a European Socialist would accept the assurances of a landed proprietor. The result in the State in which the aristocracy had been the most controlling and defiant was the appearance of TILLMAN, first as Governor of South Carolina and then as a Senator. The Senate is not very fastidious, but it seems its members have drawn the line at TILLMAN and declined to associate with him. This amazing person made a speech here the other day and gave us a taste of his quality. He made it clear both what sort of person he is and what sort of constituency he represents.

Now, it is TILLMAN alone who can make any contest with ALTGELD for the control of the majority of delegates to Chicago. It is a perfectly unexampled thing in American politics that the leaders of the National Convention of a great party should be respectively the representatives of the imported Reds, who have their grievances to avenge upon European society, and the Southern crackers, who have their grievances to avenge upon Southern society. But whoever considers this phenomenon will be forced to admit that we do possess a proletariat, and that it must be reckoned with in American politics.

July 3, 1896

BRYAN'S BID FOR FIRST PLACE.

The Silver Men Swept Away by a Flood of Prairie Oratory.

CHICAGO, July 9.—The silverites had their inning when Russell had finished and Bryan, " the boy orator " and general demagogue of Nebraska, took the platform. They yelled and raved, waved flags, threw hats into the air, and acted like wild men for five minutes.

Bryan wore trousers which bagged at the knees, a black alpaca coat, and a low-cut vest. A black stud broke the white expanse of his shirt bosom. His low, white collar was partially hidden by a white lawn tie. Bryan began fishing yesterday for the Presidential nomination. If there was any doubt of his ambition in the minds of the friends of other candidates, that doubt was dispelled to-day by his speech and the events that followed. He dwelt upon the necessity of another Andrew Jackson to rise up and crush the National banks and other agents of the " money kings " and indulged in many like utterances calculated to attract the attention of the silver fanatics to himself. The applause with which his remarks were punctuated attested to the audience's relish for his revolutionary expressions.

Bryan's chief qualification as an orator is his splendid voice. His views on public affairs are those of a wild theorist filled with a desire of personal advancement. No better evidence of the diseased condition of the minds of the silver delegates could be desired than that furnished to-day by their indorsement of Bryan's utterances. The demonstration at the close of Bryan's speech struck terror to the hearts of the

Bland and Boies and McLean and Stevenson boomers. The declaration by him that the people must not be crucified on the cross of gold was the signal for an avalanche of cheers which speedily developed into a measureless outburst. As he started for his seat one policeman stood ready to clear the way and another to prevent the crowd closing in upon him. Their efforts were unavailing.

Demonstration with a Purpose.

The silver delegates fell over each other in their efforts to reach him. The aisles became congested. Bryan found himself in the midst of a shouting, pushing mob, every man anxious to grasp his hand. He was not at all averse to the proceedings. Already the prospect of a unanimous nomination began to dance before his eyes. The storm grew intensely as he neared his seat. The Tennessee and Texas delegations gave a hint to the other fanatics by carrying their banners to the Nebraska reservation and ranging themselves about Bryan. Immediately there was a movement toward that point by the bearers of the banners of the other silver States. While the deafening din was maintained, the banners waved about the conspicuous form of Bryan, who had been lifted on the shoulders of several sturdy admirers, so that the people might look upon this new defender of the people. Bryan is heavy, and the men holding him grew tired; so he stepped upon a chair and beamed upon the assemblage. His reappearance above the sea of heads intensified the noise. Thousands in the Coliseum were shouting.

While the excitement was at its height, the man carrying the Kentucky banner, a ponderous individual, who previously had given the impression that nothing could shake his fealty to Blackburn, organized a new feature of the entertainment. Holding his banner aloft, he marched up the main aisle. Behind him came men carrying the blue banners of Alabama, Nebraska, Louisiana, Colorado, Kansas, Ohio, Indiana, Michigan, Tennessee, California, North Carolina, Texas, West Virginia, Florida, North Dakota, Georgia, Oklahoma, Nevada, Iowa, Idaho, Missouri, Montana, Indian Territory, Arkansas, Utah, Wyoming, Virginia, New-Mexico, and Washington.

The only banners not seen in the combination were those of Delaware, Connecticut, Alaska, New-Hampshire, Maine, Maryland, Minnesota, Massachusetts, New-York, New-Jersey, Rhode Island, Pennsylvania, South Dakota, Vermont, and Wisconsin.

To the accompaniment of the ear-splitting yells of the silverites, this procession moved around the confines of the delegates' reservation, the banner bearers adding to the confusion as best they could. There was no cessation of the noise for fourteen minutes. The Chairman made no effort at first to quell it, being willing to see the Hill demonstration overshadowed.

The first sign of willingness on the part of the silver yawpers to subside was met by the men in the Bryan delegation with an appeal for a fresh outburst. This was successful, and the walls again resounded to a perfect Niagara of sound, which continued five minutes. It was twenty-five minutes after the demonstration began before the business of the convention could be proceeded with.

A tribute more conclusive of the regard of the fanatics and repudiators for Bryan could not be given. As may be readily imagined, the talk of Bryan as the possible nominee of the convention took a tremendous jump as the result of this ovation. The Georgia delegation, which already had declared for Bland, decided, while confusion yet reigned, to throw its votes to Bryan. Other delegations were said to be contemplating similar action. The Bryan men were overjoyed. Their leader was quick to see the possibilities contained in the events of the last half hour and to set his lieutenants to working among the different delegations.

The constant running of delegates to him and the consultations being held had a most dispiriting effect upon the managers of the other booms.

Williams to Name Bryan.

Before order was completely restored, the convention was provided with a fresh sensation by the announcement that George Fred Williams of Massachusetts was going into the Alabama delegation as a substitute to place Bryan in nomination.

Mr. Bryan began speaking clearly and distinctly. The belief in the honor of a righteous cause was stronger, he said, than the predicitons of disaster. He would move to lay on the table the resolutions in condemnation of the Administration. This was not a question that permitted descent to personalities. This had been a great contest; never before had so great an issue been fought out. He sketched the growth of the free-silver idea in the Democratic ranks, and told of the zeal that had been injected into the party contest. The silver men had gone forth to victory after victory, and were assembled now, not to condemn, not to protest, but to enter up a judgment ordered by the people. As individuals those he represented might have been willing to compliment the gentleman from New-York, (Mr. Hill,) but they were unwilling to put him in a position where he could thwart the will of the Democratic Party. He claimed for his people that they were the equals of the people of Massachusetts, and when the people of Massachusetts came to the people of Nebraska and said, "You have disturbed our business," the people of Nebraska replied to the people of Massachusetts, "You have disturbed our business." "We say," he continued, "you have made too limited an application of the definition of the word 'business man.' The man employed for wages is as much a business man as his employer. The farmer who goes out to toil in the morning is as much a business man as the man who goes on the Board of Trade to gamble in stocks. The miner is as much a business man as the few financial magnates who, in a back room, corner the money of the world."

Mr. Bryan said those he represented were tired of submitting to the burdens which oppressed them. "We beg no longer; we petition no more; we defy them."

A New Jackson Needed.

Mr. Bryan continued:

What we need is an Andrew Jackson to stand, as Andrew Jackson stood, against the National banks. We are told that our platform is made to catch votes. We reply that changed conditions make new issues. The principles on which Democracy rests are as everlasting as the hills, but they must be applied to the new conditions as they arise.

New conditions have arisen, and we are attempting to meet them. They tell us that the income-tax question ought not to be brought in here; that it is a new idea. They find faul with us for our criticism of the Supreme Court of the United States. We have not criticised it. We have simply called attention to it. If you want a criticism of the court in the matter of the income tax, read the dissenting opinions of the Judges. They say that we passed an unconstitutional law. I deny it. The income tax was not unconstitutional, when it went before the Supreme Court for the first time. It did not become unconstitutional until one Judge changed his mind. And we cannot be expected to know when a Judge will change his mind. The income tax is a just law. I am in favor of it, and when I find a man is not willing to pay his share of the burdens of the Government which protects him, I find a man who is unworthy to enjoy the blessings of a Government like ours.

They say that we are opposing the National bank currency. It is true. Thomas Benton said that, in searching history, he could find but one parallel to Andrew Jackson; that when Cicero destroyed the conspiracy of Catiline and saved Rome he did for Rome what Jackson did when he destroyed the bank conspiracy and saved America. We say in our platform that the right to coin and issue money is a function of government. We believe that that power of sovereignty can no more, with safety, be delegated to private corporations than the power to enact penal statutes or to levy taxation. Mr. Jefferson, who was once regarded as good Democratic authority, seems to have had a different opinion from the Senator from New-York. They tell us that the issuance of paper money is the function of the banks, and that the Government ought to go out of the banking business. I stand with Jefferson and tell them, as he did, that the issue of money is a function of the Government, and that the banks ought to go out of the governing business.

A Reply to Hill.

The Senator from New-York says he will offer an amendment providing that the proposed change of law shall not affect contracts already made. Let me remind him that that is not the intention, where, under present law, contracts are made payable in gold. But, if he means to say that we cannot change our monetary system without protecting those who have loaned money before the change is made, I want to ask him where, in law or in morals, he can find authority for not protecting the debtors, when the act of 1873 was passed.

The Senator from New-York also asks about the consequence of a failure to maintain parity. My reply is that we cannot couple the platform with a doubt as to our sincerity. He says he wants this country to try to secure an international agreement. Why does he not tell us what he is going to do if they fail to secure it? They have tried for twenty years to secure an international agreement for bimetallism; and those are waiting for it most patiently who do not want it at all.

If they ask us why it is that we say more on the money question than on the tariff question, we reply that, if protection has slain its thousands, the gold standard has slain its tens of thousands. If they ask us why not embody in the platform all those things that we believe, my reply is, that when we have restored the money of the Constitution, all other necessary reforms will be possible, and that, until that is done, there is no reform that can be accomplished.

Why is it that, within three months, such a change has come over the sentiment of this country? Three months ago it was confidently asserted that those who believe in the gold standard would form a platform and nominate and elect a candidate. And they had good reason for the assertion, because there is scarcely a State here to-day asking for a gold standard that is not within the absolute control of the Republican Party. Mr. McKinley was nominated at St. Louis on a platform which declares for the maintenance of the gold standard until it shall be changed to bimetallism by international agreement. Mr. McKinley was the most popular man among the Republicans, and three months ago everybody in the Republican Party prophesied his election. How is it to-day? That man who used to boast that he looked like Napoleon shudders to-day when he thinks that he was nominated on the anniversary of the battle of Waterloo. He can fancy that he hears in the distance the sound of the waves as they beat on the lonely shores of St. Helena. Why this change?

Ah, my friends, the change is evident to any one who looks at the matter. It is because no private character, however pure, no personal popularity, however great, can protect from the avenging wrath of an indignant people. The man who would declare that he is in favor of foisting the gold standard on this people, or who is willing to surrender the right of self-government and to place legislative control in the hands of foreign potentates and powers, cannot hope for an election to the Presidency of the United States.

Confident of Success.

We go forth confident that we shall win. Why? Because there is not a spot of ground upon which the advocates of the gold standard can meet us.

You tell us the great cities are in favor of the gold standard. Burn down your cities and leave our farms, and your cities will grow up again. But destroy our farms and the grass will grow in every city of the Union.

My friends, we shall declare that this Nation is able to legislate for its people upon every question, without waiting for the consent of any other nation on earth, and upon that issue we expect to carry every State in this Nation.

It is the issue of 1776 over again. Our ancestors, when only 3,000,000, declared their independence of every nation on earth. Shall we, when grown to 70,000,000, have less courage? If they say we cannot have bimetallism until some other nation assists, we reply, we will restore bimetallism and let England adopt it because the United States has led the way.

We shall answer their demand for the gold standard by saying to them: "You shall not press down upon the brow of labor this crown of thorns. You shall not crucify mankind upon a cross of gold."

Then the applause broke forth.

July 10, 1896

PLATFORM OF THE CHICAGO CONVENTION.

We, the Democrats of the United States in National Convention assembled, do reaffirm our allegiance to those great essential principles of justice and liberty, upon which our institutions are founded, and which the Democratic Party has advocated from Jefferson's time to our own—freedom of speech, freedom of the press, freedom of conscience, the preservation of personal rights, the equality of all citizens before the law, and the faithful observance of constitutional limitations.

During all these years the Democratic Party has resisted the tendency of selfish interests to the centralization of governmental power, and steadfastly maintained the integrity of the dual scheme of government established by the founders of this Republic of republics. Under its guidance and teachings the great principle of local self-government has found its best expression in the maintenance of the rights of the States and in its assertion of the necessity of confining the General Government to the exercise of powers granted by the Constitution of the United States.

The Constitution of the United States guarantees to every citizen the rights of civil and religious liberty. The Democratic Party has always been the exponent of political liberty and religious freedom, and it renews its obligations and reaffirms its devotion to these fundamental principles of the Constitution.

THE MONEY PLANK.

Recognizing that the money question is paramount to all others at this time, we invite attention to the fact that the Constitution named silver and gold together as the money metals of the United States, and that the first coinage law passed by Congress under the Constitution made the silver dollar the money unit and admitted gold to free coinage at a ratio based upon the silver-dollar unit.

We declare that the act of 1873 demonetizing silver without the knowledge or approval of the American people has resulted in the appreciation of gold and a corresponding fall in the prices of commodities produced by the people; a heavy increase in the burden of taxation and of all debts, public and private; the enrichment of the money-lending class at home and abroad; the prostration of industry and impoverishment of the people.

We are unalterably opposed to monometallism which has locked fast the prosperity of an industrial people in the paralysis of hard times. Gold monometallism is a British policy, and its adoption has brought other nations into financial servitude to London. It is not only un-American, but anti-American, and it can be fastened on the United States only by the stifling of that spirit and love of liberty which proclaimed our political independence in 1776 and won it in the War of the Revolution.

We demand the free and unlimited coinage of both silver and gold at the present legal ratio of 16 to 1 without waiting for the aid or consent of any other nation. We demand that the standard silver dollar shall be a full legal tender equally with gold for all debts, public and private, and we favor such legislation as will prevent for the future the demonetization of any kind of legal-tender money by private contract.

We are opposed to the policy and practice of surrendering to the holders of the obligations of the United States the option reserved by law to the Government of redeeming such obligations in either silver coin or gold coin.

INTEREST-BEARING BONDS.

We are opposed to the issuing of interest-bearing bonds of the United States in time of peace and condemn the trafficking with banking syndicates which, in exchange for bonds and at an enormous profit to themselves, supply the Federal Treasury with gold to maintain the policy of gold monometallism.

AGAINST NATIONAL BANKS.

Congress alone has the power to coin and issue money, and President Jackson declared that this power could not be delegated to corporations or individuals. We therefore denounce the issuance of notes intended to circulate as money by National banks as in derogation of the Constitution, and we demand that all paper which is made a legal tender for public and private debts, or which is receivable for duties to the United States, shall be issued by the Government of the United States, and shall be redeemable in coin.

TARIFF RESOLUTION.

We hold that tariff duties should be levied for purposes of revenue, such duties to be so adjusted as to operate equally throughout the country and not discriminate between class or section, and that taxation should be limited by the needs of the Government, honestly and economically administered. We denounce as disturbing to business the Republican threat to restore the McKinley law, which has twice been condemned by the people in National elections, and which, enacted under the false plea of protection to home industry, proved a prolific breeder of trusts and monopolies, enriched the few at the expense of the many, restricted trade, and deprived the producers of the great American staples of access to their natural markets.

Until the money question is settled we are opposed to any agitation for further changes in our tariff laws, except such as are necessary to meet the deficit in revenue caused by the adverse decision of the Supreme Court on the income tax. But for this decision by the Supreme Court, there would be no deficit in the revenue under the law passed by a Democratic Congress in strict pursuance of the uniform decisions of that court for nearly 100 years, that court having in that decision sustained Constitutional objections to its enactment which had previously been overruled by the ablest Judges who have ever sat on that bench. We declare that it is the duty of Congress to use all the Constitutional power which remains after that decision, or which may come from its reversal by the court as it may hereafter be constituted, so that the burdens of taxation may be equally and impartially laid, to the end that wealth may bear its due proportion of the expenses of the Government.

IMMIGRATION AND ARBITRATION.

We hold that the most efficient way of protecting American labor is to prevent the importation of foreign pauper labor to compete with it in the home market, and that the value of the home market to our American farmers and artisans is greatly reduced by a vicious monetary system which depresses the prices of their products below the cost of production, and thus deprives them of the means of purchasing the products of our home manufactories; and as labor creates the wealth of the country, we demand the passage of such laws as may be necessary to protect it in all its rights.

We are in favor of the arbitration of differences between employers engaged in interstate commerce and their employes, and recommend such legislation as is necessary to carry out this principle.

TRUSTS AND POOLS.

The absorption of wealth by the few, the consolidation of our leading railroad systems, and the formation of trusts and pools require a stricter control by the Federal Government of those arteries of commerce. We demand the enlargement of the powers of the Inter-State Commerce Commission and such restrictions and guarantees in the control of railroads as will protect the people from robbery and oppression.

DECLARE FOR ECONOMY.

We denounce the profligate waste of the money wrung from the people by oppressive taxation and the lavish appropriations of recent Republican Congresses, which have kept taxes high. while the labor that pays them is unemployed and the products of the people's toil are depressed in price till they no longer repay the cost of production. We demand a return to that simplicity and economy which befits a democratic Government and a reduction in the number of useless offices, the salaries of which drain the substance of the people.

FEDERAL INTERFERENCE IN LOCAL AFFAIRS.

We denounce arbitrary interference by Federal authorities in local affairs as a violation of the Constitution of the United States and a crime against free institutions, and we especially object to government by injunction as a new and highly dangerous form of oppression by which Federal Judges, in contempt of the laws of the States and rights of citizens. become at once legislators, Judges, and executioners, and we approve the bill passed at the last session of the United States Senate, and now pending in the House of Representatives, relative to contempts in Federal courts and providing for trials by jury in certain cases of contempt.

PACIFIC RAILROADS.

No discrimination should be indulged by the Government of the United States in favor of any of its debtors. We approve of the refusal of the Fifty-third Congress to pass the Pacific Railroad Funding bill and denounce the efforts of the present Republican Congress to enact a similar measure.

PENSIONS.

Recognizing the just claims of deserving Union soldiers, we heartily indorse the rule of the present Commissioner of Pensions that no names shall be arbitrarily dropped from the pension roll; and the fact of enlistment and service should be deemed conclusive evidence against disease and disability before enlistment.

ADMISSION OF TERRITORIES

We favor the admission of the Territories of New-Mexico, Oklahoma, and Arizona into the Union as States, and we favor the early admission of all the Territories having the necessary population and resource to entitle them to Statehood, and, while they remain Territories, we hold that the officials appointed to administer the government of any Territory, together with the District of Columbia and Alaska, should be bona fide residents of the Territory or District in which the duties are to be performed. The Democratic Party believes in home rule and that all public lands of the United States should be appropriated to the establishment of free homes for American citizens.

We recommend that the Territory of Alaska be granted a delegate in Congress and that the general land and timber laws of the United States be extended to said Territory.

SYMPATHY FOR CUBA.

The Monroe doctrine, as originally declared and as interpreted by succeeding Presidents, is a permanent part of the foreign policy of the United States, and must at all times be maintained.

We extend our sympathy to the people of Cuba in their heroic struggle for liberty and independence.

CIVIL SERVICE LAWS.

We are opposed to life tenure in the public service. We favor appointments based upon merit, fixed terms of office, and such an administration of the civil service laws as will afford equal opportunities to all citizens of ascertained fitness.

THIRD TERM RESOLUTION.

We declare it to be the unwritten law of this Republic, established by custom and usage of 100 years and sanctioned by the examples of the greatest and wisest of those who founded and have maintained our Government, that no man should be eligible for a third term of the Presidential office.

IMPROVEMENT OF WATERWAYS.

The Federal Government should care for and improve the Mississippi River and other great waterways of the Republic, so as to secure for the interior States easy and cheap transportation to tide water. When any waterway of the Republic is of sufficient importance to demand aid of the Government, such aid should be extended upon a definite plan of continuous work until permanent improvement is secured.

Confiding in the justice of our cause and the necessity of its success at the polls, we submit the foregoing declarations of principles and purposes to the considerate judgment of the American people. We invite the support of all citizens who approve them and who desire to have them made effective through legislation for the relief of the people and the restoration of the country's prosperity.

July 10, 1896

BRYAN, FREE SILVER, AND REPUDIATION

CHICAGO, July 10.—The Populist Democrats of the United States have chosen William Jennings Bryan as their candidate for President on the fifth ballot, with 162 votes in the convention refusing to consent by participation in the nominations to the revolutionary platform previously adopted or to bind themselves to support the man who was placed upon it. Bryan's nomination was made with a whirl, in the same impetuous manner in which the platform was constructed and put through.

Worn out with excitement the convention took a recess until to-night at 8 o'clock, with the expectation that the ticket would be completed then. At the night session the delegates who had named a Presidential candidate with a rush, paused for reflection. "In order that no mistakes might be made," it was decided to adjourn until Saturday at 10 o'clock to complete the ticket that will be repudiated by all Democrats who have not lost all sense of National honor and credit.

Bryan's nomination was not a surprise to anybody who was in the convention Thursday when Bryan made the speech that stirred the convention so mightily. When Garfield in 1880 rose to name Sherman as the choice of the Buckeye State his eloquence and his presence were a greater recommendation for the speaker than for the man for whom he spoke. So it was with Bryan. But Bryan sways men of the emotional sort more readily and profoundly than Garfield did. Indeed, Garfield never was so superficial, dramatic, sophistical, as Bryan is whenever he speaks. Bryan's bearing is graceful; his face is handsome; his utterance is clear and strong, with something of the McKinley sing-song, and his style is free, bold, picturesque, and brilliant.

No wonder that his oration moved the emotional and enthusiastic silverites, and at once turned the delegates in several Southern States who had declined to pick a man, to the "Boy Orator of the Platte." But the Bland forces, represented by delegates who had insisted that Bland more fitly represented the silver cause than any other man, because he had been identified with it longer and more prominently, hung back. They had built up a boom with great care for the Missouri "Commoner," as they called him when they did not call him "Silver Dick" or "Honest Dick" Bland, and they expected Bland to win as the result of great expenditure for headquarters, bands, uniforms, and singing clubs.

When the convention met to-day the Bryan boom was the popular one. The Bland shouters were on hand, as vociferous as ever. Missouri reinforced its lines by consultation with other States, and was prepared to sweep away Bryan, if possible, by a prodigious lead at the start.

On the very first roll call the zealous silver men once more were reminded that the Democratic Party had been divided. In the States of Connecticut, Delaware, Maine, Maryland, Massachusetts, Michigan, Minnesota, New-Hampshire, New-Jersey, New-York, Rhode Island, and Wisconsin there were refusals to vote; no votes whatever were cast by New-York and New-Jersey. One gold man in Ohio refused to sit still, and he voted under the unit rule.

Gen. Bragg of Wisconsin, a fighter still, and evidently proud of it, insisted upon applying the unite rule in Wisconsin, but was prevented by the ruling of Permanent Chairman White. The ruling was forced. Wisconsin instructed her delega-

tion to vote as a unit "when and how" the majority should decide. Senator White ruled that this should not prohibit delegates from voting in spite of the will of the majority to the contrary, and according to this decision five of Wisconsin's votes were cast for silver candidates. It was not difficult for a convention that had overturned so many Democratic doctrines and practices to add this violation of the unit rule to its list of offenses.

Bland's strength never was more than 300, as ascertained by recent canvasses, and the result of the first ballot showed that the canvasses had been inflated or that Bryan had weakened Bland's line.

Boies gathered 86 votes, a ridiculously small number considering the expenditures for lithographs and the boastful confidence of the candidate's friends.

Pattison, who ought not to have been in the race, according to the opinion of some of his friends, ran up to 95, and Blackburn, with 83 votes, was closer to Boies than any Iowa boomer would have believed be could be.

The boasted strength of Teller, which was almost exclusively in the minds of a few silver Senators, Republican and Democratic, amounted to merely a handful of votes, a beggarly eight.

The stampede to Bryan was looked for at the beginning of the second ballot. All that that ballot showed, however, was that the men who secretly had objected to Bland, but who were committed to him, had put Bryan to good use in introducing him for exhibition. Alabama went over from Boies to Bland, and "Silver Dick" picked up 58 votes. Boies dropped 49 votes and Bryan gained 92. Pattison had 100 votes. Blackburn dropped half of his string. McLean, who had 53 to start with, picked up 1. Teller increased to 17. Marsden of Louisiana, who made a ridiculous attempt to drown himself the night before while making a nominating speech, boisterously attempted to have the two-thirds rule abolished offhand. Representative Richardson, who was presiding, took advantage of the house rules to send the motion to the Committtee on Rules, which disposed of it and Marsden, but did not shelter Marsden from merciless ridicule.

Again the Bryan stampede was not brought on.

The third ballot began auspiciously for Bland, but it soon turned Bryan's way. Bland's gains were 10, but Bryan increased his vote 22. Teller disappeared. Stevenson lost one of his 10 votes, and Blackburn had only Kentucky and one vote added.

When the fourth ballot began with the shifting of Alabama's 22 votes from Bland to Bryan, and California, Idaho, and Kansas gave their votes to Bryan, the end was in sight.

Bryan's friends gave themselves up to celebrating with a zeal that prevented business from proceeding rapidly, and at times stopped it altogether.

Illinois went out while the vote was being completed—everybody knew what that meant. The announcement of the fourth ballot, with Bryan leading with 280 votes and Bland next with 241, was the signal for a rumpus. It was stopped with difficulty, and after much delay the fifth and final ballot was begun.

As the roll call proceeded for the fifth ballot an exciting scene developed. Alabama, California, Colorado, Georgia, Idaho, Kansas, Kentucky, Louisiana, Michigan, Mississippi, Nebraska, North Carolina, South Carolina, South Dakota, Tennessee, Virginia, and most of the Territories enrolled their votes for Bryan.

When the fifth call was completed he still needed votes. To recruit the line a common convention expedient was adopted. Amid cheers and frantic demonstrations of delight, the Bryan men made a collection of State banners about Nebraska, organized a march about the body of delegates, and under the inspiration or infection of excitement presently were able to collect near a majority of two-thirds.

Illinois came in to swell the list with her forty-eight votes.

The stampede had come. Bulletins began to fly out of the hall announcing Bryan's nomination. Illinois did not nominate him. It was not until Gov. Stone, speaking for Missouri, hauled down the Bland standard and cast 34 votes for Bryan that the gifted blatherskite was selected as the Presidential candidate of the Democratic-Populist Convention.

Not a gold State had budged.

The gold standard States that had refused to participate in the nomination, refusing to be disgraced by committing themselves to a Populistic declaration and its revolutionary methods, did not object to the motion to make the nomination of Bryan unanimous. Pennsylvania, however, that had offered a candidate and voted for him, voted against the motion.

This action provoked some manifestations of resentment. Chairman Richardson did not notice them, and declared that the motion was carried.

July 11, 1896

W. J. BRYAN, POPULIST

Standard Bearer Named by the St. Louis Mob.

St. Louis, July 25.—In a convention lasting four days, the Populists have named a ticket and presented their platform of ad-

vanced Populist principles.

Upon this platform they have placed William J. Bryan, the candidate of the Chicago Convention, not by indorsement, but by nomination, and for the reason that he is, they say, a "good Populist and an honest Populist," chosen by the Democratic Party, perhaps, to anticipate the action of the Populists, and then secure their approval of work already performed.

Bryan's nomination, made after the candidate for Vice President had been desig-

nated by the selection of a "middle-of-the-road" Populist, Thomas E. Watson of Georgia, was also made defiantly.

Before the convention adjourned last night, even before Watson's nomination had been completed, but when it seemed to be assured, it was known in the convention hall that Mr. Bryan had sent word through Senator Jones, acting in a voluntary advisory capacity to the Populists, that he would not permit the use of his name on a ticket that did not also carry the nomination of

Arthur Sewall. But the Populists were in no humor to be dictated to by Mr. Jones. They have scant reverence for Senators, as that venerable Populist and Senatorial Pantaloon, Stewart of Nevada, discovered last night when he was hooted off the stage in a convention in which he was a delegate before he had half completed a dismal apology for Sew... Jones's advice was flung in his face. The convention believed that it had as perfect a right to select a Populist as had the convention at Chicago.

Do what he may, Bryan is now identified as a Populist, and such opportunity as the Bryan Democrats who are not Populists neglect to advertise him as a Populist will be grasped by the people who regard St. Louis Populism as an advance upon Chicago Populism to impress upon the voters the real tendencies of their Presidential candidate. In the South, where Populists and Democrats have fought each other almost with the ferocity of wild beasts, the association proposed by this St. Louis nomination may be distasteful; in the North and East and in some parts of the West there can be no doubt that if the election of Bryan is urged by the sort of people that predominated in the convention here, the personal character of its advocates will not justify the assumption that the cause is a good one.

It is inconceivable that the sober-thinking, self-respecting, clean, and orderly people of any section should be carried away by the hysterical, senseless, vituperative yawpings of orators drawn from Coxey's Army of Commonwealers, or that any body who has learned anything about the pranks of the freaky delegates to the St. Louis Convention should contemplate for a moment the casting of a vote that would give an irresponsible, unregulated, ignorant, prejudiced, pathetically honest and enthusiastic crank complete or partial control of the Government.

The convention is over, but, looking back over its course during the last four days, and particularly to-day, it is difficult not to believe that it could have gone on forever if the St. Louis Business Men's League had volunteered its expenses. In a convention where every man is a king, every man an orator, where no one pays any attention to what has been said by anybody else; where every man insists upon every chance to be heard; where each doubts the honesty of purpose of every fellow delegate, and where there is a kindred distrust of the ordinary practices in most conventions, there is sure to be loss of time. When to this generally unfavorable condition is added a gross ignorance of parliamentary law and practice, such as was betrayed by Chairman Allen, and passed without criticism by the howling, interrupting, shouting, confused aggregation of aliens over which he was chosen to preside, a prospect was afforded of a convention that might go on to the crack of doom, emptying from day to day the wells of meaningless oratory with which the Populists of all sections delight to regale each other.

For Vice President the Populists have chosen, in "Tom" Watson, a man best known in the North, East, and West for a brief Congressional service. Watson is the sort of man to delight the Southern haters of the old Democracy. As an olive branch, he will affect the South, unless a great deal is forgiven, very much with the same feeling of resentment that an infuriated bull would accept the gift of a red shirt tossed in his way.

A swashbuckling, nagging, vulgar scold, indifferent to the amenities that make it possible, by reasonable regard for them, for men of all parties to amicably and yet effectively oppose each other in Congress, Watson struck out boldly, recklessly, and shamelessly for notoriety, and he got it. Not contented with indulging in demagogic harangues, he resorted to personal vilification of associates on the floor, became the subject of an investigation, and only because the Democratic House he slandered preferred not to advertise him by sore punishment he escaped the dismissal that he deserved and should have received. In the South, among Democrats who have any regard left for dignity, honesty, and civilization, Watson's nomination is calculated to weaken rather than strengthen Bryan. In the North and East, excepting, perhaps, among the class of misguided persons who are on the way to such public institutions as are maintained at Bloomingdale, his nomination will be entitled to be regarded as a gross political joke.

July 26, 1896

THE DEMOCRATIC TICKET

Palmer and Buckner Nominated at Indianapolis.

GOOD MEN TO LEAD A GOOD FIGHT

Platform Sound in Its Financial Declarations and Strong in Denunciation of Populism.

President—JOHN McAULEY PALMER of Illinois.
Vice President — SIMON BOLIVAR BUCKNER of Kentucky.

INDIANAPOLIS, Sept. 3.—Gen. John M. Palmer of Illinois and Gen. Simon B. Buckner of Kentucky were named this afternoon as the candidates for President and Vice President of the United States by the National Democratic Party. Gen. Palmer' nomination, which was made on one ro call, Gen. Edward S. Bragg receiving about 130 votes, was the acceptance of the first intention of the party. Nothing except his unwillingness to stand, expressed positively—and, it was feared, irrevocably at the time of the conference of Aug. 7, ever made his nomination seem doubtful.

If he had been out of the contest, the warm admiration for Gen. Bragg in many States would have made him a formidable candidate, and it is probable he would have commanded so much support as to deprive Illinois of the honor of selecting Gen. John C. Black as an alternative candidate.

A Business-Like Convention.

The convention has more than satisfied those who organized the movement that brought it here, and it has surprised those who knew only of the strength of this Democratic impulse by observation in their own States. The men who made up the body of delegates were of the best type, devoted to business, not devoid of some boisterous zeal, but never carried away by their own emotions nor disposed to devote time to excessive cheering and banner carrying in procession. All the work of the convention was done with reasonable promptness.

When it came to making the nominations the disposition to unite made it easy to concentrate upon men. Nearly everybody wanted Gen. Palmer for President; absolutely everybody favored Gen. Buckner's nomination for second place. Both candidates were nominated within the same hour. From the first session of the convention Wednesday to the close of proceedings to-day the temper of the body was of the best. The enthusiasm increased as the business proceeded. The mass meeting last night, which was as large a gathering as Tomlinson Hall could contain comfortably, not only was remarkable in size, but it was one of the most thoroughly interesting, appreciative, and encouraging gatherings of enthusiastic Democrats that ever assembled in Indianapolis. Delegates were still praising the speeches of Col. Fellows and Charlton T. Lewis and Mr. Ehrich of Colorado when they took their places in the hall this morning to complete the business that brought them here.

No Nostrums in the Platform.

Diverting as was the speechmaking to-day, the convention began to be somewhat impatient before the Committee on Resolutions was ready to report the platform. When at last Senator Vilas reached the stage with the declaration of Democratic doctrines he was received with a glad shout of welcome. He reported the platform for the last Democratic Convention at Chicago in 1892, and there was a fitness in his performing a similar service in this convention, brought together to reassert Democratic doctrine.

Impressive and delightful to note was the attentive reception of the platform. Senator Vilas read it admirably, with appropriative emphasis and clearness. At every period there was applause. The assertion of a purpose to defend the honor and the welfare of the people, the denunciation of the Chicago vagrants, the defense of the Supreme Court, the rejection of the free coinage of silver, and the declaration for a gold standard, were all approved by applause as uttered, and there was prodigious acclaim as the paragraph of indorsement of the Administration of Grover Cleveland was read with deliberation and increased emphasis. As it was a Democratic platform, containing no nostrums nor invitations to experiment, and the convention was a convention of Democrats, there was no criticism of the work of the committee, and the platform was adopted almost as soon as read.

September 4, 1896

THE NATION'S VOTING HABIT.

It Has Held the Bulk of Parties Intact in Many Elections.

WASHINGTON, Oct. 7.—The National capital is one of the poorest points of observation of the campaign that can be used to convey to the rest of the country a correct impression of what the election is to bring forth. There are here, to be sure, the headquarters of the Republican and Bryanite Congressional Committees, employed chiefly in sending out Congressional literature under frank. Those committees also receive some letters purporting to give information about the conditions in the districts from which they come, but the men who write them are not all equally good observers, and most of them have reasons for seeking to impress upon the committees views that may result in the extension of unusual favors.

It is plain enough, however, that both sides are easily affected by the reports that come in from day to day of the conditions reported in distant parts of the country. The Republicans have been the more confident men up to the last week, and the sudden chill that appears to have affected them cannot be traced to any well-defined cause of information. With the assumption of a more hopeful tone of conversation at the Bryan headquarters, the free-silver people in the departments have also chirped up. It would be possible, perhaps, to prove, by a canvass, if it were made closely and carefully, that the departments contain more friends of free silver than of sound money; that there are but four heads of bureaus in the Treasury who are not for

free silver and so opposed to the policy of the Administration; but these assertions do not take into account that the departments are full of employes who were there when this Administration came in, who had in part entered the civil service before Mr. Cleveland's first term, and who naturally would be with the Republicans.

The habit of voting by the people of the United States will determine the victory in the next election unless the election is to be a contradiction of the elections of the last forty or fifty years. Take the last three Presidential elections as an illustration of the tendency of parties to vote by habit. In 1884 there were cast for Blaine and Cleveland about ten million votes, of which Cleveland had a lead of 23,005. In 1888 there were more than eleven million votes cast, and the difference between the vote for Harrison and Cleveland was 95,534 to the advantage of Cleveland, and yet Harrison was elected. In 1892, when about twelve million votes were cast, Cleveland had 5,554,226, and Harrison had 5,175,202, or a plurality for the Democratic candidate of 379,000.

In 1892 the task imposed upon the Democratic managers was to elect their candidate by the votes of a united Democracy assisted by a certain number of votes cast by low-tariff Republicans. There was no organized Republican bolt, but there was an admitted degree of desertion. The reported vote shows that the parties persisted in the main in voting as they had voted before, for the candidates of the party to which they happened to belong. Now, in 1896, the task of the Democratic managers for Bryan is to elect their candidate with a divided Democratic Party and by the assistance of such Republicans and Populists as can be induced to accept the Chicago platform and candidates.

According to the statements made by residents of the Western States not in the silver-mining districts, the disaffection of Republicans, while unmistakable, is not so great as to justify the descriptions of it conveyed in the talk about a "craze" or a "sweep." The polls taken by the parties do not find it. Democrats and Republicans, as a general thing, are enlisted under the old columns. In the middle Western States the Republicans who are inclined, or who were inclined, to be tempted by the Bryan talk of high prices and plenty of money with free coinage have largely dropped back by habit to the party to which they belong.

That there is a division of Democrats that will not be closed by the return of Indianapolis Democrats to the Chicago class, is admitted, even by Jones, the Popocrat leader, and by Bryan, the candidate. Unless the Democratic Party can recover from the Republicans enough votes to make up the loss of Democrats who still remain loyal to Cleveland and cannot vote for a man or a platform that denounces Cleveland, it is difficult to see how the Chicago cause can win. To be sure, the Populists appear to be entitled to hold about 1,000,000 of votes, and if these were all cast for Bryan, and the Palmer and Buckner vote should amount to 500,000, there might be a chance for Bryan. Still, the Populist vote is not advantageously placed. In 1892 about half of it was in the States of Alabama, Colorado, Georgia, Kansas, Nebraska, North Carolina, and Texas. McKinley may be elected without the Electoral votes of any of those States. He may get the votes of several of them, and if he does it will be because of the tendency of the voter to resume his habit of voting with his party.

One manifestation of this tendency is that in Minnesota. Within a week the Republicans have become satisfied that they have a chance to win in the State, although at the time of the nomination of Bryan the chance for the Republicans was regarded as very poor indeed. A strong set of Germans to the support of McKinley, a division of farmers into Bryanites or McKinleyites, according to whether they are exclusively wheat farmers or farmers raising a diversity of crops, and a division also of Populists into Bryanites and resentful "Middle of the Road" men, ready to vote for McKinley to rebuke the sell-out of Watson, has made more hopeful to the Republicans a condition that was recently almost hopeless.

October 9, 1896

McKINLEY

ELECTED

PRESIDENT UNITED STATES

TIMES OFFICE, Nov. 4.—4 A. M.

William McKinley and Garret A. Hobart, the Republican candidates for President and Vice President of the United States, have been elected by a tremendous majority in the Electoral College and by an enormous plurality of the popular vote.

Out of the 447 Electoral votes, the Democratic - Populist combination of Bryan, Sewall, and Watson was only able to secure 122, as against 313 for their Republican competitors, with one State in doubt.

The victory for sound money is even more strikingly shown in the popular vote. In this, the pluralities from the most trustworthy data make it appear that McKinley and Hobart lead the opposition by more than 1,000,000 ballots.

In the analysis by States, as shown in the adjoining column, the fact is made clear that the attempted coalition of the South and West has been an absolute and thorough failure.

The boasted "Solid South" has been broken. Of the States which formerly made up this mass that was regarded as Democratic under all circumstances, the Republican candidates for the Presidency have carried Delaware, Maryland, West Virginia, North Carolina, and Kentucky. In nearly all cases, moreover, the pluralities were large.

In the Middle West, which was by common consent made the principal fighting ground, the Republicans have made a clean sweep. Illinois, the pivotal State, has gone Republican by an immense pluralities. Ohio, Indiana, Michigan, Wisconsin, Iowa, the Dakotas, Kansas, and Nebraska have followed.

The three Pacific coast States and Wyoming are also to be placed in the Republican list.

In the East, every State from Maine to North Carolina, inclusive, has gone for McKinley and Hobart, with the exception of Virginia, which is in doubt.

Thirty States went Republican and fourteen Democratic and Populist.

Every record for large pluralities in the history of the country has been broken by New-York and Pennsylvania, each of which gives the Republican candidates about 300,000. Of other States in the same column, Illinois gives 150,000, Massachusetts 110,000, and Wisconsin 100,000.

The landslide for honest money came according to prediction.

November 4, 1896

MR. HANNA'S CAREER.

Successful in Both Business and Politics—Worth $5,000,000.

Marcus Alonzo Hanna, Chairman of the Republican National Committee, who will be John Sherman's successor in the United States Senate, is nearly sixty years of age, having been born in Columbiana County, Ohio, Sept. 24, 1837. He comes of a Quaker family, though he attends the Episcopalian Church almost exclusively, his wife being a member of that church.

Hanna received a very good education for a Western boy. He was graduated from the Cleveland High School, and was then sent for a year to the Western Reserve College at Hudson. He was a leader in his classes, as he has always been in business and politics.

Mr. Hanna began his commercial career as a vessel owner and grocer, in company with his father. He gradually increased his business and possessions, until he became the owner of a great shipbuilding plant and iron and coal mines, besides having large railroad and real estate interests. He is said to be worth $5,000,000.

For many years he has been the most influential business man in Cleveland, and although it is not generally understood, he has been a power in politics since Garfield's preliminary canvass for the Presidency.

Mr. Hanna was among the first to recognize the availability of both Garfield and McKinley for the Presidency, and in each case he was the power that gave direction and irresistible force to the movement which led up to the White House.

He was not known to have political aspirations for himself until after McKinley's election, when the public was informed that Mr. Hanna purposed to spend the next four years in Washington. Naturally it was supposed that he was to enter the Cabinet, but in time the fact developed that Mr. Sherman was to become Secretary of State, while Mr. Hanna would step into his place in the Senate if he could.

Mr. Hanna has been a delegate to several of the National Republican Conventions, twice going in Sherman's interests. He started the business men's movement during Garfield's campaign, which was a potent factor in the election. President Cleveland appointed Mr. Hanna one of the five Government Directors of the Union Pacific Railroad during his first term.

Mrs. Hanna is recognized as a social leader.

February 22, 1897

REPUBLICAN BELIEFS.

"Is or is not the Republican Party held together by a common belief of its members in a certain distinctive body of principles and doctrines?"—The Sun.

The leaders of the Republican Party hold firmly these common beliefs:

That the Americans are a rich and patient people.

That the existing arrangement between the Republican Party and the captains of our infant industries whereby the former supplies protective tariff rates to order in exchange for campaign contributions to keep it in power is the most astute and far-reaching political "deal" ever made by man.

That it is great sport to fool the farmer with duties on things he does not produce, while his immense crops of wheat, corn, hay, and cotton are beyond the need and possibility of protection.

That $140,000,000 a year for pensions is not too much—not enough, even, if by making it $160,000,000 more Republican votes could be got.

That the sectional issue and other questions growing out of the war were settled too soon for the welfare and comfort of the Republican Party, and, in view of the fact that the party won the Presidency on the financial issue last year, it might be bad policy to settle the currency question until some other winning issue has arisen.

There is a great deal of what Mr. DAVID B. HILL used to call enlightened self-interest in the Republican Party.

December 16, 1897

THE LEADERLESS PARTIES.

That the Democratic Party, without a helmsman, is going stern foremost a good part of the time is a trite and hackneyed remark. BRYAN no longer cuts any figure. Senator HILL is not listened to outside of this State, and only by a minority of his party here, though it is the wiser minority. Men like Senator VEST at Washington speak with no authority, and BAILEY in the House is young and not a little absurd, although our Washington correspondent says he is studious and may grow. Facing the greatest questions and the greatest opportunities that have presented themselves in a generation, the Democratic Party is without unity, without a policy, and without a leader.

But is the Republican Party much better off? By the official acts of his appointed agents at Paris the President has embarked the country in the great National venture of expansion. We are to have colonies and dependencies. But the President has not uttered a word to his party or to the country upon the subject. No keynote has been struck, no summons issued to the country to support the Chief Magistrate in his daring policy. Accordingly the Republican Party is in violent disagreement. Senator HOAR, to whose utterances the country pays as much attention as to those of any other Republican, predicts the ruin of the Republic as a consequence of the acts of President McKINLEY. It would be impossible for the most partisan Democrat to condemn an Administration policy in more vigorous language. Senator HALE of Maine is equally outspoken and almost equally emphatic. Ex-Senator EDMUNDS, one of the wisest of living Republicans, and about the most experienced, laments as perilous follies the enterprises to which we are committed. In Republican Massachusetts there is a growing organization of anti-expansionists. Mr. ANDREW CARNEGIE, to whose zeal and liberality the Republican Party owes much, is an earnest and active opponent of the President's policy.

Who is to lead the Republicans in support of the Administration? Speaker REED? Nobody believes that he is an imperialist. It would be contrary to all his principles and behavior. It might well puzzle any young Republican to say who is the leader or where the rank and file are to look for guidance.

Is it safe to follow the President himself? Is it not highly significant that he has declined to commit himself by words to the policy to which his acts have committed the country? The situation is ludicrous in a high degree. But it should be remembered that it is the lifelong habit of our Chief Executive to keep his ear to the ground. He appears to be listening. At least he is not talking. Any Republican who sets out to follow him runs a measurable risk of having to make a sharp turn and follow him on the back track. If the sounds that reach his listening ear from Boston are multiplied in other directions to a degree that would make them seem the voice of the country, the policy of expansion may presently lack the support of its originator.

December 12, 1898

M'KINLEY AND ROOSEVELT

Ticket Nominated by the Republican Convention.

TUMULT OVER THE GOVERNOR

Great Enthusiasm in the Republican Convention.

Special to The New York Times.
PHILADELPHIA, June 21. — The twelfth Republican National Convention to-day completed its work by the nomination of William McKinley for Presi-dent and Theodore Roosevelt for Vice President.

President McKinley's nomination was made with enthusiasm, the customary tumult of shouts, the frantic fluttering of banners, hats, handkerchiefs, plumes, and flags.

The demonstrations were not as pro-longed, however, as they have been in conventions where nomination has been preceded by conflict.

Gov. Roosevelt was the idol of the convention, but the idolatry was not frenzied. His speech was a model of directness and conciseness, his bearing was soldierly, dignified, and satisfactory to his most anxious friend.

The tumult over him was manifestly spontaneous, universal, and sincere. It was not overdone. His conduct plainly strengthened him in the estimation of the convention.

The work of the convention was closed up in a session less than five hours long. This was made possible by the abandonment by Senator Quay of his amendment to the rules proposing to fix future representation.

McKinley and Roosevelt were nominat-ed upon a call of the roll, as provided by the rules. McKinley received every vote in the convention. Roosevelt received 929, one delegate not voting. The delegate who did not vote was Theodore Roosevelt.

The temper of the convention was admirable. Its balance was maintained, although the hall was overcrowded, and many incapable speakers tried the forbearance of the vast, sweltering audience as well as the nerves of Senator Lodge, the presiding officer.

All the States except New York are cordially glad of the nomination of Roosevelt with McKinley. The West is sure that Roosevelt will help the party. A few Republicans are anxious about the State of New York, but they are not many.

Senator Hanna accepted the outcome not only with cheerfulness, but with enthusiasm. He waved a triple plume to spur on the cheers, and afterward consented to be re-elected Chairman of the National Committee.

June 22, 1900

BRYAN NOMINATED; 16 TO 1 PLATFORM

Resolutions Committee Votes for Silver After Long Contest.

NO FIGHT IN THE CONVENTION

Hill Accepts the Platform and Says the East Will Approve.

Special to The New York Times.
KANSAS CITY, July 5.—William Jennings Bryan was nominated to-night for President by the Democratic National Convention on a 16 to 1 platform.

The nomination was made by acclamation, after a presentation followed by scenes of delirious excitement. For more than half an hour the vast audience of 20,-000 persons gave themselves up to demonstrations of delight, cheering wildly while the delegates marched about the hall with flags, State standards, and extemporized banners with inscriptions upon them, borne high in the air.

The platform was reported by Senator Tillman of South Carolina, and was read by him with excellent effect. Its references to imperialism provoked one of the tumultuous demonstrations that have been so frequent in the convention for two days, the interest in that issue, which was declared to be paramount in the campaign, being evidently greater than the concern about trusts, militarism, and the reduction of war taxes. The free-silver plank was rapturously applauded for twenty minutes.

The platform was adopted as reported, the opponents of free silver abandoning their determination to dispute its adoption in the interest of party harmony.

Mr. Bryan is expected to be in Kansas City to-morrow and to attend the convention to accept at one time the nominations of the Democrats, Populists, and Silver Republicans, the latter to be completed as soon as the Democrats have chosen a Vice Presidential candidate.

The choice for Vice President appears to-night to lie between Towne, Stevenson, and Hill, with the chances favoring the elimination of Hill. New York will stick to Keller, its candidate, until it is apparent that he cannot be nominated. It then will probably go to Stevenson. Should Bryan indicate a preference for Towne it may bring about his nomination.

Ex-Senator Hill received a great ovation when he seconded the nomination of Bryan. He accepted the platform without criticism, and spoke hopefully of Democratic success.

It is expected that the work of the convention will be completed to-morrow in one session.

July 6, 1900

BRYAN ON ANTI-IMPERIALISTS.

Sees No Reason Why the 16 to 1 Plank Should Keep Them from Voting for Him.

LINCOLN, Neb., July 17. — William J. Bryan's attention was called to-day to the fact that some anti-imperialists had announced they would be opposed to him on account of the silver plank in the platform, and he was asked whether this fact would affect seriously the anti-imperialist vote. He said:

"Several gold-standard opponents of imperialism have already announced their intention to support the Democratic ticket, although the Anti-Imperialistic League has not acted officially. In such a matter each individual is governed by his own views as to the relative importance of the issues. The Democratic platform declares the question of imperialism to be the paramount issue.

"If any opponent of imperialism refuses to support the Democratic ticket because of the silver plank it must be because he considers the money question more important than the Philippine question; that is, he prefers a gold-standard empire to a bimetallic Republic.

"When I believe the test comes I believe that those who adhere to the doctrine that Governments derive their just powers not from superior forces, but from the consent of the governed, will support our ticket, even though they do not indorse the silver plank. A large majority of the Democrats believe that a restoration of bimetallism would prove a blessing, but the anti-imperialists who dispute this will admit that any evils that might arise from bimetallism could be corrected more easily than the evils which would follow from the deliberate indorsement of militarism and imperialism."

July 18, 1900

AN ATTACK ON BRYANISM

Charged with a Design to Pack the Supreme Court.

Republicans Issue Warning Headed, "Bryan Against Orderly Government and for Mob Rule."

The following was issued yesterday from Republican National Headquarters:

"The Republican Club of New York City, recognizing the grave danger overhanging the public from the declared purpose of the Democrats to radically alter the complexion of the Supreme Court so as to overturn its long-established conservative policy, and to obtain decisions in harmony with the revolutionary ideas of the Bryanites, has prepared and urged a careful public consideration of the following article."

The article in question is headed "Bryan Against Orderly Government and for Mob Rule." It begins by quoting Mr. Bryan's declarations before the Democratic National Convention of 1896, in which he denounced arbitrary interference by the Federal authorities in local affairs as a violation of the Constitution.

Continuing, the article attacks the Democratic Party as follows:

"The Chicago Convention condemns the Supreme Court for declaring the law levying an income tax unconstitutional. The court does not declare an income tax unconstitutional, but only the method prescribed in that law for raising one.

"If the present Constitutional provision is not wise, the remedy is by amendment of that instrument, not by an assault upon the court; yet the Democratic Convention, referring to the decision, appeals to a power 'which may come from its reversal by the court as it may hereafter be constituted.'

"If this means anything it is a threat to pack the court in case of Bryan's election by the addition of Judges pledged to reverse the decision. Such action would be fatal to the independence and fairness of the court. Confidence in courts and their usefulness are based on the idea that the Judges approach a question without preconceived opinions and ready after argument to decide according to the law and facts of the case. Argument before Judges whose minds are ready made up, appointed to render a given decision, would be a farce did it not involve a crime.

"It is not pertinent to argue, as Bryan's supporters sometimes do, that courts properly constituted occasionally become convinced that an earlier decision was erroneous and overrule it. The Supreme Court now consists of nine Judges. The number is not limited by the Constitution, and may be increased by act of Congress. In addition to filling vacancies as they might occur, Mr. Bryan, together with a Bryan Congress, could easily add Judges enough, ten if necessary, to form a majority to do his bidding. The court, so constituted, would have power to reverse any of its decisions, from the origin of the tribunal more than a century ago to this day, many of which lie at the foundation of our republican form of government. Every question touching the interpretation of the Constitution and its amendments might be reopened and disposed of in a way to suit him and his Populistic and Anarchistic allies.

"Thus, for the first time in the history of the country a National convention of any party threatened to pack the Supreme Court and condemned a President for enforcing the laws.

"The danger involved is greater and more insidious than that confronting the Republic in 1861; more insidious, because then the firing on Sumter was an object lesson visible to all, now argument is needed to arouse the people; more dangerous, because then the division of the Union was threatened, but each part would have been governed by law, now the foundations of all orderly government are assailed and Anarchy awaits."

The article concludes with an appeal for the support of McKinley and Roosevelt.

September 3, 1900

M'KINLEY RE-ELECTED

McKinley 284
Bryan 155

REPUBLICANS CARRY

NEW YORK,
INDIANA,
WEST VIRGINIA,
DELAWARE,
MARYLAND,
KANSAS,
NORTH DAKOTA,
SOUTH DAKOTA.
CALIFORNIA.
WYOMING,

DEMOCRATS CARRY

NEVADA.
KENTUCKY,

DOUBTFUL

NEBRASKA.

Total Electoral Vote	447
Necessary to a choice	224
William McKinley	284
William J. Bryan	155
McKinley over Bryan	121

The expected has happened. The Republican Presidential ticket has swept the country.

William McKinley of Ohio, the Republican candidate for President of the United States, has been re-elected to that office, and Theodore Roosevelt of New York has been chosen Vice President.

The Republicans carried twenty-seven States and the Democrats eighteen.

In 1896 the Republicans carried twenty-three States, including California and Kentucky, in each of which the Democrats secured one Electoral vote. The Democrats carried twenty-two States.

The Republicans have regained the States of Kansas, South Dakota, Washington, Utah, and Wyoming.

The Democrats have recovered the State of Kentucky.

Kentucky has given her entire Electoral vote to Bryan.

While victorious in Kentucky in securing the Electors for Bryan, the Democrats have suffered a great defeat in the election of John W. Yerkes, Republican, as Governor, over Beckham, the successor to Gov. Goebel.

Colorado's Electoral vote will be cast for Bryan.

A fusion Legislature has been elected in Colorado. It will elect an opposition Senator to succeed Edward O. Wolcott, Republican, whose term will expire March 3, 1901.

Delaware has chosen Electors favorable to McKinley and Roosevelt.

The election in Delaware of a Democratic Legislature assures the election of two Democratic Senators, one to fill a vacancy and another to succeed Senator Richard R. Kenney, Democrat, whose term will expire March 3, 1901.

Idaho's Electoral vote will go to Bryan and Stevenson.

The victory in Idaho for the fusion legislative ticket assures the election of an opposition Senator to succeed George L. Shoup, Republican, whose term will expire next March.

Kansas has decided to cast her Electoral vote for McKinley.

The election in Kansas of a Republican Legislature will give to that State a Republican Senator to succeed Lucien Baker, Republican, whose term will expire March 3, 1901.

Montana persists in its allegiance to free silver and to Bryan and will give him its Electoral vote.

Although Montana has chosen a Democratic Legislature, it is not yet certain that the partisans of William A. Clark can command votes enough to elect him. The Daly Democrats and Republicans may combine to choose Senator Thomas H. Carter, Republican, to succeed himself, and a Democrat of the Daly faction for the short term.

South Dakota has returned to the Republican column and will cast her Electoral vote for McKinley and Roosevelt.

Senator Richard F. Pettigrew, who calls himself a silver man, the most active and bitter opponent of the Administration in the United States Senate, will be succeeded by a Republican, South

Dakota having chosen a Republican Legislature.

Utah has reversed the position occupied by that State four years ago, and will give its three Electoral votes to McKinley.

Having elected a Republican Legislature, Utah will choose a Republican Senator to fill the vacancy created in that State by failure to elect.

West Virginia adheres to the Republican Party, and will give its Electoral vote to McKinley.

The election in West Virginia of a Republican Legislature will be followed by the return to the United States Senate of Stephen B. Elkins, whose term will expire March 3, 1901.

McKinley's plurality of the popular vote is about 550,000.

This is smaller than his plurality of 603,514 in 1896, which was exceeded only by Grant's plurality over Greeley, in 1872, of 762,991.

November 7, 1900

STRANGE SYMBOLS AND UNFAMILIAR HANDS.

No Democrat will be in the least surprised to learn that Mr. CLEVELAND's stirring adjuration is wholly unintelligible to W. J. BRYAN. Re-establish the old-time faith? I do not know what that means, says Mr. BRYAN. Mr. CLEVELAND must explain. Return from our wanderings? How could BRYAN be expected to understand that? He never saw the old home, and for the life of him could not tell where it stands. Nor can the nomadic adventurer comprehend the reference to strange symbols on banners borne by unfamiliar hands. He never stood beneath the old flag. Any banner, any symbols, will do for him, if they are changeable at his will, and the chieftain of a rabble army recruited on the march is never too particular about the hands that hold up the staff.

Yet how swiftly this compact and startling analysis of the party disaster penetrates the understanding of every Democrat who has studied the old creed and seen the flag:

The culmination of Democratic woe was reached when its compact with these un-Democratic forces was complete, and when our rank and file were summoned to do battle under banners which bore strange symbols and were held aloft in unfamiliar hands. The result of such a betrayal was foredoomed. This abandonment of the principles of true Democracy, this contemptuous disobedience of its traditions, and this deliberate violation of the law of its strength and vigor were, by a decree as inexorable as those of fate, followed by the inevitable punishment of stunning, staggering defeat.

It was an alien horde that overbore the old leaders at Chicago in 1896. They seized the organization, they took the name. They were never Democrats. The observing read the truth in the mongrel roster of the defeated forces after that first battle. The second disaster has made it plain to every eye. We can now trace the origin and antecedents of these Populists who forced themselves and BRYAN and staggering defeat upon the Democracy.

It was Populism that confused and betrayed the Democracy, and Populism sprang from Republican loins. It is not Democratic in parentage or blood or behavior. It took its rise and reached its high and sudden development in those States and that part of the country where Republicanism was formerly supreme and Republican majorities overwhelming. The States that were rockribbed in their devotion to the party of GRANT and HAYES and GARFIELD were precisely the States where Bryanism raged like a prairie fire in 1896, overcoming the old Republican majorities and implanting in the minds of superficial observers the false and dangerous notion that the new doctrines had made tens of thousands of new Democrats whose accession would insure ultimate triumph, even after a first defeat.

But these recruits were not Democrats, they never became Democrats, for when the causes that had made them Populists had ceased to be operative, when the hard times due to Republican silver legislation had given place to good times for the coming of which the way was prepared by the firmness and courage of GROVER CLEVELAND, in causing the vicious law to be erased from the statute book, they began to go back to the Republican Party, where they came from, reducing BRYAN's pluralities everywhere and carrying some of the Populist States of 1896 once more into the Republican column. This swinging of old Republican votes from that party over to the Democracy, for its ruin, and back again to Republicanism, is exhibited by the figures of the votes cast in five Presidential elections in the three typical Republican-Populist States of Colorado, Kansas, and Nebraska:

	Colorado.	Kansas.	Nebraska.
1876—			
Republican......	......	78,322	31,916
Democratic......	......	37,902	17,554
1880—			
Republican......	27,450	121,549	54,979
Democratic......	24,647	59,801	28,524
1888—			
Republican......	50,744	182,904	108,425
Democratic......	37,567	102,745	80,552
1896—			
Republican......	26,271	159,541	102,304
Democratic......	161,163	171,810	115,880
1900—			
Republican......	93,072	185,955	121,835
Democratic......	122,733	162,601	114,013

Here is a cycle of political change, in large part completed and evidently on its way to fuller accomplishment. Kansas and Nebraska have swung all the way back to Republicanism. In Colorado the Republicans have gained 67,000 votes, as compared with 1896, while BRYAN has lost nearly 40,000. The recruits whom BRYAN brought have deserted even him. They have no interest in the principles of the Democratic Party. They have for a brief time been Populists; they were and are Republicans. The shift over to Populism is exhibited, also, in the figures of the Presidential election of 1892. In that year the Democrats nominated no Electors in Colorado, having effected a fusion with the People's Party, whose candidate, WEAVER, received 53,584 votes, against 38,620 for HARRISON. A similar fusion in Kansas gave WEAVER 163,111 votes, against 157,237 for HARRISON. In North Dakota, Idaho, and Wyoming also Democracy was ignobly yoked with Populism, and in all but Wyoming, Weaver Electors were chosen. In that year 1,122,045 Populist votes were cast, and it was the Republican West and Northwest that contributed the bulk of them, Minnesota, for instance, giving WEAVER 110,456 votes, CLEVELAND 100,920, and HARRISON 122,823. The hell-brew of Populism was then preparing that in the next two Presidential elections stupefied and strangled the Democratic Party. It was compounded of Republican elements and mixed by Republican hands.

It is natural and quite to be expected that a proclamation of the old-time principles of Democracy should be unintelligible to the ears of these Populist outlanders. It is not to be wondered at that their leader should be mystified when Democrats speak of the strange, false symbols that defile the flag.

But to Democrats the words of Mr. CLEVELAND ring with a clear meaning. To them he sends an awakening message.

December 22, 1900

BRYAN DENOUNCES GROVER CLEVELAND

Says that He Wrecked the Democratic Party.

LINCOLN, Neb., June 23.—The absence of W. J. Bryan from the Democratic harmony dinner at New York is pretty well explained by a statement given out by Mr. Bryan this evening, commenting on the dinner.

At the outset Mr. Bryan says there is no such thing as Democratic harmony where ex-President Cleveland is concerned. He says:

"The banquet given on the evening of June 19 by the Tilden Club of New York City was advertised as a 'harmony meeting,' but it turned out to be what might have been expected of such a gathering, an ovation to the chief guest, ex-Democrat Grover Cleveland. There can be no such thing as harmony between men like him and those who believe in Democratic principles, and he is frank enough to say so.

He spent no time looking for 'middle ground,' upon which to gather together discordant elements. He boldly called upon members of the party to abandon their convictions and accept the construction which he placed upon Democratic principles. He even taunted the party with being a sort of prodigal son, and invited it to give up its diet of husks and return to its father's house.

"He spoke of his 'retirement from political activity,' and said: 'Perhaps there are those who would define my position as one of banishment instead of retirement. Against this I shall not enter a protest. It is sufficient for me in either case that

I have followed on the matters of difference within our party, the teachings and counsel of the great Democrat, in whose name party peace and harmony are to-night invoked. No confession, of party sin should, therefore, be expected of me. I have none to make; nor do I crave political absolution.'

"He not only boasted of his course, but put his brand upon those who sat at meat with him. Having asserted that his Democratic faith compelled him to leave the party, (or resulted in his banishment,) he descried the banqueters as sharing in that faith.

"He is not only defiant, but he insists that party success can be secured only by an open and avowed return to his ideas. Harmony is to be secured, not by the suppression of differences, but by the elimination of those who differ from him."

Mr. Bryan says he will print in his paper Mr. Cleveland's speech, "to show that the reorganizers do not want harmony, but control, and that their control means the abandonment of the party's position and a return to the policies and practices of Mr. Cleveland's second Administration."

He continues:

"He [Cleveland] secured his nomination in 1892 by a secret bargain with the financiers; his committee collected from the corporations and spent the largest campaign fund the party ever had; he filled his Cabinet with corporation agents and placed railroad attorneys on the United States bench to look after the interests of their former clients. He turned the Treasury over to a Wall Street syndicate, and the financial members of his official family went from Washington to become the private attorneys of the man who forced (?) the Treasury Department to sell him Government bonds at 105 and then resold them at 117. He tried to prevent the adoption of the income tax provision, he refused to sign the only tariff reform measure passed since the war, and while thundering against the trusts in his messages did even less than Knox has done to interfere with their high-handed methods.

"His Administration, instead of being a fountain of Democracy, sending forth pure and refreshing streams, became a stagnant pool from whose waters foul vapor arose—poisonous to those who lingered near.

"Having debauched his party, he was offended by its effort to reform and gave comfort to the enemy. Virginius killed his daughter to save her chastity. Cleveland stabbed his party to prevent its return to the paths of virtue.

"And now, still gloating over his political crimes, he invites the party to return to him and apologize for the contempt which it has expressed for him. Will it? Not until the principles of Jefferson are forgotten and the works of Jackson cease to inspire.

"If we are to have reorganization Cleveland himself should accept the Presidential nomination. It would be due him; his reinstatement would be poetic justice to him and retribution to those whose Democratic conscience revolted against his undemocratic conduct. Of course he would get no Democratic votes, but being closer to plutocracy than any Republican likely to be nominated, he might divide the enemy, and even Democrats would have what little consolation would come from receiving their disappointment in advance.

"A merchant about to fail invited his creditors to a dinner, and after stating his condition, secured a year's extension from all present. One of the number, a relative, waited until after the others had retired, and then accosted the debtor: 'Of course I promised with the rest to extend the time, but you are going to make me a preferred creditor, are you not?'

"'Yes,' replied the debtor, 'I'll make you a preferred creditor. I'll tell you now that you are not going to get anything; the rest won't find it out for a year.'

"Mr. Cleveland's nomination would have this advantage over the nomination of any other reorganizer; he would make the Democrats preferred creditors and tell them that they would not be benefited by his administration.

"Mr. Cleveland's speech should be read in full. It answers a useful purpose; it outlines the plan of campaign decided upon by the plutocratic elements for which the reorganizers stand. Tariff reform is to be made the chief issue, and the men who voted for McKinley, the high priest of protection, are to carry on a sham battle with their companions of 1896, while the financiers make the dollar redeemable in gold, and fasten upon the country an asset currency and a branch bank system. Trusts are to be denounced in sonorous terms, while the campaign managers mortgage the party to the trust magnates in return for campaign funds. Sometimes imperialism will be denounced, as in Mr. Hopkins's Illinois convention; sometimes ignored, as in Mr. Cleveland's speech; but whether denounced or ignored, the secret and silent power that can compel submission to the demands of the financiers and to the demands of the trust magnates can compel submission to the demands of the exploiters and the representatives of militarism.

"The fight is on between a Democracy that means Democracy and a Clevelandism which means plutocracy. Every speech made by Mr. Cleveland shows more clearly the odiousness of the policies for which he stands. We have more to fear from those who, like Mr. Hill, indorse Mr. Cleveland's views, but conceal their real purpose in ambiguous language."

June 24, 1902

THE NEGRO IN POLITICS

Congressman Bankhead Discusses Conditions in the South.

Says Disfranchisement of the Blacks Would Result in Great Gains for the Republican Party.

Special to The New York Times.

WASHINGTON, May 2.—The prospect of the elimination in the South of the negro vote and the removal of the fear of negro domination as an incident of the withdrawal of universal suffrage are leading Southern Democrats to express themselves in a way calculated to excite surprise and concern among some of the old party leaders. Several such expressions have been recently published, and now Representative Bankhead of Alabama, one of the stoutest of Democrats and a candidate in 1899 for election as Democratic leader, has contributed his opinion in some striking words, to the number already given to the public.

"I am a Democrat, and in voting the Democratic ticket vote my sentiments," he said to-day, "but I know that there are many men of wealth and social and business prominence in the South who affiliate with the Democratic Party under protest. There has been a wonderful industrial development in Alabama, and many of the wealthy and prominent men engaged in business enterprises are at heart Republicans, and if conditions were such as to admit of it, would vote with the Republican Party. As long as the negro is in politics, however, they cannot do so. They have to ignore every other consideration in politics when confronted with the danger of negro domination.

"I feel no hesitation in saying that if the negro question is eliminated, some of the most prominent men in Alabama will associate themselves with the Republican Party, and as a Democrat I say that it would be better for the South and for the whole country if conditions were such as to admit of every man voting his sentiments on great questions of public policy without being held in bondage by a disturbing local condition.

"With the negro out of politics, I believe the time would come when Alabama would be divided between two great parties of nearly equal strength, and that elections would be determined there by the candidates and the issues of the hour. This cannot be as long as the negro question remains unsettled. That question renders it impossible for many who are prominent in business affairs, progressive and respected in the community—some of the best men we have—who are in sympathy with Republican politics, from acting with that party.

"If this obstacle were removed it would conduce to the welfare of the whole country, as well as of the South, giving the South a freedom of thought and action, magnifying its influence in public affairs, while giving to the Republicans the advantage of the co-operation of all those who believe in its policy. If the elimination of the negro question results in the Republicans dominating anywhere in the South, through the expression of the sentiments of intelligent voters, we will have no reason to complain, but as long as the negro is in politics the men who are now voting the Democratic ticket under protest will continue to vote it."

May 3, 1901

MR. ROOSEVELT IS NOW THE PRESIDENT

Special to The New York Times.

BUFFALO, Sept. 14.—Theodore Roosevelt to-day became President of the United States, with a solemn promise that he would follow out the policy laid down by President McKinley.

His exact words, which produced a most profound impression upon the small company of people to whom he spoke, were: "I wish to say that it shall be my aim to continue absolutely unbroken the policy of President McKinley for the peace and prosperity and the honor of our beloved country."

A more solemn scene would be hard to conceive than was the swearing in of Mr. Roosevelt as President. It occurred in the library of the home of his personal friend, ex-State Senator Ansley Wilcox, which home is a little, old-fashioned Colonial mansion on Delaware Avenue, within a mile of the residence of Mr. Milburn, where the body of the assassinated President is lying.

There was nothing of pomp in the ceremony. It was as simple and as sanctified as a family religious service, such as a wedding. It was hard to realize that it was an event of world-wide import.

Mr. Roosevelt, as Vice President, arrived here at 1:30 o'clock this afternoon. He had been brought on, as fast as the best of horses and the swiftest of special trains could bring him, from his retreat in the Adirondacks, where he went last week, fully satisfied that President McKinley would recover.

September 15, 1901

ROOSEVELT AND FAIRBANKS NAMED

Republicans Cheer Roosevelt Twenty-one Minutes

For President — THEODORE ROOSE-VELT of New York.

For Vice President—CHARLES WAR-REN FAIRBANKS of Indiana.

For Chairman of the Republican National Committee—GEORGE B. COR-TELYOU of New York.

Special to The New York Times

CHICAGO, June 23.—With a mighty roar of human voices that swelled through Chicago's great Coliseum like the rumblings of an avalanche for a full twenty-one minutes and accompanied by a demonstration of enthusiasm delirious and picturesque, the Republican National Convention today proclaimed Theodore Roosevelt of New York as the party's choice for President of the United States. The nomination of Senator Charles Warren Fairbanks of Indiana for Vice President, which followed by acclamation, also called forth a wild outburst.

The scene witnessed in the convention today when ex-Gov. Black of New York closed his speech submitting the name of President Roosevelt to the convention seemed proof positive that the lack of enthusiasm on the part of the delegates which has been so much remarked here since last Monday was not indicative of indifferent regard for the man who was to be the party's candidate. It suggested the idea that all that was needed to dispel the sobriety of demeanor, which has marked the gathering was a drink from some fountain of real eloquence.

Obtaining that drink today, the convention at once livened up, and, as it relaxed more and more under the influence of the rhetorical spirits which were served up to it by ex-Gov. Black, Senator Beveridge, and George A. Knight, the brilliant orator from the Pacific Coast, it cast off all reserve and gave itself over to the delight of its intoxication. It subsided only when it was exhausted.

June 24, 1904

BANKERS INDORSE ROOSEVELT.

No Wall Street Criticism of Him Now, Says Speyer.

Regarding the nomination of President Roosevelt the following opinions were expressed by prominent financiers in Wall Street yesterday:

"Mr. Roosevelt," said James Speyer, who is not a Republican, "has been nominated on his merits, and the Republican Party could not, I believe, have selected a stronger candidate. It is generally known that there was a time when certain interests in Wall Street were more or less outspoken in their antagonism to President Roosevelt, but his actions in respect to certain matters which were criticised then have been completely vindicated.

"Most of his former critics are now among his strongest supporters. Those who came to scoff have remained to pray. People in Wall Street as in other parts of our country realize that in upholding and enforcing the laws against every one the President is giving the best protection to every one's interest, rich and poor alike.

"No one who has watched public opinion in the whole country doubt that the great mass of the American people approved of Mr. Roosevelt's Administration, and that they desire it to continue. I have been a sincere admirer of President Roosevelt and of his Administration, and I believe he will be elected, and that the American people will feel proud of their choice."

Jacob H. Schiff received the news with enthusiasm, so he said.

"Ex-Secretary Root," said Mr. Schiff, "in his address as Temporary Chairman in no way overdrew the great qualities of President Roosevelt; if anything he rather undervalued the services rendered to this country by the Roosevelt Administration.

"When at the instance of President Roosevelt the litigation against the Northern Securities Company was begun I thought an error of judgment had been committed, but the course of events has borne out the wisdom and justification of the President's course in this important instance. I am certain that there is a strong feeling in conservative financial circles that in any case of emergency President Roosevelt will be found on the safe side."

June 24, 1904

JUDGE PARKER SAYS IT MUST BE GOLD OR HE WILL NOT RUN

His Stand Approved by the Delegates After a Long Wait.

DAVIS FOR VICE PRESIDENT

Special to The New York Times.

ST. LOUIS, Sunday, July 10.—The Democratic National Convention adjourned sine die at 1:30 o'clock this morning.

It completed the ticket at 1:10 o'clock by nominating ex-Senator Henry G. Davis of West Virginia for Vice President by acclamation.

But that event was completely overshadowed by the remarkable action of Judge Alton B. Parker, candidate for President, in declaring that he would not accept the nomination except upon the understanding that he was uncompromisingly for the gold standard. The Convention, after an exciting conference and strong debate, indorsed the position of Judge Parker by a vote of 785 to 190.

Judge Parker announced his position in a telegram to the Hon. W. F. Sheehan of the New York delegation. This telegram was received while the convention was in session late yesterday afternoon. It's text follows:

Hon. W. F. Sheehan, Hotel Jefferson, St. Louis:

I regard the gold standard as firmly and irrevocably established, and shall act accordingly if the action of the Convention to-day shall be ratified by the people. As the platform is silent on the subject, my view should be made known to the Convention, and, if it is proved to be unsatisfactory to the majority, I request you to decline the nomination for me at once, so that another may be nominated before adjournment.

A. B. PARKER.

The convention was adjourned yesterday afternoon just as it was ready to ballot for the Vice Presidency. A conference of the leaders who had brought about the nomination of Judge Parker was called immediately. After discussion it was agreed to ask the convention to send this telegram to Judge Parker:

"The platform adopted by this convention is silent on the question of the monetary standard because it is not regarded by us as a possible issue in this campaign, and only campaign issues were mentioned in the platform. Therefore there is nothing in the views expressed by you in the telegram just received which would preclude a man entertaining them from accepting a nomination on said platform."

The motion to send this telegram was made by John Sharp Williams after the convention had reconvened at 9:10 o'clock in the evening.

Mr. Williams, Senator Tillman, Senator Daniel, and Senator Carmack spoke in favor of the agreement. William J. Bryan, who had risen from a sick bed, spoke twice in opposition.

July 10, 1904

DEFENDS REPUBLICAN RECORD.

Campaign Committee's Textbook Reviews the Last Four Years.

WASHINGTON, Aug. 14.—Tariff, prosperity, labor wages and prices, trusts, the Panama Canal, Cuba and Cuban reciprocity, expansion and its results, the investigations of the postal and land frauds and punishments of offenders, rural free delivery, irrigation, the record of the Republican Party, and the record of Theodore Roosevelt are the leading subjects discussed by the Republican campaign text book of 1904, which is just about to be issued.

The following is a synopsis of the book prepared by the Republican Campaign Committee:

" 'The four great facts,' which justified the Republican Party in asking the support of the public in 1900 were: First—That its pledges of 1896 had been redeemed; second, that prosperity had come as a result; third, that developments since 1896 had shown the fallacy of the principles upon which the Democracy then appealed for public support; and, fourth, the conditions which had come to other parts of the world and their people as a result of promises fulfilled by the Republican Party in the United States.

" These assertions made in the text book of 1900 have been fully justified by the added experiences of another four years. The pledges of 1896 and those made in 1900 have been redeemed. The protective tariff has been restored; the gold standard made permanent; Cuba freed and made independent; the Panama Canal assured under the sole ownership and control of the United States; a Department of Commerce and Labor established; rural free delivery given to millions of the agricultural community; the laws for the proper regulation of trusts and great corporations strengthened and enforced; prosperity established, commerce developed, labor protected and given ample employment and reward; intelligence, prosperity, and good government established in distant islands, and the flag of the United States made the emblem of honor in every part of the world.

" All of these great accomplishments have been the work of the Republican Party. In each of them it has met the discouragement, the opposition, and the hostilities of the Democracy. It is upon this additional evidence of the past four years, evidence that the Republican Party is the party of progress, and the Democracy the party of inaction, retardment, and fault-finding, that the Republican Party again confidently appeals for public support in the Presidential and Congressional elections of 1904."

Following this introduction the book takes up in consecutive order the tariff, prosperity, trusts, and industrial combinations, labor wages and prices, the advance in prices, the money question, the record of Theodore Roosevelt, the Panama Canal, Cuba and Cuban reciprocity, expansion and its results, the record of the Republican Party, the work of the departments under the McKinley and Roosevelt Administrations, merchant marine, pension and pension laws, rural free delivery, irrigation, public lands, and numerous other subjects liable to be discussed during the coming campaign.

The book also contains a sketch of the life and work of President Roosevelt and of Senator Fairbanks, a discussion of conditions in the island territories of the United States, a discussion on American diplomacy in the East, a series of chapters on the work of each of the executive departments during the terms of Presidents McKinley and Roosevelt, and a chapter on the investigations into the postal frauds.

August 15, 1904

WATSON QUESTIONS PARKER.

Would You Eat with Booker Washington at the White House?

ATLANTA, Sept. 1.—Thomas E. Watson, the Populist nominee for President, delivered a speech to-day to the State Convention of his party. He said in part:

" In the South we are told we must submit to the surrender to Wall Street because of ' the nigger.' What a blessed thing it is for Democratic leaders that they always have ' the nigger ' to fall back on! For thirty years they have been doing business on ' the nigger,' and to-day he is their only stock in trade.

" In the West Virginia Democratic Convention, the State of the Democratic nominee for Vice President, the ' white supremacy ' resolution was voted down, and on Aug. 1, 1904, Judge Parker himself, in writing to the negro James A. Ross, addressed him as ' My Dear Sir,' just as though Ross had been a white man.

" The South should demand to know the facts about Judge Parker. How does he stand upon this alleged negro question? Is his position at all different from that of Roosevelt? If so, in what respect? The South should demand explicit reply to the following questions before it votes for him upon the assumption that he differs from Roosevelt on the negro question:

"(1.) Would you refuse to eat at the same table with Booker Washington?

"(2.) Would you refuse to appoint negroes to office in the South?

"(3.) If elected, will you refuse to receive on terms of equality, at the White House, such negroes as Bishop Turner, Booker Washington, and T. Thomas Fortune?

"(4.) Do you approve the mixed schools of New York, inaugurated under Grover Cleveland, in which social equality is practically made a matter of compulsion?

"(5.) If such schools wherein black children and white children are educated together are a good thing for your native State of New York, would they be a good thing for Georgia and South Carolina? If not, why not?"

September 2, 1904

ROOSEVELT

Sweeps North and West and Is Elected President.

SAYS HE WILL NOT RUN AGAIN

Will Have 325 Electoral Votes—Republican Gains in Congress—Folk, La Follette and Douglas Win Governorship Fights.

Theodore Roosevelt was yesterday elected President of the United States for four years more, overwhelming majorities having been given to the Republican Electoral tickets in all of the States which had been classed as doubtful. The returns received up to midnight indicate that Roosevelt will have 325 votes in the Electoral College to 151 for his opponent, Alton B. Parker. The total number of votes in the Electoral College is 476, of which 239 are necessary to a choice. Mr. Roosevelt, therefore, will have a majority in the Electoral College of 174. The only State about whose Electoral vote there was any doubt at a late hour was Maryland. The returns indicated that it had gone Republican by several thousand, but the Democratic State Committee' had not abandoned hope.

As soon as it became certain that he had carried the country Mr. Roosevelt issued the following statement at the White House, in Washington:

Washington, Nov. 8, 1904.
"I am deeply sensible of the honor done me by the American people in thus expressing their confidence in what I have done and have tried to do. I appreciate to the full the solemn responsibility this confidence imposes upon me, and I shall do all that in my power lies not to forfeit it. On the Fourth of March next I shall have served three and one-half years, and this three and one-half years constitutes my first term. The wise custom which limits the President to two terms regards the substance and not the form. Under no circumstances will I be a candidate for or accept another nomination."

The polls closed in New York at 5 o'clock, and the people were not kept long in suspense as to the result in New York State and the Nation. As early as 7:30 o'clock August Belmont who was at the Democratic National headquarters receiving returns, conceded the election of President Roosevelt by "an overwhelming majority." By 8 o'clock those in charge of returns at Democratic headquarters were willing to concede that Mr. Roosevelt had carried every doubtful State in the country.

The figures which came in from New York, New Jersey, Connecticut, Indiana, and West Virginia were stunning to the Democratic managers. In none of the bulletins was there a single ray of hope for the Democrats, and as early as 8:30 o'clock a telegram was sent to Judge Parker informing him of his defeat.

Returns from New York State up to midnight indicated that Roosevelt would have a plurality of 186,000 in the State. His indicated plurality above the Bronx line was 223,000, while Parker's indicated plurality in New York City was 37,000. Higgins's plurality for Governor will be about 85,000.

The Republicans of the State of New York retained their hold on the Legislature, electing on the face of the returns as this edition of THE TIMES went to press, 36 members of the Senate, to 14 Democrats, and 104 members of Assembly to 46 Democrats. This is a clean Republican gain of 7 in the Senate and

7 in the Assembly. Districts that went Republican only when McKinley ran in 1896 were this year again turned into the Republican column.

The returns for Congress show that the Republicans have elected 229 members of the House, and the Democrats 157, thus giving the Republicans 72 majority.

In New Jersey the indicated plurality for Roosevelt is 60,000, and the Republican candidate for Governor, Edward C. Stokes, will have about 35,000.

Connecticut gave a plurality of 25,000 for Roosevelt. A. Heaton Robertson, the Democratic candidate for Governor, ran ahead of his ticket, but Henry Roberts, the present Lieutenant Governor, was elected by a plurality of about 20,000.

Indiana went 50,000 for Roosevelt. The latest returns indicated 50,000 plurality for the Republican Electoral ticket in Wisconsin. La Follette, the regular Republican candidate for Governor in Wisconsin, ran behind the Electoral ticket, but the returns indicate his election.

West Virginia, the home State of Henry Gassaway Davis, the Democratic candidate for Vice President, gave 23,000

plurality for Roosevelt and Fairbanks.

The latest returns from Colorado indicate that the State went for Roosevelt by a small plurality and that Peabody, the Republican candidate for Governor, won by a narrow margin.

Maryland was claimed by both sides at midnight, but the latest returns indicated that the State would be Republican by a small plurality.

Massachusetts furnished a surprise by electing William L. Douglas, Democrat, Governor of the State, although the plurality for Roosevelt and Fairbanks was in the neighborhood of 80,000.

Joseph W. Folk is elected Governor of Missouri by a plurality estimated at 40,000, but the returns indicated that Parker was running behind. He probably will carry the State by 35,000.

While complete returns were lacking at 1:30 o'clock it seemed probable that the Democrats had elected Governors in Nebraska and possibly West Virginia. In the latter State the vote is very close, but the indications are that Cornwell, the Democratic candidate, has outrun the National ticket and will pull through.

Montana also reverses her Electoral vote on State issues and elects a Democratic Governor.

November 9, 1904

IS THE REPUBLICAN PARTY DYING?

A partisan contemporary asks, "Is the Democratic Party dying?" The basis of the question is the Administration's adoption of some Democratic ideas, and the praise of the President by some Democratic leaders and conventions. Thus the Rhode Island Democratic Convention on Thursday approved Mr. ROOSEVELT's railway rate regulation ideas, and Tammany, like Mr. BRYAN, has indorsed a political opponent.

These and similar incidents suggest to us rather the question whether the Republican Party is dying, or perhaps it might better be said committing political hara-kiri by abandoning possible sources of strength and adopting extravagancies and erraticisms adapted to weaken it with conservative men of all parties. Praise by Tammany and BRYAN for the adoption of semi-Socialistic fads are doubtful signs of Republican vitality or of Democratic decease.

On the other hand, the deliberate repudiation by the Administration of measures demanded by sober Republicans certifies that it is losing strength in its own house. Thus the Ohio Republicans condemned by silence and inaction Mr. ROOSEVELT's railway rate vagaries, and the Massachusetts Republicans indorsed the tariff reform programme which Mr. ROOSEVELT rejected.

Democratic interpretation of such incidents is less authoritative than Republican. We learn from the stoutest of Republican sheets that Gov. CUMMINS tells the Iowa Republicans that Republican disruption is imminent:

Slowly but surely we are making a clear issue upon the tariff and reciprocity between the members of the Republican Party.

Reasonable revision, reasonable reciprocity, and reasonable railway regulation go hand in hand, the invincible trio of reform. If, temporarily, they do not win, mark my prediction that they will go down in defeat together.

Those are the ideas of a leading Re-

publican. They certainly are more Democratic than Republican in their quality. Those who wish may discern Democratic decease in Republican insistence upon an irrational tariff, oppressive and confiscatory railway regulation, and the denial of measures demanded by commercial bodies of no politics whatever. While the Democrats are adopting Mr. ROOSEVELT, it appears to us that Mr. ROOSEVELT is presenting the winning issues to his opponents if they will have them. The next campaign will not repeat the precedent when Democratic votes elected a Republican President. Conditions are ripening rather for repetition of the defeat of the candidate of the extremists of all parties by the coalescence of the reasonables and conservatives of all parties.

October 14, 1905

SOCIALISM ON WANE; ITS CREEDS SPREAD

The Times's Canvass of States Shows Party on Decline as Political Factor.

Socialism as a concrete political proposition and a factor in the recurring battle of the ballots is retrograding in the United States. At the same time ideas first ad-

vocated by Socialists are taken up by both the Republican and Democratic Parties in their appeals for votes and are reflected in legislation as well as in party platforms in a number of the States. These conditions were brought to light by an investigation made by THE NEW YORK TIMES through its special correspondents in every State of the Union.

That the doctrines enunciated and put into practice by President Roosevelt in his dealings with corporations are the chief source of inspiration to the out-and-out Socialists who vote under their own party emblem was another interesting discovery made. Victor Berger, the Socialist boss of Wisconsin and one of the founders of the Social Democratic Party in the United States at present, is

declaring in public speeches everywhere that President Roosevelt's attitude toward the corporations is exactly that of the the Socialists, though until the Government receivership idea was voiced abroad he admitted that the President was less of an extremist.

The declaration that President Roosevelt has annexed many of the basic principles of Socialism and is now putting them into practice on a National scale is giving Socialists in all parts of the country a great deal of comfort and, it is predicted, will give new impetus to the movement in the near future. In connection with this the statement made by a prominent Socialist in Kansas to a correspondent of THE NEW YORK TIMES is interesting. Here is what he said:

"We are resting now. Our cause is marching on under the leadership of President Roosevelt. He is doing us more good than we could possibly do for ourselves."

Show Falling Off in Vote.

The reports received by THE NEW YORK TIMES from its correspondents, while showing a distinct falling off both in the vote and the political influence of the Socialists as such, fail to show any appreciable growth anywhere, with the exception of Kansas and Missouri. Wherever strength has been added to the party it has been purely local and chiefly in the large municipalities. Even in California, which has been called the Promised Land of Socialism, where the labor element in the last few years has been strongly intrenched politically in the principal city of the State, and where our correspondent finds it extremely difficult to tell where trades unionism ends and Socialism begins, there is no locality where the Socialists have been able to obtain political control.

Of the legislation which has been characterized by the correspondents as Socialistic much is merely humanitarian, or maybe mildly paternalistic. With all parts of the country enjoying prosperity, and with wages high and work to be had for the asking, such indications of social unrest and discontent as our correspondents have been able to find have been due largely to local conditions.

Resentment against corporations of a monopolistic tendency on the other hand seems to be general throughout the country and in a great number of States has found expression in legislation both punitive and with a view of curtailing their power. Railroads and insurance companies seem to have been singled out for popular vengeance, but broadly speaking the legislation passed or merely presented has been no more radical than the legislation passed in this State with a view of curbing the insurance companies and subjecting public service corporations to a more rigid supervision and control.

Municipal Ownership Boosted.

The dispatches to THE TIMES indicate that the idea of municipal ownership of public utilities, such as water and lighting plants and telepnones in small cities, has received a boost. In some of the Western States in particular omnibus acts have been passed giving such communities the right to own and operate such plants, and in some instances local trolley lines. In Connecticut the Legislature passed an act permitting the town of Willimantic to conduct a municipal business in natural ice, and the Wisconsin Legislature gave Milwaukee authority to erect a plant for the manufacture of artificial ice.

Legislation of a tendency sufficiently radical to enlist the active support of Socialists under the following heads seems to have kept the Legislative Assemblies of a large number of States busy during their last session: Public service supervision, insurance control, two-cent fare, shortening of working hours for women and children, general labor legislation, child labor, employers' liability, old age pension.

The Bryan theory of Government ownership of inter-State railroads has not been echoed by any Legislature, nor has the idea of State ownership of public utilities come prominently before the lawmakers of any State.

The other pet doctrine of the Nebraska Commoner—that of initiative and referendum—came before the Legislature of his own State and was killed in its infancy. Legislation based on this theory was defeated in Massachusetts, New Jersey, Colorado, and Nebraska, and passed in Missouri and in Iowa in a modified form.

Two-cent fare bills were passed in Pennsylvania, Nebraska, Iowa, and New Jersey. A 2-cent fare bill was passed in this State, too, but was vetoed by Gov. Hughes, who sent a message of dissent explaining his reasons. New York, Wisconsin, Nebraska, New Jersey, and Indiana passed bills providing for public service commissions or increasing the power of existing Railroad Commissions. In Nebraska telegraph and telephone companies were included under the provisions of the Public Service Commission act, which in that State is somewhat more stringent than the laws passed by other States.

Socialistic Trend Legislation.

Massachusetts easily leads in legislation of a tendency toward Socialism, though the measures passed did not emanate from Socialists, but from either Democratic or Republican quarters. Much of the Massachusetts legislation is such, however, that it would be difficult to say whether it should be classed as Socialistic or broadly humanitarian. Nebraska, Kansas, and Missouri come next. In Nebraska scarcely a measure bearing the marks of Socialism failed of passage, though there is not a single outspoken Socialist a member of either house of the Legislature.

In Wisconsin, which has become the leader of all the States in the Union in the outspoken campaign of the Socialists to secure a new order of affairs, social and political, dozens of bills frankly Socialistic were introduced by the two Socialist Senators and the five Assemblymen of the same political color. All these measures were defeated, but the Wisconsin Socialists are nevertheless jubilant, because the serious consideration their bills received at the hands of conservative legislators prompts them in the belief that before long Wisconsin, at least, will have to figure on Socialism as a fact and not merely as a theory.

California, which in proportion to its population has the greatest Socialist vote, has seen a reaction in the growth of the party which, after doubling in number in three years, suddenly has begun to decline as rapidly as it grew. The fact that labor unionism has drawn heavily from its ranks, and that the Hearst Independence League, which draws practically its entire voting strength from the Socialists, has been busy in the State, are given as a reason by THE TIMES's correspondents for the rapid decline of the Socialist Party proper. The California Legislature was deluged with measures introduced in the interest of organized labor and of a somewhat Socialistic tendency. These bills were supported by the Socialists, and many were passed, while the Socialists and trades unionists in conjunction were enabled to kill many measures directed against labor.

Little Social Unrest in South.

The reports reaching THE NEW YORK TIMES from Southern States show a total absence of Socialistic legislation, or of any appreciable degree of social unrest. State and municipal ownership ideas have not reached the South. There is no Socialistic propaganda in any of the Southern States with the exception of Louisiana, where it centres in New Orleans. In the State of Maryland, and in its neighbor, Delaware, the Socialists are preparing to arouse public sentiment in favor of their doctrines. In Maryland the Socialists poll only 2½ per cent. of the entire registered vote of the State, but some slight growth is noticed. In Delaware, in the last election, 160 Socialist votes were cast out of a total of about 42,000. Of these, 150 were in Wilmington and the other ten in the rural districts of the same county.

In this State no Socialistic tendency was manifest in the work of the Legislature. There was much radical reform legislation in addition to the Public Service Commissions act, but practically all this legislation bore the mark of Gov. Hughes, and was passed on the strength of public confidence in the Governor, where it would not have had the slightest show had it emanated from either Socialistc or radical sources. The activity of the Independence League has caused a considerable falling off in the Socialist vote in the State, but the party lines are now in process of forming again.

In New Jersey many bills were introduced during the last session showing social unrest and extreme resentment against the trusts and large corporations, but, altogether, according to THE TIMES's correspondent, it cannot be said that Socialism has made any inroads on the New Jersey Legislature. The vote for many years has betokened a similar condition of the public mind through the victory of candidates who have run for office on an independent or reform platform. Socialism, as far as votes are concerned, has not made any headway in New Jersey. In 1904, Gubernatorial year, the New Jersey Socialists polled altogether 9,445 votes out of a total of 429,629. The next year the Socialist vote dropped to 7,501 of a total of 377,932, and again, in 1906, the Socialst vote was 7,431 out of a total of 364,464.

Utah, according to THE TIMES's correspondent at Salt Lake City, is as firmly controlled politically by the railroads as ever, and the legislation passed at the last session was reactionary, if anything. As a general thing, Utah is remarkably free from any tendency toward social unrest. The Mormon Church employs its great power toward keeping the people in ignorance regarding Socialism, where that can be done.

Observations in Other States.

Here is a summary of the observations made by TIMES's correspondents in other States:

Rhode Island—The Socialist Party in the State is apparently losing ground rather than gaining. The independent vote is becoming the deciding factor, but none of it goes to the Socialists.

Connecticut—There was a decided falling off in the Socialist vote last year. After seven months of strenuous work the Connecticut Legislature of this year has not a single Socialistic measure to show for its work.

Georgia—No such thing as Socialism in Georgia, politically speaking. The Socialists cast 20 votes in the entire State last Gubernatorial year. No social unrest and discontent is finding expression at primaries or polls. There is a growing sentiment in favor of municipal ownership of water and lighting plants.

Texas—Socialists have a weak organization in this State. Not a single one of their kind holds any office whatever in the State or any city of the State. There was no Socialistic, but some radical, anti-trust legislation.

Illinois—The cause of Socialism has no strength in Illinois. There have been spasmodic outbursts of Socialism. There has been no legislation of Socialistic trend, nor have any such bills been introduced at Springfield this year. In Chicago the party has been represented from time to time by one or two Aldermen, and twice a Social Labor Democrat has sat in the lower house from the Cook County district.

Colorado—Socialism is at present sliding along pretty close to the grass in Colorado. No member of the party is in any prominent official position. Socialists have no strong following in any city in this State. No member of the party is known to hold any municipal office. Nowhere is any city conducting experiments in municipal ownership.

North Carolina—Socialism has not yet reached this State.

West Virginia—There has been no legislation of even remote Socialistic tendency in this State. In some localities there is some public opinion trending in that direction, but it is mostly confined to talk and seldom finds expression at the polls.

New Hampshire—No legislation that could be called Socialistic was passed here by the New Hampshire General Court. No member of either branch was chosen as a Socialist or Labor Party man, and the legislative programme of the State Federation of Labor was very modest.

On the Wane in Montana.

Montana—Socialism is decidedly on the wane in Montana, judging from recent political events. The labor unions are strong, very strong, but their tendency is not Socialistic, anywhere near the degree noticeable three or four years ago.

North Dakota—There are few preachers of Socialism here, but through such active propaganda as these have carried on the Socialist vote has risen to 1,200 or 1,500 out of a total of 80,000. The recent Legislature enacted no measure of a Socialist dye. There are no Socialists in office as such. There is some slight reflection through the State of industrial unrest and of the anti-trust and anti-railroad sentiment generally prevailing, but social unrest does not appear.

Minnesota—Socialism has made some progress here during the last two years, as is shown by the increasing vote, but the last Legislature enacted none of the measures that have been advocated by the Socialists.

Nebraska—Socialistic ideas have been growing in Nebraska, though the Socialist Party has not made much progress. Socialism is yet a red flag to the Nebraska voter, yet he is coming to accept many of the principles of that party when they appear as part of the creed of the two dominant political factions. The idea of public ownership of public utilities has taken firm root in almost every city of the State. So far as known, not one Socialist holds an office in any county or municipality of this State.

Unrest Among Indiana Farmers.

Indiana—There were no avowed Socialists in the recent session of the Legislature, and the influence of that class, though apparent in some directions, was not of a very pronounced nature. There is marked unrest among the farmers, despite phenomenally high prices and much prosperity, and the same is true of some towns and villages. It was the farmer Senator and Representative, backed by the Representatives from the smaller towns and by Socialist propaganda, that were most insistent in their advocacy of anti-corporation legislation, which in most cases was enacted.

Kansas—Since the wane of the Populist Party in Kansas the tendency toward Socialism has been growing. Fifteen years ago there were but a few Socialists scattered over the State. To-day the Socialist vote is 280,000. The recent session of the Kansas Legislature, while it did not write into the new laws anything radically Socialistic, left the tinge of Socialism in many.

Missouri—The spirit of unrest flourishes in Missouri, and yet the Socialist Party is weak. It polls less than 12,000 votes in the whole State, but is growing. Socialistic sentiment in the dominant parties rather than Simon-Pure Socialistic effort is responsible for most of the radical legislation passed here this session.

August 11, 1907

TAFT NAMED; FIRST BALLOT

Throng in Galleries Vainly Makes a Great Demonstration for Roosevelt.

Special to The New York Times.

CHICAGO, June 18.—William Howard Taft of Ohio was nominated for the Presidency of the United States on the first ballot by the Republican Party assembled in convention here to-day. The roll was called in the midst of a deafening uproar and an attempt to stampede the convention for Roosevelt. The call was completed at 5:10, and at 5:16 Senator Lodge, the permanent Chairman of the convention, announced that Mr. Taft had received 702 votes. At 5:23, on the motion of Gen. Stewart L. Woodford of New York, the nomination was made unanimous. The convention then adjourned until 10 o'clock to-morrow morning.

For more than seven hours the delegates and 10,000 visitors had sweltered in the almost overpowering heat of the packed Coliseum. For many hours the task of nominating various candidates had been going on. Then at the close came the attempt at a stampede, and the ovation accorded President Roosevelt yesterday was repeated. Weary and warm though every one in the hall was, the tremendous outburst swept every one but the delegates and the Chairman from their feet, metaphorically, and had it not been for the fact that the delegates were not to be stampeded under any circumstances the result of the convention might have been different.

Delegates Not to be Stampeded.

As it was, there never was one minute when there was a chance of a real stampede; there never was an instant when Taft's nomination was in doubt. From first to last the machine worked to perfection, and nothing could have interfered with its action.

Except for the Roosevelt outburst, which followed close upon and was really a part of a demonstration in favor of Senator La Follette of Wisconsin, the whole proceedings of the session were marked with artificiality. The applause for Taft when his name was first mentioned was artificial to a large degree, coming only from those of the delegates who were of the Taft crowd, and from a few, a very few, people in the gallery. There was no spontaneity about it, and though it lasted fairly long, it was not to be compared to the enthusiasm manifested at the mention of the name of Roosevelt yesterday, nor to the outburst that followed later in the day.

This convention will probably be known for a long time to come as the most torpid gathering of its kind that was ever held.

A more disappointing convention to the novice could not well be imagined. It did not go wild when it was announced that Taft had obtained enough votes to give him the nomination. On the contrary, the long expected having happened, there was a round of cheers, and while the Ohio delegation did make a lot of noise, delegates from other sections of the country began immediately to leave the hall, and visitors in the gallery left by the hundreds.

June 19, 1908

BRYAN NAMED; FIRST BALLOT

Denver Convention Nominates Nebraskan in the Early Morning.

ANOTHER GREAT OUTBURST

Noise Is Kept Going for Seventy Minutes by Huge Crowd in the Hall.

Special to The New York Times.

DENVER, Friday, 3:05 A. M., (5:05 New York Time,) July 10.—William Jennings Bryan, twice nominated and twice defeated for the Presidency, was nominated for a third time by the Democratic National Convention early this morning.

The roll call on the nomination began at 8 A. M., (5 o'clock New York time.) The roll call had not proceeded more than four minutes before it was evident that Bryan was nominated.

The convention clock had been stopped at midnight Thursday to avoid the Friday "hoodoo."

A demonstration second only to that of Wednesday was given when Bryan's name was placed before the convention. It started at 9:06 o'clock, (11:06 New York time,) and it was 10:16, or seventy minutes later, before order was restored. It was necessary to turn out most of the lights in the hall before the Bryan boomers would give up their efforts to exceed the record of the day before.

After more than two days of wrangling over the platform the Committee on Resolutions was not ready to report at 7 o'clock, the hour set for the night session. The convention waited until 8:35 o'clock, and then was told that a report would not be made till midnight. A motion was carried to hear the nominating speeches, with the understanding that the vote on the Presidency would not be taken until the platform had been adopted.

Ignatius J. Dunn of Nebraska placed Mr. Bryan in nomination. When his speech was concluded the great outburst took place.

Gov. Johnson of Minnesota was placed in nomination by Congressman Hammond at 11:05. Immediately a big demonstration began for him, Georgia joining with Minnesota. Chairman Clayton tried to stop the cheering, but despite his efforts it went on for twenty-two minutes.

Judge Gray was placed in nomination by L. Irving Handy just before midnight. As the Resolutions Committee was ready to report the Delawarean got only a minute's cheering.

Gov. Haskell began reading the platform, on which the report was unanimous, at 12:02.

The report of the committee was adopted unanimously at 12:56, and after many seconding speeches had been made the ballot was taken.

July 10, 1908

TAFT WINS

William H. Taft will be the twenty-seventh President of the United States, having swept the country by a vote which will give him *314* ballots in the Electoral College against Mr. Bryan's *169,* or only *22* less than Mr. Roosevelt had in 1904. His majority will be *145.* William J. Bryan yesterday suffered his third and most crushing defeat in his twelve-year run for President of the United States.

To enforce his policies President Taft will have an overwhelmingly Republican Congress, the Senate being as strongly Republican as before, and the House increasing its Republican majority from *57* to *65.*

About every so-called doubtful State went Republican, though Indiana is still in doubt. It was noticeable that the majorities in the East were greater than those in the West. In New York, for instance, Taft beat the great Roosevelt majority of 1904, getting *187,902* majority, as against Roosevelt's *175,000.*

The greatest surprise of the election was the Republican victory in New York City, where Taft's majority was *9,378.* Never before this has this city gone Republican in a Presidential election except in 1900, when it voted for McKinley as against Bryan. Chanler's plurality in the city was *56,000.*

Taft's plurality on the popular vote is estimated at *1,098,000,* as against Roosevelt's plurality of *2,545,515* over Parker.

Bryan, however, has improved on Parker's run by carrying Missouri, Nevada, and apparently his own State of Nebraska, though later returns may change the last-named State's position in the Electoral College.

In his great sweep of this State Taft carried with him Gov. Hughes, though the Governor's majority fell far below his, being only *71,189.*

Speaker Cannon will be able to make the race to succeed himself, having downed his opponent in the Danville district by about *10,500* majority in spite of Samuel Gompers's efforts.

Morris Hillquit, the Socialist candidate for Congress in the Ninth New York District, was defeated by Republican votes which were cast for his opponent Judge Goldfogle.

A noticeable feature of the election was the increase of the Republican vote in the Southern States. In Florida, for example, it increased so much that early in the evening there was a report that the State had gone Republican. Everywhere in the Southern States along the Atlantic Coast there was this unusual Republican vote.

In Illinois, which Bryan's managers had claimed, there was a smashing vote against him. Cook County, where Roger Sullivan is supreme, went against him by *50,000.* The majority in the State is estimated at *170,000.*

Indiana is still in doubt, and it seems likely that Thomas R. Marshall, the Democratic candidate for Governor, has been elected, though the State may have cast its vote for Taft.

Maryland, which was claimed by the Democrats and almost conceded by the Republicans—actually conceded, in fact, by President Roosevelt—has gone Republican by a majority of about *5,000.* Kentucky is for Bryan by about *15,000*

The biggest surprise was in Senator La Follette's State of Wisconsin, where knifing of the ticket was freely predicted even by Republican observers, and where nobody looked to see Taft do more than squeeze through. He has bettered Roosevelt's 1904 majority there, and the La Follette men have apparently played fair.

Michigan may have elected a Democratic Governor. That State is still in doubt on its Gubernatorial ticket, though it has voted for Taft.

Connecticut's majority is as usual, and Representative Lilley has been elected Governor by *15,000.*

Taft carried his own State, Ohio, by *49,000,* but Harmon (Dem.) is elected Governor.

New Jersey went Republican by over *65,000.*

The city election was full of surprises, not the least being the victory here of Taft and Chanler. In Kings County McCarren made good by carrying it for Chanler by *5,241,* though it went for Taft by *22,500.* These extraordinary results led to the report that wholesale trading had been going on in the greater city.

Texas is actually in doubt on the Governorship. Cecil Lyon's prediction, at which everybody laughed at Chicago last June, that a Republican might be elected Governor this year, may come true. Col. Simpson, an old Confederate cavalryman, is Boss Lyon's candidate.

November 4, 1908

RESURGENT DEMOCRATS

A POLITICAL BLUNDER.

The Democrats Might Split the Republican Party on the Tariff.

To the Editor of The New York Times:

Was the Democratic party ever given such an opportunity for political regeneration as is hers to-day? With the Republican leaders almost avowedly breaking faith with the people, with the Payne tariff rates higher even that the Dingley rates, with protection being carried to extremes that Blaine, Garfield, and McKinley never dreamed of, what are the Democrats doing? Where is the fighting opposition that must precede a victory?

Throughout all this debate in the Senate not one Democratic Senator has risen up to fight for Democratic principles and to show the inequality of the proposed tariff. Bailey has urged his income tax, Simmons and Fletcher have urged protection, and all the rest have sat silent save for occasional questionings. And from

first to last Bryan has been as silent as the grave. It has remained for Republicans to attack the tariff, for example, Dolliver, Nelson, Clapp, McCumber, and Cummins. Has the Democratic Party ever been so humiliated? Is there no leadership, no fight, no opposition left? The Republicans are splitting on the tariff question. The difference in views between Aldrich and Dolliver, between the old leaders and the new, is as great as that which for years existed between Cleveland men and Bryanites.

And yet, not one Democrat has arisen to drive in the wedge. The party stands deaf, dumb, and blind to the first opportunity that has come its way in fourteen years, and the last probably for another decade—by the end of which time the party perhaps will be a memory.

H. A. HORWOOD.

New York, May 8, 1909.

May 16, 1909

WILSON POINTS WAY TO NEW DEMOCRACY

Old Ideal of "as Little Government as Possible" Outlived, He Declares.

ATTACKS ALDRICH TARIFF

Calls It a System of Favors—Utilities Commissions a Source of Graft, He Tells Plainfield Democrats.

Special to The New York Times.

PLAINFIELD, N. J., Oct. 29.—Dr. Woodrow Wilson, President of Princeton University, in the first political speech he has made for some time, spoke tonight before the Plainfield Democratic Club on "The Democratic Opportunity." Dr. Wilson said, in part:

"The Democratic Party is now facing an unusual opportunity and a very great duty. The party in power has become entangled with all sorts of interests, and may be said to have allied itself with something less than the Nation as a whole. The Democratic Party, on the other hand, is free from entanglements and is at liberty to choose policies suited to the National conditions as a whole. It is free to make a programme for the general good. But it should do this without allowing itself to be embarrassed by old formulas formulated for another age, which had other and very different questions to settle.

"Take the old ideal of 'as little government as possible.' The indisputable fact is that the Federal Government has in recent years been launched into many fields of activity even the existence of which previous generations did not foresee. I for one am very jealous of the separate powers and authority of the individual States of the Union. But it is no longer possible with the modern combinations of industry and transportation to discriminate the interests of the States as they could once be discriminated. Interests once local and separate have become unified and National. They must be treated by the National Government.

"Stated in general terms, our principle should be: Government not for the sake of success at whatever cost and the multiplication of material resources by whatever process, but for the sake of discriminating justice and the wholesome development as well as regulation of the national life.

"Apply these doctrines to tariff legislation. The original principle of protective tariffs in this country was that laid down by Alexander Hamilton. He thought always of the general development and never of the particular interests of those who were engaged for their own profits in furthering it.

"The principle upon which the Aldrich tariff is based is a radically different one, as sharply contrasted with the principle of Hamilton as private interest is contrasted with public benefit. The object of that tariff, and of those which immediately preceded it, is not the benefit of the country at large and the careful stimulation of its many and various industries, but the benefit of those engaged in the protected industries.

"The whole system is a system of favors, by which not the country at large is profited, but certain perfectly distinguishable beneficiaries of the Government and the party which grants the favors. The demoralization of the whole thing, its corrupting effect upon our politics. A day of reckoning upon this matter is at hand, and it will be an unjust reckoning, a mere reaction, unless we determine and insist upon the true principle of correction.

"What shall that principle be? Nothing else than the principle upon which the whole system was originally founded—namely, a studious attention to the general and public benefits to be conferred by it.

What we need is knowledge of the actual facts in respect of each industry and the honesty to act upon those facts.

"But how shall we act upon them? Certainly not by rapid and radical changes in our present tariffs, but by such a prolonged and steady change as will bring about an adaptation of the fiscal policy of the Government to the real needs and circumstances of our manufacturing and laboring classes, with a view ultimately to get upon this basis: the taxation for the support of the Government of things for which it will not be a real hardship to pay high prices, and throughout the whole process an honest seeking for the things which will yield the most revenue with the least burden to the people.

"Apply our principle of government to the trust question. We are at present trying the very hazardous experiment of regulating trusts by the compulsion of fines and penalties. These generally fall not upon the individuals responsible, but upon the stockholders. Fines also operate to take out of legitimate business large sums of money whose withdrawal embarrasses the general processes of trade and manufacture. It is a means of regulation which so far has certainly not accomplished its objects.

"The other means by which we seek control is the government of public service corporations through commissions. We have carried this method so far that we have virtually gone the length of dictating their management. We threaten them with penalties if they do not obey, the directions given them. These directions may force upon those corporations policies and measures which will render their business unprofitable, but the Government has calmly adopted the policy of rule even if it involves ruin. But the method is only in its infancy. The opportunities it offers for political influence and individual tyranny, which are the bases of graft, every man who is well read in the history of government can easily perceive.

"There is only one principle in regard to these matters which the Democratic Party can consistently or conscientiously adopt. It is this: That control shall not be managed in such a way as to increase the powers and temptations of those who administer government, but in such a way as shall make law supreme through judicial instrumentalities, by making it operate directly upon individuals and emphasizing in every item of legislation the responsibility of individuals.

"One conspicuous responsible person sent to the penitentiary for ignoring the public interest would do more to correct abuses than a thousand fines piled high upon one another, or a thousand corporate penalties for disobeying the orders of commissions."

October 30, 1909

DEMOCRATS SWEEP COUNTRY; WIN CONGRESS, MANY STATES

New York, New Jersey, Ohio, Massachusetts, Indiana and Connecticut Carried.

The Democratic Party carried the Union yesterday. The landslide put the historic Folger year, 1882, in the background and eclipsed the avalanche years of 1890 and 1892. In the language of Col. Theodore Roosevelt, the Democrats whipped the Republicans "to a frazzle" and put them "over the ropes."

Such traditionally Republican States as Massachusetts followed in Maine's lead by tremendous majorities. New Hampshire was long in doubt and finally elected Senator Bass, the Republican candidate for Governor, by a majority of only about 6,000.

New York took her place at the head of the procession, with a Democratic majority for John A. Dix of 64,074 and elected a Democratic Legislature. A Democratic Senator will succeed Chauncey M. Depew.

President Taft has got to face the one danger he most dreaded and which he besought the Republican voters to prevent—a hostile House of Representatives to nullify what remains of his legislative programme. The next House will be Democratic by a majority of 40. Whatever is to be done in the way of tariff reform will have to be done by mutual forbearance and agreement on the part of a Republican Senate and a Democratic House—unless, indeed, later returns should indicate the election of a Democratic Senate.

In the United States Senate the Democrats gain four seats certainly and probably seven.

The two great leaders of the Republican Party, Taft and Roosevelt, have received body blows. Their own States have voted for the opposition party. Harmon defeated Harding in Ohio by a great plurality, probably 40,000.

A most peculiar feature of the voting has been that in the big cities, New York excepted, the Republicans gained, while they lost in the country. In this State, for instance, the early returns from the up-State cities seemed to indicate Stimson's election. In Ohio Harmon, the Democratic candidate, lost heavily in the cities and gained in the country.

The reason is believed to be the hostility of the labor vote to the Democratic candidates. For instance, Gov. Harmon's interference with the strike in Columbus cost him thousands of votes in such labor centres as Hamilton and Franklin Counties.

Another striking feature of the election is the repudiation of Republican leaders in their own homes. Col. Roosevelt's own election district in Oyster Bay went Democratic by 60 votes. Sereno Payne, nominal author of the Tariff bill, lost his home city, Auburn, by 417. Vice President Sherman's home town, Utica, went Democratic by 3,700.

Ex-Gov. Odell's bailiwick, Newburg, turned a Republican majority of 600 into a Democratic majority of 600. Speaker Cannon's majority in the Danville district, which he represents in Congress, was reduced.

Senator Beveridge will cease to represent Indiana in the National Legislature. The Democrats have carried the State Legislature and will elect John W. Kern. Bryan's running mate in the campaign of 1908, to succeed Beveridge. "Mary of the vine-clad cottage" has lost out as an issue.

Woodrow Wilson has carried New Jersey by a majority of at least 34,000, and the outlook at the time of going to press is that the Democrats have also carried the Legislature.

November 9, 1910

PROGRESSIVES UNITE ON NATIONAL LINES

Direct Election of Senators, the Initiative, Referendum, and Recall Urged in Their Platform.

ROOSEVELT NOT A MEMBER

Although Asked to Join — Senator Bourne. Head of the League, Denies It's a Political Party.

Special to The New York Times.

WASHINGTON, Jan. 23.—Announcement was made here this afternoon of the organization of the National Progressive Republican League, composed, as its name implies, very largely of those Republicans in Congress and elsewhere throughout the country who have been referred to usually as "insurgents." Accompany the announcement of the birth of the League was a statement of the five cardinal points of its policy, which are:

Direct election of United States Senators.
Direct primaries for the nomination of all elective officers.
Direct election of delegates to National conventions, with opportunity for the voter to express his preference for Presidential and Vice Presidential nominees.
Amendments to State constitutions providing for the initiative, referendum, and recall.
A thoroughgoing corrupt practices act.
The platform does not declare whether the corrupt practices act called for is to be National, State or both.
Senator Jonathan Bourne of Oregon is the President of the League; Representative George W. Norris of Nebraska, First Vice President; Gov. Osborn of Michigan, Second Vice President, and Charles R. Crane of Chicago, Treasurer.
An Executive Committee will direct the affairs of the League composed of Senators Clapp and Bristow. Congressmen Hubbard of Iowa and Lenroot of Wisconsin; Gifford Pinchot, Congressman-elect Kent of California, George L. Record of New Jersey, and the officers of the League.
In a statement accompanying the announcement of the formation of the League Senator Bourne declares that the new organization is not to be a new political party. It is simply to fight for progressive legislation wherever such a fight is called for, in Congress or in State Legislatures. It is composed of Republicans, as its name implies, but the doors will be open to progressives of any political breed—provided they can obtain a majority vote of the members, and it will help progressive Democrats if they want its assistance, just as quickly and enthusiastically as it will help progressive Republicans.
The headquarters of the National League are to be maintained in Washington, but State leagues are to be organized as rapidly as may be.
Ever since the opening of Congress the project which culminates in this announcement has been under consideration among the progressive Republicans. Last Saturday night the final steps in organization were taken at a meeting held at the home of Senator La Follette here. In order to emphasize the contention of the league that it was not an organization in furtherance of the political ambitions of any man, Senators La Follette and Cummins, who are prominent in its affairs and had much to do with its formation, are not among its officers. It was foreseen that if either were to take an office it would at once be charged that the league had been formed as a means of furthering his Presidential aspirations.
The brief list of charter members includes practically all the progressives in the Senate and House, with about all the progressive Governors and a number of others who have made themselves prominent as progressives.
Col. Theodore Roosevelt was among those who were asked to join the League, but he has not yet done so. It was hardly expected that he would, because, as a matter of fact, no one can say surely now just where the League is going, or what will be the outcome of the movement. Among regular Republicans here the opinion was expressed forcibly this afternoon that it was an attempt to organize a new political party with especial intention to defeat the renomination and re-election of President Taft.
So far as Col. Roosevelt is concerned, it is known by those who are familiar with his views that he is not inclined to regard favorably an attempt to organize a new Republican Party. He has all along called himself a progressive as distinguished from an insurgent or a "radical." He has no sympathy with what he calls "wild radicalism," although his definition of that might differ decidedly from what some of the regular Republicans mean by the same term.

January 24, 1911

SOCIALISTS REJOICE OVER MANY VICTORIES

Head of State Ticket Leads in Mississippi, but Full Returns Will Probably Beat Him.

HAVE TEN MAYORS IN OHIO

Special to The New York Times.

CHICAGO, Nov. 8.—A rapidly forming labor-Socialist coalition, which they predict will destroy all old party lines and sweep the country in future Presidential campaigns, was described in Chicago today by National Socialist leaders, as they reviewed the final returns from yesterday's elections.

The showing in Chicago and Cook County, where 10 per cent. of the entire vote cast by all parties combined was polled by the Socialists, was declared to be as significant as any of the victories in the other States.

A new note of conservatism was sounded by the Socialist campaigners as they discussed the new element they are introducing to National politics. They warned their followers not to be so inflated over yesterday's showing that they would be unprepared for occasional reverses.

The wave which swept ten cities of Ohio, President Taft's home State, into Socialist control, and gave Socialists an important part in the administration of four other municipalities, was the subject of most of the discussion. The inroads made in the Democratic strength in Mississippi, where James T. Lester, the Socialist candidate for Lieutenant Governor, is leading his Democratic opponent, was declared almost as significant.

Gains in Pennsylvania, with Reading and Newcastle added to the list of cities having Socialist Governments, and Pittsburgh showing a gain of 100 per cent., were held by Socialists to be other important results upon which their predictions were based.

Their success in carrying Schenectady, N. Y.; gains of 25 to 30 per cent. in the Socialist vote in New York City, in spite of the bitter Republican fight against Tammany; the strong showing in Auburn, where one Socialist Alderman was elected and a second claims a victory, and other victories in cities scattered from the Atlantic to the Pacific, were pointed to as further evidence that the growing strength is not confined to any one section.

"I want to congratulate the Socialists of Chicago on the splendid showing made in the election yesterday," said Mayor Emil Seidel of Milwaukee. "We wanted to hear of a big vote in Chicago because the influence of a heavy poll would have in other cities in the country, and we are satisfied."

East Breaking from Moorings.

In referring to the showing made by

the Socialists in the East, especially in Ohio, New York, and Pennsylvania, he said:

"Nothing now can check the rapid growth of socialism. Even the conservative States are breaking loose from their moorings and drifting along with the

west toward socialism.

"The election shows that the harder our opponents fight us the more we grow."

The National Socialist Campaign Committee, whose headquarters are in Chicago, have made an appeal to the Socialist local branches throughout the country for funds to further the campaign of Job

Harriman for Mayor of Los Angeles, whom they expect to elect on Dec. 5, believing that the recent enfranchisement of women in California greatly strengthens their cause there. Funds are also solicited from the labor unions.

November 9, 1911

DEBS AND SEIDEL NOMINATED

Socialists Also Adopt Platform Denouncing Violence In Strikes.

INDIANAPOLIS, Ind., May 17.—Eugene Victor Debs of Terre Haute, Ind., was nominated to-day as a candidate for the Presidency of the United States by the National Socialists' Convention. Emil Seidel, former Mayor of Milwaukee, was named for the Vice Presidential nomination.

Mr. Debs was not in the hall when the result of the ballot was announced, but Mr. Seidel, in a few words, thanked the delegates and promised that he would make the campaign "as lively as the capitalist parties had ever seen."

Mr. Debs was opposed for the Presidential nomination by Mr. Seidel and Charles Edward Russell of New York. After the result of the first ballot, which gave Debs 165, Seidel 56, and Russell 54, had been given out, Mr. Seidel moved that the nomination be unanimous, and it was seconded by Mr. Russell.

Many candidates, including Kate Richards O'Hair of St. Louis and Anna Agnes

Mahley of Seattle were named for the second place, but only three, Mr. Seidel, John W. Slayton, Pennsylvania, and Dan Hogan, Arkansas, remained to be voted upon. Seidel, on the first ballot, received 159 votes; Hogan 73, and Slayton 24. Mr. Hogan's motion to make Mr. Seidel's nomination unanimous was seconded by Mr. Slayton.

The suffragists scored when they succeeded in amending the section of the constitution pertaining to membership in the party to read, "and unrestricted political rights for both sexes." The adoption of the amendment followed heated debate, and the voting down of a similar change in the constitution as introduced by a New York suffragist. The successful amendment was carried, 135 to 86.

The only other business was the adoption of a section of the constitution which places the party as taking a decided stand against "violence as a weapon of the working classes."

The session was the most heated of the convention and the amendment was not adopted until after several hours of debate, which frequently ran into personalities.

The new section reads:

Any member of the party who opposes political action or advocates crime, sabotage, or other methods of violence as a weapon

of the working class, to aid in its emancipation, shall be expelled from membership in the party. Political action shall be construed to mean participation in elections for public office and practical legislative and administrative work along the lines of the Socialist Party platform.

The section was opposed by the "direct action" forces who have been espousing the cause of the Industrial Workers of the World, and was favored by the so-called "yellow" or conservative faction in the party.

The report of the Constitution Committee was taken up seriatum. The most important changes made were regarding the size and duties of the National Committee and the initiation of the referendum. The new Constitution provides that the National Committee shall consist of the State Secretaries of all organized States and one additional for each State for every 3,000 members. The committee is to meet at least once a year and as often as called. The referendum must be initiated by a State organization instead of by a local one.

The new Constitution declares that no member of the Socialist Party shall vote in primary or regular election for any candidate other than Socialists indorsed and recommended by the party.

May 18, 1912

Sure Now of Victory for Taft.

By Congressman McKinley, the President's Manager.

Special to The New York Times.

CHICAGO, June 19.—President Taft will be renominated by the National Republican Convention now in session.

Theodore Roosevelt has been eliminated as a candidate. Two test votes, one yesterday and another forced by his leaders to-day, have demonstrated that he cannot be nominated. The delegates have repudiated his third-term pretensions.

His managers have resorted to every known method of political strategy, but without success. They have attempted combinations with other candidates; they have adroitly presented unfair and revolutionary plans of procedure under the pretense of honesty, and they have endeavored by every means to make Taft's delegates break their pledges and instructions. In the face of these desperate efforts, the Taft column has steadily grown. Taft's majority to-day was larger than it was yesterday.

The Roosevelt followers, knowing that their candidate can never get enough votes to give him a majority of the Convention, are now seeking in hopeless and discouraged fashion for another leader. Their search will be in vain. President Taft's demonstrated majority represents delegates who have come to Chicago determined to renominate him and they will not be swerved from that purpose. They have shown their loyalty and devotion to the President upon two occasions and their solidity was not in the least affected by a deliberate attempt to stampede the Convention through a carefully planned demonstration. They gave their answer to the demonstration by casting more votes to-day than they did yesterday.

They have shown that they propose to remain with the President until his renomination is an accomplished fact and they will receive accessions to their ranks from those who have been temporarily carried away by a noisy, braggadocio campaign. The balloon-like character of the campaign has twice been punctured by decisive majority votes.

The Southern colored delegates instructed for Taft are carrying out their instructions with courage and fidelity, in spite of money and political promises. They have shown a laudable regard for loyalty to party pledges.

Roosevelt not only lost in votes to-day, but his delegates indulged in forty minutes of continuous cheering for Gov. Hadley, one of his campaign managers, showing a decided tendency to desert the Roosevelt standard.

Roosevelt's repeated threat to bolt has not materialized, and statements are made by many of his leaders that should a bolt be attempted, it will not be participated in.

The solidarity of President Taft's lines and the wavering weakness of the Roosevelt forces tell their own story of victory for the President and the bursting of the Roosevelt bubble.

WILLIAM B. McKINLEY.

June 20, 1912

ROOSEVELT NAMED AS CANDIDATE BY BOLTERS

Roosevelt Delegates Go from the Regular to Rump Convention.

GOV. JOHNSON PRESIDES

Scores the National Committee as Thieves and Promises Them a Lesson.

NEW PARTY ON RUINS OF OLD.

Prendergast Makes the Nominating Speech He Had Prepared for Regular Convention.

COMMANDMENT AS PLATFORM

It Is "Thou Shalt Not Steal" Applied to All the Affairs of Life.

WIFE AND DAUGHTERS THERE

News That Bolting Convention Was to be Held Drew a Great Crowd and the Police Reserves.

Special to The New York Times.

CHICAGO, June 22.—Col. Roosevelt has at last openly broken off all connection with the Republican Party as represented in the National Convention.

He was nominated for President on an independent ticket to-night in the dying hours of the Republican National Con-

vention in which he had met a defeat.

The followers of Col. Roosevelt gathered in Orchestra Hall, less than a mile from the Coliseum, and pledged their support to the former President. In accepting the nomination, Col. Roosevelt appealed to the people of all sections, regardless of party affiliations, to stand with the founders of the new party, one of whose cardinal principles, he said, was to be "Thou Shalt Not Steal."

The informal nomination of Col. Roosevelt was said to be chiefly for the purpose of effecting a temporary organization. Beginning to-morrow, when a call is to be issued for a State convention in Illinois, the work of organization will be pushed forward rapidly, State by State. At a later time, probably early in August, it is intended that a National convention shall be held.

Col. Roosevelt, in accepting the nomination to-night, said he did so on the understanding that he would willingly step aside if it should be the desire of the new party when organized to select another standard bearer.

Prendergast Presents His Name.

The speech nominating Col. Roosevelt was made by Controller William Prendergast of New York, who was to have presented the Colonel's name to the regular convention. Dean William Draper Lewis of the University of Pennsylvania Law School, who was to have made one of the seconding speeches, delivered to-night the address which he had prepared for the Republican Convention.

Representatives of twenty-two States composed the Notification Committee which informed Col. Roosevelt of his nomination, and in a sense stood sponsors for the movement. The committee consisted of Controller Prendergast of New York, Meyer Lissner of California, former Congressman Richmond Pearson of North Carolina, Frank Knox of Michigan, Matthew Hale of Massachusetts, A. R. Garford of Ohio, David Browning of Kentucky, Everard Bierer, Jr., of Utah, Walter Thompson of Vermont, Judge Oscar R. E. Hundley of Alabama, Judge Ben B. Lindsey of Colorado, Andrew R. Rahn of Minnesota, Judge Stevens of Iowa, Judge W. S. Lander of North Dakota, William Allen White of Kansas, John C. Greenway of Arizona, ex-Gov. John Franklin Fort of New Jersey, Col. E. C. Carrington of Maryland, Pearl Wight of Louisiana, Lorenzo Dow of Washington, Walter Clyde Jones of Illinois, and Frank Frantz of Oklahoma.

Although no public announcement was made until very late in the day of the meeting, which was expected to result in the formation of a new party, word of the plan was then flashed about the city, and before the doors were opened a crowd had collected, extending for nearly a block on Michigan Avenue. Police reserves were summoned to handle the crowd.

When the doors were thrown open the people streamed in quickly, filling all the seats except those reserved for the Roosevelt delegates to the Republican National Convention, their alternates, and the Roosevelt delegates to whom seats in the convention were refused.

Telegraph and telephone linemen were rushed to Orchestra Hall to install wires over which news of the nomination of Col. Roosevelt was to be flashed out. A huge painting of Col. Roosevelt was hung behind the stage, which was all that was done in the way of decorations.

Roosevelt Men Gather.

Francis J. Heney, one of the most radical of Roosevelt's supporters arrived at 9:40 and as he stepped on the platform was given a hearty cheer. There were cries of "Where is Teddy?"

As the time passed the crowd in the balcony and galleries grew impatient. It broke into applause whenever there was any excuse for a demonstration. Word received from the Coliseum that President Taft had been placed in nomination was received in silence. A moving picture concern set up a machine on the rear of the platform.

Mrs. Roosevelt, Mrs. Nicholas Longworth, and Miss Ethel Roosevelt are occupying a box.

George P. Brown and Edgar Keith of the Young Men's Roosevelt League got an enthusiastic greeting as they appeared on the stage.

At 10 o'clock the meeting had not been called to order, and the crowd began to shout:

"We want Teddy."

The California delegates arrived at 10 o'clock, headed by Gov. Johnson, and were received with a great outburst of applause. Medill McCormick and Gifford Pinchot were the next to get to the hall.

The crowd outside the hall at this time was tremendous, and the police had their hands full keeping order.

Once the crowd rushed an alley and was driven back after a hard struggle. Gov. Johnson was enthusiastic and said that Roosevelt would be the big man in the coming fight.

"He will break the solid South and

be elected despite all the bosses," he declared.

Perkins Encounters Trouble.

When the Roosevelt family appeared Mrs. Roosevelt and Mrs. Longworth waved and smiled a welcome in recognition of the cheers. While this demonstration was going on some of the Ohio delegation arrived and received a tumultuous welcome.

Mississippi Roosevelt delegates entered the hall fresh from a meeting in their headquarters, and announced the election of S. D. Redmond of Jackson as the State's National Committeeman of the new party. Massachusetts delegates with their cry," Massachusetts, Roosevelt 18, first, last, and all the time," next arrived.

When George W. Perkins started to mount the steps to the stage a policeman stopped him, and he had some difficulty in explaining his right to a stage seat. Mrs. Roosevelt, who witnessed the encounter, was observed to laugh heartily.

When the hall had been packed the entire audience joined in singing "America," after which the Roosevelt delegates greeted Gov. Johnson as he opened the formal part of the meeting. The Governor was preparing to speak when the Oklahoma delegation arrived. By this time the non-arrival of the Pennsylvania delegation was causing comment.

Gov. Johnson's Speech.

"To any man with red blood in his veins," said Gov. Johnson, "it's always a pleasure to fight a fraud, and especially to fight a fraudulent convention.

"The delegates present represent a majority of the legally elected delegates to the National Republican Convention. They propose to do right here and now just what they were elected to do."

The Governor's speech was interrupted with a wild burst of cheering.

"We came here with the mandate of the people of California. You came here with the like design to carry out, not the will of a rotten boss in Pennsylvania or a crooked one in New York, or a United States Senator in Massachusetts, but to carry out the mandate of the people to nominate Theodore Roosevelt.

"By a fraudulent vote he has been robbed of what was his. We delegates, free and untrammeled, have come here to nominate him to-night."

These words brought the great audience to its feet with a shout and for some time there was an uproar of applause.

People Will Take Up Fight, He Says.

"The time has gone by when in this country any self-constituted representative of the people can deny to the people that which is theirs," Gov. Johnson continued. "The time has passed when men can foist by chicane or unfair means a candidate upon the people whom the people don't want.

"So we have come here to-night to right a wrong, and just as certain as we are here to-night the people will rule. Every man who embarks in this course understands full well the responsibility which is his, recognizes the obstacles to be overcome, but we've learned out in the West that whenever there is a great wrong to be righted, the people will take up the fight and win it.

A New Party on the Ruins of the Old

"Beyond the mere personality of the candidate," Gov. Johnson continued, "there is much to interest every person in this movement. It has come out of the West, stalking toward benighted New York, and endeavoring even in darkest Philadelphia to make understood the principle upon which this Republic was founded. This principle was trampled under foot at the Republican National Convention. Then it was that the people of all this country rebelled.

"A National committee has endeavored to assassinate the Republican party. If it has succeeded, there are left enough patriotic, honest citizens to erect upon the ruins another party that represents progress. That is the main purpose that brings us here."

Gov. Johnson described the campaign of Col. Roosevelt against the bosses and clared that the delegates assembled proposed to "see that Mr. Roosevelt gets his reward." He then introduced Senator Clapp of Minnesota, who read the resolution nominating Col. Roosevelt. It was adopted with a cheer. The resolution follows:

The Call for the Candidate.

We, delegates and alternates to the Republican National Convention, representing a clear majority of the voters of the Republican Party in the Nation, and representing a clear majority of the delegates and alternates legally elected to the convention, in meeting assembled, make the following declaration:

We were delegated by a majority of the Republican voters of our respective districts and States to nominate Theodore Roosevelt in the Republican Convention as the candidate of our party for President, and thereby carry out the will of the voters as expressed at the primaries. We have earnestly and conscientiously striven to execute the commission intrusted to us by the party voters.

For five days we have been denied justice in the National convention. This result has been accomplished by the action of the now defunct National Committee in placing upon the preliminary roll of the convention and thereby seating upon the floor of the convention a sufficient number of fraudulently elected delegates to control the proceedings of the convention. These fraudulent delegates, once seated, have by concerted action with one another put themselves upon the permanent roll, where they constitute an influence sufficient to control the convention and defeat the will of the party as expressed at the primaries.

We have exhausted every known means to head off this conspiracy, and to prevent this fraud upon the popular will, but without success.

We were sent to this convention bearing the most specific instructions to place Theodore Roosevelt in nomination as the candidate of our party for President, and we, therefore, deem it to be our duty to carry out those instructions in the only practical and feasible way remaining open to us; .

Therefore, be it Resolved, That we, representing the majority of the voters of the Republican Party, and of the delegates and the alternates legally elected to the National Republican Convention, in compliance with our instructions from the party voters, hereby nominate Theodore Roosevelt as the candidate of our party for the office of President of the United States; and we call upon him to accept such nomination in compliance with the will of the party voters;

And, be it further Resolved, That a committee be appointed by the Chair to forthwith notify Col. Roosevelt of the action here taken, and request him to appear before us in this hall as soon as convenient.

June 23, 1912

Convention Deadlock Is Broken on Forty-sixth Ballot at 3:30 P. M.

Gov. Woodrow Wilson of New Jersey

Democratic Candidate for the Presidency.

Special to The New York Times.
BALTIMORE, July 2.—Woodrow Wilson was nominated for President on the forty-sixth ballot this afternoon at 3:30 o'clock. The vote was never announced, for it was made unanimous before the clerk could finish counting it up, but on the last roll call Wilson had received 990 votes to 84 for Champ Clark and 12 for Judson Harmon

The first ballot of the convention was

taken in the early hours of Saturday morning, after an all-night session, and the convention had remained deadlocked through Saturday and Monday.

The final ballot was preceded by a sort of love feast in which the spokesmen for the other candidates pledged their hearty and enthusiastic support to Wilson, despite the fact that he had not been nominated. New York went so far as to propose, through Representative Fitzgerald, that the forty-sixth ballot be dispensed with and that Wilson be nominated by acclamation.

The only reason why this was not done was that the supporters of Clark desired to place themselves on record once more—for the purpose of demonstrating their love for "Old Champ Clark," as their spokesmen all called him.

It was 12:05 when Chairman James ascended the platform and called the convention to order in the broken and husky tones which are all that remain of the voice that a week ago sounded like a forest storm.

He immediately called for the forty-third ballot. Mr. James was weary and

worn, and although he kept himself under admirable control and won the respect of everybody for his patience and firmness in dealing with the hard task before him, he had none of that patience for the people who clogged the aisles and made the voices of the clerks inaudible.

Trouble Restoring Order.

"Please cease conversation or get out," he shouted at them, "to some place where you can talk without disturbing the convention."

Forty times during the day he had to suspend the proceedings to order the police to clear the aisles. Those wonderful Baltimore policemen only grinned sheepishly each time, and now and then one would timidly lay his hand on the shoulder of some disturber and then take it off again when he saw the disturber paid no attention to him.

This forty-sixth ballot was to be the ballot whereon Illinois was to start an expected stampede. Everybody was waiting for the vote of that State. It was, indeed, the vote of Illinois which made Wilson's nomination sure, but the other candidates managed to hold on for two more ballots, the forty-fourth and forty-fifth.

July 3, 1912

ROOSEVELT NAMED SHOWS EMOTION

"Of Course, I Accept," He Tells Progressives Who Give Him Third Term Nomination.

JOHNSON FOR SECOND PLACE

Dramatic Scene as Candidates Join Delegates in Singing of the Battle Hymn.

TAKE UP ROLE OF CRUSADERS

Colonel, Much Affected, and Happy, Plans to Open a Vigorous Campaign.

Special to The New York Times.
CHICAGO, Ill., Aug. 7.—Col. Theodore Roosevelt has attained the goal of his ambition. Before the first National Convention of his new party passed into history to-night it handed him on a silver platter the honor that Washington and Jefferson modestly declined and Ulysses S. Grant, though crowned with a hero's laurels, sought in vain. He was nominated as a third-term candidate for President of the United States.

Hiram W. Johnson, the militant and Progressive Governor of California, who was a Republican until the Republican Convention, six weeks ago, refused Col. Roosevelt the coveted glory of a third term, was chosen as his running mate. Both nominations were made by acclamation under a suspension of the convention rules and amid scenes which fluctuated strangely between the solemn and impressive and the merely spectacular and melodramatic.

The closing scenes of the first National Convention of the Progressive Party were unlike the scenes that have marked the closing of any National Convention within the memory of living politicians of any party. Amid an ovation that was as striking and sincere as it was impressive the two candidates were brought out on the platform to face the delegates and to deliver in their hearing, and with crowded galleries looking on, their pledges to fight manfully for the principles and policies of this new party for which it is claimed that it will usher in a new dispensation in politics and in public life. Both nominees, but the Colonel especially, seemed deeply affected as they stood face to face with the men and women who are to shape the destinies of the new party and who had selected them as their standard bearers to do "battle for the Lord."

Tremor in Colonel's Voice.

There was a suspicious tremor in the Colonel's voice as he acknowledged the nomination. Nor was it strange that he and his running fate should display such evidence of feeling. Wave upon wave of emotion swept over the audience as men and women joined in singing the stirring patriotic and partly religious airs which the band played. It was more like a Methodist consecration meeting than a political gathering.

It was after the Colonel's platform embodying the vast scheme for "social and industrial justice," that he has advocated in recent public utterances, had been adopted, and after a dozen men had made nominating and seconding speeches of varying length for Gov. Johnson, that Senator Albert J. Beveridge of Indiana, Permanent Chairman of the convention, declared that Col. Roosevelt and Gov. Johnson had been duly nominated for President and Vice President, respectively.

It was nearly 7 o'clock, and the delegates and spectators had been through a long and wearing day of speeches and routine business, but there was no sign of apathy in the tremendous cheer that broke when it was proclaimed from the platform that the most important business of the convention had been completed and that the hat of the new party was in the ring.

August 8, 1912

DEBS CLASSIFIES THE NEW HYBRID

Reactionary, Capitalistic, and a Mere Trap for Votes, Is the Bull Moose Party.

To the Editor of The New York Times:
The most significant thing about the Roosevelt Progressive Convention is that it represented hundreds of thousands of men who have voted the Republican ticket all their lives, and who have now quit the Republican Party forever. The progressive tendency here manifested can never be checked, but will become more and more pronounced until it finds expression in socialism.

So far as the Progressive Party itself is concerned it contains too many diverse and conflicting economic elements, and its platform is too much of a hodge-podge to give it the character and stability of a great National party. It is built largely upon the personality of one man, and no great party has ever been reared upon that kind of a foundation.

The really progressive planks in the Progresive platform were taken bodily from the Socialist platform, and even the red flag of socialism was appropriated, or at least imitated, by the red bandana of the Roosevelt followers.

As the leader of the Bull Moose Party Mr. Roosevelt must be judged by his performances and not by his pledges. He was President almost eight years, and how he dealt with the trust evil is well known to the country. It is especially well known to the trusts themselves, who financed his campaign for the nomination and are now financing the campaign for his election.

The Progressive Party as a party is not only not progressive but it is reactionary. In the aggregate it is a middle class protest against trust domination. The middle class will furnish the votes, and the trusts, in the event of Roosevelt's election, will take care of the administration.

There is no doubt that Mr. Roosevelt and his new party will start off with a great hurrah and make considerable noise during the campaign. There will be plenty of trust funds available, and with such substantial inspiration any kind of a campaign could be made a howling success. But men and women who do their own thinking and who know why political parties are organized and what they stand for, will not be deceived by the Bull Moose Party, which is neither fish, flesh nor fowl. At one end it is going to head off the trusts, and at the other end it is going to head off socialism. As a matter of fact Mr. Roosevelt has shrewdly seized upon the prevailing popular unrest and has baited his platform like a trap to catch the votes of the discontented people.

There is no room in this country for such a hybrid aggregation as the Bull Moose Party. It corresponds to the Liberal Party of Great Britain, which professed to be organized to represent the common people, and especially the working class, and turned out to be the most reactionary party in that country. If the workingmen of this country would profit by the bitter experience of workingmen in the old country, they would better give a wide berth to Mr. Roosevelt and his Progressive Party.

At bottom the Progressive Party is a capitalist class party. It stands for the present capitalist system, aiming only to mitigate some of its most glaring evils. There is nothing in the record of Mr. Roosevelt, its candidate for President, and nothing in the platform upon which he stands, some of the planks of which he denounced as treason and anarchy when he was President, that will appeal to Socialists, or to the intelligence of the working class.   EUGENE V. DEBS.
Terre Haute, Ind., Aug. 10, 1912.

August 14, 1912

WILSON WINS

He Gets 409 Electoral Votes; Roosevelt, 107, and Taft, 15.

Woodrow Wilson was elected President yesterday and Thomas R. Marshall Vice President by an Electoral majority which challenged comparison with the year in which Horace Greeley was defeated by Grant. Until now that year has always been the standard of comparison for disastrous defeats, but the downfall of the Republican Party this year runs it a close second.

The apparent results at 4 o'clock this morning gave Wilson **409** Electoral votes, Roosevelt **107,** and Taft **15.**

Wilson carried 38 States, Roosevelt 6, and Taft 4.

The Republican Party is wiped off the map. Nearly everywhere Taft ran third, with Roosevelt capturing a large majority of the old Republican vote, and in many States Taft's vote was almost negligible.

New York gave Wilson a plurality over Taft of about 206,000. Wilson's vote in the State was 698,000, Taft's 493,000, and Roosevelt's 419,000.

The Democratic plurality in the House of Representatives will not be less than **157,** and the United States Senate will probably be Democratic also.

The Democrats swept New York, electing Sulzer Governor, with Hedges running second and Straus a poor third.

Throughout the night the most interesting features were the fluctuations in Illinois and Pennsylvania, the returns from which every minute or two put first one candidate and then another in possession of the two States. This morning it is apparently certain that Roosevelt has carried them both.

New Jersey produced a majority of about **50,000** for Wilson over Roosevelt, and the Democrats have apparently gained three Congressmen. The Legislature is overwhelmingly Democratic, insuring the election of a Democrat to succeed Senator Briggs and a Democratic Governor to succeed Wilson.

In Idaho, where Senator William E. Borah is running for re-election as a Republican, though a Progressive at heart, the Legislature is badly split.

There is a close race for the Senate in Oregon, with Senator Bourne, who ran independently, utterly out of it.

Maine went for Wilson by probably 7,500, with Roosevelt second. The indications are that Wilson has 47,500, Roosevelt 40,000, and Taft 27,000.

The returns from California, which Roosevelt has been expected to carry, are naturally meagre, owing to the three hours' difference in time to New York, but Wilson has carried San Francisco by 20,000 and the State seems to have gone for Wilson. The reason, of course, is that the Taft Republicans, having no opportunity to vote for candidates of their own under the California law, have voted in a body for Wilson.

Ohio has gone overwhelmingly for Wilson, electing Cox (Dem.) for Governor. President Taft's defeat in his own State was as complete as Col. Roosevelt's in his State.

Massachusetts's not only went for Wilson by a great majority, but for the first time in her history she elected a Democratic State ticket and a Democratic Legislature. This means a Democratic Senator from the Bay State in the place of Winthrop Murray Crane.

One of the features of the election was the heavy vote Roosevelt polled in the South, particularly Alabama and Georgia. At one time it seemed as if Congressman Underwood, the Democratic leader in the House, might be defeated because of the heavy vote for the Bull Moose in his district. The first three counties to be heard from in Georgia reported that Roosevelt had carried them.

Iowa has apparently gone for Roosevelt by between 4,000 and 5,000, despite Gov. Cummins's failure to take any active part in the campaign after Mr. Roosevelt's failure to take his advice about not running a State ticket.

Nebraska, which had been expected to cast an overwhelming majority for the Democrats since Mr. Bryan took an active part in the campaign, did not do so well as had been expected. Wilson has apparently carried the State, but the fight over both the Senatorship and the Governorship is close, and it is possible that Senator Brown, (Rep.) who was looked upon as a sure loser, may win.

"Uncle Joe" Cannon went down to defeat in the Danville district, and will be missing from the Capitol for the first time since his defeat in 1890, the only other defeat he has ever met with since he began representing that district in the 70's of the last century.

Roosevelt and Taft each carried their home towns handsomely. Oyster Bay went for Roosevelt by a majority of 292, giving him 510, Wilson, 218, and Taft, 67. Gov. Wilson's birthplace, Staunton, Va., gave him 632, Taft, 287, and Roosevelt, 65.

In Vermont Taft won by 924 votes, but Roosevelt is close behind him.

New Hampshire is Democratic. Wilson carried Connecticut by nearly 7,000, and Baldwin was re-elected Gevornor.

Victor L. Berger, the Socialist Congressman from Milwaukee, is defeated by William H. Stafford, the Republican candidate. His majority was over **2,000.**

In New York City Wilson defeated Roosevelt by 123,000, but Roosevelt had 59,000 more than Taft.

Wilson lost 6,000 votes in Erie because of the double ballot. They have voting machines there, and that many voters pushed the knob for Sulzer, but did not push the knob for Wilson, forgetting that both knobs had to be pushed.

November 6, 1912

REPUBLICANS VOTE DELEGATE REFORMS

Special to The New York Times.
WASHINGTON, Dec. 16.—The Republican National Committee, in formal session at the New Willard Hotel to-day, decided to proceed direct, without the holding of a special national convention, to the reorganization of the national machinery of the party.

Without a dissenting vote the committee resolved, subject to approval by two-thirds of the Republican States of 1908, to so change the basis of representation in national conventions as to reduce the number of delegates from the South, a fruitful cause of dissatisfaction in the party for the last thirty years. The committee also decided to give full recognition to the principle of the primary in the election of delegates to national conventions.

The action taken to-day was in full accord with the conclusions reached by the members of the committee at the Hills dinner last night.

December 17, 1913

Text of Hughes's Message, Accepting the Nomination, and Attacking the Wilson Administration

WASHINGTON, June 10.—Following is the text of the message of acceptance sent by Charles E. Hughes to the Republican National Convention at Chicago:

Washington, D. C., June 10, 1916.

Mr. Chairman and Delegates:

I have not desired the nomination. I have wished to remain on the bench. But in this critical period in our national history, I recognize that it is your right to summon and that it is my paramount duty to respond. You speak at a time of national exigency, transcending merely partisan considerations. You voice the demand for a dominant, thoroughgoing Americanism with firm protective upbuilding policies, essential to our peace and security; and to that call, in this crisis, I cannot fail to answer with the pledge of all that is in me to the service of our country. Therefore I accept the nomination.

I stand for the firm and unflinching maintenance of all the rights of American citizens on land and sea. I neither impugn motives nor underestimate difficulties. But it is most regrettably true that in our foreign relations we have suffered incalculably from the weak and vacillating course which has been taken with regard to Mexico—a course lamentably wrong with regard to both our rights and our duties. We interfered without consistency; and while seeking to dictate when we were not concerned, we utterly failed to appreciate and discharge our plain duty to our own citizens.

At the outset of the Administration the high responsibilities of our diplomatic intercourse with foreign nations were subordinated to a conception of partisan requirements, and we presented to the world a humiliating spectacle of ineptitude. Belated efforts have not availed to recover the influence and prestige so unfortunately sacrificed; and brave words have been stripped of their force by indecision.

I desire to see our diplomacy restored to its best standards and to have these advanced; to have no sacrifices of national interest to partisan expediencies; to have the first ability of the country always at its command here and abroad in diplomatic intercourse; to maintain firmly our rights under international law; insisting steadfastly upon all our rights as neutrals, and fully performing our international obligations; and by the clear correctness and justness of our position and our manifest ability and disposition to sustain them to dignify our place among the nations.

I stand for an Americanism that knows no ulterior purpose; for a patriotism that is single and complete. Whether native or naturalized, of whatever race or creed, we have but one country, and we do not for an instant tolerate any division of allegiance.

I believe in making prompt provision to assure absolutely our national security. I believe in preparedness, not only entirely adequate for our defense with respect to numbers and equipment in both army and navy, but with all thoroughness to the end that in each branch of the service there may be the utmost efficiency under the most competent administrative heads. We are devoted to the ideals of honorable peace. We wish to promote all wise and practicable measures for the just settlement of the international disputes.

In view of our abiding ideals, there is no danger of militarism in this country. We have no policy of aggression; no lust for territory, no zeal for strife. It is in this spirit that we demand adequate provision for national defense, and we condemn the inexcusable neglect that has been shown in this matter of first national importance. We must have the strength which self-respect demands, the strength of an efficient nation ready for every emergency.

Our preparation must be industrial and economic as well as military. Our severest tests will come after the war is over. We must make a fair and wise readjustment of the tariff, in accordance with sound protective principle, to insure our economic independence and to maintain American standards of living. We must conserve the just interests of labor, realizing that in democracy patriotism and national strength must be rooted in even-handed justice. In preventing, as we must, unjust discriminations and monopolistic practices, we must still be zealous to assure the foundations of honest business. Particularly should we seek the expansion of foreign trade. We must not throttle American enterprise here or abroad, but rather promote it and take pride in honorable achievements.

We must take up the serious problems of transportation, of interstate and foreign commerce, in a sensible and candid manner, and provide an enduring basis for prosperity by the intelligent use of the constitutional powers of Congress, so as adequately to protect the public on the one half, and, on the other, to conserve the essential instrumentalities of progress.

I stand for the principles of our civil service laws. In every department of government the highest efficiency must be insisted upon. For all laws and programs are vain without efficient and impartial administration.

I cannot within the limits of this statement speak upon all the subjects that will require attention. I can only say that I fully indorse the platform you have adopted.

I deeply appreciate the responsibility you impose. I should have been glad to have that responsibility placed upon another. But I shall undertake to meet it, grateful for the confidence you express. I sincerely trust that all former differences may be forgotten and that we may have united effort in a patriotic realization of our national need and opportunity.

I have resigned my judicial office and I am ready to devote myself unreservedly to the campaign.

CHARLES E. HUGHES.

June 11, 1916

ROOSEVELT, NAMED BY MOOSE, DECLINES; HE'S 'OUT OF POLITICS'

MOOSE ANGRY AND BITTER

Convention Ends in Gloom After Long Fight for Roosevelt.

NAME HIM AMID CHEERS

Three Minutes Afterward They Hear of the Republican Stampede to Hughes.

Special to The New York Times.

CHICAGO, June 10.— After having nominated Theodore Roosevelt of New York for President and John M. Parker of Louisiana for Vice President, and having listened to a communication from Colonel Roosevelt, in which was embodied a conditional refusal to lead the fight, the Progressive convention dispersed at 5 o'clock this afternoon.

It was a thoroughly resentful and indignant, if not a disheartened body of men, that filed out of the Auditorium, but, apparently, they were determined that the third party must keep to the middle of the road at all costs.

The Progressive leaders had been engaged all day in a dramatic struggle with a convention plainly out of sympathy with all plans for reconciliation with the Republicans not involving the nomination of Colonel Roosevelt on the Republican ticket as well as on the Progressive. They did not dare spring the Colonel's message on the convention until the work of the final day was done and it was ready to adjourn. Then, as it was read, it came as a stunning blow to the men who had burned all their political bridges behind them four years ago to join the Colonel in his exodus and who by this time have had more than enough of their sojourn in the wilderness.

Silent, Cheerless Procession.

At the closing session of the convention there had been in evidence the first flickering away of the old Bull Moose spirit which was so conspicuous in the earlier stages of the convention. The delegates and spectators who had sat through it all did not have time to realize what it all meant before the final gavel fell and the band broke into the solemn strains of "America." The Progressives are much given to fervent singing, but even the cherished strains of that old melody held no lure for them. The Colonel's message had taken all song out of them, and they started for the doors a silent and cheerless procession. Some were complaining bitterly that after all their sacrifices, the Colonel was preparing "to run out on them."

Many of the delegates went straight from the Auditorium to the nearest telegraph offices. Tonight, and for days to come, Colonel Roosevelt will be bombarded with messages, urging it upon him as a duty to run, in language probably more direct than any to which he has been accustomed, from members of his Bull Moose flock. Everybody here seems to realize that the Colonel's "conditional refusal," hinging on the attitude of Justice Hughes with regard to Americanism and preparedness, might just as well have been made absolute, especially in the light of the published statement from Justice Hughes accepting the nomination and outlining his position on the issues.

Colonel Roosevelt's message was carried to the convention by John W. McGrath, his private secretary. It was read by Raymond Robins, who presided. Amid tense silence the convention listened. It was what it had been waiting for all afternoon. When the final session began announcement was made that the Colonel should be heard from during recess, and that his communication would be read before the final adjournment.

"I am now going to read to this convention a statement from Theodore Roosevelt," said Chairman Robins. "In accordance with a lifelong practice, he refuses to act hastily in a matter of importance to all the people of this country. He wants to hear from the people first, and I imagine he has heard from them by this time."

Then Mr. Robins read the following:

To the Progressive Convention: I am very grateful for the honor you confer upon me by nominating me as President. I cannot accept it at this time. I do not know the attitude of the candidate of the Republican Party toward the vital questions of the day. Therefore, if you desire an immediate decision, I must decline the nomination. But if you prefer it, I suggest that my conditional refusal to run be placed in the hands of the Progressive National Committee.

If Mr. Hughes's statements, when he makes them, shall satisfy the committee that it is for the interest of the country that he be elected, they can act accordingly and treat my refusal as definitely accepted. If they are not satisfied they can so notify the Progressive Party, and at the same time they can confer with me and then determine on whatever action we may severally deem appropriate to meet the needs of the country.

THEODORE ROOSEVELT.

June 11, 1916

"I Am Very Grateful," President Wilson Says, on Receiving the News of His Renomination

Special to The New York Times.

WASHINGTON, Friday, June 16.—" I am very grateful to my generous friends."

This was President Wilson's only comment when told of his nomination by acclamation this morning. The President, who earlier in the evening had taken a walk in the rain with Mrs. Wilson, returned to the White House at 10:30 o'clock.

Bulletins were sent to him from the White House offices until 11:30 o'clock, when word was returned to the executive offices that the President had gone to bed. The President was not disturbed again until 12:55 o'clock this morning, when Joseph P. Tumulty, his private secretary, telephoned to him that he had been nominated by acclamation. The secretary was talking to the President when news arrived that Vice President Marshall had also been nominated by acclamation.

President Wilson slipped out the main door of the White House at 10 o'clock last night in a driving rain when nobody was about but the ushers and policemen at the front door. With him was Mrs. Wilson. Neither had an umbrella, although the rain was coming down strongly and there was a strong southeastern wind. Both wore rubber coats and rubber hats. The Secret Service men in the executive offices were promptly advised by the policeman at the front door, and took up the trail, followed by several newspaper men. Swinging around the eastern side of the White House President and Mrs. Wilson walked briskly into the Mall and the monument grounds, following the path to the Washington Monument. They went to the base of the monument, and, after tarrying several minutes, returned to the White House. Their walk lasted about half an hour.

Returning to the White House, the President and Mrs. Wilson went to the library. The White House was in direct telegraphic and telephonic communication with the St. Louis Convention hall tonight. Over the telephone line, which ran from Secretary Tumulty's offices to the platform in the convention hall, the cheering during the demonstration at midnight was easily audible.

June 16, 1916

HUGHES IRONS OUT OPPOSITION TO ICKES

Moose and G. O. P. Must Work Side by Side, He Tells Illinois Men.

OLD GUARD SURRENDERS

Albert J. Beveridge Dines with Nominee, Says Third Party Is Dead, and May Take the Stump.

When Charles E. Hughes arrived at his Hotel Astor headquarters yesterday from his Summer home at Bridgehampton he found some old-line Illinois Republicans waiting for him with further protests against Harold L. Ickes as their State's only representative on the Campaign Committee. Mr. Ickes was the Progressive National Committeeman from Illinois.

Mayor Thompson of Chicago, Senator Lawrence Y. Sherman of Illinois, and H. R. Rathbone, President of the Hamilton Club of Chicago, were told by Mr. Hughes that all factions must work together for the interests of the party in the nation. Mr. Rathbone insisted that Mr. Ickes had repeatedly given objectionable interviews to the newspapers, in which he intimated that he (Ickes) would run the Republican campaign in Illinois. Republican leaders had taken offense at such statements. Mr. Rathbone said. Mr. Hughes replied that Mayor Thompson, Mr. Rathbone, and others must take a broader view, and subject local differences to the big national cause.

The Old Guard surrendered to the new leader. Mayor Thompson later in the day said emphatically:

" Of course we are working for Mr. Hughes."

Reunited Party His Demand.

After his talk with the nominee, Mr. Rathbone said that Chicago would turn out every Republican when Mr. Hughes went there after his speech in Detroit on Aug. 7. It had not been decided, he said, whether the address would be delivered at the Auditorium or the Coliseum.

The statement that the Hamilton Club would be unreservedly behind Mr. Hughes was received with much enthusiasm at headquarters, as it is the largest Republican organization of the kind in the State. It was accepted as evidence that the leaders of the party throughout the country were willing to follow Mr. Hughes and forget what happened in 1912.

Mr. Hughes said his principal object in the organization of the Campaign Committee was to bring together a body which would unite the Progressive and Republican parties and that he expected all past differences to be forgotten. He will remain the dominant figure in the situation. He will demand that all work together—Old Guard and Progressive—and that he shall have the last word if any dispute comes up.

The manner in which matters were handled yesterday indicated that Mr. Hughes would have his way. The members of the Old Guard on the Campaign Committee with whom he consulted went away pacified, and today he will go over the situation with Mr. Ickes. It was predicted that after that conversation the Republican and Progressive leaders in Illinois would work with one purpose and that when Mr. Hughes went to that State early in August he would be the guest of a reunited party.

Mr. Hughes saw many Republican leaders at headquarters and discussed the situation with them with the utmost frankness. He was willing to work with them, but he insisted that the Progressive Party, which had indorsed him, should have satisfactory recognition, and he made it evident that there would be no weakening on his part in that connection during the campaign.

Moose Dead, Beveridge Says.

Mr. Hughes had dinner last night with Albert J. Beveridge of Indiana, one of Colonel Roosevelt's most enthusiastic supporters, who delivered the keynote address at the Progressive convention in 1912 and then ran for United States Senator. Mr. Beveridge went over the national situation with Mr. Hughes and promised him his full support.

After the dinner Mr. Beveridge said the Progressive Party was dead. He gave out a statement in which he said:

"The Progressive Party as an organized national party no longer exists. People may have many opinions as to the causes that produced this condition, but it is useless to discuss them, for the fact itself stares us in the face.

"Therefore, Progressives must either refrain from voting for President at all or support the candidate of some other party. I shall vote for Mr. Hughes. In taking this stand I do not make nor imply any criticism of Progressives who may decide differently. I personally know large numbers of these men and women and hold them in the highest regard and esteem. Whatever they individually determine to do will be the result of their mature judgment arrived at conscientiously.

"I have known Mr. Hughes for several years and admire his ability, integrity, and courage. He is, above all else, a straightforward man, trustworthy and dependable. He means what he says and says what he means. I trust him, like him, am his friend, and shall support him.

May Stump for Hughes.

"The work on which I am engaged—the writing of the life of Chief Justice Marshall—has absolutely prevented all political activity on my part for the last eighteen months; in case the demands of this work are such as to permit me to take any part in the campaign I shall give my reasons on the stump for my conviction that the welfare of the country demands the election of Mr. Hughes."

July 20, 1916

APPEAL TO FOREIGN BORN.

Democrats Send Many Pamphlets to Naturalized Citizens.

Of the one hundred or more newspapers in this country printed in the German language President Wilson has the active support of only one, Der Staats Anzeiger, published at Bismarck, N. D. Three other German-American newspapers, it was said at the headquarters of the Democratic National Committee, while not actually pro-Wilson, are strongly opposed to Charles E. Hughes, the Republican nominee. They are the Chicago Abendpost, the Milwaukee Demokrat, and the Buffalo Demokrat.

There is little at the headquarters of the Democratic National Committee in the Forty-second Street Building to show to the casual observer that a finger is being raised to secure the goodwill of the voter of foreign birth or extraction for the President. What is being done is under the direction of a "Special Bureau," in charge of Hugh C. Wallace, Democratic National Committeeman from Washington.

The bureau is located at 6 East Thirty-ninth Street, where the Democratic National Committee is occupying the better part of three floors for the work of its Literary Bureau, which this year is doing work on a scale beyond precedent. There is a Polish, a Russian, a French, an Italian, a Spanish, a Yiddish, a Swedish, and a Norwegian Department doing campaign work under the supervision of the Special Bureau.

The principal work of these departments consists in preparing and sending broadcast pamphlets in foreign languages dealing with phases of the Wilson Administration which may be expected to appeal with particular force to voters of foreign origin or descent. In addition to this the Special Bureau employs a large number of organizers for field work among "foreign-language" voters.

One of the pamphlets is an appeal to voters of Latin-American origin. In it the policy of the Wilson Administration toward the Latin-American republics in South and Central America and toward Mexico is briefly reviewed and explained. On the title page of the pamphlet, which carries a picture of the President, he is introduced to voters of this category as "the founder of true Pan-Americanism," the "tried and true friend of the Latin Americans" and the "Protector of Mexico in her misfortune."

For the instruction of Polish voters the Special Bureau, in addition to four pamphlets, has published a four-page newspaper, Wolnosc, (Liberty.) Of this two editions were printed, one a national edition dealing with national issues and the national campaign exclusively, the other a State edition, which carries a page of matter more particularly related to the Democratic State campaign. In both editions appear the pictures of Juliusz Smietanka and Roman L. Modra, both of Polish origin, of whom the first was appointed Collector of Internal Revenue in Chicago and the other Chief Deputy Collector of Internal Revenue in this city.

October 1, 1916

VOTES OF WOMEN AND BULL MOOSE ELECTED WILSON

Western Progressives Turned to Him Almost En Masse, but Not Those of the East.

PEACE A POWERFUL ISSUE

"He Kept Us Out of War" Won Women — Hyphen Shot to Pieces—Labor Vote Divided.

NEW HAMPSHIRE WILSON'S

His Lead, Complete, 63—Gains In California—Hughes Drops in Minnesota.

On the returns up to date, President Wilson has received 8,508,085 votes and Mr. Hughes 8,090,951. Mr. Wilson's popular plurality is therefore 417,134. He is a majority President, which he was not when he went into office. In 1912 he had received 6,293,419 votes. Taft and Roosevelt had 7,604,463, so that Wilson was then in a minority by 1,311,044.

It has been said that Mr. Hughes received the votes of the most populous States of the Union and Mr. Wilson those of the less populous. There is not so much difference as might be expected. The States which voted for Mr. Hughes had, according to the last census, 45,901,739 inhabitants. Those which voted for Mr. Wilson had 47,737,643. The difference in Mr. Hughes's favor is 164,096.

The latest returns from the close States show the following results:

In California Wilson is leading by 8,431 votes, with a few scattering precincts missing; in Minnesota, where some of the militiamen's votes have been counted, Hughes is still ahead by 248 votes, with 27 districts missing; in North Dakota, with 9 districts missing, Wilson leads by 1,284 votes; New Hampshire, where the count has been completed, gives Wilson a plurality of 68 votes.

The New York Times asked its correspondents in the different States to report the causes and influences which brought about Mr. Wilson's victory in their localities. From the replies received it is possible to get a clear idea of the part played by the different group "votes" of which so much was said before election, and of the reasons which moved great bodies of voters to the decision they reached.

Progressives and the Women.

Two classes of voters, and two only, accomplished the result. They were not the German-Americans, the labor vote, or any of the groups standing for special interests. They were the Progressives and the women.

The split made in the Republican Party in 1910, which became a break in 1912, was not mended at Chicago. The dispatches now in the hands of *The Times* indicate no probability of its being mended until the cause for it is taken away. From the Hudson River to the Mississippi the bolters of 1912 were largely satisfied with Hughes, but to the East and West of those boundaries, especially to the West, they were not. And it was the West that decided the election.

In New York and Illinois the breach was apparently healed, there is no sign of anything to the contrary, and the same thing seems true of the States that generally follow the leadership of these two. That, however, was as far as Colonel Roosevelt was able to bring about a reunion.

The Progressives of Kansas, Washington, California, and the other Western States have again defeated a Republican Presidential candidate because the other wing of the party was in control and made the nominations. Minnesota and Wisconsin

voted for Hughes, but both have shown that they are as progressive as ever, Minnesota by accepting him so narrowly and Wisconsin by La Follette's victory.

The woman vote and the Progressive vote telescope each other, for in the critical States the women who turned the election were largely Progressives. But the women voted as women, too. The reports from the States where women vote show that the dream of solidifying woman as a sex and swinging her vote this way and that at the order of female political leaders is shattered forever. But the women did make up their minds as women in many Western States, and voted without regard either to how the women politicians bade them or how their own men folks voted.

The woman vote and the Progressive vote telescope each other, for in the critical States the women who turned the election were largely Progressives. But the women voted as women, too. The reports from the States where women vote show that the dream of solidifying woman as a sex and swinging her vote this way and that at the order of female political leaders is shattered forever. But the women did make up their minds as women in many Western States, and voted without regard either to how the women politicians bade them or to how their own men folks voted.

Woman's Party Failed Utterly.

The Woman's Party terrorized the two conventions and frightened them with the prospect of "four million votes," which it held over them as a club. Mr. Hughes was led to believe that it had the votes, and made his celebrated declaration for the Anthony Federal amendment. The Woman's Party tried to make its threats good and marshal the Western women for Hughes, but the dispatches received by *The Times* showed that it failed utterly.

It did have an influence, but the wrong kind. These dispatches are unanimous in recording the antagonism excited by the activities of the Woman's Party, and also by the special train of Hughes women which went campaigning from New York into the West. From many States come reports that both these things added greatly to Wilson's vote; from no State comes a report that it subtracted from that vote.

The women, where they broke away from party lines, or where they voted contrary to their men folks, voted for Wilson. They did so generally on the argument that "He kept us out of War." In some States, such as Washington, the influential argument with them was not this one, but

the legislative record which appealed to them as progressives.

The fact that in Illinois they voted as did the men of their families led to the belief that they had done so everywhere, but this now proves to be a mistake. It was so in Illinois, and in some other States, but it was not so in the Far West.

The labor vote did not go solidly to Wilson, and there was no State, except New Mexico, where it loomed large. In a number of States he got a great many labor votes as a result of the Adamson eight-hour law, but it was not the determining factor anywhere, and in most of the States it does not figure as a factor at all.

"He kept us out of war," was the great argument, East and West, but especially West. Nearly all the dispatches lay emphasis on that point. From some States came the report that it appealed to the hatred of war, but these are mostly Far Western States. In the Middle West it appealed not to theoretical pacifism or instinctive horror of war, but to the desire for continued prosperity. The States where it appealed to a moral sentiment were chiefly States where women vote. In other States the dispatches speak of it as influential with "the farmers."

In the summaries which follow *The Times* gives a birdseye view of the different ways in which different considerations appealed to the voters in different States. But out of the whole there loom two inescapable facts: The progressives hold the power to make or unmake a President, and are as unreconciled as ever, save in the East; and the women of California, Washington, and the other nine suffrage States helped them to swing this election. Deaf to all appeals to them as suffragists, they voted on the issues of the day alone, just as the men did; but they made up their minds on those issues in their own way.

November 12, 1916

DIVIDED REPUBLICANS DOMINATE

Text of President Wilson's Appeal

WASHINGTON, Oct. 24.—Following is the text of President Wilson's appeal to the nation to support his Administration by the return of a Democratic majority to Congress:

My Fellow-Countrymen: The Congressional elections are at hand. They occur in the most critical period our country has ever faced or is likely to face in our time. If you have approved of my leadership and wish me to continue to be your unembarrassed spokesman in affairs at home and abroad, I earnestly beg that you will express yourselves unmistakably to that effect by returning a Democratic majority to both the Senate and the House of Representatives.

I am your servant and will accept your judgment without cavil. But my power to administer the great trust assigned to me by the Constitution would be seriously impaired should your judgment be adverse, and I must frankly tell you so because so many critical issues depend upon your verdict. No scruple or taste must in grim times like these be allowed to stand in the way of speaking the plain truth.

I have no thought of suggesting that any political party is paramount in matters of patriotism. I feel too deeply the sacrifices which have been made in this war by all our citizens, irrespective of party affiliations, to harbor such an idea. I mean only that the difficulties and delicacies of our present task are of a sort that makes it imperatively necessary that the nation should give its undivided support to the Government under a unified leadership, and that a Republican Congress would divide the leadership.

The leaders of the minority in the present Congress have unquestionably been pro-war, but they have been anti-administration. At almost every turn since we entered the war they have sought to take the choice of policy and the conduct of the war out of my hands and put it under the control of instrumentalities of their own choosing.

This is no time either for divided counsels or for divided leadership. Unity of command is as necessary now in civil action as it is upon the field of battle. If the control of the House and the Senate should be taken away from the party now in power an opposing majority could assume control of legislation and oblige all action to be taken amid contest and obstruction.

The return of a Republican majority to either House of the Congress would, moreover, be interpretative on the other side of the water as a repudiation of my leadership. Spokesmen of the Republican Party are urging you to elect a Republican Congress in order to back up and support the President, but, even if they should in this impose upon some credulous voters on this side of the water, they would impose on no one on the other side. It is well understood there as well as here that Republican leaders desire not so much to support the President as to control him.

The peoples of the allied countries with whom we are associated against Germany are quite familiar with the significance of elections. They would find it very difficult to believe that the voters of the United States had chosen to support their President by electing to the Congress a majority controlled by those who are not in fact in sympathy with the attitude and action of the Administration.

I need not tell you, my fellow-countrymen, that I am asking your support not for my own sake or for the sake of a political party, but for the sake of the nation itself in order that its inward duty of purpose may be evident to all the world. In ordinary times I would not feel at liberty to make such an appeal to you. In ordinary times divided counsels can be endured without permanent hurt to the country. But these are not ordinary times.

If in these critical days it is your wish to sustain me with undivided minds, I beg that you will say so in a way which it will not be possible to misunderstand, either here at home or among our associates on the other side of the sea. I submit my difficulties and my hopes to you.

WOODROW WILSON.

October 26, 1918

CONGRESS WON BY THE REPUBLICANS

SENATE SEEMS REPUBLICAN

Apparent Majority Is Four, but Several Seats Are in Doubt.

HAVE HOUSE BY ABOUT 19

Ford and J. H. Lewis Defeated —Champ Clark Reported Beaten Also.

G. O. P. GAINS IN STATES

Though the returns from yesterday's election are incomplete, present reports indicate a Republican majority of four in the United States Senate and a House Republican by about 19. An astounding incident is the report by The Associated Press that Speaker Champ Clark has probably been defeated for re-election to Congress for his Missouri district.

The Republicans also gain in State elections for Governor and other offices. In this State Whitman is leading Smith slightly, but the soldier vote is counted on to elect Smith. In Ohio Governor Cox, Democrat, is ahead a little; but the Republican majorities for Governor in other doubtful States are decisive.

The Republicans may have a majority of four in the Senate, thanks largely to the defeat of Senator Shafroth in Colorado, Senator Saulsbury in Delaware, Senator Lewis in Illinois, and Senator Thompson in Kansas. Oklahoma and Kentucky are in doubt, but in Missouri Judge Selden Spencer, Republican, has evidently defeated Joseph W. Folk.

Contrary to early reports, the returns at 4 A. M. showed that the Republicans had gained an additional seat in Idaho. They have elected Gooding over Nugent, Democrat, to whom last night's reports had given the victory.

The greatest interest centred in the Senatorial fight in Michigan, where Truman H. Newberry, formerly Secretary of the Navy and now a Lieutenant Commander in it, was running as a Republican and Henry Ford as a Democrat. Mr. Ford has said that he was "commanded" by President Wilson to make the race. Newberry is elected by a majority estimated at this writing at from 30,000 to 50,000. The returns from Wayne County may reduce this, but Newberry's lead is so great that they will probably not endanger it.

The biggest sensation of the election was the complete overturn in the Kansas Congress delegation and the Republican landslide in the whole State. In the present Congress the delegation stands: Democrats, 5; Republicans, 3. In the next it will apparently stand: Republicans, 8; Democrats, 0. In addition, the Kansans have turned out their Democratic Senator, Thompson, and elected Governor Capper to his place by 100,000 majority. Henry J. Allen, Republican, who is doing war work in France and did not come home to participate in the campaign, is elected Governor by 150,000, leading the ticket. The rest of the State

ticket is Republican by about 85,000.

Senator James Hamilton Lewis, the Democratic "whip," and often referred to as the President's spokesman in the Senate, is defeated for re-election in Illinois by Medill McCormick, a Roosevelt Republican, and until lately a member of the Progressive Party. McCormick's majority is at least 50,000.

Illinois's delegation in the House, however, is unchanged, standing twenty-one Republicans to six Democrats. The two Republican candidates for Congressman at Large, Representative William E. Mason and ex-Governor Richard Yates, have carried the State.

Massachusetts elected Walsh, Democrat, over Weeks, Republican, to the Senate, but elected a Republican Governor, Coolidge.

Senator Norris, Republican, one of the "Willful Twelve," who was expected to receive the German vote, is re-elected by an increased majority. The whole State ticket goes with him, turning out a Democratic Governor.

Senator Walsh of Montana, Democrat, is re-elected over Landstrum, Republican, and Jeannette Rankin, who was running on a third ticket. She will therefore not be in either House of the next Congress.

In Rhode Island, which was in doubt and in which a severe fight had been waged against the Republican Senator, Colt, he is re-elected. The State has gone Republican on everything else as well, electing a Republican Governor and Republican Congressmen. In the present House Rhode Island has two Republicans and one Democrat; in the next it will have a solid Republican delegation.

Governor Philipp of Wisconsin is re-elected. The greatest interest in that State centred in the fight for Congress in the Fifth District, in which Victor L. Berger, Socialist, though under indictment for sedi-

tion, was running. He has been elected. The Republican candidate was Congressman Stafford, whose war record was also unsatisfactory, and the Patriotic League put in the field U. P. Carney.

New Jersey, despite President Wilson's appeal for the election of La Monte and Hennessy, has gone Republican, electing Governor Edge to the Senate for the long term and Senator Baird for the short term.

The Democratic side of the House has suffered a severe loss in the defeat of Representative Swagar Sherley of Kentucky, who is Chairman of the Committee on Appropriations, and regarded as one of the ablest men in Congress.

Senator Saulsbury, Democrat, has been defeated for re-election in Delaware by Ball, Republican, and the Republicans have also captured the Congress seat now held by a Democrat. Ex-Senator Ball's majority is large.

Governor Burnquist, loyalist Republican, the same who refused to permit the pacifists to meet in Minnesota, is re-elected. So is Senator Knute Nelson by a majority of 4 to 1. At first the Democrats agreed to make no nomination in opposition to Nelson, but at the eleventh hour they indorsed the Socialist candidate, with disastrous results.

Strange to say, Senator Owen is having a close race in Oklahoma, which is in politics virtually a Southern State, and has never given the least sign of going Republican before.

Connecticut has re-elected Governor Holcomb, Republican, by 6,000.

In Pennsylvania the Republican candidate for Governor, Sproul, is elected.

The Socialist vote in the House will not be increased. It will still be one —Berger instead of London. All the Socialist candidates in New York were defeated, including Shiplacoff, who ran against a Republican and a Democrat in the Tenth or Brownsville district because Representative Haskell, Republican, refused to agree to fusion. Haskell, is elected.

November 6, 1918

Text of the Republican Plank On the League of Nations

The Republican Party stands for agreement among the nations to preserve the peace of the world. We believe that such an international association must be based upon international justice and must provide methods which shall maintain the rule of public right by development of law and the decision of impartial courts and which shall secure instant and general international conference whenever peace shall be threatened by political action, so that the nations pledged to do and insist upon what is just and fair may exercise their influence and power for the prevention of war.

We believe that all this can be done without the compromise of national independence, without depriving the people of the United States in advance of the right to determine for themselves what is just and fair when the occasion arises and without involving them as participants and not as peacemakers in a multitude of quarrels, the merits of which they are unable to judge.

The covenant signed by the President at Paris failed signally to accomplish this purpose and contained stipulations not only intolerable for an independent people, but certain to produce the injustice, hostility and controversy among nations which it proposed to prevent.

That covenant repudiated to a degree wholly unnecessary and unjustifiable the time-honored policy in favor of peace declared by Washington and Jefferson and Monroe and pursued by all American administrators for more than a century, and it ignored the universal sentiments of America for generations past in favor of international law and arbitration, and it rested the hope of the future upon mere expediency and negotiation.

The unfortunate insistence of the President upon having his own way without any change and without any regard to the opinion of the majority of the Senate, which shares with him in the treaty-making power, and the President's demand that the treaty should be ratified without any modification, created a situation in which Senators were required to vote upon their consciences and their oaths according to their judgment upon the treaty as it was presented or submit to the commands of a dictator in a matter where the authority under the Constitution was theirs and not his.

The Senators performed their duty faithfully. We approve their conduct and honor, their courage and fidelity, and we pledge the coming Republican Administration to such agreement with the other nations of the world as shall meet the full duty of America to civilization and humanity in accordance with American ideals and without surrendering the right of the American people to exercise its judgment and its power in favor of justice and peace.

June 11, 1920

HARDING NOMINATED

Special to The New York Times.

CHICAGO, June 12.—Senator Warren G. Harding of Marion, Ohio, was nominated for President of the United States by the Republican Party represented by its delegates assembled in national convention at the Coliseum this evening. Calvin Coolidge, Governor of Massachusetts, was nominated for Vice President.

The nomination of the Presidential candidate came on the tenth ballot. In the ninth ballot the whole trend of the convention sentiment was toward Harding. When New York, with its heavy representation, went to him on the tenth, everything was over except the shouting—and the shouting began immediately.

Senator Harding's nomination was the outcome of a complex situation that did not begin to clear until last evening. After four ineffective ballots yesterday the convention had adjourned until this morning. Four additional ballots in the forenoon and early afternoon of today had developed Harding strength, but General Leonard Wood and Governor Frank O. Lowden had remained in the lead. A recess was taken for two hours, and during that short period combinations were formed that made Harding's nomination certain.

The real stampede of delegates to Harding began when Governor Lowden, abandoning his intention to address the convention, issued instead a formal announcement that his delegates were released from their pledges to him.

Interesting, and even thrilling, as the open proceedings in the convention were, moves behind the scenes, of which most of the convention knew nothing, had their dramatic side. The nomination of the candidate for President was arranged in conferences in hotel rooms. The prediction made in Washington weeks ago that the convention would get into a deadlock over candidates that would necessitate a combination arranged by a comparatively few of the party's dominating spirits was fulfilled to the letter.

June 13, 1920

Text of the Platform

STANDS FIRM FOR LEAGUE

Condemns Republican Senators for Blocking Peace of the World.

SAN FRANCISCO, July 2.—The following is the text of the platform adopted by the Democratic National Convention today.

The Preamble The Democratic Party in its national convention now assembled, sends greetings to the President of the United States, Woodrow Wilson, and hails with patriotic pride the great achievements for the country and the world wrought by a Democratic Administration under his leadership.

It salutes the mighty people of this great Republic, emerging with imperishable honor from the severe tests and grievous strains of the most tragic war in history, having earned the plaudits and the gratitude of all free nations.

It declares its adherence to the fundamental progressive principles of social, economic and industrial justice and advance, and purposes to resume the great work of translating these principles into effective laws, begun and carried far by the Democratic Administration and interrupted only when the war claimed all the national energies for the single task of victory.

League of Nations The Democratic Party favors the League of Nations as the surest, if not the only, practicable means of maintaining the permanent peace of the world and terminating the insufferable burden of great military and naval establishments. It was for this that America broke away from traditional isolation and spent her blood and treasure to crush a colossal scheme of conquest. It was upon this basis that the President of the United States, in prearrangement with our Allies, consented to a suspension of hostilities against the imperial German Government; the armistice was granted and a treaty of peace negotiated upon the definite assurance to Germany, as well as to the powers pitted against Germany, that "a general association of nations must be formed, under specific covenants, for the purpose of affording mutual guarantees of political independence and territorial integrity to great and small States alike." Hence, we not only congratulate the President on the vision manifested and the vigor exhibited in the prosecution of the war; but we felicitate him and his associates on the exceptional achievements at Paris involved in the adoption of a league and treaty so near akin to previously expressed American ideals and so intimately related to the aspirations of civilized peoples everywhere.

We commend the President for his courage and his high conception of good faith in steadfastly standing for the covenant agreed to by all the associated and allied nations at war with Germany, and we condemn the Republican Senate for its refusal to ratify the treaty merely because it was the product of Democratic statesmanship, thus interposing partisan envy and personal hatred in the way of the peace and renewed prosperity of the world.

By every accepted standard of international morality the President is justified in asserting that the honor of the country is involved in this business: and we point to the accusing fact that before it was determined to initiate political antagonism to the treaty, the new Republican Chairman of the Senate Foreign Relations Committee himself publicly proclaimed that any proposition for a separate peace with Germany, such as he and his party associates thereafter reported to the Senate, would make us "guilty of the blackest crime."

On May 15, last, the Knox substitute for the Versailles Treaty was passed by the Republican Senate; and this convention can contrive no more fitting characterization of its obloquy than that made in the Forum Magazine of December, 1918, by Henry Cabot Lodge, when he said:

"If we send our armies and young men abroad to be killed and wounded in Northern France and Flanders with no result but this, our entrance into war with such an intention was a crime which nothing can justify."

The intent of Congress and the intent of the President was that there could be no peace until we could create a situation where no such war as this could recur. We cannot make peace except in company with our allies. It would brand us with everlasting dishonor and bring ruin to us also if we undertook to make separate peace.

Thus to that which Mr. Lodge, in saner moments, considered "the blackest crime," he and his party in madness sought to give the sanctity of law; that which eighteen months ago was of "everlasting dishonor" the Republican Party and its candidates today accept as the essence of faith.

We indorse the President's view of our international obligations and his firm stand against reservations designed to cut to pieces the vital provisions of the Versailles Treaty, and we commend the Democrats in Congress for voting against resolutions for separate peace which would disgrace the nation. We advocate the immediate ratification of the treaty without reservations which would impair its essential integrity, but do not oppose the acceptance of any reservations making clearer or more specific the obligations of the United States to the League associates.

Only by doing this may we retrieve the reputation of this nation among the Powers of the earth and recover the moral leadership which President Wilson won and which Republican politicians at Washington sacrificed. Only by doing this may we hope to aid effectively in the restoration of order throughout the world and to take the place which we should assume in the front rank of spiritual, commercial and industrial advancement.

We reject as utterly vain, if not vicious, the Republican assumption that ratification of the treaty and membership in the League of Nations would in any way impair the integrity or independence of our country. The fact that the covenant has been entered into by twenty-nine nations, all as jealous of their independence as we are of ours, is a sufficient refutation of such charge. The President repeatedly has declared, and this convention reaffirms, that all our duties and obligations as a member of the league must be fulfilled in strict conformity with the Constitution of the United States, embodied in which is the fundamental requirement of declaratory action by the Congress before this nation may become a participant in any war.

July 3, 1920

COX

COX TOOK LEAD AT NIGHT

Passed McAdoo Early In Session on the 39th Ballot.

CONVENTION HALL, SAN FRANCISCO, Tuesday, July 6, 1:39 A. M. (5:39 New York time).—Governor James M. Cox of Ohio was nominated for President by the Democratic National Convention at 1:39 A. M. today.

The nomination came on the forty-fourth ballot. When the night session began, the thirty-seventh and thirty-eighth ballots were taken. Attorney General Palmer then released his delegates. In the succeeding ballots Cox gained steadily, until on the forty-fourth he had secured 699 votes and it was apparent that before the ballot was completed he would obtain more than 729 votes, the two-thirds majority required to nominate.

Vice Chairman Amidon of the Democratic National Committee, manager for McAdoo, interrupted the voting and moved to make the nomination unanimous which was done amid uproarious applause.

It was 1:43 o'clock A. M. (5:43 o'clock A. M. New York time) when Cox was declared the nominee.

Thereupon the convention adjourned until noon today (Tuesday), when it will complete the work by nominating a candidate for Vice President.

Cox was nominated by acclamation before the finish of the ballot. He had 699 votes at that time and McAdoo 270 when the motion was made to declare the nomination unanimous.

July 6, 1920

HOME PEACE BEST, HARDING ASSERTS IN PORCH ADDRESS

Attacks Covenant as Fostering Discord Among Foreign Elements in America.

DENIES BROKEN OBLIGATIONS

We Went to War as an Obligation to Ourselves, with Associates, Not Allies, He Adds.

RENEWS ARTICLE X. ATTACK

Delegation from Wayne County, Ohio, Hears Republican Candidate and Senator Watson.

Special to The New York Times.

MARION, Ohio, Aug. 4.—Industrial and social peace at home is to be preferred to international peace of all the world, Senator Harding told a delegation of 400 business men, farmers and factory workers from Wayne County, Ohio, who made a pilgrimage to the front porch this afternoon.

"Why make a covenant which violates the good faith of nations?" he asked, after emphasizing that no governmental authority other than Congress may declare war.

"Suppose the League of Nations should agree upon a military expedition which Congress should refuse to support," the Senator said. "Then, under the provisions of Article X, the President would be called upon to carry on a war without constitutional authority, or we should prove our compact to be no more than a scrap of paper."

If Germany had had the same constitutional provision that gives Congress the sole authority to declare war, the World War might have been avoided, the Senator added.

"Many advocates of pacifism think our safeguards are not enough," he went on, "that there should be a referendum to the people before a war. The other extreme is to be found among those who seriously propose that a council of foreign powers shall summon the sons of this republic to war anywhere in the world."

"No! No!" shouted the crowd standing on the gravel coated lawn in front of the Harding home.

Elaborating upon his speech of acceptance pledging a Republican administration to negotiate a new treaty, with an association of nations based on moral ties alone, Senator Harding affirmed that "we are on the side of both safety and honor to hold for ourselves the decision of our obligations to the world."

War "An Obligation to Ourselves."

"Men prate about violated obligations to the nations of the earth," he went on. "The solemn truth is that our part in the World War was an obligation to ourselves, performed in sympathy with associated, not allied, powers, and our splendid part in helping to win the war was the armed manifestation of American conscience, not the fulfilment of a written obligation."

Adoption of the League of Nations, Senator Harding intimated, would involve this country in entanglements that Washington never dreamed of. With natives of every country on earth now American citizens, should the United States he asked to attempt to settle the "jealousies and hatreds of all civilization? These adopted sons of the republic want the settlement favorable to the lands from which they came. The misfortune is not alone that it rends the concord of nations. The greater pity is that it rends the concord of our citizenship at home."

Referring to Governor Coolidge's speech of acceptance calling for rescue from the reaction of war, Senator Harding added that "we also need to be rescued from the visionary and fruitless pursuit of peace through super-government."

He then defended his slogan of "normalcy."

"That doesn't mean the old order. That doesn't mean looking backward. It is the short and easy way of saying 'again to stability,' 'once more to regularity.' There hasn't been a backward look in America for three hundred years, but the man who faces the future with highest assurance is he who has noted the paths which made his progress secure."

August 5, 1920

HARDING WINS

GIGANTIC MAJORITIES

Pennsylvania, 750,000; Illinois, 800,000; Ohio, 400,000.

MAY BE 6,000,000 IN ALL

More Than 370 Electoral Votes Won by Harding and Coolidge.

BIG GAINS IN THE WEST

Indiana, Wisconsin, Michigan, Iowa, Kansas, Nebraska and California Won.

By majorities unprecedented in American politics, Warren G. Harding was elected President and Calvin Coolidge Vice President yesterday on Senator Harding's fifty-fifth birthday. Though the addition of women to the electorate might have been expected to make the margins of successful candidates somewhat larger than in past years, it could hardly account for any such unheard of majorities as were rolled up yesterday. From coast to coast records were broken.

Harding's total pluralities in the States he carried may reach 6,500,000 and his net plurality over Cox may be 6,000,000.

This surpasses by 3,500,000 the previous record, which was that of Theodore Roosevelt's victory over Alton B. Parker.

The highest State plurality ever previously recorded, Roosevelt's margin of 500,000 over Parker in Pennsylvania in 1904, was surpassed by at least four States yesterday. New York State went for Harding by nearly 1,100,000; Pennsylvania gave him a plurality of 750,000; Illinois gave him 800,000; California, which went for Wilson four years ago by a majority of 2,700, gave Harding a plurality of perhaps 500,000 over James M. Cox. Ohio, the home State of both candidates, went for Harding by 400,000.

At 4 o'clock this morning it seemed that Harding's majority on electoral votes would equal or surpass the record-breaking landslide by which Roosevelt beat Alton B. Parker.

Cox held the solid South, and Kentucky and perhaps Oklahoma among the border States; but West Virginia and Missouri had apparently gone for Harding, as they went for Roosevelt in 1904. Late reports indicate that Cox might possibly lose Tennessee.

The latest reports give Harding 371 electoral votes and Cox 152, with eight votes—those of Arizona and North Dakota—still uncertain. This, however, seems to be due to inadequate reports; the probability is that they are all for Harding.

All over the country the Harding pluralities broke records. Boston, which has been consistently Democratic in recent years, except in 1896, when McKinley carried it over Bryan, showed the effect of the drift of the Irish vote by giving Harding a plurality of more than 20,000.

New York City, however, was even more surprising. The city went for Taft in 1908 by less than 16,000; it seems to have given Harding a plurality of more than 443,000. Buffalo gave Harding a plurality of 46,247.

The effect of the Harding sweep showed everywhere. Though the Southern States stood fast, Harding had carried two wards in Atlanta and two Louisiana parishes. In the Middle West, Indiana and Kansas each gave him more than 200,000 plurality, Iowa about the same; Michigan nearly 400,000; Wisconsin nearly 300,000.

Maine, which surprised observers last September by a Republican plurality of 70,000 in the Gubernatorial election, surpassed this figure by several thousand yesterday. New Jersey gave Harding more than 200,000.

Reports from the Far West, due to the wide extent of territory and the difference in time, were slow in coming in, but there was every indication that the Western States which had re-elected Wilson in 1916 when almost all the East went for Hughes had turned over solidly to the Republican nominee this year.

Harding carried his home precinct, 273 to 76. It was Democratic four years ago, though there has been a reapportionment since. Governor Cox's home precinct was carried by Harding by 12 votes. In Northampton, Mass., Coolidge's home town, the Republicans won by two to one. Four years ago Hughes carried it by a very narrow margin. Harding carried Hyde Park, N. Y., the home town of Franklin D. Roosevelt, Democratic nominee for Vice President, by 279 votes to 194, and he carried President Wilson's home district at Princeton, N. J., by a majority estimated at about five to one.

At 11 o'clock last night Governor Cox's newspaper, The Dayton News, conceded the election of Harding, and George White, Chairman of the Democratic National Committee, followed his candidate's example a few minutes later.

Governor Alfred E. Smith seems to have been defeated, although he ran nearly 300,000 ahead of the Democratic national ticket up-State and more than three quarters of a million ahead of the national ticket in the city. His plurality in this city at 4 o'clock this morning, was estimated at 315,000, but Judge Nathan L. Miller, the Republican candidate, had a margin of apparently 370,000 in the up-State vote. Democratic leaders, however, refused at 4 o'clock this morning to concede Governor Smith's defeat.

The Republican sweep carried with it considerable increased majorities in both houses of Congress. Indications at 2 o'clock this morning were that the Republicans would have fifty-four Senators to the Democrats forty-two, but Will H. Hays, Chairman of the Republican National Committee, was claiming a majority of fourteen. The present Senate has forty-nine Republicans and forty-seven Democrats.

In the House the Republicans will apparently have 273 and the Democrats 159. Two independents and one Prohibitionist have been elected. The present House has a Republican majority of 38 over all; it will be increased in the next to 111. It appears that the Democrats will have only 13 of the 43 seats from New York.

Ogden L. Mills (Rep.) defeated Representative Pell in the Seventeenth District here.

In each house of the New York Legislature the Democrats have lost six seats. The next Senate will have 37 Republicans and 14 Democrats; the next Assembly 116 Republicans, 29 Democrats and 5 Socialists. Four of the five Socialists expelled from the Assembly last Winter were re-elected, and the Socialists gained another seat in the Bronx.

Senator James W. Wadsworth, Jr., was elected easily, despite the opposition of the woman suffragists, who were embittered by his consistent antagonism to their cause in recent years. His plurality over Harry C. Walker, the Democratic nominee, seems to be about 365,000, although Republican headquarters are claiming 500,000.

In Connecticut Senator Frank B. Brandegee, also opposed by the woman suffragists and by some League Republicans because of his outspoken hostility to the League, will probably have a margin of 35,000 or more over Congressman Augustine Lonergan, his Democratic opponent.

From coast to coast veteran and popular Democrats fell in the general collapse. The disaster which seems to have beaten Alfred E. Smith out of the Governorship of New York has also defeated Senator James D. Phelan for re-election in California, despite his great popularity throughout the State. In Indiana, Thomas Taggart, candidate for the Senate against James E. Watson, the present holder of the seat, was thought likely a few weeks ago to win his fight; but though Watson has apparently run behind the Presidential ticket by many thousands, he seems sure of election.

Factional fights in Illinois and Wisconsin did not disturb the Republicans. The battle in the primaries between the Thompson and Lowden factions in Illinois had caused bitter animosities, and several Republican papers, including The Chicago Tribune, supported James Hamilton Lewis, the Democratic nominee for Governor, against Len Small, the Thompson Republican candidate. But Lewis was overwhelmingly defeated, and William B. McKinley, the Lowden Republican candidate for the Senate, was elected by a huge majority over Waller, his Democratic opponent.

In Wisconsin Senator Irvine Luther Lenroot, a mild reservationist on the League question, was opposed by James Thompson, a LaFollette man and representative of the bitter-end anti-League faction. But Lenroot won handily, and Paul S. Reinsch, former Minister to China, who was the Democratic candidate, did no more than beat the Socialist for third honors. In New Hampshire Senator George H. Moses, one of the bitter opponents of the League, had been disturbed in his campaign by echoes from the primary fight against a pro-League Republican, but he too won with ease.

Socialist managers claimed a vote of more than 2,000,000, as against less than 600,000 four years ago, but the early returns did not provide a basis for judging the reliability of their estimates. They seem to have a heavy vote in Illinois.

November 3, 1920

950,000 VOTED FOR DEBS.

Socialist Poll Approximately Double That of Four Years Ago.

According to an Associated Press dispatch sent out from New York yesterday, Eugene V. Debs, Socialist candidate for President in the last election, received nearly 950,000 votes — the greatest number polled by a Socialist Presidential nominee in the country's history and approximately twice the Socialist vote in 1916.

Available official and unofficial returns from all but seven States show that Debs polled 900,563, which, added to the Socialist vote four years ago in these seven States—48,366—would give him a total of 948,929. The missing States are Idaho, Louisiana, Montana, New Mexico, North and South Dakota and Texas.

Debs rolled up 204,120 votes in New York State alone, excepting the soldier vote, the unofficial returns show—more than four times the State's Socialist vote in 1916 and over three times Debs's poll in 1912.

Other States which gave Debs a sizeable vote this year included Wisconsin, with 80,635; Illinois, 74,747; Pennsylvania, 70,021; California, 64,076; Ohio, 57,147; Minnesota, 56,106; Massachusetts, 32,267; Michigan, 28,947; New Jersey, 27,141; Oklahoma, 25,638; Indiana, 24,703; Missouri, 20,243; Iowa, 16,981; Kansas, 15,507, and Connecticut, 10,335.

Of these States, however, Illinois, Pennsylvania, California, Ohio, Oklahoma, Indiana, Missouri and Kansas gave a smaller Socialist vote than in 1912.

December 8, 1920

REPUBLICANS SPLIT AS CONGRESS OPENS

Farm-Labor Group Claims It Has Gained Balance of Power During Recess.

CAN DEFY PARTY LEADERS

Likely to Make Its Presence Felt in Tariff and Ship Subsidy Legislation.

Special to The New York Times.

WASHINGTON, Dec. 4.—The Republican Party enters tomorrow upon the first regular session of Congress in the Harding Administration, seriously divided not only on important domestic questions, but with a strong faction opposed to any proposition to place the United States in a society of nations, the expected outgrowth of the Washington conference.

With legislation of the first importance in domestic and international concerns to be considered in the coming session, the Republican leaders find themselves unable to lead. The progressive farm-labor bloc is stronger than in the special session, when it defied the recognized leaders and even rejected the advice of President Harding on the surtax feature of the revenue bill. During the recess this bloc has perfected its organization and it will appear with a settled program.

It is declared that the only way this Republican group can be overcome is by a combination of the old guard Republicans with the Democrats, and that such a combination can be perfected is doubted, as in the special session the Democrats joined with the progressive bloc.

Evidences are accumulating to show that the Republican Party is entering on such a career as it did in the first session of the Taft Administration. In that session the progressive group was formed and fought stubbornly against the enactment of the Payne-Aldrich tariff. The party leaders were strong enough then to prevent the progressives having their way. The result was that the Tariff bill became a law and the progressive group finally broke away from the party and, in 1912, formed the party which had Colonel Roosevelt as its candidate for President.

With the Progressive Farm-Labor bloc controlling the balance of power it is possible for this small body of men to defy the recognized leaders and write a Tariff bill which will satisfy the progressives, but will be a bitter pill to ithe Old Guard and the conservative Republicans. One thing is certain to develop in the consideration of the Tariff and the Ship Subsidy bill, and that is that the party will be divided and without leaders. In this situation many observers believe there is not much prospect that the legislation will be any more satisfactory to the country than was the Revenue bill.

In the international sphere will appear legislation for refunding the foreign debt, and, incidental to this program, there will be a clamor for action on bonus legislation. It is stated definitely that the Republican leaders intend to pass a bonus bill. There are several plans, but the one having the most support is that which favors making the repayment of the $4,500,000,000 owed by Great Britain as the basis for issuing bonus bonds. The United States under this plan, is to guarantee to some extent the $4,500,000,000 bonds which it is proposed to float at 4 per cent. against the British foreign debt.

Exceeding in international and domestic interest the question of the forreign debt is the action which Congress will be called upon to take in some form in case the Conference for Limitation of Armament succeeds. Advisers of the Administration say that plans for limitation of naval armaments cannot be dealt with except by a treaty or a resolution. Predominant opinion favors a treaty with the powers concerned in the reduction.

While both these matters are sure to cause a long, and perhaps divided, discussion in the Republican Party, the real test of the party leadership and the strength of President Harding will come when the tariff and the legislation for a ship subsidy appear.

West Against the East.

It is expected that the Progressive-Farm-Labor bloc will show its power in a more determined form during the regular session, especially in these two matters of a distinct political character. The Progressive bloc already has declared for heavy tariff duties on farm products, with slight duties on manufactured products. It is the West against the East.

The same bloc, or, rather, the leading men in this bloc, always have opposed a ship subsidy, so there is evidence already on the surface of a bitter and uncompromising fight in the Republican Party over tariff and a ship subsidy which may have a serious effect on the Congressional elections next November.

The foreign debt refunding bill will be reported from the Finance Committee on Tuesday as it passed the House in the special session, making provision for a commission of five to be appointed by the President, one of whom shall be the Secretary of the Treasury. This commission is authorized to fix the terms and interest rates for the refunding of the foreign debt. Despite the opposition, it is believed the bill will be passed substantially as it came from the House.

Nothing of importance is before the House, which will content itself with acting on minor matters until the Senate disposes of the Tariff bill. The first proposal to come before the House tomorrow will be a move to consider the St. Lawrence River canal project.

December 5, 1921

PLAN PEOPLE'S BLOC FOR NEXT CONGRESS

Labor and Farmers Move for Nomination of Candidates for Presidency and Congress.

TO ORGANIZE IN 48 STATES

But Cleveland Convention Defeats, 64 to 52, Radical Move for a Labor Party.

Special to The New York Times.

CLEVELAND, Ohio, Dec. 12.—The organization of a "people's bloc" in the next Congress, composed of Senators and Representatives elected through the aid of the liberal elements in November, was decided upon today as part of the "people's progressive program" adopted by the conference for progressive political action.

The conference perfected a permanent organization under which it is proposed to unite all the liberal elements of the country—labor and farmer organizations and progressive and political organizations "in harmony with the progressive movement"—to participate in a nation-wide campaign to "secure the nomination and election of a President, Vice President, United States Senators and Congressmen, State Legislatures and State officers pledged to progressive policies and the interests of the producing classes and to the principles of genuine democracy in agriculture, industry and Government."

The platform of the new organization, which was declared by speakers to be the shortest platform ever adopted by a convention of this kind in the history of American politics, demanded:

The repeal of the Esch-Cummins railroad law and operation of the railroads for the benefit of the people.

The public control of water power in the interest of the people.

The direct election of the President and Vice President by the people and extension of direct primary laws in all States.

Action by Congress to end the practice of the courts of declaring legislation unconstitutional.

Enactment of the Norris-Sinclair Consumers and Producers' Financing Corporation bill, designed to increase prices farmers receive and reduce prices consumers pay for the farm products, and theh creation of an independent system of food producers' credits.

Increased tax rates on large incomes and inheritance and payment of a soldiers' bonus by restoring the tax on excess profits.

Legislation providing minimum essential standards of employment for women, equality for women and men, while improving existing political, social and industrial standards, and State action to insure maximum benefit of Federal maternity and infancy acts.

Plan for State Conferences.

The organization plan under which this program is to be carried out provides for the calling of State conferences as soon as possible in each of the forty-eight States to work along the lines of the national conference. These State conferences, with the approval of the national organization, will have authority to organize a third party in the State if they do not care to participate in the primary of the two major parties.

The following National Committee was elected to administer the activities of the national political movement:

Warren S. Stone, Cleveland, Ohio, Grand Chief of the Brotherhood of Locomotive Engineers; William Green, Indianapolis, Secretary of the United Mine Workers of America; William H. Johnston, Washington, D. C., President of the International Association of Machinists; Sidney Hillman, New York, President of the Amalgamated Clothing Workers; Joseph A. Franklin, Kansas City, President of the Brotherhood of Boilermakers; E. J. Manion, St. Louis, Mo., President of the Railroad Telegraphers; Edward Keating, Washington, D. C., editor of Labor; Morris Hillquit, New York City, member of the National Committee of the Socialist Party; Benjamin C. Marsh, Washington, D. C., of the Farmers' National Council; J. G. Brown, Chicago, National Secretary of the Farmer-Labor Party; George H. Griffith, Minneapolis, Minn., of the National Non-Partisan League; Frederick C. Howe, New York City; Alice Lorraine Daly, Non-Partisan League, South Dakota; Basil Manly, Washington, D. C.; J. B. Laughlin, Oklahoma, of the Farmer-Labor Union; H. F. Samuels, Idaho; John Baer, North Dakota; D. C. Dorman, Montana; Benjamin Schlesinger, New York, President of the International Ladies' Garment Workers of America; James Maurer, Harrisburg, Pa., President of the Pennsylvania State Federation of Labor; D. B. Robertson, Cleveland, Ohio, President of the Brotherhood of Locomotive Firemen and Enginemen.

Third Party Move Is Defeated.

A proposal for the formation of a national Labor Party, composed of the industrial and agricultural workers of the country was defeated by a vote of 64 to 52 at tonight's session. The action of the delegates, who claim to represent more than 6,000,000 workers and farmers, marked the conclusive defeat of the radical element which has been clamouring throughout the convention for the abandonment of the present non-partisan political policy and substitution of independent political action.

The fight, led by the delegates of the National Farmer-Labor Party, precipitated another stormy session of the convention. The debate developed that the supporters of the third party move were chiefly labor bodies in State Federations west and northwest of the Mississippi River. The League for Industrial Democracy and the Chicago State Federation of Labor, however, were ardent champions of the new political move. B. M. Jewell, head of the railway employes department of the American Federation of Labor, and other labor leaders in the conservative group, appealed for the defeat of the National Labor Party move and urged application of the non-partisan policy.

Delegates of the National Socialist Party, who had been heralded as advocates of the labor party movement were conspicuous by their silence on this issue. Morris Hillquit, however, before the matter came up tonight, made it clear in an address that he was in accord with the declaration of principles already adopted by the conference providing for non-partisan action.

Bars Communist Delegates.

The convention opened its second day's session by refusing to seat the delegates of the Workers' Party of America and the Young Workers' League, two communistic labor organizations. The Credentials Committee reported that these delegates could not be seated, as the policies of their organizations were not "in harmony with the declarations and principles of this conference."

C. E. Ruthenberg, National Secretary of the Workers' Party, and the three other delegates to the movement, which was denounced yesterday as "un-American and anti-labor," were barred from taking seats among the delegates by sergeants-at-arms. After several protests they took seats in the gallery, where, surrounded by several score of sympathizers, they silently watched the conference proceedings.

The report of the Credentials Committee was rushed through before the party sympathizers had a chance to register a protest. Chairman W. H. Johnston explained, "We are moving quickly today," as several delegates attempted to champion the radicals' cause.

Defeated in the convention, the four delegates of the Workers' Party and the one delegate from the Young Workers' League issued a statement attacking the action of the convention, declaring that the decision to refuse them seats had been "railroaded" through the convention and "shows how desperate these leaders are to keep the Workers' Party and the Young Workers' League, which stand for a labor party, out of the convention."

The delegates gave a big ovation to Senator-elect B. K. Wheeler of Montana, who in a brief address said that he expected to line up with the progressive Democratic and Republican members of Congress and "do what I can for the farmers, labor and the common people of the country in general." He said that this group had a road ahead and expected to have the support of the liberal elements of the country.

Mr. Wheeler charged that private detective agencies are attempting to destroy organized labor from the inside.

"If you find a man advocating sabotage and urging the taking of the law in his own hands," said Mr. Wheeler, "I am suspicious he is a detective who wants to discredit legitimate labor organizations."

B. B. Laughlin, President of the Oklahoma Farm Labor Union, said that not more than 20 per cent. of the farmers in Oklahoma had money to pay their taxes for the last two or three years. He said many of the farmers throughout the Southwest were starving, and "it is all due to the farmer getting less money for his crops than the cost of production."

"The farmer is ready to co-operate with you in economics and politics," he asserted.

December 13, 1922

MAGNUS JOHNSON'S FRIENDS AWAIT STRONG THIRD PARTY

Farmer-Labor Group Against Fusion, But Believes Progressive National Movement Is Just Ahead—How the Minnesota Organization Started and What It Has Done.

The Minnesota election has served to centre attention on the Farmer-Labor Party, which put Magnus Johnson in the Senate. The story of its origin and growth is set forth by its Chairman.

BY FREDERIC A. PIKE,

Chairman of the Farmer-Labor Party State Central Committee of Minnesota.

THE relation of the Farmer-Labor Party of Minnesota to national politics will be best understood when seen in the light of historical development. The tendencies that have culminated in the existing situation, and the character of the elements that make the new party, must be considered in any intelligent estimate of the present or forecast of the future.

Minnesota has had a share in the development of independent political thought and activity for many years. It was a fertile field for the growth of the principles of the Granger movement half a century ago and of its successor, the Farmers' Alliance, that thrived in the '80s. The political offspring of these earlier movements, which professed to be non-political, was the People's Party, led in Minnesota by Ignatius Donnelly, an outstanding character of great ability and force. Then came the stirring days of Bryan, when party lines were broken and re-formed as they had not been since the Civil War, and when there gathered in close political association and activity an influential group still known as the Bryan Democrats. In 1904 this group sent an anti-Parker delegation to the National Democratic Convention, and in 1908 almost prevented the choice of a "favorite son" delegation pledged to the then Governor, John A. Johnson.

In the first Bryan campaign labor leaders and labor organizations began to be strongly felt as political elements, and they have shared the political developments that have followed.

The Republican Party has been dominant in State politics ever since Minnesota was admitted to the Union, but within it there have been frequent commotions threatening its solidarity. Three Democratic Governors have been elected within twenty-five years, and Wilson in 1916 lost Minnesota's electoral vote by a scratch. Roosevelt carried the State in 1912, with twice Taft's vote.

The so-called radical vote in Minnesota never has been large. The views of extremists sometimes have been ably presented, but the obvious tendency in Minnesota toward progressive policies has not been of the radical type.

Such, in brief, was Minnesota's recent political history when that extraordinary organization, the National Non-Partisan League, entered the scene. Clever publicity created by political adversaries, consisting of ingenious but unjust charges of disloyalty during the war, has tended to obscure the origin and character of the Non-Partisan League. To understand Minnesota's present politics one must understand the league not as one has read about it in hostile journals, but as the league really was before the war. It had been born in North Dakota; had taken over part of the government of that State in 1916, and early in 1917 prepared to organize in Minnesota. It was an organization of farmers formed to achieve certain economic reforms, not as a political party, but through control of a selected political party already existing. Organized before the war, its program was not concerned with the issues of the war; but because its leaders asserted that predatory business interests pursuing the same iniquitous policies as in peace enjoyed during the war unjust gains and privileges, it was said by their adversaries that these leaders were un-American and pro-German.

No Brief for League.

But I am not submitting a brief for the Non-Partisan League or its leaders. As I have said, the league came into Minnesota as a farmers' movement, political but not partisan, and it found a soil well prepared for its growth. The farmers joined the league by tens of thousands. Mostly they were Republicans, and they tried to nominate candidates of their choice on the Republican ticket in the primary elections of 1918 and 1920. They failed. Meanwhile, in 1918 the farmers' battleline was augmented by recruits from organized labor. Members of the unions formed the Working People's Non-Partisan Political League, which became an ally of the farmers' league.

After two successive failures to capture the Republican ticket and organization, both leagues decided in 1922 to avail themselves of a new party name and status that had been created in 1918. In that year, after meeting defeat in the Spring primary, the allied progressive forces, the two leagues and their political associates nominated a State ticket by petition, which was supported in the November election.

There was much thought and discussion as to the name to be used in designating on the ballot the candidates who were thus nominated. None was suggested that seemed free from objection. It was finally decided that the term "Farmer-Labor" should be used. The name was unsatisfactory in this, that it might seem exclusive, not appealing to the universal citizenship of the State, and giving a too restricted aspect to the program of the new movement. But it had the advantage of indicating the two great groups of voters who were immediately responsible for the enterprise; and so the designation "Farmer-Labor" came to be used upon the ballot.

The candidate for Governor received 111,948 votes. He was defeated by 54,000 plurality by the Republican candidate, but led the Democrat 35,000 votes. The result gave legal standing to the Farmer-Labor Party, and thus that party was born.

Its status was continued by nominations made in 1920 as to a partial State ticket, and in 1922 was ready for an entire ticket and a complete campaign organization. The results of the campaign are recent history. Henrik Shipstead, Farmer-Labor candidate for United States Senator, was elected by a large plurality over Frank B. Kellogg, Republican; Magnus Johnson, Farmer-Labor, lost the Governorship to the Republican incumbent, Preus, by less than 15,000 votes; and the Democratic candidates trailed far behind.

One representative in Congress was elected as a straight-out Farmer-Labor candidate, and another, elected as independent, belongs to the same party. **The Farmer-Labor Party of Minnesota** had achieved its first success and was fairly launched upon its career.

This first success projected the new Minnesota party upon the national field, for its successful candidates became not State officers but members of the Congress of the United States. The election of Magnus Johnson in the recent special election sends another Farmer-Laborite to the Senate. What then is to be said of this new political body in its national aspects?

First, it should be noted that the Farmer-Labor Party of Minnesota and the national Farmer-Labor Party are separate and distinct organizations. There never has been any connection between them. This is emphasized, not to intimate an opinion as to whether such a connection would be desirable, but to negative a presumption that might arise from the identity of names.

As I have stated, the name "Farmer-Labor" was adopted and used by the State organization in 1918. In 1920 there were several conferences in Chicago, where an effort was made to form a new national party, and that party took the name Farmer-Labor. That national organization nominated a national ticket, and in several States Presidential electors. But this was not done in Minnesota. It could not have been done without the consent of the State organization already in possession of the name, and no proposition looking to that end was ever made or considered.

The National Farmer-Labor Party invited the State party to send delegates to the recent Chicago convention and conference. The courtesy of this invitation was appreciated in Minnesota. It was thought best, however, not to send an accredited representative, but to await the development of events. There was no delegate present from the Farmer-Labor Party of Minnesota.

Is the new Minnesota party lacking a purpose or policy of national scope? I think not. It is not easy to say just how such a purpose or policy would be ascertained or declared, for the Minnesota statutes recognize no form of party convention that would be appropriate for such an occasion. Conferences and conventions not recognized by statutes may be held, of course, and in fact are held from time to time; but at none of these, nor in any other authoritative way, has any expression been given disclosing the trend of thought among members of the State party as to what, if any, national movement should be undertaken.

It is my belief that the majority of the voters of Minnesota supporting the Farmer-Labor Party have done with all the old parties and desire that a national party be formed in 1924 with which the State organization can affiliate. Progressive voters are coming to regard the Republican and Democratic Parties as substantially the same in general tendencies, and they consider those parties unfit to be their political agents any longer, in either State or nation. Republicans can see no reason why they should leave the Republican Party to obtain economic reforms and become Democrats, and likewise Democrats will not become Republicans. Former Republicans and former Democrats are together with many thousands who were neither Republicans nor Democrats.

Fusion will have no attractions for the Farmer-Labor Party of Minnesota. Here and there progressives will control the local organizations of the Democratic or Republican Party, but the effective force of those parties will not be deflected from conservative, not to say reactionary, ends. Nor will the claims of organizations founded on narrow basis of class distinctions and demands control the policies of the Minnesota Farmer-Labor Party. It will steer between the Charybdis of class party distinction and the Scylla of fusion, the rock on which populism split and sank.

A word as to the things the Farmer-Labor party stands for, the things, speaking nationally, it is going to fight for. They are:

1. Repeal of the Esch-Cummins law and the substitution of public ownership and management of railways.

2. A graduated income tax placing the burden on those most able to pay.

3. Cash bonus to ex-service men paid by an excess profits tax.

4. Restriction of the courts in the use of injunctions in labor controversies and in the nullifying of acts of Congress.

5. A national farm products price fixing law.

6. Full Government control of the Federal Reserve banks.

7. Legislation making the constitutional right of free speech, free press and peaceable assembly effective.

8. Friendly relations with all nations, alliances with none.

July 29, 1923

COOLIDGE ASSUMES ROLE OF HARMONIZER AMONG REPUBLICANS

Special to The New York Times.

WASHINGTON, Sept. 23.—President Coolidge now appears in the rôle of a composer of differences between factions in the Republican Party, according to those who are in intimate touch with the Administration. They say he intends, if possible, to cement the party and get through a legislative program on railroads, taxation and farm aid that will represent constructive achievement.

In this program the President will be aided by his secretary, C. Bascom Slemp, who, as a recent member of the House, is believed to be able to add a sufficient personal element to the situation to aid the move for harmony and thereby help the Administration in carrying out its legislative program. This cannot be accomplished, it is argued, without a great deal of compromise.

President Coolidge has not met that situation yet, but he is preparing the way for cordial relations, at least, by holding out the olive branch to the radicals and not excluding them from the party councils as his predecessor did. One evidence of this was his invitation to Senator Borah to dinner at the White House recently to discuss the conditions among the farmers.

Hopes to Pacify Radical Bloc.

But the most difficult task the President has set for himself is in pacifying the La Follette Congressional bloc. Upon the outcome of his efforts depends to a large extent the success of the legislative program which he will present to Congress when it convenes in December, and upon the success of this legislative program depends his ability to present to the country a record of achievement which will entitle him to the Presidential nomination in 1924.

The strategy of the Administration in dealing with the complex and unfavorable situation at the Capitol has been brought to light in the past few days. As the first step in the conciliation program it is understood that Mr. Coolidge has given assurances to the followers of La Follette that he will restore their Federal office patronage rights in Wisconsin.

Early in the Harding Administration all Federal patronage was taken away from Senator La Follette and the La Follette Representatives and turned over to Senator Lenroot, to be used in the construction of a powerful political machine to smash the La Follette power. The La Follette men protested vigorously, but President Harding steadfastly refused to recognize the recommendations of men who consistently hampered his policies, and the word of Senator Lenroot was law in the distribution of Federal jobs in Wisconsin.

Word that the La Follette patronage ban is to be lifted was announced by Representative Lampert of Wisconsin, after a conference with President Coolidge. Mr. Lampert is one of the La Follette Representatives whose recommendations as to patronage were ignored by President Harding. When he left the White House he was jubilant.

White House Will Welcome La Follette.

Senator La Follette, the recognized radical leader in Congress, was on the high seas en route to Europe when President Harding died. When he returns he will be welcomed at the White House, if he calls, it is understood.

President Coolidge, some Administration leaders say, can hardly expect to bring the Wisconsin Senator and his followers into close accord with the Administration, but he may succeed in mitigating their antagonism and smooth the way for action on measures which might otherwise be blocked.

Another important move in the harmony plan was made by the President when he invited Senator Borah to dine with him at the White House. Senator Borah has already agreed to make no fight against the World Court plan, provided Mr. Coolidge adopts the conditions laid down by President Harding in his St. Louis speech.

September 24, 1923

SOUTH WINS BACK DELEGATES DROPPED BY 1920 CONVENTION

Republican Committee Restores Old Representation, and Increases Northern Membership.

OPPONENTS PREDICT REVOLT

Special to The New York Times.

WASHINGTON, Dec. 12.—The Republican National Committee reversed today the mandate of the 1920 National Convention, which fixed the apportionment of delegates for the South on the basis of one delegate for each 2,500 Republican voters, and restored the old apportionment of one delegate for each Congressional district and increased the representation of the thirty-seven Republican States by three delegates-at-large. The committee then selected Cleveland as the convention city and June 10 as the date.

The choice of Cleveland was made unanimous after the ballot showed 39 for that city, 10 for San Francisco, and 1 for Des Moines.

Under the resolutions adopted and the call issued there will be 1,109 delegates in the 1924 convention, as compared with 984 in the 1920 convention and 1,036 recommended by that convention's special committee.

Progressive Republicans, led by Senators Howell and Johnson, denounced the action of the committee, which they asserted was dictated by the Administration. This defiance of the National Convention and sentiment in progressive States, they said, would cause a revolt in the Republican Party not unlike the fight over the Southern delegates in the 1912 convention.

The action increasing the representation of Northern States and restoring the South's old apportionment, followed a long fight by the negro leaders against the resolution of the last convention. This resolution reduced the South's delegates by 23, and gave the non-Republican States 211 delegates in all, instead of 234 as heretofore. The delegates for Republican States were increased by 74.

Northern Delegates Increased.

Under the resolution offered by Senator Pepper, national committeeman from Pennsylvania, and adopted today, the delegates from Northern States are increased by eleven over the 1920 ratio, while the Southern list remains as then—234.

In revising the resolution of the 1920 convention, the leaders, after a midnight session, decided that unpleasant race struggles could be avoided at the next convention and the Northern representation increased if the committee should reach a compromise which would have the same effect as was intended by the convention's action.

Many Republican leaders have fought for twenty-five years against the Southern delegations, asserting that they did not represent any Republican votes. Another point made was that the South's delegates were usually obtained by Federal patronage and other means, and were employed to overcome the sentiment of Republican States.

After the committee and its subcommittee had heard the protests of the Negro leaders they became convinced that something must be done to satisfy them. They saw a loss of Republican votes in Illinois, Ohio, Indiana, New Jersey, Pennsylvania and New York, where the Negro vote is large. It was the threat of revolt in the North that largely influenced the party leaders to restore the South's representation.

Midnight Conference Called.

A hasty midnight conference was attended by Chairman Adams, Senator Pepper, David W. Mulvane of Kansas, Charles D. Hilles of New York, Ralph D. Williams of Oregon, Senator Ernst of Kentucky, Hamilton F. Kean of New Jersey, Mrs. Christine Bradley South of Kentucky. Mrs. Henrietta L. Livermore of New York and Mrs. George Orvis of Vermont.

The midnight conference agreed to surrender to the demands of the South, after the situation was carefully considered with due regard to the negro vote in the North. The conference appointed Chairman Adams, Senator Pepper, Mr. Kean, Mr. Hilles, Mr. Mulvane and George B. Lockwood to work out the compromise which Senator Pepper offered when the committee met this morning.

Charles D. Hilles moved to reconsider the report of the committee on apportionment. Then Senator Pepper offered his resolution which, in effect, gave every Southern Congressional District one delegate and added three delegates at large to the Republican States. This caused a long and bitter debate, but the compromise was adopted by a viva voce vote, though there was a large number of dessents.

"I am amazed at the proposal," Senator Howell of Nebraska, who was Chairman of the convention's committee which worked out the apportionment. "For twenty years we have been attempting a reform of apportionment, and now you are proposing to undo that great reform. The progressive-minded Republicans do not know what you are proposing to do or they would be here in arms.

"You remember the fatal division of 1912. The trouble at that time was caused by resentment at the control of Southern delegates who represented no Republican States and no Republican voters.

"I warn you that this is going to cause more trouble. You are about to light the train that leads to a powder barrel. There is always a suspicion that the Administration controls these Southern delegates."

Senator Pepper agreed with Senator Howell that recognition should be accorded those States which were really Republican, and said his proposal did that by giving such States three additional delegates, while it left the South with only what it had in 1920.

"The net result of my proposal," said Senator Pepper, "would accord to the States affected the principle of a basis of Congressional districts as distinguished from the conflict of the uncertain standard of a numerically constituted vote, and in order to meet the difficulty which Senator Howell has very properly called our attention to, namely, the suspicion or suggestion that a political advantage was being given to anybody, the proposal is that additional delegates shall be added to the States which gave their electoral vote to the Republican candidate for President, thus giving to that group of States an increased representation.

"The figures, I believe, are these: That the additional delegates at large would mean thirty-eight delegates at large, and the Southern States would have an increase of 23 or 25 over your proposal. So that the political significance of this thing is eliminated, and the thing that we accomplish by the resolution, if adopted, is to purge ourselves of what I, for one, believe to be an indefensible act of injustice, and that is to make representation in the Republican convention dependent upon the counting of votes in election districts which we neither control nor can make any effective effort to control.

Urges Real Representation.

"I do not believe that any group of people within the American nation, within the limits of the Republican Party, can long successfully be denied a representation based upon something that is real and not on something that is shallow.

"Senator Howell speaks of progressive minds throughout the country. Many of us feel ourselves entitled to be included in the category of such minds, and no interest of the progressive minds ought to be more earnest or more sincere than the interest of fundamntal justice in the make-up of a representative body. Our convention is a representative body. Those who are Republicans are entitled to representation in it upon a basis which is fixed, certain and genuine. That cannot be said of the present situation, and it is in order to relieve that situation that I have ventured to propose the resolution now pending.

"If you will consider for a moment justice, not merely in a theoretical sense," replied Mr. Howell, "but in an actual sense, you will realize that by the adoption of this change you are giving to South Carolina eleven votes in the next convention. And although South Carolina cast but 2,200 votes in the last election, yet in the Northern States it would require 220,000 votes to have the same number of delegates in the National Convention.

"The last National Convention directed such a change to be made. It said that the change should be made in accord with the votes cast. We have followed the injunction of the convention. I contend that the mandate of the convention cannot be overruled by this committee.

"Enough has been said about our State," exclaimed Joseph W. Tolbert of South Carolina. "I want to say that every district in South Carolina elects its own delegates, and that the four delegates at large are elected in a State convention. We don't want you to come here with your nonsense and foolishness. We don't want the people of the nation to misunderstand. We are as good Republicans in South Carolina as anywhere, as good as you, Senator Howell, or any other man in the United States."

Mrs. Patterson of North Carolina appealed to the committee to help the Republican Party in the South by giving them proper representation.

December 13, 1923

COOLIDGE AND DAWES

DAWES WINS ON 3D BALLOT

By ELMER DAVIS.

Special to The New York Times.

PUBLIC HALL, CLEVELAND, Ohio, June 12.—The Republican National Convention of 1924 adjourned at 10:35 tonight, Eastern Standard Time, having renominated President Calvin Coolidge and placed Brig. Gen. Charles G. Dawes of Illinois on the ticket with him as a candidate for Vice President.

The last day of the convention, the only one that had decently comfortable weather, the only one that saw the auditorium filled with spectators, was also the busiest and most entertaining of the three days of sessions.

The nomination of President Coolidge at the morning session, by 1,065 votes to 34 for Senator Robert M. La Follette and 10 for Senator Hiram Johnson, had, of course, long been foreseen; but the selection of a Vice President developed quite a struggle. Some of the struggling was done by gentlemen who wanted to be Vice President and much more of it was done by gentlemen who would not be Vice President under any circumstances and objected to being drafted.

General Dawes was nominated on the first ballot tonight, at the last of the day's three sessions, receiving 682½ votes, as against 234½ for Herbert Hoover, Secretary of Commerce, and 75 for Judge William S. Kenyon and a few scattering. But at the afternoon session former Governor Frank O. Lowden of Illinois had been nominated despite his frequently expressed refusal to be a candidate, and it took two or three more refusals before the convention took him at his word.

Hoover Was Butler's Choice.

General Dawes was second choice, but Mr. Hoover, whom he defeated, was not even that. Hoover was the final candidate picked by William M. Butler, President Coolidge's campaign manager, and he was defeated by Dawes, not because the delegates had anything against Hoover, but because they had a great deal against William M. Butler.

President Coolidge and Vizier Butler have ruled this convention in everything but the nomination for Vice-President, and the discontent against their domination, which has been loudly expressed in words all week, finally blossomed out into action today. The delegates couldn't beat Coolidge, nor the Coolidge platform, but they could and did beat whatever Vice-Presidential candidate was unfortunate enough to have Mr. Butler's approval. They beat one this afternoon and they beat another tonight. And neither of these was Butler's first choice, or even his fourth or fifth choice.

All the week the Administration forces have been trying to find somebody to take the Vice Presidential nomination. Borah refused, Kenyon was cold, Lowden refused; when the convention finally started balloting for a Vice President in its second session of the day Mr. Butler had been forced to recognize that though Judge Kenyon had been placed in nomination he stood small chance of being selected as the candidate of the party. In that situation Mr. Butler was forced reluctantly to give such support as he could to Representative Theodore E. Burton, Temporary Chairman of the convention, who is a Clevelander, and has, besides the support of Ohio, that of most of the leaders in the Eastern industrial States.

But the convention had a mind of its own and power to take action of its own—on the Vice Presidency.

Half a dozen other candidates had been placed in nomination at the afternoon session, among them ex-Governor Lowden. He had repeatedly refused to let himself be considered for a place on the ticket; his nomination, when first made this afternoon, brought another statement from his friends that he wouldn't take it; but he was nominated again and on the second ballot he was chosen as the Vice Presidential candidate. At the end of the roll call on the ballot he had only 412 votes, as against 286 for Burton, 555 being necessary for a choice; but there was a rush of States to change their votes before another roll call, and New York and Pennsylvania put Lowden over.

Lowden's Refusal Causes a Snarl.

Then it was learned that Lowden, foreseeing something of the sort, had given to friends at the convention a sealed letter, to be read in case he were nominated, absolutely refusing to be a candidate. The letter was read and William M. Butler began to cheer up. Maybe he had a chance to put over a Vice President after all. By this time it was half past seven and the convention recessed for two hours to give Chairman Frank W. Mondell a chance to communicate directly with Governor Lowden.

When the convention met tonight at 9:30 for the third session of the day Mr. Mondell read a telegram from Mr. Lowden reiterating his refusal to be a candidate, and this time the delegates had to take him at his word.

The refusal was accepted and balloting began again. Mr. Burton had been abandoned by both his own friends and by the Administration, which had supported him feebly in the afternoon, and Mr. Butler tried to pick up his lost leadership and put over Secretary Hoover. But in the meantime the other side had been busy—not only the Old Guard, which has been slighted in this convention by the President and the forces of the various executive departments, but even some men of the President's own faction, who are for Coolidge but not for Butler.

Lowden was out of the race, but Dawes, who had run well on the first ballot in the afternoon, was still available. The Southern States, amenable to Administration pressure, were voting for Hoover, but the rest of the country was voting, not so much for Dawes as against Butler.

Sixty votes from New York made Dawes's victory a virtual certainty and 78 from Pennsylvania gave him the necessary majority. By the time the ballot ended he had 682½ to Hoover's 234½, and the choice was thereupon made unanimous, with Wisconsin and the six La Follette delegates from North Dakota alone dissenting, as they have dissented from everything done by the rest of the party during this convention.

The few remaining formalities were hurried through, and after a session lasting a little more than an hour the convention adjourned without a day.

June 13, 1924

CALVIN COOLIDGE

LA FOLLETTE NAMED AS HEAD OF TICKET BY THE PROGRESSIVES

Cleveland Delegates Endorse Wisconsin Senator, Leaving Second Place Open.

COMMUNISTS THROWN OUT

Foster and Ruthenberg Then Call It the Most Reactionary Convention of All.

SHORT PLATFORM ADOPTED

Special to The New York Times.

CLEVELAND, Ohio, July 5.—Senator Robert M. La Follette of Wisconsin was endorsed for President of the United States at 5:30 o'clock this afternoon by the Conference for Progressive Political Action, the National Convention of which adjourned tonight. The endorsement was by acclamation and carried with it an authorization to the National Committee of the conference, acting with the La Follette for President Committee, to name the candidate for Vice President.

A great demonstration followed the presentation of Senator La Follette's name, which was placed before the convention in the form of a resolution from the Committee on Organization.

There was no nominating speech, but there were four seconding speeches, and a score of delegates were clamoring for recognition when Chairman Johnston, to make adjournment tonight certain, brought the speechmaking to an end and put the question on the adoption of the endorsing resolution.

Every delegate was on his or her feet and everybody was shouting like mad. There was no camouflage, no artificiality about it. It was a real demonstration.

There was some opposition to the proposition vesting authority in the National Committee and the La Follette for President Committee to name the Senator's running mate. It was feeble, however, and was backed by not more than a dozen of the more than 1,200 delegates who shouted "Aye" for the resolution.

The resolution of the Organization Committee states that the platform adopted was submitted by Senator La Follette himself. Textually it is not the Wisconsin platform which was rejected by the Republican National Convention, but the things advocated or denounced are the same in the main.

Vice Presidential Tangle Avoided.

There was a reason for endorsing by resolution. Had the original program, which called for a nomination speech, been followed, a snarl over the Vice Presidential problem might have resulted. By providing for the selection of a Vice President by committee and embodying the recommendation in the La Follette resolution this avenue of possible trouble was closed.

The platform on which Senator La Follette goes to the country is regarded by Progressives as a model so far as brevity is concerned. It is less than 1,000 words in length and contains fourteen specific pledges, ranging from the restoration of the excess profits tax to the public ownership of railroads and the repeal of the Esch-Cummins law.

The platform declares that the power of the Federal Government must be used to crush and not to foster monopoly; promises public ownership of the water-power resources of the nation; the public control of all natural resources, including oil, coal, iron and timber; the retention of taxes on swollen incomes "rapidly progressive taxes" on large incomes and inheritances; the reconstruction of the Federal Reserve and Federal Farm Loan systems; the passage of drastic legislation for the relief of agriculture; international action to effect the economic recovery of the world from the effects of the World War; election of Federal Judges and the curtailment of the power of the courts in the matter of injunctions, &c., and the prompt ratification of the Child Labor Amendment to the Constitution.

Foreign Policies Denounced.

So far as the foreign affairs of the country are concerned, the policies of recent Administrations are denounced as mercenary and degraded and in the "interests of financial imperialists, oil monopolists and international bankers."

The influence of these interests has been such, it is alleged, as to have degraded the State Department into "a trading outpost for those interests engaged in the exploitations of weaker nations."

The platform declares for a revision of the Versailles Treaty in accordance with the terms of the armistice.

Donald A. Richberg, general counsel for the Railway Brotherhoods, Chairman of the Platform Committee, read the document and moved its adoption.

There was no debate and not a dissenting voice. Everybody knew it was Senator La Follette's platform, and that was all they cared to know. It was adopted with a whoop.

July 6, 1924

Special to The New York Times.

DEMOCRATIC WOMEN TO HELP ON PLATFORM

Mrs. Roosevelt Heads Committee to Formulate Planks on Welfare Legislation.

WASHINGTON, March 30. — Mrs. Franklin D. Roosevelt of New York was appointed today by Cordell Hull, Chairman of the Democratic National Committee, as Chairman of an advisory subcommittee of Democratic women to formulate planks on social welfare legislation for the Democratic platform.

This advisory committee of women will submit to the Resolutions Committee of the Democratic National Convention in New York, June 24, a woman's platform of legislation, combining the requests of all women's organizations of the country.

Mrs. Roosevelt will select as members of her committee women who are nationally known as experts in various social welfare endeavors. This committee will invite all women's organizations to submit to it the planks upon which they desire to have the Resolutions Committee pass. The Women's Advisory Committee will combine the proposals into a social legislation platform and will in turn submit it to the National Committee before the convention.

Mrs. Emily Newell Blair, Vice Chairman of the Democratic National Committee, said today:

"The Democratic committee, which proved its eagerness in 1920 to welcome women voters into the party by giving them a full vote on the National Committee, now is the first political group to seek women's views on important questions of peculiar interest to them so that these social legislation planks as incorporated in the national Democratic platform may represent their ideas."

March 31, 1924

CONVENTION, BY ONE VOTE, DEFEATS PLANK NAMING KLAN

GEORGIA BEATS KLAN PLANK

Changes Vote and a Half, Some Say on Order by McAdoo Leaders.

UNIT RULE ALSO HAS EFFECT

Many States Challenged and Repolled, and One Fist Fight Mars Dramatic Session.

By ELMER DAVIS.

An effort to incorporate in the Democratic platform a plank condemning the Ku Klux Klan by name was lost early this morning by a single vote, 541 3-20 votes having been cast for it and 542 3-20 against it.

The motion was defeated largely by virtue of the unit rule, under which only one State, Alabama, with a dissenting minority, voted for it, while a number voted against.

Even so, it could not have been beaten without the forced changes of one and a half votes in the Georgia delegation, originally cast for the motion but turned against it, according to rumor, by instructions from the McAdoo headquarters.

The resolution that was beaten was offered by fourteen of the fifty-four members of the Platform Committee as a minority report. It was advocated most vigorously by William Pattangall of Maine and Edmond H. Moore of Ohio. In its place there was adopted the Klan plank recommended by a majority of the committee, which merely advocated religious liberty and equality without mentioning the name of any order which opposes them.

Struggle Lasts Four Hours.

The fight over the Klan plank lasted from 8:45 o'clock at night till nearly 2 o'clock in the morning. Before it began a minority plank, calling for immediate entry into the League of Nations, offered by Newton D. Baker of Ohio and advocated by him in a passionate speech, which won him a personal triumph, was defeated by a vote of 742½ to 353½. The majority plank which was adopted, called for a popular referendum which the Government should regard as advisory.

With the majority planks thus supported in both the controversial cases, the platform as a whole was put to the convention and declared carried by a viva voce vote, although there were loud shouts against it.

At 1:55 o'clock, after nearly ten hours of continuous session, the convention adjourned until 9:30 o'clock Monday morning, when balloting on the candidates for President will begin.

The effort to get the name of the Ku Klux Klan into the platform resulted in one of the most entertaining evenings that have been seen in recent national conventions. There was, to begin with, two hours of oratory for and against the proposal, which was closed for the defense—that is for the majority of the Resolutions Committee who did not want to name the Klan—by William Jennings Bryan, who spoke with his old-time fire and enthusiasm and very nearly with his old-time success.

Bryan Often Hissed and Booed.

Unfortunately the galleries happened to be passionately interested in the side of the case which he was against, and he was hissed and booed again and again.

Once the chorus of hoots became so loud that Senator Thomas J. Walsh, Chairman of the convention, threatened to have them cleared if the offense were repeated. That kept the galleries fairly quiet.

Mr. Bryan was perhaps the most brilliant speaker of the evening, but the hero of the session was Andrew C. Erwin of Athens, Ga., who made a three-minute speech of extraordinary fire in favor of naming the Klan and declared that Georgians who didn't support him were unworthy of their ancestry.

This provoked a wild demonstration and the parade of twenty-three State standards around the Georgian delegation, the crowd pushing in so hard that police had to protect the Georgians.

Erwin nearly saved the anti-Klan motion again when he demanded a poll of the Georgia delegation after it had been announced by its Chairman, Hollins Randolph, as having voted three ayes and 25 noes. On Mr. Erwin's insistence, the roll of the delegation was called and it was discovered that several members were absent so that the roll showed 2½ votes aye and 17 no.

Tries Hard to Get Votes.

But Mr. Randolph labored hard to get the votes for the motion changed and he finally worked on three of the five half-vote delegates who had voted for it and persuaded them to come around to the negative. Two or three delegates, who had been absent when the first vote was taken, came in later and were counted. Mr. Randolph reported two or three more as just arriving and asked that they be counted, but the Chair discovered that they had been counted already.

The computation of the vote on this final ballot took almost two hours and while it produced only one actual fight there probably would have been more but for the presence of some 200 policemen in the hall.

The one fight took place in the Philippine delegation, which was reported as voting one Aye and five Noes. The report was made by Percy M. Moir, who lives in Washington and is only an alternate. It was challenged at the end of the roll call by T. T. Ansberry, also an alternate.

In the course of the argument Mr. Moir tried to knock a man who was raising a point of order off a chair and was restrained by a police captain and several patrolmen. The industrious pointer of order from the Philippines was heard a moment later demanding a recount in New Hampshire and it was discovered that he was Lawrence F. Quigley, a delegate from Massachusetts.

He was not allowed to have New Hampshire polled again, but Ohio, Louisiana and Nevada were recounted, the last two only to develop the fact that while several of their delegates were in favor of the motion, the delegations were being voted against it on the unit rule.

There was no effort to rush the Georgians, perhaps because, though there were only a few policemen at that particular point, there were about 200 in the hall. But enthusiastic friends of Mr. EErwin presently hoisted him on their shoulders and carried him around he Garden. The standards followed him, and thus the congestion around Georgia was more or less relieved so that the speaking could go on.

June 29, 1924

75

DAVIS IS PUT OVER IN WILD STAMPEDE

Weary Delegates Jump for Band Wagon and Then All Join Big Demonstration.

By ELMER DAVIS.

The Democrats have finally nominated and gone home. John W. Davis was selected as the Presidential candidate yesterday afternoon, on the 103d ballot. At 2:25 o'clock this morning Governor Charles W. Bryan of Nebraska was nominated as Vice President.

The fierce tension had been relaxed by the long days of fruitless balloting. The two men in this convention who have inspired the bitterest ecstasies of love and hate had been driven out of the running after a struggle that had endured too long, so there was not the frenzied joy springing from the release of pent-up feeling such as greeted the nomination of James M. Cox in San Francisco four years ago. The delegates had fought each other to a standstill and themselves to exhaustion. They had no spirit left for the revival that should have come with the dismissal of the two leading candidates, the settlement by treaty of that endless war, and the turning toward more productive effort.

July 10, 1924

WHEELER BOLTS THE DAVIS TICKET

Montana Senator Declares He Will Support La Follette for President.

Special to The New York Times.

WASHINGTON, July 16.—Senator Burton K. Wheeler of Montana bolted the Democratic ticket this afternoon, announcing at the same time that he would support Senator La Follette for President.

This is the first important defection from the Democratic ranks and serves to complicate the Democratic situation in the Northwest, where the radical progressive forces are said to have many recruits and where Senator Wheeler has influence in farm and labor councils.

"I cannot consistently support John W. Davis for President," said Senator Wheeler, "but, on the other hand, I can consistently support Senator La Follette and shall do so.

"When the Democratic Party goes to Wall Street for its candidate I must refuse to go with it. The nomination of Mr. Davis was brought about in the hope it would make possible a big campaign fund, and as a result of this nomination the Democratic Party, in my opinion, has forfeited any right it may have to the support of the progressive Democrats of the country."

Mr. Wheeler declared he would not accept the second place on the La Follette ticket if it were offered to him.

Senator Wheeler said he would support his colleague, Senator Thomas J. Walsh, who is running for re-election to the Senate, and also would do what he could to help elect the Democratic ticket in Montana. He stands ready to support Senator Borah in Idaho, Senator Norris in Nebraska, Senator Brookhart in Iowa and other candidates whom he describes as representative of the progressive thought of the country.

Reverting to the Democratic nominee for President, Senator Wheeler declared that, no matter how many progressive speeches Mr. Davis made, he would not be able to overcome the "Morgan" handicap.

"What kind of a run do you expect Senator La Follette to make in the Northwest?" Mr. Wheeler was asked.

"In my opinion," he replied, "Senator La Follette will sweep that part of the country, and he is going to surprise a lot of people in other parts of the country, too."

The La Follette supporters are expecting other prominent men in each of the old parties to follow the example of Mr. Wheeler. Senators Brookhart, Norris, Ladd and Frazier are among the expected "deserters" from the Republican ranks, and there is considerable talk about the possible defection of Senator Dill of Washington, of the La Follette Democratic group.

Another Senator whose course is being watched is Hiram Johnson of California. To date he has remained silent. It is common knowledge that the Californian is out of sympathy with the Coolidge policies, and it is recalled that he stood with Senator La Follette in opposing the Mellon tax plan. He opposed the President's World Court and immigration policies and voted to override the bonus veto.

July 17, 1924

OLD PARTY POLICIES REJECTED BY LABOR

Federation Finds Republican and Democratic Candidates Unacceptable.

CALLS DAWES AN ENEMY

Report Praises La Follette Party Attitude, Especially on Domestic Issues.

Special to The New York Times.

ATLANTIC CITY, N. J., Aug. 3.—The text of the report endorsing the candidacies of Senators La Follette and Wheeler, which was adopted yesterday by the Executive Council, the supreme body in the American Federation of Labor, was made public today. A reading of its contents made plain what the labor chiefs meant when they said it was a "personal and non-partisan" endorsement.

There are three points in the report which make clear the adherence to the keynote utterance of President Gompers, uttered last Wednesday on his arrival here in advance of the meeting, namely, that the non-partisan tradition of the Federation would not be deviated from.

First, the report characterizes La Follette and Wheeler in these terms: "The first an independent Republican; the second an independent Democrat, running as such."

Second, the report, while specifically condemning the platforms of both Republican Party and Democratic Party, does not use the term "party," when defining the La Follette platform, as sympathetic to labor, but emphasizes the individual nature of the candidacies by speaking of the platform of "these candidates."

Third, the report, as if in an effort to clear up all doubt specifically, says: "Cooperation hereby urged is not a pledge of identification with an independent party movement or a third party, nor can it be construed as support for such a party, group or movement."

Reserve Choices on Congress.

In addition to these direct points relating to the present, there is another point in the report relating to future eventualities. The report says:

"The La Follette ticket has no Congressional nominees, but has indicated it will endorse Congressional candidates sympathetic toward its viewpoint of the two major parties."

"Will there be a disposition on the part of organized labor to await the La Follette Congressional endorsements and then declare for them?" was asked of a member of the council today. Here is the answer he gave:

"Absolutely not. That question is specifically covered in the section of our report which relates to Congressional nominations. We have completely reserved our own right to action on Congress."

The section referred to reads as follows:

"In the campaign to elect men to Congress, regardless of their political group or party affiliation and deserving of labor's support, there must be unity of purpose and method. Therefore leadership must lie with the only organization having the right to speak for the entire labor movement. In this the American Federation of Labor yields to none, but will maintain steadfast its leadership, guidance and direction.

"In the selection and election of men to public office within the several States, leadership must lie with our State Federation of Labor, and in city or county elections this right must rest with central labor bodies."

One reason why the members of the council so minded were able to resist the minority's demand for a complete endorsement of the La Follette cause was referred to today by an official of the convention as having found expression in the wording of the report. He pointed out the sentence which read as follows:

"Neither can this cooperation imply our support, acceptance or endorsement of policies or principles advocated by any minority groups or organizations that may see fit to support the candidacies of Senator La Follette and Senator Wheeler."

He explained that this phrase referred to Socialists and "even some outlaw unions" who have come to the Wisconsin Senator's support. It has been known that at any stage of the deliberations at which the talk of throwing in the Federation's influence behind La Follette in a Labor and Farmers' Party movement became too fervent, the more conservative members of the council were able to check it by citing to its advocates instances of groups and organizations in their own territory identified as hostile to the Federation's purposes.

It was denied specifically at the headquarters today that there would be a complete list of Senators and Representatives favored or opposed by labor. For the most part, it was said by the labor men, Congressional candidacies would be left to local jurisdiction. However, it was intimated that in some conspicuous instances in which "there could be no doubt as to the attitude of labor, either locally or nationally," statements would be forthcoming from the present meeting of the Council. For instance, rudely as the Republican Party as a whole has been dealt with in the report, it is considered likely that a Republican like Senator Hiram Johnson of California will have the official approval of labor before the meeting is over.

The report made public today is in two sections, the first devoted to the recital of the steps the Federation took in investigating candidacies and platforms and the measures it adopted as a test of fitness. The second section is devoted to "recommendations and conclusions" and tells the results of the survey.

When the text of the report was given out, the statement was made that it had been adopted by the Council in the form it had been submitted by the Non-Partisan Campaign Committee. This statement was interpreted as having the purpose of denying the reports of strife in the committee over its adoption.

The Council's Conclusions.

The second section of the report, which deals with the "conclusions and recommendations," follows in full:

The Executive Council of the American Federation of Labor National Non-Partisan Political Campaign

Committee presented labor's proposals to the Republican Convention.

The Republican Convention gave labor's representatives a brief and curt hearing. The Republican platform ignores entirely the injunction issue. It fails to deal with labor's right to organize or the right of the workers, even in self-defense, collectively to cease work. That platform sustains the Railroad Labor Board, with all that it means in the direction of governmental coercion of wage earners. It fails to recommend the ratification by the States of the child labor constitutional amendment.

The Republican Convention nominated candidates unacceptable to labor.

Its candidate for Vice President is one of the most outspoken enemies of labor and is the founder of an organization dedicated to the task of writing into all political platforms planks calling for the anti-union shop—an organization which also encouraged and supported the Daugherty injunction against the railroad shopmen.

Labor's representatives submitted to the Democratic Convention identical proposals to those submitted to the Republican Convention. At this convention an extended hearing was granted. The Democratic platform pledges that party to legislation to regulate hours and conditions of all labor, a proposal against which the American Federation of Labor has struggled throughout its whole history. It is silent as to the injunction. It does not meet the Railroad Labor Board issue. On that point it is so equivocal that the enemies of labor may well feel that their desires will be met. It, too, fails to recommend the ratification by the States of the child labor constitutional amendment.

The Democratic Convention nominated candidates unacceptable to labor.

As to the candidates and platforms, both the Republican and Democratic National Party Conventions flaunted the desires of labor, the Republican Convention in an arrogant manner; the Democratic Convention by that evasiveness which is the customary mark of insincerity.

Favors La Follette Platform.

There remains the candidacy of Robert M. La Follette and Burton K. Wheeler, the first an independent Republican, the second an independent Democrat, running as such.

These candidates have proffered a platform in which the economic issues of the day are met in a manner more nearly conforming to labor's proposals than any other platform.

This platform pledges a remedy for the injunction evil.

It pledges the right to organize and collectively to cease work.

It pledges protection of the rights of free speech, free press and free assemblage.

It pledges abolishment of the Railroad Labor Board. It pledges a measure to annul the power of the Supreme Court to declare laws permanently unconstitutional.

It declares for direct election of President and Vice President and election of Federal Judges.

It recommends prompt ratification by the States of the Child Labor Constitutional Amendment.

It pledges subsequent Federal legislation to protect child life.

On international affairs this platform does not conform to labor's proposals, but it does more fully than any other political platform meet labor's views in relation to domestic economic issues.

We cannot do other than point out this fact, together with the further and perhaps more important fact that the candidates, Mr. La Follette and Mr. Wheeler, have throughout their whole political careers stood steadfast in the defense of the rights and interests of the wage earners and farmers.

We cannot fail to observe that both Republican and Democratic Parties through manipulated control are in a condition of moral bankruptcy which constitutes a menace and a peril to our country and its institutions. Machine politicians have brought upon our country moral obliquity and unashamed betrayal. We are judging on the basis oof the conditions which exist, and this judgment will be reversed only when the conditions upon which it is based are changed.

Service to the people is a noble cause which demands consecration and the American labor movement demands that there be that consecration in candidates to whom it gives support.

Our course is clear. In pointing to the platform and records of the independent candidates, we do so with confidence that no other course can be pursued if we are to remain true to our convictions and our traditions. Those who are hostile to labor and to the people generally and who devote their energies to the service of reaction and special interests must be opposed.

Cooperation Is Uurged.

We call upon the wage earners and the great masses of the peoples everywhere who stand for freedom, justice, democracy and human progress, to rally in this campaign to the end that the representatives of faction and special interests may be defeated and the faithful friends and servants of the masses elected.

Cooperation hereby urged, is not a pledge of indentification with an independent party movement or a third party, nor can it be construed as support for such a party, group or movement except as such action accords with our non-partisan political policy. We do not accept government as the solution of the problems of life.

Major problems of life and labor must be dealt with by voluntary groups and organizations, of which trade unions are an essential and integral part. Neither can this cooperation imply our support, acceptance or endorsement of policies or principles advocated by any minority groups or organizations that may see fit to support the candidacies of Senator La Follette and Senator Wheeler.

In the campaign to elect men to Congress regardless of their political group or party affiliation, and deserving of labor's support, there must be unity of purpose and method; therefore leadership must lie with the only organization having the right to speak for the entire labor movement. In this the American Federation of Labor yields to none, but will maintain steadfast its leadership, guidance and direction.

In the selection and election of men to public office within the several States, leadership must lie with our State Federations of Labor, and in city or county elections this right must rest with central labor bodies.

Organized labor owes allegiance to no political party or group. It is not partisan to any political party or group. It is partisan to principles—the principles of freedom, of justice, of democracy.

It is the duty of trade unionists, their friends and sympathizers, and all lovers of freedom, justice and democratic ideals and institutions, to unite in defeating those seeking public office who are indifferent or hostile to the people's rights and interests. It is the duty of all to support such candidates to public office who have been fair, just and outspoken in behalf of the welfare of the common people.

We shall analyze the records and attitude of every aspirant to public office, and shall give our findings the widest possible publicity. Labor's enemies and friends must be clearly known and be definitely indicated.

In calling upon all affiliated and recognized national and international brotherhood organizations, State Federations of Labor, central labor bodies, local unions, labor's friends and sympathizers, to give united, unrestricted, loyal and active support to the non-partisan campaign now set in motion, we emphasize the imperative need of an intensive educational campaign to enable all to act with discrimination and wisdom in this election and to stand faithfully by our friends and elect them and to oppose our enemies and to defeat them.

The document is signed by Samuel Gompers, Frank Morrison, James O'Connell and Matthew Woll, the Executive Committee of the American Federation of Labor National Non-Partisan Political Campaign Committee.

August 4, 1924

LAGUARDIA BOLTS REPUBLICAN PARTY

Representative Tells Koenig He Will Run Independently and Support La Follette.

WON'T SACRIFICE PRINCIPLE

Says He Cannot Limit His Legislative Activities to "Narrow Confines" of Party Platform.

Representative F. H. LaGuardia formally withdrew from the Republican Party yesterday and announced himself a follower of La Follette.

The reasons he gave for leaving the party that frequently put him in office were that he would not sacrifice his principles for a renomination, that he did not like the Republican national platform and that he did approve the La Follette-Wheeler platform.

Mr. LaGuardia's action has been expected. He has more than once shown a determination to kick over the organization traces and when he last returned from Washington he refused to say he would run again as a Republican, although he made it clear that he would run. He states his present position in a letter to Samuel S. Koenig, Chairman of the Republican County Committee, with whom, it appears, he has been conferring regarding his renomination. His letter follows:

Hon. Samuel S. Koenig, Chairman Republican Candidate Committee.

My dear Mr. Chairman:

In our talk a few days ago you indicated that my candidacy for Congress on the Republican ticket would depend on my compliance with certain minimum requirements. Desirable and comfortable as a party nomination may be, I cannot sacrifice principle for the sake of a party nomination or anything else.

During all of my time in the House I worked hard and voted according to my best judgm.nt, and in a manner which I believed represented the wishes of the people of my district. The platform of the Republican Party as adopted at Cleveland makes no appeal to the hope of the people whom I represent. I cannot conscientiously pledge myself to support that platform and to limit my legislative activities within the narrow confines of that document.

You are correct when you say that on many of the important bills that came before the House, such as soldiers' bonus, immigration, the Mellon tax plan, postal salary increase, prohibition, Cape Cod Canal, Henry Ford and Muscle Shoals, I did not support the reactionary attitude of the Republican majority. On these issues I am willing to go before the people of my district.

If honest independence of action in the fulfillment of a legislator's duty in his representative capacity disqualifies a candidate and prevents his renomination, on that too I am ready to go before the people of the Twentieth Congressional District.

Of course, I shall hold the Republican candidate for Congress in that and in every district of the City of New York strictly to the Republican Party's platform and shall dare them to say they advocate and support those Administrative measures which I fought and voted against in the last session.

Inasmuch as a small group which now controls the party locally has seen fit to single me out, you cannot but agree that the same standard which you require for the Twentieth District will apply to all the Congressional districts in the city, so that the voters will have no difficulty in choosing their representative.

In reply to your inquiry as to whom I shall support for President of the United States, I beg to state that the platform adopted by the Conference for Progressive Political Action contains an economic and political program which comes nearer fitting our present time and conditions than any platform presented to the voters of this country since 1912, when the late Theodore Roosevelt set the example of righteousness rather than regularity. I shall therefore support the C. P. P. A. platform and the candidacy of Robert M. La Follette for President.

With kindest personal regards, I am

Sincerely,

F. LAGUARDIA.

The Twentieth District, which LaGuardia represents, is independent. LaGuardia hired a hall to give an account of his stewardship after Congress adjourned and it was filled to overflowing with a most enthusiastic audience. A short time ago, when the Socialist leaders were considering designations for Congress, they decided not to take any action as to the Twentieth, though they considered it an excellent field for their purposes, until it should appear whether LaGuardia would run on the Republican ticket. Inasmuch as he is not to run as a Republican it is almost certain he will get the endorsement of the Socialists, who are allied with the La Follette Progressives.

At Bradley Beach last night Mr. Koenig said the test of a man's Republicanism was not what measures he had voted for or against but for whom he would vote for President. Mr. LaGuardia had been given until today to make up his mind.

"He has done so and that is his affair," added Mr. Koenig.

The Republican organization in the district probably will meet today or tonight to designate a man to run in LaGuardia's place.

August 11, 1924

COOLIDGE WINS

Calvin Coolidge has been elected President of the United States in a victory of impressive proportions.

At 5 o'clock this morning the returns indicated that President Coolidge had secured 357 electoral votes, Davis 136 and La Follette 13, and that 25 votes in five Western States were still in doubt. The principal overtures in the late returns were in Kentucky and Missouri. In Kentucky, in 3,431 out of 3,971 precincts, seven-eighths of the State, Coolidge had 337,838, against 331,244 for Davis. It was the opinion of the most competent observers in the State that later returns would not take the State away from the President.

In Missouri Coolidge has 251,802, against Davis's 238,896 in 1,954 out of 4,069 precincts. Correspondents in the State believed that the Republican rural precincts were sure to give the State to the President. The St. Louis Globe-Democrat estimates that Coolidge will carry the State by 50,000.

The five States remaining in doubt are Minnesota, Montana, Nevada, Arizona and New Mexico.

In Montana Coolidge has a slight lead, but the returns are too scant to justify giving the State to him at present. Arizona and New Mexico are close, with indications of going for Davis. In Nevada Coolidge has a lead of 600 votes over La Follette, who is running second, in a little less than one-half the State.

It is not probable that Davis's vote in the Electoral College will exceed 142, which it will be if he carries Arizona and New Mexico. Apparently he has no chance in Minnesota, Montana and Nevada, where he is running third, La Follette being second. On the other hand, it is possible that Coolidge may carry Minnesota, Montana and Nevada, giving him a total of 376, or, with Arizona and New Mexico added, 382 as his utmost limit.

An extreme possibility, but not a very strong one, for La Follette, is the addition of Minnesota, Montana and Nevada, to the one State that he has surely carried, Wisconsin, which would give him a total of 32.

Senator Robert M. La Follette is leading in his home State, Wisconsin, and will undoubtedly win there and get its 13 electoral votes.

Mr. Coolidge is the sixth Vice President to become President through the death of the incumbent and the second to be elected President immediately afterward. The other was Theodore Roosevelt.

Coolidge Victory Overwhelming.

The victory which returns President Coolidge to office and elects Brig. Gen. Charles G. Dawes of Illinois Vice President is overwhelming in the East and Middle West, and early indications are that the Republicans have registered heavily even in the Far West. Such States as North and South Dakota, which the La Follettites claimed for the Third Party, have gone to President Coolidge. So also had Oregon which some expected to see in the Third Party column.

Nebraska also has apparently gone for Coolidge by about 50,000, according to the latest returns.

Mr. Davis, however, went to bed at midnight refusing to accept the fact of the returns and concede defeat for himself and his running mate, Governor Charles W. Bryan of Nebraska. Mr. Davis then believed the returns from Western States, some of which might not come in until 6 o'clock in the morning, would throw the election into the House. Mr. Davis was alone in his prediction of such a result.

Mr. Davis has carried the solid South, except Kentucky, winning Tennessee by apparently 30,000.

The Democratic national ticket appears to have made no serious inroads in the border States. West Virginia apparently is President Coolidge's by 25,000. Mr. Davis's inability to carry his own State is accompanied by failure to win Maryland, where the President seems to have triumphed by a plurality of some 12,000 votes.

La Follette's Vote Industrial.

If the heavy vote rolled up by President Coolidge be taken as an outcome fully expected and generally forecast, the surprise of the election is the heavy vote that La Follette managed to pile up in the industrial districts in the East. His estimated totals include 410,000 in New York State, nearly two-thirds of which was polled in New York City.

Senator La Follette's estimated popular vote of 4,000,000 is interesting because of the assertions of himself and his party leaders that the present campaign was waged chiefly in the interest of founding a third party and that the movement would not be abandoned after the present election. The approximate La Follette vote compares strikingly with the popular total of the last third party candidate—Theodore Roosevelt—whose Bull Moose movement away from the Republicans in 1912 resulted in a nation-wide vote for him of 4,126,024.

While Senator La Follette appears to have registered nearly as many votes as did the late Colonel Roosevelt, his Electoral College showing is much poorer than that of the 1912 third party. La Follette has carried only one State, his own Wisconsin, with its thirteen electoral votes, whereas Roosevelt carried six States—Pennsylvania, Michigan, Minnesota, South Dakota, California and Washington, with an Electoral College vote of 90.

The vote polled by President Coolidge and his Republican running mate, while naturally falling behind the landslide figures of the 1920 Harding victory, if only because the vote this year was split three ways, is one of huge totals in the East and the Middle West, topped by 920,000 in New York, 150,000 in New Jersey and 1,100,000 in Pennsylvania.

The Republican national figures in other States include Ohio 500,000; Indiana, 225,000; Illinois, 750,000; Kansas, 250,000; Michigan, 400,000; West Virginia, 35,000; Maryland, 10,000, and Delaware, 15,000. The last returns from California indicated a plurality there for Coolidge of 300,000.

In Minnesota, Magnus Johnson, one of the two Farmer-Labor Senators now in Congress, was trailing far behind his Republican opponent, Representative T. D. Schall, in the early morning returns.

Charles D. Hilles, Vice Chairman of the Republican National Committee, at 4 o'clock this morning estimated the popular vote as follows—Coolidge, 18,000,000; Davis, 8,000,000; La Follette, 4,000,000.

City Vote Elected Smith.

Alfred E. Smith has been re-elected Governor of New York, according to all indications, with three-quarters of the vote tabulated. The defeat of Colonel Theodore Roosevelt, the Republican candidate, is due to the huge majority piled up by the Democratic Governor in his race in New York City. Indications are that Governor Smith has the State by about 140,000, although Colonel Roosevelt came down to the Bronx with an up-State majority around 385,000. Governor Smith's majority in the Greater City will be about 500,000.

Of outstanding interest in the up-State result is the shift of many cities to the Republican column, although Governor Smith carried them against Nathan L. Miller two years ago, when he was elected for his second term. Of the first eight cities to report, Colonel Roosevelt carried Rome, Poughkeepsie, Buffalo, Newburgh, Binghamton, Gloversville and Syracuse. Of these eight, Governor Smith managed to keep tucked away only Troy, and his majority there dropped about two-thirds.

President Coolidge has carried New York City by probably 130,000, winning every borough, including, apparently, Manhattan, in which, however, the returns were shifting and close.

Governor Smith's majority of about 500,000 in New York apparently carries with it the whole Democratic slate.

The effect of the big Republican vote in the State, so far as the early returns showed, has been to make the State Senate safely Republican, changing its complexion from that at the last legislative session. The Republicans also will have an increased lead in the Assembly.

Congress Changes.

In the country at large the Republican sweep brings the party very close to control of both houses of Congress. The apparent complexion of the Senate is: Republicans, 50; Democrats, 38; Farmer-Laborites 1; vacancy to be filled, 1; in doubt, 6. Necessary to a majority, 49, with the Republican showing up to an early hour this morning exceeding that figure.

In the House the Republicans seem to have obtained a fairly good majority. The present tally stands: Republicans, 232; Democrats, 180; Socialists, 2; Farmer-Laborites, 2; in doubt, 19. Necessary to a majority, 218.

This gives the Republicans a present indicated majority of 48 over the Democrats, Socialists and Farmer-Laborites, whose election seem assured or 30 over the combined opposition, granting it success in all the 19 doubtful districts.

Among the outstanding results indicated in the United States Senate are the election of General T. Coleman du Pont, Republican, in Delaware; the election in Oklahoma of W. B. Pine, Republican, who contested for the seat with ex-Governor Jack Walton.

The returns from Iowa foreshadow the defeat of Senator Brookhart, La Follette Republican, by Daniel F. Steck.

Klan Defeat and Victories.

The Ku Klux Klan, which figured heavily in the political battles of several States, appears to have won most of its fights and also to have suffered one notable defeat. That defeat brings into office the first woman Governor ever to hold the executive chair of a State—"Ma" Ferguson of Texas. Mrs. Ferguson has won the office lost to her husband by impeachment, overcoming strenuous Klan-Republican opposition.

The outcome in the other Gubernatorial contest in which a woman figured still is in doubt. Mrs. Nellie T. Ross, the Democratic candidate, is running a neck-and-neck race in Wyoming with Eugene I. Sullivan, the Republican nominee. Mrs. Ross was nominated by the Democrats when her husband, then Governor, died recently in office.

The Klan, which fought altogether on the Republican side, has won a victory in Oklahoma, where W. W. Pine has been elected to the United States Senate over the Democratic opposition of ex-Governor Walton, who made a straight-out anti-Klan fight. Another Klan victory has been scored in Kansas, where the Republican candidate, Ben S. Paulen, has been elected Governor, defeating Jonathan M. Davis, the Democratic incumbent, and William Allen White, who took the field in the hope of downing the masked and hooded element.

Again in Indiana the Klan has triumphed, putting its Gubernatorial candidate, Ed Jackson, the Republican contestant, in the Governor's chair.

Opponents of a proposed amendment to the State Constitution of Michigan, which would abolish parochial schools, were far in the lead on the face of early returns.

The ranks of women in official public life probably have been swelled by the election to the national House of Representatives of Mary T. Norton of Jersey City, candidate in the overwhelmingly Democratic Hudson County. The first figures received also show that Nellie Cline, Democrat, of Kansas is endangering the seat in the House now held by Representative Tincher.

A new feature in national elections this year was the broadcasting throughout the country of the returns as fast as they were gathered. Many millions kept in touch in that way with the hour-to-hour tallying of the votes and went to bed knowing the outcome both of the Presidential race and even of the local contests in which they were interested. One result of the broadcasting was to keep down the election crowds on the streets, hordes of people gathering around loud speakers in homes, clubs and other meeting places.

Almost everywhere the balloting was carried on under favorable skies, although there were some slight showers on the Pacific Coast and in some of the Northwestern States. Early tabulations, taken in connection with the country-wide increase in registration, indicated that a record vote had been cast throughout the country. That result was attributed in part to the weather, in part to the interest aroused by the lively fight among the three principal parties and in part to campaigns by candidates, civic organizations and the press to persuade the recalcitrant or indifferent citizen to do his duty at the polls.

November 5, 1924

WEST IS AROUSED BY FARM BILL VETO

Special to The New York Times.

OMAHA, Neb., May 23.—A call for 100,000 farmers to march on the Republican National Convention at Kansas City and "demand their rights" at the hands of the Republican Party was made today by Governor Adam McMullen of Nebraska. In a statement he declared no farm relief could be obtained from the present "anti-agricultural" Administration or from any candidate like Herbert Hoover. Governor McMullen is strongly opposed to Hoover as the party candidate.

"The time has come for action by the farmers themselves," the statement reads. "They can expect no effective farm legislation from the present Administration or from any candidate like Hoover, whose only claim for recognition and whose only hope of securing the Republican nomination is based on his blind adherence to the anti-agricultural attitude of the Chief Executive.

"Let 100,000 farmers confront that convention and as American freemen demand economic justice.

"Let 100,000 farmers face their delegates and challenge their opposition.

Urges "Living Petition."

"Let 100,000 farmers march through the streets of the city that has grown into a great industrial centre through the toil of men and women who have struggled against odds to wrest a bare existence from the soil.

"Farmers, arise as crusaders of old. Defend your families, property and freedom. Go to Kansas City on June 12. Do not ask your neighbors to go instead. Go yourself and meet your neighbors there. Form a living petition of 100,000 souls and demand your rights."

An army of farmers at the national conventions, and particularly the Republican national convention, represents the only possibility for farm relief, Governor McMullen declared, asserting "the people and not classes" are representing them.

Sees Party "Killed."

Special to The New York Times.

DES MOINES, Iowa, May 23.—"The Republican Party, which found its origin in the Middle West, may find its death here," Henry A. Wallace, editor of Wallace's Farmer, said here this evening, in commenting on

President Coolidge's veto of the McNary-Haugen bill.

Mr. Wallace's sentiments expressed the attitude taken by leaders of Iowa farmers who were interviewed here today on the President's action. He said further:

"Coolidge and Hoover stand for industrializing the United States as rapidly as possible. The Administration program will tolerate nothing which will restore to the Middle West and the South the same share of the national income which these sections had before the war."

Milo Reno, President of the Iowa

Farmers' Union; Charles E. Hearst, President of the Iowa Farm Bureau Federation; Mark G. Thornburg, Iowa Secretary of Agriculture; Dan Thurner, leading Republican and national delegate, and others expressed the opinion that Coolidge has dealt a death blow to the party's chances in the Middle West unless the Kansas City convention repudiates his action.

After remarking that the equalization fee is the vital principle of the bill, Mr. Hearst said:

"It seems unfortunate that the

President could not permit the Supreme Court to determine the constitutionality of the bill rather than usurp the function of the judicial department."

Mr. Reno declared:

"It is a necessary step to be taken to completely bureauize agriculture in the United States. We must concede to President Coolidge sincerity in his position of antagonism toward the farm bill."

May 24, 1928

HOOVER

QUICK VICTORY FOR HOOVER

His Nomination Follows a Night of Long and Fervid Oratory.

LOWDEN WITHDRAWS NAME

Acts at Last Minute as Protest Over Farm Declaration He Regards as Inadequate.

BUT HE LEADS THE RIVALS

Coolidge Gets 17 Votes, Hughes 1, Dawes 4, Watson 45 and Norris 24.

By RICHARD V. OULAHAN.

Special to The New York Times.

KANSAS CITY, June 14.—Herbert Hoover of California was nominated for President of the United States by the Republican National Convention at 11:20 o'clock tonight (1:20

o'clock Friday morning, New York Daylight Saving Time).

The nomination came to Mr. Hoover on the first ballot. He received 837 votes.

The other 200-odd represented in the convention went to the various contenders for the nomination and to some whose names had not been presented when nominating speeches were made at a session that began at 7 o'clock this evening and ended just after Mr. Hoover's victory was announced officially.

The vote in detail was as follows:

Hoover	837
Lowden	74
Curtis	64
Watson	45
Norris	24
Goff	18
Coolidge	17
Dawes	4
Hughes	1
Not voting	5
Total	1,089

The convention adjourned until noon tomorrow, when it will devote itself to its concluding duty of choosing a candidate for Vice President.

Seeks Vice Presidency Solution.

When the convention adjourned, various groups of leading Republicans went into conference in the hope of being able to adjust the conflicting and embarrassing Vice Presidential situation before the convention convened for its final session.

Late tonight the chief conference was in progress in the headquarters of Secretary Mellon in the Hotel Muelhbach. Prior to the time the conferees met the understanding pre-

vailed that the principal contest over Vice Presidential honors had narrowed down to a choice between Senator Moses of New Hampshire and Senator Deneen of Illinois, with Deneen reluctant to have his name presented to the convention, and Moses seemingly having a shade the better of it.

A new name was brought into the situation in that of former Governor Channing Cox of Massachusetts, who was proposed on the ground that his candidacy on the Hoover ticket may save his State from going Democratic in the Presidential elections. The Pennsylvania delegation strongly urged that he be selected for second place on the national ticket.

Convention Quiet at Climax.

That Hoover would be chosen to lead the party in this year's Presidential campaign had been certain for days. The honor came to him at a time when the convention, tired out after two long sessions and fatigued by the cheering that marked tonight's proceedings, was not in a mood for a demonstration.

There was no outburst of enthusiasm such as might have been expected when victory perched itself at last on the Hoover banner. A cheer or two went up and then the convention was quiet while delegates from three States that had opposed Hoover's candidacy—Kansas, Oklahoma and West Virginia—moved that the nomination be made unanimous. Senator Moses, the presiding officer, called for a viva voce expression. There was a great chorus of "aye." When he called for the nays, delegates from Wisconsin shouted a loud "no." But Moses declared that the motion to make the nomination unanimous had been carried and he read to the convention a telegram which he said had already been sent to Secretary Hoover notifying him of his nomination and congratulating him in the convention's name.

Text of the Telegram.

The text of the telegram as he read it to the convention was:

The Honorable Herbert Hoover, 2,300 S Street, Washington D.C.:

The Republican National Convention by a sweeping majority,

which has since been made unanimous, amid great enthusiasm, has named you as its candidate for the Presidency in this campaign. No message of information which I have ever sent to any one has given me as much satisfaction as this to you. I send it in the name of a united enthusiastic and militant party organization, which has turned to you as the inevitable leader in the contest which confronts us.

It is not so much that we give you this nomination as that you have earned the right to it. Your training, your equipment and, above all, your character make the leader for whom the party has looked in order that there may be no halting in the progress of the United States under policies which are warmly approved by the people and to which you have contributed so much.

The convention still in session would appreciate a message from you and I hope that you may be able speedily to send it to us.

GEORGE H. MOSES, Permanent Chairman, Republican National Convention.

It was North Carolina that had the honor of casting the vote that gave Mr. Hoover the 545 necessary to be the convention's choice. It had been figured that New York, whose name on the roll of State delegations preceded North Carolina, would give the prize to Hoover. But New York's 90 votes, all of them cast for Hoover's nomination, brought the total to 537, or 8 short of the required majority. Then North Carolina cast 17 for Hoover and 3 for Lowden and the trick was done. These 17 took Hoover over the boundary line of contest into the safety of party endorsement, with 9 votes to spare. After that the recording of the ballot was a mere formality.

June 15, 1928

THE URBANITES ARE UPON US!

One effect of runaway candidacies at national conventions is to stimulate exercise in the Higher Thought. Newspaper men harassed by a total lack of suspense about HOOVER or Governor SMITH take refuge in inner meanings and ultimate significances. On the same day MARK SULLIVAN and WILLIAM ALLEN WHITE in The Herald Tribune are moved to speculate about what is behind SMITH, since it is quite obvious what is immediately before him. To both observers the issue at Houston is one between town and country. Mr. SULLIVAN sees anti-Smith sentiment rooted in a

"distaste" for New York City felt by nearly all of America outside of New York. This would make the Democratic outlook for next November dark indeed, were it not for important modifications from Emporia. To Mr. WHITE, too, Houston signalizes the passing of the old Populist Democracy typified by BRYAN and the advent of a new city leadership. But it is not New York alone. They come, the new leaders in command of the urbanite Democratic hosts, "from Kansas City, "from Detroit, from Minneapolis, "from Seattle, from Butte, from San "Francisco." From the Smith point of view, this is much better. If the battle next November is to be town

against country, the temptation is strong for Democratic pencils to get busy. In 1920 the census figures had the population of the United States 51.4 per cent. urban and 48.6 per cent. rural, thus apparently assuring the election of Governor SMITH! But, after the manner of political pencils, this is traveling a bit too fast. It is not yet true that more than half of the American people live in "cities" dominated by the new type of leader "with Irish cast of face." When the Census Bureau says "urban" it means any incorporated place with more than 2,500 inhabitants. But the small town is as rural as the farms that encompass it, and if we speak in terms of

rural-mindedness and urban-mindedness, the chances are greatly against Governor SMITH's election on the face of the census returns. The outlook is better in Massachusetts with 95 per cent. officially "urban," Rhode Island 98 per cent., Connecticut 68 per cent., New Hampshire 63 per cent., New York 83 per cent., New Jersey 78 per cent. There, if the conflict between town and country is to determine the issue, the Democratic outlook is bright.

The thing may happen; but even then it is doubtful whether it will be the victory of that new anti-Protestant, anti-individualist creed against which, according to Mr. WHITE, the voices of women are praying in the little white churches. Victory, if it comes, will be in largest measure the victory of a remarkable personality and an extraordinary vote-getter. It will be only another instance of American democracy taking its leaders where it finds them. Today it happens to

be the sidewalks of New York. It has not yet been proved by the philosophers of urbanism and ruralism that the future is closed against a great Democratic leader arising in Ohio or Tennessee and exercising the spell on popular imagination and the impression of high ability that

ALFRED E. SMITH wields. Political parties want very much to win elections. That incentive has brought a very considerable part of the rural Protestant South to the support of SMITH and will in the future rally "anti-Protestant" New York and New Jersey to a rural Protestant

candidate who has a chance to carry a large block of doubtful States. It is not so dramatic a picture as the city against the homestead or one social creed against another, but it happens to be somewhat closer to the facts.

June 26, 1928

SMITH

OHIO CLINCHES NOMINATION

Other States Rush to Switch Once Choice Is Assured.

GREETED BY WILD CHEERS

By W. A. WARN.

Special to The New York Times.

HOUSTON, Texas, June 28.—Governor Alfred E. Smith of New York was nominated for President of the United States by the Democratic National convention on the first ballot

tonight. Formal announcement of his nomination was made at 11:55 P. M., when Senator Joseph T. Robinson, Permanent Chairman of the convention, announced that he had received a total of 849 2-3 votes.

The announcement was followed by a wild demonstration. The banners of every State in the Union and every Territory were carried through the aisles of the huge auditorium while men and women, marching, cheered at the top of their voices and the bands played the east side melodies associated with Governor Smith.

Ohio Puts Smith Over the Top.

Governor Smith got the required two-thirds vote only after Ohio had changed its vote and given forty-seven votes, cast for former Senator Atlee Pomerene, to Governor Smith, who already had received the remaining one of the forty-eight votes which constitute Ohio's total. With Ohio's ofrty-eight, Governor Smith had a total of 768 2-3 votes.

Governor Smith's total after the roll-call had been ended was 724 2-3. This was exactly 9 votes short of the required two-thirds. Ohio switched

to Governor Smith almost immediately, but, owing to demands from Mississippi that its delegation be polled, there was considerable delay before the formal announcement of his nomination.

There were many shifts after Ohio had changed. Indiana gave him 25 votes, Kansas 11½, Nebraska 12 and Mississippi 9½. Twenty-three more votes which were swung to the Governor by the Tennessee delegation brought his total up to 849 2-3.

Official Result of Ballot.

The vote for all candidates on the first ballot was announced as follows:

Alfred E. Smith (N. Y....... 849 2-3
Senator George (Ga.) 55 1-2
Senator Reed (Mo.) 52
Rep. Cordell Hull (Tenn.).... 50 5-6
Jesse H. Jones (Texas)...... 43
Sen. Pat Harrison (Miss.).. 31 1-2
Gov. Vic Donahey (Ohio).... 5
Evans Woollen (Ind.)........ 7
Rep. Ayres (Kan.).......... 3
Senator Pomerene (Ohio).... 3
Huston Thompson (Cal.).... 2
Chief Justice Watts (S. C..... 18
Gov. Biblo (Miss.) 2 1-2
Total vote cast, 1,097 1-2.
Not voting, 2 1-2.

June 29, 1928

A MADE-OVER PARTY.

How powerfully personalities affect the trend of party politics has long been the theme of historians. But seldom has one man so rapidly transformed the objectives of a political organization as ALFRED E. SMITH has done in the case of the Democratic Party.

Not until he was actually nominated at Houston was the extent of his influence realized. For the past two years he had been growing rapidly. The party was developing no other leader. The death of BRYAN, and the inability of any aspirant to wear the BRYAN mantle, left the Presidential field to SMITH. With the opening of this year it was evident that no serious rival could arise. Even to the moment of the convention there was sufficient anti-Smith strength to have denied the nomination to the Governor of New York. Numerically there were enough delegates who wanted a more traditional type of candidate. But the lack of one, and the steady beat of the fact that to deny SMITH two-thirds after he had attained a majority would

mean certain defeat in November, removed the barriers. Delegates and those who choose them are politicians, and, though there were a few who sought encouragement to die for their preferences, expediency prevailed and the inevitable nomination was made.

Instantly came the transformation. A party which, at least since 1894, had chosen the radical phase of economics, the bureaucratic phase of law and regulation, and the paternalistic view of national morals, had its mind and its garb changed in two days. The head of the largest corporation in the world, himself one of the richest men in America and a member of citadel clubs of Republicanism, was put in as National Chairman by Governor SMITH. Centralization and bureaucracy, with their tendency to regulate from Washington the daily lives and habits of citizens in distant communities, were attacked in every official utterance made by the nominee and his Chairman. Prohibition was singled out as the party's chief enemy. The tariff, as part of the measures for farm relief, was accepted on a qualified basis. In

these new modern clothes the Democratic Party is a strange sight to the Southern and Western Democrats who were brought up on Bryanism and who took very little interest either in JAMES M. COX or JOHN W. DAVIS, the standard-bearers of 1920 and 1924, because of the evident lack of interest felt in these nominees by BRYAN himself.

Yet the changed party is recognizable—even by the Westerners and Southerners—as possessed of great strength, of effective attack, powerfully led. The obvious anxiety of the Republicans alone would be a complete testimonial of the accession of Democratic power. Nor are there signs that, save for a few one-idea men, there is any lamentation over the passing of the Bryanized Democracy. It had its day, and that was a long one. Parties and their policies are bound to change as old leaders pass and new ones arise. The difference between BRYAN's Democracy and SMITH's Democracy is not so great as that between JEFFERSON's Democracy and BRYAN's.

July 15, 1928

OBSERVATIONS FROM TIMES WATCH-TOWERS

ORGANIZE NEGRO VOTE

Republicans, Surprised by the Move of Raskob, Form New Colored Division.

By JOHN E. MONK.

Editorial Correspondence of THE NEW YORK TIMES.

WASHINGTON, Aug. 4.—Republican leaders are perturbed over news they have received that Chairman John J. Raskob of the Democratic National Committeee plans to organize the negro vote in Northern, Border and Central Western States in an effort to land it for the Smith-Robinson ticket.

The Republican Party always has regarded the negro vote as its own, and party leaders, therefore, were somewhat pained to learn that they would have to be up and doing this year to keep this particular segment of the voting population in line.

The campaign now being conducted on behalf of Governor Smith has taken on characteristics that tend at times to confuse the political opposition. The Raskob management is not proceeding along the conventional lines that have marked Democratic campaigns in former years. Its appeal to what is known as "big business" was a notable departure from previously accepted Democratic policy.

Mr. Raskob's bid for the negro vote was a bold challenge that Chairman Work of the Republican National Committee met by the prompt organization of a colored voters' division to resist the Democratic attempt to wean the negro in the North and West from his long-time political association.

***

Harlem Leaders Put to Work.

According to information received here, Chairman Raskob has gone after the negro vote in a most business like manner. Hoover leaders are advised that he has chosen a number of bright young men identified with the Harlem black belt, where Governor Smith is strong, to carry on the work. These young men are to be sent to other black belts to convey the message that Governor Smith is friendly to the race; that this would be a good year for the negro to demonstrate that he is capable of independent thinking and that he must no longer permit himself to be treated merely as a chattel of the Republican Party.

Definite information is lacking as to what special arguments are to be made in urging the colored voter to vote for Smith and Robinson. The Republicans have had no trouble in former national elections to hold the negro voter in leash. They have rewarded leaders of the race with public offices and recognition in other ways. It is a new experience for the Republicans to find themselves confronted by an organization that thinks it has a chance of swinging the colored vote into the Democratic column.

***

Seek Negroes in Pivotal States.

There are about 5,588,500 negroes of voting age in the United States. While the bulk of them are located in the South where they do not count, or at least are not counted at the polls, according to Republican leaders there are a sufficient number in many of the pivotal and in some of the border States to determine the result in a close election.

According to the Census Bureau the negro population of the country numbered 10,463,131 in 1920, and it is estimated that it was 11,698,000 in 1927. About one-half of the number estimated for 1927 had reached the voting age.

New York, New Jersey, Pennsylvania, Illinois, Indiana, Ohio, Tennessee, Kentucky and Missouri are States with a comparatively large negro population that are regarded as either doubtful or debatable in the political contest now under way. The census of 1920 showed that each of those States had enough negro voters that year to cut quite a figure in a national election, and Chairman Raskob has decided to capture them in whole or in part for his principal if it is possible to do so.

The census reports disclose that in 1920 there were 5,522,274 negroes of both sexes who had reached the voting age out of a total colored population in excess of 10,000,000. From 1920 to 1927 the number of negroes increased to over 11,689,000, with a corresponding increase in the number of voters of that race.

Ten States Have 1,370,000 Negro Voters.

In 1920 the census showed negro voters in the States named as follows:

New York, 142,544; New Jersey, 75,671, Pennsylvania, 191,226; Illinois, 128,090; Indiana, 53,935; Ohio, 126,940; Tennessee, 245,395; Kentucky, 143,881; Missouri, 121,328, and Maryland, 141,991.

Of the total of 5,522,524 negro voters in 1920, 2,792.006 were men and 2,730,274 women.

There are other States where the negro is by no means a negligible factor in politics. For example, there was a colored population of more than 149,000 in Oklahoma in 1920, and of these more than 76,000 had attained the voting age.

Kansas had 79,725 negroes within her borders in 1920, and of the number 37,000 were entitled to vote. In New England the 1920 population of negroes was:

Massachusetts, 45,466; Connecticut, 21,046; Rhode Island, 10,036; Vermont, 572; New Hampshire, 621, and Maine, 1,310.

In all of the Northern States, with the possible exception of New York, the negroes usually vote the Republican ticket and the same holds true in the West. Chairman Raskob knows that this is the case. He knows further that every negro vote he can attract to the Democratic ticket in either the Middle West or the border States will be so much gain.

It is apparent that Mr. Raskob's plan to go after the negro vote excited concern in the Republican National Committee. It resulted in an immediate decision by Chairman Work to organize the colored voters' division, which is officered by negroes of prominence. The division will have headquarters in Washington and will function under the watchful eye of Chairman Work and his aides. Branch offices, with negroes in charge, will be established in New York and Chicago. Chairman Work has given instructions that an intensive campaign shall be conducted for Hoover and Curtis among the negroes in all regions outside of the South. The fight may be close and if it is the negro vote may be a prize worth having in many States.

***

Hesitant Over Southern Fight.

Out of consideration for the sensibilities of the colored voter in the North and West, Chairman Work has shown some hesitancy in making a militant fight for Hoover in States of the solid South. The whites and blacks in the South have a social as well as political conflict. There is danger, the chairman considers, in a close affiliation of the Republican National Committee with Southern politics. In some States of the South "lily white" groups are in control of party organizations. In others the organizations are all black, and in still others separate white and black groups attempt to dominate.

This lack of uniformity in party management in the South makes the situation a difficult one to deal with at long range. There is always a possibility of resentments being stirred up among Southern negroes that might be conveyed to their brethren in other sections.

The Republican high command at present is disposed to let the Southern leaders, white and black, work out their own problems. If present plans are followed the Republican National Committee will not itself try to organize the South for the party ticket. It will asist the local leaders by contributing funds, distributing literature and sending in party orators if the Southern leaders want them.

August 5, 1928

SOUTH SEEMS SPLIT ON ROCK OF RELIGION

North Carolina Is Especially Stirred Up Against the Candidacy of Governor Smith.

PASTORS FOMENT FEELING

Attacks Less Sharp in Alabama and Georgia Where Papers Resent Political Preachers.

By JULIAN HARRIS.

Editorial Correspondence of THE NEW YORK TIMES.

COLUMBUS, Ga., Aug. 22.—Just a few days ago a storm swept across Northern Florida into South Georgia and on into the Carolinas. Had the velocity of the wind been a mile or two less an hour and the rainfall been an inch or two less in volume the storm stories would have failed to make top of column on the front pages of Southern newspapers. For politics has grabbed streamer space and scare-heads—dry politics, wet politics, clerical politics, Smith politics, Hoover politics, anti-Smith politics—politics, politics, politics.

Streams of politicians visit the two leaders—Governor Smith and Mr. Hoover. Out of the South go Senator George, Carter Glass and Josephus Daniels to glimpse in advance Governor Smith's speech of acceptance and assure him that Georgia, Virginia and North Carolina will be in line. And Josephus Daniels tells Governor Smith there is little to the tales of religious intolerance in North Carolina.

One may well hesitate to contradict Mr. Daniels with reference to conditions in his own State, but facts should not be kept in the background. Then let it be said that North Carolina is a hot-bed of anti-Smith religious intolerance. The very day Mr. Daniels said that prohibition was the basis of opposition to Governor Smith, I received a letter from a man known to every leader in North Carolina.

***

Preachers Oppose Smith.

He wrote, among other things, the following:

"We are having a very difficult campaign in North Carolina. It seems that a very large majority of the preachers are desperately opposing Governor Smith's election and are doing so for the reason that he is a Catholic. Quite a number of them give as a reason that Governor Smith is wet. From a rather thorough personal canvass of the State, I am convinced that the majority of our trouble results from the fact that Smith belongs to the Catholic Church. How to meet this situation is very puzzling."

One trouble in North Carolina is that the opposition to religious intolerance has not been sufficiently outspoken. In Georgia and Alabama the leading newspapers have accepted the challenge of intolerance.

In Georgia The Macon Telegraph, The Atlanta Constitution, The Savannah Press, The Americus Times-Recorder, The Greensboro Herald-Journal, The Dalton Citizen and scores of other dailies and weeklies resented openly and vigorously the intrusion of the political pastors. In Alabama The Montgomery Advertiser, The Birmingham News and The Age-Herald have led in fighting fearlessly and mercilessly the spirit of religious intolerance. As a result, the attacks on Governor Smith are less vicious, and Georgia and Alabama were never less in danger of going Republican than in the forthcoming election.

It should also be said that a number of leading ministers have not only refrained from political attacks but have been outspoken for tolerance and against the entry of preachers into the political field. This week, in Atlanta, Dr. C. B. Wilmer, formerly rector of St. Luke's of that city and now Professor of Theology at the University of the South, opened his sermon with the assertion that to preach obedience to the law is within the prerogative of the pulpit, "but denunciation by prohibitionists of those who think some other method of control would be wiser is an intolerable piece of arrogance and tyranny."

On the subject of Catholics and intolerance, Dr. Wilmer said:

"One important question is: Even supposing that the attitude of the Catholic Church may not be, as some think it is not, theoretically satisfied and thoroughly consistent with Democratic principles, whether we have not here in broad-minded America an opportunity to work out a solution of the vexed question by cooperation with those Roman Catholics who are loyal patriots.

"A very serious question is whether we are not at present in greater danger in this country from the opposite end; from Protestant violence, hatred and prejudice. I do not refer to reasoned opinions.

"The attempt of religious bodies and religious leaders to bulldoze church members into compliance with their political opinions is worse than the attempt of a reasonable person like the Pope of Rome to guide political life in the right direction would be. The worst possible theocracy is that of a religious mob.

"Prohibition is one method out of many in dealing with the evils of liquor drinking and the liquor traffic."

***

Fight Is Good for Democracy.

While it is to be deplored that the pulpit has in a number of instances entered politics, it is not bad for Democracy in the South that there is a defection to the Republican Party by certain groups.

Democracy is being revived. Many voters who have thought of the

Democratic Party as merely the party which opposes negro domination are finding out that there is something real and fundamental in Democracy. And Democrats are discovering that there is considerable exaggeration to the so-called negro menace—there are worse things, as for instance domination by the Vatican.

None but a dyed-in-the-wool, true and tried, 100 per cent. Nordic Southerner can appreciate how deep must be the anti-Catholic feeling when former delegates to the Houston convention consent to serve as Republican electors on a ticket named by the G. O. P. group controlled by Ben Davis, negro Republican National Committeeman from Georgia, until the Hooverites in this State recovered from the color blindness.

Ben Davis, who delivered the Georgia delegation to Mr. Hoover at Kansas City, is also editor of The Independent. In his latest issue he prints the names of the Republican electors—Mrs. Mary Harris Armour and Mrs. Marion Williams are on the list—and follows it with an editorial that is worth reading carefully. Says Editor Davis:

"Sometimes we may vote for a Democrat because of the man, but we can never vote for the Democratic Party, so long as it stands for ignorance, meanness and race hatred as exemplified in Memphis, Texas, Georgia and Mississippi. A vote for Al Smith is not a vote for the man, but a vote for the Democratic Party.

"Al Smith is no better than the Democratic Party. His record does not disclose a single favor that he had done for negroes in New York. He (the negro) knows that the Democratic Party is his sworn enemy.

"As infamous and as wrong and cowardly as lily-whiteism is, it is no worse than the robbery and outlawry of the Democratic Party against the American negro."

It is to be hoped that the former Democrats who are now opposing the Democratic nominee will read Ben Davis's comments.

As I have said before, the South is not solidly for Smith, but the Solid South will go Democratic. The weak spot is North Carolina. Senator Simmons, defection and religious intolerance are the obstacles. Perhaps Senator Simmons may change his views—the intolerants will not.

August 26, 1928

THRONG OF 22,000 IN THE GARDEN HEARS HOOVER ASSAIL SMITH'S POLICIES AS 'STATE SOCIALISM'; OPPOSES PUTTING GOVERNMENT INTO BUSINESS

SPECIFIES THREE ISSUES

Attacks Farm Aid, Power and Dry Plans of His Opponent.

STRIKES AT PATERNALISM

Candidate Declares It Would Cripple Energies of People and Destroy Initiative.

Speaking to an immediate audience of about 22,000, and to a vastly greater number of radio listeners, Herbert Hoover, Republican nominee for President, declared last evening at Madison Square Garden that the policies advocated by Governor Smith, his Democratic opponent, for the solution of the prohibition, farm relief and electrical power problems, constituted State socialism. Such policies, he said, are an abandonment of the traditional American policy of private initiative in business under which the United States has become the most prosperous nation in the world.

It was Mr. Hoover's first speech in New York City since his nomination. His address was an appeal for the continued support of the business element in New York City and elsewhere, which has been an important factor in Republican success in past Presidential campaigns. Declaring himself opposed to the Government engaging in business, Mr. Hoover asserted that evils that might result from great private business units could be corrected by regulation, but indicated a belief that there should not be too much of that.

Vice President Charles G. Dawes, seconded Mr. Hoover's appeal to the business element by declaring that the issue of the campaign was the maintenance of prosperity. Mr. Dawes, who had been a receptive candidate for the nomination for President, asserted that a Republican national administration meant prosperity, and declared that a revision of the tariff by its enemies, the Democrats, instead of by its friends, the Republicans, would unsettle business confidence and destroy prosperity. Mr. Dawes declared that prohibition was not an issue and that, with both major parties pledged in their platforms to attempt to bring about farm relief, this could not become a major issue.

Mr. Hoover's speech at Madison Square Garden marked the climax of a busy day, passed almost entirely under the roof of the Waldorf. During the morning and afternoon Mr. Hoover conferred with the leading party chieftains and obtained from them assurances he would carry New York State. He received delegations of those who had aided him in relief work abroad and in the food administration here, foreign-born voters, theatrical folk, disabled veterans and members of the Hoover Service League. He was entertained at luncheon by Charles D. Hilles, National Committeeman; State Chairman H. Edmund Machold and Samuel S. Koenig, Chairman of the New York County Committee, and told the men and women County Chairmen and Vice Chairmen of the State that he had no doubt of his election.

Cheered for Many Minutes.

Mr. Hoover received an enthusiastic welcome in the home city of his opponent. There were two demonstrations for him at the meeting, the first of nine minutes' duration on his appearance on the platform and the second, which lasted twelve and a half minutes, when he rose to speak.

The first ovation was the more spontaneous. A roar went up when he appeared on the platform, accompanied by James R. Sheffield, former Ambassador to Mexico and Chairman of the meeting; his son, Allan Hoover, and George Akerson, his assistant. The cheers drowned out the sound of the bands, and the waving of thousands of American flags sent a ripple of color around the huge hall which, with its arena seats and balconies, resembles a stadium. Mr. Hoover, who had come from the Waldorf by automobile, smiled and waved his hand.

The number present was estimated by the Garden management as 22,000, and of these probably about two-fifths were women, a large fraction for a political meeting. It was noticable during the cheering that the women seemed to be even more enthusiastic than the men.

There was another outburst of cheering for Mrs. Hoover, when Mr. Sheffield in his opening remarks brought her into the limelight after predicting the election of Mr. Hoover and particularly strong support for him in New York City. Mr. Sheffield said:

"New York is not unmindful of the fact that in electing him we are selecting as first lady of the land his leading lady, the gracious person who has played so prominent a part in the drama of his brilliant career."

Long continued cheering followed. Mrs. Hoover was brought to the front of the platform by H. Edmund Machold, Chairman of the Republican State Committee. She smiled and bowed as the applause continued.

Republican Régime Reviewed.

Mr. Hoover started his speech with a brief review of constructive measures brought about by the Republican national Administration during the last seven and a half years. During the World War, he said, the Federal Government became a centralized despotism which assumed autocratic powers and took over the business of citizens. Though such steps might be justified in time of war, he continued, this and other countries were confronted at the close of the war with the issue of whether or not their Governments should continue their war-time ownership and operation of many means of production and distribution.

"We were challenged with peace-time choice between the American system of rugged individualism and a European policy of diametrically opposed doctrines, doctrines of paternalism and State socialism," Mr. Hoover said, and his audience applauded. "The acceptance of these ideas would have meant the destruction of self-government through the centralization of government. It would have meant the undermining of individual initiative and enterprise through which our people have grown to unparalleled greatness."

Flings Challenge to Smith.

Without mentioning his opponent by name. Mr. Hoover flung his challenge to Governor Smith as follows:

"There has been revived in this campaign, however, a series of proposals which, if adopted, would be a long step toward the abandonment of our American system and a surrender to the destructive operation of governmental conduct of commercial business. Because the country is faced with difficulty and doubt over certain national problems—that is, prohibition, farm relief and electrical power—our opponents propose that we must thrust government a long way into the businesses which give rise to these problems.

"In effect, they abandon the tenets of their own party and turn to State socialism as a solution for the difficulties presented by all three. It is proposed that we shall change from prohibition to the State purchase and sale of liquor. If their agricultural program means anything, it means that the Government shall directly or indirectly buy and sell and fix prices of agricultural products. And we are to go into the hydroelectric business. In other words, we are confronted with a huge program of government in business."

Such a program, Mr. Hoover declared, would reach into the daily life of every man and woman, destroy self-government, create an extensive bureaucracy, cramp and cripple the energies of the people, extinguish equality and dry up the spirit of liberty and progress.

In enumerating the disadvantages of government in business, Mr. Hoover declared that effective leadership in business could be obtained only through advancement because of ability and character in the free atmosphere of competition, and that political channels were poor agencies through which to select leaders to conduct commercial business. Government in business, he added, would be subject to too many checks through the necessity of obtaining the majority of Congress or of the State Legislatures and would increase the "log-rolling" in legislative bodies.

Mr. Hoover cited the operation of the railroads during the war as an example of the incompetency of government to conduct business.

He characterized the school of thought which would put the Government into the operation of commercial business as a false liberalism. He declared that every step of "bureaucratizing" the business of the country would poison the roots of liberalism, political equality, free speech, free assembly, free press and equality of opportunity. True liberalism, he added, seeks all legitimate freedom.

Mr. Hoover said he did not intend, in his advocacy of the retention of private initiative in business and his opposition of government in business, to indicate that he would abandon any safeguards for the control of private business. He said he did not mean that the Government should part with any of its national resources without full protection to the public interest or that, when the Government engaged in public works, for the purposes of flood control, navigation, irrigation, scientific research or national defense, that it must not produce power or commodities as a by-product. He insisted, however, that these must be by-products and not the major purpose of the Government.

He spoke of the prosperity of New York City which, as the commercial centre of the United States, he said, was the outstanding beneficiary of the prosperity of the country and which would be affected immediately by any slackening of industry far more than any other section of the country.

October 23, 1928

HOOVER WINS

HOOVER CARRIES NEW YORK BY 125,000

Republican Nominee Captures New Jersey, Takes Wisconsin; Breaks Solid South. Winning Virginia, Florida

GAINING IN NORTH CAROLINA AND BAY STATE

Voting in unprecedented numbers, a myriad of American citizens yesterday chose Herbert Hoover of California for President of the United States and Charles Curtis of Kansas for Vice President.

How pronounced is the victory of these candidates of the Republican Party over their Democratic competitors, Governor Alfred E. Smith of New York, nominee for President, and Joseph T. Robinson of Arkansas, the Vice Presidential nominee, cannot be determined until the stupendous task of counting 40,000,000 or more votes is completed, but a Republican landslide took place at the polls, and it will be reflected in a heavy Hoover-Curtis majority of the 531 ballots in the Electoral College.

400 Electoral Votes for Hoover

Mr. Hoover is assured of more than 400 electoral votes. It is probable that his majority will increase as further returns are received. He has broken the traditionally Democratic Solid South. He has carried Virginia and returns from Florida indicate that he has won in that State. His tally in the Electoral College may go as high as 444 votes if North Carolina, North Dakota and Texas, which are very close, are added to his strength, or even to the stupendous total of 462, if the count now proceeding in Massachusetts turns in his favor.

Such an outcome would give Mr. Hoover a majority of 397 electoral votes over Governor Smith. It is already apparent that no Presidential candidate of any major party has been beaten as badly as Governor Smith, with the exception of William H. Taft, who got only 8 votes in the Electoral College in his contest for re-election against Woodrow Wilson and Theodore Roosevelt.

According to the latest returns received from Massachusetts, North Carolina, North Dakota and Texas, these States are still in the doubtful column either by reason of inadequate returns or on account of the closeness of contests as the count proceeds, and while Governor Smith may be shown to have carried some of them, his tally of electoral votes may not exceed seventy.

New York Spells Smith's Doom.

Governor Smith's hope of victory began to fade within a few hours after the polls closed in New York State when it was indicated that he had carried New York City, his great stronghold, by less than 450,000, which was much short of the estimate of his managers. As returns began to roll in from up-State it became apparent that the Hoover plurality in that strong Republican area would materially overcome the showing for Governor Smith in New York City, with the prospect that the Republican nominee would carry the State by a lead in the neighborhood of 125,000.

With New York's forty-five electoral votes placed in the Hoover column it became merely a matter of waiting until the full returns determined what the Republican candidates' majority will be in the Electoral College. The tremendous onsweep of the Hoover following was emphasized when State after State in which the Democrats had placed hope of victory went over into the Republican camp.

New Jersey was carried by the Republican national ticket by a heavy majority. Maryland followed suit. Late returns show that Hoover also took Missouri. Of other border States, he captured Kentucky and Oklahoma. Minnesota, which the Smith management was also hopeful of carrying on account of the defection among Republican voters because of Mr. Hoover's attitude on the McNary-Haugen bill, gave him a heavy plurality.

Smith States Only in South.

As for Governor Smith, there is no assurance that he has carried any State outside of the South. With the results in Florida and Texas still in doubt he seems to be certain of having carried only Alabama, Georgia, Louisiana, Mississippi and South Carolina. In the early morning hours late returns had Hoover forging ahead even in North Carolina. Tennessee was conceded to the Republican candidate.

His victories in Alabama and North Carolina are a setback for Senator J. Thomas Heflin and Senator Furnifold M. Simmons, who deserted their party allegiances to oppose him, Simmons on the ground of Governor Smith's anti-prohibition policy and Senator Heflin for the openly stated reason that Governor Smith was a Catholic.

In the early morning hours returns from Wisconsin indicated that the portion of the State outside of Milwaukee had voted so heavily for Hoover that Smith's lead in the metropolis made famous by beer had been overcome and that the State's thirteen electoral votes would be added to the steadily mounting Hoover column.

It was after 4 o'clock this morning before virtually complete returns from Rhode Island showed that Smith had carried Rhode Island, the only State outside the Solid South that can with certainty be placed to his credit. He seems to have carried it by a small majority, probably not exceeding 2,000.

Maine, New Hampshire, Vermont and Connecticut joined the Republican procession. At an early hour this morning the prospect was that where the eighteen electoral votes of Massachusetts would go could not be made certain until late today.

Republican Congress Assured.

The victory for the Republican national ticket is accompanied by the assurance that, as President, Mr. Hoover will have the support of a Congress controlled by those of his own party. While returns are incomplete, the indications are that the Republican majority in the House of Representatives, now thirty-six over the combined opposition, will be increased, and the mere constructive majority of the Republicans in the Senate, where Insurgent members of that party hold the balance of power, will be augmented so materially as to permit Mr. Hoover's political associates to dominate that body.

November 7, 1928

SAYS STOCK CRASH ENDED PARTY MYTH

Prof. Rogers Asserts It Showed Republican Rule Is Not Synonymous With Prosperity.

The recent stock market slump should end forever the belief that prosperity is synonymous with a Republican Administration in Washington, Dr. Lindsey Rogers, Professor of Public Law at Columbia University, told members of the Southern Women's Democratic Organization in New York at its first meeting of the season in the Plaza Hotel yesterday afternoon.

Statements linking prosperity with Republican rule, used so fluently by Republican campaign orators, are mere catch phrases which lack specification and the support of competent economists and statisticians, he declared. However, elections have proved, he said, that catch words have a considerable power in catching electorates and that the myth of a Republican monopoly of prosperity has overshadowed Republican records of corruption and malfeasance.

While the speaker placed no responsibility upon the Republicans or the administration for the break in stock prices, he declared that a careful analysis of the bull market probably would justify a severe criticism of former President Coolidge and Secretary Mellon for the reassuring statements issued periodically to keep stock prices up.

"Mr. Coolidge declared that the increase in brokers' loans was not alarming," the speaker continued. "This was the first occasion that a President of the United States made a statement on a subject as controversial, a subject on which, I claim, he was abysmally ignorant."

December 8, 1929

CHAPTER 2

Four-Party Politics
1930-1963

Senator Robert Taft (left), leader of Republican
isolationists, with Senator Arthur Vandenberg of the
party's internationalist wing.

Courtesy The New York Times

DEMOCRATIC LANDSLIDE

SEE PRESAGE FOR 1932

Democrats Are Victorious in Nearly All the Chief Battles.

PINCHOT BEATS HEMPHILL

Election of Bulkley, a Wet, as Senator in Ohio Seems Indicated.

By RICHARD V. OULAHAN.

A distinct Democratic sweep, suggesting a landslide for that party, extended across the country in yesterday's elections, held in all the forty-eight States except Maine. While the outcome of a number of contests for important public offices is still in doubt, the Democrats were victorious in most of the outstanding battles from which definite returns have been received.

The general trend of these returns up to the time this edition of THE NEW YORK TIMES went to press furnished encouraging evidence to Democracy's leaders that the sentiment expressed at the polls throughout a widespread victory for their Presidential ticket in the elections of 1932.

Democratic Governors were elected in New York, Connecticut, Massacusetts, Rhode Island and Ohio, and in States normally Democratic. In such States as Kansas, Minnesota, Nebraska, Oregan and Wyoming, where the Republicans win more often than not, the result is in doubt on account of the strong trend of Democratic sentiment.

Senate Lead Slender.

Judging by the latest returns, there is a bare chance that the nominal Republican majority in the Senate will be overthrown, although the prospect is that the Republicans may still have a slight excess of members over the Democrats. It is possible, however, that the next Senate will be a tie politically.

Democratic Senators have been elected in place of Republicans in Colorado, Minnesota, Ohio, Oklahoma, West Virginia and Massachusetts, and the chances favor a victory for the Republican Senatorial candidate in South Dakota. Only one Republican Senatorial aspirant has triumphed over a sitting Democratic Senator. This happened in Iowa.

In line with the general Democratic swing, the return showed that candidates of that party have cut heavily into the big Republican majority in the House of Representatives with a fair prospect that the Democrats will get control, though the actual outcome remains in doubt.

Based on the latest returns, the Senate line-up appears to be 45 Democrats, 47 Republicans and 1 Farmer-Laborite, with 3 contests doubtful. This line-up concedes the election of Hoidale, Democrat, over Senator Schall, Republican, in Minnesota. The doubtful contests are in South Dakota, Kansas and Kentucky. Should the Democratic candidates carry all these contests the Senate would stand:

Democrats 48, Republicans 47, Farmer-Laborite 1.

Heavy gains were made by the Democrats in the contest for 431 seats in the House of Representatives, but whether these will be sufficient to wipe out the present Republican majority is uncertain, with returns incomplete from approximately threescore districts.

Results of Latest Figures.

Counting nine vacant seats which had been held by Republicans, the majority of that party in the present House is 103. The latest definite election returns give the Republicans 189 seats, the Democrats 200 and the Farmer-Labor party 1, with 44 in the doubtful column and 1 Independent Republican.

The Democrats have 165 members in the present House and 218 are necessary to control.

Strength was given to predictions that the Democrats would carry the House by reports from Ohio that ten seats there now held by Republicans were in danger as a result of the sweep that has elected Robert J. Bulkley, wet Democratic candidate, for the Senate.

The voters of New York carried Franklin D. Roosevelt into another term as Governor through his defeat of his Republican opponent, Charles H. Tuttle, by a staggering majority, one far exceeding the highest ever given to a Gubernatorial candidate in this State. The previous record was in 1922 when Alfred E. Smith was elected by a plurality of 385,338.

Roosevelt and 1932.

Prior to the election it was generally recognized by politicians that if Governor Roosevelt was victorious in his contest for re-election he would be an outstanding contender for his party's Presidential nomination two years hence. The overwhelming character of his triumph is certain to be interpreted as placing him in a strong position to obtain his party's chief prize. While the East and portions of the West showed a strong anti-prohibition trend in what took place at the polls yesterday, the South retains its position as a politically dry area and unless there is a radical change in the attitude of the Democratic party in that section the effort to nominate Governor Roosevelt for President in the next Democratic national convention will be vigorously resisted by Southern delegates.

Maryland re-elected Governor Albert C. Ritchie for a fourth term, thus repeating its overturn of the tradition in that State that a Governor shall not serve more than two terms. Governor Ritchie, classified as a constitutional wet, is likely to be put forward by Maryland's Democracy as a contender for the Presidential nomination.

Governor Roosevelt apparently carried the State by a plurality of 730,000. His lead in New York City over Mr. Tuttle was approximately 556,000. He also carried up-State, normally Republican, by an indicated plurality of about 174,000.

The entire Democratic State ticket

Times Wide World Photo.

OVERWHELMINGLY RE-ELECTED.
Governor Franklin D. Roosevelt, Who, With His Entire Ticket, Is Returned to Office by a Record Plurality.

was swept into office on the crest of the Roosevelt tidal wave.

In Pennsylvania Gifford Pinchot, in the Gubernatorial race, was elected over his Democratic opponent, John M. Hemphill.

Tremendous interest was shown in this contest because of a revolt against Mr. Pinchot's candidacy by leaders of the Republican organization in the State, foremost of whom was General W. W. Atterbury, who resigned his position as National Committeeman for Pennsylvania to take charge of the anti-Pinchot forces within the Republican party.

Another sweeping victory for a Democratic candidate came in Illinois where Mrs. Ruth Hanna McCormick, now a Republican Congresswoman-at-Large, went down to defeat for United States Senator under a deluge of ballots for former Senator James Hamilton Lewis, her Democratic antagonist. Colonel Lewis not only swept Cook County, which includes Chicago, but ran ahead of Mrs. McCormick in that part of Illinois known as down-State, which is traditionally Republican.

The triumph of Colonel Lewis was a distinct wet victory. He ran on a dripping wet platform, and declared that if elected to the Senate he would vote wet without regard to how Illinois sentiment was expressed in today's referendum on the prohibition question. Mrs. McCormick had announced that, while she was dry personally and on principle, she would follow the dictum expressed in the referendum.

Alabama Chastens Heflin.

The voters of Alabama punished Senator J. Thomas Heflin by relegating him to private life after thirty-six years of office holding. He was defeated by J. H. Bankhead, nominee of the regular Democrats for Senator, in a party primary from which Heflin was excluded because he bolted the Democratic Presidential ticket in 1928. In yesterday's contest Senator Heflin ran as an independent under the title of Jeffersonian Democrat. Victory was also won in Alabama by V. M. Miller, the regular Democratic candidate for Governor, over Hugh A. Locke, the nominee of the Heflin party.

With the defeat of Senator Heflin that part of the country known as the Solid South emphasized its return to its old Democratic allegiance. Texas, which cast its electoral vote for Herbert Hoover, had rejected in its Democratic primaries those aspirants for office who had refused to support the Democratic Presidential nominees two years ago. North Carolina refused a renomination to its veteran Democratic leader, Senator F. M. Simmons, who also had bolted the Smith-Robinson ticket, and in yesterday's election the voters of the State gave Mr. Simmons's seat to Josiah W. Bailey, the regular Democrat who had defeated him in the party primary. Virginia had already elected a Democratic Governor in a contest with an anti-Smith Democrat who was endorsed by the Republican party.

November 5, 1930

PARTY LINES GROW FAINTER AND FAINTER

With Economic Questions as Dominant Issues, the Old Boundaries Are Crossed by Sectional and Class Interest

In recent years of economic stress the system of government by political parties has faltered in many countries. The following article surveys this unusual situation with especial reference to the United States as the Presidential election approaches. The author is Professor of History and Government at the California Institute of Technology.

By WILLIAM B. MUNRO

ARE the old political parties doomed? Can they hope to survive in the new era? Perhaps they can and will, but the breakdown of party discipline is one of the significant phenomena of these hectic days in the realm of government. This collapse of the old partisan solidarity is not confined to the United States. It is taking place over most of Europe as well. The recent election in Germany, for example, disclosed how completely the old political alignment has given way.

The coming election in the French Republic is apt to uncover a similar situation. Party divisions in France have never been very firmly stabilized, but they appear to be more shifty today than ever before. That is why France has had more than twenty Ministries since the war. It has become the fashion for a French Deputy to change his party group about as often as he changes his shoes. The habit of flitting from one faction to another has become so prevalent that it no longer calls for any comment. "To what group do you now belong?" a Deputy was asked by one of his voters not long ago. "Radical-Socialist, the same as you elected me," he replied. "You don't say so?" was the retort. "Then you are making no progress at all!"

Likewise there is England, the classic land of party regularity until a few years ago. For generations it was the English political tradition that one party should range itself unitedly behind the Cabinet while the other with equally unwavering unanimity opposed it. That tradition is now in eclipse. The existing MacDonald Ministry represents three parties with such divergent programs that the principle of Cabinet solidarity has been openly discarded. On the tariff issue the Ministers, as well as the members of the House, were given freedom to speak and to vote as they pleased. A Minister of the Crown voting against his chief and yet remaining a member of the Cabinet—such an occurrence would have been unthinkable in the England of pre-war days.

As for Italy and Russia, the party system has been thrust into the discard by both. Russia has crushed all political insurgency by branding it counter-revolution and dealing with it accordingly. Italy has not gone so far, but fascism has brooked no serious opposition during the past few years. Throughout Europe, therefore, the two-party system has disappeared. In a few countries a single party governs unopposed; in some others there are three or four parties; while in others, again, there are a dozen or more.

• • •

ONLY in the United States do we retain the practice of superficially classifying the whole electorate into two major groups. We do it from force of habit. But the term Republican is no longer descriptive. Neither is the term Democrat. There is no authentic difference between the two parties on any of the fundamental issues of today. Both have traditions, of course, and both claim to have tendencies. But neither is any longer a cohesive affair with ideas guiding its leadership or discipline restraining its ranks. They are like two bottles, as has been well said, with distinctive labels on each, but both of them empty.

Today it seems to matter little which party is in control of Congress, for neither is able to keep its ranks even measurably intact. Cleavages of all sorts are cutting across the straight party lines and making them sinuous. The Republicans are supposed to be in control of the Senate, but the leaders of the Republican party do not control or guide the Senate's deliberations. It is a law unto itself. Our Senate is not a mere branch of the national Legislature. It is an assemblage of Ambassadors from the States. Consequently it is a rare Senator who does not put the special interests of his own State above the general interests of the political party to which he professes allegiance.

Numerically, also, the Democrats are in control of the House and were able to organize it at the beginning of the session; but to say that their leaders have shown themselves able to guide the actions of the House would be to use the term in a Pickwickian sense. Insurgency, of course, is no new thing in American national government, for we have had spasms of it before, but almost invariably the revolt has confined itself to the ranks of a single party. Today the spirit of rebellion is rampant in both of them. Not for a generation has the national House of Representatives gone so completely on the rampage. It jumped clear out of hand on the sales tax and it is likely to do the same thing when it reaches the proposal to pay veterans' compensation in full. The best that the two-party system seems able to give us just now is legislation without leadership.

Political parties have usually been defined as groups of voters who think alike on public questions. That definition sorely needs to be revised, for least among the characteristics of a political party today is a consensus of opinion among its members. Nor is this surprising when one reflects for a moment upon the mottled array of shock troops which make up the party's membership. Take a look at the Democratic party, for example. Its backbone is a composite of two outstanding elements—the Solid South and a widely scattered following in the States of the North and West, but more particularly in the large industrial cities. Obviously these two elements have nothing in common.

The Southern wing of the party is native-born, Protestant, conservative, agricultural, and bone dry; while the other sections of the country is largely of foreign birth or descent, diverse in religious affiliations, predominantly industrial, more radical in its point of view, and wringing wet on what it regards as the most important issue of the day. How can one expect unity of action, or obedience to leadership, or adherence to a common program from a political party that is thus constituted?

The situation in the Republican party is not substantially different. It is merely that in this case the geographical cleavage is east and west, not north and south. The G. O. P. is also a composite of two great elements which have little in common. The Eastern wing of the party, resting on New England and Pennsylvania, gets its chief strength from citizens of native birth and Nordic ancestry. It is largely, though of course not wholly, non-Catholic; its general inclination is to conservatism; likewise it is strongly protectionist, friendly to the vested interests, and badly divided in its attitude toward prohibition.

Then, as you move toward the Middle West, the Northwest and the Far West you find the Republican party taking on a bucolic coloration. In these great agricultural regions the attitude on public questions is molded by a traditional aversion to Wall Street, the railroads, the great public utility corporations and the mobilized money power in general. This Western section of the Republican party is less hampered by any adherence to fixed principles; it inclines to be insurgent whenever the price of wheat goes down, and its restlessness gives the leaders of Republicanism almost perpetual concern.

Nor are these sectional splits the only ones. Within the ranks of each party there are progressives and standpatters, pacifists and militarists, rugged individualists and public-ownership advocates, high protectionists and tariff revisionists, wets and drys with all shades of moisture in between, inflationists and hard-money partisans, not to speak of racial, religious and vocational groups of every conceivable variety. These currents and cross-currents of interest and opinion have made each of the major parties a mosaic which is precariously held together by a rope of sand called party allegiance.

• • •

BROADLY speaking, we have no longer any political issues. Politics has become economics. The two have become hopelessly intertwined. Virtually every question that comes up in Congress is one that directly touches the pocketbook of some interest, section, class or vocation. People do not realize how enormously the functions of government have expanded during the past thirty years. Today the hand of government reaches into every nook and corner of our daily life. Its tariff laws, tax laws and banking laws, its promotions and prohibitions, its control of transportation and its vast array of administrative regulations have transformed our government into a giant paternalism.

This of course has had its repercussions on the American party system which was devised and developed in an age when life was simple, when issues were few and clean-cut, and when the functions of government were easy to understand. The system was never intended to serve the needs of an age in which the advance of technology and the spread of collectivism have made politics incomprehensible to that much overrated fellow—the plain citizen.

Nor can it hope to do so. The multifarious questions which arise in connection with our governmental activities of today cannot be settled by an appeal to historic party principles. Nor can they be wisely settled by submitting them to the reactions of a mass electorate. To refer intricate problems of bank regulation, public finance and international relations to the judgment of an unassorted populace is merely to set up a Supreme Court of Ignorance before which all varieties of self-interest, sectionalism and prejudice can plead their cause in the name of party principles.

CONGRESS is supposed to represent the States and the people, but in reality it has now become a great economic council. The primary solicitude of its members is to see that nothing is put over on the States and districts which they represent. Even more it is their business to get some economic advantages for their own areas at the expense of the others if they can. This is the first axiom in the textbook of Congressional economics—to get for your own people as much as you can and to have them bear, in turn, the least possible portion of the common burden. Any tax, according to the principles of Congressional economics, is a good tax if it falls mainly upon those who will have no part in the Congressman's re-election.

One need only follow the course of the recent revenue measure on its journey through the House of Representatives to appreciate the way in which sectional and class covetousness have managed to rupture party lines, abolish party discipline and dethrone party leadership. Republicans and Democrats from the agricultural regions joined hands with the tribunes of the proletariat in the exhilarating sport of "soaking the rich," quite unmindful of the fact that there are nearly $5,000,000,000 of outstanding tax-exempt securities to which the big incomes can readily fly for refuge.

It was characteristic of this fiery debate, moreover, that both parties agreed to saddle increased postal rates on the people but that neither suggested a curtailment of the franking privileges which Congressmen themselves enjoy. Taxation has sometimes been defined as a system of confiscation tempered by favoritism. The tempering is not to the shorn lamb but to the ram with horns, to the element that has the political power.

• • •

THE issues which are running in the minds of the American voters today are not the ones which have bulked large in the recent platforms of the two leading political parties. They cannot, in fact, be set forth in orderly planks or paragraphs, for they are subtle in their implications and reach deeply into the whole fabric of American life. They are merely the outward manifestation of great and fundamental diversities in race, religion, social status and economic self-interest.

When we have a great effervescence of economic prosperity the party in power claims the credit and usually gets it. That is unfair, of course, for the administration may have had little or nothing to do with the nation's interlude of good fortune. Likewise when the reaction comes, when the level of prices goes tumbling and the factories are shut down, when the banks go broke and the breadlines form—when these misfortunes come upon us the party in power must be prepared to take the blame. It is no answer to say that the blame is undeserved. So was the credit a few years ago. The rule must work both ways.

• • •

JUST as national prosperity was the greatest asset of the Republican party four years ago, to the same extent will the industrial depression be a Republican liability in this campaign. All other issues, even prohibition, will probably be subordinate to this outstanding one. It is an issue with many ramifications, besides being one in which the farmer and the industrial worker can join. Usually these two great elements in the American electorate do not feel a common grievance. Four years ago that was the case. But today their jeremiads are pitched in the same key. The big task of the Republican campaigners will be to convince these people that the party has done all things possible to relieve the farmer, to mitigate industrial unemployment, to succor distress, to lessen the tax burden, to support credit and to peg the general decline in prices.

It will not be an easy task, yet it is by no means an insuperable one. The country is normally Republican; in fact, it is Republican whenever it gets anything like a fair chance to be. It is more strongly inclined to be Republican in national than in State elections, and more strongly in a Presidential than in a Congressional line-up. The forecasters who are now predicting an assured Democratic landslide next November should remember that only once in the past seventy years has the Democratic candidate for the Presidency won by a wide margin, and then only as the result of a wide-open Republican split. It takes serious provocation to send the United States of America into the Democratic column. Perhaps the economic depression will continue long enough, and continue severe enough, to do it this year.

Some consolation for the Republicans may be found in the fact that a large part of the country blames New York rather than Washington for its troubles. Main Street dislikes Wall Street with greater intensity today than ever before. New Yorkers may not realize it, or may feel altogether unconcerned about it, but any Presidential aspirant who comes from the metropolis will find that he has something to live down when he appeals for support in the regions West and South.

Prohibition will be an issue in the impending campaign, as it has been in Congress, but it cannot be constrained within party lines. As indicated by recent Congressional votes it is a question which cuts right across them. In the main it is a cleavage of urban versus rural, quite irrespective of political affiliation. The rural voter is still in the majority and controls the situation on this issue. Likewise the Nineteenth Amendment serves as a shield and buckler to the Eighteenth. Both political parties are disinclined to come out straight and forthright on this question, and with good reason, for it contains more dynamite for the wrecking of party alignments than any other issue now in sight.

In a word, the old party loyalties are weakening both in Congress and in the country. This is because the old principles do not fit the new needs or help to solve the new perplexities. Those who are not familiar with the practicalities of politics are wont to inquire: "Why not scrap them both and organize new parties on a rational basis?" The only rational division of men and women in politics is that between conservatives and liberals. But such a realignment seems to be quite out of the possibilities just now. Regional traditions, the force of habit and the mountainous mass of political inertia stand in the way. Much more likely it is that the existing party organizations, having run their cycle of weakening and insurgency, will be able to revive their old solidarity once more. It would not be the first time that they have done it.

April 17, 1932

HOOVER

CHEER HOOVER 27 MINUTES

Delegates Give 1,126 1-2 Votes on First Ballot, 634 1-4 to Curtis.

NEW YORK FOR HARBORD

By ARTHUR KROCK.
Special to THE NEW YORK TIMES.

CHICAGO, June 16.—Under the disclosed domination of the President, the Republican national convention at its closing session today renominated Herbert Hoover and gave a grudging but safe majority to Charles Curtis of Kansas, renominated as the party candidate for Vice President.

Mr. Hoover received 1,126½ votes on the first ballot, his nomination immediately thereafter being made unanimous. Mr. Curtis, the beneficiary of a last-minute switch of Pennsylvania's 75 votes from its Republican State Chairman, General Edward Martin, to the Vice President, had a first ballot majority of 55¾, with a total of 634¼. His nomination also was made unanimous. Until Pennsylvania responded to the Administration goad, Mr. Curtis lacked 19¼ votes of the sum required for his renomination.

It has been twenty years since the obvious will of a Republican National Committee has been so completely and publicly subordinated to a President's program. In 1912, as today, both President and Vice President were renominated, the only time in its history that the Republican party has repeated its ticket.

But then Theodore Roosevelt bolted the convention and formed the Bull Moose party, badly defeating the regular Republicans under William H. Taft in the election and assuring the victory of the Democratic ticket headed by Woodrow Wilson.

No Prospect of a Bolt.

So far as the political elements of the Republican party are concerned, there were no prospects of a bolt as the result of the defeat of the repeal plank last night and the renomination of Mr. Curtis today. The only menacing element was the insurgency of the New York delegation. Today its members cast ninety-five of their ninety-seven votes for General J. G. Harbord for Vice President, ignoring the plain warning which lay in the fact that the two New Yorkers who voted for Mr. Curtis were the Secretary of State, Henry L. Stimson, and the Secretary of the Treasury, Ogden L. Mills.

Last night the New Yorkers cast seventy-six of their votes for the Bingham repeal plank. The administration, which made that struggle the test of its control, had only twenty-one. Had not Charles D. Hilles, the national committeeman, declined to aid the State chairman, W. Kingsland Macy, in his effort to supplant Representative Ruth B. Pratt as national committee woman, this steadfast friend of the President would have been defeated.

The church drys, and those who are dry before they are Republican or Democratic, will not be heard from until they meet in national conclave in August, after they have examined the prohibition plank which the Democrats will adopt in Chicago the week after next.

It may be that then, as they did against James W. Wadsworth Jr. and Charles H. Tuttle, they will put independent New York State and national tickets in the field. Should this happen, the effect of that action, joined to the demonstrated dissatisfaction with Mr. Hoover's program of New York's regular Republicans, may be as disastrous to the national Republican candidates as was Colonel Roosevelt's third-party movement twenty years ago.

June 17, 1932

ROOSEVELT MAY GET FARMER-LABOR AID

By CHARLES B. CHENEY.
Editorial Correspondence, THE NEW YORK TIMES.

MINNEAPOLIS, April 7.—The Farmer-Labor party of Minnesota, unique during its ten-year career as a political group with no national affiliation, is on the verge of taking part in the coming Presidential campaign. Firmly convinced that Franklin D. Roosevelt is a "progressive," as that word is understood by them, they are disposed to go Democratic this Fall. That is, assuming that Governor Roosevelt is the Democratic nominee.

Practical politicians now, the Farmer-Laborites have no idea of donating this support to the Democratic national ticket without assurance of something in return. What they want is a sort of fusion, under which Democrats here would ignore their own State ticket and support Governor Floyd B. Olson and other State nominees of the third party. This deal is also in the minds of key men in the Democratic party who are backing Governor Roosevelt.

Signs may be said to point toward some such arrangement—not complete fusion, not showing on the official ballot, but a practical working agreement to the advantage of Democrats nationally, and of Farmer-Laborites in the State campaign. Party heads do not concede this for publication, but privately the plans are well under way.

Conventions of the two parties are over, and they have left the way open to fusion of the sort outlined. Nomination of Governor Roosevelt is a prerequisite. It would be next to impossible to sell any other Democratic nominee to the Farmer-Labor organization. Another essential step is the nomination of Democratic State candidates who will fall in with the arrangement, and be willing to make only a pro forma campaign, that will be settled in the primary election on June 20. Fusion will be the issue between two Democratic factions, which are preparing their candidate slates.

Not an Easy Task.

It has been the dream of the Minnesota Democratic organization to absorb the Farmer-Laborites as once it engulfed the Populists. The present task is more difficult, however. The Farmer-Labor party sprang full-armed to a leading position in its first campaign ten years ago, when it elected Henrik Shipstead to the United States Senate. It was a secession from the Republican party, and most of its rank and file are set traditionally against the Democrats who for ten years have been a poor third in State campaigns, waiting in vain for the hyphenated party to break apart and founder. Instead the agricultural depression has built up the Farmer-Labor party as an instrument of protest, until now it has the Governor, Lieutenant Governor, one United States Senator and a member of the lower house within its ranks.

In this campaign, as one leading Democrat expresses it, the Farmer-Laborites have them "on the spot." Governor Olson has attacked President Hoover and expressed hope that there will be a "progressive" candidate to vote for. He is all ready to go out and make speeches endorsing Governor Roosevelt. It is conceded that the bulk of the Farmer-Labor vote is ready to go to Roosevelt anyway. But such a course by Governor Olson would make it hard for the Democrats to make an aggressive fight against him.

Farmer-Laborites have a weapon in a proposal for an independent electoral ticket. Urged before their State convention, it was referred to the executive committee with power to act. This really shelved the proposal, but it could be revived and electors nominated by petition next Fall, who would divide the anti-Hoover vote.

Fight Within Party.

Democrats, under the primary law, must have State candidates. The law also gives those candidates the power to name the State central committee, and two factions are contesting for that prize.

The regulars, who indorsed Governor Roosevelt in their convention, left the matter of a State ticket to a later meeting of county chairmen. A resolution locking the door against any kind of fusion or gentlemen's agreement was tabled. The bolters, who are sending a contesting delegation to Chicago, uninstructed, took strong ground against fusion and their committee is framing a slate of candidates to make a primary contest on fusion as an issue. The regulars expect to win in the primary. It will be humiliating for them to lie down in the State campaign, with a dummy ticket, and many of them are opposed to the plan, but the Roosevelt managers figure that an official Farmer-Labor endorsement will insure Minnesota's eleven electoral votes for him. The bolters will scotch fusion if they win the primary test, it is expected. They point out that Democrats always get the worst of such deals. They endorsed Senator Shipstead in 1928 and withdrew their own candidate, but Governor Olson helped to block delivery of the Farmer-Laborite vote to Al Smith by urging Farmer-Laborites to keep out of the national contest.

Again in 1930 Democrats named a man for Governor who publicly disclaimed any desire for votes. They voted almost solidly for Olson. Democrats had a golden chance to elect Einar Hoidale Senator because of the Republican split, but Farmer-Laborites failed to do their part and Thomas D. Schall was re-elected. Naturally there is great reluctance among Democrats to enter into another deal this year, but they may go in nevertheless, lured by the hope of a national victory which might depend on Minnesota. The visit of Governor Roosevelt to St. Paul on April 18 may have considerable influence on the situation.

April 10, 1932

Text of Platform Offered by Committee

Special to THE NEW YORK TIMES.

CHICAGO, June 29.—The text of the platform as adopted by the majority of the resolutions committee and presented tonight to the Democratic convention reads:

In this time of unprecedented economic and social distress, the Democratic party declares its conviction that the chief causes of this condition were the disastrous policies pursued by our government since the World War, of economic isolation fostering the merger of competitive businesses into monopolies and encouraging the indefensible expansion and contraction of credit for private profit at the expense of the public.

Those who were responsible for these policies have abandoned the ideals on which the war was won, and thrown away the fruits of victory, thus rejecting the greatest opportunity in history to bring peace, prosperity and happiness to our people and to the world. They have ruined our foreign trade, destroyed the values of our commodities and products, crippled our banking system, robbed millions of our people of their life savings and thrown millions more out of work, produced widespread poverty and brought the government to a state of financial distress unprecedented in times of peace.

The only hope for improving present conditions, restoring employment, affording permanent relief to the people and bringing the nation back to its former proud position of domestic happiness and of financial, industrial, agricultural and commercial leadership in the world lies in a drastic change in economic and governmental policies.

Believing that a party platform is a covenant with the people to be faithfully kept by the party when entrusted with power and that the people are entitled to know in plain words the terms of the contract to which they are asked to subscribe, we hereby declare this to be the

Platform
of the Democratic Party

The Democratic party solemnly promises by appropriate action to put into effect the principles, policies and reforms herein advocated and to eradicate the policies, methods and practices herein condemned,

WE ADVOCATE:

1. An immediate and drastic reduction of governmental expenditures by abolishing useless commissions and offices, consolidating departments and bureaus and eliminating extravagance, to accomplish a saving of not less than 25 per cent in the cost of Federal government; and we call upon the Democratic party in the States to make a zealous effort to achieve a proportionate result.
2. Maintenance of the national credit by a Federal budget annually balanced on the basis of accurate executive estimates within revenues, raised by a system of taxation levied on the principle of ability to pay.
3. A sound currency to be preserved at all hazards, and an international monetary conference called on the invitation of our government to consider the rehabilitation of silver and related questions.
4. A competitive tariff for revenue, with a fact-finding tariff commission free from executive interference, reciprocal tariff agreements with other nations, and an international economic conference designed to restore international trade and facilitate exchange.

Unemployment Relief

5. Extension of Federal credit to the States to provide unemployment relief wherever the diminishing resources of the States make it impossible for them to provide for the needy; expansion of the Federal program of necessary and useful construction affected with a public interest, such as flood control and waterways, including the St. Lawrence, Great Lakes deep waterways; the spread of employment by a substantial reduction in the hours of labor, the encouragement of the shorter week by applying that principle in government service; advance planning of public works.
6. Unemployment and old-age insurance, under State laws.

Agriculture

7. For the restoration of agriculture, the nation's basic industry, better financing of farm mortgages through reorganized farm bank agencies at low rates of interest, on an amortization plan, giving preference to credits for the redemption of farms and homes sold under foreclosure; extension and development of the farm cooperative movement and effective control of crop surpluses so that our

farmers may have the full benefit of the domestic market.

Enactment of every constitutional measure that will aid the farmer to receive for basic farm commodities prices in excess of cost of production.

National Defense

8. A navy and an army adequate for national defense, based on a survey of all facts affecting the existing establishments, that the people in time of peace may not be burdened by an expenditure fast approaching $1,000,000,000 annually.
9. Strict and impartial enforcement of the anti-trust laws to prevent monopoly and unfair trade practices, and revision thereof for the better protection of labor and the small producer and distributor; conservation, development and use of the nation's water-power in the public interest.

Protection of Investors

10. Protection of the investing public by requiring to be filed with the government and carried in advertisements of all offerings of foreign and domestic stocks and bonds true information as to bonuses, commissions, principal invested and interests of sellers. Regulation to the full extent of Federal power of:
(a) Holding companies which sell securities in interstate commerce;
(b) Rates of utility companies operating across State lines;
(c) Exchanges trading in securities and commodities.
11. Quicker methods of realizing on assets for the relief of depositors of suspended banks, and a more rigid supervision of national banks for the protection of depositors and the prevention of the use of their moneys in speculation to the detriment of local credits.

The severance of affiliated securities companies and the divorce of underwriting schemes from commercial banks; and further restriction of Federal Reserve banks in permitting the use of Federal Reserve facilities for speculative purposes.

The War Veterans

12. The fullest measure of justice and generosity for all war veterans who have suffered disability or disease caused by or resulting from actual service in time of war, and for their dependents.

Foreign Policy

13. A firm foreign policy including: Peace with all the world and the settlement of international disputes by arbitration; no interference in the internal affairs of other nations; the sanctity of treaties, and the maintenance of good faith and of good will in financial obligations; adherence to the World Court with the pending reservations; the Pact of Paris, abolishing war as an instrument of national policy, to be made effective by provisions for consultation and conference in case of threatened violation of treaties; international agreement for reduction of armaments; and cooperation with nations of the Western Hemisphere to maintain the spirit of the Monroe Doctrine. We oppose cancellation of the debts

owing to the United States by foreign nations.

The Philippines

14. Independence for the Philippines; ultimate, Statehood for Puerto Rico; the employment of American citizens in the operation of the Panama Canal.
15. Simplification of legal procedure and reorganization of the judicial system to make the attainment of justice speedy, certain and at less cost.
16. Continuous publicity of political contributions and expenditures, strengthening of the corrupt practices act and severe penalties for misappropriation of campaign funds.
17. [This section is the prohibition repeal plank printed on page 1.]

WE CONDEMN:

1. The improper and excessive use of money in political activities.
2. Paid lobbies of special interests to influence members of Congress and other public servants by personal contact.
3. Action and utterances of high public officials designed to influence stock exchange prices.
4. The open and covert resistance of administrative officials to every effort made by Congressional committees to curtail the extravagant expenditures of the government, and to revoke improvident subsidies granted to favored interests.
5. The extravagance of the Farm Board, its disastrous action which made the government a speculator in farm products, and the unsound policy of restricting agricultural production to the demands of domestic markets.
6. The usurpation of power by the State Department in assuming to pass upon foreign securities offered by international bankers, as a result of which billions of dollars in questionable bonds have been sold to the public upon the implied approval of the Federal Government.
7. The Hawley-Smoot tariff law, the prohibitive rates of which have resulted in retaliatory action by more than forty countries, created international economic hostilities, destroyed international trade, driven our factories into foreign countries, robbed the American farmer of his foreign markets and increased his cost of production. Conclusion:

To accomplish these purposes and to recover economic liberty we pledge the nominees of this convention, and the best effort of a great party whose founder announced the doctrine which guides us now, in the hour of our country's need, "equal rights to all, special privileges to none."

June 30, 1932

ROOSEVELT PUTS ECONOMIC RECOVERY FIRST IN HIS ACCEPTANCE SPEECH AT CONVENTION;

FAMILY FLIES TO CHICAGO

Thundering Cheers Greet the Governor at Airport and in Stadium.

'100%' FOR THE PLATFORM

"Eighteenth Amendment Is Doomed From This Day," He Declares in Speech.

PLEDGES SELF TO 'NEW DEAL'

He Calls for Enlightened International Outlook and Shorter Work Day and Week.

By ARTHUR KROCK.
Special to THE NEW YORK TIMES.

CHICAGO, July 2.—Before it adjourned tonight, after unanimously nominating Speaker John N. Garner of Texas for Vice President, the Democratic National Convention saw and heard its Presidential choice of yesterday, Governor Franklin D. Roosevelt of New York.

Mr. Roosevelt confessed that in coming here he was breaking a tradition.

"Let it be from now on," he said, "the task of our party to break foolish traditions. We will break foolish traditions and leave it to the Republican leadership * * * to break promises."

Pledges Aid to "Forgotten Man."

His speech was aggressive. He pledged his aid, "not only to the forgotten man, but to the forgotten woman, to help them realize their hope for a return to the old standards of living and of thought in the United States." He would, he said, "Restore America to its own people."

Mr. Roosevelt began with a tribute to Woodrow Wilson. He then described the economic situation from his own viewpoint, saying that swollen surpluses went into the building of "unnecessary plants and Wall Street call money." The government should be made solvent" again, said Mr. Roosevelt.

The galleries warmed to him when he firmly endorsed the platform plank advocating repeal of the Eighteenth Amendment and modification of the Volstead act, and the Southern delegations noted his pledge to protect the dry States in their wish to keep out intoxicating liquors and to prevent the return of the saloon.

Work and Security the Need.

He suggested as one means of decreasing unemployment, putting men at work on reforesting waste areas. As to agriculture, he would aid that by production planning, by the adoption of a tariff equalizing world prices and by lowering interest rates of farm loans. He expressed it as his firm conviction that the popular welfare depends on the granting of what the great mass of the people want and need.

Their demand is for work and reasonable security, he declared, and he pledged his efforts to effect them.

In concluding, he told his hearers that he intended to make a number of short visits during the campaign to various parts of the country.

Jefferson, the father of the Democratic party, rode to his inaugural on horseback, but the nominee of 1932 flew to the scene of his triumph by airplane from Albany and covered the ninefold greater distance in less time. The convention rose enthusiastically to the voyager of the skies, and accepted his method of travel and the fact that he endured its rigors so well as a proof of his venturesome spirit and fine physical equipment for the office of President of the United States.

Animosities Are Forgotten.

Governor Roosevelt, when he had reached the platform, faced a hall almost as crowded and as emotional as at any time during the convention period. Except in small groups among the galleries and the delegates the disappointment and animosity of the preceding days were buried, and it was evident that the thousands of people believed they were in the presence, not only of the nominee of the Democratic party, but of the next President of the United States.

Before Mr. Roosevelt appeared, and his appearance was delayed by bad flying weather and slow progress from the Cicero airport to the Stadium, everything had been done in the convention to promote harmony in the party. Particularly was the New York City organization the objective of tender attentions from the Roosevelt leaders.

Both John F. Curry and John H. McCooey were called to the platform to offer routine resolutions, and when a Chicago concert singer filled in part of the wait for Mr. Roosevelt her choice was "When Irish Eyes Are Smiling." The retiring national chairman, John J. Raskob, who, in company with Alfred E. Smith and others had done everything he could to prevent the selection of Mr. Roosevelt, was requested by the chairman to arise in a box across the hall from the platform and acknowledge the thanks of the party, extended to him by a resolution.

Mr. Raskob limited his remarks to an expression of appreciation for the courtesy and said nothing about supporting the ticket. This, it was learned later from one of his associates, is because he, Mr. Smith and John W. Davis have decided to talk things over in New York before making a statement of their campaign attitude.

Mr. Davis departed yesterday and Mr. Smith today, and the last of the triumvirate, Mr. Raskob, will join them in New York soon for the conference.

The attitude of the Roosevelt delegates on this subject seems to be that, since for the last three years Mr. Smith and Mr. Raskob have been asking for the retirement from public office of those "Hoovercrats," who deserted the party ticket in the South in 1928, they are not themselves likely to withhold support from the ticket of 1932.

So far as Mr. Curry and Mr. McCooey are concerned, the successful Roosevelt faction need not have been anxious about what their organizations will do. New York warmly seconded the nomination of Speaker Garner, and whatever unpleasant feelings may be harbored in the bosom of Alfred E. Smith are not likely to bring the tears of Tammany. Both Mr. McCooey and Mr. Curry said publicly today that they will support the ticket and that it is certain to be elected.

Sure to Win, Says Curry.

Mr. Curry was especially enthusiastic about the prospects, saying, "This ticket cannot possibly be defeated," and Mr. McCooey, referring to the favorable Democratic situation for any nominee this year, remarked that Mr. Roosevelt is "the luckiest man in forty-eight States."

When the Governor took his place on the platform the Kansas delegation, the members of which had all donned green kepis adorned with sunflowers, gave him what is probably known as the "Kansas salute." Senator Thomas J. Walsh, the permanent chairman, delivered a short speech, officially notifying Mr. Roosevelt that he has been nominated for President by the convention, and ended with the statement that "Republicans will get little comfort out of your nomination."

In the presence of the nominee, A. Mitchell Palmer, former Attorney General, read the platform adopted several days ago. He was chosen for this ceremony because, with only a few changes, the draft of the platform was made by Mr. Palmer, and the form in which he cast the party's views and pledges was preserved by the committee and by the convention.

As Mr. Roosevelt advanced to the rostrum the great hall seemed to surge upward, an illusion which accompanied the sight of so many thousands rising simultaneously to their feet. Encouraged by cheers, even from the galleries which have all week been so hostile to his cause, the Governor in a clear voice and with every indication of great vigor delivered his speech of acceptance.

Soon after the clear tones of Mr. Roosevelt's voice died away in echoes high in the rafters, the convention adjourned. Save for the small Eastern groups which distrust the policies of Mr. Roosevelt and feel, in addition, that he will not give their organizations political prizes, the convention was very happy over its ticket and seemed immensely confident of victory next November.

Mr. Garner's nomination for Vice President was almost an acclamation affair from the time last night, when, as California and Texas were about to vote for Mr. Roosevelt, Senator Cordell Hull of Tennessee announced that the Speaker had been offered second place on the ticket and that he would accept. After Texas nominated him today, Mayor Frank Hague of Jersey City changed his mind about making the gesture of putting Representative Mary T. Norton in the contest. General Matthew A. Tinley of Iowa, who was placed in nomination, withdrew when it was evident that the convention wanted

to make the Garner nomination unanimous.

West and South in the Saddle.

Not since 1912 have the West and the South so effectively and completely established their ascendency in the Democratic party as at this convention. The United States Senators, the Governors and William Randolph Hearst met the city bosses from the East and North on the field of battle and gave them one of the quickest lickings in history. When Mr. McCooey and Mr. Curry were led, captives in daisy-chains, to the platform today the delegates gazed upon them with interest in which much triumph was to be discerned.

Two facts came to light today which help to explain more of the circumstances preceding the shift of California and Texas from the Garner to the Roosevelt column.

It has been related in these dispatches how Mr. Hearst paid off old scores to Mr. Smith, and how Mr. McAdoo got his public revenge for what happened to him at Madison Square Garden in 1924. But today it was learned that for a time Mr. McAdoo would have conveyed to Mr. Hearst the idea that perhaps an easier concentration could be made on him than on Mr. Roosevelt.

But the publisher was taking no chances. From Los Angeles, where he has been directing his political interests here, he sent emphatic word that he did not want to run any risk of getting Newton D. Baker or possibly "Al" Smith out of a deadlock; that Mr. Roosevelt was the only candidate; that he alone had sufficient votes to offer a focal point for the needed ninety from the West and that the decision should be made that way. It quickly followed.

It was learned also that Mr. McAdoo for a time thought that he was the most available Vice Presidential candidate. But this, too, was vetoed by Mr. Hearst. The Roosevelt leaders say that B. M. Baruch of New York acted as liaison between the "stop Roosevelt" faction and Mr. McAdoo and was as much surprised and disappointed as they when the former Secretary of the Treasury became the instrument of Mr. Roosevelt's nomination.

The other report here is that when Mr. Smith learned of the decision of Texas and California, with the consequent ending of his last hope, he tried to get Speaker Garner on the telephone at Washington, and was informed by the manager of the hotel where the Speaker makes his home that Mr. Garner did not want to discuss with Mr. Smith the obvious subject of the proposed conversation.

As the convention passes into history it becomes more inexplicable how Mr. Smith ever believed that Mr. McAdoo and Mr. Hearst would make common cause with him merely to accomplish one of Mr. Smith's personal desires. So long as their involved stake seemed greater to them than Mr. Smith's they went along. But as soon as they perceived that only the Smith interest was being served they broke the very fragile connection.

The Deciding Factors.

Mr. Roosevelt's managers were informed today that Mississippi had already voted to break to Mr. Baker on the fourth ballot when it heard the news about Texas and California. Had the Western States held off one more ballot, Mr. Roosevelt's fortunes would have been in a less happy position. Tammany was prepared to give him what he needed if his own line held firm.

But a break by Mississippi in that line would have furnished Tammany with the excuse to start a movement for another candidate. But Mr. Hearst stopped all of that and left the Baker men in the Mississippi delegation with their mouths open. This pleased Senator Pat Harrison very much. He has been working for days to hold the delegation in the Roosevelt camp. Governor S. M. Conner is said to have been less enthusiastic about Mr. Roosevelt.

But when Mr. McAdoo took the platform and made his paramountly effective statement about California and Texas, the Mississippi delegation pretended that it had been born on the bandwagon.

It was explained today that Mr. Garner was willing to accept the Vice Presidential nomination because, being more than 60, he is weary of the cares and burdens of the Speakership and would enjoy the

quiet haven of the Senate chamber. Having been Speaker, the first Democrat for many years to hold that office, Mr. Garner was willing to let his future years be spent either in the Senate dais or on the pleasant plains of Uvalde County, Texas.

But he and the Texans feel that the prospect of defeat is slight. In presenting the name of Mr. Garner today, Representative John J. McDuffy of Alabama said that the ticket of Roosevelt and Garner "brings a chill to the hearts of Republicans." Some Eastern delegations which were for Mr. Roosevelt would have preferred a different type of candidate. But everything was arranged; resistance was useless and the ticket went through as planned.

Hear of Norris Support.

With mingled emotions the delegates heard that Senator George W. Norris of Nebraska in Washington had pledged his support to the Democrats. Although they passed a resolution thanking Mr. Norris and calling on "his associates" to do likewise there were some who feared that so great popularity with the Progressive Republicans would hurt the party's chances in the Fall. They were assured by Mr. Farley that when Governor Roosevelt has fully developed his legislative plans the conservative interests will not fear the Democrats and will not worry about either Mr. Roosevelt or Mr. Garner.

On its last day the convention saw one piece of satiric comedy. It was

offered by Mayor James Curley of Boston. Defeated as a Roosevelt candidate for delegate in the Massachusetts primaries, Mr. Curley appeared on the platform as a delegate "from the beautiful island of Porto Rico."

He explained that it is an old Spanish custom to do something for the "forgotten man" (himself). He grinned at the glowering Smith delegates from Massachusetts who sat beneath him and did a small jigstep as he walked by their section on the floor.

It was a fitting incident to serve as the end of a convention in which the big city organizations got a trouncing.

July 3, 1932

ROOSEVELT TO MAKE A NATION-WIDE TOUR

He Plans Trip in September That Will Probably Take Him to West Coast.

From a Staff Correspondent.
Special to THE NEW YORK TIMES.

ALBANY, July 31.—A drive in which he will seek to portray President Hoover as a sponsor of unsound "radical" experiments in government

and himself, the so-called "radical," as a supporter of practical measures for rehabilitation was mapped by Governor Roosevelt tonight.

He returned to the capital from his home at Hyde Park, elated by the endorsement of Governor Ely of Massachusetts, voiced in a statement at Boston.

The effort to turn the tables on the Republican Administration, which has been labeling him as a "radical," will be made by Mr. Roosevelt in the course of a wide swing through the nation which the Democratic candidate has now definitely decided to make. The tour will probably take him as far West as the Pacific Coast.

His radio talk last night on the party platform set the theme which the Governor will play on in several

addresses during the tour, and aides are now gathering data with which he will strike at administration policies on currency inflation, financing of railroads and farm relief.

Mr. Roosevelt, according to members of his managerial group, has already collected a vast amount of material to support a contention that Republicans have swung into dangerous paths in a vain attempt to stem the depression.

It is expected that the Farm Board will be singled out as a special example, with Mr. Roosevelt arguing along the line that through this agency the government for the first time in its existence was actually put into the business of bargaining in grain futures. The Governor will then contrast the "no government in busi-

ness" policy of the Democratic party.

On the subject of inflation, it is understood that Mr. Roosevelt will amplify his charge that currency has been expanded without a proper base.

Next Speech at Columbus.

The Democratic candidate will meanwhile take care not to alienate his own progressive support through the country. This will be achieved, according to his aides, by trying to show that President Hoover as a "safe" conservative is wearing a radical mask for disguise, whereas the Roosevelt program of "bold experimentation" would be on a sounder basis.

August 1, 1932

PROGRESSIVES START A ROOSEVELT LEAGUE

Norris Heads Group Seeking to Alienate Independent Vote From Hoover.

BASED ON ECONOMIC ISSUES

Bainbridge Colby Among Speakers—Records of President and Governor Contrasted.

Special to THE NEW YORK TIMES.

WASHINGTON, Sept. 25.—Organization of a National Progressive League to support Franklin D. Roosevelt for President was announced here today, with Senator Norris of Nebraska, independent Republican, as chairman of its national committee and Frederic C. Howe of New York as secretary.

The league is to be "non-partisan in its policy and its activities are confined to economic issues," Mr. Howe said in a statement. "Its membership includes progressives of both the Democratic and Republican parties as well as independents who

acknowledge no party allegiance."

A nation-wide campaign for Governor Roosevelt will be conducted and the league will seek to bring progressives of both parties to his support in November. The most extensive organization of progressives since the late Senator Robert M. La Follette ran for President on a third party ticket in 1924 is envisaged by its promoters.

For a slogan, this statement, made by Senator Norris some months ago at a progressive conference in Washington, will be taken:

"What this country needs is another Roosevelt in the White House."

This will be printed on stationery and publications of the new league. A recent article by Mr. Norris in Liberty magazine on "Why I Am a Better Republican Than President Hoover" will be widely distributed as a campaign document.

Headquarters with Melvin Hildreth in charge as executive secretary have been opened here, and a New York office at the Hotel Roosevelt with David K. Niles of Boston as director of organization is also ready to function. Mr. Niles will have charge of the speakers' bureau.

Senator Norris will make a coast-to-coast speaking tour, beginning Oct. 15. Other speakers for the campaign will include Mayor Murphy of Detroit, Bainbridge Colby of New York, one of the founders of the Bull Moose party in 1912 and Secretary of State in the latter days of the Wilson Administration, and Amos Pinchot of New York, another active

Progressive in 1912 and a brother of Governor Gifford Pinchot of Pennsylvania.

On the league's national committee besides Mr. Norris are Senator Edward P. Costigan of Colorado, a progressive Democrat, as vice chairman, and Frederic C. Howe, former Commissioner of Immigration at the Port of New York, as secretary.

Other members are:

Henry A. Wallace of Iowa, publisher of Wallace's Farmer; William Draper Lewis of Pennsylvania, director of the American Law Institute, who was chairman of the platform committee of the Roosevelt progressive convention in 1912; former Senator H. C. Hansbrough of North Dakota; Felix Frankfurter, Harvard law professor; John G. Maher of Nebraska, president of the Old Line Insurance Company.

Also Donald R. Richberg of Illinois, general counsel of the Railway Labor Executives' Association; James M. Thompson of Louisiana, publisher of The New Orleans Item and Tribune; Ray Stannard Baker of Massachusetts, official biographer of Woodrow Wilson; Francis J. Heney Superior Court judge in California; W. R. Ronald of South Dakota; Roscoe Fertich, District of Columbia lawyer; W. N. Polakov of New York, consulting engineer; H. S. Julian of Missouri, and H. C. Schober of South Dakota.

The plan of the league's organizers, to turn the progressive wing of the Republican party away from President Hoover, dovetails with the campaign of Governor Roosevelt, who has called upon liberals, regardless of party, to rally to his standard, and made a direct public bid in California for support of the followers of Senator Johnson.

The following declaration of its purposes and plans was issued by the new league:

"In this critical election, independent voters face a clear issue.

"They must choose whether the nation shall have four years more of indecisive autocracy and indifference to human distress, or four years of constructive administration inspired by human sympathy.

"Today 10,000,000 willing workers are unemployed; 2,000,000 farmers, deprived of their home and foreign markets, are bankrupt, and more than 100,000 banks and business houses have failed.

"In such a crisis the highest patriotism demands that voters ignore party labels in the choice of their national leader.

Assail Hoover Leadership.

"For four years Herbert Hoover has been Chief Executive of the United States. For four years Franklin D. Roosevelt has been Chief Executive of a great State. They have had similar opportunities for public service and similar tests of their capacity for statesmanship. Upon their public records in these high offices the candidates for the Presidency should be judged.

"Throughout his administration President Hoover has proved himself incapable of effective leadership. Lacking a program of conviction, he has been on both sides of vital public questions. Declaring himself for limited tariff revision, he signed and defended the unlimited Grundy tariff. Advocating the principles of the Wagner unemployment bills in public addresses, he persistently opposed their enactment.

"Formerly denouncing Federal regulation of interstate utilities, today he half-heartedly advocates it. The achievements in unemployment relief for which the Hoover Administration today claims greatest credit are those which it bitterly opposed and accepted only under protest.

"During the same period, Governor Roosevelt, faced by a hostile party majority in both branches of the Legislature, was able through expert leadership and strong popular support to secure prompt enactment of a sound, progressive program.

"This program includes relief for the unemployed, administered through non-political agencies; farm market program and drastic reduction of rural taxation; old-age security for destitute men and women; reform of the administration of justice and revision of the public utility laws; permanent planning for the reforestation of waste lands, and provision for the public development and control of the enormous power resources of the St. Lawrence River for the benefit of domestic and rural consumers.

"President Hoover seeks to rebuild the nation's prosperity from the top down by showering loans and subsidies upon great corporations in the belief that the masses may thus best be aided. Governor Roosevelt seeks to rebuild from the bottom up by restoring the employment and purchasing power of the nation's basic producers.

"In his demand for social justice, his zeal to defend and conserve the people's natural resources and his intolerance of graft and corruption, Governor Roosevelt throughout his public career has been true to progressive principles.

"Faithful to his pledges, unwavering in his decisions, his moral courage and stanch determination have met and conquered every crisis that has been presented to him.

"Upon these issues the National Progressive League calls upon every independent voter to ignore party labels and join in support of Governor Roosevelt's candidacy and the progressive principles for which he stands."

September 26, 1932

ROOSEVELT WINNER IN LANDSLIDE!

SWEEP IS NATIONAL

Democrats Carry 40 States, Electoral Votes 448.

SIX STATES FOR HOOVER

He Loses New York, New Jersey, Bay State, Indiana and Ohio.

DEMOCRATS WIN SENATE

Necessary Majority for Repeal of the Volstead Act in Prospect.

Roosevelt Statement.

President-elect Roosevelt gave the following statement to THE NEW YORK TIMES early this morning:

"While I am grateful with all my heart for this expression of the confidence of my fellow-Americans, I realize keenly the responsibility I shall assume and I mean to serve with my utmost capacity the interest of the nation.

"The people could not have arrived at this result if they had not been informed properly of my views by an independent press, and I value particularly the high service of THE NEW YORK TIMES in its reporting of my speeches and in its enlightened comment."

By ARTHUR KROCK.

A political cataclysm, unprecedented in the nation's history and produced by three years of depression, thrust President Herbert Hoover and the Republican power from control of the government yesterday, elected Governor Franklin Delano Roosevelt President of the United States, provided the Democrats with a large majority in Congress and gave them administration of the affairs of many States of the Union.

Fifteen minutes after midnight, Eastern Standard Time, The Associated Press flashed from Palo Alto this line: "Hoover concedes defeat."

It was then fifteen minutes after nine in California, and the President had been in his residence on the Leland Stanford campus only a few hours, arriving with expressed confidence of victory.

A few minutes after the flash from Palo Alto the text of Mr. Hoover's message of congratulation to his successful opponent was received by THE NEW YORK TIMES, though it was delayed in direct transmission to the President-elect. After offering his felicitations to Governor Roosevelt on his "opportunity to be of service to the country," and extending wishes for success, the President "dedicated" himself to "every possible helpful effort * * * in the common purpose of us all."

This language strengthened the belief of those who expect that the relations between the victor and the vanquished, in view of the exigent condition of the country, will be more than perfunctory, and that they may soon confer in an effort to arrive at a mutual program of stabilization during the period between now and March 4, when Mr. Roosevelt will take office.

The President-elect left his headquarters shortly before 2 A. M. without having received Mr. Hoover's message.

As returns from the Mountain States and the Pacific Coast supplemented the early reports from the Middle West and the eastern seaboard, the President was shown to have surely carried only five States with a total of 51 electoral votes. It is probable that Mr. Roosevelt has captured forty-two States and 472 electoral votes. With two States in doubt he has taken forty States and 448 votes. Only 266 are required for the election of a President. It also appeared certain that the Congress elected by the people yesterday will be wet enough not only to modify the Volstead act, as pledged in the Democratic platform, but to submit flat repeal of national prohibition.

Republican Strongholds Fall.

The States carried by the President, after weeks of strenuous appeal for re-election on his record, seemed early this morning to have been Delaware, Maine, New Hampshire, Pennsylvania and Vermont. It is possible that complete returns may deprive him of one or more of these, but Connecticut seems to have returned to the Republican standard. It will be shown that Mr. Smith,

In 1928 Mr. Hoover defeated Alfred E. Smith by a popular plurality of more than 6,300,000 and with a tally of 444 electoral votes to 87. Not only will this equation be more than reversed, according to all indications, but in the final accounting it may be shown that Mr. Smith, who aided powerfully in Governor Roosevelt's cause with especial effects in Massachusetts, Rhode Island, New York and New Jersey was a much less badly defeated candidate than his successful rival of four years ago.

Late returns indicate that such Republican fortresses as Michigan, Ohio, Indiana, Illinois, Kansas, New Jersey, Oregon, Utah, Wisconsin and Wyoming—and even the President's birth State of Iowa and resident commonwealth of California—will join New York and the eleven Southern States which led the van of Governor Roosevelt's overwhelming victory.

A message to THE NEW YORK TIMES from Ohio, which seemed for a time to be in doubt, is that it will choose the Democratic nominee by more than 200,000, and 100,000 for Mr. Roosevelt is claimed in a telegram from Michigan, where the requirement for Democratic success was to change 100 votes per precinct. In Minnesota and Washington, reporting late, Mr. Roosevelt is leading.

Votes National Grouch.

The country was voting a "national grouch" against three years of business stagnation, against farm foreclosures, bank failures, unemployment and the Republican argument that "things could have been worse." The President's single-handed fight to sustain his record, his warnings against Democratic changes in the Hawley-Smoot tariff and efforts to impress the country with fear of a change of administration were as futile in the final analysis as straw votes and the reports of newspaper observers indicated that it would be.

Mr. Hoover joins in history Benjamin Harrison and William Howard Taft as the only Republican Presidents who sought and were denied re-election. In the sum, his defeat was greater even than Mr. Taft's in 1912, for while his electoral and popular vote will be greater, he had a united party organization behind him and Mr. Taft was opposed by Theodore Roosevelt and the Bull Moose party.

Political Monuments Fall.

Illinois turned down Senator Otis F. Glenn in favor of Representative William Dietrich. New Jersey refused to re-elect Senator W. W. Barbour, giving his Senate place to Representative Percy H. Stewart. The latest word from Utah was that Senator Reed Smoot, apostle of the Republican high tariff and watchdog of the Treasury, was defeated for re-election.

California appears to have chosen for its Senator W. G. McAdoo, the Democrat who delivered to Governor Roosevelt at Chicago the votes he required to be nominated, over Reverend "Bob" Shuler.

F. Ryan Duffy, opposed as Democratic Senate nominee in Wisconsin by Mr. Hoover's protégé, John B. Chapple, apparently was successful. On every front, Republicans were falling and Democrats triumphing in one of those great reversals of party preference by which the American people occasionally signify their acceptance of the dictum that they are "sovereign voters."

The party contest was so close in some States that they veered from Hoover to Roosevelt several times throughout the night. Connecticut, which showed a substantial Democratic lead for hours, went into the Republican column at 2 A. M. The same thing was true of candidates for State offices. Thus Senator George H. Moses of New Hampshire, whom Al Smith called 'Hawkshaw the detective," was in front for a long time, but about an hour after midnight The Manchester Union conceded his defeat by former Governor Brown, Democrat.

In Wisconsin former Governor Walter Kohler and the Democratic candidate for Governor, Mayor A. C. Schmedeman of Madison, see-sawed in the tally, with the Mayor on top as dawn approached. There was at no time, however, any doubt that Missouri had elected to the Senate the son of the late Speaker, Colonel Bennett Champ Clark, or that when

Kentucky counts tomorrow Senator A. W. Barkley will have been re-elected. Pennsylvania re-elected Senator James J. Davis.

This closeness in some States and local contests may bring the popular vote of the two major candidates nearer than the distance between their electoral vote totals would suggest. Perhaps more than 40,000,000 votes were cast, but Mr. Roosevelt, the overwhelming victor, conceivably might have a plurality of not more than 6,000,000. Norman Thomas, the Socialist candidate, seems to have polled more than 1,000,000, but less than the 2,000,000 toward which goal he had set his face.

The defeat of Senator Barbour, and the possible election of a Democrat in Colorado, both victors to take office in December, would mean that the Democrats control the Senate which meets in December and would be able to organize it at once. What will be done about chairmanships for the Progressive Republicans who have helped Governor Roosevelt, and what Senator Huey P. Long of Louisiana will do with his "personal bloc," will be earlier issues than March 4 will present. It depends on Colorado.

Defeat Privately Conceded.

Before 9 o'clock, following the discouraging news from New York, Connecticut, Illinois, Massachusetts and Indiana, Republican leaders privately conceded their defeat, although they withheld official acknowledgments. President-elect Roosevelt came early to his headquarters at the Biltmore Hotel, in New York City, where, surrounded by a happy and confident group, he heard the returns and smiled when his campaign and pre-nomination manager,

National Chairman James A. Farley, reiterated his often-asserted but now disproved claim that Mr. Hoover would not carry one State.

The President was at his home in Palo Alto for the news. He had reached there this afternoon, weary after thousands of miles and active days and nights of campaigning, but expressing confidence that the people would give him a vote of confidence.

Business as represented by Wall Street has already discounted the result of the election and has expressed its confidence in the future by a general rise in stocks on Monday of this week. When the rise came, the betting was as high as 7 to 1 on Governor Roosevelt and few important members of the financial community doubted that the odds were accurate.

Democrats Elect Governors.

So tremendous a party victory as this one, accomplished by the secession of Republicans and independents from the standard to which they usually rally, insures the victory of many candidates who ordinarily would have no chance.

For this reason there is a possibility that Iowa has elected Louis R. Murphy, a Democrat, to the Senate, and that there will be a Democratic Governor in Michigan, William S. Comstock.

Massachusetts re-elected Governor Joseph B. Ely, a Democrat, and in Illinois the Governor will be Judge Henry Horner, the nominee of the party which swept the State and the nation.

In Texas Mrs. Miriam A. Ferguson successfully resisted the fusion movement in the interest of Orville Bullington, Republican nominee for Governor, and she and "Jim" will go

back as a governing team to the State Capitol at Austin.

Late returns from Tennessee, where an independent Democrat was contesting with Hill McAlister, the regular Democratic candidate for Governor, are that Mr. McAlister will have a plurality of 25,000.

Returns from Washington, on the Pacific slope, are meager, but the indications favor Homer T. Bone to succeed Senator Wesley L. Jones, author of the prohibition "five-and-ten" act. In Kansas the reports are that John R. Brinkley, the independent "goat gland" candidate for Governor, has been defeated by Governor Harry Woodring, a Democrat.

Indiana sent to its State House Paul V. McNutt, former national commander of the American Legion. Ruth Pratt, New York City's woman Representative, and Representative Fiorello H. LaGuardia went down in the shambles, but a distinguished survivor of the party rout was former Senator James W. Wadsworth of Genesee, N. Y., who was elected to the House of Representatives.

Other curiosities of the returns were that Speaker John N. Garner, the Democratic nominee for Vice President, who was also running for re-election to the House, was successful in both quests, while Governor Roosevelt carried his home district in Dutchess County, New York, but lost his "home town" of Hyde Park.

In Ohio Senator Robert J. Bulkley, a pioneer repealist, was re-elected, as was Senator Robert F. Wagner in New York. Both are Democrats. It also seemed certain that a former Democratic national chairman, Governor George White of Ohio, had successfully resisted the challenge offered by David S. Ingalls, former Assistant Secretary of the Navy for Aviation.

November 9, 1932

VOTE FOR THOMAS IS PUT AT 800,000

Total Is About 500,000 Above His Showing in 1928, but Below Expectations.

COMMUNISTS FARE BADLY

Socialist's Following in City Is 120,486, While State Aggregate Is Probably 160,000

With little more than a third of the country's election districts heard from, the vote cast for Norman Thomas, Socialist candidate for President, and his running mate, James H. Maurer, were moving close to the record established by the late Eugene V. Debs in 1920, when he polled 920,000.

The incomplete figures, as transmitted by The Associated Press last

night, indicated a gain by Mr. Thomas over his own last Presidential vote in 1928 of 500,000 or more, and may bring his vote up to between 800,000 and 1,000,000.

The Associated Press returns showed that from 44,398 of the 119,714 districts Mr. Thomas received 373,692 votes. Complete returns are not likely to be available for a few days.

William Z. Foster, Communist, did very poorly, according to the fragmentary returns as reported by The Associated Press.

160,000 in State for Thomas.

Mr. Thomas received 120,486 votes in New York City and nearly 160,000 in the State.

Outside of New York, his chief strength was in Pennsylvania, Wisconsin, Connecticut, Massachusetts, California, Maryland and Illinois, according to dispatches to THE NEW YORK TIMES.

Late yesterday afternoon his vote in Wisconsin was 34,017. In Massachusetts his total vote was 32,808. Connecticut, with nearly all returns in, showed a Thomas vote of more than 20,000, while 9,251 precincts out of 10,547 in California gave him 26,766.

His vote in Pennsylvania was 44,-

020 in 4,289 election districts out of 8,199. In Michigan the total vote indicated was about 20,000, Detroit supplying 13,000 of this total. In Illinois, for 233 districts out of 7,222, the vote was 11,251. Incomplete returns from Maryland showed a Thomas vote of 9,233, with indications that it would go above 10,500, against 1,701 in 1928. In Washington the estimated State total was 4,500.

Returns from two-thirds of North Carolina gave Mr. Thomas 3,254. With more than 160 election districts out of 1,684 missing, his vote in Virginia was 1,683. In Oregon 1,103 out of 1,783 election districts gave him 6,401 votes. Rhode Island gave him a total of 2,306 votes. His vote in Kansas is estimated at about 20,000, while in Minnesota 1,555 precincts out of 3,716 gave him 6,520 votes.

The Communist vote was exceptionally low, as indicated by 444 votes for Mr. Foster in Rhode Island, 802 in Oregon, 43 in Virginia, 2 in North Carolina, 100 in Washington, 641 in Maryland, 824 in Connecticut and 2,385 in Pennsylvania.

On the basis of these incomplete figures, with no figures for New York State available, the Communist vote appears to be insignificant.

Thomas Grateful for Showing.

Before leaving Chicago for his home here yesterday, Mr. Thomas issued the following statement, released in New York through station WEVD:

"In the light of very partial figures, I am grateful that with our exceedingly limited funds and our encouraging but still young organization in State after State, the Socialist vote in this year of an overwhelming anti-Hoover stampede is as good as it now seems likely to be.

"It is evident that what we got was the convinced Socialist. Obviously, the mass protest vote went with a great rush to Mr. Roosevelt, who may find it more of a boon in getting him elected than in helping him to face the years that lie ahead.

"In many respects it is a blessing to the cause of socialism that the Democratic party is as completely in power. It has no unifying principles, hope or program, nothing in fact to hold it together, save passion for office and a general acceptance of the status quo as against constructive change. Its inevitable failure to deal with any fundamental problems will help to educate the masses of the people to the one essential lesson: There is no hope in either old party.

"Not a man or a party has failed in these tragic years through which we have passed and which still lie ahead, but the capitalistic system. We Socialists will carry on with energy and determination, for there is no hope save in our purpose and program. I want to thank the loyal comrades who have stood by us in this fight and who will be ready to begin again tomorrow."

November 10, 1932

NEW SENSE OF DUTY GUIDING PRESIDENT, HIS CHIEF AIDES SAY

Realization of State's Obligation to All for Common Good Called His Motivation.

SECTIONALISM IS DOOMED

Old Doctrine of Laissez Faire Is Dropped for a Humanizing of Government.

A CURB ON RADICALISM

Moley, Ickes, Tugwell, Wallace and Wagner Among Those Who Interpret His Policies.

By RUSSELL OWEN.
Special to THE NEW YORK TIMES.

WASHINGTON, May 21.—The basic idea of the Roosevelt administration, its guiding conception, as expressed by members of it, is a new realization of the duty of the State to the individual and to industry, and a unification of national effort for the common good of the whole. Formulators of administration ideas have no hesitancy in saying that the old order has passed and that it will never return.

"Government has to go a new way because the old way is closed forever," said Secretary Ickes.

To these men engaged in the problems of adapting government to the new needs of a people and the world, the primary virtue of the administration, and the underlying motive in all the legislation that has been passed, is a recognition of this fact, and an attempt to translate it into practical terms of national cooperation. No future American Government, they hold, can be administered for any group, either industrial or sectional, and no government can succeed which does not offer full protection to employe as well as employer, debtor as well as creditor, and to the individual as well as the group.

It is a complete abandonment of the laissez faire policy based upon a pioneer conception of a people's relationship as expressed by these men who are forming American policies. The humanizing of government, the emphasis on the personal attitude of the State to the people, is written in nearly every expression of opinion as to what the present administration is trying to do, and what is its political and economic philosophy.

Hold Change Was Inevitable.

One of the most striking things in every statement of opinion—and it must be remembered that these are individual opinions and not reflections of President Roosevelt's ideas, although most of those quoted are so close to him that this technical distinction is not important—is their unanimity of outlook, their complete agreement on fundamental principles of government in a time which they say is changing from an old to a new order.

As they put it, what is being done is inevitable and would have occurred anyhow, the depression merely having hastened the social and industrial transformation. They see a new world evolving out of the old, carrying with it solid American principles which will check a communal radicalism—the evolution, in fact, of basic American philosophy based on cooperation and individual liberty.

In obtaining these views each member of the Cabinet or adviser of the President was asked the following question:

"To what extent do you believe that the basic policy of this administration is related to a new conception of the relation of worker to employer, debtor to creditor, the State to the people? How, in your opinion, does this conception differ from past policies, and did the depression and its effects prove the necessity for the change?"

Professor Moley Gives Views.

The first answer sought was that of Raymond Moley, Assistant Secretary of State, who spends his forenoons with the President, and has been one of his closest advisers and confidants during the past months. Mr. Moley said:

"In my opinion, the basic policy of this administration, as it is coming to be embodied in legislation and in administrative action, expresses a concept of the relation of worker to employer, debtor to creditor, State to people, which is quite unlike that of the past twelve years, at least.

"The expression of this new policy in practical governmental action was, in my opinion, destined to come because the fundamental policy of the past twelve years was destined to fail. The depression and the breakdown of business in the past months hastened the necessary expression of a new concept.

"Its formulation thus was born of necessity but the principle back of it is very old. It perhaps can best be expressed in the word partnership, used by President Roosevelt recently. It conceives of the relationship of worker and employer, debtor and creditor, State and people as a common effort to unify the people of this country, regardless of economic group or geographical distinction, into a genuine nation of equals, conserving the values of our present economic order, but at the same time recognizing a common interest in national well-being and prosperity.

"I am thinking of a great American, Walt Whitman, who spoke in terms of a nation of comrades. I regret that the term 'comrade' has been used by foreign and strange and un-American groups of social revolutionists and reformers. I do not mean comrade in the sense that they do. I mean it in the sense that Walt Whitman used it in his great poetic expressions of democratic unity among all people, rich and poor, high and low, all of them devoted to the building of a nation of happy people. We do not need

imported mathematical conceptions of social reorganization to work this out.

"It is an American purpose, older than Jefferson, and its achievement can be accomplished by American common sense, coupled with a new sense of unity born largely of the terrible distress that we have all gone through in the past few years. We have all learned the meaning of unselfishness and we are trying to translate it into practical policy.

"This is traditional Americanism of the best sort. I regret that in the scramble for economic development, actuated by a wrong concept of the right of one man to profit at the expense of another, we have departed so far from it in the days since the Civil War.

"We are going back to the faith."

Ickes Sees Old Way Closed.

Secretary Ickes, who has long been interested in the affairs of the "under dog," as he expresses it, and who calls his department the "home department," had this to say:

"Reconstruction of American industry and a revolutionary change in our concept of the relation of worker to employer were forced upon America by the break-down of the industrial and financial order in the crash of 1929. That crash, of course, marked the collapse, but did not cause it. Manifestly, the policies of the present administration were forged out of the white heat generated by the grand smash in the Fall of 1929.

"The relation of man to job, of debtor to creditor, of State to people, is pretty much one thing. It comes down to a man's relation to the source of his living.

"The source of men's living is coming under something like a social control. Life processes, by which I mean factories, farms, mines, transportation and such things, are being transformed from empires controlled by industrial and financial overlords into social enterprises in the output of which there must be a decent sharing by those who do the work, pay the bills and consume the output.

"The old concept made farmer and wage earner fair game for ruthless high finance, long-tentacled and powerful. The new concept concedes to these men a chance to live and an effective voice in their way of livelihood. This change has not been brought about by any man or set of men. It is something forced by the break-down, the utter collapse of the old way of doing things, the old way of exploitation. No government could stand today if it failed to recognize these enormous new forces, if it failed to understand the thing that has happened.

"Government has to go a new way because the old way is closed forever."

Tugwell Sees Nothing Radical.

Assistant Secretary Tugwell of the Agriculture Department, who is one of the most radical economists in the present administration, said:

"Naturally I look upon the present tendencies in government from the point of view of the economist. Many economists, not all, but many of them, have believed for some time that there should be a greater cohesion, a more far-reaching inter-relationship of industry, not only for the sake of efficiency, but so that through cooperation the community as a whole might benefit. This concept is really that of a united effort in which every individual may play a part and receive from the State the assurance that he will have his part in it.

"For fifty years the efficiency idea has been germinating and growing in America. It began as time-and-motion study. It was given the name 'scientific management' by Justice Brandeis and gradually extended as a principle

from the shop to the factory and from the factory to industries. But industries need to act coherently together no less than workers on a job.

"All the time this technique of cooperation has been growing, the government has been attempting to prevent it instead of taking advantage of it. The new Farm Bill and the Recovery Act are the first recognition that cooperation and not conflict is the better organizing principle. From the point of view of the public the old sentiment of fear of big business has become unnecessary. The advance in technique of control has been just as great as the advance in efficiency.

"It is only a problem of adapting it to the public service.

"This would be my interpretation of the basic conception on which all recent legislation has been considered. There is nothing very radical in it. As a matter of fact, some of the things which are being done, such as the suspension of the Anti-trust Laws, the legalization of trade agreements and similar provisions, seem more like Republican than Democratic doctrines.

"These things which are being done are not things which might be done ten years from now, but are things which should have been done ten years ago. They are merely the crystallization of a tendency in modern social and economic thought which was inevitable and was bound to find expression eventually.

Holds Election Was "Revolution."

"Many people were a long time realizing that what happened last Fall was not an election but a revolution, a revolution accomplished in a particularly American way. The old order has been slowly weakening for years and its foundations gave way all at once, opening the way for a completely new program. That the administration seized the opportunity is not surprising. It had to.

"The need for making government a more flexible instrument for translating the wishes of the people into action has been present in our body politic for years. The depression merely accentuated its need and gave the opportunity to put these changes into effect, so that every group, whether industrial or geographical, might find, in the government it has helped to create, the answer to each individual problem.

"That the President had in mind long before election a well-rounded plan of action to bring about this result I have no doubt. Perhaps it was not complete as to detail, but in its general outlines it existed. He certainly knew what plays were to be made, to use a football metaphor, and he knew the order in which they were to be made to realize their greatest effectiveness.

"He is remarkable in his combination of practicalness with an almost uncanny intuition. He can see a fact no matter what preconceived idea he may have had, and he does not attempt to dodge that fact. He accepts it and fits it into his plan. And when you combine with this an intuitive sense of when and how to act, you produce a mind which has an unlimited opportunity for accomplishment.

"What is going on now is frankly experimental. But with a government so flexible as has been set up in recent months, with this quality of intuition able to sense an immediate need for change, and the capacity to shift the attack on a problem instantly, such an experiment as is being undertaken seems to me to be as nearly certain of success as any human effort can be.

"It is fortunate that people imbued with the Roosevelt sense of noblesse oblige, or duty to the country, have been entrusted with the carrying out of these ideas, otherwise there might have been opportunity for damage to the public interests."

Henry Morgenthau Jr., to whom as head of the Federal Farm Board and the Farm Credit Administration have been given over the complicated details of rehabilitating the farmer, said:

"There is no doubt that the depression has caused a profound change in the attitude of the American people toward business and toward government. There is far less impatience with governmental restrictions and a great and appealing faith in the power of government to set economic matters right. Confidence in business leadership has weakened and so has the self-confidence of business leaders.

"The coming into power of a national administrtaion which is willing to accept responsibility and to assume leadership has been greeted with joy and with new hope. There has been a truly extraordinary expression of confidence and willingness to entrust the President with power to act. The people have not been so much concerned with the details of new law and new powers as with the direction in which government is moving.

"The Courage to Experiment."

"There is a new sense of social responsibility and interdependence which is implicit in the administration's policy and can be plainly seen in its recommendations for new legislation. It involves a readjustment of old ideas of commercial freedom and freedom of contract.

"It looks toward a more stable social order, but it is not doctrinaire, not a complete cut-and-dried program. It involves the courage to experiment. Behind it is the conviction that no prosperity can be permanent which is not shared with all elements of the population.

"The striking fact about what has been done since March 4 is not the wide grant of authority given to the President. It is the close harmony between President and people, the day-by-day ratification of what has been done, the sensitive response to every administrative act which seem to present a more direct functioning of popular government than anything we have seen heretofore."

Wagner Sees a New Order.

Senator Wagner, who has been closely identified with the re-employment movement, and whose public works measures were incorporated into the National Industrial Recovery Act, said:

"The social ideals to which this nation is committed involve equality of opportunity to all the people for political, social and economic well-being. That is a matter of common agreement among all shades of American public opinion. The division between the old and the new governmental policies is limited to the question of method: how to achieve these ideals?

"The past has been marked by the dominance of the laissez faire doctrine—the belief that order and well-being are best secured by the free play of individual enterprise, untouched by State action. This laissez faire dogma has produced a full measure of disorder. As our business mechanism has become infinitely more intricate, it has become impossible to coordinate its various activities. Wages to labor have been so poorly coordinated with returns to capital that recurrent failures of consumer demand have led to cyclical depressions and widespread unemployment. Such vital pursuits as agriculture and coal mining have become dissociated from any tenable position in our economic system. The present depression is the culmination of planlessness.

"The new economic policy of the Roosevelt Administration, as I understand it, introduces a changed concept of the duty of the State. It recognizes that government no longer fulfills its functions through mere inactivity.

"The administration is ready to employ the centralized resources of the government as one of the means of correcting the maladjustments in the relations between capital and labor, agriculture and industry, creditors and debtors, one business and another. Its aim is not to destroy individual initiative or to lessen the opportunity for voluntary action but rather to establish those conditions in which initiative and enterprise can effectively flourish.

"We must now generally admit that our economic life is too complicated to be run without an all-embracing plan and that government must play an important part in formulating such a plan and in supervising its execution."

Dickinson for Protection Basis.

Assistant Secretary Dickinson of the Commerce Department, who has a good deal to do not only with the Railroad Bill, but also with control of industry and public works, said:

"There is a new conception of the relationship of government to the people in the sense that it is being applied to American politics. It has been, in the minds of thoughtful people for a long time, but it has not been used. In the beginning of the Wilson administration some work was done along these lines, and in the war there was seen the united action of a people on a scale never visioned bfore. But the reaction to war brought just as definite a reaction against these ideas, and the return to normalcy not only brought back the good of the old system but also the bad.

"The old American social policy was based on the pioneer conception of rugged individualism, which has always seemed a necessary, almost a sacred virtue, to some of those reared in the old school. That idea is all right in a pioneer country, but in a complex, closely-connected, industrial system such as ours it does not work.

"I do not mean to say that labor or the farmer should be wards of the State, but they should have the same protection which has always been given to those at the top. In other words, under the modern conception of the relation of the State to the people there shall be equal opportunity and equal protection for every group within it.

An Effort to See Nation Whole.

"There is now a clearer recognition of the two-sidedness of all processes of our national life—that the purchasing power of the consumer must be protected as well as the rights of the producer, that labor has rights as well as the employer, that the debtor as well as the creditor must be protected. That does not mean that government is becoming paternalistic, but that it is becoming more representative of all the people.

"What this administration is trying to do is to look at our economic and social life as a process in which all have a partnership. We cannot look at the welfare of one without visualizing them as part of this process. Other administrations have looked at the man at the top as the important figure in the industrial scheme, in the belief that if he became rich enough something would trickle down to those below.

"In the new viewpoint government is looked upon as a great corporation to promote the general welfare. It is a tendency away from the type which looks at the parts of things, and toward a type which synthesizes. Ideas matured in the cloister, so to speak, coming to a well-rounded completion without political interference, have been taken out and put to practical application."

Wallace Sees 'Social Justice.'

Secretary Wallace, one of the most pronounced individualists in the administration, said:

"The motive behind the new administration, as I understand it, might be more simply expressed by the short phrase 'circuit flow of prosperity.' We are striving to abandon as far as possible the narrow, selfish, individualistic, departmental concepts.

"I have found the other departments exceedingly interested in the new Farm Bill because they believe that if purchasing power is restored to the farmer it will rapidly flow to the people of the cities. In like manner I have been interested in cooperation with the Departments of Commerce and Labor, &c., and as a manner of fact, in various projects in public works and the industrial control program, so as to make it as certain as possible that consumers would have purchasing power added to help the farmer out of the ditch.

"President Roosevelt, as he unfolds the different parts of his program, makes it clear that he believes the centralized power of the State should be invoked in times like these to enable people to do the common sense things, which they have long known ought to be done but which they have been unable to do during the past three years because of a purely competitive, individualistic attitude.

"I believe the administration to be animated by the highest ideals of social justice. It remains to be seen how rapidly we can cooperate with the people of the country in making the new social order work in a precise and well-balanced way."

Roper's View of New Deal.

Secretary Roper said:

"As evidenced by events since March 4, the 'new deal' functions primarily as a 'humanizing' force, involving, however, a deep and fruitful understanding of both economic and social problems. It strives for a 'broadening of the bases' of the general national well-being. It stresses the importance of equitable treatment to all with preferential condition to none. A wide diffusion of the benefit of creative labor is accordingly sought.

"The new deal recognizes that governmental aloofness from business is not feasible in such an emergency as now confronts us. A more cooperative 'set-up' had to be established. In this essential partnership and cooperative endeavor all the factors must play their parts, including the industrialists, distributers, workers of every sort, as well as consumers.

"The government is not to dictate but to coordinate, guide and stimulate all to wisely help themselves. The plan is thus to collaborate in essential planning and in national controls. It seeks less block thinking, less block action and more thought for the common good. So the new deal with this inspiring objective moves forward toward a goal of greater justice and broader happiness for all our people.

"Instead of legislation for groups, the new deal looks to the welfare of every one. Instead of special provision to a few, the new deal is designed to promote just treatment of all.

"This new era has been on the horizon of reasonable interpretation for several years and the results of antiquated systems were emphasized by the domestic and world distress of the last four years and brought leadership needed to launch the new era."

May 22, 1933

FLETCHER ASSERTS NEW DEAL IMPERILS THE CONSTITUTION

By The Associated Press.

JACKSON, Mich., July 7.—Sounding the drums of the coming campaign, two leaders of the Republican party—Henry P. Fletcher, chairman of the National Committee, and Senator Arthur H. Vandenberg—today charged the Democratic administration with taking steps toward "emasculation of the Constitution."

Other Republicans attending a celebration here of the eightieth anniversary of the birth of their party, left no doubt that one of the war cries of the coming campaign would be "Back to the Constitution."

Chairman Fletcher and Senator Vandenberg assailed the Democratic administration for the establishment of what they termed a "bureaucracy" and for a fiscal policy which they said was gathering a huge debt that ultimately must be paid "by taxation or repudiation."

"The final alternative unless we retrench," said Mr. Vandenberg, "is the 'printing press.' Whether we like it or not, this is one of the realities ahead."

George F. Getz, national treasurer, said today that the Republican party will try to raise a campaign chest of $1,000,000. As much as is necessary, he said, will be spent to elect Republican Representatives and Senators in the "off" year of 1934, and the balance will be saved for the Presidential year of 1936.

Veteran of '54 Session on Hand.

Rain and thunderstorms failed to dampen the enthusiasm of the more than 5,000 persons attending the two-day celebration which paid tribute to that little group of stalwart anti-slavery Democrats and progressive Whigs who met here in 1854, under six now historic oak trees, and, many claim, gave birth to the Republican party.

One of that group was present today—Foster Taggert, a 103-year-old Eaton Township farmer, who recalled vividly the former gathering.

A torchlight parade was one of the features of the celebration, and the flaming torches and banners carried by hundreds of men high in the party provided the rally with one of its most colorful touches.

As airplanes roared and circled overhead today, speakers of State and national repute claimed complete restoration of party harmony and voiced predictions of an early return of party members to power.

Besides Chaiman Fletcher and Senator Vandenberg, former Governors Fred W. Green and Wilbur M. Brucker spoke, and seveal candidates for State offices predicted victory for Republican standard bearers this Fall.

"Surrender" by Congress Seen.

Mr. Fletcher said in his address, which struck the keynote for the meeting, that Congress, "under the influence of a combination of fear and fascination, has undermined democracy and weakened representative government by surrendering its law-making power to the President."

The power and authority given to the President, he declared, were "comparable only to those possessed by Mussolini and Hitler."

"The President has in turn delegated the control of the livelihood, business and property of the individual American citizen to a vast maze of theorizing, meddling, directing, spending, lending and borrowing agencies, lettered on the Russian model," he said.

The New Deal, the Republican national chairman went on, "has cost to date seven billions. Congress has authorized the expenditure of at least twenty billions more. The government faces the greatest deficit in its history. Every dollar on both these budgets (ordinary and extraordinary expenditures) must be paid by the people of the United States or repudiated by the United States Government."

The Democratic party, Mr. Fletcher said, has "gone completely New Deal," and "has moved away from the faith and policies of Jefferson and Jackson, Cleveland and Wilson."

The Republican party, he declared, does not believe "that the national wealth and well-being of the whole people can be increased by restricting production and by causing an artificial and unnatural scarcity."

"We are told," he said, "that what the party in power has done is a mere suspension of the constitutional guarantees, that a great economic emergency has merely rendered the constitution 'resilient.'

"This adjective alone is a confession of the doubtfulness of the measures taken."

Itemizing some of the authority delegated to the President by Congress, Mr. Fletcher said it included among other things power to "distribute public funds at his discretion to certain groups of the population and so open the door to the debauching of the electorate," and also authority to "appoint hordes of employes, unhampered by civil service laws, and thus build up at the expense of the taxpayer a huge political machine."

"Let me cite just one example of bureaucratic compulsion." Mr. Fletcher went on, "the Congress, after a series of laws which practically dried up the capital market, passed a law appropriating $500,-000,000 for direct loans to industries needing fresh capital.

"The loans are to be made by the RFC, and this board has just issued regulations which in effect require each borrower to agree in advance not to spend any part of the funds obtained through this loan for 'machinery, articles, materials or services' supplied by a firm which does not pledge allegiance to the NRA.

"Think of the vast compulsive power thus lodged in the hands of a single improvised agency under the orders of a military martinet of the drill-sergeant type."

Both Mr. Fletcher and Mr. Vandenberg questioned the monetary policy of the administration.

"I believe," said the former, "that the government by tampering with our currency, by destroying confidence, by stopping the flow of capital into industry, by the hundred and one measures of interference and control of industry and agriculture, not only has delayed the return to sound economic principles and conditions, but has complicated and confused our entire political and economic situation."

Vandenberg Cites Payrolls.

Senator Vandenberg in his address declared the country "is honeycombed with the most gigantic system of political payrollers in the history of the United States."

"At the last published count," he said, "the direct Federal enlistment was 644,108—and still growing at the rate of about 20,000 a month."

He cited the figures in developing his warning that no easy task faces the Republican party in the coming elections.

"In 1854," said Mr. Vandenberg, "it was physical slavery that galvanized Republicans into the fighting force of American salvation. In 1934 it is the lengthening shadow of political and economic collectivism which challenges these same impulses."

Senator Vandenberg said there was "much of good in many" of President Roosevelt's programs, but that "there also is much of bad in these contemporary programs." He commended the "ending of sweatshops and child labor" and the establishment of the minimum wage principle and the shorter work week.

Warns of Drift to Inflation.

"I speak against the fatal error of attempting permanent recovery on the basis of temporary tonics," the Senator said; "against the prodigal mistake of trying to buy prosperity and the worse mistake of buying without paying for it: against our deadly drifts toward the maelstroms of uncontrolled inflation; against the gathering currents which could sweep all industry, commerce and agriculture under the dominion of the State and substitute it for the citizen as our economic reliance; against elective despotism which, no matter how nobly meditated, would mark the end and finish of free, happy, permanently prosperous, traditional Americanism."

Declaring that the government is spending "between seven and fifteen billions annually—something like $2.40 for every dollar we take in," Mr. Vandenberg went on:

"We can neither tax nor borrow ourselves into prosperity. We have already devalued our gold dollar—without appreciable advantage. The final alternative, except as we retrench, is the 'printing press.' Fiat money projects to the extent of fifty-two billions were proposed in the last Congress.

Fiat Money Held a Curse.

"Fiat money ultimately curses every man, woman and child under its régime—except the rich and the shrewd speculators who know precisely how to manipulate such a lethal lottery. Whether we like it or not, this is one of the realities ahead."

July 8, 1934

Sinclair Predicts Party Realignment; Says His Victory Shows Nation's Trend

By The Associated Press.

CHICAGO, Sept. 2.—The major political parties are in a process of complete realignment, Upton Sinclair, Democratic nominee for Governor of California, asserted here today.

Mr. Sinclair, whose spectacular primary victory focused national attention upon California's party set-up, stopped in Chicago on his way to Hyde Park, N. Y., to pay a "courtesy call" on President Roosevelt.

His success in the primary is an indication of the political trend, said the former Socialist. Reactionary and conservative elements of both Democratic and Republican parties are aligning not only against his California program, but also against the New Deal, he asserted.

"People in California are tired of starving," Mr. Sinclair said. "My victory represents the will of the people for a change."

The plan of EPIC, which stands for "End Poverty in California," he explained, calls upon the State to rent farms and factories now idle, and permit the unemployed to operate with raw materials and machinery furnished by the State.

In his call Tuesday on President Roosevelt, Mr. Sinclair said, he does not intend to seek support of national leaders for his Autumn campaign. He will confer, however, with Postmaster General Farley and Harry L. Hopkins, Federal Relief Administrator, in Washington after his trip to Hyde Park.

Mr. Sinclair praised the Rooseveltian New Deal, saying that it was a step "in the right direction, but was only the beginning."

The Agricultural Adjustment Administration drew criticism from the veteran writer, however. He termed crop reduction "an economic blunder and suicide," and said that any limitation on production while people are starving was fundamentally unsound.

As to the California election, he said:

"If Frank Merriam, the Republican nominee, is elected Governor of California, a Fascist State will be created that will put even Huey Long to shame."

The newly formed American Liberty League, whose membership includes Alfred E. Smith and John W. Davis, is Fascist, he contended.

Mr. Sinclair spent some time chatting with Mayor LaGuardia of New York, who will deliver a Labor Day address at the Century of Progress Exposition. Mr. Sinclair spoke at the fair today and then resumed his journey to Hyde Park.

September 3, 1934

PINCHOT'S ATTITUDE VEXES DEMOCRATS

Administration's Feeling for Progressives Tested by Fight on Guffey.

OTHER STATES AFFECTED

Republican Backers of New Deal Face Farley-Supported Tickets in Many Instances.

Special to THE NEW YORK TIMES.

WASHINGTON, Oct. 13.—Pennsylvania's political situation, where a Progressive Republican Governor, Mr. Pinchot, while still supporting President Roosevelt and the New Deal, has broken with Postmaster General Farley over the latter's Senatorial candidate, Joseph F. Guffey, has revived the entire issue of the administration's attitude toward Progressive leaders generally.

Political leaders in Washington are applying the Pennsylvania situation to the Western States, where Progressives have given support to the New Deal only to find themselves opposed today by the Democratic organization headed by Mr. Farley.

According to the reports in Washington, the problem is one vexing the Democratic leadership. Beginning with his acceptance speech at Chicago, President Roosevelt invited the Progressives into his camp and since then, by implication, has approved the old Republican Progressive leadership.

In spite of the President's attitude, these same Progressive leaders now find themselves opposed by the Democratic organization in every State except one where there is an election. In California, the exception, Senator Johnson has the Democratic nomination.

Farley Looks to 1936.

It is pointed out, in explanation of Mr. Farley's position, that the Democratic organization is compelled to keep the records straight by formal support, with a view to looking forward to the selection of delegates in 1936. The question arises, however, how definite is Mr. Farley's support of Democratic candidates in Progressive States?

In New Mexico Senator Cutting has real Democratic opposition; in North Dakota the same condition applies to Senator Frazier; in Minnesota Mr. Farley has openly endorsed Einar Hoidale as against Senator Shipstead, while the Democratic opposition to Senator La Follette is understood to have made the election of Senator La Follette open to question.

It is this phase that has made the Pennsylvania situation a test. Prior to the primary, Mr. Pinchot was openly entertained at the White House, and throughout that period the Governor favored the New Deal.

Meanwhile the Pennsylvania Democrats put a complete ticket in the field, keeping the Democrats in their own primary so that they could not aid Mr. Pinchot, who went down to defeat.

Governor Pinchot now says that he is for President Roosevelt, but hits at Mr. Farley and "can't stand for Guffey," which puts him in the position of supporting the conservative Republican, Senator Reed.

Penrose Links Charged.

Mr. Farley holds that Senator Reed was part of the old Penrose-Grundy organization, while the Pinchot people retort that Mr. Guffey also was part of the Grundy-Penrose organization working at the job of bi-partisan control of the State.

Mr. Farley, observers here say, met a defeat in trying to "Democratize Progressive forces in the election of Fiorella LaGuardia as Mayor of New York. However, this has not discouraged the Postmaster General, who continues his partisan management while the President has continued to show gratitude to the Progressive leaders who supported his program.

The situation has considerably embarrassed Senator Norris of Nebraska, who has gone over wholeheartedly to the administration, and now, as leader of the Progressive group, is called upon to move into Wisconsin, Minnesota and North Dakota in support of Senatorial candidates whom Mr. Farley opposes.

The Northwest Progressive groups will support one another, it is reported here, with no real help from the administration. Mr. Norris is expected to speak in favor of Messrs. La Follette, Frazer and Shipstead, and the respective candidates of the Progressive bloc, seeking re-election, will go into the States of their colleagues.

It is one for all and all for one—all of them supporting the Roosevelt administration with the implied good wishes of the President, but all meeting with the opposition of the Democratic organization headed by Mr. Farley.

Democrats here say that the trend in their favor has become so strong in the last few weeks that reports received by Mr. Farley are to the effect that the Democrats might win in North Dakota and Minnesota and perhaps in Wisconsin.

In the latter State, the Wisconsin Democratic organization is working zealously to elect John M. Callahan to the Senate.

Mr. Farley, however, is not giving Mr. Callahan strong support because of his opposition to Mr. Roosevelt in 1932, and it was learned tonight that Senator Wagner is planning to go to Wisconsin to speak for the re-election of Senator La Follette, Progressive. Some Democrats believe that he is doing this after having conferred with President Roosevelt on the matter.

Mr. Roosevelt, while in Wisconsin this Summer, spoke favorably of Mr. La Follette and did not mention Mr. Callahan.

Late reports from California are to the effect that the many Democrats in upper California are turning away from Upton Sinclair, and the outcome of the Gubernatorial election is much in doubt. Senator McAdoo, who arrived here this week, indicated that the Democrats were having a hard time because of the nomination of Mr. Sinclair. He would not admit, however, that the party would lose any House seats because of the mix-up.

October 14, 1934

NEW DEAL VICTORY IN NATION GROWS

CONGRESS GAINS LARGE

More Than Two-thirds of Each House Will Be Democratic.

---

39 OF THE 48 GOVERNORS

Progressives and the Farmer-Laborites Hold Two of the Remaining Nine.

MICHIGAN IS REPUBLICAN

By ARTHUR KROCK.

Belated details of the results of Tuesday's balloting, while they brought to the routed Republican party the information that it had recaptured three State Capitols and preserved one piece of Presidential timber, served only to emphasize the widespread triumph of the New Deal and President Roosevelt in their first test at the polls.

Democrats were shown to have increased their Senate strength from sixty to sixty-nine, having won in twenty-six of the thirty-five contests. In the House, while seats were in doubt, the probability was that the Democrats had increased their dominant majority in that branch of Congress by nine.

Thirty-nine Democrats appear to be Governors of the forty-eight States of the Union, as contrasted with thirty-eight after the elections of 1932. In the remaining States the Republicans have sunk from nine to seven, the Farmer-Labor party has retained its grasp on Minnesota, and the new Progressive party, founded by the La Follette brothers in Wisconsin in an effort to absorb the radical wing of the Republican party, has taken that State Capitol from the Democrats.

Three States Offer Only Balm.

The only balm that came yesterday to the Republicans, as the slower-counting States continued their computations, was administered by New Jersey, Maryland and Michigan. In these the current indications were that Democrats had been replaced by Republicans as Governors. But in Michigan, where the Republican party was born "under the oaks at Jackson," almost complete returns revealed that Senator Arthur H. Vandenberg had successfully met the Democratic challenge and retained his seat. The elimination of Senator David A. Reed by Joseph F. Guffey in Pennsylvania leaves Mr. Vandenberg the only nationally potential member of the regular Republican wing in that branch of Congress.

But, in order to assure his election, Mr. Vandenberg was obliged to moderate his criticism of the New Deal and approve the general aspirations of the President for social and economic reform. He was, in fact, a symbol of the failure of the Republican National Committee to achieve a unified policy or establish a national form of attack during the campaign. In the opinion of his managers, had Senator Vandenberg pursued the anti-New Deal course voiced and advocated by Henry P. Fletcher, national chairman, he, too, would have been defeated.

As the counting went into its second day the chief concern of the victorious Democrats, in addition to the cases cited above, was over Representative Dennis Chavez of New Mexico, candidate for the Senate against Bronson Cutting. In 1932 Senator Cutting supported Mr. Roosevelt. The President-elect offered him a place in the Cabinet. But when the Senator's campaign year arrived he elected to take the nomination of the party he had deserted two years before, and this lost him the tendered support of the White House, which got behind Mr. Chavez. Last night the Senator had drawn into a small lead. If he wins, it would represent a defeat for the political management of Postmaster General James A. Farley.

In choosing a Republican Governor while electing a Democratic Senator, New Jersey repeated its individual performance of 1932 when, though giving its electoral vote to Mr. Roosevelt, it certified Senator W. Warren Barbour by a narrow majority. So far as Maryland is concerned, Mr. Ritchie was cut heavily in Eastern Shore counties because of his dispatch of troops there during a lynching episode; and banking troubles in Baltimore had their repercussion on Tuesday.

In Governor Ritchie's defeat,

the senior Senator, a Democrat, Millard D. Tydings, becomes the new leader of the State. The successful Senatorial candidate, George L. Radcliffe, was his choice, after Governor Ritchie had declined to accept the Senatorial nomination which Mr. Tydings sought to prevail upon him to take. The Governor's friends said that Senator Tydings urged this course because he wanted to keep the Governor from contesting with him for the Senatorship on the expiration of Mr. Tydings's term. The Senator denied this, insisting that he feared for Mr. Ritchie's re-election as Governor.

Prohibition, a local issue for the first time in recent years, having shifted from the national scene after the adoption of the repeal amendment, was voted upon in six States. The question before these was whether to retain their State amendments prohibiting the sale and manufacture of liquor. As a mark of the trend of the times, five of the States gave commanding leads to the wets—West Virginia, Florida, Idaho, Nebraska and South Dakota—while only one, Kansas, traditional home of the drys, voted to keep legalized liquor outside the boundaries of the commonwealth.

First Democrat Since 1874.

But these were all minor aspects of an election in which the forces of the New Deal, under President Roosevelt destroyed the right and centre wings of the regular Republican party, surrounded the left wing, and successfully fought a political battle of Austerlitz in Pennsylvania. What happened there is best illustrated by the fact that the last Democratic Senator from the Keystone State was William A. Wallace, elected by the Legislature in 1874. Not in the memory of the oldest observer had a party, so recently dominant, suffered as crushing a defeat as came to the Republican party on Tuesday.

While the difficulties of comparing an off-year election with one for the Presidency are obvious, those interested in statistical contrasts as a guide for future prophecy are examining the returns of Tuesday in the light of what happened in 1932. Then Herbert Hoover carried six States out of forty-eight. These were Maine, Vermont, New Hampshire, Connecticut, Pennsylvania and Delaware (although Senatorships were lost to the Republicans in New Hampshire and Connecticut).

On Tuesday (and Maine in September) Democrats were victorious in this proportion: Maine, ½ (Governor re-elected, Senatorial candidate defeated); Connecticut, 1; Pennsylvania, 1. Republicans scored as follows: Vermont, 1; Delaware, 1; New Hampshire 1.

Away from the Eastern seaboard Michigan, California, Kansas and Minnesota drew away from the Democratic standard, as did Wisconsin, with its new party. New Jersey split, as in 1932. Maryland and New Mexico appear to have been the other backsliders. All the rest of the country was 100 per cent New Deal.

November 8, 1934

BORAH AND NYE DEMAND END OF 'BIG BUSINESS' TIE IN REPUBLICAN 'NEW DEAL'

APPEAL HERE FOR REVOLT

Urge Liberals to Seize Party in the Interest of the People.

OLD GUARD MEN HEAR THEM

Borah Scores 'Die-Hard' Stand, Declares Republicans Now Must 'Move to the Left.'

NRA POLICIES ATTACKED

Monopoly and Price-Fixing Defeat Recovery Efforts, Two Senators Say.

Carrying their fight against Old Guard leadership of the Republican party right into the heart of its Eastern stronghold, Senators William E. Borah of Idaho and Gerald P. Nye of North Dakota demanded in public speeches here last night that young and liberal Republicans get together, oust the "die-hards" from control of party machinery, set up liberal leadership and break the control of "big business" and monopoly upon the party.

Addressing Republicans from New York and other Eastern States at a mass meeting in Mecca Temple under the auspices of the New York County Committee, the two progressive Western Republicans answered demands of conservative Republicans for blueprints of their proposed liberalization of the party by advancing the main planks of a platform of "constructive liberalism." A coast-to-coast radio audience also heard their talks.

Must "Move to the Left."

Senator Borah declared his proposed party reorganization meant that the Republican party must "move to the left" in order to meet present conditions. Quoting a recent letter by Charles D. Hilles, Republican National Committeeman from New York, that "the Republican party cannot stagger to the left," Senator Borah replied:

"No, but it can move with grace and do a great service to the party and to the people of the United States. We are not going to stagger, but we are going to the left, just as sure as I am alive."

The Senator ridiculed Henry P. Fletcher, chairman of the Republican National Committee, suggesting that he be sent to Russia as Ambassador.

"He is not in favor of moving forward," Senator Borah said of the chairman. "If he moves at all, it is backward."

"Will that attitude save the Republican party?" he asked.

"No!" shouted the audience.

"Would it be rendering a proper service to the people of the United States?"

"No!" again.

Senator Borah asserted that the philosophy of standpatism exhibited in Chairman Fletcher's recent statement and Mr. Hilles's letter could not rebuild the Republican party or save the American people.

"If the American people are to keep their traditional personal liberties and their constitutional form of government in the face of new world conditions," he continued, "we must adopt a system of economic and social justice to the great body of people of the United States and of a more equitable distribution of wealth."

The insistence of the present party leaders on standing pat, he continued, made it necessary for the younger and more progressive elements in the party to revolt against their reactionary leaders and insist upon party reorganization. Therefore he called upon these groups to organize in a "united front" throughout the country to battle for control of the national party organization.

Answering those like the Republican Senator, James Couzens of Michigan, who have demanded that the revisionists offer a platform for their proposed new Republican party, Senator Borah said that it was more important to know who was going to carry out the platform than what the platform was itself, for the most liberal platform could be wrecked by reactionary leaders.

The supreme issue for a new platform, he asserted, was "protection of the rights, liberties and economic privileges of the average man and woman" against monopoly and concentration of wealth.

Senator Nye threatened the Eastern leaders now in control of the party with a bolt by Western Republicans to a new Progressive party if the Republican party was not reformed with recognition for the West in leadership and in determination of policies and platforms, and if its "big business connections were not buried and replaced by the interests of "agrarians, laborers, producers and consumers."

Both speakers paid tribute to President Roosevelt's leadership, but attacked the NRA for encouraging monopoly through price-fixing, and both the NRA and the AAA for curtailing production.

Both Senators were interrupted frequently by applause, both for their hopeful expressions of the future of the Republican party and for some of their demands for liberalization. Senator Borah's more emotional style of delivery won him the greater applause. It was noticed that in the case of neither speaker was the applause as loud or as prolonged as that which has greeted "real old-fashioned Republican doctrines" at Republican meetings here in the past.

An audience of between 2,500 and 3,000 did not tax the capacity of the hall, which was 3,600. The orchestra and first balcony were comfortably filled.

All sections of Republican sentiment were represented among the leaders who sat on the platform, including "die-hards" and liberals. George W. Sibley, president of the New York State Young Republican Clubs, a leader in the liberalization drive, and Mr. Hilles, one of the most powerful of the Old Guard, sat near each other.

Colonel Theodore Roosevelt, who recently joined the liberals, was near Colonel Lafayette B. Gleason, secretary of the Republican State Committee.

Chase Mellen Jr., youthful chairman of the Republican County Committee, who is fighting for party reorganization in both State and nation on liberal lines, made an opening address in which he announced that this was the first of a series of monthly meetings at which prominent Republicans from various parts of the country would give party members here their ideas about what should be done to revivify the party.

Attacking the New Deal, Mr. Mellen asserted that the Roosevelt administration had refused to recognize that the nation "cannot successfully exist on a basis half individualistic and half socialistic."

Melvin C. Eaton, Republican State chairman, spoke briefly.

December 14, 1934

REPUBLICANS NAME LANDON UNANIMOUSLY

LANDON SENDS TELEGRAM

To Back Constitutional Amendment if States' Wage Laws Fail.

FOR GOLD AT PROPER TIME

In His Message to Convention He Specifies Exceptions in Accepting the Platform.

BORAH WINS HIS PLANKS

Vandenberg Is Expected to Be Vice Presidential Choice at Final Session Today.

By ARTHUR KROCK
Special to THE NEW YORK TIMES.

CLEVELAND, Ohio, June 11.—An unbossed Republican National Convention, yet working like a machine, at 11:41 o'clock tonight unanimously nominated Alfred M. Landon of Kansas for President, adopted unanimously a platform embracing certain social welfare ideas of the New Deal (which otherwise is excoriated) and seated party control in a group of young Kansas politicians and editors who entered the national political field less than two years ago.

At a final session tomorrow Arthur H. Vandenberg of Michigan is expected to accept the Vice Presidential nomination.

Eighteen Borah delegates from Wisconsin and the Senator's campaign manager (Delegate Carl G. Bachmann of West Virginia) voted for Mr. Borah on the first ballot, which prevented a nomination by acclamation under the rules. But Wisconsin then moved to make the nomination unanimous, and it was done.

Hamilton Reads Message

Two dramatic events colored the night session. Before John D. M. Hamilton, the chief of staff of the nominee, presented his name to the convention, he read at Mr. Landon's request a telegram from the Governor "interpreting" three planks of the platform and stating reservations. These planks, relat-

ing to currency, civil service and State control of wages and hours, had been revised by the resolutions committee from the text submitted by the Governor as a part of the week-long effort to placate Senator Borah and win his support in the campaign.

Governor Landon "interpreted" a "sound currency" to mean a currency eventually convertible into gold, insisted that the civil service should extend as far as the government's under-secretariat and pledged himself to support a constitutional amendment to permit the States to regulate wages and hours if the statutory method were not effective. He said "in good conscience" he must make these intentions known in advance.

The other element of drama was when all the other Presidential candidates but Senator Borah, who had already left for Washington, took the platform and seconded the nomination of Mr. Landon. Mr. Borah is only fairly well-pleased with the platform, and he expects to survey Mr. Landon's speeches and the personnel of his campaign cabinet for a couple of months before deciding whether to support the candidacy. Herbert Hoover, the other eminent Republican whose opposition was feared by the Landon group, phoned here today that he was satisfied with the platform.

Senator Vandenberg was among those seconding the nomination. Colonel Knox, L. J. Dickinson, Robert A. Taft and Harry Nice, the other aspirants, followed.

Harmony the Landon Goal

Harmony among all Republicans and the support of anti-New Deal Democrats have all along been stated as the twin goals of the Landon managers, and, except for Mr. Borah, the harmony seems to have been effected.

The end of the session, amid a series of ecstatic demonstrations for Mr. Landon and Mr. Vandenberg, came after a day of anxious concern to the Kansas syndicate which, at midnight last night believed that all its worries were over. Mr. Landon's differences with the resolutions subcommittee, and with Mr. Borah, and the latter's objections to revision of planks he had been asked to submit, caused the snarl.

But by 7 o'clock tonight, except for the open reservations of Mr. Landon and the unknown future course of Mr. Borah, troubles were over. The squalls had been weathered and the covered wagon was safe.

Day of Compromises

After subcommittee sessions which endured almost all of the night and day, the platform finally

emerged at 7 o'clock and its text revealed that Senator Borah had won his battles on the foreign affairs and monopolies planks and had lost only one sentence in the currency pronouncement. This sentence—"We oppose further devaluation of the dollar"—had been forced in from Topeka by Governor Landon, who also wanted a pledge to return to the convertibility of currency into gold as soon as possible, but did not obtain it.

Mr. Borah, whose support in the campaign is considered vital by the Landon managers, demanded proscription of the World Court along with the League of Nations and got it. He will now presumably decide in due course whether, as he has further made precedent to his support, "the candidate fits the platform."

Party Pledges Are Set Forth

The platform begins with a mixture of paraphrase of the Declaration of Independence to fit modern conditions and original arraignments of the New Deal. All Americans are asked to join with the Republican party in defeating the President for re-election. The Supreme Court is defended as the sure protector of human rights and the party pledges itself to maintain its independence from the Executive. Free enterprise, free production, no hindrance to business, decreased cost of living are guaranteed under Republican rule.

The needy are assured by the platform of the necessities of life, with relief administered by non-political, local agencies, no politics, grants-in-aid to the States by the Federal Government on a fair ratio, public works separated from relief and approved on a strict basis of merit.

Social security is promised to the people on a pay-as-you-go principle, the money to be raised by a direct tax, widely distributed as grants to States, and all persons over 65 given the minimum sum they require to keep them from want.

Collective bargaining is pledged to labor, and through the statutes, rather than through a constitutional amendment; ways are to be found to give to the States powers over wages and hours. Governor Landon and Mr. Hoover wanted a constitutional amendment pledge at this point, but Mr. Borah opposed. The President in his speech at Little Rock yesterday said the country's only need was a broader view of the Constitution.

The farm plank is difficult to distinguish from the administration's soil-conservation plan, which it hails as of Republican origin. Subsidies, scientific and experimental aid and the retirement of submarginal lands are promised the farmer. He is also offered a tariff ban on imports that conflict with his own wares. Further, the platform proposes the repeal of the reciprocal

treaty system and the substitution of the flexible tariff of Mr. Hoover's day.

Present and additional laws, civil and criminal, are invoked against all forms of monopolies. Such regulatory agencies as the SEC and the Federal Trade Commission are to be placed under court review if the Republicans win and keep these platform promises, and interstate utilities are to be strictly regulated.

The platform offers to place the whole government employe group under civil service; to stop Federal spending at once, and to balance the budget through economy instead of through taxation. After that the whole tax system is to be coordinated and, generally, levies are to be spread more equitably.

Isolation Plank Adopted

A foreign policy is outlined which will forever keep the United States out of the League and the World Court and any foreign entanglements, while supporting always the principle of international arbitration. The Borah flavor at this point is highly pervasive, even to a pledge to try to collect the war-debts which William Allen White says is one "will-o'-the-wisp" that got into the platform over his futile protest.

No discrimination against women in industry, solicitude for colored citizens, provisions for flood control, and a final paragraph binding the candidate of this convention to stand by every word in the document complete the pledges.

Mr. Borah never had so much effect on a Republican platform before in his long and controversial life.

Having assured Governor Landon's nomination through the public polls of New York and Pennsylvania; having lived safely through the demonstration for Herbert Hoover, and having battled on through negotiations with Senator Borah, the managerial syndicate found itself during the day involved with its own candidate, the Governor of Kansas, over some planks, and with Senator Borah, and ex-Senators Reed, Bingham and Moses over others.

The East, as represented by the ex-Senators, was insisting on a softer money plank than was favored by Governor Landon and his chief monetary advisers—Ogden L. Mills, Eugene Meyer and Dr. Benjamin Anderson of New York City.

Mr. Hoover, before he left town last night, had ranged himself with the Kansas-New York gold bloc. Mr. Borah was in opposing alliance with the Pennsylvania-Connecticut-New Hampshire monetary liberals, and was concerned over deletions he heard had been made in his planks on monopolies and foreign affairs. There were side arguments over social security, utilities, relief and a constitutional amendment to extend the power of States over wages in which various interests, including Governor Landon, were participating—he by long-distance telephone, they by personal appearances before the committee on resolutions.

A stranger situation never had existed in a Republican convention, with the Westerner, soon to be nominated, insisting on a more progressive platform socially and a more conservative platform fiscally than representatives of the Eastern States.

But there was evidently more in it than met the eye, because the Kansas control group was obviously delighted with the response from distant areas where news of the struggle had penetrated, and expressed confidence that the platform would "suit everybody." Meanwhile, the country was having a forceful view of the Governor of Kansas it had not had before.

Mr. Hoover sent from New York a telegram giving his views on the monetary plank. This was not released by the chairman of the California delegation, to whom it was sent, but it was said that all the features in which the former President is interested were included. Mr. Hoover also phoned to make sure of that.

Borah Waits and Erupts

While some of the Landonites were working hard on the platform, interviewing at regular intervals Senator Borah, who alternately waited and erupted upstairs in his room at the Hotel Cleveland, and telephoning to Topeka, others were exerting relentless pressure on Senator Vandenberg to accept the nomination for Vice President.

Thus the convention picture clouded and cleared as the baffling day wore on, with the sunny wearers of the sunflowers, the young amateurs and professionals who have been handed what many Eastern Republicans consider a doubtful chance, confident that another twenty-four hours would see a triumphant conclusion. The convention met and recessed twice while awaiting the result of the debates and the strategies.

In the conclusion, Senator Borah is to be found with his fingers crossed, according to the best available reports about his latest intentions. He said he came to Cleveland for two purposes: To put certain things in the platform and keep others out, and then to determine whether the "candidate will fit the platform."

It might be considered that he is in a position to decide whether his platform efforts have been sufficiently satisfactory to preclude his departure from the party fold at once. But it was confidently stated on his behalf tonight that he will have to make observations of Governor Landon for several months before he will be sure whether "the candidate fits the platform." After completing his work at this session of Congress, the Senator will return to his re-election campaign in Idaho. After listening to Mr. Landon's speech of acceptance and taking note of his campaign counselors and speeches, Mr. Borah will come to a final determination.

This, if Senator Borah holds to the program as outlined, is the net result of the superhuman efforts made by the Landon managers to get his active support this year. He has been the central figure of the convention, waited on, sought after and granted more concessions than even he could have expected.

Whether or not it was a part of the Landon drama, the Governor's subcommittee last night even yielded Mr. Landon's views on the gold standard and the World Court to Mr. Borah until they were called to account from Topeka. Whatever was the strategy of this, the Senator has been courted by the Landon group as no convention leaders or agents have ever courted him before. It leaves him with his fingers crossed, but the Kansans are full of hope.

Opposition, even nominal, to the selection of Mr. Landon began to melt away yesterday afternoon with the news from the Pennsylvania and New York delegations. But by midnight the thaw had started with a rush. Senator Vandenberg released his delegates, and other candidates followed suit, or were obliged to do so. By 3 A. M. the only question left was on the Vice Presidential nomination, with the Landon group renewing their pressure on Senator Vandenberg.

June 12, 1936

COUGHLIN DEMANDS COHORTS MOBILIZE

In Opening Bid for Political Action by Followers, He Asks Independent Congress.

FOR CHECKING 'DICTATOR'

He Plans Drive for Workers, to Begin in Auto Field—Nye and Thomas at Detroit Rally.

Special to THE NEW YORK TIMES.

DETROIT, April 24.—The Rev. Charles E. Coughlin mustered his forces tonight for a country-wide drive to make his National Union for Social Justice an effective instrument for changing the present social, economic and financial structure.

The aggressive radio priest opened his campaign at a meeting of the Michigan unit of the national union in the Olympia Auditorium. Fifteen thousand persons filled every available seat in the great indoor bowl and an overflow gathering of thousands of others in Northwestern Playfield heard the speeches of Father Coughlin and others over loud-speakers.

The aims of the organization, which is to have chapters in the forty-eight States and in the District of Columbia, were outlined as follows:

To uphold and defend the right of private ownership of property within the United States, but always subordinate to the inalienable supremacy of human rights.

To protect the masses of the people within the United States against the greed and domination of and exploitation by powerful vested interests.

To promote the common welfare by securing for all of the people within the United States, irrespective of race, creed or station in life, genuine application of the principles of social justice.

Specifically, Father Coughlin announced that the union would devote its influence to supporting the Frazier-Lemke bill for the relief of farm debts; the Wagner labor bill, the Wheeler Holding Company bill, the Nye munitions bill, the Nye-Sweeney coinage bill and the veterans' bonus.

Cheers greeted an announcement by Louis B. Ward, close associate of Father Coughlin and temporary chairman of the meeting, that 8,500,000 persons qualified to vote had signed the radio priest's "sixteen principles for social justice."

More cheers rolled through the auditorium when Mr. Ward made a reference to reforming the national banking system, with abolition of the Federal Reserve Banks. A mingled chorus of applause and boos went up when Mr. Ward spoke of "the time when Father Coughlin was under attack by a certain kept General, Hugh S. Johnson."

The speakers also included Edward Kennedy, secretary of the National Farmers' Union; William Collins of the American Federation of Labor; Representative William P. Connery Jr., of Massachusetts; Representative Thomas O'Malley of Wisconsin, Representative Martin L. Sweeney of Ohio, Senator Elmer Thomas of Oklahoma and Senator Gerald P. Nye of North Dakota.

Cotton Men at Meeting.

The arrival of Robert Harriss, a member of the New York Cotton Exchange, and J. J. O'Donnell, Boston cotton broker, here today to participate in tonight's meeting was viewed in some quarters as evidence that the cotton interests, on the warpath against the AAA's cotton policy, were cooperating with Father Coughlin's National Union.

In outlining the organization's plan of campaign, Father Coughlin declared that "it is our intention to drive out of public life the men who practice the philosophy of plutocracy."

He accused the administration in Washington of having entered into speculation in farm products, after mentioning the defeat of the McCarran prevailing-wage amendment to the relief bill and the failure to provide tariff protection for farm products.

Speaking directly to the citizens of Michigan, Father Coughlin declared that the "loose mass" of workers must be woven into an organic body.

"There are at least 1,000,000 laborers either directly or indirectly employed in the automotive industry," he said. "These laborers, almost individualists, are practically devoid of bargaining power because they lack solidarity. It is here we shall begin."

For "an Amalgamation."

Father Coughlin called for "a union of organizations, a consolidation of forces, an amalgamation of scattered strengths," saying:

"The National Union in presenting to you its Michigan unit, which is devised for the attainment of our common ends through our common efforts, proposes to work under the Constitution of the United States.

"We reject atheistic communism. We disavow racial Hitlerism. We turn our backs upon industrial fascism. We have no part with plutocratic individualism and less with immoral capitalism as we find it in Michigan or in the United States today.

"We insist upon a Legislature as the fathers of our country created it, not under the dictatorship of a President, not under the dictatorship of the fear of the high commissioner of prostituted patronage which tends to make America a one party government."

Father Coughlin asserted that his organization demanded "an executive with an American concept of the Presidency enjoying the veto, if he will, but recognizing that the Constitution never merged and never intended to merge the legislative and executive branches of government."

Hits Broken Promises.

By The Associated Press.

DETROIT, April 24.—In his address prepared for delivery at the mass meeting this evening Father Coughlin said:

"It is not our desire to form a political party, but it is our intention to drive out of public life the men who have promised us redress, who have preached to us the philosophy of social justice and, then, having broken their promises, practice the philosophy of plutocracy.

"With these men we have no sympathy. They deserve to be driven from their Congressional districts, or from their Senatorial State or from the broad expanse of the Presidential nation with our undivided, united strength.

"The days of broken promises and hypocritical pledges have passed, as tonight there is born in the hearts of the members of the national union resident in Michigan the philosophy of 'united we stand or divided we fall.'

"The national union is nothing more than the hub of the wheel of social justice. Your organizations are the spokes in the wheel bound together by the steel band of the sixteen points which we share in common.

Both Parties Scored.

"Year after year the farmer has listened to the siren voice of both Democratic and Republican, who promised production at a profit. Year after year the laborer in the city has been inveigled into the ranks of either party by pseudo-champions of a just and living wage.

"By the same party one gospel was preached in agricultural sections of the country and another gospel totally contrary was professed in the industrial centres. The result has been that, too often, on the floors of the Senate and of the House of Representatives, neither the farmer nor the laborer, upon whom the entire nation depends, were treated as if they were American citizens.

"Against this immorality the National Union for Social Justice raises its voice and stands prepared to throw its united force."

Outlining legislation which the union already approved, Father Coughlin said that it would actively support "the Thomas-Massingale bill for the farmer which guarantees the cost of production; the Frazier-Lemke bill which is destined to relieve the debt burden on agriculture; the Wagner bill which is written in defense of the laborer; the Wheeler-Rayburn bill which proposes to abolish the unnecessary and wealth-sucking holding companies of public utilities; the Munitions Bill which our esteemed friend, Senator Gerald P. Nye, has prepared to take the profit out of war, and the Nye-Sweeney bill which is designed to drive the money changers out of the temple and restore to Congress its constitutional right of coining and regulating the value of money.

"These we will support," he declared, "although I have no hope of their being passed at this session of Congress, because this administration, counter to the true interests of the masses, prefers to consult wickedness in the high places.

"We are in politics in the classical sense in that we will help to prepare and to support with all our organized strength certain salutary pieces of legislation designed for the common good of the majority of the people."

Father Coughlin urged his listeners "to recapture the solidarity which you have surrendered and struggle manfully to escape from the straits which have encompassed you."

"It is your right, it is your duty, to reassemble your ranks, under our democratic form of government, and struggle morally and constitutionally to destroy an immoral control of credit and an immoral concentration of wealth, which have multiplied poverty in the midst of plenty.

"This can be accomplished only through your solidarity—only through your concentrated action.

"'Bear ye one another's burdens' is the scriptural counsel in our fight for social justice. 'United we stand, divided we fall' is the American doctrine in our struggle against concentrated wealth."

Thomas Asks Public Support.

Senator Thomas declared that Congress hesitated to act on such measures as the Banking Bill, the Silver Bill, the Farm Refinancing Bill and the Soldiers' Bonus until public opinion had made itself felt.

"The passage of these bills depends very largely upon the demands made by the people," he said. "Congress hesitates to act until public sentiment crystallizes back of the pending proposals.

"The cause of this depression has been and still is a famine of money. The only cure is a supply of money.

"I have been and am demanding that more actual money be placed in circulation, and as money becomes more plentiful money will become cheaper and the prices of commodities will rise."

He welcomed the support of the Coughlin union for his views and for the passage of the banking bill, the silver bill, the farm refinancing bill and the bonus bill.

Senator Nye dealt with his favorite subject of war and munitions, attacking the du Ponts, who testified before the munitions committee in Washington.

"Four hundred per cent profit was all the du Ponts got out of the war," said the Senator. "If it wasn't for the war, the du Ponts would not own one dollar's worth of General Motors today."

The Rev. Herbert Bigelow of Cincinnati supported Father Coughlin's program, saying:

"I am glad this gospel against the slaveries of man is being preached to us by this Catholic priest."

He added that he believed "the National Union for Social Justice is the liberation of the nation's soul."

Threat to Congress.

Referring to the present Congress, the minister said, "If this Congress

does not give us what we want, we're not going to ask it of the next Congress. We're going to take it."

Rabbi Ferdinand M. Isserman of St. Louis declared that the program of the union projected by Father Coughlin would "become a great instrument in establishing a new order of social justice in the United States and thus blaze a trail of hope for the children of men everywhere."

Edward Kennedy, secretary of the National Farmers Union, declared that the National Union was backing Father Coughlin's plan for a central bank of issue to provide complete Congressional control of money.

"This nation is still in agony," said Representative William Lemke of North Dakota, whose Frazier-Lemke bill is being backed by the National Union.

"The great Secretary of Agriculture cut the throats of 6,000,000 pigs so that the packers could profit.

"My farmer friends got two cents a pound for their meat and you are paying 45 to 60 cents a pound. The farmers are not getting the benefit of the triple A."

April 25, 1935

TOWNSEND GROUP OPENS STATE DRIVE

Headquarters Set Up Here in National Campaign to Elect the Next Congress.

An invasion of New York State by representatives of the Townsend Plan to enlist voters in support of the old-age revolving pensions was

officially started yesterday with the announcement by Max Loewenthal, State area manager, of the opening of headquarters in the Gregorian Hotel, 42 West Thirty-fifth Street.

Mr. Loewenthal said the plan now has from 2,000,000 to 3,000,000 supporters and will have between 8,000,000 and 10,000,000 voters enrolled by election day in 1936. It will be the first time since 1776 that the American people will vote individually for a cause and not as partisans, he said.

"We are going to elect the next Congress," Mr. Loewenthal declared. "We have no opponents—merely people who don't understand the plan. We are strictly in politics from now on, but strictly nonpartisan. We are going direct to the American people with our message that no one shall go to Congress next time unless he is committed to the Townsend plan."

Under a new set-up for the campaign, according to Mr. Loewenthal, there will be four regional directors throughout the country. Under

these directors there will be State area managers and then district organizers in 435 Congressional districts.

The revised bill now in the hands of the House Ways and Means Committee calls for a 2 per cent tax on all financial transactions, including small store sales; a 2 per cent inheritance tax; a 2 per cent tax on gifts above $500 and a 10 per cent increase in the income tax rate. The proceeds from these taxes, he said, would be sufficient to carry out the plan and retire the national debt in six years.

July 13, 1935

HUEY LONG TO SEEK PRESIDENCY IN 1936

With His Main Goal to 'Beat Roosevelt,' He Is Ready to Bolt the Convention.

Special to The New York Times.

WASHINGTON, Aug. 13.—Senator Long has told Senatorial colleagues that he intends to run for President in 1936 and defeat President Roosevelt if he has to wreck the Democratic party to do it. He has privately said that his plan is roughly as follows:

1. He will enter Presidential primaries wherever he thinks he has a chance, if not of winning, at least of disaffecting enough voters to affect the result in the general election. At the same time he will encourage favorite-son candidacies, to split the normal con-

vention vote for Mr. Roosevelt.

2. Should the national convention refuse to seat whatever delegates he may win, he is prepared to bolt the convention and run as an independent, at the same time trying to get himself on the ballot as the regular Democratic candidate by civil suit in as many States as possible.

3. He is prepared to throw all possible support in strategic localities to the Republican nominee; that is, he would offer to trade votes in the South for Republican support in the North and West for "share-our-wealth" candidates for Congress.

Aims Are Three Fold.

Mr. Long's aims are asserted to be three fold: first, to beat President Roosevelt; second, to put over his wealth-sharing schemes, and, third, to become President. He is said to put them in that order of importance, believing that his election as President can wait until he has made good on a national scale the system of disrupting existing parties which he has used successfully in Louisiana.

Five House Seats at Stake.

Should this not take place, he is said to be willing to go to the length of putting up "straw men" who would pose as administration candidates. Five anti-Long members of the House are up for renomination in January, and if the administration stays away, it will

Considerable weight is given here to speculation that his threats are motivated by the belief that President Roosevelt's Tax Bill has cut the ground from under his own radical wealth-sharing program, and that the only way left to preserve his instruments of publicity is to attack at once.

If he cannot stop Mr. Roosevelt in the 1936 campaign, his national star will have set, according to this view.

As springboard for his last-ditch fight, Mr. Long plans to use his own well controlled State, where he is convinced he can win 5 to 1 in the primaries. He has had the primary election moved ahead to January and hopes that the administration will enter a slate against him.

be sacrificing these supporters.

It is Mr. Long's theory that once he has carried his own State, he will be able to say that the people of Louisiana have repudiated President Roosevelt, and then he can go over into Arkansas, Georgia, Mississippi, Florida and possibly Texas in an attempt to win convention delegates.

In the case of Georgia the Senator intimates that he and Governor Talmadge have a working agreement.

As to financing his campaign, if he does not change his mind before next Spring, Mr. Long is said to believe there would be little difficulty in raising the necessary funds. He claims 5,000,000 members in his Share-the-Wealth clubs, and believes they would gladly agree to small assessments.

At the same time he is reported to plan an appeal to conservative business as a defender of the Constitution and old-fashioned Americanism, arguing that Mr. Roosevelt is leading the country into socialism, whereas the Long plan would be better for industry than for the New Deal. Thus he would play both ends against the middle.

August 14, 1935

LONG DEATH EASES ROOSEVELT'S ROAD

Senator's Power Was Viewed as Hampering, Not Blocking, the President's Prospects.

REPUBLICAN HOPES UPSET

Threat of an Ultra-Radical Independent Democratic Party Also Believed Past.

By ARTHUR KROCK.
Special to THE NEW YORK TIMES.

AUSABLE FORKS, N. Y., Sept. 10.—Whatever may be said de mortuis, the administration politicians cannot but feel that the removal of Huey Long from the 1936 Presidential equation eliminates one of those hazards in the path of a candidate over which many a sure man has stumbled on his way to office. The late Senator was on the downward path as an obstruction to legislation, even though his last Congressional exploit was to talk the Third Deficiency Bill to death a few days ago. His share-the-wealth (he always called it "share-our-wealth") program had been put into a harmless position, politically, by the enactment of an administration measure just as definite in the sense of being class legislation, but specific where Mr. Long's proposals had been wholly vague. His chief remaining importance as an administration marplot was being measured by the degree to which he could hamper the re-election prospects of such Rooseveltian stand-bys as Senators Harrison and Robinson, both of whom will ask for re-election next year in their respective constituencies of Mississippi and Arkansas; and by the extent to which he could, through his boldness and ingenuity, throw monkey-wrenches into the Farley machine at the convention which will renominate the President.

Many Feared Tales Out of School.

These, considering the grandiose statements and more canny expectations of the late Kingfish, are small fry in the political ocean of the United States. But nevertheless Chairman James A. Farley did not relish the prospect of making reasonable answers to questions which might be put at the convention by a combination of anti-New Deal Democrats and the Senator from Louisiana, who would abet them only because he wanted to embarrass the President. And those who had borne the burden in Congress of pressing through legislation in the concepts of which they did not believe preferred a local re-election campaign undisturbed by Huey Long and his destructive penchant for telling the tales of politicians out of school—a recent example being his candid account in the last hours of the session which has just ended of the deal of the cotton and wheat Senators.

To these persons and elements, the death of the Louisiana Fascist must come, whatever the good taste and natural distaste of Americans for violent action may require them to say, as a distinct relief. And those deep Republican strategists, who have believed that the 1936 election would be close, and hang perhaps on two States, with a possibility of turning it into the House of Representatives, must be thinking tonight along new lines. Despite denials that Mr. Long had ever discussed secret Republican aid, and what he would do with it, the fact is that there have been several talks of this kind. On one occasion he would say that he would rather have Mr. Roosevelt than any Republican; on others—for the Senator was mercurial—he would say that, bitter as was the dose, he would be a party to the election of a Republican in 1936 so that the Democrats might clean house of the New Deal for 1940.

His death removes the only hope of such a combination, for Father Coughlin speaks from the mountain, while Huey labored in the plain and the swamp; and William Randolph Hearst has visible and vulnerable interests which the Kingfish persuaded his followers were not his. It takes from the Senate the only member who broke all the rules of that exclusive club in the pursuit of his ambition to dominate a State and defeat a President he had greatly helped to make. It sweeps from the next Democratic National Convention the most practical politician opposed to the New Deal who was fortified with some of its secrets.

From every viewpoint the assassination of Senator Long helps to clear the way of the President to a second term. But the assassin, if one would wish to view him as a William Tell or a Charlotte Corday, history-maker or fanatic patriot, must be denied that epitaph. For the Kingfish was going the way of all dictators, and his clearance was not commensurate, from the standpoint of any of his enemies, with the elimination of Marat or the Austrian tyrant in Switzerland. His objects of attack breathe more easily without him and demagogy loses its boldest exemplar. But, save in Louisiana, politics had gone far toward isolating him and, whatever ease of minds his death may bring, it was unnecessary as well as cruel and deplorable.

There will be no successor in Louisiana, for in his own State as in Washington the Senator had no lieutenants—only vassals.

September 11, 1935

SMITH THREATENS A REVOLT ON ROOSEVELT LEADERSHIP; CALLS NEW DEAL SOCIALISM

WARNS OF CLASS STRIFE

Ex-Governor Sees Danger of Government by a Bureaucracy.

OUR RESOURCES 'DRAINED'

Middle Class Will Pay Administration's Debt by Indirect Taxes, He Says.

By TURNER CATLEDGE.
Special to THE NEW YORK TIMES.

WASHINGTON, Jan. 25.—Democracy's "happy warrior" tonight sounded the bugle call for revolt.

In a ringing speech delivered at the first annual dinner of the American Liberty League and broadcast by radio to the four corners of the United States, former Governor Alfred E. Smith gave the signal, at least for his own followers, to "take a walk" from the leadership of President Roosevelt, and in so doing completed the groundwork for an anti-administration movement which his sponsors hoped might sweep the nation in the coming Presidential campaign.

Replete with the stinging sarcasm and biting wit of which he is master but missing in the personal attack which many had expected to hear, the speech called for a return of the Democratic party to the principles enunciated in the national platform of 1932, to which, the speaker declared, no one ever made a greater commitment than did the President who was elected thereon.

His reading of excerpts from that document and the witty and sarcastic comments with which he presented them brought rounds of approving applause from the diverse audience before him, including Democrats, Republicans and independents, white and black.

Capitalists Heavily Represented.

The listeners in the dining room, who numbered 2,000, in the aggregate, represented, either through principals or attorneys, a large portion of the capitalistic wealth of the country. Foregathered in the gilded banquet hall of the Mayflower Hotel were principally those identified with the stop-Roosevelt movement.

They included Republican office-holders and those who held power before the Democratic sweeps of 1932 and 1934; former Democratic leaders who were shorn of official following as a result of the same popular tide and politically minded people in general who, as the result of Supreme Court decisions or other causes, appeared ripe for the revulsion which tonight's meeting was intended to start.

Noticeably absent were any of the leaders in the present-day Democratic party management, either Federal officials, civilian party stalwarts or members of the House and Senate.

But Governor Smith spoke only as a Democrat. Before taking his place before the audience and microphones to deliver his long-heralded address, he listened with obvious impatience to two other speeches, one by Dr. Neil Carothers, director of the College of Business Administration at Lehigh University, "a good Mississippi Democrat who went to Lehigh to teach economics to Northern Yankees," and the other by the former Federal Judge Charles I. Dawson of Louisville.

Introduced by Borden Burr, a Birmingham attorney who was toastmaster, as "Al Smith of America," the former Democratic standard bearer launched vigorously into an hour's attack on the New Deal, without once mentioning the appelation under which the present administration has proceeded or referring personally to Mr. Roosevelt.

As he spoke he could look into the faces of another Democratic candidate for President, John W. Davis, and a former prominent Republican Senator, David A. Reed of Pennsylvania, who bit the dust in the Democratic landslide of 1934. Also to his fore was his old friend, former Governor Ely of Massachusetts, who presented his name to the convention in Chicago in 1932, and to his left was the former Governor Ritchie of Maryland whose friends had hoped to run him in between Smith and Roosevelt for the Democratic nomination the same year.

Hints at "Taking a Walk."

Mr. Smith left no doubt as to what he had in mind for himself and his followers in the party during the coming months. Summing up his views of the performance of the present administration, in the light of the Chicago platform, he looked to the future:

"My mind is now fixed upon the convention in June in Philadelphia," he said. "The committee on resolutions is about to report, and the preamble of the platform is:

" 'We the representatives of the Democratic party in convention assembled, heartily endorse the Democratic administration.'

"What happens to the disciples of Jefferson and Jackson and Cleveland when that resolution is read out? Why, for us it is a washout. There is only one or two things we can do. We can either take on the mantle of hypocricy or we can take a walk, and we will probably do the latter."

This remark, made with a characteristic Smithsonian gesture as he leaned toward the microphone and twisted his mouth in a snarling expression, brought the loudest cheer from the audience. The demonstration was so prolonged that Jouett Shouse, president of the Liberty League, signaled for silence as radio time was passing swiftly.

Not Seeking Office.

Early in his address Mr. Smith had given assurance that he was not seeking the nomination for himself. He disclaimed anything personal in what he was doing. Nor, said he, did he represent any group or any man.

"I am in possession of supreme happiness and comfort," he said. "But I do speak for what I believe to be the best interests of the great rank and file of the American people, in which class I belong."

It was not easy to speak against a Democratic administration. He was born in the Democratic party and expected to die in it. "I was attracted to it in my youth because I was led to believe that no man owned it," he said.

Sees Dangers Ahead.

"What are these dangers that I see?" he asked. "The first is the arraignment of class against class. It has been freely predicted that if we were ever to have civil strife again in this country it would come from the appeal to the passions and prejudices that come from the demagogues who would inctie one class of our people against the other."

He had met good and bad industrialists, good and bad financiers and good and bad laborers, but "I also know that there can be no permanent prosperity in this country until industry is able to employ labor, and there certainly can be no permanent recovery upon any governmental theory of soak-the-rich or soak-the-poor.

"Government by Bureaucracy."

"The next thing that I view as being dangerous to our national liberty is government by bureaucracy instead of what we have been taught to look to: government by law. Just let me quote something from the President's message to Congress:

" 'In thirty-four months we have set up new instruments of public power in the hands of the people's government, which power is wholesome and appropriate, but in the hands of political puppets of an economic autocracy, such power would provide shackles for the liberties of our people.'

"Now, I interpret that to mean that if you are going to have an autocrat take me.

"The next thing that is apparent to me is the vast building up of new bureaus of government, draining the resources of our people, to pool and redistribute them, not by any process of law but by the whim of the bureaucratic autocracy.

"Now, what would I have my party do? I would have them re-establish and re-declare the principles that they put forth in that 1932 platform.

"No administration in the history of the country came into power with a more simple, a more clear or a more inescapable candidate than the party that was inaugurated on the fourth of March in 1933, and, listen, no candidate in the history of the country ever pledged himself more unequivocally to his party platform than did the President who was inaugurated on that day.

"Millions and millions of Democrats, just like myself, all over the country, still believe in that platform. What we want to know is, why wasn't it carried out?

"And listen, there is only one man in the United States of America that can answer that question."

Declaring that the Roosevelt administration had substituted socialism for democracy, Mr. Smith said "that is why the Supreme Court is working overtime throwing the alphabet out of the window three letters at a time."

Quotes From 1932 Platform.

He read the 1932 declaration pledging the party to drastic reduction in governmental expenditure, abolition of useless commissions and offices and elimination of extravagance, "to accomplish a saving of not less than 25 per cent in the cost of the Federal Government."

But "no offices were consolidated, no bureaus were eliminated" and "the alphabet was exhausted."

He quoted another declaration of 1932, the one pledging the maintenance of the national credit and the balancing of the budget.

"How can you balance a budget if you insist upon spending more money than you take in," he asked.

He summed up with the assertion that of all the important promises only two had been redeemed—regulation of the stock market and repeal of prohibition.

He suggested to his audience that they lay the creed of the Socialist party alongside of the performances of the present régime and note how they tallied.

"And incidentally," he added, "let me say that it is not the first time in recorded history that a group of men have stolen the livery of the church to do the work of the devil."

"Now, after studying this whole situation, you will find that that is at the bottom of all of our troubles," he continued. "This country was organized on the principles of a representative democracy, and you can't mix socialism and communism with that. They are like oil and water—they refuse to mix.

"And, incidentally, let me say to you, that is the reason why the United States Supreme Court is working overtime throwing the alphabet out of the window, three letters at a time."

He leaned toward the audience in a confidential manner and said:

"How do you suppose all this happened? Here is the way it happened. The young brain trusters caught the Socialists in swimming and they ran away with their clothes."

It was all right with him "if they want to disguise themselves as Norman Thomas or Karl Marx or Lenin or any of the rest of that bunch."

"But what I won't stand for," he added, his voice raising with the upthrust of his fist, "is to let them march under the banner of Jefferson, Jackson or Cleveland."

Concluding, he said there could be only one capital, "Washington or Moscow."

"There can be only one atmosphere of government, the clear, pure, fresh air of free America or the foul breath of communistic Russia. There can be only one flag, the Stars and Stripes, or the red flag of the godless Union of the Soviet. There can be only one national anthem, 'The Star Spangled Banner' or 'The Internationale.' There can be only one victor. If the Constitution wins we win. But if the Constitution—stop!

"Stop there—the Constitution can't lose. The fact is it has already won, but the news has not reached certain ears."

January 26, 1936

'GRASS ROOTS' OPEN WAR ON NEW DEAL; BOOM TALMADGE

ASSAIL ROOSEVELT AIDES

Political Events of the Day

Southern Democrats, numbering 3,500, at Georgia "Grass Roots" Convention, repudiated President Roosevelt and called on Governor Talmadge to run for President.

Governor Landon, in a Kansas Day speech opening his campaign, struck out sharply at New Deal "waste" and placed recovery before reform.

Alfred E. Smith reiterated here his demand that the President himself reply to his Liberty League speech and declared Senator Robinson's address was intended merely to becloud the issue.

Colonel Knox, in Cleveland speech, declared the 1936 issue was whether the people would become vassals or remain free citizens.

Sharp Attacks at Macon
By F. RAYMOND DANIELL.
Special to THE NEW YORK TIMES.

MACON, Ga., Jan. 29. — Here in the heart of the "Solid South," a mass meeting of 3,500 Southern Democrats, united in a common opposition to Negroes, the New Deal and the teachings of Karl Marx, adopted a platform today repudiating President Franklin D. Roosevelt as their party leader, and called upon Governor Eugene Talmadge of Georgia to lead them in a holy war to drive the "Communists" from Washington.

One speaker after another stood before the microphones beneath the Stars and Bars of the Confederacy in the half-filled municipal auditorium where the "Grass Roots Convention" of Democrats from seventeen Southern and border States was held, to denounce the President and all his works as subversive to the interests of the free white voters of the South.

Emphasis was laid upon the "Christian" duty of the white voters of the South to uphold the Constitution and the Supreme Court.

For "Horse and Buggy Days."

Fundamentalists in politics as well as in religion, they turned their backs upon New Deal "heresies" and announced their conviction that "horse and buggy" days were better.

A subtle suggestion by Governor Talmadge in his plain talk to the people, broadcast over a nation-wide hook-up of the Columbia Broadcasting System, that voters who believed as they did would find champions like former Governor Smith in the North and East, brought a restrained response from the audience of tenant farmers and

State officeholders. The real cheers were reserved for those who reawakened some of the old feeling which the war between the States and the reconstruction left as a heritage of the South.

Among the latter was Thomas L. Dixon of New York and South Carolina, author of "The Klansman," who called the National Association for the Advancement of Colored People the "worst communist organization in the United States," attacked the Wagner-Costigan Anti-Lynching Bill as "infamous tyranny," and accused Mrs. Roosevelt of encouraging the Southern Negro to embrace the tenets of collectivist philosophers.

As the "delegates" to the meeting entered the auditorium they found a copy of the Georgia Woman's World on every seat. Upon the left-hand side of this publication, printed in Atlanta, was a picture, two columns wide, of Mrs. Roosevelt being escorted to her car by a Negro member of the faculty of Howard University after a visit to that institution. Opposite it was a two-column cut of Arthur Mitchell, a Negro member of the House, described in the caption as James A. Farley's "pet and protégé."

Also on page one was an editorial, asserting that President Roosevelt at the Jackson Day dinner had compared himself to Andrew Jackson.

It went on:

"Andrew Jackson didn't appoint a Negro Assistant Attorney General of the United States.

"Andrew Jackson didn't have a Negro confidential clerk in the White House.

"Andrew Jackson didn't try to ram an anti-lynching bill down the throats of the Southern people through a Democratic Congress.

"Andrew Jackson said, 'To the victor belong the spoils,' and when Andrew Jackson got to be President he didn't put in Republicans, Socialists, Communists and Negroes to tell him how to run these good old United States."

Kirby Disclaims Responsibility.

John Henry Kirby, Texas oil and lumber man and head of the Southern Committee to Uphold the Constitution, co-sponsor with Governor Talmadge of the rally, disclaimed responsibility for the distribution of the paper. At the same time he said that such things were "not to be condemned in Dixieland."

A score of Negroes at the far left side of the almost empty balcony of the auditorium listened expressionless while the speakers denounced Negro and white leaders who would stir them to question white supremacy.

Colonel Henry Breckinridge, friend and attorney of Colonel Lindbergh and a former Assistant Secretary of War, came to Macon for the gathering but declined a seat upon the platform, saying that while he came originally from Kentucky he had lived so long in New York that he doubted his eligibility to appear as a "Grass Rooter."

Among the speakers were the Rev. Gerald L. K. Smith, organizer of the late Huey P. Long's Share-Our-Wealth Society; E. W. Porter, secretary to former Governor Ruby Laffoon of Kentucky; Joseph B. Humphries, who described himself as "a country lawyer from Texas"; Hugh Howell, who, as chairman of the Democratic Executive Committee, owes allegiance to Governor Talmadge, and a bewhiskered old fellow who, although not on the program, took the floor as the meeting was breaking up to tell the crowd that his dad had "killed a sight of Yankees," and that he wished "he'd killed some more."

Speakers Extol Talmadge.

The set talks were delivered by Governor Talmadge, Mr. Kirby, Mr. Howell and E. W. Maynard, City Attorney of Macon and a member of the Talmadge-controlled State Executive Committee. All except Mr. Talmadge joined in extolling the qualifications of the Georgia Governor for the office of President. Mr. Talmadge himself expressed regret that the press of Kansas was booming Governor Landon of that State for the Republican nomination, while the newspapers of Georgia were silent about the achievements of their own Chief Executive.

The action of the "convention," the delegates to which were seated without approval by any committee on credentials, was expected to help Governor Talmadge decide whether he would enter the Presidential race.

He said yesterday that it was not up to him to offer his name to the electorate as if he were running for Sheriff. Candidates for the high office of President, he said, were "put forward by conventions."

The platform on which the "Grass Rooters" asked the Georgia Governor to run for the Presidency, was drawn by a committee led by local leaders, but including representatives of thirteen of the seventeen Southern and border States invited to the parley. The committee made no selection of a candidate but Chairman Howell and most of the other speakers left no doubt that Mr. Talmadge was the man they wanted.

It was estimated that about 150 representatives of other States were in the auditorium during the meeting.

The ratification of the platform and the call for Governor Talmadge to become the standard bearer of the "Constitutional, Jeffersonian Democrats" was by acclamation.

Kirby Praises the Governor.

The Governor left for Atlanta without committing himself to the crusade against the "brain trust wrecking crew," but he appeared willing as he sat upon the platform. His face became wreathed in smiles when his people cheered.

Governor Talmadge was introduced to the convention by Mr. Kirby, who referred to the Georgian as a man who in the present crisis has "stood at the battle front like a MacGregor on the brow of Ben Lomond," and also described Mr. Talmadge as "a plumed knight on an errand for the Republic, refusing to bend his knee to dictatorship or barter the sovereign rights of a great people for Federal gold.

"This is the first time the South has been summoned to the task of challenging the course pursued by the party elevated to power with the voice of her citizenry," said Mr. Kirby. "But if Franklin D. Roosevelt is a Democrat, Sherman's march to the sea was a Yankee retreat. I am an old-fashioned man who believes in the political institutions established by our fathers, and I make no apology for opposing with all my heart and soul one unfaithful to those institutions."

Declaring that under the Roosevelt administration there could be no security of property, Mr. Kirby went to the New Testament and the Constitution to prove the thesis that the accumulation of wealth was a right sanctioned by the time-honored laws of God and man.

"If you permit that Constitution to die," he warned, "there will be no angel of the resurrection for that crucified document of human liberty."

Governor Talmadge made his entrance before the microphones, the news reels and the crowd as Mr. Kirby finished speaking. He wore a green double-breasted suit and a black necktie from which gleamed a sapphire pin.

"Take off your coat and pour it on," shouted a leather-lunged partisan from the balcony.

"Keep it on," shouted another. "It's too cold."

Still another shouted: "Give it to 'em, Gene."

The Governor kept his coat on, but he "gave it to 'em" and "poured it on," as the phrase has it in these parts.

As he warmed to his subject, his coal-black hair cascaded over his forehead.

"The only way the New Deal can be made to work," he shouted, "is for the Brain Trust to invent an ointment to take the place of sweat."

Governor Talmadge implored his audience to remember the fate of the slaughtered little pigs and the cotton and the wheat which had been plowed under or left unsown while men and women starved, "all in the name of the more abundant life."

The administration, with its repudiation of the platform adopted at Chicago in 1932, had caused loyal Democrats to hang their heads in shame while the agents of Moscow laughed up their sleeves, he declared.

Says States Are Tyrannized.

The New Deal, he went on, was striking a death blow at States' rights by using Federal funds to tyrannize State Legislatures and had made Governors of sovereign States "goose-step" before Postmaster General Farley and the administrators of relief and public works, Harry L. Hopkins and Harold L. Ickes.

He had dared to buck this regimentation, Governor Talmadge asserted, only to have Secretary Ickes call him a "Chain-Gang Governor" and question the reliability of his word. He left it to his people, he said, to decide whether he or President Roosevelt had shown a greater respect for promises.

The Bankhead Cotton-Control Act, he declared, was even "more unconstitutional than the NRA." If the President were sincere in his desire to help the "forgotten people of Georgia," he (the President) would telephone Secretary Wallace at once to permit the removal of "the little red tags" which were keeping thousands of bales of cotton in Georgia at the mercy of speculators, the Governor said.

Asserting that the Supreme Court had "come to the rescue" of the South with its devotion to State rights, Governor Talmadge called upon his followers to see to it that the "Communists" were prevented from enjoying a four-year respite in which to change the complexion of the tribunal.

"If the New Dealers can pick their own Supreme Court, the wheels of our democracy will catch fire and burn down our own freedom," he declared.

He asserted that the South would remain "true to the fundamentals of democracy."

In his prepared speech, Governor Talmadge had listed a number of issues for the campaign of 1936, but he omitted most of them and swung into a eulogy of the assassinated Senator Long.

"We have lost Bronson Cutting, Thomas Schall and Huey Long," the Governor said, "but we little men are still here and we say to Jim Farley and his bureaucrats and to Felix Frankfurter, who boasts that he has been in Washington from Roosevelt to Roosevelt, that all of us are not going to die or fall in airplanes between now and June 23, when the national convention meets in Philadelphia."

As Governor Talmadge finished his oration and was surrounded by an enthusiastic group of overalled cotton farmers, who clapped him on the back and promised to help him drive the "dad-gummed foreigners" out of the nation's capital, the band played: "We'll Hitch Old Dobbin to the Shay." It appeared likely that the "horse and buggy" would be the emblem of these Dixie Democrats.

Long's Aide Assails Roosevelt.

The Rev. Mr. Smith took up the denunciation of the Roosevelt régime in the name of his political mentor, Huey Long, and declared that, without pledging an amalgamation of strength, he could say as the head of the Share Our Wealth Movement in the nation that the "foes of Roosevelt are the friends of Louisiana and my lost leader." He challenged any man "to take the South without the ghost and spirit of Huey P. Long."

Mr. Smith accused followers of the New Deal in Louisiana of plotting Long's assassination, and he said that when the leader was buried the administration had poured a $100,000,000 "slush fund" into his State to defeat the Long followers.

The State chairman, Mr. Howell, appeared on the platform to declare that the "people running America today are not Americans," and to assert that an extension of Mr. Roosevelt's term to four more years would make it a penitentiary offense to "attend a meeting like this."

Mr. Dixon proclaiming his right as a free man to "sleep in the open, wear rags and starve to death rather than submit to the regimentation of the New Deal."

Declaring that the "Russian communism" exemplified by the national administration's policies reduced "the whole human race to a hog pen with a trough of black bread for its fare," Mr. Dixon took a firm stand against the Negro and the radical.

In New York, he asserted, General Hugh Johnson had "rounded up" 185 "Reds" on the Federal payroll and ordered their discharge, only to have Victor Ridder come along and approve the employment of 5,000 of them, referring critics of his policy to Washington for his authority. These "social vermin," Mr. Dixon said, were accepting a dole with one hand and handing out subversive literature with the other.

Commenting on the Anti-Lynching Bill, which, he said, Mrs. Roosevelt had supported, Mr. Dixon continued:

"I denounce the bill as an infamous outrage, as the most brazen attempt to outrage States' rights by placing Federal bayonets at our backs."

Mr. Dixon also warned that the "brain trust" had everything planned for the establishment of a dictatorship in the United States. The scheme, he said, did not entail the proclamation of an emergency, but merely the re-election of Mr. Roosevelt for a second and third term in the White House. If Mr. Roosevelt were returned to power a third time, he said, the people of the country would "never get him out without a civil war."

January 30, 1936

CONVENTION ABROGATES CENTURY-OLD TWO-THIRDS RULE

SOUTH BOWS TO CHANGE

Appeased by Promise to Reapportion as Two-thirds Rule Ends.

FIGHT ON FLOOR AVOIDED

Committee Instructs Party Heads to Work Out New Representation Basis.

ON DEMOCRATIC VOTE CAST

Southerners Will Be Relatively Stronger Than Delegates of Less 'Regular' States.

By CHARLES R. MICHAEL
Special to THE NEW YORK TIMES.

PHILADELPHIA, June 25.—The century-old two-thirds rule, born in a tragic day of American history, when Jackson was President, died today in the progressive Roosevelt era. The convention tonight adopted the report of the rules committee, which recommended its abrogation and the substitution of the majority rule for the nomination of President and Vice President.

After long consideration of this troublesome issue, the rules committee, supported by administration influences, not only succeeded in overpowering the Southern opposition to a change in the rules, but avoided a fight on the floor by unanimously adopting a resolution sponsored by Senator Tydings of Maryland, which instructed the Democratic National Committee to work out a new basis of representation in the national conventions based upon the Democratic vote cast in the respective States.

The national committee was instructed to improve the system for the selection of delegates and report to the 1940 convention. The present basis of apportioning delegates will be maintained until after the next convention.

Opponents of abrogation, led by Representative Eugene E. Cox of Georgia and Beeman Strong of Texas, announced themselves entirely satisfied with this action, which they said would maintain the prestige of the Solid South and encourage the building up of the party in other sections of the country. Sectionalism is removed by the abolition of the two-thirds rule and the proposed plan of representation in the convention based upon Democratic strength in each State.

Text of Resolution

The resolution which effected a peaceful solution and satisfied those opposing repeal reads:

"Be it resolved that the Democratic National Committee is hereby instructed to formulate and recommend to the next national convention a plan for improving the system by which delegates and alternates to Democratic National Conventions are apportioned, and be it further resolved that in formulating this plan the national committee shall take into account the Democratic strength within each State, the District of Columbia, Territories, &c., in making said apportionments."

Harmony prevailed in the committee although the Southerners fought vigorously for the retention of the two-thirds rule. They had come to the convention convinced that the rule would be abolished, however, and were prepared to accept defeat in good grace, if the apportionment of delegates was made on the basis of Democratic votes and not on population.

The leaders are hopeful that the national committee will carry out the spirit of the resolution and work out an apportionment system somewhat similar to that of the Republican party where States obtain larger representation for increasing the Republican vote.

It was apparent from the outset that proponents of abolition of the two-thirds rule were in control of the situation as the proposal for repeal was supported by President Roosevelt and Chairman Farley of the national committee. The 1932 convention had recommended ending the rule.

Since that convention Senator Bennett Clark, whose father, the late Champ Clark, lost the nomination in 1912 because of the two-thirds rule, was active in stimulating the movement for abolition of the two-thirds rule, which was brought into existence by Andrew Jackson to prevent the nomination of Calhoun as Vice President and the selection of Van Buren as his successor as President.

For more than fifty years the rule has bothered the Democratic party, but agitation for dropping it was led by a small band of Northern Democrats who were outvoted by the delegates of the Solid South. The latter contended that the rule was necessary to protect their interests and prevent the nomination of candidates objectionable to that section of the country which fifty years ago was about all that the Democratic party commanded.

With Roosevelt sweeping the country in 1932, making the Democratic party a militant organization in all sections to such an extent that only six States remained Republican, the argument of the South was wiped out. The result of the election strengthened the position of Northern and Western Democrats who had fought for years to obtain the majority rule in making the party nominations.

June 26, 1936

ROOSEVELT TO WAR ON 'ECONOMIC ROYALISTS'

CAMPAIGN ISSUE DEFINED

The President Avoids All Personalities in His Philadelphia Speech.

FIGHT FOR FREEDOM SEEN

By ARTHUR KROCK
Special to THE NEW YORK TIMES.

FRANKLIN FIELD, PHILADELPHIA, June 27.—Under a cloud-veiled moon, in skies suddenly cleared of rain, to a mass of more than 100,000 people gathered in the stadium of the University of Pennsylvania, and by radio to unnumbered millions all over the nation and world, Franklin Delano Roosevelt tonight accepted the renomination of the Democratic party for President of the United States and, avoiding personalities of any description, defined the issue of this campaign as it appears to him.

The President said that, as the fathers of the Republic had achieved political freedom from the eighteenth-century royalists, so it was the function of those who stand with him in this campaign to establish the economic freedom they also sought to establish, and which was lost in the industrial and corporate growth of the nineteenth and twentieth centuries.

Vice President John N. Garner of Texas, in this same place, renewed his pledge of allegiance to the President, made four years ago, and added a vow of fealty to the New Deal. The President was notified of his renomination by Senator Robinson of Arkansas, permanent chairman of the Democratic National Convention that closed today. Senator Harrison of Mississippi acted as proxy for Senator Barkley of Kentucky, temporary chairman, whose function it was to notify the Vice President, but who sailed for Europe on official business today.

Crowd Roars Its Enthusiasm

The arrival of the President in the stadium was greeted by a real demonstration, as distinguished from the artificial efforts of conventions. One hundred thousand people rose and roared unmistakable acclaim as Mr. Roosevelt entered the platform on the arm of his eldest son and clasped the hand of Vice President Garner while "The Star-Spangled Banner" was sung.

Thunderous cheer after cheer rolled out as the President finished, and, led by his mother, members of his family gathered about him. He mopped his brow, drank copiously of ice water and then stood waving his clasped hands above his head, while the tumult continued and the band played. Before Mr. Roosevelt left the stand on the arm of his son, James—as he entered—he waited for "Auld Lang Syne," and cheered its last echoes with the crowd. It was a personal triumph of the kind given to few men.

If the high tenor of his speech can be taken as an indication of what sort of campaign the President will conduct, Postmaster General Farley's prediction of the "dirtiest" contest of recent times will not be realized, so far as the chief protagonists of the parties are concerned, for Governor Alf M.

Landon has implied the same tactics.

For Those Who Weary of Struggle

The only conceivable reference to Alfred E. Smith and other Democrats who have attacked him that the President made was when he said that some had grown weary of the struggle and relinquished their hope of democracy "for the illusion of a living." The crowd roared approval.

Informed by Senator Robinson that the administration "has vindicated the faith of plain people in the processes of democracy," and confounded those who demanded a dictatorship in 1933, the President took up this major theme, which is also sounded in the Philadelphia platform.

The following is a summary of the President's speech, which was more of a rededication of the New Deal to obtain and secure "economic freedom" than an acceptance speech, outlining a definite program, according to custom:

This occasion is for dedication to a simple and sincere statement of an attitude toward current problems. The speaker comes not only as party leader and candidate for re-election, but "as one upon whom many critical hours have imposed and still impose a grave responsibility."

For loyalty in cooperation thanks are due the people, Democrats everywhere, Republicans in Congress, many local officials and especially those who have borne disaster bravely and "dared to smile through the storm." The rescue was not the task of one party; the rally and survival were made together.

Fear which was the most dangerous foe in 1933, has been conquered. Yet all is far from well with the world. The United States is better off than most, but "the rush of modern civilization" has created problems for solution if both political and economic freedom are finally to be attained.

The eighteenth-century Royalists sought to perpetuate their special privileges from the British Crown. They regimented the people in labor, religion and the right of assembly. The American Revolution was fought to win political freedom, and political tyranny was wiped out at Philadelphia July 4, 1776, when the Declaration was penned.

But modern industry and invention have raised new forces that produced new royalists and new dynasties, with new privileges which they seek to retain. Concentration of economic power pressed every citizen into service, and economic freedom—the twin ideal, with political freedom, of Jefferson and Washington—was lost again.

Small business men, with the worker and the farmer, were excluded from this new royalty. "New mercenaries sought to regiment the people." The average man once more confronts the problem faced by the Minute Men. He is entitled to a living that means something to live for as well as something to live by.

The collapse of 1929 revealed the new despotism for what it was. In the election of 1932 the people gave to the present administration a mandate to end it. It is being ended.

Freedom No Half-and-Half Affair

The modern royalists contend the economic slavery is nobody's business, and certainly not the government's. But the administration contends that freedom is no half-and-half affair; the citizen must be free in the market place as well as in the polling place.

To the complaint of the economic royalists that the New Deal seeks to overthrow American institutions, the President answers that what they really seek to retain is their kind of power, hidden behind the flag and the Constitution. But the flag and the Constitution stand for democracy and freedom, and no dictatorship either by the mob or the overprivileged.

"The brave and clear platform * * * to which I heartily subscribe," sets forth the inescapable obligations of the government: protection of family and home, establishment of equal opportunity and aid to the distressed. The opposition will beat down these words unless they are fought for, as for three years they have been maintained. The fight will go on as the convention has decreed.

Faith, hope and charity are not unattainable ideals, but stout supports of a nation struggling for freedom. The nation is poor indeed if it cannot lift from the unemployed the fear they are not needed in the world. That accumulates a deficit in human fortitude. The bearers of the standard of hope, faith and charity, instead of privilege, seek daily to profit from experience, to learn to do better.

The sins of the cold-blooded and of the warm-hearted are, as Dante says, weighed in different scales. The overt faults of a charitable government are preferable to the consistent omissions of an indifferent one.

This generation of Americans has a rendezvous with destiny. Some who have long fought for freedom have wearied and yielded their democracy. Success of the New Deal can revive them. The war is for the survival of democracy, to save "a great and precious form of government for ourselves and for the world."

The President accepts the nomination and is enlisted "for the duration of the war."

June 28, 1936

LEMKE'S NEW PARTY, AND THREE KEY MEN

Its Strength Depends Much on What Coughlin, Townsend And Gerald Smith Can and Will Do in the Campaign

By DUNCAN AIKMAN

A NEW American political alliance is in the making—a coalition of four colorful and diverse elements united by the decision of four powerful leaders and a single strand of mutual interest in the theory that "the more abundant life" will come with more abundant money. Not for a dozen years has a movement outside the major parties aroused such curiosity among voters, or stimulated such fear and hope among the political professionals.

The Union party, proclaimed a few weeks ago by Congressman William Lemke of North Dakota, who simultaneously announced that he would be its Presidential candidate, has definite hopes of dealing with votes in millions. If it succeeds in uniting the followers of Dr. Townsend, the members of Father Coughlin's Union of Social Justice, the survivors of Huey Long's Share-the-Wealth movement and the radical agrarian groups which have at one time or another endorsed Lemke's farm relief and currency proposals, the Unionists should poll one of the most impressive third-party votes in American history.

Whether any such strength develops, whether a Union party revolt will rival the damage done by the Greenback and Populist schisms of the Eighties and Nineties or duplicate the more recent excitement of the Bull Moose and La Follette movements depends on the men who lead its separate wings. But a step toward fusion was taken at the OARP convention in Cleveland when Coughlin and Gerald Smith pledged themselves to take the stump for Lemke, and Townsend indicated that he, too, would do so.

The coalition will be achieved and will prove effective largely in proportion to the ability of the leaders to persuade themselves and their following that "Lemke money" will give the Coughlinites the kind of social justice they want, pay Dr. Townsend's "marching soldiers" the old age pensions they seek and bestow upon the Rev. Gerald L. K. Smith's adherents the $5,000 family fortunes and the perpetually adequate incomes which the late Huey Long promised them in a world where every man is to be "a king."

No emotional swell in the "grass roots" has brought these fairly diverse blocs into a pact of union. So the 1936 third party's prognosis depends almost entirely on the ability of Coughlin, Smith and Townsend to deliver the votes of their supporters to Congressman Lemke, and on Lemke's own ability to hold this fusion together if it fuses closely.

. . .

IN Washington the gamble on William Lemke's qualifications as a welder of different interests is considered fairly even. The Union party's Presidential candidate will not bring personal magnetism to his task, or even such dramatic gifts as are possessed by most run-of-the-mine candidates.

Lemke speaks earnestly, factually and impersonally rather than caressingly. After all, he is gray, baldish, undistinguished in appearance. He would probably rather argue all night to win a hundred members of an audience by the power of conviction than coax a cheer from 10,000 by a platform trick. What Lemke will give to his cause will be hard work, a large body of economic knowledge subtly rationalized to fit his own conclusions and a cold, fierce energy in persuasion.

Lemke got these traits from a frugal German peasant ancestry, a strict Lutheran Fundamentalist upbringing and hard farm labor from his earliest childhood. He has strengthened them, perhaps, by lifelong association with causes which, initially at least, meant sacrifice to the struggling young lawyer who fought for them. Helping his parents to break ground in the Dakota prairies in the early Eighties, struggling against bitter farm poverty for a State university and Yale law education, fighting the battles of the Nonpartisan League in the days when in many places it was a byword for pro-Germanism and dangerous radicalism, all inevitably took their toll.

Lemke today is one of the most serious members of Congress. He neither smokes nor drinks, rarely skips a Lutheran Sunday service and has practically no social life. Only his most intimate friends suspect that he has a caustic sense of humor which is used at the expense of less stern characters. Life and the knowledge with which he has diligently stocked his mind are too serious to be played with. For his recreation he raises gladioli—the best gladioli in the northern tier of prairie States, his admirers insist—but a characteristically painstaking amusement.

* * *

LEMKE'S political measure, however, is to be taken from the Nonpartisan League. He was in it from the earliest days and was North Dakota's Attorney General—a key post, since he had to fight for the State's legal rights to administer banks, grain elevators, mills and insurance projects. The league has colored the Lemke political philosophy far more than any of the other movements with which he has been associated.

He would deny that either he or the Nonpartisan League is essentially collectivist or socialistic, just as he would deny that his fiscal ideas are inflationary. He probably considers himself a genuine believer in the free competitive system. But the government, he argues, must have absolute control of the people's money, of banking, natural resources and a few of the essential marketing facilities if free competition is to be kept alive. He argues that a currency system managed as a national rather than a private banker's concern, and based on other values besides gold and silver, is necessary to spare competitive business the ruinous effects of an endless series of inflations and deflations contrived in the interests of gamblers in specious values.

Lemke expounds these views to audiences as he has expounded them to Congress in his struggles for the various Frazier-Lemke farm relief measures, tirelessly, energetically, with frequent citations from statistics and the economic authorities. His flat, monotonous voice somehow claims attention, perhaps for the sheer intensity of the man's convictions. No one of his lifelong associates seems to remember his ever having attempted an oratorical flight or a fine phrase, yet he has something which many a more artful stump beguiler frankly envies. So much inner emotional sincerity is present that Lemke can often hold a mass meeting of stolid Scandinavian farmers spellbound simply by quoting statistics of world wheat shipments or the law of marketing cooperatives.

Lemke said in Cleveland that he was "100 per cent for an old-age revolving pension." He is close to the Coughlin currency theories and undoubtedly sympathizes with the Share-the-Wealth project and its general objectives. Probably he believes that a Federal bank of issue, modeled on the Nonpartisan League's Bank of North Dakota, will come much nearer to giving the Townsendites and the Share-the-Wealth followers what they want than any other dispensation that has been suggested.

Thus it is fair to conclude that if the Townsendites and the heirs of the Long crusade accept Lemke as a leader, they

will have to revise their premises in keeping with an old Nonpartisan Leaguer's plan of procedure. They will, moreover, never be quite the same after the Lemke faculties of economic criticism and the relentless Lemke logic get through with them.

If Lemke is to be the third party's leader and teacher, Father Coughlin, who roared "Franklin 'Double-Crossing' Roosevelt" at the 10,000 Townsendite conventioners and swept them into a furious Lemke party demonstration, will bear gifts to the new Unionists quite as precious as economics lessons. The "radio priest" of the Church of the Little Flower at Royal Oak, Mich., in accents now pleading and honey-toned, now booming with anger and denunciation, will give them the slogans and the spacious, exciting phrases from which Americans draw so much emotional delight in campaign politics.

* * *

FATHER COUGHLIN calls on his following in the Union of Social Justice to "march against the pagan god of gold"—meaning the gold standard. He flares out against "government by the high commission of prostituted patronage." He flays those who object to a priest's projecting his economic and political views. He denounces "plutocratic individualism and immoral capitalism and the sins of private financialism."

"Alas!" he gibed at President Roosevelt recently, "the temple still remains the private property of the moneychangers. The golden key has been handed over to them—the key which now is fashioned in the shape of the double cross." No phrase-making talent of quite this sort is likely to characterize any of the major party orators this season. Yet Father Coughlin is more than a reservoir of phrases. His words knit together confused beliefs and prejudices among the masses; he himself brings the Union of Social Justice into the third-party movement. Whether there are 1,000,000 or 5,000,000 members—estimates vary—can be told only when the November ballots are counted. But it has shown strength enough already in the 1936 primaries to unseat Congressmen in the industrial districts of the Great Lakes and to drive others to the shelter of its endorsement.

The Social Justice following, too, is responsible for much of the third party's tentative platform—the declaration for a living wage for all, the guarantee of income to youth while finding a place in business or the professions, the limitation of income and inheritance, the strong pledge of government protection for labor unions. A central bank of issue and a widening of the currency base were Coughlin and Lemke projects long before the party was considered. But there is a good deal in the picture to suggest that the "radio priest" of a great industrial city's suburban parish showed Lemke, the old-line agrarian radical, how the Nonpartisan League program could be adapted to the economic discontent of the city workers.

Dr. Townsend, founder of the OARP movement, will shortly be 70. Most of his life he has been a poor country doctor in obscure Midwestern villages. When he went to Long Beach, Calif., in the Nineteen

Twenties, following old patients who had fled the prairie Winters, his practice gradually slipped away from him. Then he lost a minor post in the Long Beach Health Department. By 1933, the bottom year of the depression, he was a physician turned part-time real estate salesman—with virtually no customers.

At this point Dr. Townsend invented his old-age pension plan of $200 a month for everybody over 60—"Every recipient has got to spend every cent of it." It took on; a shrewd organizing plan was put into effect by a promoter associate, and within a year the spare-framed, threadbare, hesitant doctor had been transformed into a kind of national folk hero.

He rode on de luxe trains and airplanes. He presided at conferences of men and women who knew the trick of sounding important. He gave orders to Congressmen and public officials and saw them respected. Tears ran down the cheeks of hundreds of old women when he stepped upon a platform and flashed his shy, benevolent smile. When he shouted his newly acquired jargon of economic terms at a mass meeting, thousands cheered.

* * *

All this changed unpretentious Dr. Townsend into a new kind of person, a man who believed—had he not experienced it?—that anything was possible. When advisers in the movement intimated that it would be unwise to be too specific in his $200-a-month promises, since that would be a lot of money to raise during the plan's experimental years, he would wave them away with: "You can't argue this idea away just with figures. Of course we'll get the money." When promoters in his suite calculated that 30,000,000 people had in one way or another showed interest in the Townsend Plan he began announcing that the OARP movement controlled 30,000 voters.

But he will hardly—no matter how sincerely he may strive—bring 30,000,000 votes into the Union party. In recent months he has dismissed his original organizing staff, broken with most of his supporters in Congress, revamped his promoting system and his political front, as it were, in the face of the enemy. When he decided to throw his prestige into winning his following for Lemke, he probably alienated OARP groups of considerable size whose leaders are still officially "Roosevelt politicians."

How much he has lost by these changes nobody knows, but the open secession of potent leaders and great segments of his following is apparent. Yet at the center of the OARP movement is a core of hundreds of thousands of old men and women to whom there is something definitely anthropomorphic about "the doctor's" status. He, too, was old, poor, shabby and hopeless. Yet he created a great movement and lifted himself, as they see it, to the heights of humanitarian statesmanship.

This is what the devout members of his following see themselves as achieving, and, in this sense, Dr. Townsend stands for greatness made in their own image. Those who feel this way about him would follow him anywhere—into Old Guard Republicanism, socialism or a movement to set up a Stuart monarchy in Kansas.

107

THE chief mathematical mystery about possible support for the Union party is the membership of the Share-the-Wealth movement. The Rev. Gerald L. K. Smith has said on numerous occasions during the past ten months that he has 9,000,000 followers and that the 9,000,000 "trust me." Yet the Share-the-Wealth organization, which was essentially a strategic device in the late Senator Huey Long's campaign for the Presidency, was liquidated by the Louisiana politicians after the Long assassination. Lacking an interest in Presidential politics and having a practically foolproof machine in State politics, they had no further use for it. Since then the movement has been without funds, headquarters, organizing staff or definite official leadership.

The Rev. Mr. Smith, so far as Louisiana politics is concerned, is out of the picture. For a few weeks after the death of his patron he tried to seize control of the Long machine, promote himself to the vacant United States Senatorship, give orders to the new bosses by sheer word power. When the smoke cleared, Smith was no longer on the roll of Long lieutenants. Since then he has been, in a way, a leader in search of an allegiance.

He tried, with only moderate success, to sweep Governor Eugene Talmadge's "grass roots" convention into his orbit last January. An old Klansman—prominent in the mystic order's ruling circle in Indiana until the Stephenson murder destroyed it in the middle Twenties, he has circulated around during the Spring among groups nursing various plans of social and economic reform through Fascist action. After Dr. Townsend's troubles last May with the Bell Congressional investigating committee, Smith settled down as strategic adviser and informal spokesman to the OARP founder. In fact, those closest to OARP affairs have considerable evidence that Smith has had more influence in giving Dr. Townsend's policy its list toward Lemkeism than any other man. Quite obviously the late Senator Long's chief pulpit apologist—he preached the Senator's funeral sermon—regards the Lemke coalition as the best available medium through which to rebuild the shattered forces of the Share-the-Wealth movement.

• • •

SMITH'S service in the Union party high command will undoubtedly be that of rabble-rousing. Others in the Long faction have patched up a truce with the White House, but Gerald L. K. Smith professes to hate President Roosevelt with intensity. "The man who smiled at the assassination of Huey Long," he calls him. "The contemptible and damnable Farley dictatorship with its fake liberal foreground and a Communist background" is one of his milder tags for the whole New Deal régime. "If Franklin D. Roosevelt is re-elected," he has pledged himself on various occasions, "I personally will lead a movement to impeach him."

A preacher of fervid evangelical style, who held a large Christian pastorate in Shreveport, La., until his connection with the Long movement brought about his resignation, he knows all the tricks of the platform. "Let's try that applause again," he shouts when he takes charge of a platform situation and begins to release his audience's emotions. "Let's have everybody that's happy stand up. Now, everybody that's mad!" "I ought to get a better hand on that one," he roars drolly when one of his favorite epigrams fails to score a bullseye. Rarely does he fail to get it.

"You who toil are nailed to the cross tonight," he assures sharecropper and relief-worker audiences, "but remember, the resurrection follows the crucifixion." "Oh, you feudal lords!" he shouts at the New Dealers and Republican Old Guards alike. "You hired tools! You lying newspapers! You damnable hypocrites! Burn your bridges! Burn our ballots! We will meet you with Jefferson and Lincoln! We will meet you with Father Coughlin and the spirit of Huey Long!"

Handsome and florid, a perfectly trained athlete in his late thirties, the Rev. Mr. Smith, once he has fused the Townsend hopes, the Coughlin social ethics and the Lemke economics in his mind, has his part cut out for him. He can be the new populism's stump evangelist.

July 26, 1936

ROOSEVELT'S ALLIES IN LABOR PROPOSE 1940 LIBERAL PARTY

By LOUIS STARK
Special to THE NEW YORK TIMES.

WASHINGTON, Aug. 10.—State chairmen and committeemen from forty-eight States today formed as a permanent body Labor's Non-partisan League, enthusiastically endorsed the candidacy of President Roosevelt and planted what speakers referred to as the possible seeds of a liberal party, if one is deemed necessary, in 1940.

Greeted warmly by President Roosevelt, who, in a letter, declared his pride in the league's endorsement, the delegates heard predictions that labor would hold the balance of political power this year in West Virginia, Pennsylvania, New York, Illinois and Kentucky and would come close to such a desired condition in other States if the organization carried on as expected.

Above and beyond the speakers' attacks on Governor Landon's labor record and on the Republican party were the repeated declarations that a new "political realignment" was under way in this country, that after 1936 it would be necessary for labor and its liberal friends to adjust themselves to such an alignment and that to that end the league was to be dedicated as a "permanent" organization for the furtherance of human progress.

The convention, the first national meeting sponsored by the league, which was organized last April with the avowed purpose of supporting Mr. Roosevelt, was held on an upper floor of the Willard Hotel. The keynote address was made by Major George L. Berry, chairman, who outlined the aims of the organization. His references to a coming political "realignment" were greeted with applause.

He was followed by John L. Lewis, president of the United Mine Workers of America, and Sidney Hillman, president of the Amalgamated Clothing Workers of America.

Mr. Lewis maintained that the organization of the league "was the most significant development in American politics that has occurred in the lifetime of most of us," and Mr. Hillman challenged "the allies of the du Ponts" to walk out of the Democratic party and work openly as they "would secretly" for the election of Governor Landon.

At the afternoon session brief speeches were made by the delegates from various States and labor organizations who reported progress in the furtherance of the league's "1936 objective, the re-election of President Roosevelt."

Organization Is Effected

Permanent organization was effected at the afternoon session when the present officers were designated to comprise the nucleus of a directorate of ten who will have charge of the campaign for Mr. Roosevelt's re-election. Messrs. Berry, Lewis, Hillman and M. S. Warfield, permanent secretary, were so designated.

In his letter President Roosevelt said that his administration had attempted "to correct through legislation certain of the evils in our economic system" and had "sought to put a stop to certain economic practices which did not promote the general welfare."

"Some of the laws which were enacted were declared invalid by the Supreme Court," said the President. "It is a notable fact that it was not the wage-earners who cheered when those laws were declared invalid.

"I greet you in the faith that future history will show, as past history has so repeatedly and so effectively shown, that a return to reactionary practices is very short-lived.

"Having tasted the benefits of liberalism, men and women do not for long forego those benefits. I have implicit faith that we shall find our way to progress through law."

August 11, 1936

PROGRESSIVES UNITE BEHIND ROOSEVELT

Permanent Organization Is Formed at Chicago for a National Campaign.

'PRINCIPLES' ARE ADOPTED

La Follette Is Made Chairman of Non-Partisan Appeal for President's Re-election.

By TURNER CATLEDGE
Special to THE NEW YORK TIMES.

CHICAGO, Sept. 11.—Progressive leaders from all parts of the United States organized themselves here today into a nonpartisan band for the re-election of President Roosevelt.

Reciting a long list of alleged economic faults in this country, the Progressive leaders urged the choice of Mr. Roosevelt as one who had recognized these evils and had made a "gallant effort to correct them," and as one who could be counted upon in the future to use the force of government to build a better life for all.

Furthermore, they said, he was the only progressive candidate for the Presidency who could be elected.

Following their endorsement with practical steps, the Progressives voted themselves into a permanent organization to be known as the National Progressive Conference; elected Senator La Follette of Wisconsin as chairman, and empowered him to appoint an executive committee of fifteen to organize the Progressive-for-Roosevelt movement throughout the country. In addition, they pledged about $10,000 with which to start the organization.

More Than 100 Attend

More than 100 men and women answered the roll-call when the conference began this morning. Among them were two Governors, four Senators, twelve members of Congress and twenty-seven labor leaders, one latter including such figures as John L. Lewis, president of the United Mine Workers of America, and Sidney Hillman, president of the Amalgamated Clothing Workers.

One of the most prominent men at the meeting was Mayor La Guardia of New York, who headed the committee that drew up the resolutions with which the group pledged support to the President.

With an eye to the future, when they regarded political realignment as assured, the Progressives specifically kept themselves separate from any party. At the same time they issued a warning to their liberal colleagues who were not present today to beware of any movement that might divide their ranks.

"In this critical situation division of liberals has only one result, and that is direct support of reaction," said the resolutions adopted by the conference.

"Progressives, regardless of good motives, who aid in dividing those opposed to reaction must share responsibility for the result."

Avoid Party Alignment

Although the resolutions at no place mentioned the Union party, Father Coughlin and Representative William Lemke of North Dakota, this was regarded as a direct warning to the liberals of the West and Northwest to continue their fight under the generals they have followed heretofore and not to be tempted off by the glittering promises of Mr. Lemke and his associates.

The Progressives likewise avoided any language which might indicate support to the Democratic party, although when they first convened this morning the pro-Roosevelt trend was so strong that it appeared for awhile that they would join with the President's own party in his support.

They urged "all progressive-minded citizens, in every walk of life, to vote for Franklin D. Roosevelt for President of the United States," and then proceeded to set up their own forces.

The final character of the new organization was credited largely to Representative Thomas Amlie of Wisconsin, a La Follette Progressive, who insisted that Democrats in many ways were as bad as Republicans. He suggested, moreover, that the time might come very soon when the Progressives would want to stand out alone in continuing their crusade for economic freedom.

He succeeded in having the resolutions committee put the declaration of principles of the conference ahead of its endorsement of President Roosevelt.

September 12, 1936

LABOR PARTY STARTS MACHINE

New York State Groups Unite in Effort to Have Ticket Placed on Ballot

By JAMES C. HAGERTY

The newly formed American Labor party of New York State, an affiliate of Labor's Non-Partisan League, is busy making plans to get its ticket on the ballot in November, to align organized labor and sympathetic groups in the State solidly behind President Roosevelt and Governor Lehman, and to serve as a spearhead in the formation of a national labor party in 1940.

Under the leadership of Mrs. Elinore M. Herrick, New York regional director of the National Labor Relations Board who obtained a leave of absence without pay from the board to act as campaign director, party leaders—officials of leading trade unions and joint trade boards—are concentrating their organization efforts on the 1,000,000 trade-union members in the State. They already claim an enrollment of nearly 400,000 and say they expect a total of more than 600,000 by Election Day.

Alliances Sought

Looking beyond 1936, the leaders hope that the new party may form an alliance with similar affiliated groups of the Non-Partisan League and Farmer-Labor movement, to the end that a strong national labor party may come into being. The new party, it is said, will continue to function here, and will present a ticket in future municipal, legislative and judicial elections.

The party has already set up machinery in practically all counties in the State and, so party leaders claim, is assured of more than sufficient signatures for petition lists, which are necessary to place its ticket on the ballot. Its official emblem will be a pair of clasped hands superimposed on a background of a gear wheel.

Party leaders have not yet decided whether they will enter a full ticket of local candidates in the city. They have, however, refused to endorse any local candidate of any other party and probably will nominate their own candidate for president of the Board of Aldermen.

List of Electors

As a matter of technical convenience, the identical list of Presidential electors will be listed in the Labor and Democratic party lines on the voting machine in order to avoid the possibility of splitting the vote. Six of the electors are labor leaders associated with the American Labor party: Andrew R. Armstrong, president of the International Printing Pressmen's and Assistants' Union, Local 2; George Meany, president of the New York State Federation of Labor; Sidney Hillman, president of the Amalgamated Clothing Workers of America; Joseph P. Ryan, president of the Central Trades and Labor Council of Greater New York; Max Zaritsky, secretary of the United Hatters, Cap and Millinery Workers, and David Dubinsky, president of the International Ladies Garment Workers Union of America.

In addition to the regular labor-union vote, the party predicts that it will be able to line up nearly 150,000 independent voters who normally would not vote for the two leading Democratic candidates.

In organizing their party, the labor forces have followed the example set by the two major political parties—with a single exception—and have, or are, establishing county and Assembly district units throughout the State. The exception is that each affiliating union pays a small per capita fee, giving it an organization voice in the control and policies of the party. In addition, union members, joining individually, pay party dues of 50 cents a year.

In New York City, where the party naturally expects to get the most of its strength, county headquarters have already been set up in all boroughs, except Queens, where five local offices have been established and a beginning has been made to build up Assembly district units.

Although organization work in up-State counties has progressed less rapidly, strong party units have been established in Syracuse, Binghamton, Schenectady, Troy, Albany and Buffalo. Party strength in Westchester, Nassau and Suffolk Counties is also reported growing, and county headquarters have been set up in all three places.

Up-State Activities

The Central Trades and Labor Council of Binghamton, at a special meeting on Sept. 2, voted to affiliate with the party, while on the same day 110 delegates of trade unions from Albany, Schenectady and Troy met in Albany and set in motion the machinery for intensive organization. In Syracuse campaign headquarters have been established with Albert W. Sherman, vice president of the New York State Federation of Labor, acting as local chairman. In Buffalo a conference of labor-union representatives voted affiliation last week.

With organized labor in the larger cities already enrolling in the party, up-State leaders started a drive last week throughout all counties to enlist labor strength in the outlying towns and villages.

Luigi Antonini of Yonkers, first vice president of the International Ladies Garment Workers Union, is State chairman of the party, while Rose Schneiderman of New York, president of the Women's Trade Union League and head of the women's division of the party, is vice chairman. Other officers include Alex Rose of New York, vice president of the Hatters, Cap and Millinery Workers International Union, secretary; Mr. Armstrong, treasurer, and Jacob S. Potofsky of New York, assistant president of the Amalgamated Clothing Workers Union of America, chairman of the executive committee.

September 20, 1936

STRESS RED ISSUE FOR REPUBLICANS

Leaders Conferring at Chicago Also Will Press Tax Fight in Closing Campaign.

ANSWER DEMANDED ON NRA

Hamilton Hints at 'Dictator' Aim of President, Citing Troop Use in Parade.

By CHARLES R. MICHAEL
Special to THE NEW YORK TIMES.

CHICAGO, Oct. 15.—High Republican leaders, conferring here today, were inclined to stress as issues in the final weeks of the campaign the administration's taxation policy and alleged radical support.

Participating in the conference were John D. M. Hamilton, chairman of the Republican National Committee, C. D. Goodspeed, treasurer of the committee, Roy Roberts, one of the leading Landon backers, and others. Plans to raise more money for use on election day also were devised.

The conference decided to urge Governor Landon to emphasize in his speeches the putting of the Farmer-Laborites on the Democratic ticket in Minnesota, and support assertedly assured President Roosevelt by the Communists. He will also be advised to continue questioning the President as to the Roosevelt program on any new NRA plans and the tax on corporation surpluses.

Commenting on the large turnout in the Roosevelt parade here last night, Mr. Hamilton said:

"Soldiers marched in line, a new custom for America, an old one with European dictators. And laboring men joined the procession, many because they were threatened with fines if they did not participate.

"Mr. Roosevelt last night was strangely silent about the unemployed 11,000,000 men and women. Maybe the omission was just another of his 'magnificent exceptions,' the phrase he so smoothly coined when he sold the Democratic party down the river in Nebraska last week after his earlier sale in Minnesota.

As to Monopoly

"Mr. Roosevelt waxed indignant about monopoly. But the NRA fostered monopoly until the Supreme Court stopped it. As THE NEW YORK TIMES put it this morning, the NRA was regulated monopoly under governmental direction, a collective action under a code system.

"THE TIMES, a great Democratic newspaper, has joined Governor Landon in asking President Roosevelt whether he intends to revive NRA, AAA and other forms of governmental control in the remote possibility of his re-election.

"THE TIMES put its finger on the sorest spot in this campaign when it said editorially, 'there are many voters who remain in doubt as to the President's convictions and intentions on the matter of the NRA * * * They do not know today precisely where the Democratic party stands on these important questions.'

"I would add that there are many voters who remain in doubt of Mr. Roosevelt's convictions and intentions on all important questions.

"And even if he promises to return to the American way, the doubt will remain in view of his long string of broken promises."

A statement issued by the Republican National Committee said the President "proved last night that he is the Kerensky of the American revolutionary movement." Continuing. the statement declared:

"The poor lamb does not realize that his fantastic, planned economy, his rapid extension of government ownership, his idea that saving for a rainy day by business is wicked and must be prevented by a confiscatory tax on surpluses, lead directly to the destruction of the capitalistic system.

Stalin Is Mentioned

"But Browder, the Communist candidate for President, knows it and is supporting him. Rexford G. Tugwell knows it, and realizes that his own muzzling until after election is in the interest of the cause. Felix Frankfurter knows it and is keeping mighty quiet for the present. Mordecai Ezekiel knows it, and you haven't heard his name for months.

"Stalin over in Russia knows it and has ordered his following in the United States to back Roosevelt. The radicals of Minnesota know it and were willing to trade support of Roosevelt for suicide of the Democratic party in that State. The radicals of Wisconsin know it and made the same deal. The radicals in Nebraska know it and have scuttled the nominee of a Democratic party primary to aid Roosevelt.

"Woodrow Wilson must have turned over in his grave. He risked his whole political future by insisting that the Democratic bosses of New Jersey stand by a Democratic primary for United States Senator, though he had no personal or political interest in the man so nominated.

"It is probable that Franklin D. Roosevelt really thinks he can save this system of free enterprise. It may be that he is sincere in the golden words of opportunity spoken to business here last night. But why are his words so different from his deeds?

"Let's analyze his sincerity right now. Is he willing to repeal the tax on surpluses which he forced through the last Congress? Does Mr. Roosevelt propose to modify it? Every one knows he does not.

"Mr. Roosevelt said expenditures are coming down. But he has spent $25,000,000,000 and there are still 11,000,000 unemployed.

"What does he propose to do about those unemployed if he cuts down this spending? Does he propose to re-establish the NRA in some new form in another fantastic experiment that will harass both labor and these individual business men for whom he is suddenly so considerate?

"He has ignored all of Governor Landon's questions."

October 16, 1936

ROOSEVELT SWEEPS THE NATION

POLL SETS RECORD

Roosevelt Electoral Vote of 519 Seen as a Minimum

NO SWING TO THE BOLTERS

By ARTHUR KROCK

Accepting the President as the issue, nearly eight million more voters than ever before had gone to the polls in the United States—about 45,000,000 persons—yesterday gave to Franklin Delano Roosevelt the most overwhelming testimonial of approval ever received by a national candidate in the history of the nation.

Except for the small corner of New England occupied by Maine, Vermont and New Hampshire—which was oscillating between Republican and Democratic in the early morning hours of Wednesday—the President was the choice of a vast preponderance of the voters in all parts of the country, and with him were re-elected as Vice President John N. Garner of Texas and an almost untouched Democratic majority in the House of Representatives. The Democratic national ticket will have a minimum of 519 electoral votes and a possible popular majority of ten millions.

The Republican candidates for President and Vice President, Governor Alfred M. Landon of Kansas and Colonel Frank Knox of Illinois, are the worst-beaten aspirants for these offices in the political annals of the United States, with the exception of William H. Taft in 1912, when Colonel Theodore Roosevelt led a formidable revolt in the Republican party and Mr. Taft carried only Vermont and Utah. Yesterday Utah was also in the President's campaign bag. He had carried forty-five States as contrasted with the forty-two he won from Herbert Hoover in 1932. And to assure his reputation as the greatest votegetter in the annals of the United States he—a Democrat—had overwhelmingly swept Pennsylvania, unfailingly Republican for generations in national elections.

The following table contains a list of the States carried by the President, with a total of 519 electoral votes, to which the four of New Hampshire may yet be added:

Alabama	11	Nebraska	7
Arizona	3	Nevada	3
Arkansas	9	New Jersey	16
California	22	New Mexico	3
Colorado	6	New York	47
Connecticut	8	North Carolina	13
Delaware	3	North Dakota	4
Florida	7	Ohio	26
Georgia	12	Oklahoma	11
Idaho	4	Oregon	5
Illinois	29	Pennsylvania	36
Indiana	14	Rhode Island	4
Iowa	11	South Carolina	8
Kansas	9	South Dakota	4
Kentucky	11	Tennessee	11
Louisiana	10	Texas	23
Maryland	8	Utah	4
Massachusetts	17	Virginia	11
Michigan	19	Washington	8
Minnesota	11	West Virginia	8
Mississippi	9	Wisconsin	12
Missouri	15	Wyoming	3
Montana	4		

After hours of hopeful waiting on rural districts in the Northeast States, Mr. Landon and the Republican national chairman, John D. M. Hamilton, announced their intentions of letting the night pass before agreeing to the fact of the stupendous party defeat. But about 1 A. M. in Topeka, Mr. Landon sent the customary message of congratulation to the President at Hyde Park, and at 1:45 A. M., at headquarters in Chicago, Mr. Hamilton followed suit. All the important newspapers supporting the Republican ticket (about 90 per cent of the metropolitan and country press) had given up many hours before.

Among the casualties in the voting, along with Governor Landon, Colonel Knox, Chairman Hamilton and a number of Republican Senators and Representatives, were Father Charles E. Coughlin and his Union for Social Justice ticket, headed by Representative William Lemke, who polled a negligible vote, even in his own State of North Dakota, and other minor Socialists. William E. Borah of Idaho and George W. Norris of Nebraska, venerable Senate leaders, were victorious; the youthful Henry Cabot Lodge 3d, Republican, was running far ahead of Governor Curley for the Senatorship in Massachusetts, and two Republican Senators who voted against the Social Security Act, on which the party managers made a last-minute attack—Hastings of Delaware and Metcalf of Rhode Island—were also rejected by the voters in their States. Another Republican casualty was Senator W. Warren Barbour of New Jersey.

The "Jeffersonian Democrats," led by such well-known and supposedly influential Democrats as Alfred E. Smith, John W. Davis and James A. Reed, and on whose rejection of the New Deal the Republicans had greatly depended to cut into Southern votes and swing the Northeast away from the President, proved as ineffectual foes as did the Republican campaign candidates and management. The South rolled up tremendous Roosevelt pluralities, and the President carried Philadelphia, Chicago, New York City and Boston by large margins.

Labor, the unemployed and the colored voters, on whose support the Democrats had counted, were visible in the stunning returns from Illinois, Pennsylvania, New York, Ohio and Michigan.

Several thousand neighbors, bearing torches and accompanied by a band playing "Happy Days Are Here Again," visited the President at Hyde Park after it appeared that his victory was established. He stood facing them in a light drizzle and said that, "while I can't say anything official, it appears that the sweep is covering every section." The President, on the arm of his son Franklin, urged press photographers to get through with him because "I've got to get back and get the returns from California."

Soon after 11 P. M. Mr. Farley issued a formal statement in which he congratulated the nation on the results of the election and praised

the President for his administrative efforts. He said the final results would show that the President had received "probably the greatest vote of confidence" ever accorded in the United States. The victory was in large measure a personal triumph for Mr. Farley himself, who takes rank as the most successful political manager in the history of the Democratic party. Since he was a steady personal target throughout the Republican campaign, his share in the outcome is particularly gratifying to his associates.

From a standpoint of sentiment there was great interest in the close contest between the President and Governor Landon in the Republican nominee's home State of Kansas. The margin was as thin as a razor's edge between them, and shifted several times as the night wore on.

Dissension in the Republican party over Chairman Hamilton's conduct of the campaign was foreshadowed early last night when Representative Hamilton Fish of New York criticized the attack on the Social Security Act, for which a large Republican majority in Congress, including the Senate and House leaders, had voted.

The first of the President's non-political leaders to issue a formal statement was John L. Lewis, president of the United Mine Workers of America, to whom is given great credit for the Democratic victory in Pennsylvania—the first in modern political history.

"The people could not be deceived," he said in part. "Labor's Non-Partisan League has justified the expectations and claims of its founders. * * * Labor's strength is being demonstrated in each of the industrial States. Without this unanimity of support the result would have been otherwise."

The outstanding events in the early returns were the colossal majority given to the President in Chicago and his foreshadowed capture of Pennsylvania. Soon after these astonishing facts were being digested, Ohio showed a pro-Roosevelt trend which could give him a majority of 200,000 in a State estimated to be "close," and where 50,000 was the private figure on both sides.

So well was the President running in New England that The Providence Journal, a Landon supporter, early conceded that State to Mr. Roosevelt by 30,000 votes.

Every sign, as the returns piled up, was that Republican campaign strategy had come to a disastrous finish. A year ago the prevailing idea among Republican leaders was to make a frontal assault on the New Deal with an outstanding Eastern candidate, such as Senator Vandenberg of Michigan. Subtler counsels, however, were adopted, and it was decided to swallow half of the New Deal in the platform and nominate a nationally unknown candidate who would provide a powerful personal contrast to the forceful personality of the President. This was done

in the selection of Governor Landon.

Although a year ago the Republicans had little or no hope of electing a President in 1936, the spirit of the Cleveland convention fired them to hope, and this was highly stimulated by the public desertions of their party by such prominent Democrats as Alfred E. Smith, John W. Davis, Lewis W. Douglas and T. Jefferson Coolidge, and by the refusal of Democratic newspapers like The Baltimore Sun, The St. Louis Post-Dispatch and The Omaha World-Herald (once edited by William Jennings Bryan) to support the President.

The result of this new-found enthusiasm was persuasion of Republican leaders that they could defeat the President, and from this viewpoint came a much more active and expensive campaign than any one would have predicted a year ago. Activity on the Republican side produced a corresponding acceleration of pace, with consequent expense, in Chairman Farley's staff.

The two national committees have and will have confessed to the expenditure of nearly $10,000,000. But, considering the sums spent personally by Republican enthusiasts of great wealth in their own communities and in the nation at large, it is perhaps no wild estimate to conclude that $50,000,000 were expended in the name of politics in the United States between the Cleveland convention in June and yesterday.

The campaign was not particularly interesting in so far as speeches and situations were concerned. But because of the strategy employed and the emotional mood in which partisans on both sides soon found themselves, it will probably stand out in American political history. The issues offered at first by the Republicans—the Presidential candidate, the Vice Presidential candidate and the national committee—were "dictatorship" and general accusations of administration designs against individual liberty; waste, extravagance, political manipulation of relief and spoilsmanship generally; and contempt for the Constitution.

But by mid-October reports from midland States which Mr. Landon had to carry to win were so unsatisfactory that the national committee discharged a petard in reserve. That was an attack in the industrial centers on the Social Security Act in an effort to win back unorganized labor. The payroll contribution of employes was stressed without mention of the employers' levy, and it was contended that, since collections were placed in a Treasury general fund, contributors were always in danger of having any Congress take their money for an extraneous purpose. This propaganda was circulated in payroll envelopes.

When word came to Chairman Farley that the attack on the Social Security Act was affecting labor—one of the President's greatest group reliances—a counter-attack was launched, led by the President himself. This dispute marked the last week of the campaign, and managing politicians were accordingly on tiptoe all last night for returns from such labor centers as Chicago, Detroit, Gary, Ind., and Pittsburgh.

"Master" Speech Seized Upon

The President himself furnished the Republicans with another eleventh-hour hope in certain passages of his speech at Madison Square Garden in New York City last Saturday night. He said that he "welcomed" the "hatred" of "organized money," and added the hope that, having found his first administration its "match," "organized money" would find his second administration its "master." These remarks, taken from their context, were reported to have alienated many Northeastern voters who were preparing to vote for the President. The campaign ended with a great deal of money being spent by the Republicans to hammer these words home with as much sinister implication as both fact and fancy could furnish.

Throughout the four months between the Cleveland convention and the election, Republican strategy was a matter of revision and change, suggesting that the President's description of the New Deal in his famous "quarterback" simile could be applied to the attack of his political foes. Governor Landon made more speeches than he had planned at first, and the "front porch" Kansas campaign plan went glimmering. In his speech of acceptance he pleaded for quiet and tolerance, but by October he was charging the President with a wish to be dictator, and in the middle of that month he made a sudden trip to California to garner votes of those expectant of the benefits of Dr. Townsend's plan to pay old people $200 a month each.

The President's managers, alarmed by the rise in Republican hopes and activities and by news that such States as Massachusetts, New York and Illinois were too close for comfort, prevailed on Mr. Roosevelt greatly to extend his speaking schedule, with the result that he almost duplicated his effort of 1932.

Several factors in addition to control of the executive branch of the government and Congress were in the balance as the voters went to the polls yesterday. The next President will in all likelihood have several appointments to make for justices of the Supreme Court. The party leadership will almost inevitably shift back to this side of the Mississippi River and Chairman John D. M. Hamilton will have to make way for another. Also Mr. Landon will not be renominated, and the star of Senator Arthur H. Vandenberg of Michigan will rise for 1940.

November 4, 1936

Digest to Seek Reason For Failure of Poll

The Literary Digest poll, which predicted a victory for Governor Landon over President Roosevelt in yesterday's voting, apparently was affected either by distribution of the ballots or by a late

shift in public opinion, Wilfred J. Funk, editor of the magazine, said last night.

"We may not have reached a representative cross-section of the population in distributing the ballots," he said.

"On the other hand, the last returns were received some weeks ago, and there may have been a

shift in voting sentiment since then. What we will do now is try to figure out which happened, as a guide to our future policy."

It is too early yet, he said, to announce whether The Digest will change its method of distributing ballots in any future polls that it may conduct.

November 4, 1936

DEMOCRATS MAKE CONGRESS RECORDS

Their Ratio Is Largest Since 1869 in the Senate and Since 1855 in the House.

By The Associated Press.

WASHINGTON, Nov. 5.—Not since 1869 has any party held such a large percentage of the Senate's membership as the Democrats won in Tuesday's election, and records as far back as 1855 show no House majority to equal that assured in the new Congress.

There will be seventy-five Democrats and seventeen Republicans in the Senate which meets Jan. 5. In 1869, when Grant was President, the Republicans hit a high mark of sixty-one members while the Democrats had only eleven. This was a ratio of 82 per cent, slightly higher than the Democratic now.

Since 1855, neither party has held so high a percentage of House strength as the 334 Democratic members elected Tuesday will provide. The new House will have only eighty-nine Republicans.

Numerically, the Democratic strength will be the greatest in the country's history in both houses. The previous high marks were the memberships of 322 Democrats in the House and seventy Democrats in the Senate last year.

Furthermore, barring a break-up in the "Solid South," or a reforming of party lines, the Democrats will have control of the Senate throughout President Roosevelt's second term, and probably until 1943.

The Democrats will maintain a majority through to 1943 unless the Republicans make almost a clean sweep of the next two elections.

Incidentally, the traditional party aisle, which has divided the opposing forces since Civil War days, may be abandoned.

It took great study and much crowding to get the old Democratic membership of seventy on one side of the aisle, but with the new additions, it will be virtually impossible.

For the past two years the Republicans have had to spread their thin ranks with care to cover their side of the chamber. With less than a score of members left, the Republicans would look lost if put in the entire space on Vice President Garner's left.

November 6, 1936

LABOR AND FARM GROUPS BIG FACTORS IN VOTING

Credit for Outcome Shared by Small Cities and Large, Negroes and Whites, New Voters and Old

By LUTHER A. HUSTON

WASHINGTON, Nov. 7.—President Roosevelt's election triumph was so overwhelming that it can hardly be attributed to any one factor or any one class of voters, but leaders in agriculture and labor circles here attribute much of its decisiveness to the backing of farmers and wage-earners.

In fact, if the claims of the labor leaders are correct, the wage-earner vote might easily account for the landslide. These claims cannot be demonstrated by accurate figures or percentages because our system of voting by secret ballot makes it impossible to "count noses" and say how every man voted. But the most authentic basic figures available indicate that nearly four-fifths of Mr. Roosevelt's total vote may have been cast by wage-earners.

The term "wage-earners" as used here includes all those who work for wages and salaries in the United States: the 4,000,000 in the organized labor movement and the many millions more who toil on farms, in stores, in offices and in the unorganized groups in industry and the skilled trades.

On the basis of Census Bureau figures of those "gainfully employed"—the wage-earners—the potential vote of the group was about 45,000,000. The best estimate is that something like more than 25,000,000 of these voted in Tuesday's elections.

Four-to-One Ratio Seen

Labor leaders predicted before the election that 80 per cent of the organized labor vote would be for Roosevelt. They also predicted that the unorganized labor vote would be almost as solidly for the President. If it is true that 80 per cent of the total wage-earner vote went for the Democratic candidate, then something like 20,000,000 voters of this category were included in the total Roosevelt vote. Governor Landon, on that basis, would have received only about 5,000,000 votes —less than one-third of his total— from the ranks of the workers. That would mean a ratio of the wage-earner vote of about 4 to 1 for Mr. Roosevelt and labor leaders insist that this estimate is not too high.

Although labor seemingly has cause for claiming the lion's share of credit for the Roosevelt victory, agriculture undoubtedly rallied with unexpected strength to the Roosevelt banner and upset the hopes of the Republicans. Much of the wage-earner vote to which labor attributes the President's landslide came from the ranks of agriculture, for Census Bureau figures show that about 8,000,000 of the potential voters among the wage-earners are employed on farms and the estimate is that probably 5,000,000 of them cast ballots —about 4,000,000 of them for Mr. Roosevelt.

Work in Rural Towns

Furthermore, agriculture claims credit for a switch in another type of rural voting strength toward the end of the campaign that enhanced the Roosevelt victory. This switch came from the element in the rural population that was generally considered to be the unknown factor in the campaign as far as agriculture was concerned.

At no time did the agricultural leaders in the Democratic ranks doubt that the dirt farmers were for Mr. Roosevelt. They were sure that the New Deal's agricultural program had the support of those who actually toiled on the farms.

The element they were in doubt about was what they term the "rural" vote, or the population of the towns and villages in the farming areas, the non-industrial communities that depend upon the farming regions for their support.

At the outset of the campaign it was believed that this rural vote leaned toward the Republican side. But the agriculturist politicians in the Democratic ranks went after it. They preached to the rural vote that its fortunes were indissolubly linked with those of the dirt farmer. The fundamental prosperity of the rural business man, they insisted, was based upon the prosperity of the farmers. If the farmers felt that the New Deal program was a good thing for them—and they were in a position to know— then did it not necessarily follow that the New Deal was a good thing for the rural business man?

Big Swing Explained

Toward the end of the campaign, the agriculturists say, the rural vote swung around to their way of thinking. It was because of this, they assert, that in many of the predominantly agricultural States Mr. Roosevelt's plurality over Mr. Landon in 1936 was greater than his plurality over Mr. Hoover in 1932. It was this shift in the rural vote, they declare, which, for instance, sent Minnesota's plurality for Roosevelt from 237,000 in 1932 to more than 370,000 in 1936 and Montana's from 49,000 to more than 125,000.

In many of the other States which gave Mr. Roosevelt a larger plurality in 1936 than they did in 1932, however, labor claims a share of the credit with agriculture. In Illinois, for instance, a Roosevelt plurality of 450,000 in 1932 became one of about 750,000 in 1936 and Michigan's margin of 132,000 for Roosevelt in 1932 became a plurality of more than 300,000 in 1936. Available figures in each of these States and others similarly constituted indicate that the Roosevelt gains were proportionate in both the agricultural areas and in the large industrial centers where the labor, or wage-earner, vote predominates.

Some interesting divisions of sentiment are shown in reports of the election received by the Department of Agriculture. Returns from Kansas, for instance, the home State of the Republican candidate, show that in the Western half of the State the farmers voted almost 3 to 1 for President Roosevelt, while those in the Eastern half voted about 2 to 1 for the President. The Western half of the State, generally speaking, was the section most afflicted by drought.

The Ohio Vote

In Ohio, where the labor vote in the large cities registered sizable gains for Mr. Roosevelt, the farmers kept pace with the trend toward the New Deal. Fourteen counties which went for Mr. Roosevelt in 1932 increased their Democratic plurality in 1936 and fourteen others changed from Republican in 1932 to Democratic in 1936.

Reports from Colorado indicated that in the cattle-raising areas the vote in favor of Mr. Roosevelt was about 2 to 1, while in the irrigated districts the ratio was 3 to 2 and in the dry farming sections 2 to 1.

The vote for Roosevelt, it was indicated, was generally heavier in those portions of the farming regions where the cooperative movements had made greatest headway. Officials of the Department of Agriculture contend that the Republican attacks upon the reciprocal trade treaties, particularly the treaty with Canada, had little effect upon the farmer vote.

Democratic pre-election predictions regarding other divisions of the electorate were quite generally fulfilled by the outcome of Tuesday's voting. The relief vote, for instance, estimated at about 3,000,-000 and comprising the qualified voters who are beneficiaries of the government's relief agencies, was believed from all available reports to have been more than 95 per cent for the President.

Negro Vote

The predictions about the Negro vote, however, may not have been entirely fulfilled. It had been estimated that there were about 1,250,-000 Negroes in the United States who would vote and that about 60 per cent would forsake the traditional Republicanism of their race and vote for the New Deal candidate. The element that makes fulfillment of this estimate doubtful was the action of Father Divine, the New York Negro religious leader, who advised the members of his sect to remain away from the polls.

In the outstanding test of the attitude of the Negro voters toward the New Deal, however, the New Deal candidate was victorious. Representative Arthur W. Mitchel, a strong Roosevelt supporter, was re-elected in the First Illinois District, where the Negro vote controls, defeating Oscar De Priest, Republican and former Representative.

The urban vote as a whole, that of the major cities of the country, was predominantly Roosevelt. All pre-election forecasts were that the President's greatest strength would come from the urban centers and the only thing wrong with the pre-

dictions was the estimates of his pluralities. In New York City, for instance, Mr. Roosevelt's plurality exceeded 1,360,000. Chicago, Detroit, Cleveland, Boston, Philadelphia, Pittsburgh and other large cities gave correspondingly large pluralities.

First Voters

Although supporting statistics are lacking, there is no reason to doubt that the voters who cast ballots for the first time in this election were preponderantly for Roosevelt. It had been estimated that probably 75 per cent of the new voters would vote Democratic, and nothing in the general results of the election would appear to make this estimate inaccurate.

Geographically, however, the result upset pre-election forecasts. There were a few, like Chairman Farley of the Democratic National Committee, who said that Mr. Roosevelt would carry all but two States, but this forecast was thought almost as over-optimistic as the Republican chairman's claim that Governor Landon would carry thirty-six States.

New England was generally regarded as Landon territory but it went for Roosevelt except for Maine and Vermont. Several of the Middle Atlantic States were considered probable Landon strongholds and some of the Middle Western States were considered debatable ground.

But as the voters from the shoe-making and textile towns of New England, from the coal mines and steel mills of Pennsylvania, from the farms and factories of the Middle West, from the mines and ranches and fruit farms of the Far West, from the cotton plantations of the South and from the sidewalks of New York marched to the polls they loosed an avalanche of Roosevelt ballots that confounded all those who professed to believe that the Kansas Governor would make a better showing in 1936 than President Hoover did in 1932.

November 8, 1936

NO CLASS WARFARE

No cry was more often heard in the Presidential campaign, or was more bitter, than the warning that this country stood face to face with a war between classes. It was specifically charged that the New Deal had developed, whether it intended to or not, class hatred in the United States to a degree and intensity never before dreamed of here. Fear was expressed that all extremist elements would get together and form a nation-wide Labor party, or Farmer-Labor party, to fight the next Presidential election strictly on the basis of one class against another. All these alarms are left looking quite needless and a little ridiculous by the results of last Tuesday's election. President ROOSEVELT's great victory was not won by class or even by party. The mass of voters who swept him into office again by overpowering majorities were more influenced by

personal and economic motives than by group appeals or arguments for party regularity.

The evident fact was that parties or movements or leaders identified with class selfishness or with excessively radical measures were treated pretty roughly by the voters. The Communist vote was negligible. That party, despite all its thundering in the index, had so few supporters in this State as to lose its right to be again on the official ballot. The vote for the candidate of the Socialist party, Mr. NORMAN THOMAS, was pitifully small—only a fraction of what he had four years ago. It now seems probable that the Socialist party, which for a long time came nearer to being a class party than any which we had ever had, will be liquidated and absorbed by other organizations. As for the Union party, led by Mr. LEMKE and Father COUGHLIN, it proved to have absolutely no at-

traction for American voters in their present mood. Even the proposed Labor party will find it hard sledding after the impressive demonstration of Nov. 3.

It was like the sudden slip of an avalanche, and efforts to trace its causes are as futile as if one were to stop at the foot of a Swiss mountain and argue that a slight fall of snow, or the explosion of a gun, had precipitated the mass of ice down the slope. In the presence of so great an outpouring of votes, petty analysis and detailed assignment of causes are out of the question. We can, however, do something in the way of judging the results. One of the greatest of these, it is now clear, is to have submerged guerrilla tactics and extremist policies under the flooding of a national, nonpartisan and unifying sentiment.

November 8, 1936

CONSERVATIVE REACTION

PRESIDENT PUTS COURT PLAN ON BASIS OF PARTY LOYALTY; SAYS PROBLEMS CAN'T WAIT

'VETO' OF LAWS HIT

By TURNER CATLEDGE
Special to THE NEW YORK TIMES.

WASHINGTON, March 4.—President Roosevelt tonight put support for his plan to make over the Supreme Court squarely on the basis

of party loyalty and responsibility.

In a speech delivered before 1,300 guests gathered at the Hotel Mayflower for the Democratic Victory Dinner, and broadcast to more than 1,100 similar dinners held in all parts of the country, Mr. Roosevelt exhorted his party, "and its associates," to "remain a natural rallying point for the cooperative effort of all of those who truly believe in

political and economic democracy."

He said again and again that the time to act was "now," and warned his supporters that if they did not have the courage to "lead the American people where they want to go, some one else will."

The President did not mention the Supreme Court by name at any point in his address. He drew such a word picture, however, as to

leave no doubt as to what he meant when he demanded a "well-matched, three-horse team" to plow the fields that hold the opportunities for human progress in the United States.

He Cites Strikes and Floods

He also pictured a serious condition in the country—of ill-nourished and ill-housed people, of farmers burdened by debt, of men and women laboring in factories for inadequate pay, of children working in mines and mills, of labor strikes costing millions of dollars, of threatening floods and blowing dust—which he said lay beneath the surface of the present appearance of prosperity.

He held that none of these problems could be adequately met by national action with the present uncertainties as to the legality of remedial legislation that might be passed by the Congress.

113

His speech was accepted as tantamount to an announcement that no new effort would be made to meet the conditions he described unless and until the court were brought into better harmony with the legislative and executive branches of the government.

"It will take courage to let our minds be bold and find the ways to meet the needs of the nation," the President said. "But for our party, now as always, the counsel of courage is the counsel of wisdom."

Makes Appeal to His Party

The President's frank appeal to his party, "and its associates," was not unexpected. Faced with determined opposition in Congress to his judiciary proposals, and with much of this coming from Democrats and "liberals" who had supported him in his last two campaigns, Mr. Roosevelt had been faced for days with what appeared to his Congressional leaders to be a necessity for dramatic action.

And in his opening remarks tonight, the President said that he would continue his discussion of the present "crisis" in his radio "Fireside Chat," scheduled for next Tuesday night.

The President recalled to his supporters tonight that they had only recently come into the responsibilities of government. Their party was now the majority party by the greatest majority any such group ever had, he said, adding:

"It will remain the majority party so long as it continues to justify the faith of millions who had almost lost faith—so long as it continues to make modern democracy work—so long and no longer."

He told his hearers that the landslide of 1936 which they were celebrating was not a final victory.

"Whether we shall celebrate in 1938, 1940 and in 1944, as we celebrate tonight, will deservedly depend upon whether the party continues on its course and solves these problems," he added.

He said that after election day in 1936 some of his supporters were uneasy lest the "false era of good feeling" be taken as an excuse "to evade our obligations."

"They were worried," he said, "by the evil symptom that the propaganda and the epithets of last Summer and Fall had died down."

But today, he went on to say, those persons might be reassured, "for the tumult and the shouting have broken forth anew—and from substantially the same elements of opposition."

Tells of His 1941 'Ambitions'

Mr. Roosevelt recalled that a few days ago a member of Congress designated as "John" had called to talk to him about national problems in general, and specifically about the problem of the judiciary. He described the conversation with the Congress member, and of the latter's reactions when he started to relate to his visitor his ambitions for Jan. 20, 1941, when his present term as President expires.

He told his Congressional caller, the President said, that his great ambition for Jan. 20, 1941, was to turn his desk over to his successor, whoever he may be, with a nation intact, a nation at peace, a nation prosperous, "a nation clear in its knowledge of what powers it has to serve its own citizens, a nation that is in a position to use those powers to the full in order to move forward steadily to meet the modern needs of humanity."

He further told his visitor that he did not want to leave to his successor the condition which Buchanan left to Lincoln.

"I spoke in the dead earnestness of anxiety," said the President. "I speak to you tonight in the same earnestness. For no one who sees as a whole today's picture of this nation and the world can help but feel concern for the future."

Mr. Roosevelt said that letters reaching his desk every day reflected the most striking feature of the life of this generation—"a feature which men who live mentally in another generation can least understand"—the ever-accelerating speed with which social forces now gather headway.

He held that these forces could not wait for forty years, like slavery, to be dealt with; that economic freedom for the wage-earner and the farmer and the small business man would not wait even for four years.

"It will not wait at all," he said. Democracy in many lands had failed for the time being to meet the needs of the hour, he continued, adding:

"People have become so fed up with futile debate and party bickerings over methods that they have been willing to surrender democratic processes and principles in order to get things done."

He insisted that democracy in the United States had "not yet" failed "and does not need to fail." But he could not say "with complete candor" that in these past few years democracy in the United States has fully succeeded.

"Nor can I tell you, under present circumstances," he continued, "just where American democracy is headed nor just what it is permitted to do in order to insure its continued success and survival. I can only hope."

"For as yet there is no definite assurance that the three-horse team of the American system of government will pull together," he went on. "If three well-matched horses are put to the task of plowing up a field where the going is heavy,

and the team of three pull as one, the field will be plowed. If one horse lies down in the traces or plunges off in another direction, the field will not be plowed."

With this the President went into a discussion of what had been attempted in the way of national action to meet the national needs but which had failed because of adverse decisions in the court. The Agricultural Adjustment Act, he said, testified to the effort to solve the farm problem.

"You know who assumed the power to veto, and did veto that program," he said.

He related, then, that in the campaign of 1936 he had said that he and his party would continue the efforts in behalf of the farmers, and he quoted from his Madison Square Garden speech the words "for all these things we have only just begun to fight."

He insisted that neither individually nor as a party could Democrats postpone "and run from the fight on advice of defeatist lawyers."

"But I defy any one to read the majority opinion invalidating the A. A. A. and tell us what we can do for agriculture in this session of Congress with any reasonable certainty that what we do will not be nullified as unconstitutional," he added.

He continued with the assertion that the Democratic administration and Congress had made "a gallant, sincere effort" to raise wages, reduce hours, abolish child labor and eliminate unfair trade practices in industry.

"You know who assumed the power to veto, and did veto that program," he said.

He recalled that the Railroad Retirement Act, the National Recovery Act and the Guffey Coal Act were successively outlawed as the Child Labor Statute had been outlawed twenty years before.

March 5, 1937

In Washington

The President and the Southern Conservatives

By ARTHUR KROCK

WASHINGTON, Aug. 17.—The House Rules Committee provides a typical cross-section of the Democratic elements which will come to grips for party control hereafter. As has often been written, the President fully realizes the Southern conservative challenge to his leadership and must therefore have been prepared for the blockade of the Wages-and-Hours bill by the Democratic committee minority, gladly made into a temporary majority by the support of four Republicans. The statement can now be added that the field on which this opening skirmish is being fought could not suit him better.

In the debate over the bill to enlarge the Supreme Court, no popularly effective reply was made to the query: "Where is your mandate?" Although it was known during the campaign that the successful Presidential candidate would probably have several vacancies

to fill on the Supreme Court, the reorganization plan formulated by the Maverick-Ashurst bill—the President's own measure—was not put forward in the election debate. Therefore, aside from the contention that Mr. Roosevelt received a general mandate to proceed with his reforms in his own way, the Administration forces were never able to prove a specific instruction on this point, and it hurt them.

A Clear Mandate

But on the question of Wages-and-Hours legislation the mandate was as clear as anything in American politics can be. The President early let it be known that such was his objective. He reiterated it most forcefully in his Madison Square Garden speech. Details were not put in issue, and the Senate changed these fundamentally from the original proposals before it passed the bill to regulate the working conditions of labor. But the objective was plainly before the people, and many Democratic candidates for Congress were pledged to vote to achieve it.

Now, if the blockade by the Democratic minority of the Rules Committee prevents the House from supplementing the Senate's action at this session of

Congress, the President will have a direct issue of a kind that greatly appeals to him. There is no question that a large majority in the House wants to act favorably on a Wages-and-Hours bill. Organized labor, having obtained the safeguarding amendments it sought, endorses passage. The group which calls itself "liberal," although it divided on the Supreme Court plan, also supports the measure. Only a bloc of Southern conservatives, temporarily dominant at this period of a session by the rules of the House, stands in the way of all these forces.

Where the Blame Lies

Since the President long has felt that the Southern Democratic conservatives must be dominated, defeated or dispersed, if future party control is to bear his brand of progressivism, the House situation is, from his viewpoint, Exhibit A for the plaintiff. A large majority is being frustrated, and a campaign mandate is being nullified. Mr. Roosevelt could not ask for a more useful group on which to place the blame.

Unless one holds with advocates of a pure democracy that a majority should always be free to legislate as it chooses, there are, of course, many good reasons for holding up this bill. It extends Federal power to invisible and cloudy limits, supporting the argument of those who hold it repugnant to the spirit, at least, of the Constitution. The bill is certainly not a perfect measure, but a collection of makeshifts, compromises and experimental provisions. In the hands of an expert commission it doubtless could be made into a more workable measure, removing all opposition save that which could be pilloried as economically selfish and socially unenlightened, or traditionally stubborn in its construction of the Constitution.

Materials for Campaign Drama

But all this, though true, does not bulk strongly in a political test. In a campaign such as the President is capable of making, particularly in the South, it would not lend itself so well to dramatization as the claim of a mandate ignored, a reform blocked, a small economic group arrayed against the welfare of the many. And in fundamentally Democratic communities, which abound in the South, the mathematical fact that only an alliance with Rules Committee Republicans has made the bloc controlling could probably be used with good political effect.

President Seems Satisfied

It may be because the alignment is so useful to his purpose that the President has sat by while the Wages-and-Hours bill was being smothered in committee. His nomination of Senator Black for the Supreme Court is viewed by many as having been partly influenced by the conservative Southern obstruction, but that is only a guess. The fact is he has personally made no drive to save one of his pet bills. Unless he does this before the session ends, which few expect, the assumption will grow that he is well satisfied with the illustration of party cleavage which has been furnished by the Rules Committee. And practically he may console himself further with the reflection that at the next session he is more certain to get a better bill.

August 18, 1937

ACCUSE NEW DEAL OF PLOT TO 'PURGE' DEMOCRATIC FOES

SENATORS TO FIGHT

Seek to Bar Defeat at Polls of Those Voting No on the Court Bill

ATTACK HOPKINS ON IOWA

Speakers Hit Intervention— Chandler Aide Says WPA Brazenly Helps Barkley

War Opened in Senate

By TURNER CATLEDGE
Special to The New York Times.

WASHINGTON, May 25.—Anti-New Deal Democrats in the Senate took the offensive today to protect themselves against what they regarded as Administration reprisals in the coming primary elections.

They acted after seeing newspaper accounts of the endorsement by Harry L. Hopkins, Works Progress Administrator, of Representative Wearin in his race to capture the Senate nomination from Senator Gillette in Iowa.

The Senate was tied up for nearly three hours while Senators Wheeler of Montana, McCarran of Nevada and Clark of Missouri, all Democrats, condemned this or any interference by Administration agents in party contests. Meanwhile these and others held numerous conversations on the floor and in the cloakrooms on plans for mutual self-protection in the precincts where the voting is to be done.

The attack on Mr. Hopkins and the Administration was accentuated by charges circulated among Congress members that Federal relief agencies in Kentucky were being used as aids to Senator Barkley in his contest against Governor Chandler for renomination to the Senate.

The Kentucky allegations, not mentioned on the floor, were made in a letter from Governor Chandler's campaign manager to President Roosevelt, a copy of which was sent to each member of Congress.

Some of the anti-New Deal Democratic spokesmen contended that the efforts of Mr. Hopkins in behalf of Mr. Wearin were only a curtain-raiser in a deliberate plan within the Administration inner-circle to rid the party of the less-than-one-hundred-per-cent New Dealers.

They said Administration scouts were now actively searching for candidates to run against Senators George in Georgia, McCarran in Nevada, Lonergan in Connecticut and Tydings in Maryland.

Representative David J. Lewis, outstanding advocate in the House of labor and social measures, is understood to have been sounded out as to his willingness to oppose Senator Tydings and is now seriously considering it.

This strategy is believed by the anti-New Deal group to have been worked out within the close circle around the President which includes Secretary Ickes, Mr. Hopkins, Thomas Corcoran and James Roosevelt. According to the Senators, it was vigorously opposed by Postmaster General Farley, who advised party harmony instead of a "purge."

Mr. Farley took no special pains, it seems, to prevent his feelings on the matter from becoming known to the Senators in question.

Those who were quickest to suspect efforts at administration reprisals, and who were loudest in their resentment of Mr. Hopkins's stepping into the Iowa situation, were Senators identified with the opposition to the President's court enlargement bill last year. They declared that loyalty on this particular issue had been made the acid test for Senators who were to be blessed or opposed by the Administration.

In their plan of counter-attack the anti-court bill leaders were explaining several possible courses to protect the men who ran afoul of the Administration on this question. They made tentative plans to organize themselves into a "flying squadron" of speakers to go into this or that State if one of their number, finding himself in trouble, might ask such aid.

"We can organize at a moment's notice and we'll do it if necessary," said Senator Wheeler, head of the Steering Committee, which stopped the court bill.

Said Senator McCarran:

"There's no question about what is going on. I know they are looking for some one to run against me. Just let them come."

In discussing the "flying squadron" idea, the anti-court bill Senators counseled caution among themselves. In some States any kind of outside interference, even a flying squadron of Senators, would be resisted, they reasoned, and in others the incumbents would need no particular aid.

They pointed to the situation in Missouri, where Senator Clark, one of the prominent figures in the anti-court fight, does not seem to be menaced, they said, in the primary.

Certain Administration spokesmen tried to minimize the import of Mr. Hopkins's statement in the Iowa situation, as well as other evidences of Washington pressure, but without much success so far as impressing the anti-New Deal group was concerned.

The recalcitrant Senators took it for granted that the Administration was now out to get their scalps and were planning their courses accordingly.

In an attempt to pour some pacifying oil, Senator Barkley told the Senators that Administrator Hopkins, in giving his statement in behalf of Mr. Wearin, might not have meant to make it so definite as it appeared. Mr. Hopkins had said that, if he lived in Iowa, he would vote for Mr. Wearin because of his record as a member of the House.

Mr. Barkley said he had made some inquiries from which he concluded that a newspaper man had somewhat casually asked Mr. Hopkins about his views on the subject, the administrator being a former resident of Iowa, and had received the apparently casual statement of his preference.

The story of how the statement was actually given, however, was about as follows:

Mr. Wearin, in answer to questions about New Deal support for him, suggested to newspaper men yesterday that they ask some of the recognized Administration leaders for their views.

He advised that they see Mr. Hopkins and inquire how he would vote if he were voting in the Iowa primary. When the correspondents visited Mr. Hopkins he at first declined to give any statement. Later, however, his office called one of the correspondents, Richard Wilson of The Des Moines Register and Tribune, and told him the administrator had reconsidered and would have something to say.

When Mr. Wilson, following Mr. Wearin's suggestion, put the question as to how he would vote if Mr. Hopkins made the reply, as attributed to him, and authorized its publication.

May 26, 1938

ROOSEVELT PLANS ACTIVE PRIMARY ROLE, SPEAKING OUT FOR 'LIBERAL' CANDIDATES; REBUKES HAGUE, LABOR AND BUSINESS

HITS 'COPPERHEADS'

Fireside Chat Assails Campaign of Defeatism in Congress

SAYS COURT FIGHT IS WON

President Asks Business Co-operation With Low Prices and High Wages

By FELIX BELAIR Jr.
Special to THE NEW YORK TIMES.

WASHINGTON, June 24.—President Roosevelt tonight brushed aside all doubt that he would take an active part in the coming Democratic primary campaigns, saying in the course of a nationally broadcast "fireside chat" that "as head of the Democratic party"—not as President—he had "every right" to speak out where New Deal principles were involved.

Speaking from the oval room in the White House just after returning from a dinner given for him by the "Little Cabinet," the President defined the political issue confronting the nation today as one transcending traditional party alignments and calling for the election of Congressional and Gubernatorial candidates who recognized "that the new conditions throughout the world call for new remedies."

After expressing the hope that all party affiliates would vote in the primary elections and would be guided by "the fundamental principles for which his party is on record," Mr. Roosevelt said that "as President of the United States" he was not calling on the country to vote Democratic in the Fall, nor "as President" was he taking part in the primaries.

Defends Right to Speak

Then he added:

"As head of the Democratic party, however, charged with the responsibility of carrying out the definitely liberal declaration of principles set forth in the 1936 Democratic platform, I feel that I have every right to speak in those few instances where there may be a clear issue between candidates for a Democratic nomination involving these principles, or involving a clear misuse of my own name."

Referring to the statistical position of the national welfare today, President Roosevelt conceded that the leaders of private enterprise, of labor, and even of government, had made mistakes. Labor had mistakenly pressed for too much after years of oppression, business had overproduced to the detriment of a market months removed, and government had displayed overconfidence of the ability of both business and labor to cooperate with government to the benefit of the entire nation, he said.

Lincoln's Time Recalled

It was in spite of the influence of the "copperheads" who had tried to drive a wedge between the legislative and executive branches that the record of the recently adjourned Congress had been made, said Mr. Roosevelt. Not even in Lincoln's time had there been such a drive to make both branches give up the fight in quest of "peace at any price," he continued.

The President remarked that "never in our lifetime has such a concerted campaign of defeatism been thrown at the heads of the President and Senators and Congressmen as in the case of this Seventy-fifth Congress."

It was against these "defeatists" that the President hurled the label "copperheads," identifying them as modern counterparts of those who, during the war between the States, opposed both Congress and the Executive with their "peace-at-any-price" policy so as to split the nation.

The President took occasion to announce to his radio audience the price reduction ordered by the United States Steel Corporation today, and to make public the private pledge of the company against any wage cut at this time. Word of the steel company's action reached the President after he had completed his draft. He commended the company for the step.

Reviewing the record of the recently adjourned Congress, Mr. Roosevelt congratulated its leaders for having responded, on the whole, to what he regarded as the will of the majority of the American people.

He recognized that it had "left many things undone," particularly in the matter of government reorganization and emergency railroad legislation, but said that barring "unforeseen events" there would be no special session of Congress, a constantly rumored Administration plan.

In what was generally regarded here as a thinly veiled reference to Mayor Frank Hague of Jersey City, President Roosevelt said he was "concerned about the attitude of a candidate or his sponsors with respect to the rights of American citizens to assemble peaceably and to express publicly their views and opinions on important social and economic issues."

"There can be no constitutional democracy in any community which denies to the individual his freedom to speak and worship as he wishes," said the President. "The American people will not be deceived by any one who attempts to suppress individual liberty under the pretense of patriotism."

It was the final third of the President's address, broadcast by all major radio chains, that was devoted to a statement of his intentions in the primary campaigns. He gave his own definitions of liberal and conservative, progressive and reactionary, and to his listeners posed the question:

"To which of these general schools of thought does the candidate belong?"

The President's announcement that as Chief Executive he would not ask for the election of Democrats as opposed to Republicans or any other political party was followed by the statement that an election could not give to the nation a firm sense of direction if it involved parties "which merely have different names but are as alike in their principles and aims as peas in the same pod."

Containing an emphatic restatement of New Deal objectives sandwiched in between a survey of the accomplishments of the last Congress and his expressed primary campaign plans, the President's address was regarded by seasoned observers as the most challenging utterance that has come from him since he declared war on the "economic royalists" in his Franklin Field acceptance speech in 1936.

Sounds Primary Keynote

Sounding the keynote of the primary contests the President said that "in simple frankness and in simple honesty, I need all the help I can get." He added the statement that he saw signs of getting more help in the future from many who "have fought against progress with tooth and nail."

Expressing a complete lack of sympathy with his opponents and some associates who, he said, had asked him to do or say something to "restore confidence," the President said it was the same group that had been demanding more and more concessions to their views before they were willing to admit the possession of "confidence."

"It is because you are not satisfied, and I am not satisfied, with the progress we have made in finally solving our business and agricultural and social problems that I believe the great majority of you want your own government to keep on trying to solve them," the President said.

With apparent appreciation of the importance of a Congressional majority to the attainment of his projected social and economic reforms, Mr. Roosevelt called for support from Democrats, Republicans, Farmer-Labor, Progressive, Socialist "or any other" schools of political thought. He wanted it "clearly understood" that his remarks tonight were addressed to them all.

Mentions Congressional Acts

In his recitation of the accomplishments of the recently adjourned Congressional session the President mentioned such enactments as the Farm Bill, wage-hour legislation, the projected anti-monopoly investigation, provision for complete Federal regulation of civil aeronautics, low-rent housing projects, authorized spending for recovery and relief, and for upbuilding of the national defense.

To these the President added "the attitude of the Supreme Court toward constitutional questions" which, he said was "entirely changed" as a result of a "lost battle which won a war." Recalling his message outlining the judiciary reorganization program, he remarked that "its real objectives have been substantially attained."

"Its recent decisions are eloquent testimony of a willingness to collaborate with the two other branches of government to make democracy work," Mr. Roosevelt continued, adding that "no single judge is any longer empowered to suspend a Federal statute on his sole judgment as to its constitutionality."

But, as the President viewed the recent Congressional session, one of its noteworthy accomplishments had been its response to "the devotion of the American people to a course of sane, consistent liberalism."

Finds Congress Understanding

To the Congress he attributed an understanding that "under modern conditions government has a continuing responsibility to meet continuing problems," and that government could not take a holiday "just because a few people are tired or frightened by the inescapable pace of this modern world in which we live."

President Roosevelt asked his listeners not to let "any calamity-howling executive with an income of $1,000 a day, who has been turning his employes over to the government relief rolls in order to preserve his company's undistributed reserves, tell you—using his stockholders' money to pay the postage for his personal opinion—that a wage of $11.00 a week is going to have a disastrous effect on all American industry."

President Roosevelt said he wanted it clearly understood that when he referred to "liberals" he had in mind believers in progressive principles of democratic, representative government and not "the wild man, who, in effect, leans in the direction of communism," which he said was just as dangerous as fascism.

After defining liberals as those recognizing the need for new remedies to meet new conditions, the President described the conservative school as those failing to recognize the need for Federal intervention to meet these problems, and proposed to leave them to "individual initiative and private philanthropy."

This latter school, he said, believed "that we ought to repeal many of the things we have done and go back to the gold standard, or stop all this business of old-age pensions and unemployment insurance, or repeal the Securities and Exchange Act, or let monopolies thrive unchecked; in effect, to the kind of government we had in the Twenties."

These were the definitions and

the standards by which the President said, as head of the Democratic party, he proposed to help the American people select their candidates in the coming primary elections. He knew, he said, that neither in the primaries or the November elections would the voters fail "to spot the candidate whose ideas have given out."

June 25, 1938

CAN ROOSEVELT DRAW NEW PARTY LINES?

His Aim to Separate Liberal and Conservative, A Historian Holds, Runs Counter to Traditions

By HENRY STEELE COMMAGER

IT is seldom that Congressional elections and the primaries preceding them arouse the intense interest which this year's campaign commands. The nation has been anxiously watching the outcome of Mr. Roosevelt's attempt to "purge" the Democratic party of conservative elements; throughout the land men and women are wondering whether the November elections will forward the President's desire to remold our chief political parties along liberal-conservative lines.

Not long ago Mr. Roosevelt, in announcing that he would make known his stand in some of the Democratic primaries, said that "an election cannot give a country a firm sense of direction if it has two or more national parties which merely have different names but are as alike in their principles and aims as peas in the same pod." In the clash within all parties between liberals and conservatives, the President aligned himself with the liberals.

Mr. Roosevelt is right in his assertion that the electorate cannot go intelligently about its political business if the major parties do not stand for clearly defined policies, do not offer real alternatives. And it is a commonplace that the major parties of today, and of the past, are in many respects "as alike in their principles and aims as peas in the same pod." Even in 1936, it will be recalled, the Republican party pledged itself to fulfill most New Deal policies—only with variations in method and cost—while in earlier years the situation was even more confused. Nor do the major parties pretend to any unity; it is a no less hackneyed observation that each of the two major parties contains all shades of political opinion, all extremes of social and economic philosophy.

Mayor La Guardia's Republicanism is as well authenticated as Senator Vandenberg's; Senator Glass glories in the title "Democrat," and so does Maury Maverick. The laborers of the great Northern cities, many of them of Southern European stock, Catholic in faith, decidedly wet on the liquor question, and tolerant on the question of racial equality, are for the most part Democrats; so too are

Southern farmers, of Anglo-Saxon stock, Protestant, dry, and skeptical of racial equality. Eastern business men, industrialists, bankers, stockholders, are for the most part Republicans; so too are Western farmers, burdened by tariffs which their Eastern allies demand and by high freight rates which Eastern investors require.

ALL this is nothing new, nor is it difficult to understand if we recall the history of political parties in the United States. Almost from the beginning our party alignments have been illogical and fortuitous, and with the passing years their illogical and fortuitous character became increasingly marked.

The Jeffersonians were, or meant to be, liberal Democrats, but the curious alliance of North Carolina farmers with the New York machine was remarked even in 1800, and Aaron Burr was as far from Jefferson in political faith as is Al Smith from Franklin Roosevelt. Nor was the confusion confined to the new Democratic party. The Federalist party was more unified, but even here there were intriguing groupings, South Carolina planters in alliance with New England merchants reluctantly supporting a candidate who had little use for either group.

Throughout the nineteenth century, with brief exceptions, the party situation remained confused. The Republicans, eager for high tariffs, railroad subsidies and new banking legislation as for free soil, chose for their standard-bearer the humble Abraham Lincoln and cemented a strange alliance of Eastern business and Western agriculture which endured until 1932; the Democratic candidate who received the largest popular endorsement was another Illinois lawyer, less interested in slavery than in railroads and the development of the West.

BUT it was after Reconstruction that the ingredients of the major parties became most bewildering. In the twenty years from 1876 to 1896 the two parties were so much alike that even their spokesmen found difficulty in discovering legitimate issues, and campaigns were fought on per-

sonalities and past records. Not political conviction, but the determination to maintain white supremacy and the hatred of carpetbaggers kept the South solid to the Democratic party; not political conviction, but the determination to enjoy office and its spoils and to prolong the punishment of Rebels, animated spokesmen of the Republican party of the North and the West.

When a real issue finally came along —free silver—it split both parties asunder. For once, in that exciting year of 1896, the parties appeared to divide along class and sectional lines. For once, they appeared to espouse clear-cut issues. But the internal wounds were quickly sutured, if not healed, and by 1900 Bryan was welcoming Tammany back into the fold and the Republicans were naming the liberal Theodore Roosevelt for the Vice Presidency. With Roosevelt's accession to the Presidency it became once more impossible to distinguish between the two great parties in principles and aims.

BRYAN, however, more fully than any other political leader, did attempt to unify his party with common political principles, to win over liberals of all classes and to purge the organization of reactionaries. This was the meaning of the dramatic fight in the Baltimore convention of 1912 when the Great Commoner tried to read out of the party all "members of the privilege-hunting and favor-seeking class." His strategy was successful, temporarily, and Woodrow Wilson, who profited by it, adopted it.

The first Wilson administration was not unlike the first administration of Franklin D. Roosevelt. The Democrats, long out of office, were willing for a time to drop factional disputes and follow an inspired Presidential leadership. In 1916 Wilson was still in undisputed control of his party, but after the election there were signs of revolt. The famous appeal of 1918 to return a Democratic Congress was rebuffed, and thereafter Wilson's leadership was discredited and his party at loggerheads.

Nor was the Republican Theodore Roosevelt more successful in welding his party into a unified progressive organization. The Old Guard never learned, but it never surrendered, and it outlasted the impetuous Rough Rider. By 1909 it was once again in control of the party machinery and in position to dictate party policies. The Progressives fought back, and in 1912 they bolted. The bolt did not last, but the Progressive bloc did, La Follette and Norris retaining the Republican label but fighting the organization.

The situation was not clarified in the decade of the Twenties. There was little to choose between the two Ohio editors whom the parties nominated in 1920, and less to choose between Coolidge and Davis in 1924. So alike were the two great parties, indeed, that the elder La Follette led a bolt of farmers and laborers which uncovered five million independent voters. By 1928 the parties managed to differ on the prohibition question, but, as if to compensate for this boldness, the Democratic candidate confessed himself a convert to the protective tariff. It took the great depression to reveal fundamental differences of policy among Americans and canalize those differences along party lines.

NEEDLESS to say, the discordant and disjointed character of the membership of the major parties has made for confusion in the political scene. It has been almost impossible to get a popular referendum on any important issue. With each party representing all shades of opinion, with each party forced to conciliate elements from all classes, all sections and all interests, it has seemed the common sense of the matter to evade or straddle every dangerous issue. Thus no voters could tell where the major parties stood on the questions of neutrality in 1916, the League of Nations in 1920, prohibition in 1924. The list of issues that the major parties have successfully evaded is an impressive one: woman suffrage, tariff, farm relief, taxation, prohibition, water power, foreign affairs are merely the most obvious.

Yet this situation is not without its compensations and advantages. It is easy to denounce the parties for being hodge-podges of opinion and interest, but we must not forget that this very incoherence has made for strength and unity. Historically the parties have been the great unifying forces in American history, and when, in 1860, the parties became sectional, the Union split.

We have escaped, in this country, the strife which seems to result from parties which represent particular sections, particular classes, particular interests.

Fitzpatrick in The St. Louis Post-Dispatch

A critic looks at the Democratic donkey.

We have not, as yet, a real labor party, a farmers' party, a business party, a party of the employed or of the unemployed, a party of the East or the West, the North or the South. We have but two major parties, and both represent cross-sections of American life. The experience of most European nations would indicate that this is a healthy situation.

YET there is no reason why the major parties cannot represent cross-sections of American life and still stand for distinct aims and principles. Few will challenge the generalization that our political problems would be simplified if the two major parties did divide along clear-cut lines, if they did represent consistent and coherent principles. This was what Bryan attempted to achieve for his own party during his years of leadership; it was what Wilson struggled for, as Governor and as President. And this is what is implied in President Roosevelt's address of last June and in his present campaign.

But the student of history may be skeptical of the effectiveness of this policy. It is not without significance that neither of our major parties has ever agreed for any length of time on a consistent body of principles, and that those parties which have been able to impose agreement upon a consistent body of principles have never achieved the status of major parties.

It would seem that Americans do not want, perhaps do not trust, parties that concentrate on particular issues and appeal to special groups, classes or sections. And nothing, apparently, is more dangerous to a party than to incur the suspicion that it represents a class or sectional

interest. It is this which will doubtless prevent either a farmer or a labor party from attaining national status. And the suspicion that the Republican party had become an upper-class business men's party was not without effect in the catastrophic defeats of 1932 and 1936.

Instinct, rather than reason, argues for parties that differ on means rather than on ends, for parties that represent cross-sections of voters, interests, classes and sections, for parties that are common denominators of the average American. Thus a party is apparently safest, a President most successful, when assailed from both left and right; when criticized by business for pro-labor policies and by labor for favoritism to business; when charged by city dwellers with favoritism to farmers and by farmers with neglect; when challenged by the wealthy for extravagance and by the poor for inadequate relief expenditures. It is suggestive that the Roosevelt Administration has thus been a target for both the left and right for six years, and that Roosevelt himself has retained his popularity almost unimpaired.

THE fact is that there is little room in the United States for parties that differ on fundamental issues. This country is fortunate beyond any other great country in that its people present a united front on almost all basic questions of the nature and purpose of government. Almost all Americans, and certainly all parties, are agreed on the necessity of maintaining democracy, and there is a very general agreement upon the nature and implications of democracy.

Republicans and Democrats

may differ upon the power issue, but the difference is one of means, not ends. Liberal and conservative Democrats may quarrel over the reorganization of the Supreme Court, but their quarrel reveals that both are concerned with effectuating democracy. Dorothy Thompson and Heywood Broun may seem far apart on questions of government finance, but the chasm which appears to separate them is in reality but a gently sloping valley.

To appreciate the superficial character of these differences we have merely to contrast the American scene with the German, the Italian, the Russian, the Spanish or even the French. The American political scene is like that in England or in the Scandinavian countries. And it is the democracies that have been able to solve their problems peaceably.

The task of party reorganization is, then, by fortunate necessity, a limited one; the area of reform a circumscribed one. In addition, the task of party reorganization is not doctrinaire or academic. It is very practical. For what, after all, are parties? They are groups of men organized to get control of the offices and run the government. This is the only definition that makes sense, historically and pragmatically. We must remember that the Federal Constitution made no provision for parties, nor were they recognized by law until almost our own time. The Fathers of the Constitution outlined an admirable form of government, and went off and left it; parties had to take over the skeleton and clothe it in flesh and blood and animate it.

IT is parties that run our government, and this is their proper business. They perform the endless, hard, prosaic job of getting out the voters, selecting candidates, drawing platforms, campaigning, and the hundred other things that we take largely for granted. In the course of performing these tasks they have built up large and powerful organizations embracing thousands of workers, and they have inspired deep-seated loyalties to themselves.

The American political parties are, indeed, the oldest and the largest in the world. They have their own organization, interests, codes of loyalty and purposes. They can, on occasion, be infused with a common idealistic purpose, directed from a common center. But such occasions are rare and, historically, brief. A party can function without a platform, if it has an organization, but it cannot function effectively without an organization, no matter how appealing the platform. Every practical politician knows this, and President Roosevelt, like his great predecessors in the party, Wilson and Bryan, is a practical politician.

President Roosevelt's determination to unify his party about a coherent set of liberal principles will excite applause from idealists, but misgivings in the minds of more realistic students. For the unification of a major party on a body of predetermined aims and principles runs counter to our historical experience. A powerful and magnetic leader can impose his own aims upon his party, whip recalcitrants into line and drive out the opposition. Bryan was able to do this—for a short time. Wilson tried it, and succeeded—for a short time.

Theodore Roosevelt was able to name his successor and dictate his platform, but within two years the successor had caved in to the Old Guard and the platform was forgotten.

FOR, as Lord Bryce pointed out half a century ago, Presidents come and go, but Congress goes on forever. Presidential leadership is ephemeral; party organization is permanent. Democratic Congressmen know, now, that they will have to satisfy their constituents as to their loyalty to the President and the New Deal. But they know, too, that within two years there will be a new President, and new problems, while the organization will

still be doing business at the old stand. It is an awkward dilemma; there is little doubt that many hardened politicians will solve it by a skillful grasping of both horns.

Nor must we forget that it takes two parties to make an issue. President Roosevelt may be able to consolidate his party around his own liberal principles, but there is no reason to believe that the Republicans will play his game by acquiescing in the hazardous role of the champions of conservatism. If the Republican party should do this, under the leadership of such a man as Hoover—then, indeed, the political atmosphere would be wonderfully cleared. But then, indeed a miracle would have oc-

curred. It is almost beyond the realm of possibility that the Republicans would permit themselves to be jockeyed into the position of the champions of reaction. All portents, indeed, point in the opposite direction, and there is ground for thought in the recent overtures of the New York Republicans to the Labor party.

It is highly probable that, regardless of Mr. Roosevelt's success this year, or in 1940, the voters will again be presented with a choice not between liberalism and conservatism but between a confused variety of "liberalisms" designed not to clarify thought but to get votes.

September 4, 1938

DEMOCRATIC FOES OF COURT BILL WIN

All Eight of the President's Opponents, Three Directly Opposed, Are Upheld

Special to THE NEW YORK TIMES.

WASHINGTON, Sept. 15.—With the failure of President Roosevelt to eliminate the Democrats marked for the "purge" in Georgia, Maryland and South Carolina, all of the party's Senators who sought renomination after having fought the Supreme Court Bill and other Administration measures have been successful in the primaries.

The eight Democratic Senators who opposed President Roosevelt's Court Bill and sought renomination have been successful. Mr. Roosevelt made a direct fight on three: Smith of South Carolina, Tydings

and George. There was no direct opposition by the Administration against Senators Clark of Missouri and McCarran of Nevada. In Iowa, defeat for Senator Gillette was suggested by Harry L. Hopkins, WPA administrator, but the Senator won in the primary. Senator Van Nuys of Indiana was renominated in convention after the State party leaders, who once read him out of the party, invited him nevertheless to stand for renomination. In Connecticut, Senator Lonergan was renominated by the State convention.

Representative O'Connor, seeking renomination in the Sixteenth New York district, is the last on the "purge" list. In many quarters his position in his primary race was considered to have been strengthened by the Administration upsets.

In any event, barring a complete rout in November, there will be in the Senate a group of independent Democrats who may be expected to scrutinize Administration measures carefully. In particular, if Senators Tydings of Maryland, George of Georgia and Adams of Colorado are elected, they will be found opposing

vast expenditures.

There have been intimations from some of the younger Administration advisers that they hoped the President would withdraw from certain conservatives the usual State patronage. Such a step would be likely to lead to the formation of a solid conservative bloc, including Senator Harrison of Mississippi, Bailey of North Carolina and Byrnes of South Carolina. Vice President Garner's sympathies most likely would be enlisted.

According to some of the Senators considered dominant in this group, serious consideration is being given to an attempt to elect a new majority leader. Friends of Senator Harrison still resent the moves that dragged away two Senators from his support at the last moment and gave the leadership to Senator Barkley of Kentucky. Senator Harrison has been told by some of the conservatives that enough votes are available to elect him leader of the next Senate if he will seek the post, but he has declared that he wished to devote himself to writing a tax bill.

The Mississippian's refusal, however, has not ended discussion on the part of some of the New Deal dissidents of moves to elect a new leader. Senator Byrnes of South Carolina, who occupies neutral ground, but favors the scaling down of expenditures, has been mentioned as a man upon whom they might center in seeking a candidate for leader. Not all of the conservatives, however, are in favor of a break with Senator Barkley. They argue that they can more effectively mold legislation by letting the leadership rest with the Kentuckian whom President Roosevelt indorsed for renomination.

The apparent victory in the Georgia primary of Representative Cox, and the renomination of Representative Howard W. Smith in Virginia, have a decisive bearing on the alignment of the Rules Committee, since their election, looked upon as a certainty, will leave the conservatives in control of the committee's powers over the progress of legislation, even if Chairman O'Connor is defeated in New York next Tuesday.

September 16, 1938

COALITION IN CONGRESS TO HALT THE NEW DEAL URGED AS THE REPUBLICANS APPRAISE VICTORY; GAIN 80 IN HOUSE, 8 IN SENATE, 11 GOVERNORS

TAXPAYERS REVOLT

By ARTHUR KROCK

The average taxpayers of the nation—the group which, for want of a better name, is called the "middle class"—restored the country's traditional two-party system in Tuesday's elections and set up an opposition to the overwhelming Administration majority in Congress

and a guard on its control of the administrative agencies of the New Deal. This was the message to be read in the almost complete returns of the polling in the forty-eight States.

Republican gains in Congressional seats, governorships and local offices were scattered over twenty-four of the forty-eight States, all outside the South. But the South, dominated by the Democratic party, had previously rejected the President's attempts to require complete

obedience from its members of Congress. Therefore the decisions of the twenty-four States on Tuesday were annexes to what the South, in party primaries, had previously indicated.

Late last night it was evident that the Republicans had gained eighty seats in the House of Representatives at Washington, fifty more than the Democratic leaders expected, added eight—perhaps nine—Senators, made great inroads in the Farm Belt and among the

Northern Negroes, and added eleven Republican Governors in the nation, a number that may be increased to thirteen.

Curb on New Deal Urged

On this news the New York stock market rallied strongly and Republican leaders in the country began to suggest a Congressional coalition to prevent any further advance of New Deal programs. Among these leaders was Herbert Hoover, whom President Roosevelt defeated in 1932.

119

The impression grew, on a study of the returns, that the President's New Deal political combination, devised in 1932 and perfected in 1934 and 1936, had been broken by the uprising of the average American citizens. This combination was made up of farmers, organized labor, the Northern Negroes, the regular Democrats, intellectual independents and a wandering group of left-wing radicals.

On Tuesday in twenty-four States many farm votes were lost; there were visible divisions in organized labor; the Negro vote divided in Ohio and Pennsylvania; and, according to Alf M. Landon, the Republican Presidential nominee in 1936, many regular Democrats broke away from their party moorings. He made a statement to that effect.

The directness of the attack on the left-wing radicals, who have been allies or members of the New Deal, was particularly to be noted in Wisconsin, Michigan and Minnesota. In these States Republican nominees for Senator or Governor upset New Dealers, Progressives and Farmer-Laborites, sounding a knell for the third party of the La Follette brothers in Wisconsin, the Democratic-C. I. O. alliance in Michigan, and the Roosevelt-Benson coalition in Minnesota.

The trend implicit in these happenings sufficiently impressed Mayor Fiorello H. La Guardia of New York, a prime mover in the New Deal radical combinations, and induced him to arrange to meet with Senator Norris of Nebraska, Governor Murphy of Michigan and the La Follette brothers soon in an effort to get the left-wing Democratic allies back into formation.

In their successful effort to regain major party status and erect a real opposition in Congress and the various States, many Republican candidates gave encouragement to the Townsend plan and other devices to pension elderly citizens. Most Republican candidates also endorsed the social objectives and many of the legislative expressions to that end of the New Deal, putting a period to Old Guard Republicanism.

They based their criticisms on New Deal methods and personnel, on government by administrative agencies, on taxation, on monopoly of office and on the budget. These arguments finally proved effective after three defeats at the polls, each one more crushing than the other.

James A. Farley, Democratic National Chairman, frankly conceding that the Republicans had shown greater gains in the States and in Congress than he had anticipated, said in a statement that "the country as a whole is still strongly behind the humanitarian policies of President Roosevelt." But, speaking privately, Democratic leaders made no secret of their fear that the country was displeased with the form and administration of those policies.

Leading Elements in Defeats

They ascribed the series of defeats to these elements of the population, all enthusiastic supporters of the first New Deal—1932 to 1984—and the second New Deal—1934 to 1936:

Small business men, resentful of increased taxation and vexatious methods of collection. Employers,

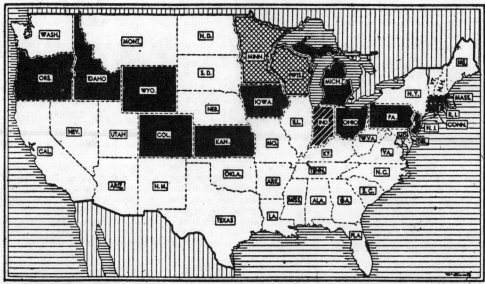

MAP SHOWING STATES RECAPTURED BY REPUBLICANS IN TUESDAY'S ELECTION

In 1936 the electoral votes of every State, except Maine and Vermont, a total of 523, were won by Franklin D. Roosevelt. Thirteen States, appearing in black on this map and casting 183 electoral votes, were carried by the Republicans Tuesday, twelve of them electing Republican Governors, and New Jersey choosing a Republican Senator. In addition Indiana (designated in black with white lines) is giving an increasing lead to Willis, Republican, running for the Senate. In the two States which appear in lighter shading, a Republican will succeed a Farmer Labor Governor in Minnesota and a Progressive in Wisconsin.

large and small, disaffected by the one-sided nature of the Wagner Act and the fiscal features of the Social Security Act. Citizens at large, distrustful of the methods and delegated powers of the New Deal agencies at Washington.

To these groups others could be added, and will be, as the final details of the voting are available and close analysis is made possible. But this explanation of what happened Tuesday is another way of saying that what the moderate Democrats have been saying to the President for six years has been accepted by the country.

Should Mr. Roosevelt agree with this analysis of the causes for what is now definitely revealed as a major political reverse, the Democratic leaders are hopeful that his future course will be definitely altered and an effective barrier placed against the Republican march toward victory in 1940. This would mean the relegation of the White House inner circle—T. G. Corcoran, Harry L. Hopkins, Harold L. Ickes, Herman Oliphant, Leon Henderson and others—and the restoration to intimate and respected counsel of Mr. Farley and the moderate Democratic leaders in Congress. It would mean a halt to extreme programs and methods, seeking to make over the country in a hurry, and an acceptance of the doctrine of "festina lente."

If the President, however, decides to ignore this counsel and move back into the battle-lines of 1937 and 1938, the argument in favor of a temporary coalition in Congress between the moderate Democrats and the newly elected Republicans will carry greater weight.

The severest blows to the President and the New Deal on Tuesday were delivered by the voters of New Jersey, Michigan, Kansas, Minnesota, Pennsylvania, Iowa, New Hampshire, Oregon, Ohio and Rhode Island. In these States particularly the President made the cause of the Democratic candidates his own. His endorsements were personal. Appeals for votes were made largely in his name. The voters were told that the issue was between

liberalism and reaction, that if they approved the New Deal they should support the Democratic ticket. The failure in each instance was signal, although the National Administration and the party committee used all the resources of the Federal establishment.

The victories of the New Deal and the President were won in New York, California and North Dakota. Senator Robert F. Wagner, the outstanding legislative standard-bearer of the regime, was re-elected, though by 350,000 less votes than in 1932, and with him went Representative James A. Mead for the short term. The "purge" of Representative John J. O'Connor was completed in the Sixteenth New York District. The Democratic ticket was triumphant in California, after the President had transferred his unsuccessful endorsement of Senator McAdoo to Sheridan Downey, the "$30-every-Thursday" sponsor. And North Dakota elected a Governor a supporter of the New Deal.

But overshadowing these marginal successes were the Republican gains in Congress, in State houses and in county offices—enumerated above. The loss of Pennsylvania, New England and the Farm Belt States broke the combination of 1932 and 1936. New Jersey voters demonstrated that the WPA could be overcome in a popular surge against a political deal, despite the vote of Hudson County. Michigan registered strongly against the administration's C. I. O. alliance and Governor Murphy's toleration of the sit-down strike. And in New York State, though the American Labor party cast about 410,000 votes, it failed to elect any candidate on its Republican coalition ticket.

Observers noted that had Mr. Farley's strategy been displaced by Mr. Hopkins's in New York and Illinois, as it was in other States, the results of Tuesday's elections would probably have mounted to a total disaster. It was on Mr. Farley's insistence that Governor Lehman was drafted to run again, and the outcome demonstrated that the

national chairman was correct in his belief that no other Democrat could defeat Thomas E. Dewey. When he first urged this the White House was still nursing its grievance against the Governor for making a point of balanced budgets and for opposing the Supreme Court enlargement bill. Had the White House vetoed Mr. Farley's plan, New York would have been in the Republican column also.

In Illinois the White House inner circle—the ones Mr. Farley calls the "amateurs"—wanted a renomination for Senator Dieterich, a faithful and 200 per cent New Dealer who was obliging enough to shift his vote for majority leader from Senator Harrison to Senator Barkley at the President's request. But Governor Henry Horner refused to accede and managed to designate for Senator a moderate Democrat, Representative Scott Lucas, over State's Attorney Michael Igoe of Chicago, an unswerving Presidential follower. On Mr. Farley's advice, the Administration did not interfere, and Mr. Lucas was elected Senator. For this reason Illinois was also missing from this election's Republican column.

As the final returns are counted, the New Deal has been halted; the Republican party is large enough for effective opposition; the moderate Democrats in Congress can guide legislation; the third-term movement has been strongly checked; Federal relief money in elections has been overcome by voters in several States; the White House circle, which invented the Supreme Court bill and the "purge," has been discredited; a barrier against New Deal extension program and candidates has been set at the gate of the 1940 Democratic Convention; the sit-down strike and the Democratic-C. I. O. alliance have been emphatically rebuked; the Farm Belt has revolted; the country is back on a two-party system; the McNutt Presidential boom in Indiana has collapsed with the McNutt State ticket, and legislative authority has been restored to Congress.

GAINS OF G. O. P. RETARD MOVE FOR THIRD PARTY

Republican 'Rebirth' Changes National Outlook, Deferring for Years the Growth of Any Minor Group

By DELBERT CLARK

WASHINGTON, Nov. 19.—In the midst of all the confused and contradictory interpretations of the Congressional elections last week, there appears one reasonably important result from the Republican gains. That is the probable deferment for several years of the rise to an influential position of any new or currently minor party.

For several years past it has seemed apparent to impartial political observers here that sooner or later, and probably sooner, some new "third" party was likely to become a potent factor in our national life. The underlying causes which would give rise to such a strong new party are not now materially altered, these observers believe, but the growth of their influence has been somewhat retarded.

The picture as it was in 1932, in 1934 and in 1936, and as it appears now in 1938, is somewhat along this line:

In 1932, inchoate liberal influences, impelled by a wave of irresistible discontent with a deepening depression, swept the Republican party out of power and into what one great Democrat once termed "innocuous desuetude."

In 1934 the Republicans, tottering but still game, but with no particular program beyond a desire for public office, took another beating in the mid-term Congressional elections, and the New Deal increased its already top-heavy majority in Congress.

The Defeat of 1936

In 1936 the Republicans tried again, this time with the rich Presidential prize in view. They suffered by far the heaviest defeat in the long history of the party.

Three successive defeats, each worse than the preceding one, gave rise again to talk of the "death" of the G. O. P.; this time with more reason than at any other time. It seemed likely that one of two things must happen: either the Democrats, with their unwieldy and unnatural coalition of liberals and conservatives, must split two ways, bringing about a natural liberal-conservative realignment, or a new and more trend-conscious party must arise to take the place of the Republicans.

A third possibility was for the Democrats to follow the historic course of parties long and securely in power and turn conservative; in which case, it was presumed, the conservative Republican remnant would gradually disappear, and left-wing elements of all parties could be expected eventually to coalesce into a new and vigorous radical opposition, in the traditional manner of political parties in Great Britain as well as in the United States.

First Blow to New Deal

Now, however, the Republicans in 1938 have gained some eighty seats in the House of Representatives and a respectable increment in the Senate. It is the first electoral setback the New Deal has suffered, and restores to at least a semblance of life the old Republican party. There appears little if any doubt that "third"-party prospects, either right or left wing, have been considerably dimmed for several years to come.

CHEERED UP

Harris & Ewing

Senator Vandenberg found G. O. P. life renewed by election result.

The reasons are not hard to find and the confusion among the left-wing groups does not lend any brilliance to their immediate outlook.

Last week, right after the election, Mayor La Guardia of New York, in a clarion call to "hold that line," invited all liberal leaders to meet with him this week in Washington. At this writing they have not met, and there has been no further word of the meeting.

The Mayor was not entirely specific as to the purpose of the conference, and some unkind ones suggested that it was to put himself in the position of a great liberal leader for 1940. Others were willing to believe that his foremost intent was to form a compact liberal bloc, regardless of party affiliation, which would try to preserve the legislative gains of the Roosevelt Administration and seek more of the same.

One reason, it seems, why the La Guardia conference has yet to be held is that the Mayor found it difficult to assemble a group of liberal leaders who would think anywhere near alike on the fundamentals of public policy.

It should be remembered that Mr. La Guardia is a member of a minor party—the American Labor party, classed as a creation of Labor's Non-Partisan League, which, in turn, is the political bureau of the C. I. O. He sought to rally to his standard a number of individuals who pay fealty to a variety of political groups, and who were far from agreement on what they wanted for the future.

Differing Desires

Some wanted to let matters alone, to permit things to work themselves out in leisurely style. Some wanted to tighten up the Democratic party and make it a compact, thoroughly liberal organism. Some wanted an entirely new party. Some didn't, but thought a third term for President Roosevelt would be a good idea. Virtually their only common ground was their sorrow that the Republicans had gained eighty House seats.

It seems reasonably evident, then, that the various leftists groups are not at all in a position to unite in any new party for awhile yet.

If the Republicans had gained control of the House, instead of merely building up their minority to a position of respectability; if the legislative achievements of the New Deal were in immediate jeopardy; if there had appeared the prospect of a national political stalemate for two years, they could be expected to be in session right now, choosing a party name and adopting a declaration of principles. But none of these things has happened. The traditional rival of the Democratic party has gained materially in strength, although considerable doubt has been expressed as to just how many real conservatives replaced just how many real liberals in the House and the Senate.

Be that as it may, the electors voted against Democrats and for Republicans, and the "go slow" signal is generally considered to have been hung out.

Still the "White Hope"

The Democratic party, for all the shaking it experienced on Nov. 8, is still the majority party by a great deal, and is still the "white hope" of the liberal nuclei all over the country. It is more so now, presumably, than it was a year ago. Then, for example, the American Labor party polled a heavy vote in New York and began looking wistfully westward toward the dissatisfied farmers. This year, for one reason or another, its recorded vote was greatly reduced. It cannot hope, on the basis of that record, to lead the nation out of the wilderness tomorrow, or even next week.

On the more conservative side, the National Progressive party of Wisconsin with its liberal name, its conservative platform, and its mysterious emblem, seems to be suffering from acute malnutrition. It has lost control of the government of its stronghold—Wisconsin—and has lost several seats in Congress. As liberal, befitting its name, or as conservative, befitting its platform, its future remains most uncertain, even though its leaders, Senator Robert M. La Follette Jr. and Governor Philip F. La Follette, insist that the recent elections marked not the end, but the "beginning" of its history.

Still on the conservative side, the little group of devoted gentlemen who agreed with Senator Vandenberg of Michigan that it were better to burn the G. O. P. and let a new, enlightened conservatism rise, like the phoenix, from its ashes, have recently found their eyes growing brighter, their hearts less heavy. May be the Republican party has yet some life in its ancient carcass, some red blood in its hardening arteries. The Senator wanted to wait until 1938 to find out. Now it is safe to wait until 1940.

All the symptoms of radical revolt from a too-mild Democracy were in evidence a year ago. John L. Lewis, whose followers and whose union funds were of great assistance to the New Deal, launched into an intermittent campaign of destructive criticism, with persistent hints of a bolt into a greener pasture. On the other side of the fence, the old-line, conservative Democrats had grown restive and were wondering how they could drop the New Deal.

A Twofold Effect

A year later, the Republican success seems likely to have a twofold effect: first, to pull the leftists together again under the only winning banner they know, in full realization that the one sure way to lose is to divide their strength; second, to calm down the conservative Democrats, who really want to keep in power in Washington.

If these latter feel that the Republican gains will slow up the New Deal, they can well afford to bite their lips for another two years until they can change leaders; if they do not find this so, they still dislike Republicans as a matter of inbred principle.

Four years from now it may be a different story. If the Democrats win again, but with a conservative platform and leadership; or if the Republicans should somehow snatch life from death and win the Presidency, then a new, strong liberal party would seem to be almost a certainty.

November 20, 1938

REPUBLICAN TREND TO LIBERALISM SEEN

Gallup Survey Indicates 55% of Members Want Party to Be Less Conservative

---

VIEWS ON 1940 ARE GIVEN

77% Believe Such a Change Would Help to Win the Next Presidential Election

---

The dominant pull of sentiment among the rank and file of Republican voters today is toward the liberal rather than the conservative side, according to a poll taken by the American Institute of Public Opinion, of which Dr. George Gallup is director.

The survey showed that a large majority of party voters believe the Republicans have a better chance of winning in 1940 with a liberal candidate and a progressive platform than with a conservative candidate. Giving the results of the poll, the institute said:

"Using sampling methods which have proved accurate in two national elections, and more than fifty State and local elections in the last four years, the institute put the following two issues to a cross-section of Republican voters in every State.

"'Do you tihnk the Republican party should be more liberal or more conservative than it was in the 1936 presidential campaign?'

More liberal 55%
More conservative 17%
About the same 28%

"'Do you think the Republican party has a better chance or a worse chance of winning in 1940, if it nominates a liberal candidate and adopts a liberal platform?'

Better chance 77%
Worse chance 14%
Makes no difference 9%

"The significance of this sentiment within the rank and file of the party is two-fold. First it indicates that Republican candidates of a liberal turn of mind are likely to go into the G. O. P. convention next year with more popular support than conservative candidates. Second, it shows that the rank and file do not at the present time agree with those Republican party leaders who think the G. O. P. should establish itself as the party of out-and-out conservatism categorically opposed to the New Deal and all its reforms. Instead, they appear to agree with the viewpoint recently expressed by both Senator Borah and Alfred M. Landon, that the party should avoid an ultra-conservative attitude.

"The desire of the Republican rank and file to liberalize the party is not new. Institute surveys a year and a half ago found the same sentiment existing. In December, 1937, for example, nearly half of Republican voters (47 per cent) wanted the party to become more liberal than it had been in the 1936 campaign.

"Among the rank and file of the Democratic party, on the other hand, previous surveys have found a tendency to move in the opposite direction—toward the conservative side. Although the largest group think the policies of the New Deal should be continued pretty much along present lines, nevertheless the number who think the Administration should be more conservative is far greater than the number who think it should be more liberal."

July 6, 1939

MAIN CAMPAIGN ISSUES NOW BEING FORMULATED

Presidential Contest, It Appears Now, Will Be Over Methods and Policies Rather Than Deep Principles

By TURNER CATLEDGE

WASHINGTON, Feb. 24—The report of the Republican Program Committee, headed by Dr. Glenn Frank, former president of the University of Wisconsin, obviously was intended to set up a chart of issues on which the Presidential and Congressional elections of 1940 might turn. How far it accomplished that end is yet to be fully disclosed, but from the report and first reactions to it, it is clear even now that this year's national political fight, as in 1936, will be waged much less over broad principles than over governmental management of policies already established.

In this regard the so-called Frank report confirmed a situation which had been indicated rather eloquently by the pre-convention Republican candidates themselves, to wit: That, with perhaps a few exceptions, the party has no thought of countering the basic purposes of the New Deal but rather to ask a mandate for change in some of the methods and personnel by which it has striven toward those purposes in the last few years.

In the matters of human relief, labor relations, social security, international affairs, national defense, farm aid and the like, the issues suggested by the Frank program, as well as by the Republican Presidential candidates, are largely questions of method and management.

Stand for Economies

Even on the subject of fiscal policy, where the division seems to run deepest, it is difficult to stretch the issue into the proportions of a principle, for regardless of President Roosevelt's frequent glorification of the policy of "spending to save," the current position of the Democratic high command is outwardly toward economies.

And on such a Republican subject as tariff-making the Republicans hesitate to go all the way and demand outright repeal of the Hull reciprocal trade agreements program. They propose the more subtle route of Senate ratification of all trade pacts as if they were treaties.

The fact is that the issues fundamental to these questions of method were settled in the election of 1932, and apparently so definitely that the titular opposition party has no stomach to raise them anew. There was a basic question raised then between Mr. Hoover and Mr. Roosevelt over the doctrine of Federal husbandry, and the country disposed of it in such a manner that, from all present appearances, most of the new functions undertaken by the central government will stay.

The margin for issues, therefore, although wide enough for a heated campaign, is not without its limitations. Attempts have been made by certain politicians and disinterested observers these last few days to work out a basic cleavage between what they conceive to be the "optimistic" approach of the Frank program, with its emphasis on greater freedom for business and encouragement of new enterprise, and what Republicans like to call the "defeatist" attitude of the New Deal, with its leanings toward control and regulation of fully matured national economy. The New Deal program is considered by its own authors as an "agglomerate," the cohesive element of which is the personality and political sagacity of Franklin D. Roosevelt.

Roosevelt the Issue

Thus it is that Mr. Roosevelt himself becomes the main issue in the campaign just now getting under way, and he will continue to be the principal point of discussion whether he runs for a third term or not. He will be attacked for his methods rather than for his principles and purposes.

Within this somewhat circumscribed sphere men like Mr. Frank and the 200 members of his program committee, and the candidates themselves, are fishing for issues upon which the election campaign next Fall may be fought. Moreover, it is up to the Republicans to point up and pursue the issues for, regardless of who is nominated on the other ticket, the Democrats will necessarily be on the defensive. Whether the Democratic nominees like it or not, they must stand, at least publicly, on the record which bears their party's label.

Under these circumstances, and considering certain specific manifestations, one of the chief campaign issues will be the fiscal policies of the Roosevelt administration. It is recognized by the New

"AIN'T HE HAVIN' FUN?"

Carlisle in The Des Moines Register

A Western comment on the third-term question.

Dealers themselves that one of their most vulnerable spots is the deficit spending of the last few years. They can get no satisfying comfort, moreover, from the fact that so many people, high and low, might have benefited personally from these unusual expenditures.

They know that some of the chief beneficiaries are among those clamoring for more orthodox government finances. They are aware, too, that the fiscal question is taking greater hold in the country at large, and well do they remember the emotional campaign made on the same subject, and on the same side now espoused by the Republicans, by Mr. Roosevelt back in 1932.

Problem of the NLRA

Another issue high on the list is the Roosevelt Administration's record in the matter of labor relations. No one expects the Republicans to go so far as to advocate repeal of the National Labor Relations Act. The authority and propriety of the Federal Government

in safeguarding the right of collective bargaining, although strictly New Dealish in its concept, is not to be questioned. But the methods and men by which and by whom the safeguarding has been attempted will certainly be brought into the controversial side of the campaign.

The question of relief must of necessity be an issue in some degree, but here again no one is seriously going to advocate discontinuance of the Federal Government's responsibilities in this regard. From all appearances the Republicans will advocate reductions in cost, divorcement of politics from the administration of relief, and greater control in the hands of local governments.

The Republicans will raise the general issue of the attitude of the New Deal toward business. And here, again, the New Dealers themselves see a weak place in their armor. They are hoping for such an upturn in business conditions that this question will be obviated.

The Republicans will likely demand repeal of the President's monetary powers, as well as numerous other authorities granted by Congress to the Executive since 1932. If Mr. Roosevelt or any one of his choosing is the Democratic nominee, this demand will be resisted with all force, and likely with the argument that in the present state of world affairs this government must be equipped to move swiftly to protect itself on all fronts, including the financial.

On Foreign Affairs

It will be hard to work up issues over national defense and international relations. In the first place the Republicans are split on the subject of international affairs. Secondly, all can agree, Republicans and Democrats alike, that this country must be kept out of war at all honorable cost. As to national defense, all are for an "adequate" measure of it, and the "adequacy" is something that no man or group

of men will hardly attempt to define in an election campaign.

If Mr. Roosevelt decides to seek a third term all other issues will most likely melt in the heat. "Traditional American government" will be made the sole question in that event, and the country likely will see the bitterest kind of campaign.

Even if another is selected to carry the Democratic banner, the election may turn more on personalities than on issues. A candidate can pack more vote-getting or vote-repulsing force into his own person than could be set down in endless volumes of party platforms. The Republican pre-convention campaign is being waged now mostly by personalities and not by slates of dogma.

In short, the Republicans are looking more for a man than for issues. Issues count, to be sure, but they cannot be divorced from the man who eventually must espouse them.

February 25, 1940

REPUBLICANS NOMINATE WENDELL WILLKIE

RIVALS WORN DOWN

Willkie Garners Votes as His Opponents Free Their Delegates

By TURNER CATLEDGE
Special to THE NEW YORK TIMES.

MUNICIPAL AUDITORIUM, Philadelphia, Friday, June 28—Wendell Lewis Willkie of New York, Indiana-born president of the Commonwealth & Southern Corporation, former Democrat who has been a foe of the New Deal, was nominated early this morning for President of the United States by the Republican party.

His nomination came on the sixth ballot of the party's twenty-second annual convention, marking one of the greatest upsets in the history of the convention system in America. A newcomer to the party, opposed by its veteran leaders, and lacking the usual organization to build up a candidate's strength, Mr. Willkie came into the picture here on the crest of a popular wave which not only did not diminish but finally asserted itself on the convention delegates themselves.

Starting out in tonight's balloting in third place, Mr. Willkie went forward in a series of thrusts until he

went over on the sixth. He first eliminated Thomas E. Dewey, who came to the convention with the largest number of delegates, then Senator Taft, who was supported by many of the regular leaders. He outran a challenge which Senator Taft's smooth-operating machine was finally able to start.

Rush to Willkie Is Begun

After the middle of the sixth ballot the convention turned into a rush for the Willkie standard. Governor Bricker of Ohio, who had led Mr. Taft's largest single block of delegates on the floor, sought at that time to make the convention's vote unanimous, but Joseph W. Martin Jr., the permanent chairman, ordered the roll-call to proceed to the end. Finally, however, the ballot was made unanimous at 998, two of the 1,000 delegates being absent from the hall.

Managers of other candidates at once offered their congratulations and those of their principals. All sought to close ranks in the spirit of the enthusiasm which swept the hall and the galleries when it became apparent that Mr. Willkie had been nominated.

The main business now left to the convention is the selection of a candidate for Vice President. Mr. Willkie will be requested tomorrow to indicate his desires as to a running mate. That the second-place candidate will come from the West is practically certain, and suggestions already were being made as to the availability of Senator

Charles L. McNary, Minority leader of the Senate, while some of the defeated Presidential candidates also were discussed.

Rivals to Support Willkie

After the nomination had been made unanimous, J. Russell Sprague, manager of Mr. Dewey's campaign, said the young prosecutor had asked him to express his thanks to his supporters and his assurance that he would give Mr. Willkie his whole-hearted support in the coming campaign.

David S. Ingalls, Senator Taft's campaign manager, said it had been a great fight and that Senator Taft and those who supported him would be behind Mr. Willkie, whom he acclaimed as the next President.

Governor James of Pennsylvania and Senator John Thomas of Idaho joined in making the nomination unanimous.

Former President Hoover sent his congratulations directly to the winner stressing that Mr. Willkie was the choice of a free convention and undoubtedly would move on to victory.

Mr. Willkie considered for a while going before the convention tonight and accepting the nomination, but canceled the plan because of extreme fatigue. He had been constantly on the move, with hardly three full hours of sleep a night since last Saturday. He sent a message, however, thanking the delegates for nominating him in "a free convention," and announcing that he was ready and willing to

fight to victory for the Republican party.

Chairman Martin, who read the message, told the delegates and spectators that the candidate was well prepared for the task, and asked the support of every delegate and every man and woman in America "who believes in American principles."

Mr. Willkie will set up headquarters in New York after a brief rest. He does not propose to step out of the role of a New York citizen or make his campaign from an Indiana front porch. He believes his nomination represents something new and dynamic in American politics.

He plans to resign as president of the Commonwealth and Southern as soon as he can place his affairs in order and devote his entire time to the campaign. He has been on a vacation status with his company during the pre-convention drive.

Mr. Willkie developed imposing strength even from the first ballot. On that vote he stood at 105, with 360 for Dewey, 189 for Taft and the remainder of 1,000 scattered among eight others. His showing was greater than had been expected.

The galleries, pro-Willkie throughout, set up the shout: "We want Willkie, we want Willkie, we want Willkie." They cheered each vote cast for their champion and when, at the end of the second vote, he had reached 171, the throng fairly roared. The delegates, however, remained calm and intent.

June 28, 1940

123

ROOSEVELT RENOMINATED ON FIRST BALLOT

BY 'ACCLAMATION'

By TURNER CATLEDGE
Special to THE NEW YORK TIMES.

CHICAGO, Thursday, July 18—President Roosevelt was renominated early this morning for a third term for President of the United States by the Democratic National Convention.

The President's renomination, which climaxed a "draft" movement carried out in contravention of one of the oldest and best established traditions in American politics, came theoretically by "acclamation," but the move to nominate unanimously or by acclamation came in a dramatic surrender by Postmaster General James A. Farley and others who had stood with him against a third-term nomination.

Mr. Farley, Vice President Garner and Senator Millard E. Tydings of Maryland all had been placed in nomination in pursuance of the third-term protest. Before the move to nominate by acclamation was made by Mr. Farley more than 150 of the convention delegates had cast votes against Mr. Roosevelt, distributing them among the three named above and Secretary Cordell Hull. Governor Cooper of Tennessee explained to the convention that Mr. Hull was not and had never been a candidate.

How the Ballot Stood

The total vote before it was made unanimous was Roosevelt 946 13/30, Farley 72 27/30, Garner 61, Tydings 9½ and Hull 5 2/3.

There was but little demonstration when the convention made its momentous decision. The first thing that happened was a song led by Phil Regan, "When Irish Eyes Are Smiling," the convention's song to Mr. Farley.

Mr. Roosevelt's nomination was clinched when New York voted, giving 64½ votes for him, 25 for Farley, 1 for Secretary Hull with 3½ missing. New York's sixty-four votes put the President over the 548 votes needed for renomination. There was no notice given by the delegates of this momentous hour.

It was shortly before 1 A. M.

Senator Barkley, Permanent Chairman of the Convention, appointed a committee composed of Senators Byrnes of South Carolina, Charles F. Sawyer of Ohio and Mayor Edward F. Kelly of Chicago to notify the President of his renomination.

The convention adjourned shortly before 2 A. M. until 2 o'clock in the afternoon, when it will meet to name a candidate for Vice President.

Acceptance Held Certain

The President is counted as certain to accept the nomination, despite a statement made to the convention in his behalf that he did not desire to run again. His acceptance is expected to come in a radio message to the convention before it adjourns.

He also will be expected now to indicate his choice for Vice President from among a growing list of potential candidates. He may also take occasion in replying to the Convention "draft" to express his ideas on a platform adopted by the party and which, it is understood, did not satisfy him completely by the language of its statement against intervention by the United States in foreign wars.

The Roosevelt "draft" had been indicated from a time long before the delegates assembled in Chicago, and it moved relentlessly to its successful conclusion under the management of inner circle New Dealers, assisted by Senator James F. Byrnes of South Carolina as floor leader.

Just before the roll-call of States started for the nomination, the convention howled down a proposal of Representative Elmer J. Ryan of Minnesota to restate the party's stand against a third term.

The crowd that witnessed Mr. Roosevelt's renomination was one of the largest ever to gather in the great Chicago Stadium. Delegates and alternates and spectators jammed every available inch of the floor and galleries. Outside, long lines of disappointed visitors, many of them ticket holders, were unable to push inside but stood by to hear the result.

July 18, 1940

ROOSEVELT ELECTED

BIG ELECTORAL VOTE

Large Pivotal States Swing to Democrats in East and West

POPULAR VOTE CUT

First Time in History That Third Term Is Granted President

By ARTHUR KROCK

Over an apparently huge popular minority, which under the electoral college system was not able to register its proportion of the total vote in terms of electors, President Roosevelt was chosen yesterday for a third term, the first American in history to break the tradition which began with the Republic. He carried to victory with him Henry A. Wallace to be Vice President, and continued control of the House of Representatives by the Democrats was also indicated in the returns.

But in many of the larger States so many precincts were still missing early this morning, and the contest in these States was so close, that Wendell L. Willkie, the Republican opponent, whose name Mr. Roosevelt never mentioned throughout the campaign, refused to concede defeat. He said it was a "horse race," and that the result would not be known until today. He went to bed in that frame of mind.

As the returns mounted there seemed little, however, to sustain Mr. Willkie's hope. New York, Massachusetts, Connecticut, Rhode Island, Pennsylvania, Ohio and Illinois, of the greater States, all appeared to have been carried safely by the President. The Solid South had resisted all appeals to revolt against Mr. Roosevelt's quest for a third term. The Pacific and Mountain States were following the national trend.

States sure or probable for the President are:

Alabama, Arizona, Arkansas, California, Connecticut, Delaware, Florida, Georgia, Illinois, Kentucky, Louisiana, Maryland, Massachusetts, Missouri, Minnesota, Mississippi, Montana, Nevada, New Hampshire, New Jersey, New Mexico, New York, North Carolina, Ohio, Oklahoma, Pennsylvania, Rhode Island, South Carolina, Tennessee, Texas, Utah, Virginia, West Virginia and Wisconsin—electoral votes, 429.

States sure or probable for Mr. Willkie:

Kansas, Maine, Michigan, Nebraska, North Dakota, South Dakota, Vermont—electoral votes 51.

States doubtful or insufficiently reported:

Colorado, Idaho, Indiana, Iowa, Oregon, Washington and Wyoming—electoral votes, 51.

The Electoral Vote

Listing as doubtful nine States, including several like California, Ohio and Indiana, which seem certain to join the Democratic column, there were at 3 A. M. only 51 electoral votes in possible dispute. The President had an apparently certain total of 429, while with more or less security in Mr. Willkie's column were only 51 votes.

No shift or series of shifts could affect the electoral result and the indications were that the President's total would reach from 420 to 470.

Either figure would be much less than the nearly clean sweeps he had in 1932, when he carried forty-two States, and in 1936, when only Maine and Vermont went Republican. And unless the Far West and the Mountain States shall be shown to have given incredible majorities and late returns from the Eastern States pile up the President's votes higher than indications seem to make possible, Mr. Roosevelt's popular majority will be far less than he had against Herbert Hoover and Alf M. Landon.

It appeared early this morning that a maximum of 5,000,000 and a minimum of 2,000,000 would represent the final difference between the popular votes cast for the two major Presidential candidates. The Associated Press tabulation at 1:50 A. M. was 14,879,930 for Mr. Roosevelt and 11,980,499 for Mr. Willkie.

The United Press figures about the same time were Roosevelt 13,-130,419, Willkie 10,726,517.

President Greets Neighbors

The President, early today, greeted a torchlight procession of his Hyde Park neighbors and, standing on the portico of his mother's house, gave a promise to continue to be "the same Franklin Roosevelt you have known."

Mr. Willkie would not accept the increasing statistics of his opponent's victory, and at 12:30 o'clock this morning he told a cheering group of his supporters assembled at the Hotel Commodore to keep stout hearts and the fight will ultimately be won. About 1,500 persons were present.

"I hear some people shouting 'don't give up!'" he said. "I guess those people don't know me."

Remembering the eye-lash finish of 1916, when the tSates west of the Mississippi River joined Ohio to re-elect Woodrow Wilson, this was a natural attitude for Mr. Willkie to take. But Ohio had aready been conceded by the Cleveland Plain Dealer, one of his chief press supporters. In Indiana, his home State, he was trailing.

In Pennsylvaria the story was the same. Connecticut, center of the defense industry, had already entered the Democratic column.

In these circumstances no set of other States can give Mr. Willkie the 266 electoral votes required for a majority.

The campaign which now has drawn to a successful conclusion for the President has been remarkable in many ways. First there was the unexpected nomination of Mr. Willkie by the Republicans. Then there was the so-called "draft" of the President at Chicago, followed by his loud inaction as a candidate.

There followed the sledge-hammer campaign of Mr. Willkie which so alarmed the Democratic strategists that they prevailed on Mr. Roosevelt to abandon his plan and to make a vigorous campaign. This he did, with the indicated result of having turned a close and possibly adverse political situation into an electoral landslide.

First Third Term in History

Mr. Willkie based his attack on "politics and incompetence" in the defense program, the spending and deficits of the New Deal, the "drift toward war" which, he said, the President was abetting and the general New Deal philosophy, and defended the two-term tradition.

The Democratic defense was that domestic issues were unimportant, that it was perilous to interrupt the foreign policy of the President and Secretary Hull, and that the Axis powers were anxious for Mr. Roosevelt's defeat.

The President not only did not mention his opponent by name at any time in the campaign; he never discussed the third-term issue or made any defense of his domestic policies or record. Everything was pitched on foreign policy and the mass benefits conferred by the New Deal, and this, plus the personality of Mr. Roosevelt, was successful in making the President the first Chief Executive in history to whom the two-term limitation was not applied. Also he is the first President in history to have been nominated for a third term.

His triumph, though great, was marked by a considerable recession of political strength from his high tide of 1936; by the defection of his own Vice President, John N. Garner, and by the long though passive insurgency of James A. Farley, twice the President's campaign manager.

Of all the voters recorded Vice President Garner was not among them, having apparently refrained from voting for the only time in his long career as a test against the third term and the "draft."

All over the country the vote was heavy and was registered early in the day. Rain, sleet, snow and cold weather here and there did not appear to have cut down the volume.

Considering the bitterness of the campaign, the personal attacks made on the Presidential candidates and one another by speakers, and also Mr. Willkie's assaults on the Democratic bosses in New York, Chicago and Jersey City, the continuous report of an orderly election throughout the country was not the least of its unusual features.

The control of the House of Representatives was also a stake in the election, but not of the Senate, since it is almost mathematically impossible—and certainly impossible politically——for the Republicans to overcome the Democratic majority there. That will endure until 1942.

November 6, 1940

PRESIDENT REJECTS A PARTISAN STAND IN CONGRESS RACE

By W. H. LAWRENCE
Special to The New York Times.

WASHINGTON, Feb. 6—President Roosevelt declared today that the United States at war needed Congressmen regardless of party who will back up their government and who had a record of backing up the country in an emergency regardless of party.

Mr. Roosevelt thus chose for himself a role in the 1942 elections different from that adopted in 1918 by President Wilson, who asked the country to return a Democratic House of Representatives and Senate—an appeal which was turned down by the voters.

Some political observers regarded the President's press conference remark as a toning down of the Monday speech by Edward J. Flynn, Democratic National chairman, who said that "no misfortune except a major military defeat could befall this country to the extent involved in the election of a Congress hostile to the President."

"Vast confusion," Mr. Flynn added, "would inevitably result if we had a President of one party and a House of Representatives, for example, of the opposition party."

Non-Partisan Stand Stressed

The President laid emphasis on the phrase, regardless of party, and he used it not once but twice in replying to a newspaper man's request for comment on Mr. Flynn's declaration, which had aroused considerable criticism by Republicans, who accused him of breaking the political truce which had been in effect since the United States entered the war.

None among his auditors believed that the President was counting himself out of participation in the Fall election campaign, and his statement suggested that he might throw his influence against any Senator or Representative up for re-election whose record would not satisfy the President as to his readiness to support the Administration in emergency matters.

February 7, 1942

Willkie Wins Republicans To His Anti-Isolation Stand

National Committee Unanimously Adopts a Resolution Affirming 'Obligation to Assist' in World Cooperation

By JAMES A. HAGERTY
Special to The New York Times.

CHICAGO, April 20—Wendell L. Willkie succeeded today in removing the brand of isolationism from the Republican party when the national committee unanimously adopted a resolution declaring its realization that the United States had "an obligation" for world cooperation.

The success of the 1940 Presidential nominee in having adopted his point of view on the necessity of the party repudiating isolationism came after an oral discussion which lasted the entire afternoon.

With his resolution referred to a committee of seven, only two members of which were regarded as favoring it and the other five believed to prefer a resolution prepared by Senator Taft of Ohio, which had no declaration on future foreign policy, agreement on a substitute resolution was not reached until nearly 6 o'clock.

The controversial paragraph, on which agreement was reached and which was substituted for the paragraph drafted by Mr. Willkie, read as follows:

"We realize that after this war the responsibility of the nation will not be circumscribed within the territorial limits of the United States; that our nation has an obligation to assist in bringing about understanding, comity and cooperation among the nations of the world in order that our own liberty may be preserved and that the blighting and destructive processes of war may not again be forced upon us and upon the free and peace-loving peoples of the earth."

In a statement telephoned to Chicago and made public here by his secretary, Lem Jones, Mr. Willkie hailed this declaration as an abandonment by the party of isolationism and a recognition of the necessity for the United States to assume a positive position in world affairs both now and after the war is over.

Viewed by Taft as Innocuous

When asked for comment, Senator Taft, whose resolution was offered by David S. Ingalls from his State, said:

"I think it was a great mistake for the national committee to express any policy at all at this time on post-war action, but the committee has drawn the teeth of the Willkie proposal so that no one can take exception to the language employed."

Senator Taft explained that the committee had taken out of the Willkie proposal a reference to "responsibilities" which sounded to him like another League of Nations.

He added that the responsibility of the United States never had been "circumscribed," that the United States always had had an "obligation" outside its own territory and that the statement in the resolution was so general that Democrats and Republicans alike could agree on it.

The rest of the resolution adopted, which was offered by Wallace Townsend of Arkansas, chairman of the resolutions committee, followed the lines of the original Willkie resolution quite closely but with changes in phraseology. There was no controversy except on the foreign policy declaration.

Willkie Consulted by Telephone

At an open session of the committee the Willkie and Taft resolutions were presented by Walter S. Hallanan of West Virginia and Mr. Ingalls.

Werner E. Schroeder of Illinois introduced a short one prepared by Senator Brooks calling for complete support of the Administration in the war effort, and Alexander Smith of New Jersey, who held the proxy of Daniel E. Pomeroy, offered another urging prosecution of the war to victory and for assumption by the United States of its full share of responsibility in insuring the future preservation of peace.

Under the rules, these resolutions were referred without debate to a resolutions committee appointed by Representative Joseph W. Martin Jr., the National Chairman, as follows: Mr. Townsend, chairman; Messrs. Hallanan, Ingalls and Schroeder; Mrs. Gladys E. Heinrich Knowles of Montana, Mrs. Horace H. Sayre of Oklahoma and Robert P. Burroughs of New Hampshire.

During this committee's seven hours of deliberation there were several telephone conversations with Mr. Willkie in New York.

Eastern and Far Western members of the committee were generally in favor of the original Willkie resolution, most of the opposition to it coming from some, but by no means all, those from States between the Rocky Mountains and the Alleghenies.

Subsequent adoption of the committee's resolution by the national group was generally recognized as a victory for Mr. Willkie and regarded by some members as a sort of preview of a 1944 national platform plank which would have an immediate effect in this year's Congressional elections.

In a statement issued after adoption of the resolution, Mr. Willkie said:

"The resolution affirms the belief of all true Americans that this war must be prosecuted relentlessly and without reservation until we have won an absolute and irrevocable victory over each and every one of our enemies. It likewise appropriately declares against any appeasement.

"But even more significant, the resolution as passed adopts principles of international relations which are essential to the survival and effectiveness of the Republican party and of this nation, namely, an abandonment of isolationism and a recognition of the necessity for the United States to assume a positive position in world affairs both now and after the war is over.

"The next job for Republicans to do is to see to it that in the coming primaries candidates are nominated not alone for Congress but for other positions of public influence who have the courage to declare and who believe sincerely these principles and their necessary implications.

"Thus the Republican party can win and become a great force for liberal enlightened government."

Besides its declaration on foreign policy, the committee's resolution demands prosecution of a relentless offensive war to complete victory with no appeasement or compromise. It pledges preservation of the two-party system and constitutional government.

The resolution also calls for elimination of political appointments in the war machinery, drastic reduction of non-essential expenditures and the elimination of non-essential domestic regulations.

With obvious reference to the Japanese attack on Pearl Harbor, the resolution demands that the government "coordinate our diplomatic, military, naval and air strategy so that we shall not be taken by surprise with further disastrous results" and calls for conduct of the war by a unified command.

Confidence in Martin Voted

In answer to suggestions that Representative Martin should resign as chairman because of his "isolationist" position before the attack on Pearl Harbor, the committee, on motion of Mr. Schroeder, adopted a resolution expressing confidence in his wise leadership and pledging continued co-operation.

In a speech to the committee Mr. Martin declared that the Republicans in Congress had kept their pledge to the President of full support and cooperation in the war effort.

"We will continue to keep it regardless of the provocations that may arise," he went on. "The safety and security of our country must come first. We are Americans above Republicans.

"The past year has been difficult for every one and it has been particularly so in the political field. Previous to the entrance of our nation into war there was a lively debate and discussion as to the best way to preserve the peace. This was an American issue and naturally divided both of the major parties.

"The dastardly attack of the Japanese on Pearl Harbor made it necessary for our country to enter the war. In our hour of national peril we as a nation have the one great objective to win the war and make secure the liberties and freedom of our people."

Martin States Role of Party

Mr. Martin then explained that full support of the war by the Republicans did not mean that they should abandon other responsibilities to the people of America.

"There is no security or freedom unless the ruthless Axis powers are crushed," he continued. "Neither is there any freedom unless we preserve the American form of government.

"We do not intend to let the two-party system of government be liquidated while we are fighting the foreign dictators. We do not intend to let constitutional government perish here in the United States.

"We do not intend to let private enterprise become a memory.

"We do not intend to let ours become a socialistic State.

"The American system of government must be upheld and it can only be sustained by a strong, vigorous, fighting Republican party."

Mr. Martin said that in preparation for the Congressional campaign he planned a meeting of State chairmen and vice chairmen in St. Louis or Cincinnati.

The National Committee elected Ezra Whitla of Idaho as vice chairman to succeed Samuel F. Pryor of Connecticut, who resigned. The Willkie forces won a minor victory by electing Mrs. Pearl Wates of Alabama as a member of the executive committee to succeed Mr. Whitla over R. B. Creager of Texas, who was the Taft floor leader at the 1940 National Convention.

The committee elected the following new members to fill vacancies: Henry Leonard, Colorado; J. Kenneth Bradley, Connecticut; C. H. McNulty, Florida; Mrs. Dudley C. Hay, Michigan; Harry Sandager, Rhode Island; George T. Hansen, Utah.

April 21, 1942

REPUBLICANS IMPERIL CONTROL OF CONGRESS

MARGIN IS NARROW

Democrats Get Nominal 220 to Rule House— G. O. P. Gains 43

By W. H. LAWRENCE

Mounting Republican gains—43 in the House of Representatives and nine in the Senate on the basis of still incomplete returns—imperiled the Roosevelt Administration's control of Congress, although the Democratic party remained nominally in the majority in both houses.

As each tabulation of the vote in Tuesday's election revealed new inroads yesterday on Democratic strength which surprised even the most optimistic Republican chieftains or pre-election prophets, the New Deal majority in the House and Senate was reduced to the lowest level since President Roosevelt took office in 1933. Frequent combinations of Republicans and conservative Democrats appeared a probable block to Presidential proposals, especially on domestic issues.

The flood of Republican ballots in the first wartime election in twenty-four years was interpreted generally as a reflection of the voters' dissatisfaction with the conduct of the war, both at home and abroad, but in no sense was it regarded as any manifestation of a desire to slacken the war pace or the preparations which must be made at home for victory.

Dewey to the Forefront

Thomas E. Dewey's 590,000-vote plurality in the race for Governor of New York led in the Republican sweep across the country, and placed Mr. Dewey in a leading position in speculation over the 1944 Presidential nominee, along with three other re-elected Governors—John W. Bricker of Ohio, Harold E. Stassen of Minnesota, and Leverett E. Saltonstall of Massachusetts, all of whom won third terms. There was a net gain of three Republican Governors, with some contests still in doubt.

But the most impressive gains were in Congress, which has been under attack consistently by both President Roosevelt and his critics for alleged failure to play its full role in the prosecution of the war.

Early this morning the indicated make-up of the new Congress which will convene on Jan. 3, as compared with the present Congress, was:

SENATE

	New.	Present.
Democrats	56	65
Republicans	38	29
Progressive	1	1
Independent	0	1
In doubt	1	0

HOUSE

	New.	Present.
Democrats	220	256
Republicans	208	165
American Labor Party	1	1
Progressives	2	3
Farmer-Labor	1	1
Independent Democrat	0	1
In doubt	3	*8

*Vacancies.

Notable New Dealers Lose

Notable was the caliber of men whom the Administration lost, especially in the Senate. Gone from the new Congress will be such New Deal stalwarts as these:

Senator George W. Norris, 81-year-old Independent and dean of Congress, who ran a poor second in a three-way race, losing to a Republican, Kenneth Wherry, despite the backing of President Roosevelt.

Senator Prentiss M. Brown, Democrat, of Michigan, leader in the anti-inflation fight, defeated by racket-busting Circuit Judge Homer Ferguson, a Republican.

Senator Josh Lee, Democrat and sponsor of prohibition for soldiers, defeated by E. H. Moore, Tulsa oil man, who is the second Republican to be elected from Oklahoma in thirty-five years.

Representative John M. Houston, only Democrat in the Kansas delegation, unseated by Representative Edward H. Rees, Republican, in a contest produced by redistricting.

Representative Richard M. Duncan of Missouri, a member of the Ways and Means Committee.

Representative Clyde Williams of Missouri, ranking majority member of the Banking and Currency Committee, who did much to put through the price control legislation.

Montana Result in Doubt

In all, the Republicans won nineteen Senate seats, taking eight of them from Democrats and one from an Independent, Mr. Norris. The outcome of the Montana contest was in doubt. It was between Senator James E. Murray, Democrat, and Wellington D. Rankin, Republican, and brother of the pacifist, Jeanette Rankin, only member of the House to vote against the declaration of war on Japan. Republicans won a short-term seat in the Senate from West Virginia, now held by a Democrat, but this term will expire with the beginnig of the new Congress.

The Democrats retained fifteen Senate seats, but took none from the Republicans.

In the thirty-two State Governor contests decided Tuesday, the Republicans elected sixteen Governors and the Democrats thirteen. Republicans will succeed Democratic Governors in New York, California, Connecticut and Michigan. The Republicans lost the Governorship of Wisconsin, held by Julius P. Heil, to the Progressive, Orland S. Loomis. With two Gubernatorial contests still in doubt, the national line-up was: Democrats twenty-three, Republicans twenty-two and one Progressive.

In the House, the turnover was general as the Republicans defeated forty-six Democratic incumbents, and lost only five themselves.

States in which the Republicans gained more than one seat from the Democrats were: California, 2; Connecticut, 4; Illinois, 4; Maryland, 2; Missouri, 5; Nebraska, 2; Ohio, 6; Pennsylvania, 3; Washington, 3, and West Virginia, 2.

The trend was general. The issue of pre-Pearl Harbor isolationism appeared to play no major part in the election, from a national point of view, as both interventionists and isolationists were elected and defeated.

Fish's Election Confirmed

Notable among the isolationists who won in campaigns in which their foreign policy votes were at issue were Representative Hamilton Fish, Republican, of New York, returned to office in President Roosevelt's own Twenty-sixth Congressional District despite the opposition of the President, Governor-elect Thomas E. Dewey, and Wendell L. Willkie; and Representative Stephen A. Day, Republican, who was elected Congressman-at-Large from Illinois.

Of 137 House members, who were marked for defeat by interventionist groups for their pre-Pearl Harbor voting record, 110 were re-elected, five were defeated and twenty-two did not participate in the election, having been defeated or failed to run in the primaries.

Notable among the new House members are Clare Booth Luce, author, playwright and advocate of a "tougher" war from the Connecticut Fourth District, and Lieutenant Will Rogers, Democrat and son of the famous humorist who appeared to have unseated Representative Leland Ford, Republican and outspoken foe of the C. I. O. leader, Harry R. Bridges, in the Sixteenth District of California.

Representative Andrew J. May, Democrat, of Kentucky, chairman of the House Military Affairs Committee, who had been marked for defeat by John L. Lewis, president of the United Mine Workers of America, squeezed through by 611 votes, with all but one of the precincts in the Seventh Congressional District reported.

Hook Defeated in Michigan

Representative Frank Hook of Michigan, a 100 per cent New Dealer and vigorous opponent of the Dies Committee, lost out to John B. Bennett, a Republican, in a district in which the party leaders had thought before election that they had only a 50-50 chance.

An influential member of the House Judiciary Committee, Representative Charles McLaughlin, Democrat, of Omaha, was beaten as Nebraska sent a solid Republican delegation to the House at the same time it was electing Wherry over Norris and re-electing Governor Dwight Griswold over Charles W. Bryan, three times Governor and brother of the late William Jennings Bryan, three-time Democratic Presidential nominee.

A colorful addition to the House is William J. Miller, Republican, from Connecticut's First district, who unseated Representative Herman P. Koppleman, a Democrat, who had beaten him in 1940. Although he lost both legs in a First World War aviation accident, Mr. Miller has been an opponent of veterans' legislation which, he contended, would "coddle" veterans excessively.

In Maryland's Fourth Congressional District, where Daniel Ellison beat John M. Wyatt, he was the first Republican elected from that district since 1896.

Romjue of Missouri Loses

Representative Milton Romjue, who had served twelve terms in the House from Missouri's First district, lost to S. W. Arnold, a Republican.

Representative James A. Shanley, Democrat, of the Third Connecticut district, who cooled on the New Deal over the foreign policy issue, was beaten by a Republican, Ranulf Compton, who made foreign policy a campaign issue.

In Indiana, Representative John W. Boehne Jr., serving his seventh term and ranking fourth in seniority on the Ways and Means Committee, was defeated by Charles N. La Follette, a Republican, in the Eighth district. Although his district had been allegedly gerrymandered and Republican leaders did not think he had a 50-50 chance to win, Representative Raymond S. Springer, Republican, came through to victory over Representative William H. Larrabee, Democrat, who made an issue of Mr. Springer's record in opposition to the Administration foreign policy.

A vacancy on the Rules Committee, which controls the flow of legislation in the House and is, therefore, important to the Administration, was created by the defeat of Representative William L. Nelson, Democrat, by Max Schwabe, Republican, in Missouri's Second district.

One of the important Ohio Democratic casualties was Representative Dow Harter, serving his fifth term and influential on the House Military Affairs Committee, where he was chairman of a special committee which recently investigated aircraft production. He led a successful fight for the War and Navy Departments to stop Leon Henderson, Federal Price Administrator, from imposing price ceilings on military matériel.

In the Far West, former Governor Walter M. Pierce of Oregon, a loyal New Deal representative from the Second district, was beaten by Lowell Stockwell, a Republican, and Knute Hill, Washington New Dealer who split with the President on foreign policy, was unseated by Hal Holmes, a Republican. Former Senator C. C. Dill, Democrat, of Washington, tried to win the House seat vacated by Charles H. Leavy, now a Federal judge, but lost to a Republican, Walt Horan, in the Fifth district.

Lost on Many Previous Tests

Even had the Republicans won only thirty to thirty-five seats in the House and a half-dozen in the Senate, which were the pre-election highs in predictions, it was evident that even minor upheavals among Democrats could cause Administration reversals and embarrassments, as experience has shown during the last decade.

In 1933, when the Democratic strength constituted 61 per cent of the Senate and 72 per cent of the House, it is recalled, President Roosevelt sustained defeats in Congress, notably in the matter of reductions in veterans' compensation. In 1934 the Administration underwent more defeats in such matters as cuts in government salaries and on the St. Lawrence waterway treaty.

With 72 per cent of the Senate and 74 per cent of the House, the Administration ran into defeat in 1935 on the World Court and in 1936 on the Soldiers' Bonus Bill and the Passamaquoddy and Florida Ship Canal projects.

The year 1937, when the Democrats had 78 per cent of the Senate and 77 per cent of the House, brought the Supreme Court program to defeat; in 1938 the repeal of the tax on undistributed corporate income, a New Deal innovation, was effected despite administration attempts to save it.

After the 1938 off-year elections, when Democratic control dropped to 7 per cent in the Senate and 60 per cent in the House, the administration fight for a naval base on the island of Guam was lost in 1939, and parity payments for farmers was written into law, while the lending-spending program underwent reverses in Congress.

Last year the Democrats still had 69 per cent of the Senate and 61 per cent of the House, after the 1940 elections, but the farm price guarantees, recently modified, were inserted into the price control legislation. Then, in an economy mood, the Congress killed the Civilian Conservation Corps (the CCC), one of the Administration's favorite and most popular projects.

November 5, 1942

NEW DEAL POWER EBBS AS WAR PACE QUICKENS

President Concentrates on Military Aims Advised by Conservatives

By W. H. LAWRENCE

WASHINGTON, April 3—In this eleventh year of the Roosevelt Administration the influence of the New Dealers on governmental policy is at its lowest ebb. Congress, through a coalition of Republicans and Southern Democrats, is anti-administration on straight-out New Deal issues, and President Roosevelt himself, though he founded the New Deal, is concentrating his energies and attention on problems military and diplomatic in character.

It has been said that the first term was concerned with recovery, the second with reform and the third with war. While this probably is an overgeneralization, it is basically an accurate index of the influence of the New Dealers in Washington. They began as the "brain trust" in 1933, and soon became known as the New Dealers, reaching their zenith somewhere in the second term. Since then their importance in government has diminished steadily.

This is not to say, of course, that the government is being run along anti-New Deal lines. The social changes which were achieved in the first and second terms remain in effect despite the contentions of some critics that they hamper all-out prosecution of total war.

Barriers to Extension

Occasionally there is an effort to extend the political principles of the New Deal, as witness the attempt to impose a $25,000 net limitation on salaries, which Congress already has voted to invalidate, and the "cradle to the grave" social security program advanced by the National Resources Planning Board, which Congress, thus far, has chosen to ignore despite the most urgent representations by the President that consideration should be given to the plan at the present session.

It is in the social security project that the New Dealers see their hope for return to power. They regard it as a perfect fourth term issue whether Congress acts on it or not, and they believe that the far-reaching economic changes visualized in this blueprint for a post-war world are of a character that would require New Dealers to administer them.

The President's principal advisers these days are, with a single exception, conservatives on economic matters or, in the case of the trained Army and Navy leaders, devoid of any clear political complexion.

Harry L. Hopkins, former Works Progress Administrator, former Secretary of Commerce and chief strategist for the Roosevelt forces at the 1940 Democratic convention, is the lone exception. He is a regular White House resident, and is closer to the President than any other man. Moreover, while Mr. Hopkins's critics would deny it vigorously his friends tell you that he has little interest these days in social change or in the progress of New Deal agencies which formerly were his pets.

Others in Inner Circle

The other men whom the President sees most frequently and to whom he has delegated considerable power in the conduct of the war are James F. Byrnes, the Economic Stabilization Director, who was never counted a radical as Senator from South Carolina; Donald M. Nelson, the War Production Board chairman who was executive vice president of Sears, Roebuck & Co.; Admiral William D. Leahy; Prentiss M. Brown, the Price Administrator and a lame duck Senator from Michigan who did not support the Supreme Court or governmental reorganization bills when they were prime New Deal issues in Congress; Chester C. Davis, the new Food Administrator who has been president of the Federal Reserve Bank at St. Louis and who did not hesitate to purge the "radicals" from the Agricultural Adjustment Administration in the early days of the New Deal; Secretary Hull, a conservative Southern Democrat, and Admiral Ernest J. King and General George C. Marshall. In the first two terms organized business as such was pretty well snubbed, but Eric A. Johnston, the young president of the United States Chamber of Commerce, is a frequent caller now.

"Cohen and Corcoran" Split

The old legal team of "Cohen and Corcoran" has broken up. Thomas G. Corcoran has a lucrative private law practice in Washington. Benjamin V. Cohen is, to be sure, general counsel for Mr. Byrnes's Office of Economic Stabilization, but it is Mr. Byrnes who makes the policy there. Leon Henderson who, alone among the New Deal economists, rose to have his own agency, the OPA, had to walk the plank because of the outcries from Congress and the threats of financial starvation for his organization.

In matters affecting business the responsibility for government action rests primarily on men drawn from the business world. One of the New Deal's strongest campaigns was the enforcement of the anti-trust laws, but business leaders complained that the threat of legal action or the necessity of defending actions in court were hampering all-out production, so Congress amended the law to give Mr. Nelson and the War and Navy Departments the power to call off anti-trust suits. Thurman Arnold, who as assistant attorney general in charge of the anti-trust division led the drive to enforce the Sherman and Clayton acts, was kicked upstairs to a position on the Court of Appeals for the District of Columbia.

Some Old Faces Present

Of the Cabinet, only three members, Secretaries Ickes, Biddle and Perkins, qualify in any degree as New Dealers, and two members of the President's official family, Secretaries Knox and Stimson, are registered Republicans.

The long-time significance of all this is not yet clear. It may be that the President, faced with the need for complete national unity to wage global war, has simply called a truce and ordered a halt, possibly temporary in nature, to the extension of the New Deal reforms. The planning board report would seem to support this thesis, and would suggest that the old battle of 1933-41 will be renewed as soon as peace returns.

April 4, 1943

REPUBLICAN STAND PLEASES BOTH SIDES

Some Say 'Mackinac Charter' Cracked Isolationism, but Old Guard Is Happy, Too

CONTINUING FIGHT IS SEEN

By TURNER CATLEDGE

Special to THE NEW YORK TIMES.

MACKINAC ISLAND, Mich., Sept. 8—Those Republicans who came to this secluded spot three days ago intent upon persuading their party's high command to adopt a forthright position in behalf of post-war international collaboration left today outwardly elated, with the assertion that they had succeeded. They conceded privately, however, that their job of obliterating isolationism as a Republican label had just begun.

Similarly happy, outwardly and inwardly, was another group, including most of the old-line organization leaders. They said that the first meeting of the post-war advisory council had come off without a crippling fight between exponents of extreme views which still exsit in the party over future foreign relations. They, too, realized that their task, of keeping the party on an even keel, was a continuing one.

The source of all this satisfaction, and the misapprehension, was the statement of foreign and domestic policy proclaimed by the post-war advisory committee in a literal "spasm" of party unity yesterday. Rereading their declaration in the cold light of dawn, as a ferry boat took them across the Mackinac Straits to the rail junction, whence they departed for their homes, the Republican leaders became more convinced that they had written something with which no one could disagree. Thus, all seemed to feel, the real test had been met: party harmony, so far as they could tell at this distance, had been achieved.

Post-war Pledge is Reviewed

The policy statement pledged support of those attending to "responsible participation" by the United States in "post-war cooperative organization among sovereign nations," to prevent future military aggressions and to attain permanent peace "with organized justice in a free world."

It demanded, however, that every proposition must be studied "with careful regard to the vital interests of the nation," and to its bearing upon "forseeable international developments." If there should be conflict between the two, the statement said, then the United States should follow that policy which would preserve its constitutionalism, as expressed in the Declaration of Independence, the Constitution itself, and the Bill of Rights, "as administered through our republican form of government."

Fuller inquiry into the sources of the language disclosed today that "the Mackinac charter," as some Republicans call it, was a compromise document, even to its declarations on domestic policy, which were rewritten and strengthened after one version had already been distributed to press and radio.

Advocates of a simpler, more direct and more specific foreign policy statement said that they had given ground under pressure of greater numbers, although they insisted that they "cracked the shell" of isolationism. This group, led mostly by New England Governors and other Eastern seaboard delegates, previously threatened to bolt and to file a minority report if the council tried to "back up" on the highly important and provocative international issue.

Minority Report Is Threatened

"I proposed myself to file a minority report if they had attemped to dodge the question," said Senator Warren Austin of Vermont, who, with the other New Englanders, was regarded as having views similar to those of Wendell L. Willkie. Mr. Willkie was not invited to attend and not represented at the conference.

"But what we did, I think, is marvelous, absolutely marvelous," Senator Austin continued. "We have broken through the old shell of isolationism. We have gone farther than we could possibly have gone had we continued the fight. For one thing, we have got away from the overworked word 'cooperation.'"

Governor Raymond E. Baldwin of Connecticut, who led the short-lived "Governors' revolt," held a similar view, and so did Governor Sumner Sewall of Maine. Governor Sewall was the most difficult to bring into the compromise, it was learned.

The Governors might have rallied around the standard of Governor Thomas E. Dewey of New York for an outright military alliance with Great Britain, but the New Yorker did not follow through. Accordingly, advocates of stronger words than were put together are on their way home to think over and plan their next step.

September 9, 1943

HIGH COURT RULES NEGROES CAN VOTE IN TEXAS PRIMARY

Decision, 8 to 1, Holds Denial of Right Because of Race Violates the 15th Amendment

STAND SINCE 1935 UPSET

Roberts, in Dissent to Reed, Chides Colleagues for 'Intolerance' in the Reversal

By LEWIS WOOD
Special to THE NEW YORK TIMES.

WASHINGTON, April 3—Negroes cannot legally be barred from voting in the Texas Democratic primaries, the Supreme Court ruled by eight to one today in a decision of far-reaching significance which upset a nine-year-old ruling and brought a lone but sharp dissent.

Southern members of Congress feared that the decision, while specifically applicable to Texas, could be extended to cover restrictions against Negroes in other States where the Democratic primary is ordinarily tantamount to election.

Senator James O. Eastland of Mississippi declared that the ruling revealed "an alarming tendency to destroy State sovereignty" and amounted to Supreme Court usurpation of Congressional functions.

The majority opinion was written by Justice Stanley F. Reed, who was born in Mason County, Kentucky, and the dissent by Justice Owen J. Roberts, a Philadelphian, the author of the 1935 finding in the case of Grovey V. Townsend, which was overruled.

Justice Roberts criticized his colleagues for reversing former opinions, showing "an intolerance" to views of the former court and assuming "a knowledge and wisdom denied to our predecessors."

Upsetting the previous opinion, he said, "tends to bring adjudications of this tribunal into the same class as a restricted railroad ticket, good for this day and train only."

The present case was brought to the court by Lonnie E. Smith, a Negro. Seeking to vote in the 1940 Texas primary, he presented a poll-tax receipt but the right to vote was denied him because of his race and color.

He sued two election officials of Harris County, asking for a declaration judgment upholding the right of Negroes to vote in the primaries. First argued last November, the issue was reopened in January to permit the State of Texas to present its views.

"Right Secured by Constitution"

In the majority opinion, Justice Reed said:

"It may now be taken as a postulate that the right to vote in such a primary for the nomination of candidates without discrimination by the State, like the right to vote in a general election, is a right secured by the Constitution.

"By the terms of the Fifteenth Amendment that right may not be abridged by a State on account of race. Under our Constitution the great privilege of choosing his rulers may not be denied a man by the State because of his color.

"The United States is a constitutional democracy. Its organic law grants to all citizens a right to participate in the choice of elected officials without restriction by any State because of race.

"This grant to the people of the opportunity for choice is not to be nullified by a State through casting its electoral process in a form which permits a private organization to practice racial discrimination in the election. Constitutional rights would be of little value if they could thus be indirectly denied."

State's View Considered

Discussing a resolution of the Texas Democratic State Convention saying that "all white citizens" are qualified to vote in the primaries, Justice Reed said that Texas had the right to conduct its elections as it wished so long as it did not run afoul of the Constitution or the Federal powers.

He cited the State's view that the Democratic party was "a voluntary organization with members banded together for the purpose of selecting individuals of the group representing the common political belief as candidates in the general election."

Conceding that the privilege of membership in a party might be no concern of the State, he added:

"But when, as here, that privilege is also the essential qualification for voting in a primary to select nominees for a general election, the State makes the action of the party the action of the State."

When the decision in the Grovey vs. Townsend case was written, he went on, the court "looked upon the denial of a vote in a primary as a mere refusal by a party of party membership."

Six years after that decision, however, the court ruled in May, 1941, in the case of United States vs. Classic, that Congress had the right to regulate primary as well as general elections. This 6-to-3 decision, written by Chief Justice Harlan F. Stone, related particularly to Louisiana but covered all primaries.

As a result, the case decided today was brought to the court to clear up "a claimed inconsistency" between the Classic and Lonnie Smith cases. Justice Reed stated the issue as follows:

"We are brought to an examination of the qualifications for Democratic primary electors in Texas, to determine whether State action or private action has excluded Negroes from participation."

Party as "a State Agency"

As Texas primaries are conducted under State authority, he continued, the political party "which is required to follow these legislative directions [is] an agency of the State insofar as it determines the participants in a primary election."

"The party takes its character as a State agency from the duties imposed upon it by State statutes; the duties do not become matters of private law because they are performed by a political party," he held. "The plan of the Texas primary follows substantially that of Louisiana.

"If the State requires a certain electoral procedure, prescribes a general election ballot made up of party nominees so chosen and limits the choice of the electorate in general elections for State officers, practically speaking, to those whose names appear on such a ballot, it endorses, adopts and enforces the discrimination against Negroes, practiced by a party entrusted by Texas law with the determination of the qualifications of participants in the primary."

He held that this violated the Fifteenth Amendment, which prohibits a State from abridging the right to vote because of race, color or previous condition of servitude.

As to "Continuity in Decision"

In conclusion Justice Reed said that the majority were not "unmindful of the desirability of continuity of decision in constitutional questions," but that the court throughout its history had felt free to "re-examine" these issues and when convinced of error had never felt obliged to follow precedent.

Justice Roberts, in his dissent, said that in another case of this term, he had expressed his views "with respect to the present policy of the court freely to disregard and to overrule considered decisions and the rules of law announced in them."

"The tendency, it seems to me, indicates an intolerance for what those who have composed this court in the past have conscientiously and deliberately concluded, and involves an assumption that knowledge and wisdom reside in us which was denied to our predecessors," he went on.

"It is regretful that in an era marked by doubt and confusion, an era whose greatest need is steadfastness of thought and purpose, this court, which has been looked to as exhibiting consistency in adjudication, and a steadiness which would hold the balance even in the face of temporary ebbs and flows of opinion, should now itself become the breeder of fresh doubt and confusion in the public mind as to the stability of our institutions."

Among Southern members of Congress commenting on the decision, Senator Walter George of Georgia said that party primaries should not be subject to court control beyond punishment of fraud, and Senator Burnet Maybank of South Carolina declared that his State would do what it could to "protect our white primaries."

Representative Nat Patton of Texas said that Texans would "find some way to work out a Democratic primary for white folks."

Biddle Called Upon to Act

The National Association for the Advancement of Colored People, through its counsel, Thurgood Marshall, sent a letter to Attorney General Francis Biddle saying:

"We are sure that the Justice Department will now recognize that criminal jurisdiction over interference with the right to vote extends to primary elections.

"The decision in this case, along with the decision in United States v. Classic, clearly establishes the illegality of the practice, in most of the States of the deep South, of refusing to permit qualified Negro electors to participate in party primary election.

"Immediately after the 1942 primary the NAACP sent to the department a large number of affidavits from Negro citizens in Texas, Arkansas and South Carolina concerning the refusal to permit them to vote in primary elections. All of these complaints have been investigated by the FBI, but no further action has been taken.

"Now that there can be no doubt that such exclusion is a Federal crime, we urge you to issue definite instructions to all United States Attorneys, pointing out to them the effect of these decisions and further instructing them to take definitive action in each instance of the refusal to permit qualified Negro electors to vote in primary elections in States coming within the purview of the two decisions."

April 4, 1944

DEWEY AND BRICKER NAMED ON 1ST BALLOT

DEWEY AT STADIUM

Says Plank on Foreign Policy Represents Big Area of Agreement

ASKS AID OF YOUTH

Military Phase of War Will Not Be Part of Campaign, He Vows

By TURNER CATLEDGE
Special to The New York Times.

CHICAGO, June 28—Thomas E. Dewey, Michigan-born, racket-breaking Governor of New York, was overwhelmingly chosen today by the Republican convention today as its Presidential candidate to meet the fourth term bid of President Franklin D. Roosevelt, who is expected to be nominated by the Democrats in this same hall three weeks from today.

The New York Governor, who until today had maintained publicly that he was not a candidate, flew from Albany with Mrs. Dewey to accept the nomination and to meet the Vice Presidential nominee, Gov. John W. Bricker of Ohio, who was named unanimously a few hours earlier.

In the final night session, which was the most crowded and most enthusiastic of the whole convention, Mr. Dewey pledged his utmost efforts to lead the party back to power in Washington and to new conquests in the States and Congress in the November election.

Answering the challenge of former President Hoover, who last night called for a new generation to take over the helm of the Republican party, Mr. Dewey exhorted his followers to a finish fight to drive out "the 'tired and quarrelsome' Administration which has ruled in Washington for eleven years.

Says War Command Will Stand

Taking a leaf out of the book of President Roosevelt, who flew to Chicago twelve years ago to accept his first nomination, Mr. Dewey responded with the same fighting type of speech.

He brought his audience up in cheers time after time as he delivered thrusts at the New Deal, but especially where he declared that "the military conduct of the war is outside this campaign."

"It is and must remain completely out of politics," he said. General Marshall and Admiral King are doing a superb job. Let me make it crystal clear that a change in Administration next January cannot and will not involve any change in the military conduct of the war."

The change in Administration, he confidently predicted, would bring "an end to one-man government in Washington."

After Jan. 20, Inauguration Day, he said, the Government would have a Cabinet of the "ablest men and women to be found in America" who would receive full delegation of the powers of their office.

He made an appeal time after time to youth—youth to win the war, youth to keep the peace.

No organization of peace can last if it is slipped through by "stealth or trickery," he said. Making and keeping the peace was "not a task for men who specialize in dividing our people."

"It is no task to be entrusted to stubborn men, grown old and tired and quarrelsome in office," he said. "We learned that in 1919."

America's duty to win the peace was parallel with its duty to win the war, he said. Recently there had been a growing area of agreement among the American people on foreign policy. Only a few, "a very few," maintained that America could remain aloof any longer, he said, and only a few believed it would be practical for America and her allies to renounce all sovereignty and join a "super state."

He would not deny those two extremes the right of opinion, he said, but he stood firmly in the great wide area of agreement.

"That agreement," he said, "was clearly expressed in the Republican Mackinac declaration and was adopted in the foreign policy plank of this convention."

One Delegate Holds Out

Mr. Dewey's nomination was by a count of 1,056 votes to 1. The single opposition ballot was cast for General Douglas MacArthur, hero of the Southwest Pacific, by Grant A. Ritter of Beloit, Wis., who held out to the end against the Dewey avalanche.

The nomination was accomplished with a mild show of enthusiasm, made the milder, no doubt, by the sweltering heat which reached a new high in oppressiveness during the roll-call. The parade for the nominee, when his name was presented, lasted about ten minutes, and was joined by fewer than those who later participated in a demonstration for Governor Bricker.

The Dewey managers maintained the appearance of a "draft" until near the end. For, until he signified his willingness to accept to a convention committee assigned to call him on the telephone, Mr. Dewey had stood on earlier assertions that he was not a candidate and that he intended to serve out his present term as Governor of New York, which runs until Dec. 31, 1946.

All of the 1,057 eligible delegates present at the twenty-third Republican convention voted for Governor Bricker. Two others, allocated to the Philippine Islands, were qualified to sit but did not appear.

The swing to Governor Bricker for the Vice Presidency started late last night after Gov. Earl Warren of California, the previous odds-on choice, had refused to accept the nomination, and after Mr. Bricker had decided that his bid for the first honor was hopelessly lost to Governor Dewey.

Governor Warren refused because, he said, he had made certain "commitments" as Governor of California which he intended to keep. The language he used in turning back the pressure of his friends cast immediate attention on assertions Mr. Dewey had made when besought to run for the Presidency about his intentions to remain on the job at Albany.

The Dewey-Bricker ticket was hailed by the Republicans as one of the best combinations the convention could have put together, although there was considerable disappointment that Governor Warren would not accept and give an East Coast-West Coast tie up which, some party leaders believed, would be more damaging to the Democrats. The Middle West is considered much safer ground by the Republicans than either coast, and the electoral votes of New York and California are therefore highly coveted.

Dewey "Gladly Accepts" Bricker

Governor Dewey was said to have "gladly" accepted Mr. Bricker as a running mate, although his managers had tried, up to the last minute, to persuade Mr. Warren to run. In fact, they had considered no other name until the Californian gave his final frowning headshake last night.

Governor Bricker's backers tried to keep up hope, and until 2 A. M., had maintained determination to put his name before the convention as the Presidential nominee. Friends of former Governor Harold E. Stassen of Minnesota had the same intention as to their man. But the one thing that motivated this convention as much as anything else was that there should be no fights, no recrimination, no last-minute deadlocks. So when it became apparent that trouble might develop over the Vice Presidency, the Bricker forces decided not to protest. Their decision was made the easier, of course, by the hopelessness of their position otherwise.

Mr. Dewey went over as the Presidential nominee before Ohio was reached on the roll call. Governor Bricker had withdrawn in the meantime, however, and made a seconding speech for Mr. Dewey which brought the day's, and possibly the convention's, greatest demonstration.

The nomination was actually accomplished about 12:15 P. M., when New Hampshire's eleven votes pushed the Dewey column over the 529 needed by a margin of six votes. Until that point the roll call had been responded to by one State after another voting its solid delegation for Dewey. It

proceeded thus until Wisconsin was reached and the delegation leader announced the single Mac-Arthur vote.

After the roll call, Wisconsin asked for recognition. Delegates and spectators expected that the State would withdraw its MacArthur vote and make the Dewey nomination unanimous. Such was not to happen, however. The delegation's leader merely announced that the four Stassen delegates had gone over to Dewey and added:

"That's all, Mr. Chairman."

The virtual unanimity of Mr. Dewey's vote was assured when Governor Bricker went to the rostrum and announced withdrawal of his candidacy.

The Ohio Governor told the crowd that what he had campaigned for most of all, in his criss-cross visits about the country, was for a Republican victory. He was more interested in that and in a repeal of the philosophy of the New Deal, he said, than in being President of the United States. Since it was obvious that a majority of the dele-

gates wanted to nominate Governor Dewey, he could, and would, do no less than join in the general acclaim.

Ohio Starts Demonstration

A demonstration broke out in the Ohio delegation, and was joined by numerous delegates in the hall and by spectators in the galleries. It was punctuated by demands that Mr. Bricker stay in the race for President. The shouting and parading continued for fifteen minutes, topping by five minutes the cheering for Governor Dewey when his name was first presented.

The New York Governor was placed in nomination by Gov. Dwight Grisfold of Nebraska, who hailed him as "youth's spokesman for the future," to supplant the Democratic party's "spokesman for the past." Placards with huge blue and black letters, "Dewey Will Win" and "Dewey the People's Choice," appeared in all parts of the hall when his name was first mentioned.

Various seconding speeches followed.

Among the speakers was Senator Joseph Ball of Minnesota, who had intended up to the time of Mr. Warren's withdrawal, to present the name of Lieutenant Commander Stassen.

Representative Everett M. Dirksen of Illinois, who had been a candidate for vice president, said during his speech that a combination of Dewey and Bricker would be "a winning ticket for next November."

Gov. Leverett Saltonstall of Massachusetts; Representative Leonard Hall of New York; Mrs. Rose Mayes of Idaho, and former Municipal Judge Patrick P. Prescott of Chicago also seconded the nomination.

"Today we bring Sir Galahad in quest of the Holy Grail, the knight in shining armor who will burst the biggest gang that has ever infested the United States," shouted Judge Prescott. "New York now gives Thomas E. Dewey to the limitless ages."

June 29, 1944

REVOLT IN SOLID SOUTH ON FOURTH TERM GROWS

Mississippi Joins Bolt and Leaders From Six States Map Strategy

By TURNER CATLEDGE

MEMPHIS, Tenn., June 10—Political unrest in the hitherto Solid South, which has shown itself in the recent Democratic State Conventions of South Carolina and Texas, flared anew this week when the Mississippi party organization jumped to the head of the Southern anti-New Deal forces with a resounding rebel yell.

Going further than their South Carolina compatriots dared to go, and with an unanimity not accomplished in Texas, Mississippi Democrats delivered an open ultimatum to the national party organization on the questions of white supremacy, States rights, the poll tax, and the two-thirds rule. They specifically absolved their candidates for electors from supporting the nominees of the national convention unless the demands which they instructed their delegates to make on these issues were met.

In the same week that the Mississippians took this action Georgia Democrats voted to exclude Negroes from the party primary, and a group of anti-New Deal leaders representing six States met at Shreveport, La., to begin welding dissident elements into a solid bloc for whatever it might accomplish during the remainder of this political year.

All these things were part of

the same picture—a confusing picture of crisscrossing currents in a part of the country which realizes rather unhappily that it is taken for granted in American politics.

Where the present Southern "revolt" will lead no one, of course, can tell at this time. Its top leadership desires with but little secrecy the defeat of President Roosevelt for a fourth term. The fact that this is not openly advocated is largely a matter of strategy. Many of the followers, however, do not seem to know specifically what they hope to accomplish practically. Throughout Southern Democracy there is an overweening desire to be noticed and a determination to reassert the South's influence in the national party councils which, the leaders maintain, the Democrats of this area surrendered when the so-called two-thirds rule governing national nominations was dropped in the politically prosperous days of the New Deal.

In Mississippi, for instance, the conservative leaders, largely business and professional men and planters, were able to frighten away any effective opposition in the convention by raising the issue of white supremacy.

In attempting again to assert themselves, Southern Democratic

"GET YOUR BADGES HERE"

Knott in The Dallas News

leaders have brought out the most explosive sectional issues ever known in America. Topmost of these is the issue of white supremacy, which today is being ridden for everything it is worth. Moreover, it seems to be worth considerably more now than for many years past, because of the

effort toward fuller emancipation of the Negro in general and the particular activities in that respect of Mrs. Roosevelt, and the recent Supreme Court decision aimed at opening Southern Democratic primaries to Negroes.

The effectiveness of the race question in certain parts of the

South, particularly in Mississippi, Louisiana, Alabama, Georgia and South Carolina, simplifies the task of the conservatives who would go all the way in abolition of the New Deal.

Race Issue Raised

However important the race problem may be in its own sphere, it appears to be the means of stirring action other than its own solution in the present political hubbub in Dixie.

The present plan of anti-New Deal Southern Democrats is to induce a goodly number of State organizations to nominate uninstructed electors to cast the electoral vote for President and Vice President following the November election. They propose to hold these footloose electors over the head of the New Deal political management as a threat. The threat, as they plan it, would be carried out in case of a close election by the electors casting this independent vote for some other Democrats than the nominees designated at Chicago, and thereby attempting to throw the Presidential and Vice Presidential election into Congress.

These leaders already claim a bloc of forty independent electoral votes in South Carolina, Mississippi and Texas and count on picking up others in Louisiana, Arkansas and possibly Virginia.

Regardless of the rabid attitude of several leaders of the revolt, many Southerners doubt that electors thus rendered independent would go all the way and vote against President Roosevelt should he be nominated again. But most of them feel that they would cast their ballots in a manner to bring about the defeat of Vice President Wallace were he again put on the ticket.

Evidence has reached the South that the fourth-term planners, especially those connected with the national committee, are becoming increasingly concerned about developments south of the Mason and Dixon Line. This makes the Southerners feel quite good, because they are already, apparently, accomplishing part of their purpose; they are being noticed again.

Strategy Laid Down

It may be quite fitting that the party's national directors are looking a bit more intently in this direction. For the anti-New Deal Southerners seem to have hit upon a formula which can be made successful if they can continue, and spread, the type of leadership exhibited this week in Mississippi.

In fact, it is no new formula. In the four-cornered Presidential race of 1824 ten of the thirteen electors from North Carolina voted for Crawford, although the popular vote of the State had gone for Jackson. Independent votes were cast by Presidential electors as early as 1796, and they were recorded again in 1836 and in 1828. The election of 1916, in which Woodrow Wilson won re-election over Charles Evans Hughes, could have been thrown into the House by a change of only twelve electoral votes. In other words, the thing can be serious.

What effect all this stewing and fretting and planning in the South will have on the party must await the Chicago convention for a determination. The report has been spread here that the New Deal wing intended trying to write social-equality and anti-poll tax planks into the platform. Whether many of these reports were true or not, the public agitation stemming from them might well provoke such attempts. The compromisers would then really be up against it. They might not be able to avoid a choice between slapping down the South and taking a chance on its threatened bolt, and alienation of the Northern Negro vote, risking the loss of such important States as New York, Pennsylvania, Illinois and others.

June 11, 1944

ROOSEVELT NOMINATED FOR FOURTH TERM

VOTE IS 1,086 TO 90

Byrd Gets 89, Farley One—President on Radio Accepts

STANDS ON RECORD

Says 'Experience,' Not 'Immaturity,' Will Win War, Peace and Jobs

By TURNER CATLEDGE
Special to THE NEW YORK TIMES.

CHICAGO, July 20—Franklin Delano Roosevelt of New York was nominated today for a fourth term as President of the United States by a noisy, irritable Democratic convention, meeting in the same hall where he was chosen for his first term in 1932 and for a third in 1940.

A few hours later, speaking to the convention directly by radio from his train at a Pacific Coast naval base, he accepted the nomination and opened his re-election bid on the note of "experience" versus "immaturity."

Mr. Roosevelt asserted that he considered the convention's action as a call upon him to serve. He said it was up to the American people in the November election to decide whether plans already made and men already serving to achieve victory and make America and the world a better place in which to live were to be continued or supplanted by an administration with no program but to oppose.

He presented a three-point program—to win the war, to secure the peace with force if necessary, and to build an economy with full employment and a high standard of living—as a promise of himself and the party which had called him again to lead.

In this election, he said, the people would not consider "glowing words or platform pledges," but would decide on the record made in the war and in "domestic achievements."

The President said he was too busy, and the emergency too serious, to permit him to engage in an active campaign for re-election.

But he added that he should "feel free" to report to the American people from time to time on the progress of their efforts and to "correct misstatements of fact" which might be made by the Republican opposition.

He disclosed that he was on the West Coast now in pursuance of his "constitutional duties" in connection with the war.

Roar of Cheering for Speech

The President's words came strong and magic-like through the loud speaker system—just as it did in his acceptance speech at his third-term nomination in this hall four years ago.

At the end the crowd in the arena and galleries broke into uproarious cheering. People were still shouting in a deafening roar when adjournment was moved. They attempted to shout down the motion.

The motion was carried, however, and the convention recessed at 10:55 o'clock until 11:30 tomorrow morning when it will reassemble to settle the Vice Presidential nomination.

The renomination of the President went through swiftly.

Mr. Roosevelt received 1,086 votes on the first roll call. Senator Harry F. Byrd, who was not a candidate, received 89, and James A. Farley, former chairman of the Democratic National Committee, who would not let his name go before the convention, received one from his home State of New York.

A telegram notifying the President of his nomination was dispatched to him immediately by Senator Samuel D. Jackson, Permanent Chairman of the Convention.

The Vice Presidential contest, growing in bitterness hourly, apparently was moving toward a showdown of strength between Vice President Henry A. Wallace, whom President Roosevelt has endorsed as his "personal" friend and choice, and Senator Harry Truman of Missouri, champion of the "stop-Wallace" forces, who also reputedly bore the approval of the first-place nominee.

Vice President Wallace received another ovation today when he appeared before the convention, as leader of the Iowa delegation, to second the nomination of President Roosevelt, and yet another tonight during the tumultous response to the President's acceptance speech.

Backers of Mr. Truman, who were having some trouble in solidifying their forces, seemed troubled by the display, but continued to predict that their man should roll up a majority on the second roll-call, when, as they further predicted, a number of "favorite son" candidates would drop out of the race.

Sectional Splits Mark Day

The nomination of Mr. Roosevelt came as afternoon turned into evening of a day which repeatedly witnessed the convention straining at the leash of its management.

Sectional differences which had flared in pre-convention phases in Texas, Mississippi and other Southern States, blazed again and again, reaching a climax in a partial walk-out of the "regular" Texas delegation late this afternoon.

Thirty-three Texans left the hall when the convention voted overwhelmingly to seat both of the two contesting delegations with a half vote for each delegate.

Bitterness also went deeply in the Vice Presidential race, and accusations of bad faith flew back and forth among spokesmen for the outstanding aspirants and certain convention officials, including Robert E. Hannegan, chairman of the National Committee and supposedly personal representative of President Roosevelt at the convention.

Mr. Hannegan, who is apparently directing the Truman drive, made public tonight a letter from President Roosevelt stating that he would be glad to run with either Mr. Truman or Justice William O. Douglas and that he believed either one would "bring real strength to the ticket."

Just before reaching the Presidential ballot, the convention adopted by voice vote the party platform of 1944, pledging the country, if the Democrats are retained in command in Washington, to participation in a world organization endowed with power to use "armed force" if necessary to preserve future peace among nations.

By the platform the party proposed to stand on its record of the past twelve years in the domestic field and to cast future actions around the particular needs of the men and women soon to return from the armed services after the victory in war.

In the vote on the platform a chorus of "nay's" came from the Southern delegations who resented a plank in the platform declaring in effect for equal voting rights among the races.

As the Southerners were able to obtain only eight of the required twelve signatures (one from each State) to force the issue to the floor, they had to content themselves with shouting their disapproval.

Senator McKellar of Tennessee and Delegate Oscar Johnston of Mississippi were able by the ruse of parliamentary inquiries, however, to put their States on record as opposed to the platform.

The walkout of the Texans came when the convention adopted the report of its credentials committee. This recommended the compromise of seating the two delegations, but some of the regulars would not agree to it.

On the roll-call for President all twenty-four votes of the "regulars" were cast by delegation leaders, twelve for Mr. Roosevelt and twelve for Senator Byrd.

Because of the confusion and mixed signals under which the convention has been operating, the action on both the credentials report and platform came between the nominating and seconding speeches for President and the balloting.

Emphasis on Commander

Throughout the speeches and proceedings of the day the dominant party spokesmen sought to keep the emphasis center on Mr. Roosevelt as "Commander in Chief."

Speakers sought time and again to counter the issue of age as raised by Thomas E. Dewey, Republican nominee, in his acceptance speech in this same hall three weeks ago. They joined the issue by pitting "age and experience" against "youth and inexperience."

Mr. Roosevelt's name was presented to the convention by Senator Alben W. Barkley of Kentucky, Senate Majority Leader, as one endowed with the "intellectual boldness of Thomas Jefferson, the indomitable courage of Andrew Jackson, the faith and patience of Abraham Lincoln, the rugged integrity of Grover Cleveland and the scholarly vision of Woodrow Wilson."

The convention broke into an ovation which continued for about forty minutes until brought to an end by Chairman Jackson.

Seconding speeches were made by Daniel J. Tobin, delegate from Indiana and president of the International Brotherhood of Teamsters; Byron G. Allen of Minnesota, candidate for Governor on the new Democratic-Farmer-Labor party; Ryburn Clay of Georgia, whose speech was read by the reading clerk, and Vice President Wallace.

Whether or not Mr. Wallace wins renomination, he established himself as a convention favorite by his appearance. He was compelled to stand for some minutes before he could proceed amid the shouts and cheers of the crowd, especially that part in the galleries.

He was interrupted repeatedly as he inferentially challenged his opponents by telling them that the only chance for their party was to keep on its "liberal" course.

He heaped praise and more praise upon Mr. Roosevelt as the leader of the "liberal" forces in America and the world, and asserted also that he was the "only man" in the United States capable of meeting on even terms with the other great world leaders in the international conferences that have taken place and others that are to come.

The only people who hate Mr. Roosevelt, he said, were "Germans, Japs and certain American troglodytes."

Florida Woman Offers Byrd

Senator Byrd was put in nomination by Mrs. Fred T. Nooney, one of the four Florida delegates pledged to the Virginian in a recent primary in her State. She praised Mr. Byrd as a man whose training and experience, both in State and national affairs, gave him outstanding qualifications for filling the office of President and whose political record showed him to be the type of Democrat which the convention should present in 1944.

She told the convention that Senator Byrd had not sought the four Florida delegates, nor had he consented that his name be presented.

The Senator expressed his reluctance to become a candidate again at a caucus of the Virginia delegation this morning, but said the decision was up to the members.

Senator Byrd's nomination was seconded by the Texas delegation—that was before some of the "regulars" walked out—and by Mississippi.

Jackson Warns Against Change

The convention listened to still another "keynote" this morning from Senator Jackson upon his taking the permanent chairmanship. The official "keynote" was delivered last night by Gov. Robert S. Kerr of Oklahoma, temporary chairman.

Senator Jackson declared that the American ballot box must not be made "Hitler's secret weapon," implying that the defeat of the Roosevelt Administration would be one of the greatest spurs that could come to enemy morale.

"A change in national administration in time of war, even when surrounded by promising circumstances, is frightening to contemplate," Mr. Jackson said. "It is dangerous."

The Indianan said that in terms of statesmanship and "comparison of dimensions," circumstances ruled out Mr. Dewey as a substitute for Mr. Roosevelt.

Speaking at the night session, Quentin Reynolds, war correspondent, assured the delegates that the "boys" overseas knew that the miracle of victory which they are now achieving, and which is backed by the all-out effort on the home front, was accomplished "under the leadership of their Commander in Chief and ours — Franklin D. Roosevelt."

Still another speaker was Mrs. Helen Gahagan Douglas of California who attacked the "double-talk" of the Republican platform.

July 21, 1944

BIG CITY BOSSES WON OVER HILLMAN

Two Presidential Letters Had Important Influence on Convention Strategy

By JAMES A. HAGERTY
Special to The New York Times.

CHICAGO, July 21—Somewhat belatedly, leaders of the Democratic organizations in a score and a half of States, headed by big city bosses, Edward J. Flynn and Frank V. Kelly of New York, Mayor Edward J. Kelly of Chicago, Mayor Frank Hague of Jersey City and Robert E. Hannegan, national chairman, of St. Louis, brought about the nomination of Senator Harry S. Truman of Missouri for Vice President by the Democratic National Convention.

By the nomination the Democratic politicians won a victory over Sidney Hillman, chairman of the Congress of Industrial Organizations Political Action Committee, who stuck to Vice President Henry A. Wallace to the last and whose influence had been sufficient to cause James F. Byrnes of South Carolina, Director of the Office of War Mobilization, to withdraw as a candidate for the nomination.

Two Letters Are Factors

Senator Truman was the victor in the battle of two Presidential letters. The earlier one was a lukewarm endorsement of Vice President Wallace and the later one announced the President's willingness to accept Senator Truman as a running mate and belief that his nomination would add strength to the Democratic national ticket.

These two letters played an important part in the contest. In the earlier letter the President wrote to Senator Samuel D. Jackson, Permanent Chairman of the Convention, that, if he were a delegate, he would vote for Mr. Wallace, but qualified this by adding that he did not want to dictate to the convention.

The second letter was from the President to Mr. Hannegan. It was dated July 19 and was made public by Mr. Hannegan on the evening of the following day. In it, President Roosevelt, in reply to a letter from Mr. Hannegan, wrote that he would be glad to have Senator Truman or Justice William O. Douglas of the Supreme Court as a running mate and that either would add strength to the ticket.

The two letters were of the greatest importance in the under-the-surface strategy of the convention. Supporters of Mr. Wallace stressed the President's declaration that, if he were a delegate, he would vote for the Vice President, his personal friend.

Backers of Senator Truman pointed out that, even though the President had written to that effect, the fact that he added that he did not wish to dictate to the convention indicated that he did not really wish to have Mr. Wallace renominated. They recalled that four years ago he had made the nomination of Mr. Wallace a "must" and did not hesitate to dictate to the convention.

In their talks with delegates and party leaders, backers of Senator Truman's candidacy stressed the President's declaration in his letter to Mr. Hannegan that the nomination of the Missouri Senator would add strength to the ticket. They asserted that Senator Truman was the President's choice for the ticket and in private conversations declared that this information came in talks with the President over the telephone.

After encountering many difficulties, the backers of Senator Truman finally convinced a majority of the delegates that he was the running-mate the President desired. It took a good deal of talking and a good deal of pressure to get a majority of the party leaders and delegates to that opinion.

Not sure of a Truman majority at the convention session last night, at which final adjournment of the convention had been hoped for, Mr. Hannegan and his associates worked through the night and by daybreak were satisfied that they had a majority for their candidate.

Mayor Kelly had great difficulty in bringing the Illinois delegation into line for Senator Truman. Mr. Wallace had considerable strength in the delegation and Mayor Kelly found it necessary to get the delegation to agree to vote for Senator Scott W. Lucas to prevent the Wallace vote having on the first ballot a substantial addition from Illinois. Similar difficulties were encountered in other States.

With ten other candidates placed in nomination, the vote was so split on the first ballot that Mr. Wallace had little chance of getting a majority. On the second ballot the way was opened for a succession of "switches" by various States before announcement of the result.

On these switches a solid vote from New York almost gave Senator Truman the nomination. A call for a poll of the delegation, when announcement was made of the switch, became irrelevant with the announcement that Illinois had changed its vote to give 55 for Truman and 3 for Wallace.

Other changes followed in quick succession and the stampede for the nomination of Senator Truman was on.

After a bad start, when they looked like novices in politics in comparison with Mr. Hillman and Philip Murray, president of the CIO, the politicians showed their skill. This demonstration of skill came late, but when it came it proved to be effective.

July 22, 1944

LABOR'S CAMPAIGN ROLE PROMISES TO BE GREAT

CIO-PAC Emerges as a Potent Force But Labor Unity Is Not in Sight

By LOUIS STARK

WASHINGTON, Aug. 12—The role of organized labor in the national political campaign is becoming clearer as the issues come into focus.

Organized labor, whatever political partisanship may exist in its ranks, is united on the idea of "getting out the vote." Each side argues that an increased vote over 1940 and 1936 will mean that its candidates will gain at the polls.

Samuel Gompers used to say that labor leaders cannot "deliver" the labor vote. Nevertheless the topflight union chieftains today act politically as if their efforts were certain to sway enough votes to make the difference between defeat and victory for their particular favorites.

Therefore, labor groups supporting both the Democratic and Republican tickets are likely to concentrate their efforts on winning the support of key minorities in various politically uncertain areas. Organized labor is itself the largest minority. Other minorities include Negroes and voters of foreign origin. In a closely contested district or area one of these groups or a combination of them may decide a local, a State and even the national election.

The Roosevelt Group

Undoubtedly, the more vocal and better organized of the labor adherents are on the side of President Roosevelt. They include the CIO Political Action Committee, headed by Sidney Hillman, as well as the labor groups around Daniel J. Tobin, president of the AFL International Brotherhood of Teamsters, and since 1932 chief of the labor section of the Democratic campaign committee.

The Republican labor leadership is dominated by W. L. Hutcheson, president of the AFL United Brotherhood of Carpenters, opposite number to Mr. Tobin. Both are members of the AFL executive council, the governing body of that organization. This is one of the reasons why the AFL council does not officially endorse either of the Presidential aspirants.

There is no such split, however, among the members of the CIO. President Philip Murray and all his associates see eye to eye on the candidates named by the Democratic convention.

Both AFL and CIO will follow the same general policy in so far as the elections concern candidates other than the chief standard bearers of the two parties. They will "support our friends and punish our enemies," an old-line policy of nonpartisanship set many years ago under Mr. Gompers.

Both labor organizations have prepared or are completing lists of the candidates for Congress and for Gubernatorial posts. They are formulating "box scores" to show how candidates now holding office voted on policies crucial to labor. On these records endorsements will

POLITICS AND LABOR

Williams in The Detroit Free Press

"The political preacher's son."

Smith in The Lynchburg News

"Something tells us it's not as easy as it looks."

be made or withheld.

The most significant thing in the labor picture in 1944 is the emergent role of the CIO-Political Action Committee. Organized a little over a year ago, this organization demonstrated its political strength and power by its maneuvers at the Democratic Convention. By its preoccupation with political realities the CIO-PAC has set the stage for a campaign, which if successful, will be far-reaching in its repercussions.

Not After AFL Leaders

It is apparent that the CIO-PAC is not intent on urging the top AFL leadership, already favoring the Roosevelt-Truman ticket, to co-operate with it directly since they have a common objective. The Hillman organization hopes to win many adherents among the lower voting ranks of the AFL instead.

As might be expected the CIO-PAC, because of its vigorous political offensive, has evoked far greater reaction to its efforts than has the AFL's conservative political activity. Representative Martin Dies threatens a Congressional investigation of the CIO-PAC. Representative Clare Luce charges the Communist party with having gone underground in the Democratic labor organization. Senator Bennett C. Clark attributes his failure to win renomination to the CIO-PAC.

Mr. Hillman is compelled to deny that the CIO-PAC wants to capture the Democratic party and Congress.

These are some of the issues thrown up so far in the campaign as a result of the prominent role of the CIO. However, even the CIO seems to recognize that the top labor leadership cannot bind any individual member of a labor union.

Newspaper Guild Stand

Although the American Newspaper Guild convention delegates favored Roosevelt and Truman, their decision to take such a vote was very narrow, 2,750 to 2,105. And, after the voice vote President Milton Murray found it necessary to say that the Guild didn't intend to bind its members to any Presidential candidate, for "no matter whom they endorse our members will retain their right to vote as citizens, regardless of any recommendation by this convention."

Not only would this indicate that within the CIO unanimity was lacking on the political field, but similar straws show which way the wind is blowing in the AFL. For example, the machinists in the San Francisco area split 70 per cent to 30 per cent on endorsement of the Roosevelt-Truman ticket.

While both AFL and CIO policy calls for a Congress sympathetic to organized labor, individual labor leaders may have personal ties that bind them to some men, while other labor leaders in the same area may be cool to these men and warm to their opponents.

While the Roosevelt Administration has not been a "labor Government" in the British sense of that term, it has nevertheless been as close to a labor Government as any this nation has ever had.

The role of labor after next November, if Mr. Roosevelt and a "sympathetic Congress" are re-elected, will be enhanced so considerably that its voice will be heard with deference in most Government departments.

Fear of Favoritism

A possible fly in the CIO ointment, however, is likely to be AFL suspicion that its rival will be more favored in the rewards that follow successful political offensives.

Whether correct or not AFL leaders do not hesitate to say—and not always privately—that the Administration leans toward the CIO. AFL suspicion of the CIO's political activity is heightened by Mr. Green's warnings to his members not to support the Murray-Hillman organization. However, this injunction may not always be heeded by the lower branches of the AFL hierarchy. Candidates, too, are a bit chary about seeking the support of one of the rival labor groups and not the other.

From the foregoing, it would appear to be apparent that progress toward labor unity is unlikely to be one of the end results of the Presidential campaign; if anything, the campaign is likely to worsen the relations between the labor factions, since underlying rivalries, now smoldering, may break out after November.

A sudden unemployment crisis arising from an end of the Nazi phase of the war and the consequent letdown of war production would stave off labor dissension. A threat to wages, jobs and union privileges would probably result in a truce to inter-union factionalism.

August 13, 1944

DEWEY TACTICS IN RACE CONFUSING HIS BACKERS

Politicians in Capital, Anxious for the Governor to Win, Fear His Position Is Too Close to Roosevelt's

EXPECTED SHARP DIFFERENCES

By ARTHUR KROCK

WASHINGTON, Sept. 23—The campaign thus far conducted by Gov. Thomas E. Dewey in his quest for the Presidency impresses a number of politicians here who wish him success as not sufficiently distinct from the Democratic position to attract the votes that must be transferred if there is to be a change in the Government.

Those voicing this criticism are Democrats and Republicans who want that change to take place. The Democrats among them are composed both of anti-New Dealers and party men who went along with it up to the point where they decided that the New Deal was a mask for creeping collectivism. The Republican critics, aside from those who more or less privately oppose the League concept of post-war international security, simply disbelieve that it is winning strategy to accept all the objectives and most of the legislative instruments of an opponent and try to make an issue over "methods" and "economic climate."

Undoubtedly Mr. Dewey's general endorsement of the Administration plan for collective security after the war, and his construction of a New Deal of his own to compare with that of the President, are the consequences of deep and prayerful thinking by him and his staff of advisers. Since he has been more assiduous than any candidate in recent history to seek the views of Republican leaders all over the country, large and small, it must be presumed that he worked out his line of campaigning with their counsel in hand. Yet these presumptions have not shaken the doubts that are being expressed here by politicians who want to see Mr. Dewey elected President.

'Middle Path' Issue

If he sticks to what is called his "middle path" for the remainder of the campaign, and wins the Presidency, then he will have proved himself a shrewder judge of vote-getting than his critics. But if he loses, their certainty will increase that a Presidential challenger must draw a sharper line between himself and his opponent than Mr. Dewey has or they think Mr. Willkie did in 1940.

Mr. Willkie had a definite idea how he would govern the country and try to keep the nation out of war, and doubtless he believed and believes that he expressed it with clarity. But even during the 1940 campaign it was being said that his whole argument was that he could "do the same things better," and this is now being repeated as an analysis of most of Mr. Dewey's speeches thus far.

The anxious ones who are voicing this opinion feared and did what they thought they could to prevent a third term, and to them the prospect of a fourth is even more ominous as a portent of one-party government, indefinitely entrenched in office. But, they are asking, if the "I-can-do-it-better" argument failed to carry the country in time of peace and with the two-term tradition adding strength to it, how can it be expected to carry the country in time of war, with the two-term tradition destroyed and a fourth term probably impressing a great many voters as no more dangerous than a third?

Mathematical Chance

Mathematically, of course, and especially if the vote is light, Mr. Dewey can be elected by attracting the blocs conscious of their recent foreign origins, and by splitting the President's support from organized labor and from Negro citizens. In so far as his strategy can be deduced by these critics, that is the objective to which it is directed. By erecting a New Deal of his own on the foundations of the Administration's, he hopes to attract those who have grievances against the President, but who philosophically favored the New Deal. By endorsing in many essentials the American plan at Dumbarton Oaks he hopes to win the support of independents and Democrats who favor a change in the Government but not at the expense of the plan. At the same time, by keeping silent on the issue of Congressional prerogative which some Republican Senators have raised, he is endeavoring to prevent a pre-election split in his party.

This is not the kind of campaign Mr. Dewey was expected to make, and perhaps that is one reason why the critics herein reflected are disturbed. Their political judgment may be confused by their surprise over his tactics, but, unless Mr. Dewey shows a change of pace and approach to his election problem, they won't know for certain until the November polls have closed.

Prestige of His Rival

The Republican candidate's description of his administrative, political and economic ideals and aspirations, and his outline of the post-war world and the part of the United States in it, are not the bases of the anxious criticism. But it is pointed out that Mr. Roosevelt has, can and will say the same things with the authority and prestige of office, even though the open record disproves him on the domestic front.

Mr. Dewey, it was supposed, would "prosecute" the Administration with the strongest possible indictment and with much evidence to sustain him. He would keep up a constant barrage against the President's alliance with big-city machines and their underworld allies. He would hit hard the vulnerable preparedness record prior to Lend-Lease. He would demand that laws, including the Wagner and Social Security Acts, be amended to prevent their being legislated at will by administrators, but at the same time defend the just protections that are a part of them. He would—and this he has done—attack the doctrine of the "indispensable man" and the incompetence and confusion so often revealed in Washington during the last eleven and a half years.

"CAN EVERYBODY HEAR ME?"

Little in The Nashville Tennessean

Expected Targets

But in addition, it was expected, he would heavily assail on behalf of the rank-and-file of labor the racketeering which has been imposed on many of the unions, and he would make effective heavy ammunition of the veto power which the President permitted Sidney Hillman to exercise against his own preference for the Vice Presidential nomination, James F. Byrnes, and his own majority leader, Senator Alben W. Barkley.

To cap this indictment, the an-

ticipation was, Mr. Dewey would stress the argument that all these conditions can be removed only by an uprising of the people at the polls, since the President, in three terms, has appointed the vast majority of Federal judges, and in the course of a fourth term would have appointed nearly every one. As a skilled lawyer he could have cited judicial decisions to emphasize the view that this represents a danger to all economic and political minorities and especially to unorganized groups, with the Su-

preme Court bill of 1937 and subsequent opinions by justices as his evidence.

In the time remaining Mr. Dewey may take an aggressive turn and seek to make a clearer distinction between his program and those which the President has led and promises. But, in the opinion reported here, he has not yet done this.

September 24, 1944

DEWEY PREDICTS 'RED MENACE' RISE IF ROOSEVELT WINS

Asserts Communists With Aid of Hillman Seek to Seize Control of Government

PERILS RELIGION, HE SAYS

By WARREN MOSCOW
Special to The New York Times.

BOSTON, Nov. 1—Governor Dewey declared here tonight that the Communists, using Sidney Hillman as a front, were trying to

seize control of the Federal Government, and if they succeed, he added, the fundamental American freedoms, particularly freedom of religion, would be endangered.

Speaking in the Boston Garden, where he received a rousing reception, Mr. Dewey devoted his address to the menace of communism and pictured it as being increased if President Roosevelt is re-elected, but disappearing under a Republican Administration.

An enthusiastic crowd of at least 24,000 persons was present in the big arena long before Mr. Dewey was introduced by Governor Saltonstall. Police estimated that between 100,000 and 150,000 additional persons were unable to gain admittance.

Communism, Mr. Dewey said, was a "pagan philosophy which is sweeping through much of the world," and he put Earl Browder and Mr. Hillman, head of the CIO

Political Action Committee, in the position of being the "highest bidders" for control of the Democratic party, control of which, he declared, Mr. Roosevelt had placed on the auction block in order to "perpetuate himself in office for sixteen years."

Predicting that Messrs. Hillman and Browder would obtain control of the Democratic party, instead of the members of the "notorious One Thousand Club," which the Governor attacked in his Chicago speech, Mr. Dewey denied that there was any connection between communism and the national origin of those connected with radical movements.

Recalls Browder Statements

He cited the fact that Mr. Browder was born in Kansas as an answer to Democratic charges that the Republicans have used the racial or national origin of Communists or alleged Communists to

arouse racial feelings.

Mr. Dewey declared that "everyone knows that communism is for State ownership of all property, including your house, your farm and the factory, the shop, the office in which you work. It stands for absolute dictatorship, the abolition of civil rights and total political and economic bigotry. It stands for something else.

"A few years ago Mr. Browder wrote a book called 'What Is Communism?'" in which, Mr. Dewey said, there was the following statement:

"'We stand without any reservation for education that will root out beliefs in the supernatural.'"

Then, the Governor added, Mr. Browder concluded, "'We Communists do not distinguish between good and bad religions, because we think they are all bad for the masses.'"

"Now," Mr. Dewey continued,

"Mr. Roosevelt in his recent speech from the White House very softly disavowed communism. But the very next day, at a meeting right here in Boston, Earl Browder made a speech for Mr. Roosevelt and a collection was taken up for the fourth term. And not a voice in the New Deal was raised in protest."

"Once in every four years, late in October," the Governor said, "my opponent announces that he believes in the enterprise system. Then, for the remaining three years and eleven months he wages war against the American enterprise system day in and day out." Mr. Dewey tied Mr. Hillman in with the Communists by quoting attacks made on him by David Dubinsky, Dean Alfange and other spokesmen for the right wing of the American Labor party in the primary fight last spring, which resulted in the Hillman-Communist combination winning control, and the right wing splitting off into the present Liberal party.

They called Mr. Hillman a front for the Communists at that time, and Mr. Dewey quoted them tonight, declaring that the American Labor party up to that time had been "respectable."

"Sidney Hillman has become the biggest political boss in the United States," the Governor declared,

"and in the words of David Dubinsky, Sidney Hillman is a front for the Communists."

Mr. Dewey called the PAC's collection of contributions from workingmen a "Roosevelt poll tax imposed by Sidney Hillman," adding that the American workers were in revolt against it.

Quoting an anonymous workingman as having said that they could take his dollar from him but he still could vote as he pleased in the secrecy of the voting booth, Mr. Dewey said:

"Now, American liberty means that every man has the right to believe and vote as he will, even to vote communistic, but liberty involves a corresponding duty to defend our country from what we consider evil."

He declared that while "it has been the fashion to brush aside the Communists as of little importance because of their small numbers, the fact is that the Communists wield an influence far out of proportion to their numbers."

Mr. Dewey pictured them as a small disciplined minority who have seized control of union organizations, seized control of the American Labor party and "now, by the self-same tried and familiar tactics and with the aid of Sidney Hillman, the Communists are seizing control of the New Deal, through which they aim to control the Government of the United States." He added:

"If they succeed the fundamental freedoms of every American would stand in gravest jeopardy."

Emphasizing the "deeply religious pattern" which went into the founding of this country, Mr. Dewey said that the totalitarian idea represented by an activated communism was out to reject those concepts.

"That danger can be surely met only by ending a situation which leaves vast power in tired hands," the Governor said, adding:

"The Republican party is not perfect. But one thing at least is sure: Neither the Communist group which Mr. Roosevelt professes to repudiate nor any other totalitarian group is making an effort to capture the Republican party. They know how useless it would be."

Mr. Dewey depicted the New Deal as "a collection of warring factions, tied together only by a consuming passion for power," adding that was why "my opponent is compelled to solicit the support of bigoted reactionaries on one hand and Communists on the other."

Taking up a Democratic charge that Mr. Dewey had injured American relations with Russia by his previous attacks on the Communists, the Governor said, "In this campaign the New Dealers attempt to smother discussion of their Communist alliance. They smear any discussion of this major question of our day.

"They insinuate that Americans must love communism or offend our fighting ally Russia, but not even the gullible believe that. In Russia a Communist is a man who supports his Government. In Amer-

ica a Communist is a man who supports the fourth term so our form of government may more easily be changed."

Throughout Mr. Dewey's address any mention of communism, Mr. Browder or Mr. Hillman brought vociferous boos.

After concluding his prepared speech the Governor waved the crowd to silence and said, "I know your appearance here is not because of any personal regard for myself or Governor Bricker. All of you are here because you believe in the mightiest cause in history, saving our country and building a future for our soldiers and our children."

Lieut. Gov. Horace T. Cahill, candidate for Governor, started a big demonstration when he referred to the resentment expressed yesterday by Senator David I. Walsh, Democrat, of Massachusetts, against being branded an "isolationist" by Senator Truman.

"If they (Democrats) can't work together for twenty-four hours of the campaign, how can they work together for four years?" asked Mr. Cahill.

Mr. Saltonstall told the crowd that the reception Governor Dewey received in the State today "proved that Massachusetts wants Tom Dewey as the next President of the United States and convinced me Tom Dewey will carry Massachusetts."

November 2, 1944

ROOSEVELT WINS FOURTH TERM

DEWEY CONCEDES

His Action Comes as Roosevelt Leads in 33 States

BIG ELECTORAL VOTE

By ARTHUR KROCK

Franklin Delano Roosevelt, who broke more than a century-old tradition in 1940 when he was elected to a third term as President, made another political record yesterday when he was chosen for a fourth

term by a heavy electoral but much narrower popular majority over Thomas E. Dewey, Governor of New York.

At 3:15 A. M. Governor Dewey conceded Mr. Roosevelt's re-election, sending his best wishes by radio, to which the President quickly responded with an appreciative telegram.

Early this morning Mr. Roosevelt was leading in mounting returns in thirty-three States with a total of 391 electoral votes and in half a dozen more a trend was developing that could increase this figure to more than 400. Governor Dewey was ahead in fifteen States with 140 electoral votes, but some were see-sawing away from him and back again. Typical of these were Wisconsin, where he overtook the President's lead about 2 A. M.; Nevada, where Mr. Roose-

velt passed him at about the same time, and Missouri.

In the contests for seats in Congress, the Democrats had shown gains of 11 to 20 in the House of Representatives, assuring that party's continued control of this branch. In the Senate the net of losses and gains appeared to be an addition of one Republican to the Senate, which would give that party twenty-eight members—far short of the forty-nine necessary to a majority. A surprise was the indicated defeat of the veteran Pennsylvania Republican, Senator James J. Davis.

Mrs. Luce's Opponent Concedes

The Congressional races were featured by a mass Democratic attempt, in which the President and Vice President Henry A. Wallace personally participated, to unseat

Representative Clare Boothe Luce of Connecticut. But shortly after 3 A. M., following a night in which the lead had swung back and forth, her election was conceded by her opponent, Miss Margaret Connors. Some hours before, to his neighbors at Hyde Park, the President had expressed rejoicing over Mrs. Luce's "defeat." Her success is the vitriol in the Democratic honey.

Despite the great general victories by the Democrats, the popular vote will evidently show a huge minority protest against a fourth term for the President. Tabulations by the press associations indicated that the disparity between the ballots cast for the two candidates will be so small that a change of several hundred thousand votes in the key States, distributed in a certain way, would have reversed the electoral majority. At 4:40 A. M. The Associated Press reported 16,387,999 for Mr. Roosevelt and 14,235,051 for Mr. Dewey from more than one-third of the country's election districts. This ratio, if carried through, would leave only about 3,000,000 votes between the candidates.

One of the most interesting struggles for the Presidency was that in Wisconsin, where Mr. Dewey took an early lead, lost it and regained it again. Wisconsin is the State where the late Wendell L. Willkie made his stand for renomination, posing the issue of "isolationism" versus "internationalism." He ran last in the Presidential primary and expressed the belief, in then withdrawing from the race, that isolationism controlled the thinking of Wisconsin Republicans.

The close race between the President and Mr. Dewey, however, supported the view of others that Mr. Willkie was defeated by a combination between the followers of Mr. Dewey and Harold E. Stassen and that his contrary interpretation was not sound.

Stiff Fight in Pennsylvania

Pennsylvania was another scene of an intense struggle. Mr. Roosevelt got a much reduced majority in Philadelphia, but Allegheny County (Pittsburgh) exceeded expectations, and at 4 A. M. the State's thirty-five electors seemed moving toward Mr. Roosevelt's list.

In Ohio Mr. Dewey's early lead was being cut sharply by the President early this morning. New York's forty-seven electoral votes are certain for Mr. Roosevelt, and, with Illinois, Minnesota, Massachusetts, Connecticut and the 127 electors of the old Confederacy plus Tennessee in his column, the President was far beyond the 266 electors who constitute a majority.

The States in which Mr. Roosevelt was leading at 4 A. M. were:

Alabama, 11; Arizona, 4; Arkansas, 9; California, 25; Connecticut, 8; Delaware, 3; Florida, 8; Georgia, 12; Idaho, 4; Illinois, 28; Kentucky, 11; Louisiana, 10; Mississippi, 9; Maryland, 8; Missouri, 15; Montana, 4; Massachusetts, 16; Minnesota, 11; New Hampshire, 4; New Mexico, 4; New York, 47; Nevada, 3; North Carolina, 14; Oklahoma, 10; Pennsylvania, 35; Rhode Island, 4; South Carolina, 8; Tennessee, 12; Texas, 23; Virginia, 11; West Virginia, 8; Washington, 8. and Utah, 4—Total of 391.

Dewey Leads in New Jersey

The States with margins for Mr. Dewey were:

Colorado, 6; Indiana, 13; Iowa, 10; Kansas, 8; Maine, 5; Michigan, 19; Nebraska, 6; New Jersey, 16; North Dakota, 4; Ohio, 25; Oregon, 6; South Dakota, 4; Vermont, 3; Wisconsin 12; Wyoming, 3—a total of 140.

To win Mr. Dewey was obliged to effect a combination of Massachusetts (or Connecticut), New York (or Pennsylvania), the Border States, the Midwestern States and Oregon on the Pacific Coast. This is because the President, despite the midsummer "revolts" in Texas, South Carolina, Mississippi and Louisiana, was sure to start with 127 certain electors—the old South, plus Tennessee. Mr. Dewey failed to come within spyglass distance of this feat.

Wallace Proves Right

The popular vote ran so close until after 11 o'clock that even the most optimistic supporters of the President were cautious in their claims. But Mr. Wallace was not so timorous. He established a national record as a forecasting statistician by announcing at 9:30 P. M. that the President had been re-elected by a large electoral majority, that he had been given a Democratic House with a "mandate" to carry out his war and post-war program and that "bipartisan isolationism has been destroyed."

When Mr. Wallace issued this statement few were ready to accept his conclusion. But an hour later he had become a major prophet.

Hillman's Group Effective

Early in the day, throughout the United States, it became evident that the heavy registration was the true portent of a larger vote than was anticipated when the campaign began. Soon after the national conventions were held the predictions in both political camps were for a vote well below that of 1940, under 45,000,000 and perhaps little more than 40,000,000.

Faced with this prospect, Democratic spokesmen openly conceded that so light a vote meant the re-election odds would be against the President and that only with a tally of 45,000,000 or more could his true strength be registered—in which event they were confident of success.

But within a few weeks after the nominations, the Political Action Committee of the Congress of Industrial Organizations, under the chairmanship of Sidney Hillman began its effort to bring out the vote. Pamphlets urging citizens to go to the polls, and making arguments for Mr. Roosevelt's re-election, were distributed in great numbers in all parts of the country, but particularly in the large cities and even more intensively in those areas where war industry had sprung up and the normal population was much enlarged.

When the registration periods arrived it was demonstrated that these activities of Mr. Hillman's group were very effective. By the end of this period a vote that may exceed 50,000,000 (including ballots from the armed services) was indicated, and Democratic hopes rose accordingly. Reports from the sections where CIO-PAC had been busiest accentuated the view that, in bringing out votes which otherwise might not have been registered, Mr. Hillman's committee had been more vigilant and more successful than the regular Democratic organizations.

One interesting phase of this new note in national political campaigns was that the Hillman group did not neglect the Solid South, where Democratic nomination is equivalent to election and the November vote accordingly is light. To make sure that the President's popular vote would represent his real November strength, and to avert any possibility of an electoral victory without a popular majority—or a

popular vote far below the electoral vote of the Democratic national ticket in percentage — the CIO-PAC besought Southern Democrats, especially the war industrial workers, to go to the polls and swell Mr. Roosevelt's general totals.

Not until the returns are all in will it be possible to make an estimate of the degree to which this innovation materialized. But there was no doubt in the minds of the professional politicians, after registration, that in the areas of normally close party division the CIO-PAC has done notable work in preventing a light poll this year.

The proof of this in every large industrial city was received with mixed feelings by the regular Democratic organizations, which hitherto have had all the credit for the votes registered and cast for their ticket. They were obliged to accept a competitor which, they were certain, would not be hesitant in pointing to its contribution in the event of the President's election to a fourth term which, on analysis, would prove to have been achieved by the voters in the large industrial areas where the CIO-PAC is strong and has been very active. This would presage a rivalry for influence and reward in the next administration to which dispute Mr. Hillman and his group could bring impressive support of their claims.

For a space in the campaign, when the Republican orators and organizers concentrated their fire on Mr. Hillman, and he was put down as a liability, the Democratic National Committee subordinated the role of his group as best it could and declined to certify its members as official spokesmen of the President's re-election.

But as the voters turned out yesterday in unusual and unexpected numbers, the dispute was suspended in the mutual wish to win, to be resumed in the event of Mr. Roosevelt's re-election by citizens in PAC territory and demonstrably responsive to its influence. Before the campaign ended Robert E. Hannegan, chairman of the Democratic National Committee, was vigorously defending Mr. Hillman from the Republican attacks and making the PAC cause his own in so far as he could.

November 8, 1944

ROOSEVELT IS DEAD; TRUMAN PRESIDENT

White House Statement

By The Associated Press.

WASHINGTON, April 12—The White House announced late today that President Roosevelt had died of cerebral hemorrage.

The death occurred this afternoon at Warm Springs, Ga. A White House statement said:

"Vice President Truman has been notified. He was called to the White House and informed by Mrs. Roosevelt. The Secretary of State has been advised. A Cabinet meeting has been called.

"The four Roosevelt boys in the service have been sent a message by their mother, which said that the President slept away this afternoon. He did his job to the end, as he would want to do.

" 'Bless you all and all our love,' added Mrs. Roosevelt. She signed the message Mother.

"Funeral services will be held Saturday afternoon in the East Room of the White House. Interment will be at Hyde Park Sunday afternoon. No detailed arrangements or exact times have been decided upon as yet."

April 13, 1945

DEMOCRATS: LEFT AND RIGHT

OLD SCHOOL DEMOCRATS TAKE BACK THE PARTY

Leaders Revamp Neglected Machinery, Looking to Victory in '46 and '48

By LOUTHER A. HUSTON

WASHINGTON, July 14—The Democratic party is in the process of being given back to the Democrats.

That does not mean that any of its non-Democrat supporters who admittedly contributed to its political success during the Roosevelt era are going to be tossed to the Republicans by the Truman regime. It does mean that party machinery which grew a little rusty between 1932 and 1944 is being lubricated with good old Democratic oil and the engineers will be Democrats.

Every trend that has developed since Harry S. Truman became President and the head of the party portends resurgence of leadership from within the party ranks. Democrats with whom the party's plans and future were discussed this week frankly conceded that the formula compounded to produce victory in the mid-term elections next year and the Presidential campaign of 1948 contains about 90 per cent of pure party ingredients.

Looking Ahead

Here, in substance, is what is happening now in the party, according to qualified spokesmen and competent observers:

The immediate objective is to build up a political machine which will give the Democrats victory in the 1946 Congressional and State elections. Party leaders believe that to win next year the biggest job is to get out the vote. That job is being handed to the party workers, all down the line, in all the States, counties and precincts.

Party responsibility for the policies and the operation of the Government and all its agencies is being acknowledged and accepted. The obvious concomitant is that Democratic responsibility is best borne by Democrats. Hence the jobs are going to Democrats—not to Republicans.

Key appointments, such as to the Cabinet and other top administrative jobs, are being made from among politicians who, along with ability, can bring to their jobs the kind of political strength that counts on election day.

Finally, patronage, the bulwark of politics, is going back into the hands of the party workers. Members of Congress, State leaders and precinct workers, as circumstances may indicate, are being asked to recommend the Democrat who should have the job that is open and that Democrat is getting the appointment.

Not even the Republicans find much fault with this formula. Most of them are believers in the doctrine of party responsibility. The prevalent belief is that what has happened in the Democratic party in the three months Mr. Truman has been at the helm has been good for it and good for politics as a whole.

Pitfalls Conceded

It is conceded, however, that there may be some pitfalls along the pathway the Democrats are following. Cognizance is taken of the fact that for a dozen years party leadership was subordinated to personal leadership, and it was that magnetic leadership which attracted independent elements and thus turned the Democratic party from a downtrodden minority into a triumphant majority. Loss of the support of some of these elements could convert the party into a minority.

The feeling of some influential Democrats is, however, that a strictly Democratic party organization can be built up and operate effectively without turning away the independent political forces which have contributed to the party's success in the last four national elections. The thing most likely to drive these elements away from the Democratic fold, it is reasoned, would be for the party, and more specifically Mr. Truman, to repudiate the foreign policies or the economic and social doctrines which were keystones of the Roosevelt Administration.

In the field of foreign policy, it is pointed out, the President is leading the country and his party along the same pathways Mr. Roosevelt charted. His statements in support of a permanent Fair Employment Practices Commission, his program for increased employment compensation introduced this week, somewhat reluctantly, by Representative Doughton as an Administration measure, and other official acts and pronouncements of the President indicate clearly that he has no intention of scuttling the domestic policies which were the foundation of the New Deal.

Next Year Is Test

The tests for which the Democrats are girding their loins will come in next year's elections. It is no political secret that since 1932 Democratic candidates, who had to seek office in years when Roosevelt was not running, often had hard sledding. Those were the years of Republican gains which often alarmed the Democrats. In the quadrennial Presidential elections it was easier to ride in on the Roosevelt coattails. It is now the feeling, however, that a Democratic victory in 1946 is essential to a victory in 1948.

In the 1944 elections there were forty-five Congressional districts which were carried by Democratic candidates with pluralities of 12,000 votes or less or by less than 10 per cent of the total vote. There were fifty-three districts carried by Republicans by the same relative margins. These ninety-eight districts will be the chief battlegrounds in 1946.

An illustration of the awakened emphasis on party responsibility is found in the case of the Office of Price Administration. The agency has been operated pretty much on a nonpartisan basis.

The way that worked out, however, was that as resentment developed against regulations and practices of the OPA, the blame fell on the Democrats, or at least the New Deal.

In consequence it has been made clear to the administrative heads of the OPA as well as other agencies, that hereafter the key jobs are to go to Democrats.

All of this is part of a program designed to return Mr. Truman to the White House and keep the party in power in 1948. Messrs. Byrnes, Anderson, Schwellenbach, Hannegan and Clark, new members of the Cabinet, Judge Vinson, who is to join soon, and others who may be appointed to the Cabinet, along with Congressional leaders and some lay advisers, will constitute a political hierarchy, with President Truman at its head, which will not lose sight of this goal during the next three years.

And every one of them is a Democrat, born, bred and believing in the doctrine that Democrats should run the Democratic party.

July 15, 1945

Senate Is Thrown Into Furor As FEPC Bill Is Called Up

By C. P. TRUSSELL
Special to The New York Times.

WASHINGTON, Jan. 17—A surprise move by Senator Chavez, Democrat, of New Mexico, put before the Senate today the controversial bill to create a permanent Fair Employment Practices Commission, and there developed at once the first signs of a filibuster which threatened to block indefinitely final action on any of the reconversion proposals on which President Truman has urged top speed in Congress.

By a vote of 49 to 17 the FEPC measure was given floor priority, after Senator Chavez had made the motion at a time when the Senate generally assumed there would be no bills up while Congress awaited the President's message on the state of the Union and during a period when debate on the FEPC question was barred. Supporting the Chavez motion were twenty-two Democrats, twenty-six Republicans and one Progressive. Opposed were fifteen Democrats, all from the South, and two Republicans, Senators Rushfield of South Dakota and Millikin of Colorado.

Thus a Senate blockade, accompanied by open and vigorous revolt by Southern Democrats against the Administration, and marked by anger directed personally at the President, was dropped into the midst of Congressional activity which was appearing to give promise of early action on strike-curbing and other measures on the Chief Executive's "must" list.

"If this is all that Harry Truman has to offer," Senator George of Georgia told the Senate, "God help the Democratic party in 1946 and 1948."

"If it is Truman's idea that this is a measure that should be taken up first in this critical hour," said Senator Eastland of Mississippi, "then I don't think he is competent to handle the job he holds today."

Off the floor, Senator Overton of Louisiana said that the reconversion program in the Senate was "stopped in its tracks indefinitely" and added, on the political side, that "the Democratic party is shot to hell."

Senator Bilbo of Mississippi said:

"The bill is so vitally against the interests of the people and so manifestly unconstitutional and un-American that I propose to exercise my right to speak twice on the measure—for thirty days each time."

The surprise with which Senator Chavez maneuvered his motion was complete. In the midst of the efforts by Senators Eastland and O'Daniel of Texas to force the labor legislation out of the hands of the Labor Committee, Senator Chavez arose and was recognized. He moved that the FEPC bill be made the order of business.

Senator Hill of Alabama, the acting majority leader, apparently aghast, said he had understood that no controversial measure would be called up today.

"The Senator is in error," Mr. Chavez retorted. "The motion still stands."

Senator Eastland asked Mr. Chavez to yield, and when he did the Mississippian moved that the FEPC bill be recommitted to the Labor Committee. Mr. Chavez said he did not yield for a motion.

With debate not permissible at that time, the vote was taken, bringing the measure before the Senate. When the result was announced Mr. Chavez began his debate. Soon he yielded to Senator George "for a statement, but not for a motion."

"Mr. President," said Senator George, addressing the chair, "the action taken by the Senate in taking up S-101, the so-called Fair Practice bill, a bill to control and regulate by state will in the field of human relations, at a time of crisis such as our country faces today, is notice to the American people that the American Senate has no concept of the responsibility resting upon it.

"Not only that. When the Senate met on Monday the distinguished majority leader (Senator Barkley) asked that nothing be done until the President's message was submitted. Many of us were laboring under the definite impression, induced by the action taken at that time, that no controversial matter of any kind would be brought up at this time.

"I do not criticize Senators who are pledged to support the FEPC bill for voting as they did. I criticize the Democratic party for bringing it up under explicit conditions that at least no controversial matter would be presented to the Senate at this time.

"My party can take whatever course it will, but there are men on this side who are free men. They will not follow the party's will. I wish to serve that notice now. I serve it in all sincerity.

"If the President of the United States has nothing more important to submit to the American people in a time of industrial crisis, when the very life of this nation is at stake, then I must say to the President of the United States that I will follow the best course that my

Senate's Vote for Action On Fair Employment Bill

WASHINGTON, Jan. 17 (P)— *Following is the vote by which the Senate agreed today to take up a bill to establish a permanent Fair Employment Practices Commission:*

FOR THE MOTION—49

Democrats—22		
Barkley	Hayden	McMahon
Briggs	Huffman	Mead
Chavez	Johnson (Col.)	Murray
Downey	Kilgore	Myers
Gerry	Lucas	Thomas (Okla.)
Gossett	Magnuson	Tydings
Green	McCarran	
Guffey	McFarland	

Republicans—26		
Aiken	Cordon	Smith
Austin	Donnell	Taft
Ball	Ferguson	Tobey
Brewster	Gurney	Wherry
Bridges	Hickenlooper	White
Buck	Langer	Wiley
Butler	Morse	Wilson
Capehart	Revercomb	Young
Capper	Shipstead	

Progressive—1
La Follette

AGAINST THE MOTION—17

Democrats—15		
Andrews	Fulbright	McClellan
Bilbo	George	McKellar
Byrd	Hill	O'Daniel
Eastland	Johnston (S.C.)	Overton
Ellender	Maybank	Stewart

Republicans—2
Bushfield
Millikin

judgment leads me to follow. If that is all that Harry Truman has to offer, God help the Democratic party in 1946 and 1948."

With the Southern Democrats once again belligerently off the party reservation, a conference on floor strategy was called to meet in the office of Senator Byrd of Virginia before tomorrow's Senate session. There were indications that a new form of filibuster was developing. Hints were dropped that the FEPC bill "may not even be mentioned tomorrow." It had been said previously, when appraisals were made of what would happen when the FEPC bill was called up, that "at least 1,000" amend-

ments would be offered if the bill was not displaced by other legislation.

On the FEPC side there was talk of attempting to apply the closure rule, to limit debate. It was recalled, though, that the Senate seldom applied the gag to itself, regardless of issues.

Meanwhile debate on the FEPC measure went on. Mr. Chavez said that the President had spoken to the people over a country-wide broadcast and urged them to get action in Congress on bills he had recommended, including the FEPC measure. Other measures covering points of the reconversion program, he said, were not ready for floor consideration, while the FEPC bill, which had been on the calendar since last spring, was.

Senator Overton told the Senate that "definite assurances" had been given him that the FEPC bill would not be called up today.

When Senator Chavez yielded the floor, Senator Eastland was recognized by Senator O'Daniel, then presiding, and he gave notice that before the debate was over he would move to send the bill back to the Labor Committee, which he contended, had reported it out after three days of hearings with only "radical" and "Communist front" spokesmen as witnesses.

"The reason the FEPC bill was called up," Mr. Eastland said, "was to block labor legislation. Labor wants the Senate tied to stop legislation that would stop strikes."

After Senator Eastland had spoken for fifty-two minutes, Senator McKellar of Tennessee, the President pro tempore of the Senate who had left his presiding bench, moved adjournment until noon tomorrow.

January 18, 1946

OLD GUARD BERATED BY SENATOR MORSE

Oregonian, Denouncing Taft's Speech, Says Only Liberals Can Save the Country

Special to THE NEW YORK TIMES.

WASHINGTON, Jan. 5—A sharp attack on Senator Robert A. Taft, Ohio Republican, and other party "reactionaries" was made today by Senator Wayne Morse, liberal Republican of Oregon.

Senator Morse fired one barrel at President Truman and "reactionary" Democrats yesterday. Today, as members of his party were asserting that President Truman's broadcast to the people would help the Republicans in 1946, he fired the second barrel into his own party's ranks.

"Senator Taft, in his radio tirade against bi-partisan-sponsored progressive legislation, demonstrated in a frightening manner why the common men and women of America cannot look to the reactionary Republicans, who are seeking to control the Republican party, to protect and improve their standard of living," Mr. Morse said.

Senator Morse made it clear that he was giving no aid and comfort to the Democratic party. He called on the millions of independent voters in his own party and other independents to make sure that the country elected a progressive Congress in 1946.

Bricker's Future Involved

Politicians and observers here saw in Senator Morse's statement the public staging of an old party fight in which the conservative group, or so-called Old Guard, has rallied around former Governor Bricker of Ohio as their candidate for President in 1948. The liberal Republicans fear their party will be pushed further toward oblivion

if Mr. Bricker is nominated, and favor, if no other liberal appears on the scene, a man like former Governor Stassen of Minnesota.

It had been rumored that Senator Morse had been awaiting a suitable "D-Day" on which he might open fire on the conservatives of his party. When, last night, Senator Taft, in attacking Mr. Truman's speech, also attacked considerable legislation which many of his own party had supported, Senator Morse, it was agreed, decided that the day had come.

He had planned definitely to start the war later, though. It was learned today that the declaration of hostilities was originally scheduled for next week in The Progressive, the weekly newspaper published by Senator La Follette, Progressive party liberal, in Madison, Wis. It was established that that declaration, even stronger than today's, would appear as scheduled.

He Recalls "Ohio Gang"

Senator Morse recalled the "Ohio gang" of the Harding Administration, and the scandals involving it, and charged that the "gang" was chiefly responsible for destroying the liberalism of the

Republican party in the Twenties. This liberalism he defined as comprised of "sound middle-of-the-road policies for championing the rights and interests of the common people."

Senator Morse's statement read, in part, as follows:

"Taft demonstrated that his political and economic philosophy is the same as that of the reactionary Democrats now in control of the Democratic party. Fortunately for the country, there is growing hope that middle-of-the-road liberals within the Republican party will be successful in returning that party to its traditional role of fighting for and advancing the best interests of all the men and women of America rather than just a privileged few.

"That fight can be won only if the millions of independent Republican voters and the millions of other independent voters make clear in the 1946 elections that they want a progressive and not a reactionary Congress.

"Until the Ohio gang, aided and abetted by other reactionary leaders, destroyed the public's confidence in the liberalism of the Republican party in the 1920's, the Republican party always stood for sound middle-of-the-road liberal policies and for championing the rights and interests of the common people.

"That is the essence of the liberal movement and to do it without destroying the legitimate rights of business and the private-enterprise economy is a test of statesmanship under our form of representative Government."

It is understood that one of the statements in the Taft speech which spurred Senator Morse to open his fight was criticism of full-employment legislation. The full employment bill had been sponsored by Senator Morse and other Republican "liberals" ranged on his side—namely, Senators Aiken of Vermont, Langer of North Dakota and Tobey of New Hampshire.

Senator Morse's anger is said to have been aroused by Senator Taft's opposition to raising the minimum wage under the Fair Labor Standards Act from 40 to 65 cents an hour, and to bills for "equal pay for equal work" which have the support of Republican liberals.

Senator Morse is ready, according to his friends, for "a fight to the finish," even if it means "taking on" the Republican National Committee.

While the view here is that Senator Taft was not necessarily speaking for the Republican National Committee when he made his broadcast from Cincinnati, it was at least cleared through the committee, which is regarded as being under control of the "Old Guard." A notice of the speech and its text were distributed to the press on the stationery of the Republican National Committee.

January 6, 1946

LA FOLLETTE LOSES HIS SEAT IN SENATE

Judge McCarthy Takes Lead on Vote From Industrial Areas of Wisconsin

By JAMES RESTON
Special to THE NEW YORK TIMES.

MADISON, Wis., Aug. 14—The La Follette dynasty in the United States Senate, prominent for forty-one years, came to an end today when 36 - year - old Circuit Judge Joseph R. McCarthy of Appleton, an aggressive former tail gunner in the Marines, defeated Senator Robert M. La Follette Jr. for the renomination in the Wisconsin Republican primary election.

Mr. McCarthy's victory is generally believed to be tantamount to election in the November test against Howard J. McMurray of Milwaukee, the unopposed Democratic nominee.

The defeat of Mr. La Follette was as unorthodox as the political record of his father, who died in 1925 after representing Wisconsin in the Senate for twenty years. "Young Bob," who was elected to succeed his father that year and who has been in the Senate ever since, went to bed last night with a lead in the rural areas, where he has usually been weak, and woke up this. morning to find that the industrial areas, where he has usually been strong, had retired him from office.

Margin Is Wiped Out

Mr. La Follette had a comfortable margin late last night in the rural areas, but as the late reports came in early today from the industrial areas in the southeastern corner of the State, and particularly from Milwaukee County, his lead was wiped out and Mr. McCarthy forged ahead.

In 3,002 of the State's 3,146 precincts Mr. McCarthy led by 196,-079 to 191,203. When this lead of 4,876 was compiled Mr. La Follette conceded defeat and thanked the voters for their support over the past generation.

The explanation of Mr. La Follette's defeat seems to lie primarily in the loss of labor support, not so much to Mr. McCarthy in the Republican primary, but to Mr. McMurray, the unopposed candidate in the Democratic primary.

Mr. McMurray received over 56,-000 votes, most of them in the industrial areas, and it was generally conceded that most of these votes would have gone to Mr. La Follette, who is opposed by some labor factions but whose support in the past has usually come from the very groups that chose to go into the Democratic primary to vote for Mr. McMurray.

The vote by counties indicates the importance of the switch from Mr. La Follette in the populous industrial counties. In the 1940 election Mr. La Follette had a majority in the three southeastern counties —Milwaukee, Racine and Kenosha —of 61,831. In yesterday's voting, while he was expected to carry these counties again, he lost them by 10,651, more than twice the majority by which he lost to Mr. McCarthy.

There is a certain irony in this situation. Mr. La Follette was elected to the Senate twice, in 1925 and 1928, on the Republican ticket. He was a leader in the formation of the insurgent Progressive party which broke away from the Republicans and he was elected to the Senate by this party twice, in 1934 and 1940.

During the life of the Progressive party the Democrats in Washington, guided by President Roosevelt, established a liberal coalition with the Progressives, agreeing not to compete too strenuously against them. When Mr. La Follette decided in March to disband the Progressive party, the Democrats in general and Mr. McMurray in particular urged Mr. La Follette to come into the Democratic party.

This he refused to do, and one result was that the Liberal and Labor vote in the State was split yesterday, enough of it going to Mr. McMurray in the Democratic primary to defeat Mr. La Follette in the Republican primary.

The CIO Political Action Committee forces contributed somewhat to Mr. La Follette's defeat. Though the forces of labor in this State are split, the left wing of the PAC continually sniped at Mr. La Follette's foreign policy record and urged the workers to vote in the Democratic primary.

The defeat of Mr. La Follette was also, of course, a victory for the record and personality of Judge McCarthy and his sponsor, Thomas Coleman, leader of the

WINNER AND LOSER IN WISCONSIN PRIMARY

Judge Joseph R. McCarthy
Associated Press Wirephoto

Senator Robert M. LaFollette Jr.
Blackstone Studios, 1944

State Republican organization and long-time opponent of the La Follettes.

Mr. McCarthy, the youngest Circuit Court judge in the history of Wisconsin, had the backing of the Republican organization. He picked up some labor and veteran support with an extremely active campaign and benefited somewhat by the growing sentiment in this part of the country against old names and old faces.

Mr. La Follette's opposition to the candidacy of Gov. Walter S. Goodland, the 83-year-old incumbent, also appears to have cost him some votes. As Governor, Mr. Goodland vetoed a bill, sponsored by the regular Republican organization, which would have prevented the Progressives from seeking office yesterday under the Republican banner. In spite of this, however, Mr. La Follette came out against Mr. Goodland and in favor of Ralph W. Immell, former Progressive.

In the Gubernatorial race, however, Governor Goodland defeated Mr. Immell by over 20,000 votes despite the fact that he was opposed not only by Mr. La Follette, but by the regular Republican organization. Besides, he did not go out of Madison to make a single campaign speech.

His margin for 2,992 of the State's 3,146 precincts was 187,033 to 166,711 for Mr. Immell, and 66,-615 for Delbert J. Kenny, West

Bend investment counselor who had the backing of the regular Republican organization.

Governor Goodland will be opposed in November by Daniel W. Hoan, former Socialist Mayor of Milwaukee, but his election seems assured.

Principles Second to Tactics

In national terms, it is easy to overestimate the effect of this campaign. The Republicans are saying the result is a protest against Mr. La Follette's support of New Deal domestic legislation.

Some of the PAC leaders are saying it is a repudiation of Mr. La Follette's speeches against Soviet foreign policy. The Democrats are saying it is one more indication that the West is tired of those who did not support the Roosevelt-Truman foreign policy.

And, finally, there are some observers who believe that the election retires an anti-Stassen candidate (Mr. La Follette) and retains in the State House a pro-Stassen candidate in Governor Goodland.

There may be a little something in all views, but the election seems to have been decided more by political tactics than by principles, and the light vote of about one-third of the eligible electorate seems to indicate apathy rather than any great conviction for or against either of the principal candidates for the Senate.

August 15, 1946

M'CARTHY'S RECORD LIKE ALGER STORY

Wisconsin Farm Boy Set Out to Conquer the World and Became a Judge at 29

Special to THE NEW YORK TIMES.

MADISON, Wis., Aug. 14—Joe McCarthy is back in the headlines out here in Wisconsin, only this time it's politics, not baseball.

This "Joe" is Joseph McCarthy of Appleton, a confident young man of 36, just as Irish as "Old Joe" of the Yankees, and he made the headlines this afternoon by beating "Young Bob" La Follette for the Republican senatorial nomination in Wisconsin.

It may be, of course, that "Young Joe" will not turn out to be a world champion, but he has made quite a start. At 36, he is the youngest circuit court judge this State has ever had, and he is certainly the only judge from these parts who stepped down from the bench, enlisted in the Marines as a private and spent part of his time during the war as a tail gunner in the Pacific.

A Horatio Alger Character

The conqueror of Mr. La Follette is a straight Horatio Alger character. He was born on a farm in Outagamie County, Wisconsin, went to country grade school there, then quit and set out, in accordance with the Alger scripts, to conquer the world.

When he got as far as Manawa Wis., he took a job in a store where it was pointed out to him that his education was scarcely complete. So, at 19, he took four years of high school in one, and went on from there to Marquette University.

Mr. McCarthy won his law degree in 1934 and five years later, at the age of 29, he was elected circuit judge in this State, a job he interrupted, despite his deferment and his $8,000-a-year salary, to offer his services as a private in the Marine Corps.

The young jurist admits that it was hard on his dignity, among other things, to get through the Marine training school at Quantico, Va., but, as he says, after taking or losing almost every hill in the State of Virginia, he won a commission and finally was shipped out to the Pacific.

There he took part in seventeen raids against the Japanese, over Rabaul, Kahili, Buka and Munda, among other places, getting himself wounded and properly cited in the process.

Candidate in Uniform

In a manner not exactly clear, Mr. McCarthy managed to compete from the Pacific for the Republican nomination for the Senate in 1944, and though he was not in the country during the campaign, he got somewhere in the neighborhood of 100,000 votes.

Yesterday he did considerably better. He went into Milwaukee, where Mr. La Follette is usually very strong, and picked up enough votes to overcome a deficit of several thousand and get himself a nomination which virtually assures his election to the Senate in November.

So long as the energy and charm of the Irish are popular in American political life, Mr. McCarthy seems assured of some success. While Mr. La Follette was in Washington working on a variety of projects, Mr. McCarthy raced around this State talking to and shaking hands with anybody who looked old enough to vote for him, and his vigorous campaign was at least one factor in his victory.

Nobody in yesterday's campaign allowed issues to get in his way very much, but the general idea seems to be that the Marine captain is for whatever Mr. La Follette was against, and vice versa. Roughly, that would make him conservative on domestic affairs and a supporter of an active American foreign policy, but, as he says, he is young yet, and the Senate will find out more about that later.

August 15, 1946

Prior Objection by Clayton To Wallace Talk Disclosed

State Department Warned of Embarrassing Byrnes—President Remains Silent— Taft Scores Bid for PAC Support

By JAMES RESTON
Special to THE NEW YORK TIMES.

WASHINGTON, Sept. 13—President Truman was in the middle of an acrimonious national and international political controversy today as a result of his endorsement of Secretary of Commerce Henry A. Wallace's lets-make-up-with-the-Russians speech of last evening.

It is known that before the speech was made on Thursday, Acting Secretary of State William L. Clayton sent a message to the President through the latter's press secretary, Charles Ross, saying that in his opinion, the Wallace speech would embarrass Secretary James F. Byrnes in the Paris peace treaty negotiations.

Abroad, Mr. Byrnes, who has been following a firm policy against the Soviet Union's political and military expansion toward the West, was reported to be disturbed by portions of Mr. Wallace's speech that seemed to oppose that policy.

Also abroad, nations on both sides of the East-West diplomatic conflict asked their missions here for information as to whether the Wallace speech indicated a re-direction of American policy toward a pro-Soviet, spheres-of-influence conception.

On the national scene, the President found himself confronted with angry attacks on his action not only from the opposition party but also from within the ranks of his own political supporters.

More criticism of the President's action is expected when it is generally learned that Mr. Clayton warned him of the implications of the Wallace endorsement before the speech was made.

The Commerce Department issued advance copies of the speech late Thursday morning. A member of the State Department press section was sent to the National Press Club here to get copies of it, and these were distributed to high officials of the Department.

The critical nature of the speech was noted at once in the Department, and when the President endorsed it at his press conference later in the day, Mr. Clayton called Mr. Ross and asked him to tell the President that the speech would embarrass Mr. Byrnes.

It is not known whether the President actually received the message before Mr. Wallace spoke late that night in Madison Square Garden, but Mr. Clayton sent the text of the speech to Mr. Byrnes in Paris with a report on when he had seen it for the first time and what he had done at the last moment in an attempt to avoid the embarrassment.

The day's actions in this controversy, which threatened to weaken the bi-partisan cooperation on foreign policy at home and confuse United States negotiations abroad, were as follows:

(1) It was learned that the State Department had informed the President, before the speech was delivered, that it felt Mr. Wallace's remarks would embarrass Mr. Byrnes in the peace treaty negotiations.

(2) Senator Robert A. Taft, Republican, of Ohio, backed by officials of the Republican National Committee in the capital, charged that by supporting Mr. Wallace's remarks the President had "betrayed" Mr. Byrnes and was bidding for the support of the CIO Political Action Committee, which, he asserted, favored appeasing the Russians abroad and promoting communism at home.

(3) Representative E. E. Cox, Democrat, of Georgia, who has been outspoken in opposition to Soviet policy for months, telegraphed Mr. Truman that the President's support of the Wallace speech was "the worst thing that could have happened to the country" because, he said, "it cuts the ground from beneath Secretary Byrnes and frightens America."

Faced with these developments, Mr. Truman adopted the strategy of silence. He was reported to have made contact with Mr. Byrnes in Paris to reassure the Secretary that he was not changing the emphasis of American policy, but there was no confirmation of this report.

The tendency at the White House and the State Department was to reassure the press and the foreign diplomats quietly that the United States policy was not veering toward the Left, but beyond that nothing was being said in public in the hope that the incident would pass.

The opposition party, stoking up for the November elections, showed no willingness to let the incident drop, however. On the contrary, it seemed likely tonight that long after the astonishment of the world over the mysteries of American Cabinet procedure had been forgotten, the Wallace speech would be an active political issue at home.

Mr. Taft, who often is mentioned as a candidate for the Republican Presidential nomination in 1948, released a statement saying the President, by approving the Wallace speech, had repudiated the Byrnes policy of fighting against zones of influence and of demanding freedom and equality for all peoples.

Appeal for PAC Vote Seen

The President, he charged, had advocated a milder policy toward communism and a less friendly attitude toward Britain in order to appeal for the support of the PAC and the Communists in the November election. The Democratic party, he concluded, was so "divided between communism and Americanism that its foreign policy can only be futile and contradictory and make the United States the laughing stock of the world."

A second statement was issued by the campaign director for the Republican National Committee, Clarence J. Brown, who recommended a comparison between Mr. Wallace's speech and Mr. Byrnes' recent speech at Stuttgart as "a perfect illustration of the confusion characterizing the Democratic Administration."

That the President's endorse-

142

ment of the Wallace speech was "discouraging" to his supporters in the capital was evident this afternoon at the State Department, where Mr. Clayton had to face up to the questioning of a curious and vaguely incredulous group of reporters.

Believes Byrnes' Views Stand

Even these reporters, who have seen the United States stumble into international embarrassments before, wanted to be sure that there was not a "new line" on this country's foreign policy. Mr. Clayton replied that so far as he knew all Mr. Byrnes' statements of policy stood.

Careful checking in the capital today indicated that the real significance of the Wallace speech lay not in the international field of politics but in the national.

In recent days there has been talk among Mr. Truman's more moderate supporters of the necessity of making another attempt for a Truman-Stalin meeting to stabilize American-Russian relations. If anything, however, such a meeting, which would have had the warm support of Mr. Wallace and the Left, seems more remote as a result of yesterday's speech and today's controversy.

In the national field, however, regardless of how much Mr. Truman now demonstrates his support of the Byrnes policies, an active political issue probably will be made, first, of Mr. Wallace's views, and, second, if these are repudiated by the Administration's acts, of Mr. Truman's endorsement of a speech that his closest colleagues agree he did not read very carefully.

September 14, 1946

Cabinet Unity Is Restored Through Exit of Wallace

Weakening of Democratic Party and Slump in Truman Prestige Are Held Costs

By JAMES RESTON
Special to THE NEW YORK TIMES.

WASHINGTON, Sept. 20—The resignation of Henry A. Wallace restored unity within the Cabinet behind the foreign policy of Secretary of State Byrnes, but in the opinion of some responsible observers here, it did so at the cost of weakening the Democratic party and impairing the prestige of President Truman at home and abroad.

The thinking of these persons on the preliminaries and implications of this morning's resignation of the Secretary of Commerce was as follows:

(1) The general belief is that Secretary Byrnes told the President he was not satisfied with the promise that Mr. Wallace should be silent until after the Conference of Paris and that while he did not ask Mr. Truman to choose between him and Mr. Wallace, he left the President to draw his own conclusions from Mr. Byrnes' "dissatisfaction."

(2) The complaints of other members of the Cabinet and influential Democrats on Capitol Hill and elsewhere about Mr. Truman's "agreement" to let Mr. Wallace renew his appeals for a redirection of American foreign policy are also believed to have contributed to the President's sudden decision.

Truman "Blames Himself"

(3) Mr. Truman told members of his Cabinet that he "blamed himself" for much of the controversy of the last few days and that he regretted having to take today's decision, but that he was convinced that this was preferable to repeated public demonstrations of Cabinet disunity during the next few months of intensive negotiation over the peace treaties.

(4) It is generally agreed, however, that Mr. Wallace does not go out of the Cabinet as a discredited dissenter but as the victim of his own sincere beliefs and of a series of errors, most of which he did not commit. He wrote his letter of dissent at the President's request, brought it into the open with the President's permission, and did everything to meet the President's wishes except confess insincerity. His beliefs were not popular but they were not the main reason of his resignation either.

(5) As a result of this sequence of events and the President's part in them, Mr. Truman has lost prestige at a critical time before the national elections, and while he is free to conduct a unified Cabinet in the foreign field, his direction is subject to the reservation that, like Woodrow Wilson, he may lose control of the lower House and be defeated himself at the next Presidential election.

There is considerable division of opinion here over the practical political results of Mr. Wallace's departure. He is a symbol and even a prophet to a vocal minority on the Left. Though the break came over views that the late Franklin D. Roosevelt had not always endorsed, he is still remembered by many as Mr. Roosevelt's personal choice as running mate in 1940 and 1944.

Consequently, on the home front, the Communists who booed some of the remarks in his Madison Square Garden speech and have since swung over to his support, may be expected to use what influence they have in transportation and industry to embarrass the Administration's reconstruction program.

Also, there is every expectation that dissatisfied "liberal" elements in both of the major parties may make another attempt to start a third party with Mr. Wallace and Senator Claude Pepper of Florida as the leaders.

Intimates of the former Secretary of Commerce said today, however, that they did not believe Mr. Wallace would leave the party, and if he remains in it and supports it in the elections, as he is generally expected to do, it is not regarded as likely that the Political Action Committee and other supporters of Mr. Wallace will vote Republican merely to punish Mr. Truman for demanding the resignation of their favorite.

The greatest fear of the Democrats is that they may lose the independent voting strength and therefore control of the House of Representatives in the Eightieth Congress and that Mr. Truman, like Woodrow Wilson, may have difficulty in governing during the critical days of peace-making abroad and reconstruction at home.

In the foreign field, this fear of a declining Administration certainly cannot help Mr. Byrnes in his negotiations. He would undoubtedly have been hampered more if the President had chosen to follow Mr. Wallace's foreign policy recommendations and had thereby lost the support of the Republicans, as he certainly would, but the departure from the Cabinet of Moscow's chief advocate is not calculated to help remove the Soviet Government's suspicion that the United States Government is taking a hostile attitude toward it.

This, indeed, is one of the paradoxes in the situation. Mr. Wallace wrote his letter and made his speech in the first place in the hope of moderating the policy of this Government in its dealings with Moscow.

The result of the speech, however, combined with Mr. Truman's handling of it, has been to confirm the policy of those Mr. Wallace opposed and to create a strong body of opinion in the country against making any of the concessions Mr. Wallace proposed.

The "Fundamental Conflict"

The "fundamental conflict" which President Truman referred to today in asking for Mr. Wallace's resignation lay not in the fact that he proposed different foreign policy objectives but that he proposed different tactics of negotiations.

He indicated that he was willing to reduce our military expenditures, cease production of long range bombers, turn over our chain of bases to the United Nations, and negotiate a loan with Moscow, among other things, as a preliminary to reaching a general settlement with the Soviet Union.

The Administration was not ready to make such concessions as a preliminary to such a settlement and was not convinced that making further concessions was the way to achieve such a settlement.

But these views would not have brought about the split today had it not been for the disorderly way in which the difference of opinion was handled. And it was this sense of disorderliness and clumsiness in the handling of the dispute at the White House that disturbs the Democrats as much as the fear of losing Mr. Wallace's supporters.

September 21, 1946

REPUBLICANS SURE OF CONTROL IN HOUSE, MAKE GAINS IN NATION IN TURN TO RIGHT

By ARTHUR KROCK

The voters in yesterday's elections for the full membership of the next House of Representatives, for one-third of the Senate and for Governors of many States, swung this nation sharply right in a left-veering world.

They placed the Republican party, the minority opposition in the United States for the last fourteen years, in control of the House by a majority of more than forty.

They put the government of twenty-five States, a majority of the Union, in Republican hands by adding Republican Governors in Ohio and Massachusetts to the twenty-three already belonging to that party.

They exchanged Democrats for Republicans in several key States—notably New York, Delaware, Massachusetts, Pennsylvania, Nevada, Idaho and Ohio—with indications that the changes will amount to the ten necessary to give the Republicans control of the Senate. Also, a Wisconsin Senate seat change from Progressive to Republican.

Control will be settled by the trans-Mississippi States of Missouri, New Mexico, Wyoming, Washington, Montana and California. In New Mexico and California the portents favored the Republicans at 2 A. M. today, and Senator Frank Briggs, the Democratic incumbent in Missouri seemed to be marked for defeat.

The voters swept Thomas E. Dewey to re-election as Governor of New York and into the front rank of aspirants for his party's Presidential nomination in 1948, though never in their history have the Republicans renominated a defeated national candidate and Mr. Dewey lost to President Roosevelt in 1944. A feature of Mr. Dewey's victory was his heavy vote against **Senator James M. Mead, his Democratic opponent, in New York City.**

The voters who turned to the Republicans in great numbers made the race for the Senate in Maryland closer than the Democratic supporters of Gov. Herbert R. O'Conor had expected after he had disavowed the programs of the radicals in the Democratic party. This disavowal will add another conservative to the Senate Democrats, and Virginia, by overwhelming majorities for Senator Harry F. Byrd and Representative Willis Robertson, nominated to fill out the unexpired term of the late Senator Carter Glass, added two more.

Kentucky, which has been a Democratic stronghold for years with the exception of 1928, pointed toward the right when John Sherman Cooper, the Republican Senatorial candidate, kept the lead over his opponent, John Young Brown, and Representative Emmet O'Neal of Louisville conceded his defeat for re-election by Thurston B. Morton. Representative Louis Ludlow, a House Democratic veteran, won in Indianapolis over Albert J. Beveridge Jr., but his deeply cut majority is another indication that the large industrial cities from which President Roosevelt drew his heavy and consistent majorities have joined the trend away from the left.

If the Middle West and the Far West reveal the same voting disposition which the East and the Central States showed last night, the Republican victory will develop into a landslide.

The only apparent success for radical voting elements in the election was the re-election of Representative Vito Marcantonio in New York City. Later returns from the West may increase this score, but it will be small. Among the CIO's major casualties was Senator Joseph F. Guffey in Pennsylvania, and Tom Sweeney, the Republican candidate for Senator in West Virginia, was running neck and neck with Senator Harley M. Kilgore, a strong champion of the CIO.

Illinois fell in with the Republican procession when the election of Representative William G. Stratton as Representative-at-large was claimed on the basis of the returns, though there was a heavy Democratic vote in another great industrial center, Chicago.

The absence of jubilation from the inner rooms of the successful candidates and from the public statements they made was reflected, so far as New York City was concerned, by the quiet in the streets and the small size of the gatherings here. The consensus seemed to be that the country knew it was making a serious decision in taking a Congressional majority away from the executive but felt that a change was necessary and overdue if, as Representative Joseph W. Martin Jr., who will be the next Speaker put it, the Government was ever to be "taken out of the people's hair."

Governor Dewey spoke over the radio in the same serious, non-triumphant vein. And B. Carroll Reece, Republican National Chairman, displayed the identical mood when he offered to President Truman full cooperation by the Republicans in Congress for the business of the nation and asked the President to give it in return.

The theme of the victors was expressed by Governor Dewey when he said that the people had voted for the political philosophy that holds Government should be the servant of the people, and not their master.

Governor Dewey, acknowledging his triumphant return to office, called the result a victory for constitutional government over radicalism. There were many evidences that this analysis correctly appraised the party reversals in many States and districts. Nebraska, for example, voted to make the closed shop unconstitutional. But the desire for a change, which appeared in the Congressional and State elections of 1938 and 1942 and were curbed first by the war abroad and then by the entrance of this nation into that war, was a major influence in the Republican gains.

At the last moment in the campaign, the Democratic management sought to cancel this desire at the risk of the bi-partisan coalition on foreign policy by asserting that the Republicans in power were more likely than the Democrats to advance the nation toward war. This argument apparently had no real weight with the voters.

The big registration throughout the country was reflected in what observers think will be one of the largest by-election votes in the nation's history. The Republican claim that the city registration meant a protest vote in their favor was completely borne out by the early returns.

The elections marked the end of twenty years in which the political fortunes of the two major parties have followed a typical cycle. In 1926, the Republicans, who had taken executive power and the House of Representatives from the Democrats in 1920, got one more member than the Democrats returned to the Senate and increased their overall House majority to 39. In 1928, the Republican Senate majority had been increased to 18 and their excess over all other parties in the House went to 99.

Democrats Won House in '30

This was the finish of the Republican cycle, for in 1930 the Democrats organized the House by a majority of one, carried the Senate and the Presidency also in 1932, and in 1936 reached their peak in modern times with a Senate majority of 54 and a House majority of 232. From that year onward the Democratic dominance in Congress and in the governing system of the States began to recede. President Roosevelt won two more elections, aided in 1940 by the shadow of war and in 1944 by the substance. But in the Congressional elections of 1938 and 1942 the Republicans made gains in both the House and the Senate, presaging the wider recovery which the prophets foretold for 1946.

The voting was the climax of an unusual campaign, in which President Truman, the head of the Democratic party, went into the silences on the advice of the campaign managers, and in which the Democratic orators shifted their ground, and hoped by so doing to shift the issues, on several occasions. And as a part of this phenomenon it should be noted that the most encouraging returns for the Democrats came from Maryland and Virginia, where the successful candidates of that party had avoided endorsement of the national Administration and sedulously avoided endorsement of programs which the Congress of Industrial Organizations and its Political Action Committee have been vigorously demanding.

November 6, 1946

WALLACE CHARTS POLICIES FOR 1948 IN LIBERAL MERGER

By WILLIAM R. CONKLIN

Charting a course of political action for the newly formed "Progressive Citizens of America" as an independent group with third-party possibilities, Henry A. Wallace, former Secretary of Commerce, declared yesterday that progressives could capture three-fourths of the country's vote if "we go all out to get it over to them."

Mr. Wallace made the final speech at a two-day convention in the Hotel Commodore, at which 300 delegates from twenty-one States voted to merge ten liberal organizations into the "Progressive Citizens of America." In addition to fusing the National Citizens Political Action Committee with the Independent Citizens Committee of the Arts, Sciences and Professions, the merger includes eight smaller groups.

Dr. Frank Kingdon, former chairman of NCPAC, and Jo Davidson, former chairman of the Independent Committee, were chosen as co-chairmen of the new organization.

Role of Liberals Stressed

Mr. Wallace, who resigned last September at President Truman's request after criticizing American policy toward Russia, was temperate yesterday in dealing with Soviet-American relations. His speech placed primary emphasis upon the role of liberals in the national scene, with Russian-American relations forming a secondary theme.

For the sake of pointing up the differences between reactionaries and liberals, he said he would prefer to see an "all-out, clear-cut reactionary" like Senator Robert A. Taft of Ohio in high office than a "lukewarm liberal."

"You should do all you can to get the issues clearly defined," Mr. Wallace told the delegates. "The lukewarm liberals are people who try to sit on not only two but three chairs at a time, and they are the people who get us into trouble. I would prefer to see an all-out, clear-cut reactionary like Senator Taft in high office than a lukewarm liberal."

The applause was unenthusiastic when Mr. Wallace told the gathering that "we should have no allegiance outside this country of any sort," but it swelled into respectable volume when he added: "Except to One World, peaceful and prosperous."

Clashes Over Russia Decried

Pleading for unity among liberals, he said:

"The fundamental progressive faith is so broad that we should not allow ourselves to be divided on any minor issues. The essence of the progressive faith as I see it is belief in the goal of peace, prosperity and freedom in one world.

"Those who put hatred of Russia first in all their feelings and actions do not believe in peace.

"Those who hold up Russian standards as a guide for us in the United States do not believe in freedom.

"As American progressives we are not interested in any fight between the Russian haters and the Russophiles. We believe that much of such fighting is engineered by the enemy. We shall not allow the attacks of the enemy to stampede us into foolish Red-baiting. Nor shall we allow those who owe their primary allegiance to some foreign power to determine our course. I still believe in a free American press, even though it lies continually about Russia and labor—and thus endangers both world peace and industrial peace.

To Reject Branding as Reds

"We shall never be against anything simply because Russia is for it. Neither shall we ever be for anything simply because Russia is for it. We shall hold firmly to the American theme of peace, prosperity and freedom, and shall repel all the attacks of the plutocrats and monopolists who will try to brand us as Reds.

"If it is traitorous to believe in peace, we are traitors. If it is communistic to believe in prosperity for all, we are Communists. If it is Red-baiting to fight for free speech and real freedom of the press, we are Red-baiters. If it is un-American to believe in freedom from monopolistic dictation, we are un-American. I say that we are more American than the neo-Fascists who attack us."

Turning to the domestic scene, the former Secretary surveyed the present situation in terms of what the progressives could do to change it.

"Belief in freedom does not mean that we stand for turning the country over to the laissez-faire big business interests and their special pleaders in the journalistic and political world," he said.

"The laissez-faire freedom of selfish big business inevitably leads to depression, higher tariffs, political confusion in many nations, revolution in some nations, and eventually, war. To prevent this we must have a certain amount of both international and national planning. Eventually the United Nations must become a world federation, but we cannot expect Russia to become part of such a federation until the United States has demonstrated her ability to eliminate the excesses of the post-war business cycle.

"The Republican leadership in Congress is in serious danger of repeating its mistakes of the 20's as it deals with tariff, taxation, and fiscal policies. To prevent the Republican Congress and the laissez-faire big business men from leading us down the high road of boom, bust, and war, is the immediate justification for our progressive existence. Our ultimate justification is a positive program of world peace, world prosperity and world freedom."

Several Names Considered

Conceding that small business and the farmers were most hostile to the liberal cause, Mr. Wallace said they could be won over by appeals using the language of the Bible, the Declaration of Independence, and other well-known quotations. As an immediate objective, he said the Democratic party should be made "out and out progressive."

Having adopted the name "Independent Citizens for Political Action," the delegates reconsidered their vote after protests from Midwest and Far West delegations that prejudice existed in their communities against the words "Political Action." Before the final vote was taken on "Progressive Citizens of America" the convention voted down "National Congress of Progressives," "Independent Progressives," "National Progressives," "Independent Citizens of America," "Independent Voters of America" and "Progressive Voters of America."

Before the final organization was completed the convention hit one snag on universal military training. After a test vote showed a majority for the Young Citizens PAC's opposition to military training, the matter was recalled from the organization's program and referred to its directors for study and a recommendation. A long wrangle on annual dues to be paid to the national treasury from local chapters was resolved on a payment of $1.50 a year out of a total of $3, with rebates to be made to local groups in appropriate circumstances.

Floor contributions started the new organization toward its 1947 goal of $225,000. Herman Shumlin, producer, and Michael Nisselson, banker, were elected secretary and treasurer respectively.

December 30, 1946

130 LIBERALS FORM A GROUP ON RIGHT

Opposition to Communism Is a Major Tenet of Americans for Democratic Action

ROOSEVELT MEN INCLUDED

Program Calls for Expansion of New-Deal Efforts and Aid for United Nations

Special to The New York Times.
WASHINGTON, Jan. 4—A group of 130 men and women committed to the propagation of liberal ideals and rejecting collaboration with Communists and their sympathizers established today a new organization called Americans for Democratic Action.

The historic significance of their decision was the cleavage which it creates in the American liberal movement. A week ago in New York another group formed the Progressive Citizens of America. The primary issue between the two is the attitude toward individuals who hew to the Communist party line in the United States.

Today's meeting was an invitation affair sponsored by the Union for Democratic Action, an organization formed nearly five years ago. The UDA nominally remains in existence, but it is expected that it will be dissolved as the new and expanded body overcomes the problems of organizational machinery. An organizing committee of twenty-five was appointed to carry on the program begun by the conference.

The conference participants included many who were associated with the administration of the late President Roosevelt, including his widow and his son, Franklin D. Roosevelt Jr. There also were leaders from unions in the American Federation of Labor and the Congress of Industrial Organizations and from independent labor groups.

First Goals Outlined

The immediate objective, it was agreed, was a reconstruction of the liberal movement, free of totalitarian influence from either the Left or the Right. The conferees agreed that no formal manifesto resolving all the problems of the nation and the world could be drafted at a one-day meeting, but reported complete harmony on these basic principles:

1. The New Deal program must be expanded to insure decent levels of health, nutrition, shelter and education.

2. Civil liberties must be protected from concentrated wealth and overcentralized government. They must be extended to all Americans regardless of race, color, creed or sex.

3. Any sound foreign policy requires a healthy and prosperous domestic economy.

4. The United States must continue to give full support to the United Nations. The conference endorses the American plan for international control of atomic energy.

5. Because the interests of the United States are the interests of free men everywhere, America must furnish political and economic support to democratic and freedom-loving peoples the world over.

6. Within the general framework of present American foreign policy steps must be taken to raise standards of living and support civil and political freedoms everywhere. These policies are in the great democratic tradition of Jefferson, Jackson, Lincoln, Wilson and Franklin D. Roosevelt. We reject any association with Communists or sympathizers with communism in the United States as completely as we reject any association with Fascists or their sympathizers. Both are hostile to the principles of freedom and democracy on which this Republic has grown great.

Henderson Is a Backer

The choice of a chairman or president was believed to lie between Leon Henderson, former OPA Administrator, and Wilson W. Wyatt, former Housing Expediter. It was Mr. Henderson who formally moved to establish the new organization. The organizing committee of which both are members was to select a chairman and other officers in week-end meetings and to draft a proposed program of action.

Although the organization has third-party possibilities eventually, sentiment for that course now was not significant. Mrs. Roosevelt was reported to have indicated in a speech that the preferable course now was to attempt to work within the Democratic party and to help shape that party's program.

Pending a decision on financing, she called for subscriptions and promptly raised $5,000, in addition to $4,300 which was contributed at a dinner last night.

Mrs. Roosevelt said the liberals were fighting both Communists and Fascists and must not lose sight of either. They are not trying to tell Russians what kind of government they should have, she

Democrats: Left and Right

said, but they do not want communism in this country or in any democratic country.

Mrs. Roosevelt also emphasized that the policy of the organization should not be merely negative, but should seek affirmatively to promote the welfare of this country and of democratic nations throughout the world.

Walter P. Reuther, president of the United Automobile Workers, CIO, said two difficulties would confront the organization. One was that some persons would be afraid to be called "Red-baiters." The other was a belief that the organization would accept anyone merely because he was anti-Communist. He said both ideas should be rejected.

While the CIO was a participant through personal representatives of President Philip Murray, the question of the CIO's position in the divided liberal movement was not clearly resolved. The PCA last week named Mr. Murray one of its vice chairmen, although he was not personally present.

Barry Bingham, editor of The Louisville Courier-Journal, answering questions at a news conference, said the primary areas of disagreement with the PCA could be found in Points 5 and 6 of the ADA statement. These referred to "the interests of free men everywhere" and to the rejection of Communist sympathizers.

Conferees named to the organizing committee were as follows:

Charles G. Bolte, New York City, chairman, American Veterans Committee.
Elmer Davis, Washington.
George Edwards, Detroit, president, Detroit Common Council.
Ethel S. Epstein, New York City.
Leon Henderson, Washington.
Hubert Humphrey, Mayor of Minneapolis.
Mrs. Clyde Johnson, Cincinnati.
Reinhold Niebuhr, New York City.
Edward Prichard Jr., Paris, Ky.
Franklin D. Roosevelt Jr., New York City.
Frank W. McCulloch, Chicago.
Mrs. Gifford Pinchot, Washington.
Bishop William Scarlett, St. Louis.
Walter White, New York City, president, Association for Advancement of Colored People.
Wilson W. Wyatt, Louisville, Ky.
Harvey Brown, president, International Association of Machinists, independent.
David Dubinsky, president, International Ladies Garment Workers, AFL.
Hugo Ernst, Cincinnati, president, Hotel and Restaurant Workers, AFL.
B. F. McLaurin, international representative, Brotherhood of Sleeping Car Porters, AFL.
James Killen, Washington, vice president, International Brotherhood of Pulp, Sulphite and Paper Workers.
John Green, Camden, N. J., president, Shipbuilding Workers, CIO.
Walter P. Reuther, president, United Automobile Workers, CIO.
Willard Townsend, president, United Transport Service, CIO.
Samuel Wolchok, president, Retail, Wholesale and Department Store Workers, CIO.
James Loeb Jr., Washington, secretary.

Committee of the Whole

Members of the Committee of the Whole were announced as follows:

Stewart Alsop, Jack Altman, Douglas Anderson, Eugenie Anderson.
George Baldanzi, Robert Bendiner, Andrew Biemiller, Barry Bingham, Genevieve Blatt, Dr. William Bohn, Chester Bowles, Evelyn Brandt, Harvey Brown, Andrew Brown.
James B. Carey, John A. Carroll, Alison E. Carter, Marquis Childs, Jerry Clifford, George Cranmore, Kenneth Crawford, Nelson Cruikshank.
Max Danish, A. Powell Davies, Elmer Davis, Charles Douds, David Dubinsky.
John Edelman, George Edwards, Margaret Edwards, Emily Ehle, Ethel S. Epstein, Hugo Ernst, Morris Ernst.
Herbert L. Fedder, Louis Fischer, Bernard Fleishman.
J. Kenneth Galbraith, Leo Gamow, Adolph Gerner, Richard Gilbert, David Ginsburg, A. P. Goldblum, Lester Granger, John Green, James Greer, John J. Grogan.
Louis Harris, Gilbert Harrison, A. J. Hayes, Mortimer Hays, Allan Haywood, Anna Arnold Hedgeman, Leon Henderson, the Rev. George Higgins, Melvin D. Hildreth, Dan Hoan, Johannes Hoeber, Sal Hoffman, Carl Holderman, Edward Hollander, Sidney Hollander, Chet Holifield, Frank Hook, Robert W. Hudgens.
Gardner Jackson, F. Ernest Johnson, Mrs. Clyde Johnson, Morse Johnson.
James S. Killen, Chester Kerr, Herman Koppelmann, Leon J. Kowal, Martin Kyne.
Joseph P. Lash, Trude Pratt Lash, Leo Lerner, Mrs. Newman Levy, Alfred Baker Lewis, Sarah Limbach, Dr. Eduard Lindeman, James Loeb, Mrs. Alex Lowenthal.
Frank McCulloch, A. M. McDowell, Jean McIntyre, B. F. McLaurin, Eugene Messner, Nathaniel Minkoff, Don Montgomery, Edgar A. Mowrer, William L. Munger.
Arthur Naftalin, Reinhold Niebuhr, Bishop G. Bromley Oxnam.
S. K. Padover, Cornelia B. Pinchot, Nelson P. Poynter, Paul A. Porter.
Joseph Rauh Jr., Florence Reisenstein, Walter P. Reuther, Emil Rieve, Mrs. Franklin D. Roosevelt, Franklin D. Roosevelt Jr., Marvin Rosenberg, William Rosenblatt, James Rowe Jr.
Alex E. Salzman, the Right Rev. William Scarlett, Harry Schachter, Arthur M. Schlesinger Jr., August Scholle, Boris Shishkin, Anthony Wayne Smith, Miss Laurence Stapleton, Tom Stokes.
Barney Taylor, Mrs. M. E. Tilly, Willard S. Townsend, Jay Turner.
Jerry Voorhis.
George Weaver, James Wechsler, Edward Weyler, Walter White, Samuel Wolchok, Wilson Wyatt.
Hortense Young, Abraham Zwerdling.

January 5, 1947

WALLACE TO RUN; PLEDGES 3D PARTY TO BAR WAR POLICY

DEMOCRATS SCORED

He Calls Insurgents to Fight 'Bipartisan' Plan for 'Armed Camps'

CONFERS WITH LIBERALS

Candidate Tells Leaders of 18 States 'Coalition Dry Rot' Makes Step Necessary

---

By LOUTHER S. HORNE
Special to The New York Times.

CHICAGO, Dec. 29—Henry Agard Wallace, backed by the Progressive Citizens of America and other liberal groups throughout the country, announced tonight that he would be a candidate for President in 1948 on a third-party ticket, pledged to "a positive peace program of abundance and security, not scarcity and war."

The 59-year-old former Vice President and former Secretary of Commerce denounced the Democratic party as a party of "war and depression" and asserted that the time had come for "a new party to fight these war-makers."

At the same time, he summoned Democratic party insurgents to take up the third-party banner to show the world that "the United States is not behind the bipartisan reactionary war policy which is dividing the world into two armed camps and making inevitable the day when American soldiers will be lying in their Arctic suits in the Russian snow."

"To that end," he said, "I announce tonight that I shall run as an independent candidate for President of the United States in 1948."

In a press conference at the end of his address Mr. Wallace stated that if either of the major parties became "a peace party" he would withdraw his name as a Presidential aspirant.

He expected that a preliminary third party organizing meeting would be held early in January and that a national convention would be assembled in the spring. He asserted that he would ask that his name be withdrawn if it were entered in Democratic primaries.

Announces Candidacy on Radio

The Iowan made his announcement over the coast-to-coast network of the Mutual Broadcasting Company, of which Col. Robert R. McCormick, editor and publisher of The Chicago Tribune, is a large stockholder.

The address was offered to more than 450 of the network's outlets. How many stations made use of it could not be learned. WGN, Mutual's Chicago station, where Mr. Wallace delivered his address, did not make it available to its listeners, however.

Ralph E. Shikes, a spokesman for the Progressive Citizens of America, charged prior to the broadcast that the advertiser holding the fifteen-minute time spot had agreed to relinquish his time, but that WGN officials had refused the offer.

In reply to this accusation, Frank P. Schreiber, manager of WGN, said that the Chicago outlet would not carry the Wallace broadcast "because the political nature of his address is in conflict with the station's policy governing broadcasting political speeches.

"For several years," he added, "WGN has maintained the policy of accepting political broadcasts by recognized candidates for national and major state offices only during political campaigns in election years.

Cites Controversial Issue

"Like most American radio stations, WGN has a well-established policy of granting equal time to both sides of controversial questions. If we were to broadcast Mr. Wallace's controversial political talk, we would be obliged to grant time to persons desiring to answer Mr. Wallace, which would be further violation of our policies on political broadcasts."

Mr. Schreiber added that "naturally, if anything that Mr. Wallace says tonight is of newsworthy character, it will be covered by the station as all news is covered."

Mr. Wallace's broadcast followed day-long conferences with liberal leaders from eighteen states and the District of Columbia.

Mr. Wallace, in an address to the group, said:

"This reminds me of a pep rally when I was in college before the big game. The important thing is support for the team after it is on the field. I shall be glad to know that in the formation of a new party we have people and support pledged to the cause of humanity. This is the cause to which I have been long dedicated. I feel that the formation of such a new party is vital because of the dry rot in the present bipartisan coalition of Republicans and Democrats.

"Perhaps one of our greatest allies in the coming year in forming a new party will be the mistakes of this reactionary coalition. We should be prepared to take full advantage of these mistakes by coming to the people with a real program for peace and abundance. it is this cause, the cause of peace for all humanity, that is closest to me."

Mr. Wallace will address a PCA rally in Milwaukee tomorrow.

The Illinois delegation handed the former Vice President a list of 100,000 signatures urging him to run for President and pledged him a minimum of 500,000 Illinois votes.

According to a PCA spokesman, Mr. Wallace told the meeting that a more accurate description of the new party would be a "second" party, contending that there was now "a bipartisan coalition of the Democrats and the Republicans." He then went on to say that the second party would soon become "the first party."

In his radio address, Mr. Wallace stressed that announcement of his third-party candidacy was a result of a failure of conferences among party leaders and himself to keep him in the Democratic fold. The former Vice President asserted that he had given his terms to the leaders of the Democratic party.

"By their actions and finally by their words," he said, "they have said: 'Henry Wallace, we welcome your support, but we will not change our policies.' In answering me, the Democratic leadership also gave its answer to millions of Americans who demand the right to vote for peace and prosperity."

Mr. Wallace added that "so far as the Republican party is concerned there is no hope," adding that "when old parties rot the people have a right to be heard through a new party."

In outlining the "terms" which he said he had given Democratic party leaders as a basis for retain-

ing his backing, Mr. Wallace listed defeat of the plan for universal training as the first political objective of the Progressives.

He blamed financial outlays for "military adventures" in Greece, Turkey and China, plus billions for armaments at home for the increased cost of living.

The former Cabinet member explained that he fought "the Truman doctrine and the Marshall plan as applied because they divide Europe into two warring camps."

"Those whom we buy politically with our food will soon desert us," he predicted.

He charged that the Administration's foreign policy was aimed at hemming Russia in and warned that the end result would be the same as that which followed England's and France's actions after the World War—"confusion, de-

pression and war."

Addressing himself to both Russian and American leaders, Mr. Wallace emphasized that "peace requires real understanding between our peoples." The United States, he said, would not be fully secure until there was real peace between the two countries and until there was an international police force stronger than the military establishment of any nation, "including Russia and the United States."

Asserting that Americanism was "betrayed" after World War I, he said that the United States now faced an even greater menace.

"That menace can be met and overcome," he added, "only by a new political alignment in America which requires the organization of a new political party."

December 30, 1947

AFL Bars Support of Wallace; Calls Him Front for Communists

By A. H. RASKIN
Special to THE NEW YORK TIMES.

MIAMI, Feb. 2—Characterizing Henry A. Wallace as a "front, spokesman and apologist" for the Communist party, the executive council of the American Federation of Labor voted unanimously today to reject Mr. Wallace's third-party candidacy for the Presidency.

The action of the AFL leaders left Mr. Wallace without the support of any of the three principal segments of the organized-labor movement. The national executive board of the Congress of Industrial Organizations and the heads of the independent railroad brotherhoods already have repudiated the Wallace drive as inimical to the best interests of American workers.

William Green, AFL president, made it clear that the federation's opposition to Mr. Wallace would extend to Congressional candidates running on his ticket. He said the AFL put no stock in the sincerity of the Wallace adherents, even though they professed to be against the Taft-Hartley Law and other restrictive legislation.

In its statement the executive council expressed confidence that the federation's 7,200,000 members were "too intelligent and too patriotic" to be misled by the "false liberalism" of Mr. Wallace's third party.

The council maintained that the strategy of the Communists in inducing Mr. Wallace to run was to split the liberal vote and bring about the election of "an arch-reactionary with isolationist leanings."

The result would be the creation of a chaotic condition in the country that would promote "the revolutionary aims" of the Communists and aid the expansionist ambitions of the Soviet Union, the AFL leaders warned.

In another development of today's council session, George Meany, the federation's secretary - treasurer, declined appointment as director of Labor's League for Political Education, the newly formed political arm of the AFL.

Mr. Meany had been urged to accept the post in the hope that he would be more successful than any outsider in mobilizing the federation's political energies for the defeat of Congressional supporters of the Taft-Hartley Law.

As a result of his declination the council decided to select a director from outside the labor movement. A dark-horse candidate whose name has not figured in previous speculation about the job was understood to have the council's endorsement. A choice will be made here Wednesday at a meeting of the league's administrative committee.

Coordinated Drives Studied

Mr. Green disclosed that the AFL might endeavor to set up a coordinating committee to tie together the political drives of the federation and such unaffiliated unions as John L. Lewis' United Mine Workers, the International Association of Machinists and the railroad brotherhoods.

The AFL president noted that all the groups would be concentrating on the same main objective —the defeat of the Taft-Hartley Law's sponsors and supporters— even though each would have its own political machinery.

The possibility of coordinating the drives may be considered at Wednesday's meeting, Mr. Green said. He gave no sign, however, that the federation would retreat from its refusal to enter into any formal political alliance with the CIO.

Confidence that the new political league would have the organized support of all AFL unions except the United Brotherhood of Carpenters and Joiners was voiced by Mr. Green. He said he did not expect other AFL groups to follow the lead of the 600,000 carpenters by carrying on independent political programs.

Mr. Green had specific reference to the International Brotherhood of Teamsters, largest union in the AFL. Daniel J. Tobin, leader of the 1,000,000 unionized truck drivers and warehousemen, was one of those who had been undecided about whether to come into the new league or to establish his own program. Mr. Green said he believed the teamsters would support the league.

Decision Is Unanimous

All fifteen members of the executive council voted against the Wallace candidacy. This compared

with a vote of 33 to 11 in the CIO executive board two weeks ago. The left-wing unions that backed the former Vice President at the CIO meeting have announced their intention of campaigning in his behalf.

The full text of the AFL statement follows:

"The executive council is completely and unanimously opposed to the Presidential candidacy of Henry A. Wallace.

"We make this formal announcement so that the members of the American Federation of Labor may not be misled by the false liberalism of Mr. Wallace and his so-called third-party organization.

"The only organization back of Mr. Wallace is the Communist party. The Communists have now taken him in, lock, stock and barrel. He has become their front, their spokesman and their apologist.

"The strategy behind the Wallace campaign is devious, but transparent. The Communists, of course, have no hopes of electing him. Their purpose is to confuse the workers of America and split the liberal vote. The object of this strategy is to bring about the election of an arch-reactionary with isolationist leanings.

"This would play into the hands of Soviet Russia's expansionist policy. It would also bring about a state of affairs in this country which would promote the revolutionary aims of the Communists. Oppression and depression provide converts to their cause.

"The executive council is confident that the members of the American Federation of Labor are too intelligent and too patriotic to be hoodwinked by the Communists. They will not support Mr. Wallace."

February 3, 1948

NEW EISENHOWER BOOM GAINS DESPITE CHECKS

Anti-Truman Democrats of All Kinds Turn to General as Their One Hope

By CABELL PHILLIPS
Special to THE NEW YORK TIMES.

"LEAP YEAR!"

Hungerford in The Pittsburgh Post-Gazette

WASHINGTON, April 3—The almost unparalleled pressure being exerted to project Gen. Dwight D. Eisenhower into the Presidential campaign is, in the opinion of some political analysts here, composed of about one part admiration for the general and two parts discouragement over President Truman.

This analysis of the situation connotes no underestimating of the manifest talents of General Eisenhower. What it does connote is the profound landslide-in-reverse that has all but engulfed Mr. Truman's prestige within his party, and the frantic desperation with which those party leaders are searching for a Moses to lead them out of the wilderness.

The Democratic pressure on General Eisenhower is, if anything, greater than that imposed a few months ago by his Republican admirers. The Republican party has not been faced, as the Democrats have, with the threat of a fatal vacuum. There is no dearth of eager and optimistic contenders for the Republican crown.

The Democrats, on the other hand, are looking for any promising man to carry their standard. And General Eisenhower, as they see it, is the one man who could take the risk.

Counting on Stampede

The switch to Eisenhower was a manifestation of some sort of spontaneous mass psychosis rather than of logic or sound political principles. He has said in the most unequivocal terms that he was both unsuited for and disinclined to accept political office. Few doubted his sincerity in saying it, and not even the most hopeful could find where he had left his foot in the door.

But an idea born of desperation can grow legs, and that apparently is what has happened in the second Eisenhower boom. It is rocketing along today, under the lash of Democratic necessity, at a faster clip than it gained under Republican auspices. Facing the reality of the general's disclaimer, reinforced only this week by Gen. Floyd Parks, the official Eisenhower spokesman, the instigators of the boom are counting upon a literal stampede to develop at the conventions that will leave the general no patriotic choice but to say "yes."

Can the Eisenhower boom develop such irresistible momentum between now and July? Is there, indeed, a possibility that this strange political fantasy will become a reality?

Some observers think that it can, particularly if the headlong progress which has become evident in the last fortnight persists into the summer.

Widespread Support

So many spokesmen for Southern Democrats have acclaimed him as to make it almost certain that he can, if he wishes, reweld that region into its traditional Democratic solidarity. A number of labor leaders, caught in the dilemma of having stemmed a drift toward Henry Wallace and suddenly finding that they have nowhere else to direct it, have turned to him with whoops of joy. Many Democratic leaders in Congress, including the former majority whip in the Senate, Lister Hill of Alabama, have openly repudiated President Truman and are reportedly ready to back the Eisenhower boom the moment it seems propitious to do so.

New York's Liberal party, after having announced some weeks ago its determination to stick with President Truman, reversed its decision last week and proclaimed Eisenhower as its man. Pressure is currently being put on both the New York State and the city Democratic organizations to follow suit. From the West Coast reports have emanated that large blocs of dissident Democrats as well as Republicans are coalescing around the dormant Republican Eisenhower-for-President clubs, intent on reviving them as bipartisan movements. Veterans-for-Eisenhower, Citizens-for-Eisenhower and Students-for-Eisenhower organizations are blossoming in new batches almost daily in various parts of the country.

Liberals' Position

Great interest currently attaches to the forthcoming special meeting of the executive board of the Americans for Democratic Action, which Chairman Leon Henderson has called in Pittsburgh for April 10. At its recent Philadelphia convention ADA significantly withheld its endorsement of any Presidential candidate. But it is no secret that many of the ex-New Dealers and Liberal independents who compose the membership of this influential body are now firmly anti-Truman.

Franklin D. Roosevelt Jr., who is an ADA vice chairman, and his brother Elliott last week formally announced their allegiance to the Eisenhower drive. In many quarters this is taken to presage a substantial, and perhaps a unanimous, endorsement for the general at the Pittsburgh meeting. Such a development would virtually close the ranks of the same Northern-liberal and Southern-conservative coalition around Eisenhower that made Franklin D. Roosevelt politically invincible through four Presidential elections.

Indeed, the very pace of the boom is now worrying some of the more thoughtful Eisenhower boosters. They are much afraid that its intensity will put the General in the difficult position of having to make another statement. They don't want to risk another renunciation, and they don't want to expose him to the embarrassment at this moment of denouncing his former renunciation. They want to keep things cozy and quiet until July.

Glamorous Record

This Eisenhower sweep is beginning to show some of the traces of inchoate mass appeal that developed in support of President Roosevelt in 1932. The man himself is attractive and compelling. His record is particularly glamorous in the political light in which it is currently viewed. He appears to have the capacity not only of healing the breaches among the Democrats, but of winning Republican and independent support too. He might turn in quite a performance on E-Day in November.

All such speculation, however, adds up to zero at present. General Eisenhower still is not a candidate and some of the soundest political prognostigators insist he will not be, draft or no draft. Roy Roberts, publisher of The Kansas City Star and regarded as the general's political mentor, said emphatically this week that "Gen. Ike Eisenhower is not going to take a Democratic nomination for the Presidency or any other nomination. That's final."

Furthermore, the Democrats still have an announced candidate by the name of Harry Truman on their hands. He has not withdrawn from the race and his intimates say he has no intention of withdrawing.

It is a pretty safe prediction at this point that if the Eisenhower boom does develop into a stampede at Philadelphia in July, it will be over Mr. Truman's body. Such a spectacle might have quite a chilling effect on the spirits of the stampeders.

April 4, 1948

DEWEY UNANIMOUS REPUBLICAN CHOICE

OPPOSITION FALLS

Taft and Stassen Join in Urging Selection of New Yorker

GOP PRECEDENT SET

Dewey Is First Defeated Candidate to Be Chosen Again

By WILLIAM S. WHITE
Special to The New York Times.

PHILADELPHIA, June 24—Thomas E. Dewey was nominated tonight by the Republicans for the Presidency of the United States.

His selection, on the third ballot of the twenty-fourth Republican National Convention, was unanimous after his forces had smashed an opposing coalition.

When two ballots had shown that the Governor of New York was not to be stopped, his erstwhile antagonists renounced their rivalries with him and pledged all their power to his success in November.

Mr. Dewey came at once to the convention hall and, before the hot and shouting delegates, accepted his nomination in a placating spirit toward his former opponents.

"In all humility," he said, "I pray God that I may deserve this opportunity to serve our country."

"Lasting Peace" Put First

Above all its efforts, he declared, the Republican party and the country must seek for the world "a just and lasting peace."

The convention will select tomorrow a Vice Presidential nominee in what is described in the most authoritative quarters as a "wide open field."

Mr. Dewey said pointedly that he was "unfettered by a single obligation or promise to any living person." It was understood that the Dewey group wanted to consider overnight the available men for second place on the ticket.

Governor Dewey is the only Republican in the party's history to be nominated for President after having been once defeated. He lost in 1944 to Franklin D. Roosevelt.

On the first ballot today the Governor got 434 votes to 224 for Senator Robert A. Taft of Ohio, his strongest opponent.

On the second ballot, he climbed to 515 votes, as compared with 274 for Mr. Taft.

The results of the three ballots for the major leaders were as follows:

First—Dewey, 434; Taft, 224; Harld E. Stassen, 157; Senator Arthur H. Vandenberg of Michigan, 62.

Second—Dewey, 515; Taft, 274; Stassen, 149; Vandenberg, 62.

Third—Dewey, all 1,094 votes.

When the second roll-call ended associates of Senator Taft, Mr. Stassen and other anti-Dewey aspirants brought about a three-hour recess to resurvey their position.

When the convention returned to work, word swept the arena that Gov. Earl Warren of California, a "favorite son" candidate, had released the fifty-three delegates of that state. It was obvious that the California delegation, or a great part of it, was getting ready to go over to Mr. Dewey.

At this point, Senator John W. Bricker of Ohio went before the microphones to announce the withdrawal of his old friend, Senator Taft.

He read on behalf of Mr. Taft a statement that it was plain that a majority was prepared to turn to Mr. Dewey on the third ballot. Senator Taft therefore not only released his forces, but asked them to vote for Mr. Dewey and himself pledged every support to the New Yorker, now and in the campaign.

Mr. Taft's gesture was followed by Senator William F. Knowland of California in behalf of Governor Warren. Then Mr. Stassen went to the rostrum, smiling determinedly, to declare that he too was dropping out and to recommend Mr. Dewey.

Mr. Stassen said that with the "permission" of his supporters, he would like to second Mr. Dewey's nomination. At this there were some cries of "No!" in the hall.

Second Ballot Victory Balked

Senator Vandenberg was withdrawn by his principal backer, Gov. Kim Sigler of Michigan.

Senator Raymond Baldwin of Connecticut, another "favorite

Thomas E. Dewey The New York Times (by Tames)

son," proposed that a roll call be dispensed with, and that was seconded by Harlan Kelley of Wisconsin, a backer of General MacArthur. The convention chairman, Speaker Joseph W. Martin Jr., ruled, however, that a ballot was necessary. It was then taken as a matter of form.

Governor Dewey might have been nominated on the second ballot had not Senator Baldwin found it impossible immediately to obtain a release from limited commitments to the stop-Dewey group by which he was to hold the Connecticut delegation for two ballots.

The first powerful factor in breaking the earlier coalition against Mr. Dewey was Senator Edward Martin of Pennsylvania, who caused a majority of that delegation two days ago to go over to the New Yorker.

With this great lift, the Dewey campaign began to roll powerfully and irresistibly as it turned out.

The anti-Dewey coalition forced a recess of nearly three hours at 4:55 P. M. in the hope that in the interim they could arrest the Dewey movement.

The Dewey forces, it appeared from all that was said in recent days, would have preferred to hold the convention in session until the nominee was chosen. Presumably they feared a defeat on a collateral issue that might have been used by the opposition to argue that they had shown weakness.

This critical day in the convention opened on the note that for three days had persisted: More gains for Governor Dewey in the real or the psychological sense.

One of the earliest of these was the withdrawal of Senator Leverett Saltonstall as the "favorite son" of Massachusetts, the consequence of which was soon to be reflected in the seventeen Massachusetts votes Mr. Dewey got on the first ballot.

Almost at the hour of Senator Saltonstall's decision, Mr. Stassen was doggedly carrying on his "stop-Dewey" campaign downtown. Cryptically, he promised "developments" in the afternoon.

The convention itself first got under way in the hottest day that Philadelphia had seen since the Republicans gathered here.

Dewey Gets 434 on First

On the first roll-call the Dewey candidacy went almost exactly as had been forecast by disinterested observers, and there was not a single genuine break in the lines.

All was tense as the second roll-call proceeded for the Dewey campaigners had not really expected anything like a first-ballot nomination, but had held cautious hope for a second.

This time Mr. Dewey went out almost at once to pick up gains far down the line of states. Iowa gave the New Yorker thirteen votes, or ten more than on the first roll call. He gained in Kansas, Kentucky, Maryland, Massachusetts, Missouri, Montana and Nebraska.

Then twenty-four of New Jersey's thirty-three votes, which on the first ballot had been thrown in for the "favorite son," Gov. Alfred Driscoll, went to Mr. Dewey. New York, as on the first ballot, gave him ninety-six votes of its ninety-seven, and Delegate Peter Wynne sat grinning as he again cast the single New York ballot for Senator Taft.

Now and again, as the balloting continued in a war of nerves among the partisans a delegate would demand that his state be polled, to learn whether its announced vote was correct. Sometimes the intention was to give publicity to delegates who had resisted the majority's will.

One such polling of a state, that of Ohio, reflected the rivalry and determination that were at work at the convention.

"No turncoat; still with Taft!" shouted one delegate as the Ohio list was called on the second ballot.

"Staying with Stassen—the people's candidate!" said a second.

"I do not apologize," shouted a third, in retort to the first, "for voting for Governor Dewey!"

June 25, 1948

TRUMAN, BARKLEY NAMED BY DEMOCRATS; SOUTH LOSES ON CIVIL RIGHTS, 35 WALK OUT

VICTORY SWEEPING

President Wins, 947½ to 263, Over Russell on the First Ballot

BARKLEY ACCLAIMED

Nominees Go Before Convention to Make Acceptance Talks

By W. H. LAWRENCE
Special to THE NEW YORK TIMES.

PHILADELPHIA, Thursday, July 15—President Harry S. Truman won nomination for a full term in the Democratic National Convention early today and promptly made the Republican record in Congress the 1948 key issue by calling a special session of Congress to meet July 26 to challenge the GOP to keep its platform pledges.

The President, selected by well over two-thirds of the Democratic delegates, although the Solid South dissented and thirty-five delegates from Mississippi and Alabama walked out, was in a fighting mood as he went before the convention with his running mate, Senator Alben W. Barkley, who was chosen by acclamation.

Confidently predicting his and Senator Barkley's election because "the country cannot afford another Republican Congress," the President said that the special session would be asked to act on legislation of various types.

He would call on it, he declared, to act to halt rising prices, meet the housing crisis, provide aid to education, enact a national health program, approve civil rights legislation, raise minimum wages, increase social security benefits, finance expanded public power projects and revise the present "anti-Semitic, anti-Catholic" displaced persons law.

The Republicans said they were for all these things in their 1948 platform, the President stated, and, if they really meant it, all could be enacted into law in a fifteen-day session.

President Truman set the convention on fire with his acceptance speech, which came at the end of a long, tiring, tumultuous session in which the north-south party split was deepened appreciably, although only a handful of southern delegates bolted.

The Southerners who remained were almost as angry as those in the "walk" about the convention's strong civil rights pledge and its overwhelming refusal to include a state's rights plank in the platform.

Senator Barkley promised to follow the President's leadership, agreed to carry out the platform and pledged himself to carry the story of Democratic accomplishments to every precinct to insure victory in November.

The acceptance speeches completed, the convention adjourned at 2:30 A. M.

Truman Margin of Victory

President Truman's margin over his chief rival, Senator Richard B. Russell of Georgia, was 947½ to 263, while Paul V. McNutt received half a vote in the final tabulation.

Senator Russell got almost the solid Southern vote remaining in the convention after the bolt by delegates from Alabama and Mississippi.

As soon as Mr. Truman was nominated, at 12:42 A. M., the convention moved ahead to the nomination of his Vice-Presidential running mate.

There was an attempt to present Senator Russell again for the Vice Precidency, but he stopped it and there was no opposition to Senator Barkley's selection.

The President, who came here by train from Washington, was waiting in a rear room of the convention hall to make a joint appearance with Senator Barkley to accept the nominations.

To the strains of "Hail to the Chief" President Truman entered the hall at 1:45 A. M. accompanied by Senator Barkley to accept his nomination before a wildly cheering crowd.

The wound to the South embodied in the strong civil rights program imposed on the party leadership by a combination of New Dealers and Northern city bosses went very deep indeed. It was a wound far deeper than had indication in the dramatic, but comparatively unimportant, demonstration by half the Alabama delegation and all of the Mississippi delegation.

For the first time in many years the Presidential nominee's selection was not made unanimous. There was not even a motion to make it unanimous, because the South, fighting mad, would have resisted it to the end. Those Southern delegations which stayed in the hall decided that "regularity" was most important, but there was no certainty that they would give all-out support to the ticket in November.

For the President, after he had been placed in nomination by Gov. Phil Donnelly of Missouri, there was a thirty-nine minute demonstration. When the roll call began his lead mounted steadily and he passed the majority required for nomination when New York cast 93 of its votes for him. New York later changed its vote to cast all 98 for him.

The name of Mr. McNutt, former Indiana Governor, who was War Manpower Commissioner, was placed in nomination for President by Byrd Sims of Florida, in a surprise move. Mr. Sims, opposed to the present party leadership and pledged to Mississippi's Governor, Fielding L. Wright, before Governor Wright bolted the convention, said that he acted without Mr. McNutt's knowledge or consent.

Ohio offered as its "favorite son" William A. Julian, Treasurer of the United States, but it was simply a courtesy gesture. Mr. Julian withdrew at once and asked the Ohio delegation to vote for Mr. Truman.

Party leaders, acting on behalf of the President, had sought to mollify the South by restricting the civil rights platform pledge to a generality, but the delegates, sparked by ex-New Dealers who had the support of big city machine bosses, insisted and won a floor fight for a plank with real teeth in it. Their margin was narrow—651½ to 582½—but earlier they had overwhelmingly rejected Southern demands for a states' rights plank by a vote of 925 to 309.

The platform was so strong that Governor Ben Laney of Arkansas, who had planned to have his name presented as a candidate for President, said he could not accept the platform. He and his Arkansas delegation did not leave the convention, however.

Senator Alben W. Barkley of Kentucky was slated to be the Vice Presidential nominee. He was the overwhelming favorite among delegates and the White House capitulated to their demonstrated attitude after trying and failing to persuade Supreme Court Justice William O. Douglas to take a place on the ticket.

Senator Barkley also was to deliver his acceptance speech before the convention.

The Southern walkout was dramatic, coming as it did just as Sam Rayburn of Texas, permanent chairman, ordered the roll-call of states for the Presidential nomination, but it lacked the numbers and spirit that Southern politicians had predicted.

Loud boos followed the mass walkout by all of the Mississippi delegates and alternates, and half the Alabama group. And they had the bad luck, too, to walk from this steamy, hot convention into a pouring rainstorm.

Cheers bounced against the rafters as Chairman Rayburn, a Texas "regular," recognized the rest of the Alabama delegation, headed by Senator Lister Hill, who

150

promptly yielded to Georgia so that Senator Russell could be placed in nomination.

The Southern delegates let go in a noisy demonstration to the martial tunes of "Dixie," after Charles J. Bloch of Georgia, nominating Senator Russell, delivered a solemn warning that "the South is no longer going to be the whipping boy of the Democratic party."

His group, he declared, were not "fools" enough to walk out, but he warned that Southern voters might desert the Democratic party and asserted that the party could not win a Presidential election without Southern support.

Then it was the turn of the Truman boosters, some of them genuinely enthusiastic but more of them lukewarm to the President and accepting him only because their efforts to draft Gen. Dwight D. Eisenhower were stopped by the general's flat refusal to accept the nomination under any circumstances.

Gov. Phil M. Donnelly of Missouri offered the President's name in the first speech to the convention in which the emphasis had been laid upon Mr. Truman's accomplishments in office.

All other speakers had talked more about the late President Roosevelt, with only passing reference to the present President.

It was understood that some White House advisers tried to have more attention paid to the late President in Governor Donnelly's speech, too, but that the Missouri chief executive refused to deliver his speech except in its original form.

When he closed, a well-planned demonstration for the President began, in which most states except the South took part.

ADA Spearheads Fight

New Dealers, organized under the auspices of the Americans for Democratic Action, led the fight to expand the civil rights pledge and got the votes to put it over from Northern big city machines which realize they must hold the Negro vote if their state and local tickets are not to go down in defeat in the prospective Republican landslide this November.

What the convention did was to make specific the directive to Congress to carry out President Truman's civil rights program—but the manner in which it was done could not have failed to displease the President because it created additional hostility in the South, increased the sentiment for a convention bolt and thus defeated the harmony moves which the Administration had initiated in recent days.

The President's lieutenants here had sought a milder, more generalized declaration.

Specifically, the convention directed Democrats in Congress to guarantee "these basic and fundamental rights: (1) the right of of full and equal political participation, (2) the right to equal opportunity of employment, (3) the right of security of person, (4) and the right of equal treatment in the service and defense of our nation."

In the fifty-eight-minute debate covering the civil rights and states' rights minority reports, the issue of race relations, as such, was never tackled.

Southern orators warned that a failure to reaffirm the constitutional rights of the states was essential to Southern confidence in and support of the party.

The Northern bloc, through Mayor Hubert Humphrey of Minneapolis as its principal spokesman, said that the country was 172 years behind the times in meeting the issue of equality. Mayor Humphrey won loud cheers and a scattering of boos for his praise of President Truman's "courage in issuing a new emancipation proclamation" and his assertion that "it is time for the Democratic party to get out of the shadow of states' rights and walk forthrightly in the

bright sunshine of human rights."

Lacking either band or organ music, which were kept silent by the control of Southerners in authority on the main platform, delegates led by the ADA group nevertheless staged a long demonstration for Mayor Humphrey when he closed his speech and kept it going for nearly ten minutes.

The delegates, who had sweltered listlessly through two and one-half days of campaign oratory while waiting for the real business of the convention, adoption of the platform and nomination of candidates, were spoiling for a fight when the preliminaries for the day finally were completed.

The galleries, crowded for the first time, were in general agreement with Northern demands for stronger civil rights measures and joined in cheering the demonstrations on the floor.

The debate was less torrid than might have been expected and nobody waved the flag of "white supremacy," although Southerners warned earnestly that if the states' rights amendment were rejected "you are voting down the Constitution of the United States."

July 15, 1948

South Beaten on Race Issue As Rights Plank Is Widened

By C. P. TRUSSELL
Special to The New York Times.

PHILADELPHIA, July 14—The Democratic National Convention, by a roaring voice vote, committed its party today to what was called a straightaway Roosevelt-Truman platform for 1948. In scenes of emotional demonstration, with Southern Democrats pleading rather than demanding as Northern liberals were firmly in the saddle, the document was changed at only one point. That was where a majority of the convention, in effect, accused its platform committee of hedging on the civil rights program which had precipitated the South into bitter revolt against President Truman.

By a roll call of 651½ to 582½, the convention demanded that four objectives of that program be spelled out: abolition of poll taxes in Federal elections, a national law against lynching, creation of a permanent fair employment practices system and non-segregation of the races in the armed services.

In another cracking-down action, the convention refused bluntly and decisively, in the face of Southern argument that the upholding or throwing down of the Constitution itself was at stake, to put a states' rights plank into the platform. The vote was 925 to 309.

Even the border states joined those of the North, East and West in denying the South's plea.

A states' rights plank such as was proposed by delegates from Texas, Alabama, Tennessee, Virginia, South Carolina, Mississippi, Georgia and Florida, it was conceded, would hurt the civil rights program. Sponsors of the Truman program called upon the convention to make its choice between "states' rights and human rights."

When that choice had been made and the platform was howled to adoption, the South was not even allowed to enter an immediate spectacular protest. Thirteen of the twenty-six members of the Alabama delegation, seeing what was coming, prepared to turn in their credentials and stalk out of the convention.

Blind and deaf to the frantic waving of Alabama banners, and the bellowing of Eugene Connor for recognition for the bolt, Sam Rayburn of Texas, House minority leader and permanent convention chairman, recognized instead Representative John W. McCormack of Massachusetts, the House Democratic whip. Mr. McCormack moved an hour and a half recess. While Mr. Connor and fellow-bolters continued their outcry and

physical gymnastics in vain, the motion was carried and Alabama still had twenty-six accredited delegates, one-half of them mutinous and awaiting a chance to break away.

After the recess the bolters walked out. They were led by Handy Ellis, chairman of the Alabama delegation, and D. Hardy Riddle, vice chairman. When they had gone, the delegation was taken over by Senator Lister Hill and former Gov. Chauncey Sparks, who had alternates waiting to step into the vacant places.

Biggest Floor Change in Years

Never since 1932 had there been such a material change in a party platform after it had reached the convention floor. This was the insertion of the plank advocating repeal of the Prohibition Amendment.

Prospective pledges for the 1948 campaign had been steadily under hearing and study for, an entire week. The document taken to the floor had undergone initial draft by a seven-member group which, as was expected, had found the civil rights plank its greatest headache.

This group's proposal was a virtual rewriting of the Democrats' 1944 civil rights plank, which had been compromised with the South. At second stage, within an eighteen-member platform subcommittee, it was "strengthened" but was viewed by liberals as still falling short of spelling out the issues.

Such a spelling out was attempted within the 108-member resolutions body, representing every state, by Mayor Hubert H. Humphrey Jr. of Minneapolis. Mr. Humphrey is national vice chairman of Americans for Democratic Action, headed by Leon Henderson, former Price Administrator, which organized demand for "putting the

issues on the line." Mr. Humphrey met defeat in committee.

The gauge was thrown down in the splashing glare of kleig lights this afternoon, as the north and south faced one another for the showdown.

How Rights Plank Did Read

Before the convention, as to civil rights, was this pledge:

"The Democratic party is responsible for the great civil rights gains made in recent years in eliminating unfair and illegal discrimination based on race, creed or color.

"The Democratic party commits itself to continuing its efforts to eradicate all racial, religious and economic discrimination. We again state our belief that racial and religious minorities must have the right to live, the right to work, the right to vote, the full and equal protection of the law, on a basis of equality with all citizens as guaranteed by the Constitution. We again call upon the Congress to exert its full authority to the limit of its constitutional powers to assure and protect these rights."

This went under dramatic assault. Offered as an addition to the resolution committee's plank was the following:

"We highly commend President Harry Truman for his courageous stand on the issue of civil rights.

"We call upon the Congress to support our President in guaranteeing these basic and fundamental rights (1) the right of full and equal political participation, (2) the right of equal opportunity of employment, (3) the right of security of person, and (4) the right of equal treatment in the services and defense of our nation."

Sponsoring this were Mayor

151

Humphrey, former representative Andrew J. Biemiller of Wisconsin and Mrs. Esther Murray of California, a fellow member of the resolutions body with M r. Humphrey Aaron L. Jacoby, a member of the New York delegation and chairman of the speakers' bureau of the New York Democratic Committee, took the platform to join them in sponsorship.

South Urged States Rights

A little while before—debate on all matters challenging the platform draft had been limited to an hour—the convention had heard the plea from the South. States' rights planks of varying composition were awaiting their tests, too.

The principal states' rights proposal, introduced as an amendment by former Gov. Dan Moody of Texas and sponsored by fourteen other delegates from eight of the eleven states of the solid south, was as follows:

"The Democratic party stands for the principle that the Constitution contemplated and established a union of indestructible sovereign States and that under the Constitution the general Federal Government and the separate States have their separate fields of power and of permitted activities.

"Traditionally it has been, and it remains a part of the faith of the Democratic party that the Federal Government shall not encroach upon the reserved powers of the States by centralization of government or otherwise. Within the reserve powers of the States, to be exercised subject to the limitations imposed by the Fourteenth and Fifteenth Amendments to the Constitution on the manner of their exercise, is the power to regulate and control local affairs and act in the exercise of the police power."

Collaterally and representing the Tennessee view of a states' rights plank, was one, offered by Cecil Sims, a delegate from that State, which proposed a plank that would read:

"The Democratic party reaffirms its adherence to the fundamental principle of States' rights as reserved in the Federal Constitution, and pledges that it will oppose any attempt, by legislation or otherwise, to invade the exclusive jurisdiction of the States in their domestic affairs."

Reception to the pleas from the South foretold the defeat that was to come to it. Both enthusiastic approbation and derisive demands for stronger stuff greeted the calls for support of the Resolution Committee's civil rights planks. Mr. Humphrey started a demonstration lasting nearly ten minutes when he threw down the gauntlet for a spelling out by the platform of what it meant by "civil rights."

For the first time since the contest began, men and women bearing state banners stepped into the aisles and started marching. Active officials and members of Americans for Democratic Action were carrying the banners. It did not become a general demonstration, but there already had been signs that the "putting it on the line" amendment was taking hold as Mayor Humphrey spoke.

'New Emancipation Proclamation'

"We are confronted by emotionalism on all sides," he said, "but there is no single religion, no single class, no single racial group. President Truman had the courage to issue a new emancipation proclamation."

There were cheers.

"We are 172 years late in acting." Mr. Humphrey continued. "It is now time for the Democratic Party to get out of the shadow of states' rights and walk forthrightly in the bright sunshine of human rights, march down the high road of progressive democracy."

Former Governor Moody of Texas approached the states' rights matter cautiously. Establishing himself as a spokesman for the proposed amendment, he made it a plea, not a demand or a threat.

"I have never scratched a ticket," he said. "I have never stayed away from the polls to avoid giving support. I have never bolted a convention and never intend to. My purpose here is an effort to appeal for restoration of harmony in the Democratic party."

Mr. Sims said he was ready to abide by the decision of the convention. In November, he said, he would support the party nominee.

"I agree with everything in the platform," he said. "I am asking only for a simple statement of reserved rights of states. Your vote will determine whether the Democratic party is to be the victor in the South. If we are defeated here today you are witnessing the dissolution of the Democratic party in the South."

Little Non-South Aid for Plank

Texas called for a roll-call on the the states' rights issue. The proposed plank received only eleven votes outside the Solid South, one and one-half from California, one-half from Wyoming, and three each from Colorado, Oregon and Alaska.

It was a different and unexpected story when the vote, asked by California, was taken on the Humphrey - Biemiller - Murray amendment to put civil rights on the line. Delegations of eighteen states which had voted unanimously, or nearly so, to reject the states rights plank, voted also in similar proportions for overriding the Resolutions Committee to make the civil rights plank stronger and more specific as to objectives.

Most of these states carried strong voting power, the strongest being New York with all of its 98 votes. The others were: California, Colorado, Connecticut, Illinois, Indiana, Iowa, Kansas, Massachusetts, Michigan, Minnesota, New Jersey, Ohio, Pennsylvania, South Dakota, Vermont, Washington and Wisconsin.

SOUTHERNERS NAME THURMOND TO LEAD ANTI-TRUMAN FIGHT

Rebellious Democrats Nominate Wright of Mississippi With South Carolina Governor

'TRUE MINORITY PARTY'

Candidates Are Wildly Cheered by 6,000 Supporters in Contest on States' Rights Issue

By JOHN N. POPHAM
Special to THE NEW YORK TIMES.

BIRMINGHAM, Ala., July 17— Gov. J. Strom Thurmond of South Carolina was unanimously chosen today by a group of rebellious Southern Democrats as a Presidential candidate to lead them in a fight to defeat President Truman in the November general elections.

An uproarious rump convention attended by 6,000 fervent followers also named Gov. Fielding L. Wright of Mississippi as a Vice Presidential running mate on a states' rights Democratic ticket. It announced a grand strategy designed to establish the group as the "only true minority party" in Congress.

Both standard bearers, whose candidacies have the effect of putting a fourth party into the national Presidential campaign, have been leading figures in the South's bitter fight against the civil rights proposals that were first introduced in January by President Truman.

From the enthusiasm of the convention crowd and the presence of several top southern political leaders it was evident that the new ticket would have a powerful attraction for the nine electoral votes of Mississippi, the eleven electoral votes of Alabama and a scattering of such votes in Florida, South Carolina, Louisiana and Texas.

Second Meeting Oct. 1

Immediately after the naming of the candidates the convention agreed to reassemble here on Oct. 1 to make further plans with reference to the electoral votes in the various states. It was requested that each state send official delegates equal in number to its votes. It was believed this was a plan to make the meeting one of Presidential electors likely to be pledged to the new ticket.

The convention ended with a burst of shouts, cheers and rebel yells, as well as countless parades on the convention floor, with a portrait of Gen. Robert E. Lee held high. These demonstrations followed speeches denouncing President Truman and his civil rights program as "threats to make Southerners into a mongrel, inferior race by forced intermingling with Negroes."

In a declaration of principles, the dissident group closed the door on the possibility of throwing their strength to the Republican party by calling for the defeat of Mr. Truman and Gov. Thomas E. Dewey.

"We call upon all Democrats and upon all other loyal Americans who are opposed to totalitarianism at home and abroad to unite with us in ignominiously defeating Harry S. Truman and Thomas E. Dewey, and every other candidate who would establish a police state in the United States of America," the declaration read.

The declaration voiced opposition to the elimination of segregation, the repeal of miscegenation statutes and set forth a four-page criticism of "Federal interference" in the field of civil rights to support its conclusion that the actions of the National Democratic Convention in Philadelphia were "totalitarian."

Generally, it was a six-hour session marked by great bursts of enthusiasm inside the auditorium as speakers drew an oratorical picture of the future of the South if segregation barriers were removed. Outside there was brief picketing by ten representatives of the Southern Progressive party, who departed under a fusillade of catcalls and boos.

Governor Thurmond is 45 years old, a veteran of the second World War, leading with paratroopers in the invasion of Normandy. On May 10 he delivered the keynote speech when the states'-rights Democrats held their first gathering.

Governor Wright, 53 years old, started the states'-rights "revolt" and on May 8 he delivered a statewide radio address to the Negroes of Mississippi in which he told them that if they envisioned social equality with whites in schools and restaurants it would be better for them to leave the state.

Candidates Popular in South

Both men have large and enthusiastic followings throughout the South, and at each of the states' rights gatherings and on public appearances during the days of the civil rights' controversy they have been acclaimed by large crowds.

Governor Wright has had many indications that he represents the sympathies of most of the citizens of his state. There has also been political unity behind him. Senators James O. Eastland and John C. Stennis, and Representatives John Bell Williams and William P. Colmar, were at today's meeting.

Thirteen states were represented by placards on the convention floor. They were Virginia, North and South Carolina, Oklahoma, Louisiana, Mississippi, Alabama, Tennessee, Texas, Georgia,

Florida, Kentucky and Arkansas.

However, only a few had representation of real political power. Many seated in delegates' seats turned out to be college students, interested onlookers, and persons who had stopped off for the show while traveling through Birmingham on business trips or vacations.

There was no question about the strong representations of Mississippi and Alabama. They dominated the convention floor, overflowing their own allotment of space and taking up seats in sections set aside for other states. In this way every seat on the floor was occupied.

In the Virginia section there were four students from the University of Virginia and a young woman from Alexandria who said she had stopped off returning from a trip to New Orleans.

Some States Not Represented

In the sections set aside for North Carolina and Kentucky no one would identify himself as from those states. Oklahoma had three of its own in its section and former Gov. "Alfalfa Bill" Murray sat in the balcony.

Louisiana and Florida and Texas had delegations of from fifteen to twenty-five persons. It was reported that ten national convention delegates from Texas, three Presidential electors from Florida and two Presidential electors from Louisiana were present.

Three of South Carolina's delegates to the Philadelphia convention were on hand. Governor Thurmond brought a large retinue.

Tennessee was represented by four students from the University of Tennessee, six students from Cumberland College at Lebanon and five persons who said they were "sympathizers." J. H. Ballew of Nashville, a delegate to the national convention, sat in the rear of the hall under a placard that read "Other States."

At the first meeting of the states' rights Democrats in Jackson, Miss., on May 10, Tennessee had a strong delegation from Memphis, home of E. H. "Boss" Crump.

Georgia, which pulled out as a participant in the states' rights movement in May, had no political representatives present. Eight men who sat in the Georgia section said they were just "interested" and "sympathetic."

Arkansas had about twelve persons present, one of them a delegate to the national convention at Philadelphia.

Some on the convention floor who explained that they were believers in the precepts of the states' rights Democrats said they were from Indiana, Pennsylvania and Illinois.

The convention got under way with a series of speeches by local political figures, all stressing opposition to President Truman and predicting national chaos if the South's segregation pattern was abolished. There was much old-fashioned oratory replete with colloquialisms that drew gales of laughter from the crowd. Said one speaker:

"We have no choice between the little man with the sickening smile and the little man with the little mustache."

One speaker kept repeating that if the civil rights proposals became laws the South would find both races "mingling in the beauty shops and the swimming pools."

For the second day in a row the officials of the states' rights Democrats displayed their principal political weakness, when former Gov. Frank M. Dixon of Alabama told the convention crowd:

"Some of the office-holders in the South are afraid of losing their jobs if they follow us and if they think they can weasel their way through this and weather the storm we will soon retire them to private life."

Several convention officials boasted that they would have "enough money behind this move to match the Republicans or the Democrats." Leaders stressed that it was their hope to insure the defeat of Mr. Truman in November and then to gain enough support for their ticket in every state to make the states' rights Democrats the actual Democratic Party minority in Congress under a Republican administration.

"This way," they said, "we will be the dominant minority group and the northern city machines will have to come to us for their committee assignments. That way we will block this trend to knife the South."

It was learned that the strategy of the new party's leaders would be to try to get the state conventions in all Southern states reconvened, if they have already been held, and have them name new slates of Presidential electors who are pledged against Mr. Truman or pledged to support Governor Thurmond.

This move to "free the electors" is regarded as the new ticket's trump card in defeating Mr. Truman in the electoral college and giving it the dominant party position in the South.

The delegates gave vent to a wild demonstration that spilled onto the speakers' platform with flags and pennants and state placards when Governors Thurmond and Wright appeared and accepted the nominations.

"We will not turn back," the Mississippi Governor said. "This is the South's big opportunity to show that we are the real Democratic party. Those who believed we would never be able to carry this fight on to a successful conclusion are beginning to tremble."

There were shouts of "no, no" when Governor Wright said he would "step down" when the states' righters met again on October "if a better candidate can be found."

Governor Thurmond said that "we have just begun to fight" and "if the South should vote for Truman this year we might just as well petition the Government to give us colonial status."

"President Truman has betrayed the South," he added, "and we Southerners are going to cast our votes for candidates who are true believers in states' rights principles. For our loyalty to the party we have been stabbed in the back by a President who has betrayed every principle of the Democratic party in his desire to win at any cost."

July 18, 1948

Text of States' Rights Platform Voted in South

By The Associated Press.

BIRMINGHAM, Ala., July 17—Following is "the declaration of principles" reported today by the Resolutions Committee of the States' Rights meeting:

We affirm that a political party is an instrumentality for effectuating the principles upon which the party is founded; that a platform of principles is a solemn covenant with the people and with the members of the party; that no leader of the party, in temporary power, has the right or privilege to proceed contrary to the fundamental principles of the party, or the letter or spirit of the Constitution of the United States; that to act contrary to these principles is a breach of faith, a usurpation of power, and a forfeiture of the party name and party leadership.

We believe that the protection of the American people against the onward march of totalitarian government requires a faithful observance of Article X of the American Bill of Rights which provides that: "The powers not delegated to the United States by the Constitution, nor prohibited by it to the states, are reserved to the states respectively, or to the people."

We direct attention to the fact that the first platform of the Democratic party, adopted in 1840, resolved that: "Congress has no power under the Constitution to interfere with or control the domestic institutions of the several states, and that such states are the sole and proper judges of everything appertaining to their own affairs not prohibited by the Constitution."

Such pronouncement is the cornerstone of the Democratic party.

A long train of abuses and usurpations of power by unfaithful leaders who are alien to the Democratic parties of the states here represented has become intolerable to those who believe in the preservation of constitutional government and individual liberty in America.

The Executive Department of the government is promoting the gradual but certain growth of a totalitarian state by domination and control of a politically minded Supreme Court. As examples of the threat to our form of government, the Executive Department, with the aid of the Supreme Court, has asserted national dominion and control of submerged oil-bearing lands in California, schools in Oklahoma and Missouri, primary elections in Texas, South Carolina and Louisiana, restrictive covenants in New York and the District of Columbia, and other jurisdictions, as well as religious instruction in Illinois.

By asserting paramount Federal rights in these instances, a totalitarian concept has been promulgated which threatens the integrity of the states and the basic rights of their citizens.

We have repeatedly remonstrated with the leaders of the national organization of our party but our petitions, entreaties and warnings have been treated with contempt. The latest response to our entreaties was a Democratic convention in Philadelphia rigged to embarrass and humiliate the South.

This alleged Democratic assembly called for a civil-rights law that would eliminate segregation of every kind from all American life, prohibit all forms of discrimination in private employment, in public and private instruction and administration and treatment of students; in the operation of public and private health facilities; in all transportation, and require equal access to all places of public accommodation for persons of all races, colors, creeds and national origin.

Proposed FBI Powers Hit

This infamous and iniquitous program calls for the reorganization of the civil rights section of the Department of Justice with a substantial increase in a bureaucratic staff to be devoted exclusively to the enforcement of the civil rights program; the establishment within the FBI of a special unit of investigators and a police state in a totalitarian, centralized, bureaucratic government.

This convention hypocritically denounced totalitarianism abroad but unblushingly proposed and approved it at home. This convention would strengthen the grip of a police state upon a liberty-loving people by the imposition of penalties upon local public officers who failed or refused to act in accordance with its ideas in suppressing mob violence.

We point out that if a foreign power undertook to force upon the people of the United States the measures advocated by the Democratic convention in Philadelphia, with respect to civil rights, it would mean war and the entire nation would resist such effort.

The convention that insulted the South in the party platform advocated giving the Virgin Islands and other dependencies of the United States "the maximum degree of local self-government."

When an effort was made to amend this part of the platform so as to make it read that the party favored giving the Virgin Islands and the several states the maximum degree of local self-government, the amendment adding the words "these several states" was stricken out and the sovereign states were denied the rights that the party favors giving the Virgin Islands.

Democrats: Left and Right

We point out that the South, with clock-like regularity, has furnished the Democratic party approximately 50 per cent of the votes necessary to nominate a President every four years for nearly a century. In 1920 the only states in the union that went Democratic were the eleven Southern states.

Notwithstanding this rugged loyalty to the party, the masters of political intrigue now allow Republican states in which there is scarcely a Democratic office holder to dominate and control the party and fashion its policies.

As Democrats who are irrevocably committed to democracy as defined and expounded by Thomas Jefferson, Andrew Jackson and Woodrow Wilson, and who believe that all necessary steps must be taken for its preservation. we declare to the people of the United 'ates as follows:

1. We bei eve that the Constitution of the United States is the greatest charter of human liberty ever conceived by the mind of man.

2. We oppose all efforts to invade or destroy the rights vouchsafed by it 'to every citizen of this republic.

3. We stand for social and economic justice, which we believe can be vouchsafed to all citizens only by a strict adherence to our Constitution and the avoidance of any invasion or destruction of the constitutional rights of the states and individuals. We oppose the totalitarian, centralized, bureaucratic government and the police state called for by the platforms adopted by the Democratic and Republican conventions.

4. We stand for the segregation of the races and the racial integrity of each race; the constitutional right to choose one's associates; to accept private employment without governmental interference, and to earn one's living in any lawful way. We oppose the elimination of segregation, employment by Federal bureaucrats called for by the misnamed civil rights program. We favor home rule, local self-government and a minimum interference with individual rights.

Convention Action Assailed

5. We oppose and condemn the action of the Democratic convention in sponsoring a civil rights program calling for the elimination of segregation, social equality by Federal fiat, regulation of private employment practices, voting and local law enforcement.

6. We affirm that the effective enforcement of such a program would be utterly destructive of the social, economic and political life of the Southern people, and of other localities in which there may be differences in race, creed or national origin in appreciable numbers.

7. We stand for the checks and balances provided by the three departments of our Government. We oppose the usurpation of legislative functions by the executive and judicial departments.

We unreservedly condemn the effort to establish nation-wide a police state in this republic that would destroy the last vestige of liberty enjoyed by a citizen.

8. We demand that there be returned to the people, to whom of right they belong, those powers needed for the preservation of human rights and the discharge of our responsibility as Democrats for human welfare. We oppose a denial of those rights by political parties, a barter or sale of those rights by a political convention, as well as any invasion or violation of those rights by the Federal Government.

We call upon all Democrats and upon all other loyal Americans who are opposed to totalitarianism at home and abroad to unite with us in ignominiously defeating Harry S. Truman and Thomas E. Dewey, and every other candidate for public office who would establish a police state in the United States of America.

July 18, 1948

New Party's Peace Plan

By The Associated Press.

PHILADELPHIA, July 25—Following is the full text of the "peace" program of the Progressive party as adopted in an amendment today to the party's platform:

"The Progressive party believes that enduring peace among the peoples of the world community is possible only through world law. Continued anarchy among nations in the atomic age threatens our civilization and humanity itself with annihilation.

"The only ultimate alternative to war is the abandonment of the principle of the coercion of sovereignties by sovereignties and the adoption of the principle of the just enforcement upon individuals of world federal law, enacted by a world federal legislature with limited but adequate powers to safeguard the common defense and the general welfare of all mankind.

"Such a structure of peace through government can be evolved by making of the United Nations an effective agency of cooperation among nations. This can be done by restoring the unity of the great powers as they work together for common purposes.

"Since the death of Franklin D. Roosevelt this principle has been betrayed to a degree which not only paralyzes the United Nations but threatens the world with another war in which there can be no victory and few survivors. Beyond an effective United Nations lies the further possibility of genuine world government.

"Responsibility for ending the tragic prospect of war is a joint responsibility o. the Soviet Union and the United States.

"We hope for more political liberty and economic democracy throughout the world. We believe that war between East and West will mean fascism and death for all. We insist that peace is the prerequisite of survival.

"We believe with Henry A. Wallace that 'there is no misunderstanding or difficulty between the United States of America and the U.S.S.R. which can be settled by force or fear and there is no difference which cannot be settled by peaceful, hopeful negotiation. There is no American principle or public interest, and there is no Russian principle or public interest, which would have to be sacrificed to end the cold war and open up the century of peace which the century of the common man demands.

"We denounce anti-Soviet hysteria as a mask for monopoly, militarism and reaction. We demand that a new leadership of the peace-seeking people of our nation—which has vastly greater responsibility for peace than Russia because it has vastly greater power for war—undertake in good faith and carry to an honorable conclusion, without appeasement or saber rattling on either side, a determined effort to settle current controversies and enable men and women everywhere to look forward with confidence to the common task of building a creative and lasting peace for all the world."

July 26, 1948

DEWEY'S CONFIDENCE GROWS

Speeches by Governor Reflect Assurance Of His Election

By LEO EGAN
Special to The New York Times.

LOS ANGELES, Calif., Sept. 25—At the end of the first week of his active campaign for President, Gov. Thomas E. Dewey of New York is acting like a man who has already been elected and is merely marking time, waiting to take office. In his speeches and in his manner there is an attitude that the election will be a mere formality to confirm a decision already made.

The basic theme of Mr. Dewey's campaign outlined in the kick-off speech last Monday in Des Moines and amplified and repeated in subsequent addresses and back-platform appearances, is that only the election of a Republican President and a Republican Congress can provide the country with the unity it needs to insure peace in a troubled world.

Factional divisions within the Democratic party have been referred to but not emphasized in support of this contention. Henry A. Wallace's third party has been mentioned only once, and then as an example of American tolerance for crackpots. Gov. J. Strom Thurmond and his States' Rights party have not even been mentioned.

The whole tone of the campaign is in sharp contrast with the strategy employed in 1944, when Mr. Dewey was running against the late President Roosevelt at a critical point in a global war. Then the New York Governor was employing every device at his command to provoke his adversary into a verbal slugging match. Now he is deliberately avoiding any sharp controversy with the Democratic incumbent.

Contagious Confidence

In appearance, in tone of delivery and in the content of his speeches, Mr. Dewey exudes confidence in his election. It is a confidence that is reflected by most of those in his audiences, by the advisers who are making the campaign trip with him and by a large group of the press corps on "the Dewey Victory Special" on which he crossed the continent.

What anxiety or misgivings are felt by Mr. Dewey or his advisers relate chiefly to the outcome of the contest for control of the next Senate.

In all of his speeches, formal and informal, Mr. Dewey has taken cognizance of the widespread and intense interest in the possibility of war because of the tense international situation. The danger of war, he has contended, will be lessened by the election of a Republican administration that will have a strong and consistent foreign policy, will support an adequate military establishment and strengthen the domestic economy.

As far as domestic issues are concerned, he promised in the first week to bring inflation under control by cutting Government expenses, reducing the Federal debt and revising tax laws to encourage production and thrift, to continue Government support of farm prices and to strengthen the soil-conservation program, to go forward with the public development of reclamation and irrigation projects and hydroelectric developments, and to institute the greatest political house-cleaning in Washington in the nation's history.

He has promised also to end the Government monopoly in atomic-energy development as soon as world conditions permit.

His audiences have been large,

154

friendly and mildly enthusiastic. In Rock Island, Ill., where he made his first back-platform appearance, the crowd appeared to be composed almost equally of factory workers from the agricultural implement plants and farmers from the surrounding countryside. In Des Moines, Denver, Albuquerque and Phoenix there was a large proportion of persons 30 years old and younger to hear his main speech of the day.

Back-platform crowds at wayside stops were notably friendly and appeared to represent a good cross-section of the communities in which they live. At most stops large parking fields filled with automobiles indicated that many had driven in from the surrounding area to see and hear him.

His back-platform talks, particularly near the end of the week, were very folksy. He exchanged quips with some in the crowd, bought tickets to a local school play, talked about crop conditions and related experiences on his Pawling farm.

In the various cities he has visited, persons who have not seen him since 1944, the last time he campaigned, remarked that Mr. Dewey was much more friendly, sociable and relaxed than he was then. It helps convince them that he has an excellent chance of winning.

September 26, 1948

TRUMAN SEES DRIVE TO RUIN NEW DEAL, ESPOUSES IT ANEW

GOP Planning 'Hatchet Job,' With Labor Law First Step, He Declares in Akron

11 OHIO POINTS HEAR HIM

He Says Rival Evades Stand on Issues Aiding the People —Thousands Cheer Sallies

By CLAYTON KNOWLES
Special to The New York Times.

AKRON, Ohio, Oct. 11—President Truman dedicated himself anew to the New Deal tonight as he made a climactic bid for Ohio's twenty-five electoral votes.

Hammering away all day at the Republicans as the servants of special privilege, the President wound up a 300-mile tour across the state, in which he made eleven speeches, with this first full-dress espousal in the present campaign of the governmental philosophy that came to life with the election of Franklin D. Roosevelt sixteen years ago.

He made no reservations as he reaffirmed his belief in this philosophy despite the fact that the note on which he bid for support might not be a popular one. Ohio, Democratic in 1932, 1936 and 1940, swung over to the Republicans four years ago.

Cheers Drown Wallace Cries

Tens of thousands of persons lined the streets of this city of 300,000 as the President and his party drove from the railroad station to the armory for his speech, and their cheers could be heard for blocks.

Inside the armory, packed to its capacity of 2,500, the audience was equally free with applause and cheers. Other thousands heard the speech outside the building.

The only dissident note was sounded by a band of pickets, perhaps two dozen strong, who stood across from the armory carrying Wallace-Taylor placards. But their cries were drowned out by the roar of the Truman crowd. Cheering in the hall reached its peak at the President's first mention of the New Deal.

"The Democratic party," the President declared, "thinks in terms of doing things for people—higher minimum wages — broader social security—protection in old age—better medical care—better schools and better homes — and a better life for the men and women who do the world's work.

"That is our basic philosophy—service for the people—the greatest good for the greatest number. And upon that philosophy we have erected during the past sixteen years a great progressive body of laws. We call those laws—and I say it proudly—we call them the 'new deal.'"

As he developed this keynote the President declared that the Republicans "have the propaganda and the money" but that the Democrats enjoyed the support of the people.

Says Corporations Back GOP

"And the people have the votes," he said. "That's why we're going to win. The Republicans have the money because the big corporations have found out that they can get what they want from the Republican party. We have the people because the people have found out that they can get what they want from the Democratic party."

While most of his appeal hinged upon the Democratic labor record and the actions of the Republican-controlled Eightieth Congress, Mr. Truman emphasized that attacks upon New Deal gains would grow if another Republican Congress and a Republican President were elected.

"The Republican politicians don't like the New Deal," he said. "They never liked the New Deal, and they would like to get rid of it.

"This is shown by their words and deeds. They have been talking for years about 'cleaning up' the New Deal. Then, in 1946, they got control of the Congress and began to whittle away at the New Deal laws.

"Now they've tasted blood and they are waiting eagerly for the time when they can go ahead with a Republican Congress and a Republican President to do a real hatchet job on the New Deal without interference."

Without mentioning his opponent by name, the President quoted Governor Dewey, whom he called "the chief prosecutor against the New Deal," Senator Robert A. Taft of Ohio, Speaker Joseph W. Martin Jr., and Representative Fred A. Hartley of New Jersey as revealing the real intentions of the Republican party.

Taking cognizance of the oft-repeated Republican charge that "so-called New Deal Democratic misrule" conspired to "strangle industry and farming," the President noted that corporate profits increased from a loss of $400,000,000 in 1933 to a profit of $17,000,000,-000 in 1947, while farm income increased from $2,500,000,000 to $18,-000,000,000.

He quoted at some length from Representative Hartley's recent book, "Our New National Labor Policy, the Taft-Hartley Act and the Next Steps," to illustrate announced Republican intentions on labor and social fronts.

Renewing his call for the repeal of the Taft-Hartley Act, Mr. Truman declared that Mr. Hartley in his book said that all such legislation "requires interim treatment."

Predicts "Bare Knuckles"

"Interim treatment," he said. "Do you know what that is? That is the Taft-Hartley Law. They call the Taft-Hartley Law interim treatment. After that, they take off the gloves and give you the bare knuckles."

The Akron speech, widely broadcast, came after the President had made talks ranging from five to twenty minutes before uniformly good crowds at Cincinnati, Hamilton, Dayton, Sidney, Lima, Ottawa, Deshler, Fostoria, Willard and Rittman.

Conservative estimates put the day's crowds before his arrival at Akron at 100,000. Upward of 50,000 were on hand to welcome him at Dayton. And the response at all points was enthusiastic as the President urged his audience to listen to his night radio speech. He promised that in it he would "take the hide" off the Republicans.

Traveling aboard the campaign train as it swung from the southwest to northeast corners of the state were former Gov. Frank J. Lausche, who is seeking to return to the State House, and other state and Congressional candidates. The President spoke warmly in their behalf at every stop.

Despite the fulsome praise by the President, there was some question whether Mr. Truman's Akron speech would be helpful in Mr. Lausche's state campaign. The former Governor is running without the support of labor, with which he has been at odds at many points in his public life.

Kroll With President

Others in the Presidential party, however, were Jack Kroll, national director of the CIO Political Action Committee, and George Harrison, chairman of a group of leading American Federation of Labor unions that are supporting the President's candidacy. Both are Ohioans and it is believed the President's speech was geared to their views.

In his night speech the President charged that the Republicans had not limited their attack upon the New Deal to passage of the Taft-Hartley Law over his veto. He cited other instances, particularly an act adopted at the last session taking Social Security insurance benefits away from almost a million people."

He reaffirmed Democratic objectives to increase the minimum wage to at least 75 cents an hour, to broaden Social Security coverage and increase benefits, and to provide health insurance and Federal aid to education while combating inflation.

In his breakfast talk at Cincinnati the President again taunted Governor Dewey for his "silence" on the issues, noting that Senator Taft at least was "frankly conservative."

"You know where I stand," he said. "I have taken a stand on every one of the issues before the country today. You know what I stand for. But just try to find out where the other fellow stands. We would be hopelessly committed to an old-fashioned Republican boom-and-bust cycle if we turned the whole Government over to the Republicans."

Grace was said at the breakfast by Archbishop John T. McNicholas, head of the Archdiocese of Cincinnati, whose appearance at political functions are exceedingly rare.

October 12, 1948

155

DEWEY FAR IN LEAD; A TIE IN THE SENATE STRONG POSSIBILITY

By JAMES A. HAGERTY

With only eight days to go before the election on Nov. 2, Thomas E. Dewey and Earl Warren, Republican nominees for President and Vice President, respectively, appear certain to defeat President Harry S. Truman and Senator Alben W. Barkley, their Democratic opponents, by a large plurality in the Electoral College. The Republicans seem likely to retain control of the House of Representatives, probably by a reduced majority, and it is certain that the fight for control of the next Senate will be close.

These are the conclusions to be drawn from reports from correspondents of THE NEW YORK TIMES in all states in which election results are regarded as doubtful. The contest for control of the Senate appears to be so close that these reports indicate a strong possibility of a tie. In this case the next Vice President, presumably Governor Warren, would be in a position to break a tie vote on the election of a president pro tempore, a post now held by Senator Arthur H. Vandenberg, and thus enable the Republicans to organize the Senate and name the chairmen of its committees.

October 25, 1948

PRESIDENT LIKENS DEWEY TO HITLER AS FASCISTS' TOOL

Says When Bigots, Profiteers Get Control of Country They Select 'Front Man' to Rule

DICTATORSHIP STRESSED

Truman Tells Chicago Audience a Republican Victory Will Threaten U. S. Liberty

By ANTHONY LEVIERO
Special to THE NEW YORK TIMES

CHICAGO, Oct. 25—A Republican victory on election day will bring a Fascistic threat to American freedom that is even more dangerous than the perils from communism and extreme right "crackpots," President Truman asserted here tonight.

Already the "gate" has been opened "just a little bit" by the Eightieth Congress to admit this totalitarian specter to the shrines of democracy, the Chief Executive told his audience in Chicago Stadium. It was in this arena sixteen years ago that Franklin D. Roosevelt was first nominated for the Presidency. Here, too, four years ago, Mr. Truman was selected as Mr. Roosevelt's running mate.

President Truman asserted that three forces of evil were conniving through the Republican party to fasten a grip on the country which might reduce the Bill of Rights to "a scrap of paper."

He identified the three forces as consisting of "men" who (1) wanted unbridled inflation to profiteer; (2) were striving to concentrate power in a few hands, and (3) were fomenting racial and religious hatred.

Says They Find "Front Man"

When a few "men" gain economic control of a country, he asserted, "they find a 'front man' to run the country for them."

The President did not identify the "evil forces" specifically, leaving this largely to implication and innuendo. An analysis of his address, however, made the cumulative effect of it even more piercing than the "gluttons-of-privilege" speech he delivered at Dexter, Iowa, on Sept. 18. That talk provoked a storm of criticism that Mr. Truman was stirring up a class war in this country.

In his reference to the "few men" manipulating a "front man," Mr. Truman cited Hitler, Mussolini and Tojo as examples, leaving the intimation that Governor Dewey fitted this role in the United States.

Mr. Dewey has pledged himself to an administration of unity and efficiency, and Mr. Truman said: "In our time, we have seen the tragedy of the Italian and German peoples, who lost their freedom to men who made promises of unity and efficiency and security.

"Today, in the United States, there is a growing—and a dangerous—concentration of immense economic power in the hands of a few men."

Great corporations are "squeezing small business," he asserted, and the "record of the Eightieth Congress is a sad tale of the sellout of the people's interest to put more and more power into the hands of fewer and fewer men."

The President quoted Mr. Dewey as saying that "the Eightieth Congress delivered as no other Congress ever did for the future of the country"; then Mr. Truman asserted:

"I'll say it delivered. It delivered for the private lobby. It delivered for the big oil company lobby. It delivered for the railroad lobby. It delivered for the real estate lobby.

"That's what the Republican candidate calls delivering for the future. Is that the kind of future you want?"

23,000 Hear Him in Stadium

President Truman spoke at 9 P. M., Central standard time (10 P. M. New York time), before a capacity audience of 23,000. He reached the Stadium after an hour-long parade of more than two miles through streets jammed with great crowds.

Everywhere was evidence that the Cook County Democratic machine had exerted the utmost effort to bring out members of unions, veterans organizations and ward political groups. The parade route blazed and echoed to the crash of fireworks.

Some political observers were of the opinion that by this speech Mr. Truman hoped to draw strength from Henry A. Wallace's third party, which, according to some forecasts, threatens to cut heavily into the normally heavy Democratic majority of Chicago.

The President asserted that this campaign was not "just a battle between two parties" but a "crusade" for "the very soul of America." He declared that the independent voters would decide the issue, and that by throwing their weight to the Democrats or Republicans "they will choose the forces which are to compose our Government."

In opening his address Mr. Truman asserted that "vicious partisan attacks" had kept this country from joining the League of Nations, the "great vision" of Woodrow Wilson. He paid tribute to President Roosevelt for his "foresight" in helping to establish the United Nations.

Sees Democracy Menaced

Leaving foreign policy at this point, Mr. Truman said that it was necessary to do more "than just avert war" because American democracy was under attack "right now inside this country." He added:

"The American way of life which most of us have been taking for granted is threatened today by powerful forces of which most people are not even aware.

"Everybody knows about the contemptible Communist minority which we detest. Everybody knows, too, about the crackpot forces of the extreme right wing. We are on our guard against them.

"The real danger to our democracy does not come only from these extremes. It comes mainly from powerful reactionary forces which are silently undermining our democratic institutions."

Mr. Truman said that he knew it was "hard for Americans to admit this danger," but that if the undemocratic forces continued unchecked, the people would awaken in a few years to find that the Bill of Rights no longer existed.

While accusing big business of posing a threat to freedom on the economic front, Mr. Truman asserted that some of those who were instigating racial and religious feeling against "Catholics, Jews, Negroes and other minority races and religions" were members of the Eightieth Congress. He referred to those who had supported the Displaced Persons Act of 1948, which, he said, "cruelly discriminated against Catholics and Jews."

President Truman's reception for his Chicago appearance began in Gary, Ind., where leading Chicago Democrats boarded his train. Among them was Jacob M. Arvey, Cook County Democratic chairman, who before the Democratic convention sought to sidetrack Mr. Truman in favor of Gen. Dwight D. Eisenhower. Others on the train were former Mayor Edward J. Kelly and Senator Scott Lucas of Illinois.

Arriving in Chicago at 3 P. M., the President was driven to a hotel for a party reception. He remained there until 8 P. M. when he joined the gigantic parade to the stadium.

Dewey Is Linked to Brooks

Earlier, Mr. Truman made two attacks on Governor Dewey and the Eightieth Congress, one of which was at Garrett, Ind., where he told a trackside crowd of 3,000 persons:

"The Republican candidate has gone from one doubtful state to another trying to bail out the campaigns of hopeless reactionaries who ran the Republican Eightieth Congress. He is trying to get them all re-elected. One of these salvage operations is being carried on right next door here in Illinois.

"The Republican candidate is hoping to save the hard-shelled isolationist reactionary Curley (C. Wayland) Brooks, who has been the Senator from Illinois for quite some time."

Making his third appearance in four months in the industrial city of Gary, the President told a labor rally there that "President Roosevelt brought the capital of the United States back to Washington from Wall Street." He said it would stay in Washington "as long as the Democratic party controls the government."

October 26, 1948

DEWEY DECLARES TRUMAN'S POLICIES HELPFUL TO SOVIET

Alternate Appeasing and Firm Stand Aided Spread of Sway Half Around Globe, He Says

CAMPAIGN THEME SCORED

Boom or Bust' Warnings Voice World Reds' Propaganda on U. S., He Tells Clevelanders

By W. H. LAWRENCE
Special to THE NEW YORK TIMES.

CLEVELAND, Oct. 27—Speaking here tonight, Gov. Thomas E. Dewey accused President Truman of helping communism at home and abroad.

In a major appeal for votes on the foreign policy issue, he charged that the Administration "did not seem to understand the nature of the Communist threat," and, by appeasing the Russians one day and standing firm the next, had "made tragic concessions in many areas of the world." "In a little

more than three years," he added, "the Soviet has extended its sway nearly half way around the world and now rules more than five hundred million human beings."

Domestically, he said, Mr. Truman's campaign warnings that election of a Republican President might lead to another depression were "voicing the world-wide Communist propaganda that America is heading from boom to bust." He asserted that the Communists can take advantage of the President's efforts "to drive our people by appeals to fear and prejudice" and by his ridicule of "the old-fashioned American idea of teamwork and unity."

The Republican nominee said there was no easy answer to the question of how peace might be secured, and that the road of "easy answers" was the road to disaster. "But," he continued, "of one thing we can be sure: we shall not achieve peace by conducting these desperately important matters on a happy-thought basis or by jovially remarking that we like good old Joe."

The "happy thought" apparently referred to the President's abortive plan to send Chief Justice Fred M. Vinson to Moscow to negotiate with Premier Stalin and "good old Joe" to Mr. Truman's remark that he liked "old Joe" but that Stalin was a prisoner of the Politburo.

The New York Governor appeared here tonight just twenty-four hours after the President had concluded his Ohio campaign in the same auditorium. And, wheth-

er Mr. Truman's tactics are winning Democratic votes or not, it seemed that Governor Dewey was stepping up the tempo and sharpening the bite of his own campaign oratory. He told his Cleveland audience tonight that he was proud that he and his running mate, Gov. Earl Warren of California, had "not been guilty of using our high responsibility to rip our country apart or to arouse fear and prejudices."

"We will win this campaign and we will win it by clean and decent methods," the Republican nominee declared.

Mr. Dewey also replied to the President's charge that a Republican victory might lead to dictatorship in America.

"Unlike our opponents, we do not assert that there is only one party in the United States that is fit to govern," he said. "We do not believe in one-party rule. That is totalitarianism."

Both great parties alternately have served the country well, he said, but after they have been in office too long they have grown weary, and become "fumbling and weak."

In his bill of indictment against the Truman Administration Governor Dewey, stressing the spread of Soviet power, said that the Russians had "swallowed up" Lithuania, Estonia, Latvia and part of Finland and subjugated as "satellites" Poland, Hungary, Bulgaria, Yugoslavia, Rumania, and Czechoslovakia and currently "are endeavoring by political strikes to paralyze France and destroy the republic even while they wage war in Greece and threaten Turkey."

His own formula to meet this threat was an administration that would work for peace "calmly and patiently, that would work day and

night to build up the strength of the cause of freedom, and, while refusing to appease Russia, would extend the hand of friendship to every country." He renewed his pledge of support to the United Nations and to the federation of western Europe. He also promised again to give more help to China.

The Governor's "victory special" bearing a group of Ohio politicians including Senator Robert A. Taft, whom he defeated for the nomination, reached Cleveland at 5 P. M., during the late afternoon rush hour, and police estimated 75,000 persons were on the streets through which the Republican candidate was driven from the Union Terminal to his hotel.

The Cleveland public hall was packed with an audience estimated at 13,000 immediately in front of Governor Dewey and with an overflow of several thousand in the music hall in the same building who listen on the public address system.

Governor Dewey received an ovation of three minutes and 20 seconds when he was introduced by Gov. Thomas J. Herbert. He was interrupted by applause twenty-five times in the course of his speech.

On his way to Cleveland from Chicago, where he had spent the night, Governor Dewey made his second unscheduled stop within twenty-four hours at Elkhart, Ind. Noticing the crowd of several thousand, he remarked jokingly that Indiana politicians apparently had made plans for him to stop there even if he didn't know it. In Indiana the closest political contest is between Hobart Creighton, Republican candidate for Governor and former Gov. Herman Schricker.

October 28, 1948

TRUMAN CONFIDENT OF A BIG VICTORY

Sees a Great Many 'Red-Faced Pollsters' Wednesday—Scores Republican High Prices

President Truman bore down hard on "Republican high prices" in his metropolitan appearances yesterday and told a night gathering of 700 in Lost Battalion Hall, Queens, that housewives understood very well the issues of the campaign.

Earlier, the President had stressed the high price theme at a luncheon of Bronx Democratic women. He coupled a prediction of certain victory with a reiteration of his belief in a strong, free Israel. Passing over the Palestine issue without mention

last night, the President concentrated on price increases, which he said had raised living costs 30 per cent in Queens.

"Every Queens Congressman voted to kill price controls when I was trying to keep them," Mr. Truman said. "They were part of the do-nothing, good-for-nothing Eightieth Congress. There will be sixty million people voting in this election. . . . "

"And fifty million for Truman," a member of the audience shouted.

Sees Many Red Faces

Joining in the general laughter, the President predicted that "there will be more red-faced pollsters on Nov. 3 than there were in 1936, when they had to fold up The Literary Digest."

"You can throw the Gallup poll right into the ashcan," he added.

October 30, 1948

TRUMAN WINS WITH 304 ELECTORAL VOTES; DEMOCRATS CONTROL SENATE AND HOUSE

OHIO POLL DECIDES

It Clinches for President in Race Called Miracle of Electioneering

NO RECORD BALLOT IS SEEN

Dedicating Himself to Peace, Prosperity, Truman Says He Wants to Deserve Honor

By ARTHUR KROCK

The State of Ohio, "mother of Republican Presidents," furnished the electoral bloc early yesterday forenoon which assured to President Harry S. Truman a four-year term in his own right as Chief Executive of the United States. Until this late accounting of votes cast in Tuesday's general election put Ohio firmly in Mr. Truman's column, after it had fluctuated throughout the night, he was certain of but 254 electoral votes, which were twelve less than the 266 required.

The historic role played by Ohio was only one of the dramatic and extraordinary phases of the election of 1948. The President, opposed by the extreme right and left wings of the Democratic party, won a minimum of 304 electoral votes as against 189 acquired by his Republican opponent, Gov. Thomas E. Dewey of New York; carried a Democratic majority in Congress along with him after the Republicans had held this for two years; and gained victory through a multisectional combination of states that did not include New York, New Jersey, Pennsylvania and four of the Southern states in normal Democratic territory.

Miracle of Electioneering Seen

In the political history of the United States this achievement by Mr. Truman will be set down as a miracle of electioneering for which there are few if any parallels. His victory made him the undisputed national leader of the Democratic party, which, though bitterly divided for the past few years, has acknowledged none since the death of Franklin D. Roosevelt, whom Mr. Truman succeeded from the office of Vice President.

When it was assured that he would have Ohio's electors and hence the majority he needed, and Governor Dewey had wired his congratulations and publicly conceded defeat, the President dedicated his official future to world peace and domestic prosperity and said to his brother, J. Vivian Truman, simply: "I just want to deserve the honor."

Mr. Truman acknowledging plaudits of a crowd outside his hotel in Kansas City. He had just received Governor Dewey's message of congratulations.

Associated Press Wirephoto

No Record Vote Indicated

In the result, unexpected by nearly everyone who qualified as a judge of elections except the President himself, there were these other attendant circumstances:

1. The popular vote, expected to reach 51,000,000 or 52,000,000 and thus break the record poll of about 49,548,000 in the Presidential contest of 1940, will probably be far short of the 1940 total.

2. It is possible that Mr. Truman's plurality over Mr. Dewey will not exceed 2,000,000 and may be less than that, which is smaller than the electoral division of 304 to 189 would ordinarily indicate. But this can be partly attributed to the fact that two splinter Democratic tickets were in the field—the States' Rights Democrats headed by Gov. J. Strom Thurmond of South Carolina, and the Progressives headed by Henry A. Wallace, which will poll almost 2,000,000 votes more than probably would have gone in large measure to the national Democratic ticket in normal circumstances.

3. To the vote cast for Mr. Wallace can be traced definitely the failure of the President to carry only one state, New York, with forty-seven electors.

4. California, after see-sawing all Tuesday night and yesterday morning as in 1916, and as Ohio did this year, ended in the Truman column as it did in Woodrow Wilson's contest with Charles E. Hughes thirty-two years ago. But then California made the drama of victory for Wilson: this year Ohio had taken the laurels by an hour or two.

5. The winning combination of states for Mr. Truman bore some resemblance to Wilson's in 1916, but there were notable exceptions, such as Iowa and Illinois which the President carried Tuesday in his group of twenty-eight states. His popular and electoral majority differed from Wilson's also in that it was supplied by an unusual combination of large popular blocks with grievances against the Republican Eightieth Congress which the President had accentuated—such as union labor—contented farmers in normal Republican territory who like the current price levels and did not want to take a chance on a new regime in which they might decline, and urban consumers who, though disturbed over prices, were more disturbed over emotional issues like "civil rights" and Palestine.

6. In the wake of the President's attacks on the record of the Eightieth Congress, centering on tax reduction and the Taft-Hartley Act, a minimum of 258 Democrats were returned to the House of Representatives (the last one had 185) and a minimum of fifty-four to the Senate which, when it recessed, contained only forty-five. The Republicans in the House exchanged 243 for 167, with more losses in sight, and, in the Senate, forty-two members for fifty-one. The fly in this ointment, however, is that under the Democratic label in Congress are two bitterly divided wings of the party which has been unable to cooperate very often for years.

Missouri Maintains Record

7. Missouri, Mr. Truman's home state, maintained the record it has had since 1904 of being on the winning side of every Presidential contest. But Maryland, which had a much longer lien on that record, lost it Tuesday by giving its electors to Governor Dewey.

8. For the first time since the death of President Roosevelt, the United States will have a Vice President and the Senate a President in the person of Alben W. Barkley, now a member of the Senate from Kentucky, the present minority and former majority leader. And Representative Sam Rayburn of Texas will be restored to the Speaker's dais in the Eighty-first Congress.

9. More than fifty members of Congress who helped to make the Taft-Hartley Act into law over Mr. Truman's veto were defeated for re-election. This will likely be reflected in the President's labor legislative policy which he will doubtless present to the Eighty-first Congress.

10. In contests for Governor, Democrats defeated Republican incumbents in eight States, were ejected in one and may be in another—Washington—a net gain of six or seven. The major parties each had twenty-four Governors on election day.

Truman Carries 28 States

The President's victory was so complete and so surprising to almost everyone except himself that analyses of the reasons will recur for years and began yesterday as soon as Ohio's decision was known. But, assuming that California will stay in his column, it was enough for his opponents temporarily to realize that Mr. Truman carried twenty-eight states, in addition to the other victories to which he led his party, and Mr. Dewey sixteen, as follows:

Truman—Arizona, Arkansas, California, Colorado, Florida, Georgia, Idaho, Illinois, Iowa, Kentucky, Massachusetts, Minnesota, Missouri, Montana, Nevada, New Mexico, North Carolina, Ohio, Oklahoma, Rhode Island, Tennessee, Texas, Utah, Virginia, Washington, West Virginia, Wisconsin, Wyoming.

Dewey—Connecticut, Delaware, Indiana, Kansas, Maine, Maryland, Michigan, Nebraska, New Hampshire, New Jersey, New York, North Dakota, Oregon, Pennsylvania, South Dakota, Vermont.

Mr. Wallace carried no state. Governor Thurmond got the 38 electors of Alabama, Louisiana, Mississippi and South Carolina, while 2 of Tennessee's 12 electoral votes are pledged to him, but are in dispute.

It was plain from the above division that the inter-sectional combination of voting groups effected by President Roosevelt after 1932 and held, by him in sufficient numbers to maintain victory through the election of 1944 has been renewed as a national majority by Mr. Truman, for the time being at any rate. This pattern was not many minutes old when Governor Dewey, summoning a press conference, said that he would never again seek the Presidency. It was his third try—twice as the Republican nominee (1944 and 1948) and once (1940) as an unsuccessful candidate for the nomination.

During the long hours of Tuesday night and yesterday morning, when it seemed possible that the Presidential contest might be carried into the next House of Representatives, many persons were deeply disturbed over the possible effects of this on the international situation and the pressing problems of the domestic economy that underlie it. But, with the decision of Ohio and California, and the establishment of the new complexion of Congress, these fears subsided in a feeling that the continuity of the American Government was one of the most definite results of the general election of 1948.

November 4, 1948

POLL ERRORS LAID TO POOR JUDGMENT

Executives Did Not Use Lessons of Their Prior Lapses, Report on 1948 Election Says

SHIFT BY VOTERS STRESSED

Pollsters Call on the Committee to Continue Inquiry Into Turnout on Election Day

The public opinion polls failed to predict the results of the recent Presidential election because the executives showed poor judgment, although they acted in good faith, it was reported yesterday by the inquiry committee set up by the Social Science Research Council. The committee was named after the election to investigate why all the principal public research organizations erroneously had predicted the election of Thomas E. Dewey as President.

The pollsters had no business making a flat prediction on the result of a possibly close election when their own past records showed no basis for such infallibility, the group of educators who conducted the inquiry declared.

In addition, the committee reported, the executives failed to apply to the 1948 election what they knew about their past errors, they failed to ascertain late campaign trends and they were unaware of major causes of error in their methods of sampling and interviewing and in their forecasting, or projecting what the samplings showed.

The survey of the polls and pollsters was made by a group that included James Phinney Baxter 3d, president of Williams College; Philip M. Hauser, University of Chicago; Carl I. Hovland, Yale University; V. O. Key, Johns Hopkins University; Isador Lubin, American Statistical Association; Frank Stanton, president, Columbia Broadcasting System; Samuel A. Stouffer, Harvard University, and Frederick E. Stephan and Samuel S. Wilks, Princeton University.

Better Methods Advised

The committee urged the pollsters to work out better methods and to avoid flat forecasts if a possibility of error existed. The investigators said that the manner in which the pre-election polls were analyzed and presented had led to a poor understanding of the lack of accuracy of polls and therefore to a greater reaction against them.

In discussing the average error of the polls in elections, the report declared that they consistently had underestimated the Democratic vote. On the basis of the errors regarding the elections from 1936 through 1948, the report said, the polls would have only one chance in four of correctly predicting the result in an election as close as in 1948, if the Democratic candidate won. If the Republican candidate were the victor, the polls would have been right three times out of four, the committee declared.

Elmo Roper, one of the leading pollsters—while accepting the report in good grace and characterizing it as "a you are honest but dumb verdict" — took exception yesterday. He said he had overestimated the Democratic vote in 1936, 1940 and 1944 in terms of percentages. However, he agreed that the average error of the Crossley, Gallup and Roper polls together did justify the committee's finding.

The inquirers noted that the average errors in previous election forecasts were about 2 points in 1944 and 1940 and 5 to 6 points in 1936. In 1948 there was a discrepancy of 4 to 5 points in the Crossley and Gallup predictions, while Roper underestimated the Truman vote by 12 points. The discrepancy came about as the result of a compounding of errors by the pollsters, the committee said.

Sampling Criticized

In sampling, the polls took too many voters with college educations and too few with only grade-school educations, according to the report. It added that the executives failed to screen out persons who were not going to vote and to detect the shift from Dewey to Truman.

"Failure to detect and measure changes of mind about voting during the closing days of the campaign accounts for a considerable part of the total error of the prediction," the committee commented.

The group dismissed the error in connection with the "undecided" vote, on the ground that the defective allocation of this potential vote among the candidates contributed less than 1.5 points to the over-all error.

The committee declared that in interpreting the results of the actual polling and presenting them to the public the "pollsters went far beyond the bounds of sound reporting." The investigators added that "final releases carried very little indication of the limitations of polling and the tendencies in past elections to underestimate the Democratic vote."

The releases also failed to provide enough information about how the polls worked for the public to decide how much confidence to place in the predictions, the committee said. The number of persons interviewed, the type of sampling employed and the "weighting" of the results in the form of corrections were not made known, the committee reported.

The inquirers said that the smallness of the samples used—3,250 by Gallup in a national poll —was not to be blamed for the poor result, since errors canceled themselves out. Polls failed to reach either the very highest or the very lowest economic segments of the population in true proportions, it was declared.

The committee found evidence of a shift of 2 to 3 percentage points to President Truman in the final weeks of the campaign. Even taking this into account, there would be no guarantee of future accuracy, the committee said, unless many reforms were made.

The group's recommendations included more reliable polling techniques, increased research on such methods, research into social psychology and political science, greater information to the public of the limitations of the polling device, more effective cooperation among research workers and greater training for students in the field.

Roper Gives Views

Mr. Roper called the committee's report a "welcome Christmas present, because anyone foolish enough to be in the business of predicting elections can't very well object to politely worded sentences which call attention to other errors in judgment."

"It's unfortunate that the brief news release the committee made doesn't do justice to the really worth-while report itself," Mr. Roper said. "The committee worked hard and achieved excellent results, particularly in view of the time they had and the money at their disposal.

"To me their major finding is the need for more work in the realm of determining turnout. The question of which groups will vote in the greatest proportion is the unsolved problem. We thought we had it licked, but we didn't. The use of better psychological methods is needed.

"Past voting behavior by groups was upset this year and the questions we used to determine intensity of feeling were not good enough to detect that fact. It is to be hoped that funds will be made available to the committee in order that they may further study this problem of turnout—which is

still unsolved and is the vital problem of election polling."

Mr. Gallup commented as follows:

"The report represents a painstaking and impartial job. The Gallup poll was glad to cooperate with the committee in every way and suggests that to get the full facts of the case the detailed report of the committee be read.

"The committee finds that a considerable part of the total error

in poll predictions was due to the failure to take last-minute polls to catch the shift to Truman during the final days of the campaign. This agrees with our own post-election analysis.

"Other factors contributed in a lesser way to poll errors, as the committee points out. But a careful study of the committee's findings shows no conclusive evidence that different interviewing methods or sampling systems would

have indicated the election of Truman.

"It is unfortunate that the committee did not go more deeply into the problem of turnout—the identification of those who vote and those who stay at home on election day. We strongly urge the committee to continue its study of this major problem which all polls face in every election."

December 27, 1948

Truman Victory Is Found To Contain Four Elements

New Deal Ideas, Truman's Faith in Them, Clifford's Tactics, Labor Held Responsible

By JAMES RESTON

The elements of President Truman's remarkable victory, it is generally agreed, were these:

1. The ideas of Franklin D. Roosevelt's New Deal and Woodrow Wilson's New Freedom.

2. The faith of President Truman in these ideas and his courage in basing his campaign on them.

3. The political tactics of Clark Clifford which won the admiration of the electorate, if not of Mr. Truman's other associates in Washington.

4. The organization of a labor movement, which acquired strength from the middle and the right by shedding the support of the ideological left.

There are many observers who believe there were other important and even decisive factors—the arid personality of Governor Dewey, the attempt of the New York Governor to sit on the fence while keeping both ears to the ground, etc.—but these four considerations, combined with the nation's unparalled economic prosperity, are generally credited with having won for Mr. Truman the most dramatic electoral victory since Wilson defeated Hughes in 1916.

Truman Held Impressed

Mr. Truman has probably never been so impressed with the strength of the New Deal philosophy among the electorate as he is this morning. Last week, despite his great show of confidence and his defiance of all his detractors, he was scarcely as confident in private as he was in public.

When his campaign train rolled into Chicago a week ago last Monday morning, he discussed his chances in moderate and even disparaging terms.

"It's worth a fight anyway," he said to one of his Illinois colleagues; and that was about the

measure of his faith.

Nevertheless, such as it was, his faith was greater than that of almost any other member of his official party with the possible exception of his handsome young secretary and political tactician, Clark Clifford.

He apparently decided that, even if he lost, he would, by embracing the New Deal, assure its future—and his own—in a world which was clearly going to the left. And in the end that philosophy evidently paid off.

"Peace, Prices, and Places to Live" was the main burden of his argument. Everywhere he went he emphasized in homespun terms the issues popularized by his predecessor: controls for "the interests"; more housing; more Social Security; equality and even privileges for labor; benefits for the farmers; conservation of the natural resources of the nation; medical security; and equality for all citizens before the law.

Many times in the forty-four months since the death of Franklin Roosevelt, Mr. Truman had been a dubious and even wavering supporter of many of the New Deal measures of the past, but in identifying himself in the end with these issues, he gained a response which was greater than anybody on his campaign train imagined.

Clifford Backed This Strategy

Almost alone among the White House advisers, Clark Clifford supported and added to this strategy. He described the President's campaign problems in these terms:

When the Democratic convention met in Philadelphia last July, he recalled, the President was abandoned by all except his most intimate supporters. The liberal wing of the party had left him; the States' Rights Democrats of the South were in rebellion; the Democratic party's organization, ac-

customed to winning without much labor, was dispirited and even hopeless.

"At that time," Mr. Clifford observed, "we were on our own 20-yard line. We had to be bold. If we had kept on plugging away in moderate terms, we might have reached midfield when the gun went off, so we had to throw long passes—anything to stir up labor, and to get the mass votes of the great cities of the Middle West, New England and the East."

This strategy — particularly the use of blunt instruments to win the racial and religious groups of the cities—met considerable opposition within the President's family. The Chicago speech—comparing Mr. Dewey and the Republicans with the totalitarian movements of Italy, Germany and Japan—was much more violent in its original draft than when it was finally delivered, but even then it did not win the support of all Mr. Truman's colleagues.

Nevertheless, the tactic worked better than its contrivers dreamed, and while these efforts at the end of the campaign are not likely to remain as a model of morality, they apparently achieved the objective of persuading the electorate that something important was afoot.

Labor did "get out the vote," as the President had pleaded with it to do. It did respond to the campaign to repeal the Taft-Hartley Act and defeat the return to power of a party which was pictured as a symbol of reaction.

What the effect of this campaign will be remains in serious doubt. By his tactics, Mr. Truman has opened up some old party wounds, but by his own stubborn courage he has at the same time won the admiration and even the allegiance not only of many members of his own party but of many of the most powerful members of the opposition party.

Men like Senator Arthur Vandenberg, for example, whose support Mr. Truman will need to implement the foreign and domestic programs he has outlined, are full of admiration for his accomplishments if not for his tactics, and at least for a time, he is expected to win their votes when the Eighty-first Congress convenes early in the New Year.

November 4, 1948

ELECTION BRINGS SHIFTS WITHIN THE TWO PARTIES

Democrats Cast Off Extremists While GOP Faces Major Changes

By W. H. LAWRENCE
Special to THE NEW YORK TIMES.

WASHINGTON, Nov. 6–The amazing victory of Harry S. Truman in Tuesday's election is bound to have a tremendous effect on the future course of America's political parties. Many of the questions raised cannot yet be satisfactorily answered; but it is clear that both of the major parties, as well as the two new minor parties, find themselves in a new and entirely unexpected situation as a result of the electoral upset.

The central fact emerging from the election is that the mighty coalition forged by President Roosevelt when he built the New Deal is a continuing thing. That coalition bids fair to give the Democratic party continuing control as the nation's majority political group. It has survived the death of President Roosevelt, and has shown that it was not, as so many persons believed, an insecure alliance based on the personality of one "indispensable man."

It has survived the defection of its extreme left wing, the Communists, the fellow-travelers, and the way-to-the-left-of-center liberals, who usually marched with Franklin D. Roosevelt, but tried to do business for themselves through the candidacy of Henry Wallace.

Loss of Southerners

It has survived the loss of the extreme right wing of Southern Democrats, who threatened rebellion on the "white supremacy" issue because of President Truman's civil-rights program, and who managed to take four states and forty electoral votes out of the Truman total.

Perhaps, most important of all, the coalition emerged from this election as a politically united group of workers, farmers, little business men and housewives with a program for the country—one that promises to preserve and, where possible, expand the New Deal.

There was no retreat in Tuesday's election—the American people, having tried the Republicans in Congress for two years, were ready to move more to the left, even though not in any abrupt manner.

The first reaction of Democrats to Tuesday's victory is that President Truman is the undisputed master of his party, at least for the time being. He is entitled to almost exclusive credit for the tenacity of his campaign and the strategy of his appeal to the electorate—the two factors which spurred the coalition to victorious efforts.

Expect Congress Backing

The President and Alben W. Barkley, Vice President-elect, believe they won because they had a program, and they are counting on the backing of their heavy majorities in both chambers of Congress to put that program through.

Senator Barkley was asked what would be done about the "Dixiecrats," and he replied, with a smile, that "we'll cross that bridge when we get to it—and there may not be a bridge when we get there."

How long the honeymoon will last between the President and those Democrats who differ with the New Deal is an open question, however. It should not be forgotten that President Roosevelt won his greatest victory in 1936, and came out of that election with the Republican membership in the House reduced to eighty-nine; but, almost as soon as his second term began, he encountered one legislative defeat after another, beginning with the court-packing bill, the governmental reorganization statute and other administration "must" bills.

There has been some talk, within the labor organizations, of a movement, immediately after election, to establish a third party, which would be a Labor party. But that talk was predicated on the probability of President Truman's defeat and the resulting disintegration of the Democratic party. Nothing succeeds like success, and it is probable that the third-party talk will diminish.

But what of the other parties which challenged this coalition? What is their future? What, if anything, can they do to have a chance to win again?

For the Republicans, this is their fifth successive defeat, and it has hit them very hard because they were certain of victory, to the point of overconfidence. But the Republicans are figuring today that they can start up the comeback trail in 1950. They have hopes of taking the Presidency in 1952. They stress that they are better off in the Senate after the 1948 election than they were after the 1944 election, and, while they are not so strong in the House, they have, on the other hand, recaptured majorities in New York and Pennsylvania, the states with the two largest electoral votes.

Considering the major-party vote alone, the Republicans got 47.75 per cent, and the Democrats 52.24 per cent, which is the closest that the GOP has come to a Presidential victory since 1928. In that year Herbert Hoover received 58.8 per cent of the major-party vote.

However, the Republicans have been so shocked by Tuesday's results that they still do not know exactly what happened, and a waiting period of a month or six weeks to think about a future course is indicated. There then will be called a meeting of the Republican National Committee to discuss the problem.

One always hears comments, after an election defeat, that the minority party is about to fall apart; that there inevitably will be a realignment of political groups, probably with one outright conservative party and one outright liberal party. These perennials are being circulated again today, in the wake of Governor Dewey's defeat, but they seem no more likely of realization now than in any previous year.

In the first place, the most likely time for the Republican party to have fallen apart would have been in 1936, after Mr. Roosevelt's smashing victory over Gov. Alf M. Landon. Then the Democrats got 523 electoral votes to eight for the Republicans, and Mr. Roosevelt had 62.5 per cent of the major-party vote.

There will, inevitably, be changes in the Republican party. In the last two campaigns, it has been a Dewey party. It has seemed to have two policies—one pursued by the Republicans in Congress, who wanted to turn the clock back; and the other pursued by Governor Dewey, who seemed to be a New Dealish sort of candidate who promised that he could do it better. Neither policy has proved popular or successful. The Republicans in the Congress took a worse licking than did Governor Dewey.

Questions for Republicans

Where will the Republicans turn? Will it become the party of the Tafts, the Wherrys, the Martins, the Tabers and the Hallecks? Or will it look for young and more liberal leadership, such as Senator Henry Cabot Lodge Jr. of Massachusetts, and continue the trend in the party best symbolized by the late Wendell L. Willkie? Who will be the caretakers for the party in its years of adversity?

These are questions which are being asked all over the country, but not enough Republicans have recovered from the shock of reading Wednesday's newspapers to come up with a clear and definitive answer. Governor Dewey, having tried twice and failed, has said he will not run again. How much strength he has in the party that can be transferred to someone else is in question. He never has been very popular as a man, even with Republicans, and his

record as a political strategist is not good.

Harold E. Stassen, former Minnesota Governor and now president of the University of Pennsylvania, proved himself a good soldier for the GOP, campaigning hard for the man who beat him for the nomination, even in areas like West Virginia, where Governor Dewey refused to help the unsuccessful effort to re-elect Senator Chapman Revercomb. Mr. Stassen still has ambitions.

Progressives' Future

The second party to be considered is the Progressive party, which was formed around Henry Wallace's candidacy and was sparked by the Communists, who dictated every change permitted in the party platform. The Progressives had high hopes, to begin with, of getting perhaps 10,000,000 votes, and even at the end most of them thought they would not get fewer than 3,000,000 votes. But the latest popular vote figures tabulated give them slightly more than 1,000,000 votes, and this amounts to only 2.3 per cent of the total.

There was nothing in that vote to give aid or comfort to the Communist bloc of eastern Europe. There was no sign of real division within the American people on the firm-but-patient policy pursued toward the Soviet Union.

The Wallace people were disconsolate after the election returns were in, but planned to go ahead with a series of meetings in Chicago beginning Nov. 12 to decide future policy. They insist they will continue in politics, but their chances of achieving any importance in the foreseeable future are extremely small.

The third group to be considered is the States' Rights party, whose vote appeal, even among Southerners, turned out to be less than expected. Backing Gov. J. Strom Thurmond of South Carolina for President and Gov. Fielding Wright of Mississippi for Vice President, the party gained victories; but only in the candidates' home states were these above question.

In Alabama, a maneuver within the Democratic party denied to the President a place on the ballot, and in Louisiana, another stratagem deprived the Truman ticket of the rooster label at the head of the ballot by which Southerners normally identify the Democratic party.

Aim of "Dixiecrats"

These four states had thirty-eight electoral votes, and two Thurmond electors were swept to victory on the Truman ticket in Tennessee. To win these forty votes, the Thurmond-Wright ticket polled about 900,000 popular votes—an average of one electoral vote for every 25,000 votes received, a statistic which by itself casts a considerable doubt on the nature of the democracy in the South. Each of President Truman's electoral votes averaged 73,-000 votes, and Governor Dewey's averaged 108,000 votes.

The announced aim of the "Dixiecrats" was to throw the election of a President into the House of Representatives and try to barter Southern votes for a promise that civil-rights legislation would not be enacted. It failed. There are many important Democrats who believe that the real leaders and financiers of the States' Rights movement were

"local Democrats and national Republicans" who really wanted to elect a Republican President.

Governors Thurmond and Wright have not announced their plans for the future, but an objective reading of the election returns gives little reason to believe the States' Rights movement has any great future, even if limited to the South. It should be borne in mind that none of the Democratic leaders in Congress openly associated themselves with the "Dixiecrat"

movement, and after the party's poor showing at the polls on Tuesday are not likely to cast their lot with them at this date. President Truman and the rest of the Democratic party, for the most part, simply ignored this limited Southern rebellion, and won despite it.

Spurned by Congressmen

Unless the "Dixiecrats" want to continue a futile, expensive, separate existence, they probably will come back to the Democratic

party. Some of the leaders, notably in Alabama, Mississippi, Louisiana and South Carolina, will be punished by losing Federal patronage and by removal from the Democratic National Committee. New, regular and loyal Democrats will get the posts of privilege in those states. But the rank and file will be welcomed back, and probably will be found voting Democratic in the future.

November 7, 1948

TUGWELL DISOWNS WALLACE'S PARTY

Leader in Progressives Says Communists Had Prominent Role in Its Activities

By W. H. LAWRENCE
Special to THE NEW YORK TIMES.

WASHINGTON, March 27 — Rexford Guy Tugwell, an original New Deal "brain-truster" and chairman of the Platform Committee at the Henry A. Wallace Progressive party convention in Philadelphia last July, admitted today that Communists were prominent in the Progressive convention and campaign and said that

he should have left the party last August.

Dr. Tugwell said that he was "truly thankful" that President Truman won the election last November because he regarded him as "at least a domestic liberal," although he still thought that the President's foreign policy "is potentially dangerous and ought to have come much earlier under complete civilian control."

The Tugwell views were presented in the April issue of The Progressive, a Madison, Wis., magazine founded forty years ago by the late Senator Robert M. La Follette. The magazine has no connection with the Wallace party of the same name.

His article reflected the dilemma of New Dealers—whether the Democratic party, with its Southern and conservative groupings, can ever be made as liberal as they would like it, or whether a new third party is necessary.

Dr. Tugwell, now a University of Chicago professor, argued for building a new third party, with Communist influence excluded. He attacked the futility of the role of Americans for Democratic Action, a non-Communist New Deal group that stayed within the Democratic party.

His views were challenged in the same issue by Senator Hubert S. Humphrey, Minnesota Democrat and A. D. A. chairman.

Dr. Tugwell said that the "fatal errors" made at Philadelphia were compounded by Mr. Wallace's "extremism," and declared that he "ought to have left the party in August."

But he criticized his fellow New Dealers of progressive viewpoint for staying out of the Wallace movement and letting the Communists assume such a prominent role with this declaration:

"The reason Communist workers were so prominent in the Wal-

lace campaign was that the Progressives were—well, where were they? Sitting it out; wringing their hands, and wailing about the wickedness of the Reds."

To this, Senator Humphrey replied that "Dr. Tugwell totally ignores the vast and tragic record of experience, which demonstrates the essential incompatibility between liberals and the Communist brethren—both in the realm of ideas and in day-to-day political operations."

The Minnesotan said that the Tugwell article was a "significant confessional," because it represented "the first public admission by a prominent member of the Progressive party that the Communists dominated the Wallace campaign and dictated the words and music of the Progressive convention."

March 28, 1949

DEWEY WARNS GOP IS SPLIT 'WIDE OPEN'; ASSAILS OLD GUARD

ADVISES IT GET OUT

Says Reactionary Rule Would Make Party 'Deadest Pigeon'

BARS COPYING NEW DEAL

By W. H. LAWRENCE
Special to THE NEW YORK TIMES.

WASHINGTON, Feb. 8 — Gov. Thomas E. Dewey of New York warned a Republican Lincoln Day dinner tonight that the party "is split wide open," with a reaction-

ary group attempting to return it to the philosophy of the Nineteen Twenties.

If they are successful, he added, "you can bury the Republican party as the deadest pigeon in the country."

To recapture national power for the first time in twenty years, he said, Republicans must live up to its position in platforms that "government today has to be more than a cold and impartial umpire."

He asked them to prove this by their votes in Congress and in legislatures in favor of unemployment insurance, increased old-age assistance, broader social security, slum clearance and public housing, public development of water power resources, and farm price supports, and in the vigorous protection of the rights of labor.

He invited those of contrary

views to get out of the party—and his declaration on this point did not differ greatly from statements of President Franklin D. Roosevelt in the 1938 "purge" effort.

Points to Platform Aims

"Those who disapprove of these principles and want to fight them ought to go out and try to get elected in a typical American community and see what happens to them," Governor Dewey said. "But they ought not to do it as Republicans. They ought not to get their personal prejudices confused with the basic aims the Republican party has repeatedly set forth in its platforms."

That, roughly, was the view President Roosevelt expressed of Senators Walter F. George of Georgia and Millard E. Tydings of Maryland, among other conservatives, when he said they should not be in office as Democrats.

This was Governor Dewey's first major political speech since his unexpected defeat for the presidency in November, and his words were carried to the nation over the Mutual Broadcasting System and American Broadcasting Company networks from the Lincoln Day dinner of the Washington Federation of Women's Republican Clubs. The event was tele-

vised in the East.

In the audience of more than 800 tonight were many who wondered whether he might try for a third presidential nomination in 1952, despite his disclaimers in the past.

As if in answer, the Governor said that he spoke in the dual capacity of titular head of the party and as a comparatively young "elder statesman," a role which he said someone else had "aptly defined as a politician who is no longer a candidate for any office." But he did not go beyond this on the question of whether he would be a candidate again.

There were echoes of the bitter battle waged at Omaha within the Republican National Committee, where an effort to oust Representative Hugh D. Scott Jr., of Pennsylvania, labeled pro-Dewey, as national chairman failed by a narrow four-vote margin.

Warning that the nation was coming dangerously close to one-party government, due to five successive defeats for Republican Presidential candidates, the New York Governor said that "without trying to find scapegoats or make excuses, I would like to bring out in the open one basic problem."

"The Republican party is split wide open," he declared. "It has been split wide open for years, but we have tried to gloss it over. We have tried to deny it to ourselves and conceal it. That doesn't work. I suggest that we face it, get it right out in the open and look at it. Then, let's see what we can do

162

about it."

He picked as the first target for his criticism Republicans who honestly oppose farm price support, unemployment insurance, old-age benefits, slum clearance and other programs, and who urge Republicans in and out of Congress to fight every Democratic proposal, regardless of merit, and who say that Republicans taking another viewpoint are "me too" Republicans and no better than New Dealers.

The other Republican faction, he said, would embrace the entire New Deal and attempt, unwisely, to "out-promise" the Democrats.

He said he disagreed with both extremes, and warned that "both courses are fatal to our party and would be fatal to the country."

"If, as a party, we try to go back to the nineteenth century, or even to the 1920s, you can bury the Republican party as the deadest pigeon in the country," he said.

He charted his own course on the 1948 Republican platform, and said its policies should be carried out by Republicans voting for Democratic-sponsored legislation without giving any thought to "political credit."

But, at the same time, he opposed the Administration's compulsory health insurance bill, which he said would "reduce our doctors to government servitude."

The capacity crowd gave Governor Dewey a thirty-nine-second ovation when he was introduced but reacted with little and often no applause for the specific points in which he criticized the Republican party and some of its leaders.

The crowd had just received a surprised spanking from Senator Margaret Chase Smith of Maine, who told the Republicans they lost the 1948 election because of the "excesses" of the Eightieth Republican Congress. She said the party needed to become the party of the people and quit being identified in the public's mind as the party of big business only.

Senator Smith said that the Republicans needed a new policy committee consisting of three Senators, three members of the House, three Governors and two members of the Republican National Committee. She specified that one of the Senators should be a member of the "young Turks" who fought Senator Taft's leadership.

Sharing the speaker's platform with Governor Dewey were Representative Joseph W. Martin Jr. of Massachusetts, Senator Smith and Mrs. Jane E. Hunter of Cleveland.

Representative Martin, who was Speaker of the last House of Representatives, vigorously promoted the record of the Eightieth Congress as the best vehicle for regaining national power, and sharply assailed the Truman Administration's legislative program, especially the request for tax increases.

February 9, 1949

DIXIECRATS REJECT G.O.P. WOOING AGAIN

'Emissaries' Make Overtures to Two Southern Leaders, Are Cold-Shouldered

By W. H. LAWRENCE
Special to The New York Times.

JACKSON, Miss., Jan. 24—Two top-ranking States Rights leaders reported today a renewed burst of activity in recent days by "emissaries" of northern Republicans attempting to transform the present Congressional coalition of Southern Democrats and the GOP into a formal party merger. They said such overtures had been cold-shouldered in Mississippi and other southern states.

The leaders were Gov. Fielding Wright of Mississippi, the States' Rights candidate for Vice President in 1948, and W. W. Wright, the Mississippi representative on the three-member national executive committee of the States Rights movement.

Mr. Wright, a Jackson businessman, said that he had refused to talk to one "emissary" last Saturday, and that another from Omaha, Neb., had called, asking permission to stop here for a conference on his way home from a meeting in Atlanta. He declined to name either man, and said he thought there was plenty of "jawboning" going on in other parts of the South.

See No Chance of Merger

Both Governor Wright and Mr. Wright emphasized that there was not the remotest chance of a Republican-Dixiecrat merger. They said the rank and file of the South never would accept a Republican label, and that there was not time enough to organize a new party on a national basis before the Presidential elections in 1952.

Neither ruled out the possibility of an eventual political realignment with new parties more accurately reflecting the nation's "conservative" versus "liberal" division, but neither saw such a prospect in the immediate future.

Both said that the best hope of the South in its "immediate emergency" was for the eleven Southern states to band together in 1952 to elect totally unpledged members of the Presidential Electoral College, and to decide only after the November popular elections on the man for whom they would cast these "balance of power" votes.

Under such a plan Presidential electors chosen under a straight Democratic label would make the Presidential choice for the Southern states without direct instructions from the people. If the regular nominees of the Democratic convention wished to challenge this program and appeal directly to the people they would have to use some designation other than the regular Democratic symbol for which Southern people habitually cast their vote.

Both Wrights seemed unwilling to repeat the 1948 performance when States' Rights Democrats nominated their own ticket, headed by Gov. J. Strom Thurmond of South Carolina. The States Rights ticket in 1948 received thirty-nine electoral votes, including all of those from South Carolina, Mississippi, Alabama, and Louisiana, plus one from Tennessee.

Neither evidenced any enthusiasm for the proposal on Saturday of Gessner T. McCorvey, chairman of the Alabama Democratic executive committee, who proposed that the southern electors should make their 1952 choice known even before the Republican and Democratic national conventions. Mr. McCorvey said that if the Southerners would promise in advance their electoral college votes to a man like Gen. Dwight D. Eisenhower, one of the major parties might take the lead and select him as their standard-bearer.

Mr. Wright said that a meeting of the principal leaders of the States' Rights movement would be called before March 1, probably in Washington, to discuss an intensive organizational and educational campaign, reaching down to the precinct level, throughout the eleven Southern states. He said the chances were "excellent" on winning more than four states in 1952, but that talk of a merger with the Republicans was injurious to his group.

January 25, 1950

G. O. P. POSES ISSUE FOR '50 AS LIBERTY VERSUS SOCIALISM

FAIR DEAL IS TARGET

By W. H. LAWRENCE
Special to The New York Times.

WASHINGTON, Feb. 6—The Republican party policy makers today proclaimed "Liberty Against Socialism" to be the major domestic issue of the 1950 Congressional elections.

But the party failed to achieve complete unity, either in its denunciation of the Truman Administration's program at home and abroad, or on the alternatives which it promised.

In all-day separate and closed meetings members of the Republican National Committee and the House and Senate Republican conferences finally gave their approval to a "statement of principles and objectives" designed to serve as a national platform for the months between now and the November elections.

Party chieftains had hoped that the declaration would demonstrate party unity and purpose and bring a new flow of financial contributions to defray campaign expenses, but a group led by Senator Henry Cabot Lodge Jr. of Massachusetts, Senator Margaret Chase Smith of Maine, Representative Jacob K. Javits of New York and Representative James G. Fulton of Pennsylvania promptly made known its dissatisfaction.

"Fair Deal" Vigorously Opposed

As was to be expected, the party declaration approved by the majority was vigorous in its opposition to enactment of the most of the Fair Deal program put before Congress by President Truman.

On foreign policy questions it found a middle ground, advocating continuance of a bipartisan attitude but sharply criticizing the administration of foreign policy with particular reference to "secret agreements" made at Yalta and Potsdam "which have created new injustices and new dangers throughout the world."

An effort made by Werner Schroeder, Illinois national committeeman, to put the party on record as opposed to continuance of the bipartisan foreign policy, was overwhelmingly defeated in the national committee. Members said that a voice vote showed support for Mr. Schroeder from only one or two others.

The party statement declared:

"We advocate a strong policy against the spread of communism or fascism at home and abroad, and we insist that America's efforts toward this end be directed by those who have no sympathy either with communism or fascism."

It asserted that "basic American principles are threatened by the Administration's program for a planned economy modeled on the Socialist Governments of Europe, including price and wage control, rationing, socialized medicine, regional authorites and the Brannan Plan with its controls, penalties, fines and jail sentences."

The Republican program "to rebuild a prosperous and progressive America" included these major planks:

A return to a balanced budget through material reductions in Federal spending.

Immediate repeal of wartime excise taxes and "reduction of taxes on small business to stimulate new industry and growth," with a policy of "general" tax reduction "to be accompanied as rapidly as reduction in Federal expenditures will permit."

A fair price for the farmer's products in the market place "aided by a system of price supports and by protection against the dumping of competitive commodities produced by underpaid foreign labor."

Continuance of the Taft-Hartley labor-management relations law with renewed efforts "to enact such improvements in the law as

have been shown to be necessary to accomplish its purposes more effectively and achieve more complete equality."

Extension of the coverage and an increase in the benefits of the Federal old-age and survivors insurance program, with studies to be made of the pay-as-you-go principle.

Limited Federal aid to the states "to assist them in affording subsistence, shelter and medical care to their citizens who are unable to provide for themselves," but with safeguards to avoid "socialization of the medical profession or of any other activity."

Prompt elimination of "all Communists, fellow travelers and Communist sympathizers from our Federal payroll."

The proposal on the civil rights issue stirred considerable controversy and brought protests from Senator Lodge and Representative Javits.

The party pledge as approved read:

"The right of equal opportunity to work, to vote, to advance in life and to be protected under the law should never be limited in any individual because of race, religion, color or country of origin. Therefore, we shall continue to sponsor legislation to protect the rights of minorities."

Senator Lodge wanted the party to declare its "forthright determination" to enact civil rights legislation at the present Congres-

sional session, "and to break a filibuster, if necessary," but he was overruled. Republicans have often found common ground with Southern Democrats in blocking Administration bills.

Since the party had picked a Lincoln Day rally to unveil its 1950 manifesto, Representative Javits said he regretted that the statement "did not declare unequivocally for FEPC, anti-lynching and anti-poll tax legislation in the best Lincoln tradition." The FEPC bill would establish a Fair Employment Practice Commission.

In the final vote on the party document as a whole, Senator Lodge, in opposing approval, had the known support of Senators Margaret Chase Smith, Irving M. Ives of New York and George D. Aiken of Vermont. There were said to be one or two others, not named, who joined in the dissent.

Mrs. Smith asserted that the platform was filled with "vague generalities," which would appeal to persons who voted Republican anyway, but which would have no special appeal to the "rank-and-file of the people who win elections." She had wanted a simple, brief but specific program and was "disappointed and unhappy with the result."

Representative Fulton declared that the declaration "blithely-ignored" the fundamental division within the party. This he defined as "whether we shall go back to Methuselah or offer alternative

programs for social progress within the framewok of a balanced budget."

Senator Lodge told his colleagues that they were overstating the case in asserting that the main issue was "liberty against socialism." He said that President Truman and his supporters were not Socialists but, on the contrary, were "opportunists" and that such extravagance of language as was used in the declaration would not make many votes for the Republicans.

There was some argument on Capitol Hill over the section discussing foreign policy, but most Republicans were better satisfied with the planks in this field than with the domestic program.

In its final form the foreign policy attitude was generally satisfactory to Senator Arthur H. Vandenberg of Michigan, who has been the principal GOP spokesman for the bipartisan foreign policy. But it also satisfied Senator Kenneth S. Wherry of Nebraska, the minority floor leader, because it denounced "secret agreements," reiterated the Senate's constitutional role in treaty making and demanded "consultation between the Executive and members of both major parties in the legislative branch of government in the initiation and development of a united American foreign policy."

February 7, 1950

G.O.P. DIGEST TRIMS 'SOCIALISM' ISSUE

Policy Stand Re-stated in 99 Words, With Soft Pedal on Slogan—Taft Dissents

By CLAYTON KNOWLES
Special to The New York Times.

WASHINGTON, April 2 — The Republican high command seemed divided tonight over a ninety-nine-word, ten-point digest seeking to popularize the 1,950-word statement of Republican principles and objectives adopted by party leaders in February.

The digest devoted just four words and relegated to tenth place the call for a showdown on "liberty against socialism" upon which, as a sort of keynote, more than 400 words were used in the original version.

Senator Robert A. Taft, Republican of Ohio, dominant among his party colleagues in Congress on most issues, immediately declared

that the digest "has no official standing whatsoever" and that, therefore, no switch in emphasis could be construed.

Chairmen's Names Used on It

Informed that the condensed version was released with the statement that it had been "prepared at the direction of Senator Owen Brewster of Maine, chairman of the Republican Senatorial Committee, and Representative Leonard W. Hall, chairman of the Republican Congressional Committee, with the cooperation of Guy G. Gabrielson, chairman of the Republican National Committee," Mr. Taft said:

"Anybody can prepare a digest. Nobody was consulted about this, except the campaign committees, and so it can't have any official standing."

The original Republican policy statement, after dealing with the party's position on foreign affairs, switched to a discussion of the domestic scene with the words: "The major domestic issue today is liberty versus socialism." It then went on for more than 400 words by way of elaboration before detailing the party's stand on specific issues.

The digest, dealing with the sub-

ject last, has as point No. 10, "safeguarding liberty against socialism."

Foreign policy position, set forth first in another 400 words in the original, became point No. 9 in the digest. It read:

"Developing a united American foreign policy for peace—world trade without undermining American living standards."

The announcement of the digest by the Senatorial, Congressional and National Committees said that they "intend to use the digest in campaign material during 1950, and it is expected that Republican candidates will incorporate it into their campaign pamphlets."

The three chairmen were out of town tonight and so could not answer the exception Mr. Taft took to the digest. Their announcement, however, credited the idea of the digest to Senator Margaret Chase Smith of Maine who, it was said, was "consulted in its preparation."

Mrs. Smith was one of several outspoken party critics of the Republican statement of principles adopted Feb. 6 as a supplement to the party's 1948 platform. She particularly objected to its wordiness.

While she also objected generally to what she called the vagueness of the original document, others were more outspoken. Representative James G. Fulton of Pennsylvania asserted it ignored the fundamental division in the party: "whether we go back to Methuse-

lah or offer alternative programs for social progress within the framework of a balanced budget."

Senator Henry Cabot Lodge Jr. said the party was overstating its case in asserting that the main issue was "liberty against socialism" and warned that the slogan would not make many votes for Republicans.

TEXT OF THE STATEMENT

The text of the digest follows:
THE REPUBLICAN PARTY STANDS FOR:

(1) Reducing taxes.

(2) Balancing budget.

(3) Eliminating Government waste, especially along lines of Hoover Commission reports.

(4) Fighting communism here instead of condoning it.

(5) Providing fair market prices on farm products aided by price supports—cooperative marketing, soil conservation, reclamation, rural electrification—no Brannan plan.

(6) Continuing and improving Taft-Hartley law to protect public from excessive power of labor and management.

(7) Developing an adequate security system that does not limit opportunity nor discourage initiative and saving.

(8) Protecting rights of veterans and minorities.

(9) Developing a united American foreign policy for peace—world trade without undermining American living standards.

(10) Safeguarding liberty against socialism.

April 3, 1950

Seven G.O.P. Senators Decry 'Smear' Tactics of McCarthy

Attack Led by Mrs. Smith of Maine, Who Also Scores Democratic 'Whitewash'

By WILLIAM S. WHITE
Special to THE NEW YORK TIMES

WASHINGTON, June 1—Seven Republican Senators denounced and repudiated today the tactics of their party colleague, Joseph R. McCarthy of Wisconsin, in his campaign to try to prove Communist penetration of the State Department.

Led by the Senate's only woman member, Margaret Chase Smith of Maine, they issued a "Declaration of Conscience" that accused "certain elements" of a design for "riding the Republican party to victory through the selfish political exploitation of fear, bigotry, ignorance and intolerance."

They attacked the Democrats as well, specifically accusing the Truman Administration of lacking leadership, of giving "contradictory grave warnings and optimistic assurances," of "complacency" toward communism, of "oversensitiveness to rightful criticism" and of "petty bitterness against its critics."

The other signers of the declaration were Senators Irving M. Ives of New York, a close political associate of Governor Dewey; Charles W. Tobey of New Hampshire, George D. Aiken of Vermont, Robert C. Hendrickson of New Jersey Edward J. Thye of Minnesota and Wayne L. Morse of Oregon.

This revolt among the avowedly liberal Republican wing of the Senate against the encouragement given to Senator McCarthy by the party hierarchy came in the midst of an effort by other Republicans to force a full-scale public investigation of the Amerasia case of 1945.

Taking the lead in this drive, Senator William F. Knowland, Republican of California, asserted that grave, "unanswered questions" remained concerning the disposition of the case, which involved the unlawful possession in wartime of secret Government documents.

Mr. Knowland accused the Democratic-controlled investigating subcommittee, which is studying the Amerasia incident as a part of Senator McCarthy's general charges, of "star chamber" proceedings and giving the impression of a "whitewash."

Amerasia, a now defunct magazine that dealt with Far Eastern affairs, was a "'transmission belt'" between the Communists and the

Senator Margaret Chase Smith
The New York Times (Washington Bureau)

State Department, Senator Knowland asserted.

Mrs. Smith read the "Declaration of Conscience" from the floor, as Senator McCarthy sat white and silent hardly three feet behind her. She accompanied the reading with a speech, in which she rebuked Mr. McCarthy, though not by name.

Mr. McCarthy heard her out, then left as she was being congratulated by several colleagues. One of these, Senator H. Alexander Smith, Republican of New Jersey, said that he found nothing in her words "with which I do not wholeheartedly agree."

The whole episode was profoundly comforting to the long-harassed Democrats. Senator Millard E. Tydings, Democrat of Maryland, chairman of the subcommittee investigating the McCarthy charges, offered no direct objection to Mrs. Smith's strictures on his own party. He called her speech "temperate" and "fair" and an act of "stateswomanship."

Asked at his afternoon press conference about the address, with special reference to Mrs. Smith's assertion that she would not like to see the Republicans win on "calumny," President Truman replied, with a broad smile, that he would not want to say anything that bad about the Republican party.

Text of the Declaration

The declaration issued by the seven Senators was as follows:

We are Republicans. But we are Americans first. It is as Americans that we express our concern with the growing confusion that threatens the security and stability of our country. Democrats and Republicans alike have

contributed to that confusion.

The Democratic Administration has initially created the confusion by its lack of effective leadership, by its contradictory grave warnings and optimistic assurances, by its complacency to the threat of communism here at home, by its oversensitiveness to rightful criticism, by its petty bitterness against its critics.

Certain elements of the Republican party have materially added to this confusion in the hopes of riding the Republican party to victory through the selfish political exploitation of fear, bigotry, ignorance and intolerance. There are enough mistakes of the Democrats for Republicans to criticize constructively without resorting to political smears.

To this extent, Democrats and Republicans alike have unwittingly, but undeniably, played directly into the Communist design of "confuse, divide and conquer."

It is high time that we stopped thinking politically as Republicans and Democrats about elections and started thinking patriotically as Americans about national security based on individual freedom. It is high time that we all stopped being tools and victims of totalitarian techniques—techniques that, if continued here unchecked, will surely end what we have come to cherish as the American way of life.

Mrs. Smith Hits Opportunism

Mrs. Smith told the Senate at the outset that there was now "a national feeling of fear and frustration that could result in national suicide and the end of everything we Americans hold dear." There was no definite leadership now, she argued, either in the White House or Congress. "I speak as briefly as possible," she said, "because too much harm has already been done with irresponsible words of bitterness and selfish political opportunism.

"The United States Senate has long enjoyed world-wide respect as the greatest deliberative body in the world. But recently, that deliberative character has too often been debased to the level of a forum of hate and character assassination sheltered by the shield of Congressional immunity.

"It is ironical that we Senators can in debate in the Senate directly or indirectly impute to any American, who is not a Senator, any conduct or motive unworthy or unbecoming an American—and without that non-Senator American having any legal redress against us—yet if we say the same thing in the Senate about our colleagues, we can be stopped on the grounds of being out of order.

"I think it is high time that we remembered that we have sworn to uphold and defend the Constitution. I think it is high time that we remembered that the Constitution, as amended, speaks not only of the freedom of speech, but also of trial by jury instead of trial by accusation.

"Whether it be a criminal prosecution in court or a character prosecution in the Senate, there is no practical distinction when the life of a person has been ruined.

"Those of us who shout the loudest about Americanism in making character assassinations are all too frequently those who, by our own words and acts, ignore some of the basic principles of Americanism—the right to criticize, the right to hold unpopular beliefs, the right to protest, the right to independent thought.

"The American people are sick and tired of being afraid to speak their minds lest they be politically smeared as 'Communists' or 'Fascists' by their opponents. Freedom of speech is not what it used to be in America. It has been so abused by some that it is not exercised by others.

"The American people are sick and tired of seeing innocent people smeared and guilty people whitewashed. But there have been enough proved cases to cause nation-wide distrust and strong suspicion that there may be something to unproved, sensational accusations."

The country, Mrs. Smith asserted, was "being psychologically divided by the confusions and the suspicions that are bred in the Senate to spread like cancerous tenacles of 'know nothing, suspect everything' attitudes.

"Today we have a Democratic Administration that has developed a mania for loose spending and loose programs. History is repeating itself—and the Republican party again has the opportunity to emerge as the champions of unity and prudence.

"The record of the present Democratic Administration has provided us with sufficient campaign issues without the necessity of resorting to political smears. America is rapidly losing its position as a leader of the world simply because the Democratic Administration has pitifully failed to provide effective leadership.

"The Democratic Administration has greatly lost the confidence of the American people by its complacency to the threat of communism here at home and the leak of vital secrets to Russia through key officials of the Democratic Administration. There are enough proved charges to make this point without diluting our criticism with unproved charges.

"Surely, these are sufficient reasons to make it clear to the American people that it is time for a change and that a Republican victory is necessary to the security of this country. Surely, it is clear that this nation will continue to suffer as long as it is governed by the present ineffective Democratic Administration.

"Yet to displace it with a Republican regime embracing a philosophy that lacks political integrity or intellectual honesty would prove equally disastrous to this nation. The nation sorely needs a Republican victory. But I don't want to see the Republican party ride to a political victory on the Four Horsemen of Calumny—Fear, Ignorance, Bigotry and Smear.

"I don't want to see the Republican party win that way. While it might be a fleeting victory for the Republican party, it would be a more lasting defeat for the American people."

June 2, 1950

Democrats: Left and Right

DEFAMATION MARKS VIOLENT CAMPAIGN

Republicans Suggest Setbacks Abroad Were Due to Stupidity and Treason in Government

By JAMES RESTON
Special to THE NEW YORK TIMES.

WASHINGTON, Oct. 30—There is unmistakable evidence in the country today that good morals could be good politics, but the fact is that this political campaign has seen the triumph of "McCarthyism."

If this term means the use of lies or partial truth to score a political point, regardless of the consequences to personal reputation or public trust, if it means public charges before proof, guilt by association and the elevation of means above ends, as its critics assert, then "McCarthyism" has been carefully planned, widely used and even institutionalized in this campaign.

Nobody but Senator Joseph R. McCarthy, Wisconsin Republican, himself has actually charged that there were more than 200 Communists in the State Department, but almost every other McCarthy charge has been made or implied in this election by many of the most distinguished candidates of the Republican party.

And the tactics of the Democrats in Ohio and New York, like the strategy of President Truman in the last week of the 1948 Presidential campaign, likewise have gone well beyond the usual bounds of political license.

Attack Is Unrestricted

Running through almost all the Republican campaign reviews of the nation's foreign policy is the theme, carefully outlined in the Republican National Committee's candidates' handbooks, that our international troubles resulted from a dark conspiracy.

This conspiracy, the Republicans argue, was put over on the Administration and the country by Alger Hiss, former State Department official convicted of perjury; Henry Julian Wadleigh, former State Department economist who admitted that he passed secret papers on to Whittaker Chambers, witness against Hiss; Prof. Owen Lattimore, who was a State Department adviser on Far Eastern affairs, and others prominent in the McCarthy charges.

The Republicans have not restricted their attack to the Administration's misjudgment of Soviet objectives at Yalta, to its acquiescence in the destruction of United States military power from 1945-49, to its military unpreparedness at the outbreak of the Korean war, or to Secretary of State Dean Acheson's public pronouncement that the United States line of defense ran just short of Korea.

All of these undoubtedly were legitimate campaign issues, regardless of the Republican party's policies at the time, but almost al-

ways in the development of these issues the suggestion is clearly left with the audience that these things were done in consequence not only of stupidity and misjudgment but because of the disloyalty and treasonable activities of men within the Administration.

Duff Cites Hiss' Role at Yalta

This theme is not the special province of a few men; one hears it all over the country; from representative Richard M. Nixon in California, who is virtually campaigning on Alger Hiss; from Senator Eugene D. Millikin in Colorado; from Everett M. Dirksen in Illinois; from Senator Robert A. Taft in Ohio; from Gov. James H. Duff in Pennsylvania, to mention only a few.

Governor Duff, one of the most respected and distinguished Republican candidates for the Senate, relates to his audiences how Soviet power was vastly increased at Yalta through the concessions of President Roosevelt. He explains that no President can hope to follow the details of all the intricate foreign policies in such an international conference, but must rely upon "four or five trusted advisers" who really do the work. And one of these "four or five" trusted advisers at Yalta, he concludes, was the convicted perjurer, Alger Hiss.

The Rev. William Alexander of Oklahoma City, running on the Republican ticket for Senator against Repersentative A. S. Mike Monroney, announced his candidacy from the pulpit on the perfectly accurate ground that Washington could do with a little more Christianity. But his campaign is based on the charge that Representative Monroney "went East and turned Left" in association with the "Maragons, the Vaughans and the Hisses."

The Rev. Mr. Alexander stood outside the barber shop in Moore, Okla., the other day and said, to the "amens" of his audience: "Your boys wouldn't be dying in Korea today if a man named Alger Hiss hadn't been at Yalta and a man named Owen Lattimore hadn't been the big adviser to the State Department."

Taft Threatened, Ridiculed

Even Governor Duff refers to the Korean war as "an entirely unnecessary war," and Senator Taft asserts that Secretary of State Acheson "gave the green light" to Stalin in Korea, a phrase widely used and attributed originally to Senator Arthur H. Vandenberg of Michigan.

There is no tactic used by the Republicans, however, that the Democrats are not using against Taft himself in Ohio.

They have printed photographs of him with Earl Browder, former head of the Communist party of the United States, and linked his foreign policy voting record to Vito Marcantonio and the Communist party line. He has been subjected to a political strike in Youngstown because he talked to workers in a factory. He has been threatened by John L. Lewis that if he went into a United Mine Workers mine the mine would be closed. He has been ridiculed and misquoted and even hit by over-ripe tomatoes.

Around the turn of the century, President William Howard Taft made the statement that every

working man should make at least $1 a day. The statement turned up in the current Ohio campaign attributed to Senator Taft and even twisted into "every working man should make no more than $1 a day."

In 1947, Mr. Taft was asked in California whether he knew of any way in which the price of meat could be brought down. He replied that one way was to eat less meat. The United Labor League of Ohio recently put out a 218-page Black Book on the Senator's record in which the above "eat less" quote was applied, not to meat but to the cost of living in general. Thus, the Senator was represented as having said that if the people wanted to reduce the cost of living, they should "eat less."

Wage Vote Misrepresented

Likewise, Mr. Taft's labor opposition is condemning him for opposing the 65 cent an hour minimum wage legislation in the last session of Congress. It is true that he voted against the 65-cent minimum, but only because he favored, and voted for, the 75-cent minimum. The Senator's opponents, however, omit that fact.

Few politicians have been accurate historians, particularly during election campaigns, but the distortion of big facts and little facts in this election is really extraordinary.

Thus, Mr. Taft repeats in speech after speech that the United States went to war against Japan in 1941 to prevent China from being dominated by a hostile power, and then turne daround and gave China to the Russians—thus skipping quite a few facts, including the attack on Pearl Harbor.

Several years ago Chester Bowles, the present Governor of Connecticut, wrote a letter to Freda Kirchwey, editor of The Nation, in which he said that he read her magazine from cover to cover every week. Some time later The Nation published a series of articles by Paul Blanshard on the Catholic Church that infuriated Roman Catholics all over this country and led to a ban of the magazine, not only in many Roman Catholic institutions but in the public schools of New York City.

Donnell Praises Opponent

In the fierce Connecticut race for the Governorship, now in progress, Mr. Bowles is being attacked as a left-winger who is soft on communism, and a Nation pamphlet containing the Blanshard articles has been reproduced and is now being circulated in the state with Governor Bowles' endorsement of The Nation on the back.

The Governor absolves Catholic church officials of any responsibility for distributing the pamphlet and does not believe the Republican organization in Connecticut got them out. But that does not relieve him of having to worry about the possible loss of some support among the very large number of Roman Catholic voters of Connecticut. His opponent is of that persuasion.

Some candidates, of course, have not departed from a high standard of campaigning. For example, Senator Forrest C. Donnell, the conservative Republican for Missouri (who goes around saying his opponent, Thomas Hennings, is "a

fine gentleman, and the son of a fine gentleman"). Also, many newspapers have deplored the low tactics of the campaign, but other newspapers have themselves been guilty of the same tactics employed by the candidates.

In California, the Democratic candidates for Governor and Senator, James Roosevelt and Helen Gahagan Douglas, have not received anything like the play in the papers that has been available to their opponents. In Ohio, similarly, Senator Taft's speeches have been far more prominently written and displayed, though in this case, it must be said that he has had much more to say than the Democratic nominee.

In general, the Dewey-Hanley "arrangement" in New York received comparatively little space in many Republican papers throughout the country and was excused on the ground that the pot had no right to call the kettle black.

Similarly, the alleged Democratic deal to get Mayor William O'Dwyer out of the mayoralty race in New York by making him Ambassador to Mexico, and the reputed offer of a judgeship to Acting Mayor Vincent R. Impellitteri (in the hope of getting him to withdraw from the same race), were passed over with surprisingly little display or comment in those papers that favor the Democratic party.

If all these incidents were merely the accidents of individual initiative, they could perhaps be put down to human frailty, but the pattern is too clear and the evidence too impressive for that.

Policies of Moderation Rejected

The Republican leadership is clearly convinced that it is fighting against an evil coalition of political forces in America. It is impressed by the success of the tactics used by President Truman in the last week of the 1948 campaign, when the President's own associates boasted that they were going out to stir up the fears and prejudices of the voters in the large urban areas of the East and Middle West.

The policy of moderation, employed by Mr. Dewey in the last Presidential campaign, has been rejected as being largely responsible for the defeat of the Republicans. In consequence, a new and fiercer strategy has been applied, not by the individual candidates on their own initiative, but by direction from the center.

This, plus the continuation of the old 1948 Democratic strategy, has given a new sharpness to the political atmosphere. The Democrats have asked the voters to believe that a vote for the Republican candidates is a vote for Herbert Hoover, depression, and isolationism. The Republicans have asked them to believe that a vote for the Democrats is a vote for socialism, bankruptcy, and war.

It is all a little like the children's Halloween game of "tricks for treats," and while most people may be indifferent or cynical about it, some are not.

"I wish I had two votes," a man in Chicago said to this reporter last week. "Then I could vote against both parties."

October 31, 1950

INTELLECTUAL LEFT SILENT IN CAMPAIGN

By JAMES RESTON
Special to THE NEW YORK TIMES.

WASHINGTON, Nov. 1—There is plenty of political thunder in the land today, but the thunder on the intellectual Left has lost something of its old fury.

The labor unions, of course, are giving forth with loud and raucous cries, particularly in the Ohio and Mahoning Valleys, but the philosophical mentors of the New and Fair Deals—the college professors and instructors who were so militant and eloquent in their support of Franklin Roosevelt—seem strangely quiet in this election, and even a little frightened.

In the last off-year election, and even in 1948, an itinerant reporter would find on almost any college campus a little group of teachers full of zeal for the Democratic party, proud of their support of the Roosevelt social revolution and eager to campaign for its development at the polls.

This is still true in some areas, particularly on the campuses of the large Eastern universities, but there is a marked timidity now farther west.

Zeal Cooled by Events

The furor on various campuses about the Communist oath; the conviction of Alger Hiss; the political campaign speeches linking New Dealers and Communists indiscriminately; the charges of Senator Joseph R. McCarthy of Wisconsin against Prof. Owen Lattimore and Philip Jessup; the hesitation of prominent Democrats to defend Secretary of State Dean Acheson against his critics, and the general atmosphere of suspicion against anybody who ever said a good word for the Russians —all these things have helped bring about a marked change upon the activities of the so-called intellectual Left.

They are much more cautious in their public statements and even in their private conversations with visiting reporters; they are less bold in their opinions about the political and economic future of the country; they are not engaging in the election with anything like the vigor they used to show, and the candidates running for office are similarly showing very little enthusiasm about trying to gain their support.

This trend is more noticeable in California than anywhere else, partly because the two principal Democratic candidates there, Helen Gahagan Douglas for Senator and James Roosevelt for Governor, are under severe attack as left-wingers. Also, the evidence of Communist infiltration in Hollywood and the tumult over the Communist oath at the University of California have brought the whole question of past political affiliations and present economic and foreign policy views very much to the fore.

These things have undoubtedly reduced the support given to Mrs. Douglas and Mr. Roosevelt by the California intelligentsia and the well-to-do artists in the movie capital. The latter, in particular, are now highly sensitive to the dangers of adverse publicity, and Mrs. Douglas' efforts to win their support in the current campaign have certainly been a disappointment to her political associates.

For example, a dinner was arranged recently to help increase the Douglas campaign treasury and get prominent artists to help draw crowds to the Douglas rallies. More than seventy of Mrs. Douglas' closest associates in the Hollywood and Los Angeles area were invited to attend. Only about twenty showed, and the excuses given by the others were regarded by Mrs. Douglas' campaign assistants as somewhat feeble.

Caution about getting involved in the election, even indirectly, is also being shown elsewhere. There has been a rule for years at the University of Illinois against allowing political rallies on the campus. In view of the key Illinois Senatorial race between the Democratic majority leader, Senator Scott W. Lucas and Everett McKinley Dirksen, however, an effort was made to have the rule lifted so that both Mr. Dirksen and Senator Lucas could address the students.

This was approved by the representatives of the student body, by the faculty and by President George E. Stoddard. The board of trustees, however, turned it down. This decision was finally taken to Gov. Adlai E. Stevenson for review, but after long meditation, the board of trustees finally decided, with the Governor's approval, that the political atmosphere at the present time was not propitious for holding political rallies on university property.

Position of Liberals

In defense of their comparative neutrality in this campaign the liberal intellectuals say something like this:

"In the present atmosphere of suspicion, no liberal can get up and pronounce his views with any vigor without being smeared as a fellow-traveler, and without causing embarrassment to the candidate he supports and the institution he represents.

"Too many men have been attacked in the last year with impunity. The defense, no matter how persuasive or complete, never quite gets as much display or attention as the charges and never quite catches up with the accusations. Therefore, participation in the campaign now would merely damage our reputations without helping the candidates we supported."

The experience of Americans for Democratic Action in this campaign also illustrates the same caution on the left. The support of this organization of young intellectuals was welcomed by many candidates in the 1948 election. In particular, it was helpful to such candidates as Senator Hubert H. Humphrey, Democrat of Minnesota; Gov. Chester Bowles of Connecticut, and Gov. G. Mennen Williams, Democrat of Michigan, among others.

Though this organization was formed to dramatize the non-Communist left, it has been widely attacked since the 1948 election as a left-wing organization, with the result that in this election, candidates are showing a distinct lack of enthusiasm for its support, and some are even repudiating it entirely.

One of the paradoxes of this situation is that the Democratic party and the Americans for Democratic Action have been placed in a more difficult political position in this election because of the success they had in 1948 in their fight against the extreme left wing as represented by Henry Wallace's Progressive party.

So long as the so-called "progressives" were in the political picture the New Dealers were able to make a distinction between their own liberals and the Wallace fellow-travelers, but with the "progressives" destroyed as a political force, the Republicans were in a much better position to argue that the Democratic party was not a liberal party of the center but a party of the left. And that has been almost the central argument of the Republicans in this campaign.

In short, the intellectual left, which has been on the offensive for more than a decade, has been placed on the defensive by the militant anti-Communist campaign of the Republican party.

In the Nineteen Thirties the liberal intellectuals in the United States took the lead in the fight against Fascist totalitarianism, but in the Nineteen Forties, unlike many European Socialists and other European left-wingers who were fighting hard at the time of Yalta, they allowed the leadership in the fight against totalitarian communism to pass to the conservatives and are now seeing the political consequences.

This does not mean that the campaign to confuse all New Dealers with fellow-travelers has succeeded in this election. On the contrary, nothing is clearer in a trip across the nation today than that the New Deal policies affecting farmers and industrial workers have struck deep roots in this country and have a very good chance of being rewarded at the polls on Tuesday. The irony of the situation is that many of the intellectuals who pioneered these policies and fought for them privately and publicly from 1936 to 1948 are now on the defensive.

November 2, 1950

REPUBLICAN SENATE GAINS HELD THREAT TO MAJOR FAIR DEAL DOMESTIC PLANS;

COALITION IS LIKELY

By WILLIAM S. WHITE

The Republicans have taken all but arithmetical control of the United States Senate in the oncoming Eighty-second Congress. They have cut deeply, though not at all decisively, into the Democratic majority for the new House of Representatives.

They have, in a net gain of five, seized forty-seven of the Senate's ninety-six seats, a number far more than enough to give them, in association with the Southern Democrats, an almost unquestioned mastery of the highest domestic issues of President Truman's Fair Deal program.

They have struck down two of the most powerful national Democratic figures in the field of legislative action, Senator Scott W. Lucas of Illinois, the Democratic Senate floor leader, and Senator Millard E. Tydings of Maryland, chairman of the Senate Armed Services Committee.

They have reduced by about two-thirds the House majority held by the Democrats in the present, and expiring, Eighty-first Congress.

All this the Republicans had accomplished last night on the showing of returns, which were nearing completion, from a very heavy balloting of Tuesday that established many areas of dissatisfaction, particularly in the Middle West, but nothing so strong as a country-wide revulsion from the Democrats.

The Republican minority, which but for the one brief period of the Eightieth Congress from 1946 to 1948 had known no grand victory since Franklin D. Roosevelt

167

started the New Deal in 1933, has reasserted its vitality with great force.

The Republicans have brought forward, or strengthened visibly, a good handful of possible Presidential contenders in 1952—Senator Robert A. Taft of Ohio, Gov. Thomas E. Dewey of New York, Gov. (and now Senator) James H. Duff of Pennsylvania, and Gov. Earl Warren of California.

All but one of these, Mr. Taft, stand well to the left of the orthodox Republican party that he rather generally, but not in every aspect, so represents, and they have not been associated with his hostility or skepticism toward the present internationalist policy of the Truman Administration.

However, in the election itself, despite the fact that it thrust upward three more or less liberal Republicans against one of an older school, whatever pattern was perceptible seemed to indicate a restless stirring in the Midwest of what the Democrats would call "isolationism."

The most impressive Republican gains came from the center of the country, first of all, then from the Far West. Illinois, Indiana, Nebraska, Ohio—these states in the Republican heartland were impressively, in this election, turning toward home again.

This news meant for Mr. Truman more than the wreck of his Senate mechanism as even a moderately effective Fair Deal force.

The loss of Senator Lucas in Illinois put him to the hard task of recommending, at least, a new Senate leader.

Mr. Lucas, it appeared from all that could be gathered after the event, was one of the chief victims of a foreign policy upon which, above all else, he had preferred to stand, though he had not been conspicuously among those who had made that policy.

His defeat by former Representative Everett Dirksen, who had the support of the "nationalist" forces, seemed to point up the strange sectional movements of an election, which was, in the last analysis, one of issues that worked both ways.

For the most welcomed victory for the Democrats was in the East —that of Senator Brien McMahon in Connecticut, who had persistently presented himself as one preoccupied with international affairs, as he had in fact been in Congress. Mr. McMahon won in Connecticut against all local political tradition of recent years.

The relative stability of the Democratic position in the East as against that in the grain country was again demonstrated in Pennsylvania, where the young Democratic incumbent Senator, Francis J. Myers, put the powerful Mr. Duff to the greatest exertions before falling at last.

Maryland a Soft Spot

Then, there was New York, where Senator Herbert H. Lehman, a Democrat supported by the Liberal party, survived handily, his vote against the McCarran anti-Communist bill notwithstanding, in a place of confused infighting where local issues, though very strong, tended to some extent to weaken each other.

Maryland, however, proved a soft spot in the Democratic second line of defense along the Eastern Seaboard. There, Senator Tydings, one of the most deeply entrenched members of the Senate, was ousted by a newcomer, John M. Butler. That campaign seemed to have turned about the Senate's investigation of the charges of Senator Joseph R. McCarthy, Republican of Wisconsin, of Communist infiltration of the State Department.

Senator Tydings—and his selection to that highly vulnerable post was made precisely because he was believed to be politically unassailable—was chairman of the subcommittee that made the inquiry, then brought in a verdict that Senator McCarthy had knowingly offered a fraudulent case.

Mr. McCarthy, and many other Republicans, took up the cry of "whitewash" against Mr. Tydings, and his high position in the Senate could not save him. Mr. McMahon was on the same subcommittee, but he was neither so active nor so symbolic of it as his senior, Senator Tydings.

Seniority, in this election, in fact was carried with peril by the Democrats and with corresponding self aid by the Republicans, so far as the Senate was concerned.

It was not the juniors who fell, but those who had all the combat skill of many years. In the House, on the contrary, the old-timers held on, serene and undisturbed, through what was in this and in other respects an oddly less severe convulsion than shook the Senate.

And, in the Senate, it was not the wholly convinced Fair Dealers who were rejected. Senator Lucas, majority leader and all that notwithstanding, was extraordinarily independent of the White House. He voted for the Taft-Hartley Labor Act. He opposed the President on two other of his biggest objectives—the Brannan farm plan and compulsory health insurance. He was accused, correctly or not, by some of the more zealous of not going all-out, as majority leader, for the Truman civil rights program.

Senator Tydings, for his part, was anything but a White House intimate. His record for twenty years had been an essentially conservative one. His greatest real interest was in military affairs, though he also was a member of the Senate Foreign Relations Committee.

That committee, though it is to remain in at least nominal Democratic control, has now lost three of the eight Democrats who sat on it at the outset of the Eightieth Congress. Senator Claude Pepper of Florida was defeated in the primaries. And Senator Elbert D. Thomas of Utah gave up one of the five seats captured on Tuesday by the Republicans.

Mr. Thomas' unsuccessful race against Wallace F. Bennett, a former president of the National Association of Manufacturers, appears to have presented, except for certain accusations attempting to link the incumbent with communism, something of a classical left-right issue. Senator Thomas was an advanced Fair Dealer.

Still another such a test, and one of the most important by the Republicans, was in Colorado. There Senator Eugene D. Millikin, a Republican veteran commonly thought in Washington to be one of the ablest and most candid spokesmen for old-time Republican views, fought it out successfully to the end with a young Fair Dealer, John A. Carroll.

Mr. Millikin's survival, though less spectacular than Mr. Taft's, was in a legislative sense almost as heartening to the Republicans. A man of immense private influence in the Senate, he is chairman of his party's caucus organization, the Republican Conference.

Again, however, as the scene shifted, this time to California, the issue was less domestic. Representative Richard M. Nixon easily picked up a Democratic Senate there, from which Senator Sheridan Downey had retired and which Representative Helen Gahagan Douglas tried to capture.

November 9, 1950

MUNDT GETS HELP TO REALIGN PARTIES

He Says 100 From 17 States Set Up Bipartisan Committee to Plan for '52 Campaign

Special to THE NEW YORK TIMES.

WASHINGTON, Sept. 17—Senator Karl E. Mundt, Republican of South Dakota, announced today that a committee, bipartisan in leadership, would carry on the effort he has been making to get a political realignment in the country for the 1952 election.

He said that the Committee to Explore Political Realignment was organized at a week-end conference of 100 "like-minded Americans" from both major parties who seek to "find a working formula for combining their voting strength to stop the encroachment of socialism and the all-inclusive centralized super-state."

At the founding conference, he stated, were persons from seventeen states, including the emissaries of five Governors. Without saying so, he left the impression that the Governors were in Southern states.

Acting chairman of the new organization is former Senator Edward R. Burke of Nebraska who served one term as a Democrat. Eventually the committee will have co-chairmen of equal authority, one Democrat and one Republican, according to the announcement.

Executive Board Members

Democrats on the executive board besides Mr. Burke are former Gov. Charles Edison of New Jersey, a former Secretary of the Navy, and Donald R. Richberg of Virginia, one-time New Deal executive, who directed the National Recovery Administration.

Republican members of the executive board are former Senator Albert W. Hawkes of New Jersey, former Gov. Horace A. Hildreth of Maine, now president of Bucknell College, and Donald J. Cowling, president of Carleton College in Minnesota.

Those who formed the committee came to Washington. Senator Mundt said, at the invitation of himself, Senator Owen Brewster, Republican of Maine, Mr. Burke and Mr. Hawkes.

The objective of the new committee, Senator Mundt asserted, was to transform the informal alliance in the Congress against "socialistic legislation" and "bureaucratic tyranny" into a reality in a presidential election.

Cites Record of Alliance

Over the past fifteen years, he said, this alliance in Congress had determined the fate of thirty-five important measures. He cited adoption of the Hatch Act, spelling out illegal political activity by Federal workers, and defeat of the bill to enlarge the membership of the Supreme Court, commonly known as the "court-packing" bill.

States represented at the week-Texas, Alabama, New York, New Jersey, Virginia, Nebraska, Minnesota, Maine, Pennsylvania, Oklahoma, Georgia, Tennessee, South Carolina, North Carolina, South Dakota, Wisconsin and Florida.

September 18, 1951

PARTY CHAIRMAN'S JOB IS A HARD ONE TO FILL

Since Farley's Time Many Have Been Called but Few Have Excelled

By CABELL PHILLIPS
Special to THE NEW YORK TIMES.

WASHINGTON, Oct. 27—The political spotlight shifts briefly away from candidates and neo-candidates next week to figures of only slightly lesser importance, the chairmen of the two big national committees.

On Wednesday, the 108 members of the Democratic National Committee come to Washington to pick a successor to William M. Boyle Jr. Boyle, who had been unhappily involved in the investigation of "influence" at the Reconstruction Finance Corporation, resigned three weeks ago because of ill health. He has been party chairman since August, 1949.

The Republican chairman, Guy George Gabrielson, has denied any intention of stepping down from his job. But there are mounting rumors that when the Republican National Committee gets together in January he will be eased out for, it is asserted, someone less tangibly oriented toward the candidacy of Senator Robert A. Taft.

Eruptions of this sort are not uncommon at this season of the political calendar. With an important election year coming up, it is natural for the politicians of

'YOU FEEL O.K.?'

Fischetti, N. E. A. Service

both camps (a) to look for a scapegoat for past failures, and (b) to succumb to the hope that "some one else can do it better." The party chairmen are the natural targets of this invidious attention since upon them rests a major share of the responsibility for the party's health and vitality.

Chairman's Major Functions

The party chairman essentially is the housekeeper and business manager of an amorphous, loosely knit, multi-million-dollar enterprise that probably is unique among all the forms of social organization. Each presides over a headquarters and executive staff of from thirty to forty employes here in Washington. But his authority derives from, and his influence is extended upon, tens of thousands of big and little party workers of voluntary and uncertain allegiance who are scattered throughout the whole fabric of the population.

In operating and holding together this incongruous sort of enterprise, the major functions of a national chairman, in the period between elections, break down about this way:

(1) *Organization.* It is primarily up to the chairman to keep the party structure, from national headquarters down to the remotest precinct, a viable and active organism. An axiom of political life is that elections are won at the grassroots. If the grassroots wither, it is the chairman's fault—or at least so the reasoning goes. He and his top aides are constantly on the move around the country whooping up party enthusiasm in the state and local leaders.

Party Needs Money

(2) *Fund raising.* The chairman has to have access to the leading clubs and counting houses in his national constituency, and a knack for prying the check books of the well-heeled party members out of hiding. Even in a non-election year, it takes upward of $1,000,000 to maintain either of the major parties. In a Presidential year the sum may be quadrupled.

(3) *Strategy.* Propaganda is the principal weapon of the national political committee. While each employs a competent staff of publicists, writers and speech-makers, it is the chairman who sets the tone and the pattern of the output. Both party headquarters issue a constant stream of criticism and invective against the other, both for general consumption and for edification of local party workers.

In addition to propaganda, there are strategic considerations regarding policy moves for which the chairman is responsible. He must have an imaginative turn of mind, and an intuitive sense of timing and of the fitness of things. When twenty-six Republicans in Congress suddenly produce a resolution condemning the President's recent security order, or when a flood of telegrams pours in on Democratic Senators from their state leaders urging support of the Administration's price support bill, a reasonable supposition is that somebody at national headquarters—presumably the chairman—is on his toes.

Role of Conciliator

(4) *Conciliation.* The wise chairman develops a bland, Solomonic neutrality as far as the clashing ambitions of the party bigwigs are concerned. He is supposed to serve the whole party, not a candidate for its leadership. But when rivalries occur on a less exalted plane, say at the state or city level, and threaten the party's stability locally, he moves in to calm the ruffled waters.

(5) *Patronage.* This is a function largely denied to the minority party, but the chairman of the party in power has next to the last (but often the controlling) say in who gets what job at the President's disposal. Thousands of ordinary Government jobs outside of civil service and hundreds of more juicy appointments to judgeships, as district attorney, for service on various boards and commissions and even to Ambassadorships are made yearly on the recommendation of the committee chairman. Patronage is one of the most potent cements holding a party together. The smart chairman knows how to use it for maximum benefit.

Campaign Manager

That's the pattern, roughly, in non-election years. Election years are the same with one important addition. The national chairman usually is his party's campaign manager, as well, and he is supposed to get his man elected President. It often happens, however, that the candidate comes from a different faction of the party from the incumbent chairman. In that event a new chairman of the candidate's choice takes over. Thus in 1948 the Republican chairman, Carroll Reece, a Taft man, was replaced by Hugh D. Scott Jr., whom Thomas E. Dewey named to pay off his debt to the Pennsylvania delegation that led the convention bandwagon into the Dewey corral.

Up to twenty years ago a national chairman was a figurehead except for every fourth year when the party organizations came back to life. It was an empty honor or passed out to whatever faithful wheelhorse seemed most to deserve it.

James A. Farley is universally credited with having rescued the job from the innocuous desuetude in which it had been submerged since the days of Mark Hanna and putting it and the whole committee organization on a dynamic, year-round basis. He did it, of course, for the Democrats, beginning with the 1932 campaign of Franklin D. Roosevelt. It took the G. O. P. another four years to catch on to the idea, but after the disastrous Landon campaign of 1936 its national committee under John D. M. Hamilton went on a full-time basis, too.

In the decade since Farley (he resigned in 1940 after breaking with F. D. R. over the third term question) the Democrats have had five national chairmen and the Re-

publicans six. For each it became virtually a full-time job, although two who were drawn from Congress—Representative Joe Martin for the Republicans from 1940 to 1942, and Senator J. Howard McGrath who served the Democrats from 1947 to 1949—did not formally relinquish their seats.

Quality of Leadership

The job calls for a capacity for hard work, a shrewd sense of po-

litical strategy and timing, a pervasive quality of leadership capable of bridging chasms of viewpoint and personal ambition, an indestructible optimism and abuse-proof loyalty.

On top of all of this, the chairman must also be capable of self-effacement. Anytime the notion gets around that he wants to run with the ball himself (Farley had such an idea in 1940) he becomes persona non grata with the man or

men at the top.

These are the paragon-like qualities which Mr. Truman is seeking as he scans the field for a successor to Mr. Boyle, and for which, it is possible, the Republicans may be looking in January. It is a difficult quest, for there aren't many Farleys around.

October 28, 1951

MODERN REPUBLICANS VS. THE OLD GUARD

G. O. P. CALLED SHY 4 MILLION VOTERS

Census Analysis of Election Trends Shows Democrats Hold Edge for 1952

WASHINGTON, Nov. 24 (UP)—If the Republicans are to win the Presidency in 1952 they may need, barring a revolt of Southern Democrats, at least 4,000,000 more votes than ever have been cast for a G. O. P. candidate, Government statisticians estimated today.

On the basis of a Census Bureau analysis of Presidential elections since World War I, the voters must come from: An increase in the number who go to the polls; a shift from the Democratic to the Republican ranks;

Republicans who have stayed away from the polls, and persons who have reached voting age since 1948.

Statistics since 1932, when Franklin D. Roosevelt defeated Herbert C. Hoover, give the Democrats a decided edge in relative party strength. Even though recent public opinion polls show President Truman's popularity at a low ebb, they still give the Democrats a numerical margin in party affiliation—41 per cent against 32 per cent for the Republicans.

Independent voters are credited with about 27 per cent, a slice of which apparently has gone to the Democrats in past years.

90,000,000 Potential

President Truman defeated Governor Dewey of New York by 2,236,525 popular votes in 1948. A Southern rebellion deprived him of another 1,169,021 normally Democratic. In addition, the Henry A. Wallace Progressives siphoned away 1,156,103 votes.

The total eligible voter potential for 1952 is estimated at about 90,-

000,000. Therein is the big "if" of the election—if that number of voters can be aroused to ballot.

The Republicans, under Guy G. Gabrielson, National Chairman, already are pressing a get-out-the-vote drive. The Democratic National Committee, urged on by President Truman, is preparing one.

The President has warned the voters several times that, unless they go to the polls, they must accept, without criticism, the candidates elected.

Both Democrats and Republicans were let down in 1948. A 60,000,000 vote had been forecast but only 48,833,680 turned out.

Both party managers are shooting at 60,000,000 again next year, but the Republicans must win more than a moderate shift from the Democrats. This reasoning rests on the Census Bureau's historical score card.

Record Set by Roosevelt

The maximum vote for the Republican candidate to date was 22,304,400 for Wendell L. Willkie

in 1940. If the G. O. P. gained 4,000,000 over this peak in 1952, their total still would be less than the vote for President Roosevelt in 1936 and 1940.

Mr. Roosevelt had an all-time record of 27,476,673 in 1936, when he defeated Gov. Alfred M. Landon of Kansas, and he had 26,826,742 when he defeated Mr. Willkie in in 1940.

According to the Census Bureau, the Republican party vote since World War I is as follows:

```
1920 (Harding elected) ...............16,152,200
1924 (Coolidge elected) ..............15,725,603
1928 (Hoover elected) ................21,391,381
1932 (Hoover defeated) ...............15,761,841
1936 (Landon defeated) ...............16,679,583
1940 (Willkie defeated) ..............22,304,400
1944 (Dewey defeated) ................22,006,285
1948 (Dewey defeated) ................21,969,170
```

The regular Democratic party vote since 1920 follows:

```
1920 (Cox defeated) ...................9,147,353
1924 (Davis defeated) .................8,385,586
1928 (Smith defeated) ................15,016,433
1932 (Roosevelt elected) .............22,821,857
1936 (Roosevelt re-elected) ..........27,476,673
1940 (Roosevelt elected third time) ..26,826,742
1944 (Roosevelt elected fourth time) .24,776,864
1948 (Truman elected) ................24,105,695
```

The Truman Democrats lost 1,169,021 votes to the States Rights party in 1948.

November 25, 1951

In The Nation

A Statistical Survey of the Republican Problem

By ARTHUR KROCK

WASHINGTON, Feb. 13—An editorial in this newspaper today, addressed to the Republican voters of New Hampshire, included the following paragraph:

The Republican party needs the support of * * * independent voters if it hopes to win this year's election.

This conclusion is amply supported by the national voting statistics of many years. The figures and their meaning were recently cited and analyzed in a paper presented to the Nittany Council of Republican Women by Dr. Ruth C. Silva of the State College of Pennsylvania. "If voting patterns remain as they have since 1932," she wrote, "and if there is no serious

Northern split in the Democratic party, the Democratic Presidential candidate is likely to win at least 173 electoral votes in [eleven] big-city states, plus another fifty electoral votes in ten other Northern states, making a total of 223, only forty-three short of the necessary 266. * * * In contrast * * * the Republicans will start out with only thirty relatively certain electoral votes in six states. "In addition to these * * * the Republicans have a chance of winning at least some of the 124 electoral votes in the ten 'uncertain' states of the North. * * * It seems rather obvious that we will need a candidate who can carry not only these doubtful states but who can also invade Democratic territory."

Of her "big-city" states the Democrats in 1948 carried California, Illinois, Massachusetts, Minnesota, Missouri, Ohio and Wisconsin. The Republicans carried Pennsylvania with a majority, but got only pluralities, or less than 50 per cent of the votes, in Maryland, Michigan and New York. And Henry A. Wallace's candidacy diverted

from the Democratic ticket in New York more than 500,000 voters in radical groups normally affiliated with that party.

In her "ten other Northern states," with fifty electoral votes, the Democrats in 1948 carried Arizona, Idaho, Montana, Nevada, New Mexico, Rhode Island, Utah and Washington; and the Republicans won Connecticut and Oregon, but with pluralities of less than 50 per cent of the votes.

The "relatively certain" Republican states in Dr. Silva's tables, with thirty electoral votes, are Kansas, Maine, Nebraska, North Dakota, South Dakota and Vermont. In 1948 the Republicans had majorities in all six.

Her "ten uncertain" Northern states include the "big-city" states of Ohio, Pennsylvania and Wisconsin in addition to Colorado, Delaware, Indiana, Iowa, New Hampshire, New Jersey and Wyoming. Of the last-named seven the Democrats in 1948 won Colorado, Iowa and Wyoming by majorities and the Republicans carried Delaware, New Hampshire and New Jersey by majorities and Indiana by a plurality.

Translating these categories into 1952 electoral units, Dr. Silva tabulated them as follows:

Likely Democratic 223
Likely Republican 30
Doubtful, North 124
Eleven Southern States......128
Kentucky, Oklahoma, West
    Virginia 26

As forecast this tabulation can be challenged in detail, some of it important. But as a cold appraisal of the voting statistics of the last three Presidential elections it is realistic. And it lends force to the argument that the Republican candidate must take over well - established Democratic voting areas in the North, or a large section of them and several big Democratic states in the South, to break up "the voting patterns as they have been since 1932."

Dr. Silva's conclusion was that Senator Taft cannot break the pattern and General Eisenhower can. "Suppose," she told her audience, "we nominate a liberal Republican who is a world leader, where will the more conservative and isolationist Republicans go? Certainly not to the Fair Deal and internationally minded Democrats. But what votes could a progressive Republican who is a world leader win? He could win the votes of independents, of * * * Republicans who have voted Democratic in recent years and even of some Democrats who. * * * are far from sold on all the Fair Deal and corruption in Washington."

The reply of the Taft supporters to this typical argument is about as follows:

1. No statistics can be produced to prove that if all or most of those eligible to vote in 1948 had gone to the polls, instead of only 49 per cent, the President would still have been elected. His margin was so narrow in the states that made the essential contribution to his electoral majority—Iowa, Illinois and Ohio—that it would have been overcome by a vigorous assault on his record that Governor Dewey failed to make and Mr. Taft would have and will. The reason is that such a campaign brings the stay-at-homes to the polls. They stayed at home in 1948 because Mr. Dewey did not offer them the issues and the alternative that Mr. Taft would have and in 1952 will.

2. Normally Democratic electoral votes in the South will be withheld because the party nominee for President, whether or not Mr. Truman, will be obliged to run on the Fair Deal platform and record. Mr. Taft may not be able to get these electors directly and maybe General Eisenhower could get some. But their withholding, in combination with the recapture of Republican states lost to the President in 1948, will assure the defeat of the Democratic ticket.

The argument of the statistics is that Mr. Taft cannot recapture these states.

February 14, 1952

TV AS A POLITICAL FORCE

This year's Presidential campaign will differ from all others that have preceded it in that television will take the voter everywhere, and put him face to face with the candidate. It is worth while, in technological as well as political interest, to pin-point the moment when TV became a major instrument of national politics. This moment was probably the beginning of General Eisenhower's first political speech, in Abilene, Kan., on June 4, 1952, to be quickly followed by his first press conference.

The TV audience is now nation-wide for the first time in a national campaign, and the camera is also newly ubiquitous. Television will watch the political conventions in Chicago. It will examine the spellbinders. It makes a goldfish bowl out of every rostrum. It applies the litmus test to shenanigans, phonies and plain bores. It separates the men from the boys.

Never before has the voter had such widespread opportunity to get the "feel" of the man he may or may not vote for to sit in the White House. Never before has he been able, with his own eyes, to take measure repeatedly of the sincerity, the goodwill and the intelligence of a candidate for high office.

It is one thing for a candidate to mount the platform and read a speech, which he himself may or may not have written. It is another thing for him to face a roomful of newspaper men and submit to informed, critical questioning. In no respect has television made a greater contribution to public service, perhaps, than in putting a press conference on the air. The public is able at first-hand to measure the forthrightness, the courage or the evasiveness of a candidate. It watches while the subject speaks on topics he might prefer to avoid. It catches all the hesitations and the nuances.

We of the newspaper press need not fear or be jealous of this comparative newcomer in the spread of information to the public. TV is a stimulant to fair, complete news reporting, a check on bias, slant and warped selection or emphasis. The camera's grasp is necessarily incomplete and selective, of itself. The public will continue to want the trained newspaper man's report, the black-and-white record of what was asked and what was replied, the background and the editorial page's opinion. But the reading public will also have the advantage of having been there, seeing it happen, and a better, more complete basis of making up its own mind. If we believe in democracy and the ability of the people to choose wisely when they have all the facts this new medium of political education is a welcome arrival.

June 8, 1952

EISENHOWER NOMINATED ON THE FIRST BALLOT; SENATOR NIXON CHOSEN AS HIS RUNNING MATE

REVISED VOTE 845

By W. H. LAWRENCE
Special to THE NEW YORK TIMES.

CONVENTION BUILDING in Chicago, July 11—General of the Army Dwight D. Eisenhower won a hard-fought first-ballot nomination today as the Republican candidate for President and Senator Richard M. Nixon of California was chosen by acclamation as his running mate for the Vice Presidency.

The former Supreme Allied Commander in Europe went before the 1,206 Republican delegates tonight to accept the nomination and pledge that he would lead "a great crusade" for "total victory" against a Democratic Administration he described as wasteful, arrogant and corrupt and too long in power. He said he would keep "nothing in reserve" in his drive to put a Republican in the White House for the first time since March 4, 1933.

The Republican convention adjourned finally at 8:21 P. M., Central daylight time (9:21, New York time) after it had heard Senator Nixon accept the Vice-Presidential nomination. He pledged a "fighting campaign" to insure election not only of a Republican President, but also a House and Senate controlled by his party.

Bitterly Divided Convention

General Eisenhower won in a bitterly divided Republican convention. In the last week the general had taken leadership in the contest from Senator Robert A. Taft of Ohio, the chief party spokesman in Congress, who was making his third unsuccessful bid for nomination to the office once held by his father, William Howard Taft.

Victory came for General Eisenhower on the first ballot. The official results were 845 for General Eisenhower, 280 for Senator Taft, 77 for Gov. Earl Warren of Cali-

Modern Republicans vs. the Old Guard

fornia, and 4 for General of the Army Douglas MacArthur.

But that figure did not represent truly the voting sentiments of these delegates as they faced the crucial and final showdown between General Eisenhower and Senator Taft.

When the first roll-call of the states was completed, General Eisenhower had 595 votes—nine short of the required majority of 604—and Senator Taft had 500. The balance of power rested with favorite-son candidates, such as Governor Warren, who had 81 votes, and Harold E. Stassen, former Minnesota Governor, with 20. General MacArthur had received only 10 votes.

Others Then Changed

And while Governor Warren's California delegation held firm for him in the hope of a deadlock, Mr. Stassen's Minnesota delegates, no longer bound because he had received less than 10 per cent of the vote, broke away and cast nineteen votes for General Eisenhower before a first ballot result could be announced.

The nineteen, added to the General's previous total, gave him 614, or ten more than a majority. Then other states began to change their votes in order to be recorded on the side of the winner.

Thus, while General Eisenhower's nomination later was made unanimous on the motion of principal backers of Senator Taft and Governor Warren, who pledged the support for their principals to the nominee, it was made clear that General Eisenhower was the choice of a divided convention, and that one of his first tasks would be to restore party unity and heal the deep wounds inflicted during the fierce competition for the nomination.

To that end, General Eisenhower's first act, after he knew he had won, was to call on Senator Taft to ask—and receive—from him assurances that the Ohioan would campaign actively for the Eisenhower-Nixon ticket.

The Republicans who picked the 61-year-old commander of the Allied invasion of Europe and the 39-year-old California Senator believed this to be their best chance of victory over the Democrats in twenty years, and their only fear was that continued bitterness over the outcome would make it possible for the Democrats to run to six their consecutive string of victories in national elections.

Starting his active campaign preparations at once, General Eisenhower asked Republican members of the Senate and House who were in Chicago for the convention to meet with him at 10 A.M. tomorrow in his Blackstone Hotel suite. This group predominately favored Senator Taft's nomination, and the invitation to its members was one more step by the general toward establishing party harmony.

General Eisenhower was the candidate of a group that believed he

had enormous appeal to the independent voter and dissident Democrats, without whom the Republicans cannot achieve victory, and that Senator Taft "couldn't win."

Eisenhower backers had charged Taft forces during the nomination campaign with improperly seeking to obtain Southern delegate strength in Texas, Georgia and Louisiana.

It was on the contested-delegate issue that General Eisenhower and Senator Taft fought before this convention after the Ohioan's challenged delegations had been upheld by the Taft-dominated National Committee.

There were two key test votes on this issue, and General Eisenhower, with the backing of pro-Warren and pro-Stassen delegates, won impressive victories on both. This started a bandwagon rolling for General Eisenhower and stopped Senator Taft, who had been the favorite before this convention met.

500 Votes for Taft

Stripped of a net of forty-two Southern delegates on whose support he had counted, and rebuffed by the convention on what were called "moral issues" affecting the integrity of the party, Senator Taft's delegate strength began to slip away.

Nevertheless on the first ballot 500 delegates voted for Mr. Taft despite the fact that it was evident by then that he could not be nominated.

After his own nomination had been formally proclaimed at 1:32 P.M., General Eisenhower returned from his brief visit with Senator Taft, went into conference with his principal political advisers and told them that his own choice for Vice President was Senator Nixon.

Since it is customary for a convention to honor the nominee's choice for running mate, there was no dissent in the convention to Senator Nixon's nomination.

Earlier plans of women delegates, led by former Representative Clare Boothe Luce of Connecticut, to place Senator Margaret Chase Smith of Maine in nomination for the No. 2 spot were abandoned at Senator Smith's request, since she did not wish to create any impression that she was dissatisfied with the team that will carry the Republican banner in the November election.

Republican strategists believe they had picked a hard-campaigning pair of nominees to carry the battle to the Democrats in the nearly four months remaining before election day, Nov. 4.

The Democrats will meet here a week from Monday to select their candidates for President and Vice President. For the first time since 1932, there is doubt about their choice for standard-bearer. President Truman has announced his refusal to accept another nomination, even if drafted, and has said that his decision is irrevocable.

The leading Democratic Presidential possibilities are Gov. Adlai E. Stevenson of Illinois, Senator Richard B. Russell of Georgia, Senator Estes Kefauver of Tennessee, Averell Harriman of New York and Vice President Alben W. Barkley. Governor Stevenson has said on many occasions he is not a candidate but, quite recently, as Republican division and dissent spread, he has said he would at least consider running if the convention is ready to draft him.

Added Votes Explained

And the Democrats were very much on the minds of the Republicans today as first they picked General Eisenhower and then set to work to close the breach between his supporters and those of Senator Taft.

The Eisenhower managers had been certain of a first ballot victory even before Chairman Martin called the convention to order at 11:31 A.M., sixty-one minutes late. The word from leaders of the Eisenhower camp was that they were sure of 590 votes when the first roll-call of states was taken, and that Harold E. Stassen would shift nineteen votes from his Minnesota delegation before the vote could be announced.

As it turned out, General Eisenhower led Mr. Taft 595 to 500 when the roll-call was finished. Minnesota's additional votes put the general over the top with a total of 614, ten more than the total needed for nomination.

"We just picked up five more votes on the way," was the explanation of William L. Pfeiffer, New York State Republican Chairman, when reporters jokingly chided him for underestimating the Eisenhower strength.

The delegates, weary after the long and tiring floor fights that have marked this most boisterous of recent Republican meetings, were ready for the showdown when they marched into the International Amphitheatre in the heart of Chicago's stockyards today. All the Presidential nominating speeches and organized demonstrations had been concluded at an early hour this morning, and now the only job remaining was to vote.

It was 11:49 A.M. when Mrs. Charles P. Howard of Massachusetts, the secretary, began to call the roll of states, leading off with Alabama which split its fourteen votes, nine for Taft and five for Eisenhower.

Cheers greeted the announcement of many state votes, and the first loud boos were heard when Gov. Thomas E. Dewey stepped to the microphone to announce New York's 92-to-4 vote in favor of General Eisenhower.

Cheers of the Eisenhower delegates, who recognized the Governor's contribution to the general's victory, quickly drowned out the boos of the bitter Taft backers, who had sought desperately in the final hours to make the issue one between the Senator and Governor Dewey, rather than between Mr. Taft and General Eisenhower.

When the roll-call was finished, and General Eisenhower lacked nine votes of a majority, Chairman Martin recognized Warren E. Burger of St. Paul, a leader of Mr. Stassen's campaign. The Minnesotan announced that his state's delegation, previously divided nineteen for Mr. Stassen and nine for General Eisenhower, wished to change its vote to twenty-eight for General Eisenhower. Loud cheers greeted the change that gave General Eisenhower his majority, and the organ blared forth "The Minnesota Rouser," the first line of which goes:

"Minnesota, hats off to you."

That began a parade of states, shifting their vote, but some of the Taft backers refused to change, and California also kept its solid

bloc of seventy votes for Governor Warren.

The first significant pro-Taft group to shift to the winner was that led by former Senator Joseph R. Grundy and Joseph N. Pew Jr. in Pennsylvania, which had cast fifteen votes for the Ohio Senator, while General Eisenhower, backed by Governor Fine, had fifty-three and General MacArthur two. Pennsylvania became unanimous for General Eisenhower, but many of the states announcing changes in their voting included a good number of Taft votes.

Martin Announces Results

At 1:32 P.M., Chairman Martin announced the results of the first ballot in this order:
General MacArthur 4.
Governor Warren 77.
Senator Taft 280.
General Eisenhower 845.

This was 241 more than needed for the general to win, but Mr. Martin did not declare him to be the party nominee until after Senators Bricker and Knowland had moved, and the convention had approved, a resolution declaring General Eisenhower nominated by unanimous vote.

It was the third time in twelve years that Senator Bricker had stepped to the rostrum of a Republican convention to concede defeat on behalf of his colleague.

He began by saying that Senator Taft had communicated with him and that he spoke with the Senator's full approval.

Declaring that he was certain the convention would understand the import of his words, Senator Bricker added:

"General Eisenhower and Senator Taft already have met. Proving to all of us his loyal devotion to his party and its principles, Senator Taft has pledged his unlimited and active support to elect Dwight Eisenhower. General Eisenhower most graciously responded by saying that he could not be elected without the wholehearted support of Senator Taft and his friends, and that he could not carry out his program when elected president, as he will be, without their support."

Bricker is Cheered

This brought loud cheers from every section of the convention hall, and Senator Bricker reminded the delegates that the permanent duty for Republicans was to "drive the plunderers out of government" and to "bring order out of chaos."

"The last vestiges of the New Deal, the Fair Deal, the ordeal, and the mink deal must be destroyed," the silver-haired Ohioan asserted.

Joining in the motion, Senator Knowland pledged to General Eisenhower the wholehearted support of Governor Warren's friends to insure a victory in November, which he termed essential not alone to the Republican party but also "to the future of this nation of ours and the maintenance of a free world of free men."

After the Bricker-Knowland resolution had been approved, Daniel C. Gainey of Minnesota, one of Mr. Stassen's managers, read a telegram from him to General Eisenhower expressing his congratulations and best wishes for a November victory "and success to you and to America in the years ahead."

Then the convention recessed at

1:49 P. M. while party leaders huddled with General Eisenhower to learn his preference as to a running mate.

It took the Republicans less than half an hour to complete the necessary formalities of nominating Senator Nixon after General Eisenhower's wishes had been made known. The Senator was placed in nomination by Senator Knowland, who last night had made the nominating speech for Gov. Earl Warren for the Presidency. Since Mr. Nixon was the only candidate, Chairman Martin declared him nominated by acclamation.

The only potential barrier to quick action on Senator Nixon's nomination had been the desire of approximately 200 Republican women delegates to symbolize the demand of their sex for political equality by proposing a woman, Senator Smith, for the Vice Presidency. But the Maine Senator, who had gone along with the idea when it seemed there would be a field of Vice Presidential candidates from whom the convention might choose, quickly let it be known she did not want to be placed in nomination if Senator Nixon was to be the only other candidate. This was announced to the convention by Mrs. Luce, the playwright and wife of Henry Luce, the publisher.

July 12, 1952

NIXON IS YOUNGEST OF G. O. P. IN SENATE

But His Relative Youthfulness Is More Than Offset by His Rich Political Record

Richard M. Nixon, who was nominated last evening for Vice President, is a California Quaker.

Thirty-nine years old, he is the youngest Republican member of the United States Senate and calls himself an internationalist in the realm of foreign policy and an "intelligent conservative" in domestic policies.

Not even in Congress until five and a half year ago, Mr. Nixon by his tenacious work as a member of the House Committee on Un-American Activities Committee won the most individual credit for breaking the Alger Hiss case and paving the way for the indictment and conviction of the former State Department official.

Mr. Nixon's fight against domestic communism as reflected in the Hiss case became the springboard, in 1950, for his plunge into the Senate contest in California after Senator Sheridan Downey, a Democrat, had decided against seeking another term. That led the way to a feat that sometimes has been overlooked by all except close students of the record books.

As a member of the California delegation at this Republican National Convention he is looked upon as having been a potent influence in aiding some of the delegate seating contest victories that led to the nomination of General of the Army Dwight D. Eisenhower for the Presidency.

Early in the convention indications pointed to Senator Nixon as the choice of the Eisenhower strategists for second place on the ticket.

Won Seat by Record Margin

After speaking all over California by plane and station wagon in a prodigious campaign he waged against Helen Gahagan Douglas, the Democratic nominee who was equally active as a speechmaker and inspector of the Golden State's landscape, Mr. Nixon won his seat by the greatest vote margin registered by any victorious Senate candidate that year.

And that was the year in which Senator Robert A. Taft of Ohio, against labor's opposition, was re-elected by about 400,000 votes over his Democratic rival, Joseph T. Ferguson, the State Auditor.

Mr. Nixon amassed a plurality of 670,000 votes over Mrs. Douglas in their battle, which, in the bitterness and sometimes viciousness with which charges and countercharges were hurled verbally and in campaign documents, has seldom seen its equal in California.

The Hiss case had thrust the second-term member of Congress into the public eye and he, with his friends and supporters, look upon his probing and prodding in that investigation as his outstanding accomplishment to date.

From the Navy to Congress

Senator Nixon had gone into the Navy in 1942 as a lieutenant, j. g., and came out three and a half years later as a lieutenant commander. He served as an air operations officer for a Marine combat air transport group in the Solomons campaign of the South Pacific. The group brought in needed supplies and took out casualties, and Mr. Nixon served with the unit at Bougainville, Guadalcanal and elsewhere in the area.

"I came right back and ran for Congress," he related.

"Back in this country I was on Navy business in Baltimore when I received an invitation to come out to California and appear on the same program with a group of others who were possible candidates."

In the group that issued the invitation were about 150 persons, representing local Republican clubs throughout the district. This committee heard all of the potential candidates and put its "money" on the lieutenant commander, who had flown out from Baltimore for his appearance and then went back to complete his Navy work.

It is this method of picking Republican candidates that after Mr. Nixon's successful campaign became known as the "Nixon plan."

That 1946 campaign took the former Navy officer to the House, and, two years later, he was able to forego a November battle by winning both Republican and Democratic nominations for Congress in the June primary.

Not So Successful at Football

These successive victories, followed by Mr. Nixon's rather spectacular triumph in the Senatorial jousting, were in contrast to the young politician's experiences on the football field as an undergraduate at Whittier College in the early Nineteen Thirties.

A liberal arts student at that small Quaker institution in Southern California, he aimed for the team in his freshman year. At game time he was left on the bench. He stayed a bench warmer for four years.

What he lacked on the football field he made up for on the public speaking platform.

After winning the Southern California championship, there and graduating from Whittier in 1934 he went on to Duke University Law School.

In both student bodies he was known as politically astute. Those who would deny it must face the fact that he was president of the student body at each institution. At Duke he served on The Law Review and was a member of the order of the COif, composed of the top ten students in the Law School.

Helped in Father's Gas Station

Senator Nixon was born in the village of Yerba Linda in Orange County, Calif., the son of a citrus rancher who became owner of a grocery store with a service station. As a youth the present Senator spent his spare time selling gasoline to former Iowans and other inhabitants of or visitors to Southern California.

Two decades later, in Congress, he was a member of the Herter Committee that went to Europe in 1947 and came back with recommendations for implementing the Marshall Plan.

He has served on the Labor Committee of both the House and Senate. He voted for the Taft-Hartley bill, but favors modification of the law now "to make it equitable."

"I am opposed to its repeal," he declared. "We've got to take steps to meet legitimate objections to the law, but the principles of the act have got to be sustained."

On his foreign affairs record Mr. Nixon offered these comments:

"I have been a strong supporter of the European reconstruction program, of the Voice of America, Point Four, and the arms-aid program. I am one of six Republicans who opposed the cut of $2,000,000,000 made in the foreign-aid program two months ago.

"With Senator William F. Knowland of California I have been a critic of the Administration's policy in the Far East."

Friends of Senator Nixon look upon his work as one of the factors leading to the resignation of William F. Boyle Jr. as chairman of the Democratic National Committee. He not only called upon Mr. Boyle to resign his post but asked Guy G. Gabrielson to quit as chairman of the Republican National Committee. He renewed his vain call for the Gabrielson resignation as recently as last January, in connection with the San Francisco meeting of the committee.

Mr. Nixon's importunities to both of the National Committee heads were the result of the investigation of political influences exerted on the Reconstruction Finance Corporation.

Although he is the youngest Republican in the Senate, Mr. Nixon has more competition among the Democrats. Senator Russell Long of Louisiana is only 33 and Senator George Smathers of Florida is Mr. Nixon's own age, 39.

When California's Junior Senator needs secretarial help in a bad way he looks around for a redheaded, very attractive, former Irish Democrat named Patricia.

As Patricia Ryan she was graduated from the University of California at Los Angeles. She taught commercial subjects at Whittier High School (the Senator now is a member of the board of trustees of Whittier College) and is recommended by Mr. Nixon as "an excellent typist." They have two daughters, Patricia, 6, and Julie, 4. In the words of Senator Nixon, she has "never been on the Federal payroll."

July 12, 1952

Text of Senator Taft's Statement

Statement by Senator

On July 17 General Eisenhower wired me that on my return from my vacation he would like to consult with me concerning campaign plans. I replied by wire that I would be glad to do so. In Chicago in July I stated that I would do everything possible in the campaign to secure his election, and in his administration after his election. I was complimented by his statement at that time that he regarded my willingness to cooperate as absolutely necessary to the success of the Republican party in the campaign and in his administration to follow.

I have never changed my intention expressed at Chicago, but, of course, I have not intended to abandon in any way the principles I have fought for the past fourteen years or abandon those countless friends who supported me in the preconvention campaign. I have felt, therefore, that I could be far more effective in the campaign if I could state to the people, after talking with General Eisenhower, my definite convictions regarding the character of his administration when he is elected and the principles by which it will be guided.

A good many of my friends have been concerned because so many of his editorial and columnist supporters, and other individuals, who have always heretofore taken the New Deal line, have been urging him to repudiate the Republican platform, approve

173

New Deal policies, and purge everyone who has fought hard for Republican principles against Truman and Acheson, and the rest of the left wingers. I have felt confident that General Eisenhower had no such intention. The expression of such a confidence can be far more effective after a personal talk with him.

One Fundamental Issue

As I see it, there is and has been one great fundamental issue between the Republican party, and the New Deal or Fair Deal or Stevenson Deal. It is the issue of liberty against the creeping socialization in every domestic field. Liberty was the foundation of our Government, the reason for our growth, the basis of our happiness and the hope of our future. The greatest threat to liberty today is internal, from the constant growth of big Government, through the constantly increasing power and spending of the Federal Government. The price of continued liberty, including a free economic system, is the reduction of Federal spending and taxes, the repudiation of arbitrary powers in the Executive claimed to be derived from Heaven and the stand against statutory extension of power by the creation and extension of Federal bureaus.

The protection of the people against any arbitrary excessive power, which may be developed by big business or big labor or other pressure groups, is also essential. I recognize that some Federal Government action is necessary simply to protect liberty in our complicated modern life, but our left-wing thinkers believe that only government can solve our problems and they present project after project, each one with plausible arguments, but all meaning a constant growth of the Federal Government.

Today, we are up against the guns. Government is taking one-third of the people's income and thereby one-third of their freedom. I wished to be sure that the new administration will be inspired with the philosophy of extending liberty before I entered into an extensive speaking campaign.

After a satisfactory discussion with General Eisenhower this morning for two hours, I am satisfied that that is his philosophy. I am convinced that he will carry out the pledges of the Republican platform, which express that philosophy adopted unanimously by Republican representatives from all parts of the country under the leadership of Senator Millikin. I recognize, of course, that the platform is not specific in every regard and that the candidate must have the right to develop the details of the program within the general spirit of the platform.

Convinced on Eisenhower Views

I am convinced that General Eisenhower believes in the words and spirit of the statement of Republican principles and objectives adopted by Republican members of Congress Feb. 6, 1950, and often approved by him, which states clearly the issue of liberty against socialism, of liberty on the farm, of free collective bargaining, of liberty for the individual workman, of liberty of the people against Federal regulations.

I cannot say that I agree with all of General Eisenhower's views on the foreign policy to be pursued in Europe and the rest of the world, but I think it is fair to say that our differences are differences of degree. We are both determined to battle communism throughout the world and in the United States. From my standpoint the essential thing is to keep our expenditures on armament and foreign aid, as long as there is no general war, at a percentage of our total income which will not destroy our free economy at home and further inflate our debt and our currency.

Our success in any war depends upon a strong fiscal and economic system able to maintain the production which has been and is the basis of our strength. General Eisenhower emphatically agrees with me in the proposal to reduce drastically over-all expenses. Our goal is about $70,000,000,000 in fiscal year 1954 and $60,000,000,000 in fiscal year 1955. That would make possible a reduction in taxes to the $60,000,000,000 level for the year 1955. Of course, I hope we may do better than that and that the reduction can steadily continue. In our opinion a free economy cannot continue successfully if the total tax burden for the purposes of all government continuously exceeds 25 per cent of the national income.

General Eisenhower has also told me that he believes strongly in our system of constitutional limitations on Government power, that he abhors the left wing theory that the Executive has unlimited powers, such as Mr. Truman's claim that he could seize steel mills and usurp other powers generally without constitutional authority.

General Eisenhower has also told me that he believes in the basic principles of the Taft-Hartley Law, its protection of the freedom of the people and union members themselves against the arbitrary use of power by big business or big labor, and is opposed to its repeal. We discussed certain amendments, which I have frequently advocated, but we agreed that they should not change the basic principles of the law, that is, the right of free and representative collective bargaining without Government dictation, the right to strike except for brief waiting periods in national emergency cases, the prohibition of unfair labor practices on the part of both management and labor, prohibition of the closed shop, jurisdictional strikes and secondary boycotts, the protection of the right to work even under legalized union shop agreement and other individual rights of the individual union member, the omission of seizure of property as a remedy for national strikes except by special legislation.

General Eisenhower agrees that the proper role of the Federal Government beyond its present activities is one of advice, research and assistance to the states, the local communities and the people.

I have been concerned about the attitude of those who apparently are urging that we should eliminate from all activity many of those who have been the most active workers for Republican principles in recent years, and who make up at least one-half of the Republican party. General Eisenhower stated without qualification that in the making of appointments at high levels or low levels there will be no discrimination against anyone because he or she has supported me, and that he is determined to maintain the unity of the entire party by taking counsel with all factions and points of view.

I am completely satisfied that General Eisenhower will give this country an administration inspired by the Republican principle of continued and expanding liberty for all as against the continued growth of New Deal socialism which we would suffer under Governor Stevenson, representative of the left-wingers, if not a left-winger himself.

I urge all Americans and particularly those who have confidence in my judgment and my principles, to vote for Eisenhower and Nixon, for all the Republican senatorial candidates and all the Republican House candidates, and to do everything possible to bring many others to the polls to do the same. I shall be glad to speak on a national broadcast or at any point throughout the country to the extent of my ability.

I believe General Eisenhower will be elected. A campaign based on the American principles in which he and I believe can arouse the enthusiasm of the people, and if that enthusiasm is properly organized we can bring to the polls 8,000,000 more voters than have ever voted the Republican ticket before. That is a sure program for success.

September 13, 1952

TRUMAN ANNOUNCES HE WILL NOT RUN AGAIN

HE BARS ANY DRAFT

President Also Maps the Party's Strategy, Says It Can Win Again

By W. H. LAWRENCE
Special to The New York Times.

WASHINGTON, March 29— President Truman dramatically announced tonight that he would not be a candidate for re-election and would not accept the nomination if he were drafted by the Democratic convention.

He made the announcement in almost dead-pan fashion toward the end of his speech before the 5,300 Democrats attending the party's traditional $100-a-plate Jefferson-Jackson Day dinner in the National Guard Armory here.

Following is the text of the statement interpolated into his prepared speech:

"I shall not be a candidate for re-election. I have served my country long and I think efficiently and honestly. I shall not accept a renomination. I do not feel that it is my duty to spend another four years in the White House."

The audience was taken completely by surprise by the announcement since there had been no indication anywhere in the earlier part of his speech nor in the advance word given to highest officials on his staff that he intended at this point to bow out of the 1952 political campaign.

"Oh no, oh no," shouted a few people on the floor.

Statement Total Surprise

But there was less demonstration than might have been expected because the huge crowd was taken totally by surprise.

Many of those in the audience appeared not to have heard or understood the import of Mr. Truman's statement. Others simply were stunned.

As soon as he had made his matter-of-fact disclaimer of any intentions to run again, Mr. Truman hurried on to finish the rest of the speech. The crowd applauded, not more vigorously than might have been expected, and the President hurriedly left the hall.

One man sitting near him said that the President's announcement, in long hand, rested on the speaker's rostrum alongside the typescript of his prepared speech.

The President inserted his statement just after he had declared that the record his administration had made would be the one on which the Democratic nominee would have to run "whoever the Democratic nominee * * * may be this year."

As the President left the armory he was stopped by reporters who asked, "Is this decision subject to any change at all?"

Any Change Ruled Out

"None whatsoever," Mr. Truman replied.

Mrs. Truman, who was with him, was asked whether she agreed with the decision.

"Of course," she said, "anything he says goes."

After the Trumans had returned to the White House Joseph Short, White House secretary, said that Mr. Truman had reached the decision to make his announcement tonight about a week ago while on vacation in Key West. Mr. Short underlined that the Key West decision was the timing of the announcement and not the basic decision itself. He would not say when Mr. Truman decided not to run again.

At his press conference Mr. Short was asked if he had any idea of Mr. Truman's plans for the time after he leaves the White House.

"I would suggest you ask him at his next press conference," Mr. Short replied.

The press secretary steadfastly refused to answer any questions as to whom the President had notified in advance of his decision to retire from the Presidency.

"That," he said, "was the President's business."

Some further disclosure of Mr. Truman's reasoning in making his decision may come when he attends a Mayflower Hotel reception tomorrow for all of the $100-a-plate contributors to tonight's dinner. The President is scheduled to speak at this reception.

Mr. and Mrs. Truman rode back alone to the White House immediately after his surprise announcement. There were no guests at the White House for the week-end.

Views in Book Are Cited

Immediately after the President had made his announcement one White House aide pointed out that the President's refusal to run again was in accord with the views he had expressed in interviews given to William Hillman in preparation of his newly published book, "Mr. President." One Page 13 of the book Mr. Truman is quoted as follows:

"There is no indispensable man in a democracy. When a republic comes to a point where a man is indispensable then we have a Caesar."

"I do not believe that the future of the nation should depend upon the life or health or welfare of any one man."

In his speech Mr. Truman peppered his political enemies with epithets, and sweepingly defended the accomplishments of his Administration both in domestic and foreign policies.

Describing his Republican opponents as "dinosaurs," "loud talkers" and users of "phony propaganda," the President accused them of belying their own campaign oratory by acts that had the effect of appeasing communism abroad and favoring "private selfish interests" at home.

The President's attack upon the Republicans and their record followed a charge by Vice President Alben W. Barkley that General of the Army Douglas MacArthur had grossly perverted the truth. Mr. Barkley struck back at the ousted Far Eastern commander for his charge before the Mississippi Legislature last Saturday that Administration policies were leading to communism at home and fomenting war in Europe.

Mr. Truman struck back at Republican charges that the Government was full of crooks and Communists and assertions that the Truman Administration had coddled communism abroad while promoting socialism at home.

His speech, carried to the country by all radio networks and one television network, was designed to turn against the Republicans their own selected campaign issues of communism and corruption.

"The real test of anti-communism," Mr. Truman declared, "is whether we are willing to devote our resources and our strength to stopping Communist aggression and saving free people from its horrible tyranny.

"That kind of anti-communism takes money and courage — not just talk. And the next time you hear some of this loud anti-Communist talk from our Republican friends, ask them how they voted—on aid to Greece, on the Marshall Plan, on the Mutual Security Program. The chances are they voted to cut or cripple these all-important measures against communism.

Warns of "Appeasers"

"I say to you in all seriousness, beware of those who pretend to be so violently anti-Communist in this country, and at the same time vote to appease communism abroad. In my book, that is talking out of both sides of the mouth at once; and I don't think the American people are going to be taken in by it."

The President had a similar counter-attack for the Republicans as he dealt with the corruption issue. He did not deny there had been dishonest men in the Government, but he accused the Republican party of trying to fool the voters into believing that "white is black" and that "the Government is full of grafters and thieves and all kinds of assorted crooks." Mr. Truman declared that he stood for "honest government" and had done more than any other President to extend Civil Service and reorganize the Government efficiently.

"I hate corruption not only because it is bad in itself, but also because it is the deadly enemy of all the things the Democratic party has been doing all these years," the President said. "I hate corruption anywhere, but I hate it most of all in a Democratic officeholder, because it is a betrayal of all the Democratic party stands for * * *."

He recalled the scandal-ridden Republican Administrations of the nineteen twenties, including those involving the Veterans Administration and Teapot Dome, and declared that these "were no worse —no more immoral—than the tax laws of Andrew Mellon or the attempt to sell Muscle Shoals to private interests." Legislation that favored "the greed of monopoly and the trickery of Wall Street," he added, "was a form of corruption that did the country more harm than Teapot Dome."

Gives a Political 'Key'

The President cited his liking for politics and said the key to the current political picture was "one simple thing: the Republicans have been out of office for twenty long years—and they are desperate to get back in control."

The Republicans, he went on, have been out of office for so long that they "can't figure out what to do."

"One theory that they have is that they ought to come right out and say they are against all the advances the country has made since 1932," the President said. "This is the dinosaur school of Republican strategy. They want to take us back to prehistoric times."

"Republicans of this school say —'Let's stop beating about the bush—let's say what we really believe. Let's say we're against social security—that we're against labor unions and good wages—that we're opposed to price supports for farmers—that we're against the Government doing anything for anybody except big business.'

"Now, I have a lot of sympathy for these Republicans. They have been hushed up for a long time. They would certainly be happier if they could tell the truth for once and campaign for what they really believe. It would be good for their souls. But it wouldn't be good for the party. The dinosaur school of Republican strategy would only get the dinosaur vote—and there aren't many dinosaurs left."

Another Republican theory, Mr. Truman continued, is that the Republicans can win if they oppose our present foreign policy, by pulling out of Korea, abandoning Europe and allowing the United Nations to fail. This strategy also would fail, he predicted, because the American people realize after two World Wars that as long as communism is lose in the world, we must resist aggression and we need allies.

"The American people are living in the atomic age, and they know that the ideas of the Stone Age won't work any more — if they ever did," the President declared.

He asserted still another school of Republicans opposed to his foreign policy advocated the "all-out" or "let's get it over with" theory.

"These are the Republicans who say they want to expand the fighting in Korea, and start dropping atomic bombs, and invite a new world war," Mr. Truman said. "They figure it's good politics to talk that way. They don't stop to count the cost. They think people don't understand that the hardest and bravest thing in the world is to work for peace—not war. But if war comes—if the showdown comes—these loud talkers would be the first people to run for the bomb shelters. And the voters know it."

None of these Republican theories of how to win an election holds much promise of success this year, he went on, but they do show that "the platform the Republicans write in Chicago in July will have to be a fearful and wonderful thing to cover all these different theories."

He said the Republicans realized that the country was strong and prosperous, that the nation was building up defenses against communism, and that the Democratic Administration had worked for the good of the people. The only chance the Republicans have, Mr. Truman asserted, is to make the people think that these facts are not true.

This, he said, is a pretty difficult way to win an election which would not appeal to anybody "but a very desperate politician." The Republicans, he argued, have "some reason" for thinking it might succeed, because "they will have the support of most of the press, and most of the radio commentators" and they may have "the professional poll-takers with them again."

"The Republicans, as always, will have a lot of money," the President said. "They have slick advertising experts. And they don't have too many scruples about how they use them. Remember the carpetbagger from Chicago who got convicted for the way he elected a Republican Senator in Maryland in 1950."

His reference at this point was to Jon M. Jonkel, a Chicago publicity man who was campaign manager for John Marshall Butler of Maryland when he won the Senate seat formerly held by Millard E. Tydings, Democrat. Jonkel pleaded guilty to violating the Maryland Corrupt Practices Act and was fined $5,000.

Mr. Truman interpolated a sharp dig at Harold E. Stassen, who has been campaigning in Wisconsin for the Republican Presidential nomination but offering to share equally with General of the Army Dwight D. Eisenhower, who is not on the Wisconsin ballot, any delegates he wins.

Declaring that the Republican leaders were so confused and divided that it would take a "circus tent" to cover their diversity of views, Mr. Truman remarked that it recently had "become fashionable for the Republican candidates to saw themselves in half."

It was a gay social gathering as well as a political rally with the male Democrats decked out in dinner jackets, women wearing their prettiest long party dresses.

On view in the crowd was one announced Presidential candidate, Senator Richard B. Russell of Georgia, who has the backing of the "Solid South." At the head table was Gov. Adlai E. Stevenson of Illinois, who is reported to be resisting overtures from Mr. Truman that he seek the nomination.

The dinner got the Democratic party off to a good start financially in its drive to retain power nationally for the sixth successive time. Limited by law to spending not more than $3,000,000 in a campaign year, the Democratic Committee netted well over $400,000 from this function after costs of the steak dinner and other expenses had been deducted.

It was the largest formal political dinner of the capital's history, filling all available floor space of the huge National Guard armory. Preparation of the food overworked the combined kitchen staffs of the Statler and Mayflower Hotels. The two hostelries prepared the meals and rushed them on charcoal broilers in trucks to the armory.

Sharing the rostrum with Mr. Truman and the Vice President were Speaker of the House Sam Rayburn of Texas, and the two top officials of the Democratic National Committee—Frank E. McKinney, chairman, and Mrs. India Edwards, executive director of the women's division.

Mr. McKinney predicted that Mr. Truman would rank in history alongside Thomas Jefferson, Andrew Jackson and Franklin D. Roosevelt as one of the party's four great leaders.

Mrs. Edwards urged the crowd to draft Mr. Truman for another term. Pointing out that the White House proper had just undergone an expensive rehabilitation job, Mrs. Edwards said that no one could expect new tenants not to alter it additionally.

"For the sake of economy that the opposition worships and that we respect, we must persuade the present occupants of the White House to remain in residence another four years!" she declared.

March 30, 1952

SOUTHERNERS SEATED

3 STATES ADMITTED

Virginia, South Carolina, and Louisiana Seated After Earlier Ban

STEVENSON FOR STEP

Desire for Unity Is Seen Behind Move—States Bar Party Pledge

By W. H. LAWRENCE
Special to THE NEW YORK TIMES.

CONVENTION BUILDING, in Chicago, Friday, July 25—Uncompromising Dixie Democratic leaders from Virginia, South Carolina and Louisiana early today were given full voting rights in the Democratic National Convention, which capitulated completely on the requirement imposed upon all other delegations for a signed party regularity pledge.

The result was announced after a second closely divided voice vote, but a roll call was demanded immediately by Senator Herbert H. Lehman of New York, who opposed the seating of the "regular," anti - Administration delegations from South Carolina and Louisiana.

Virginia's twenty-eight-vote delegation already had been given a special dispensation to sit in this convention after Gov. Adlai E. Stevenson of Illinois, the prospective nominee of this convention, had made clear his desire for a united party.

But the rollcall demanded by Senator Lehman was refused finally by Representative John McCormack, House Majority leader, who had taken over the chair from Speaker Rayburn in the final stages of the debate over the South Carolina and Louisiana seating issues.

The motion to seat Virginia once had been defeated. Later, by a vote of 648½ to 512 with 69½ absentations, the delegation was seated.

House Speaker Sam Rayburn, the convention's permanent chairman, cooperated with delaying tactics while the word spread through the convention that Governor Stevenson wanted the states to change their votes. At one point, the pro-Virginia motion had been defeated by 621 to 473½, but by the time states got through shifting, the final announced tally was 615 to 529 against.

The leader of the pro-Kefauver South Dakota delegation became so annoyed with Mr. Rayburn's conduct that he announced his delegation was leaving the floor in protest "against the grossly unfair methods" employed by the chairman.

Mr. Rayburn struck back with a defense of his impartiality and declared that never before in his many years as a presiding officer had his fairness been attacked.

The South Dakota walkout sounded serious when the announcement first was made, but it turned out to be only a comic interlude because the South Dakota group was off the floor for only a few minutes, and returned to their seats amid the cheers and laughter of other delegates.

While the "regular" Louisiana delegation with twenty votes was unseated, Senator Russell B. Long and a handful of his colleagues bolted the leadership of Gov. Robert F. Kennon and signed the party regularity pledge. Speaker Rayburn ruled that Senator Long and his group were qualified to cast all of Louisiana's votes in favor of seating Virginia.

There were no known defections in the South Carolina delegation, which has sixteen votes, and, when action on the Virginia resolution was complete, the state of which Gov. James F. Byrnes is the party leader was the only state in the convention that did not have any votes.

Repeats Bloc's Refusal

When Governor Battle took the rostrum to argue his state's case, he reiterated the delegates' continuing refusal to sign the pledge that each delegate would do all in his power to insure that the Democratic nominees would be listed on the ballot as such in the November general elections in Virginia

But Governor Battle said that Virginia law clearly required that the Democratic nominees shall be listed upon the ballot upon certification by the chairman of the national party, and that there was not in his state any plan or effort by anybody to keep the Democratic nominees off the ballot.

He thus, in effect, gave the convention verbal assurances about ballot listing, but he did not go into the business of accepting "majority rule" decisions, and he did not, of course, sign anything.

But the word passed on the floor among the delegates was that the word of the Virginia Governor ought to be trusted, and, when the Illinois delegation shifted its original vote of forty-five noes and fifteen ayes to fifty-two ayes and eight noes there was no doubt in the minds of the delegates that Governor Stevenson wanted a united party behind him when he was nominated.

It took a little time for enough states to change their votes to turn defeat into victory for the Virginia resolution, and it was there that Mr. Rayburn's handling of the gavel helped out the party peacemakers.

In New York, for example, the original vote was ninety to four against seating Virginia, after Representative Franklin D. Roosevelt Jr. argued that any other course of action would amount to surrender" by the convention to Senator Harry F. Byrd, the Virginia leader. But James A. Farley, a conservative and former National Chairman, went to work among the New York delegates, and was able to pick up three more affirmative votes for the Virginians.

The unseated South Carolinians were a little unhappy as they saw Virginia given seats that had been denied them, although both delegations had followed exactly the same tactics in clearing the way for another possible revolt against the nominees of this convention in 1952.

J. Strom Thurmond, the former South Carolina Governor who was the Dixiecrat candidate for President in 1948, wanted to know whether a seated Virginia delegation still would walk out if the convention continued to deny voting rights to South Carolina.

Governor Battle said Virginia would go the limit to try to seat South Carolina, but he would give no assurances that Virginia would walk out just because South Carolina had not been given a similar dispensation from the signed party pledge requirement.

There were evidences on the floor of some disagreement between Governor Byrnes and Senator Burnett R. Maybank of South Carolina, who was contending that this delegation also could be seated if one of them would give the convention the verbal assurances that the Democratic nominees would go on the South Carolina ballot in November. South Carolina was one of the state party organizations which used the Democratic label and symbol to choose Dixiecrat electors in 1948.

The change in the party rule to keep Virginia in the convention was acted upon squarely in the middle of the rollcall of states when names of Presidential candidates were being placed before the convention and at a time when any motion, other than one to recess or adjourn, ordinarily is not in order. But Mr. Rayburn ruled that the motion was in order and it was clear that the action that ensued had, to some degree, been prearranged with the advance knowledge of the speaker.

When Louisiana's name first was called on the roll-call with a view to determining whether it wished to make a nomination, the entire Minnesota delegation was on its feet to offer a point of order to obtain a ruling that Louisiana's delegates could not legally speak.

But though they shouted and waved the banners and finally brought them down squarely under the face of Mr. Rayburn, he could neither hear nor see the protesting Minnesotans until after Louisiana had yielded to Virginia, whose delegation chairman, Governor Battle, likewise had no legal right to address the convention at that time. But Mr. Rayburn permitted the Virginia Governor to address a parliamentary inquiry as to the rights of the three delegations in the convention.

Long Bolts Delegation

Mr. Rayburn called for an interpretation from Calvin Rawlings, chairman of the Credentials Committee, and Mr. Rawlings reported the three states had not signed the loyalty assurance, and could not therefore be seated. But, in a move to split the Louisiana delegation and any of the others where there might be dissidents, he invited any delegate individually to take the pledge and retain full privileges in the convention.

It was at this point that Senator Long deserted Governor Kennon and grabbed control of the entire Louisiana vote here after denouncing unprincipled politicians who would deny the people of their state the right to choose clearly between rival Presidential candidates.

Mr. Rayburn followed up with a formal ruling that the three delegations were out of the convention, and quickly turned to his right to recognize Lansdale G. Sasscer, a former Congressman, who argued that the assurances given by Governor Battle from the platform complied substantially with the objectives of the party regularity requirement.

Mr. Rayburn sought to rush approval of the Sasscer motion on a voice vote without any debate at all, but before he could make an announcement of the outcome of this shouting contest, he realized that there was a substantial demand for a roll-call vote that would have to be satisfied. So he accepted the roll-call request, and then allowed general debate on the issue.

July 25, 1952

STEVENSON IS NOMINATED ON THE THIRD BALLOT; PLEDGES FIGHT 'WITH ALL MY HEART AND SOUL'

By WILLIAM S. WHITE
Special to THE NEW YORK TIMES

CONVENTION BUILDING in Chicago, Saturday, July 26—Gov. Adlai E. Stevenson of Illinois was nominated early today on the third ballot for President of the United States by the thirty-first Democratic National Convention.

President Truman came here to salute him and to stand with him before the delegates.

Mr. Truman, cheerful and smiling, declared to the Convention:

"I'm telling you now Adlai Stevenson is going to win in 1952*** I am going to take my coat off and do everything I can to help him win."

Governor Stevenson told the delegates that he could never have sought such an honor, and adding, "I have asked the merciful Father of us all to let this cup pass from me. But from such dread responsibility one does not shrink in fear, in self-interest, or in false humility."

"So," he went on, quoting from the Bible, "'if this cup may not pass away from Me, except I drink it, Thy will be done'."

Huge Demonstration

Mr. Truman walked, as an enormous demonstration beat the walls of this hall, the length of the platform to greet Mr. Stevenson and take him to face the crowd.

The convention adjourned at 2:35 A.M. (3:35 A.M., New York time), to meet again at 11 A.M.

Governor Stevenson's nomination — the first genuine draft since the Republicans demanded and got James A. Garfield in 1880 — came after the withdrawal of Averell Harriman of New York had turned the great bulk of that delegation to the Stevenson standard.

Then Senator Estes Kefauver of Tennessee put over the Stevenson selection. Tennessee cast its 28 votes for the Governor, who was then a handful short of the required 615½ needed for a majority in a total of 1,230.

Senator Richard B. Russell of Georgia, after Mr. Stevenson's nomination, pledged to join in efforts for a party victory in November.

Senator Kefauver told the convention that it had been "quite apparent" that someone here had to yield. His intention, he said, had been to nominate Senator Paul H. Douglas of Illinois and Senator Douglas had intended in turn to give his favor to Governor Stevenson.

But this had been made impracticable by the Stevenson rush, Mr. Kefauver said, in effect, so he was simply retiring. It had been a good fight, he observed, "and we did the best we could."

Senator Kefauver, it appeared, was heading instead for the Vice Presidential nomination. The selection for Vice President is scheduled to be made today.

Mr. Stevenson to the end had not been a candidate.

Four aggressive aspirants—Mr. Harriman, Senator Kefauver, Senator Russell and Senator Robert S. Kerr of Oklahoma—had struggled with the Stevenson draft movement until it became apparent that there was to be no stopping it. Senator Kerr had retired early— before dinner-time last night— when his own Oklahoma delegation had left him, obviously with his consent, though he did not make it formal until nearly midnight.

Mr. Harriman's announcement of retirement from the race came after Mr. Truman, a Stevenson backer, had arrived here. The New Yorker said in a statement read to the convention by Paul E. Fitzpatrick, New York Democratic leader, that he had entered the list to sustain the records and policies of Presidents Roosevelt and Truman and to fight for a "liberal, progressive platform." All this had been accomplished, Mr. Harriman said.

Gov. Paul A. Dever of Massachusetts, who had been his state's favorite son, came out for Governor Stevenson and announced that Mr. Stevenson would be happy to accept the nomination and to stand on the party principles adopted here.

It was, at this point, actually all over. State after state began to break to the Stevenson standard— Michigan, a heretofore strong Kefauver delegation, among them.

The center of the Democratic party—standing neither with the advanced liberals—who made up most of the Kefauver and Harri-

Associated Press Wirephoto
ADLAI E. STEVENSON

man original backers nor the faction represented by the deep South —had won here in every way.

Two ballots—the first two, of yesterday—had been inconclusive, because the partisans of Senator Kefauver and Mr. Harriman, in their desperate exertions, had marshaled enough support to block any early Stevenson nomination, but not enough to hold it off very long.

Senator Kefauver had led Governor Stevenson on these two ballots—by 340 to 273 on the first and by 362½ to 324½ on the second.

Senator Russell, the South's favorite candidate, in the meantime, had done well and at this point his was the balance of power.

But there was a dinner interlude and President Truman had an opportunity to do a good deal of his private missionary work among the undecided, the hesitant, or the merely cautious.

With Mr. Harriman and Senator Kefauver out of the race and Governor Stevenson having been nominated, Senator Russell told the convention that he was going to join all the others in the party "in fighting for a great victory in November."

"I call on each and all of you to close ranks," he said, "and go forward under the banner of the Democratic party—not a party dictated to or controlled by any one segment of that party, but a party controlled by all of the American people."

Sam Rayburn of Texas, Speaker of the House of Representatives and the convention's permanent

177

chairman, clasped Senator Russell's ...

A... ... harmony here.

Orville Freeman of Minnesota called for a unanimous nomination of Governor Stevenson by acclamation. There were some "noes" whether or not seriously meant and Mr. Rayburn announced that it was by acclamation but not unanimous.

Escorted to Stand

The President did not actually enter this hall until 1:34 A. M., Central Daylight Time, or 2:34 A. M., in New York.

Mr. Rayburn escorted him to the microphone, a hand on his arm, then patted him gently, once, on the back.

In the rush by the states to Governor Stevenson Arkansas was first, thus going away from the South's candidate, Senator Russell. Before Mr. Harriman's withdrawal the position had been one in which he and Senator Kefauver's forces had had the Stevenson movement stalled At that point, Senator Russell had held the balance of power.

After the first two ballots this was the situation:

¶Governor Stevenson had the powerful support of the Political Action Committee of the Congress of Industrial Organizations and President Truman as well. The President's alternate in the Missouri delegation, Thomas J. Gavin, made Mr. Truman's support of the Illinoisan official by his vote.

¶The big minority Southern bloc that was supporting Senator Russell was standing faithfully with him so faithfully that Mr. Russell, who could not be considered a strong prospect in his own right, was in position to dominate the convention.

¶Mr. Russell's people were receptive to overtures from the forces seeking to draft Governor Stevenson. They wanted for the Georgia Senator the right to designate a Vice Presidential candidate to run with Governor Stevenson. Mr. Russell was authoritatively represented as not interested in the place for himself, preferring it to go to Senator Lyndon B. Johnson of Texas, a close friend and associate in the Senate.

¶Senator Kefauver's backers, in effect, were insisting that he be given consideration for the Vice Presidential nomination.

¶The draft-Stevenson people, therefore, were caught between two pressure—those from the Russell side and those from the Kefauver side.

The figures of the first two ballots demonstrated the committed nature of Mr. Russell's support. They were as follows:

FIRST BALLOT

Senator Kefauver	340
Mr. Stevenson	273
Senator Russell	268
Mr. Harriman	123½
Alben W. Barkley	48½
President Truman, by courtesy	6

The other ballots, in a convention total of 1,230, were scattered. Necessary to nominate are 615½ votes.

SECOND BALLOT

Senator Kefauver	362½
Mr. Stevenson	324½
Senator Russell	294
Mr. Harriman	121
Mr. Barkley	78½
Mr. Truman	6

Others scattered.

The changes occurring between the first and second ballot were in no case large or dramatic; it was rather a slow movement toward Governor Stevenson that was at work in some of the larger delegations such as Pennsylvania's and Michigan's. Some favorite-son voting still was going on and this, too, complicated matters.

Governor Stevenson instructed his alternate at the convention to vote for Mr. Harriman, an old friend with whom he had breakfast. He declined an invitation to have dinner with President Truman at the Stockyards Inn outside this hall.

The convention was brought into session at 12 noon, central daylight time (1 P. M. New York Time) for the fifth day's sessions by Speaker Rayburn. It had been in recess only since 1:55 A. M. and the dominant note was weariness as business was taken up again.

Resolution Salutes Truman

Frank E. McKinney, Chairman of the Democratic National Committee, offered a resolution saluting President Truman and Mr. Rayburn declared it unanimously approved. It said that in "seven critical years" Mr. Truman had given a "wise, fearless and stronghearted" leadership to this country and the free world.

It gave to the President the affection and best wishes of the Democratic party.

The party was more nearly united, by all visible signs, than it had been in twelve years or more. All the Southerners were back in their seats, with full rights of participation, after the early morning solution by which the three rebelling delegations, those of Virginia, South Carolina and Louisiana, had been permitted to remain even though they had refused formally to sign a new party loyalty pledge.

They had given "substantial" oral commitments to this effect; the convention accepted that as enough in what was a northern retreat for fear of a Southern bolt in the election this fall.

July 26, 1952

TEXAS DEMOCRATS BACK EISENHOWER, SCORE 'TRUMANISM'

Formally Nominate Stevenson Under 'Loyalty Pledge,' Then Bid All Aid Republicans

SPURN ANY 'DUAL TICKET'

Repudiate National Platform —Shivers Assails Trend Toward 'Socialism'

By GLADWIN HILL

Special to THE NEW YORK TIMES.

AMARILLO, Tex., Sept. 9—A wave of anti-Administration sentiment, gathering momentum in Texas for more than a decade, came to a head today when the state's traditionally dominant Democratic party formally endorsed the Presidential ticket of the Republicans.

The Democratic State Convention, after a lively factional dispute, went through the motions of placing the party's national candidates, Gov. Adlai E. Stevenson and Senator John Sparkman, at the head of the ticket in the November election.

But then the Democratic delegates turned right around, nearly 2,000-strong, and by an overwhelming voice vote declared their real sympathies to be with Gen. Dwight D. Eisenhower and Senator Richard M. Nixon.

They urged the Texas Democrats not only to jump the traditional party line and vote for the Republican national candidates, but also to work for their election.

Gov. Allan Shivers, leader of the principal anti-Administration and pro-Eisenhower faction in the party, and the convention keynoter, assured the Democrats that their party standing would not be jeopardized by such action. And, in an all-inclusive resolution of revolt, the delegates urged pro-Stevenson Democrats to "reconsider their actions and actively support Eisenhower and Nixon" to end the rule of "Trumanism."

Their action was accompanied by the most scathing denunciation and repudiation of the national party's and the Administration's platform and policies to emanate from any Democratic quarter in the present campaign.

Stevenson Stirred Resentment

The Texas antagonism to the Administration and its November ticket—brewing for more than a decade and manifested in the "Texas regular" and States Rights revolts of the 1944 and 1948 Presidential elections—was capped by resentment at the Illinois Governor's declaration Aug. 23 favoring Federal rather than state claims on Texas' coastal oil lands.

It was informally conceded by some key party figures that the convention sentiment probably was a somewhat exaggerated reflection of the feelings of Texas Democrats generally, but they contended they were far from a minority voice.

The convention was, in its composition, an outgrowth of the ardently States Rights Texas delegation led by Governor Shivers, which was finally seated at the Democratic National Convention in July over the protests of a pro-Administration "loyalist" slate.

Texas has twenty-four electoral votes, the sixth largest state bloc and nearly 10 per cent of the 266 votes needed to win the Presidency. In the 1948 Presidential election, its vote was divided 66.4 per cent Democratic, 24.4 Republican and 9.2 per cent States Rights.

The extreme pro-Eisenhower wing of the party had sought before the convention to achieve the nomination of the Republican national candidates to the exclusion of Governor Stevenson and Senator Sparkman.

This was opposed by the Shivers-led moderates as virtual "disenfranchisement" of pro-Stevenson Texans and a likely political boomerang.

They had explored instead the possibility of putting on the ballot by convention action a "dual ticket" with Governor Stevenson and Senator Sparkman labeled "National Democratic party" candidates and General Eisenhower and Senator Nixon "Texas Democratic party" candidates. But they finally discarded the maneuver as legally dubious.

Governor Shivers spoke against it in his keynote speech and recommended the formal nomination of the Democratic candidates, as distasteful as it might be, as the only "moral" course.

In opposition to this, the extremists today proposed the dual-ticket maneuver, insisting there was no evidence of its not being legal.

A debate, limited by agreement to an hour, was held on the issue. This produced the paradoxical spectacle of "moderates" from the Shivers faction, wearing conspicuous "Ike" pins, pleading with the convention to nominate Governor Stevenson and Senator Sparkman.

Chicago Pledge Cited

A roll-call vote on the issue of the dual ticket versus Stevenson-Sparkman nomination was half way through the roster of Texas' 254 counties, with the moderate view prevailing by more than two to one, when the extremists withdrew their amendment advancing the dual ticket proposal.

The ensuing resolution stated that the Stevenson - Sparkman nomination was being executed "because of the pledge given at the Chicago convention and the provision of the present Texas election code, and to give such Democrats as desire to do so an opportunity to vote for Stevenson and Sparkman."

The pledge referred to was the agreement joined in by the Texas delegation at the party's National

Convention in July to do everything possible to assure the national candidates places on the state ballots.

However, the resolution continued, "it is the recommendation of the convention that every Democrat in Texas vote and work for the election of Dwight D. Eisenhower for President and (Senator) Richard Nixon for Vice President * * *.

"We urge all Democrats who have pledged support to Stevenson and Sparkman to reconsider their actions and actively support Eisenhower and Nixon."

To lure Democratic Eisenhower votes, Texas Republicans at their recent convention adopted as their own the entire Democratic slate of state candidates.

Shivers Is Cheered

Most of those who attended the convention, which met in Amarillo's Municipal Auditorium this morning, were delegates. The 1,277 convention votes theoretically were allocated one to a delegate, but a number of counties sent oversize delegations and fractionalized their vote quotas.

The offshore oil question cropped up immediately—to a burst of laughter from the house—in a jocular reference by J. E. Wheat, state Democratic chairman, in his introductory remarks. Extolling Teaxs and the Panhandle district, where the convention was being held, he said the people were bent against anyone's taking it away under the offshore land doctrine.

of paramount Federal rights.

Governor Shivers was interrupted by applause and cheers twenty times during his fifteen-minute talk.

A loud outburst of approval greeted his declaration that "these things we have been fighting against are rolled up in a single package and plainly labeled 'Trumanism.' I want to see an end of Trumanism in this nation, and, thank God, I think the majority of the people of Texas feel the same way about it."

His announcement that no legal way had been found to have a dual Democratic ticket, with columns for both Governor Stevenson and General Eisenhower, evoked brief applause that quickly was drowned out by a chorus of "boos."

Governor Urges Fair Play

Mixed cheers and boos likewise greeted his recommendation that as "the true course of political morality" and fair play to the Texas electorate, the names of Governor Stevenson and Senator Sparkman should be placed on the Democratic ticket.

But the delegates voiced unequivocal and vociferous approval (in which many voices of pro-Stevenson "loyalists" were inaudible) when he declared that he personally would not support the Democratic national candidates, and urged the convention to disclaim any endorsement of the candidates or their platform.

Governor Shivers, who headed the conservative Texas delegation that was seated at the Democratic National Convention over the protests of a rival pro-administration "loyalist" group, made no reference to the "loyalty pledge" he had taken there to do his best to put the party's national candidates on the state ballot.

He said that putting the national candidates on the ballot was "the course which, in my opinion, is required by the laws of the state of Texas," and that "any other course would repudiate the principle of majority rule to which we are committed and disenfranchise the voters we are chosen to represent."

"I come before you today," he said, "as one who has fought as hard as he knows how against a trend in our Federal Government that is leading us toward statism or socialism.

Corruption Denounced

"I have done my best to make the voice of Texas heard against corruption, ineptness and inefficiency in high places; against infiltration of Communists into high government positions; against an unstable and stalemated foreign policy * * * against an increasing taxing and spending policy * * * against a new and dangerous doctrine of paramount rights under which, if you please, this government can take the property of individuals and states without just compensation as guaranted under the Constitution."

Of the 9,000 Texans who had responded to his solicitation of opinion on the nomination question

(and who, it was previously reported, favored General Eisenhower by more than a six to one ratio) about 30 per cent wanted an opportunity to vote for General Eisenhower on the Democratic ticket—the method he regretfully found infeasible—the Governor said.

"In this critical hour of decision, our just resentment at platform provisions and expressed views of the nominees of the Democratic National Convention should not and must not stampede us into following any course that is not right, lawful and sound," the Governor continued. "It is vital to the future welfare of the Democratic party in Texas that we at this time of all times follow a path beyond suspicion and above repoach."

Attorney General Price Daniel, Senate nominee who has been a leading legal antagonist of the Government on the offshore oil case, seconded the Governor's sentiments and, to exuberant whooping, went a bit further. He suggested that legislation could be passed to make a dual ticket feasible in future exigencies.

Wright Morrow, Democratic National Committeeman, while maintaining his hands-off position in the Stevenson-Eisenhower nomination squabble, denounced the United States Supreme Court's offshore lands decision. He called it as "alien to the jurisprudence of this country as if it canfe from Hitler's Germany."

September 10, 1952

NIXON LEAVES FATE TO G.O.P. CHIEFS

'I'M NOT A QUITTER'

Senator Says He'll Let Republican National Committee Decide

HE REVIEWS HIS FINANCES

Accepts Bid to Meet General— Cites Legal Opinions on Use of $18,235 Fund

By GLADWIN HILL
Special to THE NEW YORK TIMES.

LOS ANGELES, Sept. 23—Senator Richard M. Nixon, in a nation-wide television and radio broadcast tonight, defended his $18,235 "supplementary expenditures" fund as legally and morally beyond reproach.

He laid before the Republican National Committee and the American people the question of whether

he should remain on the Republican party's November election ticket as the candidate for Vice President.

Rising, near the end of his talk, from the desk at which he had sat, Senator Nixon urged his auditors to "wire and write" the Republican National Committee whether they thought his explanation of the circumstances surrounding the fund was adequate.

"I know that you wonder whether or not I am going to stay on the Republican ticket or resign," he said. "I don't believe that I ought to quit, because I'm not a quitter * * *

Decision 'Not Mine'

"But the decision, my friends, is not mine. I would do nothing that would harm the possibilities of Dwight Eisenhower to become President of the United States; and for that reason I am submitting to the Republican National Committee tonight, through this television broadcast, the decision which it is theirs to make. * * *.

"Wire and write the Republican National Committee whether you think I should stay or whether I should get off; and whatever their decision is, I will abide by it."

Later he accepted an invitation from General Eisenhower for a conference.

In a half-hour talk that was partly personal, including a frank exposition of his finances, and partly an appeal for support of the Republican ticket such as he has been making in his current whistle-stop tour, the Senator declared of the Southern California supporters' fund disclosed last week:

"I say that it was morally wrong if any of that $18,000 went to Senator Nixon for my personal use.

"I say that it was morally wrong if it was secretly given and secretly handled.

"And I say that it was morally wrong if any of the contributors got special favors for the contributions that they made."

But he declared that, on all three points, the factual answer was negative.

Speaks With Assurance

The candidate, clad in a gray suit and a dark tie, delivered his address in a Hollywood radio-television studio—from which the public was excluded—with composure and assurance. His wife, Patricia, was seated close to him, and he

made frequent references to her in detailing his career.

His talk also was peppered with barbed references to the Democratic opposition.

Referring to an Illinois political fund with which Gov. Adlai E. Stevenson, Democratic Presidential nominee, has been linked, Senator Nixon, while stipulating that he did not "condemn" this, suggested that both Mr. Stevenson and his running mate, Senator John J. Sparkman of Alabama, should "come before the American people" and report on their incomes.

"If they don't," he said, "it will be an admission that they have something to hide."

In support of his position, he cited two independent reports he had prepared, one on his finances and one on the legal aspects of the "supplementary expenditures" fund, for the information of Gov. Sherman Adams of New Hampshire, campaign executive of General Eisenhower, the Senator's running-mate.

The full texts of the two reports, one by Price, Waterhouse & Company, national accounting firm, and the other by Gibson, Dunn & Crutcher, Los Angeles law firm, in the form of letters to Governor Adams, were distributed by his press staff simultaneously with the broadcast.

The Senator read verbatim the conclusion of the law firm's report, which followed a half-dozen closely typed pages of legal references and citations. It said:

"It is our conclusion that Senator Nixon did not obtain any financial gain from the collection and disbursement of the fund * * * that Senator Nixon did not violate any Federal or state law by reason of the operation of the fund, and that neither the portion paid * * * directly to third persons nor the portion to Senator Nixon to reimburse him for designated office expenses constituted income to the Senator which was either reportable or taxable as income under applicable tax laws."

The Legal Report

The legal report said that in the correspondence files of the fund "we have found nothing which indicated, either expressly or by implication, that the contributors expected or received any services or assistance from Senator Nixon."

Citing Title 18 of the United States Code, 1914, making it an offense to give or for a Federal official employe to receive, "any salary" other than governmental salary, the report commented:

"Even if it be assumed that a United States Senator is a Government official or employe under this section, the section is inapplicable to the payments made to or from the D. and C. Smith fund because none of such payments constituted a salary received by Senator Nixon."

The report then cited a 1922 ruling by the Attorney General of the United States that acceptance of travel expenses from "third parties" by Government officials did not constitute "salary" under the prohibition.

The report cited several statutes against Federal legislators receiv-

ing gratuities to influence legislation, and added "there is no evidence that Senator Nixon assisted any contributors in the prosecution of any claim."

On the tax question, the report cited several court decisions to the effect that since the Senator had not performed nor was expected to perform services for the contributions, "it is our conclusion that the amounts contributed do not constitute income to the Senator under applicable Federal or state income tax laws."

In his resumé of personal finances, the candidate said that at the time of his first Congressional campaign in 1946, after his discharge from war service in the Navy, the lifetime savings of both him and his wife totaled less than $10,000, in government bonds.

He said that, aside from his Federal salaries and allowances, his only income since had been $1,600 in back payments from his suburban Whittier law firm, with which he had severed connections, $4,500 in family inheritances, and $1,600 a year from paid nonpolitical talks.

The family's current assets, he continued, consisted of a $41,000 house in Washington—on which he owed $20,000—a $13,000 house in Whittier—on which he owed $3,000; $4,000 in life insurance, his expiring G. I. insurance policy; furniture and a 1950 Oldsmobile.

Their debts, he continued, in addition to the mortgages, were a $4,500 loan from the Riggs National Bank in Washington and a $3,500 loan from his parents.

Before the broadcast, Representative Joseph W. Martin Jr. of Massachusetts, Republican floor leader on a speech-making tour in Southern California, telegraphed Senator Nixon:

"Keep your chin up. I and all my associates are standing by you to the limit. We know that when you go on the air tonight you will

win the election in a single broadcast."

The speech was delivered in the National Broadcasting Company's television studio in the El Capitan Theatre in Hollywood.

Original plans were for the Senator to speak from the main studios of the National Broadcasting Company a few blocks away, but the change was made, a campaign aide said, because of better lighting facilities in the theatre, where many large television shows have been staged.

The broadcast was carried on N. B. C.'s national television network and on the Columbia and Mutual Broadcasting Systems' radio networks. The cost, about $75,000, was paid by the Republican National Committee and the Republican Senate and House Campaign Committees.

The preparation of the speech occupied most of the Senator's waking hours during the twenty-seven-hour period from his arrival at the Ambassador Hotel yesterday until his television appearance.

He flew to Los Angeles in his chartered DC-6 from Portland, Ore., interrupting midway a ten-day campaign tour by train and plane of eleven Western and Southern states.

At dinner time yesterday, the candidate took about an hour out for a swim in the hotel's pool with his campaign assistant, William Rogers, Washington lawyer, and immediately afterward returned to his and Mrs. Nixon's three-room suite on the hotel's fifth floor.

They had their meals in the suite.

Aides Help Preparation

Senator Nixon had prepared his remarks in detail. In this, he was assisted by his campaign manager, Murray Chotiner, Los Angeles lawyer; James E. Bassett Jr., his press secretary; Mr. Rogers; and his confidant, Representative Patrick

J. Hillings, his successor in the House from his home district of Whittier, a Los Angeles suburb.

His preoccupation with the talk precluded his taking personal cognizance, at least publicly, of a published report that his office facilities in Washington had been used by Mr. Smith in connection with litigation of a $500,000 tax case. The case involved a Smith family property, the Red River Lumber Company, in Northern California.

Asked about the report, Mr. Bassett at midday issued a statement:

"The Senator himself is unavailable for comment, since he is engaged in preparing his important talk for tonight. However, we can reiterate what the Senator already made abundantly clear — he has never given any special favors either as Congressman or as Senator for special consideration."

Mr. Nixon was first elected to the House of Representatives in 1946, and to the Senate in 1950. He defeated Representative Helen Gahagan Douglas for the seat previously held by Senator Sheridan Downey.

Speech Is Transcribed

In the absence of an advance text of Senator Nixon's talk, his staff arranged for a battery of stenographers to transcribe his words from a television screen in an improvised press room off the Ambassador's ground-floor concourse, so that an "official" text could be distributed.

The Senator's party occupied thirty-two rooms on the Ambassador's fifth floor. Robert Hamilton, tour "security" officer, stood guard outside the Senator's suite.

While most of the Senator's staff were closeted with him throughout the day, virtually precluding communication between the candidate and the press, a definitely optimistic atmosphere had pervaded his temporary headquarters.

September 24, 1952

EISENHOWER CALLS NIXON VINDICATED; COMMITTEE VOTES TO RETAIN NOMINEE

CANDIDATES MEET

Airport Greeting Warm— General Calls Senator a 'Man of Honor'

TICKET HARMONY ASSURED

By JAMES RESTON
Special to THE NEW YORK TIMES.

WHEELING, W. Va., Sept. 24— Gen. Dwight D. Eisenhower said tonight that his Vice Presidential running mate, Senator Richard M.

Nixon of California, had been "completely vindicated" of charges in connection with a privately raised expense fund.

Speaking before a cheering and enthusiastic crowd here, the Republican Presidential nominee announced that the 107 members of the Republican National Committee who could be reached had all voted for retaining Mr. Nixon on the ticket. There are 138 members on the full committee.

General Eisenhower declared he believed Senator Nixon "had been subjected to an unfair and vicious attack."

"He is not only completely vindicated as a man of honor but, as far as I am concerned, he stands higher than ever before," said the general.

Thus it was plain that, although there had been no official statement sealing the California Senator's place on the ticket, the general's statement taken with the report on the national committee, made it certain that Mr. Nixon would remain the Republican party's Vice Presidential nominee.

'A Man of Honor'

General Eisenhower's remarks were:

"Ladies and gentlemen, my colleague in this political campaign has been subject to a very unfair and vicious attack. So far as I am concerned, he has not only vindicated himself, but I feel that he has acted as a man of courage and honor and so far as I am concerned, stands higher than ever before.

"I am going to ask Senator Nixon to speak a few words to you this evening, but before he comes to this podium, let me read to you two messages. The first one is a tribute. This is a telegram to me:

"'Dear General: I am trusting that the absolute truth may come out concerning this attack on Richard and when it does I am sure you will be guided right in your decision to place implicit faith in his integrity and honesty. Best wishes from one who has known Richard longer than anyone else. His mother.'

"Now, as I waited on him at the plane this evening, I received a telegram from the Republican National Committee signed by the chairman. It reads:

" 'This is to advise you that as of 9:00 this evening, 107 of the 138 members of the Republican National Committee who could be reached, either by telephone or telegram, have been asked for their reaction to the Senator's suggestion that the committee decide if it wants him to stay on the Republican ticket as the Vice Presidential candidate.

" 'I am proud to inform you that the results were 107 to 0 in support of Senator Nixon.

" 'The comment accompanying their unanimous response was overwhelmingly enthusiastic. Their telegrams reflected a deep conviction that Richard M. Nixon not only deserved the support of every American, but is worthy of the highest public trust.

" 'As a member of the Republican National Committee, it gave me great satisfaction to join with my colleagues in this stirring tribute to a truly great American who walked unafraid through the valley of despair and emerged unscathed and unbowed.

" 'Let there be no doubt about it, America has taken Dick Nixon to its heart. Every Republican is proud to have him on the ticket. (Signed) Arthur E. Summerfield, Chairman Republican National Committee.' "

The general met the Senator at 10 o'clock when his special plane arrived from the West. A crowd of about 3,000 was on hand at the airport when the Republican Presidential nominee reached the field.

The general went aboard the plane and stayed for a couple of minutes, then reappeared and shook hands warmly with Mr. Nixon for the photographers.

The pair had a chance to visit together during the twenty-minute drive from the airport to the City Island Stadium, where about 5,000 were gathered to meet him.

Senator Nixon, who flew her from Montana, listened to the general's brief statement and then, in a short speech said:

"I want you to know that this is probably the greatest moment of my life. The man whom I think will make the best President we have had in many, many years has stood before this audience and has said, 'We are going to fight for the principles in which all Americans have believed.' "

Senator Nixon criticized Gov. Adlai E. Stevenson of Illinois, the Democratic nominee, for refusing to disclose the names of the men who contributed to and benefited from the Illinois fund raised to encourage good men to remain in the Illinois Government.

If the Governor insisted on this position, he said, it would prove he had something to hide and it would cost him the election.

Crowds Cheer Nixon

The vindication meeting was held after General Eisenhower had toured the Ohio River Valley from Portsmouth, Ohio, to Wheeling. During the day he had concrete evidence that the Nixon incident, which three days ago looked like a serious handicap to the Republican ticket, had actually increased the party's popularity.

The crowds today were larger, considering the size of the towns, than at any time since the start of the twelve-day tour of the Mid-

Associated Press Wirephoto

THEY "STAND TOGETHER": Gen. Dwight D. Eisenhower and his running mate, Senator Richard M. Nixon, left, respond to cheers of crowd that greeted them after they met last night in Senator Nixon's plane at airport in Wheeling, W. Va.

dle West and border states. The people were more boisterous in their applause, and every mention of Senator Nixon brought roaring applause.

Senator Nixon was completely at his ease when General Eisenhower called on him to address the crowd. He started by saying that there were two times in his life when he was prouder to be an American than at any other time.

The first time, he said, was when General Eisenhower was hailed in a great ticker-tape parade after VE-Day and the Senator, just back from the South Pacific, watched the general ride by from Navy Headquarters on Church Street in New York.

"The other time when I think when I have had this feeling most deeply," the young Senator said, "was today."

Mr. Nixon said that after his nation-wide television broadcast last night, in which he explained how he had received an $18,235 expense fund from his followers in California and what he had done with it, his train stopped today at Denver, Colo., and there and in Wheeling he had an exciting experience.

"As we went through these places and saw the faces we heard them say both to Pat [his wife] and to me: 'Keep it up, keep fighting, we believe in you.' "

Mr. Nixon said that this made him realize that all you have to do in this country is to tell the people the truth and not try to hide anything from them.

Senator Nixon had praised General Eisenhower for the way he had handled the case. A lesser man, he said, would have treated the charges merely as a "smear" and would have refused to listen to the evidence about them.

Fortunately, the Senator declared, General Eisenhower had not done that.

"There has been too much of that in the present Administration * * * to much of this business of covering * * * clamming up whenever charges are made against those in high places," he said.

The Senator said that if General Eisenhower would do that for him, "just think what he is going to do when he becomes President—it is going to be the cleanest, the most honest Administration this country has ever had."

A great deal of the Senator's speech was a eulogy of General Eisenhower and the general's wife.

"What I want to tell you folks," he said in conclusion, "and this comes from the depths of a man's heart: This man Eisenhower is a great American and America needs him * * * So remember this folks: What is good for America, that is what Eisenhower stands for. And

what is good for America, believe me, is good for you."

In his speech here this evening General Eisenhower criticized those who had condemned him for trying to unify the divergent elements in the Republican party.

He said that in Europe, where he had served as Supreme Commander of the North Atlantic Treaty Organization, there had been a tendency for minorities within political parties to break away and form competitive splinter parties.

"This splinter-party system of Europe is what the Democrats recommend for us Republicans," he continued. "They most generously advise me which Senators I should work with and which I should disown. Just what kind of people do these Administration Democrats think we are?

"To hear them talk you would think that the Republican party was something that I invented and they own—that they can dictate to me a course of action and Republican candidates will fall in line. Well, let us be thankful that Republicans think for themselves."

For Tolerance in Party

It was the expectation of the founding fathers, the general observed, that political leaders would bring men of different points of view into a workable combination for the good of all. He added that in his judgment membership in the Republican party did not necessarily mean mutual agreement or approval other than on basic objectives and principles.

This line of reasoning, which the general is expected to develop in greater detail in a major speech at Baltimore tomorrow night, was directed at those who had criticized him because he had announced his support of all Republican candidates for Congress, including Senators Joseph R. McCarthy of Wisconsin and William E. Jenner of Indiana and others who had opposed policies favored by General Eisenhower.

He said there was general agreement within the Republican party:

¶To seek a just and lasting peace for the United States and the rest of the free world. He added that it was essential that the nation be strong in order to achieve peace.

¶To maintain prosperity in America but to do so without war.

¶To achieve a true equality of opportunity for all men in America. "I have no patience with the idea of second class citizenship," he added.

¶To seek in the United States "a government close to the people and responsive to their needs."

The atmosphere on the campaign train was different today than it had been heretofore. At the beginning of the week it seemed to the Eisenhower supporters on board that Senator Nixon was trapped behind his own goal line and the spectators on the Eisenhower side were gloomy and silent.

But, as sometimes happens in football and politics, the man with the ball suddenly got loose and now seems to be racing down the sidelines, to the astonishment of many and the cheers of the multitude.

The change was manifest in many ways. The general was visibly more confident. The farther the train traveled, the broader became his Kansas accent, the more he dropped into the vernacular, the more he talked about "Dick Nixon," the happier he looked.

At every mention of Senator Nixon the crowds whooped with delight. At every stop, stacks of telegrams addressed to "Ike" and "the Eisenhower train" were heaved aboard. There were so many of them that they were not even counted, let alone read.

Long before the general met his running mate, it was obvious that he had made up his mind.

Last night in Cleveland, he withheld his decision and indicated that he would go over the facts in greater detail after he had talked with Senator Nixon before making up his mind, but he did not sound very juridical or hesitant at the stops this morning.

At Point Pleasant, W. Va., where he was introduced as "here's the fighting son-of-a-gun Ike Eisenhower". The general appealed to the crowd not to send him any more telegrams.

Previously, General Eisenhower

had appeared worried about the criticism of Senator Nixon's actions, especially since much of it had come from newspapers supporting his candidacy.

Indeed, he had had two private meetings with reporters on the train in which he had indicated his opposition to the idea of private expense funds. But after last night's television talk by Senator Nixon and this morning's reaction to it he left no doubt that he now felt that he had a political asset on his hands.

After Point Pleasant, though the crowds kept appearing at the

stations along the way, the train didn't even slow down at Ravenswood, W. Va. There must have been 2,000 persons, accompanied by a scarlet coated high school band, along the track waving and crying, "We want Ike!" but by that time he was already behind schedule and kept rolling.

Tomorrow, General Eisenhower continues his tour of the border states. He will be in West Virginia in the morning, and will tour Maryland in the afternoon, with his major speech scheduled for Baltimore tomorrow night.

September 25, 1952

EISENHOWER SCORES PRESIDENT ON REDS; SUPPORTS M'CARTHY

In Tour of Wisconsin, General Asserts He Backs Senator's Aims Not His Methods

DENOUNCES 'VIGILANTISM'

Says Administration Tolerated Penetration by Communists —Asks Fight on 'Treason'

By W. H. LAWRENCE
Special to The New York Times.

MILWAUKEE, Oct. 3—Gen. Dwight D. Eisenhower today coupled a call for the re-election of Senator Joseph R. McCarthy, Wisconsin Republican, with a fierce attack upon Democratic Administrations for tolerating Communist penetration of the Government and "treason itself."

He told a Green Bay, Wis., audience this morning that the purposes Senator McCarthy and he had "of ridding this Government of the incompetents, the dishonest and above all the subversive and the disloyal were one and the same" and that they differed only over "methods."

And tonight, in a nation-wide broadcast, he said the future of the country belonged to courageous men and not to "those who have sneered at the warnings of men trying to drive Communists from high places—but who themselves have never had the sense or the stamina to take after the Communists themselves."

Omits Defense of Marshall

The Republican Presidential nominee warned, however, that "we would have nothing left to defend

if we allowed ourselves to be swept into any spirit of violent vigilantism" and that we must, therefore, respect freedom in combating communism.

While he significantly failed to demonstrate any great enthusiasm at having Senator McCarthy aboard his special campaign train, General Eisenhower did bow to the Wisconsin Senator's urging and eliminate from his Milwaukee speech tonight a defense of his old friend and chief, General of the Army George C. Marshall, who has been one of Senator McCarthy's targets.

General Eisenhower informed Senator McCarthy at their Peoria, Ill., conference last night that he intended to include in his denunciation of communism tonight a defense of General Marshall from some of the attacks made upon him.

'Whole Decades Poisoned'

Senator McCarthy, it was said, told the Republican nominee that he had no particular objection to General Eisenhower's saying anything that he wished to say, but that he believed a defense of General Marshall probably could be made better before another audience.

And tonight in Milwaukee, General Eisenhower said that a national tolerance of communism as a credo that believed in "economic democracy" had "poisoned two whole decades of our national life" and insinuated itself into our schools, our public forums, some of our news channels, some of our labor unions "and—most terrifyingly—into our Government itself."

"What did this penetration into government mean?" the general said, continuing:

"It meant contamination in some degree of virtually every department, every agency, every bureau, every section of our Government. It meant a Government by men whose very brains were confused by the opiate of this deceit.

"These men were advisers in a foreign policy that—on one side of the world—weakly bowed before the triumph in China of Com-

munists hailed as 'agrarian reformers.' On the other side of the world this policy condoned the surrender of whole nations to an implacable enemy whose appetite for conquest sharpened with every victory.

"This penetration meant a domestic policy whose tone was set by men who sneered and scoffed at warnings of the enemy infiltrating our most secret counsels.

"It meant—in its most ugly triumph—treason itself."

McCarthy Is Heckled

Speaking to the crowd of 8,500, which only partially filled the 13,700-seat Milwaukee arena, before General Eisenhower arrived, Senator McCarthy thanked the Wisconsin voters for his overwhelming Sept. 9 primary victory.

There were a few hecklers in the crowd, and Senator McCarthy was interrupted by other members of the audience shouting, "Throw them out." He quieted the audience by saying "Don't worry about one or two troublemakers in the crowd—I'm used to troublemakers."

General Eisenhower was introduced in Milwaukee by Gov. Walter Kohler. Sitting on the platform was Thomas E. Coleman, Madison industrialist and floor manager for Senator Robert A. Taft at the Chicago convention, who insisted that he had really retired from politics. He was aboard the Eisenhower special in Michigan on Wednesday and during the Wisconsin stops today.

Derides 'Silly Game' Charge

Without mentioning him by name, General Eisenhower sharply criticized Gov. Adlai E. Stevenson of Illinois, the Democratic Presidential nominee, for allegedly minimizing the Communist threat. Referring to a recent message by Governor Stevenson to the Veterans of Foreign Wars' convention in Los Angeles, he said "an Administration Democrat grandly declared that Communists in our national life were 'not very important' and that we should not waste time chasing 'phantoms.'"

He also asserted "the same man dismissed the quest for Communists in our Government as a kind of silly game being played in the bureau of wildlife and fisheries."

"Such comedy touches," General Eisenhower said, "do little to relieve the tragic knowledge that we have been for years the gullible

victims of Communist espionage experts. These experts in treason have plundered us of secrets involving our highest diplomatic decisions, our atomic research. Tragically, we do not know how much more our security may have been jeopardized."

The problems of combating communism and the exact manner in which he should urge Senator McCarthy's re-election were very much on General Eisenhower's mind as he stumped through Wisconsin today in quest of its twelve electoral votes that went Democratic in 1948. His five rear-platform appearances drew crowds totaling about 20,000 before he reached Milwaukee.

But he deviated at one stop—at Neenah—and held out the possibility that a Republican Administration might reduce over-all taxes paid by citizens by as much as 55 per cent. He said that "National Tax Freedom Day" now fell on May 19, because the average family worked from Jan. 1 up until that date "for the Government" and that "none of the money" earned in that period went into its own pocket or for its own maintenance.

Calling for the election of a Republican President and Congress he said that "when you get that kind of a Government, you will begin to push National Tax Freedom Day back toward the first of the year."

"We will get it back into March and we will get it back into February and back into a decent place," General Eisenhower said.

The "McCarthy problem" began for the Eisenhower staff last night in Peoria, when Senator McCarthy turned up at the last stop in Illinois along with Governor Kohler —without, it was understood, the advance knowledge of General Eisenhower.

'Differences' Are Cited

The general and Senator McCarthy had a long talk, and afterward the Wisconsin Republican confined his remarks to the statement that it had been "very very pleasant."

Senator McCarthy and Governor Kohler boarded the Eisenhower "Look-Ahead-Neighbor" special train to ride into Wisconsin with General Eisenhower, and the general's assistants made no secret of their problem as to how the McCarthy endorsement could be handled without alienating important Eisenhower supporters who would have liked him to repudiate or ignore the Wisconsin Senator.

Attempts by photographers to get General Eisenhower to pose in the rear car with Senator McCarthy were turned down.

At the first stop this morning in Green Bay, Senator McCarthy was introduced amid loud cheers from the crowd of about 3,000 persons and left the rear platform before General Eisenhower appeared.

It was at that stop that General Eisenhower made his only direct personal call for Senator McCarthy's re-election.

He said that the "positive program" he was offering to the United States required "strong party strength," and for that reason he was calling in every state for the election of the entire Republican ticket because "they must be a part of the team if we are to accept responsibility and to be the party of performance."

"It is, of course, well known, ladies and gentlemen, to you and to many others that there have been differences of opinion, sometimes on important matters, between me and other people in the Republican party," General Eisenhower said. "Indeed, it would be a miracle if there were not.

"The differences between me and Senator McCarthy are well known to others. But what is more important, they are well known to him and to me and we have discussed them," the general added. He continued:

"I want to make one thing very clear. The purposes that he and I have of ridding this Government of the incompetents, the dishonest and above all the subversive and the disloyal are one and the same.

"Our differences, therefore, have nothing to do with the end result that we are seeking. The differences apply to method.

"This is the pledge that I make: If I am charged by you people to be the responsible head of the Executive Department, it will be my initial responsibility to see that subversion and disloyalty are kept out of the Executive Department.

"We will always appreciate and welcome Congressional investigation but we certainly will not depend upon it to unearth and show where subversion exists and then after it is shown be indifferent and complacent about rooting it out. The responsibility will rest squarely on the shoulders of the executive, and I hold that there are already ample powers in the Government to get rid of these people if the Executive Department is really concerned with doing it.

"We can do it with absolute assurance that American principles of trial by jury, of innocence until proof of guilt, are all observed, and I expect to do it. So I pledge you that it will be my responsibility to be vigilant, to keep that Executive Department clean, and I make the same pledge to the Congress of the United States."

McCarthy Introduces General

The next scheduled stop was Appleton, which is Senator McCarthy's home town, and there had been speculation all through the night as to whether Senator McCarthy would introduce the Republican nominee there.

Senator McCarthy said he was not sure whether he would make the introduction. Some Eisenhower staff members indicated that the Senator probably would, and others said that he would not. Just five minutes before the train reached Appleton, a party official said that Senator McCarthy would introduce Governor Kohler and the Governor would introduce General Eisenhower.

But when the train came to a halt before a crowd of 6,000 to 7,000 persons, it was Senator McCarthy who came bouncing out of the rear car onto the rear platform to introduce General Eisenhower as "a man who is an outstanding general, who was an outstanding administrator in Europe, and who will make an outstanding President."

Before the home town crowd General Eisenhower made no reference whatever to Senator McCarthy. He confined himself instead to saying the crowds he had seen on his campaign were determined to clean out the mess in Washington "and they are going to clean it out by sending to Washington a great team in the Senate, in the Congress, in the Executive Departments, of the finest people we can draw from this whole United States to give you honesty, integrity, fairness and friendliness to try to help you and not to boss you."

"For that purpose, you need every single man we have got on the ticket here in Wisconsin from the Governor himself through the Senate and the House," General Eisenhower added. "Please give us the whole works, and we will do the job, we promise you."

After this address, the Wisconsin Senator was asked if he was satisfied with the endorsement General Eisenhower had expressed.

Senator McCarthy said that he was satisfied with General Eisenhower's endorsement, that he was sure both of them would carry Wisconsin, and that General Eisenhower would be elected and would make "a good President."

He declined to discuss the differences between himself and General Eisenhower, saying that he would leave that up to the Republican nominee.

In his Milwaukee speech tonight, General Eisenhower said that "freedom must defend itself with courage, with care, with force and with fairness."

"To defend freedom, in short, is—first of all—to respect freedom," he continued. "That respect demands another, quite simple kind of respect—respect for the integrity of fellow citizens who enjoy their right to disagree. The right to question a man's judgment carries with it no automatic right to question his honor."

Strictest Tests Promised

But General Eisenhower went on to say that "the Bill of Rights contains no grant of privilege for a group of people to join together to destroy the Bill of Rights" and that a group like the Communist party "cannot be allowed to claim civil liberties as its privileged sanctuary from which to carry on subversion of the Government.

"At the same time, we have the right to call a spade a spade," he said. "That means, in every proved case, the right to call a Red a Red."

He said that while every political voice had a right to be heard, "let each voice be named and counted." He would require every person or organization distributing political literature through the mails to disclose both its source of funds and its membership. Every political organization, he said, should be compelled to make public its finances, membership and affiliations.

He promised to apply the strictest tests of loyalty and patriotism to Federal employes, whose employment, he said, is a privilege and "not a right."

It was announced today that General Eisenhower had changed his itinerary to permit active campaigning tomorrow in South Dakota and North Dakota, which had not been included in the original plans for this trip. He will leave his train at Duluth, Minn., tomorrow, and fly to St. Cloud, Minn., for a noontime speech, to Brookings, S. Dak., for a midafternoon speech, and into Fargo, N. Dak., for a late afternoon speech. He will reboard his train at Fargo for the long Sunday ride to the Pacific Northwest.

October 4, 1952

Morse Resigns From G.O.P.; May Hold Key Vote in Senate

Oregonian Says He Acts for Good of Country— Will Be Independent

By LAWRENCE E. DAVIES
Special to The New York Times.

PORTLAND, Ore., Oct. 24— Senator Wayne Morse of Oregon announced tonight that he was resigning from the Republican party because the tenets of Abraham Lincoln no longer held in a party "dominated by reactionaries running a captive general for the Presidency of the United States." Henceforth, he said, he would be an independent.

His announcement, made on a recording played at a meeting and dance of Volunteers for Stevenson, followed by less than a week the Senator's word that he was supporting Gov. Adlai E. Stevenson of Illinois, the Democratic nominee, for President.

This was despite the fact, he said in his speech, that he was the first member of the Senate publicly to declare himself for Gen. Dwight D. Eisenhower as a potential Republican nominee.

Near the close of a seventeen-minute recording Senator Morse, who has been a controversial figure among Oregon Republicans almost since his election to his first term in 1944, declared he always had said that "a man sitting in the Senate of the United States has no right to bolt his party and not at the same time to be willing to resign from his party."

"I consider my bolt from Eisenhower and my enthusiastic support of Adlai Stevenson as a resignation from the Republican party," he said.

He added that he would call himself an "independent Republican" because he intended "to hold fast to the tenets of the political philosophy of Abraham Lincoln."

The junior Senator said he was aware that what he was doing, which he insisted was in "the best interests of my country," might be "the beginning of the end of my political career." But that, he declared, would be "small sacrifice indeed for me to make if my stand for what I believe to be right in the campaign may have some constructive influence on the course of American politics."

Scores General's Tactics

Senator Morse charged General Eisenhower with "stooping to any tactics," with "taking support from any source no matter how reprehensible" in order to win votes, and said the American people were "beginning to get wise to him."

General Eisenhower, he asserted, was running the Presidential campaign like a military campaign, whereas the voters, he went on, knew a political campaign called for "clear expression of principles and position and a sound political philosophy." He said that Governor Stevenson was "towering above Eisenhower" with a "statesmanship that augurs well for the future of the country if he is elected on Nov. 4."

"A vote for Stevenson is a vote against reaction and a vote for statesmanship," he added.

Senator Morse included these accusations in his particulars against General Eisenhower:

¶Said he was inefficient and wasteful as head of the North Atlantic Treaty Organization's military forces.

¶Said he was guilty of playing politics with "the cause of freedom in Asia."

¶Said he had compromised with reactionary forces in the Republican party.

¶Said he had turned his back on the philosophies of Theodore Roosevelt and Gifford Pinchot in the development of natural resources and in his Western development program was playing into the hands of private interests.

Fears Third World War

Senator Morse added that he feared the election of General Eisenhower would greatly increase the chances of a third world war.

He noted that he himself was a delegate to the Republican National Convention, supporting General Eisenhower, but said his "disillusionment" started soon after the nomination. He realized then, he declared, that the General was "taking us back fifty years to the time of McKinley."

As late as Aug. 19, Mr. Morse asserted, while on a European trip, he expressed his intention by letter to do what he could to help elect the Republican nominee, for he had found "high regard" for the the General's work in England.

Then, however, the Senator went on to the continent, he related, and found there evidences of "administrative deficiency" on the part of the leadership in the North Atlantic Treaty Organization and "a tremendous waste of taxpayers' money"—waste, he said, that General Eisenhower "should have prevented or taken steps to try to prevent."

"I came back to the United States," he said, "very much in doubt as to the wisdom of putting a military man in the Presidency."

Fears Army Man as President

Senator Morse said that in his opinion a third world war could be avoided with honor, but that it was his fear that "placing a military man in the White House along with the military group he would bring in with him plus the reactionary Republicans with which he has compromised, greatly increases the chances of an all-out war under an administration by Eisenhower."

In the Asian situation Mr. Morse was especially bitter. He declared that General Eisenhower "stooped in demagogic fashion to raising false hopes in the hearts of the mothers and fathers of the boys in Korea by leaving them with the impression that if he were elected President, he would bring the American boys home from Korea and train South Koreans to fight against communistic Asiatics."

"When he did that," the Senator, charged, "he reached a new low in the political campaign."

He declared that General Eisenhower, as a military man, knew there were "definite limitations to training South Korean troops" and knew that "our military experts in the Pentagon building made it clear" that if South Korean troops were assigned to holding the lines "Chinese Communist hordes would overrun them in short order."

"When Eisenhower played politics with the cause of freedom in Asia he lost my vote," the Senator added.

According to Senator Morse, one of the main reasons why General Eisenhower was ready to accept the nomination was his belief that "the election of Taft would be disastrous to the country."

"Therefore," the Senator related, "I could not reconcile his Morningside Heights surrender with what I knew was at least his pre-convention view of Taft's political philosophy." He added:

"I cannot support a candidate who has stooped to political hypocrisy."

Senator Morse said that Governor Stevenson had a "fighting chance" for election. He saw, he said, a "tremendous swing to Stevenson" and asserted that if it continued until Nov. 4 the Illinoisan would be elected.

The Volunteers for Stevenson of whom Dave Epps of Lebanon, is executive director, had its meeting in Teamster's Hall. Radio Station KPOJ broadcast the recording locally.

October 25, 1952

EISENHOWER WINS IN A LANDSLIDE

RACE IS CONCEDED

Virginia and Florida Go to the General as Do Illinois and Ohio

SWEEP IS NATION-WIDE

Victor Calls for Unity and Thanks Governor for Pledging Support

By ARTHUR KROCK

Gen. Dwight D. Eisenhower was elected President of the United States yesterday in an electoral vote landslide and with an emphatic popular majority that probably will give his party a small margin of control in the House of Representatives but may leave the Senate as it is—forty-nine Democrats, forty-seven Republicans and one independent.

Senator Richard M. Nixon of California was elected Vice President.

The Democratic Presidential candidate, Gov. Adlai E. Steven-son of Illinois, shortly after midnight conceded his defeat by a record turnout of American voters.

At 4 A. M. today the Republican candidate had carried states with a total of 431 electors, or 165 more than the 266 required for the selection of a President. The Democratic candidate seemed sure of 69, with 31 doubtful in Kentucky, Louisiana and Tennessee.

General Eisenhower's landslide victory, both in electoral and popular votes, was nation-wide in its pattern, extending from New England—where Massachusetts and Rhode Island broke their Democratic voting habits of many years—down the Eastern seaboard to Maryland, Virginia and Florida and westward to almost every state between the coasts, including California.

General Wins Illinois

The Republican candidate took Illinois, Governor Stevenson's home state. In South Carolina, though he lost its electors on a technicality, he won a majority of the voters. And, completing the first successful Republican invasion of the States of the former Confederacy, the General carried Texas and broke the one-party system in the South.

The personal popularity that enabled him to defeat Senator Robert A. Taft of Ohio in the Republican primaries in Texas, and present him with the issue on which he defeated the Senator for the Republican nomination, crushed the regular Democratic organization of Texas that was led by Speaker Sam Rayburn of the House of Representatives and had the blessing of former Vice President John N. Garner.

The tide that bore General Eisenhower to the White House, though it did not give him a comfortable working majority in either the national House or the Senate (the Democrats may still nominally control the machinery of that branch), probably increased the number of Republican governors beyond the present twenty-five.

"My fellow citizens have made their choice and I gladly accept it," said Governor Stevenson at 1:46 A. M., Eastern standard time, and he asked all citizens to unite behind the President-elect. The defeated candidate said he had sent a telegram of congratulation to General Eisenhower.

At 2:05 A. M., from the Grand Ballroom of the Commodore Hotel, General Eisenhower said he recognized the weight of his new responsibilities and that he would not give "short weight" in their execution. He also urged "unity" and announced he had sent a telegram of thanks to the Democratic candidate for his promise of support.

The issues of the unusually vigorous campaign that was waged by the candidates of the two major parties, with President Truman advocating Governor Stevenson's election, in a speaking tour throughout the country, as an endorsement of the record of his administration and that of the late President Roosevelt, were these:

¶General Eisenhower asserted that it was "time for a change" from the twenty-year tenure of the Democrats in the White House, with control of Congress for all but two years in that period, the third longest in American history. Governor Stevenson promised to "refresh" his party and the Government and said that would be all the "change" the critical world situation justified.

¶General Eisenhower forcefully attacked revelations of official corruption in the Truman Administration and charged first negligence and then tolerance of the infiltration of Communist agents in the Government. Governor Stevenson denounced both but defended the Administration as having done its full duty in the circumstances.

¶General Eisenhower demanded a "new look" at the war in Korea and promised to make an inspection trip to the peninsula if he were elected. He charged that more South Koreans could and should have been trained to man the front lines "where our boys do not belong." Governor Stevenson and the President denounced this as a "cheap trick," and as an injury to the chances for an armistice in the Korean war.

¶Governor Stevenson and the President assailed General Eisenhower because he declined to denounce Senator Joseph R. McCarthy of Wisconsin and other Republican Senators for "character assassination" and "isolationism."

They also accused him of having "surrendered" to Senator Robert A. Taft of Ohio, whom he defeated for the Republican nomination, and of abandoning his "principles" in domestic and foreign policy thereby.

Fitzpatrick Concedes State

The great majority of the voters sustained General Eisenhower's position on all these issues. Their desire for a "change" rather than a "refreshment" of the Administration was noted by Paul E. Fitzpatrick, Democratic State Chairman of New York, when at 11 P. M. yesterday, he conceded the state to the Republicans.

This was thirteen minutes after Arthur E. Summerfield, Republican National Chairman, had asserted that General Eisenhower had been elected by a "landslide" that also carried majorities in both branches of Congress.

In states where the issues of corruption and Communist infiltration had been actively debated, the voting majority also sustained the General.

And, by the defeat for re-election in Connecticut of Senator William Benton, who has made a career of attacking Senator McCarthy; the re-election of Mr. McCarthy by a huge margin in Wisconsin; and the re-election of Senator William E. Jenner of Indiana, the voting majority indicated approval of the objectives of what the Democrats and independents have assailed as McCarthyism.

Effect of Korea Issue

There is no way of estimating the effect on yesterday's voters of the angry argument over the Korean war between the two Presidential candidates, with President Truman rising to heights of bitterness hitherto unscaled even by him in his denunciation of General Eisenhower's criticism of the Administration's pre-war policies in the Far East and the General's promise to go to the scene of the war, if elected.

But ever since General Eisenhower made the promise, it had been evident that the Democrats were alarmed about its vote-getting potential for the Republican candidate. Therefore, it is reasonable to conclude that on this issue, which became the central one of the final phase of the campaign, the voting majority preferred the position taken by General Eisenhower.

On the over-all issue of the record of the Roosevelt-Truman Administrations, including the New Deal and Fair Deal programs, that the President insisted was "all Stevenson had to run on," the result of the election was taken by the Republicans as repudiation of Mr. Truman.

This undoubtedly will be the basis of the proposals to Congress that President-elect Eisenhower will make and that Congress will sustain, if it is controlled by the Republicans.

At midnight that control seemed possible but not certain. The Democrats lost two Senate seats to the Republicans in Connecticut—those of Mr. Benton and the late Brien McMahon—and that of Herbert R. O'Connor in Maryland.

The Republicans held the seats of Senator H. Alexander Smith of New Jersey, John W. Bricker of Ohio, and Irving M. Ives of New York, in addition to those of Messrs. McCarthy and Jenner. But final returns may disclose that the Democrats have taken the seat held by Senator Henry Cabot Lodge Jr. of Massachusetts by electing Representative John F. Kennedy to his place.

Since the Republicans must make a net gain of two to organize the Senate (that is to elect the chairman of its committees and its officers), and Senator Wayne Morse of Oregon, elected as a Republican, has resigned from the party and may vote on organization with the Democrats, the issue of party control of the Senate was in doubt and may be until Senator Morse decides on his course in that body.

The campaign just ended was unusual in many ways in addition to the fact that no retiring President ever had taken the stump with the intensity and activity Mr. Truman did in defense of his record.

The Republican and Democratic nominees both were reluctant candidates and powerful pressures had to be exerted on both before General Eisenhower would consent to seek the nomination and Governor Stevenson would agree to be drafted by his party convention.

Once nominated, however, each fought as hard as the most ambitious politician to whom a Presidential nomination has come as the consequence of unremitting efforts to acquire it.

General Eisenhower was persuaded to resign as Supreme Commander of the North Atlantic Treaty Organization by assurances that, if he agreed to accept the Republican nomination, he would be chosen by acclamation and elected easily.

Instead, he was obliged to wage a hard battle against Senator Taft that for a time split the Republican party wide open. And though it appeared at last midnight that his electoral and popular majorities would be large, the apparent strength of Mr. Stevenson was such that the General had to put everything he had into the campaign.

Governor Stevenson refused until the Democratic convention had been in session for three days to give the slightest encouragement to those who wanted to draft him.

He said and did a number of things calculated to discourage the effort, including a statement to the Illinois delegation that he was "temperamentally" and otherwise "unfit" to be President.

And, though he was the first Presidential candidate truly drafted in modern American history, the pattern was spoiled by the fact that he got delegate votes on the first two ballots in contest (though against his will and command) with Averell Harriman, Senator Estes Kefauver of Tennessee and Senator Richard B. Russell of Georgia.

Like the other reluctant candidate, however, Governor Stevenson fought as hard as he could to be elected. Beginning with a speech of acceptance that forecast a campaign on the highest level, he was soon trading blows—high ones and low ones—with General Eisenhower.

In the echelon of winners under the General the more conspicuous were:

Senator Harry F. Byrd, Democrat of Virginia, whose state endorsed his refusal to support Mr. Stevenson; Gov. Thomas E. Dewey, Republican of New York, who was among the early Eisenhower drafters and was most active in the successful campaign to carry the state; Senator McCarthy, who was made a national issue.

November 5, 1952

HOUSE AND SENATE G.O.P. BY NARROW MARGINS

PERSONAL VICTORY

General, Not the Party, Held Chief Reason for Wide Gains

WINS 442 ELECTORS

By ARTHUR KROCK

The overwhelming choice of Gen. Dwight D. Eisenhower for President and Senator Richard M. Nixon for Vice President on Tuesday by the largest outpouring of voters in American history was emphasized by late returns yesterday that accounted for all forty-eight states as the triumph of a person as contrasted with that of a political party. The verdict was clearly for a change, but primarily of national leaders.

That General Eisenhower, and not the Republican party, was the principal reason for the termination of Democratic tenure in the White House that had lasted for twenty years was made evident by the result of the contests for Congress.

The General and Senator Nixon obtained a minimum of 442 electoral votes to a maximum of 89 for the Democratic candidate, Gov. Adlai E. Stevenson of Illinois, and the popular vote as thus far tabulated was 31,862,042 for the Republican national ticket and 25,654,348 for the Democratic—a margin of 6,207,694.

But, though the history of American politics is that the victors in such a landslide carry into office with them sound working majorities in the Senate and the House of Representatives, the voters gave General Eisenhower only a tenuous majority of one in the Senate (which could be canceled if Senator Wayne Morse of Oregon, a former Republican, votes with the Democrats), and—on incomplete returns—a margin of three in the House.

A few hours after he returned to Washington from Missouri, President Truman offered to facilitate the transition of Executive power and called on the nation to unite behind the President-elect.

He invited General Eisenhower to send at once a representative who would be concerned with the budget of the next administration to acquaint himself with the details of the budget for the 1954 fiscal year that starts July 1. The budget is being completed by the officials under President Truman but will not be debated by the next Congress until General Eisenhower and Senator Nixon have assumed office.

Mr. Truman asked General Eisenhower to visit him at the White House soon for a review of problems.

The President-elect also was urged to designate as soon as possible his choices for Secretary of State and Secretary of Defense so that they, also, might familiarize themselves with the problems of these departments before they change hands.

Replies to President

Before leaving for Augusta, Ga., for a few days' rest, General Eisen-

Modern Republicans vs. the Old Guard

hower informed Mr. Truman that he would try to make arrangements in a few days to have a representative meet with the Director of the Budget.

The only national gain for the Republican party as such that is consonant with the huge endorsement of General Eisenhower's candidacy for President is represented by the fact that, in the party exchanges in the states, the twenty-five Republican Governors in office were increased to thirty and the Democratic Governors' score was reduced from twenty-three to eighteen.

In most instances Republican candidates for Congress in hotly disputed areas rode to victory on the General's coattails. This was especially evident in Indiana and Wisconsin, where Senators Joseph R. McCarthy and William E. Jenner, with whom the Republican Presidential candidate was on terms of armed and temporary neutrality at best, won by margins that suggested that with any other head of their national ticket they might have been retired.

This and other aspects of the popular vote in the states would seem to dispose of an issue that rent the Republican National Convention at Chicago in July. It was posed over whether Senator Robert A. Taft of Ohio could win if nominated; the convention decided he could not but that General Eisenhower could. Details of the voting sustain this thesis, that it was to the man and not the party that the Republicans must look for victory.

This was further supported by the capture of the electoral votes of four Southern States—Florida, Virginia, Tennessee and Texas—by General Eisenhower. Of the 128 electors in that rooted Democratic area he got 57.

The Southern vote cast for the Republican Presidential candidate was at least double that registered in 1928 for Herbert Hoover; and, in contrast with that, it was for and not merely against, as was the case when five Southern states rejected Alfred E. Smith, the Democratic nominee, on the issues

of Catholicism and prohibition.

In taking Virginia and Texas, and achieving the miracle of a popular majority in South Carolina (though he lost its electors because more than 8,000 wasted their votes on a separate set of Republican electors), General Eisenhower won the "heartland" of the former Confederacy and the states whose Democratic leaders are among the most powerful members of Congress.

Texas Leaders Divided

In Texas these leaders were sharply divided Speaker Sam Rayburn of the House of Representatives for the party ticket and Gov. Allan Shivers and Senator-elect Price Daniel against it. But in Virginia, though Gov. John S. Battle and Senator A. Willis Robertson were formally for Mr. Stevenson, the supreme head of the Democratic organization by which they rose to office—Senator Harry F. Byrd—determined the issue by announcing he could not support the Democratic nominee.

Political analysts are generally of the opinion that these results in the South could have been achieved only by General Eisenhower as the head of the Republican national ticket.

Though the prospect is for less than an effective Republican working majority in the House and the Senate, the changes wrought in the latter by the election indicate that it will even more strongly support the foreign policies to which General Eisenhower seems committed than it did the foreign policies of President Truman.

Senators Harry P. Cain of Washington and Zales N. Ecton of Montant, both Republican critics of the Administration's European program, were replaced by sympathizers with it—Representatives Henry M. Jackson and Mike Mansfield. W. Stuart Symington defeated Senator James P. Kem, another such critic, in Missouri. In the exchange of John Sherman Cooper for Senator Thomas R. Underwood in Kentucky the program favored by General Eisenhower in Europe suffered no loss.

Only in Massachusetts, where the General's pre-convention campaign manager, Senator Henry

Cabot Lodge Jr., lost his seat to Representative John F. Kennedy, did a more critical Senator in this field of policy supplant a strong supporter.

Moreover, the Senate changes add strength to the group which, like General Eisenhower, have made an issue with the Administration over its policies prior to the Korean war and the military stalemate there.

With the election of General Eisenhower and Senator Nixon, one of the longest political eras in American history comes to an end—the New Deal of President Roosevelt that merged into the Fair Deal of President Truman.

It was exceeded in the length of its party domination only twice—by the Jefferson-Jackson Democratic dynasty that endured from 1800 to 1848 and the Lincoln-Grant-Hayes-Garfield Republican period that began in 1860 and ended, temporarily, in 1884.

In these last twenty years the nation has been launched on social-economic and reform programs of a size and character not before undertaken, in which social security and "civil rights" programs have been foremost and deficit spending adopted as a means of ending the 1929-1930 depression.

The latter had not succeeded by 1939, and whether it would have or not became moot when the pre-war emergency of 1940, World War II and then the war in Korea changed the character of the national economy and ended or postponed the pace of a "recession."

But the Republicans, in every campaign since 1936, have felt obliged to promise the voters to preserve and, of course, "improve" many of the social-economic reforms and measures of the Fair Deal and the New Deal, and their winning campaign of 1952 was no exception.

On the issue of the "welfare state" the parties are close together on important details that are as antithetical to traditional Republicanism as they are to the political philosophies of Jefferson and Wilson.

Other Election Aspects

Other aspects of Tuesday's election include:

¶Among the leaders of organized labor, who were united behind the Democratic ticket and intensely active, only John L. Lewis, president of the United Mine Workers, was able to point to a victory for Governor Stevenson and the local Democratic candidates in the area of his chief influence—West Virginia. Philip Murray, head of the Congress of Industrial Organizations, saw his heavily unionized areas in Pennsylvania and Michigan fail notably to produce their expected votes for the Democrats. William Green, president of the American Federation of Labor, seemed to have had no great effect in the localities where his unions are strong, unless the almost unique increase in Democratic strength registered in Philadelphia could be credited in part to his followers. And in New York and Illinois, labor conspicuously split over the nominees.

¶McCarthyism was one of the wordiest, if not one of the most influential of the campaign issues, with the President and Governor Stevenson seeking to turn votes from General Eisenhower because he asked the Republican voters to elect to Congress the Republicans they had nominated, including the junior Senator from Wisconsin. But in sum Mr. McCarthy, though the concentrated attack on him resulted in his running well behind the national and state tickets, carried sixty-three of the seventy-one Wisconsin counties; got the above-normal majority of 142,000; and had the satisfaction of seeing his arch-foe, Senator William Benton, defeated in Connecticut, and his strong supporters, Senators Jenner and George Malone victorious in Indiana and Nevada.

Another McCarthy crony, Senator Kem, lost in Missouri, and the Wisconsin legislator had at times been aided by another loser, Senator Cain of Washington. But on balance he probably feels that McCarthyism was not the adverse Republican issue the Democrats tried to make it. And in the defeat of his fellow-party critic, Senator Lodge, Mr. McCarthy unquestionably felt no pain.

November 6, 1952

Eisenhower Victory Brings Start Of Two-Party System to the South

By WILLIAM S. WHITE

A century-old Democratic tradition in the Old South has been broken, for the first time in a fundamental sense, and there now are the beginnings at least of a two-party system below the Potomac.

Gen. Dwight D. Eisenhower, Republican President-elect, won among the eleven states of the old Confederacy a victory that was historic on more than one count. He carried Texas, Tennessee, Virginia and Florida, for a total of fifty-seven of the South's 128 electoral votes.

He lost in Alabama, Arkansas, Georgia, Louisiana, Mississippi, North Carolina and South Carolina, with a total of seventy-one electoral votes, but in some cases only by an eyelash.

He polled about double the highest popular vote ever before given a Republican candidate in the South—the 2,500,000 given in 1928 to Herbert Hoover, who defeated the Democratic Presidential candidate, the late Gov. Alfred E. Smith of New York.

Here and there the Eisenhower vote approached three times that polled by Mr. Hoover.

Moreover, General Eisenhower's

enormous personal victory has carried with it the loss to the Democrats of four Southern seats in the United States House of Representatives. And a fifth Democratic House seat is in doubt in Florida, and probably will be until Friday.

Three of these were lost in Virginia and, ironically, two of the three were seats denied to members of the Democratic organization of the ultra-conservative Senator Harry F. Byrd of that state.

To preserve that organization, against a challenge next year from anti-Byrd Democrats who will seek to seize Virginia's Governorship, was for Mr. Byrd a concern equal to his concern to do everything possible to aid General Eisenhower.

The fourth Democratic seat in Congress lost in the Eisenhower

sweep was in North Carolina, which had not sent a Republican to Congress since Mr. Hoover's break into the South.

These Democratic losses in Congress—immensely practical matters to politicians—furnished the indisputable evidence that the two-party system in principal had come to the South.

But even more important, General Eisenhower captured the most indispensable of all Solid South positions—Texas.

That state was one of the most bitterly contested, not alone for its bloc of twenty-four electoral votes, the sixth biggest in the country, but also as the economic and political heartland of all the South, the most populous, the richest by far.

And it was so contested, too, because it was in Texas that the old-line regular Democrats took their most determined stand, led by Sam Rayburn, Speaker of the House of Representatives. Mr. Rayburn became the very symbol of the "loyalist" Democrats everywhere below the Mason-Dixon Line.

On the outcome he had staked his great prestige, a prestige arising not only from the second most powerful office in the United States, the Speakership, but from his long and close association with the last two Democratic Presidents, Franklin D. Roosevelt and Harry S. Truman.

Mr. Rayburn thus stands now at the twilight of his long career—still the leader of the Democrats of the House of Representatives, but a leader who for all his exertions has failed to carry his own state for his party.

His mood as the campaign ended was both bitter and sorrowful—bitterness at what he considered an unfair concentration of Texas' financial and press power against his cause and sorrow in the knowledge that the South was about to step away from a past to which there might never be a return.

On the other hand, those Democrats who led the bolt in the South for General Eisenhower, men like Senator Byrd in Virginia and Gov. Allan Shivers in Texas, have reached new places of power in the now fragmented Southern Democratic party.

The place to be taken by those who stood rather in the middle, in a kind of hesitant and nominal advocacy of the defeated Democratic Presidential candidate, Gov. Adlai E. Stevenson of Illinois, remains somewhat equivocal.

These men, headed by Senator Richard B. Russell of Georgia, are held now in less than the highest esteem by the all-out Eisenhower Democrats. And they are, of course, held in bitterness by those who fought in vain to the end to save the South for the Stevenson ticket.

But the fundamental significance remains not in this three-way division within the old Democratic party in the South, but in the fact that the Republicans have broken into the South at last.

Mr. Hoover's victory there in 1928, though he won sixty-two electoral votes, had no real long-term meaning so far as the one-party habit was concerned. Mr. Smith lost these votes primarily because he was a Roman Catholic and secondarily because he was against Prohibition.

Again, the Dixiecrat revolt of 1948 cost President Truman thirty-nine electoral votes—but these went to a third party and not to the Republican candidate of that year, Gov. Thomas E. Dewey of New York.

Many Southern politicians blame President Truman for what has happened in the South because of what they contend was his long "extremism" in pushing the civil rights issue—an issue on which President Roosevelt never took so advanced a position.

Much recent inquiry in the South has convinced some observers, however, that the turn toward the Republicans is for more basic reasons—that it represents a movement among the dominant Southern white groups toward Republican thinking.

November 6, 1952

DEATH CALLED BLOW TO G. O. P. HARMONY

Taft Turned From President's Rival to Ally, Bridging Split Between East and Midwest

By WILLIAM S. WHITE
Special to THE NEW YORK TIMES.

WASHINGTON, July 31 — The death of Senator Robert A. Taft of Ohio has shaken the Republican party as it has not been shaken in half a lifetime. It has removed the one real bridge between the East and Midwest in the Eisenhower Administration.

The loss to the Administration—an Administration made possible only by Mr. Taft's third and final defeat for the Presidential nomination in the Republican National Convention last July—is beyond calculation.

[In Columbus, Ohio, Gov. Frank J. Lausche, a Democrat, maintained a firm silence on the appointment of a successor to Senator Taft, saying that "I simply will not discuss it—I refuse to talk about it."]

Senator Taft, a year ago General Eisenhower's great rival, had become President Eisenhower's greatest ally. At once a loyal and a guiding lieutenant, he was the only orthodox Republican who could consistently lead the orthodox to accept President Eisenhower's programs and could in turn fully interpret the orthodox to the White House.

With the departure of "Mr. Republican" has gone the last opportunity open to the President to make his tenure a genuinely Republican one. The clear prospect now is for a coalition Government so far as Congress is concerned, no matter which party is in nominal control, at least until the 1954 elections.

Mr. Taft's death, though technically reducing Republican control of the Senate to the vanished point, will not alter that control in fact for the foreseeable future.

He left a second Republican seat vacant, the other having been that of the late Senator Charles W. Tobey of New Hampshire. But when these two seats are filled with temporary appointees, a Democrat from Ohio and a Republican from New Hampshire, as it is assumed they will be, the party division will be 48 Democrats, 47 Republicans and 1 independent, Senator Wayne Morse of Oregon.

If and when a challenge comes to continued formal Republican control, Mr. Morse will vote with the Republicans. The result would be a 48-48 tie, which Vice President Richard M. Nixon would break in favor of the Republicans.

Intellectual Leader Lost

Beyond all these calculations of party strength in Congress, important as they are however, stands an even more basic consideration. This is that with Mr. Taft has died the intellectual leadership in Congress of a kind of Republican party that long antedated General Eisenhower as a political force.

While it is commonly believed in the Senate that Mr. Taft's deputy as Acting Floor Leader, Senator William F. Knowland of California, will now take that place formally without significant challenge, every Republican is in doubt as to where the party's ideological center in the Senate will now rest.

Inquiry among Republican factions running from extreme nationalist to the Eastern internationalist bloc that supported General Eisenhower "before Chicago" "indicates that Senator Knowland is acceptable at least to the extent that no one would go all-out against him for the leadership.

One of Mr. Taft's best friends and closest colleagues, Senator Eugene D. Millikin of Colorado, would be a powerful contender if he had not habitually indicated a lack of interest in the post.

Another who might ordinarily be expected to be put forward, Senator Styles Bridges of New Hampshire, already holds the Republican deanship of the Senate as president pro tempore.

Mr. Bridges, moreover, is up for re-election next year and is understood to have no wish to take on the floor leadership, in consideration both of this fact and the fact that he is chairman of the powerful Appropriations Committee and has there about all that he can do.

Where the essential tone of the Republican party in the Senate will hereafter be developed, however, is another matter. Senator Knowland, as a comparative youngster of 45 years, is not and has not sought to be another Senator Taft, whose immense prestige in the party had made him, to many Congressional Republicans, no less than co-equal to the President himself.

There are Republican Senators who believe now that a struggle for control of the spirit of the party in the Senate, if not for its formal leadership, will soon open in slow but rising violence.

The Republican side of the Senate is formed into three groups, into all of which Mr. Taft alone was able to move without difficulty. There is the internationalist, largely Eastern and all-out Eisenhower wing that never wanted Senator Taft for Floor Leader, but always wanted him in the Senate.

There is the isolationist, largely Midwestern, bloc that deeply wanted him for President and considered the Senate leadership as indispensably his.

Mellowness Had Set In

There is a central group—with which Mr. Taft himself usually made his residence, though he roved about by necessity from time to time—that wanted him, but less than passionately for President and gladly accepted him as Senate leader.

It was on June 10 that Mr. Taft's long service to his party and to the Senate really came to the end. Hobbling painfully about on crutches, the Senator announced that he was turning the day-to-day leadership duties over to Senator Knowland.

Although this was many days before he had to enter the hospital in New York in his fatal illness, the belief of many of his friends here was that he knew then what the end would be.

He never said, to the most intimate of his associates, that he had this knowledge, but there were, in spite of himself, some illuminating circumstances.

One of these was that the famous tartness of the Taft speech and the famous impatience that he had shown always to one and only one sort of person—any person he believed was rather a fool—began to leave him. And the more soft-spoken and seemingly jovial he became, the more his admirers were saddened.

In every one of the recent crises of his public life—and notably at the convention last July—he had mellowed and seemingly relaxed precisely to whatever degree his affairs seemed hopeless.

Whenever he lost his head it was invariably at a moment when that head was in no conceivable political danger. He never took a little view of a big issue, not even if that issue involved his whole career.

Then, and finally, during this phase of the inordinately kind and patient Taft, there came what in retrospect at least could be called a clear pointer.

Not long before Mr. Taft went to New York for the last time, he volunteered to this reporter that "I have gained back nine pounds."

"That," said the reporter, "is certainly good news. Doesn't that mean you have turned the corner?"

Senator Taft, lying on a leather lounge in his office for an after-luncheon rest, said with a smile:

"Yes—a kind of corner, I guess."

August 1, 1953

Modern Republicans vs. the Old Guard

M'CARTHY INSISTS ON RED TRADE BAR

Senator Scouts a 'Challenge' to Eisenhower Leadership—'Disagrees' With Dulles

By WILLIAM S. WHITE
Special to THE NEW YORK TIMES.

WASHINGTON, Dec. 4—Senator Joseph R. McCarthy summoned his followers today to a pressure campaign intended to force President Eisenhower to reverse himself on the issue of trade with Communist China by this country's allies.

The Wisconsin Republican at the same time denounced as "ridiculous and untrue" the widespread interpretation that he was engaged in a running challenge to the President's national and party leadership.

He declared he had "a great deal of admiration" for the President and that he would support all Republicans, though he would not halt his criticisms at his party's "mistakes."

Only yesterday, President Eisenhower had made plain in the strongest terms that the Administration would go on refusing Mr. McCarthy's demands that the allied nations, and specifically Great Britain, be cut off from all aid unless they ceased all trade with Communist China.

Dulles Gives His Views

John Foster Dulles, the Secretary of State, had described Senator McCarthy's proposal as an attack on "the very heart" of the basic foreign policy of the United States in that it would amount to an effort to give orders to free peoples elsewhere.

At his press conference yesterday, the President had declared himself in "full accord" with Mr. Dulles.

Senator McCarthy, thus facing heavy rebukes from the highest figures of the Administration, retorted this morning. He issued a statement both resuming his assault on what Mr. Dulles had called "the very heart" of United States policy and seeking to loose a postcard offensive against the White House.

The statement as handed to the press ended with an appeal by Mr. McCarthy for a "reappraisal," but in re-reading it for the cameras of television and the news reel he added this:

"Now I think President Eisenhower is an honorable man. I think he will follow the will of the American people if that will is known to him. I would like to take this opportunity to urge every American who feels as I do about this blood trade with a mortal enemy to write or wire the President of the United States and let him know how they feel so he can be properly guided in this matter."

Senator McCarthy's statement not only was a reply to the President and to Mr. Dulles on the matter of the China trade but involved a reiteration that "the question of communism will be an important issue in 1954."

Leonard W. Hall, the Republican national chairman, who had called on President Eisenhower this morning, said that he himself and "the leaders of Congress" were in full agreement with what the President had said yesterday.

TEXT OF STATEMENT

WASHINGTON, Dec. 2 (AP)—Following is the text of the statement Senator McCarthy issued today:

On Nov. 24 I discussed how Communist agents were protected, coddled, and promoted under the Truman-Democrat regime. I then pointed out a few mistakes made by my own Republican party. At that time I said:

'Before looking at some of the cases in which our batting average is zero, let me make it clear that I think this Republican Administration is doing a job so infinitely better than the Truman-Acheson regime that there is absolutely no comparison.'

I spent perhaps as much time as any other man last fall, urging the American people to elect President Eisenhower. I would do the same again as I have a great deal of admiration for the President and think he has an excellent record for the time he has been in office.

However, errors by Democrats or Republicans are equally bad. One of the reasons that the Democrats were removed from office was their failure to recognize their own errors and I feel that if we Republicans do likewise it may be fatal to our great political party and to our country.

Senator Stresses Issues

However, let me make these points perfectly clear:

1. It has been suggested by our political enemies that I am challenging President Eisenhower's party leadership. That suggestion is most ridiculous and untrue.

2. I will give my utmost support to all Republican candidates for the House and Senate next year, because it is so important to this nation that Republicans retain control of Congress.

3. The new Administration has already rid itself of 1,456 security risks inherited from the Democrat Administration—practically all of whom were removed because of Communist activities or connections or perversion. This is a fine record and a real contrast to the Communist-ridden Truman-Acheson regime.

4. I believe that the question of communism will be an important issue in 1954, because the facts have proved that the Democrats represent the party of the left, the party which is soft on communism. This will become more and more apparent as the full facts about the Truman coverup of Communists become known. This nation must stand as the leading bulwark against communism in the world and on the subject of communism the difference in attitude between the Republicans and Democrats will be the most important political issue for many years to come.

This should make it clear once and for all that I will continue to give my utmost support to the Republican party now and in the future. This does not mean that I will refrain from criticizing my party when I think it is making mistakes.

An Inherited Situation

Therefore, last Tuesday night I discussed our failure to clean up one of the foulest situations which we inherited from the Democrat Administration.

I pointed out that on Sept. 10 of this year the Army announced that some 900 American young men known to have been living prisoners of the Communists in Korea were still unaccounted for and that on Sept. 12 of this year, the Chinese Communists announced that they would not treat as prisoners of war American fliers who were shot down during the Korean war over Manchuria.

I pointed out that my party was not responsible for this situation—that we had inherited it from the corrupt, Communist-ridden Truman-Acheson regime, but that it is now our duty properly to protect those young men.

The course of action which I recommended was that we refuse to give any American dollars to any nation shipping any goods to Communist China so long as a single American remained in a Communist blood-stained dungeon.

On this matter Secretary Dulles and I are in complete disagreement.

In a republic such as ours there must be room for honest difference of opinion. I respect the honesty and sincerity of purpose of Secretary Dulles. However, I have such deep convictions on the subject that I shall continue to discuss the matter at every opportunity and I urge Secretary Dulles to reappraise our whole policy in this regard.

It is my hope that such a reappraisal may result in a change of policy in this respect.

December 4, 1953

PRESIDENT ADVISES PARTY TO TEMPER POLITICAL ATTACKS

Says Times Are Too Serious for Extreme Partisanship—Bars Specific Criticism

By JAMES RESTON
Special to THE NEW YORK TIMES.

WASHINGTON, Feb. 10—President Eisenhower suggested today that political parties with small majorities should speak softly in times of crisis.

He conceded at his crowded twenty-seventh news conference as President that political ruffianism was a well-established American tradition even in President Washington's day, but he said that the times were now too serious for extreme partisanship.

The President seemed to apply this principle to all windmill orators, name-callers and professional Democrat-baiters. Also, he applied it specifically to all members of his official family and to the Republican National Committee, which has arranged for 113 Republicans to make 288 speeches during this month's annual Lincoln Day party jamborees.

He declined to comment, however, on any of the contributions made to these celebrations by Senator Joseph R. McCarthy, Republican of Wisconsin, who is now delivering a series of speeches for the Republican National Committee, entitled "Twenty Years of Treason."

Johnson Praises President

For the last few days, leaders of the Democratic party have been protesting publicly that some Republicans are trying to charge the whole Democratic party with treasonable activities and with encouraging an economic depression.

The Democratic leader in the Senate, Lyndon B. Johnson of Texas, was the first of many opposition leaders who praised the President's news conference remarks.

"The President's attitude is one of a gentleman and an American," Senator Johnson said. "Unfortunately, some of his advisers' remarks put him in a position where he had to publicly rebuke them."

In Portland, Ore., the Chairman of the Democratic National Committee, Stephen A. Mitchell, remarked that the President had merely issued a challenge to his own leadership.

"The country will see whether he can lead the Republican party down a path of reasonableness," Mr. Mitchell said.

States Aim in Indo-China

On other subjects, the President said:

¶He was sending technicians, not combat troops, to French Indo-China, and every movement he made there was designed to avoid getting the United States involved in a hot war in that region. No one, he added, could be more bitterly opposed to such involvement than he was.

¶The Forty-fifth National Guard division, mainly from the Oklahoma region, was coming home from Korea about mid-April, and the Fortieth, from California, was returning about the middle of June.

¶There was no truth in rumors that the Administration was planning to raise the interest rates on Rural Electrification Administration loans.

¶He still was opposed to campaigning for specific candidates in state or district elections this year. This remark, however, did not seem to preclude general campaigning for his program as a whole.

¶He knew nothing about reports that a Negro choir from Howard University in Washington had had trouble getting into the Republican party rally here last week-end but he added: If the choir was barred by reason of race or color or anything of that kind, he would be the first to apologize.

The President knew in advance this morning that his first question would deal with his reaction to several public statements made recently by prominent Republicans.

Three of these statements had produced a howl of protest from the Democrats, who outnumber the Republicans in the Senate 48 to 47 (there is one Independent, Wayne Morse of Oregon), and are within five seats of controlling the House of Representatives.

Gov. Thomas E. Dewey of New York made the first of these attacks in Hartford, Dec. 16. In it he charged the Democrats with bungling the country into war, lacking the courage or capacity to win or settle the war, and leaving Americans to die on the Korean battlefield "because they did not have the ammunition to defend themselves."

The second was the statement by Herbert Brownell Jr., the Attorney General, that President Truman had knowingly appointed a "spy"—Harry Dexter White, former Assistant Secretary of the Treasury—to an even more important and sensitive position in the International Monetary Fund.

Representative Sam Rayburn, Democrat of Texas and former Speaker of the House, protested privately to the President about such statements and made one or two private speeches of protest against them, but it was not until this week that the protests came out in the open.

What started them was the third Republican speech, this one by the Assistant to the President, Sherman Adams of New Hampshire. He told the Republican National Committee last Saturday that "political sadists"—the Democrats—were spreading a "fear deal" and trying to talk the country into a depression.

When it appeared that the Republican Lincoln Week speakers, with the support of the Republican National Committee, were being supplied with this same kind of material for a nation-wide campaign against the Democratic party, the Democrats drew the issue and demanded a repudiation by the President.

The President was calm as he dealt with the first question. He was relaxed and ruddy, dressed in a brown suit, brown and white figured tie. He spoke quietly and moderately.

Well, first of all, he said, he thought it was apparent to everyone that he wasn't very much of a partisan. The times were too serious, he thought, to indulge in extreme partisanship, and he admitted—quite cheerfully, he added—that there must be Democratic support for enactment of certain parts of his program.

Having said this, however, he went on to raise a question about the extent of his authority to deal with Republicans who made such attacks. He said he knew of no way the Chief Executive could stop this sort of thing except among the members of his own executive family (Cabinet and other appointed officials).

He added that great partisanship among such officials raised doubts in his mind. He seemed to suggest that maybe the Democrats were making too much of the partisan comment, however, by saying that the people were pretty wise about such political talk and observing that, after all, it had gone on ever since the days of Washington.

The President said he didn't believe in bitter partisanship; that he never thought that all wisdom was confined to one party; and that it was not only untrue but unwise to make blanket charges against a whole party.

Who would be so foolish as to call all the members of a political party treasonous to the United States? he asked. After all, he added, all had fought for America.

President Eisenhower was asked if it would be accurate to construe his remarks as meaning that he counselled officials of the Executive Branch of the Government not to engage in extreme partisanship. The President replied that it would be accurate.

The President was reminded that he had referred recently to his responsibilities as head of the Republican party and was asked how far those responsibilities governed the operations of the Republican National Committee, which arranged the speaking tours of Senator McCarthy and others.

President Eisenhower replied that, so far as directing the affairs of that body, he had no official position at all. He then was asked whether he would expect the chairman of the National Committee, Leonard W. Hall, to follow his advice to avoid extreme partisanship. The President replied: Yes, he would.

When it came to dealing with statements by Senator McCarthy and others, specifically on the "Twenty Years of Treason" series, the President would not continue the exchange.

Without mentioning the Senators by name, a reporter asked for comment on these statements:

By Senator McCarthy: "The label 'Democrat' is stitched with the idiocy of a Truman, rotted by the deceit of an Acheson, corrupted by the red slime of a White."

By Senator William E. Jenner of Indiana, who also is making five speeches this week and next under the auspices of the Republican National Committee:

When the Republicans took over the Government in Washington they found "heaps of evidence of treason" and that the Democrats had "tampered with the security of the United States."

The President was visibly impatient as these statements were read out, then he said, with a slight edge to his voice:

Well, he wouldn't comment on anybody's statements as such. He would not engage in personalities. He thought he had stated his position quite clearly as to what he thought and believed in. He believed, he concluded, that the ordinary American was capable of deciding what was temperate and just and what was merely indulging in language for no good purpose.

A reporter noted that Chairman Hall had said he considered Senator McCarthy a political asset and asked whether the President agreed with Mr. Hall and approved the national committee's helping with the financing of the Senator's trip. President Eisenhower replied, again somewhat sharply, that he didn't think he was called on to approve or disapprove and that he wasn't going to talk about personalities.

The President's remarks, as a whole, took some of the heat out of the controversy with the Democrats, but few observers here believe they have ended either the controversy or the Republican campaign on the "Communists in Government" issue.

This is not the first time that the President has shown, first, that he personally does not like extreme partisanship, and second, that he does not think it is proper for him to try to dictate to Republican Senators and Representatives what they should say in the developing political campaign.

February 11, 1954

NIXON SAYS 'QUESTIONABLE METHODS' AND 'RECKLESS TALK' OF RED HUNTERS ARE DIVERSION FROM G.O.P. PROGRAM

BACKS 'NEW LOOK'

By W. H. LAWRENCE
Special to THE NEW YORK TIMES.

WASHINGTON, March 13—Vice President Richard M. Nixon lashed out tonight at Congressional Red hunters who by their "reckless talk and questionable methods" had divided Americans on the anti-Communist issue and diverted attention from President Eisenhower's legislative program.

The Vice President replied over a nation-wide radio and television network to charges by Adlai E. Stevenson, the Democratic Presidential nominee of 1952, that the Republican party was impotent to govern because it was divided, "half McCarthy and half Eisenhower."

Mr. Nixon said that President Eisenhower "is not only the unquestioned leader of the Republican party but he has the confidence and support of the great majority of Americans, Republicans and Democrats alike."

"Both his leadership and their support are undivided," he declared.

In attacking unfair Congressional investigations of commu-

189

Modern Republicans vs. the Old Guard

nism and appealing for fair and proper procedures governing them, Mr. Nixon did not mention Senator Joseph R. McCarthy by name but left no doubt that he was one of the men he meant.

His criticism was not confined to the Wisconsin Republican, however, because he repeatedly referred to those he attacked in the plural.

[The Associated Press quoted Mr. McCarthy in Manitowoc, Wis., as saying that he had "no comment" on Mr. Nixon's speech.]

Persons who act unfairly and irresponsibly, the Vice President said, give ammunition to those who oppose any action against communism, and give the guilty ones an opportunity to don the cloak of innocence.

Mr. Nixon had been picked by the White House and the Republican National Committee to make the answer to Mr. Stevenson. The Columbia Broadcasting System and the National Broadcasting Company gave him the same free time that had been accorded the Democratic leader and that then had been demanded by Senator McCarthy.

The Vice President challenged Mr. Stevenson to propose a better foreign or domestic program than that offered by General Eisenhower, which, he said, was the greatest presented to Americans in this generation.

Responding to Mr. Stevenson's criticism of the Eisenhower foreign policy, Mr. Nixon also asked if the Democrats would prefer to have the war in Korea still going on, or if they favored more "Korean-type wars" in the future rather than rely upon the "new look" program of massive and mobile retaliation.

The Vice President declared that the Eisenhower Administration, relying upon the President's great personal knowledge of military strategy, had decided that it would not in the future allow "the Communists to nibble us to death all over the world in little wars."

He said this nation would, in the future, rely primarily on "the massive mobile retaliatory power" it had against "major sources of aggression" at times and places chosen by itself rather than by the Communists.

The Vice President was solemn as he spoke to the nation seated behind a desk, reading from notes that had been prepared carefully during the last several days and that had been given the personal approval of President Eisenhower.

He mentioned Senator McCarthy in passing at the start when he showed a batch of letters "that says to attack McCarthy" and a batch "to attack Stevenson."

He did not mention, directly, the latest fight between the Administration and Senator McCarthy, but he did say that Congressional investigators in Congress had, in recent weeks, made themselves the issue rather than the anti-Communist crusade in

which they believed.

He drew upon his own experience in the Communist investigation field, including his part in the exposure of Alger Hiss, to say that he knew fair methods worked better and produced more lasting results.

He said he had often heard people ask why fair methods were so important "when you are dealing with a gang of traitors" or "a bunch of rats" who ought to be shot.

But he counseled moderation. He declared the Communists were "a bunch of rats," but he warned that when shooting rats "you have to shoot straight." Otherwise, if a person shoots wildly, he continued, the rats will get away, and some innocent persons may be hit.

In an obvious, but indirect, answer to Senator McCarthy's charges that the Eisenhower Administration had tried to cover up Communists, especially in the Army, the Vice President said he could assure all Americans that the Administration under the President's leadership never would tolerate disloyalty in any place.

He said that mistakes were possible, and, if made, the Administration would admit them rather than try to cover them up.

The Vice President was neatly attired in a gray single-breasted suit, a blue shirt (the color recommended for television) and a red and white figured blue tie. Pancake makeup was applied before the speech began. The tie, in the bright lights of television, seemed at times to be covered with sparkling diamonds.

As announced in advance, he had no prepared text. His careful preparation had been boiled down to nine yellow legal-sized pages of penciled notes. His only television cues were cards flashed at various intervals to indicate the time remaining.

Mr. Nixon praised the Presidential legislative and foreign policy in general, but did not go into details.

He devoted the last section of his talk to a stirring defense of President Eisenhower as one who avoided impetuous or arbitrary action and who gave leadership by example.

"We have a leader," he said, "who is not only an American leader; he is a world leader; and he's a man who is mobilizing world opinion for the free nations and for us. * * *

"I've never seen him mean; I've never seen him rash; I've never seen him impulsive; I've never seen him panic. And I've never seen him make a decision which was motivated by political purposes. His only test was the one he said he was going to use all through the campaign: What is good for America.

"I think we're lucky to have this man as President of the United States. * * * You know this is a great and a good country. Let's quit fighting. Let's join together and get behind our President in making the American dream come true."

Mr. Nixon had begun his talk with an answer to Mr. Stevenson's attack upon the Eisenhower Administration's foreign policy, and suggested that since the Democrats had offered no sub-

stitute they must be advocating a return to policies in effect when Harry Truman was President and Dean C. Acheson was the Secretary of State.

He said the Administration long ago had looked at the results of the old foreign policy and decided it had to be changed.

"What were those results?" he asked rhetorically, answering:

"Well, we found that in seven years of the Truman-Acheson policies 600,000,000 people had been lost to the Communists, and not a single Russian soldier had been lost in combat. We found when we went to Washington that we were still involved in a war in Korea that had cost us 125,000 American boys as casualties, and again not a single Russian soldier lost in that war.

"We found that we inherited a budget, a policy which if continued as recommended by the Truman Administration through the four years of the Eisenhower Administration would have added $40,000,000,000 to the national debt, and this would have meant, if we had approved that policy, more controls, higher prices for all Americans.

"We found that despite record spending for military purposes, that in our efforts to be strong everywhere, we weren't strong enough anywhere. And since our former policy failed we then asked ourselves the question what kind of a new policy should we announce.

"And in determining what that policy should be, we decided to find out what the men in the Kremlin were up to. We found that militarily their plan, apparently, was to destroy us by drawing us into little wars all over the world with their satellites, however where they themselves were not involved and where, due to our inability to bring to bear our great superiority on the sea and in the air, we were unable to win those wars.

"We found that economically their plan, apparently, was to force the United States to stay armed to the teeth, to be prepared to fight anywhere, anywhere in the world that they, the men in the Kremlin, chose."

"Well, we decided that we would not fall into these traps," Mr. Nixon continued. "And so we adopted a new plan, and that new plan, summed up, is this, rather than let the Communists nibble us to death all over the world in little wars, we would rely in the future primarily on our massive, mobile retaliatory power which we could use in our discretion against the major source of aggression at times and places that we chose."

The Vice President also took off on the Right Wing of the Republican party by praising in the highest terms John Foster Dulles, the present Secretary of State, and his performance at the recent Big Four conference at Berlin, which has come under a considerable amount of G. O. P. criticism.

"Isn't it wonderful, finally, to have a Secretary of State who isn't taken in by the Communists, who stands up to them?" he asked.

He turned from foreign policy to the defense of the Administration's record in handling the is-

sues of Communists in Government.

Mr. Stevenson had been vigorous in his complaint that the Republicans has misbranded more than 2,000 Americans as "security risks," while, in fact, it had found "only one alleged active Communist" out of more than 2,000,000 persons on the Federal payroll.

Mr. Nixon said tonight that more than 2,400 persons had left the Government, by dismissal or resignation, under the new security program.

"A great majority of these were inherited from the previous Administration," he added.

This was the first indication from any Administration source that any sizable number of these "security risks" might have gotten jobs for the first time under the Eisenhower Administration. In the past the only figure given was that five of the first 1,456 security risks had been new employes.

He said that the President recognized fully the right of Congress to investigate in the field of Communists in Government and elsewhere, but he said that General Eisenhower "is right" when he "insists" that Congress adopt rules of fair procedure.

The Vice President spoke to the nation seated behind a table from Studio 13 of Broadcast House, the new and modern home of the C. B. S. affiliate, WTOP and WTOP-TV.

He arrived at the studio a half-hour early, accompanied only by an office assistant and a Secret Service man assigned to guard him. No guests or newsmen were allowed in the studio during the broadcast.

Mr. Stevenson, addressing a Southern party rally in Miami Beach one week ago tonight, inaugurated a line of direct frontal attack upon President Eisenhower himself. While it did not please many Democrats in the Senate, it nevertheless caused deep concern at the White House and at Republican headquarters.

The former Democratic nominee charged that the Administration had begun a campaign "of slander, dissension and deception" and that "a group of political plungers had persuaded the President that McCarthyism is the best Republican formula for political success."

Mr. Stevenson also charged the Republicans with juggling figures on alleged security risks while reluctantly admitting that "only one alleged active Communist" had been found among more than 2,000,000 employes in the Federal Government.

"It looks as though the great crusade had practiced a great deception," he said. "They may consider this good politics. But it is vicious government."

His speech served to spur Republican efforts, already under way, to declare the independence of the Eisenhower Administration from domination by Senator McCarthy. White House emissaries and leaders of the Republican National Committee pleaded with Republican Senators to isolate Mr. McCarthy and to strike a direct blow at him by dismissing the chief counsel of his Permanent Subcommittee on Investigations, Roy M. Cohn.

March 14, 1954

NIXON LINKS REDS TO 'LEFT-WING' FOES

Charges Communist Alliance With Clique of A. D. A.— Lists Policy Agreements

By WILLIAM R. CONKLIN
Special to The New York Times.

CHEYENNE, Wyo., Oct. 23— Vice President Richard M. Nixon blasted away tonight at what he called the alliance between the Communist party and left-wing Democrats to defeat Republican candidates for Congress.

His views were expressed in the text of what was intended to be a major speech here. The text was released from Bozeman, Mont., where Mr. Nixon and his party were blocked by snow. It was the first time since he began his thirty-three-state campaign for G. O. P. nominees that he was weatherbound.

In his speech he enunciated four major points on which, he said, Communist party members and "the left-wing clique of Americans for Democratic Action have joined forces."

Mr. Nixon and his party of eighteen were scheduled to leave Butte by air at 10:05 o'clock this morning, New York time. Two inches of snow had fallen during the night. By morning the ceiling at Butte Airport was 700 feet and icing conditions prevailed. Between 7 and 10 A. M. the ground temperature remained at two degrees below freezing.

After waiting more than four hours to take off from Butte, the Vice President decided to drive 250 miles to Billings, where the airport was then open. The party of thirteen drove to Bozeman through snow and rain over Pipestone Pass in the Continental Divide, but the airport was closed in by the time they arrived.

The Vice President, fretting over his interrupted schedule, released his Cheyenne speech as a statement. He planned to resume his trip by air to Salt Lake City, Utah, if weather precluded his speaking in Cheyenne tonight.

Criticizes Senator Murray

Before leaving Butte Mr. Nixon criticized Democratic Senator James E. Murray for using a photograph of himself and President Eisenhower in his campaign. No member of the Senate, Mr. Nixon said, had a worse record in opposing the President than the senior Senator from Montana.

The Nixon forces made no se-

cret of their desire to start a fight with the Democrats over the communism-in-Government issue. Mr. Nixon bore down hard on this theme in his Butte speech last night when he charged that Communists were determined to infiltrate the Democratic party to control its policies. He amplified the attack today.

"It is time to talk bluntly and frankly about the most sinister development of this campaign to date," Mr. Nixon said.

"The Communist party has agreed enthusiastically with Americans for Democratic Action in the latter's position on four major points. These are:

"1. Calling for the recognition of Communist China just before the Korean war.

"2. Attacking the Eisenhower security program.

"3. Calling for the abolition of the committee which brought out the evidence which convicted Alger Hiss. [This was the House Committee on Un-American Activities, of which Mr. Nixon was a member in 1949.]

"4. Constant sniping at J. Edgar Hoover and the Federal Bureau of Investigation."

The Vice President said the majority of Democrats and Republicans were loyal Americans. He centered his attack on the Democrats associated with the A. D. A., and said other members

of the Democratic party should repudiate this group. Continuing his attack, he declared:

"The Communists know that the Democratic National Chairman, Stephen A. Mitchell, has told the American people that a Democratic Eighty-fourth Congress would go back to the Truman policies. These are the policies which meant:

"1. The Acheson foreign policy, so weak and inconsistent that it led to the loss of 600,000,000 persons to the Communists in seven years, and to the Korean war.

"2. The Truman 'red herring' attitude under which the previous Administration tried unsuccessfully to shield Alger Hiss and to cover up the treachery of Harry Dexter White.

"3. The Truman so-called 'loyalty order' under which individuals with clear Communist records in their files were retained in Government jobs and promoted rather than being fired.

"4. The Truman Administration's policy of refusing to cooperate with J. Edgar Hoover and the F. B. I., and in consistently pigeon-holing and failing to act on F. B. I. reports on Communists, and other security risks.'

October 24, 1954

DEMOCRATS CONTROL HOUSE BY 27; APPARENTLY WILL RULE SENATE; PRESIDENT PLEDGES COOPERATION

CHAIRMEN CHANGE

Rayburn to Be Speaker —No Clear Mandate Seen in Results

By WILLIAM S. WHITE

The Democrats have regained control of the House of Representatives and apparently have won a very close struggle with the Republicans for the Senate.

This is the essential position this morning, forty-eight hours after the polls had opened on one of the most desperately fought Congressional elections in the history of the United States.

Democratic seizure of the House will again elevate to the Speakership Representative Sam Rayburn of Texas, who already had served in that office nine

years, longer than any other man.

The indicated margin of the Democrats is twenty-seven seats of a total of 435.

Democratic control of the Senate will be assured if the apparent victory of Richard Neuberger over his Republican foe, Senator Guy Cordon of Oregon, is officially confirmed.

Another Senate race, in New Jersey, is undecided and is expected to remain so at least until Monday. In this contest the Republican candidate, Clifford P. Case, was leading.

Line-Up of the Senate

Assuming the election of Mr. Neuberger and of Mr. Case, the prospective Senate for the Eighty-fourth Congress is thus divided:

Democrats—48.

Republicans—47.

Independent—1, Senator Wayne Morse of Oregon.

Senator Morse has said he will vote with the Democrats on the question of which party is to

take control.

This had been the cast of the old Senate:

Republicans 49.

Democrats 46.

Independent 1 (Mr. Morse).

This was the situation in the House:

Democratic, 231; Republican 204. In the last House it was 218 Republicans, one Republican vacancy, 212 Democrats, three Democratic vacancies and one Independent.

Senate switches occurred in this order: For the Democrats, in Kentucky, Nevada, Michigan and Wyoming; for the Republicans, in Colorado, Iowa and Ohio.

In House races among those defeated were Representative Robert L. Condon, Democrat of California, who had been barred by the Atomic Energy Commission from witnessing a test, and three House Republicans who had been in the forefront as vehement anti-Communists. These were Representatives Kit Clardy of Michigan, Fred E. Busbey of

Illinois and Charles J. Kersten of Wisconsin.

No matter what the ultimate Senate division, the country will enter upon a two-year period of tensions in its Government.

At the very minimum, the White House will be estranged in the officially partisan sense from the powerful House of Representatives.

If Mr. Cordon at length is determined to have been defeated, the Democrats will command the Senate—again only nominally.

The one Independent in that body, Senator Morse, will vote with the Democrats on the question of which party is to take control.

Control of Congress is not a mere dusty housekeeping issue. The party that rules Congress controls the committee chairmanships.

Thus the ultimate Senate make-up will determine whether such Senators as Joseph R. McCarthy, Republican of Wisconsin, and William E. Jenner Republican of

Indiana, remain at the head of their controversial investigating committees.

The custody of chairmanships is equivalent to the domination of the essential tone of Congress, legislative or otherwise.

But regardless of how all this turns out, the greatest unknown factor now involved in the immediate future functioning of the Government of the United States is a human factor.

This question in the simplest terms is this: Will President Eisenhower be able to restore good bipartisan relations with the prospective House Speaker, Mr. Rayburn?

Resents Attacks on Party

Mr. Rayburn, a Southern liberal, an internationalist and a traditionalist, and moreover an old personal friend of the President's, has been deeply affronted at some Republican attacks on the patriotism of the Democratic party as a party.

He has indicated to friends that he has regarded the President's silence on these attacks as "not playing the game."

The degree of his cooperation now with the White House, it may be predicted, will depend considerably on the extent to which satisfactory personal and political relationships with the President may be restored.

The House therefore may be considered the new arena of crisis, because of this situation, because of the fact that this chamber at all events will be safely Democratic, and because the Senate Democratic leader, Lyndon B. Johnson of Texas, has not appeared to be deeply stirred by the words and the acts of the past.

To put the position in more concrete terms, Mr. Rayburn, on all his past record, will be more hospitable to a return, in part at least, to the Roosevelt-Truman days than will Senator Johnson.

This will mean, again concretely, that Mr. Rayburn will become the most powerful Democrat in the United States, with the possible exception of Adlai E.

Stevenson, the party's 1952 Presidential candidate.

What has happened in the United States, at the middle of the first Republican Presidency in two decades, is this:

¶The people of the country clearly have registered some anxiety at the course of a Republican Congress that never has exactly typified the President himself.

¶They have not given the Democrats any clear mandate in the Legislative Branch of the Government. A synthesis of political opinion probably would be that they have only set the Democrats to watch, so to speak, certain tendencies of the Republicans in Congress.

¶The election, on objective examination, has not been a total or even a general rebuke to the President, though in certain Senate races he was deeply committed to Republican candidates.

There is, in fact, no very clear pattern in it all. Right-wingers—mainly in the Republican party—have succeeded in some cases. Eisenhower-Republican liberals in

some cases—notably Senator John Sherman Cooper in Kentucky—have gone down.

The sum of the results, however, has not given any clear and firm indication as to whether the country has gone a bit Left or a bit Right.

All that is wholly clear is this:

¶The people have given a greater measure of power to a Democratic Congressional group that is in the end in the charge of basically conservative — and mainly Southern—Democrats.

¶The Republican party in Congress remains primarily in the charge of non-Eisenhower or Eisenhower Republicans, who for the most part were followers of the General's great rival for the Presidential nomination, the late Senator Robert A. Taft of Ohio.

There will be a changing of the guard in Washington. There is not likely to be any sharp and fundamental change in principles.

November 4, 1954

SWAY IN CONGRESS RETURNS TO SOUTH

Democrats in Key Posts Are Expected to Bar Revival of New or Fair Deal

By C. P. TRUSSELL
Special to The New York Times.

WASHINGTON, Nov. 4—Democratic victories at the polls on Tuesday do not mean a return of a Roosevelt New Deal or a Truman Fair Deal in Congress.

That was assured by the southern Democrats, who were given revived powers by the election returns. Their seniority status gave them automatic control of key committees that will recommend legislative action.

Congress usually follows the advice of its committees.

The southern Democrats—twenty-six in the Senate and more than 100 in the House of

Representatives—have been neither New Deal nor Fair Deal, with a few exceptions.

On the surface it might appear that a Democratic majority, assured in the House and now indicated in the Senate, could put bills through easily to build up a Democratic record for the 1956 Presidential campaign. Situations now indicate that it will not be that simple for the Democrats.

Balance of Power Shifts

Committee chairmanships in the House of Representatives were going to the Democrats without doubt, and probably in the Senate as well. Democratic control is indicated, but not New Deal or a Fair Deal control. The balance of committee power has shifted to the South.

In the House, the Agriculture Committee, for example, goes in chairmanship back to Representative Harold D. Cooley, Democrat of North Carolina, a strong opponent of President Eisenhower's plan for sliding-scales support of farmer prices. Mr. Cooley wants a fixed support at 90 to 100 per cent of parity. Parity is a formula designed to

make the farmer's receipt for his crops equal to the prices he must pay for the things he must buy.

The Committee on the Armed Services now goes to Representative Carl Vinson, Democrat of Georgia, who will take over from Representative Dewey Short, Republican of Missouri.

The Committee on Banking and Currency, now concerned with exposing scandals in the national housing program, would go to Representative Brent Spence, Democrat of Kentucky, who, as Mr. Vinson, had held his chairmanship post under Democratic rule before. The housing investigation is now pointed at a past Democratic administration.

Foreign Aid Shift Scouted

It appeared tonight that there would not be much change in the House position as to foreign affairs. Representative James P. Richards, Democrat of South Carolina, was due to take over the chairmanship of the House Committee on Foreign Affairs. Mr. Richards, however, was observed as being even more in line with the Eisenhower foreign aid program than was Repre-

sentative Robert B. Chiperfield, the Illinois Republican who had headed that committee for two years.

If the Senate goes Democratic, as it now appears, Senator Carl Hayden of Arizona will replace Senator Styles Bridges of New Hampshire as chairman of the Appropriations Committee. Mr. Hayden is a New Dealer, not afraid to spend money, and might get into disputes with Senator Harry F. Byrd, Democrat of Virginia, who may head the Committee on Finance.

The Finance Committee rules on taxes to cover appropriations. Although appropriations and taxes originate in the House under constitutional edict, the Senate decision frequently prevails at the end.

Senator Byrd, long chairman of the Joint Committee on Reduction of Nonessential Federal Expenditures, has campaigned against lusty governmental spending.

November 5, 1954

EISENHOWER WARNS G. O. P. RIGHT WING; CHIDES KNOWLAND

By WILLIAM S. WHITE
Special to The New York Times.

WASHINGTON, Dec. 2—President Eisenhower, reasserting leadership for his concept of a progressive Republican party, rebuked today the Senate Republican floor leader, William F. Knowland of California, and the

party's right wing generally.

The President did not seek to disclaim the existence of a split in the party. He said instead that the party would not long be a force in American life unless it followed a course of progressivism.

As before, he defined this progressivism as a liberal attitude in the Government's relationship with the individual and a conservative attitude concerning the national economy and the individual's pocketbook.

It was the first time since he entered the White House two years ago that General Eisenhower publicly and without apol-

ogy had criticized a leading member of his party in Congress. Always before, he had avoided such criticisms, relying frequently on the fact that the Constitution made Congress an independent branch of Government.

Even this time, the President somewhat softened his language toward the end, with the comments that while Senator Knowland sometimes made statements that certainly did not conform with the Administration's approach these normally affected method rather than principle.

China Blockade Urged

He made it clear, nevertheless, that distinctions in methods were

important, suggesting that the methods of Senator Knowland might mean the difference between peace and war in Asia.

Senator Knowland, in the face of rejections from John Foster Dulles, Secretary of State, and the President himself, has been calling for a blockade of Communist China to force the liberation of United States citizens in Communist prisons.

Yesterday, moreover, Mr. Knowland broke with the Administration on another sensitive issue, coming out against a Senate censure of Senator Joseph R. McCarthy, Republican of Wisconsin.

The President said little about his differences with Senator

Knowland over the McCarthy issue, observing only that it was up to the Senate to determine what was required for the preservation of its dignity.

On the point of the profound division within the Republican party over policy toward Red China, however, the President spoke extensively and voluntarily.

He took up Senator Knowland's proposal for a blockade and declared that in any definition known to him as a former professional military man a blockade was an act of war.

It was easy, he said, to take a "truculent, publicly bold and almost insulting attitude toward the unending harassments of China Communists.

But, he added, authorizing direct quotation, "I want to make quite clear that when one accepts the responsibilities of public office he can no longer give expression freely to such things; he has got to 'think of the results. Now that [taking the truculent attitude] would be the easy way for this reason: those actions lead toward war."

Using a phrase recently employed by Senator Knowland, "the honor of the country," the President declared:

"So far as the honor of the United States is concerned, I merely hope that I shall not live long enough to find myself accused of being insensible to the honor of the United States and the safety of her men and soldiers, no matter where we send them."

To a question asking his view of what the reporter called the unhappiness of conservative Republicans about action on Communist infiltration and the conduct of foreign policy, the President replied that one could be progressive and tough on communism at the same time.

Normally, he said, he himself had been accused of being too tough in his efforts to remove anyone in Government who might be subversive. He hoped that it would not now be necessary to defend himself from any notion that he had any love for the concept of communism.

It was here that the President went into a discussion that amounted to a warning to the Republicans that the party would die "unless it avoided extremes and took the moderate course.

He plainly implied as well that he would have no interest in leading a party that went off on those extremes.

To be useful to the country, he said, a political party must be a progressive, dynamic force; it must have a doctrine and a program, legislative and otherwise, that was moderate in its approach, avoiding extremes of right and left.

Says Party Must Meet Test

Restating his notion of a mixture of liberalism and conservatism for such a party, the President went on:

He believed the Republican party must meet this sort of test or it would not be any force long in American life. He just didn't believe that 163,000,000 intelligent Americans were going to be satisfied either with reaction or with any trend toward centralization and paternalism as to be difficult to distinguish from a socialist form.

He was not talking about conventions, he went on—presumably meaning national conventions and specifically those coming in

1956—but only about what direction the Republican party must take to survive as a useful agency for this country.

Nothing said by the President, and nothing in his attitude, suggested any effort by the Administration to take reprisals against Senator Knowland—or, specifically, to attempt to have the Senate Republicans remove him as their leader.

Some of the President's most important backers in the minority Eisenhower-Republican wing in the Senate would be prepared to advise the President, if asked, not to attempt any such course. Their conviction is that Mr. Knowland could not be displaced.

Senator Knowland himself during the day said explicitly what he often had implied—that he did not consider the McCarthy issue one to put him "at odds" with the Administration. He reiterated his view that this was "a Senate problem."

As to his contest over foreign policy with the President, Mr. Knowland several times has declared that his statements have illustrated deep-seated convictions, which he felt it his responsibility as a Senator to express.

December 3, 1954

M'CARTHY BREAKS WITH EISENHOWER; RUES 1952 SUPPORT

ISSUE IS THE REDS

White House, Accused as Weak on China, Repeats Stand

By ANTHONY LEVIERO
Special to The New York Times.

WASHINGTON, Dec. 7—Senator Joseph R. McCarthy broke his long-deteriorating relations with President Eisenhower today.

He denounced the President for his "tolerance" of Chinese Communists who were holding American war prisoners, and for congratulating two Senators who had urged the censure of the Wisconsin Republican.

Mr. McCarthy "apologized" to the American people for having urged the election of General Eisenhower in the 1952 campaign. He declared he had been "mis-

taken" in believing General Eisenhower would fight Communists vigorously at home and abroad. And he accused the President of a "shrinking show of weakness" toward Red China.

The attack by Mr. McCarthy, who was condemned only last Thursday for conduct unbecoming to a Senator, precipitated a political storm in the capital. For his sounding board, Mr. McCarthy used a hearing of his own Senate Permanent Subcommittee on Investigations.

He did not participate in the hearing. He merely appeared briefly twice, and loosed his blast the second time. Then he left with his wife, and tonight they were reported on their way out of town for a week or ten days.

He Assails President

In this first formal statement since he was condemned by the Senate Mr. McCarthy assailed the President for congratulating Senator Arthur V. Watkins of Utah, chairman of the special committee that recommended his censure,

and Senator Ralph E. Flanders of Vermont, who had sponsored the censure resolution, both Republicans.

While avoiding direct comment on the condemnation verdict of the Senate, President Eisenhower praised Mr. Watkins when he visited the White House on Saturday, for a "very splendid job." There has been no evidence that President Eisenhower indicated his feelings to Mr. Flanders.

Other political figures lashed at Mr. McCarthy or upheld him, but President Eisenhower abided by his policy of avoiding personal involvement in the McCarthy dispute.

The only reaction from the White House was to bring up to date the statistics of the Administration's fight on Communists at home and to reiterate the President's statement, made last week:

"Now, on our side we must make certain that our efforts to promote peace are not interpreted as appeasement or any purchase of immediate favor at the cost of principle, but we must, on the other hand, be steady and refuse to be goaded into actions that would be unwise."

Mr. McCarthy's frontal attack on the President and leader of the Republican party immediately revived speculation that he might seek to start a third party. A cryptic remark by Mr. McCarthy fueled the talk about the division of the Republican party.

He was asked if he would bolt the party and start a new one.

"I have no interest—at the

present time—in a third party," Mr. McCarthy replied. What was new in his position were the words "at the present time."

"I intend to work in the Republican party," Mr. McCarthy declared. "I've said all I'd better say."

Some Republican leaders felt, however, that if Mr. McCarthy continued with what they regarded as extreme tactics he might lose whatever substantial support he has in and outside Congress and find himself politically isolated.

Notable in the flood of comments that followed his explosion was the fact that some of the Senators who had defended Mr. McCarthy against censure assailed him today.

Among them was Senator Eugene D. Millikin, Republican of Colorado, one of the deans of the Senate, who has great influence in party councils.

Another was Senator Barry Goldwater, Republican of Arizona, who had assumed an active role in trying to save the Wisconsin Senator from the condemnation that was expressed by a vote of 67 to 22.

Leonard W. Hall, the Republican National Chairman, scored Mr. McCarthy with this statement:

"Senator McCarthy has made a major error. Without attempting to evaluate his fight against communism, I regret to find him in what must be strange company to him, making personal attack on the President of the United States.

"The record of the Eisenhower Administration on the Communist menace both at home and abroad speaks for itself. I do not think it is necessary to remind the people that President Eisenhower

193

was fighting the Communists quite a few years before Senator McCarthy made his maiden speech on the subject in the Senate."

Appears at Hearing

Senator McCarthy had calculated the time and setting for his statement. His subcommittee held its first public hearing in several months, with the aim of exposing alleged Communists employed in the Bethlehem Steel Company's plant in Bethlehem, Pa.

At the scheduled time, 10:30 A. M., only Senators Karl E. Mundt of South Dakota, and Charles E. Potter of Michigan, both Republicans, were on hand with staff counsel. They went ahead. Reporters were told that something important would happen and they would receive a text.

At 10:37 Mr. McCarthy walked in with his wife. She sat with the audience and he with the committee, but he took no part and Mr. Mundt continued to preside. Mr. McCarthy was still wearing a bandage on his arm for his bursitis and gave this as the explanation for not participating. At 10:50 A. M., Mr. and Mrs. McCarthy left, but they came back at 11:40 A. M.

By that time two witnesses, Joseph A. Pecucci, native of Italy, and John S. Szabo, native of Hungary, both naturalized, had invoked the Fifth Amendment to the Constitution against self-incrimination as they were questioned about alleged Communist party membership and associations.

Mr. McCarthy resumed his

seat as Mr. Szabo took refuge in the Constitution again. Senator McCarthy interrupted as the committee counsel, James N. Juliana, was asking a question. He said:

"I hate to do this. I'd like to read a brief statement."

He then read it, declaring that exposure of Communists working on secret weapons might determine whether "the sons of American mothers may live or die." He said his statement might be "my temporary swan song as chairman of the investigating committee."

He emphasized "temporary." Controll of Congress will pass to the Democrats in January and with it the chairmanships of the committees.

Then Mr. McCarthy stated that the work of this committee had been held up about ten months and the President had "taken it upon himself to congratulate Senators Flanders and Watkins who have been instrumental in holding up our work."

He went on in this vein, making his "apology" for having supported the President in 1952. He referred to the unsuccessful efforts by his friends to persuade him to apologize in their effort to prevent censure, saying he felt rather that he should "apologize" to the American people for having supported General Eisenhower in 1952.

"Unfortunately," Mr. McCarthy concluded, "the President sees fit to congratulate those who hold up the exposure of Communists in one breath and in the next breath urges patience, tolerance and niceties to those

who are torturing American uniformed men."

Flanders, Watkins Reply

Senator Flanders referred to Mr. McCarthy's statement about the thirteen Americans being held prisoners by Red China. He added:

"I cannot help feeling that the statement given out is primarily a political one, using a sad and very difficult situation as its excuse. The junior Senator from Wisconsin has declared political war."

Senator Watkins had this to say:

"Senator McCarthy's attack on the President, Senator Flanders and myself shows him to be the same irresponsible McCarthy that the Senate by an overwhelming vote condemned last Thursday."

Senator Watkins also said the Eisenhower Administration had reason to be proud of its record "in ferreting out Communists and jailing the guilty." He said he agreed with the Administration's Asian policy.

Senator Watkins called attention to his own long record of exposing Communists as a member of the Senate Internal Security subcommittee. He said that if this record was not as well known as Mr. McCarthy's it was because his investigations "were carried out without any thought of self-aggrandizement."

At first the White House would not comment on the McCarthy blast. Then it reissued a statement of last June 2, listing the results of the prosecutions of

Communists for advocating the otherthrow of the Government through violence, and the campaign to eliminate security risks.

This statement said that the "Department of Justice and the Federal Bureau of Investigation are the principal agents of the Government in dealing with subversives."

It listed eight items, including conviction of fifty Communist party leaders and indictment of forty-nine; addition of sixty-two organizations to the Justice Department's official list of subversive organizations that now total 255; indictment of one person for treason; conviction of two for espionage and ten for making false statements to the Government; deportation of 129 alien subversives; orders for 410 to be deported; orders for denaturalization of forty-nine and the barring of 172 subversive aliens.

Senator Herman Welker, Republican of Idaho and chief defender of Mr. McCarthy in the censure debate:

"I hardly think it is necessary for the Chief Executive to be warmly congratulating anyone in this very unfortunate matter. In this political trial, and that is all it was, the ninety-six Senators were not the judges. The 160,000,000 Americans were the judges of the trial of McCarthy which in my opinion blew up in the face of the author of Senate Censure Resolution 801 and those who offered amendments. McCarthy stands vindicated before the jury of the American people."

December 8, 1954

EISENHOWER PRAISES NIXON BUT DOES NOT ENDORSE HIM

2D SPOT IN DOUBT

Foes of Vice President Now May Push Drive to Block Him

By W. H. LAWRENCE
Special to The New York Times.

WASHINGTON, Feb. 29 — President Eisenhower passed up today two opportunities to give an automatic immediate endorsement to renomination of Vice President Richard M. Nixon.

General Eisenhower said he properly could not speak out on the choice of a running mate until after the Republican National Convention itself had

picked its Presidential nominee. He mixed repetition of previous high praise for Mr. Nixon with what sounded at least like indirect criticism of the Vice President for his recent effort to continue a Republican party label on Chief Justice Earl Warren. The President said he personally would never admit that any Supreme Court justice continued to have a political designation while on the high court.

President Eisenhower's failure to call at once for Vice President Nixon's renomination undoubtedly will put new steam behind an effort already under way by some influential Republicans to select another running mate. These anti-Nixon men argue that the 1956 campaign involving a President who has suffered a heart attack will place new emphasis with voters on the Vice

Presidential nominee.

In his radio-television address to the nation, the President made no mention at all of Mr. Nixon or any other possible running mate.

The omission by the President may not be meaningful, however. General Eisenhower is assured of renomination by acclamation, and the convention unquestionably will nominate any man he favors for Vice President. So he could speak up for Mr. Nixon even at the last minute and insure his renomination.

The Nixon question was raised in two ways immediately after the President had disclosed he would be available for renomination and re-election if the Republican party and a majority of the people wanted him.

He was asked directly whether he would again want Mr. Nixon as his running mate.

"As a matter of fact," President Eisenhower responded, "I wouldn't mention the Vice Presidency, in spite of my tremendous admiration for Mr. Nixon, for this reason: I believe it is traditional that the Vice President is not nominated until after a * * * Presidential candidate is nominated; so I think that we will have to wait and see whom the Republican convention nominates, and then it will be proper to give an expression on that point."

Respect 'Unbounded'

Asked whether, if nominated, he would have a personal preference for Mr. Nixon's renomination, the President responded:

"I will say nothing more about it. I have said that my admiration and my respect for Vice President Nixon is unbounded. He has been for me a loyal and

194

dedicated associate, and a successful one.

"I am very fond of him, but I am going to say no more about it."

The indirect criticism came when President Eisenhower was asked his own reaction to the Vice President's characterization of Mr. Warren as a Republican Chief Justice.

The President said he would not comment, and never had, on a comment by someone else. He added:

"But I will say this: Once a man has passed into the Supreme Court he is an American citizen and nothing else in my book until he comes out of that court, and I believe that it would be—I would never admit that

he was—longer had a political designation."

There has been sharp political controversy over the Vice President's recent contention in a New York speech that the Supreme Court's public school desegregation decision should be included among the accomplishments of the Eisenhower Administration because the court's unanimous opinion had been delivered by "a great Republican Chief Justice, Earl Warren."

There was no immediate comment from Mr. Nixon about whether he would seek renomination. It has been assumed that he would, if the President were a candidate, and that he would make his own bid for the Presidency if General Eisenhower did not run again.

Leonard W. Hall, the Republican national chairman, all

along has "assured" that the 1956 ticket would be the same as in 1952.

Mr. Nixon has potent support in the party organization, and is, of course, a certainty for renomination if President Eisenhower eventually gives him the nod.

His opponents within the party, who have not desired public identification during this period of uncertainty about General Eisenhower's intentions, have not agreed yet on a single man they would favor if Mr. Nixon could be denied renomination.

There has been talk of Gov. Christian A. Herter of Massachusetts, of George M. Humphrey, the Secretary of the Treasury, and of former Gov. Thomas E. Dewey of New York, a two-time Presidential nominee. Harold E. Stassen, the President's adviser on disarmament problems and a perennial candidate for the Pres-

idency himself, probably is not without ambitions for the Nixon Post.

From the Democratic side of the fence, Paul M. Butler, national chairman, interpreted General Eisenhower's failure to call for Vice President Nixon's support as a sign he was being dropped.

"I am not so sure but what maybe the skids aren't being greased for a dignified exit of the Vice President from the national political scene, at least at the level he now occupies," Mr. Butler told a National Press Club audience.

There have been suggestions in Republican quarters that Mr. Nixon be given a Cabinet post, perhaps as Secretary of Defense, in the next Administration if the President is re-elected with another running mate.

March 1, 1956

KNOWLAND SEEKS RIGHT-WING ROLE

Warns President to Heed Taft Republicans—Hints at Rival for Nixon

By WILLIAM S. WHITE
Special to The New York Times.

WASHINGTON, March 1 — Senator William F. Knowland of California warned President Eisenhower today that his re-election would be imperiled unless he gave heed to the wishes of the orthodox Republicans.

He declared that the Taft section of the party should be given representation in the Administration if possible and certainly within the Eisenhower campaign organization.

He suggested, moreover, that the nomination for Vice President of some member of this faction, rather than Vice President Richard M. Nixon, was not beyond the hopes of the orthodox wing.

Mr. Knowland, the Senate Republican leader, disclaimed any personal ambition for the Vice Presidential place but in no sense took himself entirely out of the reckoning. He added, however, that he "assumed" Mr. Nixon would again be the President's choice.

Takes Active Leadership

In removing himself from what had been a provisional race for the Presidential nomination, based upon the assumption that General Eisenhower would not run again, Senator Knowland took these other significant steps:

¶He publicly assumed the practical leadership of the conservative and right-wing Republicans who followed his Senate mentor, the late Senator Robert A. Taft of Ohio. This leadership has long been tacitly conceded to Mr. Knowland by many Taft men.

¶He implied that the Taft Republicans would expect from the President some sort of accommodation similar to that arranged between the two wings of the party in the 1952 meeting at Morningside Heights, New York, between General Eisenhower and Senator Taft.

¶He asserted that the campaign to re-elect the President would be "no pushover," notwithstanding what he called the "overoptimism" of White House and Republican National Committee circles. "Not a thing," he said, "can be taken for granted."

¶He declared it to be "extremely important to consolidate the party" by concessions to "those who supported Taft."

These forces, Mr. Knowland asserted, "now feel that they have not been made so much a part of the team as their long service in the party warrants."

"It is necessary to recognize the fact of this danger," he added, "and the need to unify the party."

He disclosed that he intended to "present these views" to Sherman Adams, the Assistant to the President; to Leonard W. Hall, chairman of the Republican National Committee, and to the President himself.

Senator Knowland's name had been entered for the Presidential nomination in the Republican primaries in four states where the candidate's consent is required — Illinois, Pennsylvania, Minnesota and New Hampshire —and in Alaska.

He had been prepared to go also into the primaries in Wisconsin, for which the filing deadline would have been tomorrow, and in California.

He had made clear from the start that he would be a candidate only if the President were not available for renomination.

Accordingly, the President having consented to run again, Mr. Knowland this morning arranged with Vice President Nixon and Gov. Goodwin Knight of California to support an Eisenhower slate in California.

Name Stays in Primaries

The Senator took the position that this action made it plain that he was backing the President's renomination and was no longer himself a candidate. Thus, since it was not possible in any case to withdraw his name from primaries in which it had already been entered, he took no further action.

He strongly indicated his anxiety over the fact that the President was charting a campaign of little travel and few personal appearances.

There would be "great pressure," Mr. Knowland said, for the President to appear here and there in behalf of other Republican candidates, regardless of all present plans. "Not even television," he remarked, "can substitute for the personal appearance."

It would follow, the Senator added, that a "heavy burden" of campaigning would be put in these circumstances on the Vice Presidential nominee, on Cabinet members and on "all Republican leaders," in Congress and elsewhere.

In reply to many questions about the Vice Presidency, Mr. Knowland gave this answer, in summary:

He had no reason to suppose that the nomination would be offered to him and he was not a candidate for it, since he had "always assumed" that it would go to Mr. Nixon on any Eisenhower ticket.

To the inquiry "Would you accept the Vice Presidential nomination if offered?" he replied:

"That is one of those highly 'iffy' questions. I don't assume that the situation will present itself."

March 2, 1956

Ringmaster Eisenhower: "Front—and center!"

Drawing by Tom Little

Has Eisenhower Changed the G. O. P.?

The President has acted to bind together the factions of Republicanism, with some dissent from the Old Guard. Here is an assessment of his imprint on the party.

By WILLIAM S. WHITE

WASHINGTON.

TO what extent has President Eisenhower remade the Republican party? How long will the reformation endure? As the campaign takes shape, questions such as these are increasingly asked. Not in many years, and perhaps never in history, has the highest figure of a party so dominated the essential image of that party that is projected to the public. The President's role has been, consciously or not, the role of the mediator, the binder-together, not simply of the factions within his own party but of the interests of thousands and perhaps millions in both parties.

It seems clear that to the public at large he has been a very unpartisan sort of partisan. It is a commonplace of political experience that three years after his inauguration he is to many

WILLIAM S. WHITE is chief Congressional correspondent of The New York Times.

people plainly not identified with all the acts of his Administration. Certainly this has been true in those matters—take the lowering of the farm subsidies—where there has been local or sectional or class resentment at *Administration* policy that, according to Congressional mail, usually involves little or no resentment of the President himself.

Again, not in many years, and perhaps never in history, have all the lesser politicians in all wings of a political party put such urgent and total trust in the power of a President to carry them all through. The Republicans have lost since 1952 a whole series of important political contests in which the President's name was not on the ballot, but are nevertheless almost absolutely confident that, with his name back on the ticket this time, all will be well.

Before it is possible to attempt to answer the ultimate questions as to what the President has done to the

Republican party and how long his handiwork may last it is necessary to consider history.

The shortest way, perhaps, to put the business is to say this of the Republican party: It was born and brought up in protest, passed its middle years largely in acceptance and conformity and of later years has been like an elderly man examining and re-examining the basic postulate of his life.

THE Kansas-Nebraska Act of 1854, which legally laid the Western territories open to slavery, resulted in the formulation of indignant local movements that took the name "Republican"—first, officially, in Ripon, Wis.

The seedbeds were in Indiana, Ohio, Wisconsin and Vermont, although the belligerent political liberalism of the first Republicans was within six years somewhat diluted by a concept of fiscal conservatism ("sound money") that has persisted to this day.

The Republican platform on which Abraham Lincoln won election in 1860, over a divided Democratic party that was a much older political organism, was liberal in the matter of "free soil," but conservative in the matter of high tariffs.

In fact, the least changing of all the Republican party's generally changeable and fluid characteristics is to be found at one place of great power, and one alone. That place of power is the Treasury Department.

In the lifetime of men now in middle age there have been incomparable disparities between the personalities and the philosophies of Republican Presidents. Take, for example, Calvin Coolidge and then Dwight D. Eisenhower.

But, allowing for some admitted overstatement to permit the point and allowing for the fact that time to some extent must change all frames of references, there is a considerable validity to the *(Continued)*

point that all Republican Secretaries of the Treasury are much the same. Take, for example, Andrew Mellon of Pennsylvania and the present Secretary, George M. Humphrey of Ohio.

True, they differ, but in infinitely less degree than the difference between Presidents Coolidge and Eisenhower.

THE present G. O. P., a version of a series of transformations that began at about the time of the gusty Theodore Roosevelt, is an amalgam of all these forces:

(1) Old-line orthodox Republicans, of whom Mr. Humphrey is the nearest to a perfect example in the Eisenhower Administration, although he does not fit the mold in an absolutely ideal sense.

(2) "Modern" Republicans, who have been greatly influenced in many directions by the New Deal and Fair Deal—men like President Eisenhower, who are hardly partisan at all in the ordinary sense; men like Secretary of Defense Charles E. Wilson, who are partisan only in a rather mild and institutional way, and men like Thomas E. Dewey and Attorney General Herbert Brownell Jr., who are deeply partisan but partisans of the new and not of the old form of Republicanism.

(3) Ex-Democrats, Southern as well as Northern, although mostly Northern, who have found at least a temporary home in the Republican party more or less simultaneously with a forward movement in their economic affairs that has taken them from the city flats to the ranch houses, or their equivalents, in the suburbs.

(4) What are called "Independents," a fugitive term, indeed, and one subject to much debate in the political profession. The late Senator Robert A. Taft of Ohio, perhaps because he spent the greater part of his mature political life in the common Republican frustration of the long Roosevelt-Truman years, was wryly inclined to suspect that an "Independent" was simply a crypto-Democrat whose true colors were revealed only in the voting booth on Election Day. There are, currently, some Democrats who would turn this quite about. They would suspect that the "Independent" is really a crypto-Republican—and for evidence they would point to the results of 1952.

AT all events, it is this somewhat variegated, but not necessarily inchoate, mass that now makes up the Repub-

lican party of 1956.

How did it get into this condition, and, specifically, how did the Republican party of the harshly unrewarding Thirties and Forties spring forward in this present decade to a point where, for practical purposes at least, it appears a majority and no longer a minority party?

To begin with, of course, the Democrats themselves opened many opportunities for the realizing of this state of affairs—although the wit to seize and exploit these opportunities was not, of course, among their gifts to their opposition. Anyway, the Democrats at minimum had got a bit tired, a bit fat, a bit careless and, in general, perhaps a bit noncombative. This brief summary, however incomplete, is enough for present purposes.

FROM the conventions of 1940 onward the Republicans (and here they began most clearly to appear like the introspective elderly man mentioned at the outset) were suffering a series of inner convulsions and mind-searchings of the kind that sometimes presage a recovery from illness or ineffectuality.

In 1940, in 1944, in 1948 and again in 1952 the traditional, orthodox and historically dominant Republicans—the "Taft Republicans" as they are now generally known — lost, one after another, contests of incalculable importance to the less orthodox, more liberal, more internationalist and predominantly Eastern wing of the party. Taft himself was rejected for the Presidential nomination in 1940, losing out to an erstwhile Democrat, Wendell Willkie. He stepped aside in 1944 "for John," and Senator John W. Bricker of Ohio wound up on the lower end of the ticket with Thomas E. Dewey of New York at the head.

In 1948 it was again Taft and Dewey—and Dewey won the nomination. In 1952 it was again, in many senses, Taft and Dewey, for Taft remained the undoubted choice of the orthodox Old Guard while Dewey acted as the New Guard's acute and hard-handed field marshal for General Eisenhower's nomination.

THESE victories for the New Guard—the "moderns," the relative "liberals," or whatever one may choose to call them — were fundamental. They signaled an unbroken, accumulating rise to power of a section of the Republican party that was prepared to come to some terms, to some

degree, with the liberalism that Franklin D. Roosevelt had stamped upon the general political movement in this country with an almost indelible trace and that the dogged Harry S. Truman had sought to defend to the end.

One meaning of all this in historical terms was that the locus of power in the Republican party was removed from the Midwest to this side of the Appalachians and agreeably settled into what had already for generations been the center of power in finance and in all forms of national opinion-making.

The Republican party came to have Eastern domination at the top in nearly every significant sense. And it is, of course, in the East that the Government sits, that, for the most part, the most powerful organs of the press operate, that all "mass media" have headquarters and that business itself is largely headquartered.

Another and more immediately practical meaning is that the Republican party, now in critical affairs under new control, has simply put itself into position to win national elec-

tions by accommodating itself to certain political realities rather than stolidly preparing itself to lose national elections by refusing to make any accommodation at all.

The new party has now come a long way, geographically and in certain other senses, from the prairie Republicanism of Mr. Lincoln. But in some ways it has come closer to validating his concepts than did the old Midwestern-based party, for that old party, although living in Mr. Lincoln's land, maintained the "sound money" and tariff policies of his time but had almost no trace of his liberalism in other matters.

The reformed party, the product, as it was, of the progressive rejection at four national conventions of the stand-pattism of the Old Guard, met the Roosevelt-Truman revolution not with a

simple, adamant, win-or-die resistance everywhere, but with a counter-revolution of its own.

THIS counter-revolution, based almost wholly on the pragmatic economic hopes and desires of people and their wishes for an end to vehement political disagreement in the nation, made its appeal through the centers of both political parties, moving to the right, of course, wherever it could without compromising its basic design, and straight to the ultimate mind of the predominant post-war thought of the United States. This thought had been (and perhaps it still is) characterized by what might be called a centralism of view on almost all matters.

What has President Eisenhower done to the Republican party as it now stands? He has expanded it, up to now, at least, into something far larger than it had been. For the American Center is now much larger, in the general estimates of detached viewers, than it has been in perhaps many generations, and the Right and the Left are in consequence far smaller.

President Eisenhower has fashioned this party into an instrumentality for the "moderates," who may, for practical purposes, be largely identified with the middle class. The middle class, of course, is the storied backbone of parliamentary-capitalistic countries; here and now it is not merely the backbone but very nearly the whole torso of the country.

ALTHOUGH political writers are uniquely qualified not to attempt even timid economic judgments, it does seem on common sense and inexpert observation that the middle class is vastly bigger and the so-called upper and lower classes immeasurably smaller than was the case, say, even just before the onset of the second World War. The term "class" is, of course, used here mainly in the economic sense; any other definition is thought unsuitable if not invidious in the United States.

Thus, what is at hand in the Republican party of President Eisenhower is, in its simplest terms, an enormous, a historic and, perhaps for us here, an unexampled triumph for the middle class. What the old Republicans continually feared in the Franklin D. Roosevelt days, "class warfare," has not occurred; or, if it has, the winning class has won so handily that, looking back, one can hardly see the after-marks of any conflict at all. It may be that this is so because the victorious class has been expanding at so Gargantuan a rate as more or less to blot up the other classes.

AND all this has had another, and arresting, effect on the Republican party itself as now reformed and constituted. It has inaugurated a day of great importance in politics for the rich and sentient amateur of the kind who never quite could put his modern heart into the old party, mainly because its quasi-isolationist outlook went against both his deepest interests and his more sophisticated and more hospitable view of the round world.

Along with the march into active Republican politics of this rich amateur there has been a march, in the same sense, of many not-rich but up-and-coming business and professional executives (in advertising, in communications, in law and so on). These men have enjoyed the adventure, not simply for its own sake, but for the opportunity it has offered for the exercise of their special skills.

The Old Guard has, of course, mainly held its ground in Congress, much as the Democratic Southern Old Guard held its ground all through the Roosevelt time. But in the truly national Republican party, at those moments and at those places where the highest of policy is made and where Presidential candidates are chosen, the Old Guard has been largely isolated.

Will the reforms in the Republican party made by President Eisenhower, or symbolized by him, long endure? Will this new coalition of the "moderates" survive as long as did the Roosevelt coalition of what might be called in this context the "immoderates," the alliance of the bourbon Southern planter and the Detroit auto worker?

The question is, of course, unanswerable on a score of grounds, but some considerations that would be involved in its ultimate answer might be suggested. The new coalition plainly and in the nature of things is not held together

by an absolutely impervious cement any more than was the old.

THE accommodations made within the core of the Republican party have not been made with the glad assent of the Old Guard, as any loss to the Republicans of the President's sort of popular leadership would make instantly apparent. The Old Guard has not conceded the game in any sense; it has conceded an inning or two as it has conceded that the President as of now is indispensable to the larger party success for which all Republicans hope, of course, in November.

Already there have been rumblings and grumblings from the Taft wing of the party at the limited sort of campaign, paying little heed to what the Congressional politicians see as their necessities, that Mr. Eisenhower proposes to wage. The heir of Senator Taft as the Republican Senate leader, William F. Knowland of California, has formally put these complaints in a general warning against the "overconfidence" that he sees both in the White House and in the pro-Eisenhower Republican National Committee. What Congressional Republicans fear is that an Eisenhower-Republican victory may not be otherwise a Republican victory and that the new masters of the party are not overly concerned with the fortunes of its now dispossessed masters.

There is no intention, in short, among the orthodox Republicans that the new face of the party shall endure forever —or even for any substantial number of future years. The anti-third-term constitutional amendment will in this connection be seen to be increasingly important as time goes on. If the President is re-elected for a second term he will be the first Chief Executive in history to be on prior notice that his practical influence on the party *must* begin to decline almost as soon as he takes office.

A FORMIDABLE drive by the orthodox to recover power thus almost certainly will begin within a year from next November's elections though it is probable that the old Republican will not go all out in this design until the Congressional elections of 1958.

In a curious sense, therefore, the liberal Democrats and the Old Guard Republicans have much in common: each group fears an eventual descent into something like oblivion if the Eisenhower kind of Republicanism, with its tendency ever to enlarge the center at the expense of right and left, should long prevail.

And in the current Republican discussion of the second place on the ticket—shall it be given again to Vice President Nixon or to another—lies one of a number of latently dangerous possible dilemmas.

There is no doubt whatever that the President, if he chose, could dictate the precise identity of his running mate and that the Republican convention would go along. If, however, the President should choose to leave the question open, or substantially open, an explosive contest, scattering about all kinds of cement, undoubtedly could and might develop.

AGAIN, there are more fundamental questions. To what degree can the "moderns," the "moderates," the relative liberals, keep essential control of the party in the future? To what degree will the Democrats be able to heal the party's split personality represented by the North-South wings, and to what degree will they be able to present a more coherent party front, appealing to the centrists without losing all touch with the urban liberals who are so important to it in the long slope of time?

What will be the future state of the national economy and will it continue to promote or will it begin to reduce the thus far rapidly expanding middle class? What of foreign policies and the world outside?

No, not much can be said surely of this future, as not much can be said, for certain, of any future in any sense. It can only be said now that this is the point to which the Republican party has now come and that these are some of the reasons why it has come there.

March 18, 1956

New G. O. P. Philosophy

A Study of the Idea That Republicans Have Pre-Empted the Political Center

By JAMES RESTON
Special to The New York Times.

WASHINGTON, July 11—The Eisenhower Administration is developing a philosophy for the Presidential election campaign that goes considerably beyond the slogan "peace and prosperity."

It is based on the idea that the Democratic party is a coalition of contradictory radical and conservative extremes and that the Republican party has pre-empted the center in American political life.

The task of articulating this philosophy, about which a great deal will be heard in the next three months, has been left to a brilliant young Midwestern lawyer, Arthur Larson, now Under Secretary of Labor.

Mr. Larson is a handsome, 46-year-old former Rhodes scholar from Sioux Falls, S. D., who first came to Washington during the war to serve in the Office of Price Administration. He was a Professor of Law at Cornell from 1945 until 1953 and for a short period dean of the Law School at the University of Pittsburgh. He was appointed Under Secretary of Labor on April 12, 1954.

He has written a book called "A Republican Looks at His Party"—a sequel to Dean G. Acheson's "A Democrat Looks at His Party"—in which he defines what he calls the new Republicanism. It will provoke yells of protest from the Democrats on almost every page, but it is clearly a serious contribution to the literature of the campaign.

His theme is that the winning majority in American politics lies, not at the conservative or radical extremes, or even in a combination of the two, but in the immense central block of moderates.

Old Conflicts Cited

The trouble with the New Dealers, as he sees it, is that they are out of date. They had some good ideas, and what was good in their program has been incorporated in the new Republicanism. But, he feels, they still have a tendency to think in terms of 1936—in terms of old conflicts between labor and management, old antagonisms between the farmers and the "Eastern bankers" that no longer exist in the same way.

"In the nineteenth century," he says, "there was not enough government regulation and not enough labor strength and freedom: result, unruly business expansion at the expense of the rights of the people.

"In the Nineteen Thirties, there was too much government regulation and not enough business incentive and freedom: result, deadened business activity and protracted depression, accompanied by much humanitarian concern for victims of the depression."

It was the "genius of the Eisenhower Administration's achievement," Mr. Larson contends, that "has merged and brought into balance all the positive forces in our country. It is not against any of them. It realizes that they sometimes conflict, but it has found a way to encourage them to work together to a common benefit."

Thus, he says, the political ideas of 1896 were against labor and the political ideas of 1936 were against business, but this Administration is against neither and is for both."

Mr. Larson pays tribute to Adlai E. Stevenson of Illinois for calling for an end of hostilities between the Democratic party and business, but he maintains that the very partnerships that Mr. Stevenson called for between labor and management, and the other interdependent forces in American life, actually have been achieved by the Republican Administration now in power.

Differences Diminishing

There is now so much general agreement in American life, Mr. Larson feels, that the main question in American politics is: Who deserves the credit for marshalling this consensus, and who will get its support?

Structurally, he argues, the Democratic party is not set up to be a party of the center. Its two largest blocks are represented by the most conservative element in the country — the Southern Democrats — and the most radical, the ultra-Fair-Dealers. He concedes that there are differences in the Republican party as well, but argues that the differences are not so great nor the antagonisms so fierce.

As he sees it, differences between the parties about foreign policy, about collective security abroad and social security at home, are diminishing, and political issues, once fought out at the local or state level in the United States, now are coming to the fore as national issues.

"We are entering an era, therefore," he says, "in which the views of a political group on the proper Federal-state sharing of responsibility are of crucial importance.

"If you have an Administration which lapses comfortably into the habit of applying sweeping Federal remedies for all ills, you may look for another era of concentration of power in Washington and withering away of state governments—this time perhaps forever.

"For if Washington ultimately dominates the scene in questions of water supply, roads and streets, power, houses and education, how much does this leave of the every-day responsibilities of states and municipalities?"

The Democrats reject all this as the theme of a Johnny-come-lately who got his start under President Franklin Delano Roosevelt, and is now claiming for the Republicans the fruits of the political revolution that Roosevelt started and the Republicans could not reverse.

Nevertheless, Mr. Larson has produced what is probably the most articulate argument for the Eisenhower Republicans since General Eisenhower entered politims, and the importance of his book is that it is being used already as the guide-book for the Republican campaigners.

July 12, 1956

VIRGINIANS BACK JOHNSON OF TEXAS

Byrd and Robertson Assert Colleague in Senate Is 'of Presidential Stature'

Special to The New York Times.

WASHINGTON, April 21 — Senators Harry F. Byrd and A. Willis Robertson, Democrats of Virginia, joined today in a statement describing Senator Lyndon B. Johnson of Texas, majority leader of the Senate, as a man "of Presidential stature."

The Virginians said Senator Johnson had demonstrated in his post of majority leader that he has "ability, a comprehensive knowledge of government affairs and outstanding tact and skill in reconciling and coordinating differing views."

"These qualities of Senator Johnson," their statement continued, "clearly indicate that he is of Presidential stature and we predict that when his name is offered to the Chicago convention as the favorite son of Texas he will draw support not only from the South but from other areas of the nation."

Five Other Senators on Record

Senators Byrd and Robertson through their statement today are linked with five other Democrats who have gone on record in support of the Texas Senator. One of his most outspoken backers has been Senator Alan Bible of Nevada. Others are Senators Walter F. George and Richard B. Russell of Georgia, George A. Smathers of Florida and Russell B. Long of Louisiana.

Senator Johnson had no immediate comment today on the joint statement by Senators Byrd and Robertson. Earlier he had said that he was not running for the Democratic Presidential nomination and also had made it clear that he would not become a sectional candidate if that implied any threat of a walk-out from the Democratic convention.

Particular interest attached to the fact that Senator Byrd joined in today's statement because the Virginia Senator did not support the 1952 Democratic Presidential nominee, Adlai E. Stevenson. President Eisenhower carried Virginia by 81,000 out of more than 500,000 votes that year.

Both Virginia Senators were among the signers of a recent Congressional manifesto criticizing the Supreme Court's ruling for racial integration in the country's schools.

Texan Not Manifesto Signer

Senator Johnson did not sign the manifesto. He explained that he was not asked to add his signature because those who drafted the statement did not want to involve the party's leaders in a move that had no official party sponsorship. The Texas Democrat has said, however, that he believed the integration problem was one best left to individual states to handle.

Although he is not an announced candidate, Senator Johnson has said he would be willing to accept the favorite son nomination from Texas. He is engaged in a contest with Gov. Allan Shivers for control of the state's fifty-six vote delegation to the Democratic National Convention.

April 22, 1956

JOHNSON DEFEATS SHIVERS IN TEXAS BY A WIDE MARGIN

Victory in Landslide Appears Certain for the Control of State's Democrats

By W. H. LAWRENCE

Special to The New York Times.

DALLAS, Tex., May 5—Senator Lyndon B. Johnson scored a landslide victory tonight over Gov. Allan Shivers in the battle for the control of the Democratic party in Texas.

Senator Johnson took an early lead and never was threatened as returns came in from 6,000 precinct meetings in the 254 counties.

With returns from 156 counties, measured in terms of the delegate strength they will send to the May 22 state convention at Dallas, Senator Johnson's forces appeared to have won 1,199 delegates and Governor Shivers to have the backing of 345 delegates.

With 98 of the counties still to be counted, Mr. Johnson had 248 more delegates than the absolute majority of 951 delegates required for control among the 1,900 delegates at the state convention who will ratify the decisions taken today. The Senator already has won 117 counties.

The outcome was a smashing rebuke to the retiring third-term Governor who bolted his party in 1952 and led Texas with its twenty-four electoral votes into the Republican column behind President Eisenhower. The Governor had threatened, in the course of this heated campaign, to back General Eisenhower for re-election if the Democrats again nominate Adlai E. Stevenson of Illinois.

Southern Backing Seen

The victory gave Senator Johnson, majority leader of the Senate, the support of Texas' fifty-six national convention votes as a favorite son candidate for the Democratic Presidential nomination.

He is certain to have the backing of many other Southern delegates, at least on the first few ballots at the Chicago convention, which opens Aug. 13. However, Senator Johnson said today he had "no illusions" that he would become President. A serious heart attack last year, forcing a curtailment in his official activities, has made Senator Johnson reluctant to become a serious contender for the nomination.

The apparent sweep in Texas counties strengthened greatly the prestige of the Senate leader and his ally, Representative Sam Rayburn, Speaker of the House of Representatives. Both had been brought under heavy fire by Governor Shivers, and they had retaliated in kind.

As influential, moderate Southerners, both will carry great weight in the national party convention. They hope that the Texas results will carry a stern warning to potential Democratic defectors in others states.

The voting was heavy and good weather prevailed across the state as Texas Democrats decided whether Senator Johnson or Governor Shivers would be chairman of the Texas delegation at the Chicago convention opening Aug. 13. The decisions taken today will be ratified in 254 separate county conventions on Tuesday as a prelude to the later state convention.

Rural precinct meetings in schools, garages, fire houses, private homes and stores began at 4 P. M., New York time. The larger urban meetings started at 9 P. M., New York time.

Talk of compromise on a delegation chairman—urged editorially by some newspapers—was flatly rejected by Representative

Sam Rayburn, Speaker of the House. He has been leading the campaign for Senator Johnson.

Governor Shivers leads a Democratic faction that wants to be free to participate in the national convention but then bolt the ticket if the candidate or party platform declaration on civil rights is unsatisfactory to the South. The Governor, a firm opponent of the Supreme Court decision requiring integration of Negroes and whites in public schools, has been campaigning for an "interposition" declaration.

The Johnson-Rayburn faction on the other hand, is asking for precinct resolutions instructing the Texas delegation to "vote in the national Democratic convention for the nomination of the best candidate available and * * * thereafter return and work for

the election of the nominee of the national Democratic convention."

Senator Johnson, who has been working on a reduced schedule to regain his full strength since he suffered a heart attack last year, has stumped the state intensively during the last week. So has Governor Shivers. Both sides have spent considerable sums of money for state-wide television and radio hook-ups, and for the direct mailing of campaign material.

The Texas voting system is a complicated one. Each precinct has a weighted value in the selection of delegates to the county convention on Tuesday depending upon the number of votes cast in that precinct for the Democratic gubernatorial candidate at the last general election, in November, 1954. The same system applies to the dele-

gate strength alloted each county at the state convention.

This system affords certain advantages to Governor Shivers this year. Although Texas cast 24 electoral votes for General Eisenhower in 1952, it remains strictly Democratic as far as state officers are concerned.

The big battle, therefore, always is in the Democratic primary and a major effort to defeat Governor Shivers was made two years ago. When the Governor won in a second primary, the November election became basically meaningless and many liberals and party loyalists therefore boycotted it.

Because these loyalists and liberals did not vote in large numbers, the delegate strength of the precincts they control has therefore been reduced for this year's conventions.

May 6, 1956

OLD BOSSES

"BOSS" TWEED controlled Tammany Hall, and thereby New York, in the Sixties.

BOIES PENROSE, of Philadelphia, ruled Pennsylvania between 1904 and 1921.

HUEY LONG was Louisiana's "Kingfish" before he was assassinated in 1935.

FRANK HAGUE said, "I am the law in Jersey City," and made it stick until 1948.

Exit the Boss, Enter the Leader

The old-time political chieftain, whose word was law, has become almost extinct. In his place has arisen a new type who can lead, but not command.

By CABELL PHILLIPS

WASHINGTON

AS Senator Estes Kefauver beats the bushes in the hinterlands seeking support for the Democratic nomination, he complains that apparently everybody is for him "except the Bosses." He thus conjures up a familiar caricature in American folklore of a handful of beefy, cigar-smoking, diamond-studded, Irish Machiavellis who, as masters of large and inert blocs of voters, control the political destiny of the nation.

The picture appears true to many just as does the popular image of the Wall Street Banker with a dollar sign on his paunch, the Labor Agitator holding a sizzling bomb behind his back, or the browbeaten and threadbare figure of John Q. Public.

CABELL PHILLIPS is the Washington representative of The Times Sunday Department.

Edwin O'Connor has just done a magnificent portrait of the breed in his best-selling novel, "The Last Hurrah," a portrait that bears a striking resemblance to the ineffable and indestructible Jim Curley of Boston. But the political Boss today is almost as mythical as any of these, as Senator Kefauver and every other practicing politician knows. He is a mirage, a gaudy memory out of a gaudy past, a species which time has rendered almost extinct.

THE vestigial Boss of today bears little resemblance to his ruthless, hardnosed prototype. The power he once wielded has dissipated in many directions and into many new hands. He is a far less colorful and romantic and dominating figure and he is known by the uninspiring title of Leader. There's a world of difference between The Boss of old and The Leader of

today, and in that difference lie some very significant and encouraging facts about the evolution of American political life.

What it means, in essence, is that American voters, as a whole, have matured to the point where they have pretty largely taken their political destinies into their own hands. No longer can a Frank Hague proclaim, "I am the law in Jersey City," as he did in 1937, without running the risk of being laughed out of town. And the Grand Sachem of Tammany Hall, Carmine DeSapio, found to his chagrin not so long ago that, not only could he not assure a solid slate of delegates to the Democratic convention for New York's Gov. Averell Harriman, he couldn't even deliver his own Manhattan district!

Up to twenty-five years ago, every major city, and many entire states, were political duchies under the rule of individual tyrants or cliques. New York knew in succession such powerful rulers as "Boss" Tweed, "Honest John" Kelly, Dick Croker

and "Judge" George M. Olvaney, who controlled Democratic politics in the city—and thereby the city itself—from the wigwam of Tammany Hall. Philadelphia knew the Vare brothers, Edwin and William, and, alternatively, Boies Penrose, whose Republican domains extended statewide. Chicago's Kelley-Nash machine, but recently dissolved, was the last in an almost unbroken succession of Boss-ruled political organizations which held Cook County in a firm Democratic grip.

TOM PENDERGAST, master of Kansas City for three decades, gave President Truman his start up the political ladder. "Boss" Edward Crump, perennial Mayor of Memphis, controlled the political life of western Tennessee for forty years. Frank Hague, overlord of Jersey City, was, in fact, "the law" there from 1917 to 1948. He died only three months (Continued)

NEW LEADERS

CARMINE DE SAPIO, of Tammany can't always be sure of his own district.

THEODORE McKELDIN has built an efficient Republican organization in Maryland.

RICHARD DALEY, Chicago machine man, is more a reformer at heart than a Boss.

DAVID LAWRENCE, of Pittsburgh, keeps political powers by being an effective Mayor.

ago, Jim Curley, whose loyal Boston constituency kept him in office while he was serving a term in Federal prison, still lives, though he is no longer active.

Boss rule began to emerge in the era of industrial expansion following the Civil War, when cities all up and down the eastern seaboard, and as far west as Chicago, became enormous concentrations of people living in relative poverty and virtual disfranchisement. Leaders appeared in them as naturally as flowers in a dung heap. Gaining power first in their own precincts often by being the best street fighters in the gangs they went on to dominate wards, then to run for minor offices or to form alliances with other leaders in other wards. The competitive struggle was prolonged and often brutal, but those who survived to come out on top were, almost without exception, men of superior shrewdness, human insight and intelligence.

Successful Boss rule was the perfection of minority rule. Often a Boss needed iron-clad control over no more than a single populous ward, or to have dependable infiltrators in a few key wards, or to have the whole-hearted allegiance of a particular religious or national minority, in order to gain the balance of power in city elections.

His technique was to keep a tight grip on the primary, seeing to it by whatever wiles and devices came to hand, that the right man his man got the nomination, and then turning his minions out in force to swamp the polls in the general election. He might even craftily split the opposition ticket by putting up an extra candidate as a decoy.

He was often abetted in these designs by the naiveté or the apathy of the "better element" who opposed him,

usually people to whom the business of politics was but an occasional and distasteful digression. To the Boss and his henchmen, politics was an absorbing full-time career.

The same tactics were just as applicable in state-wide contests. The highest office Frank Hague ever held was Mayor of Jersey City. But by his undisputed mastery of the city, and of Hudson County in which it lay, he could pile up such huge Democratic majorities that, coupled with the sprinkling of Democratic votes from elsewhere in the state, he could elect Governors almost at will, Democratic or Republican.

Patronage and other forms of largesse were the glue that held the Boss's machine together. When a Boss became Mayor, for example, or what was more frequently the case, put his man in the Mayor's chair, hundreds and even thousands of jobs on the public payroll fell to his use. So, also, did the distribution of other, more substantial favors such as the awarding of public contracts and the purchase of supplies. And to a great extent he was the personal dispenser of public charity, seeing to it (with an appropriate regard for the publicity factor) that there were baskets for the deserving poor on Christmas, free distribution of coal in the tenement districts when the winters were hard, summer picnics for the slum children, and so on.

Often the Boss entered an alliance with the local underworld whereby commercialized vice was tolerated in consideration of a split in the profits. And just as frequently, he might enter an alliance with the business interests for some mutually desirable quid pro quo. Reformers or other malcontents who

tried to buck the system could be quietly yoked into submission. It is said of Boston's Curley that he once threatened to have the flood gate in a sewer main running under a downtown bank opened if the bank didn't authorize a loan to the city within twenty-four hours.

Not all Bosses were crooked

"Boss" Tweed, by Thomas Nast.

(though few of them died in poverty) nor were they by any means insensible to the needs of good government—according to their lights. Most kept their cities or states in debt by extravagance, but they usually spent lavishly for parks, boulevards, school buildings and improved welfare services. The state of Louisiana is dotted today with many handsome public hospitals, the legacy of one of the most notorious Bosses of any age, Huey Long, the "Kingfish."

In their heyday, which covered roughly the period from

1890 to 1940, the Bosses could "deliver the vote" with the dependable precision of a Seth Thomas clock. And collectively, depending upon whether they were predominantly Republican or Democratic at the time, they supplied the winning balance of power in every Presidential contest from McKinley through the first election of Franklin Roosevelt.

What has happened to rob the Boss of his power and prestige?

The broad answer is the growing maturity of the American electorate. This is composed of a number of different elements.

(1) The tremendous decline in patronage has robbed the Boss of most of his purchasing power. In most cities and states the last twenty years have seen a rapid expansion in civil service and merit systems for public employes. Most jobs on the public payroll now require some demonstration of fitness, and tenure is protected by law. The Philadelphia City Hall used to abound with such well-paid dignitaries as Sink Inspector and Assistant Superintendent of Manhole Covers. But no more.

(2) Systematic public welfare services have combined with growing prosperity to deprive the Boss of much of his power over the unfortunate. No longer do supplicants for free medical care, or a food basket, or the commitment of a destitute grandparent to the County Home line up, hat in hand, at the Boss' door each morning to pray his bounty. Moreover, many other governmental activities such as schools, parks, street construction, utilities, and the like have slipped from the Boss' control to that of statutory, professional administrators.

201

(3) In the last two decades organized labor has achieved a political awareness it never had before. It has turned from an exclusive preoccupation with the familiar "gut issues"—wages and working conditions—to exert itself in the fields of social and economic policy. Political pressure

sure has become as important an instrument to the labor leader as collective bargaining, and aggressive political thinking has struck down to the local union level. Unified labor's Committee on Political Education (COPE) will be, next to the two major party organizations themselves, the biggest spender in the 1956 campaign.

(4) The flight from the cities to the suburbs has bitten deeply into the concentrations of voter strength on which the Bosses used to depend. Moreover, this symbolizes both an economic and cultural emancipation of the ignorant and subservient lower classes who composed the broad base of the Boss' empire. The new middle class does not take meekly to being pushed around or being told what to do.

(5) Finally, a higher general level of education, and the improvement in mass communication which has come with better newspapers and

with radio and television have produced a far more sophisticated and discriminating citizenry than the Boss is prepared to cope with. Politics is now a matter of general interest at almost every cultural level. More people than ever before recognize a personal stake in the modes of government and in the outcome of elections. It is impossible to deliver this kind of voter at the polls "like so many sacks of potatoes."

Thus, Boss Rule in American politics has about faded into a nostalgic limbo, and with it has gone a good deal of the corruption and the stifling of the democratic process which the Boss needed for survival. In its place has come a sort of beneficent anarchy in which more and more citizens vote as they please, wearing no man's collar. The so-called Independents—voters who ignore party labels in picking their candidates—have been decisive in the last four national elections. They are becoming more and more of a factor in state and municipal contests as well. Dr. George Gallup now estimates that approximately 25 per cent of the electorate outside of the South puts itself in the independent column. Independency is the antithesis of Boss rule.

As the Boss has faded out, the amateur in politics has leaped into the limelight. The first conspicuous manifestation of this trend came in 1940 when, seemingly out of nowhere, the Willkie groundswell rolled over the Republican National Convention at Philadelphia to snatch the carefully planned proceedings out of the hands of the professionals. Wendell Willkie was himself an amateur—who once had been a registered Democrat and his campaign for the nomination was engineered by other amateurs, Oren Root, a lawyer, and Russell Davenport, a magazine editor. Their

successful foray was made possible by their discovery of a new "secret weapon"—the citizens' clubs by which the great, dormant strength of the independent vote could be galvanized.

The demise of the Bosses has not, of course, left a power vacuum in its wake. There still are leaders at every level of the political structure through whom political power is focused. But with rare and steadily diminishing exceptions, they are not autocrats. On the whole, they are a superior breed of politicians who have abandoned the crude thuggery of the past and have adapted themselves to the more sophisticated mores of their constituencies.

Few of today's Leaders operate furtively behind the scenes. Their habitat is the goldfish bowl of public office which they have had to win and hold, not by wile but by good works. David Lawrence, the four-term Mayor of Pittsburgh, remains after twenty-five years one of the biggest Democratic wheels in the country, but he holds onto his job and his power by being a first-rate Mayor. Young Richard J. Daley, Chicago's new Mayor, was brought up in the old Kelley-Nash machine, and Cook County remains a safe Democratic stronghold under his dominion. But he is a reformer at heart rather than a Boss. None can deny the existence, even today, of a formidable "Dewey machine" in New York State; but Tom Dewey was an outstandingly capable Governor. Theodore R. McKeldin, Maryland's first two-term Republican Governor, not only is a top-ranking administrator but has succeeded in supplanting a generations-old Democratic oligarchy in his state with an efficient Republican organization of his own.

Today's leaders are still able

to influence large blocs of voters even if they have to make do without the brass-knuckles and carnival trappings of their predecessors. Big-city Mayors, Governors or United States Senators, for example, who have natural leadership roles within their states, often influence the course of political affairs simply by the exercise of personal prestige.

By granting or withholding endorsement, they can frequently make or break a candidate's prospects. Mayor Daley, for example, clipped

the nascent ambitions of Stephen A. Mitchell, former Democratic national chairman, to run for Governor of Illinois this year simply by refusing, Nero-like, to give Mitchell the nod.

But "organization support"—a euphemism for endorsement by the Leader or Leaders of a party—lacks the connotations of brute force. And it is not invincible, as Senator Kefauver so astonishingly demonstrated just recently in Minnesota.

Frank Skeffington, the hero of "The Last Hurrah!" is anything but a fictitious character. He is a faithful composite of scores of Bosses who have stridden across the political stage. But picturesque and lovable old pirate that he was, it is just as well that he died in the last chapter. For the sake of historical accuracy, there was really nothing else he could do.

April 15, 1956

DEMOCRATS HEAL 'LOYALTY' BREACH

By ANTHONY LEWIS
Special to The New York Times.

CHICAGO, Aug. 13—The "loyalty oath" issue, which tore the 1952 Democratic convention apart, was buried today in a show of party unity.

The two men who led the

North-South fight on the floor in 1952, Senator Hubert H. Humphrey of Minnesota and former Gov. John S. Battle of Virginia, jointly appealed to the convention Rules Committee to adopt a new and non-controversial "good faith" rule. The committee did so unanimously.

In another important sign of harmony, the Credentials Committee voted 52 to 2 to seat the regular delegations from Mississippi and South Carolina. These had been the only two

seating contests in this convention.

There can be no floor fight on the Mississippi and South Carolina decisions because the rules permit a minority report only if the challengers win at least 10 per cent of the Credentials Committee.

Floor Battle Unlikely

It now is certain that there will be no floor battle between North and South over any party loyalty oath or credentials. And in the important remaining area of uncertainty—the civil rights

plank—the trend also seems to be toward harmony.

The defeat of the seating challenges today upset last-minute efforts to bar Senator James O. Eastland of Mississippi from the convention.

Oregon's National Committeeman, Monroe Sweetland, said this afternoon that keeping Senator Eastland out would add 1,000,000 votes to the Democratic ticket this fall. There is widespread fear in the Northern wing of the party that Senator Eastland's outspoken views on

Negro rights, and his strategic position as chairman of the Senate Judiciary Committee, could cost many Negro votes this year.

In the 1952 floor battle, maverick Northern forces succeeded in forcing through a loyalty oath that bound all delegates to work to get the Democratic ticket on their state's ballot. This was a reaction to the Dixiecrat maneuver in 1948 of keeping the regular party ticket off the ballot in several Southern states.

As it turned out, the loyalty oath was not enforced. Its chief effect was to annoy Southern delegates. After 1952 a North-South committee succeeded in settling the issue.

The compromise discards loyalty oaths for individual delegates or delegations and "assumes" everyone is a faithful Democrat. It places on national committeemen and state organizations the responsibility of seeing that the official Democratic ticket gets on the ballot in November.

The major challenge in the Credentials Committee was to the Mississippi delegation, headed by Gov. James P. Coleman.

The challengers, labeling themselves the True Democratic party of Mississippi, charged that some members of the Coleman slate were Republicans or Eisenhower supporters in donkey's clothing.

One delegate of the Coleman slate was accused of being a Republican Presidential elector (candidate for the Electoral College) in 1952. Two were described as members of Citizens for Eisenhower. One was said to favor throwing the 1956 election into the House of Representatives.

Senator John C. Stennis of Mississippi denied the charges. Privately, some Northern members of the committee were told that they should help Governor Coleman becaus he was the one man in Mississippi with an apparent chance to win Senator Eastland's seat from him in 1960.

The issue was settled when the regular Mississippi spokesmen gave firm and repeated assurances that their delegation would support the ticket chosen at the convention. Only the two Negro members of the Credential Committee, from the District of Columbia and the Virgin Islands, voted against the motion to seat the regular South Carolina and Mississippi groups.

August 14, 1956

CIVIL RIGHTS COMPROMISE VOTED; NORTHERNERS LOSE FLOOR FIGHT

DEBATE IS BITTER

Specific Support for Court Edict Avoided —Roll-Call Barred

By WILLIAM S. WHITE
Special to The New York Times.

CHICAGO, Thursday, Aug. 16 —The Democratic National Convention adopted early today a compromise civil rights plank omitting a specific endorsement of the Supreme Court's decision outlawing segregation in the public schools.

It rejected by a howling voice vote an effort by pro-civil rights liberals to put in a harder document demanding implementation of that decision and another by the court banning segregation in transportation.

The all-out northern civil rights forces were not given a roll-call. Their proposal was declared lost by the convention's presiding officer, Sam Rayburn of Texas, Speaker of the House of Representatives.

Former President Harry S. Truman had spoken out from his convention box just before the vote to support the moderate version of the Committee on Platform and Resolutions.

His voice rough with both emotion and belligerence, he declared his civil rights record to be second to none and that the majority's plan was "the best civil rights plank we ever had."

He recalled that he had had a hand in many civil rights platforms and added:

"I've done more to implement civil rights than any other President of the United States."

The civil rights plank adopted denounced discrimination, but said of the court's anti-segregation decisions only that they had "brought consequences of vast importance."

It pledged the party to continue efforts to eradicate discrimination in employment, in security of person, in voting rights and equality of education.

It rejected "all proposals for the use of force to interfere with the orderly determination of these matters by the courts."

The defeated amendment would have pledged the Democrats to carry out the anti-segregation decisions, also not interfering "with the orderly determination of these matters by the courts."

It also would have demanded Federal legislation for fair employment, personal security, and full voting rights.

The losers took the outcome without apparent deep bitterness. One of their leaders, Gov. G. Mennen Williams of Michigan, declared:

"We accept the decision of the convention and will work for the election of the nominees."

Mr. Williams, Senator Herbert H. Lehman of New York and Senator Paul H. Douglas of Illinois were the top leaders in the minority effort.

On the southern side Gov. Marvin Griffin of Georgia made it clear that he had no deep anger at the ending of the issue.

The convention adjourned at 1:41 A. M. (2:41 Eastern Daylight Time.) Until noon tomorrow in a reasonably calm atmosphere.

Mr. Rayburn put two decisive questions to the delegates:

¶Should the convention upset the platform committee and adopt the harder plank proposed by fourteen all-out liberals?

This resulted alternately in a growling thunder of ayes and noes. Mr. Rayburn found that the noes had it.

¶Should the convention now adopt the majority version?

Again there were two choruses; again Mr. Rayburn ruled that the all-out liberals had lost.

Roll-Call Demanded

Banners were being waved out in the hall from delegations— including that of New York— indicating that they wanted a roll-call.

"No, no, now, just a minute," Mr. Rayburn responded. "I have taken the ayes and noes many times [meaning a voice vote] and I think I can tell."

But it was not the "strong" civil rights men who alone felt frustrated. One of the southern delegations, Georgia, had wanted to be recorded as holding the compromise itself to go altogether too far.

The frantic waving of the Georgia standard also was ignored by Mr. Rayburn.

At 12:45 A. M. the chairman of the committee, Representative John W. McCormack of Massachusetts, loudly and calmly read to the convention the group's middle-road civil rights declaration.

Just before 1 A. M. Robert E. Short, chairman of the Minnesota delegation, presented the minority plank, signed by fourteen members of the 108-member platform committee.

Cheers and boos rolled up alternately in the International Amphitheatre where thousands had for hours waited for this phase of decision.

Senator Lehman took the lead in supporting the minority's proposed "hard" plank.

Mr. Lehman, his voice shaking, cried out against "the massive injustice" of racial discrimination.

He complained that the convention leadership had limited to a total of ten minutes' time a dozen state delegations seeking an all-out civil rights declaration.

Mr. McCormack responded hotly that the majority, representing the vast bulk of the committee, had allowed only twenty minutes for its side and that the minority's time allocation was fair.

For some two hours the platform as a whole—which in other points supported arms to Israel, continued international access to the Suez Canal and a complex of liberal domestic legislation—had been held off the night's program.

This had been done to allow time for a series of urgent and fruitless conferences between all factions, most of them held behind the high, silken covered dais of the convention.

The bands played, the delegates whooped and cheered, while all negotiations for a compromise to avoid a floor fight were collapsing one at a time behind the scenes.

The all-out liberals, represented by party leaders from such urban states as New York, Pennsylvania and Michigan, sought some accommodation with the majority as the alternative to a fight on the floor. The New York delegation, with ninety-six votes, adopted a resolution declaring the compromise plank to be "entirely unacceptable."

Accommodation, however, was not to be had, and the liberals were informed that they must come forward to the test or go along with the plank as written.

The platform committee's paper had been adopted without a roll-call vote by that body on

203

a 12 to 5 recommendation by the platform drafting subcommittee.

Issue Sent to Floor

The issue then was sent to the floor, with its deep implications of for Democratic unity or disunity.

The facts of convention rules made the task of the dissenters difficult. To put in a minority report against the platform committee—that is, to seek to reverse it—required the support of only eleven of its 108 members.

But to force a roll-call on such an effort—and this was the decisive point—required the support of a majority of the delegates in at least eight of the state delegations.

The civil rights plank represented a substantial victory for the Southerners, although some of them bitterly denounced it. Their real minimum demand

from the start had been for no explicit approval of the school segregation ruling.

It followed the general reasoning as well of many party leaders, running from Mrs. Franklin D. Roosevelt on the left, through the center of the party and rightward toward the position of the more liberal Southerners.

This was its substance:

¶It started with a declaration for equal opportunities for all citizens.

¶It pledged the Democrats to continue their efforts to end all discrimination, and it called in this connection for unspecified Federal action.

¶It declared pride in the Democratic record of ending discrimination in the armed services, the civil services and in all areas under Federal jurisdiction.

¶It promised continued ef-

forts for "full rights to vote, full rights to engage in gainful occupations, full rights to enjoy security of the person, and full rights to education in all publicly supported institutions."

When, however, it came to the question of the Supreme Court, the document simply declared:

"Recent decisions of the Supreme Court of the United States relating to segregation in publicly supported schools and elsewhere have brought consequences of vast importance to our nation as a whole and especially to communities directly affected. We reject all proposals for the use of force to interfere with the orderly determination of these matters by the courts."

Apart from the fact that this language did not say whether the school segregation decision

was to be viewed as good or bad, it was bare of any pledge for direct implementation of that decision.

The plank went on from here to recognize that the decisions of the court were "part of the law of the land."

It ended with a condemnation of the Eisenhower Administration's "violation of the rights of Government employes by a heartless and unjustified confusing of 'security' and 'loyalty.'"

In thus making the Federal employe security program a civil rights issue, the plank accused the Administration of "a wicked and unprincipled attempt to degrade and destroy the Democratic party" by misrepresenting the facts about security risks in past Democratic Administrations.

August 16, 1956

STEVENSON NOMINATED ON THE FIRST BALLOT; OVERWHELMS HARRIMAN BY 905½ VOTES TO 210

VICTOR IS CHEERED

Wins by Acclamation Upon Motion of the Harriman Camp

By W. H. LAWRENCE
Special to The New York Times.

CHICAGO, Aug. 16—Adlai E. Stevenson won renomination for President on the first ballot at the Democratic National Convention tonight.

The roll-call gave Mr. Stevenson 905½ votes, with only 686½ required for victory. Governor Harriman of New York ran a poor second with only 210 votes despite all the help that former President Harry S. Truman could give him.

Gov. Raymond Gary of Oklahoma, who had placed Governor Harriman in nomination, moved to give Mr. Stevenson the unanimous support of the convention.

Speaker Sam Rayburn, the Permanent Chairman, put the question as one of choosing the nominee by acclamation. There was an ear-splitting roar of "ayes."

"There are no 'noes,'" announced Speaker Rayburn without asking whether there was any opposition.

Mr. Stevenson announced at once that he wanted the convention to have a free-and-open

choice of his Vice-Presidential running mate without his indicating in advance any preference. That vote will be taken tomorrow afternoon.

Cheered by Delegates

The Presidential nominee received a tremendous ovation when he appeared before the convention to express his thanks and to make his suggestion that the delegates themselves choose the Vice-Presidential nominee.

He did not say so, but it was obvious that the purpose of his move was to contrast the Democratic method choosing a Vice-Presidential nominee with that of the Republican party. The top G. O. P. leadership has joined in slating renomination of Vice President Richard M. Nixon as President Eisenhower's running mate.

Upon receiving news of the nomination, Mr. Stevenson said: "I feel relieved and happy." Later he told the delegates:

"My heart is full and I am deeply grateful but I did not come here to speak of the action you have just taken. That I shall do tomorrow night afte you have chosen a Vice President."

Mr. Stevenson said the choice of a Vice President who might succeed to the top office, as seven of the thirty-four Presidents have done, was a tremendously important one.

"I have concluded to depart from precedents of the past," he said. "I have decided the selection of a Vice-Presidential nominee should be made through the free processes of this convention so that the Democratic party's candidate for this great office

Associated Press Wirephoto

THE WINNER: Adlai E. Stevenson as he appeared last night at the convention hall, after he had been nominated.

can appear before the nation, not as one man's selection, but as the choice of the party even as I have been chosen.

"The choice will be yours. The profit will be the nation's."

Cheers and applause, in which former President Truman joined, greeted Mr. Stevenson's state-

ment that had won this nomination without making "a single commitment except faith in the program" of the party.

Senator Lyndon B. Johnson of Texas, the Senate majority leader, made his first appearance before this convention as he came in with Mr. Stevenson tonight. Senator Johnson got eighty votes for the nomination. winning the delegations from Texas and Mississippi.

The convention adjourned at 11:15 P. M. (12:15 A. M. Eastern Daylight Time) until noon tomorrow. Mr. Stevenson will make his formal acceptance speech tomorrow night from the same platform with former President Truman and the new Vice-Presidential nominee.

The convention balloting for President was a rout.

Truman 'Surprised'

In the demonstration that followed Mr. Stevenson's victory, the band struck up "The Missouri Waltz" and the crowd turned toward former President Truman and his wife to give them an ovation.

Mr. Truman told reporters he was "very, very surprised" by the first-ballot decision, but again pledged his support and cooperation in November.

Senator Estes Kefauver of Tennessee, Mr. Stevenson's hard-fighting opponent in the spring primaries, said:

"I am pleased that my supporters and I were of assistance in obtaining the nomination for Mr. Stevenson and I pledge that we shall fight with every resource to make him the next President."

A few minutes after the end of the balloting, Governor Harriman said in an interview that he wanted to congratulate Mr. Stevenson "for his great victory."

"We're going to get behind him," Mr. Harriman said. He was smiling and at ease despite his crushing defeat.

The Governor said he thought his campaign had been "worth while" because "through debate our great party gains unity and strength."

He said he and Carmine G. De Sapio had considered letting Mr. De Sapio, as head of the New York delegation, present the motion to make the nomination unanimous, but they decided it would be "more fitting" to have it come from Governor Gary.

10 Before Convention

Ten candidates were placed in nomination for the Presidency, but two withdrew before the balloting began. The first to drop out was Senator Warren G. Magnuson of Washington. The second was Representative John W. McCormack of Massachusetts.

majority leader of the House of Representatives.

Mr. Stevenson passed the required majority of 686½ votes when Pennsylvania was reached in the roll-call.

A cheer went up when Pennsylvania announced that its 67 votes had "put Mr. Stevenson over the top." His total was 741 at that time. Governor Harriman had 198½, according to a big lighted vote tabulator on which the delegates could follow accumulative totals.

The demonstration interrupted the roll-call briefly, but Speaker Rayburn stepped forward to command "no parade now."

At the end of the roll-call the totals on the big board were:

Stevenson 905½
Harriman 210
Johnson 80
Symington 45½
Chandler 36½
Davis 33
Battle 32½
Timmerman 23½
Lausche 5½

Convention delegates were in a happy, shouting mood as they prepared to ballot. They had avoided the party split that many had feared over the explosive civil-rights issue. They had lined up solidly behind Mr.

Stevenson's candidacy.

Even before the roll-call of states began, Mr. Stevenson was assured of more than the 686½ votes he needed for an absolute majority to give him a second chance to oppose General Eisenhower.

The convention convened at 12:25 P. M. (1:25 P. M., Eastern daylight time), and recessed at 7:12 P. M., to reconvene again at 9 P. M., for the balloting.

A drama-packed day preceded the roll-call of states.

A former President of the United States made a seconding speech for the nomination of a candidate, Governor Harriman of New York, who had no chance of winning.

Mr. Truman, avoiding the bitterness of his most recent attacks on Mr. Stevenson, said instead that he had come as a Democrat with some experience, to support the man he regarded as "best qualified" to be President.

"Never in history has it been as necessary for the Democrats to win an election as it is now," said Mr. Truman.

August 17, 1956

EISENHOWER AND NIXON ARE RENOMINATED; G. O. P. CONVENTION IS UNANIMOUS ON BOTH

TWO ACCEPT TODAY

Eisenhower Says That No Rival to Nixon Came Forward

By W. H. LAWRENCE
Special to The New York Times.

SAN FRANCISCO, Aug. 22—Roaring Republicans unanimously renominated President Eisenhower and Vice President Richard M. Nixon tonight.

A "dump Nixon" movement collapsed completely with the unconditional surrender of its leader, Harold E. Stassen. Mr. Stassen had tried in vain to get Gov. Christian A. Herter of Massachusetts to oppose Mr. Nixon.

General Eisenhower summoned a special, nationally televised press conference to announce that Mr. Stassen's campaign had ended and that all barriers to Mr. Nixon's renomination had been removed. Mr. Stassen later seconded Mr. Nixon's nomination.

Mr. Nixon's victory was made unanimous and complete when a Nebraska delegate, Terry Carpenter, capitulated. On the first roll-call Mr. Carpenter had passed because the convention chairman, Representative Joseph W. Martin Jr. of Massachusetts, had ignored his joking attempt to place in nomination the name of "Joe Smith." Just before the vote was announced, Mr. Carpenter gave in, and the Nixon total climbed to 1,323 votes.

Convention Is Jubilant

It was a moment of triumph and tragedy for the Vice President. He was at the bedside of his critically ill father, Francis A. Nixon, at La Habra, near Los Angeles, when the convention made him its choice for a second term. The elder Nixon is 77.

The nominating processes gave the confident delegates something to cheer and demonstrate about as they sent the victorious team of 1952 back into battle against a Democratic slate again headed by Adlai E. Stevenson of Illinois. Mr. Stevenson's new running mate, picked in an open floor fight at Chicago last week, is Senator Estes Kefauver.

Both the President and Vice President are scheduled to make their acceptance speeches at the final session of this convention tomorrow afternoon. But there was doubt tonight Mr. Nixon could leave his father's bedside. And there was talk of a special television broadcast by him from Los Angeles to the delegates in this hall.

The convention recessed tonight at 9:05 P. M. (12:05 A. M. Eastern daylight time), until 4 P. M. tomorrow when it will hear the acceptance speech of President Eisenhower at least. An organizational meeting of the new national committee was called for 11:30 A. M. tomorrow by Perry W. Howard, Mississippi committeeman who is the group's senior member.

Just before adjournment, the convention directed Representative Martin to telegraph Mr. Nixon an expression of regret over his father's illness and a statement that all were "united in prayers for his recovery."

General Eisenhower was chosen first, and then Mr. Nixon was nominated.

On the roll-call of states, every state cast its unanimous vote for President Eisenhower without a break through Nevada, and that state's vote gave him more than the 662 votes required for a majority and nomination.

At 6:55 P. M. Representative

Martin gravely declared the tally clerks had reported, 1323 votes cast, and that President Eisenhower had received 1,323 votes.

"Therefore, I declare him unanimously the nominee of the Republican party for the Presidency of the United States," he said.

A banner-waving parade then started on the convention floor. Only General Eisenhower's name was placed in nomination for the top spot. The roll-call of states began at 5:08 P. M. Alabama yielded to Indiana for the nominating speech by Representative Charles A. Halleck of Indiana.

Every other state passed up the opportunity to place any other candidate in the field. There was a brief burst of laughter as the Ohio chairman, Ray Bliss, said his state had no candidate "for the first time in twenty years."

His reference was to the continuing candidacies in the past of the late Senator Robert A. Taft and his colleague, Senator John W. Bricker.

General Eisenhower, in announcing the capitulation of Mr. Stassen, was unwilling to say whether he considered Mr. Nixon the strongest candidate the Republicans could select or whether, if a delegate from Pennsylvania, he would cast a vote for Mr. Nixon.

The 65-year-old President, who suffered a heart attack and unlerwent an emergency abdominal operation within the last year, said there were several acceptable younger men who might have been on the ticket with him. But he would give no list.

General Eisenhower, however, praised Mr. Nixon highly, and said the 43-year-old Vice President was "as good a man as you can get."

General Eisenhower said no Vice-Presidential aspirant other than Mr. Nixon had approached him for support, although his door had been open to any "who wished to make a case for himself."

On the contrary, the President said, several men mentioned for the Vice-Presidency had told him they should not be considered.

Knight Also Capitulates

Gov. Goodwin J. Knight of California also capitulated on Mr. Nixon's candidacy. He had refused before to endorse the Vice President or to remove himself as a possible challenger for the nomination. Governor Knight said:

"The President has unmistakably indicated his choice for the Vice-Presidency as Richard M. Nixon. As I have always said, I am pleased to accept the President's choice * * *"

Governor Knight declared he would enthusiastically support the Eisenhower-Nixon ticket.

A big cheer went up when Governor Knight cast his state's 70 votes for Mr. Nixon during the roll-call. The Governor headed off an effort to place his own name in nomination.

The end of the Stassen effort to displace Mr. Nixon from the ticket was announced by the President at 11:45 A. M. about four hours before the convention met to select its nominees.

Two major speeches—by former Gov. Thomas E. Dewey of New York and by Emmet J. Hughes, former White House speech writer and an editor on leave from Fortune Magazine—preceded the roll-call of states for making nominations first for President, and then for Vice President.

Governor Dewey made a fiercely partisan attack on the Democratic ticket. Mr. Hughes, who is not a Republican but who is back on the Eisenhower campaign staff, told this convention of party stalwarts why many like himself could support General Eisenhower but could not support the Republican party itself.

Mr. Hughes is a registered voter without party affiliation.

The convention erupted into a shouting, marching, banner-waving demonstration as General Eisenhower's name was placed in nomination by Representative Halleck.

It was the first real chance the confident, but generally listless, delegates had had to let off steam since the convention began Monday. The parade began with a great roar at 5:36 P. M., and fourteen minutes later Mr. Martin started trying to gavel the convention back to order.

Halleck Hails President

The President was hailed as "our greatest American today" and one who commanded support of "the overwhelming majority of all the American people" including millions in both political parties and in no party at all.

"* * * We believe, with you, that under God, it is America's destiny to go forward as a mighty leader of freedom, justice and peace for all the peoples of the world," Mr. Halleck said.

"Fellow delegates, to speed that day, for all Americans, for all the world, I now place in nomination, as the candidate of the Republican party for President of the United States, the name of the most widely beloved, the most universally respected, the most profoundly dedicated man of our times—Dwight David Eisenhower."

Eight seconding speeches reflecting support in every sector of American life followed the Eisenhower demonstration on the convention floor.

The rules were changed to allow this many, and at the same time Representative Martin

was given permission to recognize non-delegates for seconding speeches. No names were mentioned, but this amounted to authority for Mr. Stassen to appear in support of Mr. Nixon.

The Nixon nominating speech was made by Governor Herter. One of the nine seconding speeches was made by Mr. Stassen, who pledged support to the ticket he had tried to divide.

Mr. Stassen coupled his announced support of Mr. Nixon with a declaration that his surrender had not foreclosed the right of individual delegates to vote for other candidates if they wished. But he said he was reconciled to Mr. Nixon's victory. He called himself a "team player" and said he would work industriously for the ticket in November.

In a sense the drama of the convention floor and actual nominating processes became anticlimactic after the President himself summoned the news conference to announce Mr. Stassen's capitulation.

For the first time, the White House allowed a live, direct television broadcast of a Presidential conference before a crowd of reporters jammed into the Italian Room of the St. Francis Hotel.

Smiling broadly as he entered, the President became solemn as he announced that early this morning Mr. Nixon had notified him his father was seriously ill, and that it was necessary for the Vice President to fly to Los Angeles.

The President said he spoke for all Americans in expressing the hope that the illness would not prove too serious and Mr. Nixon's father would recover.

The President turned then to the Vice-Presidential race, recalling his own statements and those of Mr. Nixon expressing hopes "this would be an open convention—I said as far as it could be for the nomination of the Presidency, and he [Mr. Nixon] said certainly for the office of Vice-Presidency."

Only this morning, he continued, he had talked with Mr.

Martin and had been promised that so "there could be no suggestion of a freeze-out" the complete roll-call would be held so everybody would have a chance to speak.

The President then described Mr. Stassen as "the only individual who has made any great effort to produce another candidate" to oppose Mr. Nixon.

Stassen Is 'Convinced'

He had just talked with Mr. Stassen, he reported, and Mr. Stassen had told him that "after several days here, he had become convinced that the majority of the delegates want Nixon."

Since Mr. Stassen's proposed candidate, Governor Herter, was unwilling to run himself, Mr. Stassen now proposed to second Mr. Nixon's nomination "in order to get his own position clear before the convention and the American public," the President went on.

General Eisenhower said in response to a question he now expected Mr. Stassen to return to his duties as White House adviser on disarmament and to give his full support to the Eisenhower-Nixon team in the November campaign.

Asked if he had even considered another nominee than Mr. Nixon, the President said that he had not known for some time whether Mr. Nixon was going to run, and in that period "I thought of a whole group."

"And I told you once," he added, "the only reason I didn't name them—because I was proud of them all—is that finally someone might bring up a name I would say 'No, I don't want to run with that person.' It would be only for some reason that I couldn't think of, but I don't want to run that risk."

He said several persons mentioned for the Vice-Presidency had voluntarily told him they did not think they should be considered. Among them he mentioned Mr. Stassen and former Gov. Dan Thornton of Colorado.

August 23, 1956

EISENHOWER BY A LANDSLIDE

41 STATES TO G.O.P.

President Sweeps All the North and West, Scores in South

By JAMES RESTON

Dwight David Eisenhower won yesterday the most spectacular Presidential election victory since Franklin D. Roosevelt sub-

merged Alfred M. Landon in 1936.

The smiling 66-year-old hero of the Normandy invasion, who was in a Denver hospital recuperating from a heart attack just a year ago today, thus became the first Republican in this century to win two successive Presidential elections. William McKinley did it in 1896 and 1900.

Adlai E. Stevenson of Illinois, who lost to Mr. Eisenhower four years ago, thirty-nine states to nine, conceded defeat at 1:25 this morning.

At 4:45 A. M. President Eisenhower had won forty-one states

to seven for Mr. Stevenson. His electoral lead at that time was 457 to 74 for Stevenson, and his popular vote was 25,071,331 to 18,337,434—up 2 per cent over 1952. Two hundred and sixty-six electoral votes are needed for election.

Victory in All Areas

This was a national victory in every conceivable way. It started in Connecticut. It swept every state in New England. It took New York by a plurality of more than 1,500,000. It carried all the Middle Atlantic states, all the Midwest, all the Rocky Mountain states and everything be-

yond the Rockies.

More than that, the Republican tide swept along the border st ... .and to the South, carried all the states won by the G.O.P. there in 1952—Virginia, Texas, Tennessee and Florida—and even took Louisiana for the first time since the Hayes-Tilden election of 1876.

For the President and his 43-year old Vice Presidential running mate, Richard M. Nixon of California, who carried much of the Republican campaign, it was a more impressive victory than for the Republican party.

So close were many races for

both the House and the Senate that control of the national legislature was not expected to be decided until later in the day.

About the only consolation for the Democrats, other than that it was all over, was that they picked up strength in the Governor races and thus improved their chances of rebuilding for the post-Eisenhower election of 1960.

Starting with the advantage of holding twenty-seven state governorships to twenty-one for the Republicans, the Democrats won the state capitals yesterday in Iowa, Kansas and Massachusetts. Of the twenty-nine governorships at issue, they won twelve to ten with seven in doubt at 3:40 this morning.

The Eisenhower-Nixon sweep not only broke the Roosevelt coalition of the large urban states of the North and the "Solid South," but also carried into almost every group in the nation that was supposed to be strong for Mr. Stevenson and his running mate, Senator Estes Kefauver of Tennessee.

It clearly gained momentum in the last days during the fighting in the Middle East and Eastern Europe. It established the President as the man the nation wanted to lead it through the difficult period of transition in the Allied, Communist and neutral worlds.

The farm "revolt" was there all right in the areas where drought and falling prices had created a hardship situation, but it was not strong enough to sweep the farmers away from their natural Republican moorings.

Mr. Stevenson not only lost in the areas where his foreign policy arguments were supposed to be the strongest, as in New York, but he also lost ground on the civil rights issue in many of the Negro wards in the North.

He lost, too, in the so-called "Polish wards" of the North, no doubt because of the anti-Communist uprisings in Eastern Europe just as he was preparing to concentrate on the argument that the Administration's foreign policy had failed.

The Chicago Story

The story of Chicago illustrates what happened yesterday. Chicago, in Cook County, is the home of one of the strongest Democrat Party machines in the New Deal days, actually went for Eisenhower by a projected margin of about 16,000.

The irony of this was that Mr. Stevenson had founded his hope on the assumption that the Democratic Party machine was his main hope. Yet it failed him there, and the same trend was present, if not so marked, through most of the populous cities from the Mississippi to New York, another Democratic "stronghold," which Mr. Stevenson carried by fewer than 100,000 votes.

Outside of a few states of the Old Confederacy, Mr. Stevenson's forces broke against the combination of the President's popularity, the prosperity of the nation, and the ominous interna-

PRESIDENT EISENHOWER

VICE-PRESIDENT NIXON

tional situation, which brought out a record number of voters in a serious frame of mind.

The steel workers of Lorain, Ohio, the Negroes of Ward 32 in Philadelphia and the so-called Polish voters of Ward 21 in Buffalo, all supposed to be strong for the Democrats, shifted the other way.

They didn't "go Republican," but they cut down their margins for the Democrats. And when that happens the coalition that kept the Democrats in power for a generation in the Nineteen Thirties and Forties is badly hurt.

What was particularly impressive was the strength of the President's vote in the Northern and border state cities. Four years ago, he took Bridgeport by 314 votes. Yesterday he carried it by 16,000. He took 55 per cent of the total vote yesterday in New Haven which gave Mr Stevenson 54 per cent of that city's vote in 1952.

The President now has the opportunity to pursue the three objectives he gave in explanation of his decision to seek re-election: the maintenance of a just and stable peace in the world; the strengthening of what he has called "The New Republicanism"—that is, conservative in fiscal affairs and liberal in human affairs—and finally, the liberalization of the Republican party.

One of the most remarkable aspects of the President's victory is that he apparently was inclined not to seek re-election until after his heart attack a year ago last September. Before then, he repeatedly urged his party not to count on him but to find younger men to carry on the job he had started.

For example, when he was asked after he announced his candidacy last February what his decision was before his heart attack, he said this was something would probably not be disclosed until twenty-five years after his death. However, his associates have said privately that he finally decided to run because, after his convalescence, he felt it was too late to build up a successor who could win and he was determined to do what he could to liberalize his party and complete the program he had started.

The general expectation was that he would make a start toward rebuilding his party in his record term by changing his Cabinet at some key posts. Secretary of State Dulles is now in Walter Reed Hospital in Washington recovering from an operation to remove a cancerous section of his large intestine. He is expected to be given a new post, probably as a foreign affairs adviser to the President.

There have also been reports that Secretary of Defense Charles E. Wilson has no intention of staying on at the Pentagon through a second Eisenhower term, and Attorney General Herbert Brownell Jr. has told friends he will retire before the President's second-term inauguration on Jan. 20, 1957.

Gov. Christian A. Herter of Massachusetts, who started his federal government career in the State Department, former Gov. Thomas E. Dewey of New York, former U. S. High Commissioner in Germany, John J. McCloy, and General Eisenhower's former Chief of Staff at the North Atlantic Treaty headquarters, Gen. Alfred Gruenther, have all been mentioned as possibilities for any vacancies that

may occur in the top four posts in the State and Defense departments.

Meanwhile, Sherman Adams, the Assistant to the President, and Vice President Nixon, who carried the main brunt of the campaigning for the Republicans in the last six weeks, are expected to assume increasingly important roles in the second Eisenhower Administration. The President, who will be seventy at the end of his second term, is forbidden by an amendment to the Constitution from seeking re-election in 1960.

Accordingly, with both General Eisenhower and probably Mr. Stevenson out of the running for the 1960 Presidential election, both parties will be seeking new potential candidates before long. Mr. Nixon and Mr. Adams are expected to be high on the Republican list of G. O. P. possibilities.

The main issues of the campaign were as follows:

¶ Mr. Stevenson asserted that President Eisenhower was too old at 66 to meet the responsibilities of his office for another four years. He characterized him as a "part-time resident" who delegated his Presidential responsibilities to cabinet officials of inferior ability, and, despite two major illnesses in the last year, had chosen as his Vice-Presidential running mate a controversial politician. Mr. Nixon, he declared, would divide the country if he ever succeeded to the Presidency. President Eisenhower dissented on all counts.

¶ The Republicans contended that President Eisenhower alone had the popular following at home, and the experience and influence abroad, to guide the nation safely through a period of revolutionary transition in the world. The Democrats charged that, ever since the death of Stalin, the President had failed to understand or deal effectively with the new Soviet leaders, or the rising nationalism of the neutral nations, and had allowed the Atlantic Alliance to split wide open over the present crisis in the Middle East.

¶On the home front, the Republicans said that they had freed the national economy from unnecessary controls and not only had ended United States participation in foreign wars but also had produced the greatest era of prosperity in the history of the Republic. The Democrats, in reply, said this prosperity, like the Eisenhower "peace," was an illusion. They charged that the Republican ap-

pointments policy, tax policy, and farm policy had produced a "farm depression" and hurt "small business."

There were many subsidiary issues, including attempts by Mr. Stevenson late in the campaign to persuade the electorate that the President was remiss 1) in continuing tests of the hydrogen bomb and 2) in rejecting suggestions that the military manpower draft could be continued. However, there was little evidence that these issues had impressed the voters when they went to the polls yesterday.

The voting took place once more under pressure of extraordinary events overseas. Not since the election of 1944, when the Second World War was reaching its decisive phase with the American armies deep in Germany, have the American people gone to the polls so preoccupied with alarming foreign policy develop-

ments.

Despite the more hopeful news from Egypt yesterday afternoon. the war scare, combined with good weather over most of the nation, brought out an unexpectedly large crush at the polls.

The President drove to his home in Gettysburg, Pa. early yesterday morning after a meeting with his aides on the foreign situation. He and Mrs. Eisenhower reached the polling place at 11:15 A. M. and were applauded by their neighbors as they left the building. The President then flew back to Washington, though he originally had planned to drive back to the Capital.

Mr. Stevenson cast his ballot at Half Day, Ill., near his Libertyville farm. With him was his son, Borden, a first-time voter. Incidentally, the Census Bureau showed that 7,500,000 Ameri-

cans reached voting age between the last Presidential election and this.

The Democratic nominee was cheerful and optimistic. He bantered with a small crowd at the polling place and said he had been told that leaders in several cities had reported to him that there was "a very strong Democratic turnout."

The Democratic Vice-Presidential nominee, Senator Estes Kefauver of Tennessee, the "iron man" of the campaign, was the last to stop exhorting the voters. He was in Miami, Fla., shaking hands with everybody within reach. He finally quit campaigning late yesterday morning and flew home to Chattanooga to cast his vote. Vice President Nixon had sent his absentee ballot to his home town of Whittier, Calif., earlier. He was in Washington yesterday.

November 7, 1956

President's Power Breaks Democrats' Grip on Cities

By JAMES RESTON

President Eisenhower has produced a political revolution in the large cities of the North, fortress of Democratic strength for thirty years. This seemed to be the most significant fact of Tuesday's Presidential election. The President yesterday held his electoral margin over Adlai E. Stevenson with victories in forty-one states to seven for an electoral total of 457 to 74, and he increased his popular-vote majority to 8,982,531 with 10 per cent of the voting units still to report.

This was more than 3,000,000 greater than his plurality over Mr. Stevenson in 1952. However, what impressed the experts was that he increased his totals this time in almost all of the major cities in the nation.

In the Republican era between the end of the First World War and the election of Herbert Hoover in 1928 the Republicans held a steadily declining majority in the twelve largest cities of the nation. In 1920 that margin was 1,638,000; in 1924, 1,252,000, but in 1928 Al Smith broke the Republican hold on the cities, cutting the Republican plurality to 38,000.

Margins Dwindled

From then on Franklin D. Roosevelt put together an overwhelming coalition of the Solid South, the border states and the workers and minority groups in these Northern cities, and this was the coalition General Eisenhower cracked for the first time

in 1952 and broke wide open on Tuesday.

For example, the Democratic pluralities in these twelve cities (New York, Chicago, Philadelphia, Pittsburgh, Detroit, Baltimore, Cleveland, St. Louis, Boston, Milwaukee, Los Angeles and San Francisco) were 1,910,000 in 1932; 3,608,000 in 1936; 2,210,000 in 1940, 2,296,000 in 1944, 1,443,000 in 1948 and 1,181,000 in 1952.

The figures for Tuesday's election between General Eisenhower and Mr. Stevenson in these twelve cities are not complete, but it was obvious last night that the President not only had cut deeply into the Democratic plurality but also had almost wiped it out.

Chicago to President

The President ran ahead in Chicago, Baltimore, Los Angeles, Milwaukee and San Francisco, and while Mr. Stevenson retained a lead in New York, Philadelphia, Pittsburgh, and St. Louis, the Stevenson plurality in the ten major cities where figures were available was only 135,295.

These vast cities are thus the major battleground of American politics. If one side can capture a huge majority of the votes in the major cities, as the Republicans did in 1920 and 1924, and the Democrats did in the Thirties and Forties, it can be sure

of gaining control of the White House.

It is clear from a study of the available figures, however, that the Republicans have been gaining steadily in the cities since 1936, and have almost drawn even since General Eisenhower has headed the party's ticket.

Record of the Cities

Here is the trend in these major cities, since 1932, showing the percentage of the Democratic vote in each case:

	'40.	'44.	'48*	'52.	'56.
Baltimore	64.0	59.2	53.3	51.7	44.1
Boston	63.3	62.3	69.2	59.6	53.6
Chicago	58.5	61.4	58.6	54.4	†49.0
Cleveland	69.9	67.9	61.8	59.9	
Detroit	63.0	65.0	59.6	60.5	‡
Los Angeles	61.1	59.6	48.9	43.6	†45.6
Milwaukee	64.1	61.7	59.4	51.5	47.4
New York City	61.2	61.6	51.1	55.4	51.0
Philadelphia	60.0	58.9	49.2	58.4	57.1
Pittsburgh	61.6	60.8	60.1	58.1	52.3
St. Louis	58.1	60.4	64.3	62.0	61.1
San Francisco	60.3	60.9	48.0	47.0	48.5

*All 1948 figures except Chicago exclude the Republican and Progressive Party vote.
†Incomplete.
‡Not available.

Moreover the President's strength in the large urban areas was not nearly so impressive as his support in the suburban areas and in the small cities.

To take only two examples of many, he carried Bridgeport, Conn., a normally Democratic city, by a 16,000 plurality Tuesday (he carried it by 300 in 1952), and he won in Memphis, Tenn.

Shelby County, Tennessee, where Memphis is located, is a good illustration of what has happened to the districts once controlled by the Democratic city political bosses. and particularly of the drift of Negro voters back to the Republican party.

County Backs President

Shelby County went to Stevenson four years ago by 6,600 votes, though General Eisenhower carried the state. Tuesday, it gave the President a 3,500 plurality, and the Negro districts there voted 2-1 for him.

In the heyday of the New Deal, when Memphis politics were dominated by Edward H. (Boss) Crump, Memphis usually

gave the Democratic-presidential candidate a plurality of between 50,000 and 60,000.

Many Republicans saw in the Supreme Court's public school desegregation decision during a Republican administration the possibility of persuading the Negroes to come back to the G. O. P., where they were from the Emancipation Proclamation to the beginning of the Roosevelt Era. And there was considerable evidence that General Eisenhower had succeeded in starting that trend.

Gains in Virginia

In New York City, Baltimore, and Richmond, Va., Negroes voted much more heavily for General Eisenhower this time than last. In Harlem the swing toward the G. O. P. was between 10 and 15 per cent over '52. The Seventh Ward of Baltimore, which went for Mr. Stevenson by more than 2 to 1 four years ago, voted overwhelmingly for the President this time.

In the Richmond Negro wards, which were 70 per cent Democratic in 1952, President Eisenhower had a margin Tuesday of more than 5,000.

Some strongly organized Negro wards, particularly in Chicago, held strongly Democratic, but it now is fairly evident that many of the old assumptions about bloc voting are no longer valid.

This, of course, has been noticeable for a long time, and yet it was not obvious enough to prevent Mr. Stevenson from basing his campaign on the strength of the Democratic machine and the allegiance of voters who had marked their ballots Democratic in the past.

None of this, in the opinion of the experts. means that the Republican party can now count on doing in the old Democratic strongholds what President Eisenhower did this week. As was Mr. Roosevelt, General Eisenhower is a rule unto himself, but the vote does prove that a popular Republican candidate can break into areas heretofore regarded as impregnable.

The President's plurality was greater in every region of the nation this time than 1952 except the Pacific Coast, where the figures still were far from complete.

On the basis of about 90 per cent of the vote elsewhere, his vote in New England Tuesday was 2,858,355, or 62 per cent of the two-party vote. Last time he got 56.3 in New England.

Middle Atlantic Vote

In the Middle Atlantic States his total vote was 9,534,035, which was 59.9 per cent of the two-party vote. Last time he got 54.9.

In the Middle West his total was 11,772,937, or 58.7 per cent, as compared with 57.8 in 1952. In all three of these regions he won every state, except in the Midwest, where Mr. Stevenson carried Missouri.

In the Mountain States the President got 1,308,594 votes, or 60.6 per cent. This was three-tenth of 1 per cent higher than in 1952. And on the Pacific Coast, with a small percentage of the votes counted, he received 2,631,339, or 54.8 per cent. This was the only region where the incomplete figures showed him running behind his 1952 percentage of 57.

A study of the regional figures shows that it was in the East and in the South rather than in the Middle West and West that the President had made his greatest gains over 1952.

For example, on the basis of almost complete figures, he got 48.9 per cent of the Southern vote in 1952 but was holding 51.6 per cent yesterday.

In short, the political patterns of the past are vanishing, both in the cities and the South—or at least they are where General Eisenhower is in sight.

November 8, 1956

DEMOCRATS RETAIN SENATE CONTROL AND EXTEND MARGIN IN HOUSE BY 4; EISENHOWER IS WINNER IN 41 STATES

CLEMENTS TRAILS

Loss in Kentucky Race Would Keep Senate Edge at 49 to 47

By WILLIAM S. WHITE

The Democrats have retained Congress in the face of President Eisenhower's overwhelming re-election.

They hold the new Senate and the new House of Representatives of the oncoming Eighty-fifth Congress just as they held the departing Eighty-fourth Congress.

They increased their margin in the House by four—from twenty-nine to thirty-three.

Only four times in history, and never since 1848, has a President-elect failed to carry both the Senate and House.

And never before has any party that lost the White House by so great an electoral margin succeeded in controlling Congress.

Morton Slight Favorite

Last night this was the way the situation stood:

¶The Democrats were certain to hold the new Senate at least by the margin in which they hold the present one—49 to 47.

A single Senate race, in Kentucky between Senator Earle C. Clements, the assistant Democratic leader, and Thruston B. Morton, remained in doubt.

The lead was swaying back and forth; Mr. Morton was a slight favorite eventually to win. His success would leave the Senate margin at 49 Democrats to 47 Republicans; his failure would put it at 50 Democrats to 46 Republicans.

¶The House had gone Democratic again by about the division existing before the election. This was 230 Democrats to 201 Republicans with four vacancies. These vacancies were evenly divided—two hitherto Democratic seats and two hitherto Republican seats.

Last night the House stood: Democrats, 232; Republicans, 199; in doubt, 3.

One Democratic Vacancy

There was one vacancy, caused by the death yesterday of a victorious Democratic candidate. He was Representative Antonio M. Fernandez of New Mexico.

Some faint doubt had been raised during yesterday that the Democrats could actually organize and control the new Senate, assuming the defeat of Senator Clements and a resulting final standing of 49 Democrats to 47 Republicans.

This had arisen because the newly elected Democratic Senator from Ohio, Frank J. Lausche, had declined to say whether he would vote with his fellow Democrats in January for organizational purposes.

There was much doubt among political observers that Mr. Lausche would side with the Republicans in the showdown.

The point appeared to become academic in any event, for a newly elected Republican, Jacob K. Javits of New York, does not intend to be in the Senate in

time to vote with that side on organization.

Mr. Javits is remaining as Attorney General of New York until Jan. 9—whereas Congress meets Jan. 3—to avoid the possibility that his state office would be filled by an appointment made by Governor Harriman, a Democrat.

The New York Legislature, which is Republican-controlled, meets on Jan. 9 and it claims the power to make such an appointment.

The Democrats, still quite confident of being able to organize the Senate in the traditional way and without fuss, reached their control by upsetting Republican incumbents in three states.

Duff Beaten by Clark

Senator James H. Duff of Pennsylvania, one of the earliest of the Eisenhower backers, fell before Joseph S. Clark Jr.

Senator Herman Welker of Idaho, a far right-wing Republican wholly outside the Eisenhower school, lost to Frank Church.

Senator George H. Bender, one of the most vehement of the President's supporters, lost in Ohio to Mr. Lausche.

There was a Democratic gain in Colorado, as well, though not in an identical category. John Carroll defeated former Gov. Dan Thornton for a Republican seat left vacant by the retirement of Senator Eugene D. Millikin.

The Republicans picked up Democratic seats in New York, Kentucky and West Virginia.

Mr. Javits defeated Mayor Wagner for the place being vacated by Senator Herbert H. Lehman, Democrat-Liberal.

Former Senator John Sherman Cooper won in Kentucky over Lawrence W. Wetherby for the seat vacated by the death of Senator Alben W. Barkley.

For a hitherto Democratic seat

in West Virginia former Senator Chapman Revercomb won over W. C. Marland. This place had been opened by the death of Senator Harley M. Kilgore.

Among the Democratic survivors of many hard-fought engagements was the liberal leader, Senator Wayne Morse, who had been perhaps at the top of the Republican list of enemies.

Mr. Morse won re-election in Oregon over Douglas McKay, who resigned as Secretary of the Interior in the Eisenhower Administration to run.

The Democratic triumph had been narrowly foreshadowed, but it had been put in danger by the latecoming issue of war in the Middle East and Central Europe. A clearly perceptible national disinclination not to "change horses in the middle of the stream" had been running for about a week before Election Day.

This psychology clearly was of some aid to the Congressional Republicans and all through election night and into this morning they fought a bitter battle to return to power in the Capitol.

Organizations Cited

They fell short, it appeared on all the evidence, because of the observable power of Democratic organizations across the country and the greater institutional popularity of the Democratic party over the Republican party.

Early returns from the Eastern seaboard had shown the Democrats in trouble, in part because of this region's greater responsiveness to foreign crises.

As later reports came in from the West, Democratic fortunes rose from one succeeding time belt to another.

Farm resentment, though spotted, played a part in the party's Congressional victory.

209

Most of all, however, it appeared to reflect a phenomenon previously seen in the campaign. This was that the contest was between a popular personage, the President, and a party, the Democrats.

Democrats in Control

Among the results of an uneven race in which the President was heavily vindicated and the Democrats clung to their own Congressional position were these:

¶Democratic chairmen again will control the Congressional committees and the President will be required to deal with them as he has done in the last two years.

¶The veteran Representative Sam Rayburn of Texas again will be Speaker of the House.

¶There will be more partisan fighting between the Republican White House and the new Congress. Many right-wing Republicans, particularly in the Senate, have long not really approved the President's policies, particularly abroad.

These Republicans may be expected to begin an attack on the White House before next summer, particularly since the President is barred by the Constitution from running again and will in intra-Republican affairs be less powerful in consequence.

Some powerful Democrats already have indicated that they will be disposed to offer less cooperation to the President than formerly. Again, the main area of their complaint is in foreign policy. They will accuse the President's Administration of having split the West in its dealings with Middle Eastern problems.

The influence in Washington of the "moderate" Texan Democratic leaders—Speaker Rayburn and Senator Lyndon B. Johnson, the party chieftain in the Senate —has been increased even though their own state went for President -Eisenhower.

They have largely controlled Democratic party policy since the inauguration of President Eisenhower in 1953. They contend that policy has been responsible for two successive Democratic Congressional victories—in 1954 and now.

November 8, 1956

THE DEMOCRATIC COALITION REVIVED

DEMOCRATS PUSH LIBERAL PROGRAM

Set Up Top Advisory Unit as a Challenge to Southern Moderates in Congress

By RUSSELL BAKER
Special to The New York Times.

WASHINGTON, Nov. 27—The Democratic party will urge a program for "liberal and enlightened social progress" on its conservative Southern leadership in Congress.

This "assistance" is not expected to be greeted with enthusiasm by the conservatives and moderates who dominate the party in Congress.

[Senator Thomas H. Kuchel, Republican of California, and Senator-elect Joseph S. Clark, Democrat of Pennsylvania, announced they would join a drive by liberal Democrats to end filibusters in the Senate.]

The Democratic executive committee voted today to create a high-level advisory board to shape legislative proposals in line with the party's "progressive, forward-looking platform."

Threat to Johnson

The move was sponsored by Northern and urban elements who blamed the conservative Southern leadership in Congress for the party's collapse in its supposed industrial strongholds in the Presidential election.

It is a challenge to Senator Lyndon B. Johnson of Texas, Senate Democratic leader. He is opposed to a party legislative program and favors a compromise and cooperation with the Administration.

The resolution creating the advisory board was passed in secret session by the fourteen-member executive committee. Paul M. Butler, national chairman, said later the vote had been unanimous and without acrimony.

3 Backers Named

The proposal was backed by three men who felt that Senator Johnson's "moderation" had been politically unhealthy in their areas. They were Paul Ziffren, national committeeman from California; Mayor David Lawrence of Pittsburgh and Col. Jacob M. Arvey of Chicago.

Mr. Butler was authorized to appoint a board of no more than seventeen top Democrats that would "coordinate and advance efforts in behalf of Democratic programs and principles."

The establishment of the board was interpreted as a phase in the developing struggle between the liberal and conservative wings over the party's future.

It was regarded as an attempt to give a more authoritative voice to elements that would be largely submerged by the conservative reign in Congress.

Most observers doubted that an advisory group, no matter how high its rank, could accomplish much. With a Republican in the White House, the performance record on which the Democrats will enter the elections of 1958 and 1960 will be built by their majority in Congress.

That majority, preponderantly Southern and conservative, is composed largely of men who find themselves philosophically more at ease with President Eisenhower than with their party's Northern and urban liberals.

Their disposition in the past has been to ignore the liberal wing's proposals. Observers see no reason to assume that they will be any more eager to accommodate an advisory panel of the national committee.

It is believed that the best the liberal wing could hope for from the board would be a platform from which the party could talk about its progressivism.

This might help in counterbalancing the conservative image the Congressional Democrats are expected to put before the nation the next two years.

The executive committee also discussed the $800,000 campaign deficit. No new suggestions were offered for reducing it, beyond the usual techniques of fund dinners and appeals.

November 28, 1956

DEMOCRATS BACK ADVISORY COUNCIL AS POLICY MAKER

By W. H. LAWRENCE
Special to The New York Times.

WASHINGTON, May 3—The Democratic National Committee, by a 65-to-26 vote, sustained today the authority of its new advisory council to issue party policy declarations between national conventions.

The proposition touched off another North-South battle. Southerners generally voted to restrict the advisory council's right to speak in the name of the party on such controversial issues as civil rights.

The big margin of the vote was a victory for Paul M. Butler, Democratic national chairman, who had gone ahead with the advisory council plan in the face of opposition from the Congressional Democratic leadership headed by Speaker Sam Rayburn and Senator Lyndon B. Johnson, both of Texas.

The showdown came behind closed doors as Democrats gathered for three days of meetings designed to steam up early their campaign to retain control of Congress in 1958 and regain the White House two years later.

Former President Truman led off the partisan oratory with a charge that the policies of the Eisenhower Administration were driving him toward socialism.

Mr. Truman will share speaking honors tomorrow night with Adlai E. Stevenson, the party's Presidential nominee in 1952 and 1956, and other party leaders at a $100-a-plate dinner at the National Guard Armory. It is expected to draw more than 1,500 party faithful and raise more than $100,000 for the party.

As the Democrats gathered they had little good news to cheer them. Matthew H. McCloskey of Philadelphia, their treasurer, reported that the party deficit stood at $660,000— nearly $200,000 more than in February — and that contributions were lagging.

Governors to Confer

Mr. Butler, who had invited the twenty-nine Democratic Governors to participate in a conference, said he was "very disappointed" that only eleven

210

or twelve Governors planned to attend. Special panels for the Governors will be held tomorrow on such subjects as the shortage of money for loans and shortages of educational facilities.

On the credit side, Sam Brightman, the party publicity director, reported a 10,000 increase in circulation in The Democratic Digest since its format was changed a few months ago. Its circulation now is about 73,000. Mr. Butler said the magazine lost $86,000 in the last eleven months compared with a loss of about $100,000 in the previous year.

The National Committee public session had hardly begun when the party faced, but avoided, a renewed controversy on civil rights. It came when a communication was read from Americans for Democratic Action calling on the committee to press for what it called adequate civil rights legislation. The A. D. A. message charged that Democratic Senators had opposed the program by "delay and deceit."

Before the discussion got out of hand, however, leaders on both sides agreed to receive the A. D. A. message as "information," but to take no other action on it.

The Advisory Committee's policy-making role was questioned as the committee, in executive session, debated a new set of rules to govern National Committee actions.

Denmark Groover Jr., Georgia's National Committeeman, proposed that the Advisory Council not be authorized to formulate or declare policy of the Democratic party without the advance specific approval of the National Committee.

This led to a long debate, but when a roll-call was taken the Southern proposal was defeated 65 to 26. Voting with the Southerners was John Golden, Connecticut's National Committeeman. His was the only Far Northern vote that sided with Southern objectors.

Mr. Truman's fiery speech was not made at a party function but at a breakfast sponsored by the Electrical Consumers Information Committee.

The former President criticized the Administration's policy on money and on development of power, including peace-time uses of atomic energy.

He charged that George M. Humphrey, Secretary of the Treasury, was "trying to choke us to death with interest rates."

"I'm not a Socialist," Mr. Truman declared, "but they're driving me that way."

In addition to speaking tomorrow night, Mr. Truman will also participate Sunday in deliberations of the Advisory Council. The Democratic activities will continue through most of Sunday.

May 4, 1957

SPIRIT OF REVOLT SPREADS IN RANKS OF G.O.P.

Moderates of the Party Join Right Wing in Asserting Independence

By WILLIAM S. WHITE
Special to The New York Times.

WASHINGTON, April 27—A spirit of fundamental challenge to President Eisenhower is for the first time rising within all sections of the powerful orthodox Republican phalanx in Congress.

For four years only a handful of Republicans in the far right-wing faction of Congress—and that handful really existed only in the Senate—offered any consistently critical view toward the President and his policies.

Now a mood of questioning and resistance—a mood with clear undertones of gathering revolt—is spreading into the center section. Its manifestations, in fact, extend all the way to the outer limits of the Republican Left.

Right-Wing Core

Again, for four years, the President was able to isolate and largely to make impotent the irreducible core of the Far Right made up of such Senators as Joseph R. McCarthy of Wisconsin, William E. Jenner of Indiana and George W. Malone of Nevada.

The process of isolation is now being arrested, if not actually reversed. This is occurring not because of any accretions of strength to that core as such, but through a sharply increased spirit of restless independence within the great mass of the party in Congress.

Issues and circumstances, in short, now are making it logically possible—and politically inevitable—for the Far Right and the center of the party to draw together in common enterprises, an example being the revolt against the President's budget that is being prepared among all but the most faithful "Eisenhower Republicans."

Process of Isolation

And now these all-out Eisenhower forces, again with special reference to the Senate, are themselves being subjected, slowly but steadily, to a process of isolation. Never numerically strong, they never held posts of essential power in the Senate, simply because orthodox Republicans have retained a dominant place in the party in Congress all through the sixteen years in which comparatively liberal Republicans have held a dominant place in that party in the selection of Presidential candidates.

Thus, the already thin party influence of the liberal Republicans—those predominantly Eastern Republicans who are the President's most consistent supporters—is by the nature of the case being put under heavy erosive pressure as the orthodox Republicans increasingly speak out against the Administration's policies.

In this single week, for example, the Republican Senate leader, William F. Knowland of California, has pledged a cut "at minimum" of $3,000,000,000 in the President's $71,800,000,000 budget and has said that a continuation of present tax policies would "ultimately destroy our free enterprise system."

Senator Barry Goldwater of Arizona has, without rebuke from the party leadership, pressed a running attack on an Administration that he says is "subverting" the American economy. He has spoken of betrayal of public trust and he has thrust hard at the "Modern Republicanism" of the President.

Senator Milton R. Young of North Dakota, a member of the party hierarchy in the Senate, has declared that Administration Republicans have no understanding of the farmers' problems—"and won't understand until after another election." Mr. Young shares with other farm belt Senators a declared fear that the Republicans might lose heavily in the 1958 Congressional elections in farm areas.

Aid for Knowland

Senator Styles Bridges of New Hampshire, chairman of the Senate Republican Policy Committee, is at Mr. Knowland's side in the budget revolt.

And Mr. Knowland, apart from all this, is publicly warning the Administration not to send any military equipment to Communist Yugoslavia without further reference to Congress.

Senator Carl Curtis of Nebraska, an authentic mildand orthodox Republican, says bluntly, in a public letter to the Republican National Committee, that the "heart and core" of his party is "disappointed in the Administration's domestic policies."

These are only some of the recent manifestations from the orthodox Republicans. These now, correctly or not, are quite convinced that Senator Knowland, as an ideological heir to the late Senator Robert A. Taft

'NO THANKS—I WANT ONE JUST LIKE THIS'

Flannery in The Baltimore Evening Sun

of Ohio, will make a determined fight to keep the 1960 Republican National Convention out of the control of the Eisenhower Republicans.

Senator Knowland himself is publicly enigmatic, but he lets his friends understand that this sort of speculation in no sense makes him unhappy.

Many things in the situation are far from clear, but some indisputably suggestive points seem already to stand out. It strongly appears, for example, that many if not most of the orthodox Republicans now question the degree of coattail influence that the President may be able to exert in the 1958 Congressional elections, not to mention those of 1960, when he will be leaving office and traditionally shorn of most of the influence of the Presidency.

It seems clear, too, on the basis of private comments, that dozens if not scores of Congressional Republicans who would not have dared the thought of a break with the President last autumn are now approaching a point of being perfectly prepared to do so.

This marked change of attitude, as is usually the case when profound alterations in the Congressional-Executive relationship are in progress, most frequently appears in subtle and diverse ways. Thus, the general wave of such changes breaks only gradually on an observer's preception.

It was possible back in February, when the Senate was pointedly taking its time with th President's Middle East resolution, to sense that a great turn in this relationship was approaching. Never before, or any foreign policy issue of remotely similar attitude, had the Republican side of the Senate (or the Democratic side) been anything other than assiduously and promptly ready to please.

Battle of Budget

Then, about in mid-February, there opened the great battle of the budget, which had been only indistinctly and imperfectly foreshadowed in January when the President's message on the subject went up to the Capitol.

What had appeared in January to be the prospect of only rather routine trouble for the President began in February to look like serious trouble. Now, in late April, it looks like very grave trouble indeed; there seems real doubt that the President can maintain control over the issue in the bitter contests now approaching over the various appropriations bills.

For all this, there are several reasons.

First and foremost is the fact that the President was never gladly and in their hearts accepted by the orthodox Republicans—whose power in Congress, to repeat, is incomparably greater than that of the liberal or Eisenhower Republicans. They considered the President, from the beginning, to be dangerously close philosophically to the Democrats. They went along with him in largely resigned necessity; they would have deeply preferred Senator Taft to head their party in 1952.

They are engaged now, instinctively if not in every case consciously, upon a counter-revolution against the revolution of the "moderns"; they intend to regain the ultimate control of a party that they genuinely believe to be "ours and not theirs."

No Third Term

Then, there is the fact that the President could not constitutionally have a third term, even if he felt well and strong enough to undertake it. In this, parenthetically, there is an odd irony: when the Republicans joined the conservative Democrats in putting through the anti-third term amendment, they were striking at the incredible (to them) four terms granted to Franklin D. Roosevelt. The present President's constitutional inability even to offer a psychological threat for 1960 to the orthodox is simply a windfall to them.

Thus, in summary, here is the position: The circumstance that the President's sun is necessarily declining opens the way, in the strategic and basic sense, to party challenges to his leadership much earlier in his second term than would otherwise have been the case. Given this strategic opportunity, the orthodox Republicans, fully convinced as they are of the propriety and merit of their case, find in such issues as the budget both a tactical opportunity to rebel and a fundamental impulsion on conviction to do so.

The old monolith of the President's practical influence on the Republicans in Congress—nearly all the Republicans—still stands. But there are spreading crevices in it, small crevices, in some cases, but significant all the same.

April 28, 1957

CIVIL RIGHTS STRUGGLE POLITICALLY INDECISIVE

Republicans Hold A Slight Edge So Far But Democrats At Least Weld An Almost Solid Front

JOHNSON'S STRATEGY WINS

By WILLIAM S. WHITE

WASHINGTON, Aug. 3 — Significant battles touching Presidential aspirations have been won and lost in the Senate's great civil rights struggle. But while the field of action may be said to be strewn with wounded but not fatal casualties and with qualified but not final victors the war itself is yet to be won and lost, for individuals and for the two parties collectively.

What is relatively clear at the moment touches parties more than individuals. For one thing, the Republican party as of now is seen as the clear gainer over the Democratic party, in its far closer voting identification in the Senate with an all-out (if now highly unlikely) civil rights bill. There is substantial, if not overwhelming, detached opinion here that the mere fact that the Senate is passing an "Administration" civil rights measure, even though the President has denounced the introduction of a jury-trial provision, must on balance redound to Republican credit within the large Negro voting population.

Its favor is, of course, sought as well by all but the most adamant of Southern Democrats; the liberal Democrats as a group, therefore, are seen as at least modified losers as of now.

This unmeasurable Republican advantage, however, is not necessarily permanent. The great question in this connection is a most difficult one: What will be the effect, in political terms, if the position of the President and his Administration results in the death of civil rights legislation?

Adamant Administration insistence on a return to the Administration text as passed by the House almost certainly will mean no bill at all at this session. The political edge thus far held by the Republicans—an edge unquestionably somewhat dulled already by the repeated successes of the Johnson coalition of Western Democratic liberals, Southerners and traditional Republicans—would be critically involved in any such decision. Would this edge survive, thinly, after any Administration or general Republican decision to stand to the end for the House text, to refuse any accommodation and thus deliberately to carry the whole issue over to the Congressional election year of 1958? Would the edge enlarge in these circumstances? Or would it vanish altogether through some consensus among Negroes and other minority groups that an excess of Republican "politics" had denied them anything at all?

None of these questions can possibly find any objective answer as yet; the only answers now available are simply the answers foreordained by the identity of the politician to whom one speaks.

The Administration and the common run of the Republicans, therefore, may be said at the moment to have gained an advantage; how and whether it will be maintained only the future can tell.

Democrats Hurt

And the Democrats, as a party, clearly seem to have been hurt to some extent among the all-out civil rights voting groups. The exertions and achievements of Senator Lyndon B. Johnson of Texas, however—and the extraordinary skill of these is publicly or privately acknowledged everywhere in Washington—have made this outlook an uncertain one. At the worst estimate, by subduing the all-out Southern opposition and by bringing with him more Democratic liberals than stand in the Administration coalition led by Senator William F. Knowland of California, Mr. Johnson has kept his party casualties to an astonishing minimum while inflicting heavy, unbroken defeats on his antagonists.

At the best, from his point of view, it is conceivable that he and his party might emerge in the end as those who had accomplished (or had sought strongly if in vain) to bring off a significant, even if an unsatisfactory, advance in civil rights.

Senator Knowland, Mr. Johnson's opposite number on the Republican side, has helped greatly to bring to his party the qualified victory, in political terms, that it uneasily holds to-

212

day. In a sense, however, the exquisite dilemma heretofore confronting Senator Johnson—how far should he go and could he go effectively on civil rights and not enrage either the liberals or the Southerners—has now been transferred, though in different kind, to Senator Knowland.

Mixed Record

As to individuals, Senator Knowland, a possible Presidential aspirant in 1960 against Vice President Richard M. Nixon, has a necessarily mixed record of gains and losses. He has the credit for determined and stout-hearted efforts to put through the Administration's bill; cruelly or not, he has some considerable degree of whatever

blame will be attached to him for losing such significant parliamentary contests to Senator Johnson.

Senator Johnson—and again the estimate necessarily is no doubt somewhat oversimplified—has confirmed and enlarged his reputation as the most brilliant field general in the Democratic party.

He will reap the gratitude of those Democrats—and certainly those professional Democrats—who see how he has thus far preserved his party from chaos and disintegration and wasting internecine warfare in the Senate.

But, though he has broken with the extreme Southerners and will have the decisive imprint on the first important civil

rights enactment since Reconstruction if any enactment in fact emerges, it is hardly possible that he would be acceptable to the much more liberal big-city, industrial-state Democrats who will largely control the next Democratic convention. From their viewpoint, he has, after all, sought too soft a civil rights bill.

Nixon's Role

Mr. Nixon's activities have been less tense, less public and, so far at least, less important than those of either Senator Johnson or Senator Knowland. The Vice President nevertheless is repeatedly, and probably accurately, pictured as the source of much if not most of the "starch" in the Administration's

civil rights position.

Among the main Democratic Presidential "possibilities" only Senators Hubert H. Humphrey of Minnesota and Stuart Symington of Missouri have been "hard" civil rights bill men all the way. Each should benefit among its advocates; but each has set afire, if not wholly burnt, any possible convention bridge to the Southerners and Border State people.

Senators Estes Kefauver of Tennessee and John F. Kennedy of Massachusetts still have some sort of bridge—a stout one in Kennedy's case and a somewhat shaky one in Kefauver's case—with all the advantages and disadvantages involved.

August 4, 1957

President Assails Democratic 'Radicals,' Urges G.O.P. Congress in Coast Speech

Calls Opponents Divided and Denounces Record in the Last Session

By FELIX BELAIR Jr.
Special to The New York Times.

LOS ANGELES, Oct. 20—President Eisenhower declared all-out partisan war on the Democratic party tonight. He contended that it could offer the nation only a Government "that wages war on itself."

The President described the opposition party as dominated by "political radicals." The campaign of the Democratic "left wing" in the Northern states is as extreme as that of the more conservative Southern branch of the party, Mr. Eisenhower said. Then he continued:

"These self-styled liberals are the ones who really challenge sane, sound forward-looking Government in the United States. It is against the spread of their radical influence that we are waging this campaign."

Harsh Condemnation

Veteran political observers considered the President's talk to a capacity audience of 7,000 in Shrine Auditorium as the harshest condemnation of the Democratic party in and out of Congress in which he has ever indulged.

Some newsmen observed that the Presidential address was almost a direct paraphrase of the statement issued by Republican leaders a week ago following

their luncheon meeting with President Eisenhower in the White House. The President sought to dissociate himself from the sentiments expressed in that statement, saying that "politicians always like to make things positive."

The President said the record of the Democratic opposition in the Congressional elections next month was "one of ever higher taxes—of dollars worth 50 cents —of sky-high prices—of an economy harassed into producing fewer jobs, chronic unemployment, labor strife and fear of the future."

To this the President added his thesis on the "political schizophrenia" of the Democrats. As the President put it:

"They are hopelessly split—right down the middle.

"In Congress they crash headlong into each other on every important domestic issue.

"One wing attacks States' rights—the other defends them.

"One stands for big Government—the other for decentralization.

"One is spendthrift—the other conservative.

"In short, our opposition can offer America only deadlocked government — government that wages war on itself."

President Eisenhower told the cheering and stamping crowd of Republicans that "to a political radical, a sound program for America is an invitation for demogogic excess." He said that this had been demonstrated repeatedly during the past Congressional session.

Sees Knowland and Knight

The address followed conferences to resolve differences between Gov. Goodwin J. Knight, Republican candidate for the

Senate, and William F. Knowland, who resigned as Senate minority leader to run for the Governor's chair being vacated by Mr. Knight. There were also parades and other party business.

In his speech the President declared:

"One after another, Administration bills were mangled or mushroomed by extremists pursuing economic and political goals at odds with American tradition. We saw this in housing and public works, in agriculture and unemployment benefits—in urban redevelopment and Federal-state-community relations. It happened in every area where these self-styled liberals might have a field day."

The hard-hitting speech was generally considered the product of his new special assistant, Dr. Malcolm C. Moos, formerly Professor of Political Science at the Johns Hopkins University, now on his first political trip with the President.

The President called for the election of Mr. Knowland for Governor, Mr. Knight for Senator and Patrick J. Hillings as Attorney General. Mr. Eisenhower singled out Vice President Richard M. Nixon for a special tribute when he said:

"One of our most effective leaders in this great fight is our distinguished Vice President and your fellow Californian, Dick Nixon. He is giving us a shining example of dedication to the cause of good government."

To some it appeared that the President was trying to help Mr. Knowland's candidacy when he remarked that "parts of organized labor have long been terribly abused by hoodlums and racketeers."

Mr. Knowland and Governor Knight were present as the

President spoke. The address was carried to western states by a special radio and television hook-up.

The President was introduced by Senator Knowland to the crowded auditorium.

Senator Knowland, who was introduced by Governor Knight as "my great friend," gave the appearance of an Eisenhower diplomatic success in bringing the two men together.

Senator Knowland returned Governor Knight's compliment by saying that he was "entirely and completely in support of the Republican candidates for state and national office."

The President was cheered loud and long when he said:

"Let's have no more bickering—fancied or real. It just helps defeat what we want."

He reminded his audience that "work not done, letters not sent, phone calls not made are sins of omission against the kind of government that you and I and independent and discerning Democrats want."

The International Situation

In a completely political context, the President ignored the Communist Chinese resumption of their bombardment of Quemoy early today. An indirect reference to the Taiwan Strait area came when the President said:

"America is allergic to appeasement. There will be no appeasing Communist aggression while I am President."

Mr. Eisenhower flew to Los Angeles today from Denver after a quiet week-end there.

After a flight from Denver following a quiet week-end, the President arrived at Los Angeles International Airport about 1 P. M. and boarded a Marine Corps helicopter for a seven-minute flight to Exposition Park. There he was greeted by the gubernatorial and Senatorial candidates. The three then rode in an open limousine to the Statler Hotel in downtown Los Angeles.

As he emerged from the helicopter the President wore a blue summer-weight suit, black shoes and a gray felt hat. He grinned broadly as he was greeted by Mayor Norris Poulson and as he himself greeted Governor Knight and Mr. Knowland.

The Los Angeles police estimated that 75,000 persons had

lined the sidewalks along the route of the Presidential motorcade.

James C. Hagerty, White House press secretary, said in answer to a question that bringing together Governor Knight and Mr. Knowland, who have

differed on the "right to work" campaign issue, was a chief purpose of President Eisenhower's visit to California. This issue concerns a proposed amendment to the state constitution to outlaw the union shop, which requires union membership as a

condition of employment.

The President will make two televised addresses in San Francisco tomorrow.

October 21, 1958

SMATHERS CHIDES BUTLER ON RIGHTS

Florida Senator Bids Party Aide Avoid a Pre-Election Debate on Race Issue

By ALLEN DRURY
Special to The New York Times.

WASHINGTON, Oct. 21—A leading Southern Democratic Senator advised Paul M. Butler today to pipe down on the subject of civil rights.

In a tartly worded letter, Senator George A. Smathers of Florida told Mr. Butler, chairman of the Democratic National Committee, that he should forget the dispute over civil rights for the time being and concentrate instead on electing Democrats to Congress two weeks from today.

At the same time, however, Senator Smathers pointedly refused to join those Southerners who are clamoring for Mr. Butler's resignation.

And he said emphatically that for the South to try to

form a third party because of the rights dispute would be "a futile dead-end street for us" and "completely hopeless."

Another leading Southern Democrat, Senator Richard B. Russell of Georgia, said that it was "quite possible" that the Senate might agree in January to a rules change curtailing the Southerners' use of unlimited debate to defeat civil rights measures.

Mr. Butler touched off the latest Democratic party dispute over racial integration when he appeared on a television program over the week-end. He said that if Southerners did not like the party's official stand in favor of integration they could find asylum either with the Republicans or in a third political party.

His remarks brought a flurry of angry comment from Southerners, many of whom called for his resignation as the party's national chairman.

In his letter Senator Smathers reminded Mr. Butler that while Democratic prospects this year indicated a "substantial victory," events of the final two weeks of the campaign could seriously affect the result.

Would Avoid Dissension

He suggested to Mr. Butler that between now and Nov. 4 "at least we try to avoid allowing ourselves, or for that matter our opponents, to accentuate any division which exists in our party."

"I humbly suggest to you," the letter continued, "that you cease firing on the issues of 1960—and let's concentrate on winning the elections of 1958, which can be won or lost within the next two weeks."

"Certainly every knowledgeable Democrat recognizes," Senator Smathers wrote, "that the issue of civil rights is a delicate and difficult one because of the differing background and experience of Democrats within our party.

He went on:

"However, I am sure that you must also appreciate that it is not a general issue in the fall elections of 1958, and that a continuing discussion of it takes peoples' minds off of the virtues of the Democratic party, the reasons why our candidates should be elected in 1958, and in fact, takes the attention off of our fine candidates themselves.

"Our candidates are each running within the boundaries of his own state. Each knows best what the issues should be in his particular campaign and very properly he will pick them. We therefore should leave this decision to our candidates."

No Comment by Butler

At Democratic headquarters Mr. Butler's office said he would make no comment or reply to the Senator's letter.

Senator Smathers, chairman of the Democratic Senatorial Campaign Committee, told newsmen he felt Mr. Butler had

done "a commandable job" and should not resign. On a third party he said:

"I think it would be a very bad mistake for the South to set up a third party. It would cost us prestige in the country and in Congress. It would be a futile dead-end street for us, and it would be completely hopeless. We in the South must attempt to accommodate ourselves as much as possible within the Democratic party as it is now constituted."

Senator Russell said he felt there would be strong support in January for a change in the Senate's present Rule 22, which requires a vote of two-thirds of the full Senate membership to limit debate.

Senator Russell said such a change might allow two-thirds of the Senators actually present to apply closure, or limitation of debate, and might agree that the Senate was a "continuing" body whose rules continued from one session to the next.

Senator Russell's statement, an apparent indication of what the Southerners might be prepared to accept, would thus open the way to an easier imposition of closure, which the Southerners do not like. But at the same time, by carrying over the rules from one session to the next, it would make it more difficult to amend the rules in the future.

October 22, 1958

DEMOCRATS WIDEN CONGRESS CONTROL

National Election Picture: Democratic Tide Is Strong

By JAMES RESTON

The American people elected a more liberal Congress yesterday and confronted President Eisenhower with the largest Democratic majorities in the House and Senate since the days of the New Deal.

Nelson A. Rockefeller of New York scored the most remark-

able triumph of the day in defeating Democratic Governor Harriman in New York. But while he was running against a liberal Governor, even Mr. Rockefeller's victory was not in direct opposition to the major trend of the voting.

For most of the victories

went to Democratic liberals and Modern Republicans—to that coalition of candidates who emphasized social security at home and collective security abroad.

Here were the main events in the day's developments:

¶The Democrats gained authority to organize the Eighty-sixth Congress starting next January by winning the Senate by at least fifty-six to forty and the House by a majority of about seventy-five seats.

¶Such was the strength of the Democratic voting in New

England and the Middle Atlantic states that Connecticut, Maryland, Vermont, and Delaware were left without a single Republican in the House of Representatives.

¶As a result of one of the hardest political campaigns in recent years, organized labor succeeded in defeating the "right-to-work" legislation in the two principal battlegrounds of California and Ohio.

¶The Democrats picked up the Governorships of Ohio and Wisconsin in the heart of normally Republican strongholds,

214

and pointed toward a net gain of two or three governorships.

As an indication of the mood of the voters in the area between the Ohio and the Hudson rivers, John W. Bricker, Vice Presidential G. O. P. candidate in 1944, and a leader of the conservative bloc in the Senate, was running behind Stephen M. Young, a comparative unknown, early today and seemed likely to be defeated.

Sam Rayburn of Texas, who will be Speaker of the House for the ninth time in the eighty-sixth Congress starting in January, told The New York Times early this morning that the Democrats would not return to Washington in a punitive mood as a result of Republican charges against the Democrats during the campaign.

"All that talk about Democratic 'radicals'," he said by telephone, "may in some instances cause some trouble, but we are not disposed to punish anybody just because they are Republicans.

"We are going to try to organize and do a good job for the American people regardless of the backwash of the campaign."

To avert the Democratic gains, President Eisenhower had taken to the road last month and campaigned in Pennsylvania, West Virginia, Iowa, Colorado, California and New York. Meanwhile, Vice President Richard M. Nixon had carried the battle to the other areas where the races seemed close.

Except in New York, however, there was little evidence that his intervention had succeeded or that his efforts to defeat what he described as the "radical element" of the Democratic Party had done any good.

The Republicans went into the election yesterday with the odds against them. They held nineteen Governorships to twenty-nine for the Democrats. They were in a minority in the Senate, 47—49, and in the House, 200-235, and the recent trend of votes for Congress and the State mansions seemed to be against them.

They lost both the House and the Senate in 1954 and 1956, though President Eisenhower was re-elected in 1956 with a plurality of 9,542,354 votes. They won four of the five special House elections in 1957-58, though by lesser margins than in 1956, and they lost the three major state elections of the last two years.

More important, the Republicans had to defend twenty-one Senate seats yesterday, most of them against formidable opposition, while the Democrats had to defend only thirteen Senate seats, most of them in "safe" Democratic states.

In addition, the Democrats had the advantage of perhaps the most consistent trend of twentieth century politics in the United States. This was the tendency of the electorate to vote against the party in the White House in non-Presidential or mid-year elections.

For half a century, with one exception, the party in control of the White House has lost seats in either the Senate or the House of Representatives in the non-Presidential elections. The record is as follows:

Year.	President.	Senate.	House.
1906	T. Roosevelt	+ 3	—28
1910	Taft	—10	—56
1914	Wilson	+ 5	—66
1918	Wilson	— 6	—21
1922	Coolidge	— 6	—75
1926	Coolidge	— 7	—12
1930	Hoover	— 8	—51
1934	Roosevelt	+10	+ 9
1938	Roosevelt	— 6	—80
1942	Roosevelt	—10	—47
1946	Truman	—13	—56
1950	Truman	— 5	—28
1954	Eisenhower	— 1	—18

Thus Franklin Roosevelt, in 1934, was the only President in half a century to come out of a mid-year election with larger majorities in both the House and the Senate. The average gain in the House over this period was between twenty-five and thirty seats.

November 5, 1958

SOUTH REBUFFED IN PARTY CLASH ON CIVIL RIGHTS

Butler Hailed and High Court Stand Backed by National Committee of Democrats

COMPROMISE DISDAINED

Louisiana Loses in Move to Oust Racial Moderate as Its Committeeman

By W. H. LAWRENCE
Special to The New York Times.

WASHINGTON, Dec. 6— Top-heavy majorities of Northern and Western Democrats overrode Southern protests today on a series of civil rights issues.

Amid warnings of possible party splits and defections, the National Committee asserted the party's determination that constitutional interpretations by the Supreme Court should be enforced and made effective. It did this by a roll-call vote of 79 to 27.

The language used was stronger than that of the 1956 Democratic platform. It was offensive to Southerners still carrying on campaigns of massive resistance to the Supreme Court decisions outlawing racial segregation in the public schools.

There appeared to be no disposition to compromise with the South as the National Committee praised the conduct of Paul M. Butler, National Chairman, and refused to oust Camille F. Gravel Jr. as Louisiana's National Committeeman. A Southern-backed effort to remove Mr. Gravel because of his "moderate" stand on civil rights was defeated, 91 to 15.

Sought to Placate South

Having kept his seat with Northern and Western backing, Mr. Gravel sought to eliminate the language offensive to the South from the resolution that commended Mr. Butler for his "forthright utterances" on civil rights issues.

Gov. A. B. Chandler of Kentucky, an announced candidate for President in 1960, also pleaded with the committee to show moderation in its treatment of Southern Democrats. He appealed to his colleagues "not to press down a crown of thorns" on Southern heads.

"You may say," Governor Chandler continued, "that you can get along without the South. But for goodness' sake, don't try it. They're all good Democrats."

Paul Ziffren, California's National Committeeman, argued that the civil rights issue had to be faced "because the Democratic party cannot act as the Republican Administration had in pretending this problem does not exist."

"We are being asked to be tolerant with dishonor," Mr. Ziffren declared. "You cannot be a moderate in the face of evil."

Mrs. Murman Jensen of South Dakota told her colleagues that "if we like moderates in the South, then let us be moderate ourselves."

Compromise Disdained

But the dominant majority would not compromise, although some of its members privately said they wished the civil rights declaration had not been made so strong in the resolution commending Mr. Butler. But they also felt they had to vote for the resolution without significant change once it had been introduced by Mrs. Georgia Neese Clark of Kansas, former Treasurer of the United States.

The resolution commending Mr. Butler's conduct was carried by a vote of 84—19, with only the Southerners against it. The resolution was amended to include commendation of all the other officers of the National Committee.

At luncheon the committee heard former President Harry S. Truman urge them to work together "so we can put someone in the White House who knows where he's going and how to run the country." Mr. Truman defined his present role as one of "punching stuffed shirts."

Mr. Truman was applauded when he told the group that "the man who says 'I'm substantially a Democrat but I always vote for the man,' then you know right away that he's a damned Republican."

Approximately eighty-five of the 108 National Committee members attended, a heavy attendance for a routine committee session.

The battle got under way as the session opened at 11 A. M., with the challenge by Louisiana to Mr. Gravel's right to remain on the National Committee. The effort to replace him with Jett M. Talbott had been rejected by a 7 to 2 vote of the Credentials Committee yesterday. This was reported to the full committee today.

Mr. Talbott, who had argued lengthily yesterday, merely appealed today to the National Committee for a roll-call vote. The vote was then taken without debate.

The fifteen members supporting Mr. Talbott included both committee members or their proxies from Alabama, Arkansas, Georgia, Mississippi, North Carolina, South Carolina and Virginia. Mr. Talbott, with a proxy for the Louisiana National Committee woman, Mrs. Earl K. Long, voted for herself, and Mr. Gravel voted for himself.

Adopted by a Caucus

Southern Democrats did not press before the National Committee their demand for the removal of Mr. Gravel from the party's executive committee and his replacement by Hugh N. Clayton of Mississippi.

This demand was approved by a 14 to 5 vote at a Southern caucus last night. Mr. Butler, as party chairman, was notified by formal letter of the Southern call to remove Mr. Gravel from the Executive Committee. It is doubted that Mr. Butler will accede to the Southern proposal.

Tracy McCraken of Wyoming was one of the pro-Butler, pro-civil rights members who thought it unwise to have raised the civil rights issue in the resolution endorsing Mr. Butler.

"But the damage has been done," he added. "The press is here. The damage cannot be undone, so we should express our approval."

Claude Carpenter of Arkansas, holding a proxy, protested because Mr. Butler had spoken harshly of Gov. Orval E. Faubus of Arkansas, whom he described as "a loyal Governor of a loyal Democratic state."

215

C. Girard Davidson of Oregon retorted that Governor Faubus was a "so-called loyal Democrat," and that Mr. Butler was right in his uncompromising stand on civil rights.

The Democrats voted to hold their 1960 convention in the week beginning July 11, but put off until Feb. 27 a decision about the site. In the interim, efforts will be made to reach an agreement with the Republican National Committee on a single city for both conventions.

The Democrats have received convention invitations from New York, Philadelphia, Atlantic City, Chicago, Miami, Los Angeles and San Francisco.

To meet a $750,000 deficit remaining from the 1956 and 1958 elections, the Democrats also established today a "750 club," with a $1,000 contribution as the price of membership. Edward H. Foley, former Undersecretary of the Treasury, was named to head these fund-raising clubs. Twenty-one persons at the meeting joined at once.

December 7, 1958

A Stevenson Group Will Back Kennedy

Special to The New York Times

WASHINGTON, June 7— A group of so-called eggheads closely associated with Adlai E. Stevenson in previous campaigns is planning a formal endorsement soon of Senator John F. Kennedy of Massachusetts.

The group is small, but the significance of the joint move is that old friends of Mr. Stevenson now seem to be giving up on the idea that he might be drafted again for a third nomination after running against President Eisenhower in 1952 and 1956.

Their letter, to be sent to a large mailing list of liberals throughout the United States, will declare that Senator Kennedy is the strongest Democratic candidate and the one with the best chance of defeating Vice President Nixon, the indicated Republican nominee, in the November election.

Leaders in the group are Henry Steele Commager, Amherst historian; John K. Galbraith of Harvard, Arthur M. Schlesinger Jr. of Harvard, and Joseph L. Rauh Jr., Washington lawyer and longtime leader of Americans for Democratic Action.

All have made known their support of Senator Kennedy at various times, but they are joining in a common letter now to speed the movement of liberals to the Kennedy candidacy.

Meanwhile, Gov. LeRoy Collins of Florida, who will be permanent chairman of the Democratic National Convention, forecast here that the party would ride out its disagreements amicably and emerge from the convention stronger and more united.

Governor Collins said he did not expect any Southern delegations to walk out or to be thrown out of the convention despite earlier controversy over uninstructed electors in possible violation of convention rules.

The Florida Governor was here to confer with top party leaders on his role as permanent chairman. He met for about an hour with House Speaker Sam Rayburn of Texas, who presided at the last four conventions but retired from the post this year because he wished to work for the nomination of Senator Lyndon B. Johnson of Texas.

Sitting in with them was Representative Clarence Cannon of Missouri, the veteran parliamentarian of Democratic meetings.

June 8, 1960

Los Angeles

New Political Trends at Convention

By JAMES RESTON

LOS ANGELES, July 9 — The Democratic convention looks, sounds, and even smells exactly like every other big political blowout of the last twenty years, but it is not the same.

It has kept its appearance but lost much of its power to the states and the people.

It has not been "rigged"; it has been replaced.

Martin Van Buren noted over 100 years ago that the new political leader of the future would not worry too much about winning the support of political leaders but on winning over "the mass of the parties that he might be in a situation to displace the leaders."

This is what Senator Kennedy has done. He has won over the mass of the delegates here by fluttering the multitude in the primaries, and he has either displaced the bosses or greatly reduced their authority.

The lobby of the Biltmore Hotel is jammed at this moment with a mob of notorious political peacocks smoking cigars as big as ball bats and pretending they are going "to put Kennedy over" or stop him on Wednesday.

The Shifts in Power

But most of these gentlemen are dead and don't know it. Senator Kennedy did not come here today to negotiate the nomination with them but merely to pick up the loving cup he won and negotiated by rushing all over the country weeks and even years ago.

This convention marks not only the decline of the old political boss in America but the rise of various new types more representative of the new urban, world-minded America of the Sixties.

There has obviously been a shift in power from the men born in the nineteenth century to the new generation born in the twentieth, and from a very few all-powerful political bosses to a much larger group of younger and more intelligent political figures, many of them comparative amateurs.

There has been a shift in the type and origins of the candidates from the log-cabin or small-town politician born in Lamar, Mo., or West Branch, Iowa, to the suburban or big-city types from the populous coastal areas: Kennedy from outside Boston, Nixon from outside Los Angeles, Rockefeller from outside New York.

As world problems and Federal problems have increased there has been a shift, too, in the type of candidate from the solid administrative characters in the State Governors' mansions to the men trained in world and national affairs in Washington, most of them in the Senate.

There may finally be another shift—how much we still don't know —in the assumption of the Protestant majority of the nation that a Roman Catholic cannot win the Presidency.

Thus, Kennedy is a symbol of many new things in American life. He is representative of the spirit of an age which has emphasized good looks, personality and techniques, all of which he has in abundance.

The Old and the New

He is representative of an age which glorifies efficiency, good management, and a kind of uncommitted intellectual detachment.

Compared with Kennedy's soft speech and conservative clothes and Harvard urbanity, Lyndon Johnson with his six-gallon hat and his windmill oratory seems almost corny, and even Adlai Stevenson now appears a little old-fashioned with his genteel House of Commons manner.

All this helps explain both Kennedy's strength and weakness in this convention. The old-timers are not very happy or comfortable with him because they are not very happy or comfortable with any of the symbols and habits of this new generation or with this spirit of the new age.

All this youth, money, efficiency, all these trappings of the machine-made man, seem a little bloodless to the old boys standing cigar-to-cigar in the Biltmore lobby.

To the younger men in the delegations, however, Kennedy is the new world a-comin'. They groan when they hear the old roarers and shouters of the past on the platform but are lost in admiration at Kennedy's mastery of the art of television debate. They are ill at ease with all the clatter and hooey of the convention atmosphere, but like the cool dissecting-room efficiency of the Kennedy machine.

In short, what is in conflict here in Los Angeles is not merely Kennedy and Johnson but the old generation and the new, the country-bred boy and the city slicker, the old Model T political machine of the past and the Jupiter-C political rocketry of the Sixties.

July 10, 1960

PLATFORM WINS AFTER CLASHES ON CIVIL RIGHTS

SOUTH THE LOSER

Democrats Pledge to End Discrimination —Ask Big Budget

By W. H. LAWRENCE
Special to The New York Times.

LOS ANGELES, July 12—The Democratic National Convention overrode Southern protests tonight to adopt a "big-budget" platform that included the strongest civil-rights plank in party history.

The civil rights pledge to utilize Federal powers to end all forms of discrimination because of race, creed or color was aimed at attracting to the Democratic ticket the largest possible Northern Negro vote in November.

Although ten Southern states dissented, they did not threaten a walkout. However, there were warnings that the strong language might endanger Democratic victories below the Mason-Dixon Line.

Ready for Nomination

Approval of the platform by voice vote cleared the way for the convention to nominate tomorrow its Presidential candidate.

All signs still pointed to an early-ballot victory for Senator John F. Kennedy of Massachusetts. This remained true despite eleventh-hour efforts for Senator Lyndon B. Johnson of Texas, Adlai E. Stevenson of Illinois, and Senator Stuart Symington of Missouri.

It also remained true although the "draft" Stevenson drive took new heart from a victory over Senator Kennedy in California and a tumultuous demonstration that greeted Mr. Stevenson when he entered the Convention Hall tonight.

A split of the eighty-one votes in the California delegations, released by its favorite son, Gov. Edmund G. Brown, gave Mr. Stevenson 31½ votes and Senator Kennedy 30½ votes. The remainder were scattered.

Moreover, a final personal attack by Senator Johnson upon the experience and voting record of Senator Kennedy was interpreted generally as a failing enterprise.

Tonight's session was far less apathetic than the droning formalities of opening day.

The highlight, of course, was the spirited demonstration for Mr. Stevenson in which delegates of all shades of opinion joined the galleries in chanting. "We want Stevenson."

The hour-long debate over the civil-rights plank produced cheers and boos from North and South.

Although the delegates again milled about the floor, as they did yesterday, they were much more attentive when business was to be done than when they were listening to old-fashioned political oratory.

The galleries were better filled, but there still remained thousands of empty seats.

The convention adjourned at 9:55 P. M. until 3:05 P. M., tomorrow, both Pacific daylight saving time, which is three hours earlier than Eastern daylight time. The only scheduled business tomorrow is the selection of a Presidential candidate.

In a dramatic, nationally televised face-to-face debate before the Texas caucus, Senator Johnson criticized Senator Kennedy's absenteeism from the Senate while he was running for President and his voting record on farm, power and resources development.

Senator Kennedy responded that Senator Johnson had made a superb record as Senate majority leader and ought to be retained in that position.

Despite the support for Mr. Stevenson in the California delegation, and although Mr. Johnson forecast his own victory, there was nothing to indicate that Mr. Kennedy's grip on the convention had weakened. Nor was there anything to suggest he would fail to win the nomination on the first or second ballot.

The Kennedy claim of delegate strength mounted beyond 900 votes, with 761 needed to nominate.

In addition to the Johnson-Kennedy exchange, there were these other major convention developments:

¶Platform drafters proposed the toughest civil rights plank in party history, provoking angry Southern protests.

¶Two more Governors, Orville L. Freeman of Minnesota and Stephen L. R. McNichols of Colorado, joined the Kennedy backers.

¶A coalition of Kansas supporters of Senator Stuart Symington of Missouri and Senator Johnson prevented Gov. George Docking from withdrawing as a favorite son before the first ballot and kept all twenty-one Kansas votes pledged to him under the unit rule. The Governor, bidding for the Vice-Presidential nomination with Senator Kennedy, had wanted his state to jump to the Senator's side.

¶The Minnesota delegation, with thirty-one votes, voted again to nominate Senator Hubert H. Humphrey for the Presidency despite his releasing the delegates and despite his withdrawal from the Presidential race after his defeats by Senator Kennedy in the Wisconsin and West Virginia primaries. The withholding of a big bloc of votes from Senator Kennedy, was a maneuver to keep up the pressure on Senator Kennedy to select Governor Freeman as his running mate. But the Freeman situation is complicated by pressure from organized labor to put Senator Humprey in the second spot.

¶The consensus still was that Senator Symington was the front-runner for Vice President, though his managers continued to insist he still was running for President. Gov. James T. Blair Jr. of Missouri was known to be negotiating with the Kennedy forces in Senator Symington's behalf.

¶Mr. Stevenson began to act more and more like an eager "draftee," appearing before state caucuses where latent Stevenson sentiment was known to exist.

¶Gov. LeRoy Collins of Florida assumed the major post of convention permanent chairman, with a slashing attack upon what he called the Eisenhower Administration's failure to produce peace or prosperity.

The Johnson-Kennedy joint appearance arose from a challenge issued by the Texan, and accepted by Senator Kennedy. It appeared to be Senator Johnson's aim to demonstrate before the nation that he had superior qualities of leadership and experience to those of his young opponent, and a better voting and action record.

If his aim was to provoke Senator Kennedy to public anger by slashing at his voting and absenteeism record, without mentioning him by name, Senator Johnson failed.

The young Massachusetts Senator said simply that, since Senator Johnson had not been specific "in mentioning the shortcomings of some Presidential candidates, I will have to assume that he was referring to other candidates and not to me."

The religious issue was posed by Senator Johnson. He said that Protestants had proved they would vote for a Roman Catholic, such as Senator Kennedy, in West Virginia and he hoped that he would receive "equal treatment" in this convention by having some "Catholic states" prove they would vote for a Protestant.

Senator Kennedy bid not for the support of the Texans, already committed to Senator Johnson, but for their backing after nomination.

In taking over as permanent chairman, Governor Collins called for a "turning point" convention that would face and make the tough decisions on critical problems at home and abroad.

"An America, headed for moral bankruptcy under a self-satisfied banner of 'peace and prosperity,' never can win a world for democracy and human freedom," the Florida Governor said.

A Southerner himself, but rated as a moderate on racial issues, Governor Collins asserted that "we are not content with racial and religious prejudices which continue to stifle opportunity."

Appealing to the convention to demonstrate before the nation that which is the "best" and not the "worst" in American life, Governor Collins offered a long list of specifications of an ideal Democratic Presidential nominee.

"It is our responsibility in this convention to nominate a President who can provide the moral leadership the American people must have to meet the challenges of this revolutionary age," Mr. Collins said.

"He must be a man capable of original thought, for the Presidency is the borning-place of national policy.

Stress Put on Sincerity

"He must be a man of impelling sincerity, for the President must earn the attention of the American people by the force of his personality as well as the vigor of his ideas.

"He must be man who is not afraid to be out front, for Presidential leadership cannot await the findings of the latest opinion polls.

"He must be a man whose roots, while growing in any region, nourish a President whose vision reaches into every corner of the land and embraces all our people.

"He must know good not because he can sense it, but because he has done it.

"He must know progress not because he has seen the low ground left behind, but because he has been a part of the struggle for the high ground ahead.

"He must know injustice not because he can place the blame for wrong, but because he has righted it.

"He must know the truth not because he has heard it, but because he has spoken it.

"He must be an uncommon man with a common touch—a man who recognizes his responsibility to all the people, all the time; whose solemn commitment to the national interest and welfare he places above all else."

July 13, 1960

The Civil Rights Plank

Tougher Line Signifies Major Shift In Control of the Democratic Party

By ANTHONY LEWIS
Special to The New York Times.

LOS ANGELES, July 12— The astonishing civil rights plank in the Democratic platform signifies a major shift in the controlling forces of the party in the last four years.

At the 1956 convention the advocates of accommodation with the South were in the saddle. The nominee, Adlai E. Stevenson, had strong Southern support and was personally quite restrained on the civil rights issue.

The Platform Committee was under the control of these same believers in mollifying the South. The chairman, Representative John W. McCormack of Massachusetts, literally locked the drafters of the civil rights plank in a hotel room until they finished so that civil liberties lobbyists could not reach their friends on the committee.

The result was a pallid six paragraphs including such gems as: "The Democratic party emphatically reaffirms its support of the historic principle that ours is a government of laws and not of men."

A minority report in 1956 suggested a pledge to carry out the Supreme Court's school decision and legislation to "secure the right to equal opportunity for employment." But the amendments were overwhelmingly defeated on the floor.

In the present convention younger men, more liberal on the civil rights issue, have taken charge. The dominant forces have been those of Senator John F. Kennedy of Massachusetts, joined on civil rights by supporters of virtually every other Northern candidate.

The position of Senator Lyndon B. Johnson of Texas as the first Southerner in years with a chance at the nomination has helped to polarize the delegates on the civil rights issue, removing the area of compromise.

Kennedy's Freedom

Most significantly, Senator Kennedy has had so little Southern support that there has been no real pressure on him to take a soft position on civil rights.

In fact, Senator Kennedy is the one candidate who has run a full-scale civil rights operation out here, with a breakfast every morning and constant button-holing of delegates by civil libertarians friendly to the Senator.

Senator Kennedy was not personally responsible for the civil rights plank, but he had many men on the Platform Committee and its staff, and several sentences in the plank are taken almost verbatim from his speeches.

Moreover, the Senator's brother Robert passed the word to the Kennedy organization at a staff meeting yesterday that the civil rights plank was "great" and that the organization should give it the strongest possible support and praise.

The plank goes far beyond even the minority report of 1956. On the question of jobs, for example, it is bold enough to use the words Fair Employment Practices Commission—about the reddest flag that could be waved in front of the South.

One of the voting proposals follows, but is stronger than, a recommendation made by the three Northern members of the Civil Rights Commission.

They suggested a Constitutional Amendment to eliminate literacy tests for voters, because these tests had been used to discriminate against Negroes. The platform calls for ending literacy tests by "whatever action is necessary," not necessarily a Constitutional Amendment.

Behind this phrasing lies a theory held by some civil rights strategists that the abuse of literacy tests can be curbed by legislation, without going through the difficult process of amending the Constitution.

For example, Congress might provide that only standard, written tests be used, not subjective oral tests, and that graduation from the sixth grade be prima facie evidence of literacy. The feeling is that Congress may already have power under the Constitution to impose these restrictions to prevent racial discrimination.

Significance to North

The phrasing of this provision in the plank has significance to North as well as South. Total elimination of literacy tests—which presumably could be done only by constitutional amendment—would qualify as voters many Puerto Ricans in New York who cannot speak English.

There is also significant phrasing in the provision calling for injunction suits by the Attorney General on behalf of individual civil rights—for example, school desegregation suits, which have heretofore been brought only by individual litigants.

Proposals to authorize such suits by the Attorney General were beaten by the Southerners when the 1957 and 1960 Civil Rights Acts were passed.

But the platform does not explicitly say authorizing legislation is needed. It simply says that the Attorney General "should be empowered and directed to file civil injunction suits."

This leaves open the possibility that the President may have power, without further legislation, to direct the bringing of civil rights suits on behalf of individuals. Some of the legal thinkers in the civil rights camp would like to attempt such a suit and see how it fared in the courts.

The net impression of the civil rights plank may appear to be that the Democratic party, and especially Senator Kennedy, are writing off the South. But Kennedy spokesmen deny this.

They say the South simply must and is beginning to recognize that the dominant mood of this country today is for significant steps toward equal right rights for Negroes and that the South must live with that fact.

The Kennedy men believe that most Southern states will stay with the ticket despite this forceful civil rights plank. November will tell.

July 13, 1960

KENNEDY NOMINATED ON THE FIRST BALLOT; OVERWHELMS JOHNSON BY 806 VOTES TO 409

LONG DRIVE WINS

Wyoming's Vote Puts Bostonian Over Top Before Acclamation

By W. H. LAWRENCE
Special to The New York Times.

LOS ANGELES, Thursday, July 14—Senator John F. Kennedy smashed his way to a first-ballot Presidential nomination at the Democratic National Convention last night and won the right to oppose Vice President Nixon in November.

The 43-year-old Massachusetts Senator overwhelmed his opposition, piling up 806 votes to 409 ballots for his nearest rival, Senator Lyndon B. Johnson of Texas, the Senate majority leader. Senator Kennedy's victory came just before 11 o'clock last night [2 A. M. Thursday, New York time].

Then the convention made it unanimous on motion of Gov. James T. Blair Jr. of Missouri, who had placed Senator Stuart Symington of Missouri in nomination.

'We Shall Win'

Senator Kennedy, appearing before the shouting convention early today, pledged he would carry the fight to the country in the fall "and we shall win."

He thanked his defeated rivals for their generosity and appealed to all of their backers to keep the party strong and united in a tremendously important election. He spoke directly to Senators Johnson and Symington and the favorite sons, but made no reference to Adlai E. Stevenson.

The third session of the national convention adjourned after his speech. The next session will convene at 5 P. M. today.

Little Wyoming, well down the roll-call, provided the decisive fifteen votes that gave victory to Senator Kennedy. Two favorite-son states, Minnesota and New Jersey, waited in vain to give the on-rushing Kennedy bandwagon the final shove.

When Wyoming came in with its vote, the Kennedy total had mounted to 765 votes, or four more than the 761 votes required for nomination.

It was a tremendous victory for Senator Kennedy. Mr. Johnson, the Senate majority leader, had fought desperately to reverse a Kennedy tide that had been running for months. But Senator Johnson quickly telephoned his congratulations to Senator Kennedy and forecast his election in November.

Senator Kennedy, who chose the tough preferential primary road to victory, had demonstrated to the party's big state leaders that he could win votes.

He reasoned that only through the primaries could

218

he, as a Roman Catholic, remove the lingering fear of party leaders that he was destined for the same kind of defeat suffered by former Gov. Alfred E. Smith of New York, a Catholic, in 1928.

The convention will assemble today to ratify Senator Kennedy's choice of a Vice-Presidential running mate. Key names under consideration are those of Senator Symington, Gov. Orville L. Freeman of Minnesota and Senator Henry M. Jackson of Washington.

The Kennedy bandwagon could not be stopped despite the pressure of the combined Congressional leadership, including Speaker Sam Rayburn of Texas, and of former President Harry S. Truman. Mr. Truman had boycotted this meeting on a charge that the convention had been rigged for Senator Kennedy's nomination.

Efforts to breathe life in a "draft" movement for Mr. Stevenson, the 1952 and 1956 nominee, failed, despite a noisy, rowdy demonstration mostly by non-delegates who had infiltrated the hall by various devices.

At the end of the roll-call, Mr. Stevenson had only 79½ votes, slightly fewer than the 86 cast for Senator Symington.

Gov. Robert B. Meyner of New Jersey did not get a chance to shift his 41 favorite-son votes. Minnesota, with 31 votes cast for Senator Hubert H. Humphrey even after he had authorized their release from first-ballot obligations, also failed to put them over. The Kansas delegation, which had declined to let its Gov. George Docking join the Kennedy parade still was in caucus when the Kennedy vote passed the 761 vote total.

Nine Put in Nomination

Senator Kennedy's victory was national in scope with the exception of the solid South, which gave nearly all its votes to Senator Johnson. Of the fifty-four delegations, including the District of Columbia, the Canal Zone, Puerto Rico and the Virgin Islands, Senator Kennedy ran ahead in thirty-two of them.

All but one of the big states—New York, Pennsylvania, Michigan, Illinois and Massachusetts—gave Senator Kennedy tremendous margins. California was the exception, where he narrowly topped Mr. Stevenson by a two and one-half vote plurality, picking up 33½, or well under a majority of the state's 81-vote total.

Nine candidates had been placed in nomination, but two favorite sons—Governor Docking of Kansas and Gov. Herschel C. Loveless of Iowa—withdrew before the balloting began.

As the balloting progressed alphabetically, Senator Kennedy was well over the 100 mark after Illinois, over the 200-vote mark with Iowa, over 300 with his own State of Massachusetts, just short of 500 after New York gave him 104½ votes, and

over the 650 mark after Pennsylvania.

When West Virginia brought him to the 750 mark, the stage was set for Wyoming to move into the national limelight.

It was an orderly, swift roll-call without a challenge to any state and the resulting poll of the delegation to confirm the accuracy of the announced vote.

It had taken about six and a half hours to place the nine candidates in nomination and to allow their supporters to shout and parade around the hall in wild, but well-organized demonstrations. Only the Stevenson camp violated the convention rules limiting outside demonstrators to a maximum of 125 persons, including bands, for each candidate.

Charges Repeated

The Stevenson group passed entry badges back and forth until nearly 500 outsiders had come in, and than tried to crash through without any kind of passes, forcing a call for two-score more policemen to guard the gates.

Mr. Stevenson started out with the idea that he would not seek the nomination. But cheered by the enthusiasm of Southern Californians, he entered into the political in-fighting of the last few days.

He contributed to the faltering "stop-Kennedy" movement, which before his arrival had shown visible signs of pronounced political fatigue.

Even at the end, Senator Kennedy hoped that Mr. Stevenson would not seek a third nomination and would consent to place Senator Kennedy's name in nomination before the convention.

But finally Mr. Stevenson said that he could not reciprocate the favor Senator Kennedy had performed in 1956 when he placed Mr. Stevenson in nomination at Chicago.

There has been speculation for months that Mr. Stevenson would be Secretary of State in any new Democratic administration.

Gov. LeRoy Collins of Florida, the convention permanent chairman, gaveled the session to order at 3:16 P. M., yesterday.

The political in-fighting and maneuvering continued to the wire, with all the candidates, including Mr. Stevenson, working tirelessly to convince wavering or uncommitted delegates.

Senator Johnson slashed harshly at Senator Kennedy in what many delegates interpreted as desperation maneuvers, aimed at undermining the majority indicated for his young rival. He hit at the Senator's father, Joseph P. Kennedy, wartime Ambassador to Britain, as a friend of Prime Minister Neville Chamberlain and one who opposed American entry into the war against Hitler.

The Senate majority leader also attacked Senator Kennedy's failure to vote for censure of Senator Joseph R. McCarthy—at a time when Senator Kennedy was critically ill in Florida.

The Johnson forces contended that a "revolt" of delegates "hogtied" to Kennedy already was under way and there was no doubt that the Texan would eventually win.

However, the Kennedy camp remained cool and confident, but watchful of any developing signs of weakness in the delegations.

As the serious business of nominating a candidate began, Governor Collins angrily demanded that the milling delegates take their seats and listen with more attentiveness than they had demonstrated at the first two sessions.

Alphabetical Switches

At the outset, Mr. Collins said he would permit orderly withdrawal of non serious favorite-son candidates. He said the convention would proceed, in alphabetical order, to allow states to change their votes between the completion of the first roll-call of states and before tabulation of the final tally on any ballot. Opponents of Senator Kennedy at one stage had announced an effort to change the rules to prevent such vote switching, but this plan was abandoned.

Alabama, first on the list of states, yielded to Texas and the honor of being first placed in nomination went to Senator Johnson.

Speaker Rayburn in his nominating speech said it was the duty of Democrats to "choose the very best leader that we have," and that Senator Johnton had demonstrated "that he knows how to lead."

"This man is a winner," Speaker Rayburn declared. "He can bring together people of all walks of life, of every faith and persuasion. We must not be divided; we must be united. This man can unite us. He will lead us to reason and to work together, for over many years he has proven that he posseses the magic gift of being able to lead men in a common cause. There is no abler man in our party.

"This man belonge to no class, no section, no faction. This is a man for all Americans—a leader matured by long experience, a soldier seasoned in many battles, a tall, sun-crowned man who stands ready now to lead America and lovers of freedom everywhere through our most fateful hours."

Pour Into the Aisles

Hoisting their placards and other paraphenelia of the traditional political demonstration high, Southern supporters of Senator Johnson poured into the aisles as Speaker Rayburn concluded his nominating speech.

With a ten-minute limit for all demonstrations, Mr. Collins allowed this one to run for thirteen minutes before he began banging his gavel and eleven minutes later, it was over.

While seconding speeches were being made for Senator Johnson, the big eighty-one-vote California delegation was polled on the convention floor.

Senator Kennedy took the lead from Mr. Stevenson with a one-vote margin. Mr. Stevenson had a one-vote edge yesterday.

Alaska yielded to Minnesota, and Senator Kennedy was the second candidate placed in nomination. The principal nominating speech was by Governor Freeman, who said his candidate was a "proven liberal" and a demonstrated leader who could win in November.

An original backer of Senator Humphrey before his withdrawal, Governor Freeman said he had chosen Senator Kennedy as his candidate only after "soul searching" and long study.

Arkansas yielded to Florida, and this put favorite-son Senator George Smathers in nomination as the third candidate, coming in ahead of Senator Symington and Mr. Stevenson.

His nominating speech was made by his senior colleague, Senator Spessard Holland.

While the climactic act of the convention brought more spectators than the earlier sessions, even this was not enough to fill all of the 12,000 spectator seats in the new, gleaming Los Angeles Memorial Sports Arena. There still were hundreds of empty seats against the top of the bowl-like structure.

Govenor Blair praised Senator Symington's experience in business and government in urging the nomination of a Midwesterner who could win in November.

A new and unexpected favorite son developed during the long nominating process. He was Gov. Ross Barnett of Mississippi who chose Judge Tom Brady, author of "Black Monday," a book highly critical of the Supreme Courts' decision on racial segregation, to nominate him.

Mississippi leaders said the idea was to give Governor Barnett twenty-three complimentary votes on the first ballot then swing into line with the rest of the South behind Senator Johnson.

Wires for Stevenson

After Senator Symington, Iowa presented its favorite son, Governor Loveless who had already delivered a seconding speech in behalf of Senator Kennedy. As the Democratic nominee for the Senate, Governor Loveless had his name presented to take advantage of the wide exposure nation-wide television would give him.

Delegates reported an attempted telegraphic blitz for Mr. Stevenson, with thousands of telegrams urging his selection arriving while the nominating festivities were in progress. The clear signs also were that Stevenson fans had packed the galleries. He is perhaps stronger in Southern California than in any other place in the nation.

Governor Loveless withdrew as a candidate after the demonstration in his favor, pointing out he already had seconded the nomination of Senator Kennedy.

"I am not running against John Kennedy, so I ask the chair to remove my name from nomination," Governor Loveless said.

This set off a demonstration by Kennedy supporters, as Governor Collins announced that no further consideration would be given to the Iowan's candidacy.

Next to be placed in nomination was Gov. George Docking of Kansas, who was kept in the race against his will by the action of a delegation majority created by a combination of Symington and Johnson supporters. Governor Docking wanted to back Senator Kennedy at once.

Mrs. Franklin D. Roosevelt touched off another wild demonstration as she enterd the hall to take a balcony spectator's seat, interrupting the nominating speech for Governor Docking being made by Frank Theis, the Kansas Democratic chairman.

She was framed in a spotlight as she walked to her seat, and Governor Collins noted that the demonstration was in her honor.

"We hope you will come again, again and again," Governor Collins said.

The pro-Stevenson galleries roared with approval at Senator Eugene J. McCarthy's introduction of Mr. Stevenson.

The Minnesotan asked delegates to reconsider decisions taken earlier before "all the candidates" were in the race, and before the issues were clear.

"I say to all you candidates and spokesmen for candidates who say you are confident of your strength, let this go to a second ballot," Senator McCarthy said.

"Let it go to a second ballot when all of the delegates will be free of instructions," he added.

The cheers that went up were from the galleries and from the Stevenson demonstrators already lined up. The bulk of the delegates sat silent, or, occasionally, booed.

All-out Attack

The McCarthy speech was an all-out attack upon Senator Kennedy, using against him his own phrase about "a time for greatness."

"Power," the Minnesotan said, "is best exercised by those who are sought after."

"Do not reject this man who made us proud to be called Democrats."

"Do not reject this man who is not the favorite son of one state, but is the favorite son of fifty states and of every country on earth," Senator McCarthy said.

The big Stevenson demonstration that followed was dominated by outsiders who had infiltrated the convention hall. The great majority of delegates did not join the parading groups. It was the first major attempt of a gallery to blitz a convention since Wendell L. Willkie triumphed over other Republican hopefuls at Philadelphia in 1940.

Paul M. Butler, Democratic National Chairman, said the taking over of the convention floor by Stevenson backers was "the best answer to charges of rigging [of the convention] for Jack Kennedy."

Aided Movement

These charges have been thrown at Mr. Butler repeatedly by Senator Kennedy's opponents, including Mr. Truman.

Mr. Butler said that the Stevenson group, like all other candidates, had been granted a total of 125 "demonstrator" badges to provide bands and placard carriers for the floor shows.

But once in the hall, Mr. Butler said, the Stevenson group sent the badges back out to others, until the police had counted as many as 450 outside demonstrators.

When the ten-minute time limit had expired, Governor Collins rapped repeatedly for order, and, in his anger, told the Stevenson demonstrators to keep on with their show "if you want the name of this convention associated with hoodlumism."

"We must stop this demonstration," Governor Collins exclaimed. "I am sure that if Governor Stevenson were here he would join me in telling you to end this demonstration."

Senator Harrison A. Williams Jr. of New Jersey placed Governor Meyner in nomination, but the Governor had already ended his long hold-out and was ready to join the pro-Kennedy forces.

July 14, 1960

Some Northerners Irked By Designation of Johnson

By JOSEPH A. LOFTUS
Special to The New York Times.

LOS ANGELES, July 14—Senator John F. Kennedy's choice of Senator Lyndon B. Johnson as a campaign partner today was a swift, bold stroke to bind the wounds of the Democratic party. The new national leader from Massachusetts sought a bridge to the South. He believes that he found it by way of Texas, for the Texan was the South's candidate for President.

Senator Johnson's selection was a blow to Senator Stuart Symington of Missouri and his backers, who had had reason to believe the Missourian held top place on the "probable" list. Senator Symington, however, appeared to accept the decision as one of the realities of political life.

Senator Kennedy had faced the possibility of Southern sullenness, if not rebellion, because the convention until today had represented almost total defeat for the Southern conservative wing of the party.

Compounded Defeat

The defeat of Senator Johnson for first place had compounded the gash inflicted on the Southerners by a civil rights plank that was written by Northern liberals with scarcely a gesture of compromise.

Some Northerners felt affronted by the choice of Senator Johnson, although few were saying so for the record. In the end, it is not expected to change their determination to carry the fight to the Republicans in the fall.

At least two of Senator Kennedy's morning visitors had argued against Senator Johnson as a running mate. They were Gov. G. Mennen Williams of Michigan and Walter P. Reuther, president of the United Automobile Workers.

Informed sources said the two had come away feeling that they had made their case successfully.

Governor Williams later called the selection of Senator Johnson a "mistake" and a "disappointment."

Joseph L. Rauh Jr. of Washington, a founder of Americans for Democratic Action, used the term "double cross."

Not all of labor was opposed to the Johnson nomination. David J. McDonald, president of the United Steelworkers of America, for example, announced he would support a Kennedy-Johnson ticket.

The decision was Senator Kennedy's alone, his first as leader of his party and one that he knew would evoke, at best, acceptance without approval by many of his Liberal friends.

Dictates Statement

In mid-afternoon, the Senator sent for a press aide, Charles Roche. At that time the only other persons in the room with Senator Kennedy were his old friend, Representative Torbert Macdonald of Massachusetts, and Stephen E. Smith, a brother-in-law.

The Senator dictated a statement to Mr. Roche. When Mr. Roche handed it back in typewritten form, Senator Kennedy telephoned Senator Johnson and read it to him. The Texan approved the statement, the announcement of his designation as running mate.

Senator Kennedy then personally notified all the others who had been considered, or their sponsors, and proceeded to the news conference that had been called on fifteen minutes' notice.

As the new leader of his party, Senator Kennedy turned quickly to his new tasks of unifying those elements that for weeks had given their loyalties to rival candidates.

Some of the Senator's regular staff, helped by volunteers, worked on the preliminary drafts of the acceptance speech that the Massachusetts Senator will deliver tomorrow night at the Memorial Coliseum.

The formal selection of the party's new chairman, who will succeed Paul M. Butler, was set for Saturday. On Sunday the nominee will fly to Cape Cod to join his wife, Jacqueline. He plans a vacation of about two weeks there.

Senator Johnson made the first gesture of unity last night with a warm message of congratulation. This morning, the nominee telephoned Senator Johnson and said he would like to call on him. The Texan replied that he would go to see Senator Kennedy at Mr. Kennedy's convenience.

The insistent courtesy of New England prevailed. Senator Kennedy said he would knock at the Texan's door, two floors below him in the Biltmore Hotel, in forty-five minutes. So it was agreed. Afterward, Senator Johnson renewed his pledge of support without reservation.

When Senator Kennedy telephoned Adlai E. Stevenson to propose a visit to the Stevenson suite in another hotel, the conversation almost duplicated the one with Senator Johnson, but it ran longer. Mr. Stevenson won the courtesy-endurance contest and visited his party's new leader.

The Kennedy corner in the Biltmore resembled a subway stop at the rush hour. Callers streamed into and out of the suite, fighting their way in both directions through a great crush of newsmen, cameramen and electronic equipment. A staircase railing separated them from an open, nine-story stairwell.

Labor leaders were among the callers. The first was Mr. Mr. McDonald, who distributed copies of the seconding speech that he had hoped to make for Senator Kennedy. Mr. McDonald is a Pennsylvania delegate to the convention.

Other visitors from labor included Alex Rose, president of the Hat, Cap and Millinery Workers' Union, and Arthur J. Goldberg, special counsel of the American Federation of Labor and Congress of Industrial

Organizations.

Another group of callers included Mayor Wagner of New York, Michael H. Prendergast, Democratic chairman of New York State; Carmine G. De Sapio, national committeeman for New York; Gov. Abraham A. Ribicoff of Connecticut; John M. Bailey, Connecticut state chairman; Gov. David L. Lawrence of Pennsylvania; Representative William J. Green Jr., Philadelphia Democratic leader; Govs. Williams of Michigan, Michael V. Di Salle of Ohio, J. Howard Edmondson of Oklahome and Herschel C. Loveless of Iowa and Mayor Richard J. Daley and Jacob M. Arvey of Chicago.

By early afternoon, the city's safety authorities decided to intervene. They ordered the heavy television equipment out of the corridor.

Nearly the whole day was a succession of huddles and telephoning for Senator Kennedy. During the Kennedy-Stevenson conversation, a telephone call was placed for Mrs. Franklin D. Roosevelt. Both men talked with her, but none would reveal what had been said.

July 15, 1960

Most Southern Governors Cool To Suggestion They Bolt Ticket

Barnett of Mississippi Asks 3d Party — Others Want to Withhold Electors

JACKSON, Miss., July 19 (AP)—Some of the South's Democratic leaders, irked over the party's civil rights platform plank, are giving at least token consideration to a proposal to bolt the party.

Three Governors have rejected Mississippi Gov. Ross Barnett's idea. Others said they wanted more time to consider it.

There was less actual sympathy with a third-party movement than with a possible attempt at independent slates of electors. The elector plan, by withholding the vote from both Democratic and Republican nominees, would aim at throwing the Presidential election into the House of Representatives, where each state has one vote.

Terry Sanford, Democratic nominee for Governor in North Carolina, said he didn't know "of a single Democrat of any prominence" who would bolt the party in November.

Kentucky Backs Kennedy

Kentucky's Gov. Bert Combs said "nothing has been said to me about it and I haven't been contacted by Governor Barnett, but I can't imagine any state other than possibly Mississippi bolting the party. We are going to support the Democratic nominee and the Democratic platform in Kentucky, of course."

Governor Barnett made his suggestive on Monday night. He said he favored reconvening the state's Democratic convention to support a third-party movement.

He termed the Democratic platform "so horrible, so repulsive, so obnoxious, and so contrary to our form of government, I don't see how the people of the South can accept it."

The Democratic platform calls for "equal access for all Americans to all areas of community life, including voting booths, schoolrooms, jobs, housing and public facilities."

Senator Strom Thurmond of South Carolina, the Dixiecrat Presidential candidate in 1948, said he felt South Carolina would make some provision to name unpledged electors in the general election.

He went on to say that he did not think there would be a third party move in the South this year.

Gov. Ernest Vandiver of Georgia said that the nomination of Senator Lyndon B. Johnson for Vice President strengthened the ticket in his state but declined to say whether he felt it was strengthened enough to win. However, he opposed any shift to the Republican ticket. The alternative, he indicated, might be to withhold electoral votes from the Democratic nominees.

Under Georgia law, this may be done by having the electors pass or cast their votes for other nominees.

Gov. John Patterson of Alabama, a supporter of Senator John F. Kennedy, the Democratic Presidential nominee, opposed any Southern bolt.

Gov. Buford Ellington of Tennessee said at Nashville that he would not join in any Southern bolt and predicted the Kennedy-Johnson ticket would carry the state.

Gov. Ernest F. Hollings of South Carolina, acting chairman Arthur Watson of the Louisiana delegation to the national convention, and Gov. J. Lindsay Almond Jr. of Virginia all declined to comment on the suggestion for a Southern bolt.

Gov. Orval E. Faubus of Arkansas had no comment on a possible Southern bolt.

July 20, 1960

The Two Parties: Two Viewpoints

A Democratic View of the Republicans

By ARTHUR SCHLESINGER Jr.

POLITICAL parties acquire identities, like people; and history has endowed each of our national parties with a distinctive personality and philosophy. This character derives in great part from the relationship of the party with the interests which it represents; for, as Madison pointed out in the Federalist Papers, a variety of interests "grow up of necessity in civilized nations," and "the regulation of these various and interfering interests forms the principal task of modern legislation, and involves the spirit of party and action in the necessary and ordinary operation of the government."

Thus from the beginning, when the Virginia planters made their alliance with the workingmen of New York, the Democratic party has typically been a coalition of diverse interests, united by opposition to control of the

ARTHUR SCHLESINGER Jr., Professor of History at Harvard, wrote "The Age of Jackson" and, recently, "The Coming of the New Deal."

government by the most powerful group in the community. Everything else about the Democratic party follows from this.

So, too, from the beginning, when Alexander Hamilton declared his special faith in the "rich and well-born" and sought tirelessly to link "the interest of the State in an intimate connection with those of the rich individuals belonging to it," the conservative party, whether called Federalist, Whig or Republican, has been typically a party based on a single interest.

THE Republican party, in particular, except for the few years when it embraced the cause of anti-slavery, has characteristically identified the general welfare with the welfare of the most powerful group in our society — the business community. It has been, as Emerson once put it, "the shop-and-till party." And everything else about the Republican party follows from this.

Just as its coalition base of Southern farmers and Northern city workers determines the character of the Democratic party, so its single-interest base determines the character of the Republican party. Representing the organized wealth of the country, it has a vast stake in keeping things unchanged; this has made it the party of the status quo. Representing the most powerful private interest, it has more influence than any other group and thus less need for the protection of the state; this has made it the party of negative government.

Representing the status quo and negative government, it reveres clichés and distrusts ideas; this has made it, like the old British Conservative party, the "stupid party." Excluding labor leaders, farmers and intellectuals from its policy-making councils, it is under an irresistible compulsion to mistake a class interest for the national interest, to suppose that what is good for General Motors is good for the country; this has distorted its views of the national welfare.

LACKING the chastening experience of mingling with other segments of the population, it takes its own pretensions with the utmost solemnity; this has made it the party of stiff collars, stuffed shirts and of fogies, old and young. ("To the Republicans," Anne O'Hare McCormick once wrote, "politics is a business, while to the Democrats it's a pleasure.")

The genius of the Republican party, in short, has consisted in being the political embodiment of organized conservatism— opposed to change, to affirmative and creative statecraft, to new ideas, to interpretations of the general welfare which might conflict with vested profits or cherished platitudes.

I should point out that the basic trouble is *not* that the Republican party represents the business community. The trouble is that it represents a *single* interest. I would ob-

221

ject just as strongly to a party which addressed itself exclusively to the welfare of labor or of farmers (or, for that matter, of college professors).

NO form of single-interest government can do justice to the inexhaustible variety of a multi-interest country. It is because thoughtful business men understand this that so many of them have become valued and influential members of the Democratic coalition.

Nor do I suggest that the Republican party has been a single-interest party at every moment in its existence. It was not so under Lincoln or under Theodore Roosevelt. Twenty years ago Wendell Willkie made a gallant try at reconstructing the Grand Old Party. But the modern efforts to broaden the base of the Republican party have all ended in failure. As T. R. put it when he walked out of the G. O. P. in 1912:

"There is absolutely nothing to be said for government by a plutocracy, for government by men very powerful in certain lines and gifted with 'the money touch,' but with ideals which in their essences are merely those of so many glorified pawnbrokers."

No doubt, some future Republican leader may some day appear who can, like Lincoln and T. R., transform for a moment the single-interest tradition of American conservatism. Some day, but not in 1960. That hypothetical Republican leader does not at present exist in Washington, at least as a Presidential possibility; and those who had hoped to see him on the Albany horizon have been a little disappointed by the apparent absence there, until recently, of the fighting qualities that characterized T. R. and Willkie. The present-day Republican party, though with admirable individual exceptions, has been in the main stolidly faithful to the ortho-

dox tradition.

For seven years, the Republican Administration has given us a copybook demonstration of the meaning of single-interest government—from the moment when President Eisenhower's first Secretary of the Interior proclaimed: "We're here in the saddle as an Administration representing business and industry."

THE belief that successful business men have cornered the wisdom necessary for running an infinitely diversified country is reflected, for example, in the President's choice of his Cabinet, his advisers, even of the guests at his stag dinners. No President since Hoover has restricted his contacts to so narrow a circle; Mr. Eisenhower has even held his relations with the professional politicians of his own party to a minimum.

One shudders to think what would have happened if a Democratic President had chosen all his advisers and cronies from the trade union movement or from the universities. Yet the values of a business culture remain so dominant that few seem to mind the fact that for seven years the President of the United States has received his information and his advice from so unvaried a body of Americans.

But this would be all right, if the information and advice were good. The danger of so guileless a faith in the infallibility of successful business men is reflected most disastrously in the resulting conception of our national priorities. President Eisenhower's guiding purpose — repeatedly endorsed by Vice President Nixon—has been to maximize private spending. Everything, except the most urgent needs of national defense, has been sacrificed to this.

In 1954, the President

stated his goal: "We will reduce the share of the national income which is spent by the Government." The first result was the Revenue Act of 1954, which transferred some $7 billion ($10 billion in current dollars) from public to private spending—i. e., from schools and missiles to gadgets and gimmicks. He has repeatedly stated his conviction that private spending is always better than public spending:

"Our Federal money will never be spent so intelligently and in so useful a fashion for the economy as will the expenditures that would be made by the private taxpayer, if he hadn't had so much of it funneled off into the Federal Government."

When public action becomes inescapable, Mr. Eisenhower prefers steering our resources into things of direct benefit to business, like roads, rather than to things that do not make immediate profits for anybody, such as education and urban renewal.

All this follows from the Presidential delusion that a single interest has a monopoly of social wisdom. The business men tell him that private spending is productive and virtuous, while public spending is inflationary and wicked; that the economy can "afford" to tear down fancy office buildings in order to put up fancier ones, but that it can't "afford" to clear noisome slums and put up decent public housing; that we can "afford" as a people to spend $10 billion a year on advertising but can't "afford" to spend more than $3.5 billion a year on higher education; that Government retrenchment—i. e., freeing as much money as possible for private spending so things can be sold at a profit to consumers—is more important than providing for our military se-

curity or for meeting the social needs of a swiftly growing population.

AND all this is part of a larger delusion—that government is somehow the enemy, and that it is better to watch national defense lag, cities rot, slums multiply, segregation persist, education decay, West Virginia miners starve, pollution spread and the Soviet Union occupy the moon than to give the Government the resources to prevent these scandals or bring them to an end.

Single-interest government has starved the public needs of the nation, from our military security to our provisions for the welfare and opportunity of future generations. It has created the paradox of public squalor in the midst of private opulence. It has produced a prevailing materialism which has debased our tradition and corrupted our morals.

It has crippled our position in the world, not just by denying resources to defense and foreign aid, but above all by presenting America to the world in the image of self-righteous, complacent and sterile conservatism rather than of the clear-headed and tough-minded idealism that brought the Republic into being.

We can afford single-interest politics no longer. Government poised on so narrow a basis can never generate the sense of glowing national purpose essential to the expansion of justice and opportunity at home and to the recovery of leadership abroad. The time has come for America to have a government that will express the wonderfully various character and interests of our people and will thereby release the creative and magnanimous energies of our nation.

July 17, 1960

A Republican View of the Democrats

By RUSSELL KIRK

Rotten eggs and dead cats
Are good enough for Democrats.

NOT always has the Democratic party deserved this heroic Republican reproach of yesteryear. One of the longest-lived political factions of our egalitarian age—second in years, indeed, only to the English Conservative party—the American Democrats have been led, from time to time,

RUSSELL KIRK, Research Professor of Politics at C. W. Post College, is the author of, among other books, "The Conservative Mind."

by genuine statesmen: Calhoun, for instance, and Cleveland, and Wilson. In Jefferson they had a founder of high and diverse talents. And they have produced very colorful popular leaders, such as Jackson and Bryan and Franklin Roosevelt.

For a long while the Democratic party represented real and fairly distinct interests in the nation. It was the party, by and large, of the rural population, of the European-born in the cities, and of state and local rights. Its particular political attitudes—its hostility toward tariffs, its liking for easy-money policies, its suspicion of big business—arose from the Democrats' strength among the farmers, the immigrants and the Southerners.

Standing most of the time for what Orestes Brownson called "territorial democracy," as opposed to centralization, the Democrats were a necessary counterpoise to the centralizing tendencies of Whigs and Republicans.

SOME Democrats like to call their party "the party of the people." To judge by election returns since 1800 they have been popular only about half the time. Yet it is true enough that the Democratic party, however eccentrically, tended to represent sectional and other minorities, debtors, and the urban industrial working class. A party performing such functions is essential in a free nation.

Almost from the beginning the Democratic party really consisted of two factions in an uneasy alliance: the white rural (Continued) population of the South, and the polyglot city working people—at first, mostly Irish —of the North. Out of the latter circumstance came the allegiance of most Catholics and Jews to the Democratic leadership. Thus "Rum, Romanism and Rebellion" were curiously conjoined in the minds of ardent Republicans after Reconstruction.

With no intimate bond uniting these two factions except hostility to Whigs and Republicans, it is a testimony to Democratic loyalty and eloquence that the party has held together at all in the twentieth century.

IN 1960 we see two parties, really, both bearing the name Democratic: the Southern Democratic party, founded on white supremacy, and the Northern Democratic "liberal" party, closely leagued with the great labor unions. (The existence of some few conservative Democratic politicians in the North, and of a handful of "liberal" Southern Democratic politicians, does not much affect the general alignment.) I doubt whether a house so divided against itself can stand forever.

So it is difficult to say precisely what the Democratic party of 1960 professes or represents; Senators Byrd and Russell are odd bedfellows for Senators Humphrey and Morse. The Southern faction has clung with reasonable fidelity to Jeffersonian doctrines, notwithstanding the gulf of taste and opinion that has separated such Southern Democrats as Senator George, say, and Senator Huey Long.

But the Northern faction (excepting fundamentally conservative politicians like Senators Lausche and Dodd and the remnants of old-fashioned rural Democratic organization in such states as my own Michigan) no longer is attached to Jeffersonian traditions; even lip-service to the Jeffersonian ideas of decentralization, rural society, and self-reliance is becoming perfunctory.

WE see in the Northern "liberal" Democrats a new political faction, with roots that go scarcely deeper than the first Administration of Franklin Roosevelt. And this Northern wing generally dominates the Democratic party in a national election year—though not always in Congress, because of the seniority of Southern Senators and Representatives upon Congressional committees. In numbers, money and publicity the Northern Democratic faction is the stronger; we may expect it, increasingly, to demand of Southerners

submission or withdrawal.

What interests does this present Northern—and Western—Democratic party represent? Principally the power of the big labor unions, reinforced by the Northern Negroes and some smaller minority groups.

The union leaders aspire to exercise a veto upon candidates and measures in any degree unacceptable to them; in several states they already hold that power. The Negroes, formerly Republican, have voted overwhelmingly Democratic in the North ever since the days of W. P. A. By the promise of higher crop-price supports, the Democrats attract a good many farmers on election day; but this is a league temporary and uncertain, and in many Northern states the Democratic leaders seem to dislike rural and small-town institutions as anachronistic.

WHAT does the dominant Northern Democracy stand for? For the slogans of New Deal and Fair Deal, obviously; but that is only to stand for the dead or dying issues of the Nineteen Thirties and Forties. Their general objectives, never very clearly stated, seem to be centralization, economic planning, and increased "welfare" benefits. Suggestive now and again of English Fabian proposals of fifty years ago, the "liberal" Democratic utterances are intended to rally "the party of the people" around the standard of the central welfare state.

Not altogether paradoxically, their aspirants to the Presidency, almost to a man, are very rich gentlemen, insulated against any serious harm from the taxation which would be essential to their system; while many professors, fancying themselves in the role of philosopher-kings, see in the Democratic proposals their chance for eminence and emoluments as administrators of the new order.

Rather an old-fashioned note, evocative of the great depression, sounds in the recent speeches of "liberal" Democratic leaders. Senator Kennedy tells us that seventeen million Americans nightly go to their beds hungry. (These, some wag replied, must be the people who are too lazy to walk from the television set to the refrigerator after "The Late Show.")

Professor Samuel Beer, chairman of Americans for Democratic Action, raises the great Water-Closet Issue: multitudes of Americans, he declares, suffer the ignominy of using outside toilets. (Retreating from this bold stand after criticism in The Cleve-

land Plain Dealer, Mr. Beer protested somewhat feebly that he knew of one household in Cambridge, Mass., with its toilet in the basement, rather than on the main floor.)

REPRESENTATIVE Chester Bowles proclaims that "six million American families do not now have a balanced diet." (True: home economics teachers tell me that their charges always prefer hamburgers and French-fries to good cookery; but it is doubtful whether National Diet Inspectors would be popular.)

Professor Arthur Schlesinger Jr., let it be said, calls for a "qualitative liberalism," to replace the old "quantitative liberalism" for which the practical politicians are stumping the country nowadays; but his seems to be a lone voice in the Democratic wilderness. The general assumption of the leading "liberal" Democrats seems to be that by increase of Federal spending, and consolidation of power, we can cure all the ills to which flesh is heir. Their program is socialism without nationalizing industry.

The Democratic leaders propose to spend tremendous sums of public money—raised either by taxation or by inflationary borrowing—for free (and compulsory) medical care, schools, "depressed" regions, foreign-aid projects, and other humanitarian schemes. They imply that they will guarantee enduring and increasing prosperity through central planning and "safe" inflation. To the deeper and more pressing problems of our age, they pay no attention at all.

AND I think this a lamentable state of mind for a great party. My reasons are three: the view of the "liberal" Democrats is not progressive, but archaic; it is blind to the real needs of the nation and our civilization; and it is contrary to the former purposes and functions of the Democratic party.

First, the approach of the Democrats is out of date. At a time when the states of Western Europe are repudiating socialism and regretting certain excesses of the welfare state, the Democrats—suffering from a political lag—seem bent upon establishing in America what already has failed in Europe. The prosperity of the United States today is greater than that any people ever experienced before; and that prosperity, whatever its faults, is the work of American free enterprise.

An intelligent political party might well challenge the assumption that an abundance

of consumer goods is synonymous with national greatness and happiness. But the Democrats do not challenge that assumption. On the contrary, they are more enthusiastic about a producer-and-consumer civilization than were even the "laissez-faire" doctrinaires of the nineteenth century. A considerable annual increase of the gross national product has become almost an article of religion with the Democrats; they propose to enforce soaring productivity by positive law.

THERE was a time when American liberals and radicals used to talk about capitalistic greed and materialism. But the appetites of the "liberal" Democrats seem markedly fiercer than those of the Robber Barons. And if what the Democrats really desire is an expanding economy, to regulate that economy from Washington—to kill the goose that lays the golden eggs—seems an odd way to go about it.

Second, though for nearly eight years the Democrats have been free to criticize the national Administration without the unpleasant necessity of making hard executive decisions, they have failed to touch upon the grand difficulties of this time of troubles.

Among our actual troubles are the need for forming a coherent foreign policy, calculated to withstand communism and Soviet power; the problem that has been called "human estrangement," or social boredom, including the decay of purpose and morality in our society; and the serious decline of American education and taste, urgently demanding a qualitative reform.

But in foreign policy, no leading Democrat has proposed any convincing alternative to the Eisenhower course. The confused and uncertain response of Democrats to the recent collapse of summit negotiations and the affair of the U-2 plane suggests that the Democratic party has no notion of what policy it would pursue, if in power.

Apparently all contestants for the Democratic Presidential nomination think that Mr. Stevenson would be an admirable Secretary of State —or did before it was reported that Mr. Stevenson had confided to a Parisian journalist that the present American Secretary of State is Dr. Adenauer. Nikita Khrushchev also endorses Mr. Stevenson for high office. Both Mr. Stevenson and Mr. Bowles, who seek to be Democratic architects of foreign policy, suffer from that sentimentality and naïveté in world affairs which the late Gordon

223

Chalmers called "disintegrated liberalism."

And Senator Kennedy? Why, in one Wisconsin speech Mr. Kennedy denounced Secretary of Agriculture Ezra Taft Benson for shipping abroad foodstuffs that are the birthright of the alleged seventeen million supperless Americans, while in other utterances Mr. Kennedy is eager to give more milk to Hottentots. One may excuse a degree of inconsistency in primary campaigns; but one must feel that such politicians haven't had a glimpse of a coherent foreign policy. And the Nineteen Sixties will be a time when this nation cannot afford Yaltas.

WITH respect to the increasing monotony and purposelessness in American life, the leading Democrats have said nothing—except for Mr. Stevenson, who has touched glancingly on such matters. As for education and taste, the Democrats have done nothing but propose more classrooms and higher salaries for teachers, at national expense — which is like curing cancer by building bigger hospital wards. I know that our present discontents have no facile solutions; yet a responsible party eight years in opposition ought to have some few tentative suggestions.

Third, the dominant element in the Democratic party of 1960 seems to have abjured the old principles and responsibilities of the Democratic party. I take a brief inventory:

Formerly, the Democrats were the guardians of state and local rights. Now they are all for centralization, including a proposed policy toward the Southern states more radical than anything Republicans ever intended. They seem to be moving confusedly toward what Tocqueville called "democratic despotism." They have ceased to respect the principal success of America in politics, the federal (as distinguished from central) system of government.

Formerly, the Democrats were hostile toward concentration of economic power. Nowadays they are quite willing to allow almost unlimited economic and political power to the great labor unions, except for some gestures against racketeering; and they welcome economic planning from Washington which exceeds immensely the greatest power the trusts ever had.

FORMERLY, the Democrats stood for the interests of the small farmer, the small business man, the independent craftsman and laborer. Today they propose legislation which would tax and regulate and annoy out of existence those vital elements in American society; among the giant government, the giant unions, and the giant regulated corporations, the individual and the little private undertaking would have short shrift. The state must provide doctors for the old—in a nation that has swept away thrift and self-reliance and family responsibility and private charity. That way the Democrats are moving.

Since 1933, the Democratic party has abandoned its earlier purposes. Among its present leaders I find no trace of the high imagination that might fit their party to seek the new purposes of the dawning age.

July 17, 1960

SECRET NIXON-ROCKEFELLER TALKS DRAFT A BASIC PLATFORM ACCORD; RULE OUT GOVERNOR FOR 2D PLACE

8-HOUR MEETING

Vice President Takes Initiative in Setting Up Session Here

By WILLIAM M. BLAIR
Special to The New York Times.

CHICAGO, July 23 — Vice President Nixon and Governor Rockefeller of New York have fashioned the core of the Republican platform in an extraordinary face-to-face meeting.

They produced a set of "basic positions" on major foreign and domestic affairs during their eight-hour night conference in the Governor's Fifth Avenue apartment in New York last night and early today.

The results of their meeting were embodied in a long statement issued in Mr. Rockefeller's name and subsequently subscribed to by Mr. Nixon.

Mr. Rockefeller said the statement constituted "the basic positions for which I have been fighting." Mr. Nixon said it "defines our areas of agreement."

The ambiguity of the language in the Governor's statement indicated that he and Mr. Nixon still had differences over details of policies and how to put those policies into effect. This was later confirmed by Mr. Nixon in Washington.

[The Republican Platform Committee declared unanimously late Saturday night, according to The Associated Press, that while it welcomed suggestions such as those from Governor Rockefeller and Vice President Nixon, the committee and the convention would write the platform.]

Mr. Nixon initiated the effort to settle the differences over a Republican program. He flew secretly from Washington yesterday, arriving at the Governor's apartment at about 7:40 P. M., Eastern daylight time.

Confer With Leaders

They talked until about 3:30 A. M., interrupting their discussions for conferences by telephone with Senator Thruston B. Morton of Kentucky, Republican National Chairman, and Charles H. Percy of Chicago, the platform chairman, in Chicago.

Mr. Nixon flew back to Washington early this morning and Mr. Rockefeller flew to Chicago. Mr. Nixon's aides said the statement by the Governor had been drawn jointly by the two men.

The agreement removed several obstacles confronting platform drafters but immediately caused trouble in the panel writing a civil rights plank. Southerners and conservatives on the civil rights subcommittee protested that Mr. Nixon had abandoned his "moderate" position and bowed to Mr. Rockefeller's "ultra-liberal" stand.

The two leaders set down these basic agreements:

¶A recognition of the growing menace of communism and the "vital need" of new political creativity in foreign policy, including Mr. Rockefeller's proposal for confederations of nations in the North Atlantic area and the Western Hemisphere to meet the Soviet Union's threats.

¶Immediate resumption of underground atomic tests to improve and gain new methods of detection while discontinuing air tests.

¶A broad expansion of national defense to meet the military challenge of the next decade, including powerful retaliatory forces, balanced armed forces to put down local "brush fires," more weapons from bombers to bases and a stepped up Civil Defense program.

¶Acceleration of economic growth by policies and programs designed to stimulate the free enterprise system to achieve an annual growth rate of 5 per cent.

¶"Aggressive action" in civil rights to wipe out all forms of discrimination in jobs, schools, housing and voting.

¶Health protection for the aged through a "contributory system," meaning apparently through the Social Security System.

¶Improved procedures for ending labor disputes that endanger the national security.

◆Reorientation of farm programs on a commodity-by-commodity basis to lessen need for price supports and eliminate crop controls; doubling of the present Federal land-retirement program to cut surplus output, help for low-income farmers to find jobs in industry, expansion of the President's food-for-peace program, and creation of a civil defense food stockpile.

¶Aid to eduaction with Federal grants-in-aid for classroom and other needed facilities, expansion of student loans and establishment of Federal scholarships for able students.

Creation of two Government posts to aid the President, one for national security and foreign affairs and one for domestic affairs.

On balance, the Nixon-Rockefeller pact seemed weighted on the side of Mr. Rockefeller's views, including his implied criticisms of the Eisenhower defense and foreign policies.

However, in Washington Mr. Nixon told a news conference he still differed with the Governor on details of how to achieve adequate defense, assure economic growth, help farmers and the arbitration of labor disputes.

The Administration has insisted that defense spending has been adequate and that more would be done only if conditions dictated. Mr. Nixon has supported this position.

But the Nixon-Rockefeller agreement concluded that the "United States can afford and must provide the increased expenditures" to carry out a bigger defense program.

They left out only the amount of money to be spent. Mr. Rockefeller had proposed $3,500,000,000 more to provide more and improved bombers, an airborne

alert, speeded production of missiles and nuclear submarine, revamping of overseas bases and other programs.

Mr. Rockefeller also gained a concession in the statement that new Soviet aggressiveness made necessary "new efforts" for national defense because the country's military posture of the last ten years gave "no assurance" of survival in the decade ahead.

He bolstered his position with a call for a powerful "second-strike capacity," or the ability to retaliate against any aggressor's surprise attack.

On the domestic side, they seemed to split their differences in most areas, including economic growth, agriculture, education, and medical aid for the aged.

Growth Policy Differences

The Governor has called for Federal policies to assure an annual growth rate of at least 5 per cent to meet Soviet competition. The Administration and Mr. Nixon have avoided a target figure, downgrading such figures as a product of the game of "growthmanship," and asserting the Soviets could not

catch up with the United States in this century.

However, Mr. Nixon has mentioned the need for some Federal spending in the "public sector" as an aid to economic well-being. But he has warned against any large-scale expenditures that would increase inflation or require Federal controls.

The language of the Nixon-Rockefeller agreement was vague on economic growth and how to achieve it. It declared that the growth rate "must, as promptly as possible, be accelerated by policies and programs stimulating free enterprise."

It said only that Mr. Nixon had "pointed out" in a 1958 speech that a 5 per cent rate of growth would provide an additional $10,000,000,000 in revenue in 1962.

On health protection for the aged, the agreement appeared to combine features of Mr. Rockefeller's proposals for using the Social Security System and the Administration's plan for private insurance.

It said the program should provide insurance through a contributory system with beneficiaries enjoying an option to

purchase private health insurance.

Mr. Rockefeller has advocated using Social Security with an added payroll deduction by employes and employers to assure adequate medical care for the aged. This also is embodied in a Democratic bill sponsored by Representative Aime J. Forand of Rhode Island. The Administration called for private insurance to be financed by general taxes.

The civil rights subcommittee broke off efforts to draft a plank, with Southern members predicting a majority of the group would not accept the "strong" Nixon-Rockefeller proposals.

The conservatives made demands upon Joseph F. Carlino, Speaker of the New York Assembly and subcommittee chairman, to spell out "why Mr. Nixon changed his position overnight."

Mr. Carlino called off further meetings today and set tomorrow for another effort as emissaries of the Vice President and Mr. Rockefeller tackled individual panel members.

July 24, 1960

GOLDWATER HITS PLATFORM ACCORD

Pledges Fight in Convention on Nixon's 'Surrender' to Rockefeller Ideas

By RUSSELL BAKER
Special to The New York Times.

CHICAGO, July 23—Senator Barry Goldwater of Arizona charged Vice President Nixon today with a "surrender to Rockefeller." The Senator also promised to lead a fight on the floor of the Republican National Convention against the agreements on the platform laid down in New York this morning by Mr. Nixon and Governor Rockefeller.

Mr. Goldwater, chief spokesman for his party's conservative wing, suggested that the New York "surrender" might be part of a bargain in which Governor Rockefeller would accept the Vice-Presidential nomination.

Obviously angered and bitterly outspoken, Mr. Goldwater declared that the entire convention had been the victim of an "unprecedented last-minute attempt" to impose a platform dictated by "a spokesman for

the ultra-liberals."

If the agreement survives the convention, he said, it will "live in history as the Munich of the Republican party" and will guarantee "a Republican defeat in November."

Mr. Nixon's mission in New York, "paying court on the leader of the Republican left," could be interpreted only as "a bid to appease the Republican left," he added.

"I believe this to be immoral politics. I also believe it to be self-defeating. We will earn the scorn of the nation."

Senator Goldwater's principal objection was to what he called an attempt to impose on the party a platform worked out secretly between the two leaders, 1,000 miles from the convention.

Hopes for a Rebellion

Conversations with influential members of the Platform Committee, Mr. Goldwater told a news conference, had encouraged him to believe that the committee might rebel against "this last-minute pressure tactic."

If the committee did adopt all of the Nixon-Rockefeller points, he added, he would "be forced to fight" many of the principles when the platform came to the floor.

Whether such a fight can succeed is "hard to tell," Senator Goldwater said. But, he went on, he expects to have strong support in opposition to proposals for Federal aid to

education, Federal activity in the medical field and the liberal civil rights statement in the Nixon-Rockefeller agreement.

Mr. Goldwater told his news conference that, despite these factors, he was still supporting Mr. Nixon's candidacy.

Mr. Goldwater's open supporters here are centered in Southern delegations and far-right fringe groups. But in his protest against the platform agreement, he speaks the sentiments being privately expressed by many influential Republican conservatives supporting the Nixon candidacy.

These men, the former followers of the late Senator Robert A. Taft of Ohio, are not talking rebellion against Mr. Nixon. In private conversation, however, many are complaining that the peace of New York forebodes a Nixon turn toward "liberal me-tooism" to which they ascribe the defeat of former Gov. Thomas E. Dewey in 1948.

Losses Feared

This opinion holds that Mr. Nixon has now moved to compete with the Democratic ticket for "liberal" voters who simply cannot be won over in sufficient numbers to offset the expected loss of old-line conservatives.

The Southern Republicans, who had once held high hopes of making big gains against the Democratic ticket headed by Senator John F. Kennedy, were dismayed and gloomy about the liberal civil rights statement in

the Nixon-Rockefeller agreement.

When the news of the New York compact first broke here this morning, Senator Goldwater appeared to be in a suppressed fury.

Leaving his office in the Conrad Hilton Hotel, he complained bitterly that he talked to Mr. Nixon by telephone yesterday morning and was assured that the Republican platform would contain no recommendation for Federal action to fight racial discrimination in private employment.

Yet, he said, in the compact there was a clear implication of support for precisely this principle—in the passage approving "aggressive action" to end discrimination in employment.

Mr. Goldwater also complained with a trace of anger that he had been "told nothing about the Rockefeller meeting" when he had spoken to Mr. Nixon.

Mr. Nixon, Mr. Goldwater said, "is moving farther to the left than I ever hoped he would."

But, he added, "he'd have to go a long, long way" to match the position occupied by Senator Kennedy.

On the issue of job discrimination, Mr. Goldwater said that he was "as opposed to segregation as any man in this country," but he believed that dealing with it was a matter for the states and not the Federal Government.

July 24, 1960

225

NIXON IS GIVEN NOMINATION BY ACCLAMATION AFTER GOLDWATER GETS 10 LOUISIANA VOTES; CANDIDATE PICKS LODGE FOR SECOND PLACE

By W. H. LAWRENCE
Special to The New York Times.

CHICAGO, Thursday, July 28—Vice President Richard M. Nixon swept to a first-ballot Republican Presidential nomination last night and the right to face Democratic Senator John F. Kennedy in the November election.

Early today, Mr. Nixon chose Henry Cabot Lodge, chief United States delegate to the United Nations, as his Vice-Presidential running mate.

Mr. Nixon received 1,321 votes on the polling of state delegations. Senator Barry Goldwater of Arizona received ten votes, cast by members of the twenty-six-vote Louisiana delegation even after the Arizonan had asked withdrawal of his name from consideration.

At the end of the roll-call, Louisiana moved to make Mr. Nixon's choice unanimous, but balked at changing its ten votes from the Goldwater to the Nixon column without a poll. When the roll-call vote was announced as 1,321 to 10, the Arizona delegation then moved to make the nomination unanimous, and this was done by acclamation.

Goldwater Asks Unity

The convention decision pits the 47-year-old Vice President against the 43-year-old Senator from Massachusetts. Mr. Nixon is the first Vice President in the history of the modern two-party system to win a Presidential nomination in his own right.

Senator Goldwater made the dramatic appearance of the night, calling upon all conservatives to back Mr. Nixon in November and avoid any party split or stay-at-home nonvoting attitude that would help Democrats "dedicated to the destruction of this country."

Withdrawing his own name from consideration for the Presidency, the Arizona Senator, an avowed conservative, said he had been campaigning for Mr. Nixon's nomination for the last six years and would fight for his election in November.

"Let us put our shoulders to the wheel of Dick Nixon and push him over across the line," Senator Goldwater said.

He lectured conservatives sternly, telling them they must "grow up" and get to work "if we want to take this party back

some day—and I think we can."

He said the Democratic party no longer was the party of Jefferson, Jackson and Wilson but now was ruled by "Bowles, Galbraith and Reuther." His references were to Representative Chester Bowles of Connecticut; Kenneth Galbraith, Harvard economist, and Walter P. Reuther, president of the United Auto Workers.

The Goldwater effort was to restore unity in a party that had been torn by a platform fight in which Mr. Nixon and Governor Rockefeller of New York had insisted that the nearly finished platform be revised and tailored to reflect the substance of their fourteen-point statement of policy.

Mr. Nixon, on his own part, was demonstrating his intention to be the party's master, and not its servant.

The Nixon nomination was declared official at 11:13 P. M. (12:13 A. M. Thursday, New York time), the convention quit minutes later until 6:30 P. M. tomorrow. The Vice-Presidential choice will be ratified at that session.

The final business of the convention will be the acceptance speeches of Mr. Nixon and his running mate.

As the nominating roll-call began, every state gave its full vote to the Vice President until Louisiana was reached. There was a solid vote from every state thereafter, and the twelve votes contributed by Nevada were decisive in pushing Mr. Nixon past the 666-vote majority required for nomination.

In explaining the Louisiana defection, delegates from that state said that there was a "strong feeling in opposition to the whole platform writing process," plus a "couple of diehards who followed through on their principles."

Mr. Nixon was placed in nomination by Gov. Mark O. Hatfield of Oregon, touching off a wild, seventeen-minute demonstration on the convention floor. Senator Goldwater was also placed in nomination, but he withdrew his candidacy after the demonstration in his favor.

Earlier, the convention had approved by an overwhelming voice vote, and without debate, a party platform tailored and revised to accommodate the views of Mr. Nixon and Governor Rockefeller.

Southerners and conservative non-Southerners abandoned their plans for a floor fight on the civil rights plank. They did not demand a roll-call on final passage.

In his nominating speech, Mr. Hatfield proclaimed the Vice President "a fighter for freedom, a pilgrim for peace" who

would provide experienced leadership and make the White House a beacon for the "half-slave, half-free" world.

The surprise of the Hatfield speech was its brevity—only 288 words, and one of the shortest nominating addresses in modern political history. The nominating speech for Abraham Lincoln in this city 100 years ago was twenty-seven words.

Aiming a blow at the wealth of Senator Kennedy, whose family has been accused of having bought him the Democratic Presidential nomination, Governor Hatfield asserted that "the White House is not for sale," but that its lease was "up for renewal" for a tenant approved by the American people.

The Oregon Governor said Mr. Nixon's qualities matched "the momentous need," that the Vice President had known "awesome responsibility" and that he had "demonstrated courage in crisis from Caracas to the Kremlin."

"Never before," Mr. Hatfield continued, "has a Vice President been such a full participant in the making of national policy. Never before has a Vice President so intimately shared in the shaping of major international decisions. He has known what it is to bear the full executive burden."

Without mentioning Senator Kennedy by name, or his wealth, Governor Hatfield also declared that the Vice President had known "hard times" and "hard work" and therefore was "one of us."

A long series of seconding speeches followed. One was by Senator Jacob K. Javits of New York, considered one of the more liberal Republicans.

John A. Roosevelt of New York, who long ago turned Republican, also seconded Mr. Nixon. Mr. Roosevelt is the youngest son of Franklin D. Roosevelt.

So did Robert A. Taft Jr., son of the late Ohio Senator whose Presidential ambitions were opposed by Mr. Nixon in the 1952 convention.

Others were Senator Thomas H. Kuchel of California, Gov. Christopher Del Sesto of Rhode Island, Mrs. Jewel Rogers of Illinois, Bob Gavin, Republican nominee for Governor of North Carolina, and Mrs. Andrew Williams of Washington State.

Gov. Paul Fannin of Arizona made the nominating speech for Senator Goldwater. Mr. Fannin acknowledged that he was acting against the expressed wishes of the Senator, who had released his pledged delegates earlier.

Governor Fannin pictured Senator Goldwater as the authentic voice of Republican conservatism, courageous, fearless and "dedicated to the preservation

of our constitutional Republic."

"He is not a 'me too' person," the Governor said, and the Arizona delegation responded with cheers.

Among many delegates there remains an undercurrent of anger and resentment over what they regard as the efforts of the Vice President and Governor Rockefeller to dictate and revise their platform after its substance had been agreed on by the Platform Committee.

Governor Rockefeller followed his long-deferred endorsement of Mr. Nixon by bringing the Vice President before New York's ninety-six-vote delegation. The Governor pledged all-out support to Mr. Nixon and the "strong platform." The Governor decided that his reservations about the civil rights plank were not sufficient to warrant a floor fight.

"We want to be the first state to put the key in the lock and open it for you," Governor Rockefeller said to Mr. Nixon.

They posed with arms around each other as Mr. Nixon said Mr. Rockefeller would campaign extensively for the ticket.

President Eisenhower delayed his scheduled departure for Denver for a few hours to talk with Republican leaders and to confer again with Mr. Nixon.

Representative Charles A. Halleck of Indiana, permanent chairman of the convention, gaveled the nominating session to order at 7:14 P. M., Central daylight time.

The first business of the session was approval of the platform after its provisions were explained by the co-chairmen, Charles H. Percy of Illinois and Representative Melvin R. Laird of Wisconsin.

Then the delegates heard a smash-the-Democrats speech by former Gov. Thomas E. Dewey of New York, the Republican Presidential candidate of 1944 and 1948.

Even before the formal nomination was voted, Mr. Nixon was talking to delegates about the tough fight against the Democratic ticket of Senator Kennedy for President and Senator Lyndon B. Johnson of Texas for Vice President. He was appealing too for party unity that would close ranks for the forthcoming campaign.

Mr. Nixon compared the fierce struggle among the Democrats to the lesser battle among Republicans, saying:

"If the Democrats can get together after what Jack said about Lyndon and after what Lyndon said about Jack, publicly and privately—and privately it was a lot worse, I can tell you—then certainly we Republicans can go home united and work as we've never worked before, and, if we do, we will win."

July 28, 1960

Eyes on New York

Both Presidential Candidates Feel State Is Vital to Their Success in November

By LEO EGAN

If their actions during and since the conventions are a true indication, both Presidential candidates feel that New York has become the key to this year's national elections.

Vice President Nixon, the Republican candidate, is said to feel he cannot win without New York. This is why he went to such great lengths to win Governor Rockefeller's active support and why he insisted on a strong civil rights plank. Senator John F. Kennedy, the Democratic choice, also regards New York as vital to his success. This is why he and his brother, Robert, his campaign manager, have given so much personal attention to ending the rifts within the Democratic state organization. And this is why Senator Kennedy, too, insisted on a civil rights plank that could cost him the electoral votes of some traditionally Democratic Southern states.

Valuable as they are, New York's forty-five electoral votes are only one reason for the importance the two candidates attach to the state. Of equal concern is the conviction that the influences that determine the New York decision are present in most other populous industrial states. The repercussions of the campaign in New York are expected to extend far beyond its borders.

Minorities a Concern

Of special concern to both parties is the presence in New York of three large minority groups whose dominant attitudes and voting patterns could prove decisive in a close election, which both parties think this will be. These groups are the Catholics, the Jews and the Negroes. Together they constitute nearly half the state's potential vote.

For years, Catholic voters constituted the core of the Democratic party strength in the state and supplied the Democratic party with the bulk of its local and state leaders. Four-fifths or more of the county chairmen in the state are Catholics.

But in recent years, as they have prospered and improved their social status, large numbers of Catholics, particularly those of Irish ancestry, have been voting Republican. They were very heavy contributors to President Eisenhower's top-heavy Republican pluralities in New York in 1952 and 1956 and to Thomas E. Dewey's margins in the state as the Republican candidate for President.

One of the main foundations of Democratic hopes for winning New York and the nation this year is the expectation that large numbers of these Catholic defectors will return. This expectation assumes Mr. Kennedy will get their votes because he, too, is a Catholic.

The Republicans also are aware of this possibility. But, by emphasizing Mr. Kennedy's associations with such groups as Americans for Democratic Action and others whose orientation is to the left of the political spectrum, they hope to minimize the return of Catholics to the Democratic cause.

60% Are Catholics

One reason for Mr. Nixon's intention of waging an intensive personal campaign in the suburbs is the concentration of Catholic voters there. Nearly 60 per cent of the new families who have moved into Nassau and Suffolk Counties since World War II are Catholics.

As Catholics switched their political allegiance from the Democratic to the Republican party in the later years of the Roosevelt Administration and since, Jewish voters displaced them as the most reliable source of Democratic votes in the state. Attracted first by President Roosevelt's anti-Hitler attitude, Jewish voters in large numbers found their affections for the Democratic party increased and strengthened by its concern for minorities and its social programs.

In 1952 and 1956, the Jewish voters were large contributors to Adlai E. Stevenson's vote in New York. In the main they liked the left-of-center orientation of the Democratic party, which was a contributing factor to Catholic defections. Many Jews are suspicious of Mr. Kennedy's liberalism this year, chiefly because of his long delay in joining the opposition to the late Senator Joseph R. McCarthy of Wisconsin.

Nixon Is Disliked

But, if they are suspicious of Senator Kennedy, the great bulk of them actively dislike Vice President Nixon. This dates to his campaigns for Congress and the Senate in California and has not been mitigated by anything he has done since.

The great concern of the Kennedy managers this year is not that there will be any big shift of Jewish voters to the Republican standard, but that large numbers of them will decide to sit the election out. This is why Senator Kennedy is now placing so much emphasis on a voter registration drive. If the Democrats are able to induce large numbers of Jewish voters to register, they can count confidently in getting the bulk of their votes on Election Day.

One reason entering into the choice of Ambassador Henry Cabot Lodge for a running mate was the hope that his presence on the ticket would enable a substantial number of Jewish voters of Democratic persuasion to vote Republican this year despite their misgivings about Mr. Nixon. Mr. Lodge's defense of the Israeli position in the United Nations has brought favorable response from many Jewish groups.

Before 1932 and the New Deal, a majority of New York's Negroes usually voted Republican. The social welfare programs of the New Deal and the Roosevelt Administration's promotion of civil rights in the South converted most of them to the Democratic cause. In recent years they have been among the most consistent supporters of the Democratic cause.

Inroads Were Made

But President Eisenhower made some inroads in 1956 in the Negro vote. Governor Rockefeller enlarged the breach in 1958. They are not affected by the personal antipathy to Mr. Nixon that is so noticeable among many Jewish voters. Their big concern is the leveling of the barriers that restrict their employment, educational and housing opportunities. There is strong reason for believing large numbers would vote Republican this year if convinced the Republicans offered the better hope of accelerating the achievement of the Negroes' goals.

In the main, Negro voters are highly pleased with the Democratic plank on civil rights but are fearful its meaning may be negated by Mr. Kennedy's selection of Senator Lyndon B. Johnson of Texas as his running mate. How the Negro vote will divide is one of the big mysteries of the campaign.

The same three minorities are found in large numbers in Pennsylvania, Ohio, Illinois, Indiana, California, Maryland and many other states, although the proportions differ from state to state. They get more attention in New York because New York is a sort of showcase for the nation.

Probably the votes of these minorities will be decisive in New York. This does not mean there is likely to be a drastic change in voting patterns, in any one group, but that any changes from past patterns will be of extreme importance to the result.

August 1, 1960

Democrats to Offer 2 Mississippi Slates

By CLAUDE SITTON
Special to The New York Times

JACKSON, Miss., Aug. 16—The State Democratic Convention took steps today to withhold Mississippi's eight electoral votes from Senator John F. Kennedy.

Delegates voted to place two slates of Presidential electors on the November ballot—one unpledged and the other pledged to the Democratic nominee. Both would be identified as Democratic.

They also adopted a resolution containing a point-by-point denunciation of the national party's platform. It contained a brief rejection of the Republican platform as well.

Gov. Ross R. Barnett and his supporters, who dominated the convention, served notice that they would back the independent slate.

The state's rights faction, which the Governor heads, shouted down an attempt by loyal party members to remove "Democratic" from the title under which the free electors will be listed.

However, a step taken late today by the loyalists indicated that they might challenge the convention's action in the courts. They filed the names of the "pledged" slate with the Secretary of State, Heber Ladner.

Observers noted that if a legal test was made it might delay certification of the electors beyond the filing deadline.

There was some feeling here that the result of the dual elector slate would be to split the Democratic vote and thus enable Vice President Nixon, the Republican candidate, to carry this state.

Following the convention's adjournment, Governor Barnett sent a telegram to other Southern political leaders asking them to cooperate "in building a bloc of unpledged electors in the South." The telegram said in part:

"We urge you to join us and others in this great effort to save this nation from totalitarianism. This may be our last chance to salvage our freedoms from the selfish and ruthless hands of greedy politicians."

House Election Favored

Advocates of the free elector plan hoped that a close race would enable them to prevent either major party candidate from receiving a majority in the electoral college. This would force the election into the House of Representatives, where each state would have one vote.

If the Democratic majority in the lower chamber were substantially reduced in the election, the Southern states might exert a decisive influence, or so reason the independents.

227

However, only fourteen independent electors have won places on the November ballot. These are the eight chosen here today and six elected by Alabamians in a primary that also saw five electoral college seats go to loyal Democrats.

Party conventions in Louisiana and South Carolina have rejected the independent elector plan. Georgia voters will make their decision in a primary Sept. 14.

After approval of the elector resolution, delegates endorsed by another roaring voice vote a resolution attacking the national party platform.

It said that the platform "proposed a form of world socialism." The word "communistic" was used four times in referring to the platform's provisions.

The resolution singled out for criticism proposals dealing with Negro sit-ins, elimination of literacy tests as a voting requirement and racial segregation. It said:

"Whereas said platform places its approval on 'sit-in strikes' * * * * we reject this action as a communistic practice and approval of illegal and unlawful acts constituting a direct invasion of the personal and private property rights of our people * * *;

"Whereas said platform's proposal to eliminate literacy tests and the payment of poll taxes as requirements for voting is a communistic and socialistic proposal and a direct invasion of the sovereign and constitutional rights of the State of Mississippi * * *.

"Whereas said platform proposes to eliminate segregation in all areas of community life, including schoolrooms, jobs and housing, and proposes to empower and direct the Attorney General of the United States to file civil injunction suits in Federal courts to enforce such proposals, we recognize this as another communistic proposal similar to a plank in the Communist party platform of 1928 * * *."

August 17, 1960

Kennedy Gets Full Backing Of 10 Southern Governors

Senator's 'Control' of TV Debate Cited—Lausche Also Pledges Aid

By CLAUDE SITTON
Special to The New York Times.

HOT SPRINGS, Ark., Sept. 27—Southern Governors abandoned today their lukewarm stand in the Presidential campaign and threw their full support to Senator John F. Kennedy.

The change in sentiment grew directly out of the Democratic candidate's television debate last night with Vice President Nixon, the Republican nominee.

[Senator Kennedy was cheered by huge, enthusiastic crowds Tuesday as he campaigned through several industrial cities in Ohio. He also received the full support of Senator Frank J. Lausche of Ohio, a conservative Democrat whose enthusiasm for the ticket had been in doubt.]

In a telegram to Senator Kennedy, ten of the eleven Democratic Governors attending the Southern Governors Conference here said: "We, the undersigned Governors participating in the twenty-sixth annual Southern Governors Conference, wish to congratulate you on your superb handling of Mr. Nixon and the issues facing our country. It is the consensus of the Governors present that the masterful way in which you controlled this debate further accelerates the movement to the Kennedy-Johnson and Democratic ticket."

The signers included Govs. Buford Ellington of Tennessee, J. Lindsay Almond Jr. of Virginia, John Patterson of Alabama, Orval E. Faubus of Arkansas, Ernest Vandiver of Georgia, Bert T. Combs of Kentucky, J. Millard Tawes of Maryland, Luther H. Hodges of North Carolina, Ernest F. Hollings of South Carolina and Price Daniel of Texas.

Mississippi's Gov. Ross R. Barnett was not asked to join in the telegram because he is supporting a slate of unpledged Democratic electors.

Many observers saw this demonstration of solidarity as one of the most significant political developments in Southern terms since Senator Kennedy chose Senator Lyndon B. Johnson of Texas as his running mate.

They noted that the addition of the majority leader to the ticket had failed to bring about the desired effect among Southerners. But they believe that the Governors' action today might well start a Dixie boom for the Democratic ticket.

It was learned that the move had been conceived by two Governors among the Johnson partisans, who are in control at the conference.

Another show of support for the ticket was expected tomorrow when the conference names its chairman for the coming year. Governor Daniel is expected to receive the honor.

The theory is that this would provide a demonstration of Johnson strength on the national scene and also curry favor with voters in doubtful Texas. Moreover, it was hoped that if the move was successful it would encourage Governor Daniel to take a more active role in the campaign.

In their private conversations, the Governors said Senator Kennedy had fully proved his ability to compete with Mr. Nixon on an equal basis. Most of them contended that he had shown himself to be a master of television, a man who could remove any doubt among voters stemming from Republican contentions that he was youthful and inexperienced.

In another conference development, five prominent Southerners were named to a commission that will seek to chart a course for higher education in the region. The commission, which is the first of its kind, was established here last Sunday by the Southern Regional Education Board.

The board's sixteen-member states hope the panel's findings will enable them to meet the increasing demand for higher education without any loss in quality.

The commission members are Dr. O. C. Carmichael, a retired educator; Dr. Colgate W. Darden Jr., former Governor of Virginia and former president of the University of Virginia; H. H. Dewar, a Texas business leader; Marion B. Folsom, former Secretary of Health, Education and Welfare, and Ralph McGill, the Pulitzer-prize-winning publisher of The Atlanta Constitution.

Gov. Ellington of Tennessee, the new chairman of the Southern Regional Conference, and Gov. Cecil H. Underwood of West Virginia, its outgoing chairman, announced the appointments here.

One or two additional members of the commission will be chosen before its first meeting, which is expected to be held next January.

Key Problems Listed

In the joint announcement, Governor Underwood called attention to these problems now facing higher education in the South:

¶The prospect of doubled and tripled enrollments within the next few years.

¶The need for at least $2,250,000,000 for new buildings.

¶The necessity to raise the annual expenditure for the operation of colleges and universities in the next ten years to some $1,900,000,000.

¶"The excellence we seek can best be achieved through planning for the future," Mr. Underwood said. "Such planning rests upon the major goals the South should seek through its colleges and universities."

The Governor's Conference, which will end tomorrow, took up problems of the aging and industrial development at its business session.

September 28, 1960

3 Parties Pressing For Funds in State

By CHARLES GRUTZNER

Would you give $100 to be able to speak your name to thousands of radio listeners and tell them why you're going to vote for Senator John F. Kennedy for President?

Is it worth $100 to you to rub elbows with bankers, contractors and entertainment figures at a dinner to advance the Presidential campaign of Vice President Nixon?

For $3.50 do you want a baroque pearl brooch emblazoned "Nixon-Lodge" or a "Kennedy-Johnson" gold-plated pin?

If the answer to any of these or a hundred other similar questions is yes, you are a target of one or several of the thousands of political fund-raisers. These campaign workers are now increasing their activity in New York, which is the source of more than a tenth of all the campaign money collected throughout the country in a Presidential election year.

Campaign costs are up about 20 per cent over 1956, but the money has not been coming in as fast as during the Eisenhower-Stevenson contest that year. This is true of both major political parties and of the independent committees working here for the Nixon-Lodge or Kennedy-Johnson tickets.

While party leaders are talking publicly about ground swells of popularity for the heads of their tickets, some fund-raisers in both camps complain privately that neither Mr. Kennedy nor Mr. Nixon has yet generated whatever it is that causes people in great numbers to offer cash.

To show the extent of the problem, officials of both major parties said Friday that they were severely pinched for funds.

Lawrence F. O'Brien, Demo-

228

cratic national committee organization director, said that prime television time for Senator Kennedy had been cut back from seven to two and one-half hours, that a campaign paper had been abandoned and that campaign office expenses had been severely cut.

Leonard W. Hall, head of Mr. Nixon's campaign staff, and John Clifford Folger, Republican national finance chairman, said the party's debts exceeded its cash. The $100-a-plate dinners attended by 38,000 Republicans throughout the country on Friday night were counted on to help pull the Republican campaign account out of the hole.

Two Republican finance committees, which between them cover New York State, are seeking to collect $2,650,000, of which perhaps 90 per cent would come from residents of New York City or executives of companies with headquarters here.

The Democratic state finance committee also looks for its richest pickings downstate, with a campaign goal here of $750,000.

$65,000 From Dinner

The Democrats' principal fund-raising effort upstate was last Thursday's $50-a-plate dinner in Syracuse, which made $65,000. Aside from the dinner, the Democratic state organization has left the upstate fundraising mostly to county organizations and local candidates for their own use. The national finance committee solicits wealthy upstate Democrats directly.

The Liberal party, which is supporting Senator Kennedy and Senator Lyndon B. Johnson, his running mate, has a state-wide goal of $125,000. It mailed an appeal for contributions a few days ago to its 81,000 enrolled members, of whom 64,000 are in New York City.

The Citizens - for - Kennedy Committee has set itself a goal of $600,000 here. It will tap its own list of wealthy contributors for at least a third of this amount.

Independent Citizens for Nixon and Lodge has scaled down its original expectation of $400,000 to a more realistic state goal of $250,000, of which 80 per cent is to come from this city.

Citizens for Kennedy, which got $163,000 from 123 contributors at a dinner in the Waldorf-Astoria Hotel on Sept. 14, is faring better in gifts than are the Citizens for Nixon because more Nixon supporters are making their big contributions through the Republican organization.

Some of the anti-Tammany Democrats prefer to make their donations to the Kennedy campaign outside the party organization.

National Payment

One reason the Republican party's goal here is so much higher than the Democrats' is that the New York Republican

finance committee's figure includes a quota of $1,200,000 to be forwarded to Washington for use by the national campaign committee and the Senatorial and Congressional campaign committees.

"We are under tremendous pressure from the national committee for funds," said Arthur A. Houghton Jr., chairman of the United Republican Finance Committee here. "Our quota is 12 per cent higher than in 1956 and represents one-sixth of the combined quotas of $78,000,000 for the fifty states."

Mr. Houghton is not troubled by how the funds are apportioned, but other New York Republicans are. One high-ranking campaign aide said: "It's just like with taxes. Most of the money comes from New York and is spent in other parts of the country."

The division of effort between national and state groups is different among the Democrats.

The state organization, of which Thomas M. Cole is campaign finance chairman, does not have a quota to forward to Washington. However, the national campaign committee solicits directly those New Yorkers on its own "fat cat" lists. There are also special events, such as the $100 a-plate dinner Senator Kennedy is to address Oct. 12 at the Waldorf-Astoria, with 55 per cent of the proceeds going to the national campaign committee and 45 per cent to the state.

Who's Got the Buttons?

Both national committees are feeling the squeeze between increased costs of campaigning and not-too-ready contributions.

The Democratic national committee has cut down on the buttons, car bumper strips, posters and other supplies it formerly spread generously through the states. It has sent, instead, a token supply, along with price lists of manufacturers from whom the state organization may buy additional supplies.

"I can't get a damned thing out of Washington this year," said Michael H. Prendergast, Democratic State chairman.

A recent shipment of supplies for the state included 1,500 Kennedy-Johnson posters of the kind used in store windows. That is about the number needed for a single Assembly District here.

Harry Brandt, state campaign chairman, scanned the price lists sent from Washington. Then he shopped around and found he could buy the material for a third less because of the huge quantities required here.

The state organization bought 500,000 campaign buttons after the July convention, has since bought another 500,000, and will buy a million more in the next few weeks. It is spending more than $100,000 on these and other supplies that are a new item of expense.

The Republican and Democratic state finance committees are training their heaviest efforts on contributors who are good for $100 to $5,000. The Democrats are working also, to

a greater extent than the Republicans, to broaden their base of small contributions.

One Democratic device is the Fund for the New Frontier. A contribution of $1 or $5 gets you a "Presidential participation certificate" adorned with profiles of Senators Kennedy and Johnson over a picture of the White House, and the signatures of Mr. Prendergast and Mr. Brandt.

Both citizen committees are "giving away" cheap jewelry and other gadgets in exchange for contributions. They are careful to say they are not selling the items, but it works like this:

The trinkets are displayed on a growing number of tables in lobbies of apartment houses, office buildings, hotels and in other public places.

50c and a Joke

One must contribute at least 50 cents to get a Republican "winkie." A "winkie" is a trick button on which the face of Mr. Nixon changes to that of his running mate, Henry Cabot Lodge, as the viewer shifts his gaze.

Plastic thimbles with the slogan "Sew It Up for Nixon" are two for a quarter. Rings, pins, elephants and other kinds of ornaments command minimum contributions of from $1 to $3.50.

Citizens for Kennedy give similar items, with the donkey emblem or the names of their candidates, in exchange for contributions.

Mrs. Bernard Zisser, a former account executive turned housewife, was at the Nixon-Lodge gimcrack table in the Roosevelt Hotel lobby when a man carrying a big bag stopped to finger a two-and-a-half-inch button.

"How much for this?" the stranger asked.

"A 50-cent contribution," Mrs. Zisser said.

"I can get a Kennedy button that big for a quarter," he taunted.

"That's because he'd only make half as good a President," was the quick retort.

The man grinned, plunked down a half-dollar and said he was up from Texas for a convention and was for Mr. Nixon anyway and had just been teasing.

'Chiselers Creep Out'

No one knows, or will ever know, the total of all campaign contributions. Although all political units, campaign committees and candidates are required by law to file reports, some candidates and campaign managers fail to note some of the gifts.

All the political parties and the various other campaign groups have urged that every contributor demand an official receipt, no matter how small his donation. All legitimate groups supply such receipts to their fund-raisers.

"Every election the chiselers creep out of their holes and in Presidential years come running like ants to a picnic," one party official said.

Not many years ago a candidate for City Councilman here was promised a contribution

from a wealthy citizen. As Election Day neared the candidate called his friend to remind him that he could use some financial aid.

"Wasn't that thousand enough?" asked the wealthy New Yorker.

The candidate explained he had received nothing.

"Why, I gave it to ———— ———— weeks ago," the friend explained. "He came to my office and said you sent him as your campaign manager."

New Yorkers, especially residents of Manhattan, get more appeals for campaign contributions than persons in any other part of the nation.

Bernard Newman, New York County Republican leader, said:

"The local organization in this city has a unique problem in raising funds. People with money are more inclined to give to the national or state committees, which have them all listed. But we're supposed to give financial aid to the district clubs —I've got thirty-one of them in the county—and to help individual candidates."

The county G. O. P. gets most of its funds for campaign and year-around expenses from its $100-a-plate Lincoln Day Dinner, which this year netted $70,000. It also collects annual dues of $5 from as many as possible of its 2,728 county committee members. It canvasses all enrolled Republicans for campaign contributions, doing pretty well in the $1 to $10 category.

Many who are expected to chip in with $100 or more say they have already been tapped by the state committee. In such cases, said Mr. Newman, "we try to wring a little more out of them for the county."

Tammany Hall runs into a similar situation in trying to get enrolled Democrats to contribute at the county level.

The smoothest-working of all the New York fund-raising groups is the United Republican Finance Committee. Its chairman, Mr. Houghton, the president of Steuben Glass, Inc., runs the committee as an efficient, year-round business organization.

There is a special-gifts division, headed by John Schiff of Kuhn Loeb & Company, investment bankers. This group lands the biggest givers. A women's committee, headed by Mrs. Paul Peabody, has the names of all the wealthy widows and women stockholders. Howard Isham, retired treasurer of the United States Steel Corporation, heads a special task force for industry and business gifts.

So far this year the United Committee has taken in more than $1,000,000. The money is coming in more slowly than in 1956, but better than in 1952.

Goal of $2,400,000

Mr. Houghton is confident of reaching his goal of $2,400,000, of which $1,200,000 is earmarked for Washington, $900,-000 for the state campaign committee and $300,000 to pay year-round expenses and to provide a small surplus for starting the next fund drive.

The Republican Upstate Finance Committee is shooting for $250,000 under William L. Pfeiffer of Old Westbury, L. I., former Republican state chairman and the president of the W. L. Pfeiffer Company, Inc., a mortgage banking corporation. The Pfeiffer committee, besides using standard fund-raising methods, sets goals for each upstate county organization to raise towards its own campaign expenditure.

The Republican state and national campaign committees each take half the income from the big dinners that they sponsor jointly, such as the $100 affair last Thursday at the Astor Hotel that netted $300,-000.

The Democrats find their fund-raising for the state campaign committee made difficult by the same sort of crisscross of solicitations that is complicating Mr. Newman's task at the Republican county level. Mr. Cole, Democratic State finance chairman, finds the competition heavy from solicitors for the national campaign committee, the Liberal party and Citizens for Kennedy.

"We just don't have the big givers those other categories have," said Mr. Cole, who in private life is president of the Federal Pacific Electric Company.

The term "big giver" is, of course, relative. The Democratic state campaign may not get as many $5.000 gifts as the Republicans, but about 70 per cent of its money comes in contributions of more than $250.

Aimed at contributions of $100 to $250 is the Democrats' Minute Man project. A corps of telephone girls, using lists of selected names, asks business men and others if they would like to go on the air for Senator Kennedy.

If the prospect shows even the slightest interest, the girl hastens to explain the radio time is expensive and asks for a contribution of $100 or more.

Another Democratic project is the publication of a handsome book of selected writings of Democratic figures, "Great Writings That Have Paved the Way to the New Frontier." The book is to be published after the election with a listing of "distinguished sponsors" who give $100 now.

The Democrats expect to have at least 4,000 volunteers asking for contributions by next week in door-to-door calls, at shopping centers, at sidewalk tables, in newly opened storefront neighborhood centers and at kaffee klatches and cocktail parties in homes.

Among the methods employed by Citizens for Kennedy are a $100-a-plate dinner that Adlai E. Stevenson will address at the Commodore Hotel on Oct. 18 and a $60 Election Night "victory party" in the Astor.

Independent Citizens for Nixon and Lodge, headed by Mrs. John Loeb, is made up largely of those who campaigned as Citizens for Eisenhower in 1956. Off to a late start this year, it opened its fund-raising last Monday with a cocktail party at the 21 that produced more than $40,000.

The labor movement is using voluntary contributions from its members for direct campaigning, as when the state American Federation of Labor-Congress of Industrial Organizations supplied $10,000 to carry Senator Kennedy's speech at the Democratic dinner in Syracuse last week over a nine-station television network.

Unions, barred by the Taft-Hartley Act from using any of their dues or assessments money for political gifts or campaigning, are spending $500,000 nationally—of which at least $50,000 is from this city—in a nonpartisan drive to get all eligibles to register.

October 2, 1960

THE 'GREAT DEBATE': TACTICS ARE MODIFIED AS THE ISSUES SHARPEN

STRATEGY: Nixon Drives for Independent Vote; Kennedy Seeks to Remake F.D.R. Coalition

By W. H. LAWRENCE
Special to The New York Times.

SPRINGFIELD, Ill., Oct. 15—With little more than three weeks to go before the Nov. 8 election date, the Presidential campaign strategies of Republican Vice President Nixon and Democratic Senator John F. Kennedy still remain fluid and subject to change without notice.

Each candidate is saying the final election outcome will be close, and neither is entirely convinced that he has a surefire, demonstrable pattern of victory to make him the certain occupant of the White House after Jan. 20.

One thing is certain: the campaign is moving into a freewheeling, harder-hitting slugging match, with an intensity and vigor far above the level that had prevailed from Labor Day until now. With the indicated close result, both candidates obviously felt that a big "break" for one or the other could determine the outcome.

Both thought they had met head-to-head this week on an issue that might provide the big advantage for one or the other Presidential candidate. The issue was the defense of the tiny islands of Quemoy and Matsu, held by the Chinese Nationalists a few miles off the mainland of Communist-ruled China.

Both thought it might be potent medicine in the states with the big prizes of electoral votes —New York (45), Pennsylvania (32), California (32), Illinois (27), Ohio (25), and Michigan (20)—on which both will concentrate most heavily in the immediate pre-election period on the obvious theory that these states must provide the key to victory for any candidate however well he may do elsewhere.

But where Mr. Nixon regards foreign policy as the No. 1 issue, these highly industrialized states, plus New England, also contain major pockets of unemployment—a domestic issue on which Senator Kennedy figures to capitalize heavily.

Aside from states that are both industrial and agricultural in an important sense—such as California, Ohio, Indiana and Illinois—both candidates have about completed their farm-belt tours, and their espousal of new Federal farm programs.

So far as the Midwest is concerned, most Republicans agree that Mr. Nixon's chances of victory depend on two factors: (1) how far he successfully has divorced himself from Secretary Benson by snubbing him politically outside of Utah and (2) the anti-Kennedy vote stirred up by anti-Catholic forces in an area where Protestants predominate.

The usually Democratic South —the solidarity of which was fractured by the Republicans in the 1928 campaign against Alfred E. Smith, a wet and a Catholic, and in two campaigns by President Eisenhower—presents campaign problems for both Senator Kennedy and Mr. Nixon this year.

The heart of the Nixon strategy is to be found in his persistent appeal for the votes of Democrats and independents because of his recognition that the Republican party, nationally, is in the minority and that he could not be elected with Republican votes alone. He has yet to demonstrate that he can cut across party lines with the success demonstrated by President Eisenhower in the last two elections. Every crowd, large and small, is exhorted to put country and individual ahead of party in choosing a President in 1960. His aides thought he added important ammunition for his bipartisan drive when he announced from Beverly Hills, Calif., Friday night that President Eisenhower had agreed, on leaving the White House, to continue as a close Nixon adviser and to continue his work for world peace.

Nixon's Problems

But while Mr. Nixon pushes these efforts, he is not without his problems with the Republican right-wing — a needed source of campaign funds and a bloc of votes that might stay home in pique on Election Day even if it did not shift to the Democrats. Senator Barry Goldwater of Arizona is the foremost spokesman for this right-wing bloc, and he has been critical of some of Mr. Nixon's campaign positions. It was to appease this section of the Republican party that Mr. Nixon let it be known this week he had departed from the Eisenhower Administration recommendation for outright repeal of the Connally amendment to United States ratification of the World Court statute.

Yet the Vice President could not move greatly to the right without losing Republican liberal support, especially in key areas like New York. The electoral college arithmetic is such that no Republican can hope to win without New York. Democratic candidates, working from a substantial but not always solid Southern base, have won without New York.

230

Senator Kennedy's strategy is basically that followed by the late Franklin D. Roosevelt when he wedded the Democratic liberals from the North with their big blocs of electoral votes to the conservatives of the South. This was part of his reasoning in selecting Senator Lyndon B. Johnson of Texas, the Senate majority leader, as his Vice-Presidential running mate but on a platform that met every "liberal" demand of the North. The Massachusetts Senator, a Roman Catholic, reasons that the religious issue of anti-Catholicism may cost him some Southern states and possibly some Midwestern states, but he also believes that the religious issue may work to his benefit in the big industrial states of the North. Certainly it should bring about to the Democratic party many Catholics who have been voting Republican since about 1940.

The Democratic aim is to revive the farmer-labor alliance fashioned by F. D. R. in the depression-ridden Nineteen Thirties, and there are more than a few signs that Senator Kennedy is making progress in this direction.

October 16, 1960

KENNEDY'S VICTORY WON BY CLOSE MARGIN; HE PROMISES FIGHT FOR WORLD FREEDOM

RESULTS DELAYED

Popular Vote Almost Even—300-185 Is Electoral Tally

By JAMES RESTON

Senator John F. Kennedy of Massachusetts finally won the 1960 Presidential election from Vice President Nixon by the astonishing margin of less than two votes per voting precinct.

Senator Kennedy's electoral vote total stood yesterday at 300, just thirty-one more than the 269 needed for election. The Vice President's total was 185. Fifty-two additional electoral votes, including California's thirty-two, were still in doubt last night.

But the popular vote was a different story. The two candidates ran virtually even. Senator Kennedy's lead last night was little more than 300,000 in a total tabulated vote of about 66,000,000 cast in 165,826 precincts.

That was a plurality for the Senator of less than one-half of 1 per cent of the total vote—the smallest percentage difference between the popular vote of two Presidential candidates since 1880, when James A. Garfield outran Gen. Winfield Scott Hancock by 7,000 votes in a total of almost 9,000,000.

End Divided Government

Nevertheless, yesterday's voting radically altered the political balance of power in America in favor of the Democrats and put them in a commanding position in the Federal and state capitals unknown since the heyday of Franklin D. Roosevelt.

They regained control of the White House for the first time since 1952 and thus ended divided government in Washington. They retained control of the Senate and the House of Representatives although with slightly reduced margins. And they increased their hold on the state governorships by one, bringing the Democratic margin to 34—16.

The President-elect is the first Roman Catholic ever to win the nation's highest office. The only other member of his church nominated for President was Alfred E. Smith, who was defeated by Herbert Hoover in 1928.

Faces Difficult Questions

Despite his personal triumph, President-elect Kennedy is confronted by a number of hard questions:

¶In the face of such a narrow victory how can he get through the Congress the liberal program he proposed during the campaign?

¶Can so close an election produce any impetus for loosening the conservative coalition of Republicans and Southern Democrats which has blocked most liberal legislation in the House?

¶Will the new President be able successfully to claim a mandate for legislation such as the $1.25 minimum wage, Federal school aid and a broader medical assistance to the aged which he advocated from the stump?

In the campaign Senator Kennedy promised a "first hundred days" equal to that great period of reform in the Administration of Franklin D. Roosevelt. But the result made it more than ever likely that he would have to reach an accommodation with the conservative South, which has opposed much of his program within the Democratic party.

Senator Lyndon B. Johnson of Texas, Senator Kennedy's Vice-Presidential running mate, contributed much to Mr. Kennedy's victory and more than justified the controversial last minute tactic of putting the Texan on the ticket over the loud protests of the Northern Democratic liberals.

Without much question, he was responsible for bringing Texas back to the Democratic fold for the first time since 1948, and for helping to hold North and South Carolina, which most of the experts gave to the Republicans a month ago. Meanwhile, there was nothing to suggest that he had hurt the Democrats, as predicted, in the liberal areas of the urban North.

Not since President Harry S. Truman's surprising victory over Gov. Thomas E. Dewey of New York in the election of 1948 — and perhaps not even since Woodrow Wilson's triumph in the photo-finish election of 1916—have there been so many dramatic swings and changes of political fortune as occurred all through the night Tuesday and even into yesterday afternoon.

It is worth recalling also that Mr. Truman's victory, dramatic as it was, came with a plurality of more than 2,000,000 votes—compared with Senator Kennedy's less than 400,000 so far.

Shortly before midnight Tuesday the signs had seemed to point to a substantial Kennedy victory.

Victory Projected Into West

The Senator's national plurality of the popular vote, which had been climbing steadily all evening, was about 2,000,000. The Chicago vote had given him a big lead in Illinois, and the analysts were projecting westward his smashing triumph in the Northeast.

But actually that was the peak of Senator Kennedy's momentum. Just about midnight a slow process of attrition set in that whittled away at his "sure" win until, in the dramatic hours of the early morning, it was clear that this was the closest election in generations.

The Kennedy popular-vote margin melted to 800,000 by 5 A. M. yesterday, and the trend was still downward. The Senator's Illinois lead dropped from almost 200,000 to around 50,000, and state Democratic leaders began to sound brave when they forecast a final victory margin of "at least" 28,000.

And it became increasingly evident that the magic worked by Senator Kennedy in the East was less effective on the other side of the Mississippi. As returns began coming in from the West, the race drew closer and closer.

The returns were so close in many Western states that it became impossible to get a clear picture. Leads of a few hundred or a few thousand votes changed hands again and again in Nevada, New Mexico, Montana, Washington, Hawaii and Alaska.

By 5 or 6 A. M. yesterday, the Kennedy margin seemed to be facing a real threat in Minnesota as well as Illinois.

Nixon Finally Concedes

It became clear that Senator Kennedy had to win one of the three big undecided states —Illinois, Minnesota or California—to get his needed 269 electoral votes.

At no time did Vice President Nixon have a chance to win 269 electoral votes on his own. Even if all three of the major doubtful states and every one of the smaller western states had fallen to him, he would have been four votes short.

But in such a situation Senator Kennedy would also have been denied a majority. The power to decide the winner would then have rested with fourteen unpledged electors from Alabama and Mississippi who bolted the regular Democratic ticket as a protest against Northern Democratic views.

Throughout yesterday morning the result hung in the balance. Senator Kennedy's margin fell slowly in Illinois and Minnesota, and indeed at one point Mr. Nixon pulled ahead in the former until a last batch of Chicago votes was produced for Mr. Kennedy.

Then at 12:33 o'clock Senator Kennedy clinched Minnesota and the election. Thirteen minutes later Mr. Nixon made his formal concession.

Senators Kennedy and Johnson won by putting together their combined strength in the great cities of the North and the rural areas of the traditionally Democratic South; but they were remarkably weak elsewhere.

231

For example, they won eight of the nine so-called large decisive states, but in some of them their margins were tighter than a Pullman window: 6,000-6,500 in Illinois; 22,000 in New Jersey, 60,000 in Texas, 65,000 in Michigan, 131,000 in Pennsylvania.

Only in New York and Kennedy's home state of Massachusetts did the Democrats win by truly large majorities—404,000 in New York and 498,000 in Massachusetts. Each of these margins was larger than Mr. Kennedy's margin of victory in the nation as a whole.

The anomalies in the results were sometimes startling.

Why should Mr. Kennedy win by 131,000 in Pennsylvania and lose in neighboring Ohio, with much the same mixture of union and Catholic voters, by 263,000?

Senator Kennedy campaigned on a liberal program but could not have won without the support of conservative Catholics in the North and conservative Protestants in the South.

Contrasts in Jersey

In most areas populated by Catholics, Mr. Kennedy did well, but in some, Hudson County, N. J., for example, his showing was a great disappointment to his managers, while he did re-markably well in the more Republican territory of Essex County, N. J.

While the Senator was heavily supported in the cities of the North, Southern industrial areas such as Charlotte and Winston-Salem, N. C., went Republican. He did well in the Southern "Black Belts," as indeed did Smith in 1928, but he did poorly in the farm belts of the North, where he expected his attacks on Secretary of Agriculture Ezra Taft Benson might even swing some of the Plains States into the Democratic column.

Also, while Mr. Kennedy was regaining some of the Democratic party's lost strength in the South, he managed at the same time to pick up additional strength among Negroes, who have been complaining about the Democratic party's political associations with the South.

Senator Thruston B. Morton, the genial and relaxed chairman of the Republican National Committee, said yesterday that the main reason why Vice President Nixon had lost the election was that he had failed to hold the Northern Negro vote, which had gone so heavily to President Eisenhower in the two previous Presidential elections.

Chairman Morton's estimate was that the Vice President had got only between 10 to 12 per cent of the Negro vote, while President Eisenhower got about 26 per cent in 1952 and 1956.

Ironically, Senator Kennedy, whose political reputation rested primarily on his arresting and attractive personality, ran about 7 per cent behind the Democratic local candidates on a national basis.

This was not true in the Northeast, where he was near his home base and where his sophisticated manner was quite popular, but it was definitely true in Illinois, Minnesota, Wisconsin, and Indiana, where he ran well behind the Democratic ticket.

Nevertheless, the most striking facts of all lay in the contrasts in the voting returns from the various regions of the country.

In New England, Senator Kennedy split the six states, three to three, but built up a plurality of 592,036 votes.

He swept all six Middle Atlantic States—Delaware, Maryland, New Jersey, New York, Pennsylvania and West Virginia with another huge plurality of 684,549. Then, as the voting moved westward, his power

declined.

He split the East Central States, winning Illinois by a whisker and Michigan, but lost Ohio and Indiana, and came out of the region with a deficit of 422,904.

He lost six of the eight West central states, Iowa, Kansas, Nebraska, North and South Dakota and Wisconsin and won only two, Minnesota and Missouri. Here again, Vice President Nixon piled up a plurality for the region of 526,235.

In the Mountain states, New Mexico swung to Kennedy last night, but Mr. Nixon took six of the others, and Senator Kennedy won only Nevada. The same trend prevailed here, with the Vice President getting a plurality of at least 160,000.

Even in the Pacific Coast states, Mr. Nixon's plurality was over 22,000, and while Mr. Kennedy had a plurality of 245,000 in the South, where he won everything except Florida, Oklahoma, Kentucky, Tennessee and Virginia, the Republicans piled up a comparatively large Southern vote, 5,300,000.

November 10, 1960

Protestant and Catholic Votes Found to Offset Each Other in Kennedy's Victory

RELIGIOUS EFFECT NOT NATION-WIDE

Strategic Catholic Turnout, However, Proved Vital in the Large States

By JOHN WICKLEIN

A strong, silent "Protestant vote" cut into Senator John F. Kennedy's margin of victory, an analysis of election returns indicated yesterday. This was offset by a more strategically placed "Catholic vote," which aided the Senator in large states he needed to win.

Democratic leaders said that conservative Protestants outside the South had come out strongly to vote against the Bostonian, except in areas with large unemployment. Mr. Kennedy ran behind Protestant Democrats on the ticket in Illinois, West Virginia and several other states.

Republican leaders said the "Catholic vote" had not been

so strongly against the party as they had feared. They added their belief that the labor federation's registration drive had counted more in the defeat of Vice President Nixon.

Spotted in Some Areas

Religious prejudice in voting did not sweep the country, but could be spotted in sections.

But the singular fact in any analysis, neutral observers said, is not that religious-bloc balloting appeared, but that a Roman Catholic, in a predominately Protestant country, succeeded in knocking down the "For Protestants Only" sign outside the White House.

Senator Kennedy fared far better with the electorate than did the only previous Catholic candidate. He was Alfred E. Smith of New York, Democrat who opposed Herbert Hoover in 1928.

Mr. Smith took only Alabama, Arkansas, Georgia, Louisiana, Mississippi, Rhode Island and South Carolina, for a total of eighty-seven electoral votes.

Senator Kennedy has won all these, except possibly Mississippi, where eight unpledged electors are leading. He took seventeen more, including all states with twenty or more electoral votes except Ohio.

The Senator proved to be a far more popular campaigner

than Mr. Smith. He did not have to combat the Prohibition issue in the South, as the New Yorker did.

Increase in Catholics Noted

Another factor that made things easier for him than for Mr. Smith was the proportionately greater number of Catholics in the country now.

This worked to his advantage two ways: More Catholics might have voted for him out of religious affinity; in areas containing a higher percentage of Catholics amid a Protestant majority, prejudice against Catholics tends to decline.

In 1928, there were 19,000,000 Catholics in the country, constituting 16 per cent of the population. Today there are 40,000,000, or 24 per cent.

Although it could not be proved statistically, election returns suggested that there were more Protestant votes against Senator Kennedy because he was a Catholic than Catholic votes for him for the same reason.

The weight of numbers alone suggests this possibility. There are 61,000,000 adult Protestant church members, compared with 40,000,000 Catholics, including all persons baptized in the faith.

But Catholic voters have greater influence on the electoral result than Protestants. This is because they are con-

centrated in the populous states, often in the cities any Democrat needs to offset "downstate" Republican (and predominantly Protestant) votes.

How He Was Helped

Victory in these states weighs so heavily in the electoral outcome that the party that has them is almost assured of election.

Senator Kennedy carried eight of twelve states having Catholic populations of more than 30 per cent. These are New York, New Jersey, Pennsylvania, Connecticut, Massachusetts, Rhode Island, Louisiana and Hawaii.

In the city-rural equation, his religion also appeared to help him in Minnesota (25 per cent), Illinois (28 per cent), Maryland (17 per cent, concentrated in Baltimore), Michigan (24 per cent) and, surprisingly, Texas (19 per cent).

Protests against a Catholic for President were heard early and often from Southern Baptist preachers in Texas. There might have been a reversion to this, since a strong Protestant protest vote failed to develop.

Catholic voters in San Antonio and El Paso, however, came out heavily and might have provided the slim margin the Senator needed to take the state's twenty-four electoral votes. Ironically, the Baptist preachers apparently defeated their cause.

In the electoral balance, then, Senator Kennedy appears to have gained more than he lost from being Catholic.

But Democratic leaders think he brought off the election only by chipping steadily at the potential anti-Catholic vote against him. He did this with declarations in favor of the separation of church and state and for religious liberty. These allayed the fears of many Protestants who had been against him at the start.

However, many conservative Protestant churchmen and laymen remained resolute to the end, which probably accounted as much as anything for the Senator's narrow margin.

Anti-Catholicism seemed to be the major reason for his defeat in Oklahoma, Tennessee and Kentucky. It was a contributing factor, apparently, in Florida, Virginia, Wisconsin and Ohio.

A Democratic leader said that outside the Deep South, where party loyalty and Senator Lyndon B. Johnson, the Vice President-elect, seemed to outweigh religious factors, Senator Kennedy "just did not make it" in areas of heavy Protestant majorities.

The exceptions, he said, were in states with heavy unemployment.

"Where they're hungry," he said, "they think of their stomach and the Democrats. Where they're not, they think of the Pope."

Practical politicians in both parties were counting the "religious vote" before it came in.

Although they seldom discussed it in the two months before the election, Democratic managers 'had calculated for some time that a Catholic on the national ticket would increase the turnout among normally Democratic voters in the Northern cities, and cause many Republican Catholics to cross party lines. This apparently happened.

Toward the end of the campaign, Republican leaders in state after state were reported to be counting on the downstate "fundamentalist" vote to put Mr. Nixon across. The fundamentalists and other conservative Protestants came out in large numbers.

But the straight anti-Catholic voters were not enough to defeat the Senator. The Kennedy vote was a coalition that included labor (overlapping the Catholic vote), Negroes, Jews and many liberal white Anglo-Saxon protestants.

The Catholic vote was spotty —strong in Chicago, Pittsburgh, Buffalo and some other cities, and surprisingly moderate in places such as Jersey City.

But it tilted more than one major state into the Kennedy column, and in such a close race it would have been hard for the Senator to win without it.

November 11, 1960

LIBERALS SUFFER SETBACK IN HOUSE

G. O. P. Picks Up 22 Seats to Aid Conservative Bloc

By JOHN D. MORRIS

The House of Representatives will have a more conservative tinge in the Eighty-seventh Congress.

Inroads into the present House Democratic majority of 283 to 154 scored by the Republicans in Tuesday's elections promised to strengthen their conservative coalition with Southern Democrats.

The liberal legislative program to be submitted early next year by the new Democratic President, John F. Kennedy, may consequently face handicaps in the new Congress, which convenes Jan. 3.

In the Senate, Republicans cut the Democratic margin by two seats, to 64 to 36. That chamber remains predominantly liberal in membership, although conservatives dominate key committee posts.

Gubernatorial Shifts

The Democrats achieved a net gain of one governorship and now control thirty-four of the fifty state houses. In twenty-seven gubernatorial contests the Democrats won fifteen and the Republicans twelve, with an exchange of party control in thirteen.

In the House races, nearly complete unofficial returns showed that the Democrats had elected 257 House candidates and the Republicans 175, with five contests still in doubt.

The Republicans captured twenty-nine seats held by Democrats and lost seven of their own, for a net gain of at least twenty-two. For a bare numerical majority of 219 they would have had to achieve a net gain of sixty-five.

Among the eleven states of the Old Confederacy the Republicans maintained their hold on seven seats of the Eighty-sixth Congress. They had failed, however, to pick up any that.

The successful Republicans included two in Virginia, two in Tennessee, one in North Carolina, one in Florida and one in Texas.

Meanwhile, the Republicans also retained control of a House seat in Oklahoma and Kentucky. At the same time, a Democratic seat in each of the two states was considered in doubt.

While the Democrats easily retained numerical control, their losses exceeded both their own expectations and the pre-election forecasts of most objective analysts.

The greatest Republican inroads were made in the Midwest, where it was believed that Senator Kennedy's Roman Catholic religion was the decisive factor in a number of Democratic losses.

Republicans captured at least seventeen Democratic-held Congressional districts in Midwestern states while losing only one of their own.

Reverses Trend

Democrats found some consolation in the defeat of Representative Hamer H. Budge of Idaho, an ultra-conservative Republican member of the House Rules Committee. Mr. Budge was a member of a six-man Rules Committee coalition that blocked much liberal legislation in the Eighty-sixth Congress.

A successor of perhaps equal conservatism will be named to the committee when Congress convenes, however. The choice will be in control of the House Republican leadership.

The Democratic election losses will probably be felt mainly on the House floor, where conservatives of both parties teamed up in the present Congress to rewrite labor legislation and some other bills sponsored by liberal Democrats.

The coalition's strengthened position threatened even greater hazards for such legislation.

Republican gains in the House elections reversed a Democratic trend that began in 1954 with the recapture of Congress from Republican control.

The trend continued with a pick-up of two House seats in 1956, despite a landslide for President Eisenhower, and reached its peak in 1958 with the capture of forty-eight Republican seats and the loss of only one held by Democrats.

The triumph in 1958 gave the Democrats the biggest House majority held by either party since the peak achieved by the Democrats at the height of the New Deal in 1936. The elections that year sent 333 Democrats, 89 Republicans and 13 members of minor parties to the House.

As it turned out, the Democrats overextended themselves in untenable Republican territory in 1958 by capturing thirty-three districts held by the opposition party in twelve Midwestern states.

The seventeen Midwestern districts recouped by the Republicans Tuesday included five of the six that they lost in Indiana two years ago.

Others that switched from Democratic to Republican control in Tuesday's elections included two in Maine, two in Connecticut, one in Vermont, two in Pennsylvania, one in Maryland, one in Colorado, two in Ohio, one in Missouri, one in Wisconsin, one in South Dakota, one in North Dakota, one in Iowa, two in Kansas, two in Nebraska and one each in Montana, Oregon, California and Minnesota.

Democrats captured three Republican seats in New York and one each in New Jersey, Idaho, California and Washington.

Among the Democrats unseated was Representative James M. Quigley, whose Pennsylvania district includes the voting residence and farm home of President Eisenhower.

Symington Manager Loses

Another Democratic loser was Representative Charles H. Brown of Missouri, who managed the unsuccessful campaign of Senator Stuart Symington of Missouri for the Democratic Presidential nomination.

House leaders of both parties won re-election although the two highest Republicans, Representative Charles A. Halleck of Indiana and John W. Byrnes of Wisconsin, had unusually strong opposition. Mr. Halleck is minority leader and Mr. Byrnes chairman of the House Republican Policy Committee.

Representatives Sam Rayburn of Texas, Speaker of the House, and John W. McCormack of Massachusetts, the majority leader, were unopposed. Both are Democrats.

Of the five undecided contests, four were for seats held by Democrats and one was for a Republican-held seat.

The Democratic seats in doubt were in Kentucky, Missouri, Washington and Oklahoma. The doubtful Republican seat was in Utah.

November 10, 1960

GOLDWATER PINS LOSS ON 'ME TOO'

Says G.O.P. Must Now Rely on Conservatives—Hints Clash With Rockefeller

PHOENIX, Ariz., Nov. 9 (AP) —Senator Barry Goldwater suggested today that the Repub gested today that the Repubdential race because of a "metoo" candidate. He predicted

that the party would have to look to its conservatives in the future.

The Arizonan, leader of the Republican conservative wing, hinted at a party power fight with the liberal forces of Governor Rockefeller of New York.

"If Mr. Rockefeller can't carry New York, he can't be reckoned a figure to be contended with in the Republican party," the Senator declared.

He went on to say:

"Those who believe in the traditional philosophy of government, which is clearly identified with the conservative cause, might very well decide

the nation would benefit from a realignment of the party and a more frank disclosure of the philosophy of each group.

"We who are conservatives will stoutly maintain that 1960 was a repeat performance of 1944 and 1948, when we offered the voters insufficient choice with a me-too candidate."

Mr. Goldwater said the party would win if it took its cue from Arizona.

"Arizona is a conservative state," he explained. "Until the Democrats put up conservative candidates, they don't win."

Arizona re-elected Repub. Gov. Paul Fannin and Republican Representative John Rhodes The party scored a major vic

tory by taking the Attorney General's office from Wade Church, Democratic incumbent.

There was speculation that Mr. Nixon's defeat might pave the way for Mr. Goldwater's nomination for the Presidency in 1964. Asked about the possibility, the Senator said:

"I want to figure in 1964 not necessarily as the top candidate. But I don't want Rockefeller in that spot."

He held that Mr. Nixon had lost the election in Dixie.

"He gambled the industrial North by losing the South," he said. "I told them that at the convention."

November 10, 1960

Nixon Aides Analyze Election Patterns

Vice President's Defeat Laid to City Machines—He Is Found 'Popular'

By TOM WICKER
Special to The New York Times.

WASHINGTON, Nov. 12— Two close associates of Vice President Nixon have strongly implied that he will continue to be a powerful figure in national politics.

At a post-election news conference, Herbert G. Klein and Robert H. Finch reported "a tremendous outpouring of affection" for Mr. Nixon since his defeat last Tuesday by his Democratic opponent, Senator John F. Kennedy of Massachusetts.

"With the possible exception of the President," Mr. Klein asserted, "Mr. Nixon is the most popular man in the United States."

What about the President-elect, he was asked? "I'll just stand on that statement," said Mr. Klein, who was Mr. Nixon's press secretary in the recent campaign.

Neither Mr. Klein nor Mr. Finch, who was the Vice President's personal campaign manager, would make a positive statement about Mr. Nixon's future activities. However, they gave several indications that he did not expect to abandon politics and perhaps his Presidential ambitions.

Mr. Klein asserted that Mr. Nixon had not yet made "a very basic decision" about the future but added:

"We've never known him to

run from a fight."

Both men reported thousands of wires and telephone calls, some urging Mr. Nixon to announce his candidacy for 1964, or at least to "remain in politics," and some expressing regrets that the senders had voted for Senator Kennedy.

"In defeat," Mr. Klein said, "he is higher in the hearts of the American public than ever before."

Commenting on the "fighting mood" of many of the telegrams, they said some had urged an early start on campaigning to swing the House of Representatives to the Republicans in 1962.

Mr. Finch expressed the belief that the Vice President had waged a "strong national campaign" that had resulted in "an awful lot of vigor in our party." The election, he said, came close to making the Republicans a "national party."

In the light of Mr. Nixon's strong showing last Tuesday, when he polled almost 50 per cent of the popular vote and carried twenty-six states, the Finch-Klein news conference appeared to be designed to keep the Vice President's name in the forefront of his party's leadership.

Jab at Rockefeller

There was a tacit jab at Governor Rockefeller, who already figures in speculation as a prospective Republican nominee in 1964. Mr. Finch was asked if he were satisfied with the party campaign in New York this year.

"I think we'll just let the vote speak for itself," he said.

New York went for Senator Kennedy by a wide margin, despite the fact that the Nixon-Rockefeller pact before the Republican convention was supposed to have been an effort to swing the Governor and the state to Mr. Nixon's side.

The two Nixon aides had high

praise for the Vice President's political tactics and said they would not change any "basic decision" of the campaign. They would not concede that Senator Kennedy had won a personal victory.

The Republicans, Mr. Finch said, were beaten by "the big city machines in the North—Daley, Green and so on—tied as well with the Democratic State Houses, where they had payroll, patronage strength, plus the power of the labor unions in (A) registration and (B) delivering the vote, the great amount of money they can spend, plus Johnson's effectiveness in the South on the court houses where again you had the payroll effect."

The personal references in this analysis were to Mayor Richard J. Daley of Chicago, Representative William Green of Pennsylvania, who is regarded as the Democratic leader in Philadelphia, and Senator Lyndon B. Johnson of Texas, the Vice President-elect.

Mr. Finch said of Senator Kennedy's campaign tactics:

"One of the things he did very well was to keep emphasizing that 'I am the Democratic candidate'."

He said the Kennedy invocations of Franklin D. Roosevelt, Woodrow Wilson, et al, "pulled the diverse elements that make up the Democratic party together."

The two Nixon lieutenants made these other points about last week's election, one of the closest in American history:

¶Outside the Deep South, the Republicans won a" slight edge in the popular vote." In the South, they "made some strides toward an honest two-party system." Continuing this trend will be a "prime goal" in the years ahead.

¶In the Midwest, Mr. Nixon quelled the so-called farm re-

volt, saved some Congressional seats, and made the Republican party in that area "stronger than it's ever been before."

¶In the West, generally, the "almost complete reversal" from the Democratic trend of 1958 "particularly pleased" Mr. Nixon.

¶Neither the anti-Catholic vote nor the televised debates had as much effect as others have suggested.

¶Mr. Nixon's upset in South Carolina results from textile unemployment and "perhaps" Henry Cabot Lodge's promise that a Negro would be in the next Republican Cabinet. His unexpected victory in Ohio resulted from a "tremendous organizing job by Ray Bliss," the Republican chairman in that state.

¶"Our opinion is the Negroes voted their pocketbooks rather than on the issue of civil rights." In other words, the Democratic economic program won most Negro votes.

¶"We think the President was terribly effective" in his campaign-end speeches for Mr. Nixon. It was Mr. Nixon's decision to use President Eisenhower late in the campaign. Bringing him in a month earlier probably would have been no more effective."

¶Mr. Nixon has made no decision as to how he will earn his living and has not decided, despite reports, to practice law with William P. Rogers, the present Attorney General, in Washington. "I'm not aware he's considering anything" until after his Florida vacation, Mr. Klein said.

¶Of a reported comment by Robert F. Kennedy that Mr. Nixon had been hurt by a story of an alleged loan from Howard Hughes to Donald Nixon, the Vice President's brother, Mr. Finch snapped: "I think that's a despicable comment on his part."

November 13, 1960

234

NEGRO VOTE HELD VITAL TO KENNEDY

Dramatic Shift in South— Senator Widens Margins Scored by Stevenson

By ANTHONY LEWIS
Special to The New York Times.

WASHINGTON, Nov. 26 — New analyses of the election just made by party experts emphasize the importance of the Negro vote in the victory of President-elect John F. Kennedy.

Nor is the significance of Negro votes for Senator Kennedy confined to the big Northern cities. It is a matter of some irony that the Democratic ticket carried at least two Southern states by margins smaller than the number of Negro votes for the ticket.

The shift of Negro voters to the Democrats between 1956 and 1960 was especially dramatic in the South.

In Houston, for example, twenty-three predominantly Negro districts went for Adlai Stevenson in 1956 by 11,592 to 6,006. This year the vote there was 22,156 for Senator Kennedy and 3,393 for Vice President Nixon.

Three districts in Tampa, Fla., went for Mr. Stevenson over President Eisenhower in 1956 by the paper-thin margin of 1,011 to 995. This year the vote was 1,980 for Mr. Kennedy, 558 for Mr. Nixon.

Switch in Louisville

President Eisenhower carried five Negro wards in Louisville, Ky., in 1956 by 26,183 to 23,067. These wards went to Senator Kennedy this year, 28,613 to 23,405.

In Nashville, Tenn., three Negro wards were carried by President Eisenhower in 1956 by 3,258 to 2,861. The vote this year was 5,710 for Mr. Kennedy and 2,529 for Mr. Nixon.

Finally, among these Southern examples, there are three solidly Negro districts in Richmond, Va. They went for President Eisenhower in 1956 by 1,287 to 588 but for Senator Kennedy this year, 1,286 to 762.

The two Southern states in which Negroes can be clearly said to have accounted for the Kennedy victory — along with other blocs of votes, of course — are Texas and South Carolina.

The state-wide Kennedy margin in Texas was only 45,000. He is estimated to have polled more than 100,000 Negro votes. In South Carolina he squeaked through by less than 10,000. Here he drew more than 40,000 Negro votes.

North Carolina is another Southern state where the Negro vote was critical. Senator Kennedy won by 58,000 and is estimated to have had 70,000 Negro votes.

The same sort of statement can be made about some Northern states, notably Illinois, New Jersey and Michigan. Senator Kennedy's narrow margins in those states were far exceeded by his votes from Negroes. The same is true, though less dramatically so, in Missouri and Pennsylvania.

Negroes in Northern cities have voted overwhelmingly Democratic in recent years, so Senator Kennedy had less room for improvement there. Nevertheless, he did better in most of these areas than Mr. Stevenson had done.

Eight Negro districts in Cleveland gave Mr. Stevenson a margin of 1,231 to 993 in 1956. This year the vote was 1,992 to 506 for Senator Kennedy.

In East St. Louis, Ill., four districts went 2,342 to 761 for Mr. Stevenson and 2,734 to 534 for Senator Kennedy. In two Pittsburgh wards it was 13,940 to 8,922 Democratic in 1956 and 14,892 to 5,272 this year.

In Buffalo, four heavily Negro wards went for President Eisenhower in 1956 by 14,850 to 12,119. A big switch this year gave Senator Kennedy an edge of 21,712 to 7,329.

In New York, Manhattan's Eleventh, Twelfth and Fourteenth Assembly Districts produced a Stevenson margin of 66,527 to 32,356. This year they went for Senator Kennedy, according to figures available here, by 71,445 to 20,367.

Gets Brooklyn Vote

In Brooklyn's largely Negro Sixth Assembly District, the vote was 13,754 to 8,973 Democratic in 1956 and 22,777 to 5,808 this year.

In some Northern cities the total vote in Negro areas was lower this year than in 1956, perhaps partly because of migration due to slum clearance. Examples of such districts are those in Manhattan and Pittsburgh. But in other areas, such as Brooklyn, Buffalo and East St. Louis, the total vote was up.

Similar gains for Senator Kennedy were reported in the other big cities, though actual voting-figure comparisons could not be obtained here. The Democratic percentage of the vote rose from 74 to 84 per cent in a key Philadelphia ward, from an average of 85 to 90 per cent in four Detroit wards, from 66 to 80 per cent in six Chicago wards.

One question raised by the figures is, how did Senator Kennedy do it? Why did Negro voters shift to him?

Most analysts give a mixed answer. They think that the economic motive was one reason. Negroes have been hurt worst by unemployment, and since New Deal days they have voted for the Democrats as the party favoring the lower economic groups.

But civil rights also played an important part, most observers agree. The feeling is that Vice President Nixon did very little to identify himself with the Negro cause in the campaign and that Senator Kennedy did a great deal.

The most important single campaign move was undoubtedly Senator Kennedy's telephone call of sympathy to the wife of the Rev. Dr. Martin Luther King Jr. when the Southern integration leader was briefly in a Georgia prison on a traffic charge. Mr. Nixon made no comment on the King episode.

In the last week of the campaign, various committees and groups favoring Senator Kennedy printed and distributed 2,000,000 copies of a four-page pamphlet headed: "'No Comment' Nixon Versus a Candidate With a Heart, Senator Kennedy." It simply gave some quotes on the affair from Dr. and Mrs. King and others.

In Chicago alone, 250,000 copies of the pamphlet were handed out in the last few days before election. It could well have had a big influence on the size of the Negro turnout for Senator Kennedy in a state that he carried by 8,000 votes.

Interestingly, in one particular area where the Eisenhower Administration could claim a dramatic effort for Negro rights, the Republicans got Negro votes. Reports are that most of some 1,500 Negroes added to the registration books in Fayette County, Tenn., this year, as a result of a Justice Department suit, voted for Mr. Nixon.

Another major question suggested by the returns is how the Democrats should approach the South.

Clearly, the traditionally Democratic votes of most white Southerners were critical to Senator Kennedy. But the returns also indicate that the Democrats could profit from increasing Negro registration in the South.

In Louisiana, for example, of four parishes that have no Negro voters registered, three showed majorities for a States' Rights ticket and the fourth went for Mr. Nixon. Where Negroes could vote in Louisiana, they went heavily for Senator Kennedy.

Apparently Senator Kennedy, perhaps in part because of the King episode, overcame in part the recent tactic of some more sophisticated Negroes in Southern urban areas who vote Republican to protest the segregationist views of local Democrats.

In Atlanta, a key Negro district gave only an astonishingly small 15 per cent of its votes to the Democrats in 1956. The percentage rose to 42 this year, still a minority but a large rise —especially considering the fact that the ballot showed not Senator Kennedy's name but the names of electors known as segregationists.

November 27, 1960

Growing Dilemma of the G. O. P.

By RUSSELL BAKER

WASHINGTON.

THROUGH good times and disaster, for longer than most living men can remember, Republicans have drawn their ultimate strength from rural and small-town America. Over the last generation, with the great migration from farm and town to city and suburb, the balance of political power had been shifting glacially against them, but they survived and occasionally thrived because the rural bedrock remained secure.

But on March 26, with its ruling in the Tennessee voting case, the Supreme Court opened the door for what will surely be a historic assault on the base of the party's strength in the rural-dominated state and Federal legislatures. The Court's ruling has fallen like a spark on the already explosive debate about the party's course and leadership.

When Robert Taft was leader of the loyal opposition and spiritual trustee of the Republican faith, there was none of this nonsense about how the party should conduct itself against the Democratic colossus.

"The business of the opposition is to oppose," Taft declared. "Minority leaders," he once told an Atlanta newspaper man, "have no responsibility for presenting a program. Their role is one of opposition and criticism."

Today's Republican minority leaders—Senator Everett M. Dirksen of Illinois and Representative Charles A. Halleck of Indiana—are carrying on in the Taft tradition, often with great skill and always against tremendous odds. And yet, whereas Taft, the symbol of militant Republican opposition, won a lasting place in his party's affections and very nearly won its Presidential nomination, Dirksen and Halleck are finding that all militancy earns them is more than the leaders' normal quota of gall.

No one refers to Halleck as "Mr. Republican," though he is surely the most talented leader the party has had in Congress since Taft. Dirksen is never mentioned as a potential Presidential candidate in 1964, though his skills as an accommodator, his industry, and his performance record in the Senate leadership place him among the few who may truly be Congressional statesmen.

INSTEAD, the leaders are beset by dissident party wings with conflicting demands that would test a Solomon's wit. They are tugged and hauled by every philosopher from the John Birch Society's Robert Welch to Governor Rockefeller's Emmet Hughes.

They are scolded by the party's Madison Avenue thinkers for not properly tending the Republican "image" whatever that may be. Large, influential and ideologically hostile elements within the party are disgruntled because they have developed no program to match the Democratic White House's; two blue-ribbon committees are now embarked on projects to end this deficiency for which the overworked, undermanned leadership is held responsible.

Evidence of the general dissidence even arrives in the mail. Last winter a group of Harvard Republicans devoted the first issue of their new political journal, Advance, to an examination of what was wrong with the party in Congress. Their finding: just about everything, and Dirksen and Halleck were mostly to blame.

How different from the era, just ten years ago, when Taft could command the idolatry of the party with the simple precept that "the business of the opposition is to oppose." But why?

There are two immediate reasons. Foremost is the terrible suspicion stalking the party—in the nation, if not in Congress—that it may be atrophying into a permanent minority organ. A scared party is a party willing to take risks and try the new. The Halleck-Dirksen leadership may be good Taftian orthodoxy, but orthodoxy is small balm for the man craving strong drugs.

This leads to the second reason for the discontent, which might be called the Johnson-Rayburn example. During the eight years in which the Democrats were out of power in the White House, Lyndon B. Johnson and Speaker Sam Rayburn discarded the traditional Taft approach to two-party politics and rewrote the textbook on the art of opposition.

Theirs was a vastly complicated operation of many great political subtleties, but its basic rules were simple. First, the opposition must not risk dissipating its popular following by attacking a popular President. Second, opposition to the President is not enough; there must be an opposition program of constructive alternatives.

The theory behind the Johnson-Rayburn approach represented a small revolution in tactical political thinking. The enemy was to be destroyed with kindness. The assumption was that the electorate would no longer support a party whose prime goal was negative.

Therefore, the business of the opposition would no longer be to oppose; the business of the opposition would be to help the President govern the country.

WHILE Johnson and Rayburn were imposing their new theory of opposition, the Democrats prospered at the polls. Operating under the old theory, the Republicans had reeled from defeat to defeat through every election since 1932, with two exceptions.

For many Republicans today, the lesson seems obvious. The party in Congress must produce a program to counter the New Frontier, must deemphasize the assaults on President Kennedy with his immense popularity-poll rating, and must do something to destroy the old notion that its principal function in Washington is to block whatever any Democrat proposes.

The trouble is that, while many Republicans, notably those with urban-industrial constituencies, feel this way, many Republicans in Congress do not. The majority of the party in Congress has no stomach for abandoning the Taft way and taking up the Johnson-Rayburn theory of opposition. Alternatives to Democratic proposals have traditionally smacked to many Republicans of a surrender in basic principle, the kind of surrender stigmatized in the word "me-tooism."

"Me-tooism" is a vice generally associated with New York and the big-money Republicans. The stand against it has always centered in the rural and small-town element of the party, which gave its allegiance to Taft and sees him still as a hero martyred by the city crowd from the East.

And this element is the group that constitutes the Republican majority in Congress, dominates the Republican leadership and shapes the Republican record, being hammered out before the national audience. Halleck and Dirksen are its faithful mirrors.

DIRKSEN, though responsive to the dominating Midwestern elements, is a man of considerable political breadth, and is highly sensitive to the party's needs in the urban industrial areas. And in the foreign field, both he and Halleck have at times taken exception to the Taft doctrine of opposition. After the unsuccessful Cuban adventure of 1961, for example, both worked to prevent what might have been a disastrous partisan assault on the President, with reverberations heard around the world; but they were criticized for it by Congressional Republicans.

Usually, they do not oppose the prevailing phil- *(Continued)*

RUSSELL BAKER regularly reports on politics from the Washington Bureau of The Times.

osophy of Congressional Republicanism that the role of the opposition is to oppose. This philosophy is a mighty inertial force compounded of habit, tradition, sentiment and old faiths, which has kept the party solidly rooted in rural and small-town America.

Essentially it represents the older generation of Republicanism, preserving the principles of a country that grew up in the fresh air and open spaces with a swing on the front porch, flypaper in the kitchen and an apple tree in the back yard. Its political reactions are instinct with memories of the era when the farmer and the small business man were the representative Americans and the Negro voted Republican in homage to

ROMNEY—Victory for him in Michigan would ease Republican problems.

Lincoln. Suggestions that these principles are outmoded tend to rile it, and young men from the East offering nostrums are to be greeted with suspicion.

Thus the pressures upon Halleck and Dirksen to produce a program, to smarten up the party "image" and to forsake Taft and embrace "constructive opposition" do not stem primarily from the Congressional party. They come from the forces of both Right and Left with little influence on the Congressional party, but big stakes riding on its performance record at the Capitol.

BROADLY speaking, the two conflicting forces acting on the Congressional party from outside can be described, in the meaningless political argot of the day, as the "liberals," who are usually based in the big urban-industrial centers, and the "new conservatives," whose distribution is

national but whose political thrust is toward the South. (The vapidity of the current political vocabulary is remarkably illustrated here, for the "liberals" are in many cases to the right of Alfred M. Landon and the "new conservatives" are demanding a radical change in the entire American status quo.)

On one fundamental, both agree and both oppose the attitude of the Congressional party. In effect, both are saying that the Grand Old Party needs a new look if it is to recover the power to govern and stop the thirty-year atrophy.

THE statistics are dreary indeed: In the past thirty years Republicans have controlled Congress only four years, Democrats twenty-six. In that period, Republicans have elected only one President, a national hero with no party identification before his first campaign. Of fifty governorships, Republicans today hold only sixteen. Of 100 Senate seats, Republicans hold only thirty-six. Of 437 House seats, Republicans hold only 174. In national registrations, Republicans are outnumbered by a ratio of 60 to 40.

This, say the worried, is the fever chart of a sick party. Both the "liberals" and the "new conservatives" have prescriptions to save it. Not surprisingly, each prescriber is proposing what has succeeded for him.

The liberals insist that the party must contest the Democrats for a fair share of the mushrooming urban vote, for which the New Frontier has been hand tooled. In effect, they argue that the old rural-small-town base is no longer broad enough to support a majority national party and that the Republican party must inevitably continue to diminish with the rural-small town population unless it fights for the cities.

THE Congressional party and the National Committee agree to a point. They acknowledge serious weaknesses in urban-industrial areas. Generally, however, they tend to regard their problem as technical rather than ideological. Senator Dirksen, for example, said in a television interview a few weeks ago that the solution to the problem of the cities was to build better Republican organization.

Many of the "liberals" become vague at this point and start talking about improving the party "image." The more forthright, like Senator Jacob

Javits of New York, are candid in their insistence that new policy, rather than new organization, is the party's first need.

Javits, an isolated "liberal" among the Congressional conservatives, has single-handedly produced Republican alternatives to virtually every major New Frontier measure pitched at the cities. He proposes Republican action on medical care, civil rights, urban renewal, housing, transportation and the other issues that engage the daily emotions of the city dweller. Party support for his suggested alternatives in Congress is usually minuscule, coming usually from men like Kuchel, Scott, Aiken, Cooper and Morton in the Senate and from a handful of fifteen to twenty men in the big House delegation.

The doctrinal wrench the "liberals" are seeking to give the party, however, is mild compared to what the "new conservatives" propose. Here the argument is carried by Senator Barry Goldwater with some brilliant assistance by the editors of The National Review.

LIKE the "liberals," Goldwater accepts the argument that the party's present power base is not broad enough. He contends, however, that it would be disastrous and probably futile anyhow for the party to try competing with the Democrats for the cities. The consequence, he assumes, would be a dilution of Republican principles so complete

JAVITS—He favors Republican alternatives, not simply opposition.

that the party would lose its reason for being.

Republican revival, he reasons, will lie not in making the party more like the Democrats, but in making it more Republican. Its failures, he contends, have arisen because

it was "not Republican enough."

From this point, Goldwater lays down a program for ideological change that would dismantle a good part of the existing, laboriously constructed framework for Federal solutions to social and economic problems. For example, he has proposed new laws compelling staged Federal withdrawal from programs for agriculture, social welfare, public power and education. There would be a reaffirmation of state's rights, which appears to offer a Republican equivocation on the civil-rights issue in the South.

The "new conservatism," carried to its logical conclusion, would encourage a fundamental realignment of the parties in the European style, offering the country a choice between Left and Right. Its appeal presumably would be strong in the Democratic but conservative South, which already holds the balance of power in Congress.

Goldwater is refreshing because he does not obscure his meaning with talk about "images," but argues boldly and candidly, wherever anyone will listen, for strong ideological change. He is clearly the sentimental favorite of the Congressional Republicans, if only because his talk of old-fashioned Republicanism and a return to first principles is appealingly reminiscent of the party's more glorious days. Thus he seems to stiffen the party's will to fight.

Yet there has been no significant urging from his colleagues in Congress for him to translate his speeches and papers into legislative language. The explanation seems to be that Goldwater's program of dramatic action is essentially alien to the truly conservative temperament of the Congressional party. The essence of conservatism is its reluctance to tamper with the status quo. Goldwater proposes repealing it.

Former President Eisenhower's influence in the clash of philosophies has so far been directed toward damping any violent swing to either Left or Right. As the party's one universally respected leader, the general carefully maintains the role of elder statesman, urging the party not to tear itself apart in a squabble about labels, preaching the need for stronger organization, but standing above the ideological battle. He has had some success in persuading "attractive" candidates to run for office and he is the party's star attraction at fund-raising enterprises, but there is no evidence that he is exerting much influence on development of party philosophy.

THE clash between "liberals" and "new conservatives" may be fundamental to the issue of what kind of party is to emerge in 1964 and 1968, but it seems curiously remote from the day-to-day problems confronted by Halleck and Dirksen on the firing line where the ugly work has to be done and the hard decisions made. It is all very well to say that the party needs a program to pit against the President's, but how do you produce one that will satisfy the Javits "liberals," the Goldwater "conservatives" and the great majority between?

For the Democrats, it was comparatively easy under Eisenhower. For six of the eight years, Democrats controlled the Congress. Their committee majorities could start with an Eisenhower proposal and reshape it just enough to give it a Democratic identity. If Eisenhower did not propose, the committee majorities could. Moreover they could vote their proposals to the floor and pass them.

FOR the Republicans, it is not so simple. Being in the minority, they must operate with skeleton staffs. On some committees, Democratic technicians outnumber Republicans by a ratio of 15 to 1.

These tiny staffs, already overburdened, are a poor match for the armies of executive talent and bureaucratic manpower that the Administration can throw into preparation of programs.

On occasions when there is a Republican program, it must not be too "Republican" if it is to get the essential support of the Democratic committee majority needed for success on the floor. It was Senator Javits, for example, who devised the alternative to the President's United Nations bond-purchase proposal that was accepted by the Foreign Relations Committee. To prevent the credit from going to a Republican, however, the committee changed the Javits proposal slightly and had a Democrat sponsor it.

It is all very well, too, to say that Halleck and Dirksen ought to do something about the Republican "image." Here again the problems are staggering.

During the Johnson-Rayburn era of divided government, the Democratic Congressional leaders were an essential force in day-to-day government operations. Their plans, their decisions, their actions were headline news. Even then they were hard pressed to compete with Eisenhower for a Democratic **share of press space and TV time.**

For Halleck and Dirksen, the problem of simply com-municating with the country is poignantly acute. With their small minorities in House and Senate, they are rarely in position to control events, except when they combine with the Dixiecrats to kill some favored Presidential project. And then the headlines focus on defeating the President, which is bad "imagery."

Their attempt to retain a minority share of the communications channels through a weekly televised news conference has not been a notable success, largely because they have lacked the resources to tackle the President on the big issues and because they are inherently a weak attraction to a press corps struggling to keep tabs on the ubiquitous Kennedy family and its travels, the storm of Executive briefings, the flood of Administration "messages" and the progress of Administration bills.

WHEN the Republicans kill a Kennedy project, as they did the Department of Urban Affairs, the President can turn it into a *cause célèbre* with a news-conference needle. When the Republicans improve an Administration bill, as they did with the Manpower Retraining Act, it becomes merely an obscure detail buried in press reports that the President's retraining bill —always "the President's bill" —passed the House.

And so, the problem of Halleck and Dirksen rarely reaches the stage where they can afford the luxury of thinking about "image." The problem is usually just to break through the jamming and to communicate.

The probability is that these would be bleak days for the Republicans no matter how they ordered their opposition in Congress. For the Democrats in 1953 and 1954, it was the same. The new Administration is still young, fresh and at the peak of its post-victory flush. Republican strength is low in the Congress, and its brightest stars are preoccupied and out of the limelight around the country.

IN politics, nothing heals like success. Given some Congressional gains this fall, given the election of a bright new man or two to the Senate's Presidential hothouse, given a victory for Richard Nixon in California, George Romney in Michigan and Nelson Rockefeller in New York, and many of the Republicans' immediate problems of opposition might solve themselves.

Given another electoral disaster like 1958, and the winds of change might finally begin to sweep the Congressional party. At the moment, however, Dirksen and Halleck are representing the Republican bedrock faithfully with inadequate help, too few troops, and no coherent advice from the party about what it wants to be.

April 8, 1962

GOLDWATER BUSY BOLSTERING G.O.P.

In Speeches Across Country, He Forges Party Links

By CABELL PHILLIPS
Special to The New York Times

WASHINGTON, June 30 — During June the United States Senate was in session nineteen days. In the same month, Senator Barry Goldwater, Republican of Arizona, made twenty-three speeches away from Washington. Yet, he managed to appear at eleven of those Senate sessions in June, and to be recorded on fourteen roll-call votes.

This feat of political logistics has been matched in recent times by only one other member of the Senate, John F. Kennedy, who was a Senator from Massachusetts during the campaign year of 1960. It is the view of a good many observers here that both men have been agitated by the same virus — Presidential fever.

Many observers also assert that, next to the President, Senator Goldwater is the most exciting and provocative figure on the political landscape today.

As the leading apostle of a hard-boiled, unapologetic conservatism, he has filled the vacuum left by the late Robert A. Taft and filled it with more dash and political appeal than the dour Mr. Taft ever attained.

Senator Goldwater supplies most of the motive power for his drive. He is generously endowed with energy, charm, ambition, shrewdness and money. There is no clearly discernible brain trust or general staff leading him by the hand to a bright, Right-Wing destiny.

But neither is he a "loner." He has an organizational scaffold on which to work and a few close aides and confidantes on whom he depends for help in his political bricklaying. But as of now, at least, he dominates "Operation Goldwater" and makes it work the way he wants it to work.

The key element in this structure is the fact that Senator Goldwater is chairman of the Senate Republican Campaign Committee. He has held this job twice. His present term dates from January, 1959.

His responsibility is to get Republicans rather than Democrats elected to the Senate. This he tries to do by the grant of campaign funds and direct help in organizational and campaign strategy.

He is aided in this by a staff of two of the most talented technicians in the business—Victor A. Johnston and Irving Swanson.

Few positions afford a politician more "exposure" to other politicians throughout the country than this. Day by day, by letter, by telephone and in person, he is in touch with the Governors, state chairmen and other leaders of his party who wield the influence that counts when it come time to write platforms and pick Presidential candidates. If he is a good chairman, as Mr. Goldwater is generally conceded to be, he builds "a line of credit" with party leaders in the key states on which he can draw when the need arises.

A Sought After Speaker

If it sems anomalous that one so conspicuously identified with the right wing should hold this position of high party responsibility, it is worth noting that he is, more in demand as a speaker at political functions than any other Republican in the land— including former President Dwight D. Eisenhower and Vice President Richard M. Nixon.

Invitations have been coming into his office at the rate of twenty a day since January. He accepts, on the average, about two out of ten, bunching them as nearly as possible into Thursday-to-Monday week-ends. He has already booked himself for twenty-seven major speeches in 1962.

Roughly two-thirds of his appearances are sponsored by Republican organizations. The rest come from Chambers of Commerce, school and civic groups. The Senatorial campaign committee pays the bills for his official travel. As for the rest, he collects travel expenses only from his non-official hosts.

The Senator's mobility is aided by a private plane and crew nearly always at his disposal. It is an executive type of DC-3, the property of an old friend and political admirer, Curtis Steuart, Washington business man.

While the bulk of the Senator's expenses are borne by the committee, his exposure on these outings is not confined to party professionals. His chief audience may be a Rotary Club luncheon, or an auditorium full of the dedicated and the curious. Often a day's itinerary will include a school or college group.

Mail Flows In Heavily

As a result, he has generated a vast flow of mail to his Washington office. For the last two months this flow has averaged about 800 letters a day, about 80 per cent of it from outside the Senator's home state of Arizona.

Most are commendatory. Many writers seem to regard him as a sort of messiah of the politically dispossessed, and some plead to become foot soldiers in the ranks of his "crusade." Typical of such letters was one received this week from a young business executive in Cincinnati, who wrote in part:

"Millions of Americans are feeling pains of starvation for a spirit of national direction, for a return to some fundamental principles of democracy, liberty and challenge. Will you please advise me as specifically as possible what a young man such as myself can do to help, beginning immediately."

To handle this mountainous correspondence—as well as the other details of his Senatorial office—Mr. Goldwater has a staff of thirteen. They occupy a suite of five offices in the old Senate Office Building and two more rooms in the basement.

His staff is headed—in fact if not in title—by his cheerful but rather formidable personal secretary, Mrs. Edna Coerver, a friend of his school days in Phoenix. Two young men, Theodore Kazy and Tony Smith, are administrative assistants. All office expenses come within his Senate allowance of about $100,000 annually.

Too Much Mail to Handle

The mail has become so heavy the Senator's staff is unable to answer more than about half of the daily intake—even when using processed form letters for the less important matters. However, the office carefully keeps a card-index record of all names and addresses. A mailing list is an important asset to any politician who expects to stay in—or expand his—business.

The Goldwater staff plays a beguiling but hardly convincing game of being mystified and naive about the furor over their boss. He is not stirring things up, they insist; he is just being himself, and a lot of people have just happened to discover that he is what they have been looking for.

No, they say, there are no important advisers, just friends. And he writes all of his speeches and statements himself. "We just run them off on the typewriter for him."

They do concede, however, that there is a "ghost" for the Senator's successful newspaper column. Syndicated three times a week under the title, "How Do You Stand, Sir?," it repeats many of the strongly conservative positions on national and international affairs the Senator makes in his speeches.

The column now has 105 subscribers, including such major outlets as The Atlanta Constitution, Denver Post, Chicago's American, Detroit News, Miami News, San Francisco Examiner and others. Its monthly income of around $1,500 is given to charities in Phoenix.

Column Written by Friend

The column is written by Senator Goldwater's close friend and political ally, Stephen C. Shadegg, a Phoenix business man, who also is a mystery story writer and actor and impresario in the little theatre. He is also Republican state chairman for Arizona, although he was once a registered Democrat.

The column grew out of the Senator's only book, "The Conscience of a Conservative," which Mr. Shadegg also wrote for him. It has sold close to 700,000 copies since its publica-

tion a little more than a year ago.

Whether the ideas of "Where Do You Stand, Sir?" are more Mr. Shadegg's or Senator Goldwater's it is impossible to say. The two do confer once or twice a week by long distance telephone, and also on Mr. Goldwater's monthly flying visits back home. The prose, however, is that of the "ghost," as is that of some of Senator Goldwater's more recent speeches.

Another important figure in the Arizona wing of the group is Eugene C. Pulliam, publisher of Phoenix's two dailies and a sturdy old guard Republican, whom many regard as Mr. Goldwater's original political patron.

A frequent counselor on fiscal and economic matters is Lewis W. Douglas of Tucson, who resigned as budget director in the first New Deal in protest against President Franklin D. Roosevelt's financial policies.

Among Easterners with prominent positions in this circle are Raymond C. Moley, another former New Dealer turned conservative, who is now business columnist for Newsweek magazine; Frank C. Hanighen, publisher o fthe Human Events, a weekly newletter of strongly conservative persuasions, and William F. Buckley Jr., editor of The National Review.

Admired by Right Wing

Most of the so-called right-wing fringe groups — including nearly all of those of the "lunatic" variety — have tried to claim Senator Goldwater as their own. The Senator is wary about encouraging or disavowing this support publicly. Typical, perhaps, is his stock answer to what he thinks of the John Birch society.

"I really don't know much about it," he says with a studied casualness. "I only know that the few of them I know about in Phoenix are among the finest people in the city."

Such groups are an important factor in the build-up of the Goldwater image as the "savior" of constitutional government. He is quoted and written about admiringly by scores of extremist pamphleteers, publishers and broadcasters across the nation.

For foreign-policy guidance Senator Goldwater has a strong affinity for Brig. Gen. Bonner Fellers, retired. Currently, the

general is centering his energies on the Citizens Foreign Aid Committee, an influential lobbying organization aimed at abolishing foreign aid.

To a good many of his Republican friends who do not agree with his politics but who welcome his arousing conservative enthusiasm, Senator Goldwater's negativism on foreign policy is the most serious handicap to his own ambitions.

"What he needs," one of them said, "is an Arthur Vandenberg or a Foster Dulles to tell him a few facts of life. If he goes into the campaign of 1964 talking this kind of isolationist foolishness, people will laugh at him."

Well Liked in Senate

Washington does not take Barry Goldwater as seriously as the rest of the country. He is universally liked in the Senate, but his influence is negligible and he is not a member of its invisible hierarchy, "The Club."

When he tried last winter to get a place on the party's leadership conference, along with Senator Everett McKinley Dirksen of Illinois and Representative Charles A. Halleck, he was firmly rebuffed.

But many party spokesmen agreed that a Goldwater clique is beginning to coalesce within Republican organization ranks around the country. One highly informed person said recently that he would estimate that close to twenty state chairmen, chiefly in the South and Middle West, if polled today, would choose Mr. Goldwater as the party's Presidential candidate in 1964.

But the Senator has no intention of putting "operation Goldwater" into high gear prematurely.

"A lot of people say they want me to run," he said recently. "I tell them that electing a Republican Congress is more important to us right now than thinking about 1964.

"I tell them that I am not seeking the Presidency—and I'm not. But that's not a position you have to promise to hold right down to the wire. You never know in this business what you may have to do."

July 3, 1961

G.O.P. Asserts Kennedy Fails at Home and Abroad

By CABELL PHILLIPS
Special to The New York Times.

WASHINGTON, June 7 — Congressional Republicans made a strong attack on the Kennedy Administration today in a new statement of party principles designed as a major campaign weapon for 1962 and 1964. They accused the Administration of "incompetence" in managing the nation's economy and of "bluster" and "whimpering" in the conduct of foreign affairs.

Labeled "A Declaration of

Republican Principle and Policy," the statement has been more than four months in preparation. It was the work of a twelve-man committee, consisting of an equal number of Senate and House members, on which both the conservative and liberal wings of the party were represented.

The chairman, Representative Melvin R. Laird of Wisconsin, described the document as a "consensus" that had been adopted "with near unanimity" by the Republican membership

of both houses. It is known that two Senators voted against adoption.

Approval by House Republicans was announced as unanimous.

Mr. Laird, when asked if the statement had the approval of former President Dwight D. Eisenhower, replied that changes had been made in an earlier draft to get in some suggestions made by General Eisenhower at a recent meeting.

The statement declares that the basic political issue of 1962 is "which party acts more effectively to preserve and enlarge human freedom?"

"The current Administration," it states, "has shown little understanding of, or concern for institutions that buttress freedom at home—separation of powers, checks and balances, state and local responsibility, and a free competitive economy.

"It has demonstrated neither the wit nor the will to meet effectively the assault of international communism on freedom.

"We Republicans cannot witness the erosion of freedom without warning or protest."

The paper accuses the Kennedy Administration of a "lack of sympathy toward a free competitive economy." In an apparent allusion to the President's intervention in the steel price dispute and to the recent price plunge on the stock market, the statement asserts:

"The incompetence of the New Frontier in economic policy is manifest. It has destroyed confidence."

Encroachments Seen

The statement in several places complains that centralized Government has encroached upon the economic and political life of the country. At the same time, however, it calls for Federal action in many situations—in controlling agricultural surpluses, in encouraging economic growth, in assistance to schools and in medical care.

With respect to medical care, the paper states that Republicans reject "attempts to run a legislative bulldozer through the structure of voluntary health insurance and private medicine."

But it then adds:

"We support Government plans to increase the coverage of voluntary insurance plans and to help older citizens having difficulty meeting the costs of adequate coverage."

Some Republicans regard this clause as representing a liberalization of the party's position on this issue.

Another tendency toward liberalization was discovered by some observers in the warning that Federal intervention would have to come in the solution of the "urgent problems of urbanized areas" unless state and local governments dealt adequately with the problem. Congressional Republicans voted heavily earlier this year against the creation of a Federal Department of Urban Affairs.

Foreign Policy Criticized

The sharpest attack on the Kennedy Administration came in the section dealing with foreign affairs. The paper declares:

"Despite this nation's position as the most powerful on earth, the bankruptcy of its leadership was shown at critical times in the past year. It was shown in Berlin and Cuba. It was shown in the hesitancy to resume nuclear testing when our national security demanded it. It was shown in the bluster followed by whimpering in respect to Laos.

"Republicans demand high-powered deeds, not high-powered words. We want and expect the cause of freedom to win."

An informed source disclosed that the toughness of this language, considerably modified from earlier drafts, was insisted upon by Senator John G. Tower of Texas and other strongly conservative members of the panel.

Cooper Refuses to Sign

Senator John Sherman Cooper of Kentucky refused to sign the statement.

"The foreign policy section," he said this afternoon, "deals with several immediate areas of danger about which I believe there should be as much unity and as little partisanship as possible between the two parties." He continued:

"Berlin continues to be an area of great danger and I believe the President's policy regarding it is correct.

"Immediate and delicate decisions may be made regarding the future of Laos. . . . I do not believe that political statements are helpful at this time."

Senator Jacob K. Javits of New York said that he had threatened to withhold his signature from the report until certain language in the foreign policy section was toned down.

"I have important differences with the declaration with respect to certain of its foreign policy provisions and other matters," he said. "I am satisfied, however, that it is a consensus of the views of Republicans in the Senate, and that some progress in the crystallization of these views is better than none at all."

Senator Milton R. Young of North Dakota refused to sign. He objected to the section dealing with agricultural policy.

June 8, 1962

Eisenhower Bids Business Aid G. O. P. as Its Party

By TOM WICKER
Special to The New York Times.

GETTYSBURG, June 30—Former President Dwight D. Eisenhower said today that the Republicans were the party of business and that he was "proud of the label." General Eisenhower was speaking to about 100 party leaders who met on his farm in the first All-Republican Conference.

The conference was organized, party leaders said, to bring them together periodically, to keep party activities in the public eye, and to provide a consultative body for Republican officeholders.

In welcoming the conferees, General Eisenhower issued a strong appeal for business men to enter more fully into politics—preferably Republican politics.

"They call ours a party of business and I'm proud of the label," he said. "But business men now have to do a little waking up."

Limits for Government

They could no longer be sure, he said, that there were "well-designed and well-observed limits beyond which Government would not go."

Politics should be the first business of a business man, he said, and added that, if the business man did not realize this need, "he is not going to have a prosperous business, not in the long run." General Eisenhower declared:

"If we don't exercise the function of self-government, by golly, we'll be governed by someone else, and that I don't like."

He appealed also for Republican unity and said he had "gotten so I despise the term liberal and I have almost gotten so I hate the term conservative."

"If we can say we are for progress and for responsibility in the same breath, then I think we are going ahead," he said, continuing:

"Our country is facing a very critical period, and I believe that only some resurgence of Republican control in our Government is going to keep things on a more level keel than they seem to be going now."

The conference, under a green and white striped tent on General Eisenhower's lawn, was a new departure in Republican affairs, but the theme sounded had a familiar ring.

Former Vice President, Richard M. Nixon, a candidate for Governor of California, laid down another traditional Republican line. The party, he said, had to demonstrate to the people that "that government which spends less, taxes less and allows and encourages the people to do for themselves is the best."

General Eisenhower and Mr. Nixon were followed to the speakers stand by Senator Everett McKinley Dirksen of Illinois and Representative Charles A. Halleck of Indiana, the Congressional minority leaders.

Senator Dirksen declared that, thirty years after the election of Franklin D. Roosevelt as President, the Democrats still were trying to find the solution to "idle hands, idle acres and idle dollars."

He suggested that the answer was a return to "the old virtues that made this country great, the best weapons that this party can have."

Mr. Halleck was more specific. To end "this assault on basic American freedoms by the hip-shooting riders of the New Frontier," he said, "Get out and elect a Republican House of Representatives in November."

To President Kennedy's complaint at his news conference this week that more Democrats had to be elected before the New Frontier programs could be enacted, Mr. Halleck provided a sardonic answer.

"How many Democrats does he need, anyhow," he asked.

The present House breakdown is 263 Democrats to 174 Republicans. In view of that, Mr. Halleck said. "our accomplishments as an effective minority have been nothing short of miraculous."

Criticizes Congress

Mr. Nixon put the same point another way. The Democratic Congress, he said, has been "one of the least productive in the history of the nation."

Mr. Nixon also made a strong appeal for the election of Republican governors, but the emphasis of the conference was on victory in the House of Representatives.

William E. Miller, the National Chairman, conceded that it was mathematically impossible to take over the Senate. But it was plain that the party leaders were optimistic over their chances in the Congressional elections.

Representative Bob Wilson of California, the chairman of the House Republican Campaign Committee, reported on his committee's efforts and predicted a victory. It would take a net gain of forty-four Republican seats to take over voting control of the House.

Political leaders in both parties agree, however, that a net gain of more than ten Republican seats would be a significant legislative victory for the Republicans and a crippling blow to the Democratic legislative program.

Governor Rockefeller of New York, Senator Barry Goldwater of Arizona, and George Romney of Michigan, all regarded as potential Republican Presidential nominees of 1964, were absent, but each sent letters.

They were read by Mr. Miller, all pleading prior engagements and wishing the conference well. There were reports, however, that their absence was more nearly a gesture toward party unity and an effort to keep the conference centered on the party rather than on personalities. Mr. Nixon, another possibility for 1964, attended as the former Vice President and California gubernatorial nominee.

There were reports on the political situations in various sections of the country, made by Republican governors. All found this a salubrious year for Republicanism. President Kennedy's record, particularly his conflict with the steel industry, was repeatedly given as a cause of uneasiness in the country.

Representative Walter H. Judd of Minnesota, reporting on foreign affairs, took alarm at what he saw as a Democratic tendency to seek an accommodation with the Soviets.

Uneasiness Noted

Underneath the apparent harmony and enthusiasm of the conference, there was some uneasiness, particularly on the part of Republican members of Congress.

Chairman Miller, who organized the conference with the consent of General Eisenhower

and other non-Congressional leaders, has announced plans to set up a permanent staff and office for it in Washington, and for periodic meetings of the same general group that attended today.

Congressional leaders fear this might undermine their own prerogatives in setting party policy. No policy pronouncements were made today, however, other than the usual Republican themes.

Mr. Halleck said yesterday, in reference to the conference, "I happen to think we've been doing pretty good ourselves [in the Congress]."

Senator Dirksen, asked about the All-Republican Conference, replied:

"All I know is what I read in the papers."

This undertone of concern was not apparent today. The weather was balmy, though the sky was overcast. Far across General Eisenhower's fields, the Catoctin Mountains were blue against the horizon. A hundred yards away, his white brick house looked pleasant and comfortable, almost a symbol of security and success, under its shade trees.

'Old Home Week'

There was something of an "old home week" atmosphere as

former Eisenhower Administration colleagues greeted each other and exchanged political intelligence, and there was a constant scramble, particularly among those running for office, to sit beside the cordial and smiling General Eisenhower long enough to have pictures taken by swarms of photographers.

The oratory was pleasing to Republican ears, too, and after almost three hours of it there were fried chicken, potato salad and cold cuts eaten picnic-style in the open.

Except for the three notable absentees, the roster of those attending was a Who's Who of Republican leadership, past and present.

From General Eisenhower's Cabinet, for instance, there were former Secretary of State Christian A. Herter; the former Secretary of Health, Education and Welfare, Arthur S. Flemming; former Secretary of Defense Neil H. McElroy; former Attorney General William P. Rogers; former Secretary of the Interior Fred A. Seaton and former Secretary of Commerce Sinclair Weeks.

From Congress there were Senators Dirksen, Kenneth Keating and Jacob K. Javits of New York and John G. Tower of Texas and Representatives Halleck, Judd, Wilson, Peter Fre-

linghuysen of New Jersey and John W. Byrnes of Wisconsin.

Former Chairman Attends

Other Republican leaders included Leonard W. Hall, the former National Chairman, Dr. Gabriel Hauge, a former administrative assistant to President Eisenhower, Dr. Arthur Burns and former chairman of the Council of Economic Advisers, and a number of present and former party officals.

Henry Cabot Lodge, former United States Representative in the United Nations and Mr. Nixon's running mate in 1960, also was present.

Among notable candidates on hand were Mr. Nixon, Mr. Seaton, who is running for Governor of Nebraska, Representative William Scranton, a candidate for Governor of Pennsylvania, and Jack Cox, the Republican gubernatorial nominee in Texas.

The national Governors Conference, which opens tomorrow at near-by Hershey, Pa., brought several Republican governors to the All-Republican Conference today. They included Norman A. Erbe of Iowa, Wesley Powell of New Hampshire, Robert E. Smylie of Idaho, and John A. Volpe of Massachusetts.

July 1, 1962

Goldwater Finds Party Council Counter to G. O. P.'s Principles

WASHINGTON, July 2 (AP) —Senator Barry Goldwater, the Republican conservative spokesman from Arizona, condemned today the proposed All-Republican Conference backed by former President Dwight D. Eisenhower.

Mr. Goldwater coupled this with criticism of Eisenhower Administration policies, which he said "ran counter to the traditional principles" of the party.

It was the closest that Mr. Goldwater had come to an outright break with General Eisenhower and the moderates who back the former President.

Mr. Goldwater wrote William

E. Miller, national chairman, man, urging that he and other leaders reject the conference plan—despite the fact that Mr. Miller is an active sponsor, if not the originator, of the idea.

Mr. Goldwater told Mr. Miller that the leaders of the proposed group were "the same people who caused most of our present party troubles."

"It is unthinkable that they should be given another opportunity to lead us down the path to political destruction," he said.

Mr. Goldwater's letter did not designate by name those he referred to. Nor did he specify

what Eisenhower policies he believed violated party principles.

Mr. Miller, reached at his summer home on Lake Ontario, near Buffalo, said that he had not received Mr. Goldwater's letter. "And I don't wish to make any comment on it until I read it thoroughly," the party chairman said.

Nor was there any prompt reaction from General Eisenhower.

The All-Republican Conference concept got its biggest public support and at least the tacit blessing of General Eisenhower last Saturday in a rally of party leaders at the Eisenhower farm near Gettysburg, Pa.

The basic idea, as advanced by Mr. Miller, is that the Republicans should strive for unity and form a group of lead-

ers in and out of office, to coordinate a drive to win control of the House of Representatives and to cut the Democrats' Senate majority in this year's elections.

Mr. Miller attended the rally but Mr. Goldwater did not. Nor did Governor Rockefeller of New York, who is regarded as a leader of the party's more liberal element. Former Vice President Richard M. Nixon took a prominent part in the meeting.

The Republican Congressional leaders, Senator Everett McKinley Dirksen of Illinois and Representative Charles A. Halleck of Indiana, attended the Gettysburg meeting but neither has been counted among the most enthusiastic supporters of the conference idea.

July 3, 1962

NEW G. O. P. GROUP STIRS PARTY FIGHT

Citizens Committee Fails to Muster Wide Support

WASHINGTON, Sept. 1 (UPI) —The National Republican Citizens Committee, a pet project of former President Eisenhower, has stirred a battle among party

leaders.

The formation of the committee was revealed during the All-Republican Conference on the Eisenhower farm at Gettysburg, Pa., June 30.

A survey shows that some critics fear the project will set off warfare inside the party and drain away campaign funds. Some are worried that the committee will try to dictate the nomination of the 1964 Republican Presidential candidate.

Among these is Senator Barry Goldwater of Arizona, who protested that the organization would be a force of disunity.

Swift rebuttals came from Mr. Eisenhower and the Republican national chairman, Representative William E. Miller, who said it would help broaden the base of the party.

Long-Range Program

The committee hopes to recruit support for Republican candidates from people who are not active in the party organization. Its sponsors regard it as a long-range program to strengthen the party, but with no significant role in state and Congressional elections this November.

Both parties have had citizens' or volunteer groups in specific campaigns. The new project is set up on a permanent basis.

Republican leaders look upon Walter N. Thayer, president of the New York Herald Tribune, as the father of the movement. Some also believe Mr. Eisenhower was influential in getting it accepted at party headquarters and by the party leadership in Congress.

In the survey, forty-four Republican state chairmen and national committee members were questioned in thirty-three states.

241

Of these, twelve individuals in eleven states were critical or hostile. Six were noncommittal and fourteen in ten states said they thought the project was a good idea.

Twelve others in eleven states gave "yes, but" replies. They thought the committee could be useful if its work were coordinated with the regular party organization.

'It Can Drop Dead'

Some of the comments follow:

"We have yet to see any demonstrable evidence as to how they can help us," L. Judson Morehouse, New York State chairman, said. "We welcome new people but we want to make sure they work in a co-ordinating fashion."

"It can drop dead," Robert Pierce, Wisconsin national committeeman, declared. "I don't care whether it exists or not."

"I feel that it will be a useful tool when used as an integral part of the party itself and not to increase dissension," Winthrop Rockefeller, Arkansas national committeeman, said.

"It's basically ridiculous," Wirt Yerger Jr., Mississippi state chairman, asserted. "I think it should dry up."

The Iowa state chairman, George Nagle, said he did not want to criticize Mr. Eisenhower but he regarded the committee as "an unnecessary adjunct to the party at this time."

Some party leaders conceded the new organization could tap manpower and money not available to the regular party organization. But one summed up objections by saying that the term citizens committee "is just a dirty word" to many political professionals.

There is no evidence that the committee now favors any specific possibility for the 1964 Presidential nomination. But there is widespread belief among Republicans that it would oppose the nomination of Senator Goldwater, a conservative.

"I think the committee is concerned with the 1964 Presidential election and I think that is its only purpose," Anthony Battaglia, Florida national committeeman, asserted.

"I think the founders are too smart to back any primary candidate in the 1964 election," Joseph Martin Jr., California national committeeman, said.

Preparations for the project were made at an unpublicized meeting at Gettysburg last Dec. 12 and 13. A report on that meeting was circulated to a small group of Republicans last spring.

The participants included General Eisenhower and thirteen other Republicans. Most of them had been active in citizens committees in previous campaigns. The regular organization was represented only by the national chairman, Mr. Miller.

Leadership Not Consulted

The Republican bloc in Congress was not represented. The Senate leader, Everett McKinley Dirksen of Illinois, and the House leader, Charles A. Halleck of Indiana journeyed to Gettysburg to get a briefing from Mr. Eisenhower.

The report on the meeting said the committee would "stress, point up and articulate the fundamental and bedrock principles upon which all Republicans agree."

The report recalled that Mr. Eisenhower had praised former citizen groups and had worked to enlist people in the regular party organization.

But it said this effort had failed because local organizations often showed "no burning desire to fill their ranks with this new kind of blood" and because many in the volunteer groups were interested in politics and candidates only at the national level.

Invitations were sent June 30 by a seventeen-member organizing committee to persons who might want to join after paying dues ranging from $10 a year for junior members to $1,000-to-$3,000 contributions for founding members.

Mr. Thayer recently visited Senator Goldwater to discuss the committee. According to Mr. Goldwater, they had a pleasant conversation but parted in disagreement.

The committee is expected to open a Washington headquarters soon. General Eisenhower is honorary chairman but the working chairman is still to be named.

Vice chairmen named in the June 30 invitation were James B. Black, San Francisco; Peter M. Flanigan, New York; Barbara Bates Gunderson, former South Dakota national committee member; George Herrmann, Chicago; David O. Maxwell, Philadelphia; James L. Murphy, San Francisco; Robert A. Rowan, Los Angeles; Stanley M. Rumbough Jr., New York, and James C. Worthy, Chicago.

Joseph E. Sheffield, Camden, S. C., was listed as finance chairman, John L. Loeb Jr., New York, as treasurer and Ann Whitman, General Eisenhower's former personal secretary, as executive secretary.

September 2, 1962

DEMOCRATS KEEP CONGRESS STRENGTH

50 MILLION VOTE

President Fails to Win Larger Majorities for Program

By JAMES RESTON

The American people said O.K. yesterday to President Kennedy, hello to two new Republican Presidential prospects —William Scranton of Pennsylvania and George Romney of Michigan — and an apparent farewell to Richard M. Nixon.

Over 50,000,000 Americans went to the polls in fine weather — they were obviously in a choosy and even capricious mood. They started a Democratic tide running in New England, where the Kennedy party picked up at least three governorships and two Senate seats. They did remarkably well by the Republicans in the South, giving them four more House seats and threatening a 23-year Democratic Senator, Lister Hill of Alabama.

President Kennedy did not get everything he wanted. He got a standoff in the House (he wanted five or ten more seats). He picked up at least one seat in the Senate and might in the end get as many as four (he only asked for two).

G.O.P. Governors Named

But the Democrats lost several strongholds in the big state capitals and probably did not gain enough in Congress to assure passage of the President's liberal domestic program.

Nevertheless, the electorate was kinder to Mr. Kennedy than it usually is to most Presidents in off-year elections. The average loss to the party in power is 44 seats in the House and five in the Senate, and he did far better than that.

It was in the races for the governorships in the states that the Republicans made their most impressive gains. They apparently lost one of the biggest of these races in California, where Gov. Edmund G. Brown seemed the winner over former Vice President Richard M. Nixon.

Wiley Among Losers

But Governor Rockefeller was re-elected in New York over the Democrat Robert M. Morgenthau by about half a million votes.

And in three states that are always important in a Presidential election they took governorships that the Democrats now hold.

Thus in Pennsylvania William Scranton beat Richardson Dilworth; in Michigan George Romney beat Gov. John B. Swainson, and in Ohio James A. Rhodes beat Gov. Michael V. DiSalle.

Among the Republican Senators defeated was Alexander Wiley of Wisconsin, ranking member of the Foreign Relations Committee, who lost to Gov. Gaylord Nelson.

The election for the House was highly contradictory. For example, the Republicans picked up seats in the South—Kentucky, Tennessee, Texas and two new seats in North Carolina.

They also won surprise victories in West Virginia, Massachusetts, New York, Kansas, Illinois and Maryland. Yet the Democrats, following the capricious trend of the voting, took one Republican seat in Connecticut, and defeated Walter Judd of Minnesota, keynoter of the last Republican convention, and a principal critic of President Kennedy's foreign policy.

Many of the prominent figures in the election came through as expected. These included the President's brother, Edward M. Kennedy, who won a Senate seat from Massachusetts; J. W. Fulbright, Democrat of Arkansas, chairman of the Foreign Relations Committee; Representative Charles A. Halleck of Indiana, the Republican leader in the House, and Senator

242

Thomas H. Kuchel of California, Republican whip.

Among them also were Jacob K. Javits, Republican of New York, who won by over three-quarters of a million votes; Thruston B. Morton, Republican of Kentucky, who beat Lieut. Gov. Wilson W. Wyatt, a Kennedy favorite, and Abraham A. Ribicoff, former Secretary of Health, Education and Welfare, who had a hard race for the Senate in Connecticut.

Among the surprises were the following:

¶Democrats won the governorships of New Hampshire and Vermont and were leading for the governorships of Iowa and Nebraska, all ancient Republican strongholds.

¶Meanwhile, a Republican won the governorship of Oklahoma for the first time.

¶Senator Lister Hill, Democrat of Alabama and one of the most powerful Southerners in the South, had a remarkably tough fight with James D. Martin, a Republican—apparently because of the opposition in Alabama to the use of Federal troops at the University of Mississippi.

¶Not only did the Democrats win the governorship of New Hampshire, but Thomas J. McIntyre, former Mayor of Laconia, also won a Senate seat from Perkins Bass, Republican.

Voting on Personality

This was the kind of election it was: Republicans winning in traditional Democratic territory and vice versa. The voters seemed to be voting on personality rather than on ideology.

The son of the late Senator Robert A. Taft of Ohio, Robert A. Taft Jr., was elected to the House of Representatives, defeating, incidentally, a Kennedy —this one named Richard D. Meanwhile another Kennedy, this one a Republican named John F., was beaten in Rhode Island by a Democrat named John E. Fogarty.

There was some indication in the voting that the Cuba issue backfired on the Republicans.

The Republican leader in the Senate, Everett McKinley Dirksen, had one of the hardest battles of his political life with Sidney Yates and was still trailing early today, but the indications then were that he would pull through in the end.

There was nothing in yesterday's results to indicate any forthcoming change on basic power questions in the cold war. In the 88th Congress, as in the 87th, the President will probably get the support he requests on major defense and foreign policy questions, but he may have more trouble than before on foreign as well as domestic economic issues.

The reason for this is that in the last House, with the leadership of the late Speaker Sam Rayburn of Texas, the Democrats managed to increase the size of the all-important Rules Committee by only five votes. This was done to increase the liberal membership of that committee and assure a Rules Committee go-ahead for liberal legislation.

This is now subject to review by the 88th Congress. The Democrats appeared late last night to have lost just enough seats to enable the conservative coalition to regain control of the Rules Committee under Judge Howard W. Smith, Democrat of

Virginia.

On the other hand the Democrats apparently added one or two to their 3-2 majority in the Senate, and the prospect was that the changes in the Senate had made that body more liberal.

For the Republican party, yesterday's election was one more critical test in its effort to reverse the Democratic trend that started with the election of Franklin D. Roosevelt in 1932. Since that time, the G.O.P. has had a majority in both houses of Congress for only four years, and it has not controlled more than half of the governorships since 1954.

For the Democrats, the aim was to pick up enough new liberals in the growing urban and suburban areas above the Mason - Dixon line to overcome the conservative Republican-Southern Democratic coalition that cut deeply into the President's domestic legislative program in the last two years.

President Kennedy's two to one majority in the House and his three to two majority in the Senate were not enough in the 87th Congress to prevent the defeat of his programs of Federal aid to public elementary and secondary schools; a Cabinet Department of Urban Affairs; stiff controls on production of surplus farm crops; and standby authority to initiate public works programs and reduce income taxes to combat economic recessions.

'One-Party' Trend

To the conservative coalition, these programs, combined with the large Democratic majorities in both houses, symbolized a

trend toward "one-party" government, a planned economy and the centralization of power in Washington.

To the Administration Democrats, these programs, which will probably be introduced again next year, were essential to deal with a nation whose population was growing by more than 3,000,000 a year, whose economy was not growing fast enough to keep up with the challenge of modern electronic technology and competition from abroad, and whose unemployment figure was still 3,500,000.

Yesterday's results were not expected to have any fundamental effect on the policy of firm opposition to Communist expansion, particularly into this hemisphere and other areas vital to the security of the United States.

Cuba was a major issue in the campaign, before and even after President Kennedy's decision to force Soviet missiles out of Cuba. But the opposition to his Cuban policy came not primarily from those who wanted the President to do less to oppose Communist policies but from those who wanted him to do more.

Even in the foreign policy field, however, the President had argued that larger liberal majorities were necessary, particularly in the House because money bills, foreign aid and trade, which originate in the House of Representatives, are increasingly important to the cold war struggle in India, Africa, Latin America and other developing areas of the world.

November 7, 1962

NIXON DENOUNCES PRESS AS BIASED

In 'Last' News Conference, He Attributes His Defeat to Crisis Over Cuba

BY GLADWIN HILL
Special to The New York Times

BEVERLY HILLS, Calif., Nov. 7—Richard M. Nixon conceded defeat today. He later devoted what many observers regard as the possible valedictory of his national political career to a bitter denunciation of the press.

He also made some acid remarks about his victorious gu-

bernatorial opponent, Gov. Edmund G. Brown, in a statement to about 100 newsmen at the Beverly Hilton Hotel here. The statement was his first public utterance since the election yesterday, which dashed the former Vice President's hopes of a political comeback.

A failure to win his native state had been widely assessed before the election as impairing, probably irreparably, the 49-year-old Republican's viability in national politics.

His defeat came by a vote margin six times as large as the margin by which he carried California in 1960, when he lost the Presidential election to John F. Kennedy. The virtually unanimous opinion of political observers was that the defeat had obliterated the lingering possibility, despite his disclaimers, that he might figure in the Presidential race of 1964.

In his denunciation of the press, Mr. Nixon said to the newsmen today, "You won't have Nixon to kick around any more, because, gentlemen, this is my last press conference."

Mr. Nixon gave no hint of his plans. He has been a partner in a Los Angeles law firm. There has been speculation that he might run for the United States Senate against Senator Clair Engle, Democrat, in 1964.

The defeated candidate renounced any putative leadership of the Republican party in the state, saying that the party would have to be revitalized by others.

Blames Cuban Crisis

Mr. Nixon attributed this defeat principally to the Cuban crisis, which he said had cost his campaign impetus at a critical point. But in his denunciation of the press, he put strong emphasis on the newspapers' asserted failure to report his views fully.

November 8, 1962

G.O.P. Is Attacked for Its Aid To Segregationists in the South

By HEDRICK SMITH
Special to The New York Times

WASHINGTON, Nov 25 — A magazine published by young Republicans has attacked the party's national campaign leadership for supporting segregationist candidates in the South.

The magazine Advance said that, by "hitching the party wagon to the falling star of segregation," Republican strategists were endangering the party's long-range prospects in the South and embarrassing G.O.P. candidates elsewhere in the nation.

In a special open letter to the Republican National Committee printed in their December issue, the editors of Advance declared:

"Though a traditionally conservative appeal to the South is certainly acceptable, a segregationist appeal is totally unacceptable, both morally and politically.

Workman Is Cited

"Republican candidates like William Workman in South Carolina should receive no encouragement from the national party. Support for them plays into Kennedy's hands."

The article stated that the candidacy of Mr. Workman, a newspaper columnist known for his segregationist views, had pushed Negroes into voting for Senator Olin Johnston, the Democrat, who defeated him.

Advance also criticized the campaign management by the Republican Senate Campaign Committee, headed by Senator Barry Goldwater of Arizona, considered by many to be the party's chief right-wing spokesman.

The magazine pointed to a net Republican loss of four Senate seats this fall, commenting that "it's time for a new coach with a new approach" more sensitive to the politics of the urban centers of the north, Midwest and West.

Senator Jacob K. Javits, who compiled a majority of more than 1,000,000 votes in winning re-election in New York, was proposed as the "most talented candidate" in this respect.

Charges Exaggeration

Advance was first printed more than a year ago at Harvard College by a group of self-styled "progressive" Republicans. Since their graduation from Harvard, the group has moved the magazine to Washington.

Their article was viewed as another move in the continuing intra-party maneuvering between right-wing and moderate Republicans building up toward the 1964 Presidential election.

The Advance article accused such Republican leaders as Senator Goldwater and I. Lee Potter, head of the Republican "Operation Dixie," of exaggerating the importance of Southern election victories.

In their post-election comments, both had hailed the gain of five Congressional seats from the 12 Southern states and the close Senate race in Alabama as evidence of Republican growth and vitality.

"These were significant but hardly earthshaking achievements," the magazine said. It suggested that more stress should have been placed on "dramatic" improvement among Negro precincts in Detroit, New York, Cleveland and Philadelphia by victorious G.O.P. gubernatorial candidates.

"Is this not more worthy of cheers than a demonstration in Alabama that Republicans can almost win by betraying their heritage?" the magazine asked.

It went on to suggest that the party's right-wing was wooing the South, not "just to whistle 'Dixie,'" but to build a base of strength for itself within the party.

It added that the victories in the South, when achieved by outdoing the Dixiecrats and renouncing Lincoln, would backfire against the party and would "alienate the annually growing Negro vote in the South."

"A striking example," the article noted, "is the bald attempt of the Senatorial Candidates in South Carolina and Alabama to exploit [President] Kennedy's action in Mississippi."

See Aid Given Democrats

Such campaigns play into the hands of New Frontier Democrats in the long run, the magazine said. It pictured Democrats as adjusting slowly to Southern racial progress by retaining the votes of rural and liberal whites and adding to them the votes of newly registered Negroes.

Another problem seen in a segregationist pitch is that it will conflict with the probable platform of the Republican nominee for President in 1964.

Three likely nominees—Governor Rockefeller of New York and Governor-elect George Romney of Michigan and William Scranton of Pennsylvania—have "all expressed repugnance to a segregationist party in the South," the magazine said, adding:

"It is vital, therefore, that the party nationally make a policy decision now to concentrate on the metropolitan North, Midwest, and West, and to orient its Southern campaign—toward responsible Southern progress, rather than toward Southern prejudices and reaction."

November 26, 1962

'62 and '64

The National Committee of the Republican party is meeting in Washington this weekend for a look back at the campaign of 1962 and a look ahead to the campaign of 1964. One factor in the look both ways is the role of the party in the South.

Statistically, the Republican party did better in the South in the recently concluded 1962 campaign than it has done in many years. Republican headquarters claims, in fact, that the party's gain in the South between the Congressional elections of 1958 and those of 1962 amounted to 1,400,000 votes, compared with a Democratic gain of less than half that. A trend of this kind, projected into the future at the same accelerating pace, could bring close to realization something greatly to be desired—namely, a real two-party system in the South.

Unfortunately, however, it is clear that a substantial part of the Republican gain in 1962 was achieved by the dubious device of nominating candidates to run locally on racist and segregationist platforms. This had the immediate advantage of winning the support of some normally Democratic voters who were looking for a chance to punish the national Democratic Administration for the role it played in the "Ole Miss" affair. Short-term, this tactic may have seemed attractive, but it promises disaster.

The Republican party cannot attempt to outbid the Southern Democrats on the segregation issue without stultifying its position nationally and abandoning whatever hope it may have of winning the great urban centers of the North.

December 7, 1962

Books of The Times

By KALMAN SEIGEL
Special to The New York Times.

NEW YORK.
Early this month the nation's Representatives and Senators moved hopefully into Washington for the beginning of the 88th Congress. Already waiting was President Kennedy with an ambitious program of tax reform, foreign aid, space projects, aid to education, medical care for the aged, a farm program and other measures he deems necessary if the nation is to move ahead in an increasingly complex world.

For the successful enactment of his program the President will need the cooperation of Congress. The degree to which he gets wholehearted support or is able to weld workable coalitions will determine how much of his program he will get through. President Kennedy is prepared to fight vigorously for these measures, for as he himself has indicated, enactment of a successful legislative program is a large and sometimes seemingly impossible task.

Congress is ready to give the President's program a thorough and critical going-over. Fiscal conservatives are already looking dourly at his tax program. How the President will fare in the next two years, how much of his program he will achieve and at what cost, how he will lead his troops in the legislative battles, will occupy a large share of the future news reports from Washington. As the curtain rises on the 88th Congress, a new study of Presidential leadership relating the Presidency to Congress and to the party system comes to hand. It is "The Deadlock of Democracy: Four-Party Politics in America" by James MacGregor Burns.*

Professor Burns is the articulate chairman of the Department of Political Science at Williams College. He is the author of books on government and politics including biographies of Franklin D. Roosevelt (1956) and John F. Kennedy (1960), and a he is a successful practising politician and scholar. He worked actively in government and politics and in 1958 ran unsuccessfully for Congress on the Democratic ticket in the First Massachusetts District, an overwhelming Republican stronghold.

In his new book, Professor Burns is concerned with governmental deadlock, as Congress kills or stalls not only much of the President's program, but much of the opposition program as well. He decries the delay and immobilism inherent in our politics and finds it is the result not of something new, unexpected or extraordinary, but rather the product of a political system based on principles of James Madison, embraced 175 years ago.

As a result of the Madisonian idea, Professor Burns contends, the nation faces a four-party system "that compels government by consensus and coalition rather than a two-party system that allows the winning party to govern and the losers to oppose." The system, Professor Burns says, is rooted in our constitutional arrangements, electoral behavior, party institutions and machinery of government.

The four national parties are the presidential Democrats, the presidential Republicans, the congressional Democrats and the congressional Republicans. The Democratic parties are the oldest—the congressional Democrats began as the Madison party and the presidential party was founded and built by Jefferson. The symbolic founder of the presidential Republicans was Abraham Lincoln; the

congressional Republican party had its origins in the opposition to Pierce and Buchanan during the 1850's and with the congressional Republicans who dominated Reconstruction.

Today, says Professor Burns, the four parties are as intact as ever; the Roosevelt-Truman-Stevenson-Kennedy presidential Democrats; the Willkie-Dewey-Eisenhower-Rockefeller presidential Republicans: the John Garner-Howard Smith-Harry Byrd-John McClellan congressional Democrats; and the Allen Treadway-Robert Taft-Charles Halleck congressional Republicans.

Professor Burns points out that the results of this attachment to the Madisonian system of checks and balances, and the neglect "except furtively and sporadically" of the Jeffersonian strategy of strong leadership, majority rule, party responsibility and competitive elections, are:

¶Delays in government action.

¶Coalition government unable to generate strong political power.

¶A loss of control of our politics.

¶A lack of popular control of the policy-making process.

¶A lack of unity and teamwork in government.

¶An oscillation between deadlock and a rush of action.

¶An inability to give new leaders the means to make their leadership effective.

¶An inability to define our national purpose and mobilize our strength to meet problems and exploit our possibilities.

Professor Burns' book is an interesting and provocative record of the history of the Madisonian and Jeffersonian systems in American politics. He embraces the unorthodox and presents his impressive research in a crisp, vigorous and readable prose. Professor Burns looks at how the Presidents used their powers, how the parties were splintered; he examines the structure of coalition politics and probes such elements of change as the suburban explosion and the changes in Southern politics.

Professor Burns says we need a new kind of bipartisanship under which the two presidential parties would join forces in Congress and elsewhere long enough to workout rules for a fair, orderly and competitive battle between the two national parties. Each presidential party, he says, must convert its congressional party into a party wing "exerting a proper, but not controlling or crippling hold on party policy."

To bring about party consolidation, Professor Burns proposes that the national government control national elections; that the national parties build grass-roots memberships; that the presidential and congressional parties be merged organizationally; that new party leadership be developed in Congress; that the parties and their candidates be financed on a mass, popular, systematic basis and that the national opposition party should be better organized and given a clearer voice.

Professor Burns would not have the nation turn from the Madisonian model to the Jeffersonian, wholly and solely. He suggests that majority rule as a principle, and the party as a practical system are not enough to make the Jeffersonian system an effective model. The third requirement is leadership.

The author suggests that President Kennedy may be the first President to grasp the possibilities open to a creative party leader. Only with a man and a party who take the lead in modernizing our political system, in establishing a majority party able to govern and a minority party able to oppose, Professor Burns concludes, can we end "the dangerous cycle of drift and deadlock in our national affairs."

*THE DEADLOCK OF DEMOCRACY: FOUR-PARTY POLITICS IN AMERICA. By James MacGregor Burns. 388 pages, Englewood Cliffs, N.J. Prentice-Hall. $5.95

Mr. Seigel is a member of the staff of The New York Times.

January 24, 1963

PRESIDENT'S TRIP AROUSES TEXANS

By JOSEPH A. LOFTUS
Special to The New York Times

WASHINGTON, Nov. 19—Squabbling Texas Democrats are making a political stew out of President Kennedy's "nonpolitical" swing through their state this week.

Liberals are complaining that a $100 dinner is far beyond the reach of thousands who helped elect the President. They also want firm assurance that the dinner revenue will not be used by Gov. John B. Connally to finance opposition to Senator Ralph Yarborough in the primary next spring.

"Every faction in Texas will be taken care of," commented Pierre Salinger, the White House Press Secretary, today.

Mr. Salinger labeled the Texas trip, which starts Thursday, as "nonpolitical" except for one loop into Austin for the fund-raising dinner Friday night.

Committee to Pay

Any jet travel expense specially required by the Austin visit will be paid for by the Democratic National Committee.

Mrs. Kennedy, who has never seen Texas, will accompany her husband. They will spend Friday night at the ranch of Vice President Johnson, a 70-mile helicopter ride from Austin.

The President's appearances include a testimonial dinner for Representative Albert Thomas, Houston Democrat. Mr. Salinger said it would be a bipartisan event.

Two Democratic party officials from the San Antonio area expressed their discontent to Representative Henry B. Gonzalez. They were Maury Maverick and Mrs. Sarah McClure.

Mr. Maverick said he was taking up a collection for his $100 ticket. His wife "will have to eat chili con carne with some poor liberal friends in Austin" while he is attending the dinner, he said.

Mrs. McClure wrote to John M. Bailey, the Democratic National Chairman, saying she could not afford the $100 and that many Democrats in her district could not afford a $5 dinner.

"When brazen public recognition goes to the moneyed minority who, most suspect, vote Republican anyway, with no offsetting recognition given to the faithful, hard-working majority, it rankles in the souls

of the little man, causing bitter resentment," she wrote.

Both are members of the State Democratic Executive Committee.

Representative Gonzalez, writing to Governor Connally, noted that the Governor had said that the dinner revenue would be used to "help elect Democrats and defeat Republicans in the 1964 general election." Mr. Gonzalez said that was clear enough to him but that some of his constituents were suspicious and further comment would be appreciated.

President Kennedy may attempt to patch up the feud of Texas Democrats because of his obvious interest in the state's 25 electoral votes next year. Mr. Johnson has an identical interest as a member of the ticket, but he is one of the principals in the feud.

Senator Yarborough and his liberal backers are convinced that the Vice President's mission is to discredit him as a Kennedy Democrat, because of the Vice President's role in helping to elect Governor Connally last year over the liberal Don Yarborough. Governor Connally's record since election has been very conservative. Although he has given several board and commission positions to Negroes, he has openly op-

posed the President's civil rights program.

Even a patchwork truce would require at a minimum an assurance by Governor Connally that he will not support another Democrat in opposition to Senator Yarborough next spring, and by the same token, that Senator Yarborough and the liberals will not support a candidate against Governor Connally's second-term candidacy. Vice President Johnson would have to be a party to any such truce to make it acceptable to the liberals.

The obvious candidate against Governor Connally is Don Yarborough, who ran a close race for the post last year. Liberals expect him to run again, and the question is who can say he will not try once more.

The President has invited Senator Yarborough and a number of the Texas Democrats in the House to join him in the trip to Texas. Governor Connally, however, has not invited the Senator to the reception for the President at the Executive Mansion on the ground that the party is limited to members of the Texas Legislature.

It is a matter of protocol that the President take members of his party from Congress with him when he goes into their state.

November 20, 1963

CHAPTER . 3

Ideological Politics
1964-1974

Senator Abraham Ribicoff, while nominating Senator George McGovern for president at the 1968 Democratic Convention, has just attacked Chicago for being a police state. That city's Mayor Daley (just to the right of center, with his hand to his mouth) is calling Ribicoff "a fink," among other things.

Courtesy Compix

PARTIES' OUTLOOK FOR '64 CONFUSED

Republican Prospects Rise —Johnson Faces Possible Fight Against Liberals

By WARREN WEAVER Jr.
Special to The New York Times

WASHINGTON, Nov. 22 — President Kennedy's assassination threw the American political scene into turmoil today.

It removed at a single blow the man who would have been nominated for a second term in the White House by acclamation nine months from now.

It elevated into the Presidency and the leadership of the Democratic party an older, more conservative man still emerging from his Southern heritage.

It increased immeasurably for the leaders of the Republican party prospects of electing a President next November.

The shock of the President's death stilled the official voices of politics in the capital. But so profound was the potential effect on the Government and leadership that private consideration could not be silenced.

Before, there had been facts and strong probabilities on the national political scene: The President would run again. He would be stronger in some states, weaker in the South. He would run with Lyndon B. Johnson again. He would debate his opponent. He would be favored to win.

Now, following the tragedy in Texas, there seemed to be only questions, thrust so suddenly on the minds of political leaders of both parties that there were few answers. These were some of the questions:

Questions Raised

¶Will President Johnson be able to insure his own nomination next August, on the basis of an inherited nine months in the White House?

¶Will liberal elements in the Democratic party make any attempt to dislodge Mr. Johnson in favor of a candidate more to their liking?

¶Could Mr. Johnson, running as the first Southern Presidential candidate of this century, win support in the South despite his espousal of the civil rights cause?

¶What influence will the political motivation of the assassin, if any, have on the great wave of public revulsion against the act? Will the people turn against left-wing or right-wing extremists — or both?

¶How will the immediate prospect of fierce two-party competition in next year's Presidential election influence Republican leaders in their choice of a candidate?

Despite the many questions raised, one political consequence seemed clear in the hushed, almost ashamed, assessments that observers undertook this evening: The death of the President gave new life to Republican hopes.

Whatever political liabilities might have encumbered him, John F. Kennedy was an incumbent President, one whose person and personality had been impressed on the American electorate.

Republican leaders knew this. While they loudly scored what they saw as his weaknesses, they saw Mr. Kennedy as a figure to be reckoned with politically. Their candidate would almost surely be the underdog.

Now, in the flash of a gunshot, all that is changed. The Republican Presidential candidate, whoever he may be, will be running against a man with nine months in the White House—or none at all—instead of nearly four years of unremitting public exposure.

When the first shock of the tragedy has subsided and politicians talk again, they are sure to feel that the Republicans face a new, more favorable course next year. And this is likely to affect their choice of a candidate considerably.

Republican leaders have been saying for months that one of the powerful factors favoring the nomination of Senator Barry Goldwater of Arizona was the prevailing belief that President Kennedy would win anyway. Next year, they said, could be the one to gamble with a controversial candidate.

But now, they may reason, it may not be a time for Republican gambling. It may instead be a time to put a Republican candidate of the broadest possible appeal into the lists to challenge President Johnson or another Democratic nominee.

This conviction, if it became strong enough, could move Republican leaders strongly toward a candidate like Richard M. Nixon, or even Thomas E. Dewey.

Rockefeller's Chances

It might assist Nelson A. Rockefeller by removing his chief current rival, Senator Goldwater, from the scene, but it might also find the New York Governor too narrow in appeal for a real Presidential candidate.

The prospect of President Johnson's candidacy next year appeared also to have raised serious, if not fatal, questions about the Southern strategy on which Senator Goldwater's supporters have been relying heavily.

While Mr. Goldwater might have carried the states of the Old Confederacy against President Kennedy, there is not the same assurance that he could do so against Mr. Johnson, even with the President firmly dedicated to civil rights. Goldwater supporters may have to tally their possible electoral votes again.

Among the Democrats, the passing of the President seems sure to focus increased political attention on his brother, Attorney General Robert F. Kennedy, and the role he may play in the new administration.

If the great national wave of sadness and sympathy is still perceptible a year from now, it is the Attorney General rather than the President to whom it is more likely to attach.

Widespread Effect

Like all major political catastrophes at the highest level, the passing of President Kennedy will be measurable down through the ranks of the Democratic party among many if not all of those whose names would have shared the ballot with him next November.

Where Mr. Kennedy appeared strong, in the urban industrial states of the nation, Democratic candidates for the Senate and House must reassess their prospects. Now they must try to measure what it will mean to them to run with President Johnson, or another Democrat as yet unknown.

In these same states, Republican Congressional nominations may become more attractive to candidates who have been avoiding such a challenge in a Presidential year.

In politics, the day's appalling events demonstrated, there is only change.

November 23, 1963

ROCKEFELLER SAYS RIGHTISTS IMPERIL G.O.P. AND NATION

Attack Aimed at Goldwater Supporters —'Tactics of Totalitarianism' Scored

By PETER KIHSS

Governor Rockefeller declared war on "the radical right" wing of the Republican party yesterday with a blistering statement clearly aimed at the most vocal supporters of Senator Barry Goldwater for President.

The New York Governor asserted he was "deeply disturbed" by the "ruthless, rough-shod intimidation" and "tactics of totalitarianism" at the biennial convention of the Young Republican National Federation June 26 and 27 in San Francisco. Senator Goldwater was the convention's hero and its closing speaker.

The Governor appeared to be almost openly offering himself as an alternative for the Presidential nomination. His statement was also aimed at leaders of the John Birch Society and "others of the radical right lunatic fringe" as every bit as dangerous to America as "the radical left."

Promises Opposition

The Republican party, Governor Rockefeller asserted, would "destroy itself" if it adopted what he said was being "seriously proposed" as a 1964 campaign strategy. This, he said, would "write off" Negroes and other minority groups, the great industrial states of the North and the big cities, and appeal primarily to the South and West with "the outlawed and immoral base of segregation" and a "cloak of so-called 'states rights.'"

"The time for temporizing is over," Governor Rockefeller went on. "I for one will do everything in my power, working with others to counter the influence of these forces and to defeat their purposes."

Mr. Rockefeller refrained from naming directly Senator Goldwater, who was described in news stories as having "nearly lifted the roof" at the San Francisco convention with his attacks on "the phoneyness that has been going on under the false guise of liberalism for the last 30 years."

Potential Harm Seen

But yesterday, Fred A. Young, whom the Governor put across as state Republican chairman this spring, specifically contended that a conservative Presidential race by Senator Goldwater would hurt liberal Republicans in New York State. "I think that Goldwater would be harmful in certain areas, especially the cities, and he could affect many of the legislators running," Mr. Young said.

Mr. Young reaffirmed his "personal opinion" that Governor Rockefeller would be a candidate for the Presidential nomination. He spoke in a "Let's Find Out" interview over radio station WCBS.

A week ago, Senator Jacob K. Javits, a New York Republican, said that a Goldwater candidacy might "prove costly" to Republican Senate candidates in New York and Pennsylvania.

Statement Strongest to Date

Governor Rockefeller's 2,000-word statement, issued through his Albany office, went far beyond any previous declarations he has made on Republican affairs, even when he dropped out of the race for the 1960 Presidential nomination.

At that time, he issued a surprise statement of withdrawal on Dec. 26, 1959, announcing that "the great majority of those who will control the Republican convention stand opposed to any contest for the nomination."

He fired another shot June 8, 1960, when he demanded that Richard M. Nixon make his position clear on urgent national issues before the convention. But he refrained then from epithets such as yesterday's.

Yesterday's statement said that the future of the nation "lies in the fiscally responsible, humanely principled mainstream of American thought and leadership that the party of Abraham Lincoln, of Theodore Roosevelt, of Robert Taft has always represented and will continue to represent."

This bow to supporters of the late Senator Taft omitted any reference to Gen. Dwight D. Eisenhower, who defeated the Ohioan for the 1952 Republican nomination, or to Mr. Nixon. But associates of the Governor insisted there was no significance to the omission.

Governor Rockefeller lashed at the Democratic Administration of President Kennedy. He said it was "faltering" in allowing a Communist military base to be established in Cuba and "a general deterioration in our national security."

He contended it had been "floundering in its fiscal management" and unable to solve problems of "our stagnant economy and our millions of unemployed." He accusingly said its "inaction has plunged our country into the most soul-searing racial strife of our history."

Tenets Held in Danger

The Governor declared that there should be six "articles of faith" for the Republican party. These were freedom at home and abroad, equality of opportunity for all Americans, faith in the federal system of government, the private enterprise system, fiscal integrity and the right to know all facts.

He said that Republicans and Americans had been aware of the threats from international Communism to these principles. But, he continued, many persons had taken too lightly "the growing danger to these very same principles through subversion from the radical right."

He asserted "the vociferous and well-drilled extremist elements boring within the party utterly reject these fundamental principles of our heritage." The San Francisco Young Republican meetings, he said, had been "dominated by extremist groups, carefully organized, well financed and operating through the tactics of ruthless, rough-shod intimidation."

Such people, he declared, have no program except "distrust, disunity and the ultimate destruction of the confidence of the people in themselves." He called them "purveyors of hate and distrust in a time when, as never before, the need of the world is for love and understanding."

The Civil War, Governor Rockefeller asserted, "decided for all time that in the area of human dignity, states' rights must forever yield to the rights of the individual."

For the Republican party, he added, a task force for the national committee, headed by Ray C. Bliss, Ohio state chairman, had reported in 1961 that the party's hope lay in its willingness to deal with problems of urban areas and minority groups.

Statement Criticized

Governor Rockefeller's statement drew a comment from Senator Carl T. Curtis, a Goldwater backer, that "now is no time for either anger or name-calling among Republicans." Senator Curtis, a Nebraska Republican, said in Washington:

"Senator Goldwater is the leading candidate because he squarely challenges the New Frontier ideology and performance. I would say that one thing in his favor is that he's not a sectional candidate."

Mr. Young said in his radio interview yesterday that he believed Governor Rockefeller was conducting polls through an organization of his own on the effect of his divorce and remarriage on his Presidential chances. There had been more reaction to the remarriage than anticipated, Mr. Young said, but he predicted that this would "wear out" within another year.

July 15, 1963

Goldwater Backers Increase in Texas, Along With Republican Strength

By GLADWIN HILL
Special to The New York Times

SAN ANTONIO, Tex., Sept. 16—"Revolution" is the word on countless lips in Texas today.

You hear it from a college professor in Austin, a lawyer in San Antonio, a labor leader in the Rio Grande Valley.

What they are talking about is a bloodless, but acrimonious, upheaval in politics—with important implications for the 1964 Presidential campaign, and for race relations over a wide area.

The "revolution" has two aspects.

One is the emphatic burgeoning of Texas—where for generations practically everybody has been some kind of Democrat—into a two-party state.

The other aspect is a clearly defined threat by long eclipsed "minority" groups—liberals, labor, Negroes and Mexican-Americans—to play a decisive, if not dominant, role in a radically revamped Texas Democratic party.

What is at stake in this ferment can be seen by looking back at the 1960 Presidential election.

John F. Kennedy eked out a victory over Richard M. Nixon in 1960 in Texas by a scant 40,000 votes out of 2,000,000. And Texas's 24 electoral votes were an important block in the Kennedy victory.

The prospect for 1964 is just as tight. Mr. Kennedy has dropped in voter popularity polls from 65 to 46 per cent in less than a year. Senator Barry Goldwater's score has jumped from 22 to 39 per cent, and Texas is abuzz with Goldwater enthusiasm.

Up to a few years ago, Texas Republicans didn't even bother to have conventions.

Dissident Democrats swung Texas to President Eisenhower in 1952 and 1956, and in 1961 brought about the election of John G. Tower, Texas's first Republican Senator since Reconstruction days.

But, since the 1960 election, there has been a growing exodus of conservatives from the Democratic party to the organized Republican standard.

No precise membership figures can be cited, because Texas's election laws virtually allow a person to vote as a Democrat one day and a Republican the next. But political analysts display persuasive statistical breakdowns of voting in successive Democratic primaries, runoff primaries and general elections that indicate steady erosion of conservative loyalty to the Democratic cause.

Last weekend, the state Republican executive committee, planning next September's party convention, called for 2,000 hotel rooms and a hall seating 4,000. It also projected a drive for 600,000 new members.

This is, paradoxically, a joyous trend to many remaining Democrats. They are the liberal intellectuals and labor and minority groups that have been chronically suppressed in party affairs by conservatives. They see the defecting conservatives leaving a vacuum and an opportunity to take over the party.

This opportunity was suggested, again, in the 1960 election results. Texas, with a population matching Ohio's, had only half as big a total vote—about 2,000,000 as against 4,000,000

The "missing" votes, it is generally conceded, were those of the state's large Mexican-American and Negro populations, about 1,000,000 each.

These groups, in recent years, have not been barred from voting. Rather, it has been a matter of illiteracy, political immaturity and the poll tax ($1.50 or $1.75).

A big Democratic drive was put on in 1960 to galvanize this moribund electorate. It took the form notably of the "viva Kennedy" movement, which without question saved the day for Mr. Kennedy in Texas. His 40,000 margin can be traced many times over to unprecedented turnouts in Mexican-American districts.

The "viva Kennedy" was perpetuated after the election in a loose federation extending from Texas to California, called MAPA—the Mexican-American Political Association.

A revision of it, principally in Texas, is called PASO — the Political Organization of Spanish-Speaking People.

PASO, along with elements of organized labor, Negroes and "independent liberals," makes up a new liberal-Democrat coalition.

Its immediate objective, shared by other political groups on a non-partisan basis, is repeal of Texas's poll tax in an election Nov. 9.

This is considered by many as the key that will open the door to consummation of the "revolution" — through enlarging the electorate and dividing it into an orthodox liberal-conservative alignment, in place of the state's traditional factional strife under the Democratic banner.

September 17, 1963

249

Eisenhower Urges Choice Of Forward-Looking Man

Refuses to 'Dictate' Own Preference—Hopes for Upholder of Tradition

By DWIGHT D. EISENHOWER

Printed by permission of
The New York Herald Tribune.

Many concerned people have urged me to indicate my preference among the possible Republican candidates or to try to dictate the Republican party's choice of a Presidential nominee this July.

I do not intend to attempt this. It is not my proper role. I do fervently hope, however, that the person selected to lead our party in the coming campaign will be a man who will uphold, earnestly, with dedication and conviction, the principles and traditions of our party.

There is no mystery about Republican principles. They have been spelled out at length in our national platforms—most recently that of 1956, on which I was proud to run for re-election, and that of 1960, for which I was proud to campaign.

These platforms represented the responsible, forward-looking Republicanism I tried to espouse as President, the kind that I am convinced is supported by the overwhelming majority of the Republican party, the kind I deeply believe the party must continue to offer the American people.

We Republicans believe in limited government, but also in effective and humane government.

We believe in keeping government as close to the people as possible—in letting each citizen do for himself what he can do for himself, then making any call for government assistance first on the local government, then on the state government, and only in the final resort on the Federal Government.

But we do not shrink from a recognition that there are national problems that require national solutions. When they arise, we act.

During the Republican Administration of 1953-61 we established the Department of Health, Education and Welfare, we extended Social Security coverage and increased its benefits, we raised the minimum wage and brought more workers under its coverage than ever before. We increased aid for hospital construction, we increased aid for medical research, we introduced a new program of medical aid for the aged. We inaugurated urban renewal, passed the first depressed areas legislation, launched a new program to help low-income farmers and began the most gigantic highway building program in the history of the United States.

Positive Nature Stressed

I cite these examples not to applaud a past record but to illustrate the positive nature of true Republicanism — spotting new needs, sizing them up, and acting decisively when their national nature and scope require it.

As a party that looks to the future, not just to the present, we Republicans believe in paying now for what we need now, not saddling those yet to come with the burden of our debts. But we believe in meeting our needs.

Right now the nation's most critical domestic challenge involves man's relation to his government and also to his neighbor—the issue of civil rights.

The Republican party was born of a crusading concern for human dignity; it retains that concern today.

There is reason for Republican pride that in the eight years of its last Administration the nation made more progress in civil rights than in the preceding 80. We did this through vigorous executive action, through steadfast enforcement of court decisions and through passage of the Civil Rights Acts of 1957 and 1960—the first such acts passed since Reconstruction.

Profound Moral Obligation

Equal opportunity and mutual respect are matters not only of law but also of the human heart and spirit, and the latter are not always amenable to law. But the nation has a profound moral obligation to each of its citizens, requiring that we not only improve our behavior but also strengthen our laws in a determined effort to see that each American enjoys the full benefits of citizenship—benefits which no agency of government, national, state or local, has the right to abridge.

As the party of Lincoln, we Republicans have a particular obligation to be vigorous in the furtherance of civil rights. In this critical area, I have been especially proud of the dramatic leadership given by Republicans in Congress these last two years. With equal emphasis, I can say the same of our Republican Governors.

In the foreign field, the overriding concern of the Republican party—of either party—must be the maintenance of peace while protecting and extending freedom. This is not easily or simply done in a dangerous, volatile and uncertain world.

It requires military strength second to none, backed by a vigorous and expanding economy. Military adequacy must be our minimum. We must not, however, permit unnecessary and wasteful military expenditures to weaken the aggregate of American strength.

U.N. Support Needed

It requires loyal support for the United Nations in its peace-keeping efforts.

It requires calm, painstaking study of all the infinitely complex situations that confront us —whether in Southeast Asia, in Cuba, or wherever danger threatens or opportunity beckons—followed by firm decision and prompt but carefully conceived action. In today's nuclear-age diplomacy there is no time for indecision, but neither is there room for impulsiveness, not only to treat successfully with today's crises, but to probe into those areas where, step by step, the barriers between East and West can be lowered.

Future Approach Cited

The last Republican Administration acted both firmly and prudently in such danger areas as Berlin, the Formosa Straits, Iran and Lebanon. It acted constructively and imaginatively in such matters as enlarging its network of alliances and making them effective, evolving new concepts of social progress through foreign aid, promoting cultural and technical exchanges, and developing proposals for open skies and the peaceful use of space.

Our party's approach in the future must be no less firm, no less prudent, no less constructive, no less imaginative.

Believing in the Republican party as I so devoutly do, I have for many months urged that Republicans from coast to coast be given a fair chance to work their will, in careful deliberations, at the national convention—and therefore to make that convention truly representative of the party.

I hope they will have that chance. And I earnestly hope the party will select a nominee who skillfully and wholeheartedly would apply to our problems, both domestic and foreign, those principles which I have noted here.

© 1964, by The New York Herald Tribune.

May 25, 1964

GOLDWATER NOW HARD TO BEAT FOR THE REPUBLICAN NOMINATION

By TOM WICKER

Special to The New York Times

WASHINGTON, June 6—Senator Barry M. Goldwater of Arizona is teetering on the brink of the Republican nomination for President, and it looked until today as if the rest of his party was going to let him fall into it.

When Governor William Scranton of Pennsylvania responded to former President Eisenhower's invitation and talked with the general for 85 minutes about the possibility of rescuing Senator Goldwater from his happy predicament, a flicker of hope rose in moderate Republican hearts.

They had General Eisenhower openly on their side at last, and they had his clear indication that Governor Scranton was his choice. That could make all the difference.

Rockefeller Challenge

Until then as has been the case since the Goldwater boom began last year, only Governor Rockefeller of New York seemed openly willing to try to halt Senator Goldwater at the brink. And even the indefatigable Governor Rockefeller confessed this week that all he could do was follow someone else's leadership. But until the Eisenhower and Scranton meeting there had been no one to follow.

Since those months when Senator Goldwater charged into the lead following Governor Rockefeller's remarriage, what has been needed to stop his nomination was a high order of political skill, leadership and courage on the part of the moderate elements of the Republican party. All that ever came forward was Rockefeller's courage and Rockefeller money; and that drab history does not encourage the belief that even General Eisenhower can galvanize the moderates and lead them into effective control of the party and its national convention.

The Eisenhower - Scranton combination, if it results in forceful action, is the last hope —and at best it must be given no more than a chance to succeed.

Crippling Nomination?

How did it all happen? And can Senator Goldwater still be denied a nomination many Republicans and Democrats alike believe will cripple the Grand Old Party and cement Democratic hegemony in American politics for a generation?

Senator Goldwater's nomination now seems likely, if not assured, for two basic reasons. One was the lack of effective opposition. The other was the Senator's own strategy for victory.

These scarcely seem, in retrospect, to have been enough. The Senator is an unabashed outsider, one whose views run counter to the notions that have dominated both major parties in the post-war era. He is, if not an extremist, a radical revisionist; on the political spectrum, he is far out of that great middle area in which American political parties usually have found their success.

In addition, as the campaign has unfolded, he has demonstrated no surging popular support; he lost badly in the New Hampshire and Oregon primaries, won badly in Illinois and Nebraska, and took the crucial California primary this week not with a bang but a squeak.

Goldwater's Votes

Before the California voting, Senator Goldwater had won just over 30 per cent of all the ballots cast in Republican Presidential primaries. He had shown himself a bumbling campaigner, ineffective in crowds, inarticulate and self-contradictory, prone to off-the-cuff remarks that were in error or ill-advised. Delegate commitments to him in the major industrial states were at a minimum, and party leaders — like the Republican voters—obviously were eager for an alternative.

But moderate Republican leadership has not yet produced that alternative, unless the last-minute Scranton move develops. Governor Rockefeller gave it a hard try; but his marriage problems, the enemies he had made in the past and his political weaknesses — foggy speeches, troubles in New York, a too liberal reputation, lack of a widespread following—were too much for him to overcome.

Richard M. Nixon chose to wait for the collapse of the Goldwater movement, hoping to be its second choice. Until today Scranton chose cooly to stay in Harrisburg, waiting for all elements of the party to unite on him. Ambassador Henry Cabot Lodge chose to stay in Saigon. Other possibilities—Gov. George Romney of Michigan for example—made no moves at all, or the wrong ones.

Indecisive Leaders

Non-contending party leaders never made up their minds. General Eisenhower camped out for the winter in Palm Springs, marched up the hills against Senator Goldwater two weeks before the California primary, then marched down again the day before it. Wealthy Republican powerhouses looked longingly at Mr. Scranton but never found the nerve or skill to push him up front. Nervy and skillful political operators never found the wealth or power to keep Mr. Lodge's airy candidacy aloft. The hands of the "old pros" like Thomas E. Dewey, of the Eisenhower "team," of the state leaders like Ray Bliss of Ohio, of the Congressional chieftains, never closed firmly on either a plan or a man with which to confront Senator Goldwater.

The Senator, meanwhile, correctly read the lessons of the early primaries. He could not win by displaying massive popular support, because he had none. Midway of the Oregon primary he began concentrating on his strengths—the minor state and local party officials for whom he had made countless speeches and raised countless dollars, the right-wing faction that adored him, the ancient Republican aversion (widespread in the West and South) to another "me too" candidate put over by "the Eastern bankers."

Goldwater's Strategy

In state after state, even while losing or running poorly in primaries elsewhere, Senator Goldwater kept on picking up delegates in state conventions or through power tactics. Even in California, where he staked his chances, he concentrated on getting out his own vote, not winning Governor Rockefeller's away from him; and he effectively capitalized on the underdog role cut out for him by the Governor's victory in Oregon and the first Eisenhower statement. To hear him tell it, the East and the bosses were ganging up on him just as they had done on Senator Robert Taft of Ohio a decade before.

The result was a famous victory—no matter how thin. The

Yoes in The San Diego Union

"Used polls for sale—cheap."

86 delegates won in California gave tremendous impetus to the Goldwater total; his triumph against what the pollsters had said were big odds restored enthusiasm among his supporters and dampened the will of opponents to fight him openly. It took his only determined opponent, Governor Rockefeller, all but out of the game; it prevented Mr. Nixon—considered by some Goldwater men as the biggest threat to them—from coming foward openly as the inheritor of a bogged-down Goldwater movement.

Eisenhower Appeal

Governor Scranton wasted but a day in disclaiming any intention of taking to the field; even the Eisenhower appeal today may not persuade him to do so. Mr. Nixon said something might still be done but someone else would have to do it. And if anyone was catching a plane for Saigon to bring Ambassador Lodge home to the battles, the news was not getting into the headlines.

The obvious prediction was that no one would do anything effective to stop Goldwater— because if in the past year no one had shown the will or ability to do so, no one was likely to develop either in the final five weeks of the campaign. The general sinking feeling among Republicans that, in any case, their candidate would not be able to defeat President Johnson, made it even less likely

that anyone would step in front of the Goldwater bandwagon.

Meanwhile, on the momentum of California, Senator Goldwater seemed certain to go on adding delegates from the non-primary states (notably Texas's 56), probably up to a total of 600 or more on the first ballot. It takes only 655 for nomination.

Remaining Hope

The last remaining hope of the moderates probably was the uncertain trumpet of Dwight D. Eisenhower. If the General, after his meeting with Mr. Scranton, was to take a strong and unwavering stand for the young Pennsylvania Governor, rallying the uncommitted delegations and the favorite sons to the cause and, if Mr. Scranton went to work for the nomination, it is at least mathematically possible that the line against Senator Goldwater might be held. The huge Ohio delegation and its tough leader, Ray Bliss, would be crucial to such an effort; Governor Rockefeller, New Jersey, Pennsylvania, Michigan, New England, could chip in hundreds of delegates.

But first the trumpet has to sound. And until today everybody seemed to be listening instead of blowing.

June 7, 1964

251

Goldwater Likens Nixon to Stassen

By CABELL PHILLIPS
Special to The New York Times

WASHINGTON, June 10 — Senator Barry Goldwater gave the back of his political hand today to Richard M. Nixon, saying "he's sounding more like Harold Stassen every day."

The conservative Arizona Senator, who appears to have the Republican Presidential nomination all but sewed up, also had harsh words for the Republican Governors who, along with Mr. Nixon, mounted an abortive "stop-Goldwater" movement in Cleveland over the weekend.

"It's pretty hard to understand those fellows," he said at an impromptu news conference at the Capitol today. "A lot of them sound as if they were more intent on wrecking the Republican party than in winning an election. But they seem to have run out of 'stop-Goldwater' votes after all."

Mr. Goldwater had just returned from the Senate floor, where he cast one of six Republican votes against imposing closure to shut off the 75-day civil rights debate.

He said he did not expect this vote to hurt him politically. Many observers disagreed, however.

The Senator said he "hoped" he would be able to vote for the civil rights bill itself. He explained that his hope depended upon the present bill's being modified to avoid certain of his objections.

Mr. Goldwater's thrust at Mr. Nixon today was the sharpest he has uttered since the onset— and the collapse— of efforts by party moderates to find an opponent to challenge his claim to a first-ballot convention victory.

The latest episode in this sequence of developments, most of which have arisen at the annual Governors conference in Cleveland, occurred yesterday.

Gov. George Romney of Michigan, a sometime dark-horse possibility for the nomination himself, said he had been urged by Mr. Nixon, a visitor at the conference, to try to upset the Goldwater bandwagon.

After what appeared to have been several hours of thought, however, Mr. Romney declined and suggested that Mr. Nixon take on the job himself.

Did Not Pledge Support

Mr. Nixon said later he had not promised to support Mr. Romney as a "third force" candidate, but did not specify just what he had told the Governor. In any event, he added, he had no intention of taking on the assignment himself.

In the process, however, both men put into quite explicit language their fears of what a Goldwater candidacy might do to the Republican party.

Mr. Nixon said, for example: "Looking to the future of the party, it would be a tragedy if Senator Goldwater's views, as previously stated, were not challenged and repudiated."

It was to this and similar comments in Cleveland that Mr. Goldwater was responding in his remarks today.

He clearly had been stung by the fact that Mr. Nixon, the party's last Presidential candidate and its titular leader, had dropped the mask of neutrality.

Asked if he thought there still was a chance that Mr. Nixon might be persuaded to seek the nomination for himself, Mr. Goldwater said:

"I don't see him as an opponent. I think he has talked his way out of the running. He is sounding more like Harold Stassen every day."

A Barbed Reference

The reference to Mr. Stassen, who has aspired to the Republican nomination in every election since 1948, was especially barbed.

The former Minnesota Governor in notable among party professionals for his political naiveté, while Mr. Nixon's credentials as a "pro" are rated among the best.

Mr. Goldwater, discussing his vote against closure, said that he had always been opposed to a Senate "gag" rule, and that this position was "a matter of principle" from which he would not deviate.

He said that the closure question bore no relation to the merits of the civil rights bill, and that "I hope I'll be able to vote for it."

The Senator said he opposed certain features of the bill as it passed the House, but some of amendments proposed by the Republican minority leader, Everett McKinley Dirksen, would make it acceptable to him.

June 11, 1964

EISENHOWER SHIFT

He Indicates Refusal to Back Goldwater if Nominated

By FELIX BELAIR Jr.
Special to The New York Times

GETTYSBURG, Pa., June 11 — Former President Dwight D. Eisenhower hinted strongly in an interview here today that he would find it difficult to give his active support to Senator Barry Goldwater of Arizona if he won the Republican Presidential nomination.

His statement was viewed as a definite qualification of his early statements that he would actively support and campaign for any candidate named by the Republican National Convention.

Talking informally, General Eisenhower said it was incomprehensible to him how any candidate for his party's nomination for the Presidency could contend that civil rights was an area in which the Federal Government had no responsibility.

The former President said he did not see how he could support any man who maintained that the civil rights of citizens were entirely within the jurisdiction of the separate states when, actually, they were guaranteed in these rights by the Constitution.

Has Shifted Stand

Although Senator Goldwater has shifted his civil rights stand on several occasions, he has been consistent in upholding states' rights. He said in a statement last year, for example:

"Despite the recent holding of the Supreme Court, I am firmly convinced not only that integrated schools are not required but that the Constitution does not permit any interference whatsoever by the Federal Government in the field of education."

General Eisenhower seemed much more concerned on this point than on what he considered Mr. Goldwater's demand for repeal of the Federal income tax or his primary campaign references to him as a President who conducted "a dime-store New Deal." He remarked in passing that, as far as he was aware, the Arizona Senator had never retracted this remark.

At the same time General Eisenhower repeated his traditional position that he could and would support in the forthcoming Presidential campaign any Republican candidate who believed in the basic principles he followed during his eight years in the White House.

Specifically, he said that any candidate having his active support would have to subscribe to the 1960 Republican platform.

But the former President was emphatic in saying that he would not be a party to a movement to "stop Goldwater, or anybody else."

He also said that, the party platform aside, there was a deep conviction in the minds of many citizens that there was very little point in holding a national convention if the party candidate had been all but officially chosen before the conclave began.

General Eisenhower's apparent antipathy toward Mr. Goldwater and his hope for an "open convention" in San Francisco next month was only one of the points of political delicacy he touched on in one of his most outspoken interviews since he left the White House.

He said that as an advocate of an open convention in which opposing candidates could expose themselves and be judged on their merits there was no question but that he had suffered a real defeat so far.

But he insisted that "we're not licked yet—not by a long shot—and Bill Scranton [Gov. William W. Scranton of Pennsylvania] knows this better than most."

General Eisenhower was referring here to weekend reports that on Saturday he urged Governor Scranton actively to seek the Republican nomination and that on Sunday he had withdrawn his support.

As he explained it, he had communicated with Governor Scranton last Friday evening requesting that they meet and discuss the nomination situation.

The general said today that his basic purpose was to urge the Governor to be "less vague" on his earlier statement that he would respond only to an "honest draft."

Asks Draft Definition

The former President said he had urged the Governor, if he insisted on adhering to his original statement, at least to define what he meant by an "honest draft."

General Eisenhower went on to say that it was unwise of the Governor to insist that he be drafted by acclamation of the entire Republican convention.

As the former President recalled the interview, he had urged Governor Scranton to announce his availability if, in the opinion of the party leaders, he was the best man for the job.

General Eisenhower said that Governor Scranton had apparently taken his suggestion under consideration.

Then he added that it was certainly not his intention to imply at any point any personal preference for Governor Scranton over any other candidate. He said he had reason to believe that he was not misunderstood in this by the Pennsylvania Governor.

It was because of his astonishment on reading in the papers last Sunday morning that his conference with the Governor had been generally interpreted as supporting him over all other Republican candidates that he called the Governor on the telephone, the general said.

He went on to say that Mr. Scranton verified on the phone from Cleveland that there was no misunderstanding between the general and himself.

The former President referred in passing to the fact that reports also in last Sunday's papers that he had telephoned former Treasury Secretary George M. Humphrey about his conversation with Governor Scranton actually had nothing to do with the matter of Presidential nominations.

As General Eisenhower recalled that telephone call it was only to do with how he was to go from Akron to Cleveland, where Mr. Humphrey was to be his host for the weekend.

Of his day with Mr. Humphrey, who has been an all-out backer of Senator Goldwater, General Eisenhower said that at no time did Mr. Humphrey try to change his mind. He re-

called that the former Secretary had argued at one point that "you must not let these fellows make the party wounds any deeper."

He also recalled having said to his host that he had not given up his fight for an open convention—to which Mr. Humphrey inquired whether General Eisenhower's statement of May 24 to The New York Herald Tribune was intended as a slap at Senator Goldwater.

Notes Goldwater View

The former President recalled at this point that he had replied to Mr. Humphrey that if the shoe seemed to fit that was Mr. Goldwater's fault.

Reminded of reports that his one serious reservation regarding Senator Goldwater was that "he might take us into a war," General Eisenhower said that was not a precise statement of his views. What concerns him more, he indicated, is that a lot of people, including potential voters for the Republican ticket, might attribute such an

inclination to the Senator.

But General Eisenhower went on to say that he did have real reservations about the manner in which the Senator might conduct United States foreign affairs if elected to the Presidency.

He recalled that the leading Republican candidate had at one point suggested that the United States withdraw from the United Nations, and urged sending the United States Marines to Cuba to "turn on the water again."

Throughout the interview, the general seemed to be complaining less about Senator Goldwater than about the fact that he himself had failed to persuade other prominent Republicans to announce their open candidacy. He confirmed having conferred, beginning last November, with Ambassador Henry Cabot Lodge and since then with Governor Rockefeller, Gov. George Romney of Michigan, Senator Goldwater and, as he put it, even with Harold Stassen.

General Eisenhower said that, of course, he had a personal preference for a candidate but that nobody knew the identity of that person—not even the members of his immediate family. His son, John S. D. Eisenhower, who was present at the interview, nodded his agreement.

At one point General Eisenhower spoke of "the little guy" who wanted to feel that he was being represented at the Republican convention in July. He made the point that, as he saw it, most convention delegates were not selected on an elective basis but were really appointed by the leaders of their state delegations.

He said he thought "the little guy" would be satisfied with nothing less than a wide-open convention at which the delegates could expose themselves to each other and debate the merits of the platform and the issues.

June 12, 1964

G.O.P. GROUP FEARS GOLDWATER SLATE

Moderates Warn of Party's 'Wholesale Slaughter'

By EARL MAZO
Special to The New York Times

WASHINGTON, June 14 — A confidential eight-page memorandum being circulated to leading Republican moderates and liberals asserts that if Senator Barry Goldwater is nominated for President he probably would lose every state except Arizona and "would bring on wholesale slaughter of the Republican party."

The memorandum, prepared by the Ripon Society, a group of Republicans who teach political science and are graduate students at Massachusetts Institute of Technology, Harvard

and Tufts University, contends a moderate still can win the nomination. It also urged that in a four-week campaign to defeat the Arizona Senator "Goldwater's weaknesses should be exploited mercilessly."

The Ripon Society got its name from the Wisconsin town where the Republican party was founded.

The Ripon group, formed in January with the encouragement of several important Republican party figures, is modeled after the celebrated Bow group at Oxford-and-Cambridge, an organization of conservative oriented intellectuals, which reputedly has been influential in Britain's Conservative party.

According to the Ripon memorandum, "a carefully detailed study" indicated that with Senator Goldwater heading the Republican ticket in November, the party would lose five Senate seats, five governorships, 47 seats in the House of Representatives and an unspecified number of Republican-controlled state legislatures.

Contest Mandatory

The Senate seats the Ripon group said would be lost were those of Kenneth B. Keating of New York, Hugh Scott of Pennsylvania, Hiram L. Fong of Hawaii, J. Glenn Beall of Maryland and Edwin L. Mechem of New Mexico. The governorships, which the document said would be lost, were those of George Romney of Michigan, Archie M. Gubbrud of South Dakota, George L. Clyde of Utah, Tim Babcock of Montana and John H. Chafee of Rhode Island.

The memorandum said:

"We believe that it is possible to stop Goldwater, but we believe that, even if it were not possible to stop him, his nomination should be contested.

"Even if it is unsuccessful, a convention fight against Goldwater's nomination would give the present Republican office holders who seek re-election something to participate in which might help in their own campaigns."

The memorandum urged moderate leaders to mobilize behind a single candidate. It warned that "the diffusion of popular impact among the variety of opposition candidates defeats the whole idea of mobilizing public opinion."

Among suggestions by the Ripon group were these:

¶"The Goldwater 'Don't Wreck The Party' line must be refuted. This is simply a tactic to consolidate the Goldwater lead."

¶"Goldwater's weaknesses should be exploited mercilessly. He has an impossible task of keeping his conscience while me-tooing a moderate Republican platform."

The memorandum was signed by John S. Saloma, an assistant professor of political science at M.I.T., president of the Ripon group, and Emil Frankel of Harvard, vice president of the group.

June 15, 1964

A Fortnight of Decision: G.O.P. Faces Hard Choice

WASHINGTON, June 27 — In these last two weeks before its Presidential nominating convention, the Republican party faces an issue that can be compared only to its past great struggles over slavery, the Reconstruction of the South, isolation and industrial reform.

The issue now is whether it wishes to transfer Presidential

power from its progressive to its conservative wing for the first time in a quarter of a century; whether it wants to follow a more aggressive and nationalistic policy overseas, and whether it chooses to reduce the influence of the Federal Government in dealing with economic and social—particularly racial—problems at home.

Four times in its first hundred years, the Republican party has led the nation through periods of startling progress, only to falter at the end and stain its own remarkable history:

¶It preserved the Union but debased this, its greatest achievement, by following a vicious policy of Reconstruction in the South.

¶It presided at the end of the 19th and the beginning of the 20th century over a long and dramatic period of continental and industrial expansion and then drifted into a policy of un-

controlled exploitation.

¶It rallied from this and led the reforming impulse of the nation under Teddy Roosevelt, only to divide again over its own reforms and fall apart in the campaign of 1912.

¶It produced some of the most perceptive prophets of the new internationalism in Henry L. Stimson, Elihu Root, and Charles Evans Hughes, only to turn to isolation under Harding and Coolidge.

Seek to Bar Turn

It is clear that Governor Scranton of Pennsylvania jumped into the campaign very late, and Ambassador Henry

Struggle for the G.O.P.

Cabot Lodge came flying home from South Vienam later still, because they thought the party was about to nominate Senator Goldwater of Arizona and take another of the historic turns.

Mr. Scranton and Mr. Lodge are each symbols of the rich, Eastern, internationalist, New Dealish, reformist wing of the party. Mr. Lodge acted similarly in 1951-52, when again he thought Senator Robert A. Taft of Ohio was going to get control of the party machinery and turn it toward isolationism.

Accordingly, he flew then to Paris and helped convince General Eisenhower that he must enter the campaign to rescue the party for the progressives.

Similarly, Governor Scranton was an aide to Secretary of State John Foster Dulles when the Republicans extended the principle of collective security to the Middle East and Asia, and he has been just as progressive in domestic as in foreign policy.

Governor Scranton and Mr. Lodge, however, are merely symbols of a deep split that has existed in the Republican party in different forms and under different names since it was founded.

Started as Loose Coalition

As Clinton Rossiter, the political scientist and historian at Cornell has noted, the Republican party began life as a loose coalition of dissenting interests that were united only in trying to oppose the extension of slavery into territories.

The G.O.P. did not start primarily as a conservative business-oriented party. But in the decade of the 1860's the men of business gained the ascendancy and they have been in conflict with the more progressive Republicans ever since under various names: the Stalwarts versus the Half Breeds in the 1880's; the Regulars versus the Progressives in the early 1900's; and the Old Guard versus the Modern Republicans ever since the early days of the New Deal and before.

"Although it can be explained partly in terms of section, class, and economic interest" Prof. Rossiter says, "at bottom the split in Republicanism is one of principle.

"It is, in a word, ideological, and the dividing line runs roughly but visibly between those who, like Governor Dewey and The New York Herald Tribune, are really quite comfortably at home with the new responsibilities created by Roosevelt and Truman, and those who, like Senator Hickenlooper and The Chicago Tribune, are not.

"This split also appears as one between the sophisticated conservatism of corporation executives and the traditional conservatism of small-town leaders."

The economic reforms of Franklin D. Roosevelt's New Deal and the foreign policy reforms of Harry S. Truman's Fair Deal deepened the split between the Republican conservatives and the Republican progressives, and, while it was the Republican conservatives who dominated the party in Congress, it was the Republican progressives who got the party's Presidential nomination, beginning in 1940 with Wendell Willkie, a former Democrat who promised only to be a more prudent and efficient New Dealer than Roosevelt.

Barry Goldwater's answer to the "Me, too" cry of the Republican progressives was definitely "Not me." The fight for the Republican Presidential nomination this year is particularly sharp because Mr. Goldwater not only symbolizes the historical split in the party, but, because he is even more conservative than Mr. Taft, also widens that split.

Interested in Compromise

Most Republican political leaders, concerned to maintain as broad a supporting base as possible, have been more interested in narrowing the split by compromise, but not Goldwater.

General Eisenhower, for example, who represented the progressive wing, reached out to compromise with Mr. Taft on the conservative wing, and Mr. Taft compromised with the liberals on social policy and with Senator Arthur Vandenberg of Michigan on foreign policy.

This personal difference between Mr. Goldwater on the one hand in this election and Mr. Scranton and Mr. Lodge on the other would not justify the conclusion that a great historic issue is at stake in the San Francisco Convention.

If it were merely a struggle for personal power, or even for giving the conservative wing of the party a turn at the Presidential nomination after more than a generation of progressive Republican candidates, there would be much to be said for nominating the Arizona Senator on the first ballot.

The "historic issue," however, is whether one of the two major American political parties is now prepared to hand over the leadership and machinery of the party to a man who is in substantial disagreement with the present way of dealing with the foreign, social and economic problems of the United States—with all that that would mean in terms of domestic political tranquility and allied unity.

This general issue can be reduced to a number of specific questions that will face the Republican delegates in San Francisco in a few days:

¶Is the party that emancipated the Negroes now to be identified with the policy of leaving the Negro's battle for equal rights to the states, as Senator Goldwater proposes?

¶Is it in the interest of the Republican party, which once had the allegiance of most American Negroes, to ally itself with those who oppose the Negro battle for equal civil rights, precisely at the moment when the Negro is going to get the vote, if nothing else?

¶Does the "respectable" Republican party, which has scoffed at the cynical, immoral, spending, conniving, bloc-voting, machine - ridden, Tammany-Plantation Democrats, think Mr. Goldwater's civil-rights policy is either good morals or good politics?

Major Questions Noted

These are probably the most important political questions of the 1964 Republican nominating convention and the answers are by no means clear.

In the first place, the Goldwater policy of leaving the main Negro demands to the states, which obviously seems impractical, immoral and even wicked to many people, at the same time seems right, practical and constitutional to many members of both parties, and Senator Goldwater is therefore admired not only for his policy but for his courage in going against the contemporary trend.

Second, the Arizona Senator has an issue which stirs the emotions of many people in both parties, and this has been the main argument against the Republican progressives, namely, that their only issue was that they wanted to do most of the same things as the Democrats, only later and to a lesser extent.

It is here, however, that the major conflict arises within the Republican party. For many members of the G.O.P. to say nothing of independents and Democrats feel deeply that Goldwater is proposing a policy toward the Negro revolution, the effects of which are profoundly unjust, cynically expedient, and in the end probably politically disastrous.

These anti-Goldwater Republicans agree that he has a "good issue" for this particular campaign, but that it depends for its success on the support of many of the most prejudiced forces in the nation, from the white supremacists to the viciously anti-intellectuals.

Also, these Republicans who oppose Goldwater feel that peace, prosperity, sentiment for the murdered President Kennedy, and willingness to give President Johnson a longer chance will be the decisive elements in the campaign, and that Mr. Goldwater would not only lose the election, but weaken the future prospects of the Republican party in the process.

Opposse Present Policies

In the field of domestic economic policy, Senator Goldwater wants the Federal Government to be more restrained in interfering with private business, and in the field of foreign policy, he wants the Federal Government to be more assertive, more nationalistic, even more aggressive in waging the cold war against the Communists.

His power as President to reverse the present trend toward the welfare state at home, to scrap the economic reforms of the last generation, would obviously be far less than his authority to reverse the trend toward interdependence with the non-Communist allies and co-existence with the Communists.

It is his policy toward the allies and toward the Communists that disturbs the progressive wing of his party as much as, or even more than, his policy toward the Negroes at home.

A reversal or serious modification of the present foreign policy of the United States, upon which rests the confidence and security of the whole free world, would, indeed, be a "historic decision."

The President of the United States has the power as Commander in Chief to act on his own in foreign affairs well beyond his powers in the domestic field. The President alone has the power to order the use of atomic weapons in ways that are vital, not only to the United States, but to many other nations.

He can, for example, send the Marines at the Guantánamo Base into Cuba to turn on the water, or to invade Cuba for that matter; or, without the approval of the Congress, to use atomic weapons against the Communists in Vietnam, or order attacks on Communist North Vietnam, even if this means risking war with Communist China.

Reaction Explained

This is why there has been such a savage reaction within the internationalist wing of the Republican Party and within the allied world to the indications that the Arizona Senator was about to capture the Republican Presidential nomination.

Senator Goldwater has proposed policies in Cuba, which the Latin-American allies oppose; and in Europe, which the European allies oppose, and in Southeast Asia, which Asian allies oppose. But as President he would have authority to pursue these policies, regardless of the views of the allies, or even of the Congress.

In all these attitudes toward the Republican liberals, toward the Democrats, toward the allies and toward the Soviets and their henchmen, Senator Goldwater is no doubt expressing views that coincide with the sentiments and desires of many Americans, Democratic as well as Republican.

The question before the Republican delegates in the next two weeks, however, is whether they want to express their sentiments and desires or whether they want to define policies that will be effective and lasting; whether they want to vote for a policy they can defend over the years or one that has limited emotional appeal and happens to be popular with key voters for the moment.

In sum, Mr. Goldwater is defying the unwritten law of American politics that the parties should be as few and modest as possible; that the two parties should, as Prof. Rossiter says, "overlap substantially in principle, policy, character, appeal, and purpose—or cease to be parties with any hope of winning a national election."

Senator Goldwater defies this widely accepted view. He does not want the Republicans to concentrate on their similarities with the Democrats but on their differences. He does not want the two parties to "overlap substantially in principle, policy, character, appeal, and purpose."

In fact, he thinks the way to win elections is to go to the Right and emphasize the economic, social, and foreign policy differences with the Democrats.

And the main question is whether the Republican party agrees with him.

Mr. Scranton and Mr. Lodge are secondary—indeed they are almost incidental to this primary consideration. The policies of Mr. Goldwater, even when defined in the most moderate terms, amount to a proposal that the Republican party should let him lead it in a counter-revolution against the trend of social, economic and foreign policies of the last generation, and the "historic question" of the next fortnight is whether the G.O.P. wants to embark with him on this adventure.

June 29, 1964

PLATFORM 1964

Platform puzzle—Every group wants to include its pet plank.

Drawing by Roy Doty

Again the Platform Builders Hammer Away

The quadrennial assembly of party planks is more meaningful than some suppose— else the G.O.P. would not be so concerned about banging its thumb *this* time.

By MARVIN R. WEISBORD

TOMORROW night in San Francisco's St. Francis Hotel the Republican party platform, or resolutions, committee begins what could be one of the most agonizing weeks in G.O.P. history. Between now and the opening of the national convention next Monday, the committee is to draft a platform upon which any candidate, be he Barry Goldwater, William Scranton or Mr. As-Yet-Unknown, can be asked to put his full weight. And the draft must be approved or amended on the convention floor *before* nominations begin.

The reason all this is so agonizing is, of course, that the leading contender, Senator Goldwater, is known to disagree on most vital issues with other party leaders. Representative Melvin R. Laird of Wisconsin, the platform committee chairman, says, for example, that the document will urge vigor-

MARVIN R. WEISBORD, a freelance writer on politics, is author of "Campaigning for President: A New Look at the Road to the White House," to be published early this fall.

ous enforcement of the new civil-rights bill. He concedes that this plank "might require candidates to change their views." He mentions no names— but Goldwater voted against the bill.

Despite the evident furor caused by the G.O.P.'s dilemma, many people, as always, are likely to minimize the whole process. Criticism of platforms is as old as the writings of Lord Bryce, our friendly British observer of the eighteen eighties, who called them "a mixture of denunciation, declamation, and conciliation," whose "tendency is neither to define nor to convince, but rather to attract and confuse." It is as new as the observation of Theodore H. White that "in actual fact, all platforms are meaningless." And it is underlined by Senator Goldwater himself who has said, "At their best, political platforms are packets of lies."

YET, despite the barrage of censure, neither major party has shown any inclination to kick the platform habit. And pressure groups — farm, labor, business, religious, civil rights — con-

tinue fighting to get planks into one or both of the major-party platforms. In San Francisco, such figures as Governors Rockefeller and Romney, George Meany of the A.F.L.-C.I.O., W. P. Gullander, president of the National Association of Manufacturers, and even Senator Goldwater, are to appear as "witnesses" to try to influence the drafters.

Platforms are written by committees made up of two members from each state delegation. If a President plans to run again (as in the case of the Democrats this year) most of the platform building is done in the White House, to be ratified by the drafting committee. For the out party, the job is much harder—especially, as in the case of the G.O.P. this year, when the party's leading contenders hold antithetical views.

In such circumstances, the drafting committees strive, not always successfully, to iron out conflicts in the back rooms so that a public image of unity can be established—particularly important now that conventions are televised. Usually the platform is presented

to the full convention on the third day, as the last order of business before the Presidential nominations.

IT is hard to believe that this whole business is meaningless. "Probably no other aspect of our national political process is depreciated on the basis of so little analysis or such scanty evidence," says Dr. Edward F. Cooke of the Center for Politics at the University of Pittsburgh. As he and a few other political scientists have tried to show, platforms survive because the parties need them. For platforms help to harmonize dissident party factions, solidify support from powerful voting blocs, offer a yardstick by which a party's performance in office may be measured and, not least of all, blueprint every four years the nation's needs, goals, ideals and unfinished business. Here is how party platforms have measured up to these demands:

(1) *To harmonize the party.* In both major parties, a united front is essential to success. Yet consider the gulf of ideology on *(Continued)*

Struggle for the G.O.P.

government spending. national defense or civil rights that divides Republicans like Goldwater and Jacob Javits or Democrats like Harry Byrd and Hubert Humphrey. "The need to reconcile these clashing elements," writes Samuel Lubell, "compels each party to bring to the surface unifying compromises, without which neither the Democrats nor the Republicans could have survived this long."

THE penalty for failure to compromise can be a public feud on the convention floor. The memory of the Democrats' bitter Ku Klux Klan fight of 1924 still haunts both parties. The draft platform that year had condemned "secret societies of all kinds," but some delegates insisted the Klan be named. Others, especially from the South and Midwest, where the K.K.K. was then strong, were opposed. The issue erupted into a floor fight. Such animosities were aroused that when it came to choosing a nominee the convention deadlocked for 102 ballots before compromising on the dark horse John W. Davis. Unlike his platform, Davis denounced the Klan by name but, as a nominee of a badly split party, he was trounced by Calvin Coolidge.

Only astute bargaining by Richard M. Nixon spared the Republicans the embarrassment of a floor fight in 1960. The G.O.P.'s platform committee, weighty with conservatives, wrote a document which — especially in civil rights — didn't go nearly far enough to suit the more liberal Governor Nelson Rockefeller.

Nixon, the likely nominee, met secretly with Rockefeller in New York a few days before the convention. Next day platform committee members at work in Chicago were stunned to read in the newspapers about the "Fourteen-Point Compact of Fifth Avenue." It was said to represent Rockefeller's minimum price for supporting the ticket, to be paid in changes in the party's platform. Nixon then flew to Chicago, met with delegates behind the scenes and worked out a compromise between what Rockefeller wanted and the more conservative Republicans were willing to give. A factional dispute was avoided.

YET a similar conflict is shaping up today. This one may not be resolved so easily, especially if Goldwater goes

to the convention with enough delegates to be nominated. For 30 years the G.O.P. has run moderate candidates (Landon, Willkie, Dewey, Eisenhower) on increasingly liberal platforms. Now the Rockefeller-Lodge-Scranton wing is sure to demand the same kind of platform; but Goldwater's manager has said the Senator would never "modify his conservative philosophy — which, after all, is why he is where he is today."

Senator Goldwater not only voted against the civil-rights bill, in contrast to most G.O.P. Senators; he also voted against the nuclear test - ban treaty and the sale of wheat to Russia; he has been known to oppose the graduated income tax, suggests threatening the U.S.S.R. with withdrawal of diplomatic recognition, and felt at one time that Social Security should be made voluntary and the Tennessee Valley Authority sold to private interests. Senator Javits recently pointed out that Senator Goldwater has voiced opposition to all 25 of the most important 1960 G.O.P. platform planks.

AGAINST this background, the committee's task during the coming week seems challenging indeed. No wonder Goldwater favors abandonment of platforms in favor of a few vague statements of "principle."

For the G.O.P. to accept this suggestion would be contrary to recent practice but it would not be without precedent. The first platform written by the Democrats in 1840 (16 years before the G.O.P. was born) — might even be a model. It contained nine short resolutions favoring "rigid economy" in government, opposing the use of Federal money for internal improvements and asserting that "Congress has no power, under the Constitution, to interfere with or control the domestic institutions of the several states."

(2) To solidify voting support. As H. L. Mencken once observed, "almost innumerable cells of uplift ranging from the Mothers of America to the National Authority for the Ladies Handbag Industry" try to influence planks. So do such powerful lobbies as the American Legion, American Medical Association, A.F.L.-C.I.O., National Farmers Union, National Association for the Advancement of Colored People, and National Association of Manufacturers.

THESE groups, supported by countless voters, don't spend time and money testifying at platform hearings simply to blow off steam. They know the first step toward higher wages, lower taxes, farm-price supports, civil - rights laws or whatever they want is recognition of their aims in party platforms.

The G.O.P.'s experience with organized labor remains an expensive object lesson. In the time of William McKinley, Mark Hanna and Theodore Roosevelt, labor felt right at home voting Republican. Samuel Gompers and his American Federation of Labor could always get a respectful hearing in party councils. The Republican platform of 1900, for example, opposed "the immigration of cheap labor from foreign lands" and pledged "an effective system of labor insurance."

BUT in 1908 the G.O.P.'s most conservative wing asserted itself. Hanna had died and Roosevelt retired. The influence of big business was growing. When Gompers came to ask for an anti-injunction plank, his group was shunted to a subcommittee, then told in derision to "go to Denver" (where the Democrats were meeting). Gompers went, and labor has been in "Denver" ever since, stanchly Democratic.

The civil-rights issue makes a good case study in how a growing bloc of voters can influence party platforms and ultimately public policy. As the "party for Lincoln," the G.O.P. in 1892, when Southern states began to pass Jim Crow laws, claimed for every citizen "one free and unrestricted ballot . . . be he rich or poor, native or foreign-born, white or black. . . ." By 1900, the party also condemned lynching.

Democrats, meanwhile, as the erstwhile party of the South, considered in 1912 a so-called "white plank" proposed by Senator Francis G. Newlands of Nevada. It resolved, among other things, to deny Negroes the vote; it was argued that Negroes down South couldn't vote anyway, and those in the North voted Republican.

This anti-civil-rights plank was not adopted, but as late as 1932 the Democrats turned down an appeal by Negro leaders for a pro-civil-rights plank. Franklin Roosevelt was swept into office that year,

but without Negro votes (in Chicago three of four Negroes voted Republican). But the New Deal, which emphasized jobs, relief and equal opportunity, gradually pulled Negroes into the Democratic party. By 1944, 65 per cent of Chicago's colored population went for Roosevelt. In accepting this support, however, the party also incurred an obligation—to recognize civil rights.

FAILURE—Though each party has generally had a strong agriculture plank, none has pleased the farmer.

Hence, the Democrats underwent their own private civil-rights revolution in the 1948 convention. It took the form of a showdown between the party's Southern wing and its Northern liberals over a platform plank. President Truman's backers intended to repeat a mild 1944 plank asserting that "all citizens . . . share the rights that are guaranteed by our Constitution."

But Mayor Hubert Humphrey of Minneapolis led a fight for support of anti-poll-tax, anti-lynching and fair-employment laws, and armed forces desegregation. Defeated in committee, Humphrey took the conflict to the floor where, to everyone's surprise, his strong plank carried.

One result was the bolt of Alabama and Mississippi delegates and the formation of a short - lived States' Rights (Dixiecrat) party. When Truman won anyway, he affirmed the Democrats' commitment with an executive order ending segregation in the armed services.

Although a coalition of Southern Democrats and Republicans blocked civil rights laws then, the seeds of the present bill were planted in the 1948 Democratic platform. (It seems more than coincidence that the Democratic floor leader today was the same Hubert Humphrey, now Senator, who led the fight 16 years ago). In 1956 Republicans wrote a strong civil-rights plank, too, and a year later, with the stage set by both major platforms, Congress passed its first civil-rights law in 82 years. It set up a Civil Rights Commission and added an Assistant Attorney General to enforce voting rights.

IT hardly came as a surprise that the 1960 Democratic platform should contain a plank sponsored by the Leadership Conference on Civil Rights, a joint lobby representing not only the N.A.A.C.P. and CORE, but the American Civil Liberties Union, Americans for Democratic Action, United Auto Workers, A.F.L.-C.I.O., American Jewish Committee, Friends Committee on National Legislation and many other groups. Nor should it take a crystal ball to predict that both party platforms hereafter will declare in favor of enforcing the provisions of the new civil rights law. Senator Dirksen, in the recent debate over civil rights, pointed out to his colleagues that the G.O.P., too, had backed this cause for years. "Were these promises on rights but idle words for vote-getting purposes or were they a covenant to be kept?" he asked.

Like labor, like business, like the farmers, like veterans, Negroes at last have become, through their votes, a political force whose goals as citizens are recognized in national policy. These goals had first to be acknowledged in the major-party platforms.

(3) *To measure party performance.* The standard charge is that platforms, once adopted, are forgotten or ignored by parties in power. On the contrary, there is hardly a reform of the last 60 years that was not recognized as desirable first by one or both major parties.

Democrats began pledging freedom to the Philippines in 1900, two years after the islands were won from Spain. For 32 years the party repeated its pledge until Congress passed the Philippine Independence Act under F.D.R., granting freedom in 1946. Likewise, the G.O.P. advocated "a Cabinet post of education and relief" as early as 1924. Under Eisenhower the plank was made good in 1953 with

creation of a Department of Health, Education and Welfare.

AGAIN, the Democrats proposed a link between the Great Lakes and the sea in 1920. And the St. Lawrence Seaway Development Corporation was set up, under the G.O.P., in 1954.

The income tax, secret ballot, direct election of Senators, primary elections, woman suffrage, child-labor laws, the eight-hour day, Federal aid to education, bank-deposit insurance, closer ties to South America, regulation of railroads and utilities — all were pledged in party platforms before the year 1920.

One of General Eisenhower's first acts as President was to tell a meeting of G.O.P. leaders in 1953 he meant to redeem his campaign pledges. "To my astonishment," he reported, "I discovered some of the men in the room could not seem to understand the seriousness with which I regarded our platform provisions."

Though many consider Eisenhower's eight years static, about two-thirds of his 1952 platform was carried out, at least in part, by such measures as extension of Social Security to 10 million people, an increase in minimum wages, more funds for hospital construction, a public housing bill, a loyalty and security program, an end to wage and price controls, and the first tax-code revision in 75 years.

In his two years, 10 months

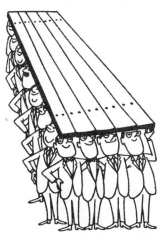

UNITY—The main function of the party platform is to iron out disputes between dissident factions.

and two days as President, John Kennedy took steps toward fulfilling a major portion of the 1960 platform upon which he had run. Lyndon Johnson quickly picked up

and pushed even harder his predecessor's tax, civil-rights, education, medical-care and arms-control programs.

(4) *To blueprint the nation's future.* "The platform," said Woodrow Wilson, running for President in 1912, "is meant to show that we know what the nation is thinking about, what it is most concerned about, what it wishes corrected, and what it desires to see attained that is new and constructive and intended for its long future."

NOT every plank in every platform becomes law, certainly not at once; but, as Wilson said, platforms do organize and tick off each four years the country's long-range goals and unfinished business. They keep us aware of needs unmet but still important to a healthy society.

For example, both parties seem doomed to fail the farmers year after year, despite strong agriculture planks. Perhaps the problem of what to do when we grow more than we can eat is beyond political solution; yet we are bound to try, and platforms affirm that the ideal has not been lost sight of. Both parties also claim to want to balance the budget, cut government spending and amortize part of the national debt. That neither party has had much success does not diminish interest in these goals or prevent their statement as public aims.

* * *

ALTHOUGH the men who write and stand on platforms care about them, not many ordinary citizens pay attention to them. Polls have shown about two-thirds to three-fourths of all voters read few planks or none. In one Gallup poll only 8 per cent of farmers and 6 per cent of working men could recall what the G.O.P. had promised them, although the platform had been released just a week before. One voter in three is sure neither party can be trusted to carry out its promises.

Dr. Gallup sees this as evidence of "a political sophistication" among voters who have concluded "that platforms of both parties are usually made up of vague promises and catchwords designed to please all groups." Yet neither he nor any other pollster has explained how people who don't read platforms know what is in them, or what good a "vote trap" is if the game ignores the bait.

The suggestion that voters

by election day probably know more about platforms than the polls show seems closer to the truth. Even when we don't realize it, many of the "issues" candidates discuss grow out of specific platform planks.

NOR should we be put off by the extravagant language of platforms (i.e., "From the wreckage of American world leadership under a Republican Administration, the great Democratic Congress has salvaged a portion of the world prestige . . ." or "In order to progress further in correcting the unfortunate results of unwise financial management during 20 years of Democrat Administrations, we pledge . . ."). Even this rhetoric, while harmless, is not meaningless. It makes party workers feel better. And the heart of each platform remains its pledges.

Platform writers respond to pressures and react to change. Their planks are like mort-

BARGAINING POWER—A pressure group will fight to get its plank into the platform by voting strength.

gages on the future, held by the voters, who expect a little reduction in the principal now and then. Like bankers lending money, we lend our votes not because we are deceived but because we have hope.

Platforms translate faith into policies which, in turn, become, in the hands of President and Congress, the programs by which we grow. Instead of accepting the idea that they are meaningless, we ought to let both parties know that we, too, are capable of taking platforms seriously, expect pledges to be realistic, and want them to be carried out.

July 5, 1964

G.O.P. DRAFTS GOLDWATER PLANKS; SCRANTON PLEDGES FLOOR FIGHT; DELEGATES BEGIN SESSIONS TODAY

PANEL ENDS WORK

Platform Asks Victory Abroad and Limit on Powers at Home

By ANTHONY LEWIS
Special to The New York Times

SAN FRANCISCO, July 12— Republican platform drafters completed their work today, pledging "victory" abroad and less Federal Government activity at home.

Like the portions released yesterday, the final sections of the platform were very much in the image of Senator Barry Goldwater. As he rolled toward the nomination, his supporters on the Platform Committee easily beat down moderating amendments.

The forces of Gov. William W. Scranton pledged to fight for changes on the floor of the convention Tuesday.

May Press 3 Issues

They will definitely move at that time for a stronger civil rights plank. They may also, depending on developments, call for a denunciation of extremist groups and for a pledge of continued Presidential control of nuclear weapons.

The convention opens at 10 A.M. tomorrow (1 P.M. Eastern daylight time) at the Cow Palace here.

The Platform Committee chairman, Representative Melvin R. Laird of Wisconsin, denied tonight the Scranton charges that the committee had produced a platform tailored to Senator Goldwater.

"It is not a Goldwater platform," Mr. Laird said. "It is a Republican platform, and I am sure it will be overwhelmingly sustained by the delegates Tuesday. This document truly represents the mainstream of this convention."

Civil Rights Plank

On civil rights the draft platform pledged "full implementation and faithful execution" of the new law. But on another page it included language apparently reflecting the "white backlash" against Negro demands for racial integration.

This was a statement of opposition to "federally sponsored inverse discrimination, whether by the shifting of jobs or the abandonment of neighborhood schools for reasons of race."

Some Negro groups have demanded racial quotas in jobs and reshuffling of school populations to overcome past discrimination. But there is no present proposal for any Federal legislation to those ends, and the new Civil Rights Act specifically excludes such Federal action.

The drafters called for a cut of at least $5 billion in Federal spending. They asked for further reduction in taxes, including the repeal of wartime excise taxes. They pledged to balance the budget.

The foreign affairs section of the platform took a strongly nationalistic position.

The platform specifically rejected "the notion that the United States should take sides" in the dispute between Soviet and Chinese Communists. It called for "eventual liberation of the Communist-dominated nations of Eastern Europe, Asia and Latin-America."

"We will move decisively to assure victory in South Vietnam," the platform said, "while confining the conflict as closely as possible.

"We will demand that the Berlin Wall be taken down prior to the resumption of any negotiations with the Soviet Union on the status of forces in, or treaties affecting, Germany."

On Cuba, the plank calls for recognition of a government in exile and for assistance to "Cuban freedom fighters in carrying on guerrilla warfare against the Communist regime" of Fidel Castro.

'Recast Foreign Aid'

There was a pledge to "recast foreign aid" so that it would not "sustain anti-American regimes." And the plank said that aid should "never be employed in support of socialism" —presumably a reference to state-run enterprise in many developing nations.

The platform followed Senator Goldwater's calls for more weapons development and great er respect for professional military opinion. It said Republicans would end "second-best" weapons policies.

The foreign affairs section had much of the strong flavor of Senator Goldwater's speech to the Platform Committee two days ago. Three times it pledged "victory" over Communism—a goal he has often stated as his foreign policy.

On the United Nations the plank reflected the Senator's revised position that this country should "revitalize" the organization but not withdraw from it.

The plank called for a change in the United Nations Charter so that votes in the General Assembly would reflect the population of member countries. This would reduce the strength of some of the smaller and newer nations.

View on Redistricting

On the other hand, on the domestic side, the platform called for overruling of the Supreme Court's decision last month that districts in each house of state legislatures must reflect population.

A proposed constitutional amendment to let one house in a bicameral legislature ignore population factors was endorsed. So was legislation to halt reapportionment by Federal courts until an amendment can be approved.

The Supreme Court's decision barring state-imposed prayer in the public schools was also a target of the draft platform.

The committee called for a constitutional amendment "permitting those individuals and groups who choose to do so to exercise their religion freely in public places, provided religious exercises are not prepared or prescribed by the state or political subdivision thereof and no person's participation therein is coerced."

Plank Evaluated

The proviso in that last clause seemed to some observers to make the proposal meaningless. The Supreme Court decision barred only officially required prayers, and some lawyers thought the plank merely stated what the law already allows.

In what was taken as another implied slap at the Supreme Court, the platform demanded tougher legislation to bar obscene material from the mails.

The over-all theme of the domestic section was "limited Government."

"We Republicans shall insist that the Federal Government have effective but limited powers," the draft said at one point. In several places it warned of excessive Federal controls and dampening of individual choice and initiative.

For example, the platform criticized what it called "ceaseless pressing by the White House, the Food and Drug Administration and Federal Trade Commission to dominate consumer decisions in the market place."

Committee members said the F. T. C. action to require health warning labels on cigarettes had been discussed in connection with this plank but had not been a "major factor." Drug controls were also said to have been involved here.

Tariffs and Trade

The platform called for "a determined drive" to remove foreign countries' trade barriers to American goods.

On our own tariff and trade barriers, it called for "meaningful safeguards against irreparable injuries to any domestic industries by disruptive surges of imports, such as in the case of beef and other meat products, textiles, oil, glass, coal, lumber and steel."

On urban problems, the platform urged the transfer of excise and other tax sources to the states to meet the growing problems of schools, housing, transportation and water systems.

There was also a demand, consistent with the call for more limited and frugal Federal activity, for a "critical re-examination" of all Federal programs of grants to states and localities.

In the farm area, the platform suggested "price supports free of political manipulation," along with other steps. There was a strong endorsement of the existing Social Security program, "with improved benefits to our people."

Medical Care

As expected, the drafters rejected the Democratic plan for Social Security financing of health care for the aged. They called instead for full coverage of medical and hospital costs out of general Federal revenue for those elderly persons who are "needy."

Last night's fuss about the failure to name either Lincoln or former President Dwight D. Eisenhower in the opening sections of the platform was settled. Each was mentioned, in tribute, twice.

Chairman Laird denied heatedly that anyone had ever wanted to keep General Eisenhower's name out.

Support for aid to education was limited to selected programs, such as "selective aid to higher education" and tax credits for college expenses. The 1960 platform endorsed general Federal aid for construction of primary and secondary schools. The 1964 draft says in general that it "incorporates into

258

this platform as pledges renewed those commitments [of 1960] which are relevant to the problems of 1964."

There were some misgivings in the Goldwater camp about this general incorporation of the 1960 platform, on the ground that Senator Goldwater had opposed a number of its planks.

But the Senator told his supporters not to object. The feeling, in any event, was that a specific plank in the 1964 platform—such as the one on education—would be read as superseding a 1960 plank on the same subject.

The process of writing the platform has produced a great deal of heat here during the

last few days. The Scranton forces have charged "railroading" and other sins several times a day, and they have announced numerous planks of their own at news conferences.

But their differences with the majority on the Platform Committee have come down to a relatively few planks. In addition to the three on which they may fight, the Scranton people wanted more liberal planks on education, immigration and labor.

There was no fight over the aggressive tone of the foreign policy section. Chairman Laird repeatedly said that the candidates were in basic agreement on foreign policy. The Cuba

plank, for example, follows Governor Scranton's proposal.

Carlino Move Beaten

The 100-member Platform Committee met through the night, until 6 this morning, to debate the draft. There was only one roll-call vote—on a civil rights amendment put forward by Joseph F. Carlino, Speaker of the New York Assembly, a Scranton man. It lost, 68 to 30.

The Carlino amendment would have toughened the civil rights plank in a number of respects. For example, it would have called for application of the voting section of the 1964 Civil Rights Act to state as well as Federal elections, and for broad-

ening of the Executive order against discrimination in federally aided housing.

Chairman Laird predicted that any effort to write the Carlino amendment into the platform on the floor would be beaten.

He said the present language would have the support of two principal figures in the writing of the 1964 Civil Rights Act. Representative William M. McCulloch of Ohio and Senator Everett McKinley Dirksen of Illinois.

"This is the soundest, the most progressive, the hardest-hitting Republican platform in years," Mr. Laird said.

July 13, 1964

GOLDWATER BACKERS VOTE DOWN SCRANTON'S ANTI-BIRCHER PLANK AND HIS RIGHTS AND A-BOMB PLANS

PLATFORM VOTED

Negro Bloc Questions Arizonan's Fitness— Rockefeller Booed

By TOM WICKER
Special to The New York Times

SAN FRANCISCO, Wednesday, July 15—The Republican National Convention sounded a thunderous "no" last night to the proposition that it should condemn the John Birch Society. Then the delegates defeated a proposal to broaden the civil rights plank of the party platform.

The roll-call vote on the civil rights question was 897 to 409, with delegates from 26 states and territories voting solidly against the broadening amendment.

Delegates supporting Senator Barry Goldwater of Arizona stayed in their seats past midnight to defeat a third proposal by proponents of Gov. William W. Scranton of Pennsylvania. It would have reaffirmed the principle of Presidential control of nuclear weapons.

The session, which ran more than eight hours, adjourned in a state of exhaustion at 12:36 A. M., after having adopted the platform by voice vote.

After the evening of defeats

for the Scranton men, Negro delegates and alternates to the convention issued a joint statement challenging Senator Goldwater's "fitness" to be President.

About 150 pickets representing the Congress of Racial Equality and other civil rights organizations organized a sit-down at two turnstiles outside the Cow Palace. They blocked some delegates as they were leaving the auditorium, but other exits were available and traffic was not badly snarled.

Rockefeller Hooted

But the high point of an unruly evening came earlier.

Spectators in the galleries and some delegates almost drowned out Governor Rockefeller with boos when he spoke strongly for a platform amendment that would have repudiated the right-wing Birch Society and other extremist groups.

Then the extremism amendment was easily defeated on a standing vote, divided roughly between the supporters of Senator Goldwater and Governor Scranton.

That vote, and the roll-call that followed on civil rights, established what everyone knew —that this convention is overwhelmingly for Senator Goldwater for President, and for the platform that was written for his campaign against President Johnson this fall.

The extremism amendment was the first offered by Scranton forces in a final platform fight, intended to salvage a

partial victory from the convention.

Nothing could have better demonstrated the hopelessness of the effort more than the howling response to Governor Rockefeller's speech.

The Governor, interrupted at every pause with a chorus of boos and catcalls, stood patiently during most of the outbursts. Finally, he snapped:

"Some of you don't like to hear it, ladies and gentlemen—but it's the truth!"

That only brought more boos.

When the amendment supported by Governor Rockefeller had been voted down, Gov. George Romney of Michigan came forward with another, milder amendment that would have condemned extremism without mentioning any organization by name. That, too, was shouted down.

At the end of the evening, the convention defeated a less sweeping civil rights amendment proposed by Gov. George Romney of Michigan.

Ironically, the defeat of the civil rights amendment was assured when two Pennsylvania delegates broke out of Governor Scranton's control and voted against it. That gave the opponents of the amendment an assured majority of 655.

Debate on both the civil rights and nuclear weapons control amendments was desultory. The spark obviously went out of the minority effort for amendments after the reception given Governor Rockefeller, although the Scranton men carried their fight through to the end.

Former Secretary of State

Christian A. Herter, a delegate from Massachusetts, presented the nuclear weapons amendment.

Senator Jacob K. Javits of New York, speaking for that amendment, drew boos from the galleries when he said the amendment was necessary because of the "position taken by a leading candidate for President."

That was a reference to Senator Goldwater, who has suggested more "leeway" in using tactical nuclear weapons for the supreme commander of the North Atlantic Treaty Organization's forces.

The uproarious debate on extremism came to a conclusion after 9 P.M., delayed to that point by a 90-minute reading of the 8,500-word draft platform.

The extremism amendment was presented by Senator Hugh Scott of Pennsylvania. Representative Abner Sibal of Connecticut and Representative Silvio O. Conte of Massachusetts also spoke in support of it.

Only Governor Rockefeller had to endure the full hostility of the galleries, however.

In general, delegates did not join heavily in the booing and catcalling, which made his speech inaudible at times. Members of the Texas delegation, for one, were enthusiastic in the noise-making.

When the Governor was introduced, a brief demonstration for him was drowned in a swelling chant of "we want Barry" from the galleries. Governor Rockefeller smiled and waited, while the chanters built up volume and a bass drum joined in with a decisive thump.

Senator Thruston B. Morton of Kentucky, the chairman, gaveled the demonstration to a close with some difficulty. But as Governor Rockefeller moved firmly into his speech, the thunder of the booing and the thump of the drum interrupted him constantly.

At one point, Senator Morton, sitting on the platform, spread his hands helplessly. On two other occasions, he quieted hostile demonstrations with the gavel, and once added:

"Now, look. The Governor has been up here 10 minutes and

he's only had a chance to talk about four."

Governor Rockefeller admonished the demonstrators at one point: "It's still a free country, ladies and gentlemen." Mostly he stood mute, sometimes smiling.

The only time applause for him seemed to overcome the hostile galleries came when he quoted Birch Society attacks on General Dwight D. Eisenhower, an earlier speaker here last night, and called for repudiation of "hawkers of hate."

Rockefeller Still Smiling

Governor Rockefeller left the podium still smiling, and was greeted immediately by Representative John V. Lindsay of New York and Speaker Joseph F. Carlino of the New York House, who gave him enthusiastic handshakes. But in the galleries, the boos were rolling up again with devastating force.

Representative John W. Byrnes of Wisconsin made the primary speech against the amendment, evoking enthusiastic applause.

He said the proposal was "dangerous, demeaning, and it has no place in a republican platform." Rather, he said, the party had to stand for "the unhampered clash of ideas."

The amendment would make Republicans appear to be "trembling in the fear of ideas," Mr. Byrnes said. The proper course, he said, was to meet the Birch Society and other extremist organizations "head-on" with the power of superior ideas.

He would not, he said, wish to see either right-wing or left-wing extremists barred from expressing their views "within framework of law."

The proposed amendment would not have imposed such a bar. It would have repudiated extremist groups but recommended no further action against them.

When the debate was concluded and Senator Morton called for a vote, delegations from New York, Pennsylvania, New England and several other areas stood up to say "aye." Senator John Sherman Cooper of Kentucky, alone in his delegation, stood with them.

When the opposition stood up, representing, as best as could be determined, most of the delegations committed to Senator Goldwater—the amendment was clearly defeated. Senator Morton's announcement set off another enthusiastic roar.

Governor Romney spoke alone on behalf of his amendment and was opposed by Senator Peter Dominick of Colorado. The delegates made short work of the proposal, first on a voice vote, then standing.

Even before the fight began, it lost some of its force by being delayed into the late hours of the night, when Eastern television viewers might be expected to tire of it all and go to bed.

Convention managers also rescheduled the speech by General Eisenhower and caused the full draft platform to be read in its entirety before the amendments were considered.

And yesterday afternoon Richard M. Nixon spoke out in favor of the platform as drafted and defended the views of Senator Goldwater adding that he expected to campaign for the Senator if he were nominated.

General Eisenhower dashed some of the hopes of the Scranton forces Tuesday when he refused to back their proposals for platform changes.

They suffered other setbacks yesterday when Senator Everett McKinley Dirksen of Illinois and Representative William M. McCulloch of Ohio, the Republican leaders in the passage of the Civil Rights Act of 1964, announced that they would speak for the platform plank on civil rights rather than for the Scranton amendment.

General Eisenhower, who has cast himself for a year now in the role of healer of party wounds, appealed in a television interview for a united effort in the fall campaign.

In his address to the convention, however, General Eisenhower gave some comfort to the Scranton forces by saying that extremism "of the right or left is bad—not simply for our party but also for America."

After his introduction by Representative Charles A. Halleck of Indiana, General Eisenhower received a two-and-a-half minute ovation. When he and Mrs. Eisenhower left the Cow Palace, to the strains of "We Love the Sunshine of His Smile," another ovation followed them.

Other business of the second day of the convention included the installation of Senator Morton as permanent chairman; just in time for him to preside over the platform fight.

Warning the delegates to "fasten your seat belts," Mr. Morton ripped into the Democrats as a "bumbling bunch of party hacks" with "one of the biggest bundles of dirty linen in history."

Earlier, the adoption of permanent rules, the approval of permanent officers and the acceptance of the report of the Credentials Committee proceeded without challenge, as did the formal confirmation of a new Republican National Committee.

Focus on Rights Plank

With the Presidential nomination virtually clinched — in the opinion of observers and delegates here — for Senator Goldwater, the moderate Scranton forces had centered their efforts more and more on the platform.

In turn, the central issue of the platform fight was civil rights, a subject on which the Scranton men were proposing a detailed and lengthy amendment to supplement what they called "the generalities of the civil rights plank" as drafted by the Platform Committee.

In a lengthy manifesto, Senator Scott and Mr. Carlino said their proposals were based on reports of the Republican Critical Issues Council and would remove "major deficiencies" in the draft plank.

Their proposals included:

More manpower for the Civil Rights Division of the Justice Department; a statement of pride in Republican support for the Civil Rights Act of 1964, which Senator Goldwater opposed, and legislation to implement the Supreme Court decision barring school segregation and to apply voting guarantees to state as well as Federal elections.

The amendment also urged "the elimination of discrimination in employment" and "positive action to promote truly open competition in the job market and to assure that the Federal-state manpower training programs and vocational education courses are in fact benefiting all citizens eligible for such assistance."

The Scranton proposals concluded with a recommendation for state and local action to protect constitutional guarantees, and for local and private civil rights action in education, housing, unemployment and public accommodations.

The much more limited draft plank written by the Platform Committee called for "full implementation and faithful execution" of this year's Civil Rights Act and previous civil rights laws, and additional administrative and legislative action, as required, to end denials of the right to work.

It also stated "the elimination of any such discrimination is a matter of heart, conscience and education, as well as of equal rights under law."

July 15, 1964

GOLDWATER IS NOMINATED ON FIRST BALLOT; HE CALLS JOHNSON 'BIGGEST FAKER IN U.S.'; SELECTS REP. MILLER AS HIS RUNNING MATE

VOTE IS 883 TO 214

By TOM WICKER
Special to The New York Times

SAN FRANCISCO, July 15— Barry Morris Goldwater, the champion of a new American conservatism, was nominated for President tonight by the 28th Republican National Convention.

The Arizona Senator, the 20th man in the line of Republican nominees that began with John C. Frémont and Abraham Lincoln, needed only one ballot to win the nomination and crush the moderate forces that had controlled his party for a quarter-century.

The only serious challenger was Gov. William W. Scranton of Pennsylvania.

At the conclusion of the ballot he appeared on the platform to move for the unanimous nomination of Senator Goldwater. The convention then adopted by acclamation a resolution making it so.

The count of the first ballot stood as follows for the two leading contenders:

Goldwater 883
Scranton 214

Will Accept Today

Senator Goldwater did not appear at the convention, which adjourned at 11:11 P.M. Pacific daylight time (2:11 A.M., Thursday, New York time). He will accept the nomination tomorrow, after his choice for Vice President, Representative William E. Miller of New York, is duly nominated.

There was never any contest from the moment Senator Everett McKinley Dirksen concluded his nominating speech for Senator Goldwater and set off a wild demonstration that thundered through the Cow Palace for 29 minutes.

Governor Scranton, who entered the race only a few weeks ago, nevertheless refused to

260

withdraw before the ballot was taken. He was on the Cow Palace grounds with his wife, waiting in a trailer for the results.

As soon as the ballot was completed, however, Governor Scranton came striding briskly down the long wooden ramp to the platform, his wife just behind him, with his campaign assistant, Walter Alessandroni, following.

He extended congratulations to Senator Goldwater and pledged: "I shall work for and fully support the ticket chosen by this convention."

"Let it be clearly understood," he said, "that this great Republican party is our historic house. This is our home. We have no intention of deserting it. We are still Republicans—and not very still ones either."

Democrats, he said, should find no comfort in the hard Goldwater-Scranton battle. Republicans, Mr. Scranton said, "have hardly begun to give them the full attention that is coming to them."

Mr. Scranton was applauded generously for his remarks, and for his plea to Republicans who had supported him "not to desert our party but to strengthen it."

The moment for which most of the delegates had been waiting since the convention opened Monday was slow in coming. It was delayed for nearly seven hours by waves of oratory and demonstrators' noise.

Eight candidates were placed in nomination, all but one with seconding speeches and noisy shows of popular support.

Finally, at 10:13 P.M. Pacific daylight time, the call of the roll for the first ballot began.

Those placed in nomination besides Senator Goldwater and Governor Scranton, were Governor Rockefeller, Gov. George Romney of Michigan, Senator Margaret Chase Smith of Maine, Senator Hiram Fong of Hawaii, former Representative Walter H. Judd of Minnesota and Henry Cabot Lodge, who sent a message of withdrawal.

Not Serious Contenders

None was regarded as a serious candidate. Governor Rockefeller was placed in nomination to keep delegates from Oregon and other states, committed to him, from swinging to the Goldwater camp.

From the moment Mrs. C. Douglass Buck of Delaware began calling the roll, after 33 nominating and second speeches, Senator Goldwater sprang into a lead he never lost. The first state, Alabama, gave him its 20 votes and the total grew steadily.

California's massive bloc of 86 votes put him over the 100 mark. Illinois threw in 56 of its 58. The Goldwater total crossed the 500 mark with 20 votes from New Jersey's total of 40.

Then, after Ohio had thrown 57 of its 58 votes into the Goldwater column, the end was at hand. It came when the chairman, Senator Thurston B. Morton of Kentucky, called for the South Carolina vote.

A flashing-light scoreboard was keeping delegates abreast of the totals and a mighty roar went up when it was realized that the South Carolina delegation, solidly Goldwater, would give him the nomination.

When the noise died away, the South Carolina chairman, in deepest Southern tones, declaimed:

"Mr. Chairman, we are humbly grateful that we can do this for America. South Carolina casts 16 votes for Senator Barry Goldwater."

What millions of American conservatives had hoped and worked toward for years had come true. Senator Goldwater had 663 delegate votes—eight more than he needed for nomination.

A mighty storm of cheering broke through the Cow Palace. Goldwater placards flew into the air. Bands broke into unidentifiable tunes. Men stood on chairs and screamed at the top of their lungs.

Walk to the Arena

In his nearby trailer, Governor Scranton stood up and, with Mrs. Scranton, began the walk to the arena and the speaker's platform.

As the ovation in the hall died away, Senator Morton came to the microphones, grinning widely, and said:

"The noise in the hall was such that the chairman could not hear what the delegate from South Carolina was saying."

But everyone knew. Senator Goldwater had won the nomination.

The balloting was concluded, with many another cheer going up for Goldwater votes—particularly when Texas threw in all its 56 votes for the Senator.

Governor Scranton, in his total of 214 votes, received his biggest bloc from Pennsylvania, which gave him 60 of its 64. But he could only break even in neighboring New Jersey, which gave him 20 and Senator Goldwater 20.

Governor Rockefeller, who polled a total of 114, got the largest single state vote. New York cast 87 votes, one over the California total, for him; five New York votes went to Senator Goldwater.

Senator Smith got 27 votes, Governor Romney, 41, Senator Fong, 5, and Mr. Judd, 22.

Sweeps Southern Votes

Senator Goldwater took virtually every Southern delegate's vote. He also swept most of the delegates from the states west of the Mississippi, and scored major breakthroughs in Ohio, Illinois and Wisconsin.

In the latter three states, he rolled up 144 votes.

Before Governor Scranton's motion for a unanimous vote could be acted upon, a number of states insisted on switching their votes to Senator Goldwater. The switching became so hurried that it could hardly be tabulated.

Eventually, however, the motion of acclamation was carried by a resounding voice vote and Governor Scranton returned to the stand to say that he and his wife were happy about the whole thing. They even managed to look as if they were.

It was the end of a long night that might have been a little longer if Mr. Lodge had

List of G.O.P. Nominees

Following is a list of Republican Presidential nominees from 1856, when the party ran its first candidate, to the present. The names in capital letters are those candidates who were elected President.

Year	Convention City	Nominee	Ballots
1856	Philadelphia	John C. Frémont	2
1860	Chicago	ABRAHAM LINCOLN	3
1864	Baltimore	ABRAHAM LINCOLN	1
1868	Chicago	ULYSSES S. GRANT	1
1872	Philadelphia	ULYSSES S. GRANT	1
1876	Cincinnati	RUTHERFORD B. HAYES	7
1880	Chicago	JAMES A. GARFIELD	36
1884	Chicago	James G. Blaine	4
1888	Chicago	BENJAMIN HARRISON	8
1892	Minneapolis	Benjamin Harrison	1
1896	St. Louis	WILLIAM McKINLEY	1
1900	Philadelphia	WILLIAM McKINLEY	1
1904	Chicago	THEODORE ROOSEVELT	1
1908	Chicago	WILLIAM H. TAFT	1
1912	Chicago	William H. Taft	1
1916	Chicago	Charles E. Hughes	3
1920	Chicago	WARREN G. HARDING	10
1924	Cleveland	CALVIN COOLIDGE	1
1928	Kansas City	HERBERT HOOVER	1
1932	Chicago	Herbert Hoover	1
1936	Cleveland	Alfred M. Landon	1
1940	Philadelphia	Wendell L. Willkie	6
1944	Chicago	Thomas E. Dewey	1
1948	Philadelphia	Thomas E. Dewey	3
1952	Chicago	DWIGHT D. EISENHOWER	1
1956	San Francisco	DWIGHT D. EISENHOWER	1
1960	Chicago	Richard M. Nixon	1
1964	San Francisco	Barry Goldwater	1

allowed his name to stay in nomination. But he sent a message withdrawing it as soon as J. Russell Squires of New Hampshire presented it.

After Senator Goldwater's floor demonstration, Senator Kenneth B. Keating of New York placed the name of Governor Rockefeller before the convention. The Governor's 22-minute demonstration, though loud, lacked the enthusiasm of Senator Goldwater's.

Demonstration for Fong

Governor Scranton was placed in nomination by Milton Eisenhower, and that set off still another shouting, screaming demonstration in the Cow Palace.

The Scranton demonstration ran 28 minutes. It fell short of the uproar that had been created by the Goldwater fans. Its enthusiasm reflected, however, the vigor with which the Scranton forces here have fought for their man.

Moving steadily through the roll of states, Senator Morton next called upon State Senator Toshio Ansai to nominate Senator Hiram Fong.

Senator George D. Aiken of Vermont then came forward to place in nomination the favorite daughter of Maine, Senator Smith—the first woman to be placed in nomination for President at a convention of a major party.

Senator Smith attended the convention session tonight. She sat calmly in a box seat while a brief demonstration in her honor rambled through the hall. Most of the demonstrators were youths, not delegates, but her bands provided the liveliest music of the night.

When Scranton forces were crushed in the previous night's platform fight, and when Wisconsin in a morning caucus threw its 30 votes to the Goldwater camp, it was all over but the shouting, which began as soon as Senator Dirksen moved to the platform.

He was able to lead off the nominations because Alabama, first on the roll of states, yielded its place to Illinois.

Senator Goldwater's nomination was seconded by Senator John G. Tower of Texas, former Senator William F. Knowland of California, Representative Charles A. Halleck of Indiana and former Representative Clare Boothe Luce of Connecticut.

Each of their speeches was punctuated with the thunderous applause of the Goldwater delegates and the spectators in the galleries—obviously an area where the Senator was a hero.

Mr. Dirksen, in a well-modulated and rumbling nominating speech, pictured Senator Goldwater as a "peddler's grandson" who had based his political career on "blazing courage."

Today, the Illinois Senator said, "it is the fashion of our critics to sneer at patriotism, to label positions of strength as extremism, to find other nation's points of view right more often than our own."

'Perhaps too long the bugles

have sounded 'retreat' in our relations with other lands," he said.

Through firmness, he said, "through the sure hand, Barry Goldwater, the grandson of that immigrant frontier peddler, could retrieve" the self-respect of America.

Galleries Take Part

Senator Dirksen described Senator Goldwater's vote against the Civil Rights Act of 1964 — of which Senator Dirksen was a chief architect — as an example of "that quality of moral courage which has won him the admiration of the citizens of this land."

As for the ideological swing of the Republican party to conservatism, Senator Dirksen declared:

"Delegates to this convention, the tide is turning! Let's give 190 million Americans the choice they have been waiting for!"

As the mellifluous Senator closed his remarks, the Cow Palace erupted in a bedlam of sound- cheering throngs, blaring bands, howling auto horns above the thump of bass drums.

Through the aisles of the great halls a mob of Goldwater supporters jammed their way, inch-by-inch, holding Goldwater placards aloft, screaming as if gone mad.

The spectators in the galleries, prevented from coming down to the floor to join the parade, added their voices, their waving banners and swaying placards and their auto horns.

Two demonstrators, carrying an eight-foot-high banner bearing the Senator's likeness, shoved their way through the mob.

Another puffed on a huge brass sousaphone. No one but a Goldwater demonstrator could move on the floor.

In the history of recent con-

ventions, few more passionate demonstrations for a candidate have been seen. It was a tribute to the zeal that Senator Goldwater inspires in his admirers—a zeal that has seemed here in the Cow Palace to take on a messianic fervor.

Fifteen minutes after the demonstration began, Senator Morton began pounding for order.

"If you want this gentleman nominated this week, you'd better clear the floor," he bellowed into the public address system. His words could hardly be heard.

Mr. Knowland, a prime mover in the Goldwater pre-convention campaign, stood proudly by Senator Morton, a smile spread across his red face, his big chest thrust out.

Seconding Speeches

When Senator Morton finally restored order to the resounding

hall, the seconding speeches, limited to four minutes each, got under way, with Mr. Knowland leading off.

He left no doubt that he, too, believed Senator Goldwater would lead the Republicans to what Senator Dirksen had called "the sweet, green valley of victory."

Mrs. Luce termed Senator Goldwater a "fearless prophet of a free and fearless America." Senator Tower said the delegates could think better of themselves "because we belong to a society that produced Barry Goldwater."

Mr. Halleck wound up the seconding speeches with a good-humored discourse in which he noted that Senator Goldwater had married a "Hoosier girl from Indiana." That brought an ovation for Mrs. Goldwater, who was in the hall.

July 16, 1964

GOLDWATER PROMISES PROGRAM TO MAKE COMMUNISM 'GIVE WAY'; MILLER IS NAMED RUNNING MATE

CONVENTION ENDS

Extremism in Defense of Liberty 'No Vice,' Arizonan Asserts

By TOM WICKER
Special to The New York Times

SAN FRANCISCO, July 16—Senator Barry Goldwater of Arizona accepted the Republican Presidential nomination tonight with a call to his party "to free our people and light the way for liberty throughout the world."

Communism, he said, must be made to "give way to the forces of freedom."

"The sanctity of private property," he said, "is the only durable foundation for constitutional government in a free society."

"Extremism in the defense of liberty," Senator Goldwater declared, "is no vice . . . moderation in the pursuit of justice is no virtue."

Thunderous Ovation

The Senator, nominated on the first ballot at last night's session of the 28th Republican National Convention, received a thunderous ovation when he appeared in the Cow Palace tonight for the closing session.

As he spoke, dedicating his campaign to what he called "the ultimate and undeniable greatness of the whole man," he was constantly interrupted by the enthusiasm of the delegates, who had never given serious thought to choosing anyone else.

Earlier tonight, the delegates nominated Senator Goldwater's choice for the Vice-Presidential nomination, Representative William E. Miller of New York, without a dissenting vote. Three delegates from Tennessee abstained, however, because they thought the convention should have made the selection.

The nomination of 50-year-old Mr. Miller was almost routine business, as the great hall waited in suspense for the appearance of its hero.

Speaks in Quiet Tone

Senator Goldwater, mild-mannered, bespectacled, speak-

ing usually in a quiet voice, and with almost no gestures, did not disappoint his hearers—the conservatives who at this convention wrested the Republican party from its quarter-century of control by moderate forces.

He laid down a strong line of active resistance to Communism abroad, and what he pictured as state planning at home.

Senator Goldwater offered no quarter to the moderate Republican forces that fought him throughout his campaign for the nomination and who succumbed reluctantly to the power of his delegates here. Some moderate delegates were reported to be angered at the militant tone of the speech and the absence of an olive branch to them.

Mr. Goldwater made no direct mention of the civil rights

issue that at times divided this convention. Instead, he laid heavy emphasis on the sanctity of property and on the necessity for maintaining law and order.

And he gave this picture of what Republicanism offered:

"We do not seek to live anyone's life for him. We seek only to secure his rights and guarantee

him opportunity to strive, with Government performing only those needed and constitutionally sanctioned tasks which cannot otherwise be performed.

"We seek a government that attends to its inherent responsibilities of maintaining a stable monetary and fiscal climate, encouraging a free and competitive economy, and enforcing law and order."

A small civil rights demonstration, involving three women from the Congress of Racial Equality, broke out during Senator Goldwater's speech, but few delegates were aware of it. The three women, wrapped in a large banner labeled "CORE," lay down in an exit and refused to move.

Senator Goldwater read his speech from a Teleprompter mounted on the speaker's stand.

At two points, indignation breaking through his composure, he burst out with the words "poppycock!" and "humbug!" in describing the policies of the Johnson Administration.

Senator Goldwater pictured the Administration as inept, lacking in integrity, and deficient in its will to resist Communism.

Senator Goldwater stated his theme early:

"The Good Lord raised this mighty Republic to be a home

for the brave and to flourish as the land of the free—not to stagnate in the swampland of collectivism, not to cringe before the bullying of Communism."

Even the theme music complemented the evangelistic Americanism Senator Goldwater enunciated in his speech. When he appeared in the Cow Palace with his wife, the band played "The Battle Hymn of the Republic." At the conclusion of his speech, while the Senator's daughters wept, the strains of "America, the Beautiful" rang through the hall. Many of the delegates were singing the words.

Mr. Goldwater's indictment of the Johnson Administration was scathing, particularly concerning foreign policy and what he saw as its failure to maintain the nation's "security from domestic violence."

History demonstrated, he said, "that nothing prepares the way for tyranny more than the failure of public officials to keep the streets safe from bullies and marauders."

Mr. Goldwater's statement that "extremism in the defense of liberty is no vice" was applauded by the delegates. The Senator's press secretary, Edward K. Nellor, said later that Mr. Goldwater, after delivering the speech, remarked in his hotel suite:

"I like that line."

As Senator Goldwater and his wife came to the platform tonight, flanked by Senators Carl T. Curtis of Nebraska and Bourke Hickenlooper of Iowa, a tremendous ovation burst through the Cow Palace.

Hundreds of balloons tumbled from the ceiling, almost inundating the candidate and his wife. Their popping rattled like machinegun fire.

Nixon Applauded

Senator Goldwater was introduced by former Vice President Richard M. Nixon.

Mr. Nixon brought applause from the delegates and galleries repeatedly with a strong appeal for party unity, and with predictions that a strengthened Republican party would win the victory in November for the "honest deal" of Senator Goldwater.

Discounting polls showing the Senator as the underdog, Mr. Nixon declared that "the only poll that counts is the one that all of us vote in and Mr. Gallup isn't going to be counting the votes, either."

Nor, he said in a reminder of Republican charges of vote fraud in the 1960 election, "will Mayor Daly [of Chicago] be counting the votes either."

His prescription for the Republicans was unity and hard work. "From this moment forward," he said, "let us think victory, and we will win victory in November."

The convention adjourned at 8:05 P.M. Pacific Daylight time, which is 11:05 New York time.

Mr. Miller's nomination was assured when Senator Goldwater, after conferring with other leaders, let it be known that the New Yorker was his choice.

After the nomination was made on a roll-call vote, Mr. Miller appeared before the convention to call for "a nationwide crusade to regain respect abroad for this land of liberty and to re-establish reason in government here at home."

In accepting what he called the "greatest challenge of my lifetime," Mr. Miller paid tribute to Senator Goldwater, whom he called "one of the most dynamic and forceful leaders in all our nation's history.'"

Senator Gordon Allott of Colorado placed Mr. Miller in nomination, terming him one with "fighting qualities to match those of Barry Goldwater." His speech set off a brief demonstration for the New Yorker.

Mr. Miller has served as Republican National Chairman since late 1961.

His selection, and Senator Goldwater's choice of Dean Burch, his assistant campaign director, as the new Republican National Chairman, completed a historic political transition. It was the delivery of party control into the hands of the conservative wing, which had been formally out of power since 1940.

Paper Unity Achieved

The conservatives will now control the 1964 campaign against President Johnson, and set the tone of the over-all Republican effort in Congressional, state and local races.

In taking over party control, the conservatives achieved at least a paper unity with the moderates whose effort they smashed down at this convention.

Symbolizing that unity was the presence in the Cow Palace last night of Gov. William W. Scranton of Pennsylvania, the late-blooming challenger who got into the race on behalf of moderate Republicans June 12.

In an emotional scene, Governor Scranton pledged his support to Senator Goldwater after he had lost on the first ballot, 883 to 214.

After switches there were 17 votes for Scranton, 3 for Governor Rockefeller and 5 New York abstentions.

The intraparty fight obviously would not end, however, even if the moderates followed Governor Scranton's advice and laid it aside for the campaign. For as he spoke for unity the Governor was also urging the moderates to "work within our party—not against it."

Calling the Republican party the "historic house" of his principles and the principles of those who supported them, Governor Scranton plainly signaled the intention of moderates to return eventually to the battle.

"We are still Republicans," he insisted, "and not very still ones, either."

His appearance recalled to many delegates a similar speech by Senator Goldwater at the 1960 convention, which nominated Mr. Nixon for President. At that time Senator Goldwater urged conservatives, outraged at the liberal 1960 platform, not to bolt the party but to work within it to gain control—a control that they have now overwhelmingly achieved.

Governor Scranton himself reminded the convention — somewhat pointedly—of Senator Goldwater's 1960 speech.

Some here were also reminded that it was a good-sport, party-unity speech by John F. Kennedy, after he lost the 1956 Democratic Vice-Presidential nomination, that helped catapult him into the front rank of the party's candidates for President four years later.

At a news conference this morning, Governor Scranton refused, however, to be specific about his intentions. Of this year's moderate collapse, he said there had been a "proliferation of moderation" — too many candidates, too little unity of purpose.

But today, moderate Republicanism was only a small, not-very-happy segment in the roaring and fervent throng of conservatives that welcomed the mild-mannered but charismatic Senator Goldwater to the smoky, banner-hung Cow Palace.

In the New York delegation— a group that with "heads high" cast 87 futile votes for Governor Rockefeller last night — there was, for instance, a muttering of discontent at the selection of Mr. Miller for the Vice-Presidential spot. Nothing practical could be done about it, however.

Mr. Miller's choice, it was reported, resulted in large part from his reputation as a hard-hitting speaker who would lay the edge of a tart tongue on the Democrats and President Johnson in the coming campaign.

That quality is not conspicuous among the assets of Representative Gerald R. Ford of Michigan, who was high on Senator Goldwater's list of possibilities for the second spot. In addition, Mr. Miller is a confirmed conservative, highly acceptable to the sensitive and volatile segment of right-wing Republicans who were the nucleus of Senator Goldwater's support here.

A question raised by some political analysts was whether Mr. Miller's Catholicism might injure the ticket in states like Tennessee and Kentucky, where Protestant voters swung heavily against Mr. Kennedy in 1960. Any such injury, it was felt, would probably be balanced by Mr. Miller's appeal to Catholic voters, many of whom are concentrated in the big urban states where Senator Goldwater, on the political form sheet, appears weakest.

The Senator apparently gave little thought to balancing his ticket with a choice of the moderate leader, Governor Scranton. The Governor said at his news conference today that the matter had never been discussed between them, even before he came out openly in opposition to the Senator.

Thus, the adoption of a Goldwater-oriented platform, the selection of Mr. Miller, the choice of Mr. Burch, all indicated that Senator Goldwater is determined to pitch his campaign squarely on the conservative themes that carried him to the nomination.

There were few indications here of any overtures to independent and liberal voters. It is a tenet of the Goldwater faith that million of Americans have been refusing to vote in Presidential campaigns until they could have a true choice between a liberal and a conservative, rather than between two liberals.

A Republican rule that prevents the switch of delegate votes before the end of a roll-call made possible an analysis of the single ballot on which Mr. Goldwater was nominated.

Before the vote for Senator Goldwater was made unanimous on the motion of Governor Scranton, most anti-Goldwater delegates switched their votes to him. Such switching is permitted at the end of a roll-call, so that states may either get on the bandwagon of a winner or shift strength to break a deadlock.

The balloting that gave Senator Goldwater the nomination as recorded before the switches reflected the power he had built up in the South and the lightly populated states of the West, as well as his dependence on adding to it some support from the urban industrial states.

The Senator received 292 of the 303 delegate votes of the 11 states of the Old Confederacy, plus Kentucky. Seven of those states voted solidly for him.

Among 19 states west of the Mississippi (exclusive of Texas and California), casting 304 delegate votes, Senator Goldwater polled 243 votes. Nine of these states voted solidly for him; only two—Alaska and Oregon—failed to give him a vote.

Thus, in these 31 Southern and Western states, of which only Texas cast a major block of votes, Senator Goldwater polled 535 out of a possible 607 votes. With the massive block of 86 California delegates, which he had captured in that state's winner-take-all primary on June 2, they gave him a total of 621 votes—just 34 under the required majority of 655.

After Senator Allott's nominating speech for Mr. Miller, seconding speeches were made by Representative Steven B. Derounian of Nassau County, former Gov. John A. Volpe of Massachusetts, Representative Bruce Alger of Texas, Representative Ed Foreman of Texas, and Gov. Paul Fannin of Arizona.

July 17, 1964

GOLDWATER GAINS IN MODERATE WING

Some Middle-Road G.O.P. Congressmen Now Give Him Nominal Support

By JOHN D. MORRIS
Special to The New York Times

WASHINGTON, July 25 — About half the Republican liberals and moderates in Congress are now planning to give at least nominal support to Senator Barry Goldwater in his campaign for the Presidency.

Four Republican Senators and two Representatives have publicly disassociated themselves from the party's national ticket. Several others may do so before the campaign gets formally under way.

Ultimately, however, it appears that the Arizona conservative will win endorsements, though reluctant or cool for the most part, from a sizable majority of his Congressional colleagues who are identified with the party's more liberal wing.

44 Congressmen Surveyed

In most cases, party loyalty and an aversion to aiding the Democratic Presidential ticket seem to be outweighing the antipathy of moderates and liberals to Senator Goldwater and his running mate, Representative William E. Miller of upstate New York.

Those conclusions are based on a survey by The New York Times of 14 Senators and 30 Representatives generally classified as liberal-to-moderate Republicans. The poll produced the following statistics:

Supporting the Goldwater-Miller ticket — Seven Senators and 14 Representatives.

Not supporting the ticket — Four Senators and two Representatives.

Undecided — Six Representatives.

Will Vote for Scranton

No comment — One Senator and three Representatives.

Unavailable for questioning — Two Senators and five Representatives.

The Senators who have disassociated themselves from the ticket are Jacob K. Javits and Kenneth B. Keating of New York, Clifford P. Case of New Jersey and J. Glenn Beall of Maryland. The Representatives are Stanley R. Tupper of Maine and James G. Fulton of Pennsylvania.

"When I vote," Mr. Fulton said, "I intend to write in the name of Gov. William W. Scranton. If he says it will embarrass him, then I'll write in the name of Bishop John J. Wright of Pittsburgh. Bishop Wright is a Catholic and I'm a Presbyterian, but at least he's not a 'new guard' Republican."

The others were less adamant and said they hoped Mr. Goldwater would modify his views on civil rights, foreign affairs and several other issues so that they could support him. However, they were not optimistic over the prospects.

Three New Yorkers were among the six Representatives who said they had not yet decided whether to back the national ticket.

One, John V. Lindsay of Manhattan, is expected to announce next week that he will not support Senator Goldwater. He may be joined by one or both of the others, Seymour Halpern of Forest Hills and Ogden R. Reid of Purchase.

Paul A. Fino of the Bronx was unavailable for questioning but was believed to be weighing a decision.

Among the 21 Senators and Representatives who indicated their support for Mr. Goldwater, many made it clear that their decision had been difficult and distasteful.

Will 'Live With Ticket'

"I'm going to live with it — support the ticket, that is," Representative Peter H. B. Frelinghuysen of New Jersey said. "I'm going to put more emphasis on my own voting record and my own views. But I don't think any of us will gain much ground by agitating at the moment."

The endorsement of Senator Winston L. Prouty of Vermont was similar.

"I have always supported the Republican Presidential nominee and I shall vote for Senator Goldwater," he said. "If he is elected, I shall support his policies when I think they are right and oppose them when I think they are wrong."

Senator George D. Aiken of Vermont said he considered himself bound by a promise to support the Republican National Convention's choice. He made the promise in his nominating speech for Senator Margaret Chase Smith of Maine.

Senator Smith could not be reached, despite repeated efforts over three days, for comment on the Goldwater candidacy. United Press International quoted her as saying in an interview last Monday that, as a Republican, "I accept the decision of the Republican majority and will support all the nominees."

Senator Hugh Scott of Pennsylvania was also unavailable. He was reported to be putting off a statement until he had consulted other Republican candidates in his state.

Senator Thomas H. Kuchel of California declined to state his position, and there was no indication whether he would do so.

Senators signifying their support for the Goldwater-Miller ticket, in addition to Mr. Prouty and Mr. Aiken, were John Sherman Cooper and Thruston B. Morton of Kentucky, J. Caleb Boggs of Delaware, Hiram L. Fong of Hawaii and Leverett Saltonstall of Massachusetts.

Representatives backing the ticket, in addition to Mr. Frelinghuysen, included Robert R. Barry and John W. Wydler, New York; Abner W. Sibal, Connecticut; Rogers C. B. Morton, Maryland; William S. Broomfield and George Meader, Michigan; John F. Baldwin, California, and James C. Cleveland, New Hampshire.

Also backing him were Charles A. Mosher, Ohio; John C. Kuchel and Richard S. Schweiker, Pennsylvania; Robert T. Stafford, Vermont, and Thor C. Tollefson, Washington.

Those undecided, in addition to Representatives Lindsay, Reid and Halpern, were Silvio O. Conte and F. Bradford Morse, Massachusetts, and Fred Schwengel, Iowa.

Representatives unavailable for comment, in addition to Mr. Fino, were George M. Wallhauser and William T. Cahill, New Jersey; Charles McC. Mathias, Maryland, and Charles E. Bennett, Michigan.

Representatives who declined to comment were Florence P. Dwyer, New Jersey, and Robert J. Corbett and Irving J. Whalley, Pennsylvania.

July 26, 1964

GOLDWATER, IN A UNITY BID, REJECTS EXTREMISTS' AID; EISENHOWER IS 'SATISFIED'

U.N. IS SUPPORTED

By CHARLES MOHR
Special to The New York Times

HERSHEY, Pa., Aug. 12 — Senator Barry Goldwater offered to Republican leaders today a sweeping set of political reassurances including a promise to consult former President Dwight D. Eisenhower on the appointments of Secretaries of State and Defense.

In a speech to a unity conference of party leaders, Mr. Goldwater made what observers considered to be a distinct shift toward the middle of the road.

The Republican Presidential candidate repudiated extremist groups and "character assassins." He expressed support of the United Nations, which he has often criticized, and of the Social Security program. He promised not to shirk Federal responsibility in the field of civil rights.

Mr. Goldwater's speech grew out of a meeting last week at Gettysburg, Pa., with General Eisenhower and former Vice President Richard M. Nixon, and it embodied "clarifications" of Mr. Goldwater's controversial opinions, which General Eisenhower had requested.

In a news conference after the unity meeting, General Eisenhower said that he had had reservations about Senator Goldwater's candidacy, that he had asked for clarifications, and was now "satisfied."

Mr. Goldwater, at the joint press conference with General Eisenhower at which Mr. Nixon, the Vice-Presidential candidate, William E. Miller, and Pennsylvania's Gov. William W. Scranton also appeared, declined to call his speech "conciliatory," or to agree that he had made "concessions."

Mr. Goldwater also said that President Johnson, in his "admonition" to naval commanders during last week's Vietnam crisis, had told "subordinate commanders to use any weapons necessary."

When asked if he was saying that it was his impression that

Associated Press Wirephoto

UNITY: Former President Dwight D. Eisenhower and Senator Barry Goldwater at news conference yesterday.

Mr. Johnson had authorized military commanders to make the decision as to whether or not to use nuclear weapons, he said his information came from the newspapers, but that "in my book" Mr. Johnson had indicated naval commanders could use "the whole inventory" of weapons if needed.

Senator Goldwater had suggested previously that military commanders be given the right to employ nuclear weapons.

Many political observers felt that today he greatly softened his stands on the issues that most disturbed liberal and moderate Republicans.

His promise, if elected, to consult General Eisenhower — and Mr. Nixon—on appointments to "critical" positions on the National Security Council including Secretaries of State and Defense was interpreted by his audience as meant to quiet fears that Mr. Goldwater would conduct a "trigger-happy" Administration.

However, Mr. Goldwater at the press conference said he still favored "interdicting" supply lines through North Vietnam to the Communist Vietcong partisans in South Vietnam, and gave the impression that he was "not necessarily" against giving United States commanders in the Pacific more authority to decide whether to use nuclear weapons in possible future conflicts in that area.

In the speech, Mr. Goldwater declared: "I seek the support of no extremist—of the left or the Right." He said of himself and Mr. Miller: "We repudiate character assassins, vigilantes, Communists and any other group such as the Ku Klux Klan that see kto impose its views through terror of threat or violence."

He supported "unconditionally the purposes the United Nations was originally intended to serve" and said that the "fullest possible use" of the world body should be made. He pledged to take "all reasonable steps" to help it to become a "more effective instrument for peace."

He rejected any suggestion that he would not carry out "faithful execution" of the Civil Rights At of 1964 and asserted that he would not "shirk any Federal responsibility to prevent any American from suppressing the rights of any other American."

He said he sought "to read no one out of" the Republican party and that he wanted to "assure a climate in the party in which all of us will feel comfortable and at home."

Backs Social Security

He pledged that under a Goldwater-Miller Administration "every American will be assured of a compassionate and understanding approach by the Federal Government" to human problems. He also said he would like to repeat "for perhaps the one millionth time" that I support the Social Security system and I want to see it strengthened."

The tone of his remarks was significantly different from the strongly conservative speech in which he accepted the Presidential nomination on July 15 in San Francisco.

Sources close to Mr. Goldwater reported that his research assistant, Edward McCabe, had been the principal draftsman of the speech. His regular speech writer is Karl Hess.

Mr. Goldwater's speech was made this morning at the Hershey Hotel to Republican Governors, gubernatorial candidates, General Eisenhower and Mr. Nixon and a few other top party officers. The meeting was closed, but a text of the speech was released.

Mr. Goldwater flew here in a chartered airplane this morning after an hour-and-one-half conference at his Washington apartment yesterday afternoon with Governor Rockefeller.

In the press conferece after the meeting, General Eisenhower said it was not merely coincidental that his own statement outlining Mr. Goldwater's views closely paralleled the Senator's speech.

Gettysburg Meeting

Mr. Goldwater said that it was a safe assumption that his speech grew out of the Gettysburg meeting with the former President.

He said that both he and General Esenhower had at that time "made notes" about what should be said and that Mr. McCabe and Bryce Harlow, a former assistant to General Eisenhower who is still close to him, had conferred with each other and with Mr. Goldwater while the Goldwater speech was being drafted.

In the speech, Mr. Goldwater not only promised to enforce the civil rights act faithfully but to "use the great moral influence of the Presidency to promote prompt and peaceful observance of civil rights laws."

Much of Mr. Goldwater's hopes for election rest on the South and there were qualifying phrases in his remarks on civil rights.

He said that he would take, "within constitutional limits, whatever action is necessary to deal effectively with situations" that "might develop in disorders, riots or other forms of mass lawlessness."

But his remarks seemed to his audience as clearly directed at reassuring Northern liberals and not Southerners.

In the speech, Senator Goldwater said the "No. 1 problem" facing Republicans in this election was the "totally wrong" charge that "the election of a Republican President in November will somehow lead to war."

Calling this the "supreme political lie," he said that a "Goldwater-Miller Administration will mean an immediate return to the proven policy of peace through strength, which was the hallmark of the Eisenhower years."

He said: "Let me say something more. Every President, if he is worth his salt will pick his own Cabinet.

"However, I can assure you that I would not appoint anyone to the offices of Secretary of State or Defense or other critical national security post until I had first discussed my plans for those appointments with General Eisenhower, Dick Nixon and other experienced leaders seasoned in world affairs."

He said that "if this amounts to an impulsive, trigger-happy approach to foreign policy, then I fear the English language has lost its meaning."

The Senator did not retract his San Francisco remarks about extremism, in which he had said that "Extremism in the defense of liberty is no vice." But he repudiated "character assassins" and vigilantes, which are descriptions Republican liberals have given to "extremist" groups.

Although Mr. Goldwater named the Ku Klux Klan and the Communist party, he did not mention the John Birch Society, which was named with the two other organizations in a liberal amendment to the Republican platform, which failed to pass at the national convention.

The reference to character assassins was, however, believed by his listeners to be directed to officers of the John Birch Society, who have called General Eisenhower a conscious agent of communism.

Explains Birch Commission

During the press conference, Mr. Goldwater said that he did not include the John Birch Society among those groups he specifically repudiated because "they are not on the subversive list," which he said the Ku Klux Klan was.

However, he noted that in the past he had "opened assailed" the society's founder-president, Robert H. W. Welch Jr., for what he called Mr. Welch's "stupid" statement that Mr. Eisenhower was associated with communism.

Mr. Goldwater also said that while civil rights could not be kept out of the coming campaign "we are agreed that backlash should not be made an issue."

The speech also contained a fighting attack on the Democrats and a prediction of Republican victory. Mr. Goldwater said that "we have some hurdles to clear and some problems on our hands."

Mr. Goldwater called the Republican party the "party of peace." He continued:

"We don't claim that the Democrats are a war party. But America might well question the caliber of leadership which has blundered into three wars in my lifetime, because it didn't understand its responsibilities for keeping the peace."

He said he wondered "if the really 'impulsive' and 'imprudent' President isn't the one who is so indecisive and vacilating that he has no policy at all" and thus encourages potential aggressors.

Although he said the United Nations needed improvement, his remarks on that subject were a considerable modification of the biting criticisms and qualified threats to pull out of the body that he had sometimes made earlier this year.

Mr. Goldwater said he was soliciting the active support of "every Republican governor" in the coming campaign.

During the press conference, Mr. Goldwater was asked by a European reporter to comment on his policies toward Europe and Germany.

Mr. Goldwater replied that, "I think that Germany originated the modern concept of peace through strength."

It was not clear exactly what was Mr. Goldwater's meaning.

Mr. Goldwater said that Mr. Johnson had taken the sting out of charges that Mr. Goldwater was impulsive by "taking an impulsive action [in Vietnam] which nobody has condemned."

Of his dispute with the press, Mr. Goldwater offered an olive branch and said, "I'll get along with you fellas all right," and

noted: "You've got to eat and I've got to eat."

Referring to the Vietnam crisis he said President Johnson has been "following my advice" and that he hoped this would continue.

In speaking of the need to interdict supply lines to the Vietcong in South Vietnam he spoke of supply lines "coming

down from Red China.

When pressed for details where interdiction should take place, he said he would ask his chiefs of staff for such advice and that, if President, would not try to run the armed forces in a detailed way.

Mr. Goldwater said he had never asked the Alabama Republican leader, John Martin, to

ask that state's governor, George C. Wallace, to withdraw as a Presidential candidate.

However, he noted that "Johnson is going to be hard enough to beat without having someone else taking votes away from me."

August 13, 1964

MIDWEST WEIGHS WALLACE IMPACT

Leaders Study Significance of White Protest Votes

By AUSTIN C. WEHRWEIN
Special to The New York Times

CHICAGO, May 9 — Gov. George C. Wallace of Alabama introduced a new political concept when he invaded the Wisconsin and Indiana primaries — "win without winning."

His 29.8 per cent showing in the Indiana Democratic primary last Tuesday, and more especially his outright victory in Lake and Porter Counties, forced Middle Western politicians to develop another theory, and that was "to win without losing."

The shock of losing heavily Democratic Lake County was compounded when the official canvas figures showed the Wallace margin was even higher than the original unofficial totals. The unofficial plurality was 1,308, but the official canvas, available yesterday, showed Governor Wallace with 42,712 votes, to be 2,527 more than the 40,185 ballots cast for Gov. Matthew E. Welsh, who ran as President Johnson's understudy.

Election night, Governor Welsh's unofficial vote was listed as 40,321, slightly more than the vote recorded in the canvas carried out by auditors hired by the election board. The board blamed clerical errors for the discrepancy.

The Wallace showing in Indiana was viewed as a setback because he ran behind his percentages in Wisconsin, but the hard fact remains that, nationally, Democratic strength is centered in large cities and industrial areas and The Gary Post Tribune commented that political strategists must take notice when an area like highly industrialized, heavily unionized

Lake County turns against President Johnson.

The vote in Lake County usually spells the difference between victory and defeat in general elections.

Oddly enough, Governor Welsh did well in counties at the foot of Indiana, which are closest to Kentucky. The clear indication, observers said, was that racial tension has long since lost regional character and depends on the actual situation. In Gary and other Lake County communities, the militancy of the civil rights movement, which was stronger than any place else in Indiana, stirred the white protest.

The questions confronting Democrats is whether the kind of white resistance shown in Indiana and in Wisconsin on April 7 will be translated into Republican votes in the general election. Although the entire Indiana House delegation voted for the pending civil rights bill and all but one of the Wisconsin Congressmen, Representative William K. Van Pelt, a Republican, supported the bill. In both states it is regarded as a Democratic measure regardless of bipartisan support.

Even slight switching could make a difference. In Wisconsin Gov. John Reynolds, a Democrat, seeking reelection, won in 1960 by 12,000 votes. In Minnesota Karl Rolvaag won after months of counting by 91 votes. Governor Welsh won by 23,000 and, although he is legally unable to succeed himself, the next Democratic nominee will face the same tight voting pattern.

Narrow Margin

Moreover, in Illinois John F. Kennedy won by 8,858 votes and a defection of less than half of 1 per cent by Democratic voters would have given Illinois's electoral vote to Richard M. Nixon.

Although Mr. Kennedy was fighting religious opposition that President Johnson would avoid in southern Illinois, there has been serious and often violent racial disturbance in Chicago.

Governor Wallace polled write-in votes in both Republican and Democratic columns in the Illinois primary. The official count just made available showed he got a combined total of 5,964 write-in votes, which was more than the write-in voters for Governors Rockefeller, Scranton and Romney together.

Political observers in the Middle West recalled that there were photo finishes in a number of non-Southern states carried by Mr. Kennedy in 1960 in addition to Illinois — such as Delaware, Hawaii, Minnesota, Michigan, Missouri, Nevada, New Jersey and New Mexico.

The problem of "white backlash" confronting the Democrats is a particularly sticky one because neither side can attack it directly.

Governors' Attack

In Indiana and Wisconsin Governors Welsh and Reynolds attacked Governor Wallace as a racist but could not attack on the same grounds, except in a very general way, voters in their own state who might support him.

The Alabama Governor offered rationalization for anybody who wanted to vote along racial lines when he insisted that the real issue was states rights and big government.

Voters in the North, except in local elections on such things as open occupancy, have traditionally not had a chance to express any racial attitudes in elections. At the same time, the Alabama Governor's supporters included people who agreed with his attacks on what he called "little pinkos and liberals" and his criticism of judicial decisions against school prayers.

In Gary precincts that are traditionally 2 to 1 and 3 to 1 Republican, Governor Wallace drew a heavy vote. In Hammond and rural areas of the Southern part of Lake County, Governor Wallace made his best showing.

There are few Negroes in Porter County, next door to Lake County, but observers interpreted the Wallace victory

there as evidence that people wanted to keep it that way.

Governor Welsh failed to carry a single all-white precinct in Gary, although the 40 per cent Negro population of the steel city carried him to victory. Gary City Councilmen representing the three districts that have large Polish or other Middle European, Southern white or Irish Catholic populations have been the backbone of a City Council bloc that has defeated proposed civil rights ordnances.

In Milwaukee, in the six city wards considered the "most Polish," the Democratic vote was to 70 per cent in 1962. However, in the Wisconsin primary, Governor Reynolds got 57 per cent of the total vote and the Wallace total exactly equalled the Democratic and Republican losses, a clear indication of a crossover.

The Democratic claim of a large crossover in Indiana was more difficult to trace, although Democrats said it was about 10 per cent. Senator Barry Goldwater's campaign manager also said the Senator suffered because of vote switching.

To what extent Republicans will be able to capitalize on the white protests varies state by state. In Illinois Republicans for practical purposes have written off the Negro vote. In Minnesota, the Negro population is only about 1 per cent concentrated in the twin cities, and the civil rights issue has not loomed as a statewide matter.

It arises indirectly through business opposition, which Governor Wallace has done his best to capitalize on. For example, in Indiana, Harold Schuman, secretary of the Indiana Manufacturers Association, attacked the civil rights bill on a radio program conducted by Clarence Manion, a John Birch Society leader.

May 10, 1964

WALLACE DROPS PRESIDENCY BID; DENIES ANY DEALS

Alabamian Was 'Committed' to Run as Segregationist —Aid to Goldwater Seen

Special to The New York Times

WASHINGTON, July 19 — Gov. George C. Wallace of Alabama withdrew today his segregationist third-party bid for the Presidency.

In a move of great political significance, he thus ended a campaign that had been expected to cut deeply into the conservative, states' rights appeal to Southern voters of Senator Barry Goldwater of Arizona, the Republican Presidential candidate.

[Senator Goldwater said at Phoenix, Ariz., that Governor Wallace's withdrawal was a "surprise" to him. "I never gave this Wallace thing much thought," the Senator said, and then refused to amplify his views.]

Mr. Wallace had been "committed" to run in 16 states.

"My mission has been accomplished," Mr. Wallace declared. He credited himself with getting "a message to the leadership" of the Republican party "to return this country to the governmental principles upon which it was founded."

The White House had no comment on the announcement. The Senate majority leader, Mike Mansfield of Montana, said:

"This draws the lines more sharply."

Finds Message Heeded

On the Columbia Broadcasting System's "Face The Nation" — a nationally televised program — Mr. Wallace said that "I was the instrument" through which "the high councils of both major political parties" had been "conservatized."

"Today we hear more states' rights talk than we have heard in the last quarter century," he said in a statement at the start of the broadcast. That his states' rights, anti-civil rights message had been "heeded and will be heeded is evident," he said.

"We shall look closely at the actions and attitudes in Atlantic City next month," he went on. The Democratic National Convention opens there Aug. 24.

Although he declined explicitly to endorse Mr. Goldwater, it seemed unlikely that the Democrats could take a position satisfactory to Mr. Wallace.

"Whoever doesn't represent the South in this campaign will not be President," he declared. "So if [President Johnson] will not represent the South in his campaign, he will not be elected."

Denies Any Arrangement

The Governor then characterized the civil rights stand of the Johnson Administration as "this political gimmick on this matter of race."

Mr. Wallace denied that he or his staff had had any communication or had made any deals with the Goldwater forces. Mr. Wallace's position until today, however, had been that any Presidential candidate who expected his support or the support of the South would have to make clear his commitment to a number of specific conditions.

These included a coalition government concept under which Mr. Wallace, representing the dissident South, would have certain powers of review over such appointments as that of the Attorney General of the United States.

The Governor had also demanded, in a speech in Little Rock, Ark., last week, that "one of the commitments would be that crowd [of Negro civil rights leaders] never would set foot in the White House again."

There seemed to be no evidence that the white-supremacist Governor had made any headway with these overtures. He implied today that he was still interested in seeking concessions from both parties.

Miller's Words Quoted

Mr. Wallace's reply to a question today asking whether persons claiming to speak for him might have approached Mr. Goldwater's staff was this:

"I cannot say what people who say that they were my representatives have done."

The Montgomery Advertiser earlier this week quoted Representative William E. Miller of upstate New York, Mr. Goldwater's running mate, as having told James D. Martin, an Alabama Republican, that "your Governor Wallace is the key to Goldwater's election in November."

The 16 states in which Mr. Wallace was pledged to run are Alabama, Arkansas, Florida, Georgia, Louisiana, Mississippi, North Carolina, South Carolina, Illinois, Indiana, Kentucky, Missouri, New York, Tennessee, Virginia and Wisconsin.

Both the Gallup Poll and the Harris Survey estimated last week that Mr. Wallace's third-party candidacy would cut more deeply into potential Goldwater votes in the South than into the loyalist Democratic vote for President Johnson. The polls agreed that the loss would be about 7 per cent for Mr. Johnson and about 12 per cent for Mr. Goldwater.

The projected 12 per cent loss was considered a serious defection from Mr. Goldwater, whom the polls showed trailing Mr. Johnson.

Mr. Wallace had been virtually incommunicado in Alabama since last Thursday night. His office had turned away questions by saying that there would be no statement until today's television appearance. The Governor flew here this morning from Montgomery.

During this 48-hour period, immense pressures were reportedly being applied to encourage Mr. Wallace to drop out. They came from Southerners in both parties who believed that Mr. Goldwater had greater national popularity than Mr. Wallace and, accordingly, had a chance to do more than force a compromise on civil rights and states' rights.

Mr. Wallace indicated that he was less than enthralled with the Republican platform or the Republican candidate. There was "no need to say anything about civil rights" in the platform, he said. "They are guaranteed under the Constitution of the United States."

Moderate Republicans have condemned the party's civil rights plank as inadequate. It calls for "implementation" and "execution" of the Civil Rights Act of 1964. The moderates' fight to include the word "enforcement" was defeated.

Mr. Wallace said he would "actively speak wherever Americans in this country would like for me to speak." It was learned, however, that he had canceled a speech before the Houston Citizens Council on Tuesday and that he may cancel an appearance Friday in Chicago before the National Conservative Council.

Although he has stated them repeatedly, Mr. Wallace's comments today on many issues underlined the similarities of his attitudes with those of the Republicans and Mr. Goldwater.

He again denounced the Federal Court system, which he predicted "is going to be put in her place."

"You cannot even arrest a criminal in New York or any place else without the Federal Court system turning him loose on the public," Mr. Wallace said.

Last Thursday in San Francisco, Mr. Goldwater said that "a rapist" in New York "is probably going to get the Congressional Medal of Honor and be sent off scot free." The man in question has been indicted and is awaiting trial.

Mr. Wallace said he thought "the American people are sick and tired of columnists and TV dudes who get on the national networks and instead of reporting the news as it is, and shame the devil, which is what they are supposed to do, try to slant and distort and malign and brainwash this country."

July 20, 1964

GOLDWATER GETS BACKING IN SOUTH

By CLAUDE SITTON
Special to The New York Times

ATLANTA, Aug. 15—Three Southern Democratic Governors have disclosed that they now plan to support Senator Barry Goldwater, the Republican candidate, in the coming Presidential race.

The Governors, all of whom have defied the Federal Courts on the school desegregation issue, are Orval E. Faubus of Arkansas, George C. Wallace of Alabama, and Paul B. Johnson Jr. of Mississippi.

They made their intentions known, according to highly reliable sources, at a closed meeting yesterday in New Orleans with Govs. John J. McKeithen of Louisiana and Farris Bryant of Florida.

Governor Bryant and the Florida Congressional delegation have long since pledged their support to President Johnson, who will receive the Democratic nomination at that party's national convention in Atlantic City the week after next. Mr. Bryant left the meeting early.

Mr. McKeithen, host for what he had hoped would be a secret conference in Room 576 of the Roosevelt Hotel, told his guests he would not attend the national convention.

But he was reported to have said he did not intend to back Mr. Goldwater, chiefly because he thought the Republicans would lose.

If the three Governors go through with their plans, it is believed that Mr. Goldwater might drive a wedge through the once-solid South from the Missouri border to the Gulf of Mexico and pick up 22 elec-

...oral votes in the process.

Mississippi and Alabama already have been considered virtually certain to go Republican in November for the first time in a Presidential race since the Reconstruction Era.

Their Governors' endorsement of the Arizona conservative, whose views on civil rights and states' rights are highly popular among Deep South whites, could remove any doubt over the election's outcome in those states.

Mr. Faubus, who has always been viewed as a Democratic loyalist despite his opposition to the civil rights policies of the Eisenhower and Kennedy administrations, is considered capable of swinging Arkansas into either camp this year.

Mr. Faubus broke precedent in 1958 by winning a third two-year term as Governor a year after he called out National Guardsmen to block, temporarily, the Court-ordered desegregation of Central High School in Little Rock.

He recently won the Democratic nomination for a sixth term and must run in the general election against Winthrop Rockefeller, the Republican candidate, who is a brother of New York's Governor.

The reported intention of Mr. Faubus to back Mr. Goldwater may indicate that he feels that the Senator's support in Arkansas combined with the popularity of Mr. Rockefeller, a millionaire cattleman, could prove too great for even him to overcome.

Governor McKeithen, heir to one branch of the political organization founded by the late Senator Huey P. Long, of "Share-the-Wealth" fame, called the conference. He wanted to work out a solution to the political dilemma they all share as a result of the Presidential campaign.

He and the others are seeking to hold their state Democratic organizations together in the face of the pro-Goldwater sentiment sweeping the strongly segregationist areas of the Deep South.

Their Congressional delegations have a crucial stake in the matter because Democratic disloyalty in response to pressure at home might cost them their committee chairmanships in Washington.

Other Southern Governors were asked to attend the conference to help establish a united front but spurned the invitation. It was learned, for example, that Governors Carl Sanders of Georgia and John B. Connally Jr. of Texas let it be known that they would hold a conference at the Democratic convention to work out "a responsible course."

Mr. McKeithen was said to have spent most of the time during the talks in an attempt to persuade Mr. Wallace to reactivate his third-party Presidential candidacy. But Mr. Wallace, who withdrew from the race suddenly, and with little explanation after Senator Goldwater's nomination, would not budge.

There have been recurring reports in Republican and Democratic circles in Alabama that Mr. Wallace has been assured that the South would hold a veto over the choice of an Attorney General under a Goldwater Administration.

A later report, given little credence outside Alabama but viewed seriously by some there, is that the Governor might receive that post.

But whatever considerations Mr. Wallace may have received in return for his agreement to pull out of the race, he was said to have made it unmistakably clear to the other Governors in New Orleans that he would not change that decision.

Mr. McKeithen reportedly felt that a Wallace candidacy would have split the segregationist vote in Louisiana and assured a Johnson victory there without open participation by the McKeithen forces.

The Governor, who is considered to favor Mr. Johnson personally, discounted the Goldwater threat at a Democratic dinner attended by Luther H. Hodges, the Secretary of Commerce, in New Orleans before the Republican National Convention.

But a friend of the Governor said the reaction in northern Louisiana to Mr. Goldwater's refusal at San Francisco to repudiate the Ku Klux Klan and the John Birch Society had forced him over to the defensive.

On the other hand, the Governor and his aides are concerned over the effects a Republican victory in Louisiana might have on the willingness of the Johnson Administration to settle the Federal-state tidelands oil dispute.

Some $600 million in lease fees now held in escrow pending an agreement over ownership of the highly productive oil fields off the mouth of the Mississippi River are involved.

The McKeithen forces also have come under the fire of the Long faction headed by Senator Russell Long, son of the organization's founder and a loyal Democrat.

The Senator is reportedly angry because the Governor's supporters helped to defeat Representative Gillis Long, the Senator's distant cousin and political protégé, in the recent Democratic Congressional primary.

The result of this dilemma, according to an intimate of the Governor, is that "John's dying a thousand deaths."

August 16, 1964

Mississippi Factions Clash Before Convention Panel

By E. W. KENWORTHY
Special to The New York Times

ATLANTIC CITY, Aug. 22—The Credentials Committee of the Democratic National Committee listened today with rapt attention to an emotion-laden confrontation between the regular delegation of the State of Mississippi and the challenging biracial delegation of the Freedom Democratic party.

The committee postponed decisions on the Mississippi contest and a challenge to the Alabama delegation until tomorrow afternoon.

A reason for the postponement was that David L. Lawrence, former Pennsylvania Governor, who is chairman of the committee, was trying to work out a formula to avoid a bruising floor battle in front of the television cameras. The chances for such a compromise were believed to be fairly good tonight.

The Freedom party contests the right of the regular delegation to represent Mississippi Democrats on the ground that

Negroes were systematically denied the right to take part in the process of selecting delegates from precinct meetings to the state convention.

Traditional Support Cited

It was an emotional session. Witnesses for the Freedom party, led by its chairman, Aaron Henry of Clarksdale, told in quiet voices of the brutality and terror they said they had experienced while trying to register and vote.

The chief spokesman for the regulars, State Senator E. K. Collins of Laurel, defended the right of his all-white delegation to be seated with an argument that relied heavily on the overwhelming support traditionally given the Democratic party in Mississippi.

Then, toward the end, the counsel for the Freedom party,

Joseph L. Rauh Jr. of Washington, told the Credentials Committee that its decision on the seating challenge would determine the course of society in Mississippi.

"If the Freedom party is once seated, Mississippi will change," Mr. Rauh said. "The regulars come here and sweet-talk you to keep the Freedom party from the seats, because if they get the seats they'll go back and build a new Mississippi that the Democratic party will be proud of."

Mr. Rauh read some bitter comments from leading Mississippi politicians on President Johnson and the national Democratic party. "Is this what we are going to approve here?" he asked.

In contrast, Mr. Rauh said, he had received his loudest applause in a speech to the Freedom party convention when he had spoken of supporting President Johnson.

"Are you going to throw out of here the people who want to work for Lyndon Johnson, who are willing to be beaten and shot and thrown in jail to work for Lyndon Johnson?" he asked in a dramatic voice. "Are we for the oppressor or the oppressed?"

Mr. Rauh predicted that the Mississippi Democratic convention would come out for Senator Barry Goldwater, the Re-

publican nominee, next month.

Mr. Collins indicated that he could not predict what the party in Mississippi would do. He pledged that he himself would support the national ticket.

Mr. Collins, who is the new national committeeman from Mississippi, said the regular delegates had agreed on a statement expressing the "hope" that the choice of a ticket and platform would "allow" them to support the national campaign.

He denied that Negroes had difficulty voting in Mississippi. He said they were "absolutely free" to participate in the state Democratic affairs, including the selection of national convention delegates.

"Categorically I assure you that Negroes did attend precinct meetings," Mr. Collins said.

Nominees on Ballot

He said further that the Democratic party in Mississippi had met one of the requirements in the Call for the Convention by guaranteeing that the party's nominees for President and Vice President would be placed on the ballot under the party symbol.

"The citizens of Mississippi will have a chance to vote for them," he declared.

Another contest, involving the Alabama delegation, was brought before the Credentials Committee.

Richmond Flowers, the Alabama Attorney General, readily conceded that Alabama electors for President next November would have to run "unpledged" because of a law passed by the Legislature at the insistence of Gov. George C. Wallace.

At one point Mr. Flowers said:

"The electors will run under the rooster [the Democratic symbol]. They could vote for Johnson. I don't think they would unless instructed by Governor Wallace."

At another point he said:

"Some said they would like to support Johnson. They are not pledged to vote against anyone. They will not support a Republican. They are pledged to vote for a Democrat [under the statute]."

Providing that the members of the regular Mississippi delegation give satisfactory assurances of their own loyalty, it is believed a formula can be devised to avoid an open floor fight like the one in 1948, when all of the Mississippi delegation and half of the Alabama delegation walked out to protest a civil rights plank.

These are the main provisions of the formula under discussion:

First, the regular Mississippi delegation would be accredited, but the Freedom party delegates would be given seats on the floor.

Second, there would be a statement commending the Freedom party for its efforts to break down the racial barriers in the Democratic party in Mississippi.

Third, guidelines would be drawn up for changing the convention rules to make clear that, in the future, deliberate discrimination in party affairs would be a basis for challenging the acceptability of a delegation.

It was not clear tonight, however, whether it would be possible to seat the Alabama delegation while state law prohibits the party's Presidential

nominee on the ballot.

In the public session held in the ballroom of Convention Hall, the drama was provided by the testimony of witnesses for the Freedom party.

Each side was allowed one hour to present its case.

Mr. Rauh concentrated on drawing a picture of Mississippi society and the actions of its officials in preventing the registration and voting of Negroes.

He called up a stream of witnesses ranging from the wife of a Negro sharecropper, who told a story of how she had been jailed and beaten for attempting to register Negroes, to the Rev. Dr. Martin Luther King Jr.

Dr. King said that no state in the union had gone to "such extremes" as Mississippi to prevent Negro participation in political life.

Turning to the Freedom delegation, which is made up largely of Negroes, he said:

"You cannot imagine the anguish and suffering they have gone through to get to this point."

What, he asked, was the alternative for the Negro — the regular democracy in Mississippi?

"This is the party which allows an atmosphere of violence and lawlessness," he said.

"If you value your party, if you value your nation, if you value the democratic process," Dr. King cried, "you must recognize the Freedom party delegation."

The wife of the sharecropper, Mrs. Fannie Lou Hamer of Rulesville, said that after she had led a group of 26 Negroes to register, the "plantation owner" had said to her:

"If you don't go down and withdraw your registration, you will have to go."

Describes Beating

She told how, on a later occasion, she and others who were engaged in the registration campaign were arrested, jailed

and beaten.

One officer, she related, said to her, "You're going to wish you was dead."

She was ordered to lie down on a bunk bed, she said, and two Negro men were ordered to beat her with blackjacks.

"Is this America, the land of the free and the home of the brave," she concluded, "where we are threatened daily because we want to live as decent human beings?"

Mrs. Rita Schwerner, wife of one of three civil rights workers murdered near Philadelphia, Miss., told briefly how she and her husband had been threatened.

Mrs. Schwerner, a slight woman with a pale, drawn face under black hair, said she had tried several times to see Gov. Paul B. Johnson Jr. after her husband's murder but was told "the Governor is unavailable."

"The State of Mississippi and the County of Neshoba have not even sent me a copy of the death certificate," she said.

The Rev. Edwin King, who is the white chaplain at Tougaloo College, said that, because of his activities on behalf of Negroes, "I have been imprisoned, I have been beaten, I have been close to death."

"The Freedom party is an open party," he said. "They [the regulars] are a closed party of a closed society."

At this point, Mr. Lawrence suggested that the witnesses for the Freedom party confine themselves to the legal issue before the committee and not expatiate on "the general subject of general life in Mississippi."

Mr. Rauh demurred, saying that the testimony of what life was like there was pertinent to the point that the Negro was deprived of participation in the Democratic party.

Mr. Collins, in reply, said he had not come here "to malign anyone." The delegation was "the creation of the Legislature and the party," he went on, and

the committee did not have "the right to invalidate the statutes of the State of Mississippi."

An assistant attorney general of Mississippi, Rubel Griffin, argued that the Freedom party was disqualified because it had not followed the laws of the state in founding the party and because it had no proof that it really was a representative party.

"These people represent no one," Mr. Griffin said.

Emotion Decried

"Do not kill our party," he concluded. "You will kill it if you do not seat the lawful delegation from Mississippi."

Mr. Collins, in his final argument, said there was "not one scintilla of evidence—only emotion—to refuse to seat the delegates sent here by Mississippi."

Meanwhile, Mr. Henry indicated that he might be willing to settle for some formula such as the committee staff had been working on. In response to a question, he said:

"We would like some formula so that all Democrats could work together."

The committee, however, faced great difficulty in devising a way to seat the Alabama delegation without violating convention rules.

Mr. Flowers, the Alabama attorney general, was asked three questions by Harold Lebenthal, the counsel to the Democratic National Committee. They were:

Will there be a place on the ballot for electors pledged to the party's nominees?

What opportunity will the voters have to vote for the convention nominees?

Can the delegates give assurance that they will support the nominees and that, if unpledged electors are chosen, they will use all "honorable means" to persuade these electors to vote for the nominees?

Mr. Flowers did not answer any of these questions.

August 23, 1964

MISSISSIPPI DELEGATES WITHDRAW, REJECTING A SEATING COMPROMISE; CONVENTION THEN APPROVES PLAN

SCUFFLE ON FLOOR

By TOM WICKER

Special to The New York Times

ATLANTIC CITY, Aug. 25— The Mississippi delegation withdrew from the 34th Democratic National Convention tonight, shattering President Johnson's effort to impose complete harmony upon his party.

Shortly after convening at 8:43 P.M., the convention overwhelmingly approved a compromise that would permit the seating of an all-white Mississippi delegation plus two members of a competing, integrated delegation from that state.

The all-white delegation had already voted to reject the compromise and bolt the convention. Only three of its members signed a required assurance of

loyalty to the party and took their seats on the floor.

[In Jackson, Gov. Paul B. Johnson Jr. said that "Mississippi's debt to the national Democratic party is now paid in full." He added that Mississippi's Democrats were now "absolutely free to take such action as we feel to be in the best interest of our state, of our nation and of our people."]

The integrated Freedom Democratic party also rejected the compromise. But the two designated members, Aaron Henry, a Negro, and the Rev. Edwin King, a white, took seats as "delegates at large." They sat with the Alaska delegation.

All told, in tonight's session, the 1964 platform was read and adopted, the permanent chairman, John W. McCormack of Massachusetts, took over the gavel and the stage was set for the nomination tomorrow night of President Johnson and his chosen running mate. But it was the seating dispute that enlivened the evening.

The three members of the Mississippi delegation who took their seats on the floor—Douglas C. Wynn of Greenville, Judge C. R. Holladay of Picayune and Fred Berger of

Natchez—did not remain for long. They left the hall after a scuffle.

About a score of the Freedom Democrats moved into the hall shortly after the Credentials Committee's report was approved and occupied seats in the Mississippi section. Two sergeants-at-arms ordered the unaccredited Freedom party members to leave, but they refused.

Finally one was ejected but the others were allowed to remain, although without official status as Mississippi delegates.

As a crush of reporters and photographers gathered, the three "loyalists" left, even though one of them had said earlier that their purpose was "to keep an unlawfully constituted delegation from having any claim to the seats."

The struggle for the Mississippi seats, heated at times, occupied the attention of most of the delegates throughout a long reading of the platform by a team of Democratic Congressional candidates.

By the time the reading came to an end and the platform was adopted, the galleries were virtually empty and not more than half of the delegates were in their seats. The convention was then adjourned, at 11:59 P. M., until tomorrow.

Approval of the seating compromise came on a voice vote. There was a shout of "no" from the section of the floor where Alabama is seated and from adjacent galleries, but Senator John O. Pastore, the temporary chairman, did not hesitate in ruling that "the ayes appear to have it, the ayes do have it."

Adoption of the compromise apparently ended the Mississippi fight, which had at one time raised the threat of a walkout by other Southern delegations or a divisive floor debate.

A subcommittee of the Credentials Committee worked out the arrangement. Senator Hubert H. Humphrey of Minnesota, the man most delegates believe will be chosen to run for Vice President, was given substantial credit for it.

His chief rival for the Vice-Presidency was still believed to be Senator Eugene J. McCarthy of Minnesota. But President Johnson, who will decide the question, maintained his long silence.

The generally successful handling of the Mississippi seating dispute appeared to many delegates to have enhanced Senator Humphrey's chances.

He worked closely with the White House and with the Credentials Committee in the matter, and the compromise was arranged at a meeting in his hotel suite this morning.

No sooner had the compromise formula been announced

by the committee chairman, former Gov. David L. Lawrence of Pennsylvania, than the Freedom Democrats voted to reject it.

When Mississippi followed with its vote to bolt the convention rather than acquiesce in the compromise, the prospect of a floor fight and a larger walkout arose again.

But Arkansas, counted on by the all-white Mississippians for support, voted to back the compromise. Tom Harper, the Arkansas chairman, said it was the best the Southern delegations could hope to gain.

J. Marshall Brown, Louisiana's Democratic national committeeman, said his delegation would vote against the compromise. But there was no suggestion of a Louisiana walkout in support of Mississippi.

On the other side of the question, the Freedom Democrats found themselves with little support for further demands on the convention.

Even their attorney, Joseph Rauh of Washington, called the compromise a significant gain for them and indicated it represented more than they had hoped initially to achieve.

Mr. Lawrence called the decision a "turning point" in the history of the Democratic party, which for most of its history has been profoundly influenced by all-white delegations from the Southern states.

But tonight the delegations from those states, following the reasoning of Mr. Harper of Arkansas, apparently felt that the formula by which the Mississippi regulars could take the loyalty pledge and be seated was as much as the reduced Southern power could command in this convention.

Speech by McCormack

With the seating dispute out of the way, the second session of the convention proceeded through a resounding speech by Mr. McCormack, who is Speaker of the House, and the adoption of a platform that had been written with few of the usual Democratic squabbles.

Senator Birch Bayh of Indiana then compared the platform with the Republican document enacted at the San Francisco convention six weeks ago. He found the Democratic platform superior down to the last whereas.

Tomorrow night, the Democrats will get their real business done—the formal nomination of President Johnson to run again, and the ratification of his choice for Vice President.

It was generally expected that Mr. Johnson would go on television following his nomination tomorrow and disclose the identity of his running mate.

Mr. McCormack, an orator of the old school, roused the Democrats repeatedly, even some of those who jammed the aisles and wandered aimlessly in the hall. He evoked one ovation with a tribute to John F. Kennedy.

His speech, however, was primarily another assault on Senator Barry Goldwater, whom he called "a trigger-happy, impulsive" candidate.

"A small band of extremists has captured the Republican party," Mr. McCormack roared.

Mr. McCormack evoked another cheer by welcoming reporters to this convention, and by praising a free press. Hostility to the press was repeatedly expressed at the Republican convention.

The major development of the day, however, was the precarious settlement of the Mississippi seating dispute with the minimum of disharmony.

Scarcely a Democrat in the hall expected that the party would carry that state next fall anyway. Thus the bolt of most of the Mississippi delegates was considered a small loss.

In addition to the seating provisions, the compromise provided that the call for the Convention in 1968 was to include language that would insure nondiscriminatory selection of delegates, and a place for Democratic electors on the ballots of each state.

A special committee was to be appointed to help state parties qualify under this call.

The loyalty pledge, or "assurance," read as follows:

"We, the undersigned members of the Mississippi delegation to the 1964 Democratic National Convention hereby each formally assure the convention of our intention to support the convention's nominees in the forthcoming general election."

Jack H. Pittman, a Hattiesburg, Miss., lawyer, read a statement explaining the Mississippi decision to bolt rather than subscribe to this statement.

He called it a "blind oath," and said the Freedom Democratic party was "an outside pressure group, which represents no one but itself."

"The Mississippi Democratic delegation did not leave the National Democratic party," Mr. Pittman said. "It left us."

A parallel case, that of the Alabama delegation, continued to offer the convention managers a problem.

Most of the Alabama delegates were in their seats tonight, although only 13 of them have signed a loyalty oath imposed on the delegation. This was the result of a law passed by their Legislature that will prevent pledged Democratic electors from appearing on the Alabama ballot.

Under the credentials rulings of the convention, only the 13 who signed the pledge are entitled to seats. No effort was made to eject the others, however.

The issue will culminate tomorrow night if the Alabamians seek to vote on the first convention roll-call. Only the 13 signers will be entitled to do so.

August 26, 1964

DEMOCRATIC TICKET: JOHNSON AND HUMPHREY; BOTH NOMINATED BY ROARING ACCLAMATION; PRESIDENT AT SCENE, BREAKING A TRADITION

JOYOUS WELCOME

Hall Erupts in Sound as Suspense Over Ticket Is Ended

By TOM WICKER
Special to The New York Times

ATLANTIC CITY, Thursday, Aug. 27—Lyndon Baines Johnson of Texas, the man who took over the Presidency last Nov. 22 in the shattering hour of John F. Kennedy's assassination, was nominated for a term of his own last night by the 34th Democratic National Convention.

Then Mr. Johnson did what he loves to do. He smashed precedent by going before a turbulent and happy gathering of more than 5,000 delegates and alternates to name Senator Hubert H. Humphrey of Minnesota as his choice for the Vice-Presidential nomination.

The happy Democrats, and thousands of spectators jammed into Convention Hall, cheered wildly for both Mr. Johnson and Mr. Humphrey.

Speech Put Off

Late in the program, after Senator Humphrey had been nominated by acclamation, it was announced that he would put off his acceptance speech until tonight. The convention then adjourned, at 12:37 A.M.

After lingering for an hour and chatting with the Texas delegation, the President finally left for Washington.

The President's nomination was also by acclamation. The motion to suspend the rules and dispense with the call of the states was offered by Mrs. Lloyd Danzig of Florida. It came after the remnants of the Alabama delegation yielded to Texas, so that Gov. John B. Connally Jr. could place the Johnson name in nomination.

It also was Governor Connally who nominated Mr. Johnson in his first abortive bid for the Presidency, at the Chicago convention in 1956.

Gov. Edmund G. Brown of California shared the nominating process, and was followed by seven seconding speakers.

Roared Into Effect

The delegates whooped the nomination into effect with a roar. Speaker of the House John W. McCormack of Massachusetts, the permanent chairman, confirmed it with a bang of his huge gavel.

The nomination set off an enthusiastic demonstration. All over the hall banners waved, balloons soared toward the lofty curved ceiling, bands played in an ear-splitting cacophony, the great organ bellowed and men struggled through the jammed aisles, screaming at the top of their lungs.

When it was quieted with much gaveling, Mr. Johnson came to the platform and set off another booming demonstration.

He stood quietly through it, smiling, waving and nodding once or twice to friends. His wife and two daughters stood with him through the thunderous ovation.

As if to symbolize his grip on this convention, Mr. Johnson himself gaveled the delegates to order.

In his opening greeting, he included a friendly salutation to "columnists and commentators." That brought a laugh, in recollection of the Republican's anger at the press at their convention in San Francisco.

Mr. Johnson also asked with a smile: "Did we really need all of these lights on?" That recalled his economy drive which included darkening many lights in the White House.

He said he and his party would begin tonight "the march toward an overwhelming victory for our party and for our nation."

Then he paid high tribute to President Kennedy, to the platform the Democrats had written under his close direction, and to the officers and delegates of the convention. He said the Credentials Committee had found a "fair answer" to the thorny Mississippi and Alabama seating disputes.

Then Mr. Johnson reached what he said was his "obligation under a very old American tradition," the recommendation of a Vice-Presidential candidate.

Mr. Johnson said he could make such a recommendation after his wide consultations with other Democrats and after "long prayerful consideration and private thought."

His "single guide," he said, had been "to find a man best qualified to assume the office of President of the United States should that day come."

Tested in Politics

The man he had found, he continued, had been tested in politics, had had long experience in public life and knew the problems of both the world and the nation.

"This is not a sectional choice," Mr. Johnson said. "This is not merely a way to balance the ticket. This is simply the best man in America for the job."

Stretching the suspense as far as it would go, the President held the name in reserve to the end. His man, he said, would make the Vice-Presidency an "important instrument of the executive" and help "carry America around the world."

His confidence in his choice, Mr. Johnson said, was not his alone but "represents the opinion of the great majority in the Democratic Party."

As if sorry to share his secret, Mr. Johnson said slowly:

"I hope that you will choose as the next Vice President of the United States my long . . . my longtime . . . " At this point laughter broke out in the hall at the lengths to which the President was carrying the suspense. " . . . My trusted colleague . . . Senator Hubert Humphrey of Minnesota!"

The name of the state was drowned in a mighty roar. As the delegates and spectators loosed their enthusiasm and vocal chords again, Senator and Mrs. Humphrey and their children came forward to join the Johnson family. Other Democrats joined the throng while the demonstration roared on.

During the demonstration that followed Mr. Johnson's nomination, his wife and two daughters, Lynda Bird and Luci Baines, sat in a special box high above the uproar. They received an ovation of their own when they appeared in the hall just before Mr. McCormack convened the session.

Late in the evening, Mrs. Humphrey joined them and also received the tribute of the crowd.

As Governor Brown was speaking, Mr. Johnson landed at the Atlantic City airport and took off by helicopter for the convention site. He reached Convention Hall about 9:30 P. M.

After climbing out of the helicopter near Convention Hall, Mr. Johnson held an impromptu news conference devoted mostly to his selection of Senator Humphrey. He said he had considered many men but "I think I've picked the best one."

He disclosed that he had invited Senator Humphrey and the Senator's wife, Muriel, to the Johnson ranch this weekend. There, he said, "under the shade of the live oak tree on the banks of the Pedernales," they would make their campaign plans.

Demonstration Under Way

Then Mr. Johnson went to a motel near the convention hall, where by then the demonstration was in progress.

He had come to settle once and for all the question that had agitated the Democratic party for months and that had provided most of the suspense at this convention. That question—Mr. Johnson's choice of a running mate—remained open all day as the President almost playfully kept up the game he seemed to be playing.

All day long yesterday, Mr. Johnson popped in and out of the White House to drop hints, spar with reporters and, moving through the chaotic situation like a broken-field runner, generally confuse the issue.

Late in the afternoon, however, after conferences with Senator Humphrey and Senator Thomas J. Dodd of Connecticut, he announced he would fly here and make a recommendation that would represent an "overwhelming consensus" of the delegates.

For several hours, Mr. Johnson refused to make his choice public. At about the time the convention session got under way, at 8:30 P. M., he disclosed it to reporters.

Many delegates did not get the official word, however, until Mr. Johnson himself gave it to them.

By then, however, Senator Humphrey had been informed of his selection and was merely helping Mr. Johnson keep the secret a few more hours.

Yesterday morning the man who had been considered the leading alternative—the junior Senator from Minnesota, Eugene J. McCarthy—had made public a wire he had sent to the President, urging the selection of Senator Humphrey.

It was Senator McCarthy who placed Senator Humphrey in nomination. Senator McCarthy took the rostrum after Alabama caused a brief flurry by placing in nomination the name of Gov. Carl E. Sanders of Georgia.

Governor Sanders hurried to the microphone to say that Mr. Johnson, "our great leader, knows who is best and who is qualified." Therefore, would Alabama please withdraw his name?

Alabama did so and yielded to Minnesota so Mr. Mc-

Carthy could nominate Senator Humphrey.

President Johnson retired to a special box with his wife and daughters and watched the seconding speakers parade to the platform to speak for Senator Humphrey.

Senator Humphrey, the assistant Democratic leader in the Senate, is a 53-year-old liberal with a long record of party service in Minnesota and nationally. He sought the Presidential nomination in 1960, but dropped out of the race after being defeated by John F. Kennedy in the West Virginia Democratic primary.

In 1956 he was a leading contender for the Vice-Presidency, but lost out to Senator Estes Kefauver of Tennessee.

As early as 1948 he was a major party figure. In that year, as Mayor of Minneapolis, he was instrumental in the liberal effort for a strong civil rights stand that caused Southern delegations to walk out of the Democratic convention at Philadelphia.

As a Senator, Mr. Humphrey has gained wide acceptance among Southern Congressional leaders and other moderate and conservative elements of the Democratic party.

He was the leader of the fight in the Senate this year for the civil rights bill, yet was able to play a peacemaking role at this convention between the Southern delegations and the liberal Northern delegates.

He is a colorful and tireless campaigner who will bring strength to the Johnson ticket in the Midwest and the Northeast, and among liberals, intellectuals and labor forces.

In addition, the Senator is widely experienced in both domestic and foreign affairs, having served for years as a member of the Senate Foreign Relations Committee.

Thus, he has been regarded from the start as one of those most capable of assuming the Presidency in the event of Mr. Johnson's death or incapacity.

Mr. Johnson, who is 56 years old today, became the first resident of a Southern state to run for President on the Democratic ticket since James K. Polk of Tennessee in 1844.

His nomination brought to a peak nine months of political drama and furious personal activity in which he took total control of the Democratic party, imposed his own style and manner on the Presidency and the Administration, and marked himself as one of the most assertive Presidents in history.

Not for a moment in those nine months was there a suggestion that the party might turn to someone else for its Presidential nominee.

Beyond that point, however, Mr. Johnson established a remarkable degree of personal sovereignty in the party, particularly for a man who had languished in the obscurity of the Vice-Presidency for nearly three years.

That sovereignty was notable

Associated Press Wirephoto

NOMINEE PRESENTS RUNNING MATE: President Johnson as he introduced Senator Hubert H. Humphrey to the Democratic convention. Mrs. Humphrey is at the left.

in the grip he kept on the convention, down to the details of its timing for television, and in the almost complete lack of any organized pressure upon him for any single Vice-Presidential possibility.

When Governor Connally rose to place Mr. Johnson in nomination, many in the great arena were given a poignant reminder of the man who had led the party until late last year. Governor Connally was riding in the same car with Mr. Kennedy in Dallas when an assassin shot and killed the President: the Governor was gravely wounded.

But this was Lyndon Johnson's night, and Governor Connally made the most of it for him.

In the sorrowful hour of Mr. Kennedy's death, he said, "under the calm, firm leadership of Lyndon Johnson, we learned gratefully that we could survive not only personal loss but national tragedy."

Mr. Johnson's record proved, Governor Connally continued, that "never in our history has any man come to the Presidency better prepared or tested for the supreme task of leadership."

The President, he said, is "a man with the steady hand of leadership to guide America and the world to new fulfillment of mankind's ageless dream."

Gibe at Goldwater

Governor Connally, a close friend of Mr. Johnson's and long his political associate, drove home one barb at Senator Barry Goldwater, the Republican nominee, whom the Democrats accuse of loose language.

"I am particularly proud that

we don't have to spend any time explaining to the American people just what [the President] means when he speaks," the Governor said. "When he speaks, it is the firm voice of common sense, the clear voice of reason, the calm voice of responsibility for this nation."

Governor Brown, serving as a conominator, piled praise even higher upon Mr. Johnson's shoulders.

He said the nine months of his Presidency had been "the most productive period of Government action since the first one hundred days of the New Deal," and he pointed to the tax reduction, the Civil Rights Act of 1964, and the antipoverty program as proof.

Governor Brown hailed the President for achieving budget reductions while still providing more money for schools, transit, roads and other programs.

But he reserved his greatest plaudits for what he called Mr. Johnson's "softspoken words of calm reason," which, in a difficult period, had "united and reassured people of every state and every section."

The Governor said that in the Gulf of Tonkin crisis, Mr. Johnson had given "a convincing demonstration that we are ready to meet any aggression."

Yet, he said, the President's record told "all mankind that we can trust him not to plunge this world into man's last war in panic or petulance."

At the conclusion of Governor Brown's speech, the great hall erupted with sound and color. For more than 20 minutes, the traditional demonstration

resounded through the arena.

Numerically, it may have been the biggest in history—this being the biggest party political convention ever held in America.

State standards, home-made placards, huge sunburst signs from California, tremendous cloth banners, waved above the heads of the sweating, screaming delegates. One home-made poster said: "We absolutely adore Lyndon."

Mrs. Johnson and her daughters waved and smiled through it all, occasionally throwing confetti on the heads of the masses below.

A California delegate banged two garbage-can lids together and a Midwestern delegation carried real cornstalks through the hall. The huge convention hall organ could be heard above it all, booming out "The Eyes of Texas" and "Happy Days Are Here Again."

Balloons rose to the ceiling—some of them six feet in diameter. Missouri mule standards lurched through the aisles.

Mr. Johnson's face, enormously magnified, gazed glumly on the scene from two photographs tall enough to mount the wall halfway to the ceiling.

Only reluctantly did the demonstrators return to their seats under Mr. McCormack's insistent gaveling.

The two Governors — the Democratic leaders of two major states that Senator Goldwater has high hopes of carrying this fall—were followed by seven seconding speakers.

They were Senator J. W. Fulbright of Arkansar, Govs. Harold E. Hughes of Iowa and Edward G. Breathitt Jr. of Kentucky, Mayors Wagner of New York and Richard J. Daley of Chicago, Senator Edmund S. Muskie of Maine and Mrs. Patricia Roberts Harris of Washington.

This group displayed again Mr. Johnson's affinity for "balancing" almost any group he appoints. He named a border state and a Midwestern Governor, and those are two areas he considers crucial to his election this fall.

Senator Fulbright, a Southerner, represented another region in which Mr. Johnson is anxious to run as strongly as possible.

The Mayors represented both the two largest Democratic strongholds and the Roman Catholics who supported the Democratic ticket so heavily in 1960. Mrs. Harris is a Negro, and Senator Muskie is of Polish extraction. The Democrats are counting on the votes of the Negroes and hoping to win the votes of Polish-Americans.

That Alabama yielded to Texas to make the nomination of Mr. Johnson reflected the fact that only "loyalist" Democrats from that state are officially seated here.

A dispute on the seating of the Alabama delegation resulted in a convention rule requiring the Alabamians to take a loyalty oath before being seated. Only nine of them were so qualified and seated last night.

At 6 P. M., sergeants-at-arms had occupied the Alabama seats and turned back the unpledged, unaccredited Alabamians who sought to take them.

Harry P. Clark of Mobile, one whom had refused the oath, tried to seize the delegation microphone but it was protected by a loyalist, Jack Sullivan, a former Secret Service agent.

Reuben Newton, a co-chairman of the loyalists, then was able to use it to yield to Texas for the Johnson nomination.

The loyalists later marched in the demonstration, carrying the Alabama standard.

Senator Muskie and Mayor Wagner had figured in Vice-Presidential speculation, but it had been apparent at this convention that they were not in the swiftly narrowing field being considered by Mr. Johnson for second place on the ticket.

The convention is scheduled to be concluded tonight, when Mr. Johnson comes here for his acceptance speech. There also will be a memorial film to President Kennedy.

Tomorrow Mr. Johnson will meet in Atlantic City with members of the Democratic National Committee, then fly to his LBJ Ranch near Austin, Tex., for a long weekend of rest and conversation with his new partner in politics.

August 27, 1964

BUSINESS LEADERS SUPPORT JOHNSON

Independent Committee Is Formed for Campaign

By FENDALL W. YERXA
Special to The New York Times

WASHINGTON, Sept. 3 — President Johnson's candidacy received the broad backing today of an influential group of the nation's business and financial leaders—three-fourth of them Republicans.

The support came at an organizational meeting in the White House of the National Independent Committee for President Johnson and Senator Humphrey.

The meeting with President Johnson was attended by 26 of the 45 men who have agreed to serve as sponsors. The membership includes two former members of Republican Cabinets as well as other members of Republican Administrations, and the heads of numerous large corporations.

Among them were Henry Ford 2d, chairman of the Ford Motor Company; Marion B. Folsom, former Secretary of Health, Education and Welfare; Robert B. Anderson, former Secretary of the Treasury; Edgar F. Kaiser, chairman, Kaiser Aluminum and Chemical Corporation; Thomas S. Lamont, New York financier, and Sidney J. Winberg, senior partner of Goldman, Sachs & Co.

The committee named as its co-chairmen John T. Connor, president of Merck & Co., who said he was an independent Democrat who "has voted for Republicans" in the past, and John L. Loeb, senior partner of Carl M. Loeb, Rhoades & Co., who said he was a "registered Republican."

Mr. Connor said after the meeting that the committee would not engage in criticism of the Republican ticket of Senator Barry Goldwater and Representative William E. Miller. Instead, he said, the "emphasis will be on the program of Johnson and Humphrey."

Mr. Connor mentioned several factors that had gone into shaping of the committee's stand. He said the group was in accordance with the procedures followed by President Johnson in the selection of his running mate. He said the committee felt the choice of Senator Humphrey gave President Johnson and the American people an "outstanding man" well qualified to succeed to the Presidency if necessary.

He said the programs followed by the Johnson Administration were beneficial "not only to the business community but to the nation as a whole," and that the prosperity of the country was due "in large measure" to these policies.

Mr. Connor declared that the committee found Mr. Johnson's foreign policies to be "firm and temperate." He said the members felt that continuity in management was wise and "conservative in the true sense" if that management was sound.

Headquarters in New York

Headquarters for the committee have been established at 99 Park Avenue in New York, Mr. Connor said, and they will be manned next week.

Henry H. Fowler, former Republican Under Secretary of the Treasury, and James H. Rowe Jr., a lawyer and confidant of President Johnson and other Democratic Presidents, are serving without membership on the committee as liaison officers between it and the White House.

Mr. Connor said an executive committee would be named and would meet early next week. The committee will consider measures for recruitment of additional members, and the raising of funds, for which no goals have been set.

President Johnson also met late today with Walter Carey, president of the United States Chamber of Commerce, and discussed with him, according to a White House spokesman, a broad range of subjects, including prices, wages and the economic outlook of the nation.

The full list of other members of the National Independent Committee follows. The official listing carried a disclaimer to the effect that the corporate and business affiliations carried no implication of their endorsement or participation.

Ford Bell, chairman, Red Owl Stores, Inc.; T. Roland Berner, chairman, Curtiss-Wright Corporation; William R. Biggs, chairman, Brookings Institute; Gordon Bilderback; Eugene R. Black, former president of the International Bank for Reconstruction and Development; Joseph L. Block, chairman, Inland Steel Company; Carter L. Burgess, chairman, American Machine and Foundry Company; Paul C. Cabot, chairman, State Street Investment Corporation of Boston; Thomas D. Cabot, chairman, Cabot Corporation of Boston; Peter Colefax, chairman, American Potash and Chemical Corporation; Donald C. Cook, president American Electric Power Company; Edgar M. Cullman, president, General Cigar Company, Inc.; Lewis W. Douglas, banker, former Congressman, ambassador and United States Budget Director; Marriner S. Eccles, chairman, Utah Construction and Mining Company.

Also, Ray R. Eppert, president, Burroughs Corporation; Samuel M. Fleming, president, Third National Bank of Nashville; William T. Gossett, Ford Motor Company executive; Walter A. Haas Jr., president, Levi Strauss & Co.; Ben W. Heineman, chairman, Chicago and Northwestern Railway Company; Harry B. Henshel, president, Bulova Watch Company; William A. Hewitt, president, Deere & Co.; George Killion, president, American President Lines, Ltd.; Mills B. Lane Jr., president, Citizens and Southern

National Bank; Ralph Lazarus, president, Federated Department Stores, Inc.; Brian P. Leeb; Robert Lehman, Lehman Bros.; Augustus C. Long, chairman, Texaco, Inc.

Also, John Mecom, Texas oil producer; Andre Meyer, partner, Lazard Freres & Co.; Arjay R. Miller, president, Ford Motor Company; Norton Simon, president, Hunt Foods and Indusries, Inc.; William C. Stolk, chairman, American Can Company; H. Gardiner Symonds, chairman, Tennessee Gas Transmission Company; S. Mark Taper, chairman, First Charter Financial Corporation; Charles B. Thornton, chairman, Litton Industries, Inc.; Charles A. Wellman, president, First Charter Financial Corporation; Fredric B. Whitman, president, Western Pacific Railroad.

Mitchell Shuns Goldwater

James P. Mitchell, a prominent Republican who served as Secretary of Labor under President Dwight D. Eisenhower, said last night he could not support the Goldwater-Miller ticket "under any circumstances."

He declined, however, to say that he would support the Democratic candidates, President Johnson and Senator Hubert H. Humphrey, declaring:

"As a private citizen, how I vote is something I have to wrestle with."

Mr. Mitchell made these statements in San Francisco in response to inquiries during a telephone interview. He was confirming statements that he was reported to have made to friends recently, including a reference to Mr. Goldwater's "defeat in November."

Mr. Mitchell, now a resident of Hillsborough, Calif., a suburb of San Francisco, is senior vice president and a director of the Crown Zellerbach Corporation, paper manufacturers. His office is in San Francisco.

September 4, 1964

THURMOND BREAK IS MADE OFFICIAL

He Will Work as Republican for Goldwater Election

By CLAUDE SITTON
Special to The New York Times

COLUMBIA, S. C., Sept. 16 —Senator Strom Thurmond confirmed tonight that he was bolting the Democratic party to work as a Republican for the election of Senator Barry Goldwater.

His break with the Democrats, the second for him in 16 years, was made public in a televised denunciation of that party and its leaders broadcast here and in seven other Southern states.

"The Democratic party has abandoned the people," he asserted. "It has repudiated the Constitution of the United States. It is leading the evolution of our nation to a socialistic dictatorship."

Senator Thurmond urged other Southerners to join him in a fight to elect Senator Goldwater and to make the Republican party 'a' party which supports freedom, justice and constitutional government."

Desk to Be Moved

In a news conference held at station WIS-TV following the taping of the 15-minute broadcast, the Senator said he had already asked that his Senate desk be moved to the Republican side of the aisle. He said he had made the request of Senator Everett McKinley Dirksen of Illinois, the minority leader.

Asked if he would lose the prerogatives of more than eight years' seniority in the Senate, he replied that this question would not come up until January, "but I think [the Republicans] will treat me right."

The Senator, who emerged from the studio with a gold elephant pin with black eyeglasses in his lapel, indicated that he might break his ties to the Republican party if he found its position too objectionable in the future.

"I've always been independent regardless of what party I've been in," he said. "I intend to maintain my independence."

Mr. Thurmond led South Carolina's delegation out of the 1948 Democratic National Convention at Philadelphia when he was Governor of the state. He later won South Carolina, Alabama, Mississippi and Louisiana as the States' Rights, or Dixiecrat, Presidential candidate against former President Harry S. Truman.

His latest departure from the Democratic fold may increase pressure on some other Southern political leaders to join him and Gov. Paul B. Johnson Jr. of Mississippi in the Goldwater camp. However, it is not expected to bring defections on the scale of those that took place 16 years ago.

Southern Republicans apparently see it as an opportunity to make political capital in the South. Newspaper advertisements calling attention to the Thurmond telecast tonight were paid for by the Republicans. It could not be learned immediately if the party also was financing the cost of the telecast in other states.

The Senator's announcement appeared to have been timed to coincide with Senator Goldwater's first campaign appearance in the state. Mr. Thurmond will introduce the Presidential candidate tomorrow for a speech at the Greenville-Spartanburg Airport.

May Campaign Outside

Senator Thurmond indicated this afternoon that he also might make future appearances in the Goldwater campaign outside the state.

The consensus among politicians and observers here was that the Thurmond withdrawal might endanger President Johnson's chances for carrying South Carolina. Many ques-

tioned, however, just how much of his following he could transfer to Senator Goldwater.

Olin D. Johnston, the state's senior Senator, Gov. Donald S. Russell and most other leading Democrats have endorsed the President and apparently will conduct a vigorous campaign in his behalf.

Mr. Thurmond conceded that he might lose his Senate seat in the 1966 election as a result of his action. But he said, "I can only follow the course which, in my heart and conscience, I believe to be in the best interest of our state, our country and the freedom of our people."

Welcomed by Miller
Special to The New York Times

DES MOINES, Sept. 16 — Representative William E. Miller today welcomed Senator Strom Thurmond "into the fold as a regular Republican if that's his intention."

The Republican Vice-Presidential candidate said that the former Democrat from South Carolina was "a fine American" and "is entitled to choose the ticket he wishes to support."

"I don't suppose anyone can say he's a member of the Ku Klux Klan or the Communist party," Mr. Miller declared. "I think he'll find a better home in the Republican party than he did in the Democratic party."

September 17, 1964

The Old Order Falling

South's Traditional Alliances Crumble, And a Two-Party System Takes Hold

By CLAUDE SITTON
Special to The New York Times

GREENVILLE, S. C., Sept. 17 —Senator Strom Thurmond's bolt from the Democratic party is not expected to change the outcome of the Presidential race here or elsewhere in the South.

This was the consensus among some Republican leaders and political observers who heard Mr. Thurmond introduce Senator Barry Goldwater today at the Republican candidate's first campaign appearance in this state. Most of the South Carolina voters who could be swayed by Senator Thurmond are thought to be Goldwater partisans already. Republican leaders think he will make his chief contribution in helping them to recruit campaign workers.

The significance of the Thurmond action appears to lie in the fact that it is symptomatic of the political crosscurrents generated by the contest between Mr. Goldwater and Presi-

News Analysis

dent Johnson, the Democratic nominee.

These forces now seem certain to bring the final emergence of a two-party system in the South this year no matter what the result of the election Nov. 3.

Divisions Likely to Remain

Even if President Johnson manages to hold a majority of the 128 electoral votes of the 11 Southern states for the Democrats, many students of the region's politics believe that deep divisions among voters will remain. Political forces being what they are, the old alliances that are being shattered now can never be restored.

There have been other defections to Mr. Goldwater's camp. C. C. Aycock, the Democratic Lieutenant Governor of Louisiana, has endorsed the Senator. Gov. Paul B. Johnson Jr. has declared that he and most other Mississippi Democrats will vote Republican.

Politicians are frequently followers rather than leaders of

public opinion, and this principle may apply here. J. Drake Edens, South Carolina's Republican chairman, said of Mr. Thurmond's switch:

"We had most of his supporters in the party already. He was just following his people."

Many of these new converts to Republicanism have long been Democrats in name only. Senator Thurmond, for example led a Democratic bolt in 1948 as the States' Rights, or Dixiecrat, Presidential candidate. He has given little evidence of having returned to the Democratic fold.

But the new willingness shown by Senator Thurmond and a large number of Southerners who do not hold public office to embrace the label as well as the conservative position of the Goldwater Republicans is significant. It reflects a polarization in Southern politics, with the two major parties exerting intense pressure on those in the middle to join one side or the other. It is this that sets 1964 apart from past Presidential-election years in the South.

The development is underscored by the failure of Gov. George C. Wallace of Alabama in his effort to construct a neo-Dixiecrat alliance behind his abortive Presidential candidacy. Mr. Wallace's failure was caused, at least in part, by the refusal of even the hard-core

third-party faction to go along after Senator Goldwater had won the Republican nomination.

The effects of the political polarization have been felt by Democratic leaders who have sought to shun involvement in the Presidential race. Dan K. Moore, the party's gubernatorial nominee in North Carolina, has come under increasing fire from ardent loyalists because of his refusal to assist in President Johnson's campaign.

An increasing number of Republican candidates for state and local office have further intensified the demand for party loyalty. Democratic officials who have become aware recently of the threat to their own positions are showing less tolerance for the maverick, thus forcing him to choose between supporting the party or joining the Republicans.

Arose During the War

The reason for the breakup of the one-party South is obvious. The disenchantment began during World War II when the Federal Government, under the Democrats, began efforts to improve the Negroes' lot. It increased even under the Republican Administration of President Eisenhower, as a result of the progressively stronger civil rights planks written into the Democratic Presidential platforms by Northern liberals.

President Kennedy, who did more than any of his predecessors to put these platform prin-

274

ciples into practice, proved to be more than many Southern white Democrats could take. The final impetus, if any were needed, was provided by President Johnson's support of the Civil Rights Act of 1964.

Civil rights is by no means the only issue today in the South, but it is generally agreed to be the most important one. From the standpoint of many Democratic whites, the position of Senator Goldwater on this issue is far more acceptable than that of President Johnson.

"The party of our fathers is dead," Senator Thurmond said in announcing his conversion to Goldwater Republicanism. What he meant, in part, was that the national Democratic party is no longer willing to give the South a relatively free hand in racial affairs in return for votes on election day.

In accepting these Democratic dissidents, the Republicans may find that they will inevitably be forced to accept some of their views as well.

September 18, 1964

GOLDWATER PUTS STRESS ON ETHICS

Shuns Orthodox Campaign to Call for a Reform in Life and Morals

By CHARLES MOHR
Special to The New York Times

PHOENIX, Ariz., Oct. 11— As Senator Barry Goldwater's campaign technique has become increasingly unusual, the reasons for the unusualness have become clearer.

In his third nationwide television appearance last Friday, Mr. Goldwater, the Republican Presidential candidate, talked about both issues and himself.

"You have probably been reading and hearing about some of the unorthodox things I have been doing," Mr. Goldwater said.

"I have gone into the heart of Appalachia, and there I have deliberately attacked the Administration's phony war on poverty."

He went on to recall how he had attacked proposals for Federal medical-care programs in Florida retirement country, the Tennessee Valley Authority in Tennessee and legislative reapportionment in urban areas.

Critical of 'Buying Votes'

"I have done all these things deliberately," he said, "for a reason that is clear in my own mind. I will not appeal to you as if you were simply pocketbooks surrounded on all sides by self-serving concerns."

He also defined political campaigning as "the science of buying votes."

He was referring to what he has called President Johnson's appeals to special interests.

Mr. Goldwater has increasingly shown that he is running for President far outside the boundaries of usual political activity in the United States.

He is not centering his arguments on the usual questions of governmental policy or expenditure for specific programs. Instead he is arguing to the voters that he will be able to reform American life and even morals.

Mr. Goldwater concedes that the nation is enjoying prosperity, and speaks instead of such issues as "the deterioration of the home, the family and the community, of law and order, of good morals and good manners."

He says that all of these things are in serious decline, and that this is "the result of 30 years of unhealthy social climate."

"I refer to the philosophy of modern 'liberalism,' the dominant philosophy of the opposition party," he said.

In speech after speech recently, Mr. Goldwater has shown that he does not want to change just laws, but to change American values as well.

He often concedes pessimism that his message will be heeded. He remarked:

"Many people are unwilling to admit they want a change. Do you remember when you were a child and crawled up in your mother's lap in a thunderstorm, needing reassurances that everything was all right? Many Americans today are reassuring one another that everything is all right by the oddly reverse method of insisting that there is no need for a change."

Thus, Mr. Goldwater, who elsewhere in his speech remarked that he was "against sin," does not always appear to be sure that being against sin is a popular idea.

As a result he has begun to scold the public in an aggressive way, as he did at Salt Lake City yesterday when he said that the American moral fiber is "beset with rot and decay."

To observers of Mr. Goldwater, this was not a surprise. The Arizona Senator appears to be a born pessimist as an election nears. In the last days before the New Hampshire Presidential primary last March he began to appear much the same way.

He would often say then that many people were more interested in the fast buck than in freedom. He told his audiences that many of the pioneer virtues of their forefathers had been lost.

And he often said, "I will only promise you one thing— not to make any promises."

It appeared to some observers then that he was warning the voters that they could vote against him if they liked, but that it would be a virtual admission of personal weakness on their part.

In recent days his campaign has been very similar.

He has scornfully dismissed political pledges of a better material life as not the proper issue of a Presidential campaign. Although many would disagree with him, he has argued that personal morals and even religious faith are the essential issues.

Mr. Goldwater, then, was quite serious when he asked:

"What place does politics have in a campaign for the Presidency?"

October 12, 1964

JOHNSON SWAMPS GOLDWATER

TURNOUT IS HEAVY

By TOM WICKER

Lyndon Baines Johnson of Texas compiled one of the greatest landslide victories in American history yesterday to win a four-year term of his own as the 36th President of the United States

Senator Hubert H. Humphrey of Minnesota, Mr. Johnson's running mate on the Democratic ticket, was carried into office as Vice President.

Mr. Johnson's triumph, giving him the "loud and clear" national mandate he had said he wanted, brought 44 states and the district of Columbia, with 486 electoral votes, into the Democratic column.

Senator Barry Goldwater, the Republican candidate, who sought to offer the people "a choice, not an echo" with a strongly conservative campaign, won only five states in the Deep South and gained a narrow victory in his home state of Arizona. Carrying it gave him a total of 52 electoral votes.

Senator Plans Statement

A heavy voter turnout favored the more numerous Democrats.

In Austin, Tex., Mr. Johnson appeared in the Municipal Auditorium to say that his victory was "a tribute to men and women of all parties."

"It is a mandate for unity, for a Government that serves no special interest," he said.

The election meant, he said, that "our nation should forget our petty differences and stand united before all the world."

Mr. Goldwater did not concede. A spokesman announced that the Senator would make no statement until 10 A.M. today in Phoenix.

But the totals were not the

only marks of the massive Democratic victory. Traditionally Republican states were bowled over like tenpins—Vermont, Indiana, Kansas, Nebraska, Wyoming, among others.

In New York, both houses of the Legislature were headed for Democratic control for the first time in years. Heralded Republicans like Charles H. Percy, the gubernatorial candidate in Illinois, went down to defeat.

Former Attorney General Robert F. Kennedy, riding Mr. Johnson's long coattails, overwhelmed Senator Kenneth B. Keating in New York.

But ticket splitting was widespread. And in the South, Georgia went Republican; never in its history had it done so. Into the Goldwater column, too, went Mississippi, Alabama, Louisiana and South Carolina—all part of the once solidly Democratic South.

But Mr. Johnson carried the rest of the South, including Virginia, Tennessee and Florida—states that went Republican in 1960. He carried his home state of Texas by a large margin and won a majority of the popular vote in the Old Confederacy.

Nationwide, the President's popular vote margin apparently would reach 60 per cent or more. His popular vote plurality had risen early this morning to more than 13 million.

The President was clearly carrying into office with him a heavily Democratic Congress, with a substantially bigger majority in the House.

The vote poured in, through the high-speed counting system of the Network Election Service, at such a rate that the leading television broadcasters were calling it a Johnson victory about 9 P.M.

But the only time the Republican candidate ever was in front was early yesterday morning when Dixville Notch, N. H., traditionally the earliest-reporting precinct in the nation, gave him eight votes to none for Mr. Johnson.

After that, in the President's own slogan, it was "L.B.J. all the way."

Election analysts thought that would be the case when the first significant returns came in from rural Kansas, where partial counts of incomplete boxes are allowed. They showed Mr. Johnson running strongly in this traditionally Republican territory.

Their early judgments were strengthened when the President swept early-reporting Kentucky, an important border state that had not gone Democratic in a Presidential election since 1948, and rolled to victory in Indiana, a Republican stronghold since 1936.

Ohio, a state counted upon as a vital part of the Goldwater victory strategy, fell to the President next, with Mr. Johnson compiling a massive lead in populous Cuyahoga County

(Cleveland). One Negro precinct there went for the President by 99.9 per cent of its vote.

In sharp contrast, Mr. Johnson at one point in the evening was carrying only 8.9 per cent of the vote in Jackson, Miss., where his civil rights stand was unpopular. Mr. Goldwater compiled an overwhelming victory in that state, winning more than 80 per cent of its vote.

But as victory after victory rolled in for the President—all New England, the big Middle Atlantic states of New Jersey and Pennsylvania, Southern states like Texas, Tennessee, and North Carolina, the Western states of Oklahoma, Colorado and Kansas—Mr. Johnson's mounting total became a triumphant march across the nation.

There was nothing spotty or regional about it and long before midnight it was apparent that the President would have the "loud and clear" national mandate

It was one of the most significant victories in Presidential history. The Goldwater campaign had posed a sharp challenge to almost the entire trend of national policy, domestic and foreign, since the Great Depression and World War II.

What He Proposed

He had proposed a sharp curtailment of Federal Government activities, particularly in the welfare field and in matters affecting the economy. He had called for a foreign policy of "brinkmanship," in which the nation's military might would be used as a threat against the Communist-bloc nations.

And he had raised doubts whether he would continue to lend Federal influence and authority to the drive for Negro equality in the United States.

Mr. Johnson, in head-on conflict with Mr. Goldwater on almost every campaign issue, thus received decisive endorsement from the nation for the general line of policy pursued by the nation for more than a quarter-century, through Administrations of both parties.

For himself, he won the distinction of being the first candidate from a Southern state to be elected to the White House in more than a hundred years.

And he won a massive vote of approval for the manner in which he had conducted its business since taking over the Presidency when John F. Kennedy was assassinated last Nov. 22.

Rapid Moves Likely

On the impetus of his imposing victory, Mr. Johnson can be expected to move rapidly on a broad front in domestic policy, and to grapple with several serious foreign problems.

He has said that a program of medical care for the aged through the Social Security system will be his first priority in legislative matters. He has also pledged to seek a major education program and to extend his "war on poverty."

In international matters, Mr. Johnson must soon seek positive answers to the problems of establishing some form of international nuclear force that would include West Germany, of reorganizing the North Atlantic Treaty Organization and its forces, and of prosecuting the anti-Communist guerrilla warfare in South Vietnam.

Mr. Johnson voted this morning in Johnson City, Tex., the hill country town where he was born on Aug. 27, 1908, and near which is located his LBJ Ranch. He and Mrs. Johnson voted, like most of the rest of

the nation, for Lyndon B. Johnson.

Mr. Johnson's remarkable victory, carrying with it such traditional Republican states as Indiana, Vermont and Kansas, produced unusual examples of ticket-splitting. These testified to the inability of Mr. Goldwater to unify the Republican party behind his conservative program.

In Rhode Island, for instance, Mr. Johnson won a victory, taking almost 80 per cent of the vote. In the same state, voters re-elected Republican Gov. John Chafee, who had fought Mr. Goldwater's nomination, by about 59 per cent of the vote.

In Vermont, Senator Winston Prouty, a moderate Republican, survived the Johnson tide. But the President's sweeping victory in Ohio endangered the senatorial candidacy of Robert Taft Jr., a pre-election favorite, who was running neck and neck with Stephen M. Young, the Democratic incumbent.

Mr. Johnson's coattails were long for some underdog Democrats, notably Gov. Otto Kerner of Illinois, who was re-elected over Mr. Percy, a Republican newcomer who had looked to many in his party like future Presidential timber.

Mr. Johnson's great victory in New York also was a prime factor in the apparent victory of Mr. Kennedy over Senator Keating.

In Iowa, however, one Democrat outran Mr. Johnson—a rare event in yesterday's election. He was Gov. Harold E. Hughes, who took about 63 per cent of the vote to about 60 per cent for the President.

Mr. Johnson's victory was solidly based in the votes of almost all religious and ethnic

The New York Times

LYNDON BAINES JOHNSON   **HUBERT HORATIO HUMPHREY**

groups, all income classes, and in every section of the nation. Nor did the so-called "white backlash" against the Civil Rights Act of 1964 materialize to any serious extent.

The backlash was apparent among Polish steelworkers in Baltimore, but Mr. Johnson piled up a heavy vote elsewhere in Maryland to add that state to his total.

In the District of Columbia, with its big Negro population, the President won by about five to one in the first Presidential election ever held in the Federal city.

Paradoxes Noted

In Kentucky, where anti-Catholic voting contributed to John Kennedy's defeat there in 1960, Mr. Johnson ran in some areas as much as 15 per cent ahead of Mr. Kennedy's totals among white Protestant voters.

In New York, he was about five percentage points ahead of Mr. Kennedy's pace among Roman Catholic voters.

New York provided another paradox. Although there was evidence of a slump in Polish-American voting for Mr. Johnson in Maryland, Indiana, Ohio, and Illinois, that ethnic group gave both the President and Robert Kennedy a heavy proportion of its vote in New York.

Even more remarkable was the situation in the South. There, Mr. Johnson carried two states, Virginia and Tennessee, that had gone Republican in 1960, and was leading narrowly in another, Florida.

Mr. Goldwater carried South Carolina, which went Democratic in 1960, and was threatening in Georgia.

PU graf beginning . . . But it

But it was an election dotted with such paradoxes. In normally Republican Nebraska, for instance, Mr. Johnson and Democratic Gov. Frank Morrison were elected—but so was Republican Senator Roman Hruska. All three carried the population center of Lincoln by a wide margin.

The explanation for such unusual voter behavior lay in the nature of the Presidential contest.

The nation was voting at the end of one of the most unusual Presidential campaigns in its history. Some called it dull, some called it dirty, some called it unenlightening, but no one disputed that there had been few like it.

It was remarkable, first, in that no Vice President had ever succeeded to office so late in the term of his predecessor as Mr. Johnson did when he took over less than a year ago—Nov. 22, 1963. As a result, almost all of his time in office, following a political "moratorium" in memory of John F. Kennedy, was spent in an intensely political atmosphere.

The campaign was unusual, too, in that Mr. Johnson was the first resident of a Southern state to be nominated by a major party for the Presidency since Zachary Taylor of Louisiana ran on the Whig ticket in 1848 and James K. Polk of Tennessee was nominated by the Democrats in 1844.

President Taylor was both the last Southern resident elected President before today and the last successful Whig candidate.

Mr. Goldwater, the President's Republican opponent, was in many ways an even more unusual candidate. As an apostle of a conservatism that was virtually uncompromised throughout his year-long campaign, he was the most ideological and factional candidate of either major party since William Jennings Bryan ran on a free silver platform in 1896.

As the candidate of a faction that had captured the Republican party, rather than the overwhelming choice of that party's consensus, Mr. Goldwater suffered sharp defections that amounted almost to a party split.

Except for a conciliatory speech to a group of Republican leaders at Hershey, Pa., on Aug. 12, Mr. Goldwater made little effort to compromise with the more moderate and liberal sentiment in his party. In Republican National Headquarters and in many of the state parties, a "purge" of non-Goldwater men was carried out soon after his nomination in San Francisco on July 15.

Appeals to Republicans

As a result, many Republicans either withheld public support of the Goldwater-Miller ticket, or defected outright to the Democrats. Mr. Johnson and Mr. Humphrey carefully refrained from attacking the Republican party as such, termed Mr. Goldwater no more than its "temporary spokesman" and openly appealed for dissident Republicans to enter the Democratic coalition this year.

Thus, a Southern Democrat once considered too conservative to win the Democratic nomination, and a small-state conservative long believed to be an isolated figure in Republican politics, made the 1964 race—the 45th Presidential campaign in the nation's history.

Although Mr. Goldwater was the challenger, his outspoken conservatism and controversial views set the tone of the campaign and largely shaped the most hotly debated issues. Most analysts and poll-takers came to believe that the central question of the campaign was not Mr. Johnson and the record of his Administration but Mr. Goldwater and the radical departures he proposed in both domestic and foreign policy.

There were few substantive exchanges between the candidates until after the nomination of Mr. Johnson and Mr. Humphrey at Atlantic City on Aug. 26. On Aug. 18, the United States Senate, with the acquiescence of the President, killed a bill that would have suspended the equal-time provision of the law governing broadcasting, and that ended all chance of an actual face-to-face debate between Mr. Goldwater and Mr. Johnson.

Nevertheless, as the campaign developed through the fall months, with both men and their running mates criss-crossing the nation and appearing frequently on television, a dialogue did develop between them on several questions, including the following:

CENTRALIZED GOVERNMENT

Mr. Goldwater contended that since 1933, the Federal Government had absorbed more and more power from the states and localities, and that within the Government itself, the executive branch and the Supreme Court had progressively usurped powers that more properly resided in Congress or with the states.

He pledged, however, that he would move slowly in terminating Federal programs and that he would honor both actual and implied commitments between the Government and the people.

Mr. Johnson vigorously defended the Federal Government as the instrument of all the people, pointed frequently to Federal programs in the welfare, conservation, medical and other fields, denied that a strong central government was a threat to the liberties of the people, and accused Mr. Goldwater of running "against the Presidency" instead of for it.

NUCLEAR WEAPONS

Mr. Goldwater argued on several fronts. He said the Administration's reliance on missiles instead of manned bombers would eventually bring a sharp reduction in deliverable nuclear capacity. He said the Supreme Commander of the North Atlantic Treaty Organization forces ought to have "more leeway" in the use of tactical nuclear weapons — weapons he said should be considered "conventional."

Later, he modified this to say that commanders in the field already had delegated authority to use nuclear weapons in certain pre-described emergency situations.

Throughout his campaign, Mr. Goldwater implied that the United States ought to have overwhelming nuclear and conventional strength, and should use it in a policy of "brinkmanship" to force Communist governments to stop disturbing the world's peace.

Mr. Johnson and other Democratic spokesmen denied that the shift to missiles endangered American security. They insisted that the nation's strength had never been greater, and that it was measurably increased over that provided in the Administration of President Dwight D. Eisenhower.

The Democrats also insisted that nuclear weapons control should and did remain executively in the hands of the President. They termed Mr. Goldwater a "trigger-happy hip-shooter" who could not be relied upon to keep his finger off the "nuclear button."

And they argued that a policy of brinkmanship was not only too risky in the nuclear era but also that the idea of forcing Communist nations to back down from their line of policy

was unrealistic and oversimplified.

CIVIL RIGHTS

Mr. Goldwater, who voted in the Senate against the Civil Rights Act of 1964, on the ground that its public accommodations and equal employment sections were unconstitutional, insisted that such legislation infringed the rights of people.

He said the solution to the problems of Negro rights could be found only "in the hearts of the people," not in legislation, and he urged that the enforcement of these rights be left to the states.

Mr. Goldwater was believed by many observers to be seeking the so-called "white backlash" vote from white persons alarmed at the pace of the Negro rights drive. His strategists conceded that they hoped to "sweep" the once solidly Democratic Southern states, and both Mr. Goldwater and Mr. Miller campaigned heavily in that region.

Mr. Johnson gave total support to the civil rights bill enacted last summer. He and his supporters derided the idea of leaving civil rights enforcement to the states.

The President campaigned extensively in the South, however, urging Southerners not to let their concern with the race problem bar them from full participation in the economic and social advance of the nation. There also was more than a hint in some Democratic campaign speeches that Southern states that remained adamantly opposed to equality for Negroes might begin to lose lucrative Federal defense contracts and other forms of subsidy.

MORALITY IN GOVERNMENT

Mr. Goldwater charged that there was "moral decay" in the nation and lawlessness in the streets; whether his reference was to hoodlums and juvenile delinquency or to Negro demonstrations was never made clear. He frequently pointed to the Robert G. Baker and Billie Sol Estes cases as examples of lax morality in the Johnson Administration.

When Mr. Johnson's top assistant, Walter W. Jenkins, was arrested on a morals charge last month, and it was subsequently disclosed that he had been arrested on a similar charge in 1959, the Republicans added his case to the others. Mr. Goldwater, however, charged only that the Jenkins case had jeopardized national security.

Mr. Goldwater's thesis was that "moral decay" in the Johnson Administration "trickled down" to the people and was affecting the fiber of the nation itself. Mr. Johnson seldom replied to these charges although he did defend Mr. Jenkins as an able public servant whose personal misconduct had not endangered the national security.

These were the main themes of the campaign—but there were others. Mr. Johnson spoke frequently of his "Great Society" concept, a plan that envisioned massive new Federal programs in education, medical care, conservation of natural resources and urban renewal in the cities.

Mr. Goldwater criticized the Democratic tax cut of 1964 as politicaly inspired "gimmickry" and offered his own five-year program of tax reduction. He also called Mr. Johnson's "war on poverty" a "cruel hoax" designed only to win the votes of the less fortunate.

Mr. Johnson, however, attributed the nation's rising prosperity to the 1964 tax cut and promised even greater efforts to eliminate poverty, illiteracy and discrimination.

Most Democratic strategists believe, however, that the most telling argument on their side was the widespread belief that Mr. Goldwater would be careless in the use of nuclear weapons, belligerent in his foreign policy, and thus would endanger the peace. This accounted, they believe, for the high percentage of women in both parties who indicated to polltakers that they feared to back Mr. Goldwater.

The two Presidential candidates campaigned in strikingly different manners, although each roamed widely in the nation by jet aircraft and made frequent speeches.

Mr. Johnson was folksy and mingled freely with the crowds; he often climbed on top of his limousine to speak to street-corner throngs through a bull horn. Mr. Goldwater almost never made sidewalk tours, handshaking expeditions and rarely came close to the sizable crowds that turned out to see him. In motorcades, he rode in a closed car, paying little attention to the increasingly sparse turnouts for these events.

On the platform, despite his hard-hitting charges, Mr. Goldwater was deceptively mild, often colloquial, and rarely made any effort to rouse his listeners to excitement. Mr. Johnson, on the other hand, sometimes roared at the top of his voice through an hour or more of almost extemporaneous speaking.

As the campaign advanced, Mr. Johnson's lead seemed at first to widen, then to shrink somewhat, then to return to approximately the level at which polltakers had first estimated it. In the final days of the campaign, for instance, Dr. George Gallup predicted that he would win 61 per cent of the vote, just about the precampaign prediction of most poll-takers.

Mr. Goldwater insisted to the last, however, that his campaign had started "moving up" before Oct. 15 and was coming to a peak that would bring him victory on Election Day. Neither he nor any of his supporters, however, ever predicted that he could win by more than a few electoral votes.

November 4, 1964

Negroes, a Major Factor in Johnson Victory, Viewed as Abandoning the G.O.P.

90% SAID TO VOTE FOR DEMOCRATS

Shift in Allegiance Is Called Long-Range — It Helped Robert Kennedy Win

By M. S. HANDLER

A preliminary national survey indicated yesterday the presence of a powerful Negro political thrust in the overwhelming election victory of the Democratic party.

Estimates from New York Times correspondents throughout the country corroborated estimates of the major civil rights organizations that between 85 and 99 per cent of Negroes' votes from state to state were cast for the Johnson-Humphrey ticket and helped elect many other candidates for Federal, state and local offices.

The Negro effort was particularly dramatic in the Northern urban and industrial states, such as New York and Illinois.

According to the Vote Profile Analysis of the Columbia Broadcasting System, this was the result largely of increased voter registration and voter participation and a massive transfer of Negroes from the Republican party to the Democratic.

In the 1960 election, it was estimated, 60 per cent of the Negroes' votes nationwide were cast for Republican candidates. On Tuesday, it was estimated, 90 per cent of the Negroes' votes went to the Democrats.

The Republican party appears to have lost most of the Negro vote for a long time, according to the Vote Profile Analysis.

The effect of the Negro shift in the North was illustrated in the victory of Robert F. Kenneddy over Senator Kenneth B. Keating in the New York Senate race. According to estimates of the National Association for the Advancement of Colored People, there were 580,000 registered Negro voters in the state for this election. Of these 508,-000 were in New York City.

While the Negro vote in the state for the Johnson-Humphrey ticket, estimated by civil rights organizations at 97 to 98 per cent, played a relatively small part in President Johnson's crushing victory in New York, it was a major factor in the Kennedy election.

According to estimates, at least 80 per cent of the 508,000 Negro voters in the city cast ballots. This meant that Mr. Kennedy received about 400,-000 votes of Negroes in the city. His statewide plurality over Senator Keating was something over 600,000.

The impact of the Negro vote for the Democrats was even more dramatically illustrated in the victory of Gov. Otto Kerner of Illinois over his Republican opponent, Charles H. Percy.

About 540,000 Negroes were registered to vote in Illinois. It was estimated that 80 per cent voted, and almost all for the Democrats. Mr. Kerner's plurality was only about 195,-000.

The N.A.A.C.P. estimated the number of Negro registrants in the nation at about 6 million. The effects of the Negro vote were most clearly visible, of course, in those areas with relatively many Negroes.

The N.A.A.C.P. said there were more than 2 million Negro registrants in the Southern states — an increase of 700,000 since the beginning of the year. This was achieved through voter registration drives conducted by the N.A.A.C.P. the National Urban League, the Congress of Racial Equality and the Student Nonviolent Coordinating Committee.

The success of the voter registration drives was sometimes remarkable. In Gadsden County ipn Florida 355 Negroes were registered to vote in 1960. This week there were 4,447.

Florida state officials estimated that 314,000 Negroes had registered. About 80 per cent voted, and of these, it was estimated 90 per cent voted for the Johnson-Humphrey ticket.

In Tennessee about 200,000 Negroes were registered. About 63 per cent voted on Tuesday, and of this number, it was believed 99.5 per cent voted for the Democratic slate — compared with 60 per cent for John F. Kennedy four years ago, when the Negro vote was estimated at 85,000.

The impact of the Negro vote was far from uniform in the Southern states.

In Georgia, Negro voter registration was estimated at 270,000 — about 80 per cent voted — and the state was carried by Senator Barry Goldwater.

But the Vote Profile Analysis pointed out one important fact relative to Negro registration. This is that increases in Negro registrations have been accompanied and sometimes surpassed by white voter registrations in the Southern states.

Thus, an increase in the Negro vote may be offset by an even greater increase in the white vote—as was the case in Georgia.

Negro voting in the District of Columbia was particularly significant. Of the 163,000 votes given the Johnson-Humphrey ticket, an estimated total of 78,500 was cast by Negroes. Senator Goldwater got virtually no support in the heavily Negro precincts.

Negro civil rights leaders hailed Negro voter participation in the election. Some indicated they believed that the massive turnout in favor of the Democrats marked a step in the direction of greater Negro political activity.

Whitney M. Young Jr., executive director of the Urban League, said of the Negroes' voting:

"For Negro citizens, it is a milestone. Thanks to the combined efforts of the responsible civil rights leadership across the nation, their unprecedented turnout is growing evidence of their desire to share in the responsibilities as well as the privileges of citizenship.

"It evinces a more sophisticated knowledge of what the vote can achieve to bring relief from poverty and despair which afflicts so many."

Roy Wilkins, executive director of the N.A.A.C.P., said:

"We impressed upon the people the importance of the vote. Younger Negroes have given more study to what can be accomplished through the vote and how political developments have an effect on civil rights."

James Farmer, national director of CORE, said:

"I think it means the beginning of genuine and effective political action."

November 5, 1964

HOW REPUBLICANS VIEW THEIR PARTY NOW

In the wake of last Tuesday's record-breaking defeat at the polls, the Republican party faced the task of reappraising its role and its image. Following are assessments made after the election by key Republicans.

SENATOR GOLDWATER: "There is a two-party system in this country and we're going to keep it. We're going to devote our days and the years ahead in strengthening the Republican party, to getting more people into it, and I feel the young people coming along will provide the army that we need . . . I will devote—being unemployed as of January 3 or thereabouts — I'll have a lot of

Sturm in The Syracuse Herald-Journal

"I love you but don't ever do that again!"

time to devote to the party, to its leadership and to the strengthening of the party, and that I have every intention of doing. I want to just ask the people in this country who worked so hard in this election not to be despondent, that we have a job to do and let's get along with it, because there are many questions that have to be answered."

DWIGHT D. EISENHOWER: "The Republican party has been hurt but not irretrievably. We need now to consult among ourselves as to methods for correcting the false image of Republicanism which, far too long, has confused so many of our citizens and led them to think of it as a political doctrine designed primarily for the rich and privileged. . . . This I believe is the proper time to remind ourselves and the country that we are the party of Lincoln. We remain true to his concepts of human liberty, dignity and equality. We share Lincoln's faith in the work of every citizen and his trust in individuals and communities to solve their own problems whenever possible, but when the problem is beyond their capacity to solve, they must be assured of Federal help generously and in-

telligently given. We believe that except in emergencies a prosperous America can and should pay for whatever she may require, avoiding piling up Federal debt upon the future. . . . Around these convictions and purposes we can unify our party, one that will refuse to be torn apart by divisive and meaningless labels."

RICHARD M. NIXON: "[Governor Rockefeller] had his pound of flesh and I do not think that he can exert leadership out of New York. . . . [He] pledged, as did Senator Goldwater, that he would support the winner. After he lost [the primary campaign] he proceeded to drag his feet. . . . He was a spoilsport . . . [and] a party divider."

GOVERNOR ROCKEFELLER: "This kind of peevish post-election utterance has unfortunately become typical of Mr. Nixon. It is neither factual nor constructive. The nomination of the Goldwater-Miller ticket divided the Republican party so severely that despite the efforts of Republican state organizations like New York, the nation rejected the national ticket by unprecedented pluralities. And it carried down to defeat, in the avalanche of protests, hundreds of Republicans — moderates, progressives, and 'true conservatives, outstanding leaders like Robert Taft, Jr., Kenneth Keating, and Charles Percy and others competing for the Congress and state and local offices across the country. . . . My differences and those of other moderate Republicans with Senator Goldwater were not personal but were matters of principle. . . . Senator Goldwater had advocated making Social Security voluntary, withdrawal from the United Nations, giving control of

the use of nuclear power to field commanders, leaving the problems of civil rights to the states, including such states as Mississippi and Alabama, selling the T.V.A., and the immediate termination of farm price supports. . . . This is a time for constructive rebuilding of the Republican party as a vital force in the mainstream of American political life. Mr. Nixon's latest maneuver is hardly calculated to advance this effort."

MR. NIXON: "I won't comment on what the Governor says. I would only suggest that it's now time for him to quit his criticism of other Republicans and his criticism of Senator Goldwater and start putting his shoulder to the wheel to get the Republicans to win in 1966. He brought on this split in the party. Now I think he should try to heal it. . . . He's continuing his vendetta against Senator Goldwater and he should knock it off. . . . I know as a loser what it means, so I urge my fellow Republicans to take into account that Goldwater deserves a cooling-off period before the great battle for leadership of the party begins. I think Senator Goldwater waged a very courageous campaign against very great odds."

GOV. GEORGE ROMNEY: "Obviously there is great need in this situation to broaden and unify the party. [But] you don't broaden the party by kicking a lot of people out."

GOV. WILLIAM W. SCRANTON: "[I intend] to join with other like-minded Republicans to make it clear' that the party of Lincoln is a great national party, eager to return to its heritage and welcome all Americans to our ranks. . . . Apparently many Americans during the recent campaign gained the impression the Republican party was opposed or indifferent to so-called ethnic or minority groups. . . . This is completely contrary to the true tradition of the Republican party. It concerns me deeply."

MEADE ALCORN (former Republican National Chairman): "The Republican party's image has been badly disfigured by the events at and since San Francisco. . . . A rebuilding job is absolutely essential and it must start now. . . . We cannot hope to shape future party victories if that rebuilding job is entrusted to the leadership of the Goldwater organization, which has brought us the most devastating defeat the party has ever suffered."

SENATOR THRUSTON B. MORTON: "If Barry sticks to his promise [of continuing his party leadership] there probably will be some blood spattered around. . . . I certainly am not arguing that we

TRENDS IN SENATE		
Democrats	Republicans	Others
Majority →		
'34	69	25
'36	75	17
'38	69	23
'40	66	28
'42	57	38
'44	57	38
'46	45	51
'48	54	42
'50	48	47
'52	47	48
'54	48	47
'56	49	47
'58	66	34
'60	64	36
'62	68	32
'64	68	32

drop the conservative label. But we have got to change the national committee, and we have got to change the party's image, by broadening the base of the party's appeal."

HENRY CABOT LODGE (1960 Vice Presidential nominee): "Voters this year rejected the idea that Republicans offered two choices, either to support some fallacious government policy or to oppose everything. We need a program that will accomplish the goals toward which the country is trying to move, and not demagoguery, and on that basis the voters were not offered a choice this time. . . . There is a small minority trying to move us back to the 19th-century system of having one party represent one point of view and the other something opposite. I don't accept the self-styled conservative's idea of what a conservative should be. A true conservative is ready to accept new developments and to innovate them."

GOV. JOHN ANDERSON of Kansas (suggested as Republican National Chairman): "We are going to have to fit with the desires of the great masses of the people in this country to survive as a party. The people are interested in tomorrow, not yesterday."

GOV. MARK O. HATFIELD of Oregon (keynote speaker at Republican convention): "Eventually [there will] be a shakeup in the national party organization. . . . I think we can make a comeback in 1966. I think there is inherent in the American mind an allegiance to the two-party system. . . . [I recommend] local councils of rank-and-file Republicans and office-holders in every part of the country . . . to help build a philosophy by talking about the party and

TRENDS IN HOUSE		
Democrats	Republicans	Others
Majority →		
'34	322	
'36	333	
'38	262	
'40	267	
'42	222	
'44	243	
'46	188	
'48	263	
'50	234	
'52	213	
'54	232	
'56	234	
'58	283	
'60	263	
'62	259	
'64	270	

helping to mold and bring in new ideas; in other words, help revolutionize the Republican party."

FRED A. YOUNG, New York Republican State Chairman: "The most noteworthy Republican victories on Tuesday were scored by progressive Republicans who survived the deadly political backwash from the disastrous, alternative course charted [by the Goldwater nomination]. The Republican party has paid a shattering price for the erratic deviation from our soundly moderate 20th-century course. That ill-advised, badly led swing to the extreme right has been decisively vetoed by the American voters, hundreds of thousands of Republicans among them."

EVERETT M. DIRKSEN, Senate Republican Leader: "Everybody will come out of his corner with a lot of ideas. Now, I intend to stand still. I intend to do a lot of thinking and get a new perspective."

SENATOR CLIFFORD P. CASE of New Jersey: "This immaturity of the candidate's position on many critical issues is not going to succeed any better in the future than it has in this campaign. We have got to rebuild the Republican party by making a realistic appeal to the intelligence of the voters."

November 8, 1964

Nixon Recommends Move to the Center—Rejects Rightist Extremism

By McCANDLISH PHILLIPS

Richard M. Nixon declared yesterday that the Republican party must choose centrist leadership that will "make a place for all responsible points of view," from conservative to liberal, while rejecting right-wing extremism.

Asking again for a cooling-off period among Republicans. Mr. Nixon declared that "the blood is still too hot and we're too close to the disaster" of Nov. 3 to take the right steps toward arranging new party leadership. He said that "the first of the year would be the time to decide" on such steps.

Ideologically, the Republican future has got to be near the center of the political spectrum, he said, and its leaders must be moderates who can draw conservatives and liberals into coalition.

"The center does not try to read anybody out of the party," he remarked. "But the farther you go in either direction, the greater the inclination to read others out—to say, 'It's my way or nothing.'"

Deploring that sort of political "cannibalism," he warned the party to avoid another massive ideological split of the sort that marked its San Francisco convention.

Mr. Nixon charged that after their victory there, the conservatives were unreasonable in "purging" the party apparatus of liberals.

"The election will be badly interpreted if it is interpreted as a rejection of conservatism," the former Vice President declared. "It was a rejection of reaction, a rejection of racism, a rejection of extremism."

He added that he did not believe the defeated candidate, Senator Barry Goldwater, had stood for those things, although he said some of the Goldwater supporters had.

Mr. Nixon aimed barbs at those on "the totalitarian right, the John Birchers and the Minutemen," and at racists and professional civil rights agitators"—all of whom he said take a rule-or-ruin attitude in the hot pursuit of their fixed ideologies.

Conservative Strength

"There is a strong conservative wing of the Republican party," Mr. Nixon said. "It deserves a major voice in party councils, and the liberal wing deserves a party voice, but neither can dominate or dictate—the center must lead."

He saw no one in the party more on "dead center" than himself, and he said he would devote all his "spare time to the political area" but he called proposals that he become the national chairman "ridiculous."

Mr. Nixon said he believed the Republican party was "through forever with any illusions" that there might be political gold in the "backlash issue," a reaction of whites against gains by Negroes.

"There were those who thought the party future might be in an anti-civil rights position, he said in an interview at his office here. "Now that's finished, and it's very much to the good."

"I think you're going to see both parties standing for responsible progress in civil rights, removing the black-white issue from national partisan politics."

Pointing out that politicians realized that the morality of an issue and its vote-getting potential were sometimes at variance, he said that the morality of the civil rights issue and its political appeal were the same —for justice and against racism.

Mr. Nixon noted that the Republican party had "lost votes in some Southern states in which it had been gaining strength" before this year, such as North Carolina, Virginia, Florida and Tennessee. "In Tennessee we would have elected two Senators if we had had some Negro votes," he said.

Urgency Emphasized

The man who led the Republican party to within a hairbreadth of a popular-vote majority for the Presidency in 1960 (Mr. Nixon got 34,108,546 votes to 34,227,096 for John F. Kennedy) now occupies a 24th-floor law office at 20 Broad Street, in the heart of the financial district.

The office is three doors from the Federal Hall national historic site at Broad and Wall Streets, which marks the first American capitol, and Mr. Nixon devoted much of the 75-minute interview to detailing the urgent need for political moderation in a nuclear age.

For almost 50 minutes he sat tipped back in his tilting swivel chair, both feet on his desk. On a table behind him in the buff-walled office were silver-framed autographed pictures of some of the world's great statesmen and royal persons.

"I'm going to write about moderation," he said, with the fingers of one hand tip to tip with those of the other. "But how do you make moderation exciting? Extremism is exciting, but moderation seems dull, bland, Pablum-like. It's got to become a cause.

"In the world in which we live today extremism—peace at any cost or victory at any price—will destroy freedom because it will destroy the world.

"A no-risk policy and an all-risk policy are both wrong. What we have to do is to take the responsible risks."

Declaring that "Republicans need an intellectual base," Mr. Nixon lamented that "80 per cent of college professors in 1960 were Democratic-oriented and the professors of political science were nearly all down that line, and they're tremendously potent people."

"We've got to get through to the eggheads," Mr. Nixon said. "The intellectual above everything else, like Aristotle, should be the reasonable man who takes the hard, tedious road of finding the right position, which may not get the easy plaudits of the snap judgment. We're sometimes the kind of people who say, 'Let's burn the schoolhouse down' or 'ban the damn book,' but that is not the way in our kind of world."

"We've got to point out to young people that it takes guts to be responsible, to reject the far right and the far left," he continued. "It takes courage to reject the wild cheering of the extremes."

Mr. Nixon counted it a good thing that civil rights leaders had alerted the nation to the need for redress of grievances, but he said that when they "take any means to the end and say they'll violate the law to redress 100 years of grievances," they encourage counterviolations by racists.

"We've got to put emphasis on the means, and intellectuals should lead the way in this," he said.

Stating that the defeated Republican Presidential candidate might be going through a difficult post-election period he suggested that "Barry Goldwater deserves a moratorium on kicking him for a while."

"But the Goldwater people have to be reasonable," he said. "They were unreasonable after San Francisco in purging the National Committee of some of the liberals."

Asked who occupied the Republican center, Mr. Nixon listed Gov. William W. Scranton ("not a rule-or-ruin type; a unifier"), Gov. George W. Romney ("slightly to the left of center, but primarily a centrist and a free enterpriser"), and most of the Governors and many Congressmen.

"Rockefeller is on the liberal side, but in some respects he pulls to the center," Mr. Nixon declared, but he ruled him out of national leadership.

"I respect the right of dissent," he said, "but Republicans in recent years have had a cannibalistic instinct. Some on the left in the party react the same way as the extreme right: 'If we can't have it our way, we're going to sit it out.'

"My quarrel with Rockefeller is not his principles. The party needs its liberals. The quarrel has to do with a basic fundamental political fact: A man who runs for the nomination, pledges his support for the winner and then takes a walk, cannot come back and say he wants to be the leader. If that happens, you reward a man in effect for deserting the party after he himself has sought the prize?"

Where does Mr. Nixon himself stand in a party needing moderate leaders? "I'm perhaps at dead center," he said.

November 11, 1964

280

BURCH WILL YIELD G.O.P JOB APRIL 1; BLISS TO GET POST

Leadership Change Backed by Goldwater in a Move to Avoid Split in Party

By The Associated Press

PHOENIX, Ariz., Jan. 12—Dean Burch will resign as Republican National Chairman April 1. The Ohio Republican chairman, Ray C. Bliss, has agreed to take over the job with the blessing of Barry Goldwater.

The move, made in an effort to avoid a party-splitting fight, was announced here today at a news conference by Mr. Goldwater, the party's 1964 Presidential nominee; William E. Miller, the Vice-Presidential nominee; Mr. Burch and Mr. Bliss.

Mr. Burch, who is 37 years old, said he would submit his resignation at a meeting of the Republican National Committee Jan. 22-23 in Chicago. Mr. Bliss, who is 57, said he had consented to become chairman if the National Committee wanted him.

Foresaw Slim Victory

Some Republican leaders promptly hailed the proposed switch as a step that would unify the party.

The announcement was made on the same patio of Mr. Goldwater's hilltop home overlooking Phoenix where the former Arizona Senator announced his candidacy for the Presidency just a little over a year ago. A warm sun beat down as Mr. Goldwater, Mr. Burch, Mr. Bliss and Mr. Miller read statements, then refused to submit to direct questioning.

Mr. Goldwater and Mr. Burch indicated that, after extensive polling, they had concluded Mr. Burch could win a vote of confidence from the National Committee at the Chicago meeting but that the margin would be insufficient to constitute a clear mandate.

Hoped to Retain Post

After the Republicans' crushing defeat in November, many party leaders began demanding the resignation of Mr. Burch, whom Mr. Goldwater personally chose for the party chairmanship last July.

The decision to avoid a showdown in Chicago came after both Mr. Goldwater and Mr. Burch made personal pleas to all members of the National Committee that Mr. Burch be given a chance to show he could unify the party.

Mr. Goldwater wrote the committee members Dec. 26 that the ouster of Mr. Burch "would be a capitulation on the part of those Republicans who have supported me and the principles for which I stood." Mr. Goldwater said it would be "a repudiation of me."

Today Mr. Goldwater termed Mr. Burch one of the most effective party chairmen in many years. "But I know, through having worked with many national chairmen, that without having the full support of the committee he could not do his job or himself justice," he said.

Mr. Goldwater urged the selection of Mr. Bliss to replace Mr. Burch and pledged his support to the Ohioan.

Mr. Bliss said that under no circumstances would he lend his name or efforts to any move to force a change in the chairmanship.

Request From Goldwater

"My own willingness now to serve as chairman after April 1, if that is the desire of the members of the National Committee, is in answer to Senator Goldwater's request that I do so and his assurance that I would have his full support in building a strong organization capable of winning Republican victories," Mr. Bliss said.

Mr. Burch said that, on the basis of a just-completed comprehensive survey of the National Committee, he had no doubt that he could win support to stay on as chairman from a majority of the committee.

But he said, "Clearly, unity cannot be achieved by forcing a vote in Chicago. Even if I won under those circumstances, neither I nor those who opposed my chairmanship would be comfortable—and my effectiveness would be impaired."

Mr. Goldwater said that, in the last few hours, he had discussed his own position on the change of chairmen with former President Dwight D. Eisenhower and Richard M. Nixon, the party's 1960 Presidential nominee.

"Each of them has concluded it as being in the best interests of our party and our country," Mr. Goldwater said. "They join us in commending this to the National Committee and both continue to be most generous in their praise of Dean Burch and the remarkable job he has done. They are equally generous in their praise of Mr. Bliss."

Mr. Burch receives $30,000 a year as National Chairman. Mr. Bliss reportedly makes $35,000 yearly as Ohio chairman.

January 13, 1965

The G.O.P. in Disarray

Why Ford's Efforts for a New 'Image' Are Often Blunted

By DAVID S. BRODER
Special to The New York Times

WASHINGTON, July 9 — Nothing so well illustrates the continuing disability of the Republican party as the plight in which the House Republican leader, Gerald R. Ford of Michigan, finds himself today.

Mr. Ford defeated Charles A. Halleck of Indiana in January with a specific pledge to "promote and communicate the image of a fighting, forward - looking party." So desperately did the Republicans want that image that they chose Mr. Ford over a man who was his acknowledged superior in parliamentary skill and at least his equal in intellect.

News Analysis

Today, Mr. Ford finds himself embroiled in a two-front war that is costly to the very cause he set out to save. With one hand, he is defending himself against Democratic condemnation of his proposal that the United States bomb Communist missile sites in North Vietnam. With the other, he is fending off Republican criticism of his leadership stance in the House fight over the voting rights bill.

It is significant that the two issues—military policy and civil rights—are the same ones that split the Republican party at its convention a year ago. The internal divisions dramatized at the time of the Goldwater nomination have yet to begin to heal.

Mr. Ford's efforts to bridge the differences with a busy effort at image-building have just served to show how serious the underlying problems really are.

The handsome former football star is popular with his colleagues and praised, even by those who did not support him against Mr. Halleck, for his industry and ingenuity in presenting the Republican cause. But the keystone of his policy—the effort to offer what he likes to call "constructive Republican alternatives" to major Administration bills, has yet to produce any significant results in either the parliamentary or the political arena.

4 Defeats in 4 Tries

Defeat of the Republican substitute voting rights bill tonight market the fourth loss in four tries for Ford-inspired alternatives.

The rejection of this carefully developed plan was particularly bitter. Twenty-one Republicans, including many of those most prominently identified with civil rights, bolted the leadership and helped balk Mr. Ford's effort to put a Republican stamp on this vital piece of legislation.

Some party leaders outside Congress are beginning to complain that the futile effort to shape legislative alternatives has kept Mr. Ford from drawing the issues against the Democrats as sharply as they would like.

In his attempt to walk a middle line between conservatives and liberals, the House leader, like Ray C. Bliss, the Republican National Chairman, is drawing fire from both flanks. Conservative G. O. P. publications complain that he and Mr. Dirksen are too soft on the Democrats, while liberal Republicans worry publicly over the influence exerted on Mr. Ford by their pet conservative target, Representative Melvin R. Laird of Wisconsin, the chairman of the House Republican Conference.

Mr. Laird, in an interview today, defended the course of "constructive alternatives" he and Mr. Ford have charted. But, he admitted, "there isn't a real issue we've developed as of this moment."

The reasons for this failure go far beyond Mr. Ford's control to the partywide weaknesses in research and publicity facilities, to the personality differences among Congressional leaders, and to the basic policy splits within the G. O. P.

The Republican voting rights and medicare bills were carefully drawn, but previous alternatives to Appalachian aid and aid to education were not.

None of these four alternatives was well publicized, even to Republican officials around the country, let alone to the general public.

Only this week did Mr. Bliss send the national committee's research and publicity directors both brand new to their own jobs—to Capitol Hill to discuss joint research and publicity work with Congressional leaders.

In the meantime, the Democrats exploit the brain power of the entire Executive Branch and Congressional committee staffs and publicize their programs through the unrivaled forum of the Presidency.

Many of the best-planned Ford ventures have been short-circuited by outsiders. A House Republican conference task force to study NATO problems in Paris, which turned in an eminently respectable report, was almost laughed offstage by Mr. Dirksen's publicly expressed incredulity when he first heard of their mission. Bad staff

281

work was to blame for that mixup, but on other occasions the Senate leader has not felt inhibited about criticizing Mr. Ford's plans.

Actually, House Republicans under Mr. Ford have been neither docile toward the Democrats nor badly divided among themselves. They have opposed the Democratic majorities on 40 of the first 81 roll-calls of the year, and on those 40 votes, an average of only 23 Republicans, of 141, have bolted the party leadership.

But the advantages the Democrats have in their massive numbers and their control of the parliamentary rules keep Mr. Ford's troops from dramatizing their fundamental disagreements with Administration views. The few Republican victories have been on trifling issues.

Whenever the Republicans have threatened to score a major victory, the Democrats have either stitched some Republican proposals into Administration bills, as they did on Medicare, or split away enough Republicans to save their skins, as they did on House rules reform and on rent subsidies.

Mr. Ford's unhappy experience suggests that the Republicans need to replenish both their numbers and their supply of ideas on the aftermath of last year's election before even the most "image-minded" of their new leaders can achieve significant success.

July 10, 1965

BIRCH SOCIETY SCORED BY G.O.P.

Republican Legislators Join in Condemning Rightist Anti-Communist Group

Special to The New York Times.

WASHINGTON, Sept. 30— Republican leaders of the House and Senate joined today in condemning the John Birch Society and disclaimed any connection between the right-wing group and the G.O.P.

Everett McKinley Dirksen of Illinois, the Senate minority leader, said at a news conference today: "The John Birch Society is not a part of the Republican party. There just isn't any room in our party for an organization that operates in secrecy to achieve its goals."

His view was echoed by Representative Gerald R. Ford of Michigan, Republican leader of the House, who said: "There's just no place for that organization in the Republican party."

Morton Charges Society

This was the most emphatic position the joint Republican Congressional leadership has yet taken in public on an issue that has bedeviled their party increasingly since the defeat of Barry Goldwater for the Presidency in 1964. Most party spokesmen have sidestepped the question of how much and what kind of influence the militant anti-Communist group has gained in a number of state G.O.P. organizations.

Yesterday, Senator Thruston B. Morton of Kentucky, who is chairman of the Republican Senatorial campaign committee, told an interview that the Birch society was attempting to "infiltrate" the party in a number of states. The group, he said, "is as dangerous as the Ku Klux Klan and the Communist party," and he urged Republicans "to kick it right square in the tail."

The Birch society opened a new regional headquarters in downtown Washington only two weeks ago. Its director is Red Benson, son of Elmer F. Benson of Utah, who was Secretary of Agriculture during the Eisenhower Administration.

Senator Goldwater was quoted from his home in Phoenix, Ariz., today in connection with Senator Morton's blast as saying: "I don't know of any Birch member who occupied a responsible position (in the party) such as state chairman or national committeeman.

"And another thing," the defeated candidate added, "Let's take a look at Birch members who are Democrats. In my state I suspect that fully 50 per cent or more of the Birch members are Democrats.

"Anyone who doesn't work for the best interest of the Republican party, whether he be a Bircher, or anybody else, should go to the other party."

Mr. Ford pursued this thought briefly during his talk with reporters today. He recalled that one of the few Birch-connected political candidates he was aware of was former Gen. Edwin A. Walker who ran for Congress in Texas last year as a Democrat "and got around 100,000 votes."

October 1, 1965

THE POLITICS OF DISORDER

REAGAN VICTORY AIDS G.O.P. RIGHT

Former Actor Is Viewed as Possible Contender in '68 With Romney and Nixon

By DAVID S. BRODER
Special to The New York Times

LOS ANGELES, June 8— Ronald Reagan's sweeping victory in the California gubernatorial primary has given the national Republican party its sharpest tug to the right in two years and placed continued Democratic control of the state in clear jeopardy.

It has also made the youthful-looking 55-year-old political novice a man to reckon with on the national scene—even, perhaps, a rival to Richard M. Nixon and Gov. George Romney of Michigan for the 1968 Presidential nomination.

Gov. Edmund G. Brown, now rated an underdog in his bid to become California's first three-term Democratic Governor, told a post-primary news conference this morning that Mr. Reagan had "taken the mantle of leadership from Barry Goldwater" in the national conservative movement.

Yorty Shows Strength

The former actor's prospects for the fall were further enhanced by Los Angeles Mayor Samuel W. Yorty's show of strength against Governor Brown in the Democratic primary. The Mayor spurned today Mr. Brown's initial plea for support.

Mr. Yorty, observers noted, could expect far more help from Mr. Reagan's conservative financial backers than he could from his old antagonist, Governor Brown, in achieving his ambition to retire Thomas H. Kuchel, a liberal Republican, from the Senate in 1968.

After yesterday's voting, no qualified California political observer would challenge Mr. Brown's statement that the current contest was "a tougher fight" for him to win than his 1958 battle with former Senator William F. Knowland or his 1962 showdown with Mr. Nixon.

Two sets of statistics measure the attrition in Mr. Brown's strength and California Republicans' steady shift to the right.

In 1958, before cross-filing was abolished, Mr. Brown outpolled Mr. Knowland in the primary by 660,000 votes. In the 1962 primary, though confined to his own party, he still outdrew Mr. Nixon by 423,000 votes.

But this year's nearly complete unofficial figures show him trailing Mr. Reagan by 68,-000 votes. No less dramatic is the shift to conservatism among California Republicans. In 1962, Mr. Nixon defeated Joseph Shell, that year's advocate of the Goldwater-Reagan philosophy, by a 2-to-1 margin. In 1964, Mr. Goldwater topped Governor Rockefeller in California by less than 2 per cent of the vote. But yesterday, Mr. Reagan rolled up a 2-to-1 margin over his rival, former San Francisco Mayor George Christopher.

Effective Campaigner

On the national Republican spectrum, Mr. Reagan's identity with the Goldwater wing is unquestioned. Not only was he one of Mr. Goldwater's most effective campaigners, but his stand on the questions that split the 1964 convention—extremism and civil rights—is also identical with the Arizonan's.

Mr. Reagan rejects any blanket condemnation of the John Birch Society and opposes as unconstitutional key provisions of the Civil Rights Acts of 1964 and 1965, as well as California's own housing law, the Rumford Act.

But his bedrock conservatism has been subordinated for the campaign to a common-man complaint about the "intellectual clique in Sacramento" he says is running the state.

Governor Brown's problem, as he defined it today, is to persuade California voters that Mr. Reagan really is "the crown prince of the extreme right" and not just a pleasant and earnest man who is giving vent to the widespread complaints that Governor Brown acknowledges to be the end-product of his 7½ years in office.

The Governor's task will not be easy, for Mr. Reagan sounds plausible insisting, as he did today, that "there is nothing in my philosophy that doesn't cross party lines."

As a citizen-candidate himself, he argues the case for a common-sense "Creative Society" partnership of individuals and government. The slogan seems tailor-made to carry into a national campaign against President Johnson's Great Society.

Finch Nominated

Whether Mr. Reagan has that in mind for 1968 is not known. But Robert H. Finch, the young Nixon campaign manager who was nominated yesterday for lieutenant governor on the Republican ticket, is one who believes that Mr. Reagan, if elected, would not and could not resist being drawn into the Presidential race.

Mr. Reagan went today as far as he has even gone in denying such a goal when he said he regarded an oath of office as "a contract with the people." But to Governor Brown, that still sounded "a little bit coy" and far from the flat disclaimer of Presidential ambitions past California candidates have given.

Whatever the outcome in November, Mr. Reagan as head of an increasingly conservative California Republican party, will be a keystone of the conservative forces at the 1968 Republican convention.

Today he is much more than that—a polished, plausible new face with what is believed to be at least a 50-50 chance of winning for Republicans their biggest victory of the year. He is the brightest hope conservatives have seen since they left the Cow Palace and the telegrams pouring in today told him that.

June 9, 1966

Washington: The New Nixon Revisited

By JAMES RESTON

WASHINGTON, Sept. 15—The man who is raising the most money, addressing the most meetings and scoring the most points for the Republican party in this year's Congressional elections is none other than that familiar figure, Richard Milhous Nixon.

At 53 he is now a little heavier, a little more relaxed, a little wiser, and a lot richer than the tense and painfully suspicious young man who served two terms as Vice President of the United States, and at this point he must be at least an even bet against any other Republican for his party's Presidential nomination in 1968.

The Early Bird Technique

Apparently this same thought has occurred to him, for he is flying through the Middlewest and the border states this week at the start of an ambitious speaking schedule that will take him into half the states of the Union, raise more than $1 million for the G.O.P., and enliven the races in the see-saw Congressional districts.

This was the technique that won the Republican nomination for Barry Goldwater in 1964. Over the previous four years he put more G.O.P. candidates, state and county chairmen in his debt than all the other Presidential hopefuls combined, and it paid off in the end. Nixon has been doing the same thing ever since 1964, and by his own estimate has already added between $4 million and $5 million to the party treasury.

Despite his humiliating defeat and bad-tempered exit in the California Governor election of 1962, also despite his temporary eclipse when he moved to New York, time has not been bad to him. The elders of the party, led by President Eisenhower, who stood in his light in '64, have now faded from the scene and the only prominent young Republican of the new generation, Mayor John Lindsay of New York City, is unacceptable to the conservative wing of the G.O.P.

Meanwhile, the only other Republican politicians of Nixon's own generation with experience in the field of foreign affairs — Govs. Nelson Rockefeller of New York and William Scranton of Pennsylvania—have retired from Presidential politics, leaving Nixon with the argument that he alone in the G.O.P. can both unify the party and challenge President Johnson's experience in the vital field of foreign policy.

It is a strange thing that a party which has held the allegiance of most of the lawyers and business executives of the United States for the last two generations should not have produced any more young political leaders, but Mr. Nixon has benefited by this failure, and we will soon be hearing the argument that anyone who came within 113,000 votes of beating John F. Kennedy in 1960 surely deserves another chance.

How to Rope Johnson

Mr. Nixon, of course, is not making this argument. He is working the hustings, and traveling the world, and exploiting the troubles of President Johnson and the Democratic Administration. He is not talking about 1968, just aiming at it, and he is just enough of a pro to know that the outcome of the Congressional and gubernatorial elections this November will greatly influence the party's political foundation in the Presidential test two years later.

His main theme has some appeal and validity. It is that the American political system is now out of balance, dominated not only by one party in the Congress and the state houses, but by one man in Washington, who is in deep trouble abroad and getting into more trouble with the economy at home.

"The leadership gap we have in Washington now in foreign policy and in dealing with inflation at home," he emphasized in his speeches in Ohio and Kentucky this week, "is because we have a one-party Congress that will go all the way with LBJ."

Mr. Nixon, who has not yet learned the art of understatement, goes on to argue that "this year will determine the survival of the Republican party and the two-party system in this country," and while this is even gloomier than the facts, there's just enough truth in it to scare the faithful to the polls.

Accent on Youth

What Barry Goldwater has put asunder no man is likely to join together in a hurry, but this is just the point about Nixon. He is starting early. He is convinced that Lyndon Johnson is in trouble with the young, with the intellectuals, and with the women, all of whom did so much to destroy Nixon's own political ambitions, so he has started down the long road again, peddling not youth but experience and looking very much the successful Wall Street lawyer.

September 16, 1966

G.O.P. WILL PRESS RACIAL DISORDERS AS ELECTION ISSUE

By JOHN HERBERS
Special to The New York Times

WASHINGTON, Oct. 3 — Republican leaders said today they had found the race issue to be of increasing concern to Americans and moved to give it more prominence in the current political races.

In a related development, the House Committee on Un-American Activities announced that it would conduct an investigation into the role of "subversive elements" in the riots that occurred in many American cities in recent months.

The race issue in various forms has been a factor in many political races this year but in most instances it has simmered beneath the surface. Many candidates have avoided mentioning it in their campaign speeches, for a variety of reasons.

Today, the Republican Coordinating Committee received the results of a poll conducted for the Republican National Committee on the sentiment and opinions of voters on various issues.

58% Cite Rights Issues

Ray C. Bliss, the committee chairman and the national party chairman, told a news conference that 58 per cent of the persons questioned considered civil rights to be one of the most important domestic problems. He said this was an increase from 44 per cent in a similar poll taken in June.

This, Mr. Bliss said, included concern over riots and racial disorders as well as the advance, or lack of it, of the civil rights of Negroes and other minorities.

The study was conducted for the party by an independent organization, Opinion Research Corporation of Princeton.

In the statements that followed Mr. Bliss's comments today, it was apparent that some

283

of the Republican leaders believed that riots and other disorders were the main cause of the increased concern on the racial issue.

Eisenhower Finds Anger

Former President Dwight D. Eisenhower volunteered a statement on law and order, saying that the public was "very rightly definitely angry" about both increased crime and violence.

"I think the Republicans ought to take the strongest possible position and pledge to remove this curse," he said.

The coordinating committee issued a prepared statement saying in part:

"Unfortunately, the Johnson-Humphrey Administration has accomplished nothing of substance to date to promote public safety. Indeed, high officials of this Administration have condoned and encouraged disregard for law and order."

Representative Gerald R. Ford of Michigan, the minority leader in the House, was asked what "high officials" the state-

ment referred to. He said that Vice President Humphrey, for example, said last summer in New Orleans that he might riot, too, if he had to live under some of the conditions in American slums.

Mr. Humphrey has since advocated law and order in his speeches condemning the results of poverty.

The committee statement also said:

"In this moral crisis, Americans are looking for leadership, inspiration and example. Example is more than exhortation, Inspiration is more than another law enforcement conference. Leadership must stand above the slightest suspicion."

General Eisenhower said he would favor Federal grants to local police departments in an effort to reduce crime and violence.

"If we are going to give grants and aid to states and cities," he said, "I would rather see us do something along this line than some of the programs they are so concerned with."

Everett McKinley Dirksen of Illinois the Senate minority leader, said the country was in danger of losing the gains made in civil rights because the Administration was "not restraining some of these people."

Mr. Bliss said that concern about civil rights and related matters had increased at a greater rate this summer than concern about rising prices.

Although the committee placed no priorities on issues, the members seemed to be trying to push "law and order" to the forefront of the campaign.

The Congressional investigation into possible subversive elements in riots was announced by Representative Edwin E. Willis, Democrat of Louisiana who is chairman of the Committee on Un-American Activities.

He said the inquiry would deal with "only one thing— planned and organized violence by subversive elements." He added that "we have no intention of investigating the civil rights movement or the opinions or positions of any individual or organization on the civil rights issue."

Mr. Willis added, however:

"If we should learn in the course of our investigation, that a certain organization which claims to be a civil rights group is actually controlled or dominated by Communists carrying out the work of the Communist party, we should not hesitate to investigate their operations."

Mr. Willis said that no public hearings had been scheduled and that the investigation would begin with a staff inquiry, the results of which will be presented to the committee, which would then determine whether to pursue the matter further.

Also today, Representative Emanuel Celler, Democrat of Brooklyn, asked Congress for $50,000 to finance an investigation by the House Judiciary Committee into school desegregation guidelines issued by the Office of Education.

Mr. Celler, chairman of the committee, is seeking to calm a controversy over the guidelines, which Southern members have said go beyond the law and have been used to harass Southern school officials.

October 4, 1966

Kennedy's Vietnam Plea Spurs Popularity on Democratic Left

By DAVID S. BRODER
Special to The New York Times

BAKERSFIELD, Calif., Feb. 20—Senator Robert F. Kennedy is becoming the new hero of the Democratic left.

Here in Bakersfield, where the strongly liberal California Democratic Council was winding up its convention today, Mr. Kennedy's public break from Administration policy on Vietnam was the chief topic of conversation.

Local newspapers headlining the suggestion he made yesterday—that the United States offer the Vietcong a share of "power and responsibility" in the Saigon Government in order to achieve a negotiated peace in Vietnam—were handed from delegate to delegate.

Gerald Hill, the newly elected president of the organization, told the delegates that the fact

that Mr. Kennedy "has enlisted in this fight" would hasten a change in American policy.

The newfound enthusiasm for the New York Senator among the liberal disciples of the late Adlai E. Stevenson is echoed among members of the Democratic left in states around the country and in the capital itself.

Talks with Democrats in a half-dozen major states during the last three weeks disclosed a shift in their attitude toward Mr. Kennedy.

Some self-described liberals who formerly regarded him as a ruthless, cold-blooded and even unprincipled political operator now look to him increasingly as the symbol and exponent of their dissatisfactions with the Johnson Administration.

"He is the only one with the

strength and independence to stand up to Johnson," a Michigan Democrat remarked last week.

In many instances the new Kennedy partisans express their disillusionment with a former hero, Vice President Humphrey. Their complaints center on his advocacy of the Johnson Administration policy in Vietnam.

Although Mr. Kennedy has done nothing to encourage such talk, some of his new supporters would like him to challenge President Johnson for the 1968 Democratic Presidential nomination. Among them is Robert Vaughn, the star of television's "The Man From U.N.C.L.E.," who delivered a speech criticizing American policy on Vietnam at a luncheon of the California Democratic Council yesterday.

Mr. Vaughn asked a reporter yesterday: "Is there any doubt in your mind that if the Vietnam war is going on in 1968 and Robert Kennedy is its leading critic, he can win the Democratic nomination and the Presidential election?"

Mr. Vaughn is typical of the liberal Democrats who regard the Vietnam war as the overriding issue in American politics. They are willing to risk a serious party split in order to

achieve a change in American policy toward the war.

Other Causes

Mr. Kennedy has identified himself with other causes of the Democratic left, as well. His Senate speeches prodding the Administration to greater efforts in the disarmament field to prevent nuclear proliferation have been warmly received by the liberals.

So have his criticisms of the Administration's actions in the Dominican crisis and his warnings that the United States is abandoning the philosophy of the Alliance for Progress in Latin America.

Mr. Kennedy has been meeting privately with Senate critics of Administration policy in Vietnam for more than a year. He has told friends that he felt he must be restrained in his own comments on that policy, for fear of identifying the policy dispute with a Kennedy vs. Johnson feud in the Democratic party.

His decision to speak out yesterday is regarded by members of the Democratic left as a major gain for their effort to escalate the Vietnam debate in intraparty politics.

February 21, 1966

Coalition Formed To Back New Left At November Polls

By PAUL HOFMANN

A new group of civil rights and antiwar militants will start raising campaign funds this

weekend for New Left candidates from coast to coast, it was learned yesterday.

The plan seemed to imply an attempt to involve the splintered and overlapping movements against the Vietnam war and for civil rights in practical politics by enlisting their support for radical politicians running for office in the November elections.

Known as the National Conference for New Politics, the new body is headed by Julian Bond and Simon Casady as co-chairmen.

Mr. Bond, a 26-year-old Negro, was barred from taking his seat in the Georgia Legislature early this year because of his antiwar sentiments.

Mr. Casady, 56, is a former president of the California Dem-

ocratic Council, a 50,000-member reform group in the Democratic party. He was ousted from his post because of his outspoken opposition to the war in Vietnam.

New Left is a grab-bag term that has come into use during the last few years to denote a proliferation of movements growing out of civil rights demonstrations and, more recently, from opposition to the Vietnam war.

Those professing adherence to the New Left—some Reform Democrats, Democratic party insurgents and groups far to the left of the party—disassociate themselves from what they call the "old" left of the Nineteen Thirties, stressing that what counts is action, not ideology.

Other promoters of the new group are pacifists, campus radicals and other left-wing crusaders against the United States involvement in Vietnam, militant civil rights leaders and Reform Democrats

One of the promoters, who did not want to be identified, said yesterday he had reason to believe that Senator Robert F. Kennedy "welcomes the formation" of the conference.

Another promoter, Arthur I. Waskow, a senior fellow of the Institute for Policy Studies in Washington, remarked yesterday that he had "a suspicion" that Senator Kennedy would react favorably to the new group. Mr. Waskow said the conference would attempt to bring together "the generation of the liberal reformers with the sit-in generation."

Senator Kennedy is touring Africa and is scheduled to return June 18. An aide, Polly Feingold, said that while she could not comment on the Senator's behalf she thought the new group "sounds very useful" as a platform for dissenting opinions.

Jerome Grossman, a Boston executive who is chairman of the comparatively moderate Massachusetts Political Action for Peace (Mass Pax) and also a promoter of the new conference, affirmed by telephone it "could enter the mainstream" of American politics sharing the outlook of Senators Kennedy and J. W. Fulbright of Arkansas on many issues. Both men have voiced various degrees of dissent with the Administration's foreign policy.

Mr. Grossman, who presided over a preliminary meeting of the new group after an antiwar demonstration at the White House in Washington last November, said the conference would function as a service organization, providing research, personnel and funds for candidates it endorsed.

An immediate goal is the raising of $500,000 to support some 50 candidates throughout the nation, it was understood.

Political Power Sought

A provisional national council of the new group said in an advertisement in The New York Times May 22:

"The killing of American and Vietnamese will not stop unless opponents of this war and of the bankrupt foreign policy which it reflects can turn their dissent into real political power."

Across the nation, the advertisement continued, "local alliances of issues-oriented liberals, student activists, peace and civil rights workers, and grassroots movements of the poor are being formed for the tangible ends of winning elections."

The advertisement listed some candidates, including Robert Scheer, who was defeated Tuesday as candidate for the Democratic nomination for the House of Representatives in California's Seventh District, and Theodore Weiss, Reform Democratic City Councilman and a candidate for the House in Manhattan's 19th District.

One New Yorker who had signed the new group's advertisement last month, Prof. Irvin Howe of Hunter College, withdrew later. Professor Howe explained yesterday that he did not agree with "Bob Scheer who has come out for the Vietcong," and would not back "candidates presenting some ambiguity."

Mr. Howe has been prominent in campaigns against the Vietnam war. His withdrawal from the new conference may be an example of dissension among the dissenters from the Administration's policies.

Members of the new conference include the national secretary of the leftist Students for a Democratic Society (S.D.S), Paul Booth, but no representatives of the W.E.B. DuBois Clubs, which the Justice Department has denounced as a Communist-front organization, and other antiwar groups to the left of the Communist Party U.S.A.

Among the sponsors of the new conference are Dr. Benjamin Spock, the pediatrician; Dr. Albert Szent-Gyorgyi, the Nobel Prize winner; Stokely Carmichael, new chairman of the Student Nonviolent Coordinating Committee, a militant Southern civil rights group, and Dick Gregory, Negro entertainer.

The new group reflects ferment and efforts at political involvement in the antiwar movement. This welter of national, regional and local organizations and ad hoc committees was the subject of a recent nationwide survey by The New York Times. More than 50 leaders and members of antiwar groups were interviewed by reporters of this newspaper.

Leaders of S.D.S., a major force in the New Left, were among those interviewed. Two of them, Mr. Booth and one of the organization's founders, Thomas Hayden, said they could imagine collaboration with Senator Kennedy. Other S.D.S. members scoffed at the Senator, asserting he was part of the "Establishment."

Speaking in an untidy walkup office in a Negro district on Chicago's South Side, the 22-year-old Mr. Booth conceded that there might be Communists in his 5,000-member organization, but he rejected suggestions that the Communist party might have infiltrated S.D.S.

He said it was the other way around. Three S.D.S. observers will attend the forthcoming national convention of the Communist party, scheduled to open in New York June 22, Mr. Booth said, and through lobbying would help the party's young generation of some 500 newly recruited members to "democratize and radicalize" the Communist party.

Mr. Hayden was the third man—together with Dr. Herbert Aptheker, the leading theoretician of the Communist party, and Staughton Lynd of Yale University—on an unauthorized and much publicized "fact-finding" mission to Hanoi last December.

Patronizing remarks about the Communist party, which was pictured as a coterie of tired bureaucrats and doctrinaires, were heard also from other young members of antiwar groups interviewed in the survey.

The study showed the following:

¶A widespread malaise over the fighting in Vietnam and fear of further escalation is resulting in a groundswell of antiwar activities in several parts of the nation, most recently in the Midwest.

¶The antiwar movement is a maze of cross-organized groups, ranging from religiously motivated pacifists to ultraleftists who condemn the fighting in Vietnam but advocate violence against "injustice."

¶Within the antiwar movement, radicals and moderates often band together in ad hoc committees for propaganda and protest. In the process the moderates usually raise most of the funds while they are maneuvered into extremist positions.

¶Rightist allegations that the antiwar movement is centrally directed and funded by a Communist conspiracy lack evidence.

¶Several antiwar factions are in touch with foreign Communist parties and with the South Vietnamese National Liberation Front, the political arm of the Vietcong guerrillas.

¶The antiwar movement is torn by internal debate over strategy, the role of civil rights issues in its propaganda, and political involvement with Reform Democratic or third-party efforts.

Students and other young people, often found to be highly motivated and articulate, are the backbone of the antiwar movement.

'Kids Run the Show'

"The kids run the show," a correspondent observed in summarizing his West Coast impressions. He continued:

"The oldtime radical stands forlornly on the fringe, wishing he could do something more, but he virtually must say 'sir' if he wants two minutes of the student leaders' time. Even in court the lawyer stands by when asked a simple question while a group of students whisper to make their decisions."

Sitting in on their bull sessions, the outsider was struck by the vehemence with which most of the antiwar and antidraft students were committed to fighting the Establishment.

"The Establishment is all that's wrong and rotten in America," an earnest girl from an affluent Long Island home asserted on a Midwestern campus in citing "President Johnson's consensus through fear, the Pentagon, the Central Intelligence Agency, foreign investment, the big business corporations, the two-party system that is really just one party, racial injustice, poverty amid prosperity."

"In this sense," she went on, "the Vietnam war has been with us for decades."

Describing the mood on the radical students' fringe, the full-time national president of S.D.S., Carl Oglesby, said here recently:

"It turns quickly from excitement to frustration and despair. The students are ready to rush to the barricades; the trouble is they don't know where the barricades are."

Mr. Oglesby, his tense face framed by a beard, comes close to the popular stereotype of the "peacenik." He toured Italy in March as a guest of a committee comprising Communists and left-wing Socialists. At about the same time, Frank Emspak of Madison, Wis., visited Budapest where, he said recently, he saw representatives of Communist China and the Vietnamese National Liberation Front.

Mr. Emspak, a zoology graduate, is chairman of the National Coordinating Comimttee To End The War In Vietnam, an umbrella organization trying to be a clearing-house for antiwar groups.

A recent visitor to the committee's Madison headquarters was shown a stack of antiwar literature published by moderate groups.

"They are sending us tons of material, neatly printed, postage paid," a student worker said. "We gratefully accept the stuff and send it out to our nearly 400 affiliates. But we don't give away our mailing lists." S.D.S. in Chicago practices a similar policy.

"A lot of fashionable money is around," Robert Pickus, the regional director of Turn Toward Peace in San Francisco, a group that produces much antiwar literature, said recently. "It's fashionable to be dissident."

June 10, 1966

G.O.P. FINDS '68 OUTLOOK BRIGHTER AS IT COUNTS ELECTION SUCCESSES: GAIN OF 47 IN HOUSE, 8 GOVERNORS

PARTY IS SPURRED

Victories Bring 4 Men to Front in Picture for Presidency

By WARREN WEAVER Jr.

After two painful years of looking back at 1964, the Republicans were suddenly looking forward to 1968 yesterday with a heady new optimism born of impressive election victories.

Tuesday's balloting, which brought the resurgent Republicans a net gain of three Senators, 47 House seats and eight Governors, also presented the party with three or perhaps four Presidential candidates for 1968. They were:

¶Gov. George Romney of Michigan, who won an impressive 500,000-vote re-election majority and carried with him Senator Robert P. Griffin and five new Republican House members, in a major display of drawing power.

¶Former Vice President Richard M. Nixon, who campaigned relentlessly for many of the Republican winners and gained further favor in the party by predicting more accurately than any other leader the campaign victories.

¶Ronald Reagan, the film star turned politician, who won the governorship of California going away to become, without a day in public office, the favorite Presidential candidate of Republican conservatives.

¶Charles H. Percy, the 47-year-old Illinois industrialist who decisively defeated Senator Paul H. Douglas and won himself immediate consideration as a national candidate with liberal support.

'New Solutions' Urged

At the same time, the election results weakened, perhaps critically, President Johnson's influence in the Congress over the next two important years and did not add luster to his reputation as a party leader

and candidate for re-election.

The net effect, politicians of both persuasions agreed, was to reconstitute the two-party system on the national level after the withering Goldwater defeat of 1964 had reduced the Republican party to a disorderly, ineffective minority.

Mr. Nixon was quick to emphasize the Republican advance. He called the size of the Democratic loss in the House "the sharpest rebuff of a President in a generation" and a "rebuke to the President's lack of credibility and lack of direction abroad."

The size of the Republican advances, the former Vice President declared, has given President Johnson "a mandate to open his mind to new solutions, to accept constructive criticism and to reinstitute the tradition of a bipartisan foreign policy."

In Texas, the President had no direct comment on the election results. His acting press secretary, George Christian, told reporters that Mr. Johnson "obviously wishes every man that he wanted elected were elected."

The press aide said that the Senate elections left the Democrats "a pretty good majority" and that the party's House margin would be in the neighborhood of 65 seats.

Political argument over what constitutes a genuine gain in House strength in an off-year by the party not in the White House seemed sure to continue unabated.

Using the most favorable time segment available—1890 to 1962—President Johnson has said that the out party should gain 41 seats just to maintain the historical average. Thus he can describe Tuesday's Republican advance as only a little better than average.

But in modern political history the fluctuation has been less pronounced and the average gain smaller. For the off-years since 1932, the average has been 33, for the last 20 years, only 31. In these terms, the Republican gain was 50 per cent above average.

Among other favorable election results for the Republicans was the promotion into political prominence of a number of relatively new faces: Governor Mark O. Hatfield of Oregon and Attorney General Edward W. Brooke of Massachusetts, who will join Mr. Percy in the Senate.

The fact that Mr. Brooke,

the first Negro elected to the Senate since the Reconstruction days of 1871, is a Republican is certainly not going to do anything to discourage Negro voters from abandoning their traditional allegiance to the Democratic party, as measurable numbers did on Tuesday.

In what was probably the election's greatest single demonstration of resilience, Governor Rockefeller of New York reoccupied his niche as a national political figure. Most Republicans had been preparing to auction off that niche to the highest bidder.

At a news conference yesterday, Mr. Rockefeller insisted "unequivocally" that he would not run for President. Close associates are convinced that even mildly encouraging circumstances could change that stand, but they do not see such circumstances developing.

Even if it did not advance his national candidacy, Mr. Rockefeller's victory was extremely important, however, to the cause of insuring that the Republican presidential nominee in 1968 be drawn from the liberal or moderate wing of the party.

New York's Cause Aided

After the Rockefeller victory, the New York delegation seems almost certain to go to the next National Convention united nominally behind Senator Jacob K. Javits as a favorite son but actually behind Governor Romney—or perhaps another liberal if the Romney cause should falter.

Had Mr. Rockefeller been defeated, freeing New York Republicans from strong central control, the convention delegation in 1968 would probably have included numbers of Nixon and Reagan supporters.

The election results accomplished a similar function for the liberal Republican cause in other big and influential states, as Republican candidates were elected Governors in Massachusetts, Pennsylvania, Ohio and Michigan and, smaller but important, in Maryland, Minnesota, Wisconsin and Oregon.

These results by no means guarantee the nomination of a liberal Republican Presidential candidate in 1968. But that prospect would have been seriously weakened if not destroyed by Republican losses Tuesday in two or three of the big states.

A governorship victory that heartened Republicans nationally, for a tactical rather than philosophical reason, was that of Mrs. Lurleen Wallace in Alabama, for it virtually guaranteed that her husband, retiring Gov. George C. Wallace, would

run for President as an independent in 1968.

Under ordinary circumstances, a Wallace candidacy could be expected to divert the electoral votes of four or five states in the Deep South from President Johnson, making him that much more vulnerable to Republican competition.

In the light of the election results, it was probably just as well for President Johnson that he canceled the political tour he had set up for the weekend before the election, in favor of a pre-operation rest.

Of ten states that were on the tentative Presidential schedule, all but Montana saw the Democratic candidates lose, which would have been a rather sorry reward for Mr. Johnson. Probably only Minnesota was close enough so that a Presidential visit might have altered the outcome.

Kennedy Not Benefited

Adverse Democratic results did little to enhance the reputation of Senator Robert F. Kennedy as a national campaigner. Many of the candidates for whom he campaigned the hardest—Frank D. O'Connor in New York, Edmund G. Brown in California, Paul H. Douglas in Illinois—lost.

Similarly, Vice President Humphrey's political prestige was scarcely enhanced when the Republican gubernatorial candidate, Harold E. LeVander, beat Gov. Karl F. Rolvaag of the Democratic-Farmer-Labor party Mr. Humphrey founded in his home state of Minnesota.

It was difficult to predict how any given member, much less a whole Congress, would vote on pieces of legislation not yet drafted. One survey indicated, however, that Tuesday's results put about two dozen more Conservatives into the House of Representatives.

The swing of 50 votes effected by these new members voting "no" where their more liberal predecessors voted "yes" could spell the difference between law and no law for controversial programs submitted by President Johnson in the next two years.

Evidence that the war in Vietnam had materially affected the election results was hard to come by. In Oregon, however, the Democratic Senate candidate, Robert B. Duncan, attributed his defeat to public dissatisfaction with the war. He had campaigned as a strong supporter of President Johnson's Vietnam policy.

The white backlash of resentment against Negro social and political advance played a real but erratic role in the election. It was estimated that 15 candidates who had advocated limited civil rights progress, most of them Republicans, won House seats among the 37 districts in which the backlash was an acknowledged issue.

Louis Harris, the public opinion analyst, said his studies indicated that inflation and rising prices had been the most effective issue underlying Republican Congressional victories.

November 10, 1966

Riots and Elections

Politicians of Both Parties Believe Johnson Has Been Seriously Damaged

By WARREN WEAVER Jr.
Special to The New York Times

WASHINGTON, Aug. 14—Political leaders here are in general agreement that President Johnson's re-election prospects have been seriously damaged by the summer's urban race riots, but some of them are puzzled by the President's response. From the evidence so far, Mr. Johnson is avoiding any immediate counter-effort—other than the appointment of his study commission—in favor of a long-range political strategy aimed at shifting the blame for the disorders to Republicans in Congress.

News Analysis

Poll figures out last weekend only serve to underscore the conviction among both Democrats and Republicans that the President has been badly hurt by the shock wave of midsummer violence that swept across the country.

The first Gallup and Harris poll samplings since the riots show public confidence in the way Mr. Johnson is handling his job dropping to a new low rating of 39 per cent. Not since Harry Truman's last month in office, after the 1952 Eisenhower election sweep, has a President's popularity registered such a sharp drop in the polls.

Mr. Johnson's only immediate response has been his appointment of the new bipartisan commission on civil disorders, with an action schedule that some of his critics inside and outside the party regard as leisurely.

The commission has been instructed to report its preliminary recommendation by next March, its final conclusions the following July. One cynic recently called this schedule "one report for the convention and one for the campaign."

Over the long haul to 1968, however, it seems increasingly clear that the President hopes to counter Republican criticism over "crime in the streets" by blaming Congress for failure to approve a number of his programs aimed at making the nation's cities more livable.

Generally, Republicans believe that their Presidential candidate stands to benefit materially from the issue of racial violence no matter who he is or what program he may put forward to end the rioting.

As the political analysts see it, the issue is one that hurts incumbent officials at every level no matter which party, on the simple theory that one of the basic responsibilities of government is maintaining public order, and a government official who cannot fulfill this responsibility has failed.

Thus, in Detroit, fearful voters are regarded as likely to support the men who next challenge, for their respective offices, Mayor Jerome P. Cavanagh, a Democrat, Gov. George Romney, a Republican, and President Johnson, a Democrat.

"It is not a question of holding the President personally responsible for local outbreaks of violence," one Democrat said. "It is a question of millions of Americans looking for some kind of new leadership, something to reverse a trend of lawlessness they just can't accept."

Some Democrats believe that Governor Romney, if he should win the Republican Presidential nomination, would be less able to capitalize on the riot issue because he was forced to request Federal assistance to quell the disturbances in Detroit.

At this stage, the two other Governors regarded as Republican Presidential contenders, Ronald Reagan of California and Nelson A. Rockefeller of New York, have not had to deal with rioting comparable to that Governor Romney tried to bring under control in Detroit.

Some Republicans believe Governor Reagan, as a Presidential candidate, would be the greatest beneficiary of the riot issue. The most conservative of the potential candidates, he would be likely to stand as the most outspoken advocate of civil order over civil rights.

The Republicans have made it eminently clear already that they will not permit the President to neutralize the issue as a political matter, which they regard as the motivation for his appointment of Mayor Lindsay of New York and other Republicans to the study commission.

The Republican Coordinating Committee has already declared publicly that Mr. Johnson must share in the blame for the series of shattering riots because he "has totally failed to recognize the problem."

Most Republicans and some Democrats doubt that an attempt by the President to "run against the Congress" on the issue of civil disturbance can effectively counter the high emotional impact that the riots have produced in the electorate.

August 15, 1967

Poll Finds Majority Would Prefer G.O.P. First Time Since '57

PRINCETON, N. J., Nov. 12 (UPI)—A majority of voters for the first time since 1957 would prefer to see Republicans rather than Democrats handle the nation's most serious problem, the Gallup poll reported today.

The poll asked 1,565 adults across the nation to name what they considered to be the most pressing problems facing the United States and which party could best handle them.

Fifty per cent cited the Vietnam war, 21 per cent civil rights and 16 per cent the high cost of living.

The poll said that 30 per cent preferred the Republicans and 26 per cent the Democrats, while 28 per cent saw no difference and 16 per cent had no opinion.

In mid-October of last year, with the same problems listed, the poll said the Democrats held a 53-to-47 edge over the Republicans.

This division was reflected in the Congressional elections in November when the vote was 52-to-48 on the Democratic side.

November 13, 1967

Skill Replaces Ideology at G.O.P. Headquarters Under Bliss

By ROBERT B. SEMPLE Jr.
Special to The New York Times

WASHINGTON, Jan. 31—Anyone visiting the headquarters of the Republican National Committee for the first time might well conclude that he had inadvertently stumbled into a modest but rather successful insurance agency.

The offices at 1625 I Street here are cramped but clean, and there is none of the noisy commotion that one would expect in the control center of a major political party in an election year. Secretaries glide down the halls and around corners. Men in white shirtsleeves bend quietly and industriously over reports, graphs and columns of figures.

Committee officials are happy to talk to visitors, but it is curiously abstract talk about the "party," and voters, and numbers and charts. Flesh-and-blood names like Rockefeller, Reagan, Nixon and Romney—living symbols of the great and real struggle for power taking place beyond the committee's walls—are rarely acknowledged. Each official no doubt has his own private preferences—but his inner loyalties remain inside.

"We are a service agency," a

committee worker remarked the other day. "We don't take sides. Our job is to build a party organization and have it ready for the nominee."

The worker's voice dropped to a reverent whisper.

"As the boss says, you don't get emotional about anybody until you have a nominee."

A Bundle of Nerves

The "boss" is Ray C. Bliss, a 60-year-old, florid-faced bundle of nerves who ran the Ohio State Republican Committee for 16 years, assumed the national chairmanship in 1965 after the resounding defeat of Barry Goldwater in the 1964 Presidential election and, for the last 33 months, has slowly wrenched the party from its consuming passion for ideological dispute and turned it toward the more prosaic but perhaps more profitable task of party organization.

Mr. Bliss is not without his critics and potential problems—problems that may stem, ironically, from his own commitment to party unity and his own endless preoccupation with the detail of party structure. But there is general agreement that the Bliss formula of work, unity and then more work has put the party on the firmest ground it has occupied for decades.

The personality of the committee's headquarters, for example, has changed dramatically. Gone are the ideologues who dominated the committee before Mr. Bliss's arrival. In their place are loyal, dedicated, essentially faceless professionals, the kind of men — and, in some instances, the same men — who surrounded the chairman in Ohio.

Meantime he has steadily strengthened all of the committee's operating divisions. For example, the Minorities Division, moribund under Mr. Goldwater, has been reactivated and placed under Clarence Lee Townes Jr., successful Negro insurance man from Virginia.

Convinced that the young Negro is politically uncommitted—"looking for a magnet around which to polarize his discontent," as he put it one day recently — Mr. Townes, along with three full-time field workers, has been swooping down on scores of Negro campuses, newspapers and neighborhoods in an effort to increase the Republican share of the Negro vote — which was only 4 per cent in 1964 and 19 per cent in 1966.

A similar transformation has seized the Arts and Sciences Division whose staff and responsibilities have quadrupled since 1965 under the leadership of John M. Hunger, a Bliss appointee.

Mr. Hunger is a 33-year-old professor of political science from the University of Wisconsin. His main responsibility is the "Opportunities Unlimited" program, the committee's principal vehicle for involving students in Republican politics.

Under the program, students from more than 250 colleges met with Republican leaders at 22 regional sessions in 1966 and 1967. Twenty-two conferences are planned for 1968.

Mr. Bliss has also done much to strengthen the party financially. Installing Gen. Lucius D. Clay as finance chairman, he raised $4-million in 1965 and $7.1-mililon in 1966, a record for a midterm election year.

'Outmanned, Outspent'

Last year the party's collection machinery raised $5.1-million — more than double the $2.2-million collected by the Democrats. At present the Republican party shows a healthy surplus, and the chairman has set his sights on a record-breaking $11-million in 1968.

Mr. Bliss's most durable contribution, however, may turn out to be his patient efforts to turn the party into an efficient political machine. Although he has always been preoccupied with organization, the subject became a fetish in 1960, when Senator Thruston B. Morton of Kentucky, then the chairman, asked him to undertake a postelection analysis of Republican efforts in the big cities during the Presidential campaign.

Mr. Bliss was horrified by what he found.

"The Republican party," he wrote, "is outmanned, out-organized, outspent and out-worked."

The Bliss report received much attention in the press but little from the Goldwater men, who were interested in the South and not the cities.

But when Mr. Bliss arrived in Washington in 1965, he took his report off the shelf and began spreading its gospel nationally through a series of workshops and seminars for state, county, big-city, small-city and suburban Republican leaders.

At each, the chairman stressed the importance of what he called the "basics" — precinct organization, finances, the selection of attractive candidates.

It was, to borrow a Bliss phrase, pure "nuts and bolts," but the results were heartening. In the 21 largest cities where state offices were contested in 1966, Republicans carried six and improved their record in nine more—a vital factor, Mr. Bliss believes, in the general Republican resurgence that year.

The chairman's critics contend that there is no accurate way of measuring the impact of his efforts, and Mr. Bliss himself concedes that other factors—issues, to take the obvious example—have as much to do with the outcome of an election as organization.

But he believes that an organized party is better than an

Ray C. Bliss

unorganized party, and in his desk there is one poll that he treasures almost as much as the 1966 results themselves. Taken after the election, it shows that in terms of personal contact between party workers and voters, literature mailed and received, candidate exposure and a variety of other indexes, Republicans outworked Democrats by a 2-to-1 margin.

Yet Mr. Bliss has problems. In an effort to bank the fierce ideological fires of 1964, he helped establish the Republican Coordinating Committee, a supergroup of Republican leaders from various wings of the party that has since turned out nearly two dozen position papers on major issues.

In the chairman's view, the Coordinating Committee offers solid proof that Republicans can get together and reach agreement. In the view of its critics, however, the Coordinating Committee has produced tepid ideological mush, robbed the party of a sharp cutting edge and kept it from developing modern policies that provide sharp, relevant alternatives to Democratic ideas.

The liberals in the party are particularly disturbed, arguing that Mr. Bliss's search for unity on ideas can only pave the way for a bland unity candidate —they offer Richard M. Nixon as an example—and inhibit the emergence of a progressive platform and a progressive candidate—such as, in their view, Governor Rockefeller of New York.

Tricky Question

The whole question of whether Mr. Bliss's efforts have helped or hurt a particular candidate is, however, a tricky one. It is argued in some quarters that the chairman's emphasis on winning elections rather than debating ideas will inevitably help a man like Governor Rockefeller, who has plenty of ideological enemies within the party but who, on the basis of current polls, is believed to have a better chance of beating President Johnson than anyone else.

In any event, the showdown for Mr. Bliss is not far off. It will come when the entire national committee assembles here Feb. 2 for a three-day meeting to discuss next summer's convention and to decide on the merits of the call by the Republican Governors for greater representation on the key platform-writing committee.

Specifically, the Governors have asked for the co-chairman-

ship of the Platform Committee, a request that so far has been met with derision from the more conservative Congressional wing of the party. Anxious to preserve their traditional policy-making functions, the Congressional members not only favor a single chairman but also back the conservative Senator Everett McKinley Dirksen of Illinois for the job.

The whole momentum of the last seven years of Ray Bliss's life—beginning with the big-city report and continuing through the workshops and seminars—would seem to indicate that de-

spite his antipathy to ideological dispute and his penchant for tried and true formulas, he might well defy his Congressional friends and grant the urban wing of the party—represented by its major-state Governors—its day in court. But only time will tell.

"The real question," says an aide, "is whether Ray can stand up in the crunch."

February 1, 1968

M'CARTHY TO FIGHT JOHNSON POLICIES IN 5 OR 6 PRIMARIES

Will Oppose Role in Vietnam in an Attempt to Prevent President's Nomination

SEEKS WAR SETTLEMENT

By WARREN WEAVER Jr.
Special to The New York Times

WASHINGTON, Nov. 30—Senator Eugene J. McCarthy announced today that he would challenge President Johnson's right to renomination in five or six Democratic primaries in 1968.

During a bantering, low-key news conference, the Minnesota Senator never actually declared himself a candidate for President or contended that he could deprive the President of the nomination.

In fact, he suggested in response to questions that it would not disturb him if his campaign against Mr. Johnson in the primaries resulted in making Senator Robert F. Kennedy of New York the Democratic candidate next year.

Crowded Conference

Senator McCarthy told a crowded morning conference in the Senate caucus room on Capitol Hill that he had decided to move against the President because "I am concerned that the Administration seems to have set no limit to the price which it's willing to pay or a military victory" in Vietnam.

Mr. McCarthy said he would run in the primary elections in Wisconsin, Nebraska, Oregon,

California and either New Hampshire or Massachusetts, possibly both. His uncertainty about the New England contests was attributed to both political and scheduling problems.

The Minnesotan, until recently a relatively relaxed figure on both the Senate and political scene, indicated he would be satisfied if his Vietnam-oriented campaign persuaded the Administration to move during the next five or six months toward a negotiated settlement.

"If not, I don't mean to draw off at any point, and I think this challenge would have to go all the way to a challenge for the nomination for the Presidency," he said.

"It may not be me at that point. It might be someone else, but so far as the end result of the effort, I think it has to go to the point of trying to change the policy and direction and also the mood of America with reference to the political problems of 1968."

Senator McCarthy said he had talked with Senator Kennedy about his decision to oppose the President and the New Yorker had not tried to dissuade him. In this regard, Mr. McCarthy indicated he was his own second choice as a Johnson challenger.

"I would have been glad if he had moved early," the Minnesotan said of Senator Kennedy. "I think if he had, there'd have been no need for me to do anything."

Senator Kennedy declined to make any further comment today on the McCarthy announcement. Two weeks ago he said such competition in the primaries would be "a healthy influence on the Democratic party," creating excitement and promoting constructive Vietnam debate.

Mr. McCarthy said Senator Kennedy had made "no commitment to stand aside all the way" and "there would surely be nothing illegal or contrary to American politics if he or someone else were to take advantage of what I'm doing."

Mr. McCarthy, a tall, tanned,

trim figure with white hair, produced nearly a dozen ripples of laughter with deadpan rejoinders. He denied that his move today was political suicide although "it might be execution," and assured reporters that his moment of decision "was nothing like St. Paul being knocked off his horse."

The Senator came a cropper, however, when he denied he was a stalking horse for Senator Kennedy and cited "that great Kentucky Derby when Coaltown was the stalking horse and Citation was supposed to win. But Coaltown didn't quit."

In the 1948 Derby, Coaltown was the pace-setter for the other half of the Calumet Farms entry, Citation, for the first mile, but Citation caught him in the stretch and won by 3½ lengths.

Dates and Prospects

Following are the primaries Senator McCarthy said he would enter, their dates and a rough estimate of his prospects:

WISCONSIN — April 2. In this last "open" primary in the nation in which voters may choose either party's contest, he could attract Republican as well as Democratic opponents of the war in Vietnam and probably enjoy sympathy if not support from Senators William Proxmire and Gaylord Nelson.

NEBRASKA — May 14. The state Democratic organization is generally conservative, reflecting an electorate that will probably prove less hospitable to the McCarthy challenge than that of other primary states.

OREGON — May 28. A Vietnam hawk won the 1966 Democratic Senate primary over a dove, but lost the election to Senator Mark O. Hatfield, a Republican critic of the war. Mr. Hatfield said today there was "a strong possibility" Senator McCarthy could defeat the President there in 1968.

CALIFORNIA—June 4. The Democratic party is already deeply split by the Vietnam issue here, with a heavy concentration of opponents of the war who would work for Mr. McCarthy against a pro-Johnson delegate slate. Much of the McCarthy financial backing is

coming from California.

Under the election laws of Wisconsin, Nebraska and Oregon, President Johnson's name will be automatically listed on the primary ballot and could be removed only by a sworn statement that he had no interest in the office. Thus, in those states, a direct contest between Senator McCarthy and the President appears certain.

In California, however, the competition would be between slates of delegates.

Others Are Listed

In addition, the Minnesotan will enter one or possibly both of these primaries:

NEW HAMPSHIRE — March 12. As the earliest primary, it is regarded as of great psychological importance. However, Democrats there tend to support the Administration's Vietnam policy. Mr. McCarthy said today a February trip to Southeast Asia might make it impossible for him to campaign.

MASSACHUSETTS—April 30. Senator McCarthy would presumably attract Roman Catholic votes, but there is little evidence that his Vietnam position would be broadly popular. Senator Edward M. Kennedy has declined to oppose Mr. McCarthy as a "stand-in" for the President but predicts his nomination.

"I am hopeful that this challenge which I am making, which I hope will be supported by other members of the Senate and other politicians, may alleviate at least in some degree this sense of political helplessness and restore to many people a belief in the processes of American politics and of American government," Mr. McCarthy said.

He told the news conference there might also be other Democrats running as favorite-son candidates on his behalf in still other primary states, mentioning Indiana and South Dakota.

Neither the White House nor the Democratic National Chairman, John M. Bailey, had any comment on the McCarthy announcement.

December 1, 1967

WALLACE IN RACE; WILL 'RUN TO WIN'

But Alabamian Also Hints One Purpose Is to Force Election Into House

By BEN A. FRANKLIN
Special to The New York Times

WASHINGTON, Feb. 8 — George C. Wallace of Alabama announced today that he would run for the Presidency and "run to win."

The 48-year-old former Governor acknowledged, however, that "certainly the odds have not been fully in favor of third-party movements in America."

Mr. Wallace, speaking at a crowded news conference here, made it clear that he had a number of objectives short of an outright popular and electoral victory.

He has himself called his frankly anti-establishment campaign that of a "spoiler," and today he said there "certainly is a prospect" that it might end by denying either the Republican or Democratic Presidential candidate the required majority of 270 votes in the Electoral College.

He indicated, and his associates confirmed, that in such a stalemate one or the other, or perhaps both, of the major-party candidates would be expected to bargain with him for the decisive portion of his electoral vote.

Nevertheless, Mr. Wallace told about 75 newsmen, "we are not running for the purpose of throwing the election into the House."

If no Presidential candidate in a multi-candidate race has at least 270 electoral votes the election must be decided by the House of Representatives from among the three candidates with the greatest number. Each state delegation would have one vote.

The relevant section of the 12th Amendment to the Constitution provides as follows:

"If no person [has] such majority, then from the persons having the highest numbers, not exceeding three, on the list of those voted for as President, the House of Representatives shall choose immediately, by ballot the President. But in choosing the President, the votes shall be taken by States, the representation from each State having one vote."

Any party with control of 26 of the 50 state delegations, accordingly, would probably control the outcome in such a so-called contingent election, and this year's House elections could thus become crucial.

An Electoral College deadlock has not occurred since 1824.

'Nothing to Lose'

Then, the House decided a four-way deadlock in favor of John Quincy Adams, although Andrew Jackson had received more popular and more electoral votes than Adams.

"If it is thrown into the House," Mr. Wallace said today, "we have all to gain and nothing to lose." That would be true, he indicated, because, at the least, the dramatic dislocation of the normal electoral process would prove that "people are tired of the interference of the central Government" supported, he said, by both the Republicans and the Democrats.

Furthermore, Mr. Wallace implied and his staff confirmed that they believed such a deadlock might well force important concessions from the Presidential candidate whose electoral vote, combined with Mr. Wallace's, would equal a majority of 270 or more.

Negotiations, staff aides said, presumably would occur between Election Day, Nov. 5, and Dec. 16, the date the Electoral College is required by law to meet, and would thus avoid a contingent election in the House.

The segregationist former Governor has several times referred approvingly to such a situation as "a kind of coalition government," and his statements today indicated that his bargaining, if it occurs this year, would be formidable.

He declared that if he were the President "we would have a different orientation on the Supreme Court than we now have."

Before he withdrew from his first third-party Presidential candidacy in 1964, Mr. Wallace spoke repeatedly of his hopes of "advising" and "consulting" on future Supreme Court appointments. And in a newspaper interview distributed to newsmen as part of a "press kit" today, he is quoted as saying:

"I might not have any chance in the House, but you must remember before you go into the House you go into the Electoral College. If we held the balance of power, we may decide the question in the Electoral College because one party may have to make a major concession to the people of our country, a solemn convenant to them."

In the interview, published last May in the Richmond, Va., News-Leader, Mr. Wallace said the "solemn convenant" would "allow representation on the Supreme Court of the people."

Mr. Wallace said he expected to announce his preference for a Vice-Presidential running mate "in a few days." He said it was likely that his American Independent Party ticket would then be ratified at a national convention this summer.

Briefcases in the River

Among other "if I were President" replies Mr. Wallace were these two:

¶"I would bring all these briefcase-toting bureaucrats in the Department of Health, Education and Welfare to Washington and throw their briefcases in the Potomac River."

¶"I would keep the peace if I had to keep 30,000 troops standing on the streets, two feet apart and with two-foot-long bayonets."

He also said that the "so-called civil rights laws are really an attack on the property rights of this country and on the free enterprise system and local government . . . and I would try to have them changed in Congress."

He said urban rioting and acts of "defiance of the national security" were led by "activists, anarchists, revolutionaries and Communists" who ought to be in jail.

February 9, 1968

M'CARTHY GETS ABOUT 40%, JOHNSON AND NIXON ON TOP IN NEW HAMPSHIRE VOTING

ROCKEFELLER LAGS

By WARREN WEAVER Jr.
Special to The New York Times

CONCORD, N. H., March 12 —President Johnson turned back a strong challenge by Senator Eugene J. McCarthy in the first 1968 Democratic primary tonight, but not before the Minnesotan had won about 40 per cent of the vote.

In the parallel Republican contest, Richard M. Nixon routed a write-in effort by supporters of Governor Rockefeller of New York, holding his only current Presidential competitor to about 10 per cent of the vote.

Although the President, a write-in candidate, was headed for certain victory in the popularity contest with nearly 90 per cent of the vote in, incomplete returns indicated that Mr. McCarthy had won about 20 of New Hampshire's 24 delegates to the Democratic National Convention.

This happened because the total Johnson vote was divided among 45 candidates for the 24 delegate openings, while the McCarthy forces had prudently limited their slate to 24, each of whom got the full benefit of the Senator's strength.

With 87 per cent of the Democratic vote cast, President Johnson held 50 per cent, or 22,272 votes, to 41 per cent, or 18,032, for Senator McCarthy, whose name was on the ballot.

Rockefeller backers had set a goal of 15,000 for their candidate. With 80 per cent of the Republican returns in, however, he had 11 per cent, or 8,610, which would give him only a little over 10,000 of the expected 102,000 total. Mr. Nixon polled about 80 per cent of the vote, or 63,325.

Despite a heavy snow that began in the late afternoon, the turnover in both party primaries was larger than expected. The projected Republican vote of 102,000 was 15,000 to 20,000 higher than many party leaders had expected, particularly after the withdrawal of Gov. George Romney had dampened competition.

The Democratic vote was estimated at 48,000. Four years ago, when a Johnson write-in was unopposed, the same figure was just over 30,000.

Mr. Nixon greeted the Republican returns jubilantly as "a very smashing victory" in a speech to supporters at his New York City headquarters. He called the small Rockefeller vote proof that "the people of this country don't like absentee candidates."

At his Manchester headquarters, Senator McCarthy said the returns had demonstrated "we can not only win but pick up delegates in nonprimary states."

He declared that the momentum of his New Hampshire showing would enable him to "go on and get the nomination in Chicago."

Senator McCarthy also received more than 1,000 write-in votes in the Republican primary, more in some areas than Governor Romney whose name had remained on the ballot.

This raised speculation that some of the Romney supporters had shifted to the Democrats because of his opposition to the war in Vietnam.

While Governor Rockefeller had kept aloof from the New Hampshire write-in, denying any sponsorship, its relatively weak showing seemed unlikely to add any momentum to his all-but-declared Presidential candidacy.

The Rockefeller share of the vote was about the same as polls had indicated he would receive two weeks ago, before former Gov. Hugh Gregg

pumped new life and money into a lackluster write-in after the withdrawal of Governor Romney from Presidential competition.

Although Senator McCarthy only led the President in the earliest scattered reports, he continued to hang fairly close to Mr. Johnson—closer than all but his most optimistic followers had believed possible—as the evening wore on.

Nixon Achieves Goal

Mr. Nixon had clearly achieved the goal he set late in his campaign after Governor Romney had pulled out and left him without active competition. The former Vice President said then that he hoped to get a higher percentage of the Republican vote than the President would get of the Democratic.

There was never any question that Mr. Nixon would win all the eight delegates to the Republican National Convention. His slate was well ahead from the beginning.

Senator Robert F. Kennedy of New York, who had tried to keep out of all competition, got some votes for both President and Vice President, but not an impressive number of either.

The New Yorker got only enough write-ins in the Presidential preference contest to total less than 1 per cent of the vote. In another write-in competition with Vice President Humphrey, he trailed the President's running-mate by 46 to 16 per cent.

In polls taken before Gov. George Romney of Michigan had dropped out of the primary contest and Mr. Rockefeller had announced his willingness to

run for President, the New York Governor had received 9 or 10 per cent of the vote.

In the last two weeks before the primary, political interest shifted from the Republican contest between former Vice President Nixon and Governor Romney of Michigan to Senator McCarthy's campaign against President Johnson.

When Governor Romney withdrew as a Presidential candidate on Feb. 28, he left Mr. Nixon with no real opponent on the ballot and only a makeshift write-in campaign for Governor Rockefeller to worry about.

Too Little, Too Late

The write-in for the New York Governor got a late infusion of financial support and professional management from Mr. Gregg, who had been Mr. Rockefeller's campaign manager here in 1964, but most politicians deemed it to be too late to have any real impact on the big Nixon advantage.

While the Republican primary became more one-sided, the Democratic contest apparently grew less so. Senator McCarthy, once conceded a paltry 10 or 12 per cent of the vote by New Hampshire party leaders, became the beneficiary of events both inside and outside the state.

As a result, the leaders of the Johnson write-in campaign predicted in its closing days that the Senator would get 35 or 40 per cent of the vote.

This estimate, it was hoped, was high enough to permit them to claim a victory of sorts in the face of expected McCarthy gains.

So encouraged were the McCarthy organizers that even their candidate, who had always concentrated on raising issues of disagreement with the President rather than defeating him, believed that he had a chance in New Hampshire.

McCarthy pollsters had advised the President that if the Democratic primary vote exceeded 45,000, there was a possibility that he could defeat President Johnson in the preferential, or popularity contest, voting.

There are 89,000 enrolled Democrats in New Hampshire, but ordinarily only about half of them bother to vote in the primary. In 1964, when President Johnson was unopposed as a write-in candidate, the turnout was just over 30,000.

When Mr. Nixon's competition abruptly narrowed down to the late-blooming Rockefeller write-in both Republican camps engaged in what the former Vice President conceded was political gamesmanship.

Mr. Gregg had said his goal for the New York Governor would be 15,000 votes, or about 18 per cent of an expected turnout of 85,000 Republicans.

Sidestepping the fact that Mr. Rockefeller's name was not on the ballot and little or no campaign had been waged for him here, the Nixon strategists had contended he should receive about 30,000 votes, or a share roughly proportional to his popularity among Republicans in the national poll.

March 13, 1968

KENNEDY TO MAKE 3 PRIMARY RACES; ATTACKS JOHNSON

CHALLENGE ISSUED

By TOM WICKER

Special to The New York Times

WASHINGTON, March 16— Senator Robert F. Kennedy of New York said today that he would seek the Democratic Presidential nomination because the nation's "disastrous, divisive policies" in Vietnam and at home could be changed "only by changing the men who are now making them."

With this severe attack on

President Johnson, the brother of President Kennedy opened what may become the most serious challenge to the renomination of an incumbent President since Theodore Roosevelt failed to oust William H. Taft in 1912.

Not since James G. Blaine won the Republican nomination from President Chester A. Arthur in 1884 has an incumbent President who sought renomination failed to win it. Mr. Johnson is generally considered a candidate this year.

Senator Kennedy said he

would actively support Senator Eugene J. McCarthy of Minnesota, another candidate against Mr. Johnson, because "it is important now that he achieve the largest possible majority next month in Wisconsin, in Pennsylvania and in the Massachusetts primaries." It is too late for Mr. Kennedy to enter any of those primaries.

He said he would enter his name in the California primary. Officials in Oregon have put his name on the ballot there and the Nebraska Secretary of State placed his name on

the ballot today. Mr. McCarthy already has announced his candidacy in all three.

Thus, there will be a three-way contest in each of them for delegates to the Democratic National Convention in Chicago next August. Mr. Kennedy left open the possibility that he might also enter the Indiana primary, where Mr. McCarthy is a candidate.

Since Indiana will vote on May 7, three weeks before the Oregon primary on May 28 and a month before the California primary on June 4, the possibility that Mr. Kennedy might compete in Indiana with Mr. McCarthy could be used as a powerful argument to win the cooperation of the latter.

Mr. Kennedy refused to pledge support to President Johnson, in the event that he was renominated at Chicago. He said he would make up his mind on that point when he had to.

He personally communicated word of his decision to run to one of the President's assistants, he said, and sent his brother. Senator Edward M. Kennedy of Massachusetts, to Wisconsin to inform Mr. McCarthy of the decision.

Fight Just Beginning

Mr. Kennedy said today that, for his part, he would "take any step that is necessary to cooperate and work with Senator McCarthy." But he made it plain that he was in the race for the nomination because "the fight is just beginning and I believe that I can win."

"I made clear to Senator McCarthy," Mr. Kennedy said, "that my candidacy would not be in opposition to his, but in harmony."

In Green Bay, Wis., where he was campaigning today, Mr. McCarthy said he would not turn down Mr. Kennedy's help in Wisconsin, but that he was "not prepared to deal with anyone."

"An Irishman who announces the day before St. Patrick's Day that he's going to run against another Irishman shouldn't say it's going to be a peaceful relationship," Mr. McCarthy said.

He is committed to the race, he said, and considers himself "the best potential candidate in the field."

Thus, an anti-Johnson, anti-Vietnam war faction in the Democratic party will be at least temporarily split between Mr. Kennedy and Mr. McCarthy —a fact that President Johnson may have had in mind when he responded jokingly to the Kennedy announcement.

"These are days when we have to take chances," Mr. Johnson said at a businessman's conference in Washington. "Some speculate in gold — a primary metal — and others just speculate in primaries."

Not in Laughing Mood

The President's campaign lieutenants were not in a laughing mood, however. James Rowe, the Washington lawyer who is chairman of the Citizens for Johnson-Humphrey organi-

zation, said pointedly:

"I'm going to watch with fascination Bobby's efforts to convince those former young supporters of his who are now supporting Gene McCarthy that he's neither ruthless nor a political opportunist."

Mr. Rowe also said there was a widespread fear among other Democrats that Mr. Kennedy's entry into the race might "destroy the Democratic party for a generation."

Mr. Kennedy, making his announcement and then answering questions in the Caucus Room of the Senate Office Building, showed himself well aware of charges that he was capitalizing on Mr. McCarthy's strong showing against the President in the New Hampshire primary this week.

The McCarthy vote, he said, has demonstrated that the party was deeply divided over President Johnson's policies; therefore, he added, the New Hampshire primary results have made it possible for him to run without being charged with the responsibility of having split the party because of personal ambition or personal animosity to Mr. Johnson.

"My desire is not to divide the strength of those forces seeking a change" in present policies, he said, "but rather to increase it."

"In no state will my efforts be directed against Senator McCarthy," he said.

'Valiant Campaign'

Praising the latter's "valiant campaign" in New Hampshire, Mr. Kennedy said that "he has strength and I have individual strength."

"I don't think that just supporting an individual delivers that . . . I know that Senator McCarthy has suggestions as to what we should do. But I also have some ideas. And I don't think that the Democratic party or the people of the United States lose at all by considering those."

"I can't believe that anybody thinks that this is a pleasant struggle from now on, or that I'm asking for a free ride. I've got five months ahead of me as far as the convention is concerned. I'm going to go into primaries. I'm going to present my case to the American people. I'm going to go all across this country.

"I'm not asking anybody to hand anything to me. I'm not asking anybody to give anything to me. I'm going to go to the people and I'm going to make an effort and I think it's worthwhile."

Mr. Kennedy conceded that he had no arrangement or agreement with Mr. McCarthy for the kind of cooperation he called for in his statement today.

One example of the emotions aroused by Mr. Kennedy's sudden decision to enter the race after Mr. McCarthy's strong showing in New Hampshire came when Mary McGrory of The Washington Evening Star asked Mr. Kennedy if he would stay out of Wisconsin if Mr. McCarthy asked him to.

"Certainly," Mr. Kennedy replied.

"So he could have the victory for himself," Miss McGrory said, audibly.

Many of Mr. McCarthy's supporters are known to feel that Mr. Kennedy took over the headlines before Mr. McCarthy had a chance to enjoy his success in New Hampshire.

Echoes of President

There were echoes of President Kennedy's prose in his brother's announcement this morning, and Theodore C. Sorensen, the late President's special counsel and speech writer, was at the New York Senator's side when he entered the crowded Caucus room.

Mr. Kennedy spoke frequently in the present tense, as his brother used to do ("I run because I am convinced, etc.,") and at one point he reverted to the theme of John Kennedy's

1960 Presidential campaign, and of Edward Kennedy's 1962 campaign for the Senate in Massachusetts.

"I think we can do better," he said.

Mr. Kennedy emphasized the war in Vietnam—although, in a jab at Richard M. Nixon, considered the leading Republican candidate, he said he could not promise to end it. Mr. Nixon has "pledged" to do so.

Mr. Kennedy said, rather, that he would stop the bombing of North Vietnam, require a greater war effort by South Vietnam, and negotiate with with the National Liberation Front, which he said would have to have a place in the future "political process" of South Vietnam.

As Mr. McCarthy has tried to do, however, Mr. Kennedy sought to avoid being tabbed as a peace candidate only.

He seeks new policies, he said, "to end the bloodshed in Vietnam and in our cities, policies to close the gap that now exists between black and white, between rich and poor, between young and old in this country and around the rest of the world."

The most immediate need in domestic policy, he said, is providing new jobs not only in the uneasy cities but also in the rural areas.

Mr. Kennedy spoke of the loyalty with which Mr. Johnson once served John F. Kennedy, and of the kindness the President had shown him after the assassination in November, 1963. Moreover, Mr. Kennedy said of the President:

"I have often commended his efforts in health, in education and in many other areas and I have the deepest sympathy for the burden that he carries today."

So the issue is not personal, he insisted, but "our profound differences over where we are heading and what we want to accomplish."

March 17, 1968

Washington: The Decline of Party Politics

By JAMES RESTON

WASHINGTON, March 26— By all the old tests of party politics, President Johnson would seem to be assured of renomination, if he wants it. But this is just the trouble, for the old tests are no longer reliable. Party loyalty and party machinery have never been weaker than they are now, and for this and many other reasons the President may be in much deeper trouble than most voters believe.

The older men, following the old party rules, are sticking with Mr. Johnson. George

Meany, head of the A.F.L.-C.I.O.; Mayor Dick Daley of Chicago and most of the other venerable "bosses" in the big cities, and even Averell Harriman of New York, who is a close personal friend of Robert Kennedy, have proclaimed their loyalty.

The Democratic Split

But even within the party structure and the labor unions, the younger leaders are in a stubbornly independent mood. Johnson can count on Meany but not on Walter Reuther. He is sure of Daley on the early

ballots, but he has already lost Jesse Unruh of California and Gov. Philip Hoff of Vermont to Kennedy, and even Gov. Harold Hughes of Iowa has threatened to leave the President unless he changes his Vietnam policy.

More than that, as Mayor John Lindsay of New York demonstrated in the last big city election, the opposition of the Democratic party bosses is no longer an insurmountable barrier. For we are now in a wholly new era of political action in America, where the television, the popularity polls and new personalities can and often do topple the old political

power structures.

This is what makes the nomination of Johnson, and even Nixon, far less certain than might appear on the surface. For under the surface deep tides of opinion are running. The war in Vietnam and the riots in the cities have startled even some of the most devoted partisans out of their normal ways of thinking and acting. Television gives the opposition candidates instant contact with vast audiences, and the ideological differences between the parties have narrowed.

Accordingly, candidates can now reach beyond the political organizations to the people. The "bosses" no longer have the same power to "boss" the "faithful" or punish the dissenters.

Thus McCarthy was able to challenge Johnson and the Democratic machine in New Hampshire, even without adequate financial support. Kennedy is infiltrating the party machinery where he can and vaulting over it where he cannot. Senator Mark Hatfield of Oregon feels independent enough to say on national television that he will not hesitate to put the issue of peace above party in the election and will vote for Kennedy rather than Nixon if Nixon does not change his Vietnam stand.

It is quite possible for this combination of great issues, television and new candidates, backed by an aroused and youthful political army, to smash all the assumptions of the old pros.

The Poll Watchers

Even many of the potential delegates to the Democratic convention are saying to the Kennedy and McCarthy people: "We are going along with Johnson for the time being, but we're waiting for Wisconsin and the late polls and then we'll decide."

Wisconsin could give the

President quite a shock. Even the wife of the Republican Governor there was in McCarthy's audience at Madison the other night. Bill Evjue's Capital Times in Madison came out for McCarthy, and one labor union leader, discouraged by the response to his appeals for Johnson, predicted that McCarthy would not only win next Tuesday but win by a substantial majority.

So the old faith in the domination of the pros, even in party conventions, may not prevail this time. McCarthy and Kennedy have made a good start. If they keep the momen-

tum, the polls will reflect their rising challenge, and even the delegates, particularly the young ones, will be hard to control.

The New Democracy

This is, thanks to television, a more representative democratic process. The idea is getting around that politics is too serious a business to be left to politicians, just as war is too serious to be left to soldiers, and if this spreads even the will of an incumbent President can be overcome.

March 27, 1968

JOHNSON SAYS HE WON'T RUN

SURPRISE DECISION

President Steps Aside in Unity Bid—Says 'House' Is Divided

By TOM WICKER
Special to The New York Times

WASHINGTON, March 31—Lyndon Baines Johnson announced tonight: "I shall not seek and I will not accept the nomination of my party as your President."

Later, at a White House news conference, he said his decision was "completely irrevocable."

The President told his nationwide television audience:

"What we have won when all our people were united must not be lost in partisanship. I have concluded that I should not permit the Presidency to become involved in partisan decisions."

Mr. Johnson, acknowledging that there was "division in the American house," withdrew in the name of national unity, which he said was "the ultimate strength of our country."

"With American sons in the field far away," he said, "with the American future under challenge right here at home, with our hopes and the world's

hopes for peace in the balance every day, I do not believe that I should devote an hour or a day of my time to any personal partisan causes or to any duties other than the awesome duties of this office, the Presidency of your country."

Humphrey Race Possible

Mr. Johnson left Senator Robert F. Kennedy of New York and Senator Eugene J. McCarthy of Minnesota as the only two declared candidates for the Democratic Presidential nomination.

Vice President Humphrey, however, will be widely expected to seek the nomination now that his friend and political benefactor, Mr. Johnson, is out of the field. Mr. Humphrey indicated that he would have a statement on his plans tomorrow.

The President informed Mr. Humphrey of his decision during a conference at the latter's apartment in southwest Washington today before the Vice President flew to Mexico City. There, he will represent the United States at the signing of a treaty for a Latin-American nuclear-free zone.

Surprise to Aides

If Mr. Humphrey should become a candidate, he would find most of the primaries foreclosed to him. Only those in the District of Columbia, New Jersey and South Dakota remain open.

Therefore, he would have to rely on collecting delegates in states without primaries and on White House support if he were to head off Mr. Kennedy and Mr. McCarthy.

Former Vice President Richard M. Nixon is the only announced major candidate for the Republican nomination, although Governor Rockefeller has said that he would accept the nomination if drafted.

Mr. Johnson's announcement tonight came as a stunning surprise even to close associates. His main political strategists, James H. Rowe of Washington, White House Special Assistant Marvin W. Watson, and Postmaster General Lawrence F. O'Brien, spent much of today conferring on campaign plans.

They were informed of what was coming just before Mr. Johnson went on national television at 9 P.M. with a prepared speech on the war in Vietnam.

As the speech unfolded, it appeared to be a strong political challenge to Mr. Kennedy and Mr. McCarthy, announcing measures that they had been advocating.

The President thus seemed to be acting in the political tradition of his office—demonstrating that his was the power to act while his critics had only the power to propose.

But Mr. Johnson was really getting ready to place himself in a more obscure tradition—

that Vice Presidents who succeed to the Presidency seek only one term of their own. Before him in this century, Theodore Roosevelt, Calvin Coolidge and Harry S. Truman followed that pattern.

'Willing to Pay Any Price'

Mr. Johnson ended his prepared speech and then launched into a peroration that had not been included in the printed text and that White House sources said he had written himself.

He began by quoting Franklin D. Roosevelt: "Of those to whom much is given—much is asked."

He could not say that no more would be asked of Americans, he continued, but he believed that "now, no less than when the decade began, this generation of Americans is willing to pay any price, bear any burden, meet any hardship, support any friend, oppose any foe, to assure the survival and the success of liberty."

This quotation from a celebrated passage of John F. Kennedy's inaugural address of Jan. 20, 1961, appeared to be a jab at Senator Robert F. Kennedy, who now is campaigning against the war in Vietnam.

The ultimate strength of America, Mr. Johnson continued, in the rather funereal voice and with the solemn expression that he had maintained throughout his 40-minute speech, is not powerful weapons, great resources or boundless wealth but "the unity of our people."

He asserted again a political philosophy he has often expressed—that he was "a free

The Politics of Disorder

man, an American, a public servant and a member of my party—in that order—always and only."

In his 37 years of public service, he said, he had put national unity ahead of everything because it was as true now as it had ever been that "a house divided against itself by the spirit of faction, of party, of region, of religion, of race, is a house that cannot stand."

Mr. Johnson spoke proudly of what he had accomplished in the "52 months and 10 days" since he took over the Presidency, after the assassination of John F. Kennedy in Dallas, Tex., on Nov, 22, 1963.

"Through all time to come," he said. "I think America will be a stronger nation, a more just society, a land of greater opportunity and fulfillment because of what we have all done together in these years of unparalleled achievement."

"Our reward," he said, "will come in a life of freedom and peace and hope that our children will enjoy through ages ahead."

But these gains, Mr. Johnson said, "must not now be lost in suspicion and distrust and selfishness and politics. . . . I have concluded that I should not permit the Presidency to become involved in the partisan divisions that are developing."

And so it was that the man who won the biggest political landslide in American history, when he defeated Senator Barry Goldwater of Arizona in the Presidential election of 1964, renounced the idea of a second term.

In American politics, a "draft" could override even words as strong as Mr. Johnson's, and he did stop short of the ultimate denial—the assertion that he would not run if nominated nor serve if elected.

But the first reaction of close associates and of other political observers here was that he meant what he said. Moreover, the candidacies of Senator Kennedy and Senator McCarthy would make a draft even of an incumbent President virtually impossible.

Still, if Vice President Humphrey does not enter the race, suspicion will undoubtedly be voiced that Mr. Johnson is only trying to stimulate a draft.

Some observers with long memories recall that in 1940, President Franklin D. Roosevelt had Senator Alben W. Barkley of Kentucky read the Democratic National Convention a message in which Mr. Roosevelt said that he had "never had, and has not today, any desire or purpose to continue in the office of President, to be a candidate for that office, or to be nominated by the convention for that office."

The convention nevertheless nominated Mr. Roosevelt for a third term, and he won.

Mr. Roosevelt was not opposed for nomination by any

candidate considered as powerful as Senator Robert Kennedy, however. In addition Senator McCarthy appears likely to win the Wisconsin primary on Tuesday, after having made a strong showing in New Hampshire.

The low point to which Mr. Johnson's political fortunes have fallen was dramatized in a Gallup Poll published today. It showed that his conduct of his office had the approval of only 36 per cent of those polled, while his handling of the war in Vietnam was approved by only 26 per cent.

The war was unquestionably the major factor in Mr. Johnson's slump in public esteem. He began a major escalation in February, 1965, by ordering the bombing of North Vietnam, just a few months after waging a Presidential campaign in which he had convinced most voters that he would not expand what was then a conflict involving only about 16,000 noncombatant American troops.

Over the years since then, the war has required a commitment of more than half a million combat troops, an expenditure of about $30-billion a year and heavy American casualties.

It limited Mr. Johnson's expenditures for domestic programs, alienated many of his supporters in Congress and provoked a widespread and sometimes violent dissent—including draft card burnings, a march of thousands on the Pentagon last year, and ultimately the candidacies of Senators Kennedy and McCarthy.

. Nevertheless, a close political associate of the President said tonight that Mr. Johnson had by no means been "forced" out of the race by his opponents, nor was it yet clear that he would fail to win renomination.

"It was going to be a nasty fight but he had a good chance to win it," was his summation of the political situation. He said that one factor in Mr. Johnson's decision probably was that "this war's upset the hell out of him" and as a result he "really didn't have his mind on his politics."

There was some speculation tonight that Mr. Johnson might believe he could work more effectively for peace in Vietnam if he were not a partisan candidate for re-election — despite the "lame duck" status that would confer on him.

Senator Albert Gore, Democrat of Tennessee, an old antagonist of Mr. Johnson, said the withdrawal was "the greatest contribution toward unity and possible peace that President Johnson could have made."

To achieve peace, he said, will require "concessions and compromises which would subject a candidate for public office to the charge of appeasement, surrender and being soft on the Communists."

In support of this thesis, Mr.

Johnson's speech on Vietnam — which came before his withdrawal announcement — was notably conciliatory, although Senator Gore pointed out that "the President did not reveal a change in war policy tonight. He discussed only tactics — a partial bombing halt."

In the wake of the President's announcement, some observers here were recalling signals that they had failed to recognize.

Theodore White the journalist interviewed Mr. Johnson earier this week and is reported to have said later that the President's remarks had a "valedictory" tone.

Others who have talked with the president lately have detected a note of "they can't take this away from me" when he discussed his domestic and other achievements.

There was little insight here tonight on why Mr. Johnson chose to announce a withdrawal rather than to fight for renomination. One clue may have been in the theme of national unity on which he chose to base his announcement.

Almost since he took office, and at least until the political pressures generated by the war in Vietnam became intense, Mr. Johnson had sounded that same theme of unity.

Early in his Presidency, he seemed to have built a "consensus" of Americans that was reflected in the more than 60 per cent of the vote he won in 1964.

As a reflection of that vote, he could work in 1965 and 1966 with a heavily Democratic, remarkably liberal Congress that passed some of the most far-reaching social legislation of the post-war era—medical care for the aged, voting rights for Southern Negroes, Federal aid to education, and a sweeping civil rights package.

Mr. Johnson campaigned on a unity theme in 1964 and as far back as when he was the Democratic leader in the Senate, from 1952 to 1960, he frequently appealed for "closing ranks" and for "working together."

In 1964, typically, he appealed to the voters to gather in "one great tent" to work together for progress and prosperity and peace.

Thus he was eminently qualified to say, as he did tonight, that "as President of all the people, I cannot disregard the peril to the progress of the American people and the hope and the prospect of peace for all people. So I would ask all Americans whatever their personal interest or concern to guard against divisiveness and all of its ugly consequences."

On that note, Mr. Johnson took his own personal step to "guard against divisiveness."

He surprised everybody, the way he always likes to do, and it probably pleased him most that the news did not leak out before he announced it himself.

April 1, 1968

294

HUMPHREY JOINS PRESIDENCY RACE; CALLS FOR UNITY

Vice President Humphrey announcing his candidacy

Associated Press

By WARREN WEAVER Jr.
Special to The New York Times

WASHINGTON, April 27 — Hubert Horatio Humphrey, who rose from South Dakota pharmacist to the Vice-Presidency of the United States, announced today his candidacy for the Democratic nomination for President.

The 56-year-old Minnesotan opened his campaign for the White House with an appeal for renewed patriotism, a stanch declaration of optimism, a pledge of maturity and a call for unity in his party and the nation.

The Vice President's well-advertised announcement came in a nationally televised speech to 1,700 friends and supporters jammed into the Regency Ballroom of the Shoreham Hotel, overlooking rain-dampened Rock Creek Park. Hundreds more watched him on television in adjoining rooms.

Known for his enthusiasm, Mr. Humphrey had never seemed quite so exuberant as he was on the threshold of his greatest challenge.

"Here we are, the way politics ought to be in America," he told the cheering audience, "the politics of happiness, the politics of purpose and the politics of joy. And that's the way it's going to be, too, all the way from here on out."

The Vice President's declaration put him officially into competition with Senators Robert F. Kennedy of New York and Eugene J. McCarthy of Minnesota for the nomination left open by President Johnson's decision not to seek re-election.

Mr. Humphrey will not compete with his two adversaries in the primaries; the deadline for entering those races has passed. Backed by an organiza-

tion whose leaders all turned out for the celebration today, he will campaign for delegates in the nonprimary states, working toward a first-ballot victory at the National Convention in Chicago in August.

He avoided any specific commitment on issues in his half-hour speech, which was carried to 11 Western European nations by satellite. He promised more detailed answers during the campaign.

The Vice President pledged to "observe the absolute priority of peace over politics." This will presumably mean a moratorium on a discussion of the Vietnam issue as long as attempts are being made to begin talks or if negotiations are under way.

Mr. Humphrey emphasized that his would be a campaign of moderation, with "maturity, restraint and responsibility" as its hallmarks. He declared that "1968 is not the year for frenzied or inflammatory rhetoric" or for "finding scapegoats for our problems."

The audience, warmed by a generous preluncheon reception and wearing plastic campaign hats, was all Mr. Humphrey's. It stood to cheer him at the beginning, interrupted his speech two dozen times with applause and drowned out the band's rendition of "The Minnesota Rouser" at the close with a rhythmic clapping.

Among the guests were George Meany, president of the American Federation of Labor and Congress of Industrial Organizations; Clarence Mitchell, Washington representative of the National Association for the Advancement of Colored People, and Democratic leaders from all over the country.

Present were Gov. Hulett C. Smith of West Virginia, who had heretofore been uncommitted in the Presidential competition, and Senators Carl Hayden of Arizona and Harrison A. Williams Jr. of New Jersey.

Among the House members on hand were Representatives James G. O'Hara of Michigan, Fred B. Rooney and William S. Moorhead of Pennsylvania, Al Ullman of Oregon, Spark M. Matsunaga of Hawaii and W. R. Poage, Richard C. White, James C. Wright Jr. and Abraham Kazen, all of Texas.

The New York delegation included Frank D. O'Connor, president of the New York City Council, and J. Raymond Jones, former New York County Democratic Chairman.

Mrs. Humphrey, blinking back tears, stood beside her husband to share in the ovations. Later, she described the day as "thrilling and exciting." Her husband's speech, she said, was "a beautiful message." "He said what we mean," she said.

There was little talk of Lyndon Johnson. No other speak-

ers mentioned the President, and Mr. Humphrey did only twice, relatively briefly.

Once the Vice President praised the President's most recent efforts to win peace in Vietnam at the expense of his political career. Then he predicted that Mr. Johnson's record "will loom large in history for its dramatic leadership toward social progress, human opportunity and peace."

The Vice President declared that "I intend to fight hard and clean for the nomination."

"But I do not and will not divide either my party or my country," he said.

Senator Kennedy's critics maintain that he is so controversial that he would have difficulty in winning the united support of his party if he should capture the nomination.

Mr. Humphrey called unity for the nation "our most urgent requirement." The huge pictures of the Vice President and his wife on the ballroom walls were topped with the slogan "United With Humphrey."

Running through the speech despair of America, he said, calling it "not a nation that has lost its way, but a restless people, a great nation striving to find a better way."

In what Mr. Humphrey called "the new American patriotism," he said that the nation "has more strength than weakness, more hope than despair, more faith than doubt, and he have more was his optimism. He did not chance than any nation in previous history to master the problems that we face."

It was clearly a time of great excitement for the Vice President. Occasionally, as he spoke, his voice thickened with emotion, or when he left his text to dwell on "this great pursuit and adventure, this cause that is ours."

Mr. Humphrey closed with a quotation ascribed by aides to an unidentified work of Victor Hugo, which he identified only as "some words inscribed in great literature."

"The future has several names," the Vice President quoted from a card he always carries in his pocket. "For the weak, it is the impossible. For the faint-hearted, it is the unknown. For the thoughtful and the valiant it is ideal. The challenge is urgent; the task is large; the time is now.

"On to victory."

The audience stood and cheered.

In Mr. Humphrey's only other bid for the Presidential nomination, he lost to John F. Kennedy in 1960.

Before the reception and luncheon, about 700 early arrivals attended a "briefing"— it was more of a rally—at which the campaign co-chairmen, Senators Walter F. Mondale of Minnesota and Fred R. Harris of Oklahoma, among others, spoke.

April 28, 1968

Revolution Among the Democrats

By WILLIAM V. SHANNON

The Democratic party is going through a political revolution. The future course of this revolution is not yet clear and its success is not certain. Since this is a rich, highly organized society, the revolution is comparatively quiet and nonviolent but its effects could be as far-reaching as the political upheaval of the 1930's over which Franklin D. Roosevelt presided.

Senators Kennedy and McCarthy are competing for the leadership of this revolution in tomorrow's Indiana primary and in the primaries to follow. One or the other is likely to be out of the running by the time the Democratic National Convention opens in late August. Vice President Humphrey, more by chance than by will, has been thrust into the role of defender of the political *status quo*.

The political revolution was born out of the civil rights drive, beginning with the Negro student sit-ins in the spring of 1960, and the protest against the Vietnam war which has been intensifying for the past three years. Both the Negroes and the antiwar groups have made use of the politics of marches, sit-ins and mass demonstrations. But those who practice this "participatory democracy" can ultimately achieve their objectives only if they work through electoral processes and win control of Congress and the Presidency.

Since the United States is not the France of 1789 or the Russia of 1917, the centers of political authority are not going to yield to peace marchers on Fifth Avenue or poor people marching on the Capitol.

Yet neither is American politics the closed "system" that many radicals envisaged. It is not really a system at all, but an amorphous and diffuse arrangement of different power centers, accessible in varying degrees to voter participation and popular opinion. Mr. Johnson's withdrawal demonstrated that even with all the power of the modern Presidency, an incumbent is still vulnerable to defeat in his own party convention.

Public Shaken by War

The Negroes, the students and the middle-class independents are together not numerous enough to make a majority. What few had foreseen before this spring, however, was the extent to which the Vietnam war has shaken up patterns of thinking on subjects having nothing directly to do with the war and among millions of quiet people who never march or turn out to jeer at public men. Politics most of the time is a matter of habit and unexamined conviction, but wars are notorious for changing habits and expectations.

Senator McCarthy is the unexpected beneficiary of this unsettled public mood. Senator

Kennedy is not much given to wasting time on regret, but at odd moments he doubtless wishes he had followed the advice of that minority of advisers who urged him to announce his candidacy against President Johnson six months ago. If he had done so, he would have pre-empted the support which in his absence flowed to Senator McCarthy and is now firmly polarized around the latter.

When Mr. Kennedy entered the race, most political writers assumed that the leadership of the anti-Administration Democrats would quickly pass to him. This is not because there is any conspiracy against Senator McCarthy in the press corps. It is rather that Mr. Kennedy alone seemed the man who not only had appeal for the Negroes, the students and the middle-class dissidents but could also organize them into a new majority coalition with some of the old political elements. He had dealt with the party bosses, local politicians and financial contributors as campaign manager and patronage dispenser for his late brother, President Kennedy.

But revolutionaries, by definition, are not realists. Or else they act upon realities that other men do not perceive. Up to now, the McCarthy supporters have not defected; they have grown stronger. And they persist in believing they can force party pros to take their man. Vice President Humphrey

meanwhile finds himself the inevitable choice of those elements in the party who resist radical change. Their powerful support is useful but he recognizes that it poses a danger. His biggest problem between now and August is to prevent his rivals from successfully depicting his candidacy as "the last hurrah" of the old order.

Although Mr. Humphrey is as liberal as Senators Kennedy and McCarthy, and fully as open-minded about the future, his past association with the Administration shadows his campaign. Style and vocabulary are also important. The Vice President is talking about unity and reconciliation when many restless voters want rapid change and see continued conflict as the only way to get it.

It is impossible as yet to know how deeply and how strongly runs this pressure for change. The Johnsonian consensus is visibly crumbling, and even if Mr. Humphrey makes it to the White House, he probably could not sustain it for long. At a minimum, the quiet revolution seems likely to transform the Democratic party, and put an end to the long-standing but illogical alliance of Southern reactionaries with Northern liberals and radicals.

WILLIAM V. SHANNON is a member of the editorial board of The Times.

May 6, 1968

A Pall Over Politics

Murder Raises Grave Questions for Presidency Races Now and in Future

By TOM WICKER

Special to The New York Times

WASHINGTON, Thursday, June 6—The murder of Robert F. Kennedy shattered the 1968 Presidential campaign and lowered a pall of uncertainty over American politics now and in the years to come. For the immediate future, it may well have assured the nominations by the Democrats and Republicans of the present front-running candidates — Vice President Humphrey and Richard Nixon. It raised grave questions, however, about the personal dangers of political campaigning in the United States.

News Analysis

It added a tragic new dimension to the near-martyrdom of the Kennedy family, which has now lost two sons to assassins' bullets.

It removed forever one of the most promising young political leaders in recent American history, one with particular appeal for the poor, the downtrodden and the alienated inhabitants of the Negro slums. That appeal had been proved in all of Robert Kennedy's primary victories this year.

These elements of society also revered the Senator's brother, President Kennedy, who was assassinated on Nov.

22, 1963. How they would react to Robert Kennedy's murder—both in the immediate future and for the long political pull—was a crucial question.

The murder added sorrowful emphasis to one of Robert Kennedy's major political themes—the necessity for orderly and just redress of grievances, in place of violent action.

Ultimately, Mr. Kennedy's death—the first assassination of an American Presidential candidate—might lead to changes in campaigning practices, even to the fundamental manner in which the nation chooses its President.

The most immediate effect, however, was that for the third —and most harrowing—time a shock wave of unexpected events had completely altered the shape of the 1968 campaign.

The first came on March 12 when Senator Eugene J. McCarthy of Minnesota won 42 per cent of the Democratic vote in the New Hampshire

primary, and Mr. Kennedy immediately thereafter became an active candidate.

The second transformation occurred on March 31, when President Johnson said he would neither seek nor accept renomination by the Democratic party. That led to the entry of Vice President Humphrey and his rapid progression to the front runner's place among Democrats.

Mr. Kennedy's death removed Mr. Humphrey's most formidable opponent for the nomination.

It leaves only Senator McCarthy as an active opponent of Mr. Humphrey. While he, as was Mr. Kennedy, is an anti-Administration candidate and no doubt will inherit some of Mr. Kennedy's strength, other elements of that strength will surely shift to Mr. Humphrey. Many Democrats who supported Mr. Kennedy do not regard Mr. McCarthy as a potential winner, and some others will find Mr. Humphrey a more congenial ideological alternative.

Any long moratorium on political activity will probably

work to Mr. Humphrey's advantage. He is the front runner and has the most delegate support; and a hiatus in the campaign will tend to let that support crystallize.

The same effect will likely be felt in the Republican party. Mr. Nixon is regarded as being so far out in front in the race for that party's nomination that Governor Rockefeller of New York needs every available campaign day to persuade favorite son candidates and delegates either to remain uncommitted or to support his candidacy.

McCarthy Statement

Senator McCarthy, appearing briefly on television and before reporters in Los Angeles, spoke cryptically of meeting with President Johnson—one of his prime targets—and Mr. Humphrey—his principal opponent —before resuming any political activity. He also said he would talk with Mr. Kennedy's "spokesmen."

These plans suggested to some observers here that Mr. McCarthy, obviously in a state of emotional upset, might be contemplating either a withdrawal or some other gesture toward unifying Democrats without further campaigning.

He was quoted by Mary McGrory in The Washington Evening Star as saying upon hearing of the shooting:

"Maybe we should do it in a different way. Maybe we should have the English system of having the Cabinet choose the President. There must be some other way."

Miss McGrory was writing what appeared to be an eyewitness account of the scene of Mr. McCarthy and his family receiving the news of the shooting in their suite at the Beverly Hilton Hotel in Los Angeles.

Another McCarthy remark suggested somber reflection upon the political meaning of the assassination. The nation is no longer a "pioneer" society, he said, but "a complex, sophisticated civilization." His implication, echoing a frequent theme of his campaign, was that the nation had to begin acting in a more rational and civilized manner if it wished to cope with its problems.

Outlook in the Slums

It was not clear whether the event would bring louder cries for law and order at any cost, or whether it would lend poignant emphasis to Mr. Kennedy's own campaign theme—his insistence that a just society must deal with its social and economic inequities if it would preserve law and order.

One bleak possibility was that Mr. Kennedy's death might provoke new disorders in the Negro sections, where he was politically and personally revered. Such outbreaks followed the assassination of the Rev. Dr. Martin Luther King Jr.

There was no real precedent for the removal by violence of a Presidential aspirant from the campaign. A would-be assassin shot and wounded Theodore Roosevelt in October, 1912, but Mr. Roosevelt was the formally nominated candidate of the Progressive party in what was by October a hopeless campaign. The shooting had little effect upon the victory of Woodrow Wilson on the Democratic ticket.

June 6, 1968

New York: The Vanishing Republican 'Establishment'

By JAMES RESTON

For years we have been hearing about a powerful and private Republican "political establishment" in New York which was supposed to have enough money and influence to control the selection of the Republican Presidential nominee. But just when we badly need some kind of outside help from somewhere to get a strong G.O.P. nominee, this much publicized and condemned "Eastern Establishment" seems to have vanished.

In any event, a few inquiries around the skyscraper underground of the party here have failed to turn up any sign of a stop-Nixon movement. The most knowledgeable Republicans in these parts think that Nixon's strength with the conservative state and county chairmen in the South, Middle West and West has all but assured him the nomination, unless an organized effort is made to get Rockefeller into the primaries, but it is hard to find any serious move in this direction.

The New Power Centers

New York is no longer the main power center of the Republican party. Other power centers have arisen in California, Texas and Ohio and their money is not on Rockefeller or any other progressive, but in general on conservatives.

Besides, there never was a Republican "Eastern Establishment" which could control Presidential nominations by raising or withholding campaign funds, though there were powerful and progressive Republicans here who were certainly influential in the nominations of Wendell Willkie in 1940, Thomas E. Dewey in 1944 and 1948, and General Eisenhower in 1952 and 1956.

The Taft Republicans raised the cry of an "Eastern Establishment" in the Willkie campaign, and the Goldwater Republicans were still carrying it on in 1964. This was popular west of the Rockies, where the Eastern bankers and Wall Streeters were symbols of everything alien and wicked.

But where is the establishment now? The same cast of characters that was supposed to have beaten Taft with Eisenhower in 1952 is still around: Henry Cabot Lodge, John J. McCloy, Gen. Lucius Clay, Douglas Dillon, Robert Lovett, et cetera. They have the same argument against Nixon that they had against Taft, namely— that he was a "loser," and Rockefeller is certainly no more reluctant to run this time than Eisenhower was eleven months before the 1952 election.

There is not now, however, anything like the same pressure on Rockefeller as there was in December of 1951 on Eisenhower. At that time, prominent Republicans were flying the Atlantic and pleading with the general to come home and save the country from the isolationists. They were using their influence on powerful Republican Governors and prominent Republican campaign contributors to "draft Eisenhower," and finally they persuaded him to accept the nomination.

The present situation is certainly not the same, but there are similarities. Rockefeller, like Eisenhower in 1952, is running ahead in the popularity polls but running behind Nixon, as Eisenhower ran behind Taft, in the polls of the potential convention delegates.

It took unremitting pressure on Eisenhower, plus a carefully planned organization of the pro-Eisenhower Republican Governors to change this situation, and even then, Eisenhower barely won the nomination at Chicago.

Three major differences exist today. Rockefeller does not have Eisenhower's popularity. The influential progressive Republicans here are not mounting a campaign to get him into the race in time, and the Republican Governors are not organizing behind him as effectively as they did behind Eisenhower in 1952.

One interesting explanation given here for this is that President Johnson has not lost all his influence with the so-called Republican Eastern Establishment. Many of them are visibly less enthusiastic about him now than they were four years ago, and they are talking rather sadly about his entrapment in the war, but there is a big difference between talking and acting.

Also many of these same influential Republicans in New York have served under Presidents Johnson and Kennedy and are now beyond the years when they can get very enthusiastic for a backstairs fight.

So the question is likely to be left largely to Rockefeller and the younger Republicans who think the country deserves something better than a choice between Johnson and Nixon. Rockefeller still thinks he can wait for a stalemate at Miami Beach to challenge Nixon, but the support for this view is steadily declining here. Even some of his closest friends are saying he must enter the race in the Oregon primary, if not before, and meanwhile let the Republican Governors know that he is available.

December 20, 1967

NIXON IS NOMINATED ON THE FIRST BALLOT

ORIGINAL VOTE 692

But Convention Then Makes It Unanimous on Plea by Reagan

By TOM WICKER
Special to The New York Times

MIAMI BEACH, Thursday, Aug. 8—Richard Milhous Nixon, the "old pro" of American politics, was nominated for President today on the first ballot at the Republican National Convention.

Mr. Nixon, only the eighth man to be renominated by the Republicans after having lost one Presidential election, triumphed over a determined "stop Nixon" drive waged from the left by Governor Rockefeller of New York and from the right by Governor Ronald Reagan of California.

Just as the Nixon forces had steadfastly contended during a week of maneuvering at this 29th Republican National Convention, the 55-year-old former Vice President, who was also the party's nominee in 1960, proved to have the 667 votes needed for nomination "buttoned up."

The first-ballot count, before the convention made the nomination unanimous, was as follows:

Nixon 692
Rockefeller 277
Reagan 182
Others 182

2 Big States Lost

Mr. Nixon's nomination came at the end of an almost interminable evening of oratory and demonstrations, in which 12 candidates were nominated and seconded; two withdrew before the balloting began at 1:17 A.M.

As the roll-call of the states proceeded, Mr. Nixon's lead mounted steadily—even though the two largest states went elsewhere. California cast 86 votes for Governor Reagan and

New York gave 88 of its 92 to Governor Rockefeller.

Wisconsin, whose 30 delegates were won by Mr. Nixon in the state primary last April, put the former Vice President over the top, giving him three votes more than the 667 he had needed.

At the completion of the roll-call, Mr. Nixon had 692 votes and the switching began with Minnesota; it had cast only 9 of its 26 votes for Mr. Nixon, but it switched all to him. One by one, the rest of the states began to fall in line.

A cheer went up when Ohio finally cast 58 votes for Mr. Nixon. Gov. James A. Rhodes had held out as a favorite son, taking 55 Ohio votes on the official roll-call.

Within minutes of the clinching votes, Governor Reagan appeared on the platform.

Reagan Barred at First

Mr. Ford, citing the convention rules, would not immediately let Mr. Reagan come to the rostrum, however.

While Mr. Reagan was waiting, the one-time front runner and a favorite son here, Gov. George Romney of Michigan, also switched his state's 48 votes to Mr. Nixon.

Meanwhile, New York representatives were trying to get recognition, apparently under instructions to move that the nomination be made unanimous. The delegation chairman Charles Schoeneck, finally shouted into the public address system that New York so moved.

Mr. Ford, however, continued to recognize the delegations one by one, rather than entertaining a motion for unanimity.

Ultimately, he entertained a motion from Virginia to suspend the rules. It was shouted through and Mr. Reagan was allowed to come to the platform, where he received an ovation.

Reagan Gets Unanimity

"This nation cannot survive four more years of the kind of policies that have been guiding us," he said.

Then he "proudly" moved that the convention declare itself unanimously behind Mr. Nixon—which it did with a roar.

Mr. Reagan had been in Convention Hall, caucusing with Southern delegates, when the roll-call began.

Governor Rockefeller was not in the hall, but in a television interview, he immediately congratulated Mr. Nixon and wished him luck. He said he had already called Mr. Nixon.

Mr. Rockefeller also said he had promised to support the campaign of Mr. Nixon.

The newly nominated candidate was not in the hall but was watching on television. He immediately called Gov. Warren Knowles of Wisconsin to thank the state for having put him over the top.

Mr. Nixon also expressed "great gratitude" to the convention and "to those who helped me win." He said this as he met the press half an hour after his nomination.

The nomination culminated a seven-month formal campaign and an informal effort that dated well back into 1967. It was a climax to a remarkable political comeback for the man who had said he was through with politics after his defeat for the Governorship of California in 1962.

The nomination came only a little more than eight years after the Republicans chose Mr. Nixon the first time. That was for what proved to be his razor-edge defeat by John F. Kennedy in 1960.

The nominating session was called to order yesterday at 5 P.M. after a final day of delegate-hunting by the three major candidates.

The long nominating process began about 5:30 P.M. when the roll of the states was called and Alabama yielded to California. That meant that Governor Reagan, disdaining prime television time either in the East or in his home state, would be nominated first by Mrs. Ivy Baker Priest Stevens.

Maine later yielded to Pennsylvania, so that state's Governor, Raymond P. Shafer, could put Mr. Rockefeller's name before the convention.

This gave him position just ahead of Mr. Nixon. Maryland claimed for its Governor, Spiro T. Agnew, the honor of nominating the former Vice President.

The other names brought before the convention were those of numerous favorite sons—the most important of which were

Gov. James A. Rhodes of Ohio and Gov. George Romney of Michigan. Their neutrality was the only hope of the "stop-Nixon" forces.

Reagan's Vote Remembered

Mrs. Stevens, a former treasurer of the United States and the first woman ever to nominate a major Presidential candidate, took the rostrum, white-haired and smiling in a blue lace dress, at 5:45 P.M.

She called Governor Reagan "a man who will confront the radicals on our campuses and the looters on our streets and say: The laws will be obeyed."

His million-vote victory for Governor of California in 1966, Mrs. Stevens said, made him a "proved winner" who could lead the party to "an even greater victory in 1968."

She pledged Mr. Reagan to a militant foreign policy in which it would be clear "that if we must fight for freedom, we will fight to win."

Her brief speech set off a 20-minute demonstration, the first of the convention, with delegations pouring into the aisle, bands playing and state standards swaying above the crowd. Veteran convention-goers rated it about average.

To tunes such as "California, Here I Come," "Dixie" and "Hey, Look Me Over," the Reagan demonstrators trooped energetically around the big convention hall. The state standards seemed to be mostly from the South and the West, the demonstrators made a lot of noise, and the placards displayed slogans such as "I'm Gone on Ron."

Favorite Sons Named

Few in the spectator galleries joined in, and when Representative Gerald R. Ford, the convention chairman, began trying to restore order the demonstrators began quietly to stack their placards and go back to their seats.

Mr. Reagan's three seconding speeches were made by Representative James C. Gardner, the Republican candidate for Governor of North Carolina, Representative Robert T. Price of Texas, and former Senator William F. Knowland of California.

After the Reagan nomination, the convention heard pro forma nominations of the following favorite sons:

Gov. Walter J. Hickel of Alaska, Gov. Winthrop Rockefeller of Arkansas, Governor Romney, Senator Frank Carlson of

Kansas, and Senator Hiram L. Fong of Hawaii.

Governor Hickel no sooner heard Representative Howard W. Pollock put his name forward than he withdrew it and said he was for Mr. Nixon. This drew an early round of shouting and placard-waving from the Nixon forces.

A fairly sizable demonstration for Winthrop Rockefeller enlivened the hall for a few minutes, with bands playing numerous printed placards swaying above the delegates who appeared generally uninterested.

Supporters of Governor Romney, once considered the front runner for this nomination and a major candidate until his withdrawal last February, utilized his left-over placards and banners for a demonstration that almost rivaled Mr. Reagan's in length, if not in enthusiasm. As it began, a leader of Governor Rockefeller's New York delegation shouted though a bullhorn:

"Everybody up. He's going for us, and we are going for him."

Whether he was hopeful or positive could not be ascertained, but many New Yorkers joined in the Romney parade.

Governor Shafer came forward for the nomination of the second major candidate, Governor Rockefeller of New York, terming him in his prepared remarks "someone who can build bridges across the deep and fragmented divisions that separate black from white, young from old, poor from rich — someone who is sincerely determined to help bring every citizen into the mainstream of American life."

The word "sincerely" was an obvious slap at Mr. Nixon. who Governor Rockefeller has accused of catering to the Southern delegations. Mr. Shafer also jibed the Democratic front-runner, Vice President Humphrey, by deriding "a politics of joy and over-optimism that unrealistically says all is well with America."

The party should nominate Mr. Rockefeller, he said, "because he is the Republican who can win" and because it is "a time in human affairs when nothing less than greatness is needed to lead us from the devastation of hatred, violence and confused goals."

Brooke Is a Seconder

Seconding speeches for the Governor were made by Senator Edward W. Brooke of Massachusetts, William E. Miller, the 1964 Vice-Presidential nominee, formerly a national chairman; Mrs. Ike Kampmann, the party committeewoman from Texas, and Georg Abbott, the Nevada State chairman.

Governor Shafer's mere appearance set off an incipient Rockefeller demonstration that Mr. Ford had difficulty in quieting. During his speech, Mr.

The New York Times

GETTING FAMILY SUPPORT: Julie Nixon, right, and her fiancé, David Eisenhower, taking part in the floor demonstration after her father's name had been put in nomination.

Shafer was interrupted by booming chants of "We Want Rocky," and he set off another loud cheer then—rubbing a little salt in Mr. Nixon's old wounds—he shouted:

"Nelson Rockefeller has never lost an election."

The demonstration following Mr. Shafer's speech roared out of control through the hall for 30 minutes, with bands striving to be heard above the bedlam, placards swaying, and the galleries joining in for the first time in any demonstration.

A huge Iowa state flag swirled down the aisles, two suspended fishnets tipped thousands of balloons from the ceiling, and their machine-gun popping at one point almost obscured the shouting and cheering.

Numerous state standards bobbed and bounced above the

heads of the demonstrators and the rhythmic chant, "We Want Rocky" emerged frequently above the deafening noise. Mr. Shafer's help had to be enlisted to get the demonstrators off the floor.

Convention guards handled some demonstrators roughly in trying to clear the floor. At least one was thrwn out of the aisle.

There was no mistaking the genuine enthusiasm of the Rockefeller demonstration, but the hundreds of Nixon signs that went up—mostly in the galleries—while it was going on made it clear that Mr. Nixon's partisans were unlikely to be outdone when their turn came.

Governor Agnew, once chairman of a "draft Rockefeller" committee, put Mr. Nixon in nomination with a series of Nixon quotations, and asked the delegates to shout back

their agreement.

Then, citing Mr. Nixon's victories in this year's primaries, he called him "a man who took his case to the people, and put his prestige on the line."

Referring to Mr. Nixon's Vice-Presidential years, Mr. Agnew said they had proved he had "the confidence to make hard decisions; the courage to keep cool before one man in Moscow or a mob in Caracas."

More Balloons Join In

Mr. Nixon, he said, had "helped lead this party to its greatest victories in the past two decades" and had stood by it "and its candidate in their darkest hour"—a jab at Governor Rockefeller, who did not support Barry Goldwater in 1964.

Recalling Mr. Nixon's campaign against John F. Kennedy in 1960 and his race for Governor of California in 1962, Mr. Agnew said he had "had the courage to rise up from the depths of defeat six years ago —and to make the greatest political comeback in American history."

That set off a tremendous demonstration for Mr. Nixon, with more balloons tumbling from the ceiling, raucous trumpets blaring, huge portraits of Mr. Nixon's familiar face bouncing above the crowds, placards proclaiming virtually every state "for Nixon" and enormous banners declaring "Nixon's The One."

A man in Uncle Sam costume staggered precariously through the mob on ten-foot stilts, holding a placard that read "Uncle Sam Needs Him."

If there was a comparison to be made between the Rockefeller and Nixon demonstrations, the former might have been ahead in sheer noise. In the galleries, however, a forest of Nixon signs and placards sprang up, a more impressive display than the Rockefeller men had managed. Some observers on the floor said more people had marched for Mr. Rockefeller.

But the Nixon demonstration left nothing to be desired in enthusiasm or length. It rambled through the hall for about 25 minutes, but proved somewhat easier for Mr. Ford to gavel to a halt than had the Rockefeller show.

Mr. Nixon's nomination was seconded by an artful "balanced ticket" of supporters—Senator Howard H. Baker Jr. of Tennessee (the South); Richard Ogilvie, the Republican candidate for Governor of Illinois (the cities); Gov. John A. Volpe of Massachusetts (ethnic groups), and Senator Mark O. Hatfield of Oregon (moderates and doves).

Senator Clifford P. Case of New Jersey, letting his name go before the convention in a stubborn effort to keep his state's delegates out of the Nixon column, was placed in nomination by Douglas Dillon, the former Secretary of the Treasury and Under Secretary of State. A small but spirited demonstration ensued.

Governor Rhodes, on the other hand, received a demonstration nearly as long as those for the major candidates—although considerably smaller in numbers of people and lower in decibel count.

Earlier in the day, Governor Reagan failed to score any major breakthroughs in the Southern delegations, and Governor Rockefeller came in with somewhat less strength than expected at caucuses in the important Pennsylvania and New Jersey delegations.

Both "stop Nixon" candidates spent active days among the delegations. At an afternoon news conference, Mr. Reagan said he had sent a telegram to each state chairman, reiterating that he would not "under any circumstances" accept the Vice Presidential nomination.

Even Barry Goldwater, the Presidential nominee in 1964, who was a strong proponent of a Nixon-Reagan ticket, had dropped his efforts for that combination, Mr. Reagan said.

Mr. Rockefeller made a sharp attack on Mr. Nixon, who he said would "unite the Democratic party as no one else in this country can do."

The New Yorker said he was 'pretty mad" at what he said were the Nixon tactics of placating the Southern delegates.

"We are not going to win nationally with a candidate beholden to Southern delegates," Mr. Rockefeller said.

At the Pennsylvania caucus, 40 delegates opted for Mr. Rockefeller, 22 for Mr. Nixon, and one for Mr. Reagan. This was five to eight more Nixon votes than had been expected.

Vice-Presidential speculation continued to be hotter than debate over Mr. Nixon's first-ballot strength. The most-talked-about possibilities for his running mate continued to be Mr. Reagan—despite his telegram—and Mayor Lindsay of New York. Senator Charles H. Percy of Illinois, Senator Mark O. Hatfield of Oregon and Senator John G. Tower of Texas were also considered.

Most observers believed that unless Mr. Nixon chose Mr. Reagan of his own free will, there would be concerted pressure by the Southern delegations to force the Californian on the ticket. Whether this could lead to a floor fight over the nomination was not clear, although a Presidential nominee's choice traditionally prevails.

Since considerable opposition to Mr. Lindsay was heard in the same delegations putting forward Mr. Reagan for Vice President, some armchair strategists here believed Mr. Nixon—if nominated—would turn to a more neutral figure, probably Mr. Percy.

The Vice-Presidential nomination is scheduled for tonight's final session, just preceding the acceptance speech of the Presidential nominee.

August 8, 1968

'New Coalition': A Nixon Gamble

His Choice of Agnew Is Traced in Part to Talk in May

By JAMES RESTON

There is obviously something wrong or at least something missing in most of the explanations of why Richard Nixon chose Gov. Spiro T. Agnew of Maryland as the Republican Vice-Presidential nominee. Mr. Nixon won the nomination and blew the election all in one day, according to some of these explanations, by appeasing the South with Agnew and affronting the urban North. By this single decision, it is said, he chose to go with the conservative minority of the country and defy the liberal majority, and in the process helped reunite the Democrats and divide the Republicans.

News Analysis

If this is so—and it may be so—Mr. Nixon, who calculated his moves with extraordinary skill until he got the Presidential nomination, suddenly wrecked it all with a calamitous blunder immediately after his victory at Miami Beach.

This, however, is not at all like Mr. Nixon. He is not a capricious man. He is a very deliberate and careful political strategist and tactician. He needed the South to win the nomination, but it is not likely that he would allow the Southern Republican leaders to dictate his choice of a running mate or even give them a veto over a liberal Vice-Presidential candidate if he really thought he needed a Northern liberal like Mayor Lindsay, Senator Charles Percy or Senator Mark Hatfield to win the election.

'New Alignment' Seen

If he is not a prisoner or a fool, then, what is the explanation of his decision? It may be that he gave the explanation himself in a nationwide radio speech last May 16, when he analyzed the temper of the nation and reached the conclusion that there was a wholly "new alignment" of political forces in America and that these forces already represented an American majority "that will affect the future of America for generations to come."

Mr. Nixon said this "new coalition" was composed of traditional Republicans, "the New South," "black militants," "new liberals" who wanted participatory democracy, and the silent millions in the middle of the political spectrum who are sore at big government—except on Election Day.

This might seem to the old power blocs like an odd collection of "strange bedfellows," Mr. Nixon said, but they all were unhappy about something, all protesting against centralized government and calling for greater individual freedom. The New South, for example, was no longer bound by "racist" ideology and was developing industrially through private enterprise.

Similarly, he added, the "black militants" were now calling for black private enterprise rather than for handouts or welfare, and the "new liberals" were demanding more participation in government, more "personal freedom and less government domination."

In short, Mr. Nixon feels that there is now a deep disenchantment among Democrats and independents with the failures of a powerful Federal Government to deal with the problems of poverty and war, and that he can exploit their grievances against violence abroad and lawlessness and poverty at home in the coming months of the campaign.

Moreover, Mr. Nixon apparently feels that he can make real progress in the South and thus turn the Republican party into an effective national rather than regional party if — and this is his immediate practical problem — he can only cut deeply into George Wallace's strength.

Even the Humphrey Democrats concede that if Mr. Nixon mounts an effective campaign on the theme that a vote for Mr. Wallace will be wasted or may even elect Mr. Humphrey —if Nixon can do this, he may very well win. And it would obviously have been hard for Mr. Nixon to do this with a John Lindsay, or a Senator Percy or some other Republican Northern progressive as his running mate.

The outlook, therefore, is for a very hard Nixon campaign appealing to all the dissident elements Mr. Wallace is now gathering and to all the others in what Mr. Nixon calls the "new coalition" — the people who are sore at big government, big unions, costly wars, etc.

Maybe he can do it and maybe he can't. It is hard to see how he can hold that part of his "new alignment" that wants to hurry up the process of change and the other forces in the coalition who are complaining that the process of change is going too fast already.

Greek Bearing No Gifts

What is clear, however, is that Mr. Nixon is not being dragged down this road by somebody else but has chosen it himself. He has been impressed by the "new alignment" theories of Stephen Hess, a young conservative writer from Harvard. He apparently believes that there is a majority coalition of frustrated and angry people in the country, and that he can gather them all together by neutralizing Mr. Wallace on the "law and order" issue.

This still leaves the question of why Mr. Nixon chose Governor Agnew as his partner in this enterprise. Mr. Agnew is one Greek bearing no gifts for anybody. For example, Senator Howard Baker of Tennessee, who is one of the most articulate of the new legislators in Washington, would obviously have articulated the Nixon thesis much more effectively.

But Mr. Nixon was not very happy with Henry Cabot Lodge as his running mate in 1960; Mr. Lodge had a mind of his own and sometimes made the voters wish he had been the nominee rather than Mr. Nixon. There will obviously be no such problem with the Governor of Maryland.

Mr. Nixon will not only be "the one" but "the only one" in the Republican race. Mr. Agnew is merely the symbol of Mr. Nixon's strategy, which is to travel a little right and South of center, gathering up the frustrated coalition as he goes.

August 10, 1968

Cleaver of Black Panthers Is Nominee of Leftists

Special to The New York Times

ANN ARBOR, Mich., Aug. 18—Eldridge Cleaver, author and a leader in the Black Panther movement in Oakland, Calif., was nominated today for the Presidency of the United States by the radical Peace and Freedom party.

He won over Dick Gregory, the comedian, on the first ballot with 161½ delegate votes to Mr. Gregory's 54.

There were 218 delegates.

Cleaver promised a vigorous campaign:

"I'm not going to let the people down that gave me this nomination. I'm going to get the job done," said the handsome Negro, who became widely known after publication of his book, "Soul On Ice."

The "job" is not winning the election. As of now his name will appear on the ballot only in California and Michigan, although supporters are trying to list it in a dozen more states. Cleaver, 33 years old, is not old enough to be President. The aim of the campaign is to use the traditional election process to win an audience and to organize for the radical movement.

August 19, 1968

DELEGATE FIGHTS TRANSFORM PARTY

Democrats Ousting Bigots and Beckoning to Youth

By MAX FRANKEL
Special to The New York Times

CHICAGO, Aug. 27 — Amid the chaos and passion that is their fashion, the Democrats took another giant stride today in the radical transformation of their party.

Not so fast as many of them would like, but more rapidly than most had ever thought possible, they were drumming out the bigots and beckoning to the young.

By the dry prose of resolution as well as the unruly cries for revolution, they were stripping the power of the back-room brokers and opening the gates to popular participation.

In the unruly hours of the opening session early today and at the start of the second session this evening, the party managers slowed this process just enough to avert a bloody rupture between North and South and young and old. And the forces backing Vice President Humphrey barely managed to protect their candidate from the great tides of change.

But the bold blacks from Mississippi and Georgia and the frustrated youngsters from the campus, supported by restive forces in New York, California and other big states, have made their mark on the Democratic party, win or lose in November, and have imposed some profound changes on its future processes.

Not only lily-white delegations from the South but also party organizations that fail to recruit Negroes, Puerto Ricans and Mexican-Americans into their ranks were put on notice that they stood to lose seats at Democratic National Conventions.

Hitherto respected and active party leaders throughout the land were warned never again to appear in conventions with delegations of hand-picked underlings, shielded by custom or law from influence or challenge by the rank-and-file party members.

End of Unit Rule

The unit rule of voting that smothers all minority opinion and forces even dissenters to vote the majority line was not only abolished at the national convention but was also declared undesirable in precinct, county and state proceedings.

The forces pressing for these changes did not win most of challenges they brought before the credentials committee over the last week and before the full convention today. But they saw such Negroes as Aaron Henry and Charles Evers casting Mississippi's votes with the North. And they cheered the turmoil attending Julian Bond's symbolic march from the balcony to an almost physical contest for at least half of Georgia's seats on the floor, and then they came within 200 votes of granting the Negro legislator the whole loaf.

Old New York liberals and Negro newcomers in this party broke even from their allegiance to Vice President Humphrey to join in the tense and emotional vote and tribute to Mr. Bond, ending in a floor demonstration that forced the unplanned recess at 2:40 A.M. today (3:40 A.M. Eastern daylight time).

The force of this drive for nationwide racial and ethnic integration haunted the Georgia regulars when they met in caucus here after breakfast.

"I guess we all feel a little like I do this morning—sore and baffled," said James H. Gray, the Georgia state chairman. "The white conservative vote in the South is not wanted by the present leaders of the Democratic party. They don't want us. I guess we are going to have to go home and make some other arrangements. Georgia has a score to settle."

About 10 of the regular Georgians quit the delegation this afternoon and two dozen more left the hall this evening soon after the convention, by perfunctory voice vote, ratified the credentials committee plan to seat loyal regulars and challengers alike and to make them divide 41 of Georgia's 43 votes.

Standard Is Rescued

But 22 of the regulars, including seven Negroes, remained behind, physically rescuing the Georgia standard from one of their retiring colleagues who made off with it toward the rostrum in protest against the compromise.

After another hour of negotiation, chairs were found for the 40-member Bond slate of challengers. The two groups mixed amicably in Georgia's section, sharing the telephone and microphone and casting their first, separately announced votes in the fight over Alabama's credentials. This was the last controversy over seats before the convention.

Alabama's regulars were challenged by two groups, one largely pro-Humphrey, which questioned the loyalty of some regulars, and one, largely favoring Senator Eugene J. McCarthy and mostly Negro, that staked its claims on civil rights issues.

Five Negro delegates from Minnesota, joined by white McCarthy supporters, walked out to protest what they considered their state's insufficient support of the Alabama Negro challengers.

Despite high emotions, the credentials committee was sustained in its compromise formula. It provided that 16 Alabama regulars who refused to certify their loyalty be replaced by some of the challengers, almost all from the pro-Humphrey group.

The roll-call vote, the fourth on a credentials issue in this convention, favored the committee position, 2 to 1. The voting showed somewhat surer maneuvering by the Humphrey forces than in the opening night credentials battles.

After all the skirmishing and testing of forces on the floor, the credentials committee was upheld in every respect. Its own delegate decisions meant a net shift of about 30 votes from Mr. Humphrey to Senator McCarthy—about 20 in Georgia and 10 in Mississippi.

Many other Southern delegations here were not challenged because they had also begun to accept the new standards, with

301

varving degrees of enthusiasm.

There were no such fights and scenes at the Republican National Convention in Miami Beach three weeks ago, and there were few Negro faces anywhere on the floor. And, while this may be useful for party unity or even victory this year, it is likely to give the Democrats the edge in the race for the loyalty of the South's new Negro electorate.

The demands for change in party processes in the North as well as the South were not so thoroughly prepared as some of the discrimination cases brought to this convention.

Moreover, while the Southern Negroes had been careful to stand a step removed from the Humphrey-McCarthy contest, the Northern reformers were all too clearly tied in one way or another to the anti-Administration forces.

Hence they failed in the specific quest for more seats in Connecticut, Washington and points in between. They failed also because in many cases they were seeking minority votes that their colleagues elsewhere had refused to yield when they attained a majority.

But their basic complaints were accepted virtually without challenge. The party managers agreed, or felt compelled to agree, that members who wish to participate in their affairs must be made welcome and that delegates to choose a Presidential nominee must reflect the up-to-date views of the members.

On the motion of Gov. Richard J. Hughes of New Jersey, the shrewd, poker-faced Solomon who presided over the credentials turmoil here, the summons to the 1972 Democratic National Convention will not only reiterate the 1968 injunction against racial discrimination but will also contain this new language:

"It is the further understanding that a state Democratic party, in selecting and certifying delegates and alternates to the Democratic National Convention, thereby undertakes to assure that all Democrats of the state will have meaningful and timely opportunities to participate fully in the election or selection of such delegates and alternates."

A special committee will be created to assist the state parties in changing state laws, and party rules to conform.

Governor Hughes said that his credentials committee felt specifically that delegates must not be chosen before the election campaign unfolds, that delegates hand-picked by leaders without primary or open convention should no longer be admitted, and that unit rules at any level worked against grass-roots sentiment.

These reforms will outlive the memory of the bitter confrontations and demonstrations here, and the sentiment for them is greater than any of the formal roll-calls on credentials issues.

The first vote last night was procedural, on a motion by anti-Administration groups to delay the credentials fight until today to give them time for maneuver. It was defeated, 875 to 1,648½.

The second, on a motion to reject charges of discrimination against the Texas delegation, developed into a major test of strength between Humphrey backers and an alliance of anti-Administration groups. The regular Texans were upheld, 1,368 to 955.

The third, early today, was on a move to give the Georgia challengers all their state's votes, instead of only half. It found many sympathizers voting "no" only because they wished to slow the pace of change and preserve some standing for the party among Southern moderates. The motion lost, 1,041½ to 1,413.

The fourth credentials roll-call came this evening on a move to upset the Alabama compromise in favor of a mostly Negro group of challengers. It was defeated, 881½ to 1,607.

August 28, 1968

HUMPHREY NOMINATED ON THE FIRST BALLOT AFTER HIS PLANK ON VIETNAM IS APPROVED; POLICE BATTLE DEMONSTRATORS IN STREETS

VICTOR GETS 1,761

Vote Taken Amid Boos For Chicago Police Tactics in Street

By TOM WICKER
Special to The New York Times

CHICAGO, Thursday Aug. 29 — While a pitched battle between the police and thousands of young antiwar demonstrators raged in the streets of Chicago, the Democratic National Convention nominated Hubert H. Humphrey for President last night, on a platform reflecting his and President Johnson's views on the war in Vietnam.

Mr. Humphrey, after a day of bandwagon shifts to his candidacy, and a night of turmoil in the convention hall, won nomination on the first ballot over challenges by Senator Eugene J. McCarthy of Minnesota and George S. McGovern of South Dakota.

The count at the end of the first ballot was:

Humphrey	1,761¾
McCarthy	601
McGovern	146½
Phillips	67½
Others	32¾

There was never a moment's suspense in the balloting, and throughout a turbulent evening, the delegates and spectators paid less attention to the proceedings than to television and radio reports of widespread violence in the streets of Chicago, and to stringent security measures within the International Amphitheatre.

Repeated denunciations of Mayor Richard J. Daley from convention speakers and repeated efforts to get an adjournment or recess were ignored by convention officials and Mr. Daley.

He sat through it all, usually grinning and always guarded by plainclothes security men, until just before the roll call. Then he left the hall. A few miles away, the young demonstrators were being clubbed, kicked and gassed by the Chicago police, who turned back a march on the convention hall.

Most of the violence took place across Michigan Avenue from the convention headquarters hotel, the Conrad Hilton, in full view of delegates' wives and other watching from its windows.

From the convention rostrum, Senator Abraham A. Ribicoff of Connecticut, denounced "Gestapo tactics in the streets of Chicago."

Julian Bond, the Negro insurgent leader from Georgia, in announcing his delegation's votes, spoke of "atrocities" in the city.

Wire services reported that Mr. Humphrey had chosen Senator Edmund S. Muskie of Maine for Vice President. Mr. Humphrey's staff denied that a decision had been made, although they would not rule out Mr. Muskie, 54 years old, a Roman Catholic of Polish extraction.

Even the roll-call of the states that nominated Mr. Humphrey could begin only over the protests of New Hampshire, Wisconsin and Mr. Conyers, all of whom moved for a recess or adjournment because of the surrounding violence and the pandemonium in the hall.

Vote Begins Amid Boos

Representative Carl Albert of Oklahoma, the chairman, ignored all the motions and ordered the roll-call to begin amid a huge chorus of boos.

When Illinois's turn came to vote, the huge old amphitheater rocked with the sounds of boos and jeers, and the recording secretary had to ask for a restatement of its vote—112 votes for Mr. Humphrey.

Early in the evening, even Mr. Humphrey got a whiff of tear gas when it was wafted through his window at the Hilton, from the street fighting below.

Mr. McCarthy saw some of the violence from his window and called it "very bad." Later, it was reported at the convention hall, he visited a hospital where some of his young supporters, wounded in the streets, were being treated.

At one point, the police broke into the McCarthy suite at the Hilton, searching for someone throwing objects out of the hotel windows.

Mr. McGovern described the fighting as a "blood bath" that "made me sick to my stomach." He said he had "seen nothing like it since the films of Nazi Germany."

Pennsylvania Does It

Nevertheless, when Pennsylvania cast the votes that put Mr. Humphrey in nomination, the convention hall broke into a demonstration on his behalf that was loud and apparently happy. Mrs.

Humphrey, watching from a box with her family, received congratulations with a gracious smile.

The day's events, moving swiftly toward Mr. Humphrey's nomination, began this morning with Edward M. Kennedy's disavowal of a draft movement in his behalf.

In an emotional afternoon debate, the delegates sealed the grip of Mr. Humphrey and Mr. Johnson on this convention by adopting a Vietnam plank drawn to the President's specifications.

They defeated by a comfortable margin a substitute proposal critical of much of the President's policy and supported by backers of Mr. McGovern, Mr. McCarthy and the "draft Ted" movement.

McCarthy's Stand in Doubt

How united this would leave the party for the fall campaign remained to be seen. Mr. McCarthy has not yet pledged his support to the ticket, the platform fight left many antiwar Democrats disappointed and bitter, and there is a pervasive fear here, based on national polls, that Mr. Humphrey cannot win against Richard M. Nixon, the Republican nominee.

The delegations of New York and California, the two biggest states, voted largely against the Humphrey-Johnson forces on all issues here, including the platform plank and the Presidential nomination.

Humphrey sources said that the nomination of a Vice-Presidential candidate would probably not be made until Thursday night, although it had been planned for tonight. Mr. Humphrey conferred with advisers this afternoon and tonight on the choice of a running mate, and numerous names were bruited about among the dele-

gates.

Two decisive breaks clinched the nomination, as well as the platform fight, for the Vice President. One was Mr. Kennedy's Sherman-like refusal to be drafted; the other was the announcement by Mayor Daley that Illinois was casting all but six of its 118 votes for Mr. Humphrey.

Of almost equal importance was Gov. Richard J. Hughes's decision to drop his favorite-son's role; that let 61 of New Jersey's votes go to Mr. Humphrey.

By mid-day Lawrence F. O'Brien, a Humphrey manager, was claiming 1,654 delegates, without any help from the Illinois delegation then in caucus.

All the Southern states, except North Carolina, abandoned favorite-son candidacies, with most Southern votes lining K. Moore of North Carolina was expected to switch to the Vice President immediately after the first ballot.

The Southern shift to Mr. Humphrey which had been generally expected from the start of the campaign, caused Gov. Lester G. Maddox of Georgia to abandon the Presidential candidacy he had announced in the late days of the campaign. He withdrew before today's sessions.

Negro delegates here put forward a black candidate, the Rev. Channing Phillips, who had been the leader of the Kennedy slate of delegates from the District of Columbia.

Mayor Joseph L. Alioto of San Francisco was chosen to place Mr. Humphrey in nomination. Selected as seconders were former Gov. Terry Sanford of North Carolina and Mayor Carl Stokes of Cleveland.

Whether these selections had any Vice-Presidential significance could not be ascertained. Both Mr. Alioto, a Roman Catholic of Italian descent, and Mr. Sanford, a Southern progressive, have figured prominently in speculation here.

Humphrey Backers Applaud

Mr. Alioto, avoiding mention of the Vietnam war, pounded out a thumping political speech that roused Mr. Humphrey's supporters to repeated roars of enthusiasm and the biggest and noisiest demonstration of the convention.

Citing the Vice President's 20 years of leadership in liberal causes, Mr. Alioto worked in the effective refrain "but he did it" after describing each of Mr. Humphrey's various achievements in terms of overcoming the impossible.

In fact, he said, in "a lifetime of courage," Mr. Humphrey had become an expert practitioner of "the art of the impossible."

The Vice President, he said, is "a leader who can be impatient" at the slow pace of progress, and he cautioned those who were calling for "new options" that they were more likely to get them from a proved man of action than from mere talkers.

Mr. Ribicoff described Mr. McGovern as "a good man without guile" and a "whole man with peace in his soul," who could bring these qualities to a nation that needed them sorely.

"He brings out of the prairies of South Dakota a new wind," Mr. Ribicoff said, "a wind that will be able to lift the smog of uncertainty from this land of ours."

His voice rising in indignation, the Connecticut Senator

then declared:

"With George McGovern as President, we would not have to have such Gestapo tactics in the streets of Chicago."

This set off a tremendous roar of approval and when it subsided briefly, Mr. Ribicoff added:

"With George McGovern, we would not have to have the national guard."

That renewed the applause but it also brought the Illinois delegates up in anger. Mayor Daley joined them in waving, catcalling and motioning for Mr. Ribicoff to sit down.

"How hard it is to accept the truth," Mr. Ribicoff replied —in a moment reminiscent of the booing of Governor Rockefeller of New York at the Republican National Convention of 1964.

Gov. Harold E. Hughes of Iowa, who was chosen to nominate Mr. McCarthy, said that "the people found Gene McCarthy for us. They found him; they follow him; he is more accurately the people's candidate than any other man in recent history."

The Governor, who seconded Lyndon B. Johnson at Atlantic City in 1964, called Mr. McCarthy "a leader who can arrest the polarization of our society—the alienation of the blacks from the whites, of the haves from the have-nots, and the old from the young."

The convention adjourned at 12:06 A.M., Chicago daylight time today. The final session is scheduled to convene at 7 o'clock tonight, Chicago daylight time (8 P.M. E.D.T.).

The session will choose its Vice-Presidential nominee and head acceptance speeches from him and Mr. Humphrey.

August 29, 1968

Defeat for Doves Reflects Deep Division in the Party

By JOHN W. FINNEY
Special to The New York Times

CHICAGO, Aug. 28 — A deeply divided Democratic National Convention, after a climactic floor clash between the Administration's supporters and its critics, adopted today a White House-dictated plank supporting President Johnson's policy in Vietnam. The whole platform was then approved.

By a vote of 1,567¾ to 1,041¼, the convention rejected a plank advanced by Democratic doves calling for an unconditional halt in the bombing of North Vietnam. Instead, it adopted a plank that called for a bombing

halt but only on conditional terms.

The vote reflected the deep, emotional division within the party over the Vietnam issue. The division manifested itself in nearly three hours of increasingly acrimonious debate, conducted against a backdrop of sporadic chants of "Stop the war!" from the galleries and the New York and California delegations.

It was a division that Vice President Humphrey, in his bid for the Presidential nomination, had hoped to avoid. But he could not avoid it when Mr.

Johnson intervened behind the scenes to toughen the language of the plank so that it would correspond to Administration policy.

In the wake of the policy confrontation, the major question was whether Mr. Humphrey, as the nominee, could heal the open rift in the party.

Even as the vote was being announced, the New York delegation, which voted 148 to 42 for the dove plank, broke into a moaning rendition of "We Shall Overcome." In a protest that continued several minutes after the convention was recessed, the singers were finally drowned out by the convention-managed band, playing with increasing volume such songs as "We Got a Lot of Living to Do."

In large measure, the debate evolved into a vote of confidence in Administration policies. But it was also a preliminary test of delegate

strength for Mr. Humphrey, who endorsed the Administration plank.

The General's Message

Again and again, as delegates milled and chanted on the convention floor, the doves protested that to approve the Administration plank was but to "rubber-stamp" and continue past policies. Administration supporters replied that the doves, with their proposed plank, were threatening to imperil the lives of American troops and to impose a coalition government on Saigon.

The debate closed not with arguments by the antagonists but with a surprise message from Gen. Creighton W. Abrams, the American commander in Vietnam, relayed to the convention by Representative Hale Boggs of Louisiana, chairman of the platform committee.

As a comparative silence fell over the convention, Mr. Boggs reported that, at a White House briefing, he had asked what additional casualties would result if the United States stopped the bombing unconditionally. The answer came back from General Abrams that within two weeks North Vietnam would be able to increase its military capacity in the south five-fold, Mr. Boggs said.

As indicated by the cheers from the front-row Texas delegation, which voted solidly for the Administration plank, the Abrams message served to support the argument of Administration backers that the doves, with their plank, were jeopardizing the lives of American troops.

But the fact that Mr. Boggs saw fit to produce the confidential message reflected the Administration's concern over the doves' attack.

With the divisive Vietnam issue finally resolved, the convention without discussion adopted its 12,000-word platform for the coming campaign.

On domestic issues, the platform is liberal in tone, committing the party, for example, to implement the recommendations of the National Advisory Commission on Civil Disorders.

At the same time, on the law and order issue, the platform pledges a "vigorous and sustained campaign against lawlessness in all its forms" while advocating an "attack on the root causes of crime and disorder."

The dove plank, drafted by supporters of Senators Eugene J. McCarthy and George S. McGovern as well as former supporters of Senator Robert F. Kennedy, called for "an unconditional end" to all bombing of North Vietnam.

In addition, it proposed negotiation of a mutual, phased withdrawal of American and North Vietnamese troops; encouragement of South Vietnam to negotiate a political reconciliation with the National Liberation Front looking toward a "broadly representative" government in Saigon; and a reduction of American offensive operations in South Vietnam. The front is the political arm of the Vietcong.

Conditions Established

The Administration plank, offered by the majority of the platform committee, called for a bombing halt only "when this action would not endanger the lives of our troops in the field" and after taking into "account the response from Hanoi."

While somewhat more loosely worded, this generally conformed to the Administration position that the bombing could not be halted so long as American lives might be endangered and until there was some reciprocal military response from North Vietnam.

In addition, the adopted plank calls for negotiation of a cease-fire with Hanoi, followed by a withdrawal of foreign troops, formation of a postwar government through "fair and

safeguarded" elections open to all major political factions and parties "prepared to accept peaceful political processes," and accelerated efforts to improve South Vietnamese forces so that American military involvement can be reduced.

The afternoon debate started off on a conciliatory note as Senator Edmund S. Muskie of Maine, striking the theme of the Humphrey camp, suggested that the two sides differed not over the objective of a negotiated settlement of the war but only over how to achieve that objective.

Senator Muskie said, "The two planks before us reflect these differences of opinion. There are real differences, but the dividing line is not the desire for peace or war; the dividing line is limited to means, not ends."

But the acrimony and the emotion built up as Administration supporters attacked the dove proposal and the doves more and more turned to assailing administration policy.

When Gov. Warren E. Hearnes of Missouri suggested the dove proposal would "jeopardize the lives of American servicemen in Vietnam," he was drowned out by hoots and boos from the New York and California delegations before he could complete his sentence with, "So don't play God with their lives."

Similarly, the convention hall echoed with hoots and jeers when Representative Clement J. Zablocki of Wisconsin reported that he had been authorized to say that Mr. Humphrey "fully supports" the majority plank.

But the suppressed emotion among the doves finally burst forth when the name of Senator Kennedy was invoked by Pierre Salinger, the Kennedy press secretary who became a campaign adviser to Senator McGovern.

"If Robert F. Kennedy were alive today, he would be on the platform speaking for the minority plank," Mr. Salinger began.

With that the first spontaneous, prolonged demonstration broke out on the convention floor. In the section where the large California and New York delegations were seated, a chant of "Stop the war!" started and was picked up by youths in the galleries. Signs bearing the same slogan were waved in the galleries and on the convention floor.

Critics Sense Defeat

Only with difficulty did Mr. Boggs silence the rhythmic chant that was to be repeated throughout the debate as the doves, sensing defeat, became more militant and more vocal.

At times the debate developed into a confrontation between the Johnson Administration and alumni of President Kennedy's Administration. Some of the sharpest criticism of the Johnson plank and policies came from such former

ON THE WINNING SIDE: Representative Hale Boggs of Louisiana, a strong supporter of the President's policy in Vietnam, waves to delegates after the convention adopted a pro-Administration Vietnam plank. Mr. Boggs was chairman of the platform committee that drafted the plank.

Kennedy aides as Mr. Salinger, Theodore C. Sorensen and Kenneth P. O'Donnell.

In essence, Mr. Sorensen said, the majority plank was a "call to affirm and continue past Vietnam policies" and "offers no way out of the present mess." In contrast, the dove plank represented "a call for a change for peace."

Domestic Planks Cited

Mr. O'Donnell said it was "the height of irresponsibility" for the party to call, in its domestic planks, for spending billions of dollars to meet the crisis of the cities. "We will not have the money unless we are able in some manner to disengage" from the "foreign adventure" in Vietnam, he said.

Describing the present Vietnam policy as "a bankrupt failure," Mr. Salinger said that adoption of the Administration plank, which he described as "indistinguishable" from the Republican platform, would be "sheer suicide for our party" in November.

Although the Johnson Administration was under attack, Mr. Johnson's name was carefully avoided, both by the doves and Administration supporters. It fell to Senator Albert Gore of Tennessee, a longtime personal antagonist of the President, to bring Mr. Johnson's name in directly.

Noting that four years ago "our nominee promised that

American boys would not be sent to fight a land war in Asia," Senator Gore said that the people "voted for Lyndon B. Johnson but got the policies of Barry Goldwater."

"The American people think overwhelmingly we made a mistake," the Senator said, "and yet in the platform we are called upon not only to approve this unconscionably disastrous policy but to applaud it."

To all the criticism Administration supporters responded with the repeated theme that the Administration plank represented a commitment to peace, while the doves would imperil American troops by their unconditional bombing halt. They also said that the doves, with their detailed proposals for a settlement, would undermine the Paris talks on Vietnam and "hamper" the President.

Crisis Blunted Campaign

Concluding the Administration case, Mr. Boggs invoked the Soviet invasion of Czechoslovakia and tensions in the Middle East in arguing that the American commitment in Vietnam was related to the general problem of maintaining peace throughout the world. "We cannot, hope as we may, disassociate ourselves from what happens in the rest of the world," he said.

In the opinion of Administration supporters, the Czechoslovak crisis, coming in the middle of the drafting of the platform, proved crucial in blunting the doves' drive to write a plank critical of the Administration.

Throughout the debate today, the Humphrey camp played an ambiguous role, confusing many of its supporters on the floor. Shortly before the Zablocki statement that the Vice President supported the majority plank, Lawrence F. O'Brien, the Humphrey campaign manager, told a news conference that the Vice President would embrace the platform adopted by the convention, even if it included the doves' Vietnam plank.

Last night, Mr. O'Brien relayed word to Humphrey delegates to oppose the dove plank. But at caucuses this morning, Humphrey representatives were passing the word that the Vice President's supporters were free to vote as they chose on the Vietnam issue.

The evident Humphrey strategy was not to bind too closely many Humphrey supporters who were restless over the pro-Administration stance assumed by the Vice President. But, in the end, as reflected in the 526-vote margin, larger than had been expected by the Humphrey camp, there were few defections among Humphrey supporters.

August 29, 1968

The Losers in Chicago

Many Democrats, Shocked by Brutality, Ponder Ultimate Future of the Party

By MAX FRANKEL
Special to The New York Times

CHICAGO, Aug. 29 — The ultimate victims of this brutalizing convention were the Democrats who thought this morning that they ought to be thoughtful about what had happened to them here.

There was the faithful member of President Johnson's sub-cabinet fighting down what he **News Analysis** called the "immoral" thought that it would be best if Richard M. Nixon were elected in November. He could not fight very well while sniffing the odor of the stench bombs in the Conrad Hilton's lobby.

There was the lifelong Tennessee Democrat declaiming over a post-convention coffee that George C. Wallace was, after all, the only hope for law and order. His colleagues insisted that he ought to be taking more satisfaction from that "wonderfully free debate" of Vietnam policy, but he wouldn't be satisfied.

'Hatred for the Young'

There was Arthur Miller, the delegate-playwright from Connecticut, who couldn't get his mind off that "aged bitterness on the platform" leading a majority in "hatred for the young."

And there were the young, with blank white buttons and armbands of black hating no one through their tears over the bloodshed, or over Eugene J. McCarthy, or themselves, they couldn't quite decide which.

And there was at least half the convention hall tonight rhythmically pounding out its defiance of the chair and everything on the rostrum of this party as it sang and sang and sang "The Battle Hymn of the Republic" in unmistakable insistence that Robert F. Kennedy's leadership was the kind they wanted.

Mr. McCarthy himself made the only sustained effort at analysis, and he produced questions rather than answers.

In asking his supporters to keep the faith and to keep raising the important issues in Congressional elections, he urged them also to think again whether they really wanted the political parties that Thomas Jefferson had added to the American system and whether they really wanted the political conventions that Andrew Jackson had added to the party system.

Symbolic Tribute

"We've forgotten the convention, we're beyond the convention," he asserted. "We've forgotten the Vice President. We've forgotten the platform. We've forgotten the national chairman of the Democratic party."

Perhaps, Mr. McCarthy mused, the party ought henceforth to nominate by absentee ballot and let the Mayor of Chicago count the ballots. It was the kindest thrust of the hundreds hurled at Mayor Richard J. Daley by Democrats who just a short time ago were competing for his favor.

But then even Senator McCarthy gave in to sentiment and sensibility and walked out of the hotel into Grant Park to offer symbolic tribute to the injured and dispirited demonstrators.

With the Kennedy men almost hoping for a Democratic defeat so that they could rebuild the party to their specifications, with the Wallace fans feeling justified now in their desertion, with the McCarthy army dispersing to the political battles on the home front, with Mayor Daley and his police force being denied even a last hurrah in the party they had so often counted into victory and with President Johnson in seclusion on his Texas ranch, there was little left of this convention to think about.

Left behind, of course, are many thoughtful or at least calculating Democrats who come away from this convention determined to save their political hides and dreams of the future.

Several hundred Negro delegates were cheered to find black men moving into the seats of Southern racists and Northern V.I.P.'s. Assembly Speaker Jesse M. Unruh and his fragmented California Democrats found unexpected unity and purpose in the convention battles against the party power brokers.

Lesson for Minority

And the large minority that tried to dissociate the party from Administration policy on Vietnam found comfort in the demonstration that there was more to dissent than a bunch of hippies, radicals or even just McCarthy fans. As John J. Gilligan, the Democratic Senatorial candidate from Ohio put it, the Vietnam debate was "unprecedented" for a major party and far beyond any war vote ever attempted in either house of Congress.

The one great value of the party convention was always said to be its ability to reconcile the irreconcilable and thus to enlist in a unified effort every four years the 50 different state organizations that otherwise barely share a single name. This value was always held to justify the tedium and noise and unseemly maneuvering that attended the selection of a Presidential candidate and gave him an opportunity to forge a winning coalition.

Inability to Coalesce

But after 35 years of majority status, the Democrats finally confessed their inability to coalesce. They spoke proudly of how the "real issues" of white versus black and war and peace came before their party, and not the Republican convention of three weeks ago. They did not even pretend, however, that conflict on those issues was still consistent with election-year collaboration.

It was because it had been so spectacularly successful that so many aspiring and dissenting Americans had looked to the Democratic party for comfort and leadership. But because it had become so many things to so many people, the party could no longer accommodate so much conflicting passion.

That discovery has been a blow more severe than any inflicted by Chicago's free-swinging police, and the Democrats were in no shape today to think about its consequences and implications.

August 30, 1968

Washington: Roosevelt, Nixon and 'The Forgotten Man'

By JAMES RESTON

WASHINGTON, Sept. 7—The capital of the United States was very beautiful this weekend: clear, cool and serene. It has survived the heat of August and the political passions of Miami Beach and Chicago. It is the great prize, waiting to be captured, half way between a period that is dying and a period still unborn, the most feminine city in the world, the last great city full of trees and close to nature, and, like most women, it knows how to wait.

Washington has been dealing with the slippery ambiguities and imponderables of life for a long time. It knows the strengths and weaknesses of its suitors, and it has heard all their arguments for many years, and hears nothing very new from Nixon or Humphrey.

Roosevelt came to power here in 1932 appealing to "the forgotten man." Nixon is seeking the Presidency now by appealing to "the forgotten people." The technique is the same, but the facts are quite different, and this is the intriguing aspect of the 1968 Presidential election.

"The forgotten man" of the 1932 election was in terrible trouble, and his trouble was physical. He was out of work. He could not provide enough food and shelter for his family. The economic system had broken down. Roosevelt argued that the Federal Government had to rescue him, and on this hypothesis he not only won the election of 1932, but he kept the Democratic party in power

305

for 28 out of the last 36 years.

Richard Nixon's argument for "the forgotten people" is quite different from Roosevelt's argument for "the forgotten man." The forgotten man of Roosevelt's day has made spectacular progress. He not only has a job a generation later, but he has property. He has benefited from the welfare state and the planned economy and has now moved out of the slums of the 'cities into the suburbs.

In fact, Roosevelt's "forgotten man," paradoxically, is now, a generation later, Nixon's "forgotten people." The vast army of the unemployed of Roosevelt's day—there were still nine million in 1937—are now employed. They have bought houses and now resent taxes, and are now indifferent and many of them even hostile, to the militant poor whites and blacks who are left behind.

Nixon's whole campaign now is directed to this "new class" of workers who have moved into the middle class as a result of the welfare state and planned economy policies the Republicans have held against Roosevelt for more than a generation. Nixon knows that there is still a "forgotten man" in the urban ghettos, black and white, but he also knows that there is a new and larger middle class, which resents the racial turmoil, the demonstrations in the cities and all the permissiveness of contemporary American life.

Nixon has been accused of appealing to racist bigots in the South, but this is not what he is really doing. He is basing his campaign on the workers who have benefited from Roosevelt's "New Deal," which his party opposed. He is saying that the workers of the middle class, liberated by Roosevelt, are now "the forgotten people," and this is his main hope of getting to the White House.

He is basing his campaign on the proposition that the blacks, the liberal intellectuals, and the liberal press are out of touch with the majority of the voters, and he may be right.

Humphrey and his aides are clearly worried about this Nixon strategy. They have lost their old allies in the universities and the press. They have the support of the labor union leaders but they are not sure of the support of the labor union voters. They have Mayor Daley of Chicago and George Meany of the AFL-CIO on their side, but not necessarily the workers or the poor who made up the Democratic labor vote of the past.

In short, the Democrats are in trouble. They are still appealing to "the forgotten man" as if this were 1932, but Nixon is appealing to "the forgotten people"—the new large middle-class workers and middle-class property owners who were the unemployed backers of Roosevelt at the beginning of the thirties.

Washington is fascinated and astonished by this political switch.

It sees the Republicans benefiting from the welfare state and planned economy policies which Taft and Nixon opposed. It sees Humphrey accused of being a conservative warmonger, though it knows him over the years to be a liberal advocate of disarmament. So it waits and wonders.

It has seen all this before, in other periods. It has heard all the predictions of disaster, now so common. It has been confronted by worse choices than Humphrey or Nixon for the Presidency; so it keeps going, cynical but hopeful, mainly through tradition.

September 8, 1968

The 'Wallace Phenomenon' Gets a Big Hand

MONTGOMERY, Ala.—Among the "left-wing liberals" and 'pseudo-intellectuals" who are the villains of George Corley Wallace's campaign for the Presidency, there has long been an assumption that the nonpolitical people he calls "the good little folks" are locked forever in a two-party system run by a group Wallace calls "the elite."

Relatively speaking—in terms familiar to the cabdrivers, beauticians, stock-car folks, auto-body repairmen, and steel and textile workers who make up Wallace's crowds—that assumption may be dead wrong.

"The other two major parties," Wallace says, including his own American Independent party in the list, contain the bureaucrats, planners, professors, preachers, judges, writers and editors who, he tells his crowds, daily affront the sensibilities of the American yeomanry with "do-good schemes," and they must go.

The common belief that Wallace's "little folks" are prisoners of the two parties is generally supported by political history, and one evidence that it is operating today is that only one national newspaper correspondent has been traveling regularly with the Wallace campaign in recent weeks.

The tendency of liberals and of the Establishment generally to dismiss Wallace's fiery pitch to popular fears, frustrations and biases as a temporary aberration is based in part, of course, on Wallace's performance as a candidate. He is stagy and corny and widely regarded as "too country."

But it is clear by now that Wallace is also injecting into the arena of public opinion ideas that have not had their times at bat in the two-party system run by "the élite folks who look down their nose at you and me." As Wallace correctly puts it, "I have been saying things that you have never heard a national candidate say before."

Assuming, as a slowly growing number of Wallace's hated "smart folks" now do, that the Wallace candidacy may carry more votes in November than any third-party has ever won before in American history, a question that demands an answer is: Is it all bad?

The liberal and moderate answer, of course, is a thousand times yes. The idea of a Wallace administration in Washington, with its promise to repeal most of the landmark social legislation of the last decade under the guise of "state's rights" and "local government," seems a nightmare.

Wallace constantly inflates the bad dream with lurid specifics. As President, he says, he is going to "call back to Washington all the pinhead, briefcase-totin' Federal harassers who've been writing the guidelines that tell you who can ride in a wheelchair in a hospital and who you have to take a shower bath with in a steel mill and throw their brief cases in the Potomac River —if it don't pollute it."

His crowds react to this kind of rhetoric as though they had been given a pleasant electrical shock. The forensic cattle prod of George Wallace "saying things you have been longing to hear" makes his people scream and stamp their feet with joy and disbelief.

His strength lies in his appeal to millions who are alienated from things as they are now and who believe Wallace is truly representing them. And if he threatens the two-party system in the process, even in losing the election—and he would like to finish off and replace one party, either one—that will be his first victory on the long road to the election of 1972.

The campaign strategy being worked out at Wallace headquarters here for the next two months shows that the candidate's staff senses that his appeal already is immense outside the South. Wallace will campaign little in the deep South, which he expects to carry without much further effort. He will concentrate in the Border states and in the great urban-industrial belt stretching from Boston to Baltimore, and west around the Great Lakes, with a frank pitch to white ethnic groups.

Although some "smart folks" have ridiculed even his Alabama English, it may be true, as the non-linguistic Wallace said the other day, that "I speak better 'Polish' than any of the other candidates."

—BEN A. FRANKLIN

September 8, 1968

Pro-Humphrey Labor Chiefs Are Worried

As the leaders of organized labor see it, the man to beat in November is George C. Wallace, not Richard M. Nixon. Labor's high command is all-out for Hubert H. Humphrey, but private polls in key industrial states indicate that he will be lucky to get even half of the rank-and-file union vote. This is a long way from the 75 per cent or better that is the normal union contribution to Democratic Presidential candidates — and that often decides which way a big state will go in the Electoral College.

"The difference between what Humphrey needs and what he seems likely to get is all Wallace," says one AFL-CIO official deeply involved in labor's vote-herding drive. "Our people know Nixon well enough. We're not worried about any big swing in his direction beyond those who always vote Republican. From here on out, we are going to concentrate on stopping Wallace."

The enthusiasm for Humphrey at the top of the union totem pole is probably keener than it ever has been for any Presidential nominee. The Vice President is a proven friend who went to bat for labor every time it was in trouble anywhere. A decade ago when the tele-vised hearings of the Senate Rackets Committee were high-lighting gangster influence and dictatorial tendencies in labor, Humphrey made a Senate speech entitled "What's Right With Labor" that is still quoted reverently in every union orientation class for new members.

So there is unlikely to be a dissenting voice when the presidents of all AFL-CIO international unions meet in New York this Thursday to give labor's blessing to the Humphrey-Muskie ticket. On Labor Day, George Meany foreshadowed the vote by walking at Humphrey's side up Fifth Avenue in the van of nearly 150,000 New York unionists, all mustered to parade in what was frankly designed as a monster election rally.

Rank-and-File Sentiment

Yet for all the claims by Harry Van Arsdale Jr., the exuberant head of the Central Labor Council, that the turnout was a sign that labor was solid behind its leaders' choice, many of his lieutenants told a very different story of sentiment in their locals.

"Sure, the business agents can get the people out to march, but their hearts are somewhere else," said the president of one of the city's biggest locals. "I wouldn't dare take a vote of our members. I'm sure we could get a majority for Wallace. We might even get one for Nixon. But not a prayer for Humphrey."

Defeatism of such dimensions is rare. But there is a general recognition that the Wallace appeal to the "white backlash" and to fears about the safety of homes and jobs is making converts among workers all over the country.

The explanation is simple enough. The worker, as the most recent arrival at a secure hand-hold on middle-class status, feels most threatened by crime on the streets, the bite of high taxes, the disintegration of the school system, the climb of the welfare rolls and the suggestion that he and his family should give up some of their prosperity to provide a better break for Negroes and others traditionally excluded from a full share of America's abundance.

Many union chiefs, convinced that they are licked before they start in the effort to counter Wallace sentiment among white workers, are putting their major thrust into getting more Negroes to the polls. There are well over a million Negroes among the nation's 17 million unionists.

Perhaps the biggest gripe of labor's rank and file—and the key to much of the Wallace attraction—was summed up two weeks ago by P. L. Siemiller, president of the million-member International Association of Machinists, in his keynote at the union's convention in Chicago. He said that "union members who have worked so hard to build this country are pretty sick of rioters, looters, peace-niks, beatniks and all the rest of the nuts who are trying to destroy it."

Labor also is stressing the "you-never-had-it-so-good" theme in pointing up the bounty that eight years of Democratic rule has brought to workers. But somehow that time-tested formula isn't working so well this year.

Maybe it's because fear—fear of a return to the great depression under the G.O.P.—has always been a main cog of labor's own political machinery that it is finding it so hard to counter a master propagator of fear.

—A. H. RASKIN

September 15, 1968

Dissident Democrats Organizing as a Permanent Power in Party

By STEVEN V. ROBERTS

Forces within the Democratic party that have opposed the Johnson Administration and its policies for the last year are organizing themselves as a permanent power in party politics.

About 200 dissident Democrats, most of whom supported Senators Robert F. Kennedy, Eugene J. McCarthy and George S. McGovern, will meet in Minneapolis on Oct. 5 and 6 to discuss plans and strategy.

Many will eventually support Vice President Humphrey to preserve their credentials as Democrats. But few are happy with their party's candidate or platform, and they are looking ahead to future elections and the campaign for the Presidential nomination in 1972.

Many members of the group, which calls itself the New Democratic Coalition, believe the techniques used so successfully by Senator McCarthy in his primary campaigns can be employed to wrest control of the party machinery from its current leaders.

Despite their dissatisfaction with the party's current status, the coalition members are essentially committed to working within the party and for specific political goals. Several members of the group's steering committee are already personally involved in party politics.

For example, Julian Bond, a former leader of the Student Nonviolent Coordinating Committee, is a state Representative in Georgia. Allard K. Lowenstein, one of the founders of the original "dump-Johnson" movement, is a candidate for Congress in the Fifth District of New York in Nassau County. David Hoeh, a young Dartmouth professor who headed Senator McCarthy's campaign in New Hampshire, is also running for Congress.

Organizers of the new coalition recognize that they face several major problems in their drive to gain power within the party. One is the immediate problem of whether to support Mr. Humphrey or not.

Some, like Mr. Lowenstein, believe they cannot support the Vice President at the moment, even though this decision is costing Mr. Lowenstein party support in his Congressional campaign.

A second problem is that people who were brought into politics by the excitement of a Presidential election might not be prepared to do grubby organizing work on a local level once the glamor and publicity of a national campaign fades.

Local organizations that formed to support Senator McCarthy and other candidates have vowed to become permanent in such states as Washington, Minnesota, New Jersey, Pennsylvania and Michigan.

A third major, but less immediate, problem, is the man who will eventually lead this force against the entrenched party regulars.

Senator McCarthy has been "kept posted" on the formation of the coalition, and if he decides to become a candidate again could undoubtedly call on a deep reservoir of loyalty among party dissidents.

A significant element in the coalition, however, retains a deep dislike of the Minnesota Senator and would not — as it did not this year — support him for President. This group, many of whom supported Senator Robert F. Kennedy, would prefer Senator Edward M. Kennedy as their future leader.

September 17, 1968

307

Study in House Finds Liberals Have Divided Into Two Blocs: 'Custodial' and 'Humanistic'

By JOHN HERBERS
Special to The New York Times

WASHINGTON, Sept. 22—The turmoil that has been boiling in the Democratic party this year is due largely to a deep and growing rift between two types of liberals, according to a study released today.

The two types, called the "custodial liberal" and the "humanistic liberal," have crystalized within the liberal bloc that was responsible for the enactment of the sweeping domestic programs under Democratic Presidents since the 1930's, the study says.

The study was based on a survey of 140 Northern and Western Democrats in the House of Representatives during July and August by the National Committee for an Effective Congress. The committee provides money and other support for Congressional candidates it considers highly motivated—mostly classed as liberals.

Until recently the Democrats under study were unified on most issues and formally banded together under an organization called the Democratic Study Group.

But in recent months, the committee said in a 3,000-word summary of its report, the liberals have been "torn apart in their search for the life force of American politics."

Defender of Johnson

The "custodial liberal" was identified as the classic, orthodox labor liberal who is a stanch defender of President Johnson's policies at home and abroad.

"He believes in the litany of welfare projects, stressing the numerical, quantitative aspects of problems and politics," the study said. "A self-styled pragmatist, he is contemptuous of intellectuals and nonconformists, of those who challenge the familiar routine of party power and Main Street morality."

There are about 100 Democrats and a dozen Republicans in the House classified as custodial liberals by the committee. These include House Speaker John W. McCormack of Massachusetts and other members of the Democratic leadership.

The "humanistic liberal," the committee said, is "passionately committed to abstract values," is strongly concerned with civil liberties and accepts protest as "an inevitable social force rather than a breach of law and order."

"His focus is on quality in education, conservation, urban design, with prime emphasis on innovation and the role and rights of the individual and less emphasis on the bread and butter goals of the old New Deal," the report said. "He has been restive under Johnson and the leadership, which he regards as out of touch with the temper of the time."

The committee placed about 50 Democrats and a dozen Republicans in that category.

Humanists For McCarthy

The committee found that "the custodial Democrats almost automatically favored Hubert Humphrey, while the humanists expressed their private preference for the politics of Eugene McCarthy or Robert Kennedy, regretting that party

and union pressure made it imprudent to express their taste and political judgment."

The two types, the study showed, "speak essentially different languages and do not speak very much to each other."

The division of the liberals, the committee said, has been identified this year in a series of roll-call votes. Included were measures dealing with the rights of dissenters, invasion of privacy, curbs against rebellious students and constitutional issues in the anticrime bill.

"In battles over the budget," the committee said, "the humanists tried to develop and advance programs for self-help among the poor, the minorities, the unorganized. The establishment forces favored cutting these 'soft' programs and continuing the appropriations for public works and engineering programs, especially those connected with the military."

The humanists, the committee said, include both "a clique of about 15 ideological protestors on Vietnam" and about 40 "operative liberals" who are "experienced and interested in the real use of power." Typical of the latter, it said, is Representative Frank Thompson of New Jersey, a leader in the Democratic Study Group."

The Democratic party, as seen through its House members, is depicted in the report as bankrupt: "The Southerners have lost their votes to George Wallace; the labor bosses go around with bags of money but can't deliver their membership; the organization blacks have

no influence, since it's the militants who stir the Negro ghettos. The Democratic party is without a great issue, without a hero and without a live constituency."

"Inability of the traditionalists to comprehend the weight of abstract and nonmaterial forces explains the Vietnam failure and debacles at home," the report continued. "Only when the new political generation enlarges its strength in the Congress will there be fundamental change. Until then, the period of transition must be one of torment, and America's entire political house will be wracked by disorder."

As for the November elections, the committee said, many of the humanists are in danger of defeat because they come from marginal districts in what appears to be a conservative year. The custodians, on the other hand, are from virtually "defeat-proof districts."

"Attrition at the polls tends to work against change," the report said, "retiring the modern men and leaving the old-timers even more in possession. The trend of 1968 politics is not yet sufficiently strong to reverse this, so the November Congressional election cannot fully reflect the depth of change in the country."

The national committee is a New York-based organization. Sidney M. Scheuer is chairman and Russell Hemenway national director. A number of its members supported Senator Eugene J. McCarthy's campaign for the Democratic Presidential nomination.

September 23, 1968

Whose Law and Order?

WASHINGTON — If there is an "issue" in this election campaign that is causing huge numbers of voters to break their traditional voting habits it is inadequately expressed by that slurred and slippery phrase, "law-and-order."

Everybody is for it, naturally, and all three Presidential candidates are trying to exploit it. Apparently, in the public mind, it encompasses everything from rising crime rates to campus disorders to the breakdown of "family structure" to the alleged-

ly excessive pace of racial integration.

"Law-and-order" as it expresses resentment or fear of the Negro is probably the major factor in the remarkably large following attracted by George C. Wallace in the North as well as the South.

"Law-and-order" as it expresses a sense of moral and legal breakdown probably accounts also for the surprisingly lopsided lead that Richard M. Nixon has developed in the opinion polls.

And, conversely, "law-and-order" probably explains Hubert H. Humphrey's loss of standing among traditional Democratic voters in the South and among union members and ethnic voters in the North. Yet as interpreted by the Vice President, it also explains the strength of his re-

sidual appeal to Negro voters and much of his strategy for salvaging victory next month.

Wallace's Pitch

Wallace has the simplest task and approach to the issue, for he seeks to register protest and grievance without too much attention to the remedy.

Insensate "bureaucrats" in Washington, he contends, are telling people where their children may go to school, how, and with whom. They are invading the serenity of local communities with hateful "guidelines" for the integration of hospitals and other facilities. They are closing their eyes to rising crime and have shown themselves unwilling to be tough in the restoration of "order" in the cities, on the campus and even in the clearing of a safe path for the President of

the United States.

What would he do? He would set a new tone of firmness in the White House, encouraging every sheriff and policeman to enforce the already adequate laws on the books, he says. He would prohibit Federal officials from telling local communities how to run their affairs. He would reverse by law the Supreme Court rulings that have gone too far in protecting the "rights" of the criminal.

Nixon sounds like Wallace when he echoes many of these same complaints against the Supreme Court, the Attorney General and the "guideline" writers. But he insists that along with firm enforcement of the law, the poor and the Negroes and other deprived citizens must be given a sense of hope and a material stake in the system that policemen seek to defend.

He would not use Federal power to force school busing and other forms of integration, Nixon says. But he would organize a nationwide volunteer effort in which private citizens and business firms would be encouraged and led in the creation of more jobs and recreational opportunities, in the refurbishing of the cities, and gradually, in the creation of opportunities for black Americans to acquire their own homes and business.

Humphrey's Approach

Humphrey approaches the issue on the defensive, contending that unrest was the result of success and rising expectations rather than the failure of Federal programs. He argues that the Republicans, by doing little in 1953-1960 are to blame for the miseries of the cities and that the Johnson Administration has imaginatively reversed the trend.

He vows, like his rivals, to enforce the law not only in the small domain of a President, in Washington, D.C., but through a "massive" program of Federal aid to local police, judicial and penal systems.

Beyond that, however, the Democratic candidate favors even more massive Federal expenditures on programs to rehabilitate and even rebuild the cities, train the unskilled and educate the ignorant, in a vast "Marshall Plan" program too large for either the private or the public sector to handle alone.

Wallace seeks to rouse the country to anger over the "law-and-order" issue. Humphrey contends that only he will find and commit the resources that are needed to change the quality of urban life. Nixon, seeking the middle, thinks the protest justified and the Democratic remedies discredited. Whether the voters want protest, costly remedy or something in between will probably determine the outcome of the contest.

— MAX FRANKEL

October 13, 1968

Million More Negroes To Vote in the South

ATLANTA, Oct. 21 (AP)— Nearly one million newly registered Negro voters in the South will be voting this fall for the first time in a Presidential election, according to the Southern Regional Council.

Negro voters could determine the outcome of the Presidential race in as many as five Southern states, a council spokesman said.

The Atlanta-based council is a private biracial research agency financed by foundation grants and dedicated to promoting equality of opportunity for all persons.

According to the study, there are now 3,124,000 registered Negro voters in 11 Southern states, compared with 2,164,000 in 1964.

The number of registered white voters increased in the same period from 14,263,000 to 15,767,000, the council said.

October 22, 1968

M'CARTHY BACKS HUMPHREY RACE; HIS PLANS VAGUE

Senator Says He Won't Run as Democrat for Senate in '70 or Presidency in '72

HE REBUKES THE PARTY

Bids Undecided Supporters Vote for Nominee—Cites His Opposition to Nixon

By JOHN HERBERS
Special to The New York Times

WASHINGTON, Oct. 29 — Senator Eugene J. McCarthy announced today that he would vote for Hubert H. Humphrey for President but said that he would not seek the Democratic nomination for the Senate in 1970 or for the Presidency in 1972.

The Minnesota Democrat, who said that he would make a speech tomorrow in the Vice President's behalf, recommended that those of his supporters who had been awaiting his announcement also vote for Mr. Humphrey.

While endorsing the Vice President's candidacy as preferable to that of Richard M. Nixon, Senator McCarthy continued to rebuke the Democratic party and left the way open for him to continue to lead his movement outside the party framework after the election next Tuesday.

Humphrey Enthusiastic

Although Mr. Humphrey received the endorsement with enthusiasm, the McCarthy statement contained more for the dissidents who had followed the Minnesota Senator's preconvention campaign than for party regulars who are desperately seeking a Humphrey victory.

The runner-up for the Democratic nomination issued the prepared statement from his office this morning, then went to the television studios in the Capitol and recited a slightly different version for broadcast. After that he answered report-

ers' questions as they trailed him through the corridors, but added little to his original statement.

Told that he had left his political future unclear, Senator McCarthy replied, "Well, that's the way it is."

"Most Americans today," he said in the statement, "I think, are quite capable of making their own decision about the Presidency. Many, if not most, of my supporters have, I believe, already made this decision. To those, however, who may be waiting for my decision, I wish to announce that on Nov. 5 I intend to vote for Vice President Hubert Humphrey and recommend that those who have waited for this statement of my position do the same."

Opposition to Nixon

Then he recited his reasons, based more on his frequently stated revulsion against Mr. Nixon's policies and conduct than an embrace of the candidacy of Mr. Humphrey, his old friend and party intimate from Minnesota.

Mr. Humphrey's position on the main issues raised in the McCarthy campaign, he said,

"falls far short of what I think it should be." But he added that the choice was between Mr. Humphrey and Mr. Nixon.

On the basis of what Mr. Humphrey has stood for in the past and what he has said in the campaign, Senator McCarthy declared, "Hubert Humphrey has shown a better understanding of our domestic needs and a stronger will to act than has been shown by Richard Nixon."

"With Hubert Humphrey as President," he went on, "the possibility of scaling down the arms race and reducing military tensions in the world would be much greater than it would be with Richard Nixon as President."

His Political Future

The rest of the statement was devoted to his future as a political leader.

He wants to make it clear, he said, to those who supported him in the primaries "after I asked them to test the established political processes of the Democratic party that I will not make that request of them again unless those processes have clearly been changed.

"I wish to assure them that I intend to work to that end, and, at the same time, to continue to discuss the substantive issues of American politics," he said.

'In order to make it clear that this endorsement is in no way intended to reinstate me in the good graces of the Democratic party leaders," he went on, "nor in any way to suggest my having forgotten or condoned the things that happened both before Chicago and at Chicago, I announce at this time that I will not be a candidate of my party for re-election to the Senate from the state of Minnesota in 1970. Nor will I seek the Presidential nomination of the Democratic party in 1972."

Thus the Senator, who entered the Presidential race almost a year ago in opposition to President Johnson's Vietnam policies and continued at odds with party leaders through the primaries and at the convention in Chicago, was still at war with those who control the party and succeeded in nominating Mr. Humphrey.

Despite the endorsement, the party continued to be divided one week before the election and Mr. McCarthy offered himself as the leader of Democratic dissidents in the future in whatever kind of political structure might materialize.

He could run as an independent in Minnesota, where, along with Mr. Humphrey, he has been a leader in the Democratic-Farmer Labor party. He could also run as an independent or third-party candidate for President in 1972.

But the Senator's associates believe that his intentions, as he said, are unclear at this time short of giving his supporters a means of continuing the movement past the election.

Lift for Humphrey Seen

Nevertheless, it was believed here that the McCarthy endorsement would give Mr. Humphrey's campaign at least a slight lift. In response to questions, Mr. McCarthy said he would speak in Los Angeles tomorrow night in Mr. Humphrey's behalf.

Previously, Senator McCarthy had spoken only in behalf of candidates for the Senate and House who shared his views on Vietnam. In California, where Mr. Nixon is reported to be ahead, the split in the Democratic party has been particularly severe and a write-in movement is under way for Mr. McCarthy.

Efforts had been made by both Humphrey and McCarthy supporters to reach an accommodation between the two men that would have brought about a much warmer endorsement.

On Oct. 9, Senator McCarthy said in a New York speech that the conditions for such an endorsement would be commitments on Mr. Humphrey's part for a new government in South Vietnam, basic changes in the military draft and reforms in the procedures of the party to make it more democratic.

The language in which the conditions were laid down made it clear that the Vice President would have to move all the way to the McCarthy position. Mr. Humphrey felt he had already moved significantly in that direction. Negotiations continued through last week, but they failed to find grounds that would bring more than a conditional McCarthy endorsement.

The Senator was asked if he intended to leave the Democratic party and continue as a political leader on another ticket.

"I didn't say that," he replied.

Then he was asked if he was saying he would not run for the Senate or the Presidency again.

"No, I'm not saying that," he replied.

It was clear, however, that Senator McCarthy was operating as he has since entering the primaries — with disregard of the established rules of politics.

October 30, 1968

NIXON WINS BY A THIN MARGIN, PLEADS FOR REUNITED NATION

ELECTOR VOTE 287

Lead in Popular Tally May Be Smaller Than Kennedy's in '60

By MAX FRANKEL

Richard Milhous Nixon emerged the victor yesterday in one of the closest and most tumultuous Presidential campaigns in history and set himself the task of reuniting the nation.

Elected over Hubert H. Humphrey by the barest of margins —only four one-hundredths of a percentage point in the popular vote—and confronted by a Congress in control of the Democrats, the President-elect said it "will be the great objective of this Administration at the outset to bring the American people together."

He pledged, as the 37th President, to form "an open Administration, open to new ideas, open to men and women of both parties, open to critics as well as those who support us" so as to bridge the gap between the generations and the races.

Details Left for Later

But after an exhausting and tense night of awaiting the verdict at the Waldorf-Astoria Hotel here, Mr. Nixon and his closest aides were not yet prepared to suggest how they intended to organize themselves and to approach these objectives. The Republican victor expressed admiration for his opponent's challenge and reiterated his desire to help President Johnson achieve peace in Vietnam between now and Inauguration Day on Jan. 20.

The verdict of an electorate that appeared to number 73 million could not be discerned until mid-morning because Mr. Nixon and Mr. Humphrey finished in a virtual tie in the popular vote, just as Mr. Nixon and John F. Kennedy did in 1960.

With 94 per cent of the nation's election precincts reporting, Mr. Nixon's total stood last evening at 29,726,409 votes to Mr. Humphrey's 29,677,152. The margin of 49,257 was even smaller than Mr. Kennedy's margin of 112,803.

When translated into the determining electoral votes of the states, these returns proved even more difficult to read, and the result in two states— Alaska and Missouri—was still not final last night. But the unofficial returns from elsewhere gave Mr. Nixon a minimum of 287 electoral votes, 17 more than the 270 required for election. Mr. Humphrey won 191.

Because of the tightness of the race, the third-party challenger, George C. Wallace, came close to realizing his minimum objective of denying victory to the major-party candidates and then somehow forcing a bargain for his support on one of them. Although he did not do nearly as well as he had hoped and as others had feared, he received 9,291,807 votes or 13.3 per cent of the total, and the 45 electoral votes of Alabama, Georgia, Louisiana, Mississippi and Arkansas.

Mr. Wallace's support ranged from 1 per cent in Hawaii to 65 per cent in his home state of Alabama, and his presence on the ballot in all 50 states unquestionably influenced the outcome in many of them. But there was no certain way of determining whether Mr. Nixon or Mr. Humphrey was the beneficiary of the third-party split-offs.

Mr. Humphrey's narrow victory in states such as Texas was probably due to Mr. Wallace's strong showing there. Conversely, Mr. Wallace's drain-off in traditional Democratic strongholds, such as New Jersey, probably helped Mr. Nixon.

Strong in the Northeast

The Vice President, staging a remarkable and highly personal comeback drive in the last three weeks of the campaign, after the opinion polls showed him 10 and even 15 percentage points behind, ran extremely well in the northeastern industrial states, including New York, and in Michigan. And he profited from large urban majorities, including Negroes, Jews and Spanish-speaking communities, to take Pennsylvania, Texas and Maryland, and possibly Missouri.

Mr. Humphrey mounted a strong challenge in California, but his only other successes west of the Mississippi were in his home state of Minnesota, Hawaii and possibly Washington, with Alaska still in doubt.

Mr. Nixon's victory, therefore, though marginal in numbers, turned out to be well spread geographically.

He established the Republican party as a formidable and probably permanent political factor in the South and Southern border states, profiting from the Wallace inroads, but nonetheless running extremely well in such states as Kentucky and Virginia. Mr. Humphrey lost everything south of West Virginia and east of Texas to his two rivals, a result that should profoundly shake the Southern Democratic parties.

Hurt in Urban Areas

Yet the broad spread of Mr. Nixon's strength clearly did not extend into the great urban areas where he must perform his works of unity and redevelopment.

After receiving Mr. Humphrey's concession, congratulations and offer of cooperation at noon yesterday, Mr. Nixon replied before television cameras with a statement that implicitly recognized this possible obstacle to his rule. Of all the signs, friendly and hostile, thrust at him on the campaign trail, he said, the one that touched him the most appeared in the hands of a teen-ager one evening in Ohio, reading "Bring Us Together."

He had not campaigned very much in Negro communities and knew of the overwhelming opposition to him by black voters. His running mate for the Vice-Presidency, Gov. Spiro T. Agnew of Maryland, had become, rightly or wrongly, a kind of symbol of white annoyance with the restiveness of the Negro community. Mr. Nixon made no mention of Mr. Agnew as he thanked all those who had contributed to his success and vowed to restore peace between the races.

Yet another challenge before the Nixon Administration will be a Congress firmly managed by the opposition party. Mr. Nixon is the first man since Zachary Taylor in 1844 to be elected President without his party's also winning control of both houses of Congress.

With the net loss to the Republicans of only four seats in the House and four, possibly five in the Senate, the Democrats will organize the legislative agendas of the 91st Congress and command all its committees. By retaining control on Capitol Hill through a change of parties in the White House, they will be in a position to exercise a powerful restraint on Mr. Nixon's budgetary priorities, which in fact means his priorities of government.

President Eisenhower, too, had to deal with a Democratic Congress for six of his eight years in office but his personal and nonpartisan standing among the opposition legislators cannot be compared with Mr. Nixon's reputation on the Hill for tough and highly partisan combativeness. Perhaps because he anticipated some of these problems, the President-elect expressed the hope in his victory statement that he could cooperate with President Johnson as Mr. Johnson dealt closely with President Eisenhower.

The Republicans took only of the 390 contested seats of the 435 in the House, and lost five seats in return, for a final line-up of 243 Democrats and 192 Republicans.

In 34 Senate races, the Democrats gained two seats, in California and Iowa, and lost seats in Maryland, Florida, Arizona, Oklahoma, Pennsylvania and Ohio, with the fate of Senator Wayne Morse of Oregon still in doubt.

The political complexion of the new Congress, however, may have shifted another few degrees from the innovative and liberal-minded spirit that prevailed in the first two years of the Johnson Administration. The concern about excessive spending on domestic social programs and about law and order that Mr. Nixon stressed in his campaign has been evident on both sides of the aisles in both Houses for some time.

Yet there was no clear ideological pattern in any of the voting, for President or Congress. Critics of the Vietnam war, for instance, lost some contests and won in others. Energetic Democratic incumbents were able to resist even strong tides to Mr. Nixon in some states while others fell victim to them elsewhere.

Survival for some created new opportunities for leadership of the now leaderless Democratic party. Mr. Humphrey indicated that he would not retire from public life, and his efforts to pay off campaign debts may in fact keep him talking for quite a while. But it will be in Congress that a new generation of Democratic leaders now begins to emerge.

Senator Edmund S. Muskie, Mr. Humphrey's running mate, became an exciting new national figure even in defeat, with a broad appeal that extended all the way from some of Senator Eugene J. McCarthy's young admirers to the hard-bitten party regulars of big-city Democratic organizations.

New Leaders Emerge

Senator Edward M. Kennedy, by loyally playing a key role in the revitalization of the Humphrey campaign, further extended his standing as a Democrat to be reckoned with in future years. Senator George S. McGovern's brief bid for his party's nomination after the assassination of Senator Robert F. Kennedy gave him new stature.

Gov. Harold E. Hughes' successful campaign for a Senate seat in Iowa will further add to his reputation as a formidable vote-getter in Republican regions and Alan Cranston of California, though a quiet and professional man, should gain stature from his defeat of the arch-conservative Superintendent of Public Instruction, Max Rafferty.

The Republicans, too, produced some vigorous new Senators such as Charles Mathias of Maryland and Richard S. Schweiker of Pennsylvania, who defeated two incumbents, Senators Daniel Brewster and Joseph S. Clark.

Of more immediate interest, however, was the question of where Mr. Nixon would turn for candidates for position in his Cabinet, his White House policy staff and other key positions. His choice of men and a few crucial appointments, such as a new Chief Justice, may well reveal how far to the right and left he intends to reach in the interests of unity and the "new coalition" of which he sometimes spoke during the campaign.

The old Democratic coalition that Franklin D. Roosevelt put together in the 1930s—united the South with the urban North, racial segregationists with Negroes, big-city machines, labor unions and the offspring of immigrants—was thought this year to be finally breaking apart.

Racial tension and the loss of interest in the economic bounty traditionally associated by the lower middle classes with the Democrats clearly threatened this political alignment, as did the physical shifting of populations out of the cities.

But Mr. Humphrey sang a vigorous last hurrah for the remnants of the New Deal and proved that the old economic arguments—or fears of Republican economic management—were strong enough to hold many Democratic voters from defection. Saddled from the start of the campaign with an unpopular President and an unpopular war in Vietnam, he also managed to wriggle loose from those burdens and held much of his party together at least one more time in opposition to Mr. Nixon.

The results suggest that in many of the big states, this remains a potent appeal. And where the Democrats remain well organized, as in Texas, Missouri or Illinois, or where the unions put their men and money to work, there was shown to be a political mechanism still worthy of the attentions of ambitious leaders.

Above all, the campaign demonstrated that the American political system as a whole could still adjust itself to the most violent strains. The bitter conflict over the war, the unexpected abdication of President Johnson in March, the shooting of the Rev. Dr. Martin Luther King Jr. and of Senator Kennedy in April and June, the riots in the Negro ghettoes and the turbulence, inside and out, at the Democratic National Convention, had spread disgust and disaffection through political ranks.

Yet the excitement of the closing days of the campaign appeared to kindle new emotions and Mr. Nixon pleaded in his victory statement with the young partisans in different branches of the Democratic party to remain within the system and to retain their enthusiasm, even if they felt compelled to continue to oppose him.

The widespread fear that neither Mr. Nixon nor Mr. Humphrey would win a clean victory and that weeks of bizarre maneuvering would result both in the Electoral College and in the House of Representatives persisted through the long night of return watching and analysis. The close escape at the end may now encourage the forces of reform who wish to alter or abandon the elector system, Mr. Humphrey among them.

But harrowing as the campaign proved to be and narrow as Mr. Nixon's margin unexpectedly came to be, the system held and turned, under the leadership of the retiring President and the defeated Vice President, to the swift and orderly passage of power.

November 7, 1968

Gallup Sampling Finds a Catholic Shift to Republicans and Negro-Jewish Democrat Tradition Holding

By PETER KIHSS

Dr. George Gallup said yesterday that there had been a shift of Roman Catholics away from the Democratic Presidential ticket in Tuesday's election, but that the Democrats had kept their Jewish and Negro voters.

He said in an interview that a sampling had indicated 62 per cent of Catholics appeared to have voted for Vice President Humphrey, 28 per cent for Richard M. Nixon, the Republican, and 10 per cent for George C. Wallace, the independent.

In 1964, Dr. Gallup said, 76 per cent of the Catholic vote went to President Johnson. the Democrat, compared with 24 per cent to Barry M. Goldwater, the Republican. His sampling, he said, included virtually solid precincts of Catholics in Boston, Hoboken, Bayonne and Philadelphia.

Dr. Gallup's indication paralleled showings from Assembly Districts in New York City and counties upstate. These showed Vice President Humphrey polling 80 to 90 per cent in area after area where Jewish, Negro and Puerto Rican voters predominated.

Votes for Nixon

Mr. Nixon won 14 of New York City's 68 Assembly Districts with 60 per cent of the vote in the 49th and 50th districts in Bay Ridge, Brooklyn. Staten Island's 58th and 59th districts gave Mr. Nixon 57 and 53 per cent, respectively;

Queen's 20th in Queens Village and 28th in Ozone Park-Woodhaven gave him more than 55 per cent; and the Bronx's 80th in Parkchester-Throgs Neck and 85th in Pelham Bay-Morris Park nearly half in the three-way contest.

While Mr. Wallace's third-party run achieved just about 5 per cent of the vote in the city and state, the former Alabama Governor's best percentages were gained in similar areas.

In the city, his highest vote was 5,156, or 9.5 per cent of the return, in Staten Island's 58th Assembly District, followed by 4,760, or 9.7 per cent, in the 30th in Elmhurst, Maspeth and Glendale, Queens, and 4,717, or 8.7 per cent, in the 80th in the Bronx.

Both Dr. Gallup and political leaders questioned in New York State believed Mr. Wallace had lost earlier professed support when voters finally got to the polls.

Dr. Gallup said three blue-collar precincts in Watertown and Middletown, N. Y., and in Philadelphia had voted for Mr. Humphrey by 47 per cent, Mr. Nixon by 45 per cent and Mr. Wallace by 8 per cent. In 1964, he said, these areas divided 67 per cent for President Johnson and 33 per cent for Senator Goldwater.

Dr. Gallup's view was that such blue-collar voters for the most part had gone back to

their normal Democratic patterns. One top Republican leader here said the last 10 days of the campaign had seen the traditional Democratic coalition of Jewish, labor and minorities voters pulling together again to provide the state's margin for Mr. Humphrey.

Upstate, Joseph Crangle, Erie County Democratic leader, celebrated an 82,000-vote county victory for Mr. Humphrey. This surpassed the 1960 margin of 65,000 for John F. Kennedy. The county embraces Buffalo.

In the nearly all-Polish Sixth Ward of Buffalo, Mr. Humphrey drew 4,119 votes to 844 for Mr. Nixon and 504 for Mr. Wallace. The area would normally be 2-to-1 Democratic, Mr. Crangle said, and he credited part of the gain to the appeal of Edmund S. Muskie, the Democratic Vice Presidential candidate, who is of Polish descent.

In the nearly all-Negro 13th Ward, strenuous Democratic efforts to get out the vote produced 6,412 for Mr. Humphrey to 466 for Mr. Nixon and 61 for Mr. Wallace. The normal Democratic edge is 6-to-1.

Negro voters showed they had learned to split their votes there — and elsewhere, — for Senator Jacob K. Javits's Republican-Liberal vote for re-election was well above Mr. Nixon's showing in Negro areas. In Buffalo's 13th Ward, the vote was 4,374 for Paul O'Dwyer, Democrat; 1,791 for Mr. Javits, and 237 for James L. Buckley,

Conservative.

In Central Harlem's 72d Assembly District, where Mr. Nixon got only 7 per cent of the vote for President, Mr. Javits polled 26 per cent. In Bedford-Stuyvesant's 55th, Mr. Nixon had not quite 10 per cent, Mr. Javits 29. In the 26th in Springfield Gardens, Queens, Mr. Nixon reached nearly 12 per cent, Mr. Javits 42.

Another indicator of Negro awareness was evident in the South Side of Yonkers, which is perhaps 95 per cent Negro. Mr. Nixon received 2,982 votes in 22 districts there, Mr. Javits 4,306 and Representative Ogden R. Reid, Republican-Liberal who has been active in slum improvement efforts, 5,240.

Dr. Gallup said his Election Day samplings of key precincts has shown such indicative areas in Trenton, Boston, Baltimore and Norfolk, which went 90 per cent for Mr. Johnson in 1964, gave 88 per cent to Mr. Humphrey.

Jewish precincts checked in Manhattan, Brooklyn and New Jersey, Dr. Gallup said, showed only a minor shift from 92 per cent for Mr. Johnson in 1964 to 87 per cent for Mr. Humphrey on Tuesday.

Dr. Gallup also reported that Mr. Humphrey appeared to have done "much better" with women voters than had Mr. Nixon. He suggested that women had been more affected by President Johnson's halting of the bombing of North Vietnam.

November 7, 1968

CAMPAIGN SHIFT BY LABOR FOUND

Gallup Says Union Members Switched Near the End

Special to The New York Times

PRINCETON, N. J., Nov. 30 —Organized labor was the big shift group in this year's election, according to a Gallup Poll analysis.

It was the swing of labor union members to Vice President Humphrey in the final days of the campaign that almost put him over the top on Nov. 5.

The Gallup Poll's analysis of the 1968 vote — based on pre-election surveys as well as

a post-election survey just completed—shows that 56 per cent of union families voted for Mr. Humphrey this year, while 29 per cent voted for Richard M. Nixon and 15 per cent for George C. Wallace.

The Democratic ticket gained 15 percentage points with the labor union group between early October and the election. Democratic gains among labor came primarily at the expense of Mr. Wallace, the candidate of the American Independent party.

Although a steady trend was recorded in the proportion of labor people who shifted back to Mr. Humphrey during the latter part of the campaign, the percentage among this group who voted Democratic is below that recorded in any election beginning with early New Deal days.

This situation presents the

Republicans with an opportunity and the Democrats with a problem.

Henceforth, labor must be regarded as a key target group for the G.O.P., since the combined Wallace-Nixon vote represents a sizable "conservative" vote among a group that is generally regarded as left of center in politics.

An important reason why the Republican party can expect to make gains among the labor rank-and-file is that a growing number of members of union families (who account for about a fourth of the electorate) are found in the income bracket of $10,000 a year and over.

The G.O.P. since early New Deal days has traditionally won heavy support from voters in the higher income evels.

About three union families out of 10 (29 per cent) have a

yearly income of $10,000 or more. This compares with 25 per cent for nonunion families.

In Presidential elections from 1936 to 1948, the vote of union labor was consistently more than 70 per cent Democratic.

In 1952, however, the appeal of Dwight D. Eisenhower drew many union members into the Republican column, and the Democratic percentage dropped to 61 per cent. In 1956, the per cent voting Democratic dropped still lower to a 20-year low point of 57 per cent.

A Return to the Fold

In the elections of 1960 and 1964 many union members returned to the Democratic fold with large majorities supporting the Democratic ticket. Sixty-five per cent in union member families voted Democratic in 1960, while 73 per cent did so in 1964.

Many of the reasons union

312

people give for shifting from Mr. Wallace to Mr. Humphrey are similar to those offered by the general public.

Chiefly they are:

¶A vote for Mr. Wallace is a "wasted vote."

¶Other candidates are more qualified.

¶Mr. Wallace is "too radical."

¶Mr. Wallace lacks the qualifications to be President.

¶"I should stick with my party."

In the 1968 election, as in earlier ones, union leadership solidly supported the Democratic ticket.

Polls taken by organized labor of its own leadership showed nearly 9 in 10 labor leaders behind Mr. Humphrey. It was the vigorous effort made by union leaders that brought many rank-and-file members back into the Democratic party fold.

December 1, 1968

The Big Givers

In America today, one of the gravest threats to democracy is inequality of access to political power. Now that civil rights laws have begun to enfranchise the Southern Negro, every citizen is equal at the polling place on Election Day. But what about an ordinary person's ability to get his own name on the ballot? Or, if it is there, of getting his political message to the public? Or of registering his potential supporters in time?

In these and many other ways, the ordinary citizen is at a severe disadvantage in gaining access to political power, compared to the small number of very wealthy individuals and corporations. Television, the preferred vehicle for political advertising, is enormously expensive and has sent campaign costs spiralling upward. Newspaper advertising, direct mailings, office rent, salaries, and all the other political expenses are also higher. These costs make it difficult for most citizens to seek major elective office.

The compilation of campaign contributions in 1968-69 recently published by the Citizens' Research Foundation of Princeton, N. J., graphically documents the importance of a relatively few big givers. Individuals who could afford to give $500 or more in 1968 accounted for a total of $17.4 million in gifts to the Republicans and $6.1 million to the Democrats. No politician doubts that in a close election money can be decisive.

The American practice of political campaigns subsidized by the rich has some bizarre side effects. The United States is surely the only major power which practically auctions off ambassadorships to political contributors. More significant is the undoubted influence which business executives and wealthy investors gain in particular spheres of public policy as a result of their political investments in winning candidates. These big givers can get the attention and often the support of Congressmen and executive officials in matters which concern them such as oil import quotas, tax bills, airline routes, drug prices, and appointments to Federal regulatory agencies.

The unions, which usually support liberal Democrats, have their own selfish aims. It is not inconceivable that the failure of Congress to enact national emergency strike legislation or of this Administration to investigate vigorously the tangled affairs of the United Mine Workers may be due to the political power of the unions.

The excessive, disproportionate power of the big givers screens many ordinary citizens out of elective politics, distorts the balance of argument in campaigns and sometimes determines their result, debases diplomacy with rich neophytes, and beclouds public policy making. Reform is long overdue. Existing Federal and state laws are lined with loopholes. There is need for a Federal commission with authority to require prompt and comprehensive public reporting of all political spending. If the power of money in politics is to be brought under democratic constraint, it is essential first to know the size and source of that power.

February 3, 1971

1968 Political Campaigns Set $300-Million Record

By R. W. APPLE Jr.
Special to The New York Times

WASHINGTON, June 19 — The campaigns of 1968 cost $300-million, more than ever before, and represented a 50 per cent increase in only four years. The Republicans outspent the Democrats almost 2 to 1.

By comparison, the increase in the 12 years between 1952 and 1964 was only 43 per cent. The jump in the cost of getting elected reflected the enormous cost of television, the fact that both major parties had Presidential primary contests and the candidacies of two multimillionaires—the late Robert F. Kennedy and Governor Rockefeller.

The cost per vote was 60 cents, also a record.

Those are the conclusions of the most extensive survey of campaign spending ever undertaken. It was carried out by the Citizens' Research Foundation of Princeton, N. J., and is detailed in "Financing the 1968 Election," a book by the foundation's director, Herbert E. Alexander. The book will be published Thursday.

Because of the looseness of the reporting laws, the tabulation is incomplete, but it contains much fresh information.

Perhaps the most surprising finding in Dr. Alexander's study is the report that former Senator Eugene J. McCarthy of Minnesota, the unsuccessful antiwar candidate for the Democratic nomination, spent $11-million. At the time, his effort was pictured as poorly financed.

Five contributions of more than $100,000 to Senator McCarthy are listed. They are: Stewart Mott, the philanthropist son of a founder of the General Motors Corporation, $210,000; Mr. and Mrs. Jack Dreyfus Jr. of the Dreyfus Fund, at least $100,000; Ellsworth T. Carrington, a 46-year-old Wall Street account executive (customer's man), who said he made his money "in the market," $100,000; Mr. and Mrs. Martin Peretz of Cambridge, Mass. — a Harvard professor who is married to a Singer Sewing Machine heiress—$100,000, and Alan Miller of Boca Raton, Fla., $108,000.

Mr. Miller, a retired industrialist from Pennsylvania, is one of the shadowy figures on the list. Not much is known about him except that he is an elderly former Republican who came forward voluntarily because of his opposition to the Vietnam war and sent two unsolicited $50,000 checks.

At one point, he came to New York in an ambulance to meet with Howard Stein, one of the principal McCarthy fund raisers. He was unable at the time to sit up because of a back ailment. Mr. Stein visited him at the St. Regis Hotel and came away with another contribution.

The campaign of 1968, Mr. Alexander writes, "brought more left-of-center or moderate money onto the political scene than at any time" in history.

Yet the third-party candidacy of George C. Wallace of Alabama was also well financed. It cost at least $9-million, most of which was raised in small sums in the most successful grass-roots fund-raising campaign ever seen in American presidential politics.

The huge McCarty expenditures in the pre-convention period helped to account for the fact that 11 of the 14 biggest contributors made most of their contributions before the parties named their candidates.

Dr. Alexander itemized preconvention spending as follows: Lyndon B. Johnson, $1-million; Hubert H. Humphrey, $4-million; Mr. McCarthy, $11-million; Mr. Kennedy, $9-million; George McGovern, $75,-000; Lester G. Maddox, $50,000; President Nixon, $10-million to $12-million; Governor Rockefeller, $8-million; George Romney, $1.5-million; Ronald Reagan,

$650,000, and Harold E. Stassen, $90,000.

Mr. Nixon's general election expenses were $24.9-million, Mr. Humphrey's $10.3-million.

The Rockefeller effort, like that of Senator Kennedy, was largely family financed. The largest single contributor in 1968 was Mrs. John D. Rockefeller Jr., the Governor's step-mother, who gave him $1,482,-625. According to Mr. Alexander's estimate, she also paid almost $850,000 in Federal gift taxes.

A total of 14 contributions of $100,000 or more are listed.

The list is full of names famous in the annals of American finance and industry—du Ponts, Fords, Pews, Mellons, Olins, Whitneys, Lehmans.

But there are others that are surprising. For example, Mrs. Margery F. Russell of Portland, Ore., an heiress to the fortune generated by Oregon's Meier and Frank department stores, contributed $94,613 to the unsuccessful campaign of Walter

Blake, a right-winger on the model of Dr. Max Rafferty of California, for Superintendent of Public Instruction in Oregon.

Dr. Manfred Clynes, director of the Biocybernetics Laboratories at Rockland State Hospital, Orangeburg, N. Y., donated $30,000 to Senator McCarthy, according to Dr. Alexander. He said in a telephone interview that he had made his money through the invention of medical computers and gave his "first and only political contribution for peace."

Bob Hope, the comedian, gave $16,000 to the Republicans; Gene Autrey, the cowboy singer, gave $15,000 to the Republicans, and Barbara Tuchman, the historian, gave $20,-500 to the Democrats, along with her husband, Lester, a New York physician.

Fourteen persons who were named ambassadors by President Nixon contributed to his campaign. The largest sum was $51,000, given by Guilford Dudley Jr., a Nashville insur-

ance man, now Ambassador to Denmark.

Democratic fund-raising for the general election campaign went so badly that the party was obliged to borrow heavily. John Factor, a real estate man once known in the Chicago underworld as Jake the Barber, lent $240,000, as did Lou Wasserman, the head of MCA, Inc. Nineteen other persons lent $100,000 each, including several New Yorkers.

They were the following:

Herbert A. Allen, New York investment banker.

The late Lester Avnet, New York electronics executive.

Jacob Blaustein, Baltimore oil executive.

Arthur G. Cohen, New York real estate man.

Robert W. Dowling, New York real estate man.

Milton Gilbert, New York trucking executive.

Milton Gordon, New York investment banker.

H. E. Gould, New York manufacturing executive.

Leon Hess, New York oil executive.

Francis S. Levien, New York manufacturing executive.

John Loeb, New York investment banker.

Arthur S. Murphy, New York distilling company executive.

Patrick O'Connor, Minneapolis attorney and former Democratic national finance chairman.

Jeno Paulucci, Duluth, Minn., food company executive.

Arnold M. Picker, New York motion picture executive.

Robert E. Short, Minneapolis trucking executive and former Democratic National Finance chairman.

Edwin L. Weisl, New York attorney and former Democratic National Committeeman from New York.

Few of the loans have been repaid, and they will probably be settled, if at all, for a few cents on the dollar. The party is still $9.3-million in debt with 1972 approaching.

June 20, 1971

DEMOCRATIC REFORM/REPUBLICAN CRISIS

Democrats Uncertain of Kennedy's Future But See Long Road Until He Regains Stature

By E. W. KENWORTHY
Special to The New York Times

WASHINGTON, July 26—"We have got to let time run on it," a Democratic party strategist said today when asked what effect he thought last weekend's tragedy on Chappaquiddick Island would have on Senator Edward M. Kennedy's chances for the 1972 Presidential nomination.

"I think it's absolutely too early to say," he said. "Anybody who tries to predict the politics of the country after 1968 and the 1970 Congressional election is out of his mind."

This was generally the view here today among Senator Kennedy's party colleagues in the Senate, their aides and workers at Democratic national headquarters.

There was nothing but praise for the Senator's bearing last night in his television statement to the voters of Massachusetts.

"He was terribly appealing, as well as sincere and straightforward," one Democratic Senator said.

Those interviewed—and all insisted that their words not be attributed — took it for

granted that the Senator's request for "advice" on whether to resign his seat would bring a many thousandfold "no" from Massachusetts voters, and that he would have no trouble being re-elected next year.

Name Is Political Magic

Since John F. Kennedy was elected Senator in 1952 in his first statewide race, the name Kennedy has carried political magic in Massachusetts. So mesmerizing was the name that an unrelated young man with the same name as the late President managed, without any discernible credentials, to be elected State Treasurer repeatedly during the nineteen-fifties.

In the 1962 primary to fill the unexpired term of John F. Kennedy, Edward Kennedy's opponent, Edward J. McCormack Jr., a nephew of Speaker John W. McCormack, said in a television debate: "Teddy, if your name was Edward Moore, with your qualifications your candidacy would be a joke."

Nevertheless, Edward Kennedy won overwhelmingly, despite a campaign disclosure that he had been forced to leave Harvard as a freshman for getting a classmate to take his Spanish exam.

That fall he beat George Cabot Lodge, son of Henry Cabot Lodge, by 284,942 votes, and two years later he was

The popularity of the Kennedy name in Massachusetts has made it difficult for the Republicans to find a candidate to oppose Senator Kennedy next year.

There have been reports that President Nixon has been trying to get the Republicans to field a candidate of stature against Mr. Kennedy, possibly John A. Volpe, a former Governor who is now Secretary of Transportation, or Elliot L. Richardson, former state Attorney General who is now Under Secretary of State.

But despite the accident and in view of the response in Massachusetts to the Kennedy telecast, it is still considered unlikely that any well-known Republican would accept this assignment.

At the same time, it was recognized that Massachusetts is not the nation, and there was agreement that Mr. Kennedy had a long road to travel before he regained the kind of national stature and approbation that would make his nomination for the Presidency a certainty, or even possible.

"I think he did everything he could do under the circum-

stances to limit the damage," another Democratic Senator said. "But I don't quite see how he can recover in time to be a candidate in 1972. He may have had some doubts about running in '72 anyway. Perhaps now he has good reason to wait until '76."

The feeling that the Senator has a long political recuperation ahead of him was based on residual doubts even after his statement last night.

Some of the doubts related to what one Senator called "the unresolved questions" about what happened, and the conduct of the Senator and two of the men who were at the cookout party—Joseph F. Gargan, a cousin, and Paul Markham, an old friend.

Questions About Friends

Thus, several of those interviewed asked why neither Mr. Gargan nor Mr. Markham informed the police of the accident and the apparent drowning of Mary Jo Kopechne. Both men, it was noted, were lawyers, and Mr. Markham once was United States Attorney for Massachusetts.

Questions were also raised about whether the two friends had stood by while the Senator leapt into the water at the ferry slip and swam the swift-flowing channel between Chappaquiddick and Martha's Vineyard or whether they left him there alone and returned to the house.

One Senator's political aide said: "I find it hard to believe they would have left him standing there. It just doesn't hang together."

More important, however, for any Presidential ambitions the Senator might have were the doubts raised by what one Democratic Senator called "his response to crisis."

Another Democratic Senator said, "That's what's going to bother the serious voter."

Effect on Senator

The resolution of these doubts, those interviewed agreed, would largely depend on the ultimate effect on the Senator of this tragedy. Would it strengthen his character? Or would it so harrow him as to weaken, resolve and inhibit decisions?

"The pressure comes from within," said the Vermont Republican Senator George D. Aiken, last night, and those interviewed today said the same thing in many different ways.

"This might toughen him, make him better," said one Democratic Senator. "Or it may reflect a flaw so that people will say, 'I have no

trouble about his being a Senator, but the Presidency is another thing."

"It must be a tremendous trauma for him," said a party politician. "It remains to be seen how resilient he is. The question is, how does this really get to the guy?"

In the background of these musings was the succession of tragedies the Senator had experienced—one brother, a pilot, shot down in World War II, a sister killed in an air crash, two brothers assassinated, an aide killed and himself badly injured in an air crash in 1964, and Mary Jo Kopechne drowned—and the Senator's own question last night: Does "some awful curse" hang over all the Kennedys?

Despite these residual doubts, it was generally agreed that, as one veteran of national campaigning put it, "He's not politically dead by any means."

Whether or not Senator Kennedy recovers to capture a Presidential nomination, it was agreed that his troubles had dealt, at least for the immediate future, a hard blow to the party, the Senate Democratic liberals and to the majority leader, Mike Mansfield of Montana.

The party will suffer, it was

emphasized, because Mr. Kennedy was not only the leading candidate for the nomination but also probably the one around whom the various elements—the party regulars, labor, Negroes, the young activists who followed Robert F. Kennedy, Eugene McCarthy and George S. McGovern—could rally after the party-riving-strife of 1968.

Also, Mr. Kennedy was the best man in a party saddled with a $6-million debt to bring out donors at a $100-a-plate dinner, and he was greatly in demand as a speaker at fund-raising affairs for Senators and Representatives.

"Now," said a politician today, "the manager of a J-J [Jefferson-Jackson Day] dinner will say to himself, 'I always wanted Teddy, but I wonder—should I bring in Ed Muskie [the Senator from Maine]?'"

Function of Whip

Senator Kennedy sought the Senate whip's job because he was convinced he could transform it from that of traffic manager for legislation into a post that would not only have a voice in party policy on issues but also serve as a rallying point for liberals frustrated by the way the aging, conservative Senate establishment shut them out of leadership posts and key

subcommittee chairmanships.

To this end, with the full support of Senator Mansfield, Mr. Kennedy set out to get more liberal representation on the largely moribund Senate Democratic Policy Committee and make the committee serve "the function that was originally conceived for it—to formulate ways and means of enacting the party platform into law."

A measure of his success was the decision of the revamped committee to demand that extension of the surtax be coupled with significant tax reform.

Today a Senate aide said: "It's tough on the liberal bloc. With Teddy, the liberals felt they'd got their first entry into the establishment."

Where Senator Russell B. Long of Louisiana, as whip, often took off on his independent, unpredictable way, or worked at cross-purposes with Senator Mansfield, Mr. Kennedy has worked closely with him. This has been most notable on opposition to development of the Safeguard antiballistic missile system.

Now, some Senators fear, Mr. Kennedy may not have for some time the influence he wielded on behalf of the leadership.

July 27, 1969

McGovern to Head Panel on Convention Reform

By E. W. KENWORTHY

Special to The New York Times

WASHINGTON, Feb. 4—Senator George S. McGovern of South Dakota will head a committee that will propose reforms in the process by which state Democratic parties choose delegates to the Presidential nominating convention.

Senator Fred R. Harris of Oklahoma, the new Democratic National Chairman, asked Senator McGovern last Friday to be chairman of the new committee. The panel was mandated by the convention last August as a result of several credentials contests centering on continentions that the delegate selection process in many states was undemocratic.

Mr. McGovern told Mr. Harris that he would be willing to serve as chairman provided his appointment had the approval of former Vice President Hubert H. Humphrey and Senator Edmund S. Muskie of Maine, the Democratic national ticket last year, and Senator Edward M. Kennedy of Massachusetts. All three are regarded as likely candidates for the Presidential

nomination in 1972, as is Senator McGovern, who was a late contender in 1968.

Mr. Humphrey, Mr. Muskie and Mr. Kennedy have signified their approval to Mr. Harris, and he is expected to name Senator McGovern along with the other members of the committee, numbering about 25, not later than next Tuesday.

The group will be called the Committee on Party Structure and Delegate Selection.

The August convention ordered the creation of a committee to study the delegate selection process with the aim of getting grass-roots participation. It then adopted a report by a minority of its Rules Committee, a minority made up chiefly of supporters of Senator Eugene J. McCarthy of Minnesota, the late Robert F. Kennedy of New York, and Mr. McGovern.

This report stated that, for the 1972 convention, the unit rule should not be used at "any stage of the delegate selection process," that each state must make "all feasible efforts" to insure that delegates "are

selected through party primary, convention or committee procedures open to public participation"; and that the delegates must be chosen within the calendar year in which the convention is held.

This minority report embodied recommendations of an ad hoc commission on the Democratic Selection of Presidential Nominees formed three weeks earlier and headed by Gov. Harold E. Hughes of Iowa.

The commission pointed out to the Rules Committee that as many as 800 of the 2,622 delegates had been chosen by methods that would be outlawed by the report. For example, delegates in many states were chosen as much as four years before the convention.

Because his proposals were adopted by the convention, Mr. Hughes, now a Senator, would have liked to head the new committee.

"I would like the job," he said today. "I made this very clear to Fred [Harris] last Friday. But I understand that I'm not acceptable to some people."

Chief among those who found

Mr. Hughes unacceptable was Mr. Humphrey. Mr. Hughes supported the candidacy of Robert Kennedy before the assassination. He put Mr. McCarthy's name in nomination at the convention because of disagreement with Mr. Humphrey over Vietnam.

Today Mr. Hughes said, "I'm not raising cain with Fred. He's got a tough job. And I think George [McGovern] would make a good chairman."

In a meeting yesterday with Mr. Harris, the leaders of the New Democratic Coalition, an organization made up largely of former McCarthy followers and supporters of Edward Kennedy, urged the national chairman to appoint Mr. Hughes.

The McGovern committee will have to move rapidly because 16 states begin the delegate selection process before the year in which the convention is held. In Arkansas, Idaho, North Dakota and Wyoming, where the Legislatures meet in odd-numbered years, laws must be enacted this year if the convention mandate is to be met.

February 5, 1969

Democratic Panel Changes Plot For Making of President 1972

By R. W. APPLE Jr.
Special to The New York Times

WASHINGTON, Dec. 7—By the time Senator Eugene J. McCarthy ran so strongly in the 1968 New Hampshire Presidential primary, more than half of the delegates to the Democratic National Convention had either been chosen or were in the process of being chosen.

That situation, which made the Minnesota Democrat's path toward the Presidency almost impossibly difficult, is one of those that may have been eliminated from the politics of 1972 by the decisions last month of the Democratic Reform Commission, headed by Senator George S. McGovern of South Dakota.

The commission's staff hopes to send out copies this week of the "guidelines" that emerged from the commission's hearings, studies and voting sessions last month. The question then will be how the state party organizations and other Democrats will react.

The commission has no enforcement powers. If a state refuses to go along with its rules, the commission must look to the convention itself to refuse to seat the offending delegation.

But a substantial number of state parties—including that of Michigan, whose delegate-selection process has long been notably archaic—have already begun reform efforts. It appears that considerable compliance will be achieved by the McGovern group.

For New York State, substantial changes will be required, but its organization is already well aware of this. John F. English of Nassau County, the national committeeman, was a member of the 26-member commission.

Last year, New York chose three delegates in primaries in each of its 41 Congressional districts, and 67 at-large by the vote of the state committee. Both parts of that procedure will be impossible for the 1972 national convention.

The new guidelines provide that no more than 10 per cent of any delegation can be selected by a state committee, which, in a 190-man delegation like the one last year, would limit New York to 19 committee choices.

Furthermore the guidelines provide that, except for at-large delegates, seats on the convention floor filled in primaries must be apportioned according to a formula that gives equal weight to population and Democratic vote in the last Presidential election.

Since Congressional districts are based solely on population, they do not meet the apportionment criteria. A preliminary study indicates that the changes might shift as many as 10 or 15 votes from upstate to the cities and suburbs in 1972.

According to commission staff members, New York is also "out of compliance" in the following party procedures:

¶It does not provide for the listing of a Presidential candidate's name along with that of a candidate for delegate in the primaries, a system that makes an insurgent's task much harder than that of the favorite of the local organization.

¶It permits both proxy voting and voting with too small a quorum at meetings of the state committee.

¶The party chairman, vice chairman, treasurer, secretary and law committee chairman are ex-officio delegates to the national convention, which is forbidden under the guidelines.

¶Eighteen-year-old are forbidden by state law to vote, so the state party must make a reasonable effort to change the law to enable the young to take part at least in primaries, if not general elections.

New York's situation is not unique; every state will have to modify party rules, state law or past practice to comply with the commission's requirements.

For example, the guideline designed to insure "timeliness" requires that the selection process not begin before Jan. 1, 1972, for delegate to a convention to be held that year. That will affect about a dozen states that would have begun to choose 1972 delegates by selecting delegate-choosing bodies early next year.

This provision is designed to make impossible a repetition of Senator McCarthy's experience early last year.

December 8, 1969

DEMOCRATIC UNIT MOVES TO REVAMP CONVENTION RULES

Reform Group Would Give Big States Larger Voice and Open All Meetings

By WARREN WEAVER Jr.
Special to The New York Times

WASHINGTON, Oct. 16—The Democratic party moved today to open up and democratize its next Presidential nominating convention.

The party's Rules Commission, adopting its first reform recommendations after more than a year of study, completely revamped the convention committee system so that the big states would have a proportionately larger voice in important decisions on the platform and seating challenged delegations.

The commission, which is headed by Representative James G. O'Hara of Michigan, also took the selection of key committee chairmen out of the hands of the Democratic National Chairman and gave it to convention committee members themselves.

Open Meetings Voted

In a day-long session in the Rayburn House Office Building, the reform group voted to make all meetings of the major convention committees — Platform, Credentials and Rules—open to the press and the public, part of an effort to dispel any atmosphere of smoke-filled-room politics.

The 30-page report on convention committee procedure, adopted with dozens of changes by the O'Hara commission today, will be circulated among party officials for their comments and then adopted by the commission in final form early next year.

The Democrats want as many of the reform recommendations as possible to be ready that early in the political schedule so that such important activities as site selection for the convention and preliminary drafting of the call can get under way next year.

Under the rules adopted today, the principal committees, which used to be composed of two convention delegates from each state, would have 150 members, a minimum of one member from each state but larger representation for states with larger Democratic votes, probably up to 15 for California.

Anti-Vietnam Plank

If such a system had been in effect at Chicago in 1968, the platform committee might well have approved a plank more critical of the war in Vietnam, with the big states, such as California and New York, holding more influence.

The commission also adopted several new rules to involve various candidates for the Democratic Presidential nomination in preconvention activity. Each candidate would be authorized to have a nonvoting representative on the subcommittee that drafts the platform.

In addition, the candidates would be invited to submit written statements to the Platform Committee.

Also adopted was a long and detailed set of rules under which the convention's Credentials Committee would decide challenges to individual delegates or entire state delegations by rival delegates or slates.

In the past, most such challenges have been based on a contention that the "regular" Democratic party discriminated against Negroes or members of other minority groups in a given state and that a racially balanced delegation should be seated instead.

A wider variety of credentials contests appears likely in 1972, however, because another Democratic reform commission, headed by Senator George S. McGovern, has provided a new set of standards for all state delegations.

These standards call for each delegation to include a number of Negroes, women and young people roughly proportioned to their representation in the Democratic party of the state involved.

The credentials machinery adopted by the O'Hara commission provides for filing notice of a challenge two months before the convention, the appointment of a hearing officer to make findings of fact, and a decision by the credentials committee based on the hearing officer's report.

In addition to today's recommendations on committee structure and function, the O'Hara commission will also make proposals on convention logistics and procedures, the apportionment of delegates among the states and new rules for the Democratic National Committee.

The commission scheduled its next meeting for Nov. 13 in Washington.

October 17, 1970

Democrats Reform Rules On Convention Delegates

By R. W. APPLE Jr.
Special to The New York Times

WASHINGTON Feb. 19 — After a day-long dispute on a relatively minor issue, marked by parliamentary bickering and impassioned speeches, the Democratic National Committee proved without debate today a far-reaching set of reforms in the selection of delegates to the party's national convention.

The committee approved without major changes the guidelines of the reform commission headed until recently by Senator George S. McGovern of South Dakota. Among other things, the guidelines outlaw the unit rule, open the delegate-selection process to broader participation by blacks, women and young people, and require that delegates be selected in the convention year.

In general, they will make it harder for party leaders to dictate the choice of a Presidential nominee — a change sought by the party's more liberal elements, particularly since the clashes at the convention in Chicago in 1968.

The party conservatives said nothing as the McGovern proposals were approved. In fact, many of those at the meeting, which was held at the Mayflower Hotel, were unaware that they had been voted upon.

For nearly the entire day, the committee debated one of the proposals of a second reform commission, headed by Representative James G. O'Hara of Michigan. It related to the apportioning of convention delegates among the states.

The O'Hara commission had recommended that the apportionment be made on the basis of each state's Democratic vote for President counting as one-half and the population of the state counting one-half. That was modified on Wednesday by the party's executive committee, which advocated a formula computed by counting the Presidential vote 47 per cent and Electoral College strength 53 per cent.

Although the differences between the formulas were not great—under one plan, the eight biggest states would have had a majority of the votes and under the other the nine biggest states would have had a majority—the executive committee proposal avoided severe losses for the smallest states.

The executive committee formula was adopted, with only John F. English of New York dissenting, after the O'Hara proposal had been beaten on a standing vote, 68 to 27.

Challenge Is Planned

Mr. English said later that he intended to challenge the formula in court, with the help of some other states and a "national reform organization." He would not identify the states or the organization.

New York's vote at the convention was cut from 301 to 278 by the rejection of the O'Hara formula. Connecticut was not affected, and New Jersey dropped from 115 to 109.

Despite the relatively small differences, tempers flared as a total of seven formulas were proposed, debated and voted upon.

The small states were unable to put across the formula that would have benefited them most. Their proposal, introduced by Grant Sawyer, a former Governor of Nevada, would have based the apportionment entirely on the Electoral College.

Voted down by larger margins were proposals for apportionment on a strict population basis, on a strict Democratic-vote basis, and two complicated compromise schemes.

Only one change in the McGovern recommendations was voted, and that came about almost by inadvertence.

At the suggestion of John Powers of Massachusetts, the committee members gave themselves the right to vote as ex officio delegates to the convention. This violated two McGovern guidelines: Prohibition of ex officio delegates, and the requirement for timely selection of delegates. Most committee members were named to their positions in 1968.

All the decisions made by the committee were incorporated into the "call" to the convention, which sets the rules for the convention itself. These can be modified by the convention after it meets, but the incorporation of the McGovern and O'Hara recommendations into the call almost intact was a triumph for the reformers.

February 20, 1971

Delegate Strength Table

WASHINGTON, Feb. 19—The following table shows the allocation of delegates to the states at the 1968 Democratic National Convention, together with the recommendations of the O'Hara reform commission for the 1972 convention and the plan for 1972 adopted today by the Democratic National Committee at a meeting here:

State	1968 Convention	O'Hara Commission Decision	Final Decision	State	1968 Convention	O'Hara Commission Decision	Final Decision
Alabama	32	36	37	New Jersey	82	115	109
Alaska	22	4	10	New Mexico	26	14	18
Arizona	19	21	25	New York	190	301	278
Arkansas	33	24	27	North Carolina	59	65	64
California	174	294	271	North Dakota	25	10	14
Colorado	35	32	36	Ohio	115	163	153
Connecticut	44	51	51	Oklahoma	41	35	39
Delaware	22	8	13	Oregon	35	32	34
Dist. of Columbia	23	12	15	Pennsylvania	130	196	182
Florida	63	83	81	Rhode Island	27	18	22
Georgia	43	52	53	South Carolina	28	28	32
Hawaii	26	11	17	South Dakota	26	11	17
Idaho	25	10	17	Tennessee	51	49	49
Illinois	118	181	170	Texas	104	139	130
Indiana	63	79	76	Utah	26	15	19
Iowa	46	45	46	Vermont	22	7	12
Kansas	38	32	35	Virginia	54	53	53
Kentucky	46	46	47	Washington	47	53	52
Louisiana	36	42	44	West Virginia	38	32	35
Maine	27	16	20	Wisconsin	59	69	67
Maryland	49	54	53	Wyoming	22	5	11
Massachusetts	72	107	102				
Michigan	96	140	132	Total	2,599	3,000	3.000
Minnesota	52	64	64	Canal Zone	5	(A)	3
Mississippi	24	21	25	Guam	5	(A)	3
Missouri	60	75	73	Puerto Rico	8	(A)	7
Montana	26	11	17	Virgin Islands	5	(A)	3
Nebraska	30	21	24	(A)—The Rules Commission			
Nevada	22	6	11	did not submit specific numbers			
New Hampshire	26	12	18	concerning the territories.			

VOTERS IGNORING THE PARTY LABEL

Elections Indicate Decline in Organizations' Stability —Polarization Grows

By JOHN HERBERS

Election returns from both major and small cities across the nation indicate a sharp decline in the stability of the political parties, further polarization of voters along racial and economic lines and increasing sophistication of the Negro vote.

The results of Tuesday's municipal elections demonstrated mounting troubles for the Democratic party, which has controlled most of the City Halls. The trend in many cities was to disregard party labels and vote according to issues and personality.

Thus, at a time when the Democrats, partly because of their strong identification with the inner cities, are losing the suburban vote to the Republicans, they also are losing their grip on the politics of the central metropolitan areas.

Although these developments have been under way for some time, they were accelerated Tuesday when about 25 cities of 100,000 or more and hundreds of smaller cities elected new Mayors and governing bodies.

In the biggest cities outside New York, where Mayor Lindsay was re-elected with about 42 per cent of the vote, there were these results:

Carl B. Stokes of Cleveland, the first Negro Mayor of a large city, a Democrat, was re-elected to a second term by a small margin over his white challenger, Ralph J. Perk, the Republican candidate. He was the only one of six Negro mayoral candidates in large municipalities to win.

In Detroit, Sheriff Roman S. Gribbs defeated a Negro candidate, County Auditor Richard H. Austin, by a vote of 257,312 to 250,020. Both candidates in the nonpartisan election were Democrats.

City Councilman Peter F. Flaherty, a Democrat, won the Mayor's office in Pittsburgh over a strong Republican contender, John K. Tabor, by a wide margin.

In Buffalo, Mayor Frank A. Sedita, a Democrat, turned back a Republican - Conservative, Mrs. Alfreda Slominski, and a Negro candidate, Ambrose I. Lane, by 20,000 votes, in a race that most clearly defined the debate over crime and civil disorders.

In Buffalo, Mayor Frank A. Sedita, a Democrat, turned back a Republican-Conservative, Ambrose I. Lane, by a margin of 20,000 votes, in a race that most clearly defined the debate over crime and civil disorders.

Beneath the facts of who won, in these and in many of the other cities, is the story of crumbling political organizations, and the other trends.

In Pittsburgh yesterday morning Mr. Flaherty, a 44-year-old populist who owes his election to the overwhelming Democratic registration and a strong labor movement, went on television and pledged to continue repudiating the Democratic ward chairmen who turned out the vote for him.

Mr. Flaherty was once an obedient member of the organization headed by retiring Mayor Joseph M. Barr, but in the spring he saw that the organization was in deep trouble due to an increase in crime, racial tensions and fiscal debt. He defeated the organization candidate in the primary, continued to repudiate City Hall in the general election campaign and toterday was promising to rule the city not through the regular party but by taking the government "to the people" in the various neighborhoods.

Although some Democratic Mayors held on and Democrats made gains in areas such as up-

state New York, there was throughout the country a number of indications of a lessening of party control.

In Youngstown, Ohio, a solidly Democratic city, voters turned out their three-term Democratic Mayor, Anthony B. Flask, largely because of labor violence seen recently in that city. Jack C. Hunter, the Republican candidate, blamed the violence on the Mayor's laxity and won the election by a small margin.

There were other examples seen outside the mayoral races. In Philadelphia, which has predominant Democratic registration, the party organization was unable to block the reelection of the District Attorney, Arlen Specter, a Republican, who is now in line for a second try at the Mayor's office.

In Tuscon, Ariz., three seats on the City Council changed from Democratic to Republican control, giving the G.O.P. a majority.

The switches appeared to be no swing to the Republican party but a disaffection with whoever was in power and a growing disregard of party.

In Connecticut, where there were elections in 156 towns and cities, 20 municipalities switched from Republican to Democratic and 16 switched from Democratic to Republican. Observers of urban politics said the switching nationally

was hurting the Democrats, because it is they who control the big cities.

Voting according to racial and economic lines was seen in a number of races. A phenomenon common to most cities is that middle-class whites have moved to the suburbs, leaving a preponderance of the poor and old within the cities. These constituencies are demanding more services, less crime and disorder and less taxes while providing a smaller tax base.

In Cleveland, Mayor Stokes put together the same combination that won for him two years ago—almost solid black support and a minority of the white vote. He managed to win 24 per cent of the white vote.

Detroit, which is even more racially tense, demonstrated intense polarization. Sheriff Gribbs, the white candidate, polled 82 per cent of the vote in the white districts around the city's borders. Mr. Austin, the Negro, won 17.2 per cent in the same districts.

In 10 districts that are predominantly Negro, Mr. Austin received 80 per cent of the vote and Mr. Gribbs 19.5

But in cities where the Negro candidates did not have a chance of winning, Negro voters showed considerable sophistication, supporting the white candidate who best represented their interests.

This was seen in Buffalo, where the Negro candidate, Mr. Lane, polled only a few thousand votes. Solid support of blacks for

Mr. Lane would have drained votes from Mayor Sedita and resulted in the election of Mrs. Smolinski, who was known as the "law and order" candidate.

The same pattern prevailed in a number of smaller cities where Negroes were running.

Although Mayor Stokes was the only Negro mayoral candidate to win election in a major city, there was an unprecedented number of Negro candidates for lesser offices and the returns indicated that a number of them were successful.

For example, William S. Hart, a Democrat, was elected the first Negro Mayor of a major New Jersey municipality, East Orange. A number of Negroes won election to City Councils, school boards and other offices.

Another aspect of the voter polarization was seen in Boston, where Mrs. Louise Day Hicks, an advocate of retaining white neighborhood schools, and Thomas I. Atkins, a Negro activist, led a list of 18 candidates for nine seats on the City Council.

Mrs. Hicks gathered 76,364 votes, mostly of low and middle-income whites, and Mr. Atkins polled 47,364, mostly from the black wards. Mr. Atkins is the only Negro member of the City Council.

November 6, 1969

G. O. P., Aided by Agnew, Surges in South

By ROY REED

Special to The New York Times

NEW ORLEANS, Dec. 6—The Agnew jokes are being replaced in the South by bumper stickers saying, "Spiro is my hero."

Six weeks ago, people down here were chuckling over such lines as "Mickey Mouse has quit wearing his Spiro Agnew wrist watch." They are not laughing any more.

A Democratic leader from Arkansas said yesterday, "It used to be that at a Democratic meeting of any kind, you were safe to lead off with a Spiro Agnew joke. But no longer."

Vice President Agnew is suddenly one of the most popular men in the South. At a meeting of Southern Republican party officials here this weekend, the hottest item in the handout packet was not the blue-and-white sticker saying, "Back the President," but the red, white and blue one proclaiming the heroism of Mr. Agnew.

But Mr. Agnew's new popularity here, a result of his attacks on the so-called Eastern Establishment, is just one of many signs of a Republican upsurge in the South that showed up in an assessment by correspondents for The New York Times during the last month.

Judging by reports from 11 Southern states, it is evident that if President Nixon is pursuing his much-discussed Southern strategy—an effort, officially discounted, to build a winning constituency out of the South, the Midwest and the West while ignoring the big Northeastern urban states—he is making headway.

Republican officials throughout the South consider Mr. Agnew the leader in the drive to expand Republican strength in the South.

Southern Democrats, from Senator Albert Gore of Tennessee on the left to former Gov. George C. Wallace of Alabama

on the right, are taking the Vice President with the utmost seriousness.

For Mr. Wallace the Agnew threat is awesome. The Vice President is cutting seriously into Mr. Wallace's base of strength in the South. Many observers believe that Mr. Agnew's Southern popularity may have surpassed Mr. Wallace's.

For loyalist Democrats, the Vice President is the cutting edge of the Republican threat that could eventually cause the once solidly Democratic South to become not just a two-party region, but predominantly Republican.

Republicans will sit in the Governor's offices of three of the Confederacy's 11 states — Arkansas, Florida and Virginia —after Linwood Holton is inaugurated in Virginia next year.

The party has four Southern Senators. Twenty-six of the region's 108 Congressmen are

Republicans.

Reaching into the grass roots, the party has more than 250 members of state legislatures and uncounted hundreds of city and county officials across the South.

In state after state the Republicans were found to be better organized than the Democrats and about as well-heeled. From El Paso to Richmond, there is hardly a Southern district left where the disorganized and dispirited Democrats are a match for the Republicans in partisan enthusiasm.

President Nixon's failure to persuade the Senate to confirm Judge Clement F. Haynsworth of South Carolina for the Supreme Court might have been expected to depress some Southerners, especially Republicans. But the Republicans here seem to feel that Mr. Nixon's heart was in the right place and that he should be praised for trying.

The conferees at the meeting here responded with a two-minute ovation yesterday when someone suggested that they show their appreciation to Judge Haynsworth.

The reports from across the South showed that contrary to a suspicion of Northern liberals, the Southern Republican party is not basing its expansion solely or even primarily on the Wallace brand of race exploitation.

The party is as diverse as Dixie, and Dixie has always been more complex than some Northerners thought. If the new Southern G.O.P. were searching for a human symbol, it would be hard put to choose between Senator Strom Thurmond, the South Carolina conservative, and Representative George Bush, the young moderate from Texas.

The Republicans did a little muscle-flexing here this weekend. The party chairman and other officers from across the south, gathered here to discuss organization and issues, brought with them about 1,000 party workers.

Mr. Agnew was the main speaker. He said to a resounding cheer that the conference was three times larger than any other regional party conference held this year.

Other National Leaders

Other national party leaders here included Postmaster General Winton Blount, Rogers C. B. Morton, the national chairman, and Harry S. Dent, special counsel to the President. Mr. Dent is the South Carolinian who, rightly or wrongly, gets much of the credit for the President's much-denied Southern strategy.

The President himself flew to Fayetteville, Ark., today to attend the football game between the Universities of Texas and Arkansas, the first- and second-rated teams in the nation.

Mr. Dent told the crowd here yesterday, with mock seriousness, "I'm sure that because he tries to enjoy that No. 1 football game tomorrow, someone will impute a 'Southern Strategy' to it."

Whether by strategy or accident, the Nixon Administration has showered attention on the South this year. Cabinet and sub-Cabinet officials have made dozens of visits, and the President has been to the region three times, if one counts a visit to the border state of Kentucky to attend the Kentucky Derby.

A state Republican chairman remarked yesterday, "A little attention to the South goes a long way."

Even the bluntly anti-Nixon Arkansas Gazette at Little Rock said editorially this week that "any President who plans to fly to Fayetteville for the Arkansas-Texas game can't be all bad."

Mr. Agnew's soaring popularity in the South can be traced directly to his recent speeches denouncing antiwar demonstrators, the television networks and the press.

His speech against "impudent snobs," which began the series, was made in New Orleans Oct. 19.

Mr. Wallace indirectly acknowledged the Agnew inroads recently with a wry comment on N.B.C.'s "Meet the Press."

"I wish I had copyrighted my speeches," he said. "I would be drawing immense royalties from Mr. Nixon and especially Mr. Agnew."

Southern Democrats now speak out against Mr. Agnew at their peril. Some speak openly for him, as Senator Russell B. Long of Louisiana did last week when he said he agreed with the Vice President's criticism of the television networks.

Some party officials assume that Mr. Agnew is speaking for the President.

A Texas party official, noting that Mr. Agnew was being sought for speeches in Galveston, Houston, Corpus Christi, Dallas, Fort Worth and Austin said, "The leaders feel he is saying what Nixon would like to say."

A Georgia party leader said, "I don't think it makes a lot of difference whether he speaks for Nixon. . . . People down here are buying what Agnew's saying and think it's about time somebody in Washington spoke out in blunt terms."

Gore Race May Be Test

There is a growing suspicion that Mr. Agnew is considerably more popular than Mr. Nixon among Southerners.

Clarke Reed, chairman of the Mississippi party, said a man told him recently, "I'm going to vote for Agnew."

Mr. Reed said he asked the man, "What about Nixon?" and he replied, "Well, I've got to vote for him to vote for Agnew."

Senator Gore of Tennessee may provide a test of Mr. Agnew's influence in the South. Mr. Gore is up for re-election next year and the Republicans are looking for a strong opponent for him.

Mr. Agnew, whom Mr. Gore once called "the nation's greatest disaster, second to Vietnam," has promised to go to Tennessee and campaign against Mr. Gore.

The Republicans are increasingly well organized in almost all the Southern states, but their organizing effort is geographically selective.

They are concentrating, first, on the cities and their growing middle class. They also have a small heritage of strength in the hill country, dating to the 19th Century. Only in the rural counties of the Black Belt, where most Negroes and "Dixiecrats" still live, are they n oving slowly.

For example, North Carolina's

Republican party has increased its registration from 344,700 in 1966 to 448,637 this year. That compares to a decline in Democratic registration from 1,540,499 in 1966 to 1,415,432 this year.

The switch is attributed to strong Republican organization, down to the precinct level, in the major Piedmont cities of Charlotte, Winston-Salem and Greensboro and in some of the Western mountain counties.

Avoiding Black Belt Areas

The G.O.P. has little more than paper organization in 29 eastern counties that include the state's Black Belt. In conservative, segregationist Jones County, there are 3,502 registered Democrats and 264 Republicans.

Several white officials recently pulled out of the Democratic party in Greene County, Ala., a predominantly Negro county. They declined to join the Republican party, saying they preferred to operate as independents.

The Republicans do not seem eager to invade the rural Black Belt. They apparently have been studying history.

Mississippi had 38 counties in 1940 that were more than half Negro. In 1960, it had only 29, and the number is undoubtedly lower now. The same loss of rural Negroes has been taking place in all the Southern states.

That means that the Black Belt areas, which once exercized disproportionate power through their race-centered politics, are no longer as important. The Republicans are willing to leave those areas for the most part to the old-line Democrats and the followers of Mr. Wallace.

The Republican rhetoric, even Mr. Agnew's, is aimed at a somewhat more moderate audience than Mr. Wallace and the conservative Democrats have traditionally served. If it contains racism, it is usually camouflaged, in the Northern manner.

Some Southern Republican office-holders are notably to the left of many Democrats in their states. Gov. Winthrop Rockefeller of Arkansas has been elected twice with heavy Negro support. Mr. Rockefelle publicly criticized Mr. Nixon for permitting a relaxation of school desegregation guidelines early this year.

The Texas G.O.P. is actively working for the support of Negroes and Mexican-Americans. Norman Newton, executive director of the state Republican executive committee, whose staff includes Negroes, said recently:

"We are making for the first time a real effort with the Negro voters. We want to find out what is bothering the Negro voter, with the idea that we will get the percentage of their vote moved up to 25 to 30

per cent over a period of 10 years."

The party has the same kind of strong moderate wing in Tennessee and Virginia.

Even the Mississippi party appears to be a little to the left of many Democratic officeholders. The state chairman, Mr. Reed, is kiown as a moderate on the race issue.

He said at a news conference here yesterday that Mr. Wallace in 1968 had been merely a "way station" for some Southerners.

"Standing in the schoolhouse door is not a very popular position anymore," he said.

Different Stands

The Southern G.O.P. is no more monolithic on other issues than it is on race. Mr. Rockefeller is striving to raise taxes in Arkansas, while the Republicans in North Carolina plan to make a major issue of opposing a recent tax rise engineered by the Democrats.

The Republicans are beginning to shock the once complacent Democrats with their organizing ability.

The Arkansas Republicans, financed largely by Mr. Rockefeller's personal fortune, use computers. The machines reportedly have a file on about 500,000 voters. The information includes their voting habits, political preferences and willingness to work in campaigns.

"We now have a filing cabinet," Representative David H. Pryor said ruefully, speaking for the Arkansas Democrats. Before the Republican onslaught the state's Democrats did not even keep an office.

Neither the Democrats nor the Republicans are much disturbed over the long-range threat of Mr. Wallace. Most of the Wallace state organizations outside of Alabama are non-existent or falling apart. A Tennessee correspondent reports that the Wallace organization in that state is more a state of mind than a political party.

The Democrats are distinctly disturbed over the Republican threat, however. Robert S. Vance, state Democratic chairman in Alabama, appointed a 50-member committee last June to study the Democrats' weaknesses. Other state Democratic officials have made similar moves.

The Republicans took control of the Tennessee House this year after last year's election left it with 49 Democrats, 49 Republicans and one Republican-leaning independent.

Howard "Bo" Calloway, who almost defeated Lester G. Maddox for Governor of Georgia in 1966, is thinking of seeking the Governor's office next year.

South Carolina Democrats are worried that they may lose the Governor's office next year to Albert W. Watson, a Congressman who, along with Senator Thurmond, is a Democrat-turned-Republican.

Conversion is a favorite tool of the Republicans. They have recently proseletized five state officials in Georgia and five legislators in Mississippi.

The G.O.P. is expected to make concerted efforts to capture the seats of from one to three "weak" Democratic Congressmen in each Southern state next year. It is expected to make a similar drive for state legislative seats.

Money becomes less of a problem for the Republicans each year. Mr. Holton reportedly spent more than $500,000 to win the Virginia Governor's office this year. He had only $100,000 to spend when he first tried for the office in 1965.

The Republicans of Florida have invented a variation on the fund-raising plan that brings the national heroes to the faithful. The faithful are taking themselves to the heroes.

About 175 Republicans chartered a plane in Florida last month, at $600 per single and $1,000 per couple, with the profit going to the party, and flew to Washington to rub elbows with Mr. Agnew and other dignitaries.

A Florida correspondent's memorandum reported:

"So successful, junket now planned to Las Vegas. If that works, California next."

December 7, 1969

Harris Survey Finds Democratic Party Is Not a Majority

A poll by Louis Harris published yesterday in the New York Post finds that, "for the first time in the modern political era, the Democratic party has lost its position as the majority political party."

The poll said that, in a sampling of the national electorate, "those who call themselves Democrats have slipped to 48 per cent, down from 52 per cent in 1968."

Mr. Harris added: "Although those who think of themselves as Republicans come to only 33 per cent, the 19 per cent who classify themselves as independent now make it impossible for a national Democratic victory along straight party lines."

Mr. Harris said the recent poll, like one taken in 1968, asked a national cross-section of persons, "What do you usually consider yourself—Republican, Democrat or Independent." The findings for the two polls were:

	1970	1968
Democrat	48%	52%
Republican	33	31
Independent	19	17

February 13, 1970

Kevin Phillips, the most controversial political analyst of the Right, works over source material in his Bethesda, Md., home. Above, a map from his book, "The Emerging Republican Majority." By presenting a conservative image, argues Phillips, the Republicans can capture the votes of both the "projected" and "contingent bastions," and enough of the "battlegrounds," to stay in power for years, while ignoring the liberal Northeast.

Nixon's Southern strategy

'It's All In the Charts'

By JAMES BOYD

THE Grand Old Party still lay buried under the debris of the latest Democratic landslide—1964—when a young, self-taught ethnologist named Kevin Phillips emerged from his charts and maps to avow to skeptical hearers that just around the corner was an inevitable cycle of Republican dominance that would begin in the late nineteen-sixties and prosper until the advent of the 21st century. To the pure of heart it all sounded spooky and a bit repugnant because it was premised on the alleged hostility of Irishmen, Italians and Poles, whose ethnic traits were conservative, toward Jews, Negroes and affluent Yankees, whom history had made liberal. There were more of the former and they were ineluctably trending Republican.

"You'll see it working in the 1966 elections," promised Phillips. "It's all in the charts."

Election night, 1966, came to the Bronx in a purple gray autumn dusk that hovered over streets strewn with curling leaves. The polls were closing. It was the hour of the butterfly in the stomachs of politicians, the hour of interregnum when they wait to learn whether fate and their current concoction of principle, guile, commitment and fakery has landed them in or out of the offices and spoils for another biennium. A different kind of butterfly fluttered in the stomach of 25-year-old Phillips, by then administrative assistant to Congressman Paul Fino, the Bronx Republican leader, as the Fino retinue started its traditional tour of the polling places. Phillips's theory, to which he had devoted 12 years of research and two years of practical experimentation, was at stake.

A 6-FOOT, gangling, **dark**-haired, bespectacled, long-faced prodigy with a pedantic manner and a visage that looked half scholar and half black-Irishman, Phillips had grown up in the Bronx. His observations of life in this polyglot borough had convinced him that all the talk about melting-pot America was buncombe. Most voters, he had found, still voted on the basis of ethnic or cultural enmities that could be graphed, predicted and exploited. For instance, the old bitterness toward Protestant Yankee Republicans that had for generations made Democrats out of Irish, Italian and Eastern European immigrants had now shifted, among their children and grandchildren, to resentment of the new immigrants—Negroes and Latinos—and against the national Democratic party, whose Great Society programs increasingly seemed to reflect favoritism for the new minorities over the old. No matter that only 29 per cent of Americans would admit to being Republicans; Phillips could show you 50 Congressional districts where working-class Catholics were leaving the Democratic party in droves. This would accelerate if only dense Republicans would learn to read the portents.

Phillips had seen to it personally that the Bronx G.O.P. could read them. In 1965, he had mapped a gerrymander there for a special State Senate election so artfully that it withstood court challenge, added a Republican senator and earned a grudging accolade from columnist Murray Kempton:

"The result is . . . a profile of Catherine De Medici, her chin receding slightly to avoid contact with a labor-union housing development, her Florentine nose thrusting after one Italo-American enclave and the whole adorned by a hat whose brim extends just far enough to include what is still Republican in the upper-middle-income Riverdale area."

And Phillips had turned Paul Fino's 24th Congressional District, which had the largest Italo-Irish vote in the nation, into a laboratory of ethnic politics. Under Phillips's guidance, Fino had broken with his routinely liberal past to oppose Great Society programs for ghetto minorities—rent subsidies, school busing, welfare liberalization, model demonstration projects, Office of Economic Opportunity community action programs; moreover, Fino had begun vociferously to assault the liberal establishment that furnished the ideology of both major political parties in New York, drawing a clear distinction between himself and Republicans like John Lindsay, Ogden Reid and Jacob Javits, or Democrats like Benjamin Rosenthal, Richard Ottinger and Theodore Sorensen.

Phillips *knew* he was right; it was all in the charts. But theory is one thing and election returns are another. Hence the butterfly, as the Fino entourage approached the polling places where, before a word was spoken, its members would learn the trend from the faces of Italian and Irish precinct leaders—the euphoric gleam of hidden treasure found, or the perplexed frown that bespoke a mysterious shortage in the company books. This time the looks were all gleams. Italian Assembly districts were reporting in more strongly than ever for the durable Fino; more significant, the most recalcitrant Irish precincts, red-flagged by Phillips for their century-old steadfastness behind the party of Richard Croker, Tammany and Al Smith, were today reporting whopping Fino majorities.

So far, so good; but the Bronx could offer only local vindication of a continental thesis. Between stops of the Fino car, Phillips's ear was cocked for scattered radio returns from other regions which, till he could get home to his phone and his voting tables, could give at least sketchy confirmation of predicted defections from the Democratic party by older ethnic blocs in a score of Southern, border and Southwestern states. For two years Phillips had been measuring a rising revolt in these areas against Great Society legislation; and his charts also showed an erosion of hostility to Yankee Republicanism, which for a century had been the key to Democratic predominance.

Phillips had not long to wait. In Maryland, Tennessee, Arkansas, Georgia, Kentucky and Missouri, Democratic governors, senators or congressmen were being toppled by Republicans.

Late that night, at home on Metropolitan Street with his yellowed election canvasses and his dog-eared maps of ethnic migrations, Phillips experienced one of those ecstacies of discovery permitted to anthropologists, like the uncovering of the jawbone fossil you always knew must be nearby but had never found until, suddenly, there it was. Random television reports mentioned that a California district centered in Bakersfield and another in the Oklahoma dustbowl had just elected Republican congressmen for the first time in their history. A check of the maps verified that the Bakersfield constituency was the progeny of Okies who had migrated west from the dustbowl district 30 years before and who today had switched from Democrats to Republicans at the exact moment their long lost cousins half a continent away were also making the shift. So, too, the maps showed that in parts of Wisconsin, Washington and Minnesota, descendants of New England Yankees were forsaking the Republican party of their fathers and voting Democratic in unconscious duplication of their parent stock, which back in Maine and Vermont was making the same switch on the same day. But, alas for the Democrats, the mystic chord of ethnic impulse was transmitting a one-sided directive. By the time Phillips went to bed, his figures showed a net G.O.P. gain of 47 House seats. Only two were from the retrograde Northeast; the rest were from the areas he had years ago marked as the seats of a new political dominance—the border states, the South, the interior states and California. On awakening, Phillips started to sketch the outline of a book that he would call "The Emerging Republican Majority." It would lead him to a place on the Nixon campaign staff and make him the most controversial political analyst of the right.

INTELLECTUALS in politics usually get a good press, but the early chroniclers of the Nixon era have come down pretty hard on Kevin Phillips, who has just concluded a 16-**month stint as special assistant to Attorney General John Mitchell, resigning last month to become a syndicated newspaper columnist. Author Joe McGinnis, in "The Selling of the President 1968," portrays Phillips as a quack, an absurdly misprogrammed human computer filled with sawdust. Richard Harris, in "Justice," depicts him as a bumptious ass, an insensitive Neanderthal with almost sadistic social concepts. Senate Republican Leader Hugh Scott dismisses his book as "baloney," and 10 other senators, including Charles Percy, George McGovern, Marlow Cook and Charles Mathias, have joined in a bipartisan assault on his theories. The Administration feigns to disown him, though during the 1968 campaign Nixon press chief Herb Klein covertly circulated key segments of the Phillips book.**

THE reason for this low public estate had only in part to do with Phillips. The rationale of practical politics, when candidly stated, is always more cynical and disreputable than ites practitioners are willing to own up to, so a certain isolated odium surrounds anyone who articulates it, however scholarly his approach. Had one of Franklin D. Roosevelt's brain trusters promulgated in 1932 a thesis that explained how Democrats were conniving to build a majority coalition out of plantation owners and urban Negroes, Ku Kluxers and immigrants, courthouse gangs in the South and corrupt ward machines in the North, anti-union farmers and antifarmer laborers, he would have been drummed out of the party and his name would today be as reviled as is Machiavelli's. So it is with Kevin Phillips, his defenders say, for contending that political success goes to the party that can cohesively hold together the largest number of ethnic prejudices, a circumstance which at last favors the Republicans.

But Phillips's bad-guy image is compounded by the balloon-pricker's aggression he brings to his researches, by a kind of grim satisfaction he takes in the incorrigible meanness of the American voter, and by an undisguised scorn for "sentimentalists" who resist his findings.

"I've seen him in debate make a monkey out of a highly respected pollster," says one Phillips acquaintance, "but there's a dead quality about him. I know people who show great relish in demonstrating a total immorality or in being a prophet of gloom. But Phillips sketches the most horrendous developments without a trace of emotion."

For a political expert, Phillips is the most impolitic of men. Sitting in his office three doors away from the Attorney General (the only subordinate's office in the Attorney General's suite entirely closed off and suitable for private conversations), Phillips was wont to deliver himself of acerbities that Martha Mitchell would prudently forbear.

On the 1968 Nixon campaign:

"It was a catastrophe—millions of dollars spent by Madison Avenue lightweights who converted certain victory into near defeat. The soap salesmen drained all of the issues out of the campaign that would have won it big. McGinnis should have called his book 'The Unselling of the President.'"

On his campaign associates:

"I respect John Mitchell. He and Murray Chotiner were the real people in the campaign, not the artificial public-relations phonies who called Nixon 'the product' as if he were some kind of underarm deodorant."

On conservatives:

"I wish we could drop into the Potomac all those obsolescent conservatives who are still preoccupied with Alger Hiss and General MacArthur, and who keep trotting out *laissez faire* economics and other dead horses. They make the Republican party look musty to millions of ignored working-class people who are looking for a party that relates to their needs."

On liberals:

"Liberalism has turned away from the common people and become institutionalized into an establishment. Its spokesmen are driven around in limousines and supported by rich foundations, the television networks and publishing houses, the knowledge industry, the billion-dollar universities and the urban consulting firms which profiteer from poverty. Liberalism is dominant only in the Northeast, which is always the last bastion of a dying order of privilege. The Northeast resists the populist surge of our day just as it fought the revolution of Jefferson, Jackson, Bryan and Roosevelt. The states that Humphrey carried in 1968 were roughly the states that Hoover carried in 1932."

On the Republican party of the Northeast:

"It's run by Yankee silk stockings like Josiah Spalding, who send their kids 2,000 miles to look for poverty in Mississippi but won't travel one subway stop to help poor whites working for $1,800 a year. As long as they are in charge, the Republican party won't do well there. But the upper crust is gradually leaving us to become Democrats. The Republicans are getting thousands of Irish and Italian working-class switchovers and the Democrats are getting Chub Peabody."

On Negroes and the G.O.P.:

"All the talk about Republicans making inroads into the Negro vote is persiflage. Even 'Jake the Snake' [Senator Jacob K. Javits] only gets 20 per cent. From now on, the Republicans are never going to get more than 10 to 20 per cent of the Negro vote and they don't need any more than that . . . but Republicans would be shortsighted if they weakened enforcement of the Voting Rights Act. The more Negroes who register as Democrats in the South, the sooner the Negrophobe whites will quit the Democrats and become Republicans. That's where the votes are. Without that prodding from the blacks, the whites will backslide into their old comfortable arrangement with the local Democrats."

Such candor in the Attorney General's office is air-clearing, but, like ammonia, it does not endear. And besides, nobody likes learning worldly lessons from an *enfant terrible*; in an old man's game like politics, an under-30 sage is tough to take.

YOUNG Phillips grew up in the Bronx in an education-conscious middle-class family. His father, William Phillips, a career civil servant, is the chief executive officer of the New York State Liquor Commission. Kevin began his researches into the ethnic roots of politics at the age of 13. He was peculiarly sensitive to the impact of ethnic influences on life, because the Bronx was full of mutually hostile nationality

groups and because Phillips suffered the deprivation of not really belonging in any of them. His forebears were divided among Irish, English and Scotch, as well as between Democrats and Republicans. His father was a Catholic and his mother a Protestant, so, as he says, "My religion was reading the Sunday papers." He was an outsider in a community made up of blocs of closely knit insiders—Jews, Germans, Irish and Italians. Hurt by this exclusion, he turned it into a scientific phenomenon and began to study it.

He does not recall the early influences that pushed him toward Republicanism, a circumstance which bears out his contention that submerged factors often shape voting habits. All he knows is that he was for Ike in the first Presidential election he remembers (1952). Four years later, at age 15, he was chairman of the Bronx Youth Committee for Eisenhower, and went about the streets haranguing pedestrians from a sound truck.

His parents sent him to the Bronx High School of Science despite his lack of interest in scientific subjects because it was one of the finest and most academically exclusive public schools in the country and because he was a precocious boy. He did well enough in the subjects he didn't like to become a National Merit Scholar. But it was out of school that his real academic development occurred. "I guess my after-school study of ethnic political behavior was a natural progression from taking zoology in the classroom," he observes.

He devoured old National Geographics and read all the college textbooks on political science, geography and history that he could find in the school library. When, at the age of 16, he entered Colgate University as a political science major, his mastery of these self-taught subjects was so impressive that he was permitted to skip them and to choose areas of research that particularly interested him. On the way to a Phi Beta Kappa Key, a Magna Cum Laude award and an honors thesis on ethnic and religious voting patterns in the Presidential elections of 1928 and 1960, Phillips spent his junior year in Scotland at the University of Edinburgh, where he outranked his Scottish classmates in the study of their own history, a distinction that was also attained later by his younger brother, Steven. While in the British Isles he continued to indulge his Professor Higgins passion for ethnic peculiarities and their effect on politics. "I'm still an avid follower," he says, "of whether the Tory majority is up in South Edinburgh or down in South Aberdeen."

After the cosmopolitanism of the British Isles and weekend holidays on the continent, Phillips found the return to Colgate, in the dreary reaches of the Shenango Valley, so unsatisfactory that he arranged to spend half his senior year in a special academic project in Washington, D.C. There his intolerance for what he terms mediocrity surfaced in schoolboy intrigues against the professor in charge, almost causing Phillips's expulsion.

At 20, he joined the staff of Congressman Fino and became the youngest legislative assistant in the House of Representatives. At 22, he was a one-man "nationalities department" of the Republican National Committee. At 23 he was the youngest administrative assistant in the House, and at 24 creator of the Florentine 38th State Senatorial District in the Bronx.

"I claim no unique insight into the art of the gerrymander. Every good ward politician has an instinctive flair for it. There can be a wonderful mutuality of interest when Democrats and Republicans sit down together to fix an area. The Democrats surrounding the 38th were just as anxious to get rid of Republicans as I was to squeeze them in. The only fights came over some conservative Catholic neighborhoods the Demmies wanted to keep to help them preserve party control in their primary fights."

In between political stints, Phillips went to Harvard Law School. He was not really interested in the law any more than he had been interested in science, but he believed a Harvard Law degree would help a political career. In his final year, 1964, he won the Bureau of National Affairs Award for a dissertation that predicted civil-rights progress through the courts would cease as soon as the locus shifted from the South to de facto segregation in the North.

After the redoubtable Fino, now a judge of the New York State Supreme Court in Manhattan, swept the Irish wards in 1966, and Phillips found his jawbone fossil in Bakersfield, Calif., he figured he had delivered enough for the congressman and thereafter used his Congressional post as "a sort of Ford Foundation grant" to finance the research and writing of "The Emerging Republican Majority." The initial version was finished in late 1967, but the publisher, Arlington House, decided to hold up publication until the election of 1968 had either confirmed or invalidated its main premise. In early 1968, Phillips circulated a boiled-down version of his book among the Nixon political command. On the strength of it he was offered a post by campaign chief John Mitchell as an ethnic expert and analyst of voting patterns and trends. Phillips, at 27, had developed a formidable expertise.

"You could ask me about any Congressional district in the country," he recalls, "and I could tell you its ethnic composition, its voting history and the issues that would appeal to its electorate."

FOR a man of Phillips's definite views, the purposefully over-generalized campaign of Richard Nixon was a continuing frustration. "There are 20 important ethnic voting groups in the country, and about 20 lesser groups. Each of these groups can be reached and I know how to reach them, but it requires a sharp delineation of issues, whereas the Nixon campaign contrived by the Madison Avenue crowd called for a blurring of the issues. . . . Nixon knew his campaign stunk. He wanted to be himself and he knew he should have fought the campaign on the issues Middle America was ready for—the Agnew issues of today. But he had this big lead in August and didn't want to change a winning game plan. It was Oct. 28 before he found out from the polls that he was blowing it. And it was too late then to do anything but hang in there and hope."

Phillips had one conspicuous campaign success—the urging of an Outer South Strategy aimed at capturing Florida, Tennessee, North Carolina and Virginia, as opposed to the Deep South Strategy that had carried Wallace territory for Goldwater in 1964, but at the cost of frightening away millions of potential voters elsewhere.

"My argument was this: Your outer Southerners who live in the Ozark and Appalachian mountain ranges and in the Piedmont upcountry—and now in urban-suburban Florida and Texas—have always had different interests than the Negrophobe plantation owners of the Black Belt. This is a less extreme conservative group. It adheres with other Republican constituencies across the country and can be appealed to without fragmenting the coalition. When you are after political converts, start with the less extreme and wait for the extremists to come into line when their alternatives collapse."

THAT Kevin Phillips is not the sawdust-filled computer of the campaign chronicles is evidenced by the fact that, while he was plotting his charts and maps for Mr. Nixon, he was also wooing and winning the charming Martha Henderson, a long-stemmed, hazel-eyed beauty who worked in the office of Congressman Melvin Laird when Phillips began pursuing her. Talking seems to have been his main tactic in romance.

"He's quite witty, you know, in a wry, caustic, cyni-cal but pleasant way," says Martha, a native Washingtonian with a master's degree from Columbia Teachers College, now doing research on child problems for the House Republican Conference. Martha and Kevin were married in September, 1968. They honeymooned briefly in Boston, where Phillips contemplated the backwardness of the South Boston Irish compared with their New York kin in making the inevitable switch to the Republican party: "It's because there aren't enough Negroes and Jews in Boston to take over the local Democratic organizations and send the other ethnics whooping into the Republican party. But it will come."

A beautiful and agreeable wife is just one of the signs that the sure-footed Phillips has not allowed the cold rigors and hot contentions of political analysis to siphon away the good life. He and Martha enjoy periodic vacations at smart hideaways in Europe and the Caribbean. They are renovating a newly purchased home on affluent Mooreland Lane in Bethesda, Md., where Senator John Tower of Texas, an early hero of the Outer South Streategy, is a neighbor. And his ethnic researches are leavened by respectable quantities of Guinness Stout and by a notable record collection of Irish and Scottish ballads. "I would like to collect Welsh ballads, too," he laments, "but the Welsh have only one decent song— 'Men of Harlech.'"

Though Phillips's ideas for an aggressive antiliberal campaign strategy that would hasten the defection of working-class Democrats to the Republican line did not prevail in the balloon-floating atmosphere of the 1968 campaign, he won the lasting respect of John Mitchell. It was Phillips whom Mitchell sent to Washington in December, 1968, to arrange the transition of the Justice Department from the benevolent era of Ramsey Clark to the somber regime of today. As special assistant to the Attorney General for almost a year and a half, Phillips served in a role much to his liking: political adviser to the man who, more than any other save the President himself, is shaping the Republican party of the future.

MOST Americans feel that when they enter the voting booth they are making a free, contemporary judgment on an issue, a man, a record, or a party philosophy. They delude thmselves, says Kevin Phillips. In his view, the outcome of a Presidential election (he always distinguishes between Presidential and Congressional elections) rarely hinges on such ephemera as an issue, a personality, or a campaign technique. At most, the costly scenarios of Madison Avenue, a disaster such as Vietnam, the L.B.J. repellency, the Kennedy style and organization, the Eisenhower charm —even the Depression—are marginal stimuli or depressants that are usually indecisive and at most advance or retard a trend by a mere quadrennium. When the average voter steps into the booth he registers the prejudice or the allegiance bred by a mix of geography, history and ethnic reaction which stems from a past he knows only murkily.

Three such mixes have determined the Presidential elections of the 19th and 20th centuries: the North-South cleavage that culminated in civil war; the slow assimilation into the Democratic party of the urban working class; and the Negro socioeconomic revolution, with its counterreaction.

The most important influence was the Civil War, the great divisor of American politics for a century. Only now is its influence beginning to wane, making possible the "emerging Republican majority." Phillips's book is a major work of research and, considering the stodginess of the subject matter, a surprising literary achievement. His findings are supported by 143 charts, 47 maps, 482 pages. His main themes are hedged by a hundred caveats, exceptions, qualifications. To summarize is to risk distortion, but one must summarize:

The roots of modern American politics, Phillips contends, lie in the contrasting geographies of rocky New England and the lush Southern delta that dictated different life styles and economic interests for North and South; hence, the historic enmity, the birth of the Republican party as the protagonist of a Northern amalgam of acquisitiveness and Puritan morality and the climax of the Civil War. Victory in that convulsion, together with the mantle of the Lincolnian causes, however ill-fitting, gave the Yankee Republicanism a patina of moral superiority, along with bayonet-point control over the ballot boxes of the Democratic South, the majority loyalties of the populous North and title to exploit the vast undeveloped resources of a continent. On these foundations, with all their advantages of prestige, power, allegiance and wealth, the Republicans built a dominance that came to full flower in the first third of the 20th century. The multiplying, colonizing descendants of the Grand Army of the Republic migrated across the Northern half of the country and continued to vote the straight Republican ticket; and millions of immigrant laborers, come to man the Yankee factories, voted for the party that could promise a full dinner pail or threaten a dismissal slip.

BUT just as Herbert Hoover was prophesying perpetual

Republican dominion, a new cycle, long a-building, took over. The very sources of Republican ascendancy had conspired to bring it down. For the Civil War victory and its carpetbag aftermath had politically mummified the offspring of the old Confederacy, now spread across the lower half of the United States, into an unreconstructed, anti-Republican bloc, and thus had split in two the conservative vote on which the Republican party had come to depend; while the Catholic and Jewish immigrants of the Northern cities, naturally resentful of their scornful Protestant overseers, but lacking a political alternative, had at last found one in a Democratic party that was evolving beyond mere Tammany spoilsmanship to embrace the liberal causes of the urban masses. This ethnic ganging up on the Yankees had long been retarded by inter-ethnic animosities. The Irish politicians—chauvinistic, conservative, peculative—controlled the Democratic party of the North for their own myopic ends, and the Jewish, Italian, Polish and Slavic newcomers detested the Democratic Irish as much as the Irish detested the Republican Yankees.

But by the nineteen-twenties, mounting pressures from below, the leadership of Alfred E. Smith and Franklin D. Roosevelt and the logic of events were pushing the Democratic party toward a programmatic championship of the working class, while the South—immobilized between its resentments against Republicanism and its hostility toward New Deal reforms—stayed under the Democratic tent, adding its conservative electroral votes to the liberal tally of the Northern Democracy. This gave the Democrats a majority that endured throughout the middle third of this century and statistically endures still.

But it was a Janus-like majority, Phillips asserts, and the side facing left developed a liberal over-thrust disproportionate to the ethnic and geographic realities that underlay the coalition. A new ethnic disturbance—the emergence of the Negro-Latino—finally shattered it. The Democratic party, veteran accumulator of minorities that it was, tried to accumulate by rote the Negro minority and trumpeted its cause through the tried formulae of patronage for its spokesmen, government aid, social planning and bureaucratic intervention. But since the grievances of the colored minorities were caused in part by the exploitation and exclusion practiced against them by older Democratic constituencies, something had to give, and did. The two bulwarks of the old coalition, working-class Catholics and the descendants of the Confederacy, began to defect from the Democratic party because of its identification with the newcomers.

These defectors have not yet lodged permanently in the suspect G.O.P. Many of them are in way stations—the Conservative party of New York, the Wallace movement. But they have left the Democrats and Phillips feels they have no place to go in the end but the Republican party. Hence, the emerging Republican majority that will dominate American politics until the year 2004.

"Political hegemony for a generation is a matter of minor slippages," says Phillips. "The difference between majority and minority is only a few percentage points. When I say that Yankees are turning Democratic or that the Irish are turning Republican, I mean only that, instead of continuing to be 75 to 80 per cent supporters of their traditional party, that percentage has now dropped nearer to 60 per cent. It is this slippage, this crossover, by 10 or 20 per cent of a few groups, that ends eras and begins cycles."

“Political hegemony for a generation is a matter of minor slippages. The difference between majority and minority is only a few percentage points.”

Sterilized and scientific as are the terms by which Kevin Phillips plots the emerging Republican majority, its common denominator is hostility to blacks and browns among slipping Democrats and abandonment of the Democratic party because of its identification with the colored minorities. In the Northeast, the slippage is among blue-collar Catholics who find their jobs threatened and their neighborhoods and political clubhouses overrun by invading Negroes, while their erstwhile party seems to cluck approval. In the Outer South, the national Democratic party has begun to replace the G.O.P. as the symbol of alien causes—the Negro politicians and Federal interference with local autonomy. Hence, the shift to Republicanism, a trend which for the same reasons has engulfed the milder border states and will, Phillips insists, capture the perfervid Deep South when events force the abandonment of the more extreme Wallace alternative.

In the "Latin crescent"—lower Florida, Louisiana, Texas—the political emergence of the Cuban and Mexican-American minorities, joined with Negroes and white radicals in a Democratic alliance, will drive the majority constituency of traditional white Democrats into the G.O.P. Phillips sees California and "the heartland," the 25 interior states, many of which are dominated by Southern immigration patterns, as the great electoral bastion of a Republicanism that is against aid to blacks, against aid to big cities and against the liberal life style it sees typified by purple glasses, beards, long hair, bralessness, pornography, coddling of criminals and moral permissiveness run riot.

WHAT of the Democratic party? It will retreat to the Northeast corner, where there is a high percentage of liberal Jews, Yankees, Negroes and, Phillips believes, masses of subsidized radicals employed by the liberal establishment. The only other Democratic area will be the Pacific Northwest, which historically follows the electoral patterns of the Northeast.

Phillips regards the approaching Democratic famine as a logical aftermath of the long feast. "For a long time the liberal-conservative split was on economic issues. That favored the Democrats until the focus shifted from programs which taxed the few for the many, to things like 'welfare' that taxed the many for the few. In the future, the liberal-conservative division will come on social issues; Middle America and the working class are socially conservative. The two issues are: Will there be a continuation of bureaucratic do-gooder interference in neighborhood patterns of life, symbolized by the school-busing issue; and will there be a continuation of permissive, criminal-coddling, anarchy-indulging attitudes? The new majority answers a vehement 'no' to both questions, but the national Democratic party has been pushed to the minority side by the thrust of its ideology."

REVOLT against the liberal intellectual élite of the Northeast by the resentful commoners of South, West and Midwest is at the heart of the Phillips diagnosis. Richard J. Barnet, co-director of the Institute for Policy Studies in Washington, D. C., and author of "The Economy of Death," is representative of that elite. He is Ivy League, wears granny glasses, has been to Hanoi, assails the military-industrial complex, runs a think-tank foundation and is surrounded at his institute by bearded men and an occasional braless woman. Barnet believes the coalition envisioned by Phillips is possible, but disputes its character.

"Phillips may be right. If people don't take his theory seriously enough to come up with alternatives — and the Democrats haven't yet — the forces he mentions, together with the national security-military institution, may well produce the nightmare he describes.

"But the analogy is not with Jefferson; it is with Hitler. The elements are all there —deep-rooted social cleavage, insoluble problems, rhetoric which attempts to legitimize and encourage hate, a phony genetic and geographical underpinning, a despised minority to blame for everything. It all adds up to scapegoat politics, which is a tactic of fascism.

"The new gains of the Republican party are based upon preserving the status quo by stopping the civil rights advance. But the status quo is racist. The Administration tries to legitimize this by saying it will carry out the orders of the courts against *de jure* segregation. But it's an old tactic to use the courts as a way of avoiding executive or political action. The courts, even before the Nixon Administration alters their composition, cannot go very far by themselves in bringing about equality between the races. The South, for instance, is just beginning to emerge from a society that was totally racist. Such small gains as have been made involved huge expenditures of energy, moral authority and political risk. To say we are to stop now, to pervert the moral authority of the Presidency in order to make people feel more comfortable with their prejudices —and that's what's happening today—is to say that we accept racism. And to build a political majority based on racism is taking a long step toward fascism."

Barnet feels that the Phillips analysis ignores a series of desperate problems looming that threaten not only a Republican majority but the existence of free government as we have known it. "The collapse of our environment, the drift toward nuclear annihilation, the need for re-allocation of resources, urban disintegration—we can't have a free elective government over the next 20 years which does not start to resolve these problems, and this Administration has scarcely even admitted that they exist. The alternative is some kind of repressive rule. That is possible, but the American people would have to abandon their central traditions of freedom and equality, and I don't think they are quite as apathetic and cynical as the Phillips theory is betting on."

Historian-journalist Milton Viorst has a background that in some ways parallels Phillips's. Familiar with the ethnic patterns of the Northeast, he is a former aide and campaign adviser to New York liberals of both major parties and a student of the political process. Viorst wrote a book in 1967 about the evolution of the Republican party ("Fall From Grace: The Republican Party and the Puritan Ethic") which anticipated a number of the trends later described by Phillips. But Viorst looks at those trends from a different perspective.

"The division between whites and blacks is, without a doubt, a profound split rooted deep in the human soul in a way we only dimly understand. No nation has ever created a successful multiracial society, and it may be possible to exploit this and put together a long-term political majority based on covert racism. But I doubt it. For one thing, it would split the Republican party. The Hatfields and Percys and Javitses and Brookes couldn't possibly stand for it. And the blacks just won't sit still for it. There would be perpetual chaos that would make effective government impossible.

"The youth revolution may be overstated, but it cannot be ignored. Historically, when a youthful intellectual elite revolts against the standards of its society, that society is in for bad trouble.

"The choice before us is order with justice or order under repression and some kind of semi-apartheid. I don't think the American people will accept apartheid; with all our faults, there has been too much of a moral evolution for that. I think instead we will have a movement toward justice—gradual, imperfect, but a continuation of the trend of the last 10 years.

"We are witnessing in Virginia and Florida the beginnings of an indigenous liberal takeover of the Democratic party in the South, as Phillips says. But that does not necessarily mean long-term Republican dominance there. For the first time the people of that region will have a genuine choice of two alternatives—liberal and conservative. Who knows what will happen? This thing will build. Wait till we see what changes hard times may make. Economic interests will supplant the one issue of the past—race. The Democrats are bound to win some of the time, and when they do a new national coalition comes into effect."

Viorst doesn't see any signs today that anything so dynamic as a shift of political trends is taking place. "So far, this is a caretaker Administration, not a coalition builder. . . . I have a certain amount of skepticism about politics, but I don't think great coalitions can be built on cynicism. They have been built by men who cared about the country enough to put into it the things needed to build a country. And that's what builds a party. To succeed, a coalition builder must be able to appeal to decent men, to idealism, and a policy rooted in the acceptance of inequality cannot do that."

PHILLIPS rejects much of this critique, but acknowledges that some of it could prove valid. He is supremely confident of his demographic ground.

Eastern-liberal Republicanism has lost its power to dictate party policy, he says; that's the meaning of the Goldwater and Nixon nominations. Liberals within the party will be on increasingly weak ground. "Rockefeller has had to turn rightward to meet the conservative revolt and Lindsay can no longer win a Republican primary. This will spread."

The youth revolution is a myth, according to his data; the New Left, a passing footnote to history. "Most young people out in the heartland are overwhelmingly conservative and the Young Republican clubs are the hottest thing on Southern campuses. Forget Harvard and Columbia and the long-haired kids driving Jaguars their permissive dads gave them; concentrate on the kid working his way

through Eastern Kentucky University — he's for Nixon and social conservatism. Out there the juke boxes don't play 'New World Coming'; they play 'Welfare Cadillac.' In the heartland, it's all Agnew put to music."

Phillips agrees that the new conservative majority should not ignore the problems of the poor, but he thinks of them not in terms of the inner city ghettos but as "sharecroppers, Appalachian mountaineers, fishing villages where the catch is getting smaller each year, dairy country where the farms are getting fewer, valleys full of redundant industries and company cottages, Portuguese waterfronts, Italian vegetable gardens, forgotten mining communities." It is the concept of the deserving poor.

Phillips does not accord moral primacy to the Negro demands; he scorns "the Episcopal Church, which pays reparations to blacks but ignores a century of sweated labor in Catholic mill towns," and "limousine liberals in Massachusetts who are more interested in integrating South Carolina than in helping Chicopee or Central Falls."

But he is concerned that the Nixon Administration has not moved effectively to build

the coalition open to it, and he agrees with Viorst that coalitions are built by putting something into the country.

"I have some ideas of my own for positive programing: Federal grants-in-aid for better fire and police protection; street lighting and sanitation assistance in slum neighborhoods; a new Civilian Conservation Corps to take kids out of slums and put them to work cleaning up the country—maybe it could be a National Ecology Corps and we would have a chance to see if the young people will put their muscle where their mouth is; massive redevelopment programs for Appalachia and the industrially redundant reaches of New England; large-scale Works Progress Administration - type guaranteed employment with the work force to be used to rebuild, reconstruct or clean up America's historic lands and historic buildings for the Bicentennial in 1976; some kind of National Health Insurance or Medicredit; full-fledged Federal aid to parochial schools. This sort of thing should replace the social gimmickry of the sixties —rent subsidies, metropolitan planning, school busing, the antipoverty program's subsidy of community agitation —

which have demonstrably failed."

This is a program tailored to the lower middle class, which Phillips argues is the "action constituency" of America and the new base of the Republican party.

He doesn't dismiss liberal fears that there is a potential for fascism in the new conservative majority. "The popular conservative majority now taking shape, like past popular movements, is vulnerable to aberration. With its important component of military, apprehensive bourgeois and law-and-order-seeking individuals, there is a proclivity toward authoritarianism and over-reaction to the liberal-engendered permissiveness and anarchy of the sixties. This is a danger the Administration should watch carefully."

But such an apocalypse, Phillips contends, would result only from the failure, not the success, of Nixon and Agnew to satisfy the yearnings of the new majority.

"Nixon could survive a failure in Vietnam, inflation, continued crime and rioting. Those are problems that originated with the Democrats and the voters would not turn back to the gang that caused the mess in the first place.

A depression, however, would be disastrous to Republicans because of their association with the last one. But whatever catastrophe might befall Nixon, and I don't think any will, it won't help the Democrats. Their string has run out. A frustrated majority would turn to a super-Wallace, a real authoritarian of the Huey Long stripe. If you're interested in real revolutionaries, wait till you see the $12,000-a-year truck driver or electrician, who is now caught up in his own revolution, of rising expectations, if the bottom ever falls out. But we won't have a depression. The politician's first preoccupation is still saving his own skin."

Phillips plans to tackle such questions in two forthcoming books, "The Nixon Revolution" and "The Unassimilated." For now, he feels that his past analysis is not advocacy but rather parallels the role of market research in an advertising campaign.

"This is not a strategy or a blueprint," insists Phillips, "just the deciphering of an inexorable trend that will run its course and then be displaced by a new cycle whose origins are already with us, somewhere." ■

May 17, 1970

C.B.S. Offers Free Time To Critics of White House

By JACK GOULD

The Columbia Broadcasting System set a precedent last night by offering free time over the company's television and radio networks as a regular practice to whatever principal political party was not in occupancy of the White House.

In a telegram to Lawrence F. O'Brien, chairman of the Democratic National Committee, Dr. Frank Stanton, president of the company, further agreed that the opposition party could use radio and TV to raise funds outside the normal months of campaigning after the national political conventions.

At the same time yesterday, the Democrats asked the Federal Communications Commission to guarantee opponents of a President's policies free time on the television networks to respond to his televised advocacy of those policies.

It was learned that Dr. Stanton had in mind at least four broadcasts by the opposition party, each running 25 minutes and followed by five minutes of news analysis by commentators

of C.B.S.

This would be in addition to the President's delivery of the State of the Union Message, which has been followed by opposition arguments.

Dr. Stanton, who reached Mr. O'Brien in Louisville, said that the Democratic chairman had expressed thanks but otherwise withheld comment.

Mr. O'Brien had previously asked the Federal Communications Commission to require networks to sell time to the opposition party that disagreed with the views of President Nixon.

President Nixon's frequent appearances on television, which as head of state he can obtain free upon request have prompted a charge from his opponents that he has "captured" the major machinery for expression of opinion and locked out opponents, save for nightly newscasts or weekend interviews.

In response to this complaint, Mike Mansfield, the Democratic majority leader in the Senate, was offered 25 minutes, from 12:30 to 12:55 P.M. tomorrow, by the National Broadcasting Company. The American Broad-

casting Company yesterday offered 25 minutes of free time from 12 noon to 12:25 P.M. on the same day.

Instead of offering 25 minutes around the lunch hour, Dr. Stanton told Mr. O'Brien that the Democratic National Committee could have 10 P.M. on July 7, which would place the opposition reply against re-runs of the popular "Marcus Welby" series.

These time offers came after President Nixon's speech last Wednesday at 9 P.M. on the state of the national economy.

Dr. Stanton's plan could conceivably be a cause of controversy among Democrats since they have not been able to agree on a single spokesman to reply to President Nixon.

In Washington, it was described as no secret, for instance, that neither Senator Mansfield, Mr. O'Brien nor Senator J. W. Fulbright would agree to let one Democrat speak for all.

In his telegram to Mr. O'Brien, Dr. Stanton said that C.B.S. wished to "maintain fairness and balance in the treatment of public issues, including the disparity between Presidential appearances and the opportunities available to the principal opposition party."

Dr. Stanton said that the network rejected Mr. O'Brien's proposal to the communications commission that networks be compelled to sell time to the opposition party. At the same time, he said, the network recognizes that the President has

"certain constitutional duties whose performance is enhanced by his ability to communicate directly with the people."

The offer of C.B.S. to accept fund-raising spot announcements—up to one minute in length—might find more unified favor among Democrats. When recently five Senators bought time on N.B.C. to oppose Mr. Nixon, they spent nearly $70,000 and received voluntary contributions of about $600,000.

If an opposition party could use broadcasting to raise funds, many TV observers agreed such a procedure might over several years materially affect the controversy over the high cost of campaigning.

From Washington it was reported that Herbert G. Klein, Director of Communications for the Administration, was wary of the C.B.S. proposal but noncommittal on how he might feel if there were currently a Democratic rather than a Republican President.

Also in Washington, a spokesman for the Democratic National Committee said that it would accept the offer of time on July 7 but hoped Dr. Stanton would make the period available to Senator Mansfield as reflecting the Congressional attitude in contrast to that of the White House.

The spokesman added that he hoped the willingness of C.B.S. to accept fund-raising spot announcements would be made mandatory for all stations.

June 23, 1970

Republicans Seek To Win Ethnic Vote

By BILL KOVACH
Special to The New York Times

CHICAGO, Oct. 20—The Republican party, after 40 years of standing wistfully by, this year is pursuing the white ethnic vote with a vigor that is making ethnic politics a major matter in many of the nation's large industrial centers.

In districts like those on the Northwest Side of Chicago, there is for the first time a sprinkling of names ending in "ski" and "wicz" on tickets traditionally dominated by Anglo-Saxon names. And in the Republican party headquarters there is a special organization to define and cater to separate units of hyphenated Americans.

"'There is a feeling of having been exploited by the Democrats," explained a member of the Republican Nationalities Committee. "They appeal to the ethnic identity during election year, but the rest of the time they pretend there is no such thing as ethnicity. We think we can capitalize on the frustration this sort of politics has developed in the ethnic communities."

This drive is stirring political counterthrusts in Chicago, Pittsburgh, Cleveland and other Northern cities as the Democratic party strives to retain the dominant position it has held among ethnic voters since the days of Franklin Delano Roosevelt.

Daley Aides Comb Suburbs

Here in Chicago, for instance, Mayor Richard J. Daley has ordered precinct captains out into the suburbs to find the ethnic voters who have fled the city and try to reverse the slow Republican growth that threatens to surround and smother the Daley organization's power in Cook County.

Because of a deep-seated belief in the "melting pot" theory of America, few statistics have been compiled on ethnic Americans, and figures are hard to come by. Most authorities seem to agree that the identifiable ethnic population includes about 40 million people, concentrated mostly in the 58 major industrial cities of the Midwest and North.

Throughout the country politicians have been forced by reaction to a decade of civil rights agitation to take another look at the white urban community, and they have found that the "melting pot" has not done its job. Angry, frustrated and fearful collections of voters who had been welded to the Democratic party in the nineteen thirties are looking for new answers to new questions.

In Pittsburgh, this reawakening of ethnic identity has taken the form of a renewal of the Pan Slavic Alliance, which seeks Government-sponsored ethnic cultural and research centers and is making itself felt as a political pressure group.

Who the "Ethnics" Are

In Cleveland, an Italian-American president of the City Council is attempting to rebuild the Italian community of the city and an ethnic task force is demanding representation on policy-making boards and commissions.

"Ethnic American" is a term almost as old as the country but one that needs to be redefined each generation or so. Those so defined in the current political struggle are largely eastern and southern Europeans — Italians, Poles, Hungarians and the welter of Slavic nationalities from the Balkan states.

They are considered by most political strategists as the largest identifiable group now ripe for political exploitation.

There was a time when a politician could win an ethnic presence on Election Day by appearing at the fraternal hall on feast day to be photographed with leading citizens, by praising the value of the voters nationality, by donating to a local cause, and by maintaining a permanent representative who could "speak in their language" in the community. But the social dislocation of the nineteen-sixties ripped away the cocoon that the ethnic communities had wrapped around themselves and they now fear loss of their identity in a still-alien world.

Calling a Pole a Pole

Today the ethnic voter is waiting to see who will talk to him about law and order (without accusing him of a racism he thinks is best reflected by those who left the city) and who will cater to his ethnic pride with programs like cultural research and American history text books that call a Pole a Pole.

Curiously, politicking among ethnic Americans is a secretive thing — as though to admit it would be to deny the American dream of a melting pot.

The appearance of a spate of ethnic-Americans on the Republican ticket here, for example, is strenuously argued as "just a happenstance."

According to Peter Piotrocicz, deputy chairman of the Republican state committee in Illinois and himself a candidate for a local office and a moving force in the ethnic-oriented thrust of the G.O.P. "You don't need a Serb to attract a Serb anymore — the 'skis' are not necessarily on the ticket because of their names."

Yet at the national and local level the Republicans have spent two years developing an intensive appeal to white ethnic Americans.

Volpe on Mission to Chicago

Secretary of Transportation John A. Volpe was sent on "a goodwill mission" to Chicago early this month. His sole purpose in visiting Chicago, in the words of The Italian American News, a leading ethnic newspaper, "was to have members of the sponsoring organization [including all major Italian-American organizations in the city] to meet first-hand the leading ranking U.S. official of Italian heritage."

Then there is Vice President Agnew, whose heritage and rhetoric speak to the white ethnic Americans' pride and frustrations, and Gov. Richard B. Ogilvie who regularly finds space in the ethnic press to catalogue the ethnic Americans he has appointed to posts in his administration.

Joseph Sable, Republican Mayor of Duquesne, a suburb of Pittsburgh, who is himself a leader in the Pan Slavic Alliance in that area, expects his party to achieve some success, but only some.

"In practice the community has always been Democratic," Mr. Sable says. "Little by little they are beginning to break away or see an advantage to the other side. Mr. Agnew's speeches have had some impact, but as a group I would guess they are still 75 to 80 per cent Democratic."

The Democrats, who have practiced the art since early Irish immigrations showed the way to power through patronage politics, still seem to maintain their basic hold on the ethnic vote.

"To function in the ethnic community" explains a Cleveland Democrat whose job is to keep the ethnic vote in line, "you have to understand how it works. Our most effective weapon is word of mouth. I go to a store or restaurant where the old folks hang out and I plant my message. These people spend their entire day visiting and talking. For each one I tell, 40 will know by the end of the day."

Nevertheless, professionals in the shadowy world of ethnic politics agree that these old formulas are dissolving.

October 21, 1970

NET GAINS FOR DEMOCRATS SEEN; NIXON STRESSES SENATE RESULT

By R. W. APPLE Jr.

The Democrats emerged yesterday with more gains than losses in a mid-term election in which Americans voted in kaleidoscopic patterns.

In the struggle for control of the Senate, the Republicans gained at least two seats. But they lost at least nine seats in the House of Representatives, lost as many as 11 governorships and suffered serious reverses in state legislatures.

The Democrats will have 54 or 55 seats in the Senate in January, 1971; the Republicans, 45 or 46. The Democrats will have either 255 or 256 seats in the House; the Republicans, 179 or 180. The Democrats will have at least 27 Governors and perhaps 29.

With the breathlessly close Senate race in Indiana undecided, and likely to remain so for days or weeks, the Republicans had gained two seats in that house. If Democratic Senator Vance Hartke maintains his lead over his Republican challenger, Richard L. Roude-

Democratic Reform/Republican Crisis

bush, the Republican gain will stay at two.

But if Mr. Roudebush, who trailed by 3,698 votes with three precincts still out, should win, the gain would be three.

Aim Not Achieved

In neither case would President Nixon have achieved either his primary goal, Republican control of the Senate, or his secondary goal, a pronounced ideological shift to the right. Despite the defeats of Democratic Senators Albert Gore of Tennessee and Joseph D. Tydings of Maryland and Republican Senator Charles E. Goodell of New York, the rightward swing was limited.

In mid-term elections since 1934, the party out of power in the White House has gained an average of 34 House seats. But such gains are usually made at the expense of Representatives pulled into office of a President's coattails, and Mr. Nixon pulled in almost no one in 1968. Thus the precedent is somewhat misleading.

For the political future, the most important results may well have been those in the races for governorships and state legislatures, and the Democrats did very well in those.

With Democrats holding slim but indecisive leads in Maine and Rhode Island, the Democrats had taken control of 13 Governors' mansions from the Republicans and the Republicans had recaptured two—a net Democratic gain of 11.

Democratic successes in major states such as Florida, Pennsylvania and Ohio will give the party's 1972 Presidential nominee a good organizational base. The new Democratic Governors will have a voice in the Congressional reapportionment that begins next year.

The legislatures will also be deeply involved in reapportionment. The Democrats took control of both houses in Pennsylvania, one in Utah and one in Wisconsin. More important, they seized both in California,

which gains five seats. If the Republicans had held both the legislature and the governorship, the Democrats might have lost as many as 12 seats.

Mr. Nixon asserted yesterday afternoon at his home at San Clemente, Calif., that he had scored an ideological gain of four seats in the Senate. But his aides indicated, among other things, that he was counting Connecticut in that computation — and most observers consider Representative Lowell P. Weicker Jr., the Republican victor, more liberal than the incumbent Democrat Thomas J. Dodd.

Moreover, there were signs that Mr. Nixon would find it harder than ever to work with liberal Senators of his own party, many of wh n were incensed by the White House "purge" of Mr. Goodell of New York.

What counted with the voters?

In the Northeast, the social issues — drugs, pornography and violence—apparently accelerated the shift of working-class voters, particularly those of Irish and Italian ancestry, to the Republicans.

Shift Toward G.O.P.

Mr. Goodell's defeat by James L. Buckley, the Conservative party candidate, was one instance of this; others were the Republican sweep in Connecticut and the crushing defeat suffered by former Gov. Philip H. Hoff of Vermont in his Senate bid.

Similarly, in Boston, Italian voters in the north end and poor Irish voters elsewhere — whose fathers would have never considered voting for a Yankee Republican — deserted Mayor Kevin H. White, a Democrat, to back Gov. Francis W. Sargent.

Across the Middle Atlantic and Middle Western states, however, the economic issues apparently took precedence.

In Akron, with its concentration of rubber plants, a Democratic neophyte, John F Seiberling, beat a 10-term Republican, Representative William H. Ayres. In Racine and Kenosha, Wis. where the unemployment rate is running above 8 per cent, Leslie Aspin, also a Democrat, ousted Represertative Henry C. Schadeberg.

Economic dislocation, made worse by the General Motors Corporation strike, clearly helped elect Milton J. Shapp Governor in Pennsylvania and John J. Gilligan Governor in Ohio.

In the race where the social and economic issues most nearly met head-on, the Senate contest in Indiana, the result was a dead heat—as forecast at least a month ago by one poll, which showed each of the candidates with 39.4 per cent.

Special Local Issues

But many contests, as always, turned on local issues and circumstances—a Republican split in Florida, Senator Tyding's aloofness from his own hardest workers, a Republican scandal in Ohio, an unexpectedly large turnout in Texas, stimulated at least partly by a referendum on liquor-by-the-drink.

Among the Governors in the Western States, the heavy Democratic incursions—Republicans lost in South Dakota, Oklahoma, Idaho, Nebraska, Nevada, among other states—resulted in large part from incumbents' inability to solve tax problems.

In big states such as California and New York, where broad-based taxes have long since been enacted, the problem is not so severe, and incumbents were re-elected. But Gov. Norbert T. Tiemann of Nebraska, who felt compelled to institute for the first time both a sales and an income tax, was unable to survive.

The Democrats' strong showing in Southern gubernatorial races — they ousted Republicans in Arkansas and Florida and withstood strong Republican challenges in Georgia, South Carolina and Texas—reflected the gradual decline of race as the exclusive focus of politics and a group of bright, young, articulate nominees.

For Mr. Nixon, who has labored diligently to expand his party's base in the once-solidly Democratic South, the results in that region must have been a disappointment. Only in Tennessee, with the defeat of Mr. Gore and the election of a Republican Governor, Winfield K. Dunn, did

the "Southern strategy" produce results.

New Democratic Faces

Among the new Democratic faces on the national scene are the following.

Dale Bumpers, a country lawyer from the Ozarks, Governor-elect of Arkansas; Lawton Chiles, Senator-elect from Florida; Adlai E. Stevenson 3d, Senator - elect from Illinois; John V. Tunney, Senator-elect from California, and two spokesmen for the New Left—Representative Ronald V. Dellums from the northern area of California and Bella Abzug from Manhattan.

Mr. Dellums is one of four new black members of the House. Three of them — Mr. Dellums, Parren J. Mitchell of Baltimore and George W. Collins, all Democrats — will represent districts formerly represented by white men. Each district has either a white majority poulation or a large white minority.

The fourth new black Representative is Ralph Metcalfe, also a Democrat, who succeeds William L. Dawson in a district on Chicago's South Side.

For the students who hoped last spring to produce a more liberal new Congress, and for antiwar casualties generally, it was not a particularly successful election.

Representative Allard K. Lowenstein of Nassau County, one of the originators of the dump-Johnson movement in 1968, was defeated, as were the Rev. Joseph D. Duffey, the Democratic Senate candidate in Connecticut, and Gerry E. Studds, the Democratic nominee in the Massachusetts Congressional district including Cape Cod.

The Rev. Robert F. Drinan, an antiwar Jesuit priest, won only narrowly to become the first Roman Catholic clergymen ever elected to Congress. He will represent the third Massachusetts district, which includes Boston's western suburbs.

However, a number of lesser known antiwar nominees won, including James Abourzek in South Dakota, John G. Dow in the suburbs north of New York City, and Teno Roncalio in Wyoming.

November 5, 1970

Democrats' Money Woes Expected to Grow Worse

By BEN A. FRANKLIN
Special to The New York Times

WASHINGTON, Nov. 27 — The Democratic party is so deeply in debt that the American Telephone and Telegraph Company, with an unpaid bill

for $1.5-million, is demanding a bonded guarantee of payment for telephone service at next year's Miami Beach convention.

The party's deficit now totals

$9.3-million, and even if Congress passes next week the Democratic-sponsored Senate plan to make available $20.4-million in public funds for each major party's 1972 Presidential campaign, the Democrats' money crisis is almost certain to get worse.

The new money could not be legally applied to the party's debt, and it could not be applied practically, either, if the

Democrats are to mount more than a matchbook and bumper sticker campaign.

The Senate-passed proposal to give every American taxpayer an opportunity to earmark $1 from Federal funds to the party of his choice by checking a box on his 1971 income tax return is to be considered next week by a Senate-House conference committee.

Amid uncertainty that the

conferees, or later the House of Representatives, will support the campaign financing plan of the Senate's Democratic majority—it cleared the Senate Nov. 18 on a tight, party-line vote of 49 to 46 — or that President Nixon would sign it should it survive a House test, the Democrats face what authorities call the worst financial crisis in American political history.

Even with the checkoff, the debt of the Democratic National Committee—not counting those of individual pre-convention contenders for the party's 1972 nomination—could reach $16-million to $18-million by the end of next year, according to Dr. Herbert E. Alexander, director of the Citizens' Research Foundation of Princeton, N. J., who is a leading expert on the huge costs of campaigning.

The $1 checkoff plan would give the Republicans, as well as the Democrats, the option of accepting $20.4-million in Federal funds and spending only that amount or of relying on private and business contributions.

The Republicans, as the party in power, could perhaps raise twice the checkoff amount. They see little merit in a plan that would hand their otherwise bankrupt adversaries an amount about equal to Democratic Presidential election expenditures in the lean year of 1968.

But Senate Democrats have attached their plan to President Nixon's sorely needed tax reduction bill. If he vetoes the measure for its campaign finance feature, he vetoes the tax cut, too.

For Mr. Nixon to face this choice, the House, which has passed a tax bill without the campaign finance provision, must first accept the Senate rider. It has usually declined to approve Senate amendments to tax measures.

The telephone cut-off threat was described in an interview this week by Robert S. Strauss, the Democratic National Committee treasurer, as "almost

impossible to believe." For the moment, however, it is clearly the sharpest point in the Democrats' fiscal bed of nails.

Phone Bill Overdue

In a letter to Mr. Strauss and Lawrence F. O'Brien, the Democrats' national chairman —with copies to the Republican-dominated Federal Communications Commission—A. T. & T. has told the Democratic National Committee that the company must receive by next July 1 the $1.5-million due, and overdue, chiefly from the 1968 convention and campaign.

Otherwise, the party will be required to post a $2-million guarantee-of-payment bond before the company will extend any of the essential communications lines and services to the Miami Beach convention.

Mr. Strauss, a deceptively calm Dallas lawyer who is struggling to make the Democratic debt possible to live with, said it was "impossible that a major, Government-regulated monopoly like A.T. & T. could deny us the use of a public utility."

Most observers of the Democrats' fiscal decline believe it would be unlikely that the Democratic National Committee could obtain a $2-million bond, the equivalent of an insurance policy covering payment of the party's 1972 telephone bill, if the company could sustain its demand in court.

The national committee's $9.3-million debt, which is a record, breaks down into roughly equal thirds owed to the following:

¶About 20 big contributors who lent $150,000 each and others who provided smaller amounts to put Hubert H. Humphrey, the party's Presidential nominee, on television during the 1968 campaign.

¶Government-regulated corporations such as A.T. & T., other telephone and telegraph companies and airlines. American Airlines, in a tally last June for the Civil Aeronautics Board,

reported that the Democrats owed it $1.1-million. The Republicans then owed American Airlines $221,000, largely from 1968.

¶Auto rental companies, hotels, printing concerns, caterers, security forces at the 1968 Chicago convention and other "general trade" companies.

The convention debt alone is $750,000 to $850,000, according to Mr. Strauss.

Analyzed by source of debt —by who incurred it—the national committee debt includes about $6.1-million from Mr. Humphrey's post-convention 1968 campaign, $1-million each assumed by the party from the pre-convention debts of Mr. Humphrey and the late Robert F. Kennedy and $400,000 to $500,000 in month-to-month operating deficits of the national committee from January, 1969, until Mr. O'Brien and Mr. Strauss stopped that drain in March, 1970.

Mr. Strauss said severe financial stringencies had been imposed on the 55-member national committee staff.

"We operate lean; we look at every expense account," the treasurer said.

Even so, the cost of maintaining the party apparatus is running $2-million a year, $160,000 a month.

"We are going to keep current," Mr. Strauss said, "and that's a chore in itself, operating with great prudence. People who contribute to our party are getting their money's worth, I'll tell you that."

Whether the creditors will do so, at least until the Democrats recapture the White House, is extremely doubtful, the Democratic treasurer said.

"What you need to pay off these debts is the romance and the majesty of the White House," Mr. Strauss observed. "That's what it is going to take. A number of our 1968 television fund contributors are giving us forgiveness. They forgive some of our debt to them every year, $10,000 or $15,000. But we not only still owe them, it takes 20 very

substantial contributors right out of circulation. They are giving us back some of what we owe them, but we don't get any cash."

Many — mostly Republicans — believe the situation raises serious philosophical and conflict-of-interest questions when the Democratic creditor is a regulated corporation whose welfare and profits may well depend on the decisions of Government agencies such as the Federal Communications Comision, Civil Aeronautics Board and Federal Power Commission These agencies would come under a Democratic President's appointive influence should the White House change hands.

Existing law is supposed to prohibit corporations from making loans or advances to any candidate for Federal office. Hugh Scott, the Senate Republican leader, made a fruitless attempt four months ago to outlaw the extension of air carrier or telephone company credit to a Federal candidate.

"If he fails to pay the bill he has, in effect, received an involuntary campaign contribution," Senator Scott said.

To Senator Scott's argument that "regulated businesses are placed in a position of unlawfully, unavoidably and unintentionally subsidizing political campaign expenses," Mr. Strauss replies that to A.T.&T. and the airlines "we are very good customers."

"Obviously, they'd like to have their money," Mr. Strauss said. "I wish we could pay it, but we can't. But we want to continue to buy their services, keeping current on bills. We'll pay our current bills, and they'll be glad to have our business."

"It creates some problems, certainly," he added wistfully. "It's going to take some real skills to conduct the business of our campaign next year. But you have to remember one thing: we are good customers of these people, and I think they'll want our business."

November 28, 1971

Nixon Signs a Law to Curb Spending on Campaigns

By BEN A. FRANKLIN
Special to The New York Times

WASHINGTON, Feb. 7— President Nixon signed into law today the first important reform in nearly half a century in the controversial process of financing election to Federal office.

In a three-paragraph statement distributed to newsmen at the White House, Mr. Nixon hailed the new law, which repeals and replaces the Federal Corrupt Practices Act of 1925, as a "realistic and enforceable bill, an important step forward in an area which has been of great public concern."

Asked if the Administration would actually enforce the new law—the old one has been ignored by prosecutors from both parties for 47 years—the White House press secretary, Ronald L. Ziegler, replied, "Yes."

No Public Ceremony

Mr. Nixon placed his signature on the Federal Election Campaign Act of 1971 without a public bill-signing ceremony. Such displays are customary in marking the final act of major legislation, and a score or more of members of Congress and other officials had been alerted privately for a week for the

possibility of a signing ceremony.

The White House offered no explanation for the apparent change in plans.

Supporters of campaign spending reform also hailed the final passage of the act. The National Committee for an Effective Congress, one of the principal groups behind the new law, declared in a statement that "today marks the end of the era of secrecy, duplicity and double-talk surrounding American political money."

Representative Torbert H. Macdonald, Democrat of Massachusetts and a principal spon-

sor of the measure in the House, said that the new law would cure "media blitz" campaigns and end "the buying of elective office."

For the first time, a candidate's personal investment in his own campaign is limited in Federal elections to $50,000 for President, $35,000 for the Senate and $25,000 for the House.

Noting that among the chief provisions of the new law, when it goes into effect in 60 days— on April 7—will be "full reporting of both the sources and uses of campaign funds," Mr. Nixon's statement said that "by giving the American public full access to the facts of political financing, this legislation will guard against campaign abuses and will work to build public confidence in the integrity of the electoral process."

However, the 60-day delay inserted in the act by the Democratic leadership in the House meant that the new law would not begin to apply until after the primaries in New Hampshire on March 7, Florida on March 14, Illinois on March 21 and Wisconsin on April 4.

A bill Mr. Nixon vetoed two years ago would have limited spending for television only. The new one limits a candidate's spending for all media—television, radio, newspapers and magazines, and voter solicitation by paid telephone callers (volunteers are not covered)—to $50,000 or 10 cents for each person of voting age within the nation, state or Congressional district being

contested at the polls, whichever figure is larger.

Based on an estimate of the national voting-age population, each major-party Presidential candidate would be limited this year to total advertising expenditures of about $13.9-million. The law sets no limit on other, noncommunications expenditures — travel, staff, mailing, rallies and so on.

The new law specifies that no more than 60 per cent of the prescribed media total may be spent on radio and television. The broadcast ceiling for each Presidential candidate would thus be about $8.4-million.

In 1968 the Republicans spent about $12.1-million on post-convention broadcast campaigning for Mr. Nixon. Mr. Nixon's Democratic opponent, Senator Hubert H. Humphrey of Minnesota, who was then Vice President, spent about

$6-million.

The limit would apply anew to each stage of the electoral process — to a primary first, to a primary runoff if required and finally to the general election.

The most effective curb is expected to be the stringent public reporting requirements of the new law.

The loopholes in the expiring law that will be closed include the exemption from public reporting of contributions in primary elections, of gifts to so-called dummy finance committees operating only in one state or in the District of Columbia, and of transfers of funds from such committees to candidates' treasurees.

Also, for the first time, contributions from corporation executives must be identified by name, address and "principal place of business."

Conservatives File Suit

A suit challenging the constitutionality of certain sections of the new law was filed in Federal District Court in New York yesterday in behalf of three local Conservative party officials.

The plaintiffs contend that enforcement of the act "would impair [their] constitutional rights to espouse Conservative party views on behalf of other candidates, and would hinder them in collecting money and strengthening the organization necessary to espouse these views."

The plaintiffs are Mario Pichler, a Conservative district leader in the Bronx; Donald J. Walsh, chairman of the George S. Patton Conservative Club in the Bronx, and George C. Smith, a party district leader in Queens.

February 8, 1972

Party Fund-Raisers Rush To Beat New, Tough Law

Anonymous Gifts Sought Before Rules on Public Reports Become Effective

By BEN A. FRANKLIN
Special to The New York Times

WASHINGTON, March 25—Political fund raisers are exploiting loopholes in Federal campaign financing regulations to enrich their election treasuries before a new and stricter law takes effect in two weeks.

As a result, the spirit if not the letter of the law is being broken on a broad scale.

Maurice H. Stans, President Nixon's chief campaign fundraiser, has been urging contributors to make their gifts to the

Primaries in April

Wisconsin	4th
Massachusetts	25th
Pennsylvania	25th

Republicans before the new Federal Election Campaign Act takes effect April 7, three days after the Wisconsin primary, the fourth of the year.

The delay in the effective date of the new law plus the fact that the old law did not require independent campaign committees to report contributions have jointly created a situation made to order for an intensive month of anonymous fund-raising.

Although they deny it—and the Republicans do not—it is believed from the nature of the

opportunity that some Democratic fund-raisers, particularly for individual candidates for the Presidential nomination, are following the plan now in use by the Republicans.

But five of the major Democratic contenders — Senators George McGovern of South Dakota, Hubert H. Humphrey of Minnesota and Edmund S. Muskie of Maine and Mayor Lindsay of New York and Gov. George C. Wallace of Alabama —have made or are committed to make full disclosure of their contributions in any case.

The Republican apparatus supporting the re-election of the President has made no such moves toward voluntary disclosure. And it appears to be actively seeking to maximize the advantages of contributor anonymity.

Under the expiring law, political finance committees were required to disclose their contributions unless they operated in one state or jurisdiction, leading to a proliferation of dummy committees in the District of Columbia. About 50 of these committees appear to have been set up here by the Republicans to facilitate anonymous fund raising.

Under the Federal Election

Campaign Act of 1971, contributions of more than $100 must be publicly reported, with the donor's name, occupation and address.

Mr. Stans, the former Secretary of Commerce who was also Mr. Nixon's chief fund raiser in 1968, has had a series of unannounced meetings with wealthy Republicans. In addition, through some of his state finance chairmen, Mr. Stans's fund-raising operation, headquartered here at the Committee for the Re-election of the President, has been providing information on how to give large sums privately before the new law takes effect.

Nixon Cites Public View

In signing the campaign act last Feb. 7, President Nixon said in a statement:

"It [the law] provides for full reporting of both the sources and the uses of campaign funds, both after elections and during campaigns. By giving the American public full access to the facts of political financing, this legislation will guard against campaign abuses and will work to build public confidence in the integrity of the electoral process.

"The Federal Election Campaign Act of 1971 is a realistic and enforceable bill, an important step forward in an area which has been of great public concern. Because I share that concern, I am pleased to give my approval to this bill."

A spokesman for the Committee for the Re-election of the President said that Mr. Stans was "engaging in normal fund-raising activities—raising money both before and after April 7—which everybody knows is his reason for being." Mr. Stans, who grants few interviews, could not be reached for comment.

Press aides at the Committee for the Re-election of the President said they could not

provide Mr. Stans's itinerary in recent weeks. A spokesman said only that the finance chairman had recently visited Illinois, Missouri and Texas.

But it is known that he has traveled continuously and widely, meeting for example, with about 35 wealthy contributors at the Casino Restaurant in Chicago on Feb. 28, advising a similar group at the St. Louis Club in St. Louis on March 9, and conferring with executives at the Olin Corporation Gunning and Game Preserve near Brighton, Ill., on the weekend of March 11-12.

According to persons who attended the Chicago and St. Louis meetings, the audience for Mr. Stans's talk about early and anonymous Republican giving included scores of wealthy corporate executives.

Guests In Chicago

The Chicago gathering reportedly included Robert D. Stuart Jr., president of the Quaker Oats Company and chairman of Mr. Nixon's Illinois campaign; John Henry Altorfer, a Peoria industrial real estate developer and former Washington assistant of Mr. Stans who is now the downstate Illinois campaign chairman for Mr. Nixon; and Robert Athay, an associate of W. Clement Stone, the Chicago insurance millionaire who gave more than $150,000 to Mr. Nixon's 1968 campaign.

In St. Louis, Mr. Stans is reported to have urged a group of large contributors to parcel out their gifts before April 1 in $3,000 to $4,000 donations to a number of Republican "front" committees in Washington. Such groups would not have to disclose their donors under the old law, even if its reporting requirements were still in effect.

The audience in St. Louis was said to have included Leif J. Sverdrup, head of the engineering firm of Sverdrup & Parcel

328

and Associates; Spencer T. Olin, a director of the Olin Corporation and former treasurer of the Republican National Committee; Howard Stamper, president of the Banquet Foods Corporation of St. Louis; Harold E. Thayer, chairman and president of the Mallinckrodt Chemical Works; G. Duncan Bauman, publisher of The St. Louis Globe-Democrat; James P. Hitckock, former chairman of the First National Bank of St. Louis, and Donald Wolfsberger, president of the United Food and Packaging Corporation and chairman of a Missouri fund-raising committee for Mr. Nixon.

Mr. Stamper, confirming the St. Louis meeting in a telephone interview today, said that Mr. Stans, in telling the executives how to avoid public disclosure of their gifts, was "not urging, he was simply pointing out how it could be done."

But the St. Louis food executive also said that Mr. Stans had not mentioned President Nixon's stated view that "full access to the facts of political financing" would restore "public confidence in the integrity of the electoral process."

Such meetings were described by one Republican fund raiser as "much more successful than just sending a letter." But letters are being used to carry the Stans message, too.

One such letter was sent recently from Los Angeles by Thomas P. Pike, a drilling machinery manufacturer, vice chairman of the Fluor Corporation in California and a donor, with his wife, of $10,000 to Mr. Nixon's 1968 campaign. The letter spoke openly of methods to circumvent the public reporting of Nixon contributions, "which," it said, "we all naturally want to avoid."

Mr. Pike, who was an Assistant Secretary of Defense from 1953 to 1956, later served as Mr. Nixon's California campaign chairman in the election of 1960 and as vice chairman of his Los Angeles County finance committee in 1963. His Los Angeles office said he was in France and he could not be reached to confirm the language of his letter, a copy of which was obtained by The New York Times. But other ranking California Republicans said they had received the identical letter and had discussed it with Mr. Pike. The letter said:

"At the request of former Secretary of Commerce Maurice Stans, I have agreed to serve with Leonard Firestone and Taft Schreiber and others as California co-chairmen of the Committee for the Re-election of the President, to raise the necessary funds.

"I am personally committed to give and secure a total of $50,000 from family and friends for this vital campaign.

"My plan is to secure from members of my family and a few friends approximately one-half of this amount and then give the balance myself.

"The simplest and most painless way to do this is by giving appreciated low-cost securities to several committees (whose names I can supply) in amounts of $3,000 to each committee. In this way neither the gift tax nor the capital gains tax liability is incurred, and I can easily explain to you the mechanics of doing it.

"The standard of giving suggested is one-half per cent, more or less, of net worth. This makes for a very substantial campaign contribution which will actually have a minimal effect on your life-style and personal estate, but will have a tremendous effect on your family's personal stake in the future of our economy and our country. I can't emphasize too strongly that the protection of your stake and my stake is precisely what is at stake here.

"We have a deadline of April 7th to meet for this important gift phase of the drive, because that is the effective date of the new Federal campaign law which will require reporting and public disclosure of all subsequent campaign contributions in excess of $100, which we all naturally want to avoid."

Mr. Pike's letter closed by saying that "you may rest assured that he [Mr. Nixon] will be personally apprised of your support."

March 26, 1972

Transcript of Mayor's Statement on Party Switch

Following is a transcript of the statement by Mayor Lindsay announcing his switch in political parties, as recorded by The New York Times:

This morning at Gracie Mansion Mrs. Lindsay and I enrolled in the Democratic party.

In a sense, this step recognizes the failure of 20 years in progressive Republican politics. In another sense, it represents a renewed decision to fight for new national leadership.

I was born into a Republican family—Lincoln, Theodore Roosevelt and La Guardia were my political heroes. As a Republican, I worked for progressive goals through seven years in Congress and almost six years as Mayor.

And those times when I thought my party wrong I followed an independent course. From battle to battle that course became more necessary.

G.O.P. Is Assailed

Today the Republican party has moved so far from what I perceive as necessary policies for our city and for the country that I can no longer try to work within it. It has become clear that the Republican party and its controlling leaders in Washington have finally abandoned the fight for a government that will respond to the needs of most of our people and of those most in need.

I joined the Democratic party today because it offers the best hope for a change in national direction and national leadership in the 1972 election.

I consider this decision a reaffirmation of my commitment to the needs of this great and vital city and all American cities—men without jobs, families without hope, indecent housing, blighted neighborhoods, crowded hospitals, crime, poverty, polarization. These are real. And again and again I have seen them on our streets.

Every day they multiply, spreading into suburban communities that once thought themselves isolated from the agony of the central city. There is no escape.

These are the harsh, sometimes ugly, facts of our national life. They require national action, not the indifference shown by Washington.

While drug addicts go untreated and children go hungry to school, while people in trouble go without help, Washington votes hundreds of millions of dollars to bail out a single corporation. The richest country the world has ever known refuses to so shape its course that its children can be taught, its sick healed and its environment cleansed.

Our community of New York and every community is ravaged by inflation, and simultaneously there is less for our families and less for basic government services.

The expense of living is imprisoning our people; con-

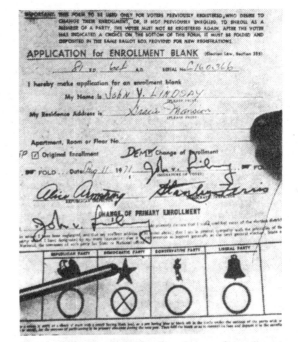

Mayor Lindsay's application for change of enrollment from Republican to Democratic party, dated yesterday.

fidence in the dollar, basic to America's world leadership, is at an all-time low. And still the Administration refuses to act to control prices and wages, to rebuild our economy.

Policemen are shot in the streets of our cities; holdups increase daily and a gun is sold every two seconds. But Washington rejects the strict Federal gun controls that are crucial to a realistic war on crime.

And so by such choice the Government reveals its priorities—the corporation before the sick person, the man of comfort before the wage-earner, the special interest before the safety of the city.

When Mr. Nixon campaigned in 1968, he was supported by virtually all Republicans, including myself, mainly because he promised to stop the debilitating war and to end the divisions that were tearing us apart.

Yet in Indochina the killing of Americans, Vietnamese, Laotians and Cambodians goes on, and our remaining soldiers and their families wonder what in God's name it's all about.

And at home we have a deeper sense than ever before of our nation fragmented by class and race and age. To me, the most troubling development has been the Government's retreat from the Bill of Rights.

Washington has tapped telephones without court order; spied on our citizens with military agents; arrested thousands of people, protesters and bystanders alike without legal authority; given minimum enforcement to the rights of minorities, and even tried to censor what we see on television and read in our newspapers.

I believe that America deserves better than this, and I regret that new directions cannot emerge from a Republican party that has finally become a closed institution. It has stifled dissent and discouraged first voters, and it has rejected internal reform so grassroots Republicans cannot challenge their present leadership.

Coalition Sought

I have no illusions about the Democratic party, and I will work as a Democrat without abandoning my personal independence. That party, too, is far from perfect. But in contrast the Democratic party has sought, since the travesty of 1968, to diversify and reform itself.

The 1972 Democratic Convention should be as open as any in American history. And this gives Republicans, Democrats and independents a chance to build a coalition that can work for peace and justice.

This at long last must be a time of realignment. Progressive Republicans, independents and Democrats must stand together in fighting for common goals. We must join together freely instead of struggling vainly against each other in the net of party alignment.

Millions of Americans believe that we have lost our way, that something more than political drift is needed to restore our lost sense of shared beliefs and goals and our lost willingness to tackle hard jobs.

For my part I will start now to help this new coalition. Whether this means "ll run for President, I do not know. But it does mean that I'm firmly committed to take an active part in 1972 to bring about new national leadership.

I believe this country can find its way again

August 12, 1971

Parties, Not Ideologies

Mayor Lindsay's departure from the Republican ranks can have a harmful and unnecessary consequence if it encourages a polarization of the two major parties along ideological lines. Persuasive as were the factors that seemed to the Mayor to deny him a future as a liberal Republican, they did not add up to the proposition, implied in his farewell statement, that liberalism itself has no future in the G.O.P.

Certainly that proposition is not the view of liberal Senate Republicans like Hatfield of Oregon, Percy of Illinois, Javits of New York or Brooke of Massachusetts, all of whom have expressed regret at the Lindsay action. Nor can it be the view of other practitioners of Republican liberalism like Case of New Jersey, Mathias of Maryland, Schweiker of Pennsylvania or Packwood, also of Oregon. In the House there are a score of Republicans who rate high in the voting-record compilations of Americans for Democratic Action, a litmus test for liberalism that hardly errs on the side of indulgence.

We believe this is a politically healthy state of affairs. The idea of two major parties cleanly divided along ideological lines has long appealed to theorists who like their politics tidy. But in practice it would not be tidy at all. It would mean drastic upheavals in policy with each shift in party control; it would dangerously transfer to the general election the kind of battling that now resolves issues within the two parties at an earlier stage.

Undeniably, there are powerful forces for conservatism in the Republican party that do from time to time discourage its more progressive members. An Administration for which Vice President Agnew is often the spokesman and Attorney General Mitchell a guiding light is bound to tempt the party's moderates to leave the reservation. But where they can effectively make common cause with others on particular issues and still remain Republicans, they do the country a service to stay and do their battling from within.

Otherwise, by the very fact of abandoning their party, by leaving it in sole possession of its most conservative elements, they would doom it to permanent minority status—a danger to which the liberal Ripon Society alluded on the eve of the Lindsay switch. Nationally, the country would then be in effect a one-party state—in the long run less likely by far than today's flexible bipartisan system to meet the Mayor's laudable standard of "government that will respond to the needs of most of our people and of those most in need."

August 15, 1971

Rep. Reid Quitting G.O.P.; Plans Race as a Democrat

By RICHARD L. MADDEN
Special to The New York Times

WASHINGTON, March 21 — Representative Ogden R. Reid of Westchester County, whose family's involvement with the Republican party dates back almost a century, will announce tomorrow his switch to the Democratic party.

Friends of the 46-year-old liberal Republican said that among the factors involved were a decision that he could not support President Nixon for re-election, the prospect of a difficult Republican primary fight in his newly drawn Westchester district, and a feeling that his chances for advancement to statewide office, such as Governor, were blocked on the Republican side.

Mr. Reid, who is completing his 10th year in the House and who has been increasingly critical of the Nixon Administration, scheduled a news conference for 10:30 A.M. tomorrow at the Carlyle Hotel in New York City to make what his office called "an important political announcement."

Mr. Reid was reported by his office to be in New York and unavailable for comment. However, other political figures — Republican as well as Democratic — who have talked to him in recent days said they were convinced that he would announce his candidacy for re-election as a Democrat.

Such a shift would follow by seven months the move by Mayor Lindsay, a political ally of Mr. Reid, into the Democratic party and would further weaken the ranks of the so-called progressive wing of the Republican party in New York State.

In anticipation of Mr. Reid's announcement, the Westchester County Republican organization, which had been scheduled to hold a convention in White Plains tomorrow night to designate Congressional candidates, postponed its meeting. Republican officials began discussing potential candidates who might make a strong race against the Representative.

Persuasion Said to Fail

It was understood that John N. Mitchell, the former Attorney General who is now directing Mr. Nixon's re-election campaign, met with Mr. Reid last weekend in an apparently unsuccessful effort to talk the Representative out of bolting the Republican party.

At a news conference in Albany today, Governor Rockefeller acknowledged that he had discussed the matter with Mr. Reid "over the last two or three weeks." The Governor indicated that he expected a party switch.

Mr. Rockefeller said that any statement should come from Mr. Reid, whom he praised as a "long and old friend" who had been a strong supporter of previous Rockefeller campaigns for the Presidency and Governor. The Governor added:

"Now I know, and have known for quite a while, that he [Mr. Reid] has been frustrated with getting—the problem of getting things done—in Congress, and that his rate

of progress onto the statewide scene in the state has not been as rapid as I think he would like to see it. So I understand the considerations he faces."

'The Wrong Party'

Mr. Rockefeller continued: "Now, my personal feeling would be that for anyone to switch his allegiance from the Republican party to the Democratic party would be joining the wrong party at the wrong time, but that is a personal feeling."

Two years ago Mr. Reid scored only a narrow victory in the Republican primary, but

he won handily in the general election, with his traditional drawing of Democratic and independent votes.

Max Berking, the Westchester County Democratic chairman, declined comment on Mr. Reid's intentions, but he said that he thought the Representative would be welcomed by Democratic officials, who are scheduled to meet Thursday night to designate candidates.

While Mr. Reid has been increasingly critical of the Nixon Administration, a decision to leave the party was regarded as somewhat uncharacteristic

for the Representative, whose ties to the Republicans have been strong.

His grandfather, Whitelaw Reid, was the unsuccessful Republican nominee for Vice President on Benjamin Harrison's ticket in 1892. Mr. Reid, a former president and editor of the now defunct New York Herald Tribune, was the United States Ambassador to Israel in the Eisenhower Administration.

If Mr. Reid is re-elected as a Democrat, his 10 years of seniority in the House also might be endangered.

March 22, 1972

WALLACE ASSERTS HE'LL RUN IN '72

Barring 'Meaningful Change' in Major Party, He Says He Is in Race 'to Win'

By JAMES T. WOOTEN
Special to The New York Times

MONTGOMERY, Ala., Aug. 5 —George C. Wallace says he has decided to run again for the Presidency in 1972.

"The only thing that would keep me out is a meaningful change of direction in the Nixon Administration or the Democratic party," he said here yesterday in an interview, adding: "I have no realistic hopes that such miracles will come to pass."

"I will be running to win," he said. "Some people think I just like to run just to run—but I'll be a serious candidate in 1972 because I believe that a victory for me is quite possible."

In a wide-ranging conversation, the third-party champion of state's rights and segregation confirmed what many of his friends and foes have believed for some time — that he has never really ceased an active pursuit of the Presidency since he captured 10 million votes in the election three years ago.

It was, however, his first outright affirmation that he will again be a candidate. Since 1968 he has couched his discussions on next year's election in terms of the possibility or the probability of his candidacy.

His previous hesitance to speak candidly about his political plans has been attributed by some knowledgeable sources to his narrow victory in last year's gubernatorial election in Alabama and his anxiety about a continuation of the financial support that made his 1968 campaign possible.

The Governor and close associates have now interpreted his slim margin over the incumbent, Albert P. Brewer, as an indication of strength rather than a reflection of weakness, a logic they base on the opposition raised against him by many of the state's organized political blocs.

Moreover, the circulation of a monthly newsletter published by Mr. Wallace's still active campaign office (the address of which is Post Office Box 1972) has now reached nearly 300,000, an increase from 100,000 in the last year.

The newsletter is a prime source of income for Mr. Wallace's political enterprises, and its current distribution is estimated to provide almost $2-million a year for the campaign office.

During the interview in his office at the State Capitol, Mr. Wallace, now in his second four-year term as Governor, also reiterated his now familiar critique of the Nixon Administration and other favorite targets, including the United States Supreme Court and the country's more prominent tax-exempt foundations.

But the primary thrust of his conversation was a positive declaration of his 1972 Presidential campaign coupled with a lively interest in the primary elections of North Carolina, Florida and Tennessee.

The Southern primaries, all new to the national political picture, "will be a perfect opportunity to show the national parties just how the people really feel about the important things," he said.

Included in his list of issues considered most important by the citizens are the busing of students to achieve racial balances in public school systems, the economy and the nation's tax schedules.

He said that President Nixon had "performed badly" in all of those fields and accused him of "standing forthrightly on both sides" of most questions.

The Governor singled out for particular scorn the President's new position on relations between the United States and Communist China.

Mr. Nixon's announced intention to visit Peking, the Chinese capital, is "a colossal mistake," Mr. Wallace said, historically akin to Neville Chamberlain's trip to Munich to discuss international affairs with Adolf Hitler.

"What if President Roosevelt had gone to Berlin to talk with the Fuehrer?" he asked with a chuckle. "I think this China thing could very well be a disaster."

Mr. Wallace will be 52 years old on Aug. 25. The dark hair coloring he has regularly applied since he became Governor last January has now been discarded as well as an over-the-ears hair style. He looked much as he did in the 1968 campaign.

When questions on the possibility that he might decide not to seek the Presidency next year were raised, he bristled with indignation and attributed such inquiries to "propaganda machines" of both major parties.

When asked about current speculation among a substantial number of state politicians that he has softened his views on the President, he quickly responded by referring to Mr. Nixon as a "double-dealer, a two-timer and a man who tells folks one thing and does another."

He was especially critical of the Nixon Administration's role in Southern school desegregation and the appointments the President has made.

"Nixon said he was against busing," Mr. Wallace commented. "That helped him get elected, but then he appointed [United States Chief Justice Warren E.] Burger to the court and he helped write the decision that makes busing pseudolegal. If I were President, I'd make sure whoever I appointed was against busing too."

The President's latest word on the controversial issue of busing — a disavowal of a desegregation plan in Austin, Tex. devised by the Department of Health, Education and Welfare — is not "a reflection" of any significant changes at the White House, Mr. Wallace said.

"He just keeps on saying he's against busing, and our children just keep on getting bused," the Governor added.

The primaries in the three Southern states offer him an opportunity to show the national parties "just what the rank and file in this country really feels, just as I did in 1968," Mr. Wallace said.

August 6, 1971

Jackson Sees Peril Of Party Take-Over By Democratic Left

By DAMON STETSON

Senator Henry M. Jackson warned yesterday that the Democratic left was trying to take over the party and that if it succeeded the Democrats would lose in 1972 and be in "deep trouble" for years thereafter.

The Washington Senator, who is frequently mentioned as a possible candidate for the Democratic Presidential nomination next year issued his warning in a speech before 1,700 delegates and alternates to the convention here of the state American Federation of Labor and Congress of Industrial Organizations.

A Standing Ovation

He received a standing ovation when he entered the ballroom of the New York Hilton and when he left, with delegates crowding around him to shake hands or have their picture taken with him.

After the Senator's speech, which was interrupted 13 times by applause, Raymond R. Corbett, president of the federation, said that the labor movement looked at Senator Jackson as "one of the brightest stars in the political arena."

"You may very well be the answer to the American people's prayers," he added.

"There are some people in the Democratic party, who intentionally or not, have turned their backs on the working man," the Senator said. "They are either indifferent to him or downright hostile. Their cocktail parties abound with snide jokes about 'hardhats' and 'ethnics.' They mouth fashionable clichés about how workers have grown fat and conservative with affluence, and how their unions are reactionary or racist.

"They ignore the fact that in the last two decades unions have been in the forefront of everything decent in this country—from civil rights to education to national health insurance. In fact, if it were not for the labor movement, many of these so-called liberals would not enjoy the affluence they now take for granted."

Law and Order Cited

What most typifies the outlook of "these absolutists on the left," the Senator said, is their attitude toward law and order. They seem to regard the whole issue as "phony, demagogic, unclean," he said.

A small but vocal minority of Democratic politicians, Senator Jackson charged, "are pandering" to the views of those on the left and are thereby alienating working people who have traditionally provided the mass electoral base for liberal Democratic victories and programs.

These Democrats, he said, are telling working people that liberals aren't interested in protecting them from crime and disorder, from disruption, from muggers and drug addicts. They are telling working people to wait until all of the nation's sociological and political problems are solved before they can expect personal safety and security, he said.

"This is the message that I am afraid is coming across to many traditional Democratic voters," Senator Jackson declared. "Well, I am a liberal Democrat, and I am not soft on law and order."

The comment brought applause from delegates and more applause followed when he said: "Right now the common man sees two pocketbook issues: Nixon is draining his pocketbook and the muggers are swiping it."

Senator Jackson, who is chairman of the Senate Interior and Insular Affairs Committee, was also critical of the way in which he said the "absolutists on the left" were perverting the environment issue into an attack on working people.

What the "emotional absolutists" want, he said, is to stop economic growth, to turn off technology, shut down factories, turn workers out and go back to the agrarian age. He charged that these leftists were contemptuous of the material aspirations and needs of working people and the poor for whom they profess compassion.

"I strongly believe that these contemptuous attitudes have no place in the Democratic party, not so long as it is a party of the people. . . . I do not want to see the Democratic party become a party which gives any comfort whatever to people who applaud Vietcong victories or wave Vietcong flags. Our party has room for hawks and doves, but not for the mocking birds who chip gleefully at those who are shooting at American boys."

Earlier in his speech, Senator Jackson asserted that the American worker and his family had also been assaulted from the right under the Nixon Administration "game plan" that had blamed excessive wage gains for inflation, engineered a recession and raised interest rates to record-breaking heights in an effort to bring prices down.

Senator Jackson called the efforts of the Nixon Administration to bring inflation under control a "dismal failure." He said he believed the time had come for wage and price controls, but he warned that controls should not discriminate against wage-earners.

At a later news conference, Senator Jackson declined several times to name any individuals of the Democratic left, saying that he did not want to get into personalities.

In commenting on his own prospects, Mr. Jackson said he had been encouraged by recent trips through the nation and that many people were urging him to go into key Presidential primaries.

On Vietnam, he proposed that President Nixon appeal to Premier Chou En-lai of China to bring about an immediate cease-fire, that the President insist that all candidates and all parties have a chance to appear on the ballot in the October election in South Vietnam and that all American offensive troops be removed from South Vietnam by the end of the year.

Convention delegates approved a constitutional change that raised per capita dues from 3 cents a month to 5 cents a month. The federation's statement of income and expenses, for the fiscal year ended June 30, showed income of $386,441.01 and expenses of $433,275.99, with a deficit of $46,834.98.

Delegates also adopted, with no discussion except in two or three cases, about 100 resolutions detailing the federation's legislative goals. Other speakers included Attorney General Louis J. Lefkowitz, State Controller Arthur Levitt and Robert B. McKersie, dean of the New York State School of Industrial and Labor Relations at Cornell University.

August 11, 1971

Reforming The Democrats

By WILLIAM V. SHANNON

WASHINGTON, Sept. 28—Without anyone noticing, this country has moved remarkably close to choosing one of its Presidential candidates by a national primary.

When the Democrats meet in Miami Beach next July, two-thirds of the delegates will have been chosen in primaries. Since voters in 22 states including New York, Pennsylvania and California are to choose their delegates, the primaries have become the crucial battlegrounds.

Up to now, the primaries have chiefly been held in small and medium-sized states — New Hampshire, West Virginia, Wisconsin, Oregon. The results were important for their psychological, propaganda, and money-raising effects but most of the big-state delegations were not directly affected. Political managers used the primary votes as talking points in their bargaining with uncommitted kingmakers. While candidates were pumping hands and trudging through small towns in Nebraska and Oregon, the really important delegations were being put together behind the scenes and the deals made by a relatively few leaders in the big states like Pennsylvania, Illinois and Texas. As Hubert Humphrey proved in 1968, if a candidate had the support of key people, he could avoid the primaries and still win the nomination.

That can no longer happen in the Democratic party. Only if the successive state primaries produce a bewildering variety of winners will the kingmakers have an opportunity to determine the outcome.

This considerable shift in the locus of power has taken place as a result of the upheavals which occurred within the Democratic party in 1968. When President Johnson unexpectedly withdrew as a candidate in late March, the delegate selection process was already far advanced in 38 states. These pro-Johnson delegations became free agents, which is another way of saying the voters could not control where they went. Most of them began drifting to Humphrey but the issue was still in doubt until early June when Robert Kennedy was assassinated.

Kennedy's death made Humphrey's nomination certain because the power brokers would not accept Eugene McCarthy. Some Kennedy supporters could not accept him either and switched their energies to structural reform. They whipped together a package of reforms which Senator Harold Hughes of Iowa presented to the convention as a minority report of the Rules Committee.

Movement for reform was already under way in the party. The Credentials Committee recommended and the convention approved the setting up of a party commission to improve delegate selection. When the convention went on to adopt Hughes' minority report, the effect was to give this commission specific instructions.

The commission, first headed by Senator George McGovern and more

recently by Representative Donald Fraser of Minnesota, has adopted stringent guide lines for the state parties based on those proposed by Senator Hughes in 1968. The unit rule is abolished so minority voices will be represented in the delegations chosen to go to the national convention. The delegates have to be selected in the calendar year of the Presidential election to make certain that they reflect the current thinking of the party. Previously, many delegates were chosen by state committees which in turn had been elected two or four years earlier. In an effort to conform with these new rules, several states have either introduced primaries or made their primaries more meaningful.

By any reasonable standard, the Democratic party has made long strides toward self-reform. The danger now is that the best will become the enemy of the good. There are elements

in the party who are prepared to challenge every delegation that is not in full compliance with every last requirement in the new guide lines. These credentials contests would lay the moral basis for the cry, "We were robbed!" The dissidents could then go out into the night to assert their purity in a new fourth party.

In reality, the delegate selection process has already been made so democratic that candidates from now through next June face nine months of unremitting, physically exhausting and financially ruinous primary campaigns. The old methods of choosing most delegates by state committees and state conventions had their evils, but in opting for an endless round of primaries, the Democrats have not found the ideal answer.

September 29, 1971

WALLACE GETS 42%, HUMPHREY 2D, JACKSON 3D, MUSKIE 4TH IN FLORIDA; LINDSAY EDGES M'GOVERN FOR 5TH

NIXON MARGIN BIG

Governor Captures 75 of 81 Delegates in Dramatic Victory

By MARTIN WALDRON
Special to The New York Times

MIAMI, March 14 — Gov. George C. Wallace of Alabama scored a dramatic victory in the Florida Presidential primary today, capturing 75 of the state's 81 delegates to the Democratic National Convention.

Riding the issue of school busing and promising to tax the rich and crack down on crime, Mr. Wallace finished far ahead of 10 other Democrats who had spent $3-million in an effort to defeat him.

Senator Hubert H. Humphrey of Minnesota, who ran here to revive his national political fortunes, finished second. Mr. Humphrey led the field in the 11th Congressional District, including parts of Miami and Miami Beach, and won six convention delegates.

Senator Henry M. Jackson of Washington ran third, firmly ahead of Senator Edmund S. Muskie of Maine, who had entered the Florida contest with strong support from party officials.

Mr. Muskie's poor showing was a major setback, even more damaging than last week's showing in New Hampshire for the man deemed the "front runner" for more than a year. There are still 21 primaries remaining.

In the Republican primary, also held today, President Nixon easily won Florida's 40 delegates to the Republican National Convention. The President did not campaign in the state.

With 99 per cent of the state's 2,841 precincts reporting, the tally was:

DEMOCRATS

Wallace	514,722	(42%)
Humphrey	231,015	(18%)
Jackson	167,539	(13%)
Muskie	109,461	(9%)
Lindsay	81,075	(7%)
McGovern	74,832	(6%)
Mrs. Chisholm	44,770	(4%)
McCarthy	5,842	(0%)
Mills	4,618	(0%)
Hartke	3,536	(0%)
Yorty	2,576	(0%)

REPUBLICANS

Nixon	357,143	(87%)
Ashbrook	35,977	(9%)
McCloskey	16,982	(4%)

Governor Wallace, who spent election day sunning himself atop an Orlando hotel, smoking cigars and reading old copies of the National Geographic magazine, said he was surprised at the margin of his victory.

He said none of the other candidates "can take any comfort from being second or third."

However, Senator Humphrey's staff took considerable comfort from his second-place finish.

A happy Mr. Humphrey said at his headquarters: "My campaign is off and it's off to a good start. I think this gives us a great boost."

Mayor Lindsay finished fifth in the primary, coming in ahead of Senator George McGovern. The Lindsay strategy had been to try to beat the South Dakota Senator to illustrate that the Mayor could run ahead of the candidate who did so well in New Hampshire's primary.

Representative Shirley Chisholm of Brooklyn, who campaigned without an organization and with a campaign fund of less than $20,000, was running seventh.

Votes for the other four Democrats who did not campaign in Florida—Mayor Sam Yorty of Los Angeles, former Senator Eugene J. McCarthy of Minnesota, Senator Vance Hartke of Indiana and Representative Wilbur D. Mills of Arkansas—were negligible.

On the Republican side, President Nixon overwhelmed his two opponents, Representative John M. Ashbrook, Ohio conservative, and Representative Paul N. McCloskey Jr. of California, who stopped campaigning after getting only 20 per cent of the vote in the New Hampshire primary last weeks.

A special New York Times cross-section survey conducted today by Daniel Yankelovitch, Inc., asked 400 voters to explain their ballots as they emerged from the polls. The survey found that the economy was an issue equal to that of school busing.

Governor Wallace, Senator Humphrey and Senator Jackson had all emphasized economic issues as well as the busing controversy.

Three of every five Wallace voters in the survey thought he could defeat President Nixon this fall, but only one in ten said they voted for him for this reason.

Busing Most Important

They said they thought it more important to vote their

views than to try to choose a winner. The Wallace voters told interviewers they considered the busing issue the most important one, followed by crime. As a group, they were so zealous that more than one-third did not even have a second choice in the primary. About one-third named Senator Jackson as their second choice.

Senator Humphrey's supporters termed him "experienced." One-third of them said he could best unify the country and understood the problems of "common people."

The most important issue to Humphrey voters was the economy, but even that was an issue to only one out of four.

Three out of every four who voted for the former Vice President thought he could beat President Nixon this fall. About one-third of them picked Senator Muskie as their second choice among the candidates.

Economy Biggest Issue

About half of the Jackson supporters said they had voted on the basis of issues. By far the most important issue to them was the economy.

The Muskie supporters were unable to give interviewers a clear reason for their choice. Five out of six thought the Maine Senator would beat President Nixon, but they did not identify Mr. Muskie with any major issue. They thought he was "experienced," could win the nomination, and could

unify the country.

Very few of those interviewed were Lindsay voters, but two out of three of those thought he could defeat Mr. Nixon. There was no clear second choice for the Lindsay backers.

More than one-half of the supporters of Senator McGovern emphasized issues, above all the Vietnam war, with the economy a poor second Two out of every three said he could beat Mr. Nixon.

Over-all, the survey showed that none of the candidates had succeeded in taking advantage of the strong feelings in the state about the economy. Florida has a 4 per cent unemployment rate and a much higher rate of underemployed people with low-paying marginal or part-time jobs.

Governor Wallace's vote closely paralleled what he got in Florida in 1968 when he ran for President on the American Independent party ticket, but he was stronger in Miami this year. He is entered in a number of other Democratic primaries.

The turnout in Florida was not as high as had been predicted by state-elected officials, who had forecast that 70 per cent of the state's 2,130,000 Democrats would vote. The final total was not expected to be more than 1,150,000, about 54 per cent of registered voters.

The Republican turnout was about 60 per cent.

The Florida vote was cast

under almost ideal weather conditions, a drastic contrast to the snow and frigid weather that gripped New Hampshire during the state's primary.

A heavy Negro turnout of voters was reported all over Florida. About 15 per cent of the state's 2,130,000 Democrats are Negroes. Of the 773,000 registered Republicans, only 11,000 are Negroes.

Both Senator Humphrey and Senator Jackson had said they would finish second behind Governor Wallace, and Senator McGovern said it was not inconceivable that he could, too.

The assertions by Humphrey and Senator Jackson that they had passed him were ignored by Senator Muskie, the pre-campaign favorite among the regular Democrats.

Governor Wallace is not considered a regular Democrat because of his campaign for the Presidency on the American Independent party ticket in 1968.

Many politicians tended to downgrade the importance of the Florida primary, feeling that the heavy tide of support for Mr. Wallace and the large number of contestants made the state meaningless as a test of a candidate's potential.

As a Springboard

Senator Jackson, who began stumping the state before Christmas, hopes to use the Florida primary as a springboard for future primaries.

He said that only 6 per cent of the people polled in the United States recognized his name before he started the Florida campaign, and that now not only do people recognize his name — and face — but they also know "what I stand for."

Senator Humphrey had said his own chances of winning the Democratic nomination for President at the national convention in Miami Beach in July would be much greater if he could finish second today.

Senator Muskie's minor setback in New Hampshire when he got 46.4 per cent of the vote, along with obvious signs of physical fatigue, raised the questions whether he could compete in all of the 23 state primaries in the nation.

The seven major contestants in the 11-candidate Democratic field did not do any serious campaigning on election day, apparently feeling that the outcome had already been decided.

All of the candidates except Governor Wallace expected to remain in Miami until tomorrow, when most of them plan to head for primaries in Illinois and Wisconsin.

Governor Wallace went to Orlando, the center of right-wing Democrats and Republicans in Florida, to watch the returns.

March 15, 1972

'You Can't Believe'

ABROAD AT HOME

By ANTHONY LEWIS

CHICAGO, March 17—In a lower-middle-class suburb of Miami, two days before the Florida primary, a 60-year-old widow was explaining why she was going to vote for George Wallace. "These politicians," she said, "you can't believe 'em. You put a good man in there, and he's a crook when he comes out."

Her bitterness toward the politicians carried over from one issue to another. Asked about Vietnam, she said: "Anybody who'd end that war, I'm with him: but they're all liars." Asked what was her main reason for favoring Wallace, she said:

"He's for the poor people. The others have just lied to the old people. It's getting where a person can't live. You take someone on Social Security like me. They come in here and put in new sewers and raise taxes, but where do

we get the money? The older people are fed up with this Government."

The widow was being questioned as part of an in-depth attitudinal survey by Oliver Quayle, the polling expert. Her mood of antagonism toward politicians turned up repeatedly in two streets of modest houses. One questioner asked people what President they had really respected, and he kept getting the same answer: John F. Kennedy.

It was only a small sample, but it did show something real. For the result of the Florida Democratic primary indicated, more clearly than anything else, an anti-Government vote, a vote against the established order, a vote by frustrated people tired of politicians taking them for granted.

At a typical rally for George Wallace, the sophisticated observer looks around the crowd of angry people and sees them as life's losers, working out their resentments. Well, it turned out in Florida that there are an awful lot of Americans who feel like losers—and they are not likely to be found only in Florida.

The significant thing, politically, is that it has become respectable for people who are not racists to express their frustration by voting for George Wallace. The Alabama segregationist who once said he would never be "out-niggered" in a campaign has

succeeded in softening that old image.

Of course "forced busing" helped Wallace mightily as an issue, and most of the other Democrats played into his hands in Florida on that question. But busing is a symbol for a lot of other things that bother Americans these days: high taxes, inflation, disorder, the despoiling of our surroundings.

The challenge to the would-be Democratic nominees is to deal with those real issues as the primary campaign goes on—to offer a positive alternative to the destructive Wallace strategy. As it happens, the general choice of direction was rather well defined in two statements in Florida as the returns came in.

Senator Henry Jackson said Florida showed that the Democratic party had to get back to "the vital center, not go out into left field." The "great center of the party is angry," he said, "that the politicians won't face up to the issues: law and order and justice, busing, the security of this country."

The other view was put by Senator George McGovern. He saw the Florida vote also as an expression of discontent, and he said "I don't like the way things are either." But as an example of an issue raised, he said, "We have to recognize that there are millions of people sick and tired of a tax system that favors the rich over the ordinary people."

334

In short, the time seems to be right for a new populism. The question is whether it is going to be a populism of the left or, as it has usually turned out in this country, a populism of the right. George Wallace read the Florida returns as signaling the Democrats to become again "the party of the people," and Senator Jackson's reading was only a politer version of the move to the right.

In addition to issues, the Florida primary said something about the personalities in the Democratic party: The voters are evidently looking for fresh ones, unmarked by what is per-ceived to be the cynical taint of national office.

In those terms, hardly any of the candidates can be proud of his Florida campaign.

There was Hubert Humphrey, the great liberal, denouncing "lazy welfare chiselers" and hinting that he would protect industry against imports. There was Henry Jackson, ducking the question of his campaign contributions with a deceitful swipe at Mrs. Robert Kennedy. There was John Lindsay, using his plastic media campaign for such cheap shots as a claim that George McGovern had "voted to compromise the Bill of Rights" by supporting a mild anti-busing amendment in the Senate in order to stop worse.

It is not exactly an encouraging campaign so far for those who worry about this country's wounds. Senator Edmund Muskie was right to say, after the Wallace victory in Florida, "I still believe in the perceptibility of my fellow man." But where is the candidate who can reach the discontented Americans with a healing program?

March 18, 1972

On McGovern and Goldwater...

By CHRISTOPHER LYDON
Special to The New York Times

WASHINGTON, May 5—The assertion that Senator George McGovern is a "Goldwater of the Left" is one of the hardier clichés of the 1972 campaign, likely to persist even after its chief political advocate, Senator Henry M. Jackson, has withdrawn from active competition in the primaries. There are indeed some striking comparisons between Mr. McGovern, the insurgent Democratic candidate from South Dakota, and the Barry Goldwater of 1964, who won a deeply divisive fight for the Republican nomination but carried only six states in the election.

News Analysis

Both men came forth as party reformers—Senator Goldwater to purify Republican thinking, Mr. McGovern to reconstitute the Democratic membership and operating rules.

Each man sought to capture his party, but also, in some measure, to repudiate the party's past—Mr. Goldwater with his gibes at the Eisenhower Administration as a "dime-store New Deal," and Mr. McGovern with a nearly nine-year attack on the Vietnam war going back to its origins in the Kennedy Administration.

Engaging the most zealous workers of his party early in the race, each man overcame some of his opinion-poll handicaps through mastery of the complex business of selecting convention delegates.

Differences Also Seen

There are some equally obvious differences between the Goldwater movement and the McGovern campaign. The campaign for Mr. Goldwater's nomination had the help of friendly state and local party officials against the manifest doubts of the Republican rank and file. Mr. McGovern, on the contrary, has only scattered party support and had none until he scored significantly in popular primaries.

Mr. Goldwater entered only three major primaries in 1964 and won only one of them (California). Mr. McGovern says that he should add four more important primary victories (Nebraska, Oregon, California and New York) to the two in hand (Wisconsin and Massachusetts) on his way to the nomination.

Mr. Goldwater was a much purer ideologue who wanted primarily to reclaim the Republican party for conservatism and, according to Theodore H. White in "Chronicle of Presidential Campaigns," decided early on that he would be satisfied to come within five percentage points of his Democratic opponent, not to win the presidency.

Mr. McGovern, by contrast, is viewed by more and more observers as an ambitious pragmatist. A liberal Democrat from a conservative Republican state, he has long practiced in the art of political accommodation and seems likely to adjust his stance, not stiffen it, as the campaign wears on.

Beyond all the points of similarity or difference, the heart of the argument henceforth will be whether or not a McGovern nomination would doom the Democrats to the sort of crushing defeat that Mr. Goldwater suffered at the hands of Lyndon B. Johnson.

Analogy Decried

Thus, for obvious reasons, Mr. McGovern rebels at the entire Goldwater analogy. Mr. Goldwater recoiled at the suggestion that he was a "McGovern of the Right" but he seems to sense that history is repeating itself, inside out.

"I find the whole concept ridiculous," Mr. McGovern commented the other day. "I think I've tapped the grass-roots of this country in a way Goldwater never did. Goldwater was appealing to the most reactionary elements of his party and won in a vacuum. I always thought that if Nelson Rockefeller had moved in early and hard, he'd have taken the nomination away."

"The comparison won't stand up," Mr. Goldwater said this week in apparent agreement. The Arizona Senator still feels that his conservatism was nothing more or less than the essential Republican faith, whereas "McGovern's philosophy is entirely outside the Democratic party," he said.

"For example, his belief in a $30-billion defense cut; no radical in either party could believe in that; you'd be cutting into salaries and troop strength."

Yet Mr. Goldwater does see Mr. McGovern as his Democratic counterpart on two essential points.

First, he says, there is the power of political moralism in both campaigns: "That's what's catching on for McGovern, especially among the kids. I don't like to say it but that's what I had going for me in 1964. That's the group that got Nixon elected. They're still gung-ho."

Second, he adds, Mr. McGovern would be demolished by President Nixon in November. "No question about it," he said.

Public opinion polls, which have not been an accurate advance gauge of the McGovern strength so far, suggest some danger of Democratic defection from the McGovern ticket, but scarcely more than from tickets led by Senator Hubert H. Humphrey or Senator Edmund S. Muskie, the Democrats who have called themselves "centrists."

In the Gallup organization's straw polls against President Nixon, taken periodically on a random national sample, Mr. McGovern has been running about 15 percentage points behind the President. In April the score was 46 to 31, with 15 per cent favoring a third-party candidacy by Alabama Governor George Wallace and 8 per cent undecided.

Mr. Humphrey trailed Mr. Nixon by 11 percentage points in the latest trial heats; Mr. Muskie trailed by 10. But Mr. McGovern does not do so much worse than other Democrats, according to George Gallup Jr., to warrant comparison with Barry Goldwater in 1964.

Mr. McGovern runs at a much more pronounced disadvantage in the Louis Harris polls. In the Harris trial heats last month there was an 18 point gap between Mr. Nixon (47 per cent) and Mr. McGovern (29 per cent), compared with a 6 point spread (42 to 36) against Mr. Humphrey and an 11-point spread (44 to 33) against Mr. Muskie.

Mr. McGovern's performance in the next month or so could be crucial. Mr. Harris noted, because "only now are the American people focusing attention on George McGovern."

May 6, 1972

GUNMAN'S ATTACK CLOUDS CAMPAIGN

Uncertainty Created Both by Wallace's Status and Impact of Shooting

By MAX FRANKEL
Special to The New York Times

WASHINGTON, May 15—The bullets that felled George C. Wallace on the eve of his greatest achievements in national politics will also upset both the conduct and the calculations of the 1972 Presidential campaign.

If he could recover in time to resume some form of campaigning, and his press secretary says he will, the Alabama Governor may find an even more aroused constituency rallying to his cause. And some degree of sympathy vote may further swell his expected victories tomorrow in the Democratic primaries of Michigan and Maryland.

The Governor had 210 delegate votes of the 1,509 needed for nomination when he was struck down.

If he is forced out of the campaign, there is no one now in sight to pick up the banner of populism, tinged with an overtone of segregation, that brought the Governor 9.9 million votes, or 13.5 per cent of the total cast for President, in 1968 and seemed to promise him an equally strong following this year.

No one has ever quite agreed on whether the building Wallace candidacy this year was a bigger threat to Republicans or Democrats. President Nixon has figured that he would run better in the South without an independent Wallace challenge. The Democratic National Committee had all but decided that it could fare much better in the big industrial states of the North without a third-party Wallace challenge.

But mathematically, at least, Mr. Wallace had an even better chance this year to win 70 or 80 electoral votes and deny his major party rivals the absolute majority that is needed for a clear election by the Electoral College. All the available signs suggested that he coveted such a result and was preparing to revive his American Independent party, in many if not all states.

Regardless of the Governor's chances of recovery, his shooting has undone four years of effort and brave self-exposure by President Nixon and all those who coveted his job. From the President down, politicians had tried to pretend that the passions and the madness that struck down two Kennedys and Martin Luther King belonged to a remote and unhappy past, that the country was recovering its balance and that controversy could again be argued out in a civilized manner.

Now, yet another huge constituency of American voters has been made to feel that it cannot, after all, safely present controversial views and electric personalities to the electorate. That is how the New Frontiersmen felt when President John F. Kennedy and later his brother, Robert, were gunned down by assassins at the peak of their political promise. That is also how vast numbers of black citizens felt when Dr. King, the militant but nonviolent leader, was slain.

President Nixon, Senators Hubert H. Humphrey, George McGovern and Edmund S. Muskie and all the other candidates this year, like Mr. Wallace himself, had taken enormous chances since then to expose themselves once more to the crowds at airports and in shopping centers to help the country regain its pride and confidence in orderly political competition. They were heavily protected, but they knew that there really was no protection against the enraged act of a suicidal assailant.

President Nixon's first instinct, to revive security protection for Senator Edward M. Kennedy, symbolized the first reaction everywhere in Washington that the violence of the nineteen-sixties was not over. It also dramatized the fear of Senator Kennedy and many members of his family that whatever other calculations he might make, he ought not to tempt fate by exposing himself to a national campaign.

It was thought here that Mr. Kennedy would almost certainly be confirmed in his decision not to seek the Presidency this year, no matter how great the pressures that were building up.

Mr. Wallace was widely expected to win strong pluralities in the primary contests tomorrow for 132 convention delegates in Michigan and 53 delegates in Maryland. But his indicated success—in a Northern industrial state where school busing has been a particularly intense issue, and in a border state that gave him 42 per cent of the Democratic vote eight years ago—also promised to be the peak of his showing inside the party.

In all, he had won 210 delegates to the Democratic convention and stood to gain fewer than 100 more. Since even some of the delegates required to vote for the Governor have been eager to bolt to another candidate, it seemed impossible that he would even come near to the 1,509 votes needed for nomination and increasingly likely that he would organize a third-party challenge.

In the race for the nomination, the delegates formally pledged to Mr. Wallace, if released, were expected to move in almost equal numbers to Mr. Humphrey and Mr. McGovern.

In the general election, Mr. Wallace appeared to have a dual power: first, to gather the electoral votes of six or seven Southern states with which to bargain in case neither President Nixon nor his Democratic rival obtained a majority in the Electoral College; and second, to draw enough votes from the Republicans in such states as Texas or Florida or from the Democrats in such states as New Jersey and Michigan to confound the results.

Gun Loe Defeated

A further consequence of today's shooting is bound to be yet another effort to write stringent Federal laws against the indiscriminate sale of guns. Many of the voters who passionately resisted such legislation were in Mr. Wallace's constituency and President Nixon, fearful of those votes, has long resisted the pressure for gun registration and limitation from urban communities.

Paradoxically, Governor Wallace was struck in a state that only two years ago defeated the re-election bid of Senator Joseph D. Tydings, a Democrat who had aroused the ire of the groups opposing gun control.

The Johnson Administration tried to write tough gun controls after the King and Robert Kennedy assassinations in 1968, but the final version left huge loopholes leading to vastly increased imports of foreign gun components. Mr. Wallace has favored tougher penalties for criminals toting firearms, but he has been sympathetic to the demand that law-abiding citizens be spared from all restrictions or inconveniences in the acquisition of weapons and ammunition.

How the Secret Service and the Federal Bureau of Investigation will react to the shooting was not yet evident tonight, but they will almost certainly reimpose severe limitations on the conduct of the President and his challengers in uncontrollable environments. Mr. Nixon had gone so far as to defy unruly crowds in 1970 by exposing himself to their taunts to demonstrate that politicians were free to face their people people again.

May 16, 1972

Democratic Convention Reform: More Blacks, Women and Youth

By R. W. APPLE Jr.
Special to The New York Times

WASHINGTON, June 2—A study of the first one-third of the delegates chosen for the Democratic National Convention shows that the proportion of women is running at three times the level set in 1968, that the proportion of blacks is nearly double and that of other minorities is higher.

But the study also indicates that the convention's make-up as a whole will fall short of the reform guidelines established by the party.

These data emerge from a New York Times computer analysis of the first 1,034 delegates selected in 21 states and the District of Columbia. There will be 3,016 delegates at Miami Beach when the convention opens July 10.

The survey documents earlier indications that the group will be unlike any before, with more blacks, women, youth and Chicanos. But it also shows that the delegate selections are falling below the guidelines, which require that groups be represented in rough proportion to their share of the population.

The guidelines were framed by a commission headed during its most active period by Senator George McGovern.

Following are some of the principal findings:

¶Of the 1,034 delegates, 358, or 34.6 per cent, are women—almost three times the total in 1968, when 13 per cent of the delegates were women. Roughly 51 per cent of the total population is female, according to the Census Bureau. The National Women's Political Caucus has filed challenges in some states where the percentage is unusually low.

¶139 of the 1,034, or 13.4 per cent are black—more than double the 1968 total of about 5 per cent. According to data assembled by the Joint Center for Political Studies, 9.2 per cent of the national voting-age population is black, so in this category the guidelines are being exceeded. But the Congressional Black Caucus has asked that 20 per cent of the delegates be black, on the assumption that blacks provide that percentage of the Democrats' vote.

There are nine Chicanos, three Puerto Ricans and four American Indians among the delegates.

¶123 of the 1,034, or 11.9 per cent, identified themselves as members of labor unions, 57 of whom are committed to Senator Hubert H. Humphrey. National union leaders have predicted that they will have between 350 and 500 delegates. If their present pace continues, they will meet their goal with about 370.

¶239 of the 1,034, or 23.1 per cent, are 30 years of age or under. Of the voting-age population nationally, about 31 per cent are between the ages of 18 and 30. No exact figure

is available for youth representation in 1968, but in a number of state delegations, no one was under 30 years old.

¶Only 111 of the 1,034, or 10.74 per cent, attended the 1966 convention, and of those, many are members of the Chicago organization of Mayor Richard J. Daley. Without the 22 Daley stalwarts who served as delegates four years ago, the percentage of veterans would dwindle to 8.6. In any event, the number of repeaters is astonishingly small and bodes ill for those who are relying on old alliances.

¶Only 357 of the 1,034 — 34.5 per cent, just over a third — hold any party or governmental office or formerly held

one. Again, the Daley contingent inflates the figure, but it is still far below past years.

Minnesota's is the best balanced delegation, with 49 per cent women, 20 per cent youth, 19.6 per cent black (though the state is only 3 per cent black) and two Indians and one Chicano. Arizona is the best on youth.

Illinois, over all, is the worst again reflecting the Daley influence. The Mayor's slates are currently being challenged before a hearing examiner because, among other things, they fall so far short of the guidelines in almost every category.

The backers of Mr. McGovern—the front-runner and the man most responsible for the

reform rules—come closest to meeting the guidelines.

For example, he has 111 young people to 25 for Mr. Humphrey and 147 women to 53 for Mr. Humphrey. The Minnesotan has proportionately the most blacks, however, reflecting his electoral strength in black neighborhoods. Mr. Humphrey and Mr. McGovern both have 29 pledged black delegates, but Mr. Humphrey's total is smaller, so his black share is larger.

Gov. George C. Wallace of Alabama has only 10 black delegates pledged to him in the states covered by the preliminary computer analysis.

June 3, 1972

McGovern's Route to the Top

By CHRISTOPHER LYDON
Special to The New York Times

WASHINGTON, June 10—"I honestly don't think there has been a major surprise in the last two years," said Gary Hart, the 34-year-old manager of Senator George McGovern's Presidential campaign, speaking calmly of a revolution in Democratic party politics that caught almost everyone else unawares.

He suffered one dark moment last January, Mr. Hart confessed. Watching the virtual parade of Democratic leaders to endorse Senator Edmund S. Muskie, he had looked ahead to the first primary and pictured himself and Joe Grandmaison, his New Hampshire coordinator, standing alone on a street corner passing out leaflets as the candidate drove his own car around to the state's college campuses.

But depression passed quickly, and only three days after Mr. McGovern's remarkably strong second-place showing in the March 7 New Hampshire primary, Mr. Hart finished a reconnaissance of Florida and declared unemotionally: "It's all over. Ed Muskie has got to get off the ground here and he isn't doing it. John Lindsay has got to get off the ground and he isn't doing it either. That means the race through the rest of the primaries is going to be us against Hubert Humphrey, and that means we're going to win."

George McGovern's candidacy was still being widely discounted three months ago when the feeling of anticlimax settled on Mr. Hart. Even now the blossoming of George Mc-

Govern—a baldish, former minister and rural radical who campaigned for a full year without exceeding 5 per cent in the Democratic preference polls and is now on the verge of winning the nomination—is generally considered mysterious. How did he do it?

Some of the critical elements in the emergence of this onetime 500-to-1 long shot were beyond his control, including the acceleration of the war in Vietnam at the culmination of his all-important drive in Wisconsin; the heavy damage that Gov. George C. Wallace of Alabama inflicted on the Democratic establishment, and Senator Humphrey's inroads against Senator Muskie.

But George McGovern, who suspects that but for his own hesitation in 1967 he might be President today, had decided, at all events, to be prepared for opportunity this year. And he was.

The most obvious of the ironies about Mr. McGovern's unheralded triumph is that the candidate and his staff predicted almost all of it—early, often and in detail. It is also striking that the same professionals who laughingly dismissed his chances last winter say now that it has been a triumph of basic political skills—the political equivalent of the late Vince Lombardi's "back-to-fundamentals" football.

'Went After Delegates'

"McGovern understood something that Muskie and Humphrey didn't: that the way you win conventions is to win delegates," says Joseph Napolitan, the political consultant and author. "He went after delegates in the nonprimary states. In addition to grass-roots organization, he had the best commercials on television—and

more of them. He mastered the mechanics."

The premises that Gary Hart outlined to disbelieving newsmen last summer, where Senator Muskie was widely thought to be unbeatable for the Democratic nomination, proved sound and relevant.

"Jack English can talk to county chairmen till hell freezes over," Mr. Hart said of Mr. Muskie's chief delegate scout. "But Big Ed isn't going to excite those housewives and those students who spend nights and days organizing their neighborhoods. That's what wins primaries."

The main lines of the McGovern strategy were agreed upon at a meeting at the Senator's Maryland farm on July 25, 1970, and they were never significantly changed.

Announced Early

Unlike Senator Humphrey, who planned originally to enter the race late, after his opponents had destroyed each other in the early primaries, Mr. McGovern knew he had to start early, and announced formally on Jan. 18, 1971. A single winner would emerge from the primaries, he thought, and the real meaning of party reform, in which he had played a large part, was that the man with the best primary score could not be denied the nomination.

Primaries would be won by grass-roots organization, he and his staff decided, not by familiarity and the endorsements of local officeholders and party officials, as Senator Muskie's managers seemed to expect, nor by television, as Mayor Lindsay planned.

"Ours would have to be the best organization in the field," Mr. Hart said, and its power should be decentralized — outside Washington and outside the capitals of each of the key primary states.

The vital primaries, they decided two years ahead of time,

would be in New Hampshire, Wisconsin, Massachusetts, Nebraska, Oregon, California and New York — Ohio would be added later, and Oregon subtracted—but not Florida, where Mayor Lindsay gambled almost all to win only 7 per cent of the vote.

Unlike Senator Fred R. Harris of Oklahoma, who announced a populist candidacy but relied heavily on Wall Street backing, Senator McGovern saw that a people's campaign would have to find popular financing. More than two-thirds of his first $1-million was solicited through the mail; the average mail contribution was under $20.

And unlike Senator Harold E. Hughes of Iowa, who called off an undeclared candidacy in July, 1971, the McGovern campaign sensed that obscure Senators from small states had to move early and be prepared for months of adversity. There would be no way to judge progress, Mr. McGovern believed, and similarly no reason to give up, until the public had had a chance to express itself in the primaries.

More important than anything else, friends and rivals all now agree, he embraced two general feelings, both larger than what is commonly meant by "issues"—a revulsion against the war in Vietnam and a vaguer longing for what he called "fundamental change." They were to attract volunteers and later voters beyond his most hopeful plans.

Shunned One Issue

An opponent of the war as early as September 1963, he wearied of his reputation as a "one-issue candidate," and doubted publicly at times that the war would be an issue in 1972. Last August he announced that he would not talk of the war any more, and asked newsmen to give attention to his economic ideas.

But the electric response of audiences around the country kept confirming the special passion about Vietnam, and by September he was off again on a publicized trip to Saigon.

Senator Harris calls Mr. McGovern's "the best organization of individual workers in the history of Presidential politics."

"We have never seen a general election campaign like this one will be—that even approached a smidgin of this organizational work," he said. But "the ability to implement the method flows from the substance," Mr. Harris said yesterday, meaning Senator McGovern's "unassailable position against the war."

Mr. McGovern's specific ideas under the heading of "change" have tended to embarrass him. His proposal for a $32-billion defense cut by 1975, largely ignored when he issued it in January, evidently cost him votes when Senator Humphrey hammered at its impact on jobs and security in the California primary.

He is now discounting, if not actually changing, his ambitious assault on tax loopholes; his staff is also redrafting the $1,000-per-person welfare substitute that was the heart of his plan for the "redistribution of income."

At the same time, his association with a change, translated in mid-March into an assertion that he was as "fed up" as anyone in America with the drift of affairs, helped him touch many varieties of unhappiness, including the anger of George Wallace's supporters.

Just as conveniently, the strength of his identification with change and against the war covered a multitude of omissions and inconsistencies on concrete issues, including most notably the matter of school busing for racial integration.

Early in the primary season he dismissed busing as "number 92" on his list of issues; at other times he endorsed busing. But during the Michigan primary in May, he hoped publicly that the courts would reconsider and reject the cross-busing of children between core cities and their suburbs.

He has also sought to dampen earlier impressions that he supported the legalization of marijuana and liberalized abortion laws, but he does not seem to have suffered yet from charges of opportunism or inconsistency.

"Muskie's problem was that

he was clearly seen as a guy with vague positions," says a bemused professional. "McGovern has been vaguely seen as a guy with clear positions."

Insiders were fooled about Mr. McGovern's progress as well as outsiders. Richard Leone, a Princeton political scientist, signed on in 1969 as Mr. McGovern's national political director, and helped target New Hampshire and Wisconsin as the key primaries. But he quit in January, 1970, and two years later joined Senator Muskie as, he said, "the only one who could put it together."

"Everybody said Ed Muskie was the obvious 'acceptable' candidate, someone a divided country could live with," Mr. Leone observed this weekend. "Basically, what we found was that people didn't want somebody acceptable; they wanted an alternative. McGovern and Wallace were the only ones.

"George McGovern became the candidate of circumstance, noticed: first he was a more but suddenly two things were substantial candidate—a better campaigner, thinker, speaker, organizer — than people had thought he was; and second, when opportunity knocked he had the structure all ready."

A critical element in Mr. McGovern's planning, Mr. Leone suspects, was his memory of rejecting the invitation, later grasped by Eugene J. McCarthy, to run against President Johnson in 1968.

"The one thing he was not going to do in 1972 was to wake up some day and say, 'If only I had stayed with it I might have been the nominee,'" Mr. Leone commented. "The genius of the McGovern campaign was understanding the 'you never know' factor in Presidential politics. It was not that they knew the scenario was going to work; just the opposite, they knew it was a long shot but they were going to be prepared."

Ohio was an extreme example of McGovern preparedness and of the daring and dedication it required. The basic planning, the recruitment of Robert McAlister, a young political lawyer, as state chairman, and the mapping of county officers was done on Memorial Day weekend in the spring of 1971.

It was, if anything, even more presumptuous for the national campaign staff to order an exhausting statewide signature drive to nominate delegate slates in January, 1972. Mere survival of the campaign to the Ohio primary in May seemed unlikely at that point, and if perchance the campaign continued, Ohio was almost certainly too big and expensive a state, too much under the control of organized labor, to risk a serious McGovern effort.

Reversed Decision

Mr. McAlister filed delegate slates in 22 of Ohio's 23 Congressional districts anyway. From October on, a young organizer named Gayle Channing had been working 18 hours a day perfecting a reserve organization.

On the weekend after the Senator's April 4 victory in the Wisconsin primary, Washington headquarters decided that there would be virtually no Ohio campaign; but on the following Tuesday, April 11, with only three weeks to go, Mr. McAlister won a reversal—a commitment of $200,000 and at least six days of the candidate's time. Virtually overnight, the reserves were mobilized and 53 offices around the state were humming.

Mr. McGovern's near-tie in Ohio was a body blow to Hubert Humphrey's claim of industrial support, the beginning of the end of the campaign. In Ohio and elsewhere Mr. Humphrey complained that George McGovern had a year's head start on him, but he got little sympathy.

"Hell," said Mr. Napolitan, who had managed the Humphrey media in 1968, "Hubert knew when the election was."

Mr. McGovern's immovable standing around 5 per cent in the Democratic preference polls through 1971—and he actually dipped to 3 per cent in one national poll during January, 1972 —would have crippled most candidates financially. But the Senator had organized direct-mail appeals—common among conservatives, but almost unprecedented on this scale among liberal Democrats. That was producing $25,000 a week even in the darkest days of last December.

The money situation was chronically desperate, as in al-

most all campaigns, but it never threatening. In addition to the steady mail flow, now averaging $40,000 a day, a handful of rich men had sworn that the campaign would not sink for lack of funds.

Max Palevsky, who sold electronics concern to the Corporation for close to $100 million, gave more than $300,000 to the McGovern campaign. Henry Kimelman, a merchant and developer in the Virgin Islands, gave substantially, raised more and lent the campaign another $200,000 at the start of the Wisconsin effort in mid-March.

The other key to financial survival was economy of operations. Henry Kimelman likes to note that Robert F. Kennedy spent over $8-million in a campaign that lasted two and one-half months in 1968, the same year that Eugene McCarthy spent $11-million.

The two-year McGovern campaign, still operating out of a tiny hive of offices on Capitol Hill—4,000 square feet at $1,200 a month—will have cost less than $6-million through the Miami Beach convention.

The more striking economy, in contrast with those of this year's Democratic rivals, was the low cost for each delegate won—something under $4,000. The sweep of California's 271 delegates this week cost around $7,000 for each convention vote; but in the nonprimary states, grass-roots activity was getting delegates at less than $50 apiece.

Victory, says Frank Mankiewicz, the chief strategist, will not necessarily prove that he and others knew what they were doing but that "we knew the only way it could be done."

"Our scenario worked because other things broke right —mainly the weakness of other candidates, Muskie's lack of organization, the fact that Humphrey and Muskie were competing for the same constituency, and a lean one at that; the fact that John Lindsay turned out to be a 1968 charisma candidate."

But had Mr. Mankiewicz believed from the start—which was, for him, the spring of 1971 —that the McGovern effort would win?

"Oh, yeah!" he purred.

June 11, 1972

DEMOCRATIC RAID TIED TO REALTOR

Alleged Leader Said to Have G.O.P. Links and to Have Aided C.I.A. on Cuba

By TAD SZULC

Special to The New York Times

WASHINGTON, June 18—The apparent leader of five men

arrested yesterday for breaking into the headquarters of the Democratic National Committee here was identified today as an affluent Miami real estate man with important Republican party links in Florida.

He was also said to have been one of the top planners of the Central Intelligence Agency's abortive invasion of Cuba in 1961.

Five men were arrested at gunpoint in the raid. The police said that they possessed

sophisticated eavesdropping devices and photographic equipment.

The five alleged raiders are being held at the District of Columbia jail. Private and official sources who know the five suspects and their background said that the leader was Cuban-born Bernard L. Barker, who, under the code name of "Macho," acted for the C.I.A. in planning the Bay of Pigs operation.

One of the other men arrested

is James W. McCord, a former employe of the C.I.A. who is currently employed as a security agent by both the Republican National Committee and the Committee for the Re-Election of the President.

The police said that file drawers in the committee headquarters had been opened and that ceiling panels near the office of the committee chairman, Lawrence F. O'Brien, had **been** removed. Presumably, it would have been possible to place the eavesdropping equipment behind the panels and to

338

photograph the contents of the files.

Neither the police nor the committee could cite any motive for the 2 A.M. raid. Nor could they say what kind of confidential information could be obtained by bugging the headquarters or rifling the files.

Calls for Investigation

The suspects were caught after the police had been summoned by a building guard. Mr. O'Brien called today for a thorough investigation by the Federal Bureau of Investigation.

At the time of his arrest, Mr. Barker gave his address as 955 First Street Southwest, Miami. That is the office of Miguel R. Suarez, a Cuban exile lawyer prominent in Republican politics in Florida.

Mr. Barker is president of Barker Associates, Inc., a real estate company. That address is 2301 Northwest Seventh Street, Miami. But he is also Mr. Suarez's partner in a separate venture.

The C.I.A. dissociated itself from all aspects of the pre-dawn raid. However, the agency did identify Mr. McCord as a former employe who resigned in August, 1970.

John N. Mitchell, former Attorney General and now chairman of the Committee to Re-Elect the President, said in a statement that Mr. McCord "is the proprietor of a private security agency who was employed by our committee months ago to assist with the installation of our security system."

"He has, as we understand it, a number of business clients and interests, and we have no knowledge of those relationships," Mr. Mitchell said.

"We want to emphasize that this man and the other people involved were not operating either on our behalf or with our consent. I am surprised and dismayed at these reports.

"There is no place in our campaign or in the electoral process for this type of activity, and we will not permit or condone it."

Dole Deplores Action

Senator Robert Dole of Kansas, chairman of the Republican National Committee, issued a statement saying that Mr. McCord's actions "were not on our behalf nor with our consent."

"We deplore actions of this kind in or out of politics," he said.

A reconstruction of the backgrounds of those allegedly involved in the raid on the Democratic headquarters suggested that all at different times had had links with the C.I.A. and anti-Cuban operations.

The most prominent among them appeared to be Mr. Barker. According to Miami sources, politically active during the Bay of Pigs period, Mr. Barker was one of the principal links be-

ARRESTED AT GUNPOINT: Men allegedly caught in office in Washington police photos. From left: James W. McCord, Bernard L. Barker, Eugenio R. Martinez, Frank Sturgis and Virgilio R. Gonzales. Mr. McCord is from New York and the others are from Miami.

tween the C.I.A. headquarters and the Cuban exile army during the pre-invasion period.

Mr. Barker was said to have a role in establishing the secret invasion bases in Guatemala and Nicaragua and to have served as one of the conduits for C.I.A. money to the exile army.

Mr. Barker, now a United States citizen, is closely associated with Capt. Manuel Artime Buesa, the military leader of the invasion. Captain Artime, who now lives in Miami, is reported to have business connections with prominent Cuban exiles in Miami who in turn have links with the Republican party.

According to his acquaintances, Mr. Barker started a real estate venture four years ago, specializing in the sale of lots. Later, he entered into association with Mr. Suarez, who heads a law firm in Miami, for the sale of condominium apartments.

Their condominium company is situated in Mr. Suarez's offices whose address Mr. Barker gave the Washington police when he was arrested.

Not Linked to Raid

Mr. Suarez represented the Cuban community in Florida in dealings with Claude R. Kirk Jr., the former Republican Governor of the state. Mr. Suarez said in a recent article in a Cuban magazine published in Miami that he was a "Nixonian."

There was no evidence to indicate that Mr. Suarez or Captain Artime was in any way connected with the Washington raid.

As for Mr. McCord, he had played, according to his former associates, a relatively minor technical role in the preparations for the Bay of Pigs. He joined the C.I.A. in 1951.

The third alleged raider, Frank Sturgis—also known as Frank Fiorini—was reported to have been involved in the Bay of Pigs preparations in an active manner but in a lesser capacity than Mr. Barker.

He is an American and a former Marine.

The two other alleged mem-

bers of the raiding party—Eugenio R. Martinez and Virgilio R. Gonzales, both of Miami—were also reported to have been active in anti-Cuban movements.

Mr. Martinez is a real estate agent and a Florida notary public. Mr. Gonzales is a locksmith.

Miami sources said that the suspected raiders, except for Mr. McCord, arrived here from Miami on Friday and checked in at the elegant Watergate Hotel. The Democratic headquarters are housed in an office building in the Watergate complex on Washington's Virginia Avenue overlooking the Potomac.

Persons in Miami familiar with the backgrounds of the five could offer no explanation for their involvement in the apparent attempt to install listening and transmitting devices in the Democratic offices and to photograph files.

Telephone interviews with Cuban leaders in Miami produced expressions of concern that the raid might reflect adversely on the standing of the large Cuban community in Florida.

The more affluent members of that community are supporters of Mr. Nixon's re-election, but they are split into at least two pro-Republican groups.

In Washington, Manuel R. Giberga, the Cuban-American coordinator of the Republican National Committee, could not be reached for comment.

Following Mr. Mitchell's statement, Mr. O'Brien urged Richard G. Kleindienst, the Attorney General, to order a thorough investigation by the F.B.I.

He said that only "the most searching professional investigation can determine to what extent, if any, the Committee for the Re-Election of the President is involved in this attempt to spy on Democratic headquarters."

"No mere statements of innocence by Mr. Nixon's campaign manager will dispel these questions," he said. Mr. O'Brien added that the investigation should continue "until we know beyond a doubt what organization or individuals were behind

this incredible act of political espionage."

Mr. McCord was held in $30,000 bail and the four others in $50,000 bail.

The police said that the Saturday raid was the third incident to occur at the Democratic headquarters. On May 28, an attempt was made to unscrew a lock on the office's door. On June 7, $100 in cash and checks was stolen after the office was broken into during the night.

According to the police, the four alleged raiders from Miami registered at the Watergate Hotel under fictitious names and occupied two rooms. They dined at the hotel restaurant.

Tape On Lock

The five men were arrested at 2:30 A.M., about 40 minutes after a building security guard observed that a tape had been placed on a door connecting a stairwell with the hotel basement to prevent its being locked.

The guard removed the tape, but he found more tape on the same door 10 minutes later. He called the police and the officers found that every door from the stairway to the hallway had been taped.

On the sixth floor, where the committee has its offices, the police discovered that the door had been jimmied.

The five suspects were then found in one of the inner offices. They had burglary kits and electronic equipment, the police said.

In court, they were charged with felonious burglary and possession of implements of crime.

Representing Mr. Barker at the arraignment yesterday was Douglas Caddy, a Washington lawyer. Mr. Caddy, who said that Mr. Barker's wife had called him after the arrest, told newsmen that he had first met the Miami realtor at cocktails at the Army-Navy Club in Washington about a year ago. He did not say who had introduced them.

June 19, 1972

Panel Denies Convention Seats to 59 Daley Delegates

Their Places Awarded to a Slate Dominated by McGovern Backers

By WARREN WEAVER Jr.
Special to The New York Times

WASHINGTON, June 30 — Mayor Richard J. Daley and 58 other Chicago delegates to the Democratic National Convention lost their seats tonight as a result of a fiercely debated decision by the convention's Credentials Committee.

By a vote of 71 to 61, the committee awarded the places to a slate of challengers dominated by backers of Senator George McGovern. The new Chicago delegation was chosen, in part, because it is much more representative of women, blacks, Latin Americans and young people than was its predecessor.

The startling decision — no one could recall a Democratic leader of comparable power being turned away from a convention with all his followers— is subject to being overturned in two forums within the next 10 days.

The move was all the more dramatic because Mayor Daley has become a symbol of the tumultuous Chicago convention of 1968. That convention led to the party reforms that in turn led tonight to Mr. Daley's repudiation, at least temporarily.

In Chicago, Mr. Daley called the vote "a great disservice to the Democratic party" and said that it had the effect of "disenfranchising over 900,000 voters who elected the Illinois delegates."

In a brief statement, he said that he would continue to fight for party principles but made no mention of an appeal.

Daley attorneys threatened to renew their argument in the United States Court of Appeals that the reform guidelines on which the Chicago slate's rejection was based were unconstitutional. On the basis of earlier arguments there, a favorable decision for the Mayor is within the realm of possibility.

In any event, the convention will have the last say as to who represents Chicago at Miami Beach.

One of the major arguments against the Daley delegation was summed up by Matthew J. Troy Jr., a New York McGovern backer, who told the committee, "Either we're going to be a party with rules for

The New York Times

AT CREDENTIALS COMMITTEE SESSION: Jo Chapman, a Wallace supporter from Michigan, with Stanley Bregman, a Humphrey backer, and Billy Joe Camp, press secretary to Governor Wallace, before the debate on Mayor Richard J. Daley's Chicago group.

everyone or a party with rules for everyone but Richard J. Daley."

The Mayor and his leaders had been accused of breaking the reform guidelines in a number of areas besides delegate balance, notably in holding closed nominating sessions for favored delegate candidates and then improperly promoting their election over the competition.

The heart of the opposition to Mayor Daley in tonight's committee vote came from the McGovern - oriented members joined by a few backers of Senators Hubert H. Humphrey and Edmund S. Muskie. In addition, seven members who had been anti-McGovern at one time or another abstained on the vote, this lending a measure of help to unseating the Chicago regulars.

Make-up in Doubt

The political composition of the new Chicago delegation remained in some doubt, but its sponsors said that it included more than 40 declared McGovern supporters and a dozen or more uncommitted members, with traces of support for Senator Muskie and Eugene J. McCarthy.

The committee's action up-

held a strongly worded report by its hearing officer, Cecil Poole, a black lawyer from California, who found that the Democratic party of Illinois had no publicly available rules for selection of delegates and thus gave people outside the organization little chance to participate.

Mr. Poole also found that blacks, Latin Americans, women and young people were "grossly under-represented" in the Daley delegation "in disregard of the clear purpose" of the party's new reform guidelines that are designed to open up its deliberations to those previously excluded.

3d Group Unseated

The Daley delegation was the third Illinois group unseated by the Credentials Committee today as supporters of Senator McGovern went back on the offensive after their California defeat of yesterday.

The McGovern forces reasserted their control of the committee on the first Illinois case, winning a 70-to-65 decision that completely reshaped delegations from four downstate Congressional districts and gave the South Dakota Senator seven more convention votes.

Taken together, the 26 original delegates from the 17th, 19th, 22d and 23d Districts included only two women, one person under 30 years old and

one black. The party's reform guidelines call for a representation of these groups in rough proportion to their share of the state's population.

In addition, party leaders in all four districts were accused of nominating delegate candidates at closed, controlled meetings and then bringing about their election, again in violation of the guidelines.

The plan that the committee adopted for the four districts proportionally reflects the relative primary vote given the candidates in all of them taken together. As a result, the Muskie delegate vote dropped from 17 to 12.5 and the uncommitted vote from 8 to 5.5, while the McGovern vote rose from 1 to 8.

At the same time, under a complicated realignment and allocation of split votes, none of the challenged delegates was deprived of going to Miami, and women, blacks and young people were added to the group to give it balance.

Chosen by the People

Counsel for the challenged delegates argued that they should retain their seats, independent of the guidelines, because they had been chosen by the people.

"I don't believe you have the right," John R. Riley, an attorney for the regular delegates, told the committee, "to tell the voters of Illinois that people they selected are not acceptable to you. These challengers are asking that you throw out the winners and replace them with losers."

Claude Holman, the Chicago Alderman who is Mayor Daley's chief spokesman on the committee, argued that the

challengers were hindering Democratic unity against President Nixon by introducing "dissension, disorganization and venom" into the convention and its preliminaries.

2d Illinois Case

In the second Illinois case, the committee voted, 76 to 63, to seat two women challengers and one additional woman in the Sixth Congressional Dis-

trict, which includes Oak Park in the Chicago suburbs. Disqualified in the process were three regular organization delegates who had won the election.

There was no immediately discernible gain for any Presidential candidate, as all persons involved were listed as uncommitted.

This challenge also hinged on

underrepresentation of women—there were none among the six delegates elected in the district, although seven had run—and on charges that the local party organization had arranged for the nomination and privately promoted the election of its own slate, discouraging all competition.

July 1, 1972

M'GOVERN NOMINATED ON THE FIRST BALLOT

A STUNNING SWEEP

Senator Seeks Unity—Wallace Rules Out Third-Party Race

By MAX FRANKEL
Special to The New York Times

MIAMI BEACH, Thursday, July 13—George Stanley McGovern was proclaimed the Democrats' candidate for President here early this morning to complete a stunning sweep of the party's processes and national convention.

Without suspense, but with many raw wounds of battle, the convention registered on a single ballot the victory that was sealed in a tense credentials battle 48 hours earlier.

Inexorably, to triumphant cheers, the Senator from South Dakota, who had defied the polls, the odds and the established techniques and the established power centers of his party, cashed in his three years of dazzling organization effort.

One week before his 50th birthday, and barely three months after he first vaulted to prominence in the grass-roots primaries, Mr. McGovern claimed the prize of a reformed, restructured but also partly resentful convention. He also won the platform he had sought and gave to the party's many skeptics and holdouts a promise of conciliation and unity by November for the expected race against President Nixon.

At the moment of victory, he learned that Senator Edward M. Kennedy of Massachusetts was firm in his refusal to run

for Vice President and that Gov. George C. Wallace of Alabama had firmly decided to stay out of the Presidential race this year.

The formal tally at the end of the first ballot gave Mr. McGovern 1,715.35 votes, comfortably beyond the 1,509 needed for nomination. The hall exploded with joy when the decisive ballots were cast by the bitterly disputed Illinois delegation.

TV Set Proves Balky

Mr. McGovern was fiddling with a balky television set in his hotel suite and barely got back to his chair before the moment of climax. His staff burst out with applause but he merely smiled, remarked that it was a long-awaited moment and retreated to take a telephone call from his stoutest rival, Senator Hubert H. Humphrey of Minnesota.

Mr. McGovern also received a congratulatory call from Senator Kennedy at Hyannisport, Mass., during which he formally asked the bearer of a famous name to join him as his running mate. The nominee later announced that Mr. Kennedy declined for "very personal reasons."

Expressing regret, Mr. McGovern said that he fully understood because the Kennedy family "has already made great sacrifices to the nation." He asked Mr. Kennedy to play an unspecified role in the campaign and Mr. Kennedy agreed to consider it.

Mr. McGovern also asked Mr. Kennedy, Mr. Humphrey and Senator Edmund S. Muskie of Maine to suggest possible running mates to him by later today.

Mrs. McGovern, in a front-row box in the convention hall said merely, "It's unbelievable, really—I feel a little bit of anxiety, too — it means a great

change in our lives."

Four other names were placed in nomination. They were the favorite sons—and one daughter—not of states or regions, as in past conventions, but of ideological segments of Democrats everywhere that were unreconciled to the McGovern candidacy, the McGovern approach to both foreign and domestic issues, the McGovern habit of circumventing old-line party regulars and the McGovern following of the young and other outsiders clamoring for a share of power.

Governor Wallace was proposed as the starkest alternative, with a demonstrated appeal as an independent in 1968 and in the primaries this year.

Wallace Pledge Reported

Mr. Wallace won the convention vote of Dolph Briscoe, the leader of the delegation from Texas and candidate for Governor there, with the explicit promise, Mr. Briscoe said, that he would not conduct an independent campaign for the White House this fall.

The man who nominated Mr. Wallace said that he was under instructions to relay that pledge to the convention, but forgot to do so.

Senator Henry M. Jackson of Washington was put forward as the clearest ideological opponent, with the diehard support of big labor, big industry and others committed to a militant defense posture.

Terry Sanford, the president of Duke University and former Governor of North Carolina, let his name stand part-way through the balloting as a symbol of Southern moderates who fear that Mr. McGovern will cost the Democrats further losses throughout their region.

Representative Shirley Chisholm of Brooklyn became the first black woman ever offered to a major convention—as the bearer of the hopes of both women and blacks who resent being taken for granted by liberal political movements.

Before switches distorted the

result, the first - ballot totals read as follows:

McGovern	1,715.35
Jackson	534.50
Wallace	385.70
Chisholm	151.95
Sanford	77.50

In addition, there were 66.70 votes for Mr. Humphrey, 33.80 for Representative Wilbur D. Mills of Arkansas, 24.30 for Senator Muskie, 12.70 for Senator Kennedy, 5 for Representative Wayne L. Hays of Ohio; 2 for Senator Eugene J. McCarthy of Minnesota, 1 for Senator Walter F. Mondale of Minnesota, and 1 for former Attorney General Ramsey Clark. There were 5 votes abstaining from the total vote of 3,016.

After switches, Mr. McGovern's total, as announced by the rostrum, stood at 1,864.65. There was no move to make it unanimous.

Mr. Mills, the chairman of the House Ways and Means Committee, withdrew his name in the closing hours, following the example of Mr. McGovern's principal rivals, Senators Humphrey and Muskie, the 1968 standard-bearers.

Mr. Mills said that he would be glad to talk about the Vice Presidency, if asked, but the word from McGovern headquarters was that the candidate would prefer someone more in his ideological "ball park."

Mr. McGovern had come to regard Senator Kennedy as the man who could most quickly help unite the party and as probably the only one who could measurably enhance the prospects of election in November.

Shriver Is Mentioned

Right through the nominating session, the McGovern forces were still juggling any alternative names. Sargent Shriver, the former director of the Peace Corps and anti-poverty program and a brother-in-law of Mr. Kennedy, was said now to have been added to the list. So were Gov. Reuben Askew of Florida, the keynoter of this convention, who again declined interest, and Senator Thomas F. Eagleton, a liberal Roman Catholic from Missouri.

341

But Mr. McGovern's private thoughts were unknown to anyone. He held himself in seclusion yesterday after breakfast with five troubled Southern Governors and yet another clarification of his Vietnam peace plan for equally troubled supporters on his left flank.

Forecasts of Defeat

Even before the formality of nomination, the pressures of candidacy — indeed, pressures commensurate with those felt in the Presidency—bore in on Mr. McGovern's entourage.

Senator Jackson was voicing the conviction of many party regulars that Mr. McGovern was destined for defeat and the warning that he would drag down members of Congress and other officeholders.

I. W. Abel, president of the United Steelworkers of America, joined George Meany, president of the American Federation of Labor and Congress of Industrial Organizations, and other big labor leaders by wondering whether Mr. McGovern's followers were seeking "to deliberately lose."

The exclusion of Mayor Richard J. Daley of Chicago from this convention, under the McGovern reforms, still rankled in many quarters, some of them in the McGovern camp. And the passionate proponents of stronger promises on defense policy, on abortion, on the rights of homosexuals and other issues were raising fears of betrayal as the McGovern forces tried to move toward the center of the party they had seized.

The South Dakotan's answer was given, in effect, in the nominating speech of Senator Abraham A. Ribicoff of Connecticut—indeed, in the very choice of Mr. Ribicoff to be the principal proposer.

Sen. McGovern telephoned Governor Wallace and urged him to attend the convention's closing ceremony tonight. An aide to the Senator said that Mr. Wallace had replied that he would participate in the traditional unity ceremony if his doctor would permit him.

Mr. Ribicoff said that he spoke for "the finest political organization in the history of American politics," and his first pledge was that it would be available in November "for every Democratic candidate in

this land." He spoke, he said, for a candidate who had read the mood of the country when others had read public opinion polls and who had shown, contrary to all the dire predictions tonight, that "he is a winner."

It is only with a plausible promise of victory over President Nixon in the fall that the McGovern forces expect to regain the support of some of their most bitter opponents, and a demonstration of that promise will be their first mission in the weeks ahead.

Senator Ribicoff listed the issues that he said would dominate the McGovern drive—an immediate end of all American involvement in Vietnam; a determination to protect the "real interests" of the United States in Europe and "the survival of Israel"; a reversal of Republican economic policies that were said to have caused "high unemployment, widespread inflation and escalating food prices"; a reordering of priorities to rebuild the country through prosperity while reducing hunger and poverty; and a Presidency that would "be honest" about problems and trust the "inherent decency and common sense of the people."

The difficulties anticipated for Mr. McGovern in his own party rested not only on the expectation of a formidable campaign by a sitting President. His problems will also be compounded, it is thought, because he is the first Democrat in 40 years to have come to the nomination without any signficant support from the established barons of regional, racial, business or labor power.

Never before has a major party nominated a candidate from a state with only four electoral votes, reflecting a population of 666,257. That historical oddity alone is evidence of the transformation of American politics upon which Mr. McGovern counts so heavily. The big states, the big unions, even the big names, are vulnerable as never before in this era of overnight television fame and ideological fragmentation.

The crucial but no longer suspenseful third session of the Democrats' 36th quadrennial convention opened an hour late at 8:01 P.M., but no one begrudged the managers this tardiness after the record-breaking meeting of more than

10 hours Tuesday night, devoted largely to writing a platform.

Despite the passions represented in the hall, the dominant McGovern forces set a pattern of remarkable decorum and attentiveness. They listened politely to Governor Wallace's appeals for serious changes in their party planks, before voting them down. They listened to avowed homosexuals plead for more active support, before voting them down. They yielded easily, and on instruction, to Mr. Jackson's plea for a warmer pledge to Israel. They fought back a more open endorsement of abortion by a margin of 3 to 2.

Though there were many more young people, many more blacks, many more women, many more Indians, many more beards, blue jeans and other informal clothes in the hall, there was none of the hostility or rowdiness that many had feared from such a gathering. All points of view were made to feel welcome and all the delegates held their seats so as to assure a voice and a defense of their interests.

When the final gavel fell for adjournment of the second session at 6:21 A.M., the Democratic National Chairman, Lawrence F. O'Brien, announced that 95 per cent of the delegates were still on hand and praised them for their maturity.

The nomination last night, in a final innovation, came in an order determined by lot rather than roll-call: Wallace, Sanford, McGovern, Chisholm and Jackson.

The Alabama Governor was proposed by State Senator Robert Wilson of Jasper, Ala., and was seconded by Hall Timanus, a lawyer, who is chairman of the Texas Democrats for Wallace, and Dr. Helen Calvin, a physician from Indiana.

Speaking for Mr. Sanford were Hodding Carter 3d, editor of The Greenville (Miss.) Delta Democrat Times; Andrew Miller, the Attorney General of Virginia; and Howard Lee, Mayor of Chapel Hill, N. C.

Seconding Mr. Ribicoff's nomination of Senator McGovern were Walter Fauntroy, the District of Columbia's non-voting delegate in Congress, who is a leader of the blacks who gave their convention votes before Miami Beach; and

Mrs. Valerie Kushner, an alternate delegate from Danville, Va., the wife of an Air Force pilot imprisoned in North Vietnam.

Mrs. Chisholm was put forward by Percy Sutton, the Borough President of Manhattan, and was seconded by Barbara Amran, a party leader from Minneapolis, and Charles Evers, the Mayor of Fayette, Miss.

Senator Jackson was offered by Gov. Jimmy Carter of Georgia, with seconds from Mrs. Lynn Sommerer, the daughter of Gov. Warren E. Hearnes of Missouri, and Mr. Abel, the steelworkers' leader.

In a final departure from precedent — among so many at this convention — the party moved with dispatch through the routine of nominations and demonstrations. One minute of music greeted Mr. Wilson's mention, at 9:45 P.M., of Mr. Wallace as "the most popular vote-getter on the American scene today" and as "the man who will take the ownership of the people away from the Government."

Time was running out. Mr. O'Brien reminded the Governor's cheering supporters, and after another minute the next speaker was on. Ten minutes per candidate was the rule, and the fact.

Mr. Carter presented Mr. Sanford with these words: "While others were blocking schoolhouse doors, Terry Sanford was opening them to all races."

Mr. Humphrey, appearing rested and refreshed after his withdrawal from the race yesterday, was among the many delegates who greeted this honorary presentation with applause. But there was no one in the huge arena who did not know that Mr. Ribicoff, the next speaker, was bearing to the rostrum the name of the victor in this long nominating season.

The standards of dozens of states came out of their moorings for the first time this week and the roars, though brief, were the convention's loudest. Mr. Humphrey stood and clapped before waves of blue McGovern placards.

July 13, 1972

Democrats Feel Impact Of Women's New Power

By NAN ROBERTSON
Special to The New York Times

MIAMI BEACH, July 14— Mrs. Martha Clampitt McKay of North Carolina had a drink with a national polling expert Tuesday afternoon to

find out how the country felt about abortion. Louis Harris, the pollster, told her that the majority of the voters in the South and Midwest were

against it.

Twelve hours later, after intensive proselytizing by Mrs. McKay and others, 48 members of the North Carolina delegation to the Democratic National Convention voted for a pro-abortion plank in the party platform and only nine voted "no."

It was apparent that some of the pro-abortion votes from the North Carolina delegation

reflected an attempt by supporters of Gov. George C. Wallace to embarrass Senator George McGovern, but others seemed to have been swayed by Mrs. McKay and her associates on the merits of the case.

The proposal lost by 472 votes out of a total of 2,673, but the fact that this explosive, emotional issue got to the floor and that its supporters were willing to fight for it across candidate lines and against the advice of professional politicians is one illustration of the impact that women had upon this convention. Time and again the 1,000 women delegates showed their clout, even though 88 per cent of them had never been to a national political convention before.

They showed it simply by being here in force, with 38 per cent of the troops as against 13 per cent in 1968. They showed it by pushing through, for the first time, a sweeping plank on women's rights. They showed it in the persons of Patricia Harris, a black woman who managed the thorny credentials challenges from the podium Monday night with toughness and skill, and Yvonne Braithwaite, another black woman who stood on the same spot Tuesday night to preside over the platform debates that did not end until sunrise.

And they showed it with the first women floor managers for a Presidential candidate — Anne Wexler and Jean Westwood—who helped to seize the prize for George McGovern.

Today, the Democratic National Committee, with 303 members, unanimously voted to make Mrs. Westwood its chairman. It was the first time either the Democratic or Republican party had given this job to a woman.

The convention's 15-point women's rights plank included pledges supporting the equal rights amendment; the elimination of discrimination against women in public accommodations and jobs; equal access to educational opportunities, tenure, promotion and higher salaries; the availability of maternity benefits to working women and the appointment of women to positions of top responsibility in all branches of the Federal Government.

The women's political caucuses outpulled the luaus and the lunches—and other caucuses, including one for those under 30 years old.

Presidential candidates made a point of appearing before women delegates' meetings to discuss the issues. "That's a revolution right there," said Gloria Steinem. the women's liberation movement leader.

But it was not really the celebrated personalities such as Miss Steinem (who was not a delegate) and Representative Bella Abzug (who was) that made the difference. It was the women who mainly had not been visible before, both the seasoned campaigners and the novices. They won some and they lost some, but all of them said "we learned a lot" in July, 1972.

And they planned to apply those lessons in the four years that lie between this Democratic convention and the next.

A Result of Reforms

There were more women, more minorities and more young people at the 1972 gathering because of party reforms that made delegate selection more democratic and representative of the people as a whole. Those reforms were drafted by a commission formed in 1968, of which Mr. McGovern was the original chairman.

The initial test for women came quickly, at the very beginning of this convention last Monday night. As with the abortion plank, delegates were voting on a new subject.

A man who has attended many conventions commented: "Only four years ago, it would have been inconceivable that the first substantive issue to come up in a national political convention would be whether to seat more women on a delegation."

The National Women's Political Caucus had fought for a minority report that would have added nine women to the South Carolina delegation for a total of 16 and shaved the number of male delegates from 25 to 16, thus giving the women a voice proportional to their numbers in that state.

It lost, by 1,555 votes to 1,429, but the outcome would have been even closer if the backers of Senator McGovern had not changed their votes late in the tally for strategic parliamentary reasons.

The second test, as far as the women's political caucus was concerned, resulted in a victory. That too came on Monday night. The convention upheld a Credentials Committee decision that ousted Mayor Richard J. Daley of Chicago, one of the last of the big city bosses, and 58 others, and seated a delegation with more women and more blacks.

The women's caucus believes its fervent lobbying helped contribute to the vote.

The third test, producing tears, shouting, fist-shaking and husband-wife splits on the floor in the middle of the night on Tuesday, was the minority abortion proposal. The word "abortion" did not appear anywhere in the proposed amendment to the 15-point "rights of women" plank adopted by the convention.

The amendment read: "In matters relating to human reproduction, each person's right to privacy, freedom of choice and individual conscience should be fully respected, consistent with relevant Supreme Court decisions."

Both "abortion" and code phrases such as "the right of a woman to control her own body" were used as the battle raged on for two hours. There was talk of a Humphrey-Wallace coalition to vote "yes" for a plank that could discomfort and ultimately defeat Mr. McGovern's race for the White House.

Meantime the McGovern forces were moving around the floor, urging delegates to vote against the plank. In the end they won and it was jettisoned.

"We were outmaneuvered and outmanipulated" said Betty Friedan, a convention observer who had been present at all the women's political caucuses.

The McGovern supporters were convinced that if the pro-abortion minority plank were adopted, it would brand the South Dakota Senator as extremist.

Today the delegates began streaming away from Miami Beach, and many of the women among them expressed hope and determination for the future rather than disappointment at this week's events.

They seemed to agree with Miss Steinem that "The convention is only the tip of the iceberg. A lot of hard important work was done before women could go through the system—a system not created to help them. The major changes are going to endure no matter what happened in Miami. It's like pushing marbles through a sieve. It means the sieve will never be the same again."

July 15, 1972

A.F.L.-C.I.O. Chiefs Vote Neutral Stand on Election

By PHILIP SHABECOFF
Special to The New York Times

WASHINGTON, July 19—The Executive Council of the A.F.L.-C.I.O. voted today to refrain from endorsing either President Nixon or Senator George McGovern for the Presidency. This was the first time that the merged labor federation, which was formed on Dec. 5, 1955, did not support officially the Democrats' nominee. The council, by a vote of 27 to 3, decided to adopt a position of neutrality but reiterated that individual member unions had a right "to support any candidate of their choice.'

Interviewed in South Dakota, Mr. McGovern said that he was disappointed by the action but indicated that he expected to get many rank-and-file votes. Clark MacGregor, Mr. Nixon's campaign manager, said that "it is obvious now that the American workingman is disenchanted with the Democrats."

A brief statement read to newsmen by George Meany, president of the American Federation of Labor and Congress of Industrial Organizations, said that, "under the circumstances," maximum concentration would be placed on efforts to elect Senators and Representatives "whose records commend them to the working people of America."

Mr. Meany declined under heavy questioning to state what "circumstances" had led to the decision of the federation to remain neutral in 1972.

Speaking for himself, the 77-year-old labor leader declared: "I will not endorse, support or vote for Richard Nixon as President. I will not endorse, support or vote for George McGovern as President."

At a news conference at federation headquarters, where the Executive Council held its meeting, Mr. Meany would only say in explanation of the decision to remain neutral that it "was better for the trade union movement."

"It is quite obvious that there are divisions among the rank and file," he said. "Let them

343

The New York Times/George Tames

George Meany, left, A.F.L.-C.I.O. president; I. W. Abel, center, United Steelworkers' president, and Jerry Wurf, president of the American Federation of State, County and Municipal Employes, after the A.F.L.-C.I.O. Executive Council voted against endorsing a Presidential candidate. Mr. Wurf called the decision a "mistake."

vote for whom they please. COPE [the Committee on Political Action of the A.F.L.-C.I.O.] will work like the devil for candidates in the House and Senate."

After the news conference, a political adviser to Mr. Meany said that the neutrality decision represented a repudiation of the "new politics" which, he said, had taken over the Democratic party and "arrogantly excluded" members of the old Democratic coalition, particularly organized labor.

"This is our showdown with the new politics," the adviser said. "The timing of the showdown was chosen by McGovern, not by us, but at some point the movement within the Democratic party had to be stemmed, and this is it."

The showdown was made necessary when a "small élite of suburban types and students took over the apparatus of the Democratic party," the adviser said.

Other officials at federation headquarters cited the "shabby treatment" accorded labor leaders, including I.W. Abel, the president of the United Steelworkers, at the Democratic convention in Miami Beach, as reasons for distrust of the Democratic ticket.

One federation official said

that one reason the A.F.L.-C.I.O. was remaining neutral was that it did not want any part of the "debacle of the McGovern candidacy." Federation leaders believe that the Democratic ticket will cause widespread defections by workers, Catholics and Jews and lead to "catastrophe" for the Democratic party in November, the official said.

Immediately after the Executive Council meeting, however, a number of A.F.L.-C.I.O. unions made strong statements of support for the McGovern ticket.

Machinist Support Affirmed

Floyd Smith, president of the International Association of Machinists and Aerospace Workers, reiterated his support for Senator McGovern's candidacy to reporters at federation headquarters. Mr. Smith said that his union would devote money and effort to elect Mr. McGovern.

"I don't think the decision to remain neutral will hurt McGovern," said Mr. Smith who voted for the resolution to keep the federation neutral. "I don't think it will help Nixon. I don't think it will have any impact at all."

Joseph A. Beirne, president of the 500,000-member Communications Workers of America and a close associate of Mr. Meany's, made public parts

of a letter to Mr. Meany in which he said:

"I think it would not be prudent to establish a political program which ignored McGovern and Eagleton. McGovern has made a damn good race and proved he has an excellent disciplined organization."

Senator Thomas F. Eagleton of Missouri is Mr. McGovern's running mate.

Mr. Beirne's letter continued:

"I think the Executive Council should recommend the endorsement of the Democratic national ticket to the general board. Endorsement of the Democratic candidates is the only way to keep A.F.L.-C.I.O. unions united in their political activity.

"It is obviously in the self-interest of the A.F.L.-C.I.O. to do so, and, without going into additional detail, I think it would be terribly wrong, after building up the COPE apparatus to its present strength and prestige, to act in such a way as to fragment that great strength."

Mr. Beirne was one of five members of the Executive Council to favor the McGovern candidacy who did not attend today's meeting.

The only votes against the neutrality resolution came from Jerry Wurf, president of the

American Federation of State, County and Municipal Employes; A. F. Grospiron, president of the Oil, Chemical and Atomic Workers, and Paul Jennings, president of the International Union of Electrical, Radio and Machine Workers.

Another resolution to delay a vote on neutrality until a meeting in August of the general board of A.F.L.-C.I.O. presidents, put forward by Mr. Wurf, was defeated by a vote of 25 to 5.

Mr. Wurf later issued a statement calling the decision of the Executive Council a "mistake" and said that the vote reflected "personal loyalties within the A.F.L.-C.I.O. rather than a true index of support for the Democratic ticket by American trade unionists."

Mr. Wurf hailed the reforms within the Democratic party, saying that they had given the labor movement "an opportunity to have substantial influence within the party independent from party bosses and local machines."

"We can and should be a major force in the campaing to defeat Richard Nixon," he said.

Senators McGovern and Eagleton, meanwhile, issued a statement expressing "regret" over the decision of the Executive Council and saying that they expected to receive the endorsement of many of the federation's member unions.

McGovern's Disappointment

Interviewed when returning from a horseback ride in Custer, S.D., where he is resting, Senator McGovern said that he was disappointed and had hoped the council would endorse him.

"Frankly, I don't want to feud with President Meany," he said, but added that if the Democratic ticket did not get Mr. Meany's support, "we will just have to get along without it."

"The important thing is where the rank-and-file vote is, and we think we are going to do very well with them," he said.

Mr. McGovern is flying back to Washington tomorrow to vote against an amendment to proposed legislation to increase minimum wages and extend

their coverage. Organized labor has strongly opposed the amendment, which would reduce the proposed new minimum wage and have it apply to fewer workers. The Nixon Administration is supporting the amendment.

Mr. MacGregor issued a statement saying that the action by the federation "reflects and reinforces the decision of most workers in the rank and file of organized labor not to support that élitist minority which seized control of the Democratic convention and nominated George McGovern as its candidate."

Calling today's action a "historic step," Mr. MacGregor said, "It is obvious now that the American workingman is disenchanted with the Democrats and tired of being taken for granted."

In what may become a recurring theme in Mr. Nixon's campaign, Mr. MacGregor asserted that today's vote meant that

workers had seen "a new McGovern élite accepting within its ranks radical professors, student agitators, professional welfarists, extremists of virtually every sort, an élite which makes the ordinary working man feel unwelcome and unwanted."

One official at federation headquarters pointed out that it was 20 years ago, in 1952, that the American Federation of Labor endorsed Adlai E. Stevenson against Dwight D. Eisenhower, thus departing from what had been a policy of official neutrality.

At the federation's convention that year, a resolution was adopted saying that it would be wrong to remain neutral in a Presidential election "because the stakes are so high."

The C.I.O. Political Action Committee was formed in 1943. In 1944 it endorsed Franklin D. Roosevelt, in 1948 Harry S. Truman and in 1952

Mr. Stevenson.

Meanwhile, several more A.F.L.-C.I.O. unions have formally endorsed the Democratic Presidential ticket In Honolulu yesterday a convention of the American Federation of Technical Engineers endorsed Senators McGovern and Eagleton and called its action a "repudiation of the Nixon Administration and endorsement and support of the alternative offered by the Democratic party's nominees."

Directors of the 125,000 member International Printing Pressmen and Assistants of North America voted its full support to the McGovern-Eagleton ticket. So did the executive board of the Oil, Chemical and Atomic Workers, whose president, Mr. Grospiron, had already endorsed Mr. McGovern. The union has 182,000 members.

July 20, 1972

EAGLETON QUITS AT REQUEST OF M'GOVERN; SAYS HE DOES NOT WANT TO 'DIVIDE' PARTY

SUCCESSOR SOUGHT

O'Brien and Muskie in Running – Dakotan to Address Nation

By JAMES M. NAUGHTON
Special to The New York Times

WASHINGTON, July 31 — Senator Thomas F. Eagleton, yielding to a request from Senator George McGovern, withdrew tonight from his campaign for the Vice-Presidency. He said that he did not wish to "divide the Democratic party" by continuing as its nominee.

Eighteen days after choosing Mr. Eagleton as his running mate, Senator McGovern, the Democratic Presidential nominee, announced that they had agreed that the "best course" would be for Mr. Eagleton to step aside and thereby terminate a national debate over his health.

Thus Mr. Eagleton became the first Vice-Presidential nominee ever to withdraw from candidacy, other than by death.

Democratic leaders across the country, after learning of Mr. Eagleton's withdrawal, said

that while the action was sad personally, it would strengthen the party's chances in the November election.

May Pick O'Brien

Senator McGovern said that he did not have a new nominee in mind, but there were reports that he would recommend to the Democratic National Committee that it select its former chairman, Lawrence F. O'Brien, to take Mr. Eagleton's place.

Among other names mentioned was that of Senator Edmund S. Muskie of Maine, whose associates said that he would be available if Mr. McGovern were to ask him to become the new Vice-Presidential nominee.

Mr. McGovern said at a news conference at which he and Mr. Eagleton announced the decision that "health was not a factor" in making it. But he added that Senator Eagleton's disclosure, six days ago, that he had been hospitalized in 1960, 1964 and 1966 for treatment of nervous exhaustion and fatigue had "dominated the political dialogue of the country" and threatened to obscure the real issue of the campaign.

Committee to Choose

Mr. Eagleton said he would write a letter in the morning officially informing Mrs. Jean

Westwood, the chairman of the national committee, of his decision. Mrs. Westwood will then convene a meeting of the committee, which has the responsibility of choosing a new candidate.

Mr. McGovern announced that he would go on nationwide television at 9 P.M. tomorrow "to discuss the events of the campaign to date." But he said he did not expect to announce a Vice-Presidential nominee tomorrow.

It was clear that Senator Eagleton had yielded to Senator McGovern in agreeing to withdraw at a two-hour private meeting in the Marble Room off the United States Senate chamber earlier tonight.

"I would have preferred to remain on the ticket," Mr. Eagleton said at a news conference an hour later in the high-ceiling Caucus Room of the Old Senate Office Building.

He said that he had "marshaled my arguments in lawyer-like fashion" in seeking to persuade Mr. McGovern that his continued candidacy would be a plus for the Democratic ticket. But he and Mr. McGovern both noted that there had been, as the Presidential nominee described it, "growing pressures" both for and against Senator Eagleton's presence on the ticket.

"I will not divide the Democratic party, which has already too many divisions," Mr. Eagleton said.

Grim-faced as he began to read from a prepared statement, Senator McGovern disclosed for the first time that he discussed Mr. Eagleton's health with three doctors who had treated the 42-year-old Missourian for mental depression.

"I am fully satisfied that his health is excellent," he asserted. Nonetheless, he said, "the public debate over Senator Eagleton's past medical history continues to divert attention from the great national issues that need to be discussed."

To Campaign for McGovern

Both men spoke of the need to unite the Democrats for the campaign against President Nixon, and Mr. Eagleton said that he would campaign on Mr. McGovern's behalf.

In addition to Mr. O'Brien and Senator Muskie as possible choices for the Vice-Presidential nomination, several other possibilities were being mentioned tonight. They included Gov. Patrick J. Lucey of Wisconsin, Gov. John J. Gilligan of Ohio and R. Sargent Shriver, the brother-in-law of Senator Edward M. Kennedy and a former Ambassador to France.

But a senior executive of the McGovern campaign said this morning that Mr. O'Brien, who is now the national chairman of Mr. McGovern's campaign, was the "fallback choice" if Mr. Eagleton should step down.

345

Technically, the decision to withdraw was Mr. Eagleton's. Nothing in the Democratic party's rules would permit his removal against his will. And although he had spoken in the last several days of being adamantly committed to remaining a candidate, members of his staff said that he could not refuse a direct request to step down.

Mr. Eagleton was red-eyed and nervous as he made the announcement.

"My conscience is clear, my spirits are high," he said, and he managed to joke with well-wishers when they interrupted his prepared statement with applause.

"I've got more to say," Senator Eagleton interjected, forcing a smile. "Please be patient, the best is yet to come."

Senator McGovern said that the final decision was not made until he and Mr. Eagleton, joined by Senator Gaylord Nelson of Wisconsin, sat in the Marble Room to weigh the fate of their joint campaign.

But an authoritative Senate source said when the meeting began that Mr. McGovern had told him earlier today, "Unhappily, Tom has to go."

Furthermore, it was known that Mr. Nelson was attempting throughout the day—when Mr. McGovern was attending the funeral in Houma, La., of

Senator Allen J. Ellender and Mr. Eagleton was marshalling support here in Washington—to work out an agreement for Senator Eagleton to withdraw.

Representative Henry S. Reuss of Wisconsin and Senator Nelson had met separately with Senator Eagleton this morning, after Mr. Reuss had told friends that he would propose that Mr. Eagleton drop out of the race but continue to campaign for Mr. McGovern.

Mr. Eagleton told newsmen that he had attempted to persuade Mr. McGovern that the issue of his past health would have "run out of gas" in two or three weeks.

But Mr. McGovern reportedly stressed the narrowness of any likely victory margin in November and the compulsion to avoid any risk that the health issue might thus endanger the prospects of winning.

Although Mr. McGovern asserted tonight that he had "consistently supported Senator Eagleton," he began hinting on Friday that the pledge of "1,000 per cent" support for his running mate was being reassessed.

Mr. McGovern told newsmen Saturday night, aboard the chartered airplane that brought him to Washington from a working vacation in his native South Dakota, that he was un-

sure how voters would react to Mr. Eagleton's health disclosures.

"The one thing we know about Eagleton," he said, "is that he's been to the hospital three times for depression."

But tonight, Mr. McGovern said he had been assured—he did not say when—by Senator Eagleton's doctors that "they felt he has made a full recovery" from the depression that had hospitalized him three times.

In response to questions about the factors that led to his decision to seek Mr. Eagleton's replacement, Mr. McGovern said: "As the days went on, it became clear to me that Senator Eagleton's past medical history has literally dominated the news, it has dominated the political dialogue of the country."

But Mr. Eagleton said that he wanted, in the words of President Nixon, to "make one thing crystal clear—this is definitely not my last press conference and Tom Eagleton is going to be around for a long, long time."

The prospects were that Mr. McGovern, in his television appearance tomorrow, would appeal to Democrats and others for understanding of the reasons behind the withdrawal of Mr. Eagleton. And it was clear that there were some within his own party who would have to

be persuaded.

At the funeral in Louisiana, Senator McGovern spent most of his time in the company of Senator Edward M. Kennedy of Massachusetts, who had been offered the Vice-Presidential nomination and had declined it. Mr. Kennedy was consulted by Senator McGovern before Senator Eagleton was chosen as the nominee, and the speculation today was that Mr. McGovern was again seeking advice, rather than a commitment to become a candidate, from Mr. Kennedy.

In his office this afternoon, Mr. Eagleton showed newsmen a copy of a book titled "Not Exactly a Crime" about the Vice-Presidency.

"Needless to say, I won't need this much longer," he said, holding up the book. Then he paused and said, "Or maybe I will."

Despite his apparent and accustomed buoyancy, members of Mr. Eagleton's staff were less charitable toward Senator McGovern. One aide said that Mr. McGovern appeared to have pulled the rug out from under Mr. Eagleton just when the tide of public opinion was turning his way.

"I don't really know whether I want to see him in the White House or not," another Eagleton aide said of the Presidential nominee.

August 1, 1972

SHRIVER IS CHOSEN BY M'GOVERN TO FILL SECOND SPOT ON TICKET AFTER MUSKIE DECLINES OFFER

DECISION HAILED

Successor to Eagleton Called Favorite of Nominee's Staff

By CHRISTOPHER LYDON
Special to The New York Times

WASHINGTON, Aug. 5—Senator George McGovern chose Sargent Shriver as his Vice-Presidential running mate today after Senator Edmund S. Muskie had rejected his invitation to join the Democratic ticket.

Mr. Shriver, the first director of the Peace Corps under his brother-in-law, President Ken-

nedy, and of the antipoverty program under President Johnson, will be put in nomination before an expanded 303-member Democratic National Committee here Tuesday night.

He will succeed Senator Thomas F. Eagleton, who resigned from the race last Monday after disclosing that he had been hospitalized three times in the nineteen-sixties for nervous exhaustion and depression.

Mr. Muskie, the Democratic Vice-Presidential nominee in 1968 and the early front runner for the Presidential nomination this year, cited family considerations in becoming the sixth man to reject Mr. McGovern's offer.

Earlier this week, Mr. McGovern had been turned down by Senators Edward M. Ken-

nedy of Massachusetts, Hubert H. Humphrey of Minnesota and Abraham A. Ribicoff of Connecticut. In addition, Senator Gaylord Nelson of Wisconsin and Gov. Reubin Askew of Florida were thought to have been given chances to express interest but declined.

Mr. McGovern made his announcement for television cameras, sitting before a wooden desk in front of a false marble fireplace in a small room in the Capitol.

Mr. Shriver, who had sailed this morning off Hyannis Port, Mass., was playing tennis at the Kennedy family compound there when he received Mr. McGovern's firm offer.

Before leaving for Washington from the Barnstable, Mass., airport Mr. Shriver said he

was "very happy and very proud" to have been chosen.

Staff Favorite

Mr. Shriver had been the choice of several factions within the McGovern organization at the Democratic National Convention three weeks ago, and was the staff's favorite after Mr. Eagleton's candidacy collapsed.

He has political roots in Chicago, where he once managed the Merchandise Mart, one of the world's largest office buildings, for the late Joseph P. Kennedy, and in Maryland, where he considered running for Governor in 1970. But he has never been a candidate before, a point that his advocates felt confirmed the antipolitics or beyond-politics air that the McGovern campaign began.

Mr. Shriver was recommended to Mr. McGovern at the convention at Miami Beach by the black members of his campaign staff and by Pierre Salinger, the White House press secretary during the Kennedy Administration.

But he was also thought to be an attractive figure in most of the Democratic party—a friend of Mayor Richard J. Daley of Chicago, for example, and warmly endorsed to Mr. McGovern last week by Senator Humphrey.

Last week, his outspoken backers came to include Congressional figures as diverse as Representatives Shirley Chisholm of Brooklyn, Wayne L. Hays of Ohio, Sam M. Gibbons of Florida and Lester L. Wolff of Nassau County.

"He is attractive, personable and well-liked by a broad cross-section of groups," Mrs. Chisholm wired Mr. McGovern last week. "He knows the Hill and is an experienced and respected businessman, but he is equally at home with the poor and minority groups whose affection and support he earned during his tenure as head of the Office of Economic Opportunity."

Wife Foe of Abortion

There had been suggestions that the determined views of Mr. Shriver's wife, the former Eunice Kennedy, against abortion would be an obstacle in his selection. Senator McGovern has tried to keep the abortion issue out of the national campaign, saying It was a matter for the states to decide.

It had also been thought that Senator Kennedy, who discouraged Senator Humphrey's interest in Mr. Shriver as a running mate in 1968, might veto his selection this year.

But Mr. Kennedy was reported not to have involved himself in the consideration of Mr. Shriver this year. And on the abortion issue, Mrs. Shriver's strong convictions and her independence were considered to have an appeal even to people who disagreed with her.

Some ranking members of the McGovern staff indicated, without attribution, that they were delighted with Mr. Muskie's refusal and hinted that they had worked purposefully at discouraging him.

Told to Stay Available

Even before Mr. Muskie made up his mind, word was circulating here that Frank Mankiewicz, the McGovern campaign's chief strategist, and Henry A. Kimelman, its finance director, had called Mr. Shriver on Cape Cod and told him to keep his hopes up and remain available as the next choice.

One of the men who had met with the Muskie staff yesterday to consider details of the prospective campaign said with relief this morning that Mr. Muskie's decision was "the best thing that ever happened to this campaign."

"They were interested in all the really vital issues facing the country, said the sarcastic McGovern staff members, "like the configuration of Muskie's airplane, whether he could

have his own advanced staff, and what his headquarters office would look like. It was preposterous."

Stewart Mott, the young General Motors heir who has contributed hundreds of thousands of dollars to the McGovern campaign, commented this afternoon: "I don't know a single member of McGovern's staff that was enthusiastic about Muskie. The offer to Muskie is one of the greatest conundrums of our time. I expected that after the offer to Humphrey, McGovern would give it to Lyndon Johnson or Richard Daley."

Excerpts from Mr. McGovern's address tonight that were released at campaign headquarters this afternoon made no mention of Mr. Shriver or the Vice-Presidential selection process.

'Sense of Uneasiness'

Reviewing the Eagleton affair, Senator McGovern asserted that although the Missouri Senator had triumphed over his illness, "disclosure of psychiatric treatment stirred a powerful sense of uneasiness in many Americans." The medical question, he said, "might obscure and confuse the real choice of this Presidential year."

In a fresh statement of his purpose, Mr. McGovern agreed with President Nixon that the 1972 campaign offered "the clearest political choice of a century." He gave briefer attention to the war in Vietnam than in most of his speeches to date, though he said again that ending the war was his first priority.

The fundamental choice, he said, is "between the belief that political power exists to serve private power, and the conviction that political leadership must take up the people's cause against those who seek advantage at their expense."

Echoing the theme of the late Robert F. Kennedy's 1968 campaign, he declared: "It is a decision between the desire to preserve things as they are against the confidence that this nation can do better, that life in this nation can be more rewarding—for every citizen."

"The chronicle of America, like some great river, sweeps into the future," he said toward the close of a speech that was crafted by Richard N. Goodwin, a Kennedy speechwriter. "It cannot be mastered by clinging to threatened banks, but only by those who, unafraid and desiring, set out upon powerful and uncertain currents —transforming shifting dangers and unimaginable change into a trail for a new American journey.

"This time not a journey to a distant coast, but inward toward the most powerful aspirations of the human heart: to make this society—its factories, institutions, government —serve each person's right to extend all the powers of his humanity to the limit of possibility. That is what Thomas Jefferson meant when he claimed for us the pursuit of happiness."

August 6, 1972

Johnson Backs McGovern Despite Their Differences

Special to The New York Times

FREDERICKSBURG, Tex., Aug. 16—Former President Lyndon B. Johnson said today that he would support and vote for the entire Democratic ticket, from the courthouse to the White House. He endorsed Senator George McGovern for President in a statement sent to weekly newspapers here, with the request that it be released to the news services.

His statement came six days before Senator McGovern is to visit him at his ranch on the Pedernales River 32 miles east of here.

Speaking at a reception for state Democratic candidates in Springfield, Ill., today, Senator McGovern said that he welcomed Mr. Johnson's support.

He also gave an example of why he welcomed it.

Commenting on President Nixon's veto today of an appropriation bill for the Labor Department and for the Health, Education and Welfare Department, Mr. McGovern said:

"I had my differences with President Johnson over the war, but I can tell you that if L.B.J. had been in the White House today, there would have been no veto of the H.E.W. bill. So I welcome his support. I welcome the support of other Democrats with whom we may have had some differences."

The Johnson endorsement of the McGovern ticket was foreshadowed last Saturday with the announcement that the

Senator would visit Mr. Johnson next Tuesday, the day the Republicans are expected to nominate President Nixon for re-election in Miami Beach.

Although Mr. Johnson indicated a pronounced coolness toward Senator McGovern through the Democratic National Convention, which Mr. Johnson did not attend, he apparently was somewhat mollified by the selection of Sargent Shriver as the Vice-Presidential nominee.

Mr. Johnson's statement made it clear that he and Senator McGovern remained far apart on such foreign policy issues as the war in Vietnam.

"It is no secret that Senator McGovern and I have widely differing opinions on many matters, especially foreign policy," Mr. Johnson said, adding that "the Democratic party can accommodate disagreement."

The former President's statement ended any speculation that the defection of former Gov. John B. Connally, a Johnson protégé, to head the Democrats for Nixon implied approval from Mr. Johnson.

Mr. Johnson's statement was delivered by an aide to Arthur H. Kowert of The Fredericksburg Standard at about 10 A.M. today, just barely in time for it to get into this week's edition. Mr. Kowert relayed the information to his competitor, Norman J. Dietel of The Fredericksburg Radio-Post, but not in time for Mr. Dietel to get it into this week's issues of his newspaper.

Following is Mr. Johnson's statement, as obtained from The Standard:

"I believe the Democratic party best serves the needs of the people. Therefore I intend to support the 1972 Democratic ticket.

"I shall vote for George McGovern and Sargent Shriver for President and Vice President of the United States.

"I shall vote for Dolph Briscoe and Barefoot Sanders for Governor of Texas and United States Senator and for all the nominees of the Democratic party.

"It is no secret that Senator McGovern and I have widely differing opinions on many matters, especially foreign policy. Senator McGovern has not refrained from criticizing policies of mine with which he disagrees. Neither shall I refrain from stating my disagreements with any positions of his when I believe that the public interest demands such action.

"The differences between us need not be minimized. The Democratic party can accommo-

date disagreement.

"Since returning to private life, I have taken no active role in political affairs. Nonetheless, I have welcomed and supported — in retirement as I always did in public service — the growing participation in the affairs of the Democratic party by the young, by women,

by blacks, by Mexican-Americans and others who have far too long been outside the political system. Such participation represents fulfillment of goals for which I worked throughout my public career.

"I believe that the people of America — all the people of America — will best be served

by election of a Democratic President and a Democratic Congress in 1972. Accordingly, I shall support and vote for candidates of the Democratic party."

August 17, 1972

Daley Calls on Chicago to Back McGovern, 'the Next President'

By SETH S. KING
Special to The New York Times

CHICAGO, Sept. 12—"Hello, Chicago," cried Mayor Richard J. Daley today, and the crowd jamming the corner of State and Madison Streets cheered.

Standing beside the Mayor on the damp platform were Senator Edward M. Kennedy and Senator George McGovern, whom Mr. Daley introduced as "the next President of the United States."

It was the Mayor's second public testimonial within an hour that he and the Democratic Presidential nominee had finally achieved a pragmatic peace.

Earlier, at the Sherman House Hotel, in a gesture even more important to Mr. McGovern, the Mayor presented the South Dakotan to the 80-member Cook County Democratic Central Committee, many of whom, including Mr. Daley, had been humiliated in July when McGovern backers supplanted them at the Democratic National Convention.

Whatever animosity may have remained toward Senator McGovern was hidden from the crowds of reporters and cameramen who watched as

the Mayor led the committee members in cheering for Mr. McGovern.

"This has been an unusual election," Mr. Daley acknowledged to the committeemen. "But that's all behind us now. Today we're interested in electing all the ticket. Articulation of the issues in this election will be brought to every home in Cook County. The unity and solidarity of the Democratic party will be demonstrated."

A Signal From the Mayor

With these hopeful words and his later appearance with Mr. McGovern at the lunchtime rally, Mr. Daley gave a clear signal to the party's apparatus that it was now all right to endorse Mr. McGovern publicly.

It was also a warning to the loyal party workers that a tepid effort for the Democratic nominee could aid in a Nixon landslide that could easily bury the rest of the county ticket.

The Mayor did not have to remind them that Cook County politics builds from the bottom up, and nothing is more important to Cook County Democrats than holding on to the offices of state's Attorney, with its

limitless investigative powers, and the post of Clerk of the Circuit Court, with its 1,200 patronage jobs.

Need for Carrying Illinois

Both Senator McGovern and Senator Kennedy, in their exhortations to the committeemen, repeated a familiar political litany: A Presidential candidate cannot win if he does not win big in Chicago and Cook County.

The more recent political polls in Illinois show Senator McGovern running behind President Nixon, even in Cook County. Far more unsettling to the Mayor are polls showing the State's Attorney, Edward V. Hanrahan, running only 4 or 5 percentage points ahead of Bernard Carey, his Republican opponent, with the sentiments in the mushrooming suburbs of Cook County looking even more uncertain this year.

Mr. Hanrahan took a few minutes off today from his own trial on charges of obstructing justice to speak at the committee meeting. He delivered a ringing endorsement of Mr. McGovern, assuring him that he had "a tremendous element of strength in this county."

Trouble for Organization

But the Daley organization is having its own troubles, right at home. The Rev. Jesse Jackson, leader of the new black action group called Peo-

ple United to Save Humanity (PUSH) and one of the insurgents who supplanted a Daley delegate at Miami, is waging a new campaign against the Chicago Board of Elections Commissioners, pressing for a greater effort to register blacks.

There are more than one-million blacks in Chicago, nearly a third of the population. Mr. Jackson is certainly supporting Mr. McGovern. But he is also an avowed enemy of Mr Hanrahan, whom he is not supporting.

Even though this threat is lurking behind the Daley machine, long-time students of Chicago and Illinois politics still doubt that ticket splitting will be widespread this year.

In most past elections not more than 10 per cent of the ballots have been split between the parties, regardless of which one carried the state.

One observer said he expected this year's splits to be somewhat higher, perhaps as much as 20 per cent.

"That means McGovern has somehow got to close the current gap before November," he said. "If he can get as much as 45 per cent of the vote, the Democrats on local tickets will probably be safe, even if Nixon wins. But if McGovern drops to 40 per cent or less, the Democrats are in real trouble clear down to the bottom of the ticket."

September 13, 1972

NIXON IS RENOMINATED BY 1,347-TO-1 VOTE; LIBERALS LOSE FIGHT OVER RULES FOR 1976

A JUBILANT PARLEY

President Appeals for Support of Youths at Key Biscayne Rally

By MAX FRANKEL
Special to The New York Times

MIAMI BEACH, Aug. 22 — The Republican party formally and jubilantly proclaimed Richard Milhous Nixon here tonight

as its candidate for another term as President.

In an atmosphere of celebration, even coronation, marred only by the harassment of delegates by antiwar demonstrators outside the hall, the party's 30th national convention designated Mr. Nixon as the party's leader for the third time in 12 years. It acted with only a murmur of opposition and with hardly a doubt that he would be re-elected by a huge majority in November.

The final tally was 1,347 votes for Mr. Nixon and one, as required by New Mexico's

primary law, for Representative Paul N. McCloskey Jr. of California. The projected picture tally called him "others."

Debate Over 1976

The nomination came after an afternoon session that brought the only open debate and the only contested roll-call of the week's events — over party rules for the 1976 convention. But the dissenters were heard and decisively voted down, leaving the delegates with nothing more to do than cheer.

Mr. Nixon, who flew to Miami

this afternoon from Washington, watched the ritual of nomination at his nearby seaside home in Key Biscayne and then made his first appearance as candidate at a youth rally at Miami's Marine Stadium. He thus devoted all his public statements today to special appeals for the still elusive support of young people.

Introduced there by Sammy Davis Jr., Mr. Nixon said he did not think the youth vote "was in anybody's pocket."

The convention watched him on television monitors as the

President called attention to the celebrities working for his election, particularly Mr. Davis, whom he welcomed also as a Democrat, a friend of the Kennedy family and a symbol of equal opportunity for black Americans, another constituency leaning toward the Democrats.

"I believe in the American dream," the President asserted. If re-elected, he added, he would be working for young people to make them look back on their first votes for him as among their best.

Governor Rockefeller of New York, who had twice failed to wrest control of the party from Mr. Nixon, rendered the ultimate tribute of placing the President's name in nomination and describing the duty as an honor.

"We need this man of action, this man of accomplishment, this man of experience, this man of courage," he said. "We need this man of faith in America."

The seconding was done by 11 other citizens, including some Democrats, to symbolize Mr. Nixon's appeal for defectors, and even including Walter J. Hickel, who was dismissed from the President's Cabinet two years ago.

The convention moved gleefully from the routine of the first three business sessions. At the last of these this afternoon, it routinely gave the President the platform the White House had wanted, recounting a "saga of exhilarating progress" since 1968 and condemning his Democratic challenger, Senator George McGovern, as the leader of a "radical clique."

But the controversy over delegate apportionment in 1976 brought at least a brief time of open argument and the convention's only contested roll-call. Liberal and urban delegates argued with some heat for a compromise that would give the more populous states a larger share of the voice when Mr. Nixon's successor as party leader is chosen four years hence.

Their cause was lost, however, on the floor as in the Rules Committee. The party's establishment, including most Southerners and all conservatives, outvoted the challengers, 910 to 434, despite the threats of younger delegates to take their case to the courts.

It was at all times a decorous contest, without booing of the rival speakers and almost no visible floor lobbying for support by either side.

The only threat of real disruption hovered outside the hall, where different groups of dissenters chose different tactics to condemn the continuing war in Vietnam and to bring the Republicans a mes-

sage of "shame" for American involvement in the war.

More than 1,000 veterans paraded peacefully in Miami Beach this afternoon. But several hundred radical youths who favor stronger tactics broke some windows, harassed the delegates and burned some bunting near Convention Hall to provoke the first mass arrests of the week.

With all due respect for legal formalities, the police isolated the presumed offenders and hauled them off in buses and trucks. Most of the Republican delegates experienced only traffic delays, which together with the three-hour runover at the afternoon session shortened the dinner hour.

One conspicuous exception, however, was New York's Senator James L. Buckley, who was recognized by some of the demonstrators as he emerged from Wolfie's Restaurant and was jeered and chased down the street with some of his aides.

The party managers were determined to nominate Mr. Nixon in prime time and to avoid what they saw as the Democrats' mistake of staging some of their most desultory business in prime television time while wasting the excitement in the predawn hours.

The nominating speeches took 45 minutes and were concluded by 10:30. The alphabetical calling of the roll, without any of the suspense that usually attends that routine at political conventions, took 30 minutes, but the running tally on television monitors in the hall showed the President nominated with more than the required majority of 675 once Missouri had cast its votes. The convention adjourned at 11:43 P.M.

Incoming as well as outgoing television has been dominating this convention.

This afternoon's meeting was interrupted at 4 P.M., for instance, when the giant screens behind the podium showed Mr. Nixon arriving at Miami's International Airport to be greeted by his family, Cabinet aides and several thousand cheering young fans — apparently the same enthusiastic claque that led the cheering in the hall last night and left the galleries almost entirely empty this afternoon.

The mere sight of the President brought shouts that the lights be lowered. His wave from the airplane ramp brought the delegates to their feet with applause and they remained standing while he displayed a confident grin to the airport crowd.

The delegates did not, however, hear Mr. Nixon's brief speech of greeting, which offered a special plea to young people, who by all accounts remain reluctant about this candidacy and prefer Mr. McGovern in larger proportion than

most other identifiable voter groups.

Mr. Nixon said he knew that youth was troubled by the desire to participate in politics and eager for peace and greater equality. He said he intended to satisfy these demands, adding:

"We want an Administration, after the election—in the next four years—in which we can be worthy of the enthusiasm and the trust and the hopes and the ideals of young Americans."

Inside the convention hall, however, there was no need for even that much defensiveness and promise. The adoration of the President appeared to be universal, and the stage effects added by his managers, including tens of thousands of red, white and blue balloons and colorful visual aids hammering home slogans of progress and confidence on the giant screen.

The rival speakers during the rules debate vied with each other in expressions of fealty to Mr. Nixon's cause. The film tribute to the President—which the delegates saw by mistake last night but which went to the television audience this evening—pictures a sure-footed and decisive manager presiding with humor and force over adoring aides and a grateful country.

Mr. Rockefeller fully caught the spirit of the occasion in his nominating speech.

Recalling the divisions of war, the riots on campuses and in cities, he said the nation had regained its confidence and renewed the confidence in the United States abroad.

"This has been due importantly to one man, our President," the Governor declared.

He stressed the diminished involvement in Vietnam, the declining rate of inflation, the new agreements with the Soviet Union, the new contact with China, the hope for peace in the Middle East and what he called the aversion of "environmental disaster."

Mr. Rockefeller also cited the still pending proposals for reforms such as revenue sharing, welfare spending and reorganization of the Federal bureaucracy. He said no President had done so much to meet the needs of the great cities and suburban communities.

"This country and the world need the continued leadership of our President," he concluded.

In a political and procedural innovation, the convention managers then distributed the seconding honors to a diligently balanced panel, whose members had 30 seconds to add their voices to the paean.

There was Jody E. Smith,' at 19 the nation's youngest Mayor, a delegate from Ayrshire, Iowa. Then Mr. Hickel and Miss Dedra Geran, a black 18-year-old student from Las Vegas, an alternate delegate.

Buckley Speaks

From New York also came the voice of Senator Buckley, followed by John McCarrell, also not a delegate but a Democrat and president of Local 544 of the United Automobile Workers in a Pittsburgh suburb.

To add a few words in Spanish there was Representative Manuel Lujan Jr., chairman of the New Mexico delegation. And from Milwaukee there was one of the party's special prizes this year, Mrs. Henry Maier, the wife of the city's Democratic Mayor.

There was also a Vietnam war veteran, John O'Neill of San Antonio, Tex.; Representative Edward Derwinski, a Polish-American Republican from South Holland, Ill.; Anne Smith Bedsole, a housewife from Mobile who is an Alabama delegate, and the President's special friend, Frank Borman, the former astronaut.

No Conservative Rival

The tugs of unity have been so strong at this convention that most dissent has been forced or shamed into silence.

Mr. McCloskey, who opposed Mr. Nixon in the primaries in protest against his war policies, came here with only a single vote. It was dutifully cast by the New Mexico delegation, but it was a disembodied vote as all that state's seats were assigned to Nixon loyalists.

There was no trace at all here of the equally modest conservative primary contest waged against the President by Representative John M. Ashbrook of Ohio.

Although there is known to be opposition in some delegations to the renomination of Vice President Agnew, it too has no political sponsorship here. The ticket is to be completed formally tomorrow evening, just before Mr. Agnew and Mr. Nixon deliver their acceptance speeches.

To preserve the aura of harmony, the White House had tried for a week to arrange a compromise on the rules issue, which spurred the only intense debate here, in or out of the hall.

But the deals offered to the liberal challengers were deemed to be so modest that the delegations of New York and other states, urged on by Governor Rockefeller and Senator Charles H. Percy of Illinois, insisted on a public airing.

The liberals wanted an apportionment system that would give some reward for electing Republican officeholders even if the state were carried by a Democratic Presidential candidate.

The conservatives produced a proposal that would reward mostly a heavy Presidential turnout, and the reward would be more generous in smaller states. New York's stake in the argument, if the plans were in effect now, was the difference between 18 and 126.

The liberals' compromise, offered by Representative William A. Steiger of Wisconsin, appeared unacceptable the moment debate began. It was scorned by a series of speakers, ending with Gov. Ronald Reagan of California, who said it sounded as if the Democrats were back and imposing reforms like those sponsored by Mr. McGovern in his party.

Mr. Percy, who is thought of here as one possible challenger of Mr. Agnew for the Presidential nomination in 1976, had fought for the change but refused to join the futile floor fight, apparently in fear of alienating many delegates.

The convention also took a series of other voice votes. After a few minutes of debate, and with the approval of party leaders, the delegates inserted a paragraph into the platform promising preference for Indians in the hiring and promotions for Indian affairs programs. They shouted down a Utah delegate's wish that the platform oppose the deficit budgets that Mr. Nixon has been using to prod the economy back to life.

As finally adopted, it still remained Mr. Nixon's platform, including his terms for peace in Vietnam, his concept of the proper defense budget, his strong opposition to school busing for integration and to stronger Federal laws controlling gun sales and his strong pitch to the no longer solidly Democratic ranks of organized labor.

Although many past Republican planks, concepts and principles have been tossed overboard in the years of the Nixon Administration, the transformation was recorded enthusiastically here today.

August 23, 1972

McGovern Accuses Nixon Of Whitewash on Break-In

By DOUGLAS E. KNEELAND
WASHINGTON, Sept. 16 — Senator George McGovern accused President Nixon today of having ordered a "whitewash" in the Federal grand jury investigation of the alleged bugging on June 17 of the Democratic national headquarters at the Watergate complex.

Yesterday the grand jury indicted two former White House aides and the five men seized by the police inside the headquarters in the early morning on charges of having conspired to break into the offices.

Although his first reaction yesterday to the indictment was measured, the Democratic Presidential candidate called a news conference today at his $110,000 Japanese-style house in a fashionable section of this capital to make one of his strongest condemnations of his Republican opponent.

"From the first count to the last, the Federal grand jury indictment returned yesterday in the Democratic bugging case spells whitewash," Senator McGovern declared, standing in the shade of his porch as newsmen gathered in the sunlit driveway.

"And I suggest," he continued, "that this blatant miscarriage of justice was ordered by the White House to spare them embarrassment in an election year."

Later today, the Justice Department vigorously countered Mr. McGovern's charges, describing them as "a grievous attack on the integrity of the 23 good citizens of the District of Columbia" who served on the grand jury.

In a statement of rebuttal, Henry E. Petersen, Assistant Attorney General in charge of the Criminal Division, said the department's investigation of the Watergate case had been "among the most exhaustive and far-reaching in my 25 years in the Justice Department," with 333 agents involved in the operation.

Before reading a prepared statement for the television cameras, Mr. McGovern said that he had interrupted what was supposed to have been a day of rest after two weeks of intensive campaigning from coast to coast.

The reason, he said, is that he believes the implications of the Justice Department's announcement that the indictments have ended the investigation of the case are of "the gravest importance."

"I think it goes right to the heart of the moral standards of this nation," he said. "There has been a growing pattern of immorality associated with the Russian wheat deal, with the I.T.T. case, with the handling of campaign funds, and now the latest revelation with regard to the invasion of the Democratic headquarters at the Watergate."

The two former White House aides who were indicted were G. Gordon Liddy, a former Presidential assistant on domestic affairs who at the time of the break-in was counsel to the finance committee for the Committee for the Re-election of the President, and E. Howard Hunt Jr., a former White House consultant and associate of Mr. Liddy.

"The questions left unanswered by that grand jury are staggering," Mr. McGovern said today. He went on to list them as:

¶"Who ordered this act of political espionage?

¶"Who paid for it?

¶"Who contributed the $114,-000 that went from the Nixon campaign committee to the bank account of one of the men arrested, and that paid off the spies for their work?

¶"Who received the memoranda of the tapped telephone conversation?"

Continuing, he said that the "Nixon Administration asks us to believe that the Watergate Five, plus two lowly White House operatives, dreamed up and carried out this shabby scheme to spy on the Democratic party all on their own, with no authority from above."

"The Administration, with its total control of the grand jury," he went on, "asks us to ignore the diversion of $114,-000 in secret campaign funds into the hands of this political espionage squad."

A $1-million suit by the Democrats has charged that Maurice H. Stans, chairman of the finance committee of the Committee for the Re-Election of the President, delivered the $114,000 to finance a spy squad. Mr. Stans has filed a countersuit of $2.5-million against the Democrats for what he called using the courts as an instrument "for creating political headlines."

Mr. McGovern renewed his request that Mr. Nixon appoint an "impartial" investigator such as former Chief Justice Earl Warren or J. Lee Rankin, counsel for the City of New York. If the President does not, he said, it will "be a very serious dereliction of duty, indeed."

Senator McGovern, as he has stumped around the country, has been increasingly sharp in his criticisms of the Nixon Administration.

He and his advisers are known to believe that they must get President Nixon to engage in some political dialogue, rather than maintain his stance of being above the battle, if they are to make up what appears to be a large Republican lead.

To that end, Senator McGovern has repeatedly mentioned the Watergate case in speeches. The immediate and angry response that such references have drawn from partisan Democratic crowds has surprised even his leading strategists.

However, when the indictments were handed down yesterday, Mr. McGovern merely said that they "point up the seriousness in the matter and what now needs to be pursued is how it [the break-in at the headquarters] was funded and whether there are violations there, which there seem to be."

By today, it was apparent that Senator McGovern and his senior advisers had decided they had a much larger issue in the Watergate case than they had hoped for. This was manifested in the calling of the news conference at a time when coverage of it would make the evening television news shows and be published in Sunday newspapers.

And Mr. McGovern left no doubt that he intended to make the case a major issue in his campaign for the Presidency.

"I charge that at all stages of this investigation," he said, "it remained a political case under the total direction and control of Mr. Nixon's political operatives, working through Mr. [Attorney General Richard G.] Kleindienst."

Concluding, he said, "The President of the United States can and must summon this nation to a higher moral standard than these sorry events have indicated. And that is why I intend to pursue this case the length and breadth of the land."

The statement by Assistant Attorney General Petersen countering Senator McGovern's charges follows:

"Senator McGovern's charges are completely unfounded and are a grievous attack on the integrity of the 23 good citizens of the District of Columbia who served on the Watergate grand jury faithfully and well.

"The investigation has been conducted under my supervision. In no instance has there been any limitation of any kind by anyone on the conduct of the investigation.

"Indeed, the investigation by both the F.B.I. and the grand jury has been among the most exhaustive and far-reaching in my 25 years in the Department of Justice.

"The F.B.I. investigation was carried out by 333 agents operating from 51 field offices in the United States and in four foreign capitals. They developed 1,897 leads, they conducted 1,551 interviews and expended a total of 14,098 man-hours.

"The grand jury held sessions for 125 hours over a period of 35 days. These jurors were scrupulously conscientious and thorough in their examination of some 50 witnesses. All aspects of the alleged break-in and bugging were studied in detail, including questions about the source and distribution of any funds relating to the incident, and the jurors were vigorous in their own questioning of witnesses.

"As the trial goes forward, the thoroughness of the grand jury investigation will become apparent."

September 17, 1972

G.O.P. Discloses Corporate Aid on Convention

By BEN A. FRANKLIN
Special to The New York Times

WASHINGTON, Oct. 18— Nearly half the $1.8-million reported cost of the Republican National Convention earlier this year was paid for by defense contractors, other large corporations doing business with the Government, and businesses regulated by Federal agencies, according to a financial disclosure statement required by law and filed here by the Republicans today.

The $860,000 in contributions, made by a total of 60 corporations, was in the form of payments for advertising space in the Republican National Committee's convention program book, at $10,000 or more a page, a practice also pursued by the Democratic National Committee, but with far less success.

According to less complete financial data filed last month with the Government by the Democratic National Commit-

tee, the Democrats netted only about $700,000 from the sale of ads in their convention program, about half of it remitted by corporations with major Government contracts or under Federal regulation. The Democratic Convention, held in Miami Beach last July, was reported to have cost $2-million.

The financial report filed today by the treasurer of the Republicans' Convention arrangements Committee, Mrs. J. Willard Marriott, said that the sale of all ads in the program book had brought in a total of $1,664,601, less the $218,386 reported production costs of the magazine-style program. The net was $1,446,115, or 78 per cent of the party's cash outlay for the Miami Beach convention from Aug. 21 to Aug. 24.

A separate group, the Finance Committee to Re-elect the President, Mr. Nixon's chief campaign finance organization, has been fighting an attempt

in Federal Court here to force disclosure of donors who made contributions before April 7, the effective date of the new Federal Election Campaign Act.

But the Republican National Committee's convention report today included a letter from Mrs. Marion Marriott, the wife of the hotel and restaurant chain owner, saying that all convention transactions back to last Jan. 1 were being voluntarily disclosed.

In an interview, Mrs. Marriott said that no policy conflict with the Finance Committee to Re-elect the President had been intended. "I didn't check it out with them," she said. "We did our report this way for our own bookkeeping convenience."

A spokesman for the Finance Committee to Re-elect the President declined to comment, saying that the committee's position on pre-April 7 disclosure had been given in court. The committee's lawyers have contended that such disclosure, if

required by the court, would impinge on the constitutional rights of Republican donors.

The Republican convention statement itemized expenditures of from $10,000 to $11,500 a page for program ads placed by such companies as General Motors, Ford, Chrysler, International Telephone and Telegraph, the Aluminum Company of America, North American Rockwell, Ingersoll-Rand, Todd Shipyards, the McDonnell Douglas Corporation and a long list of electronics, basic manufacturing, heavy construction, airline, railway, petroleum and communications companies.

The Republicans said that they would close the books on their 1972 convention with a surplus of about $100,000, to be transferred to a fund for planning the 1976 convention. The Democratic National Committee, already carrying more than $9-million in debts from the 1968 campaign, said last month that their convention this year had added $127,000 to the outstanding debt.

October 19, 1972

Nixon Vows to Back Individualist Values In a Second Term

By ROBERT B. SEMPLE Jr.
Special to The New York Times

WASHINGTON, Oct. 21— President Nixon set forth today his vision of the moral values that animate the nation and pledged to champion those values in a second term.

In the third of a series of campaign radio addresses, he set aside what he called "current issues" to focus on his "philosophy of government" and to sketch in general terms "the principles which will guide me in making decisions over the next four years."

He did not mention his opponent, Senator George McGovern of South Dakota. But taken as a whole, his speech— the product of several weeks of work with William Safire, White House speechwriter, constituted an effort to draw a distinction between the values he holds and those he perceives to be held by Mr. McGovern and his followers.

Mr. Nixon's explicit message was that the majority of Americans still believe in individualism, the virtue of hard work, the rightness of receiving rewards for achievement and a sense of community and family.

His implicit message—reminiscent of some of the earlier speeches of Vice President Agnew—was that his opponents were élitist, "self-righteous" and scornful, that they had only contempt for basic values and were trying to make those who subscribed to them feel guilty.

The essential passages in the speech were as follows:

"To them," he said of his unnamed opponents, "the will of the people is the 'prejudice of the masses.' They deride anyone who wants to respond to that will of the people as 'pandering to the crowd.' A decent respect for the practice of majority rule is automatically denounced as 'political expediency.'

"I totally reject this philosophy.

"When a man sees more and more of the money he earns taken away by government taxation, and he objects to that, I don't think it is right to charge him with selfishness, with not caring about the poor and the dependent.

"When a mother sees her child taken from a neighborhood school and transported miles away, and she objects to that, I don't think it is right to charge her with bigotry.

"When young people apply for jobs—in politics or in industry—and find the doors closed because they don't fit into some numerical quota, despite their ability, and they object—I don't think it is right to condemn those young people as insensitive or racist.

"Of course, some people oppose income redistribution and busing for the wrong reasons.

But they are by no means the majority of Americans, who oppose them for the right reasons.

"It is time that good, decent people stop letting themselves be bulldozed by anybody who presumes to be the self-righteous moral judge of our society.

"There is no reason to feel guilty about wanting to enjoy what you get and get what you earn, about wanting your children in good schools close to home or about wanting to be judged fairly on your ability. Those are not values to be ashamed of; those are values to be proud of; those are values that I shall always stand up for when they come under attack."

'New American Majority'

Mr. Nixon identified himself with principles that he had found "deep in the American spirit" and portrayed himself as unusually sensitive to those principles. As evidence, he offered the positions and actions that he had taken on containing taxes, controlling inflation and on school busing and preserving the nation's national security.

"The new American majority," he said, "believes that each person should have more of the say in how he lives his own life, how he spends his paycheck, how he brings up his children.

"The new American majority believes in taking better care of those who truly cannot care for themselves, so that they can lead lives of dignity and self-respect.

"The new American majority believes in taking whatever ac-

tion is needed to hold down the cost of living, so that everyone's standard of living can go up.

"The new American majority believes in a national defense second to none, so that America can help bring about a generation of peace.

"These are not the beliefs of selfish people. On the contrary, they are the beliefs of a generous and self-reliant people, a people of intellect and character, whose values deserve respect in every segment of our population."

In some passages, Mr. Nixon seemed almost to claim victory in advance, suggesting that Americans who shared his views represented a "new American majority" that would give him a second term in office.

The President said that he would take unpopular positions when necessary and would neither tailor his actions to the public opinion polls nor "follow the opinion of the majority down the line."

But, in what he perceived as a happy coincidence, he said that he had found that "what the new majority wants for America and what I want for this nation are basically the same."

Mr. Nixon's address was broadcast from his Camp David retreat in the Maryland mountains, where he is spending the weekend. He will deliver a Veterans Day radio address at 10:36 A.M. tomorrow over the Columbia Broadcasting System, the National Broadcasting Company and the Mutual Broadcasting System.

October 22, 1972

351

The 'Secret' Key Issue

Study of Polls Shows Racial Attitudes To Be Critical, With Nixon the Gainer

By JACK ROSENTHAL
Special to The New York Times

WASHINGTON, Nov. 5—Like the dog that, as Sherlock Holmes observed, did not bark, what may be the underlying issue of the Presidential campaign of 1972 never really came out into the open. The surface talk has been about bombing or bugging or inflation. But close analysis of the endless rows of computer tabulations from The New York Times/Yankelovich political polls indicates that the decisive issue might have been race—not racism, perhaps—but certainly race. The beneficiary, hands down, is Richard Nixon.

News Analysis

Race-based controversies, to be sure, have appeared sporadically, as in the desegregation turmoil in the Canarsie section of Brooklyn or in earlier busing disputes in Michigan. But even these were only fragmentary signs.

"The real issue," as the Rev. Jesse L. Jackson tells his black followers in Chicago, "is not the bus. It's us."

The accuracy of his insight is bolstered by the subtler finding of The Times/Yankelovich surveys. They strongly suggest that race has been a dirty little secret that is neither little nor

secret, but central to current politics.

Reluctance to Talk

Americans do not like to talk candidly about race to strangers. Usually, when polltakers ask about equal opportunity or civil rights, people dutifully give answers that certify them as good citizens.

But occasionally a survey question is accepted as neutral and then the answers provide a rich core sample of deeper racial feelings.

For example, The Times's surveys asked, "Do you feel that minority groups are receiving too much, too little or just about the right amount of attention?"

Even after four years of what black leaders have assailed as "benign neglect" of minority needs, four of every ten voters answered "too much." And of this group, almost 80 per cent said they would vote for President Nixon.

Light on Democrats

Many of these voters are Republicans, already committed to vote for Mr. Nixon. But the responses cast fuller light on Democrats, whose party has been, for a decade, a flagship of civil rights and equal opportunity.

That tradition is reflected by

Democrats who say that they will vote for George McGovern Tuesday. Less than 25 per cent of them think that undue attention is being paid to minorities.

On the other hand, a third of the Democrats—twice the usual rate—say they will defect and vote for President Nixon. Of this group, more than half the whites say that minorities, particularly blacks, have been getting "too much" attention.

The parallel is hard to escape. There are twice as many Democratic defectors as usual, and the defectors are twice as likely to resent minority group gains.

Support for Wallace

A large share—but still less than half—of those apparently defecting for reasons of race say that they would vote for George C. Wallace if the Alabama governor were a candidate again.

Were Mr. McGovern able to hold the defection rate down to normal, the polls now would not be showing a Nixon landslide, but only a slight Nixon lead.

There is a series of issues that, for many voters, add up to race—welfare, job quotas, education, crime. On these, the Democratic defectors express strikingly different views from those of the loyalist Democrats.

Who would do the better job of cleaning up "the welfare mess"? Among the defectors, 54 per cent say Mr. Nixon. Among the McGovern Democrats, 8 per cent say Mr. Nixon.

Who would do more for minorities? Among the defectors, 43 per cent say Mr. Nixon. Among the loyalists, the figure for him is 7 per cent.

Who would do best at reducing crime? The Nixon figure among the defectors is 58 per cent, among the loyalists only 25 per cent.

There is a technical explanation for such contrasts, something that analysts call a "halo effect." Having decided to vote for Mr. Nixon, the defectors are likely to justify their choice by giving him favorable ratings on issues.

A Puzzling Campaign

But the halo effect is only a partial explanation. The fact remains that, from the very beginning of the general election campaign, twice the usual proportion of Democrats have decided to vote Republican.

That is one of the major phenomena of the whole puzzling campaign. Another puzzle is why there was so little change over the months. In August, the Gallup Poll gave Mr. Nixon 64 per cent. Today, it gives him 62.

Still another puzzle has been the voters' seeming indifference to the more publicized campaign issues. Only a bare majority cite even the Vietnam war as a major national concern.

The veiled amalgam of race issues offers an answer to all these anomalies. It is as though large numbers of white voters decided, quietly and early, that Jesse L. Jackson was right and that the fundamental issue is "them."

November 6, 1972

The Campaign Issues

Many Questions of Interest to Voters Never Got Past Convention Debate

JOHN HERBERS
Special to The New York Times

WASHINGTON, Nov. 6 — A young salesman stood on a corner in Cheyenne, Wyo., a few days ago and expounded at length on the need for tax reform, especially in the closing of loopholes that benefit the rich. It was almost precisely the argument advanced by Senator George McGovern all this year in the Presidential race, and to the salesman it was the most burning national issue of the day. Yet he expected to vote for President Nixon, he said, because he did not quite trust

News Analysis

Senator McGovern and he thought that real tax reform would have to await the arrival of a more convincing candidate on the national scene.

His outlook was indicative of what happened to many important issues this year. They never got enmeshed in any meaningful sense in the campaigns. While some, such as the economy and Vietnam, were mitigated by developments of recent months, the extent of interest in the issues throughout the year suggests that after the election many of them will still be there, unresolved by the strange 1972 campaign.

According to both sides at the outset, it was to have been an important year for the issues. The two parties were to present a clear choice — on the war, the economy, military spending, social and urban programs, agriculture, health, philosophy of government, busing and others.

Borne Out for a While

For a while the forecast was borne out. For example, hearings that the Democrats held around the country in preparation for drafting the party platform showed an outpouring of interest. A diversity of individuals and groups lined up to show that they felt deeply about national policies and practices.

Many of these concerns found their way into the Democratic platform and the Republicans, although conforming to the wishes of the White House, sought to promote policies to fit the public demand on issues.

But the issues never survived the conventions. There-

after, the Presidential campaign swung on personalities as the issues faded into the background. Some issues had an indirect impact. For example, Senator McGovern had been so closely identified with the New Left on such matters as amnesty and abortion—with the Republicans constantly keeping that image of him before the public—that his credibility was damaged on more substantive matters as tax reform, Vietnam, jobs and military spending.

Some of the issues became silent ones, working mostly to Mr. Nixon's advantage, according to the public opinion surveys. His opposition to busing and "forced integration" of suburban housing, although rarely discussed by either side, worked to President Nixon's favor in many communities.

Issues Confused

A number of the issues became thoroughly confused as the campaign progressed. The Democrats began the year convinced that health would work

352

to their advantage. Senator Edward M. Kennedy and Leonard Woodcock, president of the United Automobile Workers, wanted Senator McGovern to come out strongly for their national health insurance plan, as the Democratic platform had done.

But Senator McGovern shied away from anything but token support of the plan, because it would have added billions of dollars to his list of spending programs, which were already under fire from the Republicans as an excessive drain on the Federal Treasury. For

their part, the Republicans pointed to health legislation that the White House had proposed, half-heartedly, and let it go at that.

Therefore, when the new Congress opens next year, the health issue will be right back where it was at the beginning of this year, as will the debate over what to do about chronic unemployment, tax loopholes, property taxes, racial divisions and other things that have been worrying people.

Impact on Congress Races

Yet the issues did cut, in a sense, on one level this year

—in the races for the House and Senate. All across the country, Democratic candidates who had been associated with the social programs of the 1960's were thrown on the defensive as their Republican opponents sought to identify them, not with their own stands on the issues, but with Senator McGovern's positions.

With few exceptions, there was, on the part of Democrats who had been known as Liberals, backpedaling on racial integration, busing, a guaranteed income, social programs with Federal controls and other matters that national Dem-

ocrats had endorsed in recent years. The campaigns were generally devoid of idealistic appeals and pleas for unity and healing. They focused instead on such matters as reducing property taxes for the middle class and cutting Federal spending.

As a result, whichever party prevails in the Congressional elections, the promises that the winners must keep can be expected to follow the tone and direction that have been set by President Nixon.

November 7, 1972

NIXON ELECTED IN LANDSLIDE; M'GOVERN IS BEATEN IN STATE; DEMOCRATS RETAIN CONGRESS

MARGIN ABOUT 60%

Massachusetts Is Only State to Give Vote to the Dakotan

By MAX FRANKEL

Richard Milhous Nixon won re-election by a huge majority yesterday, perhaps the largest ever given a President.

Mr. Nixon scored a stunning personal triumph in all sections of the country, sweeping New York and most other bastions of Democratic strength.

He was gathering more than 60 per cent of the nation's ballots and more than 500 electoral votes. He lost only Massachusetts and the District of Columbia.

The victory was reminiscent of the landslide triumphs of Franklin D. Roosevelt in 1936 and Lyndon B. Johnson in 1964, although it could fall just short of their record proportions.

Tickets Are Split

Despite this drubbing of George Stanley McGovern, the Democratic challenger, the voters split their tickets in record numbers to leave the Democrats in control of both houses of Congress and a majority of the nation's governorships. Mr.

Nixon thus became the first two-term President to face an opposition Congress at both inaugurals.

The turnout of voters appeared to be unusually low, despite jams at many polling places. Projections indicated a total vote of 76 million out of a voting-age population of 139.6 million, or only about 54 per cent. If accurate, that would be the lowest proportion since 51.4 per cent in 1948. The percentage had been over 60 per cent in every election since then.

May Claim Mandate

The President seemed certain, however, to claim a clear mandate for his policies of gradual disengagement from Vietnam, continued strong spending on defense, opposition to busing to integrate the schools and a slowdown in Federal spending for social programs. These are the issues he stressed through the campaign.

The 59-year-old Mr. Nixon, who will be 60 before inauguration on Jan. 20, could also claim a resounding personal vindication against the strong charges of corruption brought against him personally by the opposition.

By coincidence, the greatest triumph of his 26 years in national politics came on the 10th anniversary of his defeat for Governor of California — the time he told newsmen they would not have Nixon to kick

around anymore.

Mr. McGovern, 50, conceded defeat before midnight in the East with a telegram of support for the President if he leads the nation to peace abroad and justice at home.

The South Dakotan took credit for helping to push the Administration nearer to peace in Indochina and assured his cheering supporters at the Sioux Falls Coliseum that their defeat would bear fruit for years to come.

The President responded in a brief address from the White House, expressing appreciation to his supporters and respect for the supporters of Mr. McGovern, whose name he pronounced for the first time in months. He promised rapid progress toward peace and prosperity.

Mr. Nixon carried into office again his running mate, Vice President Spiro Theodore Agnew, who will now be regarded as a formidable candidate for the Republican Presidential nomination four years hence.

His opponent, Robert Sargent Shriver Jr., has left many with the impression that he, too, will seek to lead his party. Both will celebrate birthdays tomorrow, Mr. Agnew his 54th, Mr. Shriver his 57th.

Unlike four years ago, when he became the 37th President by the slenderest of margins, Mr. Nixon did not suffer even a moment's suspense last night. As predicted by the public opinion polls, he gathered three votes or more for every two for his opponent.

Indeed, in state after state, Mr. Nixon's margin was remarkably close to the combined total won by him and the third-party candidate, George C. Wallace, in 1968. Had Mr. Wallace not been eliminated from contention this year by a crippling bullet, the 1972 contest would have been much closer.

But in the clear field against Mr. McGovern, the President swept almost everything in sight. Projections based on early returns showed him getting between 55 and 60 per cent in the cities, 70 per cent in suburbs and nearly 80 per cent in rural regions.

Mr. Nixon's margins of victory in the states ranged from 52 per cent in Rhode Island and Wisconsin to an estimated 75 per cent in Oklahoma.

Mr. McGovern carried Massachusetts by a margin of 5 to 4. Hubert Humphrey triumphed there by 2 to 1 four years ago.

The South Dakotan carried the District of Columbia and its black majority with a decisive 72 per cent.

The President appeared to have improved his standing with all identifiable groups in the electorate, even blacks and Jews who still gave majorities to Democrats.

The first-time young voters, upon whom Mr. McGovern had counted throughout his long struggle for the nomination, appeared to have divided their votes 50-50.

The bonds of party loyalty were shattered in every part of the country. The defections of Democrats from New York to California and overwhelmingly in the once solidly Democratic South were so great that

353

the computers projecting early returns for the television networks had no difficulty marking state after state in the Nixon column.

Many Lost Interest

The unanimous verdict of the opinion polls and political analysts had deprived the campaign of much of the customary suspense. Many voters were found to have lost interest in the race, in part because they felt sure of the outcome, often because they felt no enthusiasm for either candidate.

Yet the contest was fiercely fought.

It was by far the most lavishly financed Presidential campaign, with Mr. Nixon's forces spending nearly $50-million and Mr. McGovern's at least $25-million.

The President was the beneficiary of many huge individual contributions, including two of at least $1-million each. Mr. McGovern compensated for the loss of many traditional big Democratic contributors with mail solicitations that evoked an estimated 650,000 individual responses.

And the charges exchanged by the two parties were not lacking in bite.

Mr. Nixon set an idealistic tone at the start, seeking "four more years" to complete what he called the works of peace in the world.

But without mentioning his opponent by name, he accused him of wishing to "stain the honor" of the nation by settling for "surrender" in Vietnam and of proposing a fatal weakening of the country's defenses.

Senator McGovern's lofty appeal was that Americans should "come home" to the ideals of the past, home from foreign adventure and back to a concern for the poor.

But he combined this with bitter attacks upon the President, accusing him of barbaric tactics in Indochina, of corruption and big-business favoritism and of deception of the voters.

The fundamental contrast between the contenders lay in their style of campaigning,

clearly reflecting their own agreement with the conventional finding that Mr. Nixon was far in front from the outset.

The President pleaded the press of business at the White House and left most of the stump-running to Vice President Agnew and dozens of other stand-ins.

He held only one news conference during the campaign, ventured into only a few well-prepared urban parades and topped a series of radio speeches with only one long television speech.

Mr. McGovern, by contrast, kept criss-crossing the country, seeking crowds and enthusiasm and money and concentrating his energies on the most populous states with the large blocks of electoral votes.

He and his running mate, Mr. Shriver, made a daily pitch for free time on television news shows and combined rally appearances with a heavy use of purchased television time.

With the outcome so widely taken for granted, the principal questions on election night turned on the size of Mr. Nixon's majority and the question of how many other Republicans, particularly candidates for the Senate, he could pull along to victory.

The President, in his last bid for national office—and his fifth in 20 years—was also competing against the statistics of history.

A landslide as such is not an unusual phenomenon. The term has been applied to cases in which a Presidential candidate lost no more than 10 states or carried 80 per cent of the electoral votes or at least 53 per cent of the total popular vote. By those standards, there have been 24 landslides in the previous 46 Presidential contests.

George Washington twice and James Monroe in 1820 won the electoral votes of all states. In this century, the record belongs to Franklin D. Roosevelt, who lost only Maine and Vermont in 1936.

The modern records for total

electoral votes are Mr. Roosevelt's 98 per cent in 1936 and Lyndon B. Johnson's 90 per cent in 1964.

Johnson the Leader

The data on popular votes date back to 1824. Mr. Johnson's share of 61.1 per cent in 1964 topped Mr. Roosevelt's 60.8 per cent in 1936, Warren G. Harding's 60.3 per cent in 1920 and Herbert Hoover's 58.2 per cent in 1928.

In view of his demonstrated interest in historical firsts, Mr. Nixon was probably also aware of some other possible records that were within his reach.

Since Jefferson, no man who had served as Vice President was ever elected to two full terms in his own right. And no two-term Vice President had ever been elected to two terms as President.

Also, there have been five previous teams that were elected to two terms as President and Vice President, and only one previous Republican team, that of Dwight D. Eisenhower and Mr. Nixon. The others were George Washington and John Adams, James Monroe and Daniel D. Tompkins, Woodrow Wilson and Thomas R. Marshall and Franklin D. Roosevelt and John N. Garner.

Since the creation of the modern major parties in 1854, only two Presidents had begun terms of office with the opposition in control of Congress: Mr. Eisenhower in his second term in 1956 and Mr. Nixon on his first in 1968. No President had ever begun two terms against an opposition Congress.

Mr. Nixon was ambivalent throughout the 1972 campaign about whether to seek the largest possible mandate for himself or to risk offending some Democratic voters by supporting Republican candidates for Congress.

For the most part, he stressed his own contest, making only token appearances in the closing weeks in states where Republican Senate candidates had complained of the lack of help.

The President yielded to the

calculation of his strategists that the Senate might be within reach but that the House was not.

At the same time, he appeared to believe that with a huge popular vote and the ideological support of many Southern and conservative Democrats he would be able to work almost as well with an opposition Congress as with one whose leadership and committees were in the control of Republicans.

Mr. Nixon had drawn much criticism for the partisan vigor with which he tried to capture control of Congress in 1970. In his own cause this year, he remained aloof and serene to the end.

Nixon's Vote on Coast

The President and Mrs. Nixon voted when the polls opened at 7 A.M. yesterday at a schoolhouse near their villa at San Clemente, Calif., and then flew across the coutry to await the returns at a private dinner in the White House.

Mr. and Mrs. McGovern voted in a church in the Senator's home town of Mitchell, S.D., and then drove to Sioux Falls to await the verdict.

In many states, yesterday's Presidential ballot also carried the names of one or more minor-party candidates.

They were:

American Independent party—John G. Schmitz for President and Thomas J. Anderson for Vice President (33 states).

People's party—Benjamin Spock and Julius Hobson (10 states).

Socialist Workers' party—Linda Jenness and Andrew Pulley.

Communist party—Gus Hall and Jarvis Tyner.

Socialist Labor party—Louis Fisher and Genevieve Gunderson.

Libertarian party—John Hospers and Theodora Nathan.

Prohibition party—Earl Munn and Marshall Inchaper.

Universal party—Gabriel Green.

America First party—John V. Mahalchik.

November 8, 1972

Nixon Landslide Is Traced To Democratic Defections

Desertion Rate Doubles

By JACK ROSENTHAL

As indicated by the major political polls, more than twice the usual proportion of Democrats abandoned their party's nominee Tuesday and voted for President Nixon.

The Democratic defectors were so numerous, in fact, that

they alone could be said to have given Mr. Nixon his sweeping landslide victory, according to the findings of an extensive post-election survey.

The survey was conducted by George Fine Research, Inc., a New York marketing research company, for C.B.S. News. A total of 17,405 voters were interviewed as they left their poll-

ing places in a national sample of 143 precincts. The total is about 10 times that usually employed in national surveys.

The C.B.S. survey indicated that more than a third of all Democrats—an estimated 36 per cent—voted for Mr. Nixon. This compares with an average defection rate of 16 per cent for the previous five elections.

If Mr. McGovern had been able to hold his Democratic losses down to normal, Mr. Nixon might still have won, but the race would have been very close. Without so many defec-

tors, Mr. Nixon could not have come close to a landslide.

The CBS survey findings closely paralleled what voters had said they would do when interviewed by the Gallup, Harris and Times/Yankelovich political surveys. The final standings compiled by all three organizations almost exactly anticipated the final popular vote.

Among such findings were the following:

¶For the first time in history, Roman Catholic voters, taken as a whole, voted Republican.

354

Previously, they came close to doing so only in 1956, when, according to the Gallup organization, they split 51 to 49 for Adlai E. Stevenson over President Eisenhower. This time, the CBS survey showed, Catholics chose Mr. Nixon by about 53 to 46.

¶For the first time, at least in recent history, blue-collar voters went Republican. They voted 5 to 4 for Mr. Nixon. In the last five elections, they have voted 5 to 4 Democratic.

¶Union families appeared to split evenly. The survey, subject to sampling error of about 2 percentage points, found them 50 per cent for Mr. McGovern, 48 per cent for Mr. Nixon

¶As expected, Mr. McGovern won easily among black and Jewish voters, but among both blocs his majorities appeared somewhat smaller than those estimated for recent Democratic candidates.

¶Mr. McGovern appeared to win the youth vote, but narrowly. The major polls had found first-time voters, aged 18 to 24, about evenly split or slightly favoring Mr. Nixon. The

CBS post-election survey reported a 52-to-46 McGovern margin. This was far from the decisive margin predicted by his strategists.

Projection Recalled

Early in the campaign, they projected a youth vote of 18 million, with Mr. McGovern winning 13 million. The CBS findings indicated, however, that only about 12 million young people had voted. That would mean that about 47 per cent of the 25.7 million new young voters turned out. This is well below the participation rate of about 60 per cent averaged by other adults.

The final findings of the national polls this year came almost as close to the results as in 1968. Then, the Gallup Poll came up with its closest result—43 per cent for Mr. Nixon, 42 for Senator Hubert H. Humphrey. Mr. Nixon's actual margin was 43.4 to 42.7 per cent.

With the total vote count almost complete, the 1972 result was about 61 per cent to 38 per cent. The last Gallup finding published Monday, was 62 to 38. The last Harris finding, also published Monday, was 61 to 39.

The Times/Yankelovich survey, designed to assess elec-

toral vote patterns in the 16 largest states, found a 60-to-40 margin in those states. The estimated total result in those states was 60 to 38.

At least two state polls predicted the outcome in their states with precision. The California Poll, conducted by Mervin Field Research, Inc., found a 14-point Nixon lead as of Nov. 1. The final result in California appeared to be 14 points.

10-Point Forecast Upheld

A state survey in Massachusetts, the only state won by Senator McGovern, produced a similarly exact result. The survey, conducted by Becker Research for the Boston Globe and published Sunday, found a 10-point McGovern lead. Mr. McGovern appears to have won the state by 10 points.

The final Minnesota Poll, published Sunday in The Minneapolis Tribune, found a 17-point Nixon lead. The final result appeared to be a 5-point Nixon margin.

In Detroit, the final finding of a poll by Market Opinion Research for Monday's Detroit News found a 6-point Nixon lead. The President's winning margin in the state appeared to be 13 points.

What the CBS post-election

survey most dramatically validated in the national pre-election polls was the massive shift of Democrats into the Nixon column.

The first clue to the potential magnitude of the defections came in a Times/Yankelovich survey conducted immediately after the California primary last June. It found that 40 per cent of the Democrats who had supported Senator Humphrey in the primary said that they would vote for Mr. Nixon if Mr. McGovern ended up as the Democratic nominee.

High defection rates were found in later Times surveys and by both the Gallup and Harris organizations. The last Gallup estimate was that 32 per cent of the Democrats would vote for Mr. Nixon—very close to the 36 per cent figure reported today by CBS.

Both the CBS survey and the pre-election polls found that, as is customary, virtually all Republicans remained loyal to their party's candidate. The only recent exception was in 1964, when 20 per cent of the Republicans voted for President Johnson.

November 9, 1972

MODERATES START DEMOCRATIC GROUP

WASHINGTON, Nov. 12 (AP) —Nearly two dozen veteran Democratic officeholders, authors and strategists, upset by what they call Senator George McGovern's "new politics," are

starting an organization for "restoring the party to its rightful place of leadership."

Called the Coalition for a Democratic Majority, the organization is envisioned as a base through which moderate and so-called "old-line" Democrates would influence the party's structure and Democratic members of Congress.

Among the sponsors are Ben J. Wattenberg, the author and political analyst; Representatives Richard Bolling of Missouri and Thomas S. Foley of Washington; Patricia Roberts Harris, chairman of the Credentials Committee at the party's convention last July; Max Kampelman, a Washington lawyer and former aide to Senator

Hubert H. Humphrey, and Nathan Glazer and Seymour M. Lipset, the authors.

Mr. Wattenberg said Senators Humphrey of Minnesota and Henry M. Jackson of Washington are "encouraging" the group.

November 13, 1972

INVESTIGATORS TERM G.O.P. SPYING A WIDESPREAD ATTEMPT TO INSURE WEAK DEMOCRATIC NOMINEE IN 1972

Drive Viewed as Way to Help McGovern Get Nomination

By SEYMOUR M. HERSH
Special to The New York Times

WASHINGTON, May 2—Government investigators say they now have evidence that Republican sabotage and espionage efforts in the election cam-

paign last year were far more widespread than was previously known and were designed to help Senator George McGovern win the Democratic nomination for President.

Republicans viewed Senator McGovern, the eventual nominee, as the weakest candidate President Nixon could face, the investigators said. They added that there was no way of determining how much over-all impact the major Republican

intelligence effort, organized at a cost not yet fully estimated, had upon the 1972 primaries.

The investigators said that the espionage program, initially authorized by H. R. Haldeman, the White House chief of staff, who resigned Monday, included at its peak three networks of agents controlled by the White House and the Committee for the Re-election of the President.

The Federal investigators said they had confirmed that

at least some allegations about Republican disruption voiced last year by Democratic candidates were substantially correct.

Muskie Camp Infiltrated

These sources said there was now evidence that a Nixon supporter was infiltrated into the campaign offices of Senator Edmund S. Muskie, Democrat of Maine, in early 1972. Once there, he intercepted a variety of confidential documents that were subsequently leaked to the press.

The basic Republican strategy was worked out in early 1971, investigators said, when Mr. Nixon was running behind Senator Muskie in public opinion polls. The Harris survey, for example, showed that by early May, 1971, Mr. Muskie had a 47-to-39 per cent lead over the President, an increase of 3 percentage points in three months.

The investigators emphasized that there is no evidence thus far that Republican leaders had held a formal meeting at the White House or elsewhere in which they discussed plans to defeat Senator Muskie so as to increase the chance of Senator McGovern, a South Dakota Democrat.

"Nonetheless," one source said, "there was a definite strategy worked out before the election. They tried to make sure that the Democrats nominated their weakest candidate."

In this context, the source said, the bugging of the Democratic National Committee headquarters in the Watergate complex here in June, 1972, was only a small part of the over-all effort.

"The Republicans had people in all of the campaigns," one investigator said, "but not at high levels. They had little people nobody would suspect."

"They started playing tricks with the avowed goal of heavily influencing the nomination of the Democratic candidate," he added.

It was widely known in the last campaign that Republican strategists considered Mr. McGovern the most vulnerable Democratic candidate because of his liberal views.

Intelligence operations are commonplace in political campaigns and usually include efforts to collect all published information about an opponent along with occasional efforts to obtain advance copies of speeches, travel schedules and the like.

The Justice Department's fraud unit is known to be investigating the Republican espionage activities for possible violations of Federal law.

The prime espionage target throughout late 1971 and in early 1972, investigators said, was Mr. Muskie, whose campaign was repeatedly jarred by inexplicable incidents — such as the disappearance of vital polling data, the misrouting of the candidate's personal plane, and the "Canuck" letter in the New Hampshire primary that accused Mr. Muskie of casting ethnic slurs on French-Canadians.

"We do have evidence that there was infiltration of the Muskie campaign and that many documents were stolen or photographed," one investigator said.

Letter to Muskie Cited

He specifically cited a private staff letter to Senator Muskie calling on him to stage hearings on a proposed tax bill in California because it would get him "favorable publicity."

The letter, the investigator said, was stolen by an espionage agent and sent to an official in the Republican re-election headquarters who then sent it on to a Washington columnist. When a column about the letter was published a few days later, the source said, an embarrassed Mr. Muskie canceled the proposed hearing.

In a private meeting with a group of Republican Congressmen a little more than a month ago, Mr. Haldeman was reported to have acknowledged being personally responsible for organizing a political intelligence operation in 1972. He was quoted as saying, however, that the project had involved no illegal activities.

The New York Times quoted Government investigators today as saying they had evidence that Mr. Haldeman and John D. Ehrlichman, Mr. Nixon's chief domestic adviser who also resigned Monday, along with John N. Mitchell, former Attorney General, conspired with at least three other officials to arrange a cover-up story to obstruct a Federal investigation into the full ramifications of the Watergate break-in.

Mr. Mitchell issued the following denial today: "A story appearing in today's New York Times alleging that I conspired with H. R. Haldeman, John Ehrlichman and John Dean [the former White House counsel] to obstruct justice in the Watergate case is absolutely false and without factual foundation."

Mr. Ehrlichman and Mr. Haldeman, meanwhile, were scheduled to testify tomorrow before the Federal grand jury investigating the Watergate break-in and cover-up. Both men have denied any wrongdoing.

Investigators, cautioning that their inquiry was far from complete, provided the following account of how the Republican espionage and sabotage operation developed:

Officials around the President, believed to have been led by Mr. Haldeman, began to become concerned about the 1972 elections in early 1971. At some point, Mr. Haldeman decided that a well-planned and well-financed espionage campaign was needed to insure the nomination of the weakest Democratic candidate.

By that time, Herbert W. Kalmbach, Mr. Nixon's personal attorney, who was a chief campaign fund-raiser, was beginning to collect cash that would later be set aside for the espionage operation.

In June, 1971, when The New York Times began publishing the secret Pentagon papers on the history of the Vietnam war, a White House group, called the "plumbers," was assigned to discover who had made the papers available to the press. E. Howard Hunt Jr. and G. Gordon Liddy, two leading members of the eventual Watergate team, were assigned to the operation.

Hunt, a former agent for the Central Intelligence Agency, is known to have begun researching the background of potential Democratic Presidential candidates and recruiting a number of former colleagues and associates for his political operation while working with the "plumbers," so named because their job was to stop leaks of information. Hunt coordinated his political activities with Charles W. Colson, a White House special counsel and its chief political operative.

At the same time, Dwight L. Chapin, a Haldeman protégé who was then Mr. Nixon's appointments secretary, got in touch with Mr. Kalmbach to arrange for payments to Donald H. Segretti, a former college classmate who was recruited to direct the espionage operation.

Agents Organized

Over the next 10 months, Mr. Segretti made more than 20 known contacts in his attempt to recruit fellow informers and agents and established a loosely organized network of about 10 agents. Investigators have determined that many of those received substantial cash payments from Mr. Kalmbach. Others were apparently paid in cash by Mr. Segretti.

By early 1972, both Liddy and Hunt had been reassigned to the Republican re-election committee, where they continued to recruit fellow saboteurs, along with a string of informers and obstructionists who were assigned specific campaign targets, investigators said. One key operation was in Florida, where Miami-based anti-Castroites became involved in the state's primary.

In early February, Hunt and Liddy flew to Miami for a meeting with Mr. Segretti that was arranged by Gordon Strachan, another Haldeman aide who helped direct the Segretti operations in the field.

Two Groups Merged

Mr. Haldeman, working through Mr. Strachan and Mr. Chapin, directly controlled the Segretti operation until the Miami meeting. Afterward, Hunt and Liddy both began to direct more of Mr. Segretti's movements, with Mr. Strachan reduced to a monitoring role.

The merging of the Hunt-Liddy operation with the Segretti - Kalmbach - Chapin group, each with its separate informers and agent provacateurs, was considered an important step, making the over-all operation more manageable, investigators said.

As the campaign picked up steam in 1972, hundreds of persons were added to the re-election committee staff and massive infiltration of other campaigns began, using mostly the young.

At least 30, and possibly 40, paid informers were recruited by March by the re-election campaign and were assigned to various Democratic headquarters and offices. Their basic target initially was Senator

Muskie, but after his setbacks in the early primaries the youths were assigned to infiltrate the campaigns of the other Democrats believed to be among the leading contenders for the nomination — Senators Hubert H. Humphrey of Minnesota and Henry M. Jackson of Washington, investigators said.

The over-all goal of attacking Senator Muskie was quickly revised; instead the new aim would be to do as much damage as possible to the other leading candidates so as to improve the position of Mr. McGovern.

The Times's sources said the Republicans believed that their biggest triumph came in the Florida primary in March, which was won by Gov. George C. Wallace of Alabama.

A few days before the election, a flyer was distributed throughout the state on Muskie stationery accusing both Senator Humphrey and Senator Jackson of illicit sexual activity. That flier has not yet been traced to the re-election effort, the sources said, although that aspect of the inquiry is still going on.

May 3, 1973

Southern G.O.P. and Goldwater Critical of Nixon on Watergate

By BILL KOVACH
Special to The New York Times

WASHINGTON, May 16 — President Nixon's handling of the Watergate scandal was strongly criticized today by leading Republicans, who warned that dwindling confidence in the Government was damaging both the country and the party.

Some 25 Republican party leaders from the Southern states, meeting here privately, concluded that the party might function better by divorcing itself from the Administration unless there was quick action "to restore confidence and reorganize the White House."

Also today Senator Barry Goldwater of Arizona, who was the first and most prominent Republican to urge the President publicly to act in the matter, said today that the President had not gone far enough to restore confidence in his Administration.

"It is not easy for me to say this about my country or my President," Senator Goldwater said in a statement to the press, "but I think the time

has come when someone must say to both of them, let's get going."

Apparently unrelated, the two reactions clearly indicate a rapidly spreading dismay among Republicans over the lingering nature of the scandal and its accompanying paralysis of both the Administration and the party structure.

That concern was expressed by Clarke Reed, Republican state chairman of Mississippi, who has been a key element in the Southern strategy painstakingly constructed by the party over the last several years.

As chairman of the closed meeting, Mr. Reed said it was his judgment that the group "wants this thing absolutely out in the open and completely straight, no matter who is involved, including the President."

Reflecting the bitterness of party professionals that developed during last year's campaign because they were ex-

cluded from the national campaign, and from access to the President by H. R. Haldeman and John D. Ehrlichman, Mr. Reed said that, unless the White House is reorganized soon with "some good political people, the whole thing is up for grabs."

"We have been banging on the door too long," Mr. Reed said. "We hope the President will be with us, but if he isn't and he shows he isn't; if he doesn't change now, after all that we've seen — then we're going to have to go about our business and just not worry about the White House."

Underlying the urgency felt by the party leaders, some of whom are recent converts from the Democratic party like himself, Mr. Reed said that they believe the White House has no more than 30 to 60 days within which to act to restore confidence in the reorganization of the White House and the functioning of the Administration.

He also endorsed Senator Goldwater's statement which was issued earlier in the day.

Senator Goldwater's remarks involved domestic and international signs that confidence in the Nixon Administration had plummeted. Citing the recent sharp increase in the price of gold and a drop in prices on the stock market, the Senator said the "sordid" affair had dominated all action at the top level of government.

Further, he said: "A visit to the Pentagon, which is the seat of our ability and responsibility to maintain peace in this world, leaves one with the impression that these services are suffering from a lack of civilian direction because of the vacancies not yet filled at the secretariat levels."

"A reorganization of bureaus is a decided must for the continuance of our form of government."

While urging that Watergate, which he described as a "blot upon the political records of the United States," should be cleaned up immediately, Senator Goldwater deplored its domination of the entire machinery or government.

"And it is to this end," he said, "that I urge my President to start making moves in the direction of leadership, which has suffered from lack of attention because of an understandable concern about Watergate."

The meeting at the Sheraton-Carlton Hotel of the Southern party chairmen was designed specifically to analyze the impact of Watergate on the party's political future and reflected a radical shift in attitudes in recent weeks. Two weeks ago, Mr. Reed was asked about the political impact of the Watergate scandal and said, at that time, he could see none.

May 17, 1973

Watergate Costing G.O.P. Political Help and Money

By STEVEN V. ROBERTS
Special to The New York Times

LOS ANGELES, July 21—The political organizers at the Republican National Committee in Washington cannot afford a secretary.

In Polk County, Iowa, the

party's annual, door-to-door fund-raising campaign is down 50 per cent, and as one official said, "A lot of our members are embarrassed to go out and ask their friends and neighbors for

money for the Republican party."

Here in California Robert H. Finch, once one of President Nixon's closest advisers, is worrying that his connection with the White House will hamper his political career.

Many Republican officials are incensed at the Presidential advisers involved in Watergate and agree with Gov. Winfield Dunn of Tennessee, who said the party might have to "dis-

avow [the] narrow-minded people who acted to embarrass the President."

Publicly, most Republicans remain stanchly behind President Nixon. But in private, some agree with the California politician who said, "Obviously there is a loss of confidence in the President. It just has to hurt him. I'll say this, I'm glad I'm not running his campaign this November."

Many politicians were watch-

357

ing and waiting before they gauge the ultimate effects of Watergate. But a survey of G.O.P. leaders in more than a dozen states makes it clear that the burgeoning scandal—and its constant repetition on national television—is hurting the Republican party in a variety of ways.

As the Republican National Committee put it recently in an urgent fund-raising appeal:

"As you know, the Republican party is in trouble. We need your help. The deplorable Watergate scandal has cast a pall of suspicion over the activities of the entire Republican party."

All the omens, however, do not presage disaster for Republicans. Such party figures as George Bush, the national chairman, and Vice President Agnew have been barnstorming around the country, stressing the distinction between the party and the Committee for the Re-election of the President and urging voters not to blame the entire party for the "bad judgment [of] a few misguided political adventurers."

Party fund raising is actually running ahead of schedule in a few states like Tennessee, where contributors are getting a guarantee that their money will be used only for local elections.

Republican leaders such as Senators Barry Goldwater of Arizona and Charles H. Percy of Illinois, who spoke out early against Watergate are finding that the scandal holds some political benefits. In California, Republican candidates for the State Legislature have won five of six special elections this year, sometimes in Democratic districts.

But if these bright spots can lighten the gloom, they cannot erase it, and the place most in need of illumination these days is the Republican National Committee. Contributions have dropped so sharply that last week Mr. Bush had to order a 25 per cent cut in staff and the elimination of such extras as leased cars and copying machines.

Staff members offer several explanations, including the following:

⬥The media keep reporting that the re-election committee has a surplus of $4.5-million. But that money is being kept by the re-election committee in case it has to pay damages in several pending lawsuits and is unavailable to the national committee.

⬥Many large Republican contributors gave a lot more than usual to President Nixon's campaign, and do not want to donate again so soon.

⬥Many donors feel betrayed by tales of secret payoffs and cover-ups. As one national committee official put it, "across the board there is deep resentment" about the way campaign funds were used.

⬥This is all compounded by the confusion between the re-election committee, an independent operation set up by the White House, and the formal party structure, which was largely ignored during the Presidential campaign but is now taking the heat for the re-election committee's misdeeds.

The most cautious givers in the current atmosphere are big-money types, the ones who were already bothered by the new campaign financing laws. One good example is W. Clement Stone, the Chicago insurance man who has given nearly $7-million to the Republicans since 1968.

In a recent interview, Mr. Stone said he would be more careful about his contributions and demand a more detailed accounting of their use. "In the future, one has to be certain—no ifs and ands—as to where the money goes," he said.

California, like Tennessee, is meeting its quota on the state level, but contributions to the Los Angeles County party apparatus are down almost 70 per cent. Polk County in Iowa, which includes Des Moines, is only slightly better off. Greg Orcutt, assistant to the county chairman, explained, "We've been working in the county for years to create trust in people, but Watergate is just destroying that trust."

The political outlook is less tangible and harder to evaluate. Mr. Finch is now leaning against entering a race for either Governor or Senator, and as he complained recently, "Every time they show an organization chart of the White House [at the Watergate hearings] I'm on it."

In Utah, Desmond Barker, a former White House aide, has reportedly delayed plans to run for Congress. In Philadelphia, District Attorney Arlen Specter's chances for the gubernatorial nomination have apparently been hurt by his role last year as President Nixon's Pennsylvania campaign manager. In Tennessee the Republicans are worrying about a report that Ken Reitz, formerly Senator Bill Brock's chief political strategist, helped engineer "dirty tricks" against the Democrats.

On the other hand, Senator Edward J. Gurney's national exposure as a member of the Senate Watergate committee is apparently shoring up his political base in Florida. And some observers believe that the scandal will work against all incumbents, not just Republicans.

Here in California, The Sacramento Bee analyzed a recent election won by the Republicans and found that the voter turnout averaged only 27 per cent. Its conclusion was that voters of all persuasions had been "turned off" by Watergate. And since a higher percentage of Republicans normally vote than Democrats, Watergate actually helped the G.O.P., the paper said.

Probably the most persuasive sentiment among Republicans these days is the anger they feel toward the men who served as President Nixon's key White House aides and then guided his re-election campaign. Names such as Haldeman, Ehrlichman and Mitchell are almost as much anathema as George McGovern and Abbie Hoffman.

On one level, the Republicans are angry because the Committee for the Re-election of the President ignored local politicians while draining out most of the available cash. The Iowa party is even contemplating a lawsuit to recover $450,000, the amount it contends was raised in the state but spent elsewhere.

On a second level, many of these politicians admire President Nixon and think he was badly served by his assistants. State Senator Richard Rogers of Manhattan, Kan., quoted an associate who said that "the President has assembled the darndest group of dingalings he'd ever heard of."

Clifford Jones, the state chairman in Pennsylvania, added:

"We are terribly sorry for the President, but good God, how could such an incredibly naive staff have misplaced the Presidential trust with such an arrogance of power?"

Moreover, many veteran Republicans feel considerable loyalty to their party. But Mr. Nixon's aides, they believe, cared little for the party, only for the personal triumph of the President — and themselves. Senator Goldwater expressed widespread feelings this way:

"I have spent over a third of my life trying to build the Republican party, adding my little bit to it, having been successful in the South and the Southwest, and then all of a sudden, as I near the end of my time in politics, I wonder—what the hell's it all been for?"

Perhaps most importantly, these men are professional politicians. They take pride in their work and in their reputations. And they feel that the men who planned Watergate, and then covered it up, have demeaned them and their chosen profession.

"The whole thing," said a leading New York Republican, "gives me a sort of hollow feeling in my gut."

Often, the resentment stops at the Oval Office.

"There is little condemnation of the President," said Marshall Cain, minority leader of the South Carolina Legislature. "There is a tendency to give him the benefit of every doubt because they don't want to believe he is involved in the cover-up."

But some feel, often with sadness, that the President must share the blame. In Maine, a leading party figure said: "The way the White House has responded to this [Watergate] has been so inappropriate and so unsatisfactory, almost contemptuous. I don't think the President has talked about the office as the office. I think he's talking about Richard M. Nixon's skin."

In Mankato, Minn., a young lawyer named James Manahan last year ran President Nixon's campaign in the Second Congressional District. This year, he called for the President's impeachment.

July 22, 1973

Agnew-Nixon Exchange

October 10, 1973

Dear Mr. President:

As you are aware, the accusations against me cannot be resolved without a long, divisive and debilitating struggle in the Congress and in the courts. I have concluded that, painful as it is to me and to my family, it is in the best interests of the nation that I relinquish the Vice Presidency.

Accordingly, I have today resigned the office of Vice President of the United States. A copy of the instrument of resignation is enclosed.

It has been a privilege to serve with you. May I express to the American people, through you, my deep gratitude for their confidence in twice electing me to be Vice President.

Sincerely,
SPIRO T. AGNEW

●

October 10, 1973.

Dear Ted:

The most difficult decisions are often those that are the most personal, and I know your decision to resign as Vice President has been as difficult as any facing a man in public life could be. Your departure from the Administration leaves me with a great sense of personal loss. You have been a valued associate throughout these nearly five years that we have served together. However, I respect your decision, and I also respect the concern for the national interest that led you to conclude that a resolution of the matter in this way, rather than through an extended battle in the courts and the Congress, was advisable in order to prevent a protracted period of national division and uncertainty.

As Vice President, you have addressed the great issues of our times with courage and candor. Your strong patriotism, and your profound dedication to the welfare of the nation, have been an inspiration to all who have served with you as well as to millions of others throughout the country.

I have been deeply saddened by this whole course of events, and I hope that you and your family will be sustained in the days ahead by a well-justified pride in all that you have contributed to the nation by your years of service as Vice President.

Sincerely,
RICHARD NIXON

October 11, 1973

G.O.P. Revives Policy Unit Independent of President

By CHRISTOPHER LYDON
Special to The New York Times

WASHINGTON, Nov. 12 — The Republican party established today what it hoped would be a policy voice independent of President Nixon just as the White House said it was beginning to win the counter-offensive against its Watergate critics.

A revived Republican Coordinating Committee, dormant since the party's recovery from the Goldwater defeat of 1964, listened this morning to a 40-minute speech from the President, promising full cooperation and several specific items of evidence to the Watergate investigators.

In its first resolution, the party panel said it "welcomed" Mr. Nixon's pledges of "full disclosure." But some members of the coordinating committee said later that the President was still in grave political trouble, that pledges alone were not sufficient for his recovery, and that the party had to reassert its sperate identity before the Congressional elections next year.

In a broad statement of purpose, the 28-member committee of party elders, Congressional leaders, Governors and other Republican officials assigned itself the role of seeing the party through the crisis of con-

fidence in Mr. Nixon. The group said it would try, among other things, to "develop positions" on national policy questions, meet the practical needs of local party workers, study election reforms and "actively involve itself in assessing and developing issues of major importance in future campaigns."

Seldom has the party of a President in power made such a sweeping assertion of its responsibility for leadership. And the origins of the coordinating committee, in the days after President Johnson's landslide victory when many Republicans worried about the party's survival, underlined the gloom in the party as President Nixon's popularity was reported again at about a third of the American electorate.

Ronald L. Ziegler, the White House press secretary, said at a news briefing this morning

that Mr. Nixon's continuing meetings with Republican leaders showed his determination "to meet the Watergate matter head on."

Late this afternoon, the President discussed the Watergate case with six Southern Democratic Senators and Senator Harry F. Byrd Jr. of Virginia, an independent, in the Nixon family quarters in the White House.

The Democrats were Senators James O. Eastland and John C. Stennis of Mississippi, John J. Sparkman and James B. Allen of Alabama, Russell B. Long of Louisiana and John L. McClellan of Arkansas.

All Republican members of both houses of Congress have been assured of an opportunity to hear the President's new outline of the Watergate situation. Other meetings are planned for later this week.

November 13, 1973

FORD SWORN AS VICE PRESIDENT AFTER HOUSE APPROVES, 387-35; HE VOWS EQUAL JUSTICE FOR ALL

LOYALTY TO NIXON

By MARJORIE HUNTER
Special to The New York Times

WASHINGTON, Dec. 6 — Gerald R. Ford, pledging "equal justice for all Americans," took office just after dusk tonight as the 40th Vice President of the United States.

With President Nixon standing right behind him, he was sworn into office in the 116-

year-old House chamber, which has been his political home for the last 25 years.

Only an hour earlier, the House completed action on his nomination by voting 387 to 35 for confirmation. He was confirmed Nov. 27 by the Senate by a vote of 92 to 3.

Mr. Ford, 60 years old, resigned his House seat before assuming the Vice-Presidency. He has been minority leader of the House since 1965.

It was clearly Jerry Ford's

day, and not even President Nixon's appearance overshadowed the new Vice President. The waves of applause and the smiles of his colleagues were seemingly beamed at him alone as he stood, in a trim navy blue suit, his right hand held high in recognition of old friends.

And, as he spoke, it was the Jerry Ford many of them had listened to through the years, speaking in a flat tone, declaring his love for his wife and his country and pledging his

loyalty to his President.

The historic ceremony ended a Vice-Presidential vacancy that had existed since the resignation on Oct. 10 of Spiro T. Agnew just before he pleaded no contest to a charge of income tax evasion.

First Use of Amendment

This is the first time that a Vice President was chosen under the 25th Amendment to the Constitution. The amendment, ratified by the states in

The New York Times/George Tames

Gerald R. Ford being sworn in as Vice President of the United States as his wife, Elizabeth, held Bible and Chief Justice Warren E. Burger administered oath. Ob- serving were President Nixon, at right, and at rear, Carl Albert, left, Speaker of the House, and James O. East- land, right, who is the President pro tem of the Senate.

1967, provides for Presidential succession and for filling Vice-Presidential vacancies.

The 25th Amendment was adopted to deal with situations such as that which existed following the assassination of President Kennedy in 1963. At that time, the Vice-Presidency stood vacant 13 months after Vice President Johnson succeeded to the Presidency.

Mr. Ford heard none of today's five hours of House debate, nor did he vote. He arrived in the chamber just minutes after the final vote had been cast and was greeted by thunderous cheers and applause—the first of many such ovations that he received today.

He then went to the White House to inform President Nixon of the vote, and the two men returned to the Capitol an hour later for the official swearing-in.

They were greeted by tumultuous applause as they entered the House chamber together.

A capacity crowd of 1,500 persons—Senators, Representatives, members of the Cabinet and of the Supreme Court, ambassadors and other foreign dignitaries and visitors—witnessed the brief ceremony.

Mrs. Nixon, accompanied by White House aides, sat with the four Ford children in the executive gallery.

As Chief Justice Warren E. Burger administered the oath, Mr. Ford rested his left hand on a Bible held by his wife, who wore a tangerine wool crepe dress. The Bible was purchased for the occasion by their son Michael, a theological student.

Later, in a brief speech, Mr. Ford drew a burst of applause from the Republicans as he pledged his full "support and loyalty" to the President. He also bade a "fond good-by" to his colleagues in the House.

"I am a Ford, not a Lincoln," he said, smiling. "My addresses will never be as eloquent as Lincoln's. But I will do my best to equal his brevity and plain speaking."

Mr. Ford pledged his dedication "to the rule of law and equal justice for all Americans" and declared, "I am not discouraged."

Later, he led the Senators across the Capitol to the Senate chamber where he will serve in the one job given to a Vice President under the Constitution—president of the Senate.

The Vice-Presidency has been vacant 17 times in this nation's history, due to death, resignation or succession to the Presidency.

It was just 57 days ago that a stunned nation learned of the abrupt resignation of Vice President Agnew. Two days later, on Oct. 12, President Nixon announced to Congressional leaders and others assembled in the East Room of the White House for a gala evening of champagne and laughter that he had chosen his old friend and fellow Republican, Mr. Ford, to be Vice President.

Earlier, there had been few surprises during the long hours of floor debate over the nomination. Democratic liberals, as expected, accused the nominee of lacking the qualities of leadership. Other Democrats and Republicans, also as expected, praised him as a man of honor, honesty, dedication and integrity.

The only unexpected development came as Representative Peter W. Rodino Jr. of New Jersey, chairman of the House Judiciary Committee, which handled the Ford hearings, announced that he would vote against confirmation.

"During the weeks that I spent reviewing Jerry's public and private life, I have only grown to respect his character and integrity more." Mr. Rodino told the hushed House.

Weeks of Hearings

However, asserting that his Newark district "typifies the plight which the cities of our nation face today," and accus- ing the Nixon Administration of failing to meet the needs of the poor and disadvantaged, Mr. Rodino said:

"I vote, not against Gerald Ford's worth as a man of great integrity, but in dissent with the present Administration's indifference to the plight of so many Americans."

In mid-afternoon, as the debate dragged on, Representative B. F. Sisk, Democrat of California, broke into the proceedings to announce that the National League owners had voted to transfer the San Diego Padres baseball team to Washington.

Mr. Sisk and Representative Frank Horton, Republican of upstate New York, who together had led a Congressional effort to secure a new baseball franchise for Washington, paid tribute to Mr. Ford, a onetime football star and still a sports enthusiast, for his support of their effort.

Mr. Ford's nomination reached the House floor this morning after weeks of hearings and exhaustive investigations by both the Senate and the House. The Federal Bureau of Investigation alone had detailed 359 agents to dig into his background, and the F.B.I. data covered 1,700 typewritten pages.

The nominee's tax records, personal finances, family connections, political campaigns and voting record were examined in detail.

Today, praising the thoroughness of the investigations and hearings, Representative Jack Brooks, Democrat of Texas, told his colleagues, "We know more about Jerry Ford than I ever wanted to know."

While all other blacks present voted against the nomination, Representative Andrew Young, Democrat of Georgia, said shortly before the five hours of debate ended that he would support the nominee.

Mr. Young said that he was troubled by Mr. Ford's efforts to weaken civil rights legislation but added that he also had doubts about the civil rights voting records of Presidents Kennedy and Johnson. He expressed hope that Mr. Ford would rise to his new job.

Pressure on Nixon

The debate was low key, even on the part of the nominee's severest critics, who had known from the start that they could not block the confirmation.

But the drama of the day was heightened by the realization of those present that with Mr. Ford installed as Vice President, sentiment for impeachment of Mr. Nixon—or pressure on him to resign—would intensify.

Many Democrats have openly called for impeachment, but until now most Republicans have spoken of it guardedly and usually only among themselves. Yet there are strong indications that many Republicans are becoming increasingly concerned over the tarnished image of their party because of the Watergate scandals; the Agnew affair and allegations of various political campaign

misdeeds by the Nixon Administration.

The possibility that Mr. Nixon might not serve out his term was raised repeatedly by both Democrats and Republicans during the debate.

Representative Clarence D. Long, Democrat of Maryland, suggested that the Republicans would do well to take his advice by moving swiftly to make Mr. Ford the next President.

Declaring that the Republicans would have to take the lead in forcing Mr. Nixon out of office, he said:

"Any partisan Democrat would have to be out of his mind to take that millstone off the back of you Republicans. If you keep the present incumbent in for three more years, the Democrats could win with the Boston strangler."

This was greeted by cheers and laughter from the Democrats and good-natured roars from the Republicans.

Representative Jerome H. Waldie, Democrat of California, spoke of "the shambles that the Nixon Presidency has become" and said that the situation would become worse as it proceeded "to its inevitable result"—either impeachment or resignation.

Critical of Mr. Ford's attempts three years ago to impeach Associate Justice William O. Douglas "for strictly political reasons," Mr. Waldie said, "Is the rule of law supreme? When Gerald Ford is President, I trust he will ask that question himself."

Representative John B. Anderson, Republican of Illinois, also appeared to be suggesting that Mr. Ford might succeed to the Presidency when he quoted the nation's first Vice President, John Adams, as having said, when asked what it meant

to be Vice President, "'I am nothing, but I may be everything.'"

And Representative Charles W. Sandman Jr., a Republican who recently lost his bid to become Governor of New Jersey said in a speech praising Mr. Ford, "Some feel that the President will be impeached or will resign."

The handful of Democratic liberals, including most of the blacks in the House, based their opposition to Mr. Ford's nomination on a number of issues.

The blacks decried his attempts to weaken civil rights legislation. Others protested his votes against Medicare, food stamps, housing for the poor, Federal aid to education and other social welfare programs and his unswerving support of the war in Vietnam.

Representative Elizabeth Holtzman, Democrat of Brooklyn, said that Mr. Ford's vote this year for a bill to liberalize retirement benefits for Government employes might have rendered him ineligible for the Vice-Presidency.

Constitutional Prohibition

The Constitution bars anyone from taking an office if during his term in Congress he voted to increase the emoluments of that office. However, the American law division of the Library of Congress and various consitutional experts have said that the Vice President is not a civil officer and is not covered by that constitutional prohibition.

Even the nominee's severest critics agreed with his supporters that Mr. Ford was honest, candid, hard-working, competent and a man of integrity.

"I have known Jerry for 11

years," Representative Don Edwards, Democrat of California, said. "He has always been kind to me personally. I like him as a person and as a colleague. I know he is candid, a good family man, sober and hard working."

But Mr. Ford "does not measure up" as a leader, Mr. Edwards said. He called upon the President to "provide us with a more suitable choice" to lead a divided nation.

Later, while Mr. Ford was being sworn into office, several hundred persons from his home town of Grand Rapids and elsewhere in Michigan listened to the ceremony over loudspeakers in nearby Statuary Hall. The special listening post was set up after the supply of gallery passes had been exhausted.

It was in Grand Rapids that Mr. Ford won his first race for Congress 25 years ago. He was born in Omaha July 14, 1913, but was taken to Grand Rapids as a baby after the divorce of his parents.

He was graduated in 1935 from the University of Michigan, where he played center on the undefeated national championship football teams in 1932 and 1933. He received his law degree from Yale University in 1941 and served in the Navy in World War II, emerging in 1946 as a Lieutenant-Commander.

He is married and has four children, Michael, John, Steven and Susan. He is an Episcopalian, a member of the American Legion and the Veterans of Foreign Wars and a 33d-degree Mason.

December 7, 1973

Nixon's 'New Majority' Seems Shattered for Him and the G.O.P

By CHRISTOPHER LYDON
Special to The New York Times.

WASHINGTON, Jan. 20—At his second inauguration a year ago, President Nixon still enjoyed being compared with Franklin Delano Roosevelt as a coalition builder, an architect of realignment in American politics.

The importance of 1972, he had told Theodore H. White, the campaign chronicler, was that it had "shifted allegiances" in the South, among workingmen and Catholics. He had won unusual Republican majorities among union members, manual workers and voters with grade-school educations—the rank and file of Mr. Nixon's middle America. "The new majority," the President told

Mr. White, "was what this election was all about."

Now, at the start of a new election year, the new majority appears shattered by White House scandals, inflation and the oil shortage. It is gone, clearly, not only for President Nixon, whose popularity has dropped 41 points in the Gallup Poll since the start of 1973, but also for his party—the choice now of less than a quarter of the American electorate.

The new-majority converts to the Nixon coalition in 1972 were the first to leave it in 1973. Most of them still call themselves Democrats. And most of them are inclined to vote Democratic this year in what pollsters project

as a historic sweep of Congressional races, if the current mood holds.

Straw Poll

The puzzle for analysts is a national straw poll by Louis Harris late last month that showed Gerald R. Ford, the Republican Vice President, leading Democratic Senators Edward M. Kennedy of Massachusetts and Henry M. Jackson of Washington in soundings about the 1976 Presidential campaign.

Does that mean, as some Republicans argue, that the new majority is intact, in hiding? Does the poll reflect rather the political harmony and favorable publicity that attended Mr.

Ford's confirmation last fall? Is it more important that Mr. Ford's voting record through 25 years in the House of Representatives was conservative, or little known? Most important, does Mr. Ford symbolize continuity with Nixon Administration policies or a departure from Nixon scandals?

Those are the questions confronting political strategists trying to discover whether a "new" new majority will emerge in Presidential politics. But there is a base of evidence that the "old" new majority is dead.

First, with respect to Mr. Nixon, the decline of his popularity is steepest among the new-majority groups he courted and won in 1972. The Gallup Poll found that among Catholics, approval of Mr. Nixon dropped from 71 per cent to 22 per cent during 1973—down almost to the small share of the Catholic vote that Mr. Nixon won in 1960 against John F. Kennedy, the nation's first Catholic President.

Among labor union members and their families, another new-majority target in 1972, Mr. Nixon's approval has dropped from 61 per cent to 20 per cent in the last year. George Meany, the labor leader, who was neutral in the President's last campaign, is now calling for Mr. Nixon's impeachment.

And among independent voters, a mobile, rapidly growing group that includes conservative former Democrats and liberal former Republicans, Mr. Nixon's approval has dropped from 73 per cent to 25 per cent.

Second, with respect to party identification, the Gallup Poll has reported that voters who call themselves Republicans are down, after a four-point drop last year, to 24 per cent of the electorate, the smallest share for a major party in this century.

Far from "the emerging Republican majority" that Kevin P. Phillips, a conservative analyst, divined in the Nixon victory of 1968, the Republican party now seems to be contracting on an aging, white Anglo-Saxon Protestant base.

In Illinois, for example, in the latest examination by Market Opinion Research of Detroit, a polling company that works mainly for Republican candidates, only 22 per cent of a statewide sample labeled itself Republican.

Among those Republicans,

according to Robert M. Teeter, president of the research agency, a quarter are over 65 years old; half are over 50; three-quarters are over 40. By race, 98.5 per cent are white. In contrast, 87 per cent of the electorate are white. Only 27 per cent belong to union-member families. About 80 per cent are Protestants (58 per cent is the statewide figure) and about 80 per cent are homeowners, 9 points higher than the state total.

Third, with respect to political choices, voters appear to be turning sharply against the Republicans.

A Gallup Poll late last year found that Democrats were favored over Republicans for election to Congress by 58 per cent to 30 per cent. A national survey by Louis Harris found a 53 to 31 per cent split in favor of Democratic candidates for Congress, the largest margin in a decade of Harris surveys.

Survival of the Nixon "new majority" in Presidential politics is debatable. To some of the Republican tacticians who organized the "new majority" campaigns of 1970 and 1972, Vice President Ford's lead in the Harris straw poll confirms their old analysis that, as one said: "If we have an attractive candidate who's conservative on the social issue, the new middle-class, traditionally Democratic vote will go Republican."

In the White House, Patrick J. Buchanan, a speech writer, says, "It's oversimplifying it to say the new majority was add-

ing Southern Protestants and Northern Catholics to the solid Republican base, but that's a significant portion of it, and it's still out there."

Opposition to Abortion

Charles W. Colson concurs, and if he were shaping Gerald Ford's appeal to that new majority, as he did for President Nixon, he would urge the Vice President to stress his opposition to abortion and his support for aid to parochial schools, as Mr. Nixon did in 1972.

To many other analysts, including Mr. Teeter, who did the polling for the Nixon campaign in 1972, the "new majority" was a dubious description to begin with and is unlikely to be reconstituted as a political coalition.

Presidential races will mostly be close battles between "two minority parties" over a volatile middle group of voters, contends Richard M. Scammon, the political statistician and writer. Even if the second Nixon term had prospered, Mr. Scammon believes, the class identification" with the Democratic party would have prevented Mr. Nixon from consolidating a new majority for the Republicans.

Louis Harris, the pollster, is sure that the Nixon majority in 1972 was never the "new majority," as described. Mr. Nixon's strongest appeal, the Harris surveys found, was in foreign policy where the emphasis of Mr. Nixon's trip to China and détente with the Russians was change, not conservatism. On economics and the "social issue," including forced school busing, Mr. Nixon did not have majority approval at election time, Mr. Harris asserts.

Mr. Harris adds that "new majority" elements, like union members and aging ethnics, are shrinking fractions. Union members that formed 23 per cent of the vote in 1968 will be only 15 per cent of the vote in 1976, he writes in his new book, "The Anguish of Change."

Mr. Harris believes that a year of Watergate shocks has hastened the rearrangement of symbols and issues in American politics. "When a candidate runs a law-and-order campaign today, people think: 'chances are he'll turn out to be a crook.'"

"In 1967," Mr. Harris observed in an interview, "substantial majorities of our sample—60 to 75 per cent—thought the following people were 'dangerous or harmful to the country:' people who didn't believe in God, black militants, student demonstrators, prostitutes, homosexuals. In the fall of 1975 we couldn't find a majority to say that any one of those groups was dangerous.

"Today," he continued, "the people considered 'dangerous' by a majority of Americans are these: people who hire political spies (52 per cent); generals who conduct secret bombing raids (67 per cent); politicians who engage in secret wiretapping (71 per cent); businessmen who make illegal political contributions (81 per cent); and politicians who try to use the Central Intelligence Agency, the Federal Bureau of Investigation and the Secret Service for political purposes or to try to restrict freedom (88 per cent). "That," Mr. Harris said, "is what has happened in America."

January 21, 1974

Voter Choice of a Political Party Reaches New Low in Gallup Poll

Voter identification with a partisan political party is at the lowest point in the 34 years such readings have been taken by the Gallup Poll.

Only 24 per cent of those responding to a recent poll identified themselves as Republicans, the smallest percentage to do so since the first poll in 1940, when 38 per cent identified with the G.O.P.

Forty-two per cent of those polled classified themselves as Democrats, also the lowest since 1940, when the Democratic figure was also 42 per cent.

The biggest increase in identification of the voters has been with those calling themselves independents. Thirty-four per cent of those polled

did not align themselves with a political party. This is a gain of 8 percentage points since 1970 and of 14 percentage points since 1940.

Immediately after the 1972 Presidential election 27 per cent of the voters called themselves Republicans. The three-point decline to 24 per cent came initially last May and August when the Watergate hearings were being shown on television.

The Democrats were unable to capitalize on this slackening of Republican party allegiance, however. The entire three-point Republican loss over the last year has shown up among voters labeling themselves independents.

In the last 10 years, the Democratic party has shown a

substantial drop in voter allegiance, falling from a high of 53 per cent following the assassination of President Kennedy to the current 42 per cent.

Since before 1940, the Democratic party has been the majority party in the United States. Until 1967, the Republican party was second in affiliation, but it was then passed by those calling themselves independents. The two groups reversed positions again before the independents went ahead in 1971, in the first poll in which 18-year-old voters participated.

The question asked of the 12,306 adults 18 years of age or older interviewed nationally in eight surveys taken from September, 1973, to January, 1974, was:

"In politics, as of today, do you consider yourself a Republican, Democrat or independent?"

February 10, 1974

NIXON RESIGNS

HE URGES A TIME OF 'HEALING';
FORD WILL TAKE OFFICE TODAY

The New York Times/William E. Sauro
Vice President Ford meeting with newsmen last night

United Press International
President Nixon on TV as he announced his resignation

The 37th President Is First to Quit Post

By JOHN HERBERS
Special to The New York Times

WASHINGTON, Aug. 8—Richard Milhous Nixon, the 37th President of the United States, announced tonight that he had given up his long and arduous fight to remain in office and would resign, effective at noon tomorrow.

At that hour, Gerald Rudolph Ford, whom Mr. Nixon nominated for Vice President last Oct. 12, will be sworn in as the 38th President, to serve out the 895 days remaining in Mr. Nixon's second term.

Less that two years after his landslide re-election victory, Mr. Nixon, in a conciliatory address on national television, said that he was leaving not with a sense of bitterness but with a hope that his departure would start a "process of healing that is so desperately needed in America."

He spoke of regret for any "injuries" done "in the course of the events that led to this decision." He acknowledged that some of his judgments had been wrong.

The 61-year-old Mr. Nixon, appearing calm and resigned to his fate as a victim of the Watergate scandal, became the first President in the history of the Republic to resign from office. Only 10 months earlier Spiro Agnew resigned the Vice-Presidency.

Speaks of Pain at Yielding Post

Mr. Nixon, speaking from the Oval Office, where his successor will be sworn in tomorrow, may well have delivered his most effective speech since the Watergate scandals began to swamp his Administration in early 1973.

In tone and content, the 15-minute address was in sharp contrast to his frequently combative language of the past,

363

especially his first "farewell" appearance—that of 1962, when he announced he was retiring from politics after losing the California governorship race and declared that the news media would not have "Nixon to kick around" anymore

Yet he spoke tonight of how painful it was for him to give up the office.

"I would have preferred to carry through to the finish whatever the personal agony it would have involved, and my family unanimously urged me to do so," he said.

Puts 'Interests of America First'

"I have never been a quitter," he said. "To leave office before my term is completed is opposed to every instinct in my body." But he said that he had decided to put "the interests of America first."

Conceding that he did not have the votes in Congress to escape impeachment in the House and conviction in the Senate, Mr. Nixon said, "To continue to fight through the months ahead for my personal vindication would almost totally absorb the time and attention of the President and the Congress in a period when our entire focus should be on the great issues of peace abroad and prosperity without inflation at home."

"Therefore," he continued, "I shall resign the Presidency effective at noon tomorrow. Vice President Ford will be sworn in as President at that hour in this office."

Then he turned again to his sorrow at leaving. Although he did not mention it in his speech, Mr. Nixon had looked forward to being President when the United States celebrates its 200th anniversary in 1976.

"I feel a great sadness," he said.

Mr. Nixon expressed confidence in Mr. Ford to assume the office, "to put the bitterness and divisions of the recent past behind us."

"By taking this action, I hope that I will have hastened the start of that process of healing which is so desperately needed in America," he said. "I regret deeply any injuries that may have been done in the course of the events that led to this decision. I would say only that if some of my judgments were wrong — and some were wrong — they were made in what I believed at the time to be the best interests of the nation."

Further, he said he was leaving "with no bitterness" toward those who had opposed him.

"So let us all now join together in affirming that common commitment and in helping our new President succeed for the benefit of all Americans," he said.

As he has many times in the past, Mr. Nixon listed what he considered his most notable accomplishments of his five and half years in office—his initiatives in foreign policy, which he said had gone a long way toward establishing a basis for world peace.

Theodore Roosevelt Is Quoted

And, at the end, he expressed his own philosophy — that to succeed is to be involved in struggle. In this he quoted Theodore Roosevelt about the value of being "the man in the arena whose face is marred by dust and sweat and blood" and who "spends himself in a worthy cause."

After spending himself in a long political career, Mr. Nixon is scheduled to fly to his home in San Clemente, Calif., and retirement tomorrow while Mr. Ford is being sworn in in the Oval Office.

A White House spokesman said tonight that Mr. and Mrs. Nixon and their family would bid farewell to Cabinet members and staff personnel at 9:30 A.M. tomorrow in the East Room. Then they will board a helicopter at 10 A.M. for the short trip to Andrews Air Force Base, where they will emplane on the Spirit of '76, a jet aircraft, for their flight to San Clemente.

Ronald L. Ziegler, the Presidential adviser and press secretary, also said that Mr. Nixon's letter of resignation would be delivered to the office of Secretary of State, Kissinger in th Executive Office Building adjacent to the White House by noon tomorrow.

Mr. Nixon's announcement came only two days after he told his Cabinet that he would not resign but would let the constitutional impeachment process run its course, even though it was evident he would be removed from office after a trial by the Senate.

In the next 48 hours the pressures for him to resign and turn the reins of the Government over to Mr. Ford became overwhelming.

His chances of being acquitted were almost hopeless. Senator Barry Goldwater, the Arizona conservative who was the Republican Presidential candidate in 1964, told him that he had no more than 15 votes in the Senate, far short of the 34 he needed to be sure of escaping conviction. Members of his own staff, including Gen. Alexander M. Haig Jr., the White House chief of staff, strongly recommended that he step down in the national interest.

In the end only a small minority of his former supporters were urging him to stay and pledging to give him their support. It was his friends, not his legions of enemies, that brought the crucial pressures for resignation.

Seventeen months of almost constant disclosures of Watergate and related scandals brought a steady attrition of support, in the country and in Congress, for what many authorities believed was the most powerful Presidency in the history of the nation.

However, a Presidential statement of last Monday and three transcripts of Presidential conversations that Mr. Nixon chose to make public ultimately precipitated the crush of events of the last week.

In that statement, Mr. Nixon admitted, as the transcript showed, that on June 23, 1972, he ordered a halt to the investigation of the break-in at the Democratic headquarters in the Watergate complex here six days earlier by persons in the employ of agents of Mr. Nixon's re-election campaign. He also admitted that he had kept the evidence from both his attorneys and the House Judiciary Committee, which had recommended that the House impeach him on three general charges.

Then came the avalanche. Republicans, Southern Democrats and others who had defended Mr. Nixon said that these actions constituted the evidence needed to support the article of impeachment approved by the House Judiciary Committee charging obstruction of justice. And it gave new support to other charges that Mr. Nixon had widely abused his office by bringing undue Presidential pressures to bear on sensitive Government agencies.

As the pressures mounted and Mr. Nixon held publicly to his resolve not to resign, the capital was thrown into a turmoil. A number of Senators anxious for a resignation began publicly predicting one.

At the White House yesterday, Mr. Nixon met in his White House offices with Mrs. Nixon and his two daughters, Mrs. David Eisenhower and Mrs. Edward F. Cox, and with his close aides. Members of his staff, acting independently of the Congressmen, sent him memorandums he had requested as to their recommendations. Most called for resignation rather than taking the country through a painful impeachment debate and vote in the House and a trial in the Senate.

Last night, Raymond K. Price and other speech writers were ordered to prepare a resignation statement for use tonight. Secretary of State Kissinger met with the President late in the evening and Mr. Nixon told him that he would resign in the national interest.

At 11 A.M. today, as crowds for the third day gathered along Pennsylvania Avenue outside the White House, President Nixon summoned Mr. Ford to his Oval Office and officially informed him that he would submit his resignation tomorrow to the Secretary of State, as provided by Federal law, and that Mr. Ford would become President.

Shortly after noon, Mr. Ziegler, the President's confidant and press secretary, his face saddened and weary, appeared in the crowded White House press room and announced that the President would go on national radio and television tonight to address the American people. As with most previous such announcements, he did not say what the President would talk about.

But by that time, other Presidential aides were confirming that Mr. Nixon planned to resign, and the tensions that had been building for days subsided.

At 7:30 P.M. Mr. Nixon met in his office in the Executive Office Building with a bipartisan Congressional leadership group—James O. Eastland, Democrat of Mississippi, President pro tem of the Senate; Mike Mansfield, Democrat of Montana, the Senate majority leader; Hugh Scott, Republican of Pennsylvania, the Senate minority floor leader; Carl Albert, Democrat of Oklahoma, the Speaker of the House, and John J. Rhodes, Republican of Arizona, the minority leader. The meeting was to give them formal notice of his resignation.

Among the White House staff today there was a sadness but there were no tears, according to those there. Mr. Nixon, who was described as wretched and gray yesterday while wrestling with his decision, was described today as relaxed. To some, he appeared relieved.

He ordered Mr. Price to begin drafting the resignation speech yesterday, even before he made his decision to resign, aides said. Five drafts of it were written before it was turned over to Mr. Nixon to make his own changes.

It was exactly six years ago last night that Mr. Nixon was nominated on the first ballot at the Republican National Convention to be the party's nominee for President, a note of irony that did not escape members of the President's staff.

That evening marked the beginning of an ascension to power that was to put the Nixon mark on an important segment of history. After a first term marked by innovations in foreign policy and a return of resources to the state and local governments in domestic policy, Mr. Nixon in 1972 won re-election with 60.7 per cent of the vote.

In early 1973, as he ended American military involvement in the Vietnam war and as he moved to strengthen the powers of his office in a multitude of ways, his popularity rating in the Gallup Poll registered 68 per cent. But as the Watergate disclosures broke his rating dropped quickly and was below 30 per cent before the end of the year.

Mr. Nixon made a number of counterattacks to win back his lost popularity. He campaigned from time to time across the country as if he was running for office. He disclosed information about his taxes and property. He hired a succession of lawyers to defend him in the courts and in Congress.

He made television and radio appearances. He ordered his subordinates to step up their activities to show that the Government's business was moving ahead. He made foreign trips to show he was still a world leader.

Cheered in Tour of Middle East

In the Middle East in June he was cheered by vast throngs, and he held a summit meeting with Soviet leader, Leonid I. Brezhnev, in Moscow.

Yet, when he returned to the United States, the Gallup Poll showed his rating at 24 per cent and the Watergate charges broke anew as the House Judiciary Committee stepped up its impeachment inquiry. His Administration was tottering when he made his remarkable statement last Monday, apparently in an effort to put his own interpretation on information that was expected to have been made public at the Watergate trials as a result of a Supreme Court decision upholding a court order for the information.

When the decision to resign came, Mr. Nixon moved to achieve an orderly transition of power to Mr. Ford. General Haig, who has had broad delegated authority in recent months, met frequently with the Vice President to brief him on policy, as did other Administration officials.

Mr. Kissinger gave a number of assurances that the nation's "bipartisan foreign policy" would remain firmly in place. The Defense Department announced that American military forces around the world would continue under normal status. And across this city thousands of Federal employes performed their chores as if nothing was happening

August 9, 1974

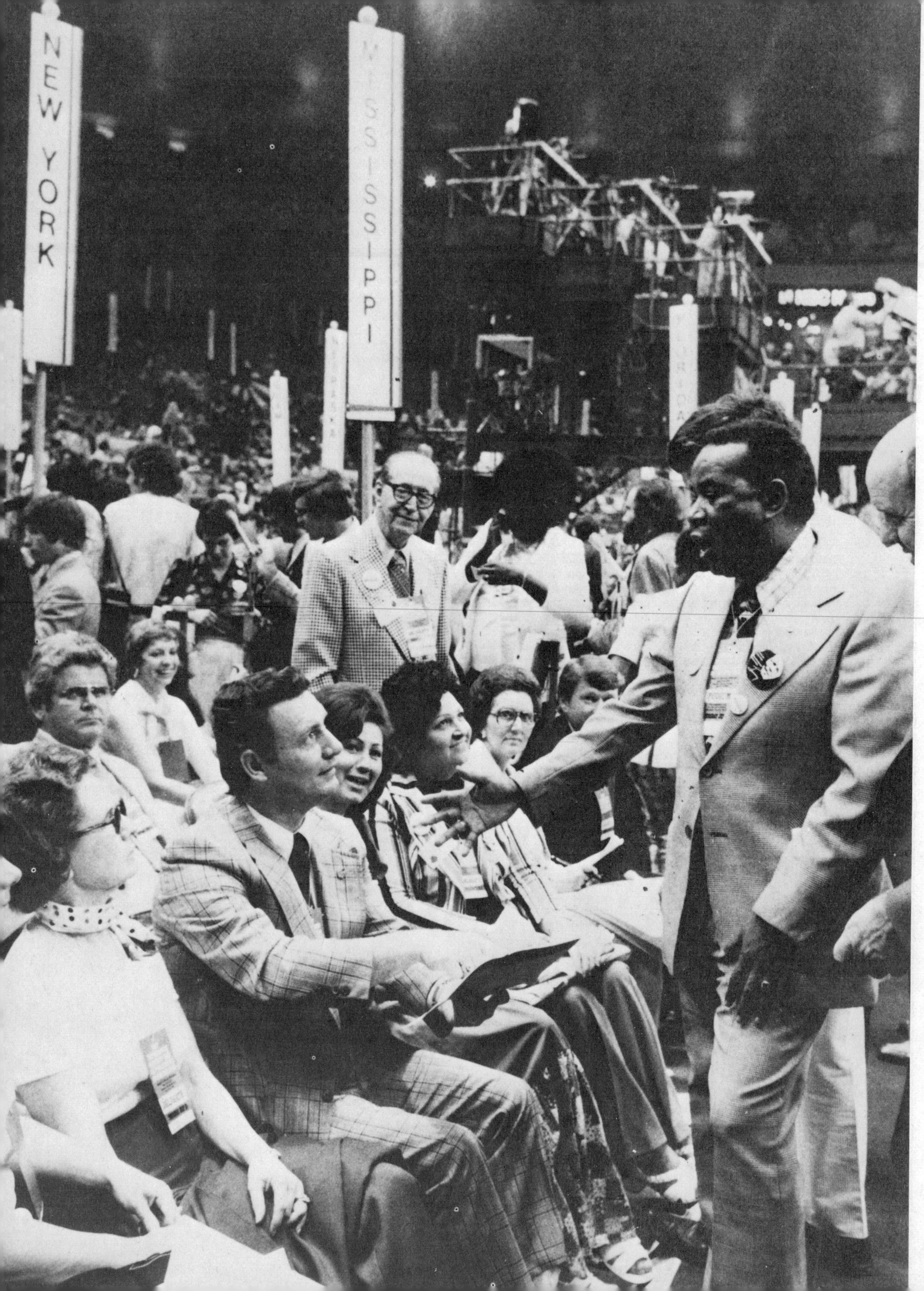
NEW YORK
MISSISSIPPI

CHAPTER 4

Politics As Usual

Aaron Henry, civil rights activist, chats with Ross Barnett Jr., son of the segregationist former governor of Mississippi. Both were members of the Mississippi delegation to the 1976 Democratic Convention.

Courtesy The New York Times

STRAUSS ELECTED DEMOCRATS' HEAD AND VOWS UNITY

'I Belong to No Man,' Dallas Lawyer Says, and Pledges to Save Party Reforms

MRS. WESTWOOD QUITS

She Makes Decision to Step Down After Bid to Oust Her Loses, 105 to 100

By CHRISTOPHER LYDON

Special to The New York Times

WASHINGTON, Dec. 9—Robert Strauss of Texas was elected chairman of the Democratic National Committee here this afternoon and immediately pledged to reconcile his opponents and to preserve reforms that had broadened participation in the party.

"I belong to no man; I am owned by no organization," said Mr. Strauss, a 54-year-old lawyer and businessman from Dallas. "I am centrist, a worker, a doer, a putter-together, and those talents belong to you," he told the committee.

Mr. Strauss won the chairmanship on the first ballot against George Mitchell of Maine and Charles T. Manatt of California hours after Jean Westwood, the chairman since Senator George McGovern's nomination for President, announced her retirement. The vote on a new chairman was 106½ for Mr. Strauss, 71¼ for Mr. Mitchell and 26 for Mr. Manatt.

Mr. Strauss had the support of labor leaders, Southerners and some Congressional figures who opposed Mr. McGovern's nomination last summer. He picked up scattered liberal and black votes today.

Ouster Effort Defeated

Mrs. Westwood's resignation and Mr. Strauss's election came shortly after Mrs. Westwood had defeated an effort by the Strauss forces to oust her. The vote against the motion to declare the chairmanship vacant —in effect to impeach Mrs. Westwood—was 105 to 100 and was an apparent setback for Mr. Strauss. Yet a number of the votes for Mrs. Westwood in that original test were based on her promise to step aside today.

Mrs. Westwood had earlier said that she would not resign until Mr. Strauss had withdrawn as a "symbol" of the party's divisions — or alternatively unless a compromise candidate could demonstrate majority support to succeed her.

But Mr. Strauss stayed in the race this afternoon, and none of the "unity" candidates showed any commanding strength.

The decision by the former chairman, Lawrence F. O'Brien, not to stand for nomination this afternoon appeared to have given potentially crucial votes to Mr. Strauss on the first ballot.

Mr. O'Brien had been expected to draw 20 or more votes for himself if he had been nominated, but a number of his supporters moved to Mr. Strauss when Mr. O'Brien stepped aside.

Among the public backers of Mr. O'Brien who voted for Mr. Strauss this afternoon were Don Anselmi, the party chairman in Wyoming; Patrick Cunningham, the Democratic chairman in the Bronx; Theodora Martinez of Brooklyn, and Dr. Mildred Ostenasek of Maryland.

Senator McGovern made a tentative move this morning to intervene on behalf of his running mate, Sargent Shriver, after other compromise candidates had failed to get together in a united front against Mr. Strauss

Late this morning, Senator McGovern told Joseph Crangle, the state chairman in New York and a possible compromise national chairman, that Mr. Shriver might be the best man to unite the party and would accept the job if it was offered.

Lee C. White, the manager of Mr. Shriver's vice presidential campaign, appeared outside the meeting hall this morning and confirmed that Mr. Shriver "would not say no if the party turned to him."

But Mr. Mitchell, still hoping to win a majority for himself, declined to step aside for Mr. Shriver, and the Shriver boomlet collapsed.

Voting on the motion to oust Mrs. Westwood underlined the regional and ideological division in the party among people who had supported and opposed Senator McGovern at the Democratic National Convention in Miami Beach last summer.

Vote on Mrs. Westwood

Mrs. Westwood, the 48-year-old mink farmer from Utah, who was installed by the McGovern forces in July, won 9 of the 11 votes from New York, 10 of the 11 from California and substantial support across the industrial Northeast. Her opposition—that is, Mr. Strauss's hard-core support—came from the South and West,

with help from the regular party organization in Connecticut and Illinois and scattered votes in the Middle West.

Almost all of the black vote went against the motion to oust Mrs. Westwood.

The most dramatic of many intense maneuvers on that vote came toward the end of the ouster roll-call, with the outcome still uncertain, when Carol McClendon of Cleveland changed her vote from "no" to "yes."

She had consulted before the change with William Lucy, a National Committee member from the District of Columbia and a leader of the Black Caucus and also with Joseph E. Cole of Cleveland, a banker and major contributor to Senator Hubert H. Humphrey's unsuccessful Presidential campaigns.

Miss McClendon repeatedly declined to explain why she had switched her vote. But she reappeared this afternoon to second the nomination of Mr. Strauss.

Gov. Reubin Askew of Florida nominated Mr. Strauss, who was also seconded by Don Peterson, a national committeeman from Wisconsin and a prime mover in Senator Eugene J. McCarthy's antiwar Presidential campaign in 1968.

Immediately after Mr. Strauss's election, the National Committee voted unanimously to adopt a list that Mrs. Westwood had prepared of 107 members of a commission to revise the party's basic charter and prepare for an off-year convention in 1974.

But the meeting postponed action on the election of 25 additional at-large members and the election of a new executive committee.

Shortly before 7 P.M., the meeting was recessed—rather than adjourned — to keep the present temporary executive committee in office to manage the affairs of the party with Mr. Strauss.

December 10, 1972

Democrats Vote to Abolish '72 Quotas for Delegates

WASHINGTON, Oct. 27 (AP) —The Democratic party's reform commission unanimously approved today new delegate selection guidelines eliminating the so-called quotas that caused a deep party division last year.

The voice-vote passage of a compromise package of party rules was one of the firmest signs of healing since the Democrats began fighting five years ago over efforts to open up the process by which delegates are selected to their national conventions.

The chief change in the new set of rules over the controversial McGovern guidelines of 1972 comes in the retreat from mandatory quotas for women, youth and minorities in state delegations to the national convention.

The new rules retain a requirement that state parties seek the participation of these groups but stipulate that these efforts will not be measured by the proportions they produce in delegations.

The old rules had been interpreted as requiring mathematical proportions of minorities and women in delegations matching their presence in the population. The resulting quota requirements split the party bitterly between reformers and old guard elements.

Other important relaxations of the 1972 rules will guarantee Democratic Governors and members of Congress seats at the convention, but not as voting delegates unless they run for election.

Another provision, allowing state parties to name up to 25 per cent of their delegations, was designed to assuage party regulars who were shut out last year when forced to stand for election.

The remaining sore point likely to produce a fight when the full Democratic National Committee considers the guidelines is a provision that delegate strength be apportioned among Presidential candidates at each stage of the selection proces down to hte precinct level. Proportional representation down to the lowest level had been a key goal of the reform element, but party regulars still want it cut off at the Congressional district level.

Some form of proportional representation was required by mandate of the 1972 convention, which outlawed winner-take-all primaries and convention systems that allow a can-

didate to get a disproportionate share of a state's delegates.

Robert S. Strauss, the party chairman, has declared his opposition to the precinct level cutoff, but the strong action of the reform commission is expected to place heavy pres-

sure on him to accept it as part fo a broader compromise.

The national committee is considered unlikely to tamper with the reforms against Mr. Strauss' wishes. However, at a meeting in Louisville this week it voted its intention to review

the commssion's report before translatng it into the rules of the 1976 national nominating convention and the 1974 midterm convention.

October 28, 1973

John B. Connally speaking in Houston yesterday

Associated Press

Connally, Joining G.O.P., Calls It More Responsive

By MARTIN WALDRON
Special to The New York Times

HOUSTON, May 2—Former Gov. John B. Connally of Texas, who was Treasury Secretary during the first Nixon Administration and was a political disciple of the late President Johnson for many years, announced today, as forecast, that he had become a Republican.

Many politicans believe that this is the first step in a campaign by Mr. Connally to try to win the Republican Presidential nomination in 1976.

He said he had decided to leave the Democratic party because he thought the Republican party was more nearly responsive to the needs and thoughts of the people. He said he could not remain a Democrat and still take part in national affairs.

"I think it is fair to say that the Democratic party has moved so far left that it has left behind the majority of Americans who occupy the great middle ground of this country," he said, adding that the Republican party now occupies "the broad middle ground where we are going to have to find the solutions to the many problems we have."

Mr. Connally's conversion was greeted as bright news at the troubled White House and at the otherwise gloomy headquarters of the Republican National Committee in Washington.

National political observers regarded the announcement

as further confirmation of Mr. Connally's intention to run for the Presidential nomination, and, its timing appeared carefully designed to impress party regulars, dispirited by the Watergate scandal, with their convert's dedication.

Vice President Agnew, who has held a commanding lead over other Republican Presidential contenders in opinion polls of party members, called Mr. Connally "a talented and personal man, an effective and articulate spokesman for traditional American values. I know that all Republicans will join me in welcoming Mr. Connally aboard."

The silver-haired Texan, who counts many of the state's rich oil men as his supporters and friends, said, "I seek no office, political or appointive."

In a small first-floor room in the First City National Bank Building of Houston, surrounded by so many bankers, lawyers and friends that some members of the press were unable to get into the room, Mr. Connally dismissed the current Watergate scandal as a "silly, stupid, illegal act" whose impact on the 1974 and 1976 elections was probably being overestimated.

"I think that by '74 the people will have an opportunity to put into better perspective what this incident was," Mr. Connally said. "One of the things we need to put into perspective was that [Watergate] was an act of individuals. The Republican party didn't do it."

Timing Held Coincidental

Alluding to speculation that he and President Nixon had timed his conversion to Republicanism to gather praise from party regulars stinging from the Watergate criticism, Mr. Connally said the timing was coincidental and said he had talked to the President only three times in the last three weeks.

"I called him this morning and told him of what I was going to do," Mr. Connally said. "I called him the other night after his speech just to commend him. But I have not discussed my political future, and I did not discuss this press conference with him before I announced it."

Mr. Connally said he also conversed at some length with the President three weeks ago.

Changing political parties in Texas is quite simple. Voters do not register by parties, so

a voter becomes a full-fledged Republican or Democrat by voting in a party's primary. Mr. Connally voted in the Democratic primary last year.

Mr. Connally served three two-year terms as Governor as a Democrat. In the middle of his first term, he was seriously wounded by rifle shots while riding with President Kennedy in Dallas when Mr. Kennedy was assassinated.

Before running for Governor, he was Secretary of the Navy in the Kennedy Administration. He served in the Nixon Administration as Treasury Secretary at a time of monetary crisis, a crisis that he said today is still with the nation.

"We ought not to let ourselves become so enmeshed in Watergate that we forget the fact that we have great problems in restructuring the monetary system of the world," he said and continued:

"We have great problems in dealing with international trade matters. We have great problems in bringing about fiscal responsibility. We need all the strength of this nation, combined strength on a nonpartisan basis, to fight inflation that plagues the nation.

"We must concern ourselves with the energy crisis which we are in the midst of, and which is going to become worse in this country. All of these things, we have to deal with and we ought to deal with them in the most objective and the most intelligent and the most effective way we can, and it is toward that purpose that I am going to direct my efforts."

Last fall, Mr. Connally headed a national Democrats for Nixon Committee, which raised hundreds of thousands of dollars for Mr. Nixon's re-election campaign. Mr. Connally said he "hoped" that none of this money went to pay for Watergate.

"Watergate was long over and done with before Democrats for Nixon were even organized," he said.

Mr. Connally said he considered political spying and espionage carried out by supporters of President Nixon to be a "very reprehensible thing." He continued:

"I feel very strongly about Watergate. I think too much of it goes on in this country in and out of Government. And I think it ought to be stopped. And I feel more strongly about it than any member of the press here. I'm convinced of

369

that. I think this illegal act and those who participated in it ought to be punished for it, but I don't think we ought to let it blind us to the realization that we have great problems in this country.

"And I don't think that incident, however reprehensible, ought to be used as a shield against what the President has done that has been so much in the interest of this country.

"I think the President has done an incredibly effective job in dealing with the foreign relations of this country and has shown great courage in dealing with our domestic problems."

Mr. Connally said that Watergate "has done great damage to the political processes of this country and those who were responsible for it must

be punished, no question about that."

He said he did not see anything wrong with having an outside prosecutor to investigate the Watergate incident if it should prove to be necessary.

"The President clearly said that Elliot Richardson has that authority, and if he feels that it can best serve the country to have someone brought in from the outside, I think Elliot Richardson will do it," he said.

Mr. Connally said he did not know if his changing parties would have any effect on Texas politics, adding that if anyone would follow him, he had not heard about it.

TEXT OF STATEMENT

I believe that every American has an obligation to par-

ticipate in our political system. This I have done all of my adult life and shall continue to do.

Regardless of past political history and traditions that many of us hold dear, I have reached the personal conclusion that my future activities should be within the framework of the Republican party.

In recent history it is the Republican party which has invited broader participation from people in all walks of life; which has worked more effectively for economic growth and fiscal responsibility; which has sought opportunity for all without the burden of bigger government and higher taxes; and which stands for expanded international trade, more realistic

monetary policies and responsible American leadership in the free world.

I believe that in our time the Republican party best represents the broad views of most Americans whatever their former political affiliation. I believe that it can best provide the strength and stability to unite our people to deal effectively with our problems. I know that it now best represents my own personal convictions.

Accordingly, I am today announcing my decision to affiliate with the Republican party, and make any contribution I can to help it meet the needs and aspirations of all Americans.

May 3, 1973

DEMOCRATS PILE UP CONGRESS GAINS

Senate and House Margins Are Substantially Enlarged

By JAMES M. NAUGHTON

Democrats swept yesterday toward domination of the next Congress as voters across the nation apparently blamed Republicans for the Watergate scandal and for economic disruption.

With 34 Senate seats and all 435 House districts at stake, the Democrats were substantially enlarging the majorities by which they already control the Congress.

Three Democrats captured Senate seats now held by Republicans in Florida, Colorado and Kentucky. A Democrat appeared to be on the verge of election to the Senate from Vermont for the first time in more than a century. And Democrats were in close, indefinite contests for Republican-held Senate seats in North Dakota, Utah and New Hampshire.

In the House, the Democrats picked up at least 22 Republican seats in states as disparate as Massachusetts, New Jersey, North Carolina, Texas, Virginia, Indiana and Colorado. Republi-

cans were considered potential losers in as many as 25 more House districts they new control.

This would give the Democrats a two-thirds majority in the House, enough to override Presidential vetoes.

The outcome was a stinging rebuke to the Republican patry, its worst showing in a Congressional election in a decade.

Moreover, the returns represented a bitter frustration for President Ford's campaign, which he carried to 20 states, for a cooperative, even if Democratic, Congress next January.

Mr. Ford declared just before midnight last night that he "accepted the verdict" of the electorate. But he pointedly challenged the Democrats to live up to the responsibility inherent in their national victory.

The President said that inflation had emerged as the dominant issue of the election, and added:

"The mandate of the electorate places upon the next

Congress a full measure of responsibility for resolving this problem."

Robert S. Strauss, the Democratic party's national chairman, called the outcome a victory for, and revitalization of, "the old Democratic coalition" created by President Franklin D. Roosevelt. Mr. Strauss added that, for his party, "The victory isn't tonight. The opportunity begins tonight."

The trend, with most of the Senate elections and a majority of the House contents decided, was toward a Congress with nearly twice as many Democrats as Republicans. Currently, Democrats have a 58-to-42 margin in the Senate and a 248-to-187 edge in the House. CBS News forecast a Democratic House majority of 295 to 140.

The tone of the election was reflected in the defeat of several Republicans on the House Judiciary Committee who had steadfastly opposed the impeachment of President Nixon. They were Representatives Wiley Mayne of Iowa, David W. Dennis of Indiana, and Charles W. Sandman and Joseph J. Maraziti in New Jersey.

"I didn't believe that Watergate would carry this far," Mr. Sandman said, "but it has and there is nothing I could do about it."

In the Michigan district that Mr. Ford had represented in the House for a quarter-century, the Democrat who won a

special election earlier this year, Richard Vander Veen, won a full term last night.

Kentucky voters refused to return Senator Marlow W. Cook, the Republican incumbent, replacing him with Gov. Wendell H. Ford, a Democrat.

Another incumbent Republican, Senator Peter H. Dominick of Colorado, was defeated by Gary W. Hart, the Democrat who managed Senator George McGovern's unsuccessful bid for the Presdency two years ago. Senator McGovern was easily re-elected in South Dakota.

In Florida, Richard Stone, the Democratic nominee, defeated his Republican opponent, Jack Ekerd, in the race to succeed the Republican Senator, Edward J. Gurney, who is retiring.

The most dramatic possible upset in the making was in Vermont, where Patrick J. Leahy, the Democratic nominee, was in a tight race with Representative Richard W. Mallary, the Republican nominee, to succeed another Senate retiree, George D. Aiken. Not since the Republican party was formed in 1854 has a Democrat been elected to the Senate from Vermont.

Throughout the country, the pattern was repeated. Democrats handily won re-election to Congress while most Republicans, including incumbents, had to struggle for survival.

Among the veteran Republicans turned out of the House yesterday were Joel T. Broyhill of Virginia, John N. (Happy) Camp of Oklahoma, William J. Scherle of Iowa, Earl F. Landgrebe of Indiana, Paul W. Cronin of Massachusetts and William B. Widnall of New Jersey.

Five women candidates were elected to the House to increase by one, to 171, the number of women in the House.

The number of black members of the House also grew by one, also to 17, with the apparent election in Tennessee of Harold E. Ford, a Democrat, over veteran Representative Dan Kuykendall, another Republican ally of Mr. Nixon. Mr. Kuykendall, who had been the beneficiary of redistricting by a Republican majority in the Tenneessee Legislature, said that he would seek a recount.

In Connecticut, Christopher J. Dodd, the son of former Senator Thomas J. Dodd, won for the Democrats the seat currently held by Representative Robert H. Steel, the Republican candidate for Governor, who

lost to Ella T. Grasso. Another Connecticut Republican, Representative Ronald A. Sarasin, apparently survived after trailing his Democratic challenger, William R. Ratchford.

Against the Democratic tide, Republican Senators Robert Dole of Kansas and Henry Bellmon of Oklahoma appeared headetd for re-election by wafer-thin margins. Former Gov. Paul Laxalt, a Nevada Republican, also stood a chance to pick up for his party the seat of retiring Democratic Senator Alan Bible.

The Republicans entered the election hoping merely to hold their losses to a minimum in both the Senate and the House of Representatives but anticipating another substantial erosion of their Congressional minority.

Not since the country gave President Johnson "Great Society" Democratic majorities of 68 to 32 in the Senate and 295 to 140 in the House in the elections a decade ago had the Republicans' prospects been considered so bleak by political observers.

Virtually every factor influencing the 1974 national campaign, from the lingering stigma of Watergate to the continuing burden of a faltering economy, was viewed by observers as working to the Republicans' disadvantage.

Able Republicans who had planned to seek office or to run for higher positions decided, months ago during the filing periods around the country, that the Watergate scandals made 1974 an inauspicious year for candidates of their party.

Thus, in Illinois, for instance, Representative John B. Anderson, a popular and respected Republican House veteran, decided against challenging Senator Stevenson, the Democratic incumbent. Mr. Stevenson thus had as his opponent for re-election George M. Burditt, who never before sought elective office.

Even the initial Republican euphoria at the Aug. 9 resignation of President Nixon faded when, on Sept. 9, President Ford granted his predecessor an unconditional pardon, which quickly became controversial.

Moreover, as the nation's attention gradually shifted from the Watergate matter, it appeared to fix on yet another political problem for the Republicans, the combination of inflation at a rate exceeding 10 per cent a year and economic stagnation.

President Ford stumped 20 states, appealing for the retention of at least enough Republicans to give him the opportunity to put his economic programs into effect. He warned that the election of twice as many Democrats as Republicans would create a "vetoproof" Congress that could block his domestic economic programs and imperil his international policies.

But Democrats, confident that they would continue to control Congress, sought to enlarge their majorities to an extent that might ease their efforts to enact such legislation as tax reform or national health insurance.

November 6, 1974

National Vote Pattern: A Sweep If Not a G.O.P. Debacle

By R. W. APPLE Jr.

The American electorate vented its wrath on Republican candidates across the nation on Tuesday, striking hardest at state legislators and United States Representatives — those theoretically most responsive to the public will. The Democrats made marked gains in state legislatures, posting truimphs in states as diverse as New York, Tennessee, Illinois and Wisconsin. They did equally well in the House of Representatives, picking up two or more seats each in California, Illinois, Indiana, Iowa, Michigan, New Jersey, New York, North Carolina, Oregon, Tennessee, Virginia and Wisconsin.

The Democratic advances in the Senate and in the governorships were more modest, about four in each case, but were still substantial.

By the measurement of most politicians, including President Ford, the results, taken together, constituted a Democratic sweep, if not quite the utter debacle some Republicans feared earlier this year.

There are a number of ways to look at the over-all picture, including the following:

Measured against the recent past, the Democratic gains were above average but not extraordinary. In the postwar era,

News Analysis

the party out of power in the White House has gained in a off-year elections an average of four Senators (as against three or four this year), six Governors (as against four or five this year) and 30 members of the House (as against 42 or 43 this year).

But the comparison is misleading. The underlying reason for the long-term trend is that most Presidents pull in many members of their party in the Presidential years. But Richard M. Nixon did not do that in 1972, so the Democrats began this year from a much stronger position than usual for the party out of power.

Thus, it may be fairer to look at the levels the Democratic majorities attained. In the House the Democrats will hold at least 290 seats, a level reached by either party only five times in this century. In the Senate, they will hold at least 61 seats, a level reached only nine times since 1900.

In terms of the popular vote, according to computer projections by the television networks, the Democrats pulled 60 per cent, probably a twentieth-century record.

In an era when it had supposedly become all but impossible to dislodge incumbents in the House and Senate, three Republican Senators and 36 Republican Representatives were ousted, more House members than both parties lost in the

three previous elections combined. Only four House Democrats lost and not a single Senate Democrat was voted out.

Big Democratic Reversal

In terms of stunning reversals, the Republicans had all the worst of it. The Democrats' one real heartbreaker was the loss of Gov. John J. Gilligan in Ohio. But the Republicans had many—the loss of a Senate seat in Vermont for the first time since the founding of their party, the loss of their coastal bases in Albany and Sacramento, the devastation of their House delegations in Oregon and Indiana and New Jersey.

In regional terms, the Democrats accomplished their goals, but not with the decisiveness they would have liked. They checked but did not wholly reverse their slippage in the South (a net gain of seven House seats and two Senate seats). They made substantial inroads as well into the Republican heartland — the Middle West and the Mountain States.

Here, too, Ohio was the anomaly. Not only did Mr. Gilligan lose; he lost to former Gov. James A. Rhodes, the living symbol of the old-politics, low-tax, low-services style that the Democrats thought they had buried forever. And, with a good chance to gain three House seats, they gained only one and lost one—that of Thomas A. Luken of Cincinnati, the

only victor in a 1974 special election to lose Tuesday.

Apart from the size of the Democratic triumph, the returns were shot through with other patterns.

Turnout: The trend toward lighter and lighter voting, disturbing to most political theorists, apparently continued. Although computer projections differed, it is safe to say that those who stayed home could have reversed the result in almost every race if they had decided to vote.

Money: Despite the Watergate-induced flurry of concern about campaign financing, there was the usual overwhelming correlation between big spenders and big winners.

Women: As advertised. For the first time, a woman was elected Governor of a state her husband had not previously governed (Connecticut). Chief Justice of a State Supreme Court (North Carolina) and Mayor of a city of more than 500,000 population (San Jose) Calif.). And, in a year when four women Representatives retired, six new ones were apparently elected.

Moderate Republicans. Contrary to some predictions, the party's left and center survived nicely, in the person of Governors such as William G. Milliken of Michigan, Senators such as Robert W. Packwood of Oregon and Jacob K. Javits of New York and Charles McC. Mathias Jr. of Maryland, Representatives such as William S. Cohen of Maine and Alan Steelman of Texas and Ronald A. Sarasin of Connecticut.

The liberal Republican organization in the House, the Wednesday Group, lost only one of its 36 members, while the so-called Republican Regulars lost at least 30 of its 70 members, according to party sources.

Hurt by Watergate

Watergate: It clobbered the Republicans. Four of Mr. Nixon's stanchest Judiciary Committee defenders lost. So did Representative Earl F. Landgrebe of Indiana, who had vowed to stick with the former President "until they take me out and shoot me," and Representative Richard G. Shoup of Montana, who described the impeachment proceedings as a "cheap partisan witch-hunt." Many a Democratic cakewalk (the Illinois and California Senate races, for example) resulted from the refusal of strong Republican candidates to run.

Economy: Reports from candidates across the country showed that most Republican losers blamed inflation as a major factor in their defeats. In at least two cases, local economic dislocations cost the Republicans House incumbents: Representative John Dellenback of Oregon, who represents a district whose timber industry has been crippled by the housing slump, and Representative William Scherle of Ohio, apparently victimized by farm problems.

Suburbs: Voters in middle-income and upper-income suburbs, perhaps more offended than some other groups by the corruption issue, turned out Republican incumbents in Long Island (two), the Chicago area (two), and elsewhere.

'Heat' on the Democrats

Mr. Ford and his fellow Republicans face a trying time, a time when they must rebuild their party for 1976 and try to work out a modus vivendi with the Democratic Congress.

But, paradoxically, the smell of success may not prove to be entirely sweet for the Democrats in the next two years.

As Senator Walter F. Mondale, the Minnesota Democrat, put it yesterday morning, "Now the heat's on us." By that he meant that unless the chronically disorganized Democrats on Capitol Hill can somehow find a way to give shape to an alternative program, especially on the economy, they may find themselves blamed for inflation and recession in 1976.

The same point was made, directly or indirectly, by other party leaders. Representative John J. Rhodes of Arizona, the House Republican leader, who survived the toughest re-election fight of his career, said, "The ball is in their court now." And Robert S. Strauss, the Democratic chairman, said pointedly, "The opportunity begins tonight."

Even though the new Democratic contingents in the Senate and the House appear to be somewhat more liberal, and therefore probably more prepared to support wage and price controls, for example, there is no guarantee of orthodoxy.

Even if they are able to ameliorate the economic situation, in concert with the President, the Democrats are far from assured of an easy ride into the White House in 1976.

For one thing, most of the pre-election polling by both parties indicated that much of the vote for Democratic candidates this year would, in fact, be anti-Republican, a slap on the wrist for Watergate and high prices, just as much of the 1972 Nixon vote was at least partly anti-McGovern.

So, the Democrats, in their more realistic moments, can consider Tuesday's swollen majorities neither permanent or even a short-term "mandate."

In addition, they are about to confront once again the problem that has bedeviled them since the death of Franklin D. Roosevelt; namely, that it is easy enough for them to find candidates who can appeal to relatively narrow constituencies, such as states or Congressional districts, but terribly difficult to find one who can appeal across all the regional and ideological gulfs of the national party.

Candidate May Emerge

There is no such candidate in sight now, although one may emerge from among those already running — Senators Mondale, Lloyd M. Bentsen of Texas and Henry M. Jackson of Washington—or those thrust forward on Tuesday—Hugh L. Carey in New York, John H. Glenn Jr. in Ohio, Edmund G. Brown Jr. in California, Gov. George C. Wallace of Alabama, Senator Birch Bayh of Indiana.

The path to the convention is strewn with obstacles, including the mini-convention in Kansas City next month, a bewildering series of two dozen primaries and the unpredictable course of events in the nation and in the world.

But at least the Democrats have regained the initiative. They have a strong base in the governorships, bigger majorities in both houses of Congress and a plethora of new talent. The Republicans would probably be glad to trade places with them.

November 7, 1974

DEMOCRATS ADOPT A PARTY CHARTER; WALKOUT AVOIDED

Compromise Is Reached on Challenges in Selection of Convention Delegates

MINORITY ROLE ACCORD

McGovern Is Cheered as He Appeals for Ideologically Aggressive Group

By R. W. APPLE Jr.
Special to The New York Times

KANSAS CITY, Dec. 7—The Democratic mid-term conference adopted the first national party charter in American history tonight after a last-minute compromise averted the possibility of a walkout by militant blacks.

In a daylong session uninterrupted by luncheon or dinner breaks, the 1,911 delegates successfully negotiated the shoals of factionalism, following the course charted by their Rules Committee on most issues. Then they adjourned in euphoria with comments of self-congratulation, unity and unbounded relief.

The change from Miami Beach, 1972, to Kansas City, 1974, was summarized when Jesse Jackson, the black activist from Chicago, threw his arms around Mayor Richard Daley as the final vote neared.

12-Article Charter

In 12 articles, the new charter provides a party structure encompassing such matters as convention delegate selection, party officers, a judicial council to arbitrate disputes and so on.

"I took my best shot today," said Robert S. Strauss, chairman of the convention and of the Democratic National Committee, "and I think we did well."

For the most part, it was a disciplined meeting with dozens of relatively minor amendments debated and voted up or down as the proceedings droned on. There was a brief display of passion when Senator George McGovern of South Dakota, the party's standard bearer in 1972, called for an ideologically aggressive Democratic party.

Walkout Threatened

But outrage among blacks and women over a single paragraph of the charter dealing with minority participation in party affairs threatened to boil over into a disruptive floor fight and possibly a walkout. After a series of caucuses and negotiating sessions that lasted all through the night and into this afternoon, enough legalistic hairs were split to restore at least a semblance of intra-party harmony.

In effect, the changes in the paragraph make it ever so slightly easier for blacks and others to mount effective challenges when they feel they have been discriminated against in the choice of national convention delegates.

For the blacks, their struggle was as much symbolic as real— an assertion of their determination "not to be left out," as one of their leaders said. They therefore counted the fact that they forced any change as their most important accomplishment.

For more than 12 hours, Mr. Strauss and the nation's Democratic Governors dug in their heels and refused to accede to the demands of the blacks and women, arguing that any tinkering with the controversial language on participation would undo a series of carefully balanced previous compromises.

Intensive Negotiations

But finally, after some intensive liaison work by liberal labor leaders headed by Leonard Woodcock of the United Automobile Workers, Mr. Strauss was able to find a way out. It was suggested by Gov. Reuben Askew of Florida and by Edward Bennett Williams, the Washington trial attorney who serves as the party's national treasurer.

Only one other question was closely contested today. That involved the choice of a single word in Article Six: should the charter provide that the party "may" or "shall" hold future midterm conferences?

James McGregor Burns, a Williams College professor who once ran for Congress, appealed to regular Democrats to join with him in mandating future conferences that would, he said, "invigorate and renew our party at the grass roots."

In rebuttal, Payton McNight of Texas argued that it would be "imprudent" to lock the party into future conferences because of their high cost. This year's meeting, he declared, had cost the party about $685,000.

On a roll-call vote, the effort to institutionalize mini-conventions fell short. The vote was 1,006 to 823.

With the galleries half empty and debate carefully structured to minimize friction, with live television cameras absent and no brass bands or ballons to help whip up emotions, the proceedings had little of the tumult of traditional political conventions.

But there was a brief burst of passion before and after the speech of Mr. McGovern, who carried only Massachusetts and the District of Columbia as the Democratic Presidential nominee two years ago.

Mr. McGovern brought cheers from the crowded floor of the Kansas City Municipal Auditorium with a rousing appeal for a fighting, ideologically aggressive party. In a year when centrism has become a Democratic rallying cry, he gave the miniconvention a new dose of 1972.

"The forces of privilege will oppose reform as they always have," Mr. McGovern said in his flat, Middle Western accent. "The voices of timidity will caution against any substantive effort toward change, as they always do. And the hard-eyed cynics will again call down distortion and ridicule.

"But to avoid issues is to invite disaster. Our survival as a party is at stake. The people will no longer accept a politics whose only purpose is power. When they ask, 'What is the Democratic program?' we cannot simply answer, 'To not be Republicans.' That is no answer at all. We cannot be bland in what we say and blind to the evils before us. If we are, we will be united but defeated; we will be in the center but a dead center."

Song of 1972

Mr. McGovern closed as he had closed in Miami Beach in 1972, when his Presidential candidacy still seemed full of bright promise, with the words of Woody Guthrie's folk song, "This Land is Your Land."

Among those seated beneath the state placards as Mr. McGovern spoke were many who had been absent two years ago, including Mayor Daley. Early this afternoon, Senator Edward M. Kennedy of Massachusetts took his seat with the Massachusetts delegation in the rear of the flood-lit, bunting-bedecked hall.

Having taken a formal position on the state of the economy last night, the delegates again today heard references to mounting inflation.

The statement on the economy, the only issue on which the convention has taken a formal stand, supported controls on wages, prices and profits; a "mandatory system of energy conservation"; an expanded program of public service jobs; tax reductions for low-income and middle-income families; a "general easing of credit" by the Federal Reserve Board and a strengthening of the antitrust laws.

Former Gov. Terry Sanford of North Carolina, now the president of Duke University, drew the arduous task of presiding over the marathon article-by-article charter debate. As chairman of the Charter Commission, he oversaw the year-long process of drafting the 3,500-word document.

The central question that the charter sought to answer, Mr. Sanford reminded the delegates in an allusion to the schisms of 1968 and 1972, was: "Can the Democratic party eliminate the squabbles that have caused us to lose?"

Standing before a blue banner emblazoned with huge gold letters spelling out the motto: "We The Democrats Of The United States Of America," Mr. Sanford led the delegates through consideration of each of 12 articles while, outside the main arena, Democratic Presidential hopefuls were making pitches for support in 1976.

In the most ambitious of those vote-seeking efforts, Senator Henry M. Jackson of Washington talked with almost 500 delegates in his white headquarters trailer. Many of his rivals were also at work, including Senator Lloyd M. Bentsen Jr. of Texas, Representative Morris K. Udall of Arizona and Gov. Jimmy Carter of Georgia.

But Gov. George C. Wallace of Alabama, who evoked chuckles at a reception Thursday night when he called out from his wheelchair: "Make way for the front-runner," returned to Alabama before today's session.

The dispute involving the blacks and women, which had been foreshadowed by heated conflicts at earlier stages of the charter-writing process, flared up last night at a cocktail party given by Mr. Strauss in his Hotel Muehlebach suite.

Seek Article's Deletion

Led by the outspoken Willie Brown of California, the small group of blacks demanded that the chairman support the excision of Section 6 of Article 10 of the draft charter. It in effect puts the burden of proof on the challengers to show that a national convention delegation is racially or otherwise imbalanced through a failure to seek full participation.

Section 6 had become the focal point of the long and bitter struggle between advocates of quotas for blacks, young people, women and others and those who oppose them. The struggle was waged prior to the 1972 convention, during the convention and in the months that followed Senator McGovern's defeat.

Ultimately, the issue was resolved through the adoption of a program of "affirmative action" — meaning that there would be no mandatory quotas but that party officials must work actively to see that full participation was guaranteed.

Among those who reportedly played a part in working out the arrangement were Lieut. Gov.-elect Mary Anne Krupsak of New York and Gov. Reuben Askew of Florida. It was adopted in a room behind the podium after some legal carpentry by Mark Siegel, one of Mr. Strauss's aides.

When Mr. Strauss reappeared at the podium to announce a recess for caucuses at which the compromise would be explained some delegations were stunned. And when he descended to the floor in the most dramatic confrontation of the convention, Mr. Strauss's path was blocked by John Tuohy, chairman of the Illinois delegation.

"You double-crossed us," Mr. Mr. Tuohy shouted. "We'll never trust you again."

During the recess, other party conservatives muttered angrily. too, but by the time Mr. Sanford called for a two-thirds vote to suspend the rules and adopt the compromise, he got the votes with ease.

December 8, 1974

Democrat in House Criticizes Liberals And Shifts to G.O.P.

By RICHARD D. LYONS
Special to The New York Times

WASHINGTON, Jan. 23— John Jarman, a 12-term conservative Representative from Oklahoma, switched his party affiliation today from Democratic to Republican because of what he termed the liberal excesses of the Democratic Caucus.

Mr. Jarman charged that there had been a liberal "takeover." He said that liberals were trying to force their views "on this Congress and on this country by nullifying the seniority system and punishing those who do not adhere to the liberal party line as laid down by the caucus."

The reference was to yesterday's Democratic Caucus action deposing three long-term Southern committee chairmen and replacing them with Democrats from Northern states. The caucus vote was formally approved today by the full House.

While several Republicans in Congress have in recent years changed their affiliations to Democratic, Mr. Jarman's action was the first the other way around since Senator Strom Thurmond became a Republican in 1964.

In recent weeks, some conservatives in Congress had spoken of a new alignment, with the Republicans taking in the Democratic right wing and the Democrats the Republican left wing, but until today no formal changes had come about.

President Ford hailed Mr. Jarman's action, saying that it was "the sincere conviction of a dedicated member of Congress."

January 24, 1975

Labor to Shun Role In Political Parties

By DAMON STETSON
Special to The New York Times

BAL HARBOUR, Fla., Feb. 18 —In what appeared to be a major policy change, George Meany asserted today that the A.F.L.-C.I.O. would no longer involve itself in political party affairs and would take no part in the selection of delegates to the Democratic National Convention next year.

Although Mr. Meany has frequently proclaimed the political independence of the American Federation of Labor and Congress of Industrial Organizations in the past, leaders of the federation's political arm, the Committee on Political Education, have involved themselves intensively in Democratic party politics.

For more than a decade Alexander Barkan, the director of the political committee, has been regarded as a major behind-the-scenes figure in Democratic politics at the local, state and national levels. Today's declaration, on its face, would curb his role considerably.

In 1972, Mr. Barkan worked diligently and unsuccessfully in Democratic primaries and state conventions to block the selection of delegates favorable to Senator George McGovern of South Dakota who won the Presidential nomination and was defeated by President Nixon.

Last December, at the Democrats' charter-drafting convention in Kansas City, Mr.

373

Barkan was an active participant in a dispute over procedures to insure significant minority-group representation among delegates to the 1976 convention. The dispute ended in a compromise that most observers considered another setback to Mr. Barkan, who argued against any form of quota system.

Today's declaration, which Mr. Meany, the federation's head, said was supported unanimously by the A.F.L.-C.I.O.'s Executive Council, was described as a "de facto" change of significance by one high labor official here. Another union leader warned, "We could wind up in 1976 with no one we could support—just as we did in 1972." In 1972, the A.F.L.-C.I.O. remained neutral in the Presidential election.

Policy Described

At a news conference after a council meeting today, Mr. Meany described the policy of noninvolvement as follows:

"We came to a unanimous conclusion that the A.F.L.-C.I.O. has no desire to influence the internal structure of either the Republican or Democratic parties and we have no desire to allow the Republican or Democratic party to interfere with our internal affairs.

"We have a political party and it's known as COPE, and we are going to continue to improve it, strengthen it, maintain it, in order to try to elect labor's friends to the House and to the Senate and to the state legislatures, irrespective of political parties."

Asked whether party officials who are officers of the A.F.L.-C.I.O. would be expected to give up their positions in the Democratic party, Mr. Meany said, "Positively not.

"The officers of the A.F.L.-C.I.O., the officers of our state federations, the officers of the central bodies, are all American citizens and they are Democrats, some of them are Republicans, some of them are independents and they can do as they please, insofar as political participation is concerned," Mr. Meany said.

"Those who are active in the Democratic National Committee, that seems to be the subject of a lot of discussion, se-cured their seats on the committee as Democrats from local areas. They were not put on there by the A.F.L.-C.I.O. The A.F.L.-C.I.O. did not recommend that they go on there, and, if they desire to stay on, they stay on. If they desire to get off, they get off without any regard to any influence from the A.F.L.-C.I.O."

Questions on '76 Delegates

The A.F.L.-C.I.O. president was then asked about the election of delegates to the 1976 Democratic National Convention.

"That's the local unions," Mr. Meany said. "Some international unions take part in that. We've had a lot of auto workers, we've had a lot of steelworkers, we've had a lot of building trades workers who are delegates to the convention. They are there as Democrats to the Democratic National Convention. Maybe some even go to the Republican National Convention, although I've never heard of one. But they go as Democrats, as American citizens and that's their business and that's not the business of the A.F.L.-C.I.O.

"The federation takes no part whatsoever in it. When they name their candidates, then the federation's political machinery goes into action."

Jerry Wurf, president of the American Federation of State, County and Municipal Employes, was reported by union sources to have raised a question at today's Executive Council meeting about the policy of noninvolvement in political party affairs. According to these sources, he warned that labor might find itself confronted with two candidates that it could not support—such as President Ford for the Republicans and Gov. George C. Wallace of Alabama for the Democrats.

On other matters today, Mr. Meany said that in the face of widespread unemployment there should be consideration of a shorter (35-hour) workweek to make more jobs available. He proposed, too, that the minimum wage be raised to $3 an hour.

February 19, 1975

The Two Majorities

By William Schneider

CAMBRIDGE—There are now two majorities in American politics—a conservative majority and a Democratic majority. But aren't the Democrats the "liberal" party?

As Max Lerner observed in 1974, "The paradox of American politics is that the voters are increasingly Democrats but not liberals, increasingly conservatives but not Republicans." How can we have two majorities at the same time? It all depends on the issue.

The conservative majority is built on the white racial resentment that for fifteen years has been steadily eroding the New Deal Democratic coalition. First the Deep South was chipped away in 1964. Then in 1968 the split became nationwide, as George C. Wallace made substantial inroads into areas of traditional Democratic strength, North and South.

The 1972 election was the ultimate triumph of the conservative majority, when fully one out of every three voting Democrats cast his ballot for the Republican. "Race," The New York Times concluded after the 1972 election, "has been a dirty little secret that is neither little nor secret, but central to current politics."

It is central no more. Since 1972, the Democratic majority has apparently reconsolidated—and this with very little effort on the part of the Democrats. What has happened is that the agenda of politics has shifted.

Voters no longer name race or law-and-order as their major political concerns. They name the economy. In a 1974 New York Times poll of New York state voters, race was considered a major political issue by fewer than one in a hundred whites and only one in ten blacks and Puerto Ricans. "Integration," one black voter replied, "has been pushed into the background because of inflation."

The message of the 1974 election

Voters now name the economy as their major political concern.

was that the Democrats can do pretty well as long as they don't have to come up with a Presidential candidate. Liberals did well in 1974 because they were Democrats. Democrats did not do well because they were liberals.

But what about the many Republican liberals who managed to hang on in the midst of a party catastrophe? Republican liberals survive in politics only by getting substantial support from liberal Democrats and independents. Well-educated, ideological, middle-class liberals, dedicated Nixon-haters, all continued to vote for liberal Republicans in 1974, particularly those Republicans identified as Richard M. Nixon's bitterest enemies.

But the big Democratic gains in 1974 did not come from liberals. The big gains came from the working-class conservatives and moderates, the critical swing group in the electorate. They were the traditional Democrats who in recent years had been defecting, not to liberal Republicans, but to conservative, law-and-order Republicans, as well as to George Wallace and to "cop candidates." Their symbol and hero was Spiro T. Agnew. It was these voters who were once most fearful about race and crime, and who are now most fearful about the economy. Thus it is Hubert H. Humphrey and Edward M. Kennedy—the most traditional regular Democrats—whose support has been increasing most rapidly in the 1975 polls.

Ideology had very little to do with the voters' return to the Democrats.

Consider, for instance, the parallel between 1968 and 1974. In 1968, Mr. Nixon avoided all ideological identification as either a dove or a hawk. He said he had "a secret plan" to end the war. Hadn't Dwight D. Eisenhower gotten us out of Korea? "End the war," the voters seemed to say, "no matter how." In 1974, the Democrats liked to think they had "a secret plan" to end the recession, though no one knew exactly what it was. Hadn't Franklin D. Roosevelt gotten us out of the Depression?

Mr. Nixon's secret Vietnam plan was to be a dove and a hawk at the same time—fewer troops and more bombs.

Apparently the Democrats' secret

374

plan for the economy is to cut Government spending and to increase Government spending at the same time. Thus we were treated to the unlikely spectacle of newly elected Democratic governors in New York, California and Massachusetts attacking the spendthrift ways of their Republican predecessors while struggling to keep their campaign promises to maintain social-welfare support.

Before Watergate, many Republicans asserted that the "emerging" majority was a Republican majority. It was not. It was a conservative majority, or, more precisely, a coalition of all non-liberals against the disruptive threats of liberalism.

A comparable misconception can be found among many liberals today, including many liberals in Congress—namely, that 1974 signified the emergence of a new liberal majority. It did not. The voters in 1974 were recalling to office the party of Franklin D. Roosevelt to revive the economy, "no matter how."

As Mr. Nixon realized in the closing days of the 1972 campaign ("peace is at hand"), sooner or later the people are going to expect some results.

William Schneider is assistant professor of government at Harvard.

September 12, 1975

G.O.P.'S '76 RULES UPHELD BY COURT

By WARREN WEAVER Jr.
Special to The New York Times

WASHINGTON, Oct. 4 — The power of political parties to manage their affairs without court interference, even in the face of charges of unconstitutional discrimination, was reaffirmed this week by the United States Court of Appeals for the District of Columbia.

In its second ruling on a four-year-old Republican party dispute, the court held, 8 to 2, that delegate strength at Presidential nominating conventions need not be apportioned among the states on a strict one-person-one vote basis.

The majority thus upheld the delegate formula that the Republican party plans to use for its 1976 convention, despite the fact that its "bonus" provisions give some large states such as New York and California less than their numerical share of voting strength.

In a broader political context, the decision appeared to give the controlling faction in any political party authority to adopt rules limiting the influence of a minority faction as long as the rules "rationally advance some legitimate interest of the party in winning elections or otherwise achieving its political goals."

Democrats Affected

In this sense, the ruling almost certainly strengthens against possible legal attack Democratic party regulations aimed at encouraging the representation of women, young people and minorities in all state delegations to the party's national convention.

The lawsuit was brought by the Ripon Society, an organization of younger Republican liberals, and nine individual party members, contending that the delegate apportionment formula approved in 1972 for the 1976 G.O.P. convention unfairly discriminates against some large states by cutting their influence.

The Republican formula awards bonus delegates to states that gave a majority to the last Republican Presidential candidate and elected Republican governors and members of Congress in the last election.

As a result, California, with 9.8 per cent of the nation's population and 9.8 per cent of the 1972 Republican vote, only gets 7.5 per cent of the 1976 convention delegates. New York, with 9 per cent of the population and 8.9 per cent of the Republican vote, has 6.8 per cent of the delegates.

Historically, this kind of apportionment has tended to reduce the influence of the Republican party's liberal wing, which is generally stronger in the larger states that lose delegates, thus favoring the conservative leadership of the smaller states that are awarded a disproportionate share of convention strength.

In recent years, this effect has been less pronounced, with conservative organizations in control in such large states as California and Florida.

The Ripon Society first sued in 1971 and won a partial victory in Federal District Court, but that ruling was stayed by Associate Justice William H. Rehnquist, and the 1972 convention was held on the basis of the old formula. Then the suit was renewed with respect to the 1976 convention.

This time, the Federal District court ruled against the uniform allocation of five bonus delegates to each state carried by the party's national ticket. A three-judge panel of the Court of Appeals declared all the victory bonuses unconstitutional by a 2-to-1 vote.

But that ruling was vacated by the full appellate court, which ordered the case reargued before all its members. It was their decision this week that reversed the previous rulings and upheld the delegate formula in all respects.

Suit Is Supported

The Democratic National Committee, appearing as a friend of the court, supported the Republican party against the Ripon Society on the theory that the courts should not interfere in internal party affairs, despite the fact that the Democrats do not use victory bonuses in their convention formula.

Democratic party officials believe the decision will help the party defeat two pending legal challenges, one a challenge by Wisconsin Democrats who challenge the party's rule against an open primary and the other a Texas challenge to the delegate apportionment formula.

Even if the Ripon Society should decide to appeal, it is extremely unlikely that a Supreme Court ruling could be handed down in time to affect the selection of 1976 convention delegates, which will begin in party primaries early next year.

October 5, 1975

Bill to Reform Campaign Funds Signed by Ford Despite Doubts

By JOHN HERBERS
Special to The New York Times

WASHINGTON, Oct. 15—President Ford signed with reservations today legislation for the most extensive reform of Federal campaign-financing practices in American history.

In a signing ceremony in the East Room of the White House, Mr. Ford said that although he had doubts about the use of Federal funds to finance campaigns and was concerned that restricting contributions might interfere with First Amendment rights of citizens, "the times demand this legislation."

"There are certain periods in our nation's history when it becomes necessary to face up to certain unpleasant truths," the President said in a written statement accompanying the signing. "We have passed through one of those periods. The unpleasant truth is that big money influence has come to play an unseeming role in our electoral processes."

Members of Congress who had worked for many months on the legislation, representatives of public interest groups who had lobbied for it and the chairmen of the two major parties looked on and applauded as Mr. Ford signed the bill.

In formal remarks to the guests, Mr. Ford made it clear that, whatever his reservations, the legislation was a response to public indignation over Watergate and related scandals.

"The American people want this legislation" he said, saying that his mail had been filled with demands for reform.

The new law is designed to limit the political influence of special-interest groups and wealthy individuals. It provides for public financing of Presidential primaries and elections. In addition, it will restrict the amount of money that contributors may give to candidates for President, Vice President and Congress and the amount that these candidates may spend in their campaigns.

"Although I support the aim of this legislation, I still have some reservations about it, especially about the use of Federal funds to finance elections," Mr. Ford said.

The provisions of the new law go into effect the first of next year. Under the public-financing provision, a candidate in a Presidential primary would be limited to an over-all outlay of $10-million in public and private funds plus $2-million for strictly fund-raising activities. In the general election for President, each major party candidate would receive $20-million.

Under the limits on contributions, no in individual could contribute more than $25,000 to all Federal candidates and organizations in an election year.

October 16, 1974

HIGH COURT UPHOLDS PUBLIC FUNDS FOR PRESIDENTIAL ELECTION RACES, REMOVES MOST LIMITS ON SPENDING

LANDMARK RULING

30-Day Deadline Is Set for Restructuring of Federal Commission

By LESLEY OELSNER
Special to The New York Times

WASHINGTON, Jan. 30 — In a landmark ruling on how political campaigns are to be waged, the Supreme Court today upheld public financing for Presidential contests, limits on how much individuals may contribute directly to a candidate in any Federal election race, and strict requirements for reporting both contributions and expenditures.

At the same time, the Court struck down as unconstitutional all limits on how much can be spent in a campaign for Congress by a candidate or in his behalf, and struck down nearly all limits on spending in a campaign for President.

One Exception Permitted

The Court permitted one exception regarding unlimited spending for Presidential contenders: In upholding the public financing system, it also upheld the requirement that candidates who accept Federal financing must in return abide by limits on expenditures.

The spending limits had been a major part of the broad campaign financing reform legislation that was enacted last winter to prevent abuses and illegalities in campaigns of the kind disclosed by the Watergate scandal.

The Court also ruled that the new Federal Election Commission, created to implement the reform legislation, must either be restructured or, 30 days from now, cease exercising all but a few of its powers.

Lack of Authority

The Court ruled that many of the powers and duties that the new law gave to the commission—such as the power to initiate civil lawsuits to enforce the law—were powers and duties that could be constitutionally exercised only by Federal officers appointed by the President.

The majority of commission members are named by officials of Congress. As a result, the Court said, the commission lacks authority to exercise those powers.

The Court stayed the effect of its ruling for 30 days to give Congress a chance to enact remedial legislation.

The current contenders in the Presidential primaries have already been operating under the new contribution, disclosure and public financing provisions. Since each has accepted public financing, each is bound by spending limits as a condition of that financing. The restructuring of the Federal Election Commission is all that must be done, at this point, as a result of the ruling.

The long-range effect of the ruling, though, is vast—both in terms of the practical rules for campaigns, and in terms of the extent of the guarantees that the Constitution, especially the First Amendment, have now been interpreted to contain.

While the Court did strike down portions of the new law, it sustained more than it knocked down. The new law drastically changed the rules for political contenders.

The law was enacted largely to prevent corruption and the appearance of corruption in the political process. It was challenged, in the lawsuit that led to today's ruling, by 12 persons and groups, including former Senator Eugene J. McCarthy, on the ground that it violated a series of constitutional provisions and particularly the First Amendment's guarantee of free speech.

What the Court did in today's ruling was balance the governmental interests underlying the law against constitutional guarantees—the need to prevent abuses such as Watergate, for example, against possible infringements by the law on free speech.

Possible Problems Seen

The Court found that various portions of the law, particularly the limits on spending and contributions, but also the requirements regarding reporting and disclosure, posed possible First Amendment problems. But, except in the case of spending limits, it found that the interests underlying the legislation outweighed the need to prevent the First Amendment violation.

Speaking of the limits on contributions and spending, for instance, the Court majority—in an unsigned opinion, joined in some parts by five Justices and in other parts by six, seven, or eight—said:

"The present act's contribution and expenditure limitations impose direct quantity restrictions on political communication and association by persons, groups, candidates and political parties."

However, the Court went on to distinguish between contributions and elections.

Limiting expenditures, the Court said, is a "substantial" restraint on speech, adding that the limit of $1,000 on what an individual may spend relative to a clearly identified candidate—for example, such as placing an newspaper advertisement advocating that person's election—"would appear to exclude all citizens and groups except candidates, political parties, and the institutional press from any significant use of the most effective modes of communication."

Limiting the amount an individual may contribute to a candidate or party, however, the court said, is only a "marginal" restriction, for the "quantity of communication by the contributor does not increase perceptibly with the size of his contribution."

After making that distinction, the court then weighed each of the limits against the governmental needs underlying the law.

In the case of contributions, it held that "it is unnecessary to look beyond the act's primary purpose—to limit the actuality and appearance of corruption resulting from large individual financial contributions"—to find sufficient justification.

"To the extent that large contributions are given to se-

Highlights of the Decision

Special to The New York Times

WASHINGTON, Jan. 30—Following are the highlights of today's Supreme Court decision on the Federal campaign law:

Presidential candidates who have not accepted Federal matching payments to help finance their primary campaigns can reject them and spend as much as they can raise before the party conventions. Previously, they were limited to $10 million, as are those receiving subsidies.

Candidates for Senate and House seats will not be subject to any spending limits. Under a provision stricken by the Court, most House candidates had a $70,000 ceiling for both the primaries and the general elections, Senate limits were higher.

An individual citizen will be able to spend any amount in an independent effort to elect or defeat any candidate through advertising of any kind. Before, he was limited to $1,000 per candidate in any election year.

Candidates for President who do not accept Federal funds and all candidates for Congress can spend as much of their own money or that received from their immediate families as they desire. The previous limits were $50,000 for Presidential candidates, $35,000 for Senate candidates and $25,000 for House candidates.

The Federal Election Commision is stripped of all its important reguatory and policy-making functions, effective in 30 days, if Congress does not revise the system under which Congress, rather than the President, designated four of its six members.

The Court upheld these provisions of the law: the $1,000 ceiling on contributions by an individual directly to any candidate in a primary and $1,000 in the general election, the system requiring detailed reporting of expenditures and contributions, and the public financing of Presidential candidates who qualify for such funds.

cure political quid pro quos from current and potential office holders, the integrity of our system of representative government is undermined," the Court said. "Although the scope of such pernicious practices can never be reliably ascertained, the deeply disturbing examples surfacing after the 1972 election demonstrate that the problem is not an illusory one."

Speaking of limitations on expenditures, however, the Court said:

"The First Amendment denies Government the power to determine that spending to promote one's political views is wasteful, excessive, or unwise. In the free society ordained by our Constitution it is not the Government but the people—individuals as citizens and candidates and collectively as associations and political committees—who must retain control over the quantity and range of debate on public issues in a political campaign."

Criticism in Dissents

The distinctions drawn by the majority drew some criticism from dissenting Justices—criticism that sometimes seemed ironic in that at least some of it expressed what might be considered a "civil libertarian view," urging more stringent First Amendment protections than did the majority, and it came from Justices who have been categorized as conservative.

Chief Justice Warren E. Burger, for example, said, "For me contributions and expenditures are two sides of the same First Amendment coin." Neither, he added, should be limited.

The majority opinion was a "per curiam," or by-the-Court, ruling that was not signed by any one Justice as the author.

A summary attached to the ruling indicated which Justices joined which parts; separate statements by five Justices also indicated points of agreement and disagreement. Eight Justices participated — Chief Justice Burger, and Justices William J. Brennan Jr., Potter Stewart, Thurgood Marshall, Lewis Powell Jr., Harry A. Blackmun, William H. Rehnquist and Byron R. White. John Paul Stevens, who was sworn in after the arguments in the case, did not participate.

The voting breakdown was as follows:

¶Sustaining limits on contributions: The vote was 6-2, with Justices Burger and Blackmun dissenting.

¶Striking down limitations on expenditures: The vote was 6-2 on limiting expenditures by a candidate or his family, with Justices White and Marshall dissenting; for other spending limits, the vote was 7-1, with only Justice White dissenting.

¶Sustaining disclosure and reporting requirements: All the Justices agreed, with the exception that the Chief Justice opposed the requirements for reporting names and addresses of contributors of more than $10 and reporting names, addresses, and business occupations of those who contribute more than $100.

¶Sustaining public financing: All but Chief Justice Burger agreed on the general principle; Justice Rehnquist dissented on the specifics of the financing plan under which, he said, minor party and independent candidates are discriminated against.

¶The structure of the commission: All agreed, except that

Chief Justice Burger dissented from the Court's sustaining the validity of actions the F.E.C. has taken to date.

In addition, there was disagreement among several Justices on the rationale of various parts of the holding. The only Justices who were in complete agreement on the entire majority opinion were Justices Brennan, Stewart and Powell.

The Court's ruling regarding the Federal Election Commission was generally based on the constitutional principle of separation of powers, and specifically on the so-called "appointments clause" of the Constitution, which provides for Presidential apointment of Federal officers.

The Court held that only some of the commission's powers could be considered legislative — such as information-gathering and investigating. Other powers, the Court said, such as rule-making, initiating civil lawsuits designed to enforce the statute, and deciding which matters to refer to the Justice Department for criminal prosecution, were powers reserved for other branches of Government.

To perform these latter non-legislative kinds of duties, the Court reasoned, the commission membership must be selected in accord with the appointments clause. So, the Court said, because the majority of the commission members are not now selected in this manner but are instead selected by legislative officials, the commission must cease performing all but the legislative type of work.

In discussing the requirements for disclosure and reporting, for example, the Court cited these purposes: To provide the electorate with information as to the source and use of po-

litical funds; to "deter actual corruption and avoid the appearance of corruption by exposing large contributions and expenditures to the light of publicity"; and to gather the data necessary for detecting violations of the law.

The Court conceded, as the various challengers had contended, that disclosure requirements might deter some people from giving money.

"It is undoubtedly true," it said, "that public disclosure of contributions to candidates and political parties will deter some individuals who otherwise might contribute. In some instances, disclosure may even expose contributors to harassment or retaliation."

The Court said, however, that serious infringements of First Amendment rights was still "speculative."

It also suggested that if a "reasonable probability" of harassment as a result of the disclosure requirements could be made out, the courts would undoubtedly be sympathetic to such contentions. Presumably the Court was thus opening the way for further litigation of the issue at a later date.

The matter is significant, for according to the challengers who brought the case to the high court, minor parties are particularly vulnerable to this provision.

The majority also agreed that the thresholds of $10 and $100 for the amounts of contributions that must be reported were "low." It said, however, that this was a determination for Congress to make.

Justice Burger, on the subject, said, "Congress has used a shotgun to kill wrens as well as Hawks."

January 31, 1976

New South Raising Crop of '76 Prospects

By ROY REED
Special to The New York Times

NEW ORLEANS, Sept. 26—Senator Edward M. Kennedy's withdrawal from the 1976 Presidential race has focused renewed attention on the unusually large number of Southern politicians who have begun to develop national ambitions and, more broadly, on the new brand of politics they espouse.

Some of them—at least nine are being discussed with varying degrees of realism—had hoped to win second place on a Democratic ticket headed by a nationally known figure like Senator Kennedy. Now it is considered possible that one or more could emerge as a serious contender for the top spot.

Who are these Southerners,

what do they stand for and how have they distinguished themselves from the older Southern politicians who never permitted themselves to think seriously of running for President?

Almost all have been classified as "new South" politicians, meaning that they have come to power in the post-segregationist era since race has declined as the No. 1 issue in this region.

Some Possible Candidates

Those being discussed for national office, at least in their own state capitals, include Govs. Reubin Askew of Florida, Dale Bumpers of Arkansas, Jimmy Carter of Georgia, Edwin W. Edwards of Lonisiana and George C. Wallace of Alabama.

All those except Mr. Wallace, who is still considered in this

region to be a symbol of segregation, are in the "new South" category.

Others who have been mentioned are Senator Lloyd M. Bentsen Jr. of Texas, a Democrat, whose ties to the Texas economic and political establishment give him only conditional "new South" status; Julian Bond of Atlanta, the black state legislator who first came to national attention during the 1960's as a youthful spokesman for black causes and former Gov. Terry Sanford of North Carolina, now president of Duke University, whose progressive gubernatorial administration from 1961 to 1965 was a hallmark of an earlier period of "new South" politics.

The lone Southern Republican in the Presidential sweepstakes, Senator Howard H. Baker Jr. of Tennessee, seems to have had

his hopes dashed for 1976 by the advent in his party of a new President and Vice President. Another Southern Republican, former Gov. John B. Connally of Texas, apparently was taken out of the running by his indictment for bribery in the milk fund scandal.

Except for Mr. Wallace and possibly Mr. Bond, any Southerner who might make it on to a national ticket in 1976 can be expected to trade heavily on the respectability that has been conferred on the South by the coming of one more "new South."

Difference From Past

There have been "numerous new Souths" since the Civil War. Two or three have seized the nation's attention since World War II featuring such stars as Leroy Collins, the liberal former Governor of Florida,

377

Southern Possibilities for 1976

Lloyd M. Bentsen Jr.
Texas Senator

George C. Wallace
Alabama Governor

Howard H. Baker Jr.
Tennessee Senator and only Republican

Dale Bumpers
Arkansas Governor

Terry Sanford
Former Governor, North Carolina

Reubin Askew
Florida Governor

Edwin W. Edwards
Louisiana Governor

Julian Bond
State Senator, Georgia

Jimmy Carter
Georgia Governor

and Sidney McMath, the angry war veteran who rode a reform wave into the Governor's chair in Arkansas.

The current new South is distinguished by a condition the others did not have, one that has national implications. Since the civil rights movement of the 1960's, race is no longer the leading overt issue in the South. Public policy is no longer determined by a minority of white segregationists from the Black Belt.

Without the albatross of race, Southern politicians now enter Presidential politics on essentially the same footing as politicians from elsewhere.

The common thread tying together almost all of the latest "new south" officeholders—including a number of other Governors, Senators, Representatives, Lieutenant Governors and Attorney General, as well as some gubernatorial nominees—is that they have come to power fairly recently from outside of the political establishment or at least with a reputation for being nonestablishment.

They share, for the most part, a political philosophy that is sometimes called neo-populist but is more accurately a confused expression of middle-class discontent. The grievances to which they give voice vary from high prices to gun

control. Some are beginning to add corporate bureaucrats to government bureaucrats in their list of public devils. Several of the aggressive young Attorneys General are battling for consumer interests.

They are virtually all respectable and socially acceptable. Most were elected, with the votes of the poor as well as the middle class, but their campaigns were not pitched primarily to the poor.

Moderation for Most

Race has been a prominent issue for only two of them, Mr. Wallace and Mr. Bond. Most are known as moderates, meaning usually that they do not advocate busing for school desegregation but on the other hand do not approve of stoning buses, as white people have been doing in Boston this fall.

One, Mr. Askew, has spoken in favor of busing. He won renomination with 74 per cent of the vote earlier this month. The next day he was elected chairman of the Southern Governors Conference at Austin, Tex.

He accepted with a short speech in which he said, looking straight at Mr. Wallace, "And let it be recorded that in 1974 a clear and final message went out which said that the people of the South were too busy and concerned about serious problems to be preoccupied with and diverted by a political

issue of the dark past."

The "new South" Governors have taken advantage of the decline of the race issue in varying ways. Some, including Mr. Carter and William L. Waller of Mississippi, are known mainly as sharp contrasts to the segregationists they succeeded, Lester Maddox and John Bell Williams. They have worked at attracting industry and taking the rough edges off the institutions of government.

Mr. Carter has raised pay for teachers, shifted the emphasis of the penal institutions from punishment to rehabilitation, expanded a kindergarten program and obtained a new law setting stricter standards for the development of coastal marshes.

Mr. Waller has lowered the maximum interest rate on small loans and has exempted older homeowners from the property tax. Both he and Mr. Carter have tried to reorganize the agencies of state government.

Many Problems Remain

Mr. Carter and Mr. Waller typify most of the "new South" Governors in the things they have achieved. They have spurned the selling of ax handles to remind the voters of the days of white supremacy, as Mr. Maddox did, but they have not broken new ground in solving the region's ancient problem of poverty.

None of the new leaders has made real headway in providing industrial jobs for the multitudes of poor people who still live in the Black Belts. None has found the answers to newer problems such as urban blight and the growing concentration of economic power in fewer hands.

Some of the new Governors have made inroads on a few fundamental problems. One of the greatest of these problems has been state tax structures in the South that placed disproportionate burdens on those less able to pay. For generations, the regressive sales tax has been the main source of revenue in this region. That is beginning to change.

In Louisiana, Governor Edwards, the state's first French-speaking Roman Catholic Governor in about 100 years, persuaded the legislature to more than double the severance tax on oil and natural gas. The proceeds went mainly to the public schools. At the same time, he led in removing the 2 per cent sales tax on food. He also led the fight for adoption of a new constitution that would make it possible to increase corporate income taxes.

Mr. Bumpers persuaded the Arkansas legislature to raise the state income tax minimum from 5 to 7 per cent and to make the tax more progressive. The income tax was removed from low incomes. This year, for the first time, the income tax is expected to produce more revenue for Arkansas than the sales tax. Mr. Bumpers has guided the proceeds into better pay for teachers, broadened educational facilities, and financial aid for the working poor under the Medicaid program.

In Florida, Mr. Askew pushed through that state's first corporate income tax.

Mr. Askew, Mr. Bumpers and Mr. Edwards are taking advantage of more than just the decline of the race issue. The political base in the South has broadened significantly since World War II. Better education, improved communications, television and the removal of legal restraints on black voting have resulted in greatly increased voter turnouts in recent years.

During the same years, the number of organized interest groups has expanded. Every Southern capital used to be dominated by one conspicuous economic interest, such as the utilities in Arkansas and the oil business in Texas. Those interests now have to share at least a small part of their power with labor unions, education lobbies, environmental groups and others. One consequence has been a change in political financing.

"The utilities dominated because they had the money," Mr. Bumpers said in an interview at Austin. "Now, candidates can get along without them. The sources of money are more scattered and they have become more idealistic. I consider this one of the best things that has happened in Southern politics."

In spite of a growing consumer anger and a mounting distrust of any "establishment," a Southern politican still cannot afford to be suspected of loyalty to Washington or New York.

It is still fatal in this region for a politician to call himself a liberal. In the white Southern mind, liberalism means encouragement of "welfare cheaters," gun control and "Government giveaways" such as food stamps. It means "coddling criminals."

· The more progressive new Southern officeholders either keep quiet on those issues or finesse them. Mr. Bumpers, for example, was accused during one election campaign of being for gun control. He found it advisable to advertise a picture of himself in hunting clothes carrying a shotgun.

September 27, 1974

How a Man Decides He'll Run for the Presidency

By CHRISTOPHER LYDON

ATLANTA—How does a Presidential candidacy get born? Mysterious forces that Russell Baker embodied in The Great Mentioner used to draw up a handicapped list of contenders for any nomination. Nowadays candidates are their own mentioners.

Everyone has seen how George McGovern transformed a 3 per cent standing in the polls, and the operative question toward 1976 is, "Why not me?" Lloyd M. Bentsen Jr., a less-than-one-term Senator from Texas, has mentioned himself widely enough to make every list of Democratic candidates. Representative Morris K. Udall of Arizona, a nice mixture of brashness and self-deprecation, found that he couldn't get elected speaker or majority leader in the House, or Senator from Arizona, and then announced last fall for the Presidency.

So, too, Jimmy Carter, moving out of the Governor's mansion here next week after a single four-year term in the Georgia Statehouse, had studied all the conventional liabilities of his position—as a southerner, soon to be out of office, minimally experienced in foreign affairs and in national policy — and considered whether each deficiency could be an asset in an improbable run for the nomination. And three weeks ago, publicly deciding in his favor, he announced—at the Statehouse, at the National Press Club and on the Today show—that he was running.

"The main difficulty I had to overcome," Jimmy Carter confessed the other day, "was embarrassment, telling folks I was running for— you know, for President."

His announcement, of course, was only the public punctuation of an incomplete evolution. It generated more front-page news, and even more editorial comment, than Governor Carter had hoped. Otherwise, the status of declared candidate has not changed his life much yet: His only out-of-state trip since the 12th of December was to San Francisco for a speech to a conference on alcoholism. His main business last week was cleaning out his office and getting his family back to his farm at Plains, Ga. But where did the Presidential idea begin?

The governor's mansion here was a special sort of hatchery. It is a grand new palace of golden red brick, with Greek columns around the outside and authentic Federal furnishings inside, and Mr. Carter made it both his school and his stage. Starting early in 1972, most of the once and future Democratic Presidential candidates came to visit, mostly Senators like George McGovern, Edmund S. Muskie of Maine, Henry M. Jackson of Washington. "For the first time," Mr. Carter said, "I started comparing my own experience and knowledge of government with the candidates, not against 'the presidency' and not against Thomas Jefferson and George Washington. It made it a whole lot easier."

He told his family he would run at Christmas time, 1972, and by the spring of 1973 he was quietly at work. Robert S. Strauss, chairman of the Democratic National Committee, had put him in charge of an inauspicious task force on the 1974 campaign. That was Mr. Carter's ticket not only to a tour of 32 states and 60-some campaign organizations this year but also to install Hamilton Jordan, his executive assistant, for a year of listening and watching at national party headquarters.

The real foundations of modern nominating campaigns are mailing lists, stored on computer tapes, and Jimmy Carter has more than one might expect. For every national group that held its big meeting in Atlanta over the past four years, the standard price of a speech from the governor has been a list of the members present. Those names and addresses have been added to lists of as many plausible constituencies as a resourceful staff can get its hands on—lists of fellow Naval Academy graduates, of fellow Lions Club members, of fellow farmers, engineers and scientists. As a result, even before the Carter campaign got to using hired magazine and fund raisers' lists, a letter announcing his candidacy has gone out to 50,000 people he calls friends around the country.

And what is he telling them now? The hardest part is explaining how four apparently solid but unspectacular years in the Georgia governor's office recommend him for the White House.

Governor Carter claims concrete achievement in bureaucratic reform: zero-base budgeting and the consolidation of 300 executive agencies into 22 departments. But they did not seem to revolutionize real power over the delivery of services in the state of Georgia, and they will hardly ignite a national following either.

It is too early to declare just what he would do as President. He admits a Navy man's instinct to "build up the Navy," but otherwise he is certain that vast amounts of military spending are wasted, especially on nuclear weaponry. He cannot believe that a "simplified, fair and compassionate welfare program" is beyond the nation's capacity—and he will offer some detailed thoughts later, he says.

'Thoughtful Idealist'

The more important thing now, he believes, is to suggest who he is and specifically to stake his claim as the thoughtful idealist in this race—to tell disillusioned citizens that "I'd like to be the personification of their hopes and ideals" and to echo John F. Kennedy's "A time for Greatness" with an equally brazen slogan: "For America's third Century, why not the Best?"

But the big strategic secret of the Carter design is its conscious resemblance to the early McGovern campaign: the dashes of moralism, the challenge of anti-establishment activists, the faith in an ink-blot organization for primary victories against better-financed candidates.

Governor Carter cannot quite describe what substitute for 1972's anti-war passion will fuel his campaign. But the first flock of letters to his three-room headquarters here suggests that some people are getting the message.

"I am a resident of Austin, Texas and a member of the Allandale Baptist Church," wrote David L. Jones, a mathematics and chemistry teacher in the public school system. "I was privileged to hear you speak when you addressed our congregation. I wish to express my desire to be of service to you in your campaign for the Presidency of the United States.... It is only because I have respect for you as a man that I want to become involved at this time...."

Every candidate, of course, gets letters like that, and no one in the Carter entourage is drawing hopeful conclusions yet. Even Jody Powell, Governor Carter's press secretary, senses that most people who read or heard the Carter announcement still have little impression of the man. But Mr. Powell believes that thousands of Americans have a vaguely pleasant feeling that there is a fresh face that deserves a second look. In the coming months, Mr. Carter will be doing everything he can to make sure they get it.

Christopher Lydon is a political reporter in the Washington bureau of The New York Times.

January 5, 1975

All the Candidates Fall Short on Defining Issues

By CHRISTOPHER LYDON

WASHINGTON—Even Jimmy Carter's admirers are heard to wonder now and then, "but what does he stand for? They are not exactly knocking him but are openly puzzled about the real content of all those good vibrations emanating from the likable former Governor of Georgia.

The question applies as well, in varying degrees, to others in the Presidential field, with the exceptions perhaps of Gov. George C. Wallace of Alabama whose game has always been racial antagonism, and former Senator Fred Harris, who presents a reasonably neat vision of an oppressed majority of Americans rising up against the concentrations of wealth and power.

For the rest, a Democrat running for President is generally a fellow who enjoys picking on Earl Butz, the Nixon-Ford Secretary of Agriculture; who repeats that détente has got to be more of a two-way street than it has been under Henry Kissinger; who looks relieved that more and more questions about personal life, including abortion and homosexual marriage, are being put outside the pale of public controversy; who finds a way to knock bigness, assaulting big oil, perhaps, with the notion of public energy development, or making antitrust threats against big business.

But none of them have much to say about the central dilemma facing Democratic politicians at the start of 1976: the fact that short-term cures for 8 percent unemployment are commonly viewed as a potential cause of higher inflation, an economic disease that affects many more voters than unemployment.

Jimmy Carter is as vague as his rivals on the issues, perhaps even more so. No one made more progress in 1975 on so slender a public record or so little profession of ideology. No one has recruited serious political help from so many different directions.

In conservative Florida, the Carter campaign is the hope of all liberals, mainly because the liberal-labeled candidates for the nomination defaulted in that first-round test against Governor Wallace. In maverick New Hampshire, Jimmy Carter built his first beachhead around Lucille Kelly of Manchester, who is on the conservative side of the Democratic Party, and he continues to hold that ground against Birch Bayh, Morris Udall, Fred Harris and Sargent Shriver.

In liberal Iowa, where precinct caucuses on Jan. 19 will provide the first scorable event of the nominating campaign, Jimmy Carter has what looks like a lead and certainly the most impressive variety of local backers. James Schaben, a cattle farmer, the Democratic nominee for governor last year and a conservative by Iowa standards, is a Carter man because "he's got two feet planted firmly on the ground."

Charles Hammer, a theoretical physicist at Iowa State University and a pillar of the McCarthy and McGovern movements of 1968 and 1972, is backing Jimmy Carter because all the other candidates sound to him like legislators, not executives.

Neither of those men has much idea about the Carter program for the country, but they both find a certain indefiniteness part of Carter's political charm. Avoiding the issues and getting away with it is no simple trick in politics. Jimmy Carter's success at it so far reflects several things.

First, he has always been careful to summarize his appeal in a wide brace of ideas. Sometimes it is "decency" and "competence;" sometimes it is the statement that Jimmy Carter is liberal on social issues and a fiscal conservative. But always he combines imagery of compassion with a line about administrative toughness, a vagueness that allows Democrats on the right and left to choose their own emphasis.

Second, he generally avoids details (and never talks about legislation, the way the Congress-based candidates perpetually do) but talks about symbols that people understand, such as 100 percent full employment and zero-base budgeting. Mr. Carter has no more hope than any other Presidential candidate of eliminating unemployment soon, but he has said what his goal is. And although he knows that the budgeting of Government programs cannot start from scratch every year, he has found a relatively non-demagogic way of saying that most Government programs live too long.

Third, when a specific statement stirs trouble, Jimmy Carter bends gracefully. He was against Federal aid to help New York avoid default, but then he conceded that Atlanta would be bankrupt, too, if it had to pay a quarter of its welfare bill from local taxes. When he took some liberal criticism for opposing amnesty for Vietnam draft-resisters, he thought it over and said he would grant the exiles pardons instead.

In strategic terms, Mr. Carter has stuck with his early guess that the center of the party is the only root to the nomination. The double lesson of the McGovern campaign of 1972 was that specific issue-mongering on the left wing of the Democratic Party was the way first to win the nomination and then to make the prize next to worthless in the fall campaign.

To a lot of Democratic professionals and semi-professionals involved in the campaign so far Jimmy Carter has "character," the nineteen-seventies' successor to "charisma" and the magic ingredient that turns disagreement with a candidate into respect for his "honesty." Politicians like to say that Watergate elevated the importance of personality and "character," but this is also the old game (more normal, really, than the issue battles of 1968 and 1972) of charming people away from narrowly political questions. Nobody did it better than John F. Kennedy in his 1960 campaign for the Democratic nomination.

If Jimmy Carter gets really close to the nomination, that personal magic will become harder to sustain, especially with the institutional blocs—including labor, business and various minorities—that may want concrete commitments on policy.

At this point, however, the Carter campaign is borne along nicely by a mystery of personality.

"People don't know what Jimmy Carter will do," says Frank Mankiewicz, who managed the McGovern campaign, "but they sense he'd do it well."

Christopher Lydon is a political writer for The New York Times.

January 11, 1976

FORD DEFEATS REAGAN IN FLORIDA; CARTER IS WINNER OVER WALLACE IN DEMOCRATIC VOTE, JACKSON 3D

By ROY REED
Special to The New York Times

MIAMI, March 9—President Ford defeated Ronald Reagan in Florida's Republican Presidential primary election today, gaining his fourth victory in as many primaries.

Jimmy Carter, the former Governor of Georgia, won the hotly contested Democratic primary. Gov George C. Wallace of neighboring Alabama finished second, suffering his worst political setback since he was shot and seriously wounded by an assassin while campaigning at a shopping center in Laurel, Md., on May 15, 1972. The shooting ended his 1972 campaign.

Senator Henry M. Jackson of Washington, the winner of the Massachusetts primary a week ago, ran third, well behind Mr. Wallace. Next in order were "no preference," Gov. Milton J. Shapp of Pennsylvania, the only other Democrat who campaigned actively here, and Representative Morris K. Udall of Arizona.

Seven other Democrats brought up the rear.

With 3,308, or 97 percent, of 3,420 precincts reporting, the tally was:

REPUBLICANS

Ford 303,975 (53%)
Reagan 268,607 (47%)

DEMOCRATS

Carter 429,230 (35%)
Wallace 385,785 (31%)
Jackson 285,613 (23%)
No Preference 36,581 (3%)
Shapp 28,644 (2%)
Udall 25,321 (2%)

The President's victory seriously damaged the candidacy of the former California Governor as a challenger for the Republican nomination. However, Mr. Reagan has said that he intends to continue campaigning until the Republican National Convention next

381

August in Kansas City, Mo.

In Washington, the President said he was "overjoyed" at the outcome, but he declined to tell reporters whether he thought Mr. Reagan should withdraw from the race.

Mr. Ford's campaign advisers were also said to be sending signals to Mr. Reagan to end his insurgency—and perhaps to become the President's running mate. [Page 18].

With 97 percent of the precincts reporting, the contest for Florida delegates to the national conventions looked this way:

Republicans, 66 delegates—Ford 43, Reagan 23; Democrats, 81 delegates—Carter 35, Wallace 26, Jackson 20.

Mr. Carter's showing would seem to re-establish his position as the front-runner of the Democratic Party's center. It helped to counter the one defeat of his campaign, his fourth-place finish in the Massachusetts primary last week.

Mr. Wallace's failure to match his 1972 showing in this semi-Southern state, which adjoins his native Alabama, was a serious blow to his candidacy in this, his third try for the Presidency.

He won the 1972 Florida primary with 42 percent of the vote. Until Mr. Carter's well-organized campaign began to take effect recently, Mr. Wallace had been expected to lead the field again, although perhaps with a smaller percentage of the vote.

Mr. Reagan and Mr. Jackson carried Dade County (Miami). A strong Latin vote in Dade County apparently accounted for Mr. Reagan's margin, and a heavy Jewish vote for Mr. Jackson's.

Both Governor Wallace and Mr. Reagan said that in their second-place finishes they

found reason enough to stay in the race.

'Win Some, Lose Some'

"I'm still in," Governor Wallace said. "You win some and lose some."

Mr. Reagan said he was "delighted" at the Florida outcome and added that he would continue his attack on the Ford Administration "with increased encouragement."

A New York Times/CBS News poll of 1,680 voters who had just cast their ballots showed that Mr. Carter repeated his Massachusetts performance among black voters, although the number here was relatively small. He won them solidly, thus confounding further those liberals of the party who have begun to portray him as unacceptably conservative.

The poll showed that Senator Jackson swept the Jewish vote along the east coast of South Florida, as had been expected. There had been speculation that Mr. Shapp, who is Jewish, might cut into the Jackson support there.

Eight other Democratic candidates appeared on the Florida ballot, but only Mr. Carter, Mr. Wallace, Mr. Jackson and Mr. Shapp campaigned here.

Those who ignored Florida included Representative Udall, now considered the liberal leader in the Democratic race.

The others on the ballot were former Senator Fred R. Harris of Oklahoma; Senator Frank Church of Idaho, who is expected to announce his candidacy later this month; Ellen McCormack, the anti-abortion candidate from Long Island who, along with Governor Wallace, advocates a constitutional amendment to prohibit abortion except to save a mother's life; Senator Birch Bayh of Indiana, who has suspended his campaign; Senator Robert C. Byrd of West Virginia; Sargent Shriver, the Democratic Vice-Presidential candidate in 1972,

and Arthur O. Blessitt, a Florida evangelist.

As the voters went to the polls, a succession of sunny days gave way to blustery weather, and many had to risk getting wet to cast their ballots.

Jackson's Campaign

Two tornadoes were spotted in northern Florida near Jacksonville. But in the Miami area, the sun came out about noon.

Two candidates, Mr. Reagan and Governor Wallace, deserted the state today and went on to Illinois, where the next primary will be held next Tuesday.

Mr. Carter campaigned in North Carolina, preparing for the primary there on March 23. He appeared in Asheville, Hickory and Morganton, the last being the home of former Senator Sam J. Ervin Jr., who has endorsed Senator Jackson.

Senator Jackson's first aim in Florida was to win as many delegates as possible. He did not expect to win much of the popular vote. After his plurality victory in Massachusetts last week, however, he began an intensive news media campaign and tried to cut into Mr. Carter's acknowledged lead.

Many political experts felt that both the Democratic and Republican races had gotten closer in the last days of the campaigning.

Mr. Reagan, responding to what he and others regarded as an erosion of his lead, began a series of sharp attacks on the President's policies in the last week of the campaign.

The Administration's policy of détente with the Soviet Union came under attack from Mr. Reagan and Mr. Jackson. Mr. Reagan also criticized Mr. Ford's approach to Cuba, contending that the President had been moving closer to an accommodation with the Castro regime until politics intervened in recent days.

Mr. Ford came to Miami

in the last stages of the campaign and severely criticized Prime Minister Fidel Castro, describing him as an "international outlaw." The attack was regarded here as an attempt to cut into Mr. Reagan's strength in the Latin community.

Court-ordered busing to achieve racial integration of public schools, a hot issue in the 1972 Florida primary, was ignored this year by all the candidates except Mr. Wallace. He has denounced it, along with welfare cheaters and Federal bureaucrats, at almost every stop recently.

Busing, like Prime Minister Castro, has had no defenders. Mr. Carter has criticized Senator Jackson, however, for having used the busing issue, which Mr. Carter regards as "emotional," in the Massachusetts campaign.

One of Mr. Jackson's main issues in Florida has been unemployment, which is more than 11 percent here. He has advocated government help in creating more jobs.

This week, Governor Shapp seized on a secret meeting in Panama City between a representative of Saudi Arabia and about 50 representatives of Exxon, Mobil, Standard Oil of California and Standard of Texas, who are negotiating to sell the American companies' interest in the Arab-American oil company to the Saudi Government.

Mr. Shapp said the President should call for the nationalization of the major American oil companies if the agreement at Panama City was not satisfactory.

For the first time, the ballots in Dade County were printed in Spanish as well as English. Latins make up about 15 percent of the registered voters of the county. Most are Cuban refugees.

March 10, 1976

CARTER WINS THE DEMOCRATIC NOMINATION

A QUICK VICTORY

By R. W. APPLE Jr.

Jimmy Carter of Georgia won the Democratic Presidential nomination last night.

By an overwhelming margin, the Democratic National Convention ratified Mr. Carter's

startling electoral ascendancy of the last six months, made him the first major-party nominee from the Deep South since Zachary Taylor in 1848 and installed him as the early favorite to capture the White House in November.

It seemed appropriate when Ohio put Mr. Carter over 1,505 votes — a majority — for it

was the Georgian's sweep of that state's June 8 primary that started the stampede of party leaders toward him.

Shouts and Cheers

When Christine Gitlin, the Ohio delegation chairman, announced the vote, the hall burst into shouts and cheers, and Robert S. Strauss, the national chairman, signaled the band to

strike up "Happy Days Are Here Again."

An unofficial tabulation by The New York Times gave Mr. Carter a total of 2,238½ votes when the somewhat muddled roll-call ended.

The other candidates who were officially nominated—Gov. Edmund G. Brown Jr. of California, Representative Morris K. Udall of Arizona and Ellen McCormack, the anti-abortion candidate—trailed far behind, as did a handful of other contenders.

Standing in the midst of his delegation, Mr. Brown switched California's votes to the former Georgia Governor, remarking, "This is the beginning of a Democratic sweep across this country that comes none too soon."

Nominee Is Declared

Gov. George Busbee of Georgia then moved that Mr. Carter, his predecessor, be declared nominated by acclamation. After a brief contretemps that prevented Massachusetts from voting, the chairman of this 37th Democratic convention, Corinne C. Boggs, declared Mr. Carter the nominee at 11:43 P.M.

In the tumult on the floor, Hamilton Jordan, Mr. Carter's campaign manager, told an interviewer: "We waited four long, hard, wonderful years for this experience and this moment."

Mr. Carter's name was placed before the convention in Madison Square Garden by Representative Peter W. Rodino Jr. of New Jersey, who two years ago this month presided over the impeachment hearings that led to the resignation of President Nixon.

"With honest talk and plain truth," he said, "Jimmy Carter has appealed to the American people. His heart is honest, and the people will believe him. His purpose is right, and the people will follow him."

Alluding several times to Watergate, Mr. Rodino said of Mr. Carter:

"As he has brought a united South back into the Democratic Party, he will bring a united Democratic Party back into the leadership of America and a united America back to a position of respect and esteem in the eyes of the world."

Then the diminutive, gray-haired legislator, orthodox in all things, proclaimed to the convention the name of "the next President of the United States."

The seconding speeches were delivered by Vice Mayor Margaret Costanza of Rochester and by Representative Andrew Young, the Atlanta Democrat whose support encouraged other blacks and white liberals to back Mr. Carter.

"I'm ready to lay down the burden of race," Mr. Young said, "and Jimmy Carter comes from a part of the country which, whether you know it or not, has done just that."

Following long-standing tradition, Mr. Carter absented himself from the convention hall at his moment of greatest triumph.

But in a speech yesterday afternoon to a caucus of Mountain State delegates, he promised to reunite conservative and liberal Democrats, and said, "I never did intend to lose the nomination, and I guarantee you I don't intend to lose the election."

Last night Mr. Carter watched the proceedings on television in his 21st-floor suite at the Americana Hotel. With him were his mother, Lillian; his daughter, Amy; a number of other relatives, and several members of his staff.

Mr. Carter's wife, Rosalynn, was at the convention.

Mr. Carter wore a serious expression when Mr. Brown announced the California switch, then burst into laughter when the young Governor, unable to explain what had happened to two votes in his delegation, explained with characteristic vagueness that "we'll just leave those two floating."

A Subdued Scene

The scene at the climatic moment when Ohio cast its votes was strangely subdued. Mr. Carter smiled, but it was not the famous campaign grin of the last several months.

Then he leaned over to his 78-year-old mother and embraced her tightly.

The three other candidates placed in nomination were the survivors of the dozen who sought vainly to halt Mr. Carter's surge through the primary elections.

But there was not a scintilla of doubt in the minds of 5,000-odd delegates and alternates in the Garden, nor in the minds of the spectators who filled every available seat, that the winner was the man christened James Earl Carter Jr., now known all across the land simply as Jimmy.

There were many doubts, however, about his choice of a Vice-Presidential running mate. Although the Democratic leaders were telling one another that Senator Walter F. Mondale of Minnesota would be the choice, none of them professed to know for certain.

So successfully had Mr. Carter masked his intentions that there were still many who thought he might name Senator Edmund S. Muskie of Maine or even one of the four other possibilities on his final list at his news conference scheduled for 10 A.M. today.

Mrs. McCormack, the anti-abortion crusader from Long Island, was nominated second, with the main speech in her behalf by James Killilea, a McCormack delegate from Boston.

He delivered a strong attack on Mr. Carter, whom he called "Mr. X," accusing him of lying about his views on abortion. But in the constant hum of conversation rising from the floor, very few heard him.

Next in line was Representative Udall, the lanky, witty liberal who stayed the primary course, right through the finale on June 8, despite his failure to win a single victory.

In his speech nominating Mr. Udall, Archibald Cox, the Harvard Law School professor who is a former Watergate special prosecutor, called the Arizonan "a candidate beloved among his constituents and admired among his colleagues in the House."

Mr. Cox then presented Mr. Udall to the convention, and the frustration of the liberals burst through the restraints placed upon it at this convention.

While the gavel sounded futilely from the podium, the Udall supporters cheered, waved placars, blew whistles and released clusters of blue balloons in the closest thing to a floor demonstration seen last night.

In the interest of greater dispatch for television purposes, the raucus demonstrations of the past have been discarded. When Mr. Carter was nominated, for example, not a note of music was heard, and order was restored after a few desultory shouts of pleasure.

Finally, Mr. Brown's name was advanced by Cesar Chavez, the charismatic leader of the United Farm Workers Union.

The 38-year-old Governor insisted on going through with a roll-call vote, without even a symbolic withdrawal such as Mr. Udall's. He said his supporters wanted it and that it would help provide "diversity."

But he repeatedly urged delegates to work hard for the Georgian in November, and seemed reconciled to the failure of his own late-starting campaign.

There were brief flurries of resistance to inevitability during the afternoon as states held their final caucuses prior to the balloting last night.

In Massachusetts, for example, Landon Butler, the Carter political director, had to make amends for an overzealous volunteer who had threatened to "blacklist" delegates who refused to back Mr. Carter.

And at a meeting of the Black Caucus, it was decided to nominate Representative Ronald V. Dellums of California for Vice President so that he could "articulate some of the issues that have not been addressed."

The roll-call went smoothly after a bumpy start.

Attempting to make a speech in behalf of Gov. George C. Wallace of Alabama before casting most of its votes for Mr. Carter, the chairman of the Alabama delegation, State Senator Robert Wilson, was drowned out by boos and was reprimanded by the chairman before giving up and announcing the vote.

At the end, after California switched, Mrs. Boggs handled the motion for acclamation before Massachusetts, which had passed, had a chance to vote.

Finally, Charles Flaherty, the delegation chairman, drew Mrs. Boggs's attention by frantically waving the state placard. Recalling his state's lonely support of George McGovern in 1972, he said, "Oh, how soon we forget!"

July 15, 1976

Democratic Winner-Take-All Primaries Abolished Despite Opposition by Carter

By WARREN WEAVER Jr.

Delegates at the Democratic National Convention voted yesterday to abolish winner-taker-all primaries in which a Presidential Candidate who carries a Congressional district receives all its delegates instead of a share proportional to his vote.

The decision was a minor setback for supporters of the party's new Presidential nominee, Jimmy Carter, who had argued for withholding judgment at this time on the question of closing what reformers regard as a "loophole" in delegate selection reform.

In a four-hour debate in the afternoon the liveliest up to then at the convention, the Carter forces were also outvoted by reform delegates on the issue of adopting ground rules for the party's 1978 mid-term conference, but prevailed anyway when the reform vote fell short of the required majority.

An attempt to open the 1980 convention for more floor debate by easing current restrictions on minority reports on controversial issues was defeated, with the Carter forces taking the lead.

Perhaps the most important Democratic rules change, which was not debated at the convention, will put into effect for the 1980 convention a revised system for encouraging more representation of women, young people and racial minorities in state delegations.

The new plan requires national and state Democratic organizations to set "specific goals and timetables for achieving results" for the "affirmative action" programs designed to produce convention delegations more representative of various groups' participation in party affairs.

Percentages to Be Estimated

In effect, this will mean that a Democratic state organiza-

tion will be required to estimate the percentage of women, young people, blacks an Indians who vote Democratic and set these figures as "goals" to be met by a specified election.

But these figures will differ from "quotas," a very unpopular term among Democrats currently, because they will be enforceable only by public pressure, and any state that fails to achieve them on time cannot be refused seats at the Presidential convention, as was true in 1972.

In preparation for the convention that closed in Madison Square Garden last night, 13 states were permitted to choose delegates on a winner-take-all basis within Congressional districts, among them New York and New Jersey. The party outlawed this system on a statewide basis in 1972 in favor of proportional division of delegates among competing candidates.

By voice vote, the convention defeated a proposal backed by the Carter forces that would have given the party's new Commission on Presidential Pri-

maries free rein to study the issue and make any recommendations it chose.

As a result, the majority rules report prevailed. It requires the commission to recommend a plan "to bar the use of delegate selections systems in primary states that permit a plurality of votes at any level to elect all of the delegates from that level."

Mr. Carter's backers waged their strongest floor fight yesterday against a minority proposal that would have sent a minimum of 2,000 delegates to the 1978 mid-term convention, at least two-thirds of whom would have been elected from jurisdictions no larger than a Congressional district.

Such a plan could have created a forum for criticism of the first two years of a Carter Administration if the Democrats won in November.

Women Participation

Also incorporated in the majority rules report adopted yesterday afternoon was a compromise involving women delegate participation in the 1980 convention. It required the call

to future conventions to "promote equal division" between men and women as delegates and required the national party to "encourage and assist" state parties, should they become laggard.

Originally, women's groups had favored language to "require" equal representation, but that proposal was defeated by the convention rules committee last month following opposition by Carter lieutenants, and the unopposed compromise was sent to the floor instead.

The revisions in the affirmative action plan for delegate selection were not debated because there had been no opposition in committee and thus no minority report submitted.

Reformers believed that the new system of numerical "goals" backed by a timetable would be much more effective in broadening representation in future conventions than the looser set of ground rules in effect for this year's convention.

July 16, 1976

Ford Urges G.O.P. Enroll 'All Who Care' About U.S.

By R. W. APPLE Jr.
Special to The New York Times

WASHINGTON, March 7—President Ford appealed tonight for a broadened Republican party embracing "all who care about this great country," implicitly rejecting conservative demands for greater ideological purity.

"We must discard the attitude of exclusiveness that has kept the Republican party's door closed too often while we give speeches about keeping it open," the President said in a speech at a Republican leadership conference.

He coupled his plea for diversity with his strongest declaration to date regarding his plans for 1976.

"I can tell you without equivocation tonight that I fully intend to seek the nomination of the Republican party as its candidate for President in 1976," he said. "There is nothing iffy about that statement.

"I intend to seek the nomination. I intend to win. I intend to run for President. And I intend to win that, too."

Mr. Ford's comments were part of a general counterattack by party leaders on advocates of a third party, on conservatives who have criticized the President's moves toward the center and, in some cases, on

former Gov. Ronald Reagan of California, the leader of the Republican right wing.

At a luncheon attended by more than 2,500 party workers from across the country, Vice President Rockefeller sounded a similar note.

"Let us keep two parties in this country with broad spectrums in both parties," he said. "I don't want to see one party of the right and one of the left."

"Everybody can't take the position that their solution is the only solution, and if their solution isn't adopted, they're not going to play," he added. "That's anarchy."

Gov. Christopher Bond of Missouri said:

"I'm a little tired of reading about Republicans meeting to discuss the so-called third party option or organizing committees to 'watch' the President. This good and decent man doesn't need watching. I think we ought to be applauding President Ford for the spirit of his openness, conciliation,

cooperation and compromise."

During afternoon panel discussions, Senators Jacob K. Javits of New York and Charles H. Percy of Illinois, two leading liberals—struck back at Mr. Reagan for suggesting that he would not be disturbed if they would leave the party.

"This is no time for politics and no time for politics among Republicans," Mr. Javits said. "It makes no sense for any Republican to attempt to read any other Republican out of the Republican party."

Mr. Percy, in a spirited performance, asserted, "We don't build strength by subtraction—we build it by attracting unhappy Democrats and independents."

"We won't win in the Plains and the West," he said, "by flailing away at that tired straw man, the Eastern establishment. We won't win votes in the South or anywhere else by turning our backs on blacks."

When the comments of Mr. Reagan, who is to speak here tomorrow, came up in the discussion, Mr. Percy snapped, "There's nothing like a former Democrat telling a lifelong Republican where he should take his party affiliation."

Mr. Reagan was once a fervent New Deal Democrat.

Party officials were ecstatic about the turnout for the leadership conference, the first since 1971. They had expected no more than 1,500 participants as recently as a week ago, but the total registration exceeded 2,700, with each paying his own way plus $36.50 in registration fees.

"Maybe at last we've washed

Watergate and all of that out of our system," said Edward Mahe Jr., the party's executive director. "I know this much: we couldn't have done this a year ago without having a total, disastrous bomb."

The meeting, at the Washington Hilton Hotel, came against a backdrop of disastrous defeat in the 1974 election, poll figures showing that the Republicans hold the allegiance of only 18 per cent of the public and calls for a third party from leading conservative spokesmen.

Both Mr. Ford and, to an even greater extent, Mr. Rockefeller, have been under concerted fire from the right, and the President's standing in the polls has sagged.

But Mr. Ford was confident, telling the conference in an after-dinner speech in the hotel's vast underground ballroom that "the standing of our party has hit its lowest point" and that a rebound was "imminent."

In an indirect slap at former President Richard M. Nixon, whose 1972 campaign was run independently of the party apparatus, Mr. Ford renewed his pledge to "never again permit an élite guard serving a single purpose to exclude and ignore the regular party organization."

"I will be in the middle of the 1976 campaign not only for the Presidency," he said, "but also on behalf of Republican candidates for the House as well as the Senate and for state governors and other elective offices across the country."

The President also continued his pressure on Congress to enact measures he has proposed, telling his critics: "If you don't like my program, show me a better one."

But his emphasis was on the necessity for a two-party system that included a "revitalized" Republican organization.

"We must erect a tent that is big enough for all who care about this great country and believe in the Republican party enough to work through it for common goals," he said.

"This tent must also be kept open to the growing number of independent voters who refuse to wear any party label, but who will support the strong candidates and good programs we present. These voters must be welcomed and won to our

cause."

Mr. Rockefeller, whose rulings as presiding officer of the Senate during the current debate on closure have revived old antagonisms toward him, urged the conference participants to "argue, discuss, debate, fight" within the party, but then to "go forward united." Mr. Rockefeller himself refused to support Senator Barry Goldwater of Arizona for President in 1964 after Mr. Goldwater beat him for the nomination.

Third-Party Intimations

WASHINGTON, March 7 (UPI)—A group of conserva-

tive Republican leaders agreed today to begin researching state election laws in preparation for a possible third party.

The Committee on Conservative Alternatives, a group of House and Senate members and other political activists, voted unanimously to establish a three-member subcommittee to study ballot laws in each of the 50 states.

The committee, headed by Senator Jesse A. Helms of North Carolina, was created last month at the conservative political action conference held here to explore the possibility of establishing another party.

The subcommittee is to be headed by William A. Rusher, publisher of the conservative magazine National Review.

Among those who attended the meeting were Representatives Philip M. Crane of Illinois and Steven D. Symms of Idaho; M. Stanton Evans, Editor of The Indianapolis News; Eli Howell, a political consultant to Gov. George C. Wallace of Alabama, and Robert Walker, a political aide to Ronald Reagan, when he was California Governor.

March 8, 1975

REAGAN REJECTS FORD PLEA TO G.O.P. TO BROADEN BASE

Urges Party Leaders Not to Compromise Republicans' Conservative Principles

TALK STIRS DELEGATES

Speech Follows Appeals by President and Rockefeller for Moderate Approach

By R. W. APPLE Jr.
Special to The New York Times

WASHINGTON, March 8 — Former Gov. Ronald Reagan of California took a firm stand today against President Ford, Vice President Rockefeller and others who called this week for a Republican party broad enough to include moderates and liberals as well as conservatives.

"A political party cannot be all things to all people," the California conservative said in a speech to the closing session of the Republican leadership conference. "It cannot compromise its fundamental beliefs for political expediency, or simply to swell its numbers.

"It is not a social club or fraternity engaged in intramural contests to accumulate trophies on the mantel over the fireplace."

Speech Viewed as Rebuttal

The significance of Mr. Reagan's speech lay not so much in what he said; his message

differed but little from the one he has been delivering across the country in recent months. But it took on new significance as a rebuttal to Mr. Ford and Mr. Rockefeller.

Perhaps because he was speaking to a forum that Mr. Ford had addressed only last night, Mr. Reagan dropped from his standard text criticisms of the President's budget and his agreement with the Soviet Union at Vladivostok.

He did not mention Mr. Ford a single time.

Mr. Reagan repeatedly brought the crowd of more than 2,000 grass-roots party leaders to its feet with his old-time Republican religion — a sermon on the desirability of a balanced budget, strong national defense, individual freedom and domestic law and order.

Like virtually all the speakers at the conference, he called for a revitalized Republican party—he called it "a new second party"—rather than the third party some conservatives have been advocating.

But the vision offered by Mr. Reagan was different. He argued that the Republicans did badly in 1974 partly because of Watergate, but also because the mass of the electorate was unable to see any differences between the two major parties and chose to stay at home.

"No one can quarrel with the idea that a political party hopes it can attract a wide following," he said, "but does it do this by forsaking its basic beliefs? By blurring its own image so as to be indistinguishable from the opposition party?

"Does any Republican seriously believe that any Democrats who subscribe to the profligacy, the big government policies of the present Democratic leadership will be won over to our side if we say these are our policies, too?"

The former Governor quoted the late Senator Robert A. Taft as saying in 1953, "The only parties that have died are those which have forgotten or aban-

doned the principles upon which they were founded. A party kills itself and removes any excuse for its existence when it adopts the principles of its opponents."

Mr. Reagan ridiculed Republican moderates and liberals who have proposed during the conference new programs to reach organized labor, minorities and the elderly. All should be appealed to on the basis of conservative principles and programs, he argued.

Working people, he said, should be reached over the heads of "the hierarchy of organized labor"; minorities should be promised equal opportunity, "not more soup from a Federal soup kitchen"; senior citizens should get not bigger Social Security payments but "the assurance that a dollar will buy as much tomorrow as it bought yesterday."

Mr. Ford was received enthusiastically last night in his appearance at the conference and Mr. Rockefeller was greeted warmly yesterday noon. But there was little doubt that Mr. Reagan and his conservative message were the favorites of the delegates who gathered here to find ways to put the party back on its feet.

Purpose of Conference

The leadership conference, which followed an occasionally uproarious two-day meeting of the Republican National Committee here, was conceived by the party's national leadership as a major element in the effort to recover from losses last year. It concluded early this afternoon with reports on finances and activities planned for this year.

Later, at a meeting of college Republicans that followed adjournment of the leadership conference, Senator Howard H. Baker Jr. of Tennessee aligned himself with the President on the question of the party's base. It is not the time, he said, for "a conservative party, a liberal party or any other party with a specific ideology."

March 9, 1975

385

ROCKEFELLER BARS RACE ON FORD TICKET

The New York Times/Teresa Zabala

President Ford at his televised news session in the White House last night. He told of high-level changes.

The New York Times/Tyrone Dukes

Vice President Rockefeller answering a question during an appearance here Sunday on a television program.

MUTUAL DECISION

Vice President's Letter Gives No Reason for His Withdrawal

By PHILIP SHABECOFF
Special to The New York Times

WASHINGTON, Nov. 3—Vice President Rockefeller added today to the sudden upheaval within the Ford Administration by saying that he would not be the President's running mate in 1976.

At his news conference tonight, President Ford said that Mr. Rockefeller had not been requested to withdraw as a candidate for election. He said the Vice President had "done a superb job" and had made "a decision on his own" not to seek the election next year.

Mr. Ford said that Mr. Rockefeller had "assured me categorically that he will support me in 1976."

However, the President declined to give any reasons for the Vice President's action. Administration sources said, meanwhile, that the decision had been reached through a mutual understanding between Mr. Ford and Mr. Rockefeller.

Resignation Not Asked

These sources said that while the President had not pressed Mr. Rockefeller for a resignation, neither had he asked the Vice President to reconsider. In fact, they said, the President had been aware for about two weeks of Mr. Rockefeller's plan for a public withdrawal from the Vice-Presidential race.

Mr. Rockefeller publicly disclosed the move by releasing a letter to President Ford, which he delivered to the Oval Office of the White House at 10:30 this morning. The President and Vice President met for 20 minutes in an atmosphere described as "extremely cordial" by Ron Nessen, the White House press secretary.

The letter gave no reason for Mr. Rockefeller's action, and aides did not rule out the possibility of his running for President himself.

One White House source close to the President said that Mr. Rockefeller would have inevitably had to step aside because his presence had become "detrimental" to Mr. Ford's efforts to win the Republican Party nomination.

The White House official said that Mr. Rockefeller had been unable to make his peace with the right wing of the Republican Party. He was, therefore, regarded as a liability by the President Ford Committee, which is seeking to win the party's Presidential nomination for Mr. Ford in the face of an expected strong challenge by former Gov. Ronald Reagan of California, the official explained.

Mr. Reagan is a favorite of the Republican right.

'The Proper Time'

President Ford said recently that he would announce "at the proper time" whether or not he wanted Mr. Rockefeller as his running mate in 1976.

Meanwhile, Mr. Rockefeller has grown increasingly uncomfortable in his Vice-Presidential role, according to members of his staff and others familiar with his activities. Senator Jacob K. Javits, Republican of New York, said in a telephone interview today that he had been expecting Mr. Rockefeller's decision for several months.

Senator Javits said that Mr. Rockefeller's position in an Administration tailoring its policies to the most conservative elements in the Republican Party was becoming "untenable." As four-term Governor of New York State, Mr. Rockefeller had found President Ford's decision to withhold Federal aid needed to keep New York City out of bankruptcy as particularly "hard to stomach," Senator Javits added.

Mr. Ford at his news conference described the differences between him and Mr. Rockefeller on the issue of aid to New York City as "minimal."

A former aide considered to be close to the Vice President said that Mr. Rockefeller had grown increasingly unhappy in his role as a loyal "Number Two" in the Ford Administration and also felt that he could be a counterpoise to the right wing drift of the Administration after renouncing any intention to seek the Vice-Presidency next year.

This former aide also said

386

that Mr. Rockefeller had probably made up his mind to resign before the President told him he was not wanted.

In his letter, Mr. Rockefeller praised Mr. Ford for his "dedication to the Presidency," and for his "courage, resolution and forthrightness."

He also said that he had made it clear to the President and the public that he had not been a candidate for the Vice-Presidency and that "realistically" it is up to the Presidential candidate to recommend a Vice-Presidential candidate to the national convention.

"After much thought," Mr. Rockefeller wrote, "I have decided further that I do not wish my name to enter into your consideration for the upcoming Republican Vice-Presidential nominee. I wish you to know this for your own planning."

Vows to Carry On

Mr. Rockefeller added that he would, of course, continue to carry out his constitutional duties as Vice President and "to assist in every way I can in carrying on to cope with the problems that confront the nation until the installation once again of a President and Vice President duly elected by the people of this great Republic."

Several members of Mr. Rockefeller's staff pointed to what they said was the "cold" tone of the Vice President's letter and the fact that Mr. Rockefeller had neither praised Mr. Ford's leadership as President nor supported his nomination next year.

These aides also noted that the letter did not rule out the possibility that Mr. Rockefeller

might run for President next year. They carefully avoided suggesting that Mr. Rockefeller would seek the Presidency but pictured him as disengaging to wait and watch for new power struggles within the Republican party.

They also made it clear that Mr. Rockefeller's friends consider the party to be in grave danger. One aide commented that the Vice President had been concerned about the "lurch to the right" and the letter to Mr. Ford was designed for "clearing the air and setting some counterforces in motion."

Public statements about the letter were also noncommittal. Mr. Nessen, speaking informally to reporters this morning, said that "the letter speaks for itself" and added that there was "a complete understanding" between the President and Vice President. Mr. Rockefeller and his spokesmen were not available for comment before President Ford's news conference. But a statement put out by the New York State Republican Committee was couched in language almost identical to that used by Mr. Nessen.

White House officials said that Mr. Rockefeller discussed his decision with President Ford last Thursday. A senior Republican political operative who has long been personally close to the President said that although the timing of Mr. Rockefeller's announcement had been prearranged, he was "not pushed" by the President, adding that the decision to step aside had been reached by "mutual agreement."

Mr. Rockefeller's action throws open the contest for the

Republican Vice-Presidential nomination next year. It also adds to the disarray of President Ford's campaign to win the Presidency in his own right, following the resignation of two key figures—David Packard the chief fund raiser, and Lee Nunn, deputy director—from the committee seeking the Republican nomination for Mr. Ford.

Mr. Ford and Mr. Rockefeller are the nation's first President and Vice President to come to office without having been elected. Both came to office under the 25th Amendment to the Constitution. Mr. Ford became President after the resignation of Richard M. Nixon, who selected Mr. Ford as his Vice President after the resignation of Vice President Agnew.

Mr. Rockefeller, one of the heirs to the great Rockefeller fortune, who had been Governor of New York for 15 years, was sworn in as Vice President on Dec. 19, 1974. Regarded for many years as a leader of the liberal wing of the Republican Party, he was seen as a political counterpoise to Mr. Ford, a conservative from Grand Rapids, Mich.

However, Mr. Rockefeller was never accepted by the ultra-conservatives who exercised increasing power within party circles. And Mr. Ford, faced with the necessity of turning back a challenge from Mr. Reagan, moved steadily closer to the right wing of the party.

This chasm between the two men widened greatly when the Vice President called for Federal aid for New York City while the President was ruling

out such aid.

Today, Senator Barry Goldwater of Arizona, who defeated Mr. Rockefeller in an acrimonious battle for the Republican Presidential nomination in 1964, praised the Vice President's decision and called it a "commendable recognition of today's political realities."

However, Senator Charles McC. Mathias, a liberal Republican from Maryland, said that the Vice President's decision meant that the Republican Party would "now be perceived as an even narrower-based" conservative party. Senator Mathias, indicated last week he might challenge the conservative candidacies of President Ford and Mr. Reagan. Today, he said he believed this kind of challenge is now more necessary than ever.

In the context of his letter today, Mr. Rockefeller's answers about possible Presidential aspirations on yesterday's "Issues and Answers" television program, seemed somewhat more significant.

Asked on the show what he would think of a challenge to Mr. Ford and Mr. Reagan, "from the liberal wing of the party that used to be called the Rockefeller wing," the Vice President replied, "Well, this is a free country and who knows what is going to happen."

He also pointed out that President Kennedy had said that he would have been beaten in 1960 "if Nelson Rockefeller had been nominated by the Republican Party."

November 4, 1975

Decision on Rules To Leave Nominee Free to Maneuver

By WARREN WEAVER Jr.
Special to The New York Times

KANSAS CITY, Mo., Aug. 17 —The first attempt by a national political party to impose any restrictions on a Presidential candidate's method of choosing his running mate was defeated tonight by the Republican National Convention.

Backers of Ronald Reagan had proposed that each would-be Presidential nominee be required to identify his Vice-Presidential selection 10 hours before the Presidential balloting begins, to give convention delegates a full picture of the ticket they were choosing.

But supporters of President Ford, applying strong political discipline in the first critical confrontation of the conven-

tion, defeated the proposition after insisting during noisy debate that it was not a valid reform but a tactical move to gain personal advantage for Mr. Reagan.

As a result, Mr. Ford will remain free to ponder his Vice-Presidential choice in private tomorrow. If he wins the nomination tomorrow night, he will announce his running mate the following morning in the traditional manner of Presidential candidates.

Then it will be up to the delegates to ratify that decision, as conventions virtually always do, or reject it in favor of another nominee.

Warns of Division

Arguing for the Ford position, Senator Robert P. Griffin of Michigan said that the proposed rule change would "drive a wedge of division in our party" at a time when unity against the Democratic ticket was essential.

"I don't know if President Ford will choose Ronald Reagan as his running mate or not," the Senator said, "but I want President Ford at least

to have that opportunity."

Had the rule been approved, Mr. Ford would have been forced to choose someone other than his opponent for the nomination, because the rule specifies that the running mate selected must agree to serve on the ticket, and Mr. Reagan has said he would not do so.

Closing the vigorous debate for the Reagan forces, Richard Derham of Washington asked the delegates, "Why should the Vice Presidency continue to be a decision of the back room?"

"I want to know if a candidate is going to make a mistake," he continued. "And I want to know that when I can still do something about it."

Reagan strategists had hoped to build a majority on the procedural issue by adding some Ford delegates and independents to their delegate count for the Presidential nomination, which was running about 90 short of the required figure. They succeeded in increasing their total of 1,040 in The New York Times nomination count by 29, but the Ford backers increased their total of 1,140 by 40, to carry the day.

After the roll-call was completed, the rest of the rules were approved by a routine voice vote. The Reagan supporters did not bother to contest a new provision they had debated in committee for a week or more that binds delegates chosen in primaries to vote as required by state law in early ballots.

The new rules approved tonight are likely to make party reform even harder to achieve during the next four years than it has been in the past.

Under the new code, continuing review of the way the party runs its conventions and picks its national candidates will be assigned to members of the Republican National Committee, rather than to the present composite group of elected officials and party professionals.

The convention's Rules Committee rejected yesterday, 54 to 42, a proposal to continue the broader party reform committee that has operated since 1972. Instead, it created a new 54-member group on rule changes consisting entirely of members of the National Committee.

387

The new rules also freeze, with only minor changes, the plan under which the relative strength of the states in the nominating convention is determined and continue to limit the role of women in party affairs.

The focus of attention tonight was on two areas of the party rules that might affect the nomination contest between President Ford and Ronald Reagan: new proposals for selecting Vice-Presidential candidates and for binding convention delegates from primary states to vote according to state law.

But the great majority of the rules submitted to the delegates, which will control party operations long after the convention and the 1976 election are over, demonstrate the prevailing insistence of conservative leaders that Republicans continue to rely on the old methods that brought them to power.

Representative William A. Steiger of Wisconsin, chairman of the present Rules Review Committee, pleaded with the convention rules group to retain a committee with Governors, members of Congress and political scientists as its members as well as those serving on the party's National Committee.

Generally, National Committee members are older men and women,- some of them party professionals and others fund raisers or contributors. They tend to be more conservative and more responsive to the active party leadership than are elective officials and working politicians.

The Republican formula under which convention strength is apportioned among the states remains essentially unchanged. It still gives the smaller states greater proportional influence in the party than either their population or their share of the Republican vote warrants on a strict arithmetical basis.

It still preserves the "victory bonus" that awards additional delegate strength to states that recorded majorities for the Republican national ticket in the last previous election.

The convention's Rules Committee voted to increase Puerto Rico's delegation to 14 delegates from 8 in 1980, on the ground that its population had increased radically and the level of Republican activity there merited special recognition.

A proposal that the Republican National Committee be given the right to revise between conventions the formula on delegate apportionment was defeated by that committee last week and is not part of the revised code that went before the convention.

Changes in the Republican rules that affect the role of women in the party were largely negative. A requirement that women have half the seats on the party Finance Committee was eliminated before the rules reached the floor.

Despite protests by women's groups that the move undercut their position, the new rules provide that the requirement that states "endeavor" to give women equal representation in their convention delegations cannot be "the basis of any kind of quota system."

As drafted by the Steiger committee, all the party rules referred to "chair" instead of "chairman," but this was changed to the old nomenclature in committee.

August 18, 1976

FORD TAKES NOMINATION ON FIRST BALLOT

2 RIVALS MEET

Reagan Not Running for No. 2 Spot but Doesn't Bar Draft

By R. W. APPLE Jr.
Special to The New York Times

KANSAS CITY, Mo., Thursday, Aug. 19—Gerald Rudolph Ford, who struggled for seven grueling months to avoid rejection by his party, was nominated in his own right early this morning at the 31st Republican National Convention on the first and only ballot.

The party sent Mr. Ford, a political insider who has held elective office for 28 years, into combat against Jimmy Carter, the political outsider chosen by the Democrats, after Gov. William G. Milliken of Michigan hailed him as the nation's "present and future President."

Unlike most Presidents, Mr. Ford, who inherited the White House after Richard M. Nixon resigned, will enter the general election campaign as the underdog.

West Virginia, the scene of intensive combat for the loyalties of delegates, gave the President 20 votes—as promised by Gov. Arch A. Moore Jr. for months—and put him over the top at 12:29 A.M. Central daylight time.

In the gallery at the south end of the hall, Betty Ford rose to her feet and waved her hands above her head in evangelistic style. Then she and her three children hugged and kissed each other.

The final count gave Mr. Ford 1,187 votes and Ronald Reagan 1,070. John J. Walsh Jr., an Illinois alternate from River Forest, abstained, and Ralph DeBlasio, a Greenwich Village district leader, voted for Commerce Secretary Elliot L. Richardson.

Despite a scattering of "noes," mainly from the pro-Reagan Texas delegation, Representative John J. Rhodes of Arizona, the convention's permanent chairman, declared Mr. Ford nominated by acclamation.

27-Minute Meeting

Mr. Ford then drove to Mr. Reagan's hotel for a 27-minute meeting with his vanquished adversary. They discussed the Vice Presidency. Mr. Reagan said at a subsequent news conference that he stood by earlier statements that he would not run with the President, but it was unclear whether he had been asked.

The Californian said he would not permit his name to be put in nomination for the Vice Presidency, but he left open the door for a draft by the delegates, many of whom appeared to want a Ford-Reagan ticket. The President, who was to announce his choice later today, smiled as Mr. Reagan responded to questions about a draft.

Describing the former Governor as "the most effective campaigner in America" and complimenting him on his organization, Mr. Ford said there would be a place in his administration for Mr. Reagan.

Until the meeting, Senator Howard H. Baker Jr. of Tennessee and William D. Ruckelshaus had been at the top of the President's list of prospects. But Mr. Ford introduced an element of uncertainty with his visit to Mr. Reagan, who waged the most powerful intraparty campaign of this century against an incumbent President.

Mr. Ford's name was placed before the delegates after that of Mr. Reagan, was presented by Senator Paul Laxalt of Nevada, his campaign manager. While Mr. Reagan watched grim-faced in his hotel suite, the Senator called Mr. Reagan "the man who can whip the irresponsible Congress into line."

The calling of the roll was delayed beyond prime television time in the East, South and Middle West by unscheduled demonstrations from the frustrated Reagan delegates, who knew they could delay if not determine the outcome.

Uncommitted delegates by the dozens broke ranks during the day, with most of them swinging behind the President. After weeks of agony, the Mississippi delegation, once considered the key to the nomination, voted before the balloting to discard its unit rule and to give 16 votes to Mr. Ford, 14 votes to Mr. Reagan.

Before the roll-call began, the 63-year-old Mr. Ford. the first unelected President in American history, was assured of the votes of 1,179 delegates, only 49 more than a majority, according to the final New York Times tabulation. Mr. Reagan had 1,068.

Only 12 diehard delegates—including Eliza Sprinkle, the 79-year-old grandmother from Virginia, one of the minor stars of this convention — remained uncommitted right up to the time the clerk called the states.

Mrs. Springle finally voted for Mr. Reagan.

The extraordinary closeness of the race was reflected by the fact that Mr. Ford would not go over the top until the roll-call reached the final two or three states.

There were no signs that the hard-fought contest between the two conservative Republicans would leave a legacy of bitterness like that generated by the 1964 showdown between Nelson A. Rockefeller and Senator Barry Goldwater of Arizona.

Reagan Shows No Anger

Mr. Reagan expressed no anger as he doggedly made the rounds of the state delegations. He declined the offer of his prospective running mate, Senator Richard S. Schweiker of Pennsylvania, to withdraw, calling his retention of Mr. Schweiker "a matter of principle."

The Reagan forces scarcely masked the conviction that they were beaten. John P. Sears, the witty and innovative campaign manager, spoke of "a very uphill struggle," and Mr. Reagan said he was "in the same old business until tonight goes by."

The delegates gathered for the third evening session in Kemper Arena speculated endlessly, and with little hard information, on Mr. Ford's Vice-Presidential selection.

Because he has never run a national campaign before, the President is something of an unknown political quantity. So politicians were looking to his selection of a running mate for clues as to his ideological and geographical strategy.

Mr. Milliken, an old political colleague of the President, made a brief and unconventional nominating address, mentioning Mr. Ford's name almost at the outset.

Customarily, the name is coyly withheld until the last line.

The Governor credited the President with having "reestablished our leadership, revived our economy and restored our honor . . . brought strength in time of crisis, order in a time of chaos." He contrasted his fellow Michigander with the "maybe-I-will, maybe-I-won't nominee of the other party," Jimmy Carter.

In Mr. Reagan's behalf, Mr. Laxalt said the former California Governor had challenged the entire Republican political establishment, including the occupant of the White House and all but nine of 535 members of Congress, and compiled "a track record" that proved he could win.

"I would dearly love to see Ronald Reagan debate Jimmy Carter," the Senator said. "After about one round of debating with Ronald Reagan he would have to go back to shucking peanuts — if that's what you do with peanuts."

Pro-Reagan political professionals said they had nothing to do with the horn-blowing that gave this convention its distinctive sound—a sound that will be remembered as long as the cowbell rung by George Bender of Ohio for Senator Robert A. Taft at Chicago in 1952.

Ray Barnhat of Texas said, for example, that he had been trying to persuade his solidly Reaganite delegation to "shut up." And the horns blew even for Senator Jesse A. Helms of North Carolina, who had to wait for more than 15 minutes to make a seconding speech for Mr. Reagan.

But the horns were all of the same make, and it appeared unlikely that they had appeared spontaneously.

Backers' Response

The Ford response to the horns was a cascade of multicolored beach balls and streamers from the balconies, which the President's campaign aides had packed with supporters. The President's partisans controlled the convention management, and they used it to good advantage in the distribution of tickets.

The Reagan demonstration lasted 43 minutes, but the Ford partisans, more restrained, kept their show going for only 28 minutes.

Seconding speeches were delivered by Mr. Helms and Dr. Gloria E. A. Toote of Manhattan for Mr. Reagan. Those for Mr. Ford came from no fewer than 19 persons, including Richard M. Rosenbaum, the New York Republican chairman; William L. Stubbs, a delegate from Newark, and Representative Ronald A. Sarasin, a Connecticut delegate.

Earlier yesterday, Mr. Sears attributed the President's success in the previous night's tense and pivotal rules fight largely to the decision of the Mississippi delegates to cast all of their votes against the Reagan attempt to force Mr. Ford to name a running mate by early this morning.

When the vote at the Mississippi caucus (31 to 28, with one delegate absent) became known, Mr. Sears contended, votes on which Mr. Reagan had counted in other delegations failed to materialize.

"When Mississippi bailed on us, most of the other did, too," the strategist said at the last of his daily news briefings. "We lost three or four here, three or four there, and by the time we got to the actual balloting, the issue was no longer in much doubt."

Compared with The Times's count as it then stood, Mr. Ford made important gains in Georgia, Hawaii, Indiana, Minnesota, New York, Pennsylvania, and Tennessee, in addition to Mississippi.

Mr. Reagan was able to score offsetting gains only in Illinois, Kentucky, Maryland, West Virginia and North Carolina. They were insufficient for him to close the gap.

"This was the ball game," said Harry S. Dent, President Ford's chief Southern delegate-hunter, after the Florida vote clinched the victory. "They put everything on this vote, and we put a great deal into it on our side."

August 19, 1976

Aground On A Rock

By Anthony Lewis

KANSAS CITY, Mo., Aug. 18—As theater, the 1976 Republican convention has been good value: spirited, funny, above all human compared to the Nixonian plastic of 1972. No onlooker can fairly complain about a political meeting at which Alf M. Landon tells the hall: "It warms the cockles of my heart—whatever that means."

But it would be a mistake to take the drama too seriously: to believe, for example, that the contest between Gerald Ford and Ronald Reagan was a desperate struggle for the soul of the Republican Party. There were flashes of bitterness. But this was no 1964 festival of hate, no great clash of ideologies.

The Republicans' ideological war is about over, in fact, and this convention showed that the conservatives have essentially won it. Their views dominate the platform: on economics, social issues, the environment, foreign policy. And apart from such far-out cases as Senator Jesse Helms of North Carolina, they act like winners now, relaxed and self-confident.

The party's moderate and liberal figures were lost souls at this convention. Representative John Anderson of Illinois, Senators Edward Brooke of Massachusetts, Charles Mathias of Maryland, Mark Hatfield of Oregon and their like did not hide their sense of isolation.

The moderates worked extremely hard for President Ford in the delegate-hunt out here, and that fact itself indicates the shift in the party's center of gravity. They would have found it hard to believe a few years ago if they had been told that they would be on the barricades for a man as deeply conservative as Gerald Ford. The best they can hope for now is that he will swing a little back toward the center to compete with Jimmy Carter.

The country has moved to the right in the last decade, so it is natural

---

ABROAD AT HOME

enough that the Republican Party has. But those who remember the Eisenhower victories, or before that the Willkie-Dewey years, will want some further explanation for the extent of the G.O.P. shift. And I think one reason was in evidence here in Kansas City: Vice President Rockefeller.

Nelson Aldrich Rockefeller has dominated what used to be the Dewey-Eisenhower wing of the party for sixteen years now. In that time it has been difficult, perhaps impossible, for any of the younger moderates to emerge as national figures. Several surely had outstanding potential, but they have remained local or regional personalities.

It would be one thing if Mr. Rockefeller had been making a tenacious fight on issues of principle. But most of his supposed liberal principles have long since proved nonexistent. As Governor of New York he turned out to be the scourge of welfare, the author of the country's most punitive drug laws, the man who allowed mass slaughter at Attica and never regretted it.

No, Mr. Rockefeller was not engaged in defending the tradition of liberal Republicanism. He was on an extended ego-trip. As he increasingly became a divisive figure in the party, its moderate forces paid dearly for his ambition. And he remained oblivious to it all—as was so wonderfully clear when he spoke to the convention the other night.

There was Nelson Rockefeller, unyielding supporter of the Vietnam

389

war, deploring the sad cost of that war. There was the man who took New York State near bankruptcy with his grandiose building schemes now denouncing big government. One close Rockefeller observer remarked that the only thing he left out was a denunciation of his friends the construction unions.

The Rockefeller speed may not quite have won the chutzpah award here. That honor probably goes to John Connally, who made his way to power and wealth in the Democratic Party and now attacked it, in Joe McCarthy's ugly locution, as "the Democrat Party." But there was a special quality of obliviousness in Mr. Rockefeller's ig-

noring of his own past. The truth is that he probably did not even know he was being inconsistent.

The amazing thing about Nelson Rockefeller is how he managed to persuade so many reasonable people for so long that he was a good-government man, humane, a sensible liberal. As it happens, that reputation is visibly crumbling nowadays in his home state. Even his great legislative monument, the drug law, has been found unworkably vindictive and been amended by bipartisan agreement.

The perfect symbolism of Rockefellerism is the "Empire State Plaza," his $2 billion marble mall in Albany.

An art critic, Thomas B. Hess of New York magazine, appraised the mall recently in the following terms: "You seem to have stumbled into the capital of a two-bit, Latin-American dictatorship, suddenly become prosperous, run by a tinhorn colonel who's decided to show who's boss—in marble."

The Nelson Rockefeller saga may of course not be over. He could be Secretary of State or Defense in a new Ford Administration. His resilience should never be underestimated. But he has probably completed his most important contribution: to the right-wing movement of the Republican Party.

August 19, 1976

Campaign '76: Barren and Petty

Lack of Dialogue on Issues Is Called Deliberate In Election That Focuses on Series of Mishaps

By R. W. APPLE Jr.

Special to The New York Times

COLUMBUS, Ohio, Oct. 19—The Presidential candidates, complained Senator George McGovern of South Dakota last week, have spent far too much of their time on "demagoguery, brainwashing, cardiac lusts, the wit and wisdom of Earl Butz and freedom in Poland." The 1972 Democratic Presidential nominee said he doubted that he had "ever seen an emptier campaign, a pettier campaign."

News Analysis

His judgments might be dismissed as the spiteful view of a man who tried to run on the issues and lost humiliatingly, were it not for the fact that Senator McGovern was saying publicly what many Republican and Democratic leaders have been murmuring behind closed doors.

A prominent Republican here in Ohio commented gloomily this week that "neither one of them is giving the voter anything to vote for," and a Democratic Senator from the East said the Presidential contest had "all the issue content of a student-council race."

Because both major parties in the United States attempt to build coalitions that transcend ideological considerations, American politics is seldom as issue-oriented as politics in Britain or France. But even by the standards of this country, 1976 is proving to be unusually barren of serious dialogue on the issues.

The New York Times/CBS News polls have consistently shown that partisanship is the strongest determinant in how most people plan to vote this year; more than 80 percent of all Republicans and Democrats—no matter where they live, no matter what their ideology—expect to stay with their parties. Only the vola-

tile and rapidly expanding mass of independents has given the Presidential race its constantly changing visage.

To a considerable degree, the revival of partisanship and the decline of ideology result from the virtual disappearance of the two issues that gave such an acidulous tone to the politics of the era that lasted roughly from the assassination of President Kennedy to the resignation of President Nixon: Vietnam and race. But both President Ford and Jimmy Carter consciously avoided issue-oriented campaigning from the start, calculating (correctly, as it turned out) that by doing so they could defeat their more ideological primary opponents.

Theme Is Trust and Pride

In the general election campaign, both men set out to deal not so much in issues as in "themes," as their strategists put it. Both have tried, with the memory of Watergate all too fresh, to sell themselves as men worthy of trust, as men who could reawaken American pride. Trust and pride—the words pop up again and again in speeches and television commercials.

But neither nominee has maintained thematic consistency. Mr. Carter, who usually pictures himself as the quintessential outsider, spent a week early in the campaign claiming his kinship with Harry S. Truman, an insider's insider, and more recently, he stated his faith in the Daley machine in Chicago. Mr. Ford, who prides himself on the prudent management of the Federal purse, boasted in Yonkers about the money Washington was pouring into New York State and gave a windfall of millions of dollars to wheat farmers.

The President promised last week that he would do what he could to elevate the tone of the campaign, then stumped through the Middle West on the assertion that Mr. Carter would do or say almost anything to be elected. Mr. Carter, meanwhile, was telling reporters that he was going to try to avoid criticizing his adver-

sary in the final two weeks, complaining that the news media had overemphasized his recent attacks, which even his own advisers had been describing as much too shrill. Neither nominee appears able to decide whether he wants to be a nice guy or a rabbit puncher.

Strange Series of Mishaps

In the confusion produced by thematic and stylistic contradictions, and in the absence of substantive discussion of most issues, the campaign has focused on a strange series of mishaps, most notably Mr. Carter's interview with Playboy magazine and Mr. Ford's comments about Eastern Europe. It is not possible to say whether the news media or the candidates themselves have had the most to do with the creation or perpetuation of these controversies, but both have certainly contributed, the candidates reaching for headlines and television time, the reporters seeking to enliven a pallid campaign.

The curious thing about these controversies, many politicians believe, is that neither was what it seemed to be. Few people if any who know Jimmy Carter thought his comments about lust betrayed any loose morality; he is, in all probability more strait-laced than most recent Presidential candidates. Indeed, he has been criticized for excessive and excessively displayed piety in some quarters.

Likewise, it would be difficult to conclude, on the basis of his record over a quarter of a century, that Mr. Ford is "soft" on Eastern Europe—not after all those ringing statements of support for Captive Nations Week.

What was really at issue was the question of whether Mr. Carter had shown poor judgment by his choice of rather earthy language and his agreement to be interviewed by Playboy, and whether Mr. Ford had shown a lack of poise and precision in fumbling a question about Eastern Europe. That so much could be read into such relatively trivial episodes is perhaps the best evidence of the superficiality of the campaign.

Statistics or Rhetoric

If there is one issue, short of war, that has always counted in American elections, it is economics. This year, both parties agree that it ought to matter, but neither is sure that it does. When economics has been discussed at length, it has either been submerged in statistics, as in the first Presidential debate, or wrapped in the same rhetoric—jobs vs. inflation, government activisim vs. private enterprise—that has served Democrats and Republicans since 1932.

But rarely has there been much discussion of what many analysts consider new realities: public distrust of programmatic solutions, the growing inability of older cities to provide essential services, and an era of shortages of vital national resources, especially energy resources.

The result, it seems to thoughtful politicians across the country, is an electorate with no real commitment to either candidate, neither of whom began the campaign with a national following. With exactly two weeks to go until Election Day, a sixth or more of the voters call themselves undecided, and the leanings of millions of others are tentative. Particularly in the big states, party leaders say that either man can still win but that neither seems sure how to do it.

October 20, 1976

Fund Shortage Cools Enthusiasm Of Those Taking Part in Campaign

By JON NORDHEIMER
Special to The New York Times

SANTA BARBARA, Calif., Oct. 20— "People expect a lot from a Presidential race," Robert Handy remarked the other day as he prepared to climb aboard the stationary bicycle he keeps in his office at Democratic headquarters here to work off the tensions of the campaign.

"When they don't see anything going on they chew me out," said Mr. Handy, a mild-mannered former sailor who is head of the Carter-Mondale campaign in Santa Barbara, on the Pacific coast about 90 miles north of Los Angeles.

Like the exercise bike, the Carter-Mondale campaign in Santa Barbara does not give the appearance of going any place. Nor does the Ford-Dole ticket.

Around this city and across the nation, the Presidential campaign this fall has been stripped like a stolen luxury car of its customary glitter and ornaments. Under the new Federal financing laws, it has become a no-frills campaign, a shoestring campaign, and, to some extent, a remote, cool-to-the-point-of-bloodless campaign.

Lack of interest in the Presidential race has been attributed to several causes: The absence of galvanizing issues, a pervasive cynicism about politics in the post-Watergate era and the charge that neither of the major party candidates possesses the charisma to stir passions, even among the party faithful.

But it has become increasingly clear that the new model of national campaigning imposed by Federal financing reform has significantly changed both the appearance and structure of Presidential electioneering.

The decision by both candidates to spend for media advertising about half the $21.8 million given them by the Government has served to heighten and perhaps extend this effect. The personal travel expenditures of the candidates and their running mates have taken another large piece out of the budget, leaving little to be spread around the 50 states as seed money to generate enthusiasm at the grass-roots level.

While the lack of large sums of money for field operations has encouraged wider participation of citizen volunteers at the local level, the tight budget has virtually guaranteed at the same time that their enthusiasm would be dampened by the absence of anything to occupy their time.

"What's happening now," observed Mr. Handy, "is that people want to get involved and feel part of the process again, but we're so strapped for funds that we can't give them anything to do.

"It might be good for a volunteer to go door to door on behalf of a candidate, but unless he can drop off a piece of campaign literature it's a waste of time."

He showed a visitor a metal index card file stuffed with the names of volunteers. "We put most of these names together in August," he said, "but we haven't been able to give them anything to do until these last two weeks of the campaign when headquarters in Los Angeles sent the first batch of literature."

Across the continent, Mr. Handy's analysis was echoed by other frustrated campaign workers.

They lamented the disappearance of campaign buttons and banners and bumper stickers this year. They also uniformly said that the absence of fund-raising activities—no money beyond the $21.8 million given each candidate by the Government can be raised or spent—had deprived the campaigns of fund-raising activities that normally energize a national election and give it zest.

"People from local political organizations don't seem to understand this when they come to our headquarters asking for bumper stickers, literature and buttons," said Thomas H. Kean, director of the Ford-Dole campaign in New Jersey. "These are the trimmings of a campaign that fuel local enthusiasm, and when somebody wants to go door to door with literature and can't get it, the situation certainly doesn't help our image at all."

And Marie LeGrand, who was a McGovern fund raiser in 1972 and now keeps track of expenditures for the Carter campaign in New York, put it this way:

"There just aren't as many people able to get involved. Fund raising used to generate a lot of activity: bazaars, concerts, cookouts, the little old ladies making Swedish meatballs—a lot of nickel and dime events that got people excited. The new regulations make it almost impossible to do this now and I miss it."

And Noreen Walsh, a state volunteer coordinator in New York for the Democratic ticket said, "There are a lot of people sitting back waiting who would like to be out there working."

The problem, she said, is that there is nothing for them to do. It has only been recently that the state drive has been given Carter literature to hand out for the final push of the campaign, and Carter headquarters were so short of space that phone work, when there were phones available, and envelope-stuffing, when there were envelopes, have been severely limited. "It's a two-week campaign," she continued. "We'll have things for everybody to do when we come down to the wire."

Campaign buttons and bumper stickers and other traditional campaign paraphernalia are so scarce they become instant collector's items in some states. In Texas, after a thin supply of metal buttons was exhausted, Ford workers resorted to printing the Republican team's names on paper with gum-sticker backs and plastering them on a voter's coat or dress, a substitute "button" that disintegrated after a few hours.

Mass mailings have been sharply curtailed, especially since the cost of postage has increased by about 60 percent since the last Presidential campaign. In New Jersey, with nearly four million registered voters, a mailing to only 100,000 of them would reduce the total Democratic field budget for the state by one-tenth.

The lack of money to communicate directly by mail has scrambled traditional tactics in crucial swing states like Texas, Florida and California, all of which have large Spanish-speaking groups that require bilingual reading materials or broadcasts.

"We're operating on less money in the campaign here in Florida than any state or gubernatorial candidate ever has, and even with less than the candidate for state treasurer is right now," said David Dunn, state coordinator of the Carter-Mondale campaign.

For Philip H. Weinberg, New York State coordinator for Ford-Dole, the new austerity is particularly frustrating after his personal experience with the past campaigns of Richard M. Nixon and Nelson A. Rockefeller, all of which were sumptuously funded.

An Unseen Campaign

"Everybody here says they don't see a campaign taking place," Mr. Weinberg noted with a touch of weariness in his voice, "but what they're used to costs a lot of money. We can't afford things like sound trucks and bunting and a lot of brass bands at rallies."

He said the Ford-Dole operation in New York had the services of one car, one station wagon and a truck rented on a day-to-day basis for upstate deliveries.

"The regular Democratic activists really aren't involved in this campaign," said Miles Rubin, who was the central figure in the Presidential campaign of George McGovern in California in 1972, when more than $2 million was spent for the Democrat from South Dakota in the California primary alone. This year, the entire Carter field budget for California is $283,000 his largest operating budget for the campaign in any state.

"People here got spoiled during the McGovern campaign," Mr. Rubin said, adding that many who might have been expected to take part this year have "thrown up their hands and are sitting this one out."

391

More important, perhaps, there are reports that blue-collar and lower-income groups who have not had a high profile in campaigns of the past, have come forward, encouraged by the Carter campaign, but have been turned away disappointed when they find there is no place for them.

Some nonpartisan experts in the field of campaign costs are reluctantly concluding that the campaign spending reforms will need considerable revision by the 1980 election.

Herbert E. Alexander, director of the Citizens Research Foundation in Princeton, N.J., who has been studying the role of money in American politics since 1958, is critical of the flat grant method of Government financing in the general election.

Challenger at a Disadvantage

In the first place, Mr. Alexander said in an interview, the figure of $21.8 million is far too low to adequately finance a national campaign, and it places the challenger at a distinct disadvantage against an incumbent President.

The obvious advantages of the incumbency, with a President's freedom to use of the White House and all its powers,

mean that a challenger has to spend more money in a campaign just to compete effectively, he said.

When both campaigns are starved for funds, this advantage is magnified, he said.

In 1972, the two party nominees spent an aggregate that approached $100 million on their campaigns, the excesses of which led directly to the reforms that set limits on this year's spending. In 1972, the defeated Democratic nominee, Senator George McGovern of South Dakota, saddled with fund-raising difficulties and unpopular with powerful elements within his own party, still managed to spend more than $30 million in the period between his nomination and the election.

Mr. Alexander suggests that $40 million might be a reasonable budget for a Presidential campaign today, and he believes that a matching program similar to the system used in the primaries this year be used. In other words, the Government would pay up to $20 million in funds to match campaign contributions raised by a party's nominee.

While complaints about the dullness of this campaign are commonplace, it is difficult to contemplate what the nature of the race might have been without the

televised debates between the candidates, which have been roundly deemed "boring" by most Americans but nevertheless have supplied the campaign's only signficant clashes.

The lack of other resources has also magnified the impact of the images created by these debates. In past campaigns, a mistake similar to President Ford's gaffe on the Communist role in Eastern Europe could have been partly overcome by the quick mass mailing of an explanation to ethnic voters concerned by the misstatement. But the cost of the mass mailing—first-class postage today is 13 cents as against 8 cents only four years ago—is too prohibitive for today's tight budgets. There has been a comparable increase in third-class mail costs.

Compliance with the Federal election law has also been a costly item in campaign budgets, mostly in the bookkeeping chores it has created and in the man-hours spent making sure each expenditure conforms with the statute, a process that engages the energies of campaign aides from the lowliest county unit to the candidate himself.

October 25, 1976

The Two-Party Freeze

By Tom Wicker

The difficulties Eugene McCarthy has experienced in trying to wage an independent campaign for the Presidency have made clear the extent to which the two major parties have been built into the political system, while everyone else is rather effectively shut out.

What inherent right to privileged status do the Democratic and Republican Parties and their nominees have? For what reason do the states and the Federal Government make it so hard for so-called minor parties or independents to compete?

To ask these questions is not necessarily to argue against the two-party system. Two "umbrella" parties, each striving for at least some support in all regions and among all shades of opinion, have been well demonstrated to be the most likely instruments for putting together winning, workable coalitions in a sprawling and varied democracy.

But minor parties and independents have a useful and important role to play. They can threaten and thus move one or both of the major parties; they may bring otherwise neglected issues to the fore, or serve as an outlet for segments of opinion and interest unknown to the majors; less often, they can put forward programs or candidates with a real chance to win.

But this year Mr. McCarthy and other non-major party candidates find

themselves handicapped not only by the usual financial difficulties and by complex and restrictive election laws, varying from state to state, which often leave no recourse but costly court action. They also were shut out of the debates that gave the major party nominees four and a half hours of free prime-time television.

They were penalized by the campaign financing laws, which provided $20 million subsidies apiece to the Republican and Democratic nominees, and more than $3 million apiece to the major parties just to finance their conventions. Last spring, even Democratic and Republican aspirants in the primaries could receive substantial Federal subsidies. Minor party and independent candidates will get no help from the Government until after the election, and then none unless they poll sufficient votes—which their lack of funds now will make it difficult to do.

It's true that it would be hard to include Gene McCarthy in the debates, or in some form of subsidy, without including Lester Maddox and others. But that is merely a difficulty in opening up a democratic political system—not really a reason for closing it to all but Democrats and Republicans. It's certainly no justification for some states actually to have laws that don't permit independents to run for office, or that make it substantially more difficult for them to do so than for a party nominee.

Mr. McCarthy, of course, is an inconvenience for the Democrats, a presence in the race who conceivably could take enough Democratic votes in important states to throw them to the Republicans. For that reason, a number of people who probably would support his abstract right to run both fear and denounce his actual candidacy.

He is hurting himself further by his

strange insistence that there's no real difference between Gerald Ford and Jimmy Carter, and that therefore he doesn't care which of them wins. Mr. Carter and Mr. Ford do seem unhappily alike on the substance of foreign policy, and Mr. McCarthy flashed one of those cutting insights of his when he told Brock Brower: "On defense, for example, you have nothing now between cut-the-budget-to-save-money or pacifism." Certainly not in Jimmy Carter, if the campaign is a guide.

Nevertheless, there are clear-cut differences between Mr. Carter and Mr. Ford that everyone but Gene McCarthy has little trouble seeing—on unemployment, for the best example, the continuing problems of racial discrimination, arms sales abroad, the proliferation of nuclear materials, draft resisters, criminal justice.

Richard Nixon, it should be remembered, appointed more Federal judges than any President in history, including four to the Supreme Court. *That* made a difference. Besides, when Mr. McCarthy lumps Mr. Ford and Mr. Carter together as two peas in a pod, the obvious implication is that Mr. McCarthy *is* different.

Most Americans probably don't know, however, what Eugene McCarthy stands for in 1976. And there's a paradox—without sufficient funds, without participation in the debates, without attention from the press for anything but his supposed "spoiler's" role, he has had nothing like the opportunity of the major candidates to justify his candidacy on its own merits.

In the long run, that's the real problem Mr. McCarthy has posed—not so much that he's a threat to the Democrats as that two-party dominance gave him little chance to be anything else.

October 26, 1976

Labor's Drive for Carter Is Biggest It Has Made in a Presidential Race

By WARREN WEAVER Jr.
Special to The New York Times

CLEVELAND, Oct. 25 — In the drab, dusty basement of Sidney Hillman Hall, a continuous murmur of overlapping female voices is punctuated by the squeak of telephone pushbuttons and the scratch of pencils on green and white computer printouts.

"Mr. Krupa?" Esther Yarbrough asked on one of the 20 phones. "I'm calling from the union office. We're taking a poll of voter opinion. What do you think is the biggest problem facing us today? I see, inflation. In the election on Tuesday, Nov. 2, do you think you'll vote for the Democratic candidate, Carter, or the Republican candidate, Ford?"

Possible Key for Carter

A brief pause, then Mrs. Yarbrough said: "Oh, you're going for a change. Well, don't forget to get out and vote. Thank you, goodbye." Then she checked off a vote for Jimmy Carter on the precinct printout and moved down to the name and telephone number of Walter Malaski.

That call was an almost infinitesimal part of the biggest, most expensive, best organized and most sophisticated campaign that organized labor has ever conducted in support of a Presidential candidate.

If it succeeds, most national political authorities agree, Jimmy Carter will be the next President of the United States. If it fails, he very likely will not.

The Democratic national chairman, Robert S. Strauss, says that organized labor's ability to produce votes on Nov. 2 is critically important for Mr. Carter and his running mate, Senator Walter F. Mondale. "Labor has to turn out where it is strong," Mr. Strauss declared.

"The labor vote is crucial," Stephen Schlossberg, general counsel of the United Automobile Workers, said. "It includes large numbers of blacks and retired workers and families of union members. The question is whether they'll vote. If they do, the Republicans are finished."

Relations between the Carter campaign and the labor bosses, like those with other elements of the old Democratic coalition, do not appear warm and personal as yet; after all, few of them backed him before his nomination. But political cooperation with labor's hierarchy seems as regular and carefully tended as the new campaign law and vestigial antagonisms will allow.

The pro-Carter status of Stanley Krupa, identified by the Cleveland phone-bank worker, was transferred to a computer-produced 3-by-5-inch card already carrying his name and address, which, in turn, was sorted into a small stack for canvassing along East 71st Street on Election Day. Then, some 900 labor volunteers will pay as many as three visits each to the homes of thousands of certifiable Carter voters in Cuyahoga County.

The labor campaign here, as in many other parts of the country, is sharply focused on precincts statistically identified as the most promising: they all have large numbers of union members, a high ratio of registered Democrats and relatively low voting turnouts in the past. Simply increasing the turnout almost automatically increases the Democratic majority.

Union Districts Stressed

The printouts and canvassing cards used here came from the in-house computer of the American Federation of Labor and Congress of Industrial Organization's Committee on Political Education, on the seventh floor of labor's nerve center two blocks from the White House. Stored there are the names, addresses, wards and precincts of most of the 14.5 million members of the giant labor organization, available for the first time in any national campaign.

Matched with registration, party enrollment and telephone numbers in a painstaking process over the last year, this massive information bank almost certainly represents the most powerful logistical weapon ever available to a Presidential candidate.

For the labor federation, not only the computer but the purpose that it is serving are new. For in 1972, led by an intransigent George Meany, the A.F.L.-C.I.O. withheld the endorsement it traditionally gives Democratic Presidential candidates from Senator George McGovern, and its campaign support was confined to Senate and House candidates.

Centrist labor leaders had backed Senator Hubert H. Humphrey for the nomination, and Mr. Meany, a hawk on the Vietnam issue, was not prepared to align himself with the amateurs, perceived radicals and young people who had managed to engineer the McGovern nomination.

A.F.L.-C.I.O. leaders estimate that about half their members, lacking any union directive, voted for Richard M. Nixon in 1972. But next week, they say, four out of five who go to the polls will support the Carter-Mondale ticket, reflecting labor's renewed moral and organizational commitment to the Democrats.

Perhaps the most important aspect of the 1976 labor drive is that it comes at a time when the Republican national candidates, for the first time in political history, are limited in the amount of money they can spend on their campaign.

In the past, labor has traditionally invested large amounts of money and manpower into Democratic campaigns, but the Republicans were able to compensate by raising and spending more money. Now, under the new campaign law, both parties are operating under $25 million ceilings for the general election, but the supplementary labor campaign remains completely legal.

The law specifically exempts from campaign spending limits the cost of "communications by a corporation to its stockholders and executive or administrative personnel and their families or by a labor organization to its members and their families on any subject."

With only a week to go in the campaign, few if any corporations have taken advantage of this opportunity to support President Ford and Senator Robert J. Dole with mailings or telephone calls to their stockholders and executives, but labor is pouring millions of dollars and manhours into just such "communications."

At the President Ford Committee in Washington, activity aimed at winning a share of the labor vote has not risen above the perfunctory.

Ned Shreve, who is the one-man People for Ford operation, has distributed more than one million copies of a two-page leaflet showing the President talking with a hard-hat worker and stating that the Administration has reduced the inflation rate, increased total employment, opposes forced busing and favors capital punishment. The word Republican does not appear.

"We've only gotten a couple of labor endorsements," Mr. Shreve said, "but in my travels around the country, I'm not finding any strong feelings for Carter, particularly in the more conservative unions. We're taking the position that Ford has the working man's point of view and should get the working man's vote."

Auto Workers Active

While the A.F.L.-C.I.O. effort is by far the largest, a number of other unions, some inside the federation orbit and others outside, are conducting intensive political drives of their own. The United Automobile Workers, for example, are also operating phone banks in the states in which the bulk of their 1.4 million members are situated.

Leonard Woodcock, the auto workers president, was one of the first labor leaders to endorse Mr. Carter during the primaries, and personal enthusiasm for the Democratic ticket appears to run somewhat higher in this union than in some others.

The U.A.W. makes considerable use of many of its 250,000 retired members as campaign workers in the canvassing and telephone programs. They have continuing stake in the union, which bargains for higher pension benefits for those already retired, and they also have plenty of free time to volunteer.

The National Education Association, with its 1.8 million teacher members becoming more politically active, endorsed the Carter-Mondale ticket last month, the first time the organization has endorsed as ticket in a national election. The move was made by the group's 8,000-member Representative Assembly, which voted more than 80 percent for the Democratic candidates.

Breaking new ground for labor political activity, the N.E.A. conducted videotaped interviews with President Ford and Mr. Carter on education issues and then spliced their contrasting replies together into a film that has been circulated to all their state organizations.

Direct Mail for Teachers

Teachers present different sorts of campaign problems than do trade union members, according to Vaughn Baker, political organizer for the N.E.A. She said, for example, that direct mail was very effective because the teachers read more of what they receive than do other voters.

Another union developing into a political force, the American Federation of State, County and Municipal Employees, is conducting a separate computer-generated campaign operation, similar to the COPE project, among its 750,000 members, with telephone calls first identifying registered Carter voters and then prodding them on Election Day.

Generally, under the new campaign law, union political activity must be self-generating. If, for example, a union reprinted and circulated generally an official piece of Carter-Mondale literature, the act would constitute an illegal private contribution to the Democratic candidates.

Under last January's Supreme Court ruling, any person or group can spend any amount of money to support a candidate, as long as the effort is "independent" of his regular campaign and com-

pletely uncoordinated. Some unions have tried to go the independent route while others have shied away.

Al Zack, information director of the A.F.L.-C.I.O., said the federation had not produced any billboards, buttons or bumper stickers on behalf of the Carter-Mondale ticket to avoid any possibility of making an illegal contribution.

The labor organizing effort has apparently reinforced a party registration drive that Mr. Strauss, the Democratic national chairman, calls "the most successful ever made in American politics." While the unions were conducting parallel efforts,

the national committee spent $1.7 million registering some three million new voters in 14 major states, more than twice its goal for the project.

Both party and union leaders caution, however, that registration drive figures are almost always higher than actual net gains, because large numbers of names are purged from the voting rolls periodically in many states and registration sometimes only reflects voters who have moved to new districts.

October 26, 1976

DOLE DENIES TALKING OF 'DEMOCRAT WARS'

By DOUGLAS E. KNEELAND
Special to The New York Times

TERRE HAUTE, Ind., Oct. 27—Senator Robert J. Dole, the Republican Vice-Presidential candidate, insisted today that he had never referred to the four wars in which the United States has been involved in this century as "Democrat wars."

Mr. Dole has been under rather widespread criticism, even among some members of his own party, since he used the phrase in his nationally televised Oct. 15 debate in Houston with Senator Walter F. Mondale, his Democratic counterpart.

Yesterday, in Troy, Ohio, he appeared to go out of his way to withdraw the statement by declaring that World War II and Vietnam were not "partisan wars" or "Democrat" wars, although he continued to maintain that they were the result of "indecision" and "weakness."

Today in an airport news conference here, Senator Dole began to discuss what he termed the Democrats' dependence on wartime economies to cure unemployment.

Asked if he had not meant to back off yesterday from what appeared to be an accusation that the Democrats were responsible for the last four wars, he said:

"No, I'm going back to my premise. I didn't want the media to be confused. I said in the debate, if they want to dredge up the past we can dredge up some of the past."

Pressed as to whether he was still going to refer to "Democrat wars," he replied sharply:

"Never did, I never did."

Later the Senator's press secretary,

Larry Speakes, was asked to show the candidate a quotation from the Oct. 15 debate in which he was responding to a question about Senator Mondale's use of the Watergate issue during the campaign.

The quotation read:

"It is an appropriate topic, I guess, but it's not a very good issue any more than the war in Vietnam would be or World II or World I or the war in Korea— all Democrat wars, all in this century. I figured up the other day, if we added up the killed and wounded in Democrat wars in this century, it would be about 1.6 million Americans, enough to fill the city of Detroit."

Mr. Speakes was asked to inquire why the candidate would have denied using the phrase.

A few moments later, Mr. Speakes returned and said:

"He said you have to look in context at the whole thing. He did not recall this specific quote."

He also quoted Mr. Dole as having repeated that "If it's fair to blame Ford for Watergate, then it's fair to blame the Democrats for the wars."

Asked if Senator Dole had not been arguing that it was not fair to blame the President for Watergate, Mr. Speakes replied:

"That's right."

Then asked if it was therefore unfair to blame the Democrats for the wars, Mr. Speakes said:

"Oh, that's what he's been trying to say all along."

But still later, Mr. Speakes sought out reporters who had been questioning him about the "Democrat wars" issue and wanted to know what he had said.

After being told, Mr. Speakes said cryptically before leaving the room:

"That's not what I meant to say. I meant I didn't want to answer the question."

Insiders in the Dole campaign have acknowledged that they were aware of the criticism that had been evoked by the Senator's remark about "Democrat

wars."They also have said that it had been discussed with the candidate and with their counterparts at the President Ford Committee in the White House.

However, they insist that the Senator has been under no pressure from President Ford or his political advisers to retract the statement.

Here in Terre Haute, Senator Dole spoke before an audience of more than 1,500 students and townspeople at Indiana State University. The crowd was largely enthusiastic, but he encountered a handful of hecklers for one of the few times in his campaign, which usually seeks out friendly Republican audiences.

At one point, a member of Kappa Sigma, the candidate's old fraternity at the University of Kansas, presented him with a plaque that he said showed "the Wabash cannonball chasing a peanut," an allusion to Jimmy Carter, the Democratic Presidential candidate who is a Georgia peanut farmer.

A male voice in the balcony called out: "Chasing him all the way to the White House."

Minutes later Senator Dole was saying, "We're talking about military strength and military spending for only one reason."

"Money," a voice interupted.

"To keep the voice you have just heard free." Senator Dole went on to loud applause.

Another voice called out: "Buy a Ford, Nixon did."

"I suggest you drink some pineapple juice," Mr. Dole replied, drawing laughter with a often-used line.

"It's a lot better for you than peanut butter," he went on, "it doesn't stick to the roof of your mouth."

As the applause rolled from that one, he threw in the stopper:

"Come to think of it, maybe peanut butter would be better in his case."

October 28, 1976

INDEPENDENTS' SWING SPURS FORD COMEBACK

By ROBERT REINHOLD

A sudden swing toward President Ford among independent voters who have hovered in indecision until the final rush of the campaign has helped the President make the most stirring political comeback in decades.

Although both Harry S. Truman in

1948 and Hubert H. Humphrey in 1968 made strong, surging finishes, neither was ever so far behind as Mr. Ford, who trailed Jimmy Carter by 33 points in the opinion polls of late July and by 18 points in late August, on the eve of the heavy campaigning.

The final poll of the campaign by The New York Times and CBS News disclosed that Mr. Ford's stand on the issues, including his vows to combat inflation, and his advantages of experience and incumbency, that had apparently brought about the critical shift among independents.

The evidence indicated that all voters,

especially those who insist they lean toward neither party, now see the two candidates as more sharply divided on issues than previously and are aligning themselves with the candidate whose positions they favor.

Sharp Decline for Carter

All signs in the final poll by The New York Times and CBS News, as well as other major surveys, point to an extraordinarily close election, possibly as tight as the race between John F. Kennedy and Richard M. Nixon in 1960.

The Times/CBS News poll, in which 2,025 registered voters selected at random were interviewed by telephone from Oct. 24 to 27, was not designed to predict the outcome of the election. But it reflects Mr. Carter's precipitous decline, showing that his lead over Mr. Ford has been cut to about a third of what it was when the campaign began around Labor Day and about half what it was at the beginning of October.

The poll showed Mr. Carter still slightly ahead but by a margin so slim that, for the first time in the campaign, it falls within the range of possible error inherent in a sample of this size—about 2.5 percentage points either way.

Moreover, interviewing for the survey was completed before an unusually large percentage of voters—12 percent of the total—had made up their minds. Their last-minute decisions, as well as actual voter turnout, stand to have a significant effect on Tuesday's voting.

In addition to the trend among independents, the survey suggested that the following other factors had contributed to the sudden closeness of the race:

¶President Ford has surged ahead in suburban and small-town areas. While Mr. Carter held a comfortable lead of 8 to 10 points in these areas at the beginning of October, he now appears to be trailing Mr. Ford in the suburbs and running dead even in small towns. This trend is partly offset by gains for the Democrats in the cities.

¶Mr. Ford has reversed the standings in the Eastern states, where he was substantially behind on Labor Day. Mr. Carter has gained slightly in the Middle West in the last few weeks, but there has been little change in the West, which is evenly divided, or in the South, where the Georgian is well ahead.

¶Young voters, surprisingly to some analysts, appear to be losing interest in Mr. Carter. While he was the favorite by 9 points among these under 29 years back around Labor Day, President Ford now seems to hold a slight edge. This

seems to corroborate campus soundings that have detected unexpected sympathy for Mr. Ford among students.

¶The undecided voters among Roman Catholics appear to be going heavily for Mr. Ford. He has gained especially among Eastern Catholics, although Mr. Carter is still ahead nationally among Catholics by about 46 to 40, a slim margin for a Democrat.

¶A possible softening of support for Mr. Carter among blacks, his strongest group. The poll shows that his lead among black voters, which was 76 to 6 a few weeks ago, has been cut to 62 to 13, with many more than before saying they are undecided. Historically, blacks tend to have a much lower turnout than whites, particularly if they are undecided. This could be a critical factor since the survey shows the Ford-Carter race almost dead even among whites.

¶The effort by organized labor to get out the union vote for Mr. Carter may be crucial to the election. Mr. Carter's slight overall edge is derived from his strong 55-to-32 lead among union members.

In a race that has seemed to be dominated by personalities and often by trivialities, the survey suggests that the electorate has finally become more sharply divided on a broad range of issues and has a clearer perception of the philosophical differences between Mr. Ford and Mr. Carter.

Some Go Back to Party

This greater clarity helps to explain the behavior of the independents, who have created the extraordinary shift documented over the last several weeks. The three waves of national polls conducted by The Times and CBS News since early September have witnessed no significant shift among "hard-core" Republicans or Democrats. Republicans have consistently backed Mr. Ford by about 7 to 1, while Democrats have favored Mr. Carter by about 5 to 1.

Independents who said they usually leaned to the Republicans have gradually cast aside any doubts about the President and now support him strongly, by 6 to 1. Similarly, independents leaning

Democratic have come around to Mr. Carter, although less enthusiastically, about 3 to 1.

So the balance has rested in the hands of the "pure" independents, those who insist they prefer neither major party. Back in early September this group was closely divided, but heavily (34 percent) undecided. Since then about half of these undecided voters have made up their minds, and almost all have chosen Mr. Ford, who leads 52 to 31 percent among these independent voters.

The explanation for this seems to be, in part, that these independents are essentially conservative and, as the issues crystallized, they have gravitated toward Mr. Ford. This is particularly true on economic matters; they were more likely than other voters, for example, to feel inflation was a greater problem than was unemployment.

Today those independents are twice as likely to say they agree with Mr. Ford rather than Mr. Carter on the issues, whereas they perceived much less difference two months ago. At the same time, the data show, Mr. Carter is seen as more of a liberal than he was in September.

If the patterns discerned in the survey hold up in the election Tuesday, it may well be that, despite years of political upheaval, 1976 will witness a return to the political divisions of the 1960 election. When the respondents in the Times/CBS poll who are considered most likely to vote and have decided are examined, they break down remarkably like the voters in the 1960 Nixon-Kennedy contest.

For example, Democrats in The Times/CBS sample divide 83 to 17 for Carter. In 1960, according to the Gallup Poll, they voted 84-16 for President Kennedy. Republicans in the new survey prefer Mr. Ford, 88-12; in 1960 they divided 95-5 for Mr. Nixon. And independents this year divide 58-42 for Mr. Ford. In 1960 they preferred Mr. Nixon, 57-43.

In the 1960 election the popular-vote margin for Mr. Kennedy was less than half of one percent of the national vote.

October 31, 1976

CARTER VICTOR IN TIGHT RACE; FORD LOSES NEW YORK STATE; DEMOCRATS RETAIN CONGRESS

By R. W. APPLE Jr.

Jimmy Carter won the nation's Bicentennial Presidential election yesterday, narrowly defeating President Ford by sweeping his native South and adding enough Northern industrial states to give him a bare electoral vote majority.

Three of the closely contested battleground states slipped into Mr. Carter's column shortly after midnight—New York, Pennsylvania and Texas. The President-designate lost New Jersey and Michigan, Mr. Ford's home state, while Ohio, Illinois and California were still up for

grabs.

New York teetered between the rivals for hours, contrary to all expectations, before delivering a small majority to Mr. Carter—a majority that gave the Democrat a bonanza of 41 electoral votes.

When Mr. Carter finally carried Hawaii by a far narrower margin than customary for Democratic candidates in that Democratic stronghold, it gave the Georgian 272 electoral votes in 23 states, two more than a majority. Mr. Ford had 160 electoral votes in 23 states, and five states were still in doubt.

A Southern Victor

Mr. Carter was the first man from the Deep South to be elected President in a century and a quarter, and Mr. Ford, the nation's first appointive President, was the first incumbent to lose a Presidential election since Herbert Hoover.

Although the President dominated the Plains and Mountain regions, he lost several middle-sized states that he had counted upon. Among them were Louisiana and Mississippi on the Gulf Coast, and Wisconsin, which went to the Democrats for only the second time in a quarter-century as the result of an outpouring of votes from industrial Milwaukee and liberal Madison.

Mr. Carter owed large debts to Mayor Frank L. Rizzo of Philadelphia, who produced the 250,000-vote margin Mr. Carter needed to carry Pennsylvania; to Robert S. Strauss, the Democratic national chairman, who worked tirelessly to put together the Texas operation, and to the South and the Border states as a whole. The Georgian won every Border state and every Southern state except Virginia, which seemed headed for the Ford column.

Division of Popular Vote

The popular vote, which was swelled by a relatively heavy turnout to roughly the same level as four years ago, appeared likely to split 51 percent for Mr. Carter, 48 for Mr. Ford and 1 for others.

With 81 percent of the nation's precincts reporting, the vote was:

Carter ..... 33,684,344—51 percent
Ford ...... 31,665,958—48 percent

In the metropolitan area, Mr. Carter lost both New Jersey and Connecticut, as his backers had feared he would.

All 25,000 voting machines in New York were ordered impounded by State Supreme Court Justice Edward S. Conway. Acting at the request of state Republican officials, with the approval of White House officials, he said the closeness of the vote made the impoundment necessary.

Mr. Carter and Mr. Ford were running a dead heat in Ohio, but the voting pattern in Cuyahoga County (Cleveland) suggested that the Democrat might be able to pull out a very narrow victory. He ran strongly in the Appalachian area.

In Illinois, Mr. Ford's vote in the suburbs and Mr. Carter's vote in the city of Chicago closely matched the figures in the fianl Chicago Sun-Times straw poll, which showed a virtual tie. But Mayor Richard J. Daley reportedly assured Democratic leaders that the state would tip Democratic.

As advertised, the race was harrowingly close in a large number of states. With the count nearly complete in Iowa, Mr. Carter held a 141-vote lead. As the tabulation wore on in Maine, Mr. Ford led by 31 votes. At one point, Mr. Carter led in Hawaii by 877 votes.

Former Senator Eugene J. McCarthy of Minnesota, running as an independent candidate, appeared to hold the balance of power in at least two hard-fought states, Ohio and Oregon.

From the beginning of the count, most of the states fell as they had been expected to. Kentucky and Indiana, the first

two to report substantial returns, appeared to be following the predictions closely, with Mr. Carter approaching 55 percent in Kentucky and Mr. Ford the same figure in Indiana.

Partial returns and interviews with party leaders indicated that the former Georgia Governor was holding his Southern base and leading in the East. But the President was narrowly ahead in the Middle West and the two nominees were virtually deadlocked in the West.

Mr. Carter appeared to be winning enormous margins among both blacks and Latin-Americans; in fact, early figures indicated that Mr. Ford was narrowly ahead among white voters, according to early results of a CBS News survey of voters as they left their polling places.

The CBS News poll, which covered about 10,000 voters and was made available to The New York Times under a special arrangement, indicated that the Presidential balloting was breaking along partisan lines, with nearly 90 percent of the Republicans backing Mr. Ford and more than 80 percent of the Democrats backing Mr. Carter.

Independents held the key, and they were going to the President by a narrow margin. But it was not clear early last night if the trend would continue or be strong enough to give Mr. Ford a victory. Almost a quarter of the independents said they had made up their minds in the last five days of a campaign that perplexed much of the electorate.

Reports from a number of states indicated that labor unions, which had supported the Carter campaign with an unusually sophisticated, computer-designed vote-pulling operation, were playing a major role in the surprisingly large turnout.

The weather was splendid across the country, and reports of jammed voting places poured in from state after state. In New York, the turnout was said to be "astonishingly heavy"; in Minnesota, voters appeared at the polls in "fantastically high" numbers; in Rhode Island, there were long lines. Mr. Carter's Illinois manager, Paul Sullivan, declared that "apathy is dead" and said he was "jumping for joy."

Mary Singleton, director of elections in Florida, was saying, before the polls closed, that voting in her state would reach the highest level since 1952, despite months of predictions that as little as half of the voting age population might choose to vote.

President Ford cast his ballot at an elementary school in his old Congressional district in Grand Rapids, Mich., said an emotional farewell to his fellow townspeople and returned to Washington to await the verdict of the voters.

He wept as he watched the unveiling of an airport mural depicting his life and

told the audience, struggling to maintain his composure, that he owed everything to his mother and father. He was obviously completely exhausted.

Mr. Carter was the 11th person to vote in Plains, Ga., the rural hamlet he left 22 months ago to begin a quest for the Presidency that was dimissed as an absurdity by the elders of his party until he won his first primary victories. He spent five minutes marking the long Georgia ballot, then commented that he had voted for "Walter Mondale and his running mate."

"I feel a sense of satisfaction," the slight, 52-year-old peanut farmer said. "I did the best that I could."

Senator Mondale voted in Afton, Minn., and Senator Robert J. Dole, Mr. Ford's running mate, in Russell, Kan.

Mr. Carter, a former naval officer who served a single term as Governor of Georgia, started as a lonely campaigner, short on money, staff and national recognition. But he was relentless in his early effort, meeting voters in two's and three's, and it slowly began to pay off in his campaign against such better-known figures as Senators Birch Bayh and Henry M. Jackson, Representative Morris K. Udall and Gov. George C. Wallace.

He won the Jan. 19 caucuses in Iowa and that gave him a bit of publicity. Then he proved that he could win a primary in New Hampshire, and he dispatched Mr. Wallace in Florida. Finally, victories in two of the big industrial states—Pennsylvania and Ohio—brought the party leaders to his side.

Mr. Ford took office in the shadow of Watergate and won high marks for restoring a measure of candor to the White House. But as the first appointed President, he lacked the strong hold on voters' emotions that most incumbents have, and he had to battle for more than six months to beat back a challenge from former Gov. Ronald Reagan of California, a telegenic conservative who came within a hair's breath of beating him.

It seemed after the conventions that Mr. Carter would win in a walk—or at least it seemed so from the polls.

But Mr. Carter found the general-election campaign more difficult than the primary campaign, and his lead began to shrink after Labor Day. An interview with Playboy magazine in which the Georgian used earthy language and a lackluster performance in the first of three televised debates hurt his cause.

By the time the President emerged from his passive, Rose Garden campaign for 11 days of furious stumping to conclude the campaign, it appeared that he had a chance of pulling off an upset. And when the campaign ended on Monday, the national polls showed the race a toss-up —too close to call.

November 3, 1976

Carter Victory Tied to Democrats Back in Fold, Plus Independents

By ROBERT REINHOLD

Jimmy Carter, in the final analysis, won the Presidency by holding together the basic elements of the old Democratic coalition, drawing back many of those who had strayed in recent years and chipping away at enough independent-

minded Republicans to compile a slim margin over President Ford.

Fundamentally, the result reflected the classic partisan and social class divisions known to American voters of a generation ago. The volatile election boiled

down to a contest between incumbency and artisanship, and ultimately party loyalty prevailed to the Democrat's advantage.

But Mr. Carter was apparently able to retain enough of his image as an iconoclastic independent to make substantial dents in some traditionally Republican segments of the electorate, like white Protestants, as well as draw back many of those who have strayed from the Democratic Party in recent years, like Southerners and conservative Democrats. Surveys suggest that had Senator Hubert H. Humphrey of Minnesota run instead of

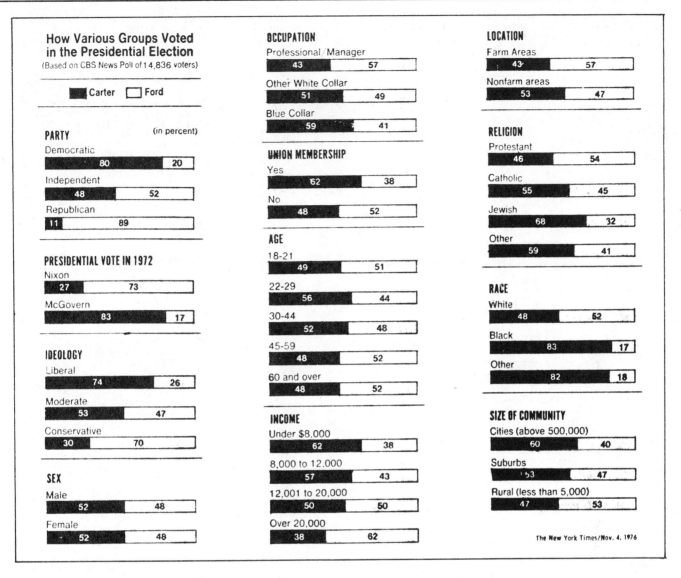

How Various Groups Voted in the Presidential Election
(Based on CBS News Poll of 14,836 voters)

■ Carter □ Ford

PARTY (in percent)

Democratic — Carter 80, Ford 20
Independent — Carter 48, Ford 52
Republican — Carter 11, Ford 89

PRESIDENTIAL VOTE IN 1972

Nixon — Carter 27, Ford 73
McGovern — Carter 83, Ford 17

IDEOLOGY

Liberal — Carter 74, Ford 26
Moderate — Carter 53, Ford 47
Conservative — Carter 30, Ford 70

SEX

Male — Carter 52, Ford 48
Female — Carter 52, Ford 48

OCCUPATION

Professional/Manager — Carter 43, Ford 57
Other White Collar — Carter 51, Ford 49
Blue Collar — Carter 59, Ford 41

UNION MEMBERSHIP

Yes — Carter 62, Ford 38
No — Carter 48, Ford 52

AGE

18-21 — Carter 49, Ford 51
22-29 — Carter 56, Ford 44
30-44 — Carter 52, Ford 48
45-59 — Carter 48, Ford 52
60 and over — Carter 48, Ford 52

INCOME

Under $8,000 — Carter 62, Ford 38
8,000 to 12,000 — Carter 57, Ford 43
12,001 to 20,000 — Carter 50, Ford 50
Over 20,000 — Carter 38, Ford 62

LOCATION

Farm Areas — Carter 43, Ford 57
Nonfarm areas — Carter 53, Ford 47

RELIGION

Protestant — Carter 46, Ford 54
Catholic — Carter 55, Ford 45
Jewish — Carter 68, Ford 32
Other — Carter 59, Ford 41

RACE

White — Carter 48, Ford 52
Black — Carter 83, Ford 17
Other — Carter 82, Ford 18

SIZE OF COMMUNITY

Cities (above 500,000) — Carter 60, Ford 40
Suburbs — Carter 53, Ford 47
Rural (less than 5,000) — Carter 47, Ford 53

The New York Times/Nov. 4, 1976

Mr. Carter, President Ford would very likely have won Tuesday.

Interviews After Vote

From interviews with tens of thousands of voters sampled by CBS News as they emerged from the voting booths across the country, the following are some of the major factors that contributed to Mr. Carter's edge in the popular vote:

¶The massive effort for the Democratic ticket by organized labor apparently succeeded. President Ford led by 52 to 48 percent among the three-quarters of voters in the survey who come from nonunion households. But Mr. Carter's 61-to-38 margin among those from union backgrounds was enough to tip the balance.

¶Mr. Carter's 5-to-1 advantage among blacks may well have been crucial. President Ford would probably have won in an all-white America, by 51 to 48. Although Mr. Carter's margin among blacks, a group he carefully courted, was a little higher than average for a Democratic candidate, he did not do so well as Senator George McGovern did four years ago or Hubert H. Humphrey in 1968.

¶The presence of Senator Walter F. Mondale on the ticket for Vice President, along with Mr. Carter's performance in the debates, seems to have helped offset voter doubts and misgivings about Mr. Carter as a person. The many voters who cited the Vice-Presidential choice as a major factor in casting their votes went overwhelmingly for the Democratic ticket.

¶Mr. Ford was unable to pile up enough of a lead among the growing independent segment of the electorate, which is crucial to any Republican because Democrats outnumber Republicans by two to one. The President won only 51 percent of the independent vote, while previous Republican candidates have received 61 percent on average since 1952. Republicans have needed about two-thirds of the independents to win in recent years.

¶Mr. Ford, who campaigned on the argument that he had restored faith in government, clearly managed to snatch that issue from Mr. Carter. Half of all voters said that was a major issue in their minds and he won, 51-49, among them.

¶The Democrats who defected to Richard M. Nixon in 1972 returned in droves. Six of every 10 such Democrats voted fo Mr. Carter, along with 90 percent of the McGovern Democrats. At the same time, a quarter of the Republicans who said they voted for former Gov. Ronald Reagan of California in the primaries defected to Mr. Carter.

¶Mr. Carter did extraordinarily well, 55-44, among young voters between 22 and 29, while losing the 18-to-21-year-old vote. Just why this should be so is not clear, but one possibility is that these voters' political attitudes were shaped during the turbulent years of protest against the Vietnam war.

Coalition Is Receding

While a Democratic Presidential candidate can normally expect to do well among such traditionally Democratic groups as blue-collar workers, liberals, Catholics and the like, the real question is how well, because the old Franklin D. Roosevelt coalition has been shrinking in recent years with growing affluence and suburbanization.

The answer is that Jimmy Carter did about average with regular Democrats—not spectacularly well, not badly. He won 79 percent of the Democratic vote, which is the average performance of Democrats since 1952. But he won 48 percent of the independents, 10 points higher than average.

The return to old partisan alignments, forecast in pre-election polls by The New York Times and CBS News, emerges clearly in the union vote. Mr. Carter won 61 percent of that vote, about average for Democrats over the years but dramatically better than the 46 percent won by Senator McGovern four years ago.

The power of organized labor is illustrated by the fact that Mr. Carter won 63 percent of the blue-collar workers' vote if they were unionized, but only 54 percent if they were not. Over all, the Georgian won 59 percent of the blue-collar vote, about average, but much better than the 43 percent for Senator McGovern.

The Catholic Vote

Among Catholics, another basic pillar of Democratic strength but a matter of special worry to Mr. Carter during the campaign because of his own Southern Baptist religion and the abortion issue, there was some evidence of weakness. Fifty-four percent of Catholics voted for him, about four points lower than average, if even the vote for John F. Kennedy, the first Catholic President, is excluded.

Mr. Carter succeeded in eating into groups that normally tend to vote Republican. For example, he did better among professional and managerial people than any Democrat in the last quarter century except Lyndon B. Johnson. He won 43 percent of this vote, still a minority but better than the 38 percent average for Democrats over the years. Similarly, he won 50 percent of the vote of other white-collar workers, as compared with a 43 percent previous average.

Protestants, another typically Republican group, also provided Mr. Carter with unusually good support for a Democrat. Whereas Democrats averaged 39 percent of the Protestant vote since 1952, Mr. Carter won 46 percent. This was not merely a reflection of his Southern strength because he did well among Protestants in all regions, particularly the West, suggesting that while his religion may have hurt him among Catholics it may have helped among the majority Protestants.

The Carter candidacy also reversed the long-term Democratic decline in his home region, the South. He earned a larger share of the Southern vote, about 54 percent, than any Democratic candidate in a generation and nearly twice the portion (29 percent) won by Mr. McGovern in 1972.

But the basic core of the Carter support rested on traditional partisan allegiances. And this is well illustrated by examining the "normal vote" one would expect of various groups solely on the basis of party loyalty, excluding short-term factors in the campaign.

When this is done, the "expected" vote conforms fairly closely to the actual in many groups. For example, union members would be expected to vote 62 percent for Mr. Carter; the actual margin was 61 percent. The corresponding figures for Catholics are 58 and 54 percent, Protestants, 56 and 46 percent, Jews, 67 and 68 percent.

November 4, 1976

South's Blacks Credit Their Votes With Winning Election for Carter

By THOMAS A. JOHNSON
Special to The New York Times

COLUMBUS, Miss., Nov. 5—Several black laborers and domestic workers fortified themselves against the 50-degree chill this morning with country sausages, eggs and grits cooked by Mary Johnson at Smith's Cafe, a tiny place that clings unobtrusively to this town's small shopping center. They compared stories about how they had "elected ourselves a President."

"The woman I work for told me to make sure that I voted for President Ford," a domestic worker said, "and I said 'Yes, ma'm, I certainly will.'"

The breakfast crowd laughed loudly, knowing what was coming.

"I went straight to the polls and voted for Carter," the woman said. And when the laughter died down, she added, more quietly, "I've worked for that white woman for as long as I can remember, and she still thinks I'm a damn fool."

Whether secretly or openly, blacks in the Deep South gave President-elect Jimmy Carter more than 95 percent of their vote. More than 65 percent of registered black voters went to the polls, according to the Atlanta-based Voter Education Project.

Praises President Johnson

"I was scared to death when Johnson, a Southerner, became President," said A. L. Henderson, a farmer who lives south of Reform, Ala., "but he turned out to be just about the best President for the colored folks."

They expressed neither fear nor elation about Mr. Carter's Southern ties, but rather hoped aloud that, as a Southerner, he "might turn out to be like L.B.J."

Several people in the cafe said that Mr. Carter had a better understanding than President Ford of the need to rid the nation of racial prejudice, especially "that deep down 'I-hates-a-nigger-and-would-rather-die-than-change' kind of prejudice," as C. T. Gilmore, a lumber worker near West Point, Miss., put it.

Blacks account for about 40 percent of the population in the Mississippi-Alabama border region, dominating districts where their great-grandfathers had been slaves on vast cotton plantations.

As the white landowners mechanized their farming and diversified into soybeans, cattle and pine trees, the poorer blacks became surplus labor. They now constitute the majority of the region's numerous unemployed workers, and many have moved from the region.

In the heavily black rural communities along the Mississippi-Alabama border, black voters saw Mr. Carter as "the only hope to change things," "an end to the Nixon-Ford scoundrels and their foolishness" and, repeatedly, as representing "a chance for black folks to get some jobs."

William B. Harris, a recruiter of rural blacks for jobs in the construction industry, expressed black voters' thoughts this way: "Of course we don't know what Carter will do in the final analysis, but we had to kick those other fellows out because they didn't do what they should have done when they had the chance."

A decade ago the civil rights movement concentrated here in "the black belt," named for both the color of some of its soil and the size of its black population, and blacks have increasingly involved themselves in politics since that time.

And since the region, like much of the "Sunbelt," expects a major economic boom, black political activism has been extended to the demands that blacks share equally in the region's economic development. This region is particularly concerned with the $2.6 billion in new industry that the 253-mile Tennessee-Tombigbee Waterway is expected to bring.

With his widely publicized vetoes of employment bills, President Ford has been compared in this region with "the rich white folks who don't really care whether black folks improve themselves or not," said Albert Temple, a mechanic just south of this town.

But since whites do control black incomes in this region, deception, like that used by the domestic worker, has long been an accepted practice among blacks.

A young professional woman in Meridian, Miss., said this was "the South's most valued tradition—hypocrisy. She added. "You see white folks can condemn what they call 'Federal giveaways' like poverty programs while they get rich on Federal farm subsidies and Government building programs. In this atmosphere, black folks see nothing wrong with lying to white folks—it's almost our sacred ethnic duty."

November 6, 1976

The Future of the G.O.P.

After the debacle of the recent election, the Republican Party—at the grassroots level—would seem to have no place to go but up. Although Mr. Ford managed in the end to turn the Presidential campaign into a close race, his party suffered a severe disappointment at every other level.

The hard-fought Senate contests ended in a standoff with the Democrats retaining their 62-to-38 margin. Instead of regaining all or many of the seats they lost in the House of Representatives two years ago, Republicans—if present trends hold in undecided elections—will actually have suffered a net loss of two seats. Democrats will once again have a 2-to-1 majority.

In the voting for governors and state legislators, the

results were equally poor. The G.O.P. in this election continued its post-Watergate slide and now has one less governorship than before Nov. 2 instead of making the net gain of two or three that many observers had expected. Beginning in January, the G.O.P. will have only 12 governorships instead of the 17 it held a dozen years ago, after the Goldwater debacle.

Throughout the Middle West from Ohio to Iowa, Republicans began losing town and county offices and state legislative seats in 1964—and many of them have never been regained. This trend has now spread to New York and California, where in the aftermath of the Rockefeller and Reagan administrations, the party is weaker than ever before.

*   *   *

What do these grim statistics portend for the G.O.P.? For the immediate future, they mean that the party heads toward 1980 with aging, battle-scarred leaders. At 65, Ronald Reagan would seem too old to contemplate another Presidential race in four years' time; but with the defeat of Senators William Brock of Tennessee and James Buckley of New York, he is still the only widely known conservative.

His chief rival is likely to be ex-Democrat John B. Connally. Although he was hurt by his inability to carry Texas for the Ford-Dole ticket, Mr. Connally convinced his new party that he—unlike Mr. Reagan—did make a maximum effort to achieve victory.

The 1976 election proved, however, what moderate Republicans had long contended. With a good campaign, their party can still win at the Presidential level, or at least make a close race in the East and the industrial Middle West. Mr. Ford carried Connecticut, New Jersey,

Michigan and Illinois, and came very near in New York and Ohio. Had he adopted somewhat more progressive policies in the last two years and chosen a more sympathetic running mate, he might easily have reversed the outcome. If Mr. Ford, a drab campaigner, was able to do as well as he did, the opportunity obviously exists for a more exciting and constructive candidate making a moderate appeal.

But the ideological fanaticism of conservative Republicans is so intense that such moderate conservatives as Senator Percy of Illinois and Secretary of Commerce Richardson have become stigmatized in many party circles as hopelessly liberal. In these circumstances, a totally new figure such as Governor-elect James R. Thompson of Illinois probably has better prospects.

*   *   *

If President-elect Carter can turn his personal triumph in the South into a viable biracial coalition, the Republican Southern strategy will stay wrecked for a long time to come. In that event, Republicans will have to emulate Mr. Ford's course in the recent campaign, building upon G.O.P. strength in the Great Plains and the Mountain States and trying to pull out victory in the East and Middle West. That would augur well for a genuinely competitive two-party system.

But a "big state" strategy can succeed only if Republicans prove themselves responsive to the actual problems of the declining cities and the inflation-strained suburbs. As the defeat of President Ford and Senator Buckley demonstrated, neither an amiable personality nor an orthodox conservatism is sufficient to rebuild the decayed bases of the once-dominant G.O.P.

November 10, 1976

REPUBLICANS SELECT BROCK AS PARTY HEAD

Tennessean Defeats Four Others —Victory Appears to Assure Control by Conservatives

By WARREN WEAVER Jr.
Special to The New York Times

WASHINGTON, Jan. 14—Bill Brock, a 46-year-old conservative from Tennessee, was elected chairman of the Republican National Committee today, winning a spirited five-man competition that required three secret ballots to resolve.

Mr. Brock, who was a Senator until he lost his seat in last November's election, defeated Richard Richards of Utah, a national committee member supported by adherents of Ronald Reagan. Mr. Richards was never able to advance beyond his 48 first ballot votes, with 81 needed for election.

Of the five candidates for the post, Mr. Brock was regarded by many committee members as the best qualified to represent the party as a national spokesman. His competitors generally emphasized their qualifications as political technicians rather than as charismatic leaders.

Conservative Choice

The choice of Mr. Brock as national chairman appeared to insure that the Republican Party would remain under firm conservative control in the year ahead, with its moderate and liberal elements effectively cut off from any position of real influence.

However, the former Senator was a supporter of President Ford against Mr. Reagan during the long 1976 primary fight, and it remains to be seen whether his leadership will prove satisfactory to the followers of the former California governor.

With the selection of Mr. Brock for a one-year term, the Republicans completed the triumvirate of new party leadership, which includes Senator Howard H. Baker Jr., also of Tennessee, and Representative John J. Rhodes of Arizona, the Congressional minority leaders.

Policy Committee Formed

Tomorrow the national committee is expected to authorize creation of a new Republican policy committee, whose chairman will rank with the Congressional and committee leaders. That group will include a broad range of elected officials, senior strategists and theoreticians.

In addition to Mr. Richards, Mr. Brock defeated Robert S. Carter, now co-chairman of the national committee; Arthur Fletcher, a White House aide believed to be the first black ever to seek the post; and Kent B. McGough, the Ohio state chairman.

Buehl Berentson, former executive director of the Republican Governors Association, and Thomas S. Milligan, the Indiana state chairman, dropped out of the race before this morning's nominating session. Frederick K. Biebel, the Connecticut chairman, who had considered running, never came to the point of announcing his candidacy.

A number of moderate party leaders ended up supporting Mr. Brock today, not because they shared his ideological position but because they believed that Mr. Richards was too closely identified with the Reagan wing of the party.

With 161 national committee members voting, Mr. Brock got 54 votes to Mr. Richards's 48 on the first ballot. On the second, the Tennessean rose to 70 while Mr. Richards remained at 48. On the third, Mr. Brock won with 90 while his chief rival fell off to 46.

In a brief acceptance speech, Mr. Brock said that the Republican party had "the makings of the greatest new majority this country has ever seen" in the 48 percent vote that President Ford received in November, plus new recruits among nonvoters and disaffected Democrats.

'Awesome Responsibility'

The fact that Democratic candidates occupy such a large share of state and Federal public offices, the new chairman contended, gives Republicans "an incredible opportunity and the most awesome responsibility this party has faced in the last 50 years."

As for black voters, Mr. Brock said, "We must intensify our efforts for their support, because we care deeply about those individuals who have been discriminated against."

January 15, 1977

MAYOR RICHARD DALEY OF CHICAGO DIES AT 74

Last of the Big-City Democratic Bosses Has Heart Attack

By PAUL DELANEY
Special to The New York Times

CHICAGO, Dec. 20—Mayor Richard J. Daley, head of this city's Democratic machine and one of the most powerful Democrats in the country for more than two decades, died today of a heart attack.

The 74-year-old Mayor, last of the big-city bosses, was stricken after 2 P. M. and collapsed on his way to lunch on the Near North Side. He was taken to the office of his private physician, at 900 North Michigan Avenue, where he was treated as emergency equipment and vehicles stood by. He was pronounced dead at 2:55 o'clock.

Earlier in the day, Mayor Daley attended the annual Christmas breakfast for department heads, where they surprised him with round-trip tickets to Ireland for him and Mrs. Daley. At noon, during dedication ceremonies for a new gymnasium on the Far South Side, he was asked to shoot the first basketball. He sank the shot on his first try.

The portly, red-cheeked Irish-American was elected in 1975 to his sixth four-year term. The previous year he had suffered a stroke that kept him from his civic duties for four months, leading to speculation, even among close associates and friends, that he would not be able to run again. He not only won, but scored overwhelming victories in the primary and general elections, as usual.

The Mayor will be immediately succeeded by Alderman Wilson Frost, president pro tem of the City Council. Mr. Frost, who is black, will serve until the council convenes a special meeting to elect an acting Mayor from among the Aldermen. Then, a special election will be set within three months for the remaining two-and-one-half years of Mayor Daley's term.

However, confusion set in immediately over the procedure for succession. Mr. Frost, arriving at City Hall, was asked whether he was now the Acting Mayor, in accordance with the law.

"Yes, I am," remarked the top-ranking black associate of Mayor Daley.

But Deputy Mayor Kenneth Sain said it was his understanding that there would be no Acting Mayor until the council holds its election.

The death leaves the city's Democratic machine in disarray. There never was a successor because the Mayor never allowed a line of succession to develop. Therefore, political observers expect a pitched battle among the Democrats not only for Mayor, but for party chairman, a post Mr. Daley also held. The battle is seen developing among the following factions:

¶Some of his old contemporaries and possibly one of his sons will make a try at taking over. They include his son, Senator Richard M. Daley; Secretary of State Michael J. Howlett, the Mayor's hand-picked candidate in a losing effort in the gubernatorial race last month; Lieut. Gov. Neil F. Hartigan, another of the Mayor's losers last month, and Alderman Michael A. Bilandic.

¶Younger machine politicians frustrated over the tight-fisted control of the party machinery by the Mayor are a factor. Among them are Alderman Edward R. Vrdolyak and Edward M. Burke.

¶The independents, who bitterly opposed Mayor Daley, are not expected to be much more of a threat with his death.

¶Blacks represent the biggest single block of voters in the city, and are crucial to the success of the machine. But they are severely divided, with some tied tightly to the machine.

In Command Since 1955

The Mayor had dominated politics in this city since his first term, in 1955, after working his way up from precinct politics. He also became a force in national Democratic politics as Illinois was one of those key, big industrial states that have been crucial to Democratic Presidential aspirants.

But recent times showed a definite decline in his power. He lost several posts that helped him maintain that power, including the Governor's seat and the office of State's Attorney. The decline could also be seen in the state legislature, where his forces have suffered several major setbacks, including attempts to seek additional funds for Chicago's schools.

As in life, a veil of secrecy surrounded the events of the Mayor's last minutes. For two hours, the nature of his illness was left to unconfirmed reports of his choking on food while eating with friends to collapsing on the sidewalk. The police closed off the section around the office building as throngs of holiday shoppers on the avenue talked about the unknown illness.

Doctors from Northwestern University's Hospital, four blocks away, were called in and emergency equipment, including an ambulance, stood by as reports circulated that the ill Mayor would be taken to the hospital. And at Northwestern, there were reports that medical personnel were standing by awaiting his arrival.

Then the Announcement

This went on for nearly two hours, and even when the ambulance wheeled away, its rear window covered, many persons thought it was taking him to the hospital. It was finally announced at about 4 P.M. by Mr. Kenneth Sain that Mayor Daley had died.

Later, the Mayor's physician, Dr. Thomas J. Coogan Jr., said Mr. Daley had come to his office complaining about chest pains. The doctor said he took a cardiogram and left the examining room to alert the hospital that the Mayor would be coming over. When he returned to the room, Dr. Coogan said he found that Mr. Daley had been stricken.

The doctor worked on the Mayor, assisted by his associate. They were joined by fire department paramedics and doctors from Northwestern University. They worked on him until 3:40.

Dr. Coogan said while he was out of the room the Mayor spoke to his son, Richard M. Daley, on the telephone. The Mayor's wife, Eleanor, and their three daughters and four sons and their wives were with him at the time of death.

Dr. Coogan said the Mayor died of ventricular fibrillation, a disordered heartbeat that he termed "one of the lethal rhythms of the heart."

Unchallenged Leader

By SETH S. KING

In any case study of America's great political machines, it is commonly accepted that the Cook County Democratic organization is the largest, richest and the last in the nation still at full thrust.

For more than 20 years the unchallenged driver of this awesomely powerful vehicle was Richard J. Daley.

From the day in 1953 when he seized its controls until he died, Mr. Daley drove the Cook County machine, and the machine directed virtually every municipal function performed for the people of Chicago and many of those offered residents of the suburbs in Cook County that surround Chicago on three sides.

Knew Ward Functions

He understood every bolt and gear in the machine, and how to utilize its power. No detail of its functions was too small for him to bother with, even after 20 years at its head. He understood the block by block development of the machine, beginning with the precinct captains, who held card files on every resident in their precinct and who called on every one of them before Election Day to make certain that each understood whom the organization was supporting.

He knew the workings of the ward committeemen, who directed the precinct captains and stood ready to see that the garbage of the faithful voters was picked up and the potholes in their streets were filled.

And he understood the use of the more than 35,000 city and county jobs (non-civil service) available to those machine's workers who delivered the vote in their precincts.

The wealthy captains of Chicago's industry and real estate, most of whom are Republicans and live in the suburbs, knew little of Richard Daley 20 years ago. But they soon learned that he was as eager for their prosperity and expansion as they were, and they soon put aside philosophical differences they may have had with him and became reliable sources of funds and approval. In return, they could count on the machine for the best of tax breaks and the least of zoning problems.

For almost all of those 20 years, Mr. Daley was also the dominating force among Illinois Democrats. And with his tight grip on the state's large convention delegation, he had been one of the most potent figures in the selection of the Democratic Party's Presidential candidates.

"Daley means the whole ball game" the late Senator Robert F. Kennedy once said when assessing the deciding factors in Democratic conventions.

The Mayor did indeed play a major role in gaining the Democratic Presidential nominations in 1952 and again in 1956 for Adlai E. Stevenson, whose election as Governor of Illinois had depended heavily on Mr. Daley's efforts.

The Mayor, who already had an abiding friendship with Joseph P. Kennedy, a fellow Irish-American whom he understood and appreciated, was certainly the decisive force in nominating John F. Kennedy in 1960 and electing him President that fall.

The Mayor delivered a 465,000-vote plurality in Cook County for Mr. Kennedy, and many political scholars still insist that the Cook County machine's ability to produce badly needed votes from the graveyards was what won Illinois for Mr. Kennedy, who carried the state by a feeble 8,858 votes and thus defeated Richard M. Nixon in the nation.

Rowdy Convention

Mr. Daley savored his convention roles and he was delighted, in 1968, when Chicago was once again selected as the site of the Democratic National Convention. But this pleasure turned sour when the already divided and disorganized Democrats belabored each other in the party's worst brawl and the Chicago police bloodied the strident young antiwar activists outside the Amphitheatre in teargas turmoil.

Few who followed these antics will ever forget the televised sequence showing Mr. Daley drawing a finger across his jowls in a signal to the podium to cut the microphones as Senator Abraham A. Ribicoff spoke of things the Mayor did not want heard.

Hubert H. Humphrey, Mr. Daley's candidate, won the 1968 nomination. But the Democratic Party was left in shambles and Mr. Daley was looked upon by many in the national party as an anachronistic ogre. While the Democrats in Chicago, as well as many of his nonpolitical constituents, still regarded their Mayor with admiration, his standing in the national party suffered still further.

Senator George McGovern and the young liberals in the party who supported him were alien to Mr. Daley and so were the organizational reforms Mr. McGovern pushed onto the national party. The Mayor ignored these reforms and in 1972 suffered the ignominy of rejection when Alderman William Singer, a brash young independent Democrat, joined with the Rev. Jesse L. Jackson, the black leader of Operation PUSH, to unseat the Daley-controlled convention delegation. The Mayor went to the convention in Miami, but its doors were closed to him.

Back in the Fold

The aging Mayor was welcomed back to the National Democratic fold in the wake of Mr. McGovern's defeat. He was once again courted by the nation's party regulars at the Democrats' miniconvention in Kansas City in 1974.

But last November's election showed clearly that his influence in statewide politics was eroding. He turned out 65 percent of the city's vote for Mr. Carter, but he could not pull in enough downstate support to win Illinois for the former Georgia Governor.

No one was a more thorough product of his environment than Richard J. Daley. He was born on May 15, 1902, in a modest brick house in the Bridgeport neighborhood of Chicago, the son of an Irish-American sheet-metal worker and union activist. He grew up on that same block and when he died he was still living in another modest brick bungalow at 3536 South Lowe Avenue, a few doors down from his birthplace.

Bridgeport was a tough, blue-collar area of Irish-Catholics, part of the "Back of the Yards" district west of Chicago's odorous stockyards and packing houses.

Mr. Daley attended the neighborhood parochial schools and De La Salle Institute, a Catholic secondary school. Short and powerfully built, he played hard, fought hard in the neighborhood gangs, and from an early age worked hard, delivering papers and later pushing cattle through the stockyard pens.

But the stockyards were no place that young Daley wanted to spend his life, and he quickly recognized that in Chicago, an Irish Catholic boy could find happiness and a good living in politics.

Mr. Daley became a precinct captain when he was 21 and shortly thereafter, putting the stenographic training he had received at De La Salle to good use, he became a clerk in the City Council.

His friends and even his detractors agree that he worked hard, stayed sober and never appeared to lose his vision of power at the top of the political heap. He held city jobs while he became a ward committeeman and then a legislator, spending nearly 10 years in the State Assembly and State Senate. There he was known as the man who would always attend meetings as he was supposed to, always behaved himself by abstaining from the fleshpots of Springfield, and who became a recognized expert on finance and taxation.

He had also put himself through De-Paul University and its law school. And he had married a neighborhood Irish-American girl named Eleanor Guilfoyle, whom he and everyone else who knew her called "Sis."

As he became a member of the Cook County Democratic Central Committee and his political weight increased, he threw it behind some atypical figures. Mr. Daley was an active force in Adlai Stevenson's successful campaign for Governor in 1948, the election to the Senate that same year of a Chicago University economist named Paul Douglas, and in the surprising victory of Harry S. Truman in Illinois.

Kept on Winning

A grateful Governor Stevenson named Mr. Daley Director of State Revenue. But in 1953, he rose to a far more important pinnacle: Cook County Democratic chairman, the top of the political heap and a position that he would jealously guard until his death.

Two years later, in 1955, when the machine had tired of the amateurish reforms of Mayor Martin J. Kennelly, a Democrat, Mr. Daley led the move to dump Mr. Kennelly. He got himself "drafted" for Mayor and, after a rough primary, smothered Mr. Kennelly.

He then went on to win a free-swinging, Chicago-style general election, replete with the familiar charges of vote fraud, against Republican Alderman Robert Merriam. Every four years after that Mr. Daley ran again and won, each time by an increasingly larger margin as the machine prospered and the Republican opposition became more enfeebled.

In the 22 years that he headed Chicago's municipal government, Mr. Daley became synonymous with the city's image:

burly, rough, powerful, restless and, except for its burgeoning black residents, a study in middle-class prosperity. He quickly became known as a brick and mortar man, and for most of his tenure Chicago grew upward in a continuous building boom.

Not all of this time was smooth. The Mayor suffered the embarassments of periodic police scandals. In his later terms Chicago's whites began fleeing to the suburbs at a rate of 55,000 a year.

As the city's black population grew larger, the machine's control over it slipped. Mr. Daley weathered the painful period of the open-housing marches of the late Rev. Dr. Martin Luther King Jr. in 1966.

But he was emotionally shaken and furious at the rioting and destruction in the city's two black ghettoes in the wake of Dr. King's assassination in April 1968. It was then that he issued his "shoot to

United Press International

At the 1968 convention in Chicago, he physically controlled events.

kill" order on arsonists and placed himself beyond the touch of the blacks.

In his final term the machine still had the city's throttle in its grip. It still tolerated nothing more than verbal opposition from without and maintained the strictest obedience from within. The Mayor had the unwavering support of virtually all the 50 aldermen on the City Council. Nonetheless, there were misfires that injured his pride and peace of mind.

In the primary of 1972, Dan Walker, a highly successful corporation lawyer, upset all the form sheets by beating Paul Simon, the choice of the Mayor and the regular Democratic organization, in the race for Governor. That fall Mr. Walker, who made many caustic remarks about machine politicians before he made a pre-election peace with Mr. Daley, edged the incumbent Republican, Richard Ogilvie, and became Governor. He also became a rival in Democratic politics to Mr. Daley.

Even more damaging was the machine's defeat in the fall of 1972 in the election for state's attorney, the county chief prosecutor.

Equally as bad, with the election of Richard M. Nixon in 1968, the United States Attorney for the Chicago district was now a Republican. The machine did not rest easily in the Mayor's last years.

Several of the machine's top gears, some of them Mr. Daley's oldest and closest political associates, were indicted on Federal and county charges of conspiracy and bribery, and some were convicted. While none of this implicated Mr. Daley directly, he did suffer the embarrassment of the disclosure of his youngest son John representing a local insurance firm that suddenly got more than $3 million in city insurance premiums, after young Mr. Daley had come to work for the firm as a beginning agent.

Even so, Mr. Daley seemed both politically and physically indestructable as he began his 72d year and his 20th year in office. When he suddenly entered the hospital in early May 1974, it was learned he had suffered a mild stroke and that, while he had appeared as robust and vigorous as ever, he had also been suffering from a mild form of diabetes and high blood pressure.

Mayor Daley is survived by his wife, Eleanor, and by seven children—Richard, Michael, John, William, Mary Carol, Eleanor, and Patricia, and by 10 grandchildren.

December 21, 1976

Alex Rose of Liberal Party, A Power in Politics, Is Dead

By A. H. RASKIN

Alex Rose, leader of a tiny millinery union, who built the Liberal Party into a significant and often-decisive force in New York City, State and national politics, died yesterday at his home in Washington Heights. The 78-year-old confidant of Presidents, governors and mayors had been ill for nearly a year, first with septicemia, a blood infection, and in recent weeks with viral bronchitis, but cancer was the cause of death.

His last public appearance was at the Liberal Party's $125-a-plate campaign dinner, with Jimmy Carter, the party's nominee for the Presidency, seated at his side. For Mr. Rose the dinner, three weeks before Election Day, was a characteristic personal triumph, with notables of both the Democratic and Republican Parties crowding the grand ballroom of the Americana in tribute to the clout of a man who performed major and minor political miracles as vice chairman of a party with only 108,000 enrolled members.

On Election Day, Mr. Rose awoke too ill to go to the polls, the first time he had failed to cast his vote in a half century. He was scheduled to go to Albany Dec. 13 to cast an Electoral College vote for Mr. Carter. It would have been his fifth experience as a Presidential elector, but illness obliged him to designate a substitute.

His choice was another reflection of his power—Raymond B. Harding, former Bronx Liberal leader, who now serves as special assistant to Governor Carey, a Rose intimate.

Mr. Rose's death leaves cloudy the future of a party that increasingly has been shaped in his image. Whom the Liberal Party will back in next year's election for Mayor may become a pivotal element in its development. An even bigger question is whether the Liberal nomination will mean as much as it once did without Mr. Rose's political skills to reinforce it.

Through all his months on the sick list, Mr. Rose kept in touch with the Governor and other close political associates, notably former Mayor Robert F. Wagner, whom he rescued from political annihilation in 1961 by masterminding a successful beat-the-bosses campaign after Tammany Hall decided to deny Mr. Wagner a third term at City Hall.

Mr. Rose also maintained daily phone communication with his offices as president of the United Hatters, Cap and Millinery Workers International Union. Hatlessness and intensified import competition have shrunk that union, which once had a membership of close to 100,000 to a present level of only 16,000.

In recognition of that precipitous cut in union size, Mr. Rose in the mid-1960's rejected a convention proposal that his own salary be increased by $10,000 a year. Instead, he cut his $20,000 pay to $17,500, the lowest salary for any international union president in the country.

He continued to draw that amount through all the inflationary years until

The New York Times
Alex Rose

his death. Since he passed his 72d birthday, the financial strain was eased by his ability to receive his full Social Security entitlement of roughly $7,000 a year for himself and his wife. He received no salary from the Liberal Party.

His Last Project, a Book

For 35 years, the Polish-born unionist and political strategist lived with his wife, the former Elsie Shapiro, in the apartment where he died at 200 Cabrini Boulevard, overlooking the Hudson River, north of the George Washington Bridge. He had hoped to write a book recounting his political experiences, but had dictated only a few pages before he was hospitalized in Florida last January. He could never get back to the project on a sustained basis.

The funeral will be at 11 A.M. Thursday at the Metropolitan Synagogue, 40 East 35th Street. Former Mayor Wagner will deliver the eulogy.

Mr. Rose is survived by his wife of 56 years; a son, Herbert, a New York lawyer; a daughter, Mrs. Carmi Schwartz, whose family moved last year from Scarsdale, N.Y., to Israel, and four grandchildren.

A shrewd blend of idealism, intelligence and political cunning enabled Alex Rose to make much out of little in both politics and labor. He was never able to command the entrenched loyalties of mass movements such as the major parties founded on ingrained party ties. He had no vast financial resources or wealthy backers to call on in bucking the dominant Democrats in New York City or the dominant Republicans upstate.

Yet, even when the Liberal Party's sturdiest supporter, the International Ladies Garment Workers Union, broke away from he party after the retirement of David Dubinsky 10 years ago, Mr. Rose remained skillful enough at political manipulation to elect John V. Lindsay to a second mayoral term in 1969 on the Liberal line alone. He played a vanguard role in winning national labor support for the Democratic Presidential candidacy of John F. Kennedy long before the 1960 nominating convention in Los Angeles. And at his death he was deeply involved in complex maneuvers affecting the 1977 New York City mayoral designation.

The organization Democrats in city and state always hated him because they felt his party was "stealing" their votes. They called him the last of "the big-city political bosses" and ridiculed his contention that the Liberal Party existed only to advance good government—in Mr. Rose's words, "the watchdog and the conscience" of the political process.

Even within his own party Mr. Rose was often regarded as autocratic and, increasingly in recent years, as old-hat, out of touch with such new waves in politics as the youth and women's movements. Eldon R. Clingan, who had been elected minority leader of the City Council as a Liberal, led a revolt within the party six years ago in protest against the Rose policies. In the last campaign, many progressives in the party grumbled at Mr. Rose's decision to deliver its Senatorial nomination to Daniel Patrick Moynihan after the former United Nations Ambassador defeated Representative Bella S. Abzug for the Democratic designation.

Mr. Rose's influence was almost as consequential within the general labor movement, even though his international union was smaller than most local unions in the mass-production and civil-service fields.

He was a pattern-setter in labor-management cooperation, a reflection of his belief that job security of union members depended on the economic health of their industries.

To combat the adverse trade conditions that were killing the hat industry, Mr. Rose in 1960 sponsored a promotion fund aimed at fostering fashion shows and other spurs to increased hat sales for both men and women. The union's members are still contributing 2 percent of their wages to that fund.

When the Merrimac Hat Company in Amesbury, Mass., an important maker of felt hat bodies, was threatened with liquidation, he saved the jobs of its workers by arranging for the company's purchase by the millinery union. For a decade, the company was kept alive, with Mr. Rose serving as chairman of the board and negotiating contracts that gave regular wage increases to the Merrimac employees.

However, a flood of Czech imports finally forced it to close. "It was the one victory the Commies ever had in our union," Mr. Rose used to tell his associates, many of whom had worked alongside him in routing Communist elements from the union in the 1930's.

Ouster of the Teamsters

His strong stance against racketeering in organized labor led George Meany, president of the American Federation of Labor and Congress of Industrial Organizations, to designate Mr. Rose as chairman of a special committee in 1957 to consider whether the scandal-scarred International Brotherhood of Teamsters should be expelled for gangster domination.

Jimmy Hoffa had just been elected president of the truck union, the federation's biggest and strongest affiliate. The five-member Ethical Practices Committee of the A.F.L.-C.I.O., on the basis of its own inquiry into corruption and disclosures by a Senate antiracket committee, had called on the teamsters to clean up or get out.

The function of the Rose group was to review the ouster recommendation. Mr. Rose joked about his role as "Lord High Executioner," but behind the scenes of the A.F.L.-C.I.O. convention in Atlantic City he sought to negotiate an accommodation that would have made it possible

Associated Press

Alex Rose, who built the Liberal Party into a force in city, state and national politics, was the center of attention for the New York Democratic leadership. From the left, at the Liberal Party dinner in 1975: Governor Carey, Arthur Levitt, State Comptroller, Mr. Rose, Patrick J. Cuningham, state chairman, and Robert F. Wagner.

for the teamsters to stay in the federation.

That accommodation would have involved Mr. Hoffa's stepping down as president, and other reforms. The teamster chief was on trial for wiretapping in New York at that time, but arrangements were made for him to drive to the convention one night to confer with Mr. Meany. Snow kept his car from getting through, and the next day the convention endorsed a Rose call for expulsion.

"If Hoffa had done what we told him to, the teamsters would still be in the federation and he would still be alive," said Mr. Rose shortly after the Detroit unionist disappeared last year under circumstances indicating gangland murder.

Mr. Rose was born Olesh Royz on Oct. 15, 1898, in Warsaw, the son of a well-to-do Polish tanner and dealer in raw hides. One advantage his father could not give him was a college education, since Jews in Poland in that Czarist period were not often admitted to the universities. At the age of 15, Alex was sent to New York, with the thought that he would prepare for a career in medicine.

The outbreak of World War I forced his father to stop sending funds for his support. The youth, now using an English transliteration of his Polish name, took a job as sewing-machine operator in a millinery shop at $6 a week and also became active in the Labor Zionist movement. In 1918 he enlisted in the Jewish Legion of the British Expeditionary Forces for duty under Viscount Allenby, fighting to free Palestine from Turkey.

Responsibility Delegated

On his return to New York two years later, he married Elsie Shapiro, a Russian-born colleague in the Zionist movement. She was short and retiring; he was tall and assertive. It made for a durable marriage.

In 1927, he became vice president of the hat union, and assisted its president, Max Zaritsky, in repelling incursions by Communists and racketeers. In 1950, Mr. Rose moved up to the presidency in his own right.

Mr. Rose took his first important plunge into the political mainstream in 1936, when he joined in the formation of the American Labor Party in this state. The American Federation of Labor and the Committee for Industrial Organizations had split a year earlier on the issue of craft versus industrial unionism, and fear was felt that their civil war would interfere with the mobilization of labor votes in support of a second term for President

Franklin D. Roosevelt.

The American Labor Party also provided a vehicle for enabling old-line Socialists, strongly represented in the leadership and rank and file of New York City's powerful needle-trades unions, to register their enthusiasm for the Roosevelt New Deal without violating their life long aversion to voting on the "capitalist" line of either the Democrats or Republicans.

The success of the American Labor Party in both respects caused its sponsors to decide to make the party a permanent "balance-wheel' in metropolitan politics, but internal politics quickly intervened.

Mr. Rose and his principal ally in the party, David Dubinsky, whose garment union was the largest of New York labor organizations, became increasingly distressed at the influence within the party of left-wing elements. The Transport Workers Union and National Maritime Union, both products of what became the Congress of Industrial Organizations were viewed by the Rose faction as leaders in Communist infiltration of the American Labor Party.

Sidney Hillman, president of the Amalgamated Clothing Workers of America, who was devoting most of his energies to wartime duty with the Roosevelt Administration, opposed any showdown

December 29, 1976

Suggested Reading

Binkley, Wilfred E. *American Political Parties*. Rev. ed. New York: Alfred A. Knopf, 1963.

Burner, David. *The Politics of Provincialism: The Democratic Party in Transition, 1918-1932*. New York: Alfred A. Knopf, 1968.

Campbell, Angus, et al. *The American Voter*. Reprint of 1960 ed. Chicago, Ill.: University of Chicago Press, 1976.

Foner, Eric. *Free Soil, Free Labor, Free Men: The Ideology of the Republican Party Before the Civil War*. New York: Oxford University Press, 1970.

Goldman, Eric F. *Rendezvous With Destiny*. New York: Alfred A. Knopf, 1952.

Haynes, Frederick E. *Third Party Movements Since the Civil War*. Reprint of 1916 ed. New York: Russell and Russell, 1966.

Hofstadter, Richard. *The Age of Reform: From Bryan to F.D.R.* New York: Alfred A. Knopf, 1955.

Key, Vladimir O., Jr. *Southern Politics in State and Nation*. Gloucester, Mass.: Peter Smith.

Keylin, Arleen, ed. *If Elected...Presidential Campaigns From Lincoln to Ford*. New York: Arno Press, 1976.

Leuchtenburg, William E. *Franklin D. Roosevelt, A Profile: The New Deal, 1932-1940*. Columbia S.C.: University of South Carolina Press, 1969.

Lubell, Samuel. *The Future of American Politics*. Rev. ed. New York: Harper & Row.

Mayer, George H. *The Republican Party, 1854-1966*. 2nd ed. New York: Oxford University Press, 1967.

Moos, Malcolm. *The Republicans*. New York: Random House, 1956.

Roseboom, Eugene H. *History of Presidential Elections: From George Washington to Richard M. Nixon*. 3rd ed. New York: Macmillan, 1970.

Schlesinger, Arthur M. Jr., and Fred L. Israel, eds. *History of American Presidential Elections*. 4 vols. New York: Chelsea House, 1971.

Shannon, David. *The Socialist Party of America*. New York: Macmillan, 1955.

Sprout, John G. *"The Best Men": Liberal Reformers in the Gilded Age*. New York: Oxford University Press, 1968.

Stein, Leon, ed. *Politics and People: The Ordeal of Self-Government in America*. A reprint series of 58 books. New York: Arno Press, 1974.

Viorst, Milton. *Fall From Grace*. New York: Simon and Schuster, 1971.

White, Theodore H. *The Making of the President 1960*. New York: New American Library, 1967.

Woodward, C. Vann. *Origins of the New South, 1877-1913*. Rev. ed. Baton Rouge, La.: Louisiana State University Press, 1972.

Index

spending, 192; and Lyndon Johnson, 199; re-elected, 144

Byrnes, James F., 128, 136, 142-43, 176

Cain, Harry, 186

campaign: contributions, 313-14; costs, 228-29; funds, 375-77, 391-92; issues, 122-23, 352-53; spending, 327-29; see also Democratic Party National Convention; elections; presidential race; Republican Party National Convention; voter returns

Carmichael, Stokley, 285

Carpenter, Claude, 215

Carrington, Ellsworth, 313

Carroll, John, 168, 209

Carter, Jimmy, 342, 377-78; black votes and, 398; and Democratic Convention, *1972,* 342; and labor, 393-94; presidential race, *1976,* 379-84, 395-96

Casady, Simon, 284-85

Case, Clifford, 264, 279, 300

Catholicism, 81-82, 232-33

Cavanagh, Jerome, 287

CBS, 324

Celler, Emanuel, 284

Chambers, Whittaker, 166

Chandler, A. B., 215

Chavez, Senator, 139-40

Chicago, Democratic Convention (1968), 302-3, 305

Chinese Nationalists, 230-31

Chisholm, Shirley, 341-42

CIA, 338-39

CIO-PAC, 135, 138

civil rights: as campaign issue, *1964,* 256-57; Democratic Party and, 150-52, 203-4, 214-17; Negro vote in 1960 election, 234-35; and political parties, 212-13; and Republican Party, 244; see also Negroes

Civil War, 17-18

Clardy, Kit, 191

Clark, Joseph, 210

Clayton, William, 142-43

Cleaver, Eldridge, 301

Clements, Earle, 209

Cleveland, Grover, 25-28, 30-31, 49-50

Clifford, Clark, 160

Cohen, Benjamin, 128

Coleman, James, 203

Colfax, Schuyler, 11

Collins, E. K., 268-69

Collins, LeRoy, 217, 219

Commager, Henry Steele, 117-19

Communism: and Dwight Eisenhower, 182-83; and Harry Truman, 142-43, 156; and Henry Wallace, 144-45, 147; and Joseph McCarthy, 165, 166; and labor, 135; liberal opposition, 145-46; and Progressive Party, 161-62; and Republican Party, 110; and Richard Nixon, 189-90; and Thomas E. Dewey, 136-37

Communist China, 188

Condon, Robert, 191

Congressional elections, *See* voter returns

Conkling, Roscoe, 22, 23

Connally, John, 245, 369-70, 377

Connor, Eugene, 151

Connor, John T., 273

Cooley, Harold, 192

Coolidge, Calvin, 70, 73-74, 78

Cooper, John Sherman, 144, 186, 209

Copperheads, 4-5, 12, 13, 116

Corcoran, Thomas, 128

Coughlin, Charles E. (Father), 100-102, 106-7

court rulings, 375, 376-77

Cox, Eugene, 105

Cox, James M., 69

Cuba, 243, 338-39

Curry, John, 90

Curtis, Carl, 211, 249

Daley, Richard, 202, 302, 340-41, 343, 348, 400-401

Daniel, Price, 186

Davis, Henry G., 51

Davis, John, 76, 90

Davis, Sammy, Jr., 348-49

Dawes, Charles, 73-74, 82

Day, Stephen, 127

Deadlock of Democracy: Four-Party Politics in America (Burns), 244-45

Debs, Eugene V., 59, 62, 76

Democratic Party: abrogation of two-thirds rule, 105; advisory council, 210-11; and Alfred E. Smith, 80; assailed by Dwight Eisenhower, 213-14; break-in at National Committee, 338-39; charter, 372-73; delegate quotas, 368-69; civil rights, 203-4, 215-17; coalition, *1948,* 161-62; in Congress, 8-9, 26-27, 86, 97-98, 112, 127, 144, 214-15, 242-43; convention reform, 315-17, 336-37, 387-88; Copperheadism, 4-5; debt of, 326-27; described, 222-24; dissident members, 307; and Dwight Eisenhower, 148, 178-79, 188-89, 208-9; and Edward Kennedy, 314-15; fund-raising, 229-30; Harris poll, 320; and Henry Steele Commager, 117-19; and Huey Long, 101; Ku Klux Klan and, 75; and leadership of Harry Truman, 139; and League of Nations, 68; left-wing, 332; liberalism, 210; loyalty oath, 202-3; and Margaret Chase Smith, 165; Negroes in, 278, 301-2; Negro-Jewish vote, 312; and New Deal, 95-96, 115, 116-17; reconstruction and, 13; reform of primaries, 332-33; Republican Party spying on, 355-57; revolution in, 296; and Richard Daley, 340-41; Richard Nixon Landslide, *1972,* 354-55; and Robert Kennedy, 284; and Robert Strauss, 368; slavery and, 3-4; and Supreme Court, 119; Tammany Ring, 13; and tariff reform, 34-35; television fund-raising, 324; third party, 121; transformation of, 301-2; urban vote, 317-18; and Vietnam War, 303-5; women power, 342-43; and Wayne Morse, 140; and Woodrow Wilson, 57; see also Freedom Democratic Party; political parties; Southern Democrats; voter returns

Democratic Party National Convention: *1860,* 2-4; *1864,* 6; *1868,* 12-13; *1872,* 14; *1876,* 17; *1880,* 21; *1884,* 25; *1888,* 28; *1892,* 30-31; *1896,* 40-45; *1900,* 47; *1904,* 51; *1908,* 55; *1912,* 61; *1916,* 64; *1920,* 68; *1924,* 75; *1928,* 80; *1932,* 88-91; *1936,* 105; *1940,* 124; *1944,* 132-33; *1948,* 150-52; *1952,* 176-77; *1956,* 204-5; *1960,* 216-20; *1964,* 269-73; *1968,* 302-3, 305; *1972,* 340-42; *1976,*

Greenback Party, 32
Green, William, 147
Gregory, Dick, 301
Gribbs, Roman, 317-18
Griswold, Dwight, 127, 131
Grossman, Jerome, 285
Gruenther, Alfred, 207
gubernatorial elections, 233
Guffey, Joseph, 97, 144

Hague, Frank, 116, 133
Hall, Leonard, 189
Halleck, Charles, 205, 226, 236-38, 242, 261
Hamilton, John, 110-11
Hamlin, Hannibal, 3, 4
Hanna, Marcus Alonzo, 46
Hannegan, Robert, 133-34, 138
Harding, Warren, 68-70
Harriman, Averell, 177-78, 204-5
Harris, Fred, 315
Harris, Patricia, 343
Harris poll, *See* public opinion polls
Harrison, Benjamin, 28, 30
Hart, Gary, 337-38
Harter, Dow, 127
Hatfield, Mark, 226, 279, 286, 300
Hayden, Carl, 192
Hayden, Thomas, 285
Hayes, Rutherford, 16-17
Haynsworth, Clement, 318-19
Hearnes, Warren, 304
Hearst, William Randolph, 102
Henderson, Leon, 145, 148, 151
Hendricks, Thomas, 25
Herter, Christian, 195, 207
Hewitt, Abram, 33
Hickel, Walter, 298-99
Hicks, Louise Day, 318
Hill, Gerald, 284
Hill, Knute, 127
Hill, Lister, 150, 151, 243
Hillman, Sidney, 133-35, 136-38
Hiss, Alger, 166
Hobart, Garret A., 38-39, 45
Hollings, Ernest, 221
Holtzman, Elizabeth, 361
Hook, Frank, 127
Hoover, Herbert: and Franklin Roosevelt, 91; presidential races, 73-74, 78-79, 83-84, 88; and Republican convention, *1936,* 99-100
Hope, Bob, 314
Hopkins, Harry, 115, 128
Horan, Walt, 127
Houghton, Arthur, 229
Houston, John, 127
Howe, Frederic C., 92
Howe, Irving, 285
Hughes, Charles Evans, 64, 65
Hughes, Richard, 302
Humphrey, George, 195, 211
Humphrey, Hubert, 151; and civil rights, 213; and Democ-

ratic Party, 202; and Harry Truman, 151; and labor, 307; presidential races, 293-97, 302-3, 305-10, 333-34; and Southern Democrats, 301; vice presidential candidate, 271-73

Ickes, Harold, 65, 94-95
Independent Citizens for Political Action, 144-45
independents, 394-95
Indo-China, 188-89
Ingalls, David, 123, 125-26
isolationism, 125-26, 127-29

Jackson, Andrew, 39-40
Jackson, Henry, 186, 219, 332-34, 341-43, 381-82
Jackson, Samuel, 133
Jacoby, Aaron, 152
Jarman, John, 373
Javits, Jacob, 163, 209, 226, 237, 243, 249, 286
Jenner, William, 186, 189, 211
Jessup, Philip, 167
John Birch Society, 259-60
Johnson, Andrew, 7-11
Johnson, Hiram, 60-62
Johnson, John A., 72
Johnson, Lyndon, 210, 215; and Allan Shivers, 199-200; and Barry Goldwater, 262; business support of, 273; and civil rights, 212-13; Democratic conventions, 204-5, 217-20; and Democratic Party, 236, 238; Freedom Democratic Party, 268-70; and George McGovern, 347-48; and Harry F. Byrd, 199; and political parties, 188-89; presidential races, 271-78, 290-92; and race riots, 287; and South, 274-75; strength of, 248; vice presidential candidate, 221-22, 231-32; withdrawal from 1968 presidential campaign, 293-94
Johnson, Paul, 269
Johnston, Eric, 128
Judd, Walter, 242
Julian, William, 150

Kansas, 2
Keating, Kenneth, 264
Kefauver, Estes, 77, 176, 213
Kelly, Edward, 133-34
Kelly, Frank, 133
Kennedy, Edward: and George McGovern, 346; political future, 314-15; presidential race, *1976,* 377-79; and vice presidential slot, *1972,* 341
Kennedy, John F.: and Adlai Stevenson, 216; assassination of, 246-48; debates with Richard Nixon, 228, 23-31; fund-raising for, 229-30; and Negro vote, 235; presidential race, *1960,* 216-20, 231-32; religious factor, 232-33; and Republican Party, 239-40; and Southern Democrats, 227-28; in Texas, 245
Kennedy, Robert F.: death of, 296-97; and Democratic left, 284; presidential race, *1968,* 291-96
Kennon, Robert, 176

Socialism, 53-55, 58-59, 163-64
Sorensen, Theodore, 304
South: and Alfred Smith, 81-82; and Barry Goldwater, 261,
    267-68; and Democratic Party, 27, 131-32, 161-62;
    and Lyndon Johnson, 274-75; and Negro vote, 81;
    and Richard Nixon, 357; presidential prospects,
    1976, 377-79; and Republican Party, 27, 318-20; and
    Spiro Agnew, 318-20; states' rights, 153-54
Southern Democrats: anti-New Deal, 131-32; on civil
    rights, 150-52; conservatism of, 114-15, 215-16; and
    Dwight Eisenhower, 186-87; and Harry Truman,
    152-53; and John F. Kennedy, 227-28; National
    Convention, *1952*, 176-77; platform, *1960*, 221; and
    Rutherford Hayes, 18; split in, 150-154; *see also*
    Democratic Party
Soviet Russia, 142-43, 145
Sparkman, John, 178
Sparks, Chauncey, 151
Speakes, Larry, 394
Spock, Benjamin, 285
Stans, Maurice H., 328-29
Stanton, Frank, 324
Stassen, Harold, 126, 149-50, 161, 172, 195, 206
states rights, 153-54, 161, 163, 178-79
Stein, Howard, 313
Steinem, Gloria, 343
Stennis, John, 203
Stevens, Ivy Baker Priest, 298
Stevenson, Adlai E., I, 30-31
Stevenson, Adlai E., III: and Democratic Party, 199; and
    Dwight Eisenhower, 189-90; and John Kennedy,
    216; presidential races, 176-79, 184-85, 204-5, 217-
    18; and Wayne Morse, 183-84
stock crash, 83
Stockwell, Lowell, 127
Stokes, Carl, 317-18
Stones, W. Clement, 328
Stratton, William, 144
Strauss, Robert, 368
Suarez, Miguel, 339
Supreme Court: campaign funding, 376-77; Democrats in,
    119; and Franklin D. Roosevelt, 113-14, 119; Negro
    vote in Texas, 129-30
Sutton, Percy, 342
Sweeney, Tom, 144
Sweetland, Monroe, 202
Symington, Stuart, 186, 213, 217, 219

Taft-Hartley law, 147
Taft, Robert, 166; campaign tactics, 243; death of, 187; and
    Dwight Eisenhower, 173-74; and Henry Wallace,
    145; isolationism, 125-26; reactionary, 145; Republi-
    can convention, *1952*, 171-72; Republican digest,
    164; tradition of, 236; and Wayne Morse, 140
Taft, Robert, Jr., 243
Taft, William Howard, 55-56, 59, 60, 63
Talbott, Jett, 215
Talmadge, Eugene, 103-4, 108
Tammany Ring, 13, 15-16, 229
tariffs, 28-29, 34-35, 57
television, 171, 324

Texas, 245, 249
Thayer, Walter, 241-42
third-party tickets, 37, 146-47
Thomas, Elbert, 168
Thomas, Norman, 93
Thurmond, Strom, 152-53, 176, 221, 274
Tilden, Samuel, 17
Tobin, Daniel, 134
Tower, John, 261
Townsend, Wallace, 106-8, 126
Tribune, 2, 9-10
Troy, Matthew, 340
Truman, Harry: assumption of presidency, 138; civil
    rights, 150-53, 215; denunciation by Republican
    Party, 163-64; and Dwight Eisenhower, 148, 185-86;
    and FEPC, 139-40; and Henry Wallace, 142-43; as
    leader of Democratic Party, 139; New Deal, 155-56;
    presidential races, 150-51, 155-60, 174-76; and Texas
    Democrats, 178-79; and Thomas Dewey, 156, 157;
    vice presidential nominee, *1944*, 132-34; and Wayne
    Morse, 140
Tugwell, Rexford G., 94, 110, 162
Tuttle, Charles, 86
Tydings, Millard, 98, 124, 165, 167

Underwood, Thomas, 186
Union of Social Justice, 106-7
Union Party, 106-8
United States Steel Company, 116

Vandenberg, Arthur H., 95-97, 99, 121, 160
Vandiver, Ernest, 221
Vaughn, Robert, 284
Vietnam, 284, 292, 302-5
Vinson, Carl, 191
Volpe, John, 300, 314
voter returns: *1896*, 45; *1910*, 57-58; *1912*, 63; *1916*, 66;
    1918, 67; *1920*, 70; *1924*, 78; *1928*, 83; *1930*, 86; *1932*,
    92-93; *1934*, 97-98; *1936*, 110-13; *1938*, 119-20; *1940*,
    124-25; *1942*, 126-27; *1944*, 137-38; *1946*, 144; *1948*,
    158-59; *1950*, 166-68; *1952*, 185-86; *1954*, 191-92;
    1956, 209-10; *1958*, 214-15; *1960*, 231-32; *1962*, 242-
    43; *1964*, 275-78; *1966*, 286; *1968*, 310-12; *1970*, 325-
    26; *1972*, 353-54; *1974*, 370-72; *1976*, 395-98

Wadleigh, Henry, 166
Wagner, Robert, 95
Waldie, Jerome, 361
Wallace, George: presidential races, 266-67, 290, 306-8,
    333-34, 341-42, 381-82; shooting of, 336; support for,
    274, 334-35
Wallace, Henry: American Federation of Labor and, 147;
    presidential races, 132, 133-34, 137-38, 144-47, 161;
    resignation of, 143; and Soviet Union, 142-43; as
    vice president, 124
Wallace, Lurleen, 286